PRIZE MEDAL,

VIENNA, 1873.

BORNHARDT'S

PATENT

ST PRIZE SILVER MEDAL.

BRUNSWICK, 1877.

ELECTRICAL FIRING MACHINE,

FOR FIRING BLASTING CHARGES IN MINES, QUARRIES, &c.

BEDFORD McNEILL,

LATE

JOHN DARLINGTON,

25A, OLD BROAD STREET,

LONDON, E.C.

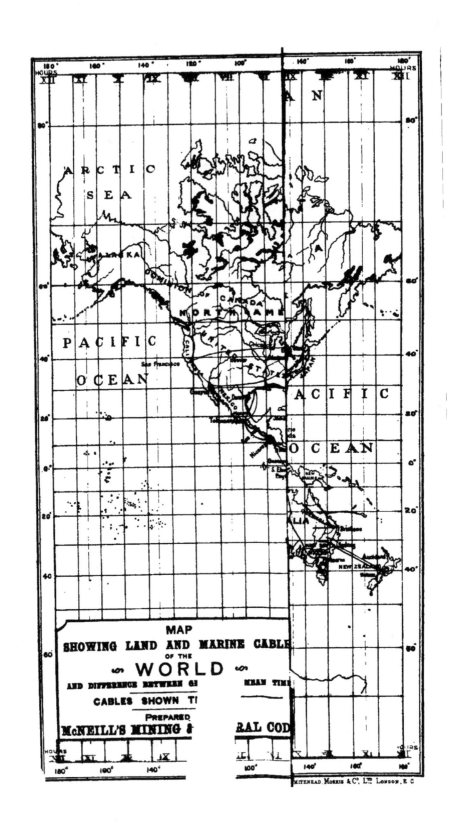

MAP

SHOWING LAND AND MARINE CABLE
OF THE
WORLD

AND DIFFERENCE BETWEEN G   MEAN TIM

CABLES SHOWN T

PREPARED

McNEILL'S MINING   RAL COD

D

McNEILL'S CODE.

Arranged to meet the Requirements of

MINING, METALLURGICAL AND CIVIL ENGINEERS; DIRECTORS OF MINING,
SMELTING AND OTHER COMPANIES; BANKERS; STOCK AND SHARE BROKERS;
SOLICITORS, ACCOUNTANTS, FINANCIERS AND GENERAL MERCHANTS.

SAFETY AND SECRECY.

BY

BEDFORD McNEILL, Assoc. M. Inst., C.E..

Associate of the Royal School of Mines;
Member of the Institution of Mining and Metallurgy and of the
North of England Institute of Mining and Mechanical
Engineers; Fellow of the Geological Society,
&c., &c.

London:
PRINTED AND PUBLISHED BY WHITEHEAD, MORRIS & CO., LIMITED,
9, FENCHURCH STREET, E.C.

New York:
THE SCIENTIFIC PUBLISHING COMPANY,
253, Broadway.

Australia:
E. S. WIGG & SON,
Adelaide, Perth, Broken Hill.

Cape Town:
E. R. MORRIS & CO.,
13, Burg Street.

1899.

CONTENTS.

PREFACE.

In the present volume the Author has endeavoured to include the technical terms and sentences required by the Mining, Metallurgical and Civil Engineer, by the Mine Director, and by those connected with the direction or management of Mining and Smelting Companies. Particular attention has also been paid to the financial part of mining, needs of Financiers generally, negotiations for effecting the sale or purchase of mineral and other properties, as well as to the requirements of Stock Exchange transactions. Legal, Banking and General Phrases are also largely included.

The Code is alphabetically arranged, with but one exception, viz. :— "Sundry Weights and Measures" on pages 774-775.

On pages 373—376, under the word "Mineral," will be found a list of the more commonly occurring Minerals; and on pages 533—535, under the word "Rock," will be found a similar list of Rocks. Both "Minerals" and "Rocks" are arranged alphabetically.

The Cipher Words have been carefully selected with a view of eliminating such as may be identical in their telegraphic signals, or otherwise liable to error in transmission. On the next page will be found General Suggestions as to the use of the Code, also for securing accuracy in messages received, for the prevention of errors in transmission, and for deciphering mutilated words when such occur.

The First Part contains over forty-four thousand Mining, Legal and General Phrases; while the Second Part includes Numerals, Measurements, Weights and Currencies.

A Schedule embracing the phrases required when surveying or reporting upon a mineral property is also added.

Any suggestions will be most cordially received.

BEDFORD McNEILL.

General Suggestions for using McNEILL'S CODE; and for the Prevention and Correction of Errors in Messages.

I.—Use of Code.

In numerous instances one or more alternative readings, separated by brackets, are given; as for instance:—

> Page 2. *Abdicacion,* meaning " you (they) (——) must abide by the decision of "

It is recommended, whenever it is not within the knowledge of the Sender, that the Receiver of the message will be able from the context to discriminate as to which alternative is intended, that one of the cipher words given under the head of *Alternative* (page 32) should be employed, to render misconception impossible.

When there is any chance of doubt arising as to whether the " singular " or the " plural " number is intended to be conveyed, one of the cipher words under the heading *Number* (page 401), or *Word* (pages 733—734), should be used. On page 734 will also be found cipher words for indicating that the word is employed in its ordinary sense, and is not to be translated as conveying the meaning that may be attached to it in the Code.

The cipher word *Aufschluss* (page 72), meaning " Blank," should invariably be employed whenever its use would be likely to obviate error. It is found most convenient to fill in the " Blanks " in a message consecutively, and immediately after the cipher word in which they are required.

Tables on pages 748 to 751, and pages 776 to 779.—The method of using these Tables is to translate the cipher word found in any of the vertical columns of cipher words by the meaning given at the head of the same vertical column *plus* the meaning given horizontally in the final right-hand column.

> Thus on page 748, *Tithing* is translated : " Need not pay attention to value of ore in sight."
>
> Whilst *Toddlers* is translated : " Report by cable as to value of ore in sight."
>
> Similarly, on page 776, *Watermark* is translated : " Have you received my (our) letter dated the 1st ? "
>
> Whilst *Waveringly* is translated : " Have received your (——'s) letter dated the 1st."

It may happen that it is wished to substitute another word for the cipher word actually occurring; for this purpose additional cipher words are given in the Substitution Tables, pages 786 to 791. These tables also afford opportunity of making the necessary record of such substitution.

As the Code contains 45767 cipher words, each of which has a consecutive number, it follows that any individual number from 1 to 45767, inclusive, is available; but in such case one of the cipher words under the heading *Numeral* (page 401) should be interpolated.

Increased secrecy when cabling can be secured if it is mutually agreed between any two correspondents to employ the cipher words not in their actual order, but in some other and prearranged order. The advantage of changing this order from time to time is obvious.

II.—The Prevention and Correction of Errors in Messages.

Errors in telegraphic messages may be due to one of several causes; such as want of care on the part of the sender when writing his original cipher message.

Failing the employment of a typewriting machine, Roman characters should be employed for the cipher words.

Another fruitful cause of error is owing to the fact that each individual letter of the Alphabet is telegraphically transmitted by means of a certain number of "dots" or "dashes," such "dots" or "dashes" being separated by suitable "time intervals." Hence it is possible, by a slight variation on the part of either the Transmitting or the Receiving Clerk, to alter considerably the word intended to be conveyed.

For example, the signals for the letter C are — . — .

Whilst those for the letters T E N are respectively { T E N .

It follows, therefore, that the words " cable " and " tenable " may be so transmitted as to be not very readily distinguishable.

	C	A	B	L	E
T E N					

The omission of a signal, the conversion of a "dot" into a "dash," and the improper lengthening or shortening of the "time interval," are responsible for many of the errors in cipher messages.

The same observations apply also to figures.

Thus the signal for the figure 1 is . — — . — — ., which by a variation of the time intervals may become { A   O   or   W   M   or   J   T

On receipt of an undecipherable word, a reference to the Morse Signals for letters and figures, with some possible substitutions (see next page), and the exercise of a little patience, will often be found sufficient to indicate the word sought after.

It being also remembered that the cipher word may not have been distinctly written in the original message, an imperfect " i " may have been read by the Transmitting Clerk as an " e," or a " t " may have been mistaken for an " l " or a " b."

Most of the cable companies will courteously repeat undecipherable words " free of cost," or on application will make such suggestions as may lead to the correct interpretation of them.

It is strongly recommended that any one when beginning to use this Code should study it whenever occasion may serve, as by such means great facility will be gained in selecting those sentences which most nearly convey the meaning of the sender of the message.

[v]

MORSE SIGNALS, ALPHABET, AND FIGURES, with some Possible Substitutions.

Letter.	Morse Signal.	Some possible Substitutions.
A	· —	ET
B	— · · ·	DE NEE NI TEI TIE TS
C	— · — ·	KE NN NTE TAE TEN
D	— · ·	NE TEE TI
E	·	
F	· · — ·	EAE IN ITE NE
G	— — ·	ME TEE TN
H	· · · ·	EEI EIE II SE
I	· ·	EE Y
J	· — — —	ATT EO EMT ETM
K	— · —	NT TA
L	· — · ·	AE AI ENE ETI RE
M	— —	TT
N	— ·	TE
O	— — —	MT TM TTE
P	· — — ·	AN ATE ETN WE
Q	— — · —	MA MET TK TTA
R	· — ·	AE EI ETE
S	· · ·	EEE IE EI
T	—	
U	· · —	EA EET IT
V	· · · —	IA ST
W	· — —	AT EM
X	— · · —	TEA DT NA
Y	— · — —	I TEM MM NTT
Z	— — · ·	GE TNE TTI
CH	— — — —	MM

Figures.

0	— — — — —	T OM
1	· — — — —	A AO WM
2	· · — — —	IO U UM
3	· · · — —	SM V VT
4	· · · · —	SA HT
5	· · · · ·	EH HE IS
6	— · · · ·	DI TH
7	— — · · ·	B GEE MS
8	— — — · ·	D OI MD
9	— — — — ·	N ON

For Places WEST of Greenwich DEDUCT from GREENWICH Time to find ACTUAL Time.

	H. M.		H. M.
Acapulco	6 39	Lisbon	0 36
Bahia	2 33	Madeira	1 7
Baltimore	5 5	Madrid	0 15
Barbadoes	3 58	Mexico	6 36
Bogota	4 57	Milwaukee	5 50
Boston	4 45	Minneapolis	6 10
Brest	0 18	Montevideo...	3 45
Buenos Ayres	3 53	Montreal	4 50
Callao	5 8	New Orleans	6 0
Cayenne	3 29	New York	4 56
Charlestown	5 20	Panama	5 18
Chicago	5 50	Pernambuco	2 20
Conception	4 52	Philadelphia	5 0
Copiapo ... ...:.	4 42	Porto Rico...	4 26
Coquimbo	4 45	Quebec	4 45
Denver	7 0	Rio de Janeiro	2 52
Detroit	5 30	Rio Grande do Sul ... ..:	3 29
Funchal	1 8	Saint John (N.B.)... ...	4 25
Galveston	6 20	Saint Thomas	4 19
Georgetown	3 53	Saint Vincent, Cape de Verd ...	1 40
Gibraltar	0 21	Salt Lake City, Utah	7 28
Grahams Town	1 46	San Francisco	8 10
Guatemala	6 2	Sierra Leone	0 35
Guayaquil	5 19	Toronto	5 20
Halifax	4 15	Trinidad	4 6
Havana	5 29	Valdivia	4 53
Honolulu	10 31	Valparaiso	4 46
Indianapolis	5 45	Vancouver's Island ...	8 14
Jamaica	5 10	Vera Cruz	6 25
Kansas City	6 15	Vigo	0 35
Kingston, Jamaica ...	5 7	Washington	5 8
Lima	5 8	Winnipeg	6 30

For Places EAST of Greenwich ADD to GREENWICH Time to find ACTUAL Time.

	H. M.		H. M.
Adelaide	9 14	Madras	5 21
Aden	3 0	Malacca	6 49
Agra	5 11	Malta	0 58
Alexandria	1 59	Marseilles	0 21
Algiers	0 11	Mauritius	3 50
Algoa Bay	1 44	Melbourne	9 40
Amoy	7 52	Nagasaki	8 40
Auckland	11 38	Natal	2 2
Bangkok	6 40	Odessa	2 2
Batavia	7 7	Otago	11 38
Bathurst, N.S.W.	9 16	Paris	0 9
Berlin	0 53	Pekin	7 46
Bombay	4 51	Penang	6 42
Borneo	7 39	Perth (West Australia)	7 43
Brisbane	10 13	Port Darwin	8 44
Bushire	3 23	Rangoon	6 20
Bussorah	3 11	Saigon	7 6
Calcutta	5 53	Shanghai	8 5
Canton	7 33	Singapore	6 55
Cape Town	1 13	Smyrna	1 49
Christchurch, N.Z.	11 32	St. Petersburg	2 1
Colombo	5 19	Suez	2 10
Constantinople	1 56	Sydney	10 5
Dunedin	11 22	Tunis	0 40
Galle	5 20	Vienna	1 5
Hobart Town	9 50	Warsaw	1 24
Hongkong	7 36	Wellington	11 38
Invercargil	11 12	Yeddo	9 18
Jerusalem	2 21	Zanzibar	2 37
Kurrachee	4 27		

PART I.

20

Aalen	... **00001**	**A**
Aalfang	... 00002	**Abandon**
Aasig	... 00003	To abandon
Ababa	... 00004	Must abandon
Abacial	... 00005	Refuse(s) to abandon
Abactor	... 00006	Consent(s) to abandon
Abacus	... 00007	Shall abandon
Abadenar	.. 00008	Before I (we) abandon
Abadenjo	... 00009	When did you (they) abandon
Abadessa	... 00010	Why did you (they) abandon ——
Abadiado	... 00011	Abandon all thought of
Abaft	... 00012	Shall abandon all thought of
Abaisance	... 00013	Have been obliged to abandon
Abajador	... 00014	Do you still advise me (us) to abandon
Abalado	... 00015	Advise you to abandon
Abalanzar	00016	Do not now advise you to abandon
Abamcar	... 00017	Provided that you abandon
Abanderung	00018	Do you propose to abandon
Abandono	... 00019	Do not propose to abandon
Abangeln	... 00020	Should you abandon
Abanitto	... 00021	Can I (we) abandon
Abantico	... 00022	Do not abandon
Abaque	... 00023	Will probably abandon
Abarloar	... 00024	Not at all likely to abandon
Abarrado	... 00025	Abandon the mine
Abarrisco	... 00026	Abandon the project
Abarrotar	... 00027	Just as I was (we were) about to abandon
Abarten	... 00028	**Abandoned**
Abase	... 00029	Was (were) abandoned
Abasement	00030	Has (have) abandoned
Abashed	... 00031	Has (have) been abandoned
Abasourdir	00032	I (we) have abandoned
Abastanza	00033	Should you have already abandoned
Abastar	... 00034	Should you not already have abandoned
Abastecer	... 00035	Have since abandoned
Abastionar	00036	Have not abandoned
Abasto	... 00037	Have not yet abandoned
Abatable	... 00038	Was (were) not abandoned until
Abatardir	... 00039	Abandoned after consultation with
Abatino	... 00040	Before actually abandoned
Abattage	... 00041	Might be abandoned for the present
Abattement	00042	The——was (were) abandoned because of
Abattis	... 00043	Write full particulars why you (they) abandoned
Abattoir	... 00044	——level under water. Mine abandoned
Abatudo	... 00045	You (they) should have abandoned——on account of
Abatvert	... 00046	**Abandonment**
Abbaccare	00047	What is your view as to the abandonment of
Abbachiere	00048	Advise abandonment of
Abbacinato	00049	Do not advise abandonment of
Abbacy	... 00050	As regards abandonment my present view is that
Abbadessa	00051	**Abate**
Abbadia	... 00052	To abate
Abbaglio	... 00053	Consent(s) to abate
Abbajante	00054	Refuse(s) to abate
Abbajato	... 00055	Cannot abate
Abballare	... 00056	Expect will abate
Abbassarsi	00057	Unless is (are) willing to abate
Abbatissa	... 00058	Likely to abate
Abbatre	... 00059	Unlikely to abate
Abbaye	... 00060	Vendors will abate

Abbeizen ...	00061	You (they) must abate at least ——
Abbellito ...	00062	Can you (they) induce vendors to abate
Abbenche...	00063	How much can you (they) abate in consideration of
Abbersten...	00064	**Abated**
Abberufen	00065	Has slightly abated
Abbess ...	00066	Has (have) not abated in the slightest degree
Abbeverare	00067	**Abatement**
Abbiente ...	00068	Can you obtain any abatement of
Abbiettare	00069	Cannot obtain any abatement of
Abbiezione	00070	Have obtained an abatement of
Abbigliare	00071	Must make some abatement
Abbild ...	00072	Unless a considerable abatement is made
Abbinden	00073	An abatement of at least
Abbitte ...	00074	Consider terms excessive; must have considerable abatement
Abblasen ...	00075	**Abeyance**
Abbluhen ...	00076	Is for the present in abeyance
Abboccato	00077	Cannot remain any longer in abeyance
Abbolire ...	00078	The matter has been in abeyance since
Abbominare	00079	The matter has been left in abeyance because of
Abbonarsi	00080	The matter must remain in abeyance
Abbondanza	00081	The matter must remain in abeyance until
Abbordare	00082	Can the matter remain in abeyance
Abborgen ...	00083	The matter cannot remain in abeyance after ——
Abbot ..	00084	Leave it (this) in abeyance meanwhile
Abbraccio...	00085	Leave it (this) in abeyance until
Abbraciare	00086	Left for the present in abeyance
Abbrevio ...	00087	Will be left for the present in abeyance
Abbringn ...	00088	**Abide**
Abbronzato	00089	To abide
Abbrostire	00090	Will you abide
Abbruhlen	00091	Consent(s) to abide
Abbrunarsi	00092	Refuse(s) to abide
Abbruten ...	00093	If you will abide
Abbujarsı	00094	If you wish me (us) to abide
Abcesso ...	00095	Provided that —— will abide by
Abdachung	00096	Am (are) unable to abide by
Abdampfen	00097	Abide by the decision of
Abdankung	00098	If —— is not willing to abide by
Abdicacion	00099	You (they) (——) must abide by the decision of
Abdicate ...	00100	Will you (they) abide by
Abdienen ...	00101	Will abide by your (——'s) decision
Abdingen ...	00102	Refer to —— and abide by his (their) decision
Abdiquer ...	00103	**Ability(ies)**
Abdonnern	00104	——'s abilities are not known to me
Abdorren ...	00105	Is a man of considerable ability
Abdrehen...	00106	Do you regard him (——) as possessing sufficient ability
Abdrucken	00107	Believe he possesses great abilities
Abduccion	00108	What ability has he for
Abduct ...	00109	I (we) require a man of tried ability for
Abduttore	00110	What is his (their) reputation for ability
Abecedario	00111	**Able**
Abeille ...	00112	Able to
Abejar ...	00113	Not able to carry
Abejaruco	00114	Able to carry
Abejon ...	00115	Am (are) not able to
Abejonozo	00116	Am (are) quite able to
Abellacado	00117	Hope to be able not later than
Abellar ...	00118	In the event of your not being able
Abelmosco	00119	Are you (they) able to
Abemolar ...	00120	When will you be able to

Abend ...	00121	Quite able to
Abendlied...	00122	Do not hesitate to say so if you are not able
Abendmahl	00123	When do you expect to be able to do this (the——)
Abendmusik	00124	Shall not be able to start in earnest until
Abendroth	00125	As soon as you are able telegraph
Abendsegen	00126	Can you (they) tell when you (they) will be able
Abendsonne	00127	Have only been able (to)
Abendstern	00128	Are you able to control
Abenola ...	00129	Are you likely to be able to control
Abenteuer...	00130	I am (we are) not able to control
Abenuz ...	00131	Shall only be able to (if)
Abermalig...	00132	Have you been able to
Aberrant ...	00133	I (we) shall be able to
Aberration	00134	Has (have) he (they) been able
Abertura ...	00135	When do you (they) think you (they) will be able
Aberwitz ...	00136	I (they) will not be able unless
Abestiar ...	00137	I shall (they will) not be able without
Abetaja ...	00138	If you are not able telegraph to
Abetting ...	00139	When will you be able to telegraph respecting
Abettor ...	00140	**Aboard**
Abetunado	00141	On board
Abfahren ...	00142	I go aboard on
Abfallig ...	00143	The whole consignment will be on board not later than
Abfarben ...	00144	——not permitted on board
Abfassen ...	00145	**Abolished**
Abfloten ...	00146	Has (have) been abolished
Abfolgen ...	00147	Not yet abolished
Abfragen ...	00148	Likely to be abolished
Abfullen ...	00149	Is it (are they) likely to be abolished
Abgehen ...	00150	Not likely to be abolished
Abgelebt ...	00151	Should it (they) be abolished
Abgerben ...	00152	**About**
Abgethan ...	00153	About a month longer
Abgleiten ...	00154	About a week longer
Abgraben ...	00155	About the
Abgrund ...	00156	About the beginning
Abharmen	00157	About the middle of
Abheben ...	00158	About the end of
Abhobeln ...	00159	About——days longer
Abhorrent	00160	About when
Abhulsen ...	00161	About what
Abigarrar...	00162	Expect will be about
Abigeato ...	00163	At or about
Abigotado...	00164	Estimated at about
Abihares ...	00165	Can you (they) say anything about
Abilitade ...	00166	Cannot say anything about
Abilmente...	00167	——can tell you about it (this)
Abimer ...	00168	Should be with you about
Abiosa ...	00169	What is about the quantity you have
Abirrung ...	00170	I (we) have about
Abismar ...	00171	Shall see——about it (this) on——
Abismo ...	00172	When will you see——about it (this)
Abispon ...	00173	You must see——at once about
Abissare ...	00174	I (we) will telegraph you about——as soon as I (we) have positive
Abitabile ...	00175	There is not the slightest suspicion about [information
Abitacolo ...	00176	Have you any suspicion about
Abitadura	00177	Do you (they) know anything about
Abitaque ...	00178	I (we) know nothing about——
Abitatore ...	00179	There is nothing known here about
Abitazione	00180	Look about for

Abitevole ...	00181	Will look about for
Abituale ...	00182	What will be about the cost
Abitudine...	00183	Cost will be about
Abjected ...	00184	What will be about the charges
Abkarten ...	00185	Charges will be about
Abkochen...	00186	**Above**
Ablandar ...	00187	Above the
Ablandecer	00188	Above the average
Ablassen ...	00189	Should not be above
Ablative ...	00190	Should it (this) be above
Ableben ...	00191	Why is this (are they) above
Ablentar ...	00192	Whether above or below
Ablesen ...	00193	Likely to be above
Ablohnen ...	00194	Not likely to be above
Abmalen ...	00195	Above ground
Abnehmen	00196	Do not give above
Abnormal ..	00197	Will have to give above
Abnutzen ...	00198	**Abroad**
Abobado ...	00199	Is at present abroad
Abocardado	00200	——is at present abroad, but is expected to return about
Abochornar	00201	I shall go abroad on
Abocinado	00202	Has——gone abroad
Abofellar ...	00203	When do you go abroad
Abofetear ...	00204	——is likely to go abroad
Abogacia ...	00205	**Absence**
Abogadear	00206	Get leave of absence
Abohetado	00207	Leave of absence
Aboiement	00208	Can I (we) have leave of absence until
Aboleza ...	00209	You may have leave of absence until
Abolibile ...	00210	—— has applied for leave of absence
Abolire ...	00211	May have leave of absence
Abolitus ...	00212	Cannot have leave of absence
Abolizione	00213	In the absence of further instructions respecting
Abollonar ...	00214	In the absence of all instructions
Abolsado ...	00215	Provided that your absence
Abordable...	00216	Now on leave of absence
Abordador	00217	In the absence of——await further instructions
Abordnung	00218	Arrange for the efficient conduct of works during your absence
Aborigeni...	00219	Have arranged for efficient conduct of works during my absence
Aborrecer ...	00220	Your cable (letter) arrived during my absence at
Aborrevole	00221	In the absence of any particulars
Abortere ...	00222	During my (our) unavoidable absence
Abortion ...	00223	**Absent**
Abortive ...	00224	Whilst you are absent
Aborto ...	00225	Whilst——is absent
Abotinado	00226	How long do you expect to be absent
Aboucher ...	00227	How long will —— be absent
Aboutir ...	00228	How long are you (is——) likely to be absent
Aboyato ...	00229	How many days will you be absent
Aboyeux ...	00230	Shall be absent about —— days
Abqualen ...	00231	Better absent yourself during
Abracijo ...	00232	You should not be absent more than
Abrahmen	00233	Shall not be absent after
Abrahonar	00234	Is (are) now absent
Abrasador...	00235	Will be absent for some months
Abrasilado	00236	Will be absent for some time
Abrasion ...	00237	Is at present absent but will return in a few days
Abrathen ...	00238	Has (have) been absent
Abrazador	00239	Is absent on account of
Abrechnung	00240	**Absolute(ly)**

Abrege ...	00241	Absolutely decline
Abreiben ...	00242	Before you absolutely decline
Abreise ...	00243	To absolutely control
Abreuver ...	00244	Will enable you to absolutely control
Abrevadero	00245	Can you absolutely control
Abreviador	00246	Give —— absolute control
Abricotier...	00247	I (we) must absolutely control
Abridero ...	00248	It is absolutely necessary to control
Abridge ...	00249	Unless I (we) can absolutely control
Abridgment	00250	Leave the matter absolutely in your hands
Abrigadero	00251	Do you leave the matter absolutely to me (us)
Abrigano ...	00252	**Abstract**
Abrimiento	00253	Get abstract of
Abrinnent	00254	Abstract of
Abrivent ...	00255	When will you mail abstract of
Abrochador	00256	Mail abstract of accounts
Abrogacion	00257	Mail full abstract of title
Abrogare ...	00258	Full and complete attested copy of abstract of title must be sent
Abromado	00259	Cannot send abstract before ——
Abrotano ...	00260	Please forward abstract of profits of (for)
Abrupfen ...	00261	Telegraph (cable) when abstracts are mailed
Abruptio ...	00262	Send abstract of your intended report by mail
Abrupturus	00263	Telegraph abstract of your report
Absagen ...	00264	Telegraph abstract of returns of (for)
Abscess ...	00265	Submit abstract of title to ——
Abscission	00266	Telegraph abstract of report
Absemio ...	00267	Abstract of title defective
Absenden ...	00268	Abstract of title quite satisfactory
Absenzia ...	00269	Abstract shows title is vested in
Absieben ...	00270	Mail abstract of agreement
Absinthe ...	00271	Will mail abstract of agreement
Absitzen ...	00272	Have mailed abstract of agreement
Absolucion	00273	**Abundance**
Absolver ...	00274	Is there an abundance of
Absondern	00275	There is an abundance of
Absorcion...	00276	In abundance
Absorption	00277	I (we) have sufficient but not an abundance
Absorvido...	00278	I (we) find there is an abundance of
Absoudre ...	00279	**Abundant**
Abspanen ...	00280	There is an abundant water supply
Abspanstig	00281	Is (are) not very abundant
Absperren	00282	Will become more abundant
Abspulen ...	00283	An abundant supply of
Abstaining	00284	Abundant water supply at a distance of —— miles ; easy grade
Abstampeln	00285	Is there an abundant supply of [for tramway
Abstecken	00286	Timber for fuel abundant
Abstehlen...	00287	Timber for mining and fuel purposes abundant
Abstenerse	00288	Fuel, timber and water are abundant
Abstenir ...	00289	Fuel, timber, water and labour are abundant
Absterben...	00290	**Accede**
Absterge ...	00291	To accede
Abstossen...	00292	Consent(s) to accede
Abstracto ...	00293	Refuse(s) to accede
Abstrafen...	00294	Is (are) likely to accede
Abstraire ...	00295	Is (are) not likely to accede
Abstruso ...	00296	Provided that —— will accede
Absturz ...	00297	Will accede to your (their) wishes
Abstutzen...	00298	I (we) cannot accede to
Absurdite...	00299	Better accede to ——'s wishes
Absurdness	00300	Cannot accede to terms named

Absurdo	...	00301	Am (are) unable to accede to your (their)
Abtheilen	...	00302	Can you persuade —— to accede to
Abtraufeln		00303	Can you possibly induce vendors to accede to reduction of ——
Abtreten	...	00304	**Accelerate**
Abubilla	...	00305	To accelerate
Abultar	...	00306	Endeavour to accelerate
Aburelado		00807	Will do all I (we) can to accelerate
Aburujar	...	00308	Can you suggest anything to accelerate
Abusivo	...	00309	Cannot suggest anything to accelerate
Abuso	...	00310	Might perhaps accelerate
Abuttal	...	00311	**Accept**
Abuzzago	...	00312	To accept
Abwandeln		00313	Accept terms
Abwarten	...	00314	Accept proposal
Abwehren	...	00315	Accept my (our) best wishes
Abzahlen	...	00316	Accept my (our) congratulations
Abzehrung		00317	Accept my (our) sincere condolence
Acabable	...	00318	I (we) accept
Acabador	...	00319	Do not accept
Acaballado		00320	Consent(s) to accept
Acabit	..	00321	Refuse(s) to accept
Acabronado		00322	Do you advise me (us) to accept
Acacian	...	00323	Advise you strongly to accept
Academia	...	00324	Do not advise you to accept
Academical		00325	Accept no liability
Academique		00326	Accept offer
Acagnarder		00327	Accept under protest
Acalonar	...	00328	Accept subject to approval of terms
Acampar	...	00329	Accept immediately—promptness imperative
Acamuzado		00330	Decline(s) to accept
Acanalado		00331	Believe——would accept
Acanchar	...	00332	Cannot accept until
Acantalear		00333	Cannot accept ——'s bills
Acanthe	...	00334	Cannot accept under any conditions
Acantonar		00335	Can you accept if
Acaponado		00336	Can I (we) accept
Acariatre	...	00337	Delay to accept conditions until you have seen ——
Acariciar	...	00338	If you can agree respecting —— accept at once
Acaulous	...	00339	If you are likely to accept telegraph
Acayoiba	...	00340	Instruct me (us) by telegraph if I (we) shall accept
Accablant	...	00341	I am (we are) unable to accept
Accadersi	...	00342	May I (we) accept on your behalf
Accaffare	...	00343	Must accept in full settlement
Accalorare		00344	Shall I (we) accept proposition
Accamparsi		00345	You should not accept without
Accanalare		00346	You (they) may accept
Accanire	...	00347	You had better accept offer if no probability of doing better
Accaparer	...	00348	Will not accept less than
Accappiare		00349	Will you (they) accept part payment in shares
Accarnare	...	00350	Will you (they) accept part payment in shares balance in cash
Accatteria	...	00351	You should not accept unless [payable on——
Accattone	...	00352	Do you (they) accept our terms
Acceder	...	00353	Cannot accept less than
Accennare	...	00354	Would be very likely to accept if offered
Accented	...	00355	Accept if you cannot do better
Accento	...	00356	Only accept if absolutely compelled
Accentual	...	00357	Telegraph (cable) whether likely to accept
Accepteur		00358	Are we bound to accept
Accertanza		00359	Bound to accept
Accertello	...	00360	I am (we are) not bound to accept

Accessare ...	00361	Do not accept unless (until)
Accessibly...	00362	Had I (we) not better accept
Accessit ...	00363	**Acceptance**
Accessoire...	00364	Cable acceptance at once
Acchetare ...	00365	Acceptance for —— honoured to-day
Acchinare ...	00366	By three months' acceptance
Acchindere	00367	By —— months' acceptance
Acciacco ...	00368	Subject to your acceptance before
Acciajuolo...	00369	Subject to my (our) acceptance before
Acciarino ...	00370	Acceptance doubtful
Acciarpare	00371	**Accepted**
Accidence ...	00372	Has (have) been accepted
Accidiato ...	00373	Has (have) not been accepted
Acciecare ...	00374	Will most likely be accepted
Accignersi...	00375	Not at all likely to be accepted
Accioche ...	00376	Provided that offer is accepted by
Accionista...	00377	Goods will not be accepted without certificate as to
Accismare	00378	If proposal is accepted telegraph (cable)
Acciuffare...	00379	Have not accepted on account of
Acciuga ...	00380	Proposition not accepted
Accivirsi ...	00381	Proposition accepted
Acclaimer ...	00382	Have accepted draft for ——
Acclamare...	00383	Terms accepted; documents lodged " in escrow "
Acclimater	00384	We (they) accepted under protest
Acclivity ...	00385	When is offer likely to be accepted
Acclivous ...	00386	Will be accepted subject to approval of ——
Accloyed ...	00387	Your offer has not been accepted
Accodato ...	00388	What liability have you accepted
Accogliere...	00389	ⱡ Telegraph (cable) whether accepted
Accolade ...	00390	**Access**
Accolarsi ...	00391	Easy of access
Accomanda	00392	Allow no one to have access to
Accommiare	00393	Am denied access
Accommoder	00394	Can you get access to
Accomplir ..	00395	Can I have access to
Accomunare	00396	Demand access on account of ——
Acconcezza	00397	If you cannot get access apply to ——
Accoppare...	00398	Vendor or Vendor's agents only to have access to workings
Accoratojo	00399	Formally demand access on account of ——
Accordanza	00400	Allow —— to have free access to workings
Accordeul ...	00401	Free access to workings underground must be given
Accordion ...	00402	**Accident**
Accordoir ...	00403	Cause of accident
Accorgere ...	00404	Cause of accident unknown
Accostable	00405	Owing to an accident at
Accoster ...	00406	Has met with a very serious accident
Accouple ...	00407	Fear accident will be fatal
Accourcir ...	00408	Accident was entirely due to
Accoutred...	00409	I (we) have just learned by accident that
Accoutume	00410	Am compelled to return on account of accident
Accovonare	00411	Accident not so serious as was thought
Accrescere	00412	Accident will cause —— days delay
Accrocher ...	00413	Accident to flume; machinery idle
Accroire ...	00414	Has any accident happened? Telegraph
Accroupir ...	00415	Accident happened to —— on ——; fear will be most serious
Accudire ...	00416	Met with an accident; not likely to be serious
Accueillir ...	00417	Mine stopped owing to accident in engine house
Accumbent	00418	—— drift stopped —— owing to accident in compressor house
Accumuler	00419	Mill idle owing to accident to
Accurato ...	00420	In case of accident

Accursed ...	00421	No delay will be caused by accident
Accusare ...	00422	Quite by accident
Accusateur	00423	Telegraph time required to repair accident
Accusatore	00424	The cause of the accident was found to be
Acebuchal...	00425	No accident whatever has occurred
Acechador...	00426	In the event of accident
Acedamente	00427	Accident at the mill
Acefalita .	00428	Accident at engine house
Acefalo ...	00429	Accident at the mine
Aceiterazo...	00430	**Accommodate**
Aceitunada	00431	To accommodate
Aceitunil ...	00432	Will accommodate
Acemilar ...	00433	Refuse(s) to accommodate
Acemile ...	00434	Consent(s) to accommodate
Acendrar ...	00435	If you do not accommodate
Acephalous	00436	Accommodate if possible
Acepillar ...	00437	Can you accommodate me (us)
Aceptador .	00438	You should not accommodate
Acequiado	00439	**Accommodation**
Acera ...	00440	Would be a considerable accommodation
Acerbetto ...	00441	Give —— all the accommodation you can
Acerbidad...	00442	Will give —— all the accommodation I (we) can
Acerbitv ...	00443	What accommodation is there for
Acercano ...	00444	Should there not be sufficient accommodation
Acerino ...	00445	There is ample accommodation for
Acerosus ...	00446	There is only accommodation for
Acertador ...	00447	It will be necessary to provide sufficient accommodation for
Aceruelo ...	00448	Decline(s) all accommodation
Acescent ...	00449	**Accompanied**
Acetabulo ...	00450	Do not go unless accompanied by ——
Acetify ...	00451	—— is accompanied by —— (his ——)
Acetimetry	00452	Must be accompanied by —— for the purpose of ——
Acetique ...	00453	You may be accompanied by
Acetone ...	00454	You should be accompanied by a reliable lawyer
Acetosilla ...	00455	I should be glad if I could be accompanied by
Acetrero ...	00456	**Accompany**
Achacoso ...	00457	To accompany
Achalande	00458	Arrange to accompany
Achaque ...	00459	Has (have) arranged to accompany
Acharner ...	00460	Unable to accompany .
Acharolar ...	00461	Should be very glad to accompany
Acheminer	00462	**Accomplish**
Acheteur ...	00463	To accomplish
Achevement	00464	It will be very difficult to accomplish
Achicador ..	00465	It will not be very difficult to accomplish
Achicoria ...	00466	So as to enable me (us) to accomplish it
Achievable	00467	Do you see your way to accomplish it (this)
Achispa ...	00468	How much will you be able to accomplish (by)
Achitto ...	00469	Have only been able to accomplish
Achtbar ...	00470	Will endeavour to accomplish
Achtelnote	00471	Expect to accomplish within next —— days
Achten ...	00472	Try your very best to accomplish this
Achtsam ...	00473	Difficult to accomplish on lines laid down
Achtzehn ...	00474	Cannot accomplish within the time
Achuchar ...	00475	Do you think you could accomplish
Acibarar ...	00476	If you cannot accomplish telegraph reason
Acicalador	00477	I hope to accomplish all within ——
Acides ...	00478	Could not accomplish it
Acidify ...	00479	**Accomplished**
Acidulate ...	00480	Have you accomplished

Aciduler ...	00481	How much has been accomplished
Acidulous	00482	Has (have) been accomplished
Acierie ...	00483	Has (have) not been accomplished
Acimboga...	00484	Can be accomplished (if)
Acinoso ...	00485	Can easily be accomplished within
Aciolein ...	00486	Has (have) readily accomplished
Acionero ...	00487	Will readily be accomplished
Ackerbau ...	00488	Cannot be accomplished except
Ackerland	00489	Cannot be accomplished until
Ackerzins	00490	This is now nearly accomplished
Aclarar ...	00491	**Accord**
Aclocado ...	00492	Am (are) quite in accord with——
Acobardar	00493	Am (are) quite in accord with your views
Acochinar...	00494	Am (are) not in accord with
Acodalar ...	00495	Are you (is——) acting in accord with
Acogedizo	00496	So that we may act in accord with each other
Acogollar ...	00497	Do not think we are likely to be in accord
Acogotado	00498	Does not at all accord with report received
Acolchar ...	00499	Does it accord with ——'s report
Acombar ...	00500	Refuse(s) to act in accord with me (us)
Acomodado	00501	**Accordance**
Acompamar	00502	Is not in accordance with
Acomunalar	00503	In accordance with
Acongojar	00504	Not quite in accordance with
Aconitic ...	00505	In accordance with agreement
Acopado ...	00506	In accordance with arrangement(s)
Acoplar ...	00507	In accordance with the understanding
Acoquiner	00508	In accordance with mining code
Acorchado	00509	In accordance with my (our) instructions
Acordaga ...	00510	In accordance with your instructions
Acordelar ...	00511	In accordance with his (their) instructions
Acornear ...	00512	Act strictly in accordance with
Acortadizo	00513	Why have you (they) not acted in accordance with
Acostado ...	00514	Have acted in accordance with
Acotillo ...	00515	Provided that——will agree to act in accordance with me (us)
Acoustics ...	00516	Now acting in accordance with
Acoustique	00517	Refuse(s) to act in accordance
Acquaccia	00518	Is not acting in accordance with
Acquaforte	00519	Are you acting in accordance with
Acquajuolo	00520	Am (are) not acting in accordance with
Acquatile ...	00521	Acting in strict accordance with
Acquavite...	00522	Is——acting in accordance with
Acquazzone	00523	——is acting in accordance with
Acquedotto	00524	**According(ly)**
Acquerella	00525	According to
Acquerir ...	00526	According to my (our) advices
Acquetare...	00527	According to all accounts
Acquidoso	00528	According to circumstances
Acquirente	00529	According to——'s plans and specifications
Acquisto ...	00530	According to reports everything favorable
Acquitrino	00531	Shall be guided accordingly
Acquolina...	00532	According to agreement
Acredine ...	00533	According to arrangement
Acremente	00534	**Account(s)**
Acribar ...	00535	Does (do) the account(s) include
Acrid ...	00536	All accounts will be settled on ——
Acriminar...	00537	The latest accounts show (state)
Acrimonie	00538	An account of
Acrisolar ...	00539	Very gradually on account of
Acritude ...	00540	Am (are) informed no account has been kept

Acrobato ...	00541	Accounts unreliable
Acronicto ...	00542	Accounts most encouraging
Acronycal	00543	Accounts very discouraging
Acrostiche	00544	Accounts overdrawn to the extent of——
Acrostico ...	00545	Accounts will be sent without unnecessary delay
Acrotera ...	00546	Please forward accounts for the year ending——of——
Acrylate ...	00547	Account(s) forwarded by mail
Acrylic ...	00548	Am (are) now making up accounts
Acryloid ...	00549	According to all accounts
Actionary ...	00550	The accounts are so involved as to be worthless
Actionner ...	00551	Accounts received, further details required with regard to
Actitud ...	00552	Accounts received
Activar ...	00553	Accounts very good
Activeness	00554	Accounts will be mailed on——
Actividad ...	00555	Accounts were mailed on——
Actriz ...	00556	Account sales of ore should be sent with least possible delay
Acttunes ...	00557	Accounts forwarded unsatisfactory. Further details required
Actuado ..	00558	The accounts are very misleading [respecting
Actuality ...	00559	Have presented account(s)
Actuante ...	00560	Open an account at
Actuario ...	00561	For our joint account
Acubado ...	00562	On joint account
Acuerdo ...	00563	On what account
Aculeate ...	00564	On account of advance
Acumbrar...	00565	Render final account(s)
Acuminato	00566	Render accounts up to (including ——)
Acumulacio	00567	Send account current
Acusable ...	00568	Send account current showing total disbursements
Acusativo ...	00569	Mail vouchers and account current up to
Acustica ...	00570	Have mailed vouchers and account current
Acutezza ...	00571	Mail account current from
Adacquare	00572	Account current
Adagiare ...	00573	Accounts for the current year
Adagietto...	00574	Account current for last month
Adagio ...	00575	Account current for this month
Adamado ...	00576	Account current to date
Adamant ...	00577	Will mail accounts and vouchers for month ending——on——
Adamantine	00578	Forward a duplicate of accounts by following mail
Adamascar	00579	Forward annual accounts at earliest moment possible
Adaptado...	00580	Accounts forwarded by——continue satisfactory
Adapter ...	00581	Accounts forwarded by——are not so satisfactory
Adaraja ...	00582	Account is already overdrawn by
Adargazo ...	00583	Has (have) overdrawn the account
Adasperare	00584	Has (have) overdrawn his (their) account
Adasprire...	00585	Has (have) not overdrawn the account
Adastarsi ...	00586	A very bad account of
Adatoda ...	00587	Awaiting accounts
Adattanza	00588	Should not be destroyed on any account
Addebilire	00589	Tell——on no account whatever to
Addecimare	00590	Accounts very incomplete
Addendum	00591	Am (are) without any account since
Adder ...	00592	Can you account for
Addestrare	00593	Employ competent auditors to examine accounts
Addiacente	00594	Forward accounts and cost sheets as promptly as possible
Addiction	00595	Have you any account of
Addiletto ...	00596	I (we) have opened an account with
Adding ...	00597	Several amounts appear in revenue account that should have [been charged to capital account
Addiren ...	00598	Has (have) discovered serious discrepancy in the accounts
Addiscere...	00599	I learn only an indifferent account of

Additatore	00600	On no account whatever
Addivenire	00601	On account of
Addled ...	00602	On account of the
Addobbato	00603	On whose account
Addogliare	00604	Not an account of the
Addolorare	00605	On your own account
Addomanda	00606	There is no account yet of
Addoparsi...	00607	The account current shows only a balance of ——
Addoppiato	00608	Cannot account for
Addormire	00609	Can only account for it on the supposition that
Addrieto ...	00610	To take charge of accounts
Adducere ...	00611	Who has charge of the accounts
Adduttore...	00612	—— has charge of the accounts
Adecuado ...	00613	Accounts urgently required
Adega ...	00614	Forward account sales of ore
Adeguare ...	00615	Accounts show a credit balance of
Adehala ...	00616	Accounts show a debit balance of
Adelanto ...	00617	In order to close all the accounts
Adelig ...	00618	Mainly on account of
Ademador...	00619	Partly on account of
Adempiere	00620	Have all the accounts been settled
Adenologia	00621	The accounts have all been settled
Adentellar	00622	The outstanding accounts amount to
Adenzione	00623	Please mail statement of accounts showing
Adeptuous	00624	Has (have) mailed statement of accounts on
Aderbare ...	00625	Will mail statement of accounts on ——
Aderezo ...	00626	You should open an account with ——
Aderig ...	00627	Your accounts must show
Aderlass ...	00628	You must inspect all accounts both at mine and at ——
Adescatore	00629	You must distinguish between revenue and capital account
Adestrar ...	00630	The last account was only up to ——
Adherent ...	00631	Serious omissions in the accounts
Adhesive ...	00632	How do you account for
Adiacenza...	00633	The account you have had is a complete fabrication
Adicion ...	00634	**Accountant**
Adiettivo ...	00635	As accountant
Adimarsi ...	00636	A competent and reliable accountant essential
Adinerado ..	00637	Can you recommend a reliable accountant
Adipocere ...	00638	May I (we) engage an accountant
Adipous ...	00639	You should engage an accountant at once
Adirato ...	00640	**Account(ed)**
Adissie ...	00641	Accounted for
Adivinado...	00642	Has (have) been accounted for
Adivinar ...	00643	Has (have) not been accounted for
Adjective ...	00644	Provided that the deficiency is accounted for
Adjoindre...	00645	Should the deficiency not be accounted for
Adjourning	00646	Accounted for by
Adjuger ...	00647	How is this (it) to be accounted for
Adjunto ...	00648	Can it be accounted for by
Adjuration	00649	Must be accounted for
Adjured ...	00650	Not yet accounted for
Adjustment	00651	Must be held accountable for
Adjutancy	00652	This is to be accounted for by
Adjutorio ...	00653	**Accumulate(d)**
Adjutrice ...	00654	Do not let —— accumulate
Adjuvant ...	00655	How much have you accumulated
Adlaboro ...	00656	I (we) shall allow concentrates to accumulate
Admetiate...	00657	Should have enough water accumulated by —— for a run of
Admettre ...	00658	Tailings have accumulated and stopped sluicing [—— days
Adminiculo	00659	Water accumulates slowly; not enough yet for a run

Admirable	00660	Better allow it (them) to accumulate for the present
Admiracion	00661	Had better not be allowed to accumulate
Admirador	00662	**Accumulating**
Admiral ...	00663	Has (have) been accumulating since
Admirante	00664	**Accumulation**
Admiration	00665	Cannot prevent accumulation of tailings
Admirative	00666	Have you any accumulation of
Admired ...	00667	There is no accumulation whatever
Admonester	00668	There is a great accumulation of
Admonitor	00669	As soon as there is sufficient accumulation
Adobado ...	00670	**Accuracy**
Adoberia ...	00671	Considerable want of accuracy
Adocchiare	00672	Have reason to doubt accuracy of——'s statement
Adocenado	00673	In ——'s report there is great want of accuracy
Adolescent	0C674	**Accurate**
Adombrare	00675	Is (are) perfectly accurate
Adonamento	00676	Not altogether accurate
Adonestare	00677	Do you consider ——'s report accurate
Adoniser ...	00678	Do not consider ——'s report accurate
Adontarsi...	00679	Strictly accurate
Adoperato...	00680	Please send accurate figures
Adoppiare...	00681	As nearly accurate as I (we) can give (it) them
Adoptador	00682	To be accurate
Adoptet ...	00683	Can I (we) regard it (this) as being accurately correct
Adoptiren...	00684	—— maintains the statement to be accurate
Adoptivo ...	00685	—— maintains that the statement is not accurate
Adorable ...	00686	—— in my hearing maintained the accuracy of statement
Adoracion...	00687	**Accusation**
Adorador ...	00688	There is (was) no truth whatever in the accusation
Adorateur...	00689	The accusation was proved
Adoratorio	00690	The accusation was only proved to the extent of
Adoratrice	00691	Accusation unfounded
Adorer ...	00692	Can you discover any truth in the accusation
Adormecido	00693	**Accused**
Adornanza	00694	Was (were) not accused of
Adornatura	00695	Has (have) been accused of
Adornezza	00696	Was (were) accused of —— but no proof was forthcoming
Adorno ...	00697	**Accustomed**
Adottativo	00698	Accustomed to
Adottatore	00699	Is he accustomed to
Adovrare ...	00700	Must be accustomed to
Adozione ...	00701	To be accustomed
Adquirir ...	00702	Has (have) always been accustomed
Adrento ...	00703	As soon as the men have become accustomed to
Adressant...	00704	Not yet accustomed to
Adressbuch	00705	**Acicular**
Adressiren	00706	**Acidic**
Adrieto ...	00707	**Acknowledge(s)**
Adroit ...	00708	To acknowledge
Adrubado...	00709	Please acknowledge this as soon as possible
Aduana ...	00710	Please acknowledge draft
Aduendado	00711	—— acknowledges to have
Adufero ...	00712	Have to acknowledge receipt of your letter dated ——
Aduggiare	00713	**Acknowledged**
Adujadas ...	00714	Letter posted from here on —— not yet acknowledged
Adulacion...	00715	Was (were) acknowledged on
Adulatore ..	00716	—— has (have) not yet acknowledged my letter (cable)
Adulatrice	00717	**Acknowledgment**
Adult ...	00718	Cannot get any acknowledgment from
Adulterant	00719	Have not yet received any acknowledgment from you of ——

Adulterio ...	00720	Has (have) received acknowledgment from
Adumbrate	00721	Give —— him (them) formal acknowledgment
Adunacion	00722	**Acquaint**
Adunamento	00723	To acquaint
Adunarsi ...	00724	Shall I (we) acquaint
Aduncity ...	00725	Do not acquaint
Adunghiare	00726	Better acquaint —— (him) (them)
Adunque ...	00727	Advise you to acquaint
Adustezza...	00728	**Acquainted**
Adustion ...	00729	Have acquainted
Adventaja...	00730	Have not acquainted
Adventual...	00731	Have you acquainted
Adverb ...	00732	Are you (is ——) acquainted with ——
Adverbial ...	00733	Can you get acquainted with ——
Adversario	00734	Must be perfectly acquainted with ——
Adversed ...	00735	Shall try and get acquainted with ——
Adversite ...	00736	Try and get acquainted with ——
Advertency	00737	**Acquiesce**
Advertido...	00738	Please cable whether you acquiesce in
Advizory ...	00739	Quite acquiesce in what you have done
Advocated	00740	Do not acquiesce
Advogado...	00741	Shall I (we) acquiesce
Advokat ...	00742	Provided that —— will acquiesce
Advowee ...	00743	Would acquiesce if
Advowson...	00744	**Acquiesced**
Adzed ...	00745	Has (have) acquiesced
Aebtissin ...	00746	Has (have) not acquiesced
Aederchen...	00747	Why has (have) —— not acquiesced
Aederig ...	00748	—— has (have) not acquiesced because of
Aefferei ...	00749	**Acquire**
Aehrenlese	00750	To acquire
Aeltern ...	00751	Am (are) able to acquire
Aeltlich ...	00752	Am (are) not able to acquire
Aendern ...	00753	Would it be well to acquire
Aengstigen	00754	It would not be well to acquire
Aequator ...	00755	It would certainly be judicious to acquire
Aergern ...	00756	To enable me (us) to acquire
Aerify ...	00757	Cable whether it is possible to acquire
Aerimante...	00758	To acquire a controlling interest
Aerimetria	00759	I (we) ought to acquire the right to
Aermel ...	00760	It would be very difficult to acquire
Aermlich ...	00761	Acquire all the knowledge you can respecting ——
Aerolite ...	00762	Acquire as quickly as possible controlling interest in
Aerometry	00763	By this purchase I (we) shall acquire
Aeronaut ...	00764	Must acquire controlling interest in [able property
Aeroscopy...	00765	We shall (you will) acquire to the best of my belief a most valu-
Aerostatic...	00766	What are the adjoining locations that we should acquire
Aesche ...	00767	Have reason to suspect —— of trying to acquire —— location
Aestig ...	00768	I (we) can strongly advise you to acquire the property
Aether ...	00769	Do you recommend —— to acquire
Aetzen ...	00770	**Acquired**
Afanador ...	00771	Have I (we) acquired
Afanoso ...	00772	Have acquired
Afatuccio ...	00773	Have not acquired
Afectacion	00774	Property to be acquired is of small actual value
Afectador ...	00775	Property to be acquired has considerable prospective value
Afectillo ...	00776	Can be acquired for
Afectivo ...	00777	Can be acquired if you wish it
Afectuoso ...	00778	Can be acquired at present time without much difficulty
Afelpado ...	00779	Provided that I (we) have acquired

Aferrado ...	00780	The adjoining locations could be acquired at a cost of
Affability ...	00781	Should be acquired at once
Affacciare ...	00782	Has (have) already acquired
Affadir ...	00783	**Acquisition**
Affaiblir ...	00784	Not much of an acquisition
Affaitato ...	00785	A very valuable acquisition
Affaldare ...	00786	By no means a desirable acquisition
Affamare ...	00787	It is a very desirable acquisition
Affamen ...	00788	Do you recommend the acquisition of
Affangare ...	00789	Cannot recommend the acquisition of
Affannato ...	00790	I (we) feel sure it will prove a very desirable acquisition
Affannone ..	00791	**Acquit**
Affascare ...	00792	Do you acquit —— of all blame
Affaticare ...	00793	Acquit you of all blame
Affectueux	00794	Can acquit —— entirely
Affegatare...	00795	**Acquitted**
Affermato...	00796	Likely to be acquitted
Affermer ...	00797	Is (are) not likely to be acquitted
Afferrare ...	00798	Was acquitted on —— of ——
Affeterie ...	00799	Has (have) —— been acquitted
Affetto ...	00800	Has (have) been acquitted
Affettuoso ..	00801	**Acre(s)** (See also " Area.")
Affezione ...	00802	How many acres
Affiance ...	00803	The property covers —— acres
Affibbiare ...	00804	Am offered —— acres additional for dumping
Affichage ...	00805	A total of —— acres
Affidarsi ...	00806	—— acres covered with
Affiggere ...	00807	—— acres consist of
Affilatura ...	00808	There are —— acres of forest
Affilier ...	00809	There are —— acres of farming land
Affinato ...	00810	**Acreage** (See also " Area.")
Affinche ...	00811	What is the total acreage of the property
Affineur ...	00812	The total acreage of the property is
Affiocare ...	00813	Can acquire a total acreage of
Affiquets ...	00814	What is the total acreage proposed to be sold
Affirmeth ...	00815	What is the additional acreage required
Affitatore ...	00816	**Across**
Affixment ...	00817	Right across
Afflamare ...	00818	Have you come across
Affleurer ...	00819	I (we) came across
Affliceas ...	00820	Might across the ——
Affliche ...	00821	**Act**
Afflictus ...	00822	To act
Afflizione ...	00823	Act as per instructions
Affluenza ...	00824	Act as soon as you receive this
Affluer ...	00825	Do not act until you have seen ——
Affogate ...	00826	Act as you think best
Affollato ...	00827	Act without delay
Affourche ...	00828	Act with caution
Affragnere	00829	Act according to agreement
Affralire ...	00830	Act on my (our) behalf
Affranchi ...	00831	Act in concert with ——
Affrappare	00832	Can I (we) act
Affreteur ..	00833	Do not act until —— is with you
Affrettate ...	00834	For whom do you (they) act
Affrettoso ...	00835	Get legal advice before you act
Affriander...	00836	—— will not act unless he is (they are) guaranteed as to ——
Affright ...	00837	Please advise me (us) how I (we) shall act
Affrioler ...	00838	Provided that you act at once
Affrontare ..	00839	To enable me (us) to act promptly

Affubler ...	00840	Delay no longer, act
Affumicato	00841	You must act promptly
Affuori ...	00842	Are you (is——) in a position to act promptly
Affuscare ...	00843	Have received your dispatch too late to act upon
Affusolato	00844	Act as quickly as you can
Affutage ...	00845	Did you act
Afianzar ...	00846	Did not act on account of
Aficion ...	00847	Could not act
Aficionar ...	00848	Could not act on account of your limit
Afilado ...	00849	Do not act hastily
Afincable ...	00850	Decline(s) to act
Afinidad ...	00851	Decline(s) to act as suggested
Afirmar ...	00852	Should —— decline to act as suggested
Afirmeth ...	00853	Act as per my (our) letter of
Afistoler ...	00854	As soon as you receive cable act
Aflamar ...	00855	Cable if he (they) will act
Aflicto ...	00856	He (they) cannot act
Afligir ...	00857	Will act on my (our) behalf
Aflorado ...	00858	Would you be willing to act in capacity of
Afollado ...	00859	Would not be willing to act in capacity of
Afondar ...	00860	Would be quite willing to act in capacity of
Aforrador...	00861	It will be necessary to act promptly in order to avoid
Afortunado	00862	I (we) propose to act for the present simply as
Afrailar ...	00863	As soon as you (they) decide how to act
Afrenta ...	00864	Should act accordingly
Afretar ...	00865	It is very urgent that I (we) should act at once
Afronitro ...	00866	Consent(s) to act
Afrontar ...	00867	Refuse(s) to act
Afterages	00868	—— will not act unless indemnified
Aftercrop...	00869	If you can withdraw the act do so
Aftermath	00870	It will be necessary to act very discreetly
Afterpacht	00871	**Acted**
Afterpains	00872	Has (have) not acted according to promise
Afterpeice...	00873	I (we) do not think that you have acted altogether wisely in
Afterwit ...	00874	I (we) think that you have acted wisely
Afuera ...	00875	I (we) consider that you have acted precipitately
Afumada ...	00876	Wish you had acted otherwise
Agacant ...	00877	Has (have) acted very
Agacement	00878	Has (have) acted exceedingly well
Agacerie ...	00879	Acted entirely in good faith
Agalibar ...	00880	Has (have) not acted in good faith
Agalla ...	00881	Has (have) not acted very discreetly
Agalluela...	00882	**Acting**
Agamitar ...	00883	Can I (we) incur legal expense before acting
Aganippe ...	00884	Proceed with caution in acting with
Agapeti ...	00885	Telegraph who you are acting for
Agaping ...	00886	Telegraph who is acting on behalf of
Agarbado...	00887	You are acting rightly
Agarbanzar	00888	You are acting wrongly
Agarico ...	00889	—— is acting as manager
Agarrar ...	00890	I am (we are) acting for
Agasajo ...	00891	**Action**
Agasonis ...	00892	Speedy action required
Agatara ...	00893	Have you (has ——) commenced action
Agavanza...	00894	Has (have) not yet commenced action
Agencer ...	00895	Threaten(s) legal action
Agenciar ...	00896	Action already commenced
Agenzia ...	00897	Cable what action you wish me (us) to take
Agestado ...	00898	When is action likely to be heard
Agevolare...	00899	Action is postponed until ——

Agevote ...	00900	Action is fixed for hearing on ——
Aggaffare...	00901	Have you (they) commenced action
Aggecchire	00902	Should you (they) commence action
Agghiadare	00903	As yet —— has (have) taken no action
Aggiacere...	00904	Action withdrawn on ——
Aggiogato	00905	Abandon action
Aggiornare	00906	Before taking any action consult ——
Aggirarsi ...	00907	Commence action for damages
Aggiugnere	00908	Cannot get action postponed
Agglomerer	00909	Cannot withdraw the action
Aggradire...	00910	Endeavour to avoid an action at law
Aggrandize	00911	Endeavour to get action postponed
Aggraver ...	00912	Has (have) commenced action for damages against us
Aggressor...	00913	I (we) approve of the action you (they) have taken
Aggrezzare	00914	If you can withdraw the action do so
Aggroppato	00915	Is it possible to effect a compromise of action
Aggrumato	00916	On account of the action of ——
Agguaglio	00917	Stop action
Agguerrito	00918	Should like to consult —— before taking action
Agguindolo	00919	Suspend further action ; instructions posted on ——
Aghast ...	00920	The action you have taken is not approved of
Agherbino	00921	Advise you to defend the action
Aghetta ...	00922	You must defend the action
Aghiaccio...	00923	Defend action
Agiamina...	00924	You had better take action at once
Agibilibus	00925	What action shall I (we) take
Agile... ...	00926	What action do you (does ——) propose to take
Agilidad ...	00927	By this action I (we) shall own
Agiliter ...	00928	Did you get desired action
Aginator ...	00929	**Actionable**
Agiotage ...	00930	The offence is an actionable one
Agioteur ...	00931	**Active(ly)**
Agiotiren ...	00932	Have not yet actively begun to
Agitable ...	00933	Shall begin actively
Agitandus	00934	This work should be actively proceeded with
Agitateur...	00935	Work is being actively proceeded with
Agitatus ...	00936	All works now actively in progress
Agitazione	00937	**Act of Parliament**
Aglette ...	00938	Acts of Parliament
Aglowing ...	00939	Certified copies of Acts of Parliament by Queen's printers
Agnails ...	00940	Send certified copies of Acts of Parliament
Agnation ...	00941	Certified copies of Acts of Parliament by Queen's printers
Agneau ...	00942	Have copies of Acts of Parliament been mailed [mailed on
Agnelet ...	00943	Copies of Acts of Parliament have been mailed
Agnellino ...	00944	Copies of Acts of Parliament will be mailed on
Agnocasto	00945	**Actual**
Agnomen ...	00946	What are the actual facts
Agobiare ...	00947	The actual facts are
Agognatore	00948	Cannot ascertain what the actual facts are
Agonisant	00949	**Adapt(ed)**
Agonism ...	00950	Specially adapted for
Agonistic ...	00951	Not well adapted for
Agonizar ...	00952	Is (are) not adapted for
Agonizing	00953	Only adapted for
Agonizzare	00954	Not at all adapted for
Agony ...	00955	**Add**
Agoreria ...	00956	To add
Agostar ...	00957	To add to
Agostino ...	00958	It will be necessary to add
Agraceno ...	00959	Can you (they) add to

Agraciar ...	00960	Unable to add to at present
Agradable	00961	I (we) shall thus add largely to
Agradecer...	00962	Will add largely to
Agrafer ...	00963	Expect to add largely to
Agramente	00964	It will be necessary to add largely to
Agranadera	00965	**Addition**
Agrandir ...	00966	Bring in addition to —— the following, viz. :—
Agranilar ..	00967	In addition to
Agrarian ...	00968	What addition have you made to
Agraticum	00969	The only addition made is
Agravador	00970	Has (have) not made any addition
Agrazada ...	00971	Will it be in addition to
Agregativo	00972	It will not be in addition to
Agrestic ...	00973	Will it cause an addition to our (your) expenses
Agrestume	00974	It will be an addition to my (our) expenses of
Agricole ...	00975	The addition will be very small
Agricultor	00976	The addition will be considerable
Agridulce...	00977	Do not at present advise any addition
Agrifoglio	00978	Would suggest in addition that
Agrimonia	00979	Require in addition
Agriotta ...	00980	Some small additions
Agripalina	00981	For small addition(s) allow say ——
Agrisetado	00982	We only require additions
Agronomia	00983	**Additional**
Agropila ...	00984	Additional expense
Agrostis ...	00985	Send additional information respecting —— by letter
Agrume ...	00986	Send additional information respecting —— by cable
Agrupar ...	00987	Provided it does not entail any additional expense
Agrypnias	00988	For additional work
Aguacero ...	00989	For additional improvement(s)
Aguacil ...	00990	**Address**
Aguada ...	00991	The address you require is
Aguaderas	00992	Following address is sufficient
Aguadocho	00993	Shall I (we) give your address to ——
Aguaitador	00994	You can give my (our) address to ——
Aguaitar ..	00995	Do not give my (our) address to ——
Aguamanos	00996	Keep me (us) informed of any change in your address
Aguamiel ...	00997	Address all letters to
Aguanafa ...	00998	Have not as yet found —— at address given
Aguanoso ..	00999	Cable the present telegraphic address of ——
Aguantar ...	01000	Address given incorrect, have not yet been able to communicate
Aguardo ...	**01001**	My (our) address is [with —— can you make suggestion
Aguarras ...	01002	My (our) cable address is care of —— at ——
Aguarsi ...	01003	Telegraph me (us) your address at
Aguastare	01004	Write full postal address of ——
Aguatocha	01005	Write full telegraphic address of ——
Aguazal ...	01006	Telegraph full postal address of ——
Agucchiare	01007	——'s postal address is care of —— at ——
Agudeza ...	01008	My (our) cable address is
Agudillo ...	01009	Let me know your permanent cable address
Aguerrido	01010	Telegraph ——'s address, letters addressed to —— have been
Aguglia ...	01011	**Addressed** [returned
Aguila ...	01012	How was (were) cable(s) addressed
Aguileno ...	01013	Cable(s) was (were) addressed as follows
Aguinaldo	01014	How was (were) letter(s) addressed
Aguisar ...	01015	Letter(s) was (were) addressed as follows
Aguishness	01016	Was (were) insufficiently addressed
Agunentare	01017	**Adequate**
Agunto ...	01018	What would you consider an adequate remuneration
Aguretero	01019	Consider an adequate remuneration

Aguron ...	01020	Remuneration named not considered adequate
Agusanarse	01021	Should this remuneration not be considered adequate
Agustino ...	01022	By no means sufficiently adequate
Agutello ...	01023	Do not consider it adequate
Aguzadera	01024	Do you (they) consider it (this) will be adequate
Aguzanieve	01025	I (we) do not consider it will be adequate
Aguzar ..	01026.	Is it of adequate power
Aguzonazo	01027	Is of adequate power
Aguzzatore	01028	Is not of adequate power
Aguzzino ...	01029	Not sufficiently adequate
Ahebrado ...	01030	Sufficiently adequate
Ahenipes ...	01031	**Adhere(s)**
Aheurter ..	01032	To adhere
Ahijado ...	01033	To adhere to
Ahilarse ...	01034	Do you (they) (does——) still adhere to
Ahilo ..	01035	Do(es) not now adhere to
Ahincote ...	01036	Still adhere(s) to
Abitera ...	01037	I (we) cannot adhere to
Ahnen ...	01038	You (they) must adhere to
Ahmundan	01039	You (they) should not adhere to
Ahnung ...	01040	——will not adhere to
Ahocinarse	01041	Cable whether you (they) can adhere to
Ahogadero	01042	Provided that you (——) adhere(s) to
Ahojar ...	01043	I (we) (——) adhere(s) firmly to what has been already stated
Ahombrado	01044	I (we) adhere to my (our) original statement
Ahondar ...	01045	Do you adhere to your original statement
Ahorcado ..	01046	I (we) also adhere to
Ahorcadura	.01047	Do not adhere to
Ahormar ...	01048	**Adhered**
Ahorn ...	01049	Must be adhered to
Ahorrado ...	01050	Has (have) always adhered to
Aborrativo	01051	Must be adhered to or I (we) shall be placed in a false position
Ahossic ...	01052	Has (have) never really been adhered to
Ahuchador	01053	Division must be adhered to
Ahumada...	01054	**Adit** (*See also* "Level.")
Aiglon ...	01055	Adit level
Aigrefin ...	·01056	Old adit
Aigrelet ...	01057	New adit
Aigrement	01058	Adit driven during —— month —— feet
Aigremoine	01059	Adit is —— in length
Aigrette ...	01060	—— feet below adit
Aiguiere ...	01061	—— feet above adit
Aiguillon ...	01062	From adit
Aiguiser ...	01063	Proposed deep adit will be —— feet in length
Aijada ...	01064	Adit is driven upon the vein
Aileron ...	01065	Adit intersects the vein at a distance of —— feet
Aillade ...	01066	What are the dimensions of the adit
Ailleurs ...	01067	Dimensions of the adit are ——
Aimant ...	01068	Adit is well timbered and laid with —— rails
Airballs ...	01069	Adit requires no timbering whatever
Airboat ...	01070	Adit requires but little timbering
Aircellate...	01071	Old adit has entirely caved in [——feet
Aircushion	01072	Adit is now in——feet. Driven for the month ending——
Aireado ...	01073	Adit intersects vein——feet below outcrop
Airecico ...	01074	Telegraph present length of adit [in feet
Airguns ...	01075	Telegraph present length of adit and rate of driving per month
Airholing ...	01076	By the intersection of the vein by the deep adit the available backs
		[will be increased by —— feet
Airily ...	01077	Workings consist simply of an adit driven to intersect vein
Airiness ...	01078	**Adjoin(ing)**

Airless	...	01079	I (we) advise purchase of adjoining location(s) namely ——
Airosidad	.	01080	If time permits write fully your reason for suggesting [increased outlay on adjoining claim(s)
Airoso	...	01081	The mine adjoins
Airplant	...	01082	The adjoining property(ies) [name(s) of which is (are) ——
Aisance	...	01083	Vein(s) traverse(s) the adjoining location(s) to the —— the
Aisdur	...	01084	Which is (what are) the adjoining property(ies) you refer to
Aislado	...	01085	Near the adjoining claim(s)
Aisles	...	01086	**Adjourn**
Aismoll	...	01087	To adjourn
Aissare	...	01088	Has (have) decided to adjourn
Aisselle	...	01089	Consent(s) to adjourn
Aitorio	...	01090	Refuse(s) to adjourn
Aizoon	...	01091	Should —— be induced to adjourn
Ajada	...	01092	**Adjourned**
Ajamiento		01093	Has (have) been adjourned for —— days
Ajedrez	...	01094	Has (have) been adjourned until
Ajenabe	...	01095	Do all you can to get case adjourned
Ajesuitado		01096	Will do all I (we) can to get case adjourned
Ajicola	...	01097	Could you get case adjourned until
Ajillo	...	01098	Has (have) arranged for case to be adjourned —— days
Ajimez	...	01099	Has (have) arranged for case to be adjourned until
Ajobar	...	01100	The matter cannot be adjourned
Ajofaina	...	01101	Can only be adjourned on the understanding that
Ajonc	...	01102	If adjourned would be very serious; try to prevent
Ajonjera	...	01103	Will try to prevent being adjourned
Ajoqueso	...	01104	**Adjust**
Ajornalar	...	01105	To adjust
Ajourner	...	01106	How do you (they) propose to adjust
Ajudiado	...	01107	Propose to adjust by
Ajudicare	..	01108	To enable me (us) to adjust
Ajudo	...	01109	How will you adjust
Ajustado	...	01110	Can you not adjust matters with —— (them)
Ajustar	...	01111	**Adjusted**
Ajustement		01112	Cannot the affair be adjusted in some way
Ajutarsi	...	01113	Cannot be adjusted
Ajutatore	...	01114	Is (are) now being adjusted
Ajutervole		01115	As soon as it (this) has been adjusted
Ajutrice	...	01116	Consider would be satisfactorily adjusted by
Akademish		01117	Has (have) not been adjusted
Akenium	...	01118	Do not see how the matter could be adjusted without
Akimbo	...	01119	**Administered**
Aktie	...	01120	Estate is now being administered by
Akustisch	...	01121	**Administrator(s)**
Alabado	...	01122	By the administrators of the estate
Alabanza	...	01123	Acting for the administrators of his (——'s) estate
Alabarda	...	01124	Administrator(s) consent(s) to
Alabaster	...	01125	Administrator(s) refuse(s) to
Alabastrum		01126	To enable administrator(s)
Alabega	...	01127	Provided that administrator(s) will
Alabetis	...	01128	Should administrator(s) refuse
Alabiado	...	01129	**Admission**
Alacran	...	01130	Should I (we) grant admission to
Alacranera		01131	Cannot grant admission
Alacribus	...	01132	Refuse(s) admission to all
Alacrity	...	01133	Can grant admission to
Aladares	...	01134	**Admit**
Aladierna	...	01135	To admit
Aladrada	...	01136	Do you (they) admit
Aladro	...	01137	Do(es) not admit anything of the sort

Alafiante ...	01138	Take care not to admit
Alaga ...	01139	Does ——'admit
Alagadizo...	01140	—— only admit(s) that
Alagariado	01141	Does not admit anything
Alaica ...	01142	You (they) must admit
Alajor ...	01143	Am (are) willing to admit
Alamaima	01144	Is (are) ready to admit
Alamar ...	01145	May go so far as to admit
Alambicado	01146	Better not admit
Alambique	01147	Admit no liability(ies)
Alambre ...	01148	—— admit(s) being in the wrong
Alameda ...	01149	Do(es) not admit of delay
Alamina ...	01150	I (we) do not admit
Alamire ...	01151	May I (we) admit —— to see mine and works
Alamparse	01152	Will not admit

Advance(s)

Alancear ...	01153	
Alanguir ...	01154	To advance
Alanina ...	01155	Do not advance from
Alano ...	01156	At an advance
Alantine ...	01157	At an advance of
Alanzar ...	01158	As soon as present advance(s) has (have) been repaid
Alarbe ...	01159	Consent(s) to advance
Alardear ...	01160	Refuse(s) to advance
Alargador...	01161	—— refuse(s) to make any further advance(s)
Alargama ...	01162	Provided that you (they) will advance say
Alarguez ...	01163	Expect(s) —— will advance
Alaridant ...	01164	Is there likely to be any advance in
Alarife ...	01165	There is not likely to be any advance
Alarmbell...	01166	Advance imminent
Alarmega ...	01167	Am (are) not prepared to advance more (than)
Alarmiren...	01168	What are you willing to advance
Alarmist ...	01169	Cannot advance owing to
Alaterno ...	01170	Cannot advance more
Alatore ...	01171	Could you advance matters personally
Alatron ...	01172	Do not make any further advance to ——
Alaun ...	01173	Endeavour to advance matters all you can
Alavanco ...	01174	Has (have) arranged the advance of cash required
Alazon ...	01175	I (we) do not see that I (we) could advance matters much
Albacete ...	01176	Must have an advance of ——
Albada ...	01177	Must limit advance to ——
Albagioso...	01178	Must not advance more than
Albanega ...	01179	No further advance has taken place in the price of
Albanil ...	01180	Shall require an advance of —— before ——
Albaquia ...	01181	Telegraph terms upon which you can get an advance of ——
Albarant ...	01182	Endeavour to get an advance (of)
Albarazo ...	01183	Owing to the advance in
Albardado	01184	The advance has been
Albardent...	01185	The advance has not been
Albarderia	01186	The advance made with works is very considerable
Albardon ...	01187	The advance made with works is very small
Albarejo ...	01188	Will advance
Albarillo ...	01189	Will not advance more than
Albarrada...	01190	Will —— advance anything
Albatara ...	01191	—— will advance cash required
Albatoza ...	01192	Will —— advance —— for examination and report on property
Albatre ...	01193	Unless you can advance matters
Albazano ...	01194	Must have an advance of —— on account of ——
Albear ...	01195	Shall be able to advance
Albedine ...	01196	In order to advance [will send
Albedrio ...	01197	Should you require an advance of money, cable, and I (we)

[20]

Albeggiare	01198	Am (are) willing to advance an additional
Albeitar ...	01199	Am (are) not willing to advance additional funds
Albenda ...	01200	**Advanced**
Albengala	01201	Has (have) advanced
Alberca ...	01202	Has (have) not advanced
Alberchiga	01203	Price(s) of——has (have) advanced
Albercocca	01204	Has (have) been advanced
Alberella ...	01205	Has the bank advanced amount
Alberetto ...	01206	Bank has advanced amount
Albergador	01207	Bank has not advanced amount
Albergue ...	01208	**Advantage**
Alberino ...	01209	For our mutual advantage
Albern ...	01210	Is it to my (our) advantage
Alberquero	01211	It is to my (our) advantage
Albescent ...	01212	It is not to my (our) advantage
Albesian ...	01213	Will any advantage be gained by
Albicante ...	01214	No advantage would be gained by
Albihar ...	01215	The only advantage gained by
Albillote ...	01216	Unless there is a decided advantage
Albino ...	01217	A small advantage
Albitana ...	01218	A considerable advantage
Albitrare ...	01219	Has (have) a great advantage over
Albogue ...	01220	Is there any advantage in
Alboheza ...	01221	I (we) consider there is no advantage
Alborada ...	01222	The advantage would be that
Alborear ...	01223	The advantage would be mutual
Alborga ...	01224	What is the advantage of (to)
Albornia ...	01225	Would there be any advantage
Albornoz ...	01226	What advantage will accrue
Alborocera	01227	Will it be any advantage to——
Alboroque	01228	It would be to my (your) (our) advantage
Alborotado	01229	Take advantage of
Albotin ...	01230	**Adventurer(s)**
Albrin ...	01231	At a meeting of the adventurers
Albruiar ...	01232	A party of mining adventurers
Albucum ...	01233	Adventurers have decided
Albudeca ...	01234	Adventurers have not decided
Albugo ...	01235	Have adventurers decided
Albulus ...	01236	**Advertise**
Albumen ...	01237	To advertise
Albures ...	01238	Shall I (we) advertise
Alcabala ...	01239	Better advertise at once for
Alcabor ...	01240	I (we) await your permission to advertise for
Alcacel ...	01241	Before you (they) advertise for
Alcachofa ...	01242	Should advertise for
Alcaduz ...	01243	Should not advertise for
Alcahest ...	01244	Why not advertise
Alcaico ...	01245	**Advertised**
Alcaidia ...	01246	I (we) have advertised for
Alcalde ...	01247	Have not advertised for
Alcalino ...	01248	Has (have) advertised
Alcam ...	01249	Has (have) been advertised for sale since
Alcance ...	01250	Have you yet advertised for
Alcandara ...	01251	Why have you not advertised
Alcandial ...	01252	Have advertised ; replies unsatisfactory
Alcanfor ...	01253	Have advertised and received the following replies
Alcanzado...	01254	Has (have) advertised ; so far no result
Alcaparra ...	01255	Has (have) advertised ; the result is
Alcaravan ...	01256	**Advice(s)**
Alcarcena ...	01257	By advice of

Alcarmes	01258	By whose advice
Alcatifa	01259	Apply to —— for advice
Alcatriz	01260	Do not apply to —— for advice
Alcaudon	01261	Shall I (we) apply to —— for advice
Alcedon	01262	Legal advice
Alchemist	01263	Procure best legal advice
Alchimie	01264	You had better have legal advice at once
Alcino	01265	Have secured legal advice
Alcobilla	01266	What is your (——'s) advice
Alcohol	01267	My (our) (——'s) advice is
Alcoholate	01268	Consult with —— and take his advice
Alcoholera	01269	Have consulted with ——, his advice is
Alcoholise	01270	What are the latest advices respecting
Alcoran	01271	Are advices from the property satisfactory
Alcornocal	01272	Advices from the property are very satisfactory
Alcovo	01273	Advices from the property are not satisfactory
Alcrebite	01274	When may I (we) expect advices regarding
Alcribis	01275	May expect advices about ——
Alcubilla	01276	Do not expect further advices until
Alcunotta	01277	Advices are generally unsatisfactory
Alcurnia	01278	Advices are more encouraging
Alcuzado	01279	Advices are most encouraging
Aldaba	01280	Latest advices are to the effect that
Aldabear	01281	No advice(s) received since ——
Aldeano	01282	No advice as yet respecting
Aldebaran	01283	Last advice(s) is (are)
Aldehydo	01284	Are your advices by mail favourable
Alderman	01285	Advices received —— distinctly favourable
Aldizo	01286	Advices received from —— slightly discouraging
Aldran	01287	Advices received from —— altogether discouraging
Aleador	01288	**Advisability**
Aleatoire	01289	As to the advisability of
Alebrewer	01290	**Advisable**
Alebrias	01291	Not advisable
Alechigar	01292	Most advisable
Aleconner	01293	It is very advisable that
Alectoria	01294	It cannot be advisable
Aledano	01295	It might be advisable to
Alefris	01296	Do you (does ——) consider it advisable
Alegar	01297	I (we) do not consider it advisable to
Aleggere	01298	I (we) consider it very advisable
Alegorico	01299	Should you (——) consider it advisable
Alegria	01300	As soon as it may be advisable
Alehoof	01301	It is not advisable for the present
Alehouse	01302	Provided that it is advisable
Alema	01303	Consider it very advisable at once to ——
Alemanisco	01304	Do not consider it advisable to do it (this) at present
Alembic	01305	Have you acted altogether advisably
Alenamento	01306	It will soon be advisable to
Alenguar	01307	It was considered advisable to
Alentado	01308	**Advise(s)**
Alentour	01309	Do not advise
Aleonado	01310	Do not advise that
Alepardo	01311	Do not advise it
Alerce	01312	Do not advise you to
Alerione	01313	Did you advise
Alertar	01314	What would you advise
Alertness	01315	Advise me (us) immediately
Alesnado	01316	Continue to advise
Aletada	01317	Continue regularly to advise me (us) as to

Aletear	...	01318	Do you still advise that we should obtain
Alevats	...	01319	Advise you to
Alevosa	...	01320	To advise
Alfabeto	...	01321	What do you (does ——) advise
Alfagia	...	01322	I (we) should advise its
Alfahar	...	01323	I (we) should advise
Alfalfa	...	01324	Can you advise anything
Alfana	...	01325	I (we) should not advise you to
Alfanjazo	...	01326	I (we) should advise you to accept
Alfaque	...	01327	I (we) strongly advise you to keep clear of ——
Alfardon	...	01328	If any alteration takes place advise me (us) at once
Alfarero	...	01329	Hope to be able to advise you within —— days of the result of
Alfeizar	...	01330	Advise you strongly to
Alfenicado		01331	Continue to advise by cable
Alfenique	...	01332	Please advise —— as to
Alferecia	...	01333	Do not see how I (we) can advise under present circumstances
Alfiere	...	01334	**Advised**
Alfoli		01335	Has (have) been advised by
Alfombra	...	01336	Has (have) not been advised by
Alfombrero		01337	Who advised you to
Alfoncigo	...	01338	Who has advised you respecting it (this)
Alfondega	...	01339	Do you know who advised —— (him)
Alfonsina	...	01340	Keep me (us) well advised as to progress
Alforja	...	01341	Keep me (us) well advised respecting
Alforjilla	...	01342	Has (have) already advised
Algalaba	...	01343	Am (are) advised that
Algaliar	...	01344	Unless you are otherwise advised
Algarabia	...	01345	—— advised on —— that he had ——; is this correct
Algarade	...	01346	Correct as advised
Algarroba		01347	**Aerial**
Algazara	...	01348	Aerial ropeway
Algebra	...	01349	By means of an aerial ropeway —— ft. long
Algebraist	...	01350	The only method is by means of an aerial ropeway
Algendum	...	01351	Cost of aerial ropeway would be say
Algensis	...	01352	**Affair(s)**
Algerine	...	01353	What is the state of affairs
Algidus	...	01354	General state of affairs is
Algificus	...	01355	Better not interfere in ——'s affairs
Algosum	...	01356	A settlement of affairs
Alholva	...	01357	A most unfortunate affair
Alhorma	...	01358	It could never become a large affair
Alhostigo	...	01359	Is it likely to become a large affair
Aliacan	...	01360	It is likely to become a large affair
Aliagar	...	01361	Is it a large affair
Alianza	...	01362	Present state of affairs
Aliarse	...	01363	Political affairs unsettled
Alibilis	...	01364	The whole affair is utterly disorganized
Alicaido	...	01365	The whole affair is but small
Alicante	...	01366	The affair must be considered at an end
Alicastrum		01367	Affairs are in a very bad state
Alicatado	...	01368	Affairs have gone from bad to worse
Alidada	...	01369	State of affairs improving [imminent
Alidamente		01370	Affairs have considerably improved; bankruptcy no longer
Alieggiare	...	01371	Unless affairs should considerably improve
Alienabile	...	01372	I (we) consider you have handled the affair well
Alienarsi	...	01373	I (we) do not consider you have handled the affair well
Alienatore	...	01374	**Affect**
Aliento	...	01375	To affect
Alifar	...	01376	Will it (this) affect
Aligaiate	...	01377	It will affect

Aligerar ...	01378	It will not affect
Alighting ...	01379	It will not affect me (us)
Alignement	01380	It may affect
Alijarero ...	01381	Should it affect
Alilla ..	01382	What will it affect
Alimentar ...	01383	Who will it affect
Alimony ...	01384	Will affect price(s)
Alindado ...	01385	Will not affect price(s)
Alinde ...	01386	Will affect proposed purchase
Alinear ...	01387	Will not affect proposed purchase
Alionin ...	01388	Provided that it does not affect
Aliquant ...	01389	It does not affect
Aliquot ...	01390	It is not likely to affect
Alisador ...	01391	It is almost certain to affect
Alisadura ..	01392	I (we) do not see how it can affect me (us) at all
Alisma ...	01393	So long as it does not affect
Alistado ...	01394	Bound to affect sooner or later
Alituoso ...	01395	Before it has time to affect
Aliveloce ...	01396	Does it affect
Aliviador	01397	Does your letter contain anything likely to affect
Alivio ...	01398	**Affected**
Alizier ...	01399	Has (have) been affected
Aljadrez ...	01400	Has (have) not been affected
Aljama ...	01401	Considerably affected
Aljerife ...	01402	Not affected in the slightest
Aljibero ...	01403	Very seriously affected
Aljofar ...	01404	**Affidavit(s)**
Aljofifa ...	01405	It will be necessary to file an affidavit
Aljuba ...	01406	It will not be necessary to file an affidavit
Alkaline ...	01407	Will it be necessary to file an affidavit
Alkoven ...	01408	The affidavit should state
Allabor ...	01409	The affidavits stated
Allacciare...	01410	Did the affidavit(s) state
Allacrimus	01411	The affidavit(s) did not state
Allagare ...	01412	Would —— swear an affidavit
Allaiter ...	01413	Would swear an affidavit
Allanador ...	01414	Decline(s) to swear an affidavit
Allargando	01415	Sworn affidavit(s) mailed
Allariz ...	01416	Has affidavit been made
Allarmare...	01417	Has affidavit of labour been filed
Allattante...	01418	We must have an affidavit showing
Allaudant...	01419	Affidavit received
Allavorare	01420	Send properly legalised affidavit
Allda ...	01421	**Affirmative**
Alleanza ...	01422	Can you (they) answer in the affirmative
Allecher ...	01423	Endeavour to get answer in the affirmative
Alleficare ...	01424	In case I (we) receive an affirmative answer
Allegador ...	01425	Reply is affirmative
Allegans ...	01426	Is your reply affirmative
Allegement	01427	Provided that your reply is affirmative
Allegiant ...	01428	**Afford**
Allegorize...	01429	To afford
Allegory ...	01430	How much can you (they) (——) afford
Allegresse...	01431	Can afford
Allegretto .	01432	Can only afford to
Alleguer ...	01433	I (we) cannot afford to
Allein ...	01434	Can you (——) afford the time to inspect
Alleluia ...	01435	Cannot afford the time
Allemal ...	01436	This will afford a capital opportunity for ——
Allende ...	01437	Would it afford any opportunity for ——

Allenire ...	01438	**Afraid**
Allentato ...	01439	I am (we are) afraid
Allenzare ...	01440	I am (we are) not afraid
Aller ...	01441	What are you afraid of
Allerdings	01442	Why are you afraid to
Allerhand	01443	Unless you are afraid to
Allestire ...	01444	There is no reason at all to be afraid
Allevatore	01445	I am (we are) only afraid to
Alleviare ...	01446	Not afraid in the slightest of
Allezeit	01447	Provided that you do not feel afraid
Allezza ...	01448	Quite afraid to
Allgemein...	01449	**After**
Allgewalt ...	01450	After allowing for
Allgutig ...	01451	This is after deducting
Allhier ..	01452	This is not after deducting
Allibbito ...	01453	Is this after deducting
Allibrare ..	01454	After sending my (our) letter
Alliderent...	01455	After sending my (our) cable
Allievarsi ...	01456	After what has been done
Allievo ...	01457	After what has taken place
Alligate ...	01458	After you have seen ——
Allinguato	01459	After you have heard from
Allisciare ...	01460	**Afterdamp**
Allium ...	01461	Owing to the afterdamp
Allividare...	01462	On account of the presence of afterdamp
Allmacht ...	01463	Progress greatly impeded by afterdamp
Allobroge ...	01464	**Afternoon**
Alloccare ..	01465	Each afternoon
Allocutio ...	01466	Only in the afternoon
Allodetta ...	01467	This afternoon
Allodiale ...	01468	To-morrow afternoon
Allodola ...	01469	Yesterday afternoon
Allogatore	01470	Not until the afternoon
Alloggeria	01471	**Again**
Allogliato	01472	Again as soon as you can
Allonger ...	01473	Am (are) unable to go again
Allopathe...	01474	Am (are) unable to see —— again
Allophylus	01475	Endeavour to see —— again
Allorino ...	01476	Has (have) been again to
Allouette ...	01477	Has (have) not been again to
Allourdir ...	01478	Has (have) again
Alloyage ...	01479	Has (have) risen again
Alloyed ...	01480	Has (have) not risen again
Alloza ...	01481	I (we) shall not again
Allspice ...	01482	I am (we are) again
Allubesco ...	01483	It is useless again to attempt it
Alluciare ...	01484	Is not likely to be offered again
Alludel ...	01485	Is —— likely to be offered again
Alludente...	01486	Is again likely to be offered for sale
Allumatore	01487	—— is again in the market
Allume ...	01488	It must not occur again
Alluminare	01489	Must go again to
Allungato...	01490	Ought to see —— again with reference to
Allupare ...	01491	See —— again as soon as possible
Allured .	01492	Working(s) is (are) again
Allusive ...	01493	Pumps have again given way
Alluvius ...	01494	Until I (we) hear again from
Allylene ...	01495	Until you hear again from
Allylic ...	01496	Shall not do so again
Almacen ...	01497	Shall not be allowed to happen again

Almacenero	01498	Is not likely to happen again
Almacigar	01499	Should it happen again you had better
Almadia ...	01500	**Against**
Almadiero	01501	Against my (our) wishes
Almadina ...	01502	Do not act against the advice of ——
Almadreno	01503	Proceed at once against ——
Almagacen	01504	Shall I (we) proceed against
Almagesto	01505	I (we) shall have —— against me (us)
Almagral ...	01506	You will do so against my (our) advice
Almaizal ...	01507	**Agent(s)**
Almanach	01508	Employ as agent(s)
Almanaque	01509	The agent(s) is (are)
Almancebe	01510	Can you (——) suggest reliable agent(s)
Almanguena	01511	I (we) would advise you to appoint —— as your agent(s)
Almarada ...	01512	Is it necessary to appoint an agent
Almario ...	01513	It is necessary to appoint an agent
Almastiga	01514	Have you an agent at
Almatrero	01515	Has (have) —— an agent at ——
Almatriche	01516	My (our) agent(s) is (are)
Almazara ...	01517	Only an agent; cannot act in the absence of principal
Almear ...	01518	——'s agent is absent
Almecina ...	01519	Only acting as agent
Almejia ...	01520	Only acted as agent
Almena ...	01521	**Aggregate(d)**
Almendra ...	01522	To aggregate
Almendrero	01523	Have aggregated
Almendrica	01524	Aggregated together
Almendron	01525	Aggregated with
Almenilla ...	01526	In the aggregate
Almibar ...	01527	**Agree**
Almidon ...	01528	If you (they) do not agree to this
Almidonado	01529	If you (they) do not agree to this come over at once
Almidonero	01530	Agree with you on all points
Almighty ...	01531	I (we) quite agree with ——
Almiraglio	01532	I (we) do not agree with ——
Almirez ...	01533	To agree
Almocafre	01534	Can you agree to
Almocati ...	01535	Cannot agree
Almocrate...	01536	Will —— agree to
Almodrote	01537	Will agree (to)
Almogama	01538	Will not agree to
Almohadon	01539	Shall agree (to)
Almohatre	01540	I (we) do not agree to
Almohazar	01541	You ought to agree
Almond ...	01542	In case —— will not agree
Almonedear	01543	Waiting for —— to agree to
Almoner ...	01544	Agree(s) to the proposition
Almoronia	01545	Agree(s) to all demands
Almorrefa...	01546	Agree(s) to all that is essential
Almorzador	01547	Do not agree with —— unless —— concur(s)
Almosen ...	01548	If I (we) agree to your (their) proposition will you agree to
Almotacen	01549	Will you (——) agree to (this) [reduction of
Almshouse	01550	Agree to everything except
Almudada	01551	Cannot agree as to
Almudi ...	01552	If you (they) cannot agree
Almuerza ...	01553	Shall I (we) agree to what they ask
Aloaria ...	01554	Shall (I) we agree to terms stated
Alobunado	01555	Do you (they) agree to terms of our letter of ——; if so, cable
Alodial ...	01556	Cannot agree to the terms of your ——
Aloes ...	01557	I (we) agree to your proposition provided time extended to

Aloetical ...	01558	I (we) agree to your proposal
Alogiatis ...	01559	Do you agree to deduction of
Alojero ...	01560	Vendor(s) agree(s) to reduction of——
Alomado ...	01561	Vendor(s) agree(s) to take —— in fully-paid shares [bond
Aloncillo ...	01562	Write fully the conditions upon which you (they) will agree to
Alondra ...	01563	Cable essential conditions upon which you will agree to bond
Aloof ...	01564	Quite agree with what you suggest
Alopecia ...	01565	Quite agree with you, except respecting
Aloquin ...	01566	While I (we) agree with you, think it would be better that
Alosna ...	01567	**Agreed**
Alotar ...	01568	Has (have) agreed to
Alpaca ...	01569	Has (have) not agreed to
Alpanata ..	01570	Have you (has——) agreed to
Alpechin ...	01571	Has (have) agreed to refer the matter to
Alpenhorn	01572	You should not have agreed to
Alpestre ...	01573	Should you not have already agreed to
Alphabet ...	01574	Have agreed provisionally
Alpigiano ...	01575	Have agreed subject to your concurrence
Alpistero ...	01576	**Agreement**
Alquanto ...	01577	Provisional agreement
Alqueria ...	01578	Draft agreement
Alquermes	01579	Pending definite agreement
Alquez ...	01580	According to agreement
Alquicel ...	01581	Not according to agreement
Alquilon ...	01582	Has (have) signed preliminary agreement
Alquimia ...	01583	Is agreement signed
Alquimista	01584	Agreement was signed on——
Alquinal ...	01585	When do you expect to get agreement signed
Alquitira ...	01586	Expect to get agreement signed on
Alquitran	01587	Provided that the agreement has not already been signed
Alrededor	01588	As soon as agreement is signed telegraph
Alrota ...	01589	Can you get —— to cancel agreement
Alsbald ...	01590	Do not on any account enter into a formal agreement
Alsdann ...	01591	Has (have) violated —— clause. Consider agreement cancelled
Alsine ...	01592	If you accept terms formal agreement can be sent by mail
Altabaque	01593	If you can enter into a special agreement
Altalena ...	01594	It is not in accordance with the agreement
Altamisa ...	01595	Original agreement signed and mailed to-day ; duplicate will be
Altan ...	01596	What was the agreement as regards [sent on——
Altaneria ...	01597	The agreement was that I (we) should
Altarcloth	01598	The agreement was that —— should
Altarello ...	01599	Please mail copy of agreement to
Altarico ...	01600	No actual agreement was ever signed
Altarpiece	01601	Was there any legal agreement as to
Altarwise ...	01602	There was no written agreement whatever as to
Alterar ...	01603	Prepare agreement and post in duplicate without delay
Alterateur	01604	Solicitors object to signing agreement [abstract of title
Alterativo...	01605	Send with draft agreement full complete and attested copy of
Altercador	01606	Submit proposed agreement to —— who is (are) my (our) [solicitor(s) in ——
Altercasti ...	01607	Terms of proposed agreement unacceptable ; writing fully
Alterigia ...	01608	As per my (our) agreement
Alterim ...	01609	According to the original agreement
Altern ...	01610	Agreement shall be sent for your signature
Alternar ...	01611	Was (were) bound by the agreement to
Alterthum	01612	Is an undoubted violation of my (our) agreement
Altesse ...	01613	Makes the agreement null and void
Alteza ...	01614	Will release me (us) from my (our) agreement
Altezzoso ...	01615	Can you release me (us) from my (our) agreement
Altgeige ...	01616	The original agreement was fraudulent

[27]

Alticcio ...	01617	Violation of agreement [with —— bank " in escrow "
Altimetro .	01618	Three copies of agreement will be required as one must be lodged
Altisono ...	01619	When will agreement be ready for signature
Altissimo ..	01620	—— is (are) willing to enter into an agreement
Altista ...	01621	Previous to signing agreement
Altitonans	01622	So as to fulfil agreement with
Altitudine	01623	Do not consider my (our) agreement binding
Altivarse ...	01624	Consider my (our) agreement binding so long as
Altivo ...	01625	My (our) agreement is binding
Altobasso ..	01626	**Aid**
Altoclef ...	01627	To aid
Altoviola ...	01628	Do not aid
Altozano ...	01629	Would it aid me (us) to
Altramente	01630	Would materially aid me (us) to (if)
Altrettale ...	01631	Would aid me (us) very little if at all
Altricem ...	01632	You could materially aid by
Altroche ...	01633	Can I (we) aid
Altstimme	01634	You could aid at this juncture by
Altura ...	01635	**Air**
Altutto ...	01636	Air machine
Altzeichen	01637	Air very foul
Alucinar ...	01638	On account of bad air
Aludel ...	01639	Air pipe(s)
Aluene ...	01640	Air hose
Alufrar ...	01641	Slight accident to air compressor will delay us —— days
Alumbrador	01642	Air compressor
Alumbre ...	01643	Send new —— for air compressor [tion
Aluminis ...	01644	Can only drive another —— feet before we must rise for ventila-
Alumno ...	01645	Shall utilise winze in —— level as an air shaft
Alunado ...	01646	I am (we are) prevented from working at —— on account of
Alusion ...	01647	Air compressor working most satisfactorily [bad air
Alveario ...	01648	Air compressor not working very satisfactorily
Alveolate ...	01649	Air pipes are now completed down to
Alveole ...	01650	I am (we are) much hindered with foul air
Alveum ...	01651	**Airway(s)**
Alvino ...	01652	Airways considerably diminished by
Alzada ...	01653	Airways completely blocked by
Alzadera ...	01654	Must improve airways
Alzamento	01655	As soon as I (we) have completed improvements to airways
Alzando ...	01656	**Aitchpiece** (*See also* " Pumps.")
Alzapano ...	01657	Aitchpiece for
Alzar ...	01658	**Alarm**
Amabilatis	01659	Do not alarm
Amabile ...	01660	**Alarmed**
Amabilidad	01661	Do not be alarmed, no matter what you may hear
Amabilita ...	01662	**All**
Amable ...	01663	Remit all you can
Amacena ...	01664	Send all the news you can
Amadoner	01665	Is it all you have
Amador ...	01666	I (we) have sent all I (we) can
Amadriada	01667	**Allege(d)**
Amaestrado	01668	Do you (does ——) allege
Amaestrar	01669	—— has alleged that you
Amagar ...	01670	Cable what has been alleged
Amaigrir ...	01671	Has (have) alleged that
Amainar ...	01672	Is it alleged that
Amaitinar...	01673	It is alleged that
Amajadar...	01674	It is not alleged that
Amalgama	01675	What has been alleged
Amamantar	01676	**Allot(ted)**

Amamblucea	01677	Has (have) allotted
Amancebado	01678	Has (have) not allotted
Amancillar	01679	Are the shares allotted
Amandatis	01680	The shares are all allotted
Amandus ...	01681	—— shares have not yet been allotted
Amanecer ...	01682	How many shares have been allotted to me (us)
Amanerado	01683	—— shares have been allotted to you
Amanojar ...	01684	When will the shares be allotted
Amansador	01685	Shares will probably be allotted about
Amansar ...	01686	Shares will be allotted on
Amantia ...	01687	—— has been allotted —— shares
Amantillo ...	01688	I (we) have applied for —— shares, but only wish —— to be
Amanuense	01689	**Allotment** [allotted
Amanza ...	01690	When will the allotment be made
Amapola ...	01691	Allotment will be made on ——
Amaracino	01692	No allotment has been made
Amaraco ...	01693	No allotment whatever will be made
Amarame ...	01694	Pending allotment of shares
Amaranthus	01695	What is the amount due on allotment
Amaranto ...	01696	Amount due on allotment is —— per share
Amaresco ...	01697	Please pay amount due on allotment
Amarefacio	01698	Will pay amount due on allotment
Amarevole	01699	Has (have) paid amount due on allotment
Amarezza ...	01700	Allotment to be made to me (us) or my (our) nominees
Amargaleja	01701	Letters of allotment were posted on ——
Amargoso...	01702	Letters of allotment will be posted to-night (on ——)
Amarguillo	01703	Letters of allotment and regret will be posted to-night
Amargura...	01704	Letters of allotment and regret were posted on —— [(on——)
Amaricado	01705	The Company is not likely to go to allotment
Amarillazo	01706	Will join the Board after allotment
Amarillejo	01707	Your application was too late for allotment
Amarillez ...	01708	**Allow** *(See also " Allowed.")*
Amarissimo	01709	To allow
Amarognolo	01710	To allow for
Amarore ...	01711	Should you allow
Amarrido ...	01712	Should you not allow
Amartelar	01713	Allow —— per cent. discount
Amartillar	01714	Allow —— per cent. rebate
Amasadera	01715	Allow no discount or any deduction whatever
Amasador...	01716	Can I (we) allow
Amasadura	01717	Do not allow any discount
Amasar ...	01718	How much shall I (we) allow
Amasijo ...	01719	How much do (did) you allow
Amasium ...	01720	How much will you (they) allow
Amatorio ...	01721	I (we) should not allow
Amatrice ...	01722	I (we) should like to allow
Amauris ...	01723	I (we) did not allow for travelling expenses
Amazona ...	01724	In order to allow
Amazorcado	01725	Cannot allow more than
Ambages ...	01726	Ought to allow at least
Ambagioso	01727	Have you (they) decided what to allow
Ambara ...	01728	Have decided to allow
Ambarilla...	01729	Have not decided to allow
Ambarino...	01730	In order to allow workmen to
Ambarvalia	01731	In order to allow miners to
Ambasceria	01732	Impossible to allow
Ambassade	01733	Unable to allow
Ambederas	01734	Why did you (they) allow
Ambedue ...	01735	You may allow
Ambergris	01736	You (they) (——) must allow

Ambesas ...	01737	You (they) (——) must not allow
Ambicio ...	01738	Do not allow it (them)
Ambicionar	01739	**Allowance**
Ambidens ...	01740	Making no allowance for
Ambidexter	01741	Make full allowance for [corrected to the extent of
Ambiente ...	01742	No allowance was made for ——, ——'s estimate must be
Ambigebas	01743	Allowance is too large
Ambiguedad	01744	Allowance is very fair
Ambiguo ...	01745	Allowance is too small
Ambiquita	01746	What do you (they) consider a reasonable allowance
Ambitieux...	01747	What allowance have you (they) made for
Ambiviun ...	01748	I (we) have made an allowance of —— for
Ambizioso...	01749	I (we) have made no allowance for
Amblador ...	01750	With an allowance of —— for travelling expenses
Ambladura	01751	Exclusive of allowance for
Ambleo ...	01752	Inclusive of allowance for
Ambligonio	01753	Make every allowance necessary for
Ambliopia...	01754	Had previously made an allowance of —— for
Ambonis ...	01755	An increased allowance
Amboss ...	01756	Cannot make any increased allowance
Ambra ...	01757	You need not make any allowance for
Ambracan...	01758	Ample allowance should be made for
Ambretta ...	01759	Some allowance will have to be made for
Ambrogina	01760	**Allowed**
Ambrollar...	01761	Have you (they) allowed for
Ambrosiano	01762	Has (have) allowed —— for
Ambrosius	01763	Have allowed —— for
Ambrotype	01764	Provided that this has not already been allowed for
Ambsace ...	01765	Already allowed for
Ambulante	01766	Was (were) not allowed for
Ambulating	01767	If this has (these have) not been already allowed for
Ambulatory	01768	Has (have) not already been allowed for
Ambuscade	01769	Has (have) already been allowed for
Ambush ...	01770	Have you allowed for ——
Ambushment	01771	I (we) have not allowed for it
Ambustione	01772	Must be allowed for
Amebeo ...	01773	Something must be allowed for
Amedrentar	01774	What have you allowed for
Ameise ...	01775	**Allowing**
Amelgado ...	01776	After allowing for
Ameliorer ...	01777	After allowing for all expenditure in connection with
Amellus ...	01778	**Alloy**
Amelo ...	01779	An alloy of
Amelonado	01780	Employ(s) an alloy of
Amenaza ...	01781	Suggest that you employ an alloy of
Amenazador	01782	Ascertain composition of alloy
Amender ...	01783	The composition of alloy is
Amendune	01784	**All right**
Amenes ...	01785	No need to fear, matter(s) will be all right
Amenguar	01786	Is everything all right
Amenidad ..	01787	Everything is all right
Amenity ...	01788	**Alluvial** (*See also* " Hydraulic," " Gold.")
Amenizar ...	01789	The alluvial contains diamonds
Amentaceo	01790	Alluvial deposit(s) occur(s) on the property
Amentans ...	01791	Alluvial is payable
Amentum ...	01792	Alluvial is worthless
Amenuiser	01793	Test the alluvial [of bed rock to be —— ft.
Amerar ...	01794	Area covered by alluvial —— acres, I (we) judge average depth
Amercement	01795	Alluvial contains——dwts. per cubic yard but water for sluicing [is only available —— months in the year

Amercer ...	01796	There are—— acres of alluvial. By trial pits have proved depth to average —— ft. By hand washing should yield when sluiced —— per cubic yard
Amerimnon	01797	What is the value of the alluvial [to —— month, both inclusive
Amerina ...	01798	Water for sluicing the alluvial is only available from——month
Amertume	01799	We shall commence working on the alluvial at once
Amesitis ...	01800	**Alluvium**
Ametalado	01801	**Almost**
Amethyst ...	01802	I (we) think vendor(s) has (have) almost decided to accept
Ameublir ..	01803	It is almost unheard of
Ameuloner	01804	The vein has almost disappeared
Amfibio ...	01805	The ore has almost come to an end
Amfractum	01806	Our capital is almost expended, practise greatest economy
Amia ...	01807	**Along**
Amianto ...	01808	Along the outcrop
Amicabilis	01809	Along the boundary
Amicamente	01810	Along the hangingwall
Amicarsi ..	01811	Along the footwall
Amichevole	01812	Along the adit
Amicizia ...	01813	Along the drive
Amicus ...	01814	Along the No. —— level
Amidon ..	01815	Along the face of the drive
Amidonnier	01816	I am (we are) now driving along
Amiga ...	01817	I am (we are) now driving along it (the)
Amigable ...	01818	**Alphabetical**
Amigdale ...	01819	In alphabetical order
Amigote ...	01820	Send alphabetical list of
Amiguillo ...	01821	Alphabetical list mailed on
Amillarar ...	01822	Not in alphabetical order
Amillonado	01823	Must it (this) be in alphabetical order
Amimar ...	01824	Should be in alphabetical order
Amincir ...	01825	Need not be in alphabetical order
Amiserabat	01826	**Already**
Amissurus	01827	If already decided
Amistad ...	01828	Already decided
Amistanza...	01829	Already completed
Amistoso ...	01830	Already talking of
Amitini ...	01831	I think we are already near the vein
Amitinorum	01832	How much have you completed already
Amito ...	01833	Spots of ore show that we are already approaching ore body
Amittendus	01834	I (we) have begun already to
Ammaccare	01835	I (we) have already driven —— feet
Ammagrire	01836	I (we) have already completed
Ammainare	01837	**Also**
Ammajato...	01838	Also as regards
Ammaliato	01839	Also as to
Ammansato	01804	Also particulars of
Ammarcire	01841	To enable —— also
Ammassarsi	01842	Provided that you (they) also
Ammattito	01843	Provided that —— is (are) also willing
Amme ...	01844	When —— will also
Ammenda...	01845	Is (are) also
Ammenstube	01846	Has (have) also
Ammettere	01847	**Alter**
Ammiccare	01848	To alter
Amminicolo	01849	Please alter
Amminutare	01850	Am (are) unable to alter
Ammiraglio	01851	Can I (we) alter
Ammirando	01852	Can you alter
Ammirativo	01853	Do not alter unless obliged

Ammisurato	01854	I (we) should like to alter
Ammitto ...	01855	I (we) propose to alter
Ammium ...	01856	It has been necessary to alter
Ammodytes	01857	If needful you must alter
Ammoinare	01858	This will materially alter
Ammollato	01859	I (we) have been obliged to alter
Ammollire	01860	**Alteration(s)**
Ammoniacus	01861	Several alterations
Ammoniate	01862	Making several alterations
Ammonitore	01863	What alteration(s) has (have) been made
Ammonitrum	01864	Have made several alterations
Ammorbare	01865	Have not made any essential alteration(s)
Ammortato	01866	What alteration(s) would you suggest
Ammoscire	01867	What alteration(s) do you consider necessary
Ammovere	01868	I (we) suggest the following alteration(s)
Ammuffare	01869	I (we) think the following alteration(s) is (are) àbsolutely
Ammuricare	01870	But little alteration is required in order to [necessary
Ammusarsi	01871	Was received too late to make any alteration
Ammutinato	01872	To enable me (us) to make necessary alteration(s)
Ammutolire	01873	Pending completion of alterations
Amnacibus	01874	Any alteration would mean increased cost
Amnestie ...	01875	I (we) hope no important alteration(s) will be necessary
Amniculus	01876	I (we) have made no alteration whatever
Amnigenus	01877	Is (are) any alteration(s) essentially needful
Amnion ...	01878	No alteration has occurred in
Amnistia ...	01879	No alteration in price need be apprehended
Amodita ..	01880	Observe closely any alteration in
Amodorrado	01881	Great alteration(s) has (have) taken place
Amogotado	01882	Some alteration is necessary with regard to
Amohecerse	01883	Telegraph what is the alteration in price
Amohinar ...	01884	The alteration in the character of the rock renders progress
Amoindrir...	01885	Alteration has given rise to great friction [slower
Amojamado	01886	The alteration(s) mean(s) greater economy
Amojonar ...	01887	Postpone alteration(s) until
Amoladera	01888	**Alternative**
Amolador ...	01889	Can you (they) suggest any other alternative
Amolar ...	01890	I (we) suggest as an alternative
Amolior ...	01891	I (we) have no other alternative but to
Amolitio ...	01892	The only other alternative is
Amolletado	01893	The only alternative I (we) know is
Amomo ...	01894	Is there no other alternative
Amonceler	01895	There is no other alternative
Amonestar	01896	The latter alternative
Amontarse	01897	The first alternative
Amontonar	01898	The second alternative
Amonxe ...	01899	The third alternative
Amoraccio...	01900	The —— alternative
Amoras ...	01901	Which alternative
Amoratado	01902	Which alternative do you (does ——) mean
Amorcer ...	01903	In the word —— which alternative do you mean
Amorcillo ...	01904	In the word —— I (we) mean the first alternative
Amoretto ...	01905	In the word —— I (we) mean the second alternative
Amorevole	01906	In the word —— I (we) mean the third alternative
Amorgado ..	01907	In the word sent by you I (we) mean the first alternative
Amorio ...	01908	In the word sent by you I (we) mean the second alternative
Amoriscado	01909	In the word sent by you I (we) mean the third alternative
Amorosello	01910	**Although**
Amoroso ...	01911	Although I (we) have
Amorously	01912	Although I (we) have not
Amorphous	01913	Although he (——) has

Amortajar	01914	Although he (——) has not
Amortiguar	01915	**Altitude**
Amortizar...	01916	On account of the high altitude
Amoscar ...	01917	The altitude is —— feet
Amoscina ...	01918	The mine is situated —— feet above the sea level
Amotina ...	01919	**Altogether**
Amotinador	01920	Is altogether out of the question
Amouracher	01921	If taken altogether
Amourette	01922	Must be taken altogether
Amoureux	01923	**Alum**
Amous ...	01924	Alum stone
Amovebat...	01925	Alum schist
Amovendus	01926	The Alum schist contains —— per cent. of Alumina
Amover ...	01927	**Alumina**
Amovible ...	01928	Silicate of Alumina
Amoxyl ...	01929	Sulphate of Alumina
Amparador	01930	**Aluminium**
Ampelidis...	01931	—— per cent. of Aluminium
Ampelita ...	01932	Aluminium bronze
Ampelos ...	01933	Aluminium bronze containing —— per cent. of aluminium
Amphibian	01934	**Always**
Amphibious	01935	You (they) (——) should always
Amphibolic	01936	Always if possible
Amphigouri	01937	I (we) always do so
Amphimacer	01938	I (we) always
Amphippi...	01939	As often as possible, if not always
Amphitane	01940	So long as you always
Amphitryon	01941	**Amalgam** (*See also* "Retort.")
Amphoralis	01942	—— ozs. of amalgam
Amplabatur	01943	Gold amalgam
Amplamente	01944	Silver amalgam
Amplectens	01945	Have retorted amalgam, yields —— ozs. retorted gold
Amplesso ...	01946	Forward —— lbs. solid sodium amalgam
Ampleur ...	01947	Sodium amalgam, solid, forwarded on
Amplexans	01948	Shall retort amalgam on ——
Amplexor ...	01949	The yield is—— ozs. of amalgam, or say —— ozs. retorted gold
Ampliacion	01950	**Amalgamate**
Ampliador	01951	Is (are) trying to compel us to amalgamate
Ampliativo	01952	Could amalgamate properties
Amplificar	01953	Wish to amalgamate; am (are) writing full particulars
Amplio ...	01954	The gold is "rusty" and difficult to amalgamate
Amplissime	01955	The gold amalgamates readily
Amplitud ...	01956	**Amalgamated**
Ampolla ...	01957	Are amalgamated together
Ampolleta...	01958	Have amalgamated with
Ampolloso	01959	The two firms are now amalgamated
Ampolluzza	01960	It is rumoured are already amalgamated
Ampoule ...	01961	**Amalgamation**
Amputantor	01962	Electro-silvered copper plates are required for amalgamation
Amputar ...	01963	Ore base, amalgamation can only be effected in pans
Amputating	01964	Require amalgamation pan(s) —— feet diameter [wide
Amputiren	01965	Send electro-silvered copper plates —— ft. long and —— inches
Amsanctus	01966	**Amalgamator** [amalgamator? Name salary
Amthaus ...	01967	Can you recommend for —— a competent millman and
Amtlick ...	01968	Competent millman and amalgamator will leave on ——
Amtmann	01969	Must have a competent amalgamator
Amtsaltar...	01970	Do you (does ——) know a good amalgamator engagement ——
Amtsbote ...	01971	**Ambiguous** [years; salary —— per annum
Amtsbuch...	01972	Your (——'s) cable is too ambiguous
Amtseid ...	01973	Your (——'s) letter is too ambiguous

Amtseifer ...	01974	**Amended**
Amuchiguar	01975	Can be amended
Amueblar ...	01976	Cannot be amended
Amugerado	01977	If can be amended
Amugronar	01978	But can be amended
Amularse ...	01979	But cannot be amended
Amulatedo	01980	If cannot be amended
Amuleto ...	01981	Cable whether can be amended
Amurcario	01982	**Amendment**
Amurco ...	01983	Suggest as an amendment that
Amusette ...	01984	Amendment was proposed by
Amusgar ...	01985	Amendment was carried by a majority of
Amusive ...	01986	Amendment was defeated by a majority of
Amygdale	01987	Amendment to —— has been adopted
Amylaceous	01988	**Among**
Amylare ...	01989	Among which
Amylon ...	01990	You will find it among
Amystis	01991	Is (are) not among
Anabaptism	01992	Would it be among
Anabasius	01993	**Amorphous**
Anabatista	01994	**Amount(s)**
Anacalifa ...	01995	Amounts to
Anacarado	01996	What is the amount
Anacardel ..	01997	What is the gross amount
Anacardina	01998	The gross amount is
Anachorete	01999	What is the net amount
Anacoluth...	02000	The net amount is
Anaconda ...	**02001**	Half the amount
Anacoreta	02002	Two-thirds of the amount
Anacosta ...	02003	Twice the amount
Anadear ...	02004	The total amount is
Anadematis	02005	What does it really amount to
Anadino ...	02006	Does not amount to much
Anadiplosi	02007	Find out what is the amount due to
Anadir ...	02008	The whole thing only amounts to
Anadon ...	02009	The amount at present in hand
Anafaya ...	02010	The ore in hand amounts to
Anafora ...	02011	Telegraph what amount
Anagalide ..	02012	Only a small amount available
Anagaza ...	02013	A large amount has already been lost
Anagiris ...	02014	A large amount will be saved
Anaglifo ...	02015	Amount(s) to —— tons
Anagnoste	02016	What is the largest amount
Anagoge ...	02017	This amount
Anagogico	02018	Large amount
Anagrama	02019	Small amount
Analectris ..	02020	Explain cause of large amount (of)
Analejo ...	02021	What is the amount owing
Analepsia...	02022	Cable what amount (if any) you have in hand belonging to me
Analeptico	02023	Such amount to be deducted from [(us)
Anales ...	02024	When it amounts to ——
Analetti ...	02025	Does it amount to ——
Analista ...	02026	Cable at once amount required
Analitico ...	02027	What amount do you require in addition
Analizador	02028	The amount due on —— for wages is
Analizar ...	02029	The amount due on —— is
Analogia ...	02030	The future amount is very uncertain
Analogical	02031	Can you (they) increase amount
Analogique	02032	Cannot increase amount
Analogised	02033	Can you (they) decrease amount

[34]

Analogismo	02034	Cannot decrease amount
Analogizar	02035	Endeavour to increase amount
Analogue ...	02036	Endeavour to decrease amount
Analytica ...	02037	Only a small amount
Ananciten...	02038	The exact amount is ——
Anapaestus	02039	What is the exact amount
Anapelo ...	02040	What amount of concentrates have you on hand
Anaquel ...	02041	Total capital is £ —— of which amount £ —— is for working
Anaranjado	02042	Total amount of capital is £ —— [purposes
Anarchique	02043	Will not amount to more than a trifle
Anarquico...	02044	Amount not yet paid is
Anasarca ...	02045	What is the amount not yet paid
Anascote ...	02046	**Amounting**
Anastrofe ...	02047	Amounting to
Anatema ...	02048	**Ample**
Anaticula ...	02049	Would be ample
Anatinorum	02050	What do you (does ——) consider would be ample
Anatocismo	02051	I (we) consider that —— would be ample
Anatomia ...	02052	Ample time must be allowed for inspection and report
Anatomical	02053	Ample for all legitimate purposes
Anatomista	02054	Must get in an ample supply for the winter
Anaudiam...	02055	This is considered ample
Anavajado	02056	Time allowed considered ample
Anbeginn ...	02057	I (we) have an ample supply of
Anbei	02058	I (we) have ample funds
Anbellen ...	02059	**Amygdaloid**
Anbequemen	02060	**Analysis**
Anbetung ...	02061	The analysis is as follows
Anbieten ...	02062	Analysis gives
Anbinden ...	02063	Certificate gives the following analysis in 100 parts
Anblasen ...	02064	Complete analysis should be made
Anblick ...	02065	Send analysis of accounts
Anbloken ...	02066	Analysis of accounts mailed
Anbrechen	02067	Sample should be analysed for
Anbringen	02068	The analysis gives only a trace (of)
Anbruch ...	02069	Telegraph if result of analysis is good
Anbrullen...	02070	What is the result of the analysis
Ancado ...	02071	**Ancient**
Ancajone ...	02072	Can you discover any ancient workings
Ancalites ...	02073	Ancient workings are all caved in; very dangerous
Ancestor ...	02074	There are plenty of evidences of ancient workings
Ancestral ...	02075	Mark any ancient workings on the plan
Ancestress	02076	So as to unbottom the ancient workings
Ancestry ...	02077	**Andesitic**
Ancetres ...	02078	**Angle(s)**
Anchamente	02079	At right angles
Ancharia ...	02080	At what angle
Ancheta ...	02081	At an angle of
Anchialus...	02082	An angle-bob
Anchicorto	02083	The vein dips at an angle of —— from the horizon
Anchoic ...	02084	The angle-bob at —— gave way on —— will take —— days to
Anchorage	02085	The shaft is inclined at an angle of [repair
Anchoralia	02086	**Anhydrous**
Anchorite ...	02087	**Announce**
Anchovy ...	02088	To announce
Anchuelo ...	02089	Shall I (we) announce
Anchuroso	02090	Do not announce
Anchusae ...	02091	Announce officially
Ancianar ...	02092	Unable to announce any dividend
Anciditore	02093	We shall announce a dividend of —— on ——

Anciennete	02094	We shall announce a dividend of ——
Ancilias ...	02095	When are you likely to announce a dividend
Ancilibus ...	02096	We authorize you to publicly announce
Ancillary ...	02097	Directors propose to announce
Ancipes ...	02098	We must announce
Ancipital ...	02099	**Announced**
Anclabris ...	02100	Not yet announced
Ancladero...	02101	Has (have) announced
Anclage ...	02102	Has (have) been announced
Anclote ...	02103	Has it been announced that
Anclotillo ...	02104	Should be announced immediately
Ancoraggio	02105	As soon as it has been officially announced
Ancoralis ...	02106	A dividend of —— per cent. has been announced
Ancorero ...	02107	A dividend of —— per cent. was announced on —— last
Ancoretta ...	02108	It is officially announced
Anculat ...	02109	It must be announced at ——
Andabata ...	02110	Will not be announced before ——
Andachtig...	02111	**Announcement**
Andaderas	02112	Pending announcement of
Andador ...	02113	Advise you to make public announcement of
Andadura...	02114	Now awaiting announcement of
Andalia ...	02115	Authorize you to publicly contradict announcement as regards
Andaluzzo	02116	**Annoyed**
Andamiado	02117	Much annoyed
Andamio ...	02118	I am (we are) more than annoyed that
Andana ...	02119	It is no use being annoyed
Andanada...	02120	—— is (are) very annoyed that
Andancia ...	02121	—— is (are) very much annoyed with ——
Andanino ...	02122	Must not be annoyed
Andante ...	02123	Somewhat annoyed
Andantesco	02124	The Board is annoyed
Andarage ...	02125	Is (are) much annoyed with ——
Andariego...	02126	I (we) regret the annoyance caused
Andario ...	02127	**Annual**
Andarivel ...	02128	The annual accounts
Andarsene	02129	Our annual meeting is fixed for ——
Andas ...	02130	Require this information for our annual meeting
Andataccia	02131	Shall inform the shareholders at annual meeting on —— that
Andatore ...	02132	What is the date of annual meeting of shareholders
Andauern ...	02133	Will be determined at our annual meeting to be held on ——
Anden ...	02134	Will be determined at our annual meeting; date not yet fixed
Andenken...	02135	Annual accounts mailed on
Andentung	02136	Have not yet received annual accounts
Anderseits	02137	An annual income of
Anderswo ...	02138	An annual profit of
Andianne ...	02139	An annual statement
Andichten	02140	**Annually** (*See also* " Yearly.")
Andiron ...	02141	Published annually
Andola ...	02142	Accounts made up annually
Andolina ...	02143	If annually or otherwise
Andorga ...	02144	**Annul** (*See also* " Cancel.")
Andorrear...	02145	To annul
Andosco ...	02146	**Another**
Andouille ...	02147	Please forward another
Andrajero...	02148	Has (have) forwarded another
Andrajo ...	02149	**Answer**
Andrang ...	02150	To answer
Andremas...	02151	Do not answer
Andringen	02152	Do not answer anybody's questions about
Andrino ...	02153	Do not answer by cable, but write

Androgynal	02154	Do not answer except by McNeill's code
Androhen ...	02155	Please send an answer as quickly as possible
Androidess	02156	Why do you (does ——) not answer
Andronem	02157	Have you had any answer from
Androsaces	02158	Have received the following answer from
Androsenio	02159	Has (have) not received any answer from
Androtomia	02160	As no answer came to hand
Andrucken	02161	As no answer came to hand I (we) considered the matter at an
Anduar ...	02162	Answer the question(s) in my telegram of —— [end
Andularios	02163	Answer the question(s) with reference to
Andulencia	02164	Answer at once
Andullo ...	02165	Answer as soon as possible
Aneantir ...	02166	Answer urgently required
Anecdota ...	02167	Answer by telegraph
Anecdotist	02168	Answer by mail
Aneddoto ...	02169	Cannot wait for definite answer after ——
Anegacion	02170	Cannot get an answer
Anegadizo	02171	Cannot give an answer yet (until)
Aneignen ...	02172	The latest date for definite answer is
Anekeln ...	02173	What is the latest date before which definite answer must be
Anelanza ...	02174	Will communicate answer as soon as possible [sent
Anelletto ...	02175	It is most unfortunate your (——'s) answer was not clearer
Anellus ...	02176	Must receive definite answer within next —— days
Anelo ...	02177	Has (have) cabled to —— and will inform you as to his answer
Anemometro	02178	Will it (this) answer your purpose
Anemone ...	02179	Will answer my purpose
Anequn ...	02180	Will not answer my purpose
Anerbieten	02181	Useless to answer unless you cable "yes" or "no"
Anethum ...	02182	Have received your dispatch; will answer as soon as possible

Answered

Aneurism ...	02183	
Anexar ...	02184	Answered in my (our) letter dated ——
Anexion ...	02185	Answered in my (our) letter dated ——; will send a duplicate
Anfachen ...	02186	Has (have) already answered [by next mail
Anfahren ...	02187	Has (have) not yet answered clearly enough
Anfallen ...	02188	Has (have) not yet answered decisively enough
Anfanare ...	02189	Has (have) answered affirmatively
Anfanatore	02190	Has (have) answered negatively
Anfang ...	02191	What has —— answered
Anfaulen ...	02192	I (we) answered by mail on ——

Anthracite

Anfechten...	02193	
Anfeinden...	02194	Anthracite exists in quantity at a distance of —— miles
Anferibene	02195	Anthracite is available at a cost here of —— per ton of 2,240 lbs.
Anfertigen	02196	Anthracite has been discovered at
Anfeuern ...	02197	Good anthracite
Anfibio ...	02198	Fair anthracite
Anfibraco ...	02199	Poor anthracite

Anticipate(s)

Anfimarca...	02200	
Anfion ...	02201	To anticipate
Anfisbena...	02202	I (we) anticipate that
Anfiscios ...	02203	Do (did) not anticipate that
Anfiteatro...	02204	Provided that you (they) do not anticipate any change
Anfitrite ...	02205	Should you (——) anticipate
Anflicken ...	02206	Should you (——) not anticipate
Anfodern ...	02207	Anticipate(s) difficulty with regard to
Anfodillo ...	02208	Do you (they) anticipate any difficulty.
Anforetta ...	02209	Do(es) not anticipate much difficulty
Anfraco ...	02210	I (we) anticipate rise in
Anfractus ...	02211	I (we) anticipate fall in
Anfragen ...	02212	I (we) did not anticipate
Anfressen ...	02213	You need not anticipate difficulty(ies)

[87]

Anfrieren ...	02214	The anticipated difficulty has been overcome
Anfuhren ...	02215	**Anticipation(s)**
Angaffen ...	02216	Buy —— in anticipation of rise
Angariabat	02217	Sell —— in anticipation of fall
Angariare ..	02218	Shall I (we) buy in anticipation of rise
Angarillon	02219	Shall I (we) sell in anticipation of fall
Angarior ...	02220	**Anticline(al)**
Angaripola	02221	Anticlinal axis
Angaro ...	02222	Form(s) one side of an anticline
Angarus ...	02223	Form a regular anticline
Angebamur	02224	**Antimony**
Angeben ...	02225	Antimony mine
Angeboren	02226	Crude antimony has been sold recently at
Angebot ...	02227	Telegraph latest quotation for French Star
Angel ...	02228	On account of the antimony contents
Angelegen	02229	Auriferous sulphide of antimony carrying gold —— silver ——
Angelica ...	02230	To-day's quotation for regulus is [per ton of 2,240 lbs.
Angelique...	02231	To-day's quotation for Cookson's Brand is
Angellus ...	02232	To-day's quotation for Ordinary Brand is
Angelon ...	02233	Sulphide of antimony (stibnite)
Angelote ...	02234	The ore contains —— per cent. of Sulphide of Antimony
Angeluccio	02235	The ore is antimonial
Angenehm	02236	**Anxious**
Angerona ...	02237	Am (are) anxious to leave for
Angersi ...	02238	Am (are) anxious to leave before
Angesehen	02239	Am (are) anxious to return before
Angheriare	02240	Am (are) anxious to know your opinion. Please telegraph
Angina ...	02241	I am (we are) most anxious to learn
Angiolella...	02242	I am (we are) becoming anxious
Angiolino ...	02243	I am (we are) becoming anxious with regard to
Angiologia	02244	—— is anxious to know your opinion. Telegraph
Angiporto...	02245	Very anxious to receive your report quickly
Anglaiser ...	02246	Very anxious to know how matters are proceeding
Anglers ...	02247	Very anxious to get matters definitely settled
Anglicano...	02248	Very anxious to hear from you
Anglicised	02249	Am (are) anxiously looking forward to
Anglicismo	02250	There is no reason to be anxious
Angling ...	02251	Should there be any reason to be anxious
Angllie ...	02252	What is it that you are anxious about
Anglomanie	02253	Very anxious to have letters from you
Anglotzen...	02254	Very anxious to hear from you respecting matters referred to in
Angoisse ...	02255	I am (we are) very anxious that [letter dated ——
Angoletto ...	02256	I am (we are) very anxious to begin
Angonia ...	02257	**Any**
Angosciare	02258	I (we) have not any more
Angostar ...	02259	Is there (are there) any
Angostilla...	02260	Have you any more
Angostura	02261	**Anything**
Angra ...	02262	Anything extra
Angranzen	02263	Disappointed you (they) have not done anything
Angreifen ...	02264	Is anything further necessary
Angriff ...	02265	Can you suggest anything further
Angrinsen...	02266	Cannot suggest anything further
Anguarina	02267	Anything in reason
Anguibus ...	02268	**Apart**
Anguila ...	02269	Apart from
Anguilero ...	02270	Apart from all other considerations
Anguillade	02271	Apart from personal considerations
Anguineal...	02272	Cannot be considered apart from
Anguipedes	02273	Considered apart from

Anguish ...	02274	Must be considered apart from
Angulado ...	02275	The two are altogether apart from
Angulaire...	02276	**Apex**
Angulated	02277	Apex of lode
Angulema	02278	From the apex
Anguloso ...	02279	The apex of
Angulum ...	02280	It is alleged that the apex of the lode is not in property
Angustans	02281	Send plan(s) showing boundary marks and apex of lode
Angustiado	02282	Apex of lode is not in property
Angustius	02283	Apex of the lode is undoubtedly in property
Angustorum	02284	The law with regard to the apex
Anhaften ...	02285	We can undoubtedly claim under the law with regard to the
Anhakeln ...	02286	Examine carefully the question of apex [apex
Anhaltend	02287	—— claim(s) that he (they) possess apex
Anhangig...	02288	Endeavour to discover ——'s views as to apex
Anhanglich	02289	**Apparatus**
Anhangsel	02290	Send full particulars respecting the necessary apparatus
Anhaufen ..	02291	The necessary apparatus
Anheim ...	02292	What apparatus is necessary
Anhelar ...	02293	**Apparent(ly)** *(See also "Appear(s).")*
Anhelavit...	02294	It is not at all apparent
Anhelito ...	02295	It is (has been) quite apparent
Anheloso ...	02296	It has been apparent all along
Anhemeles	02297	Is apparent in the bottom of shaft
Anher ...	02298	Is apparently in our ——
Anhetzen ...	02299	The intersection is apparent
Anhina ...	02800	**Appeal**
Anhohe ...	02801	Leave to appeal
Anhorca ...	02302	To appeal
Aniaga ...	02303	Appeal to
Anicetum ...	02304	Verdict of Court of Appeal in my (our) favour
Anicos ...	02305	Verdict of Court of Appeal is against us
Anicroche...	02306	Cannot appeal
Anieblar ...	02307	If you see any chance of success; appeal at once
Anifala ...	02308	Is —— (are they) likely to appeal
Aniline ...	02309	I am (we are) advised to appeal
Anility ...	02310	I am (we are) advised to appeal; success of suit almost certain
Anillejo ...	02311	I am (we are) advised that it is a forlorn hope to appeal
Animable...	02312	I (we) have appealed to —— for his (their) assistance
Animacion	02313	—— has (have) given notice of appeal [once
Animado ...	02314	Take competent advice, and if any chance of success appeal at
Animadvert	02315	Notice of appeal has been lodged
Animal ...	02316	Notice of appeal was lodged on
Animalazo	02317	On no account make any appeal to ——
Animalcule	02318	Shall I (we) appeal
Animalejo...	02319	Should you (they) appeal I (we) recommend
Animalism	03220	Shall I (we) appeal against decision [Plaintiff
Animalon ...	02321	The appeal case has been heard and decision given in favour of
Animans ...	02322	The appeal case has been heard and decision given in favour of
Animatus ...	02323	Appeal has been dismissed with costs [Defendant
Animazione	02324	**Appear(s)**
Animero ...	02325	To appear
Animosidad	02326	Appear(s) as if
Animosity	02327	Does it appear to you
Animoso...	02328	It does not appear
Animosorum	02329	Should it appear
Animuccia	02330	Should it not appear that
Aninarse ...	02331	It appears to have been
Aniquilar ...	02332	It appears to me (us) that
Anisado ...	02333	How does it appear to you

Anisetto ...	02334	Endeavour to make it appear that
Anisillo ...	02335	I (we) shall try to make it appear
Anisocycla	02336	It must not appear
Anisum ...	02337	I (we) do not care for my (our) name(s) to appear
Anitraccio	02338	——'s name should not appear
Anitrino ...	02339	There does not appear to be
Anitrocco...	02340	There appears to have been
Ankampfen	02341	Who appear(s) for

Appearance(s)

Ankern ...	02342	
Ankertau ...	02343	Present appearance(s)
Anketten ...	02344	The appearance of
Anklager ...	02345	There is only a slight appearance of
Anklammern	02346	There is every appearance of
Anklang ...	02347	Shall I (we) put in an appearance at (on)
Ankleben ...	02348	Do not put in an appearance
Anklingen	02349	Take care to put in an appearance
Anlacheln...	02350	Appearance(s) favourable
Anlanger ...	02351	Appearances exceedingly favourable
Anlass ...	02352	All appearance of
Anlauf ...	02353	Do not judge from appearances
Anlegen ...	02354	From the present appearance of things
Anleitung...	02355	From present appearance the future is very encouraging
Anlocken ...	02356	I (we) can detect no appearance of
Anmalen ...	02357	Judging from appearances only
Anmassen...	02358	To all appearances
Anmelden...	02359	To all appearances everything is
Anmerken	02360	The general appearance of the mine is
Anmuth ...	02361	The appearance of the mine is most satisfactory
Annacquare	02362	The appearance of the mine is unsatisfactory
Annaffiare	02363	The present appearance of the mine is not encouraging
Annageln ...	02364	The appearances of the —— level is most encouraging
Annahen ...	02365	What is the present appearance

Appeared

Annalist ...	02366	Who appeared for ——
Annaspare	02367	—— appeared for ——
Annealing	02368	Has (have) not appeared as yet
Anneau ...	02369	

Append

Annebbiare	02370	To append
Annerato ...	02371	Can append
Annexation	02372	Would it not be well to append
Annidarsi...	02373	What do you propose to append
Anniegare	02374	

Appended

Annieten ...	02375	Could be appended
Annihilate	02376	Is (are) appended to
Annitrire ...	02377	Appended to report
Annobilito	02378	Must be appended
Annodatura	02379	

Appendix

Annonario	02380	As an appendix to
Annoncer...	02381	Might be given as an appendix
Annotate ...	02382	Appendix will be mailed on
Annoter ...	02383	Could you not give us an appendix
Annottirsi	02384	I (we) shall deal with —— in the appendix to my (our) report
Annovale ...	02385	Appendix to my report mailed on ——
Annoverare	02386	
Annuaire ...	02387	**Appertain** (See also "Belong.")
Annugolare	02388	**Appliances** (See also "Apparatus," "Tools," "Tackle,"
Annullosis	02389	Assaying appliances for gold should be sent ["Outfit."
Annuitant	02390	Am (are) without appliances for
Annulet ...	02391	Assay appliances for —— should be sent
Annullato...	02392	Appliances for —— altogether wanting
Annulose ...	02393	All appliances will be ready

Annunziare	02394	Complete appliances are required for
Annunzio ...	02395	Complete with all appliances
Anoblir	02396	Have you (has ——) any appliance for
Anoche ...	02397	Has (have) no appliance by which he (they) can deal with
Anodinar ...	02398	Should bring with him assay appliances
Anodyne ...	02399	When are your appliances to be ready
Anointer ...	02400	What is the state of the mill and appliances
Anointing	02401	Have they the necessary appliances for
Anointment	02402	What milling appliances have you
Anomalidad	02403	What hoisting appliances have you
Anomalism	02404	What appliances have you available for
Anomalo ...	02405	What appliances do you (they) consider necessary
Anomalous	02406	Bring necessary appliances
Anomaly	02407	Appliances will be provided
Anomia ...	02408	Have no appliances for
Anonadar ...	02409	I (we) shall require to have the necessary appliances for
Anonillo ...	02410	All our appliances are now ready

Applicant

Anonium ...	02411	
Anora ...	02412	Am an applicant for
Anordnen ...	02413	Do you care to recommend an applicant
Anorexy ...	02414	—— is an applicant
Anotacion...	02415	Applicant can be permitted
Anotador ...	02416	Applicant cannot be permitted to

Application

Anotar ...	02417	
Anotomia...	02418	Support the application of
Anotomista	02419	Cannot support the application of
Anpacken	02420	Application received, but list closed
Anpassung	02421	Application to be made by
Anprallen...	02422	Can list of applications be kept open until
Anpreisen	02423	If —— makes an application to
Anproben...	02424	Has (have) made an application
Anqueta ...	02425	Make immediate application to ——
Anquirens	02426	Owing to the nature of the application
Anquiseco...	02427	Application has been granted
Anquisitus	02428	Application has not been granted
Anrathen ...	02429	The sooner you (they) make application the better
Anrecht ...	02430	Has (have) made application for
Anregen ...	02431	To whom should application be made
Anreissen ...	02432	Application should be made to
Anreizung	02433	Make immediate application to —— for his support
Anrichte ...	02434	Notice has been given that list of applications will close on ——
Anrufen ...	02435	Refuse any applications that may be made to you by ——
Anruhren	02436	Am I (are we) to refuse or accept ——'s application
Ansagen ...	02437	The applications exceeded
Ansamento	02438	Application cannot be entertained for the present
Ansarero ...	02439	——'s application cannot be entertained
Ansarino ...	02440	Has (have) made application to meet for
Ansaron ...	02441	Has (have) made application to meet for ——; cable what I am

Applied

Ansassig ...	02442	[(we are) to do
Ansatum ...	02443	Fear shall be applied to (for)
Anseatico ...	02444	If you are applied to, refuse
Ansehen ...	02445	If you are applied to, consent
Anserculus	02446	Has (have) not yet been applied to
Anserine ...	02447	—— has applied to me (us) for
Ansiar ...	02448	Must be applied in part payment of ——
Ansiedler ...	02449	Must be applied exclusively for ——
Ansieta ...	02450	Has (have) applied to me (us) for
Ansimare ...	02451	Has (have) not applied
Ansina ...	02452	Unless you (they) have already applied
Ansinnen ...	02453	Have you applied

Ansioso ...	02454	Have not applied
Anspannen	02455	Have applied
Anspeien ...	02456	**Applies**
Anspiessen	02457	The same applies to-day
Anspornen	02458	**Apply**
Ansprache	02459	Apply to
Anspucken	02460	It would be no use to apply to
Anstalt ...	02461	You (they) can apply to —— if you (they) think proper
Anstand ...	02462	Before you (they) apply
Anstarren	02463	Only apply to —— as a last resource
Anstechen	02464	Better apply at once for
Ansteigen	02465	Shall apply at once for
Anstellung	02466	To whom shall I (we) apply
Anstieren ...	02467	You must apply to ——
Anstiften ...	02468	Apply to —— in my (our) name
Anstimmen	02469	Apply this only to ——
Anstopfen	02470	Apply this to all
Anstoss ...	02471	Do your remarks apply to both —— and ——
Anstossig ...	02472	If necessary apply to
Anstreben	02473	For further instructions apply to
Anstrengen	02474	For information and funds apply to
Anstrich ...	02475	For information apply to ——
Ansturmen	02476	To whom shall I (we) apply for information
Ansuchen ...	02477	You cannot do better than apply to ——
Antaceo ...	02478	You may apply to —— for funds
Antachates	02479	Expect —— will apply to you for ——
Antalgic ...	02480	**Appoint**
Antanazo ..	02481	To appoint
Antartico ...	02482	Shall I (we) appoint
Antasten ...	02483	Might appoint —— meanwhile
Anteactum	02484	Can I (we) appoint
Anteado ...	02485	Do not appoint
Anteayer ...	02486	Should like to appoint
Antebrazo	02487	Whom do you suggest I (we) should appoint
Antecamara	02488	I (we) strongly advise you to appoint —— as ——
Antecanis	02489	At any place you may appoint
Anteceder ...	02490	**Appointed**
Antechinos	02491	Has anyone as yet been appointed
Anteco ...	02492	No one has been appointed as yet
Antecoger	02493	Was appointed on ——
Antecoluna	02494	Was officially appointed as
Antecoro ...	02495	I (we) have been officially appointed as ——
Antecristo	02496	Can you inform me (us) who has been appointed
Antedata ...	02497	Is —— likely to be appointed
Antedicho	02498	—— is likely to be appointed
Antedote ...	02499	—— is not likely to be appointed
Antehac ...	02500	Might be appointed
Antelacion	02501	Have appointed —— to look after my (our) interests
Antelope ..	02502	Some one should be officially appointed to look after my (our) [interests
Antelucano	02503	**Appointment**
Antemano ..	02504	Decline the appointment
Antemural	02505	Has (have) received the appointment
Antennato	02506	Has (have) not received the appointment
Antennetta	02507	Appointment as
Antenoche	02508	Has the appointment been filled yet
Antenombre	02509	The appointment has not been filled
Anteojera ...	02510	As soon as I (we) receive your instructions I (we) shall fix the [appointment
Antepagar	02511	Do you care to apply for the appointment
Antepasado	02512	Is the appointment still open
Antepecho	02513	—— has received appointment .

Antepenult	02514	May I apply for the appointment
Anteponer	02515	Would you advise me to accept appointment
Anteporre...	02516	Unable to advise you to accept or decline appointment
Antequam	02517	Advise you to accept appointment
Antequino	02518	Advise you to decline appointment
Anterius ...	02519	The only appointment open is the one of
Anteroom...	02520	What is the appointment worth per annum
Antesala ...	02521	The appointment is worth —— per annum
Antestatus	02522	Have you fixed any appointment with —— to discuss
Antetempo	02523	When can I (we) fix an appointment with you to discuss
Antever ...	02524	The appointment is fixed for
Antevolat ...	02525	**Appraise** (*See also* " Value.")
Antheil ...	02526	**Appreciate**
Anthemis ...	02527	Do you (they) (does ——) fully appreciate the effect
Anthericus	02528	I wish you could appreciate the value of the property
Anthology	02529	I (we) appreciate your offer which I (we) accept
Anthrax ...	02530	I (we) appreciate your offer which I (we) regret unable to accept
Anthyllis ...	02531	The Board fully appreciate what you have done
Antiandare	02532	We appreciate your conduct
Anticaglia	02533	**Apprehend**
Anticamera	02534	To apprehend
Antichetto	02535	Do you (they) apprehend
Anticipo ...	02536	Do not apprehend
Anticlimax	02537	Apprehend considerable danger
Anticorte ...	02538	Apprehend considerable difficulty
Anticpada...	02539	Do not apprehend any danger
Antics ...	02540	Do not apprehend any serious difficulties
Anticuado...	02541	Do you still apprehend difficulty
Anticuario	02542	Still apprehend considerable difficulty
Anticuore...	02543	**Approach**
Antidetta ...	02544	Can you approach
Antidire ...	02545	Can you approach —— with respect to a compromise
Antidoral ...	02546	Will endeavour to approach
Antienne ...	02547	So far any attempt to approach has been unsuccessful
Antier ...	02548	Try to approach
Antifato ...	02549	**Approbation**
Antifebril ...	02550	Does not meet with the approbation of ——
Antifona ...	02551	Has this your approbation
Antifonero	02552	Subject to the approbation of ——
Antifrasi ...	02553	**Appropriate**
Antigerio ...	02554	To appropriate
Antiguar ...	02555	How much shall I (we) appropriate for
Antilogia ...	02556	Appropriate at least —— for
Antimurare	02557	You have authority to appropriate —— for
Antinomia	02558	Appropriate at least £ —— monthly in development
Antinoo ...	02559	Can I (we) appropriate
Antipapa ...	02560	Do not appropriate
Antipasto ...	02561	In case you can appropriate
Antipates ...	02562	In case you cannot appropriate
Antipathie	02563	You had better appropriate as you think best
Antipatia ...	02564	**Approval**
Antiphony	02565	Subject to approval
Antiphrase	02566	Subject to your approval
Antipoca ...	02567	Subject to the approval of the Directors
Antipodal...	02568	Subject to the approval of
Antipodes...	02569	Until formal approval is received
Antipope ...	02570	Telegraph if this meets with your approval
Antiquatio	02571	If this does not meet with your approval
Antiquite ...	02572	You have the full approval of the Board
Antirrino ...	02573	**Approve**

Antisapere	02574	To approve
Antisaputa	02575	Quite approve of
Antiscios ...	02576	Do not altogether approve of
Antisocial...	02577	I (we) fully approve of
Antispodio	02578	Provided that the Board approve of it
Antistrofa...	02579	**Approximate(ly)**
Antitesis ...	02580	What is the approximate weight (of)
Antitipo ...	02581	The approximate weight is
Antiveduto	02582	Approximate value
Antlia ...	02583	It is approximately correct
Antojadizo	02584	It is not even approximately correct
Antojado ...	02585	Is the (this) statement approximately true
Antojarse ..	02586	The approximate value may be taken at ——
Antojera ...	02587	The statement is not even approximately true
Antologia ...	02588	The approximate distance is ——
Antoniano	02589	What is the approximate tonnage of ore in reserve
Antorcha ...	02590	What is the approximate value of supplies in hand
Antrace ...	02591	What is the approximate value of next month's returns
Antrag ...	02592	What is the approximate amount of your monthly expenditure
Antreffen ...	02593	What is the approximate amount required for the next three
Antreten ...	02594	What do you consider the approximate value of [months
Antrieb ...	02595	The approximate value of —— is
Antritt ...	02596	What is the approximate cash value of
Antroare ...	02597	The approximate cash value of —— is
Antroavit ...	02598	State approximately
Antruejar ...	02599	**April**
Antrum ...	02600	About the middle of April
Antuvion ...	02601	At the beginning of April
Antwort ...	02602	During the entire month of April
Anualidad	02603	For the entire month of April
Anublado ...	02604	Last April
Anublar ...	02605	Next April
Anuencia ...	02606	Near the end of April
Anuente ...	02607	1st day of April
Anulable ...	02608	2nd day of April
Anulacion...	02609	3rd day of April
Anulador ...	02610	4th day of April
Anularis ...	02611	5th day of April
Anulata ...	02612	6th day of April
Anulativo ...	02613	7th day of April
Anuloso ...	02614	8th day of April
Anunciada	02615	9th day of April
Anuncio ...	02616	10th day of April
Anverso ...	02617	11th day of April
Anwachsen	02618	12th day of April
Anwalt ...	02619	13th day of April
Anwandeln	02620	14th day of April
Anwehen ...	02621	15th day of April
Anweidern	02622	16th day of April
Anweissen...	02623	17th day of April
Anweisung	02624	18th day of April
Anwenden	02625	19th day of April
Anwerben ...	02626	20th day of April
Anxiare ...	02627	21st day of April
Anxietatem	02628	22nd day of April
Anxitudina	02629	23rd day of April
Anzeige ...	02630	24th day of April
Anzetteln ...	02631	25th day of April
Anzicheno	02632	26th day of April
Anzivenire	02633	27th day of April

Anzolado ...	02634	28th day of April
Anzuelito ...	02635	29th day of April
Anzuelo ...	02636	30th day of April
Anzunden...	02637	April expenses amount to
Aocar ...	02638	April shipments amount to
Aocchiare ...	02639	**Aqueous**
Aojado ...	02640	**Arbitrate**
Aojadura ...	02641	To arbitrate
Aolsharfe ...	02642	Could you (they) get —— to arbitrate
Aoncinare...	02643	Endeavour to get some fully competent person to arbitrate
Aoriflus ...	02644	It is necessary to appoint an arbitrator.—Whom do you wish
Aoristo ...	02645	In case —— cannot arbitrate [to name
Aormare ...	02646	Unable so far to get a competent person to arbitrate
Aovillarse ...	02647	Have agreed to arbitrate
Apabilar ...	02648	Have not agreed to arbitrate
Apace ...	02649	**Arbitration**
Apacible ...	02650	Agree to arbitration
Apaciguar...	02651	Arbitration reversed
Apagable ...	02652	Decline(s) arbitration unless
Apagesis ...	02653	Refuse(s) all offers of arbitration
Apagogico...	02654	Arbitration is decided in our (your) favour
Apainelado	02655	Arbitration is decided against us
Apaiser ...	02656	Arbitration has been decided in favour of ——
Apalabrar...	02657	Can you submit the matter to arbitration
Apalam ...	02658	Have submitted the matter to arbitration
Apalancar...	02659	Submit the matter to arbitration if —— agrees
Apaleado ...	02660	Shall I (we) submit the matter to arbitration
Apaleo ...	02661	Is it wise to submit the matter to arbitration
Apalmada...	02662	I (we) do not think it wise to submit matter to arbitration
Apanagiste	02663	What is likely to be result of arbitration
Apanar ...	02664	**Arbitrator(s)**
Apancora ...	02665	Arbitrators have disagreed
Apandillar	02666	Do you approve of —— as arbitrator
Apanojado	02667	I (we) do not approve of —— as arbitrator
Apantanar	02668	Fully approve of —— as arbitrator
Apanthropy	02669	When are arbitrators to declare their award
Aparadura	02670	Expect arbitrators' award on
Aparatoso ...	02671	Arbitrator(s) has (have) postponed award pending
Aparceria ...	02672	Endeavour to get —— to act as arbitrator
Aparctias ...	02673	**Arborescent**
Aparecer ...	02674	**Arch(ed)**
Aparecido...	02675	In the arch of ground
Aparejar ...	02676	In the crown of the arch
Aparejo ...	02677	Arch over
Apareilar ...	02678	Require(s) to be arched over
Aparentado	02679	**Archæan**
Aparente ...	02680	**Area** (*See also* " Acres," " Surface.")
Aparicion ...	02681	Covers a considerable area
Apariencia	02682	Covers the entire area
Aparine ...	02683	The entire area
Aparrado ...	02684	Only a small area of country is
Apartadero	02685	**Arenaceous**
Apartadijo	02686	The country is arenaceous
Apartment	02687	Arenaceous beds
Apasionado	02688	**Argentiferous** (*See also* " Bullion," " Silver.")
Apasionar...	02689	The ore is an argentiferous sulphide of lead, carrying —— [ounces of silver per ton of 2,240 lbs.
Apasturar...	02690	The ore is an argentiferous sulphide of copper; carrying —— [ounces of silver per ton of 2,240 lbs.
Apathetic ...	02691	Argentiferous iron pyrites

Apathiaris	02692	Auro-argentiferous
Apathie ...	02693	Highly argentiferous
Apathique	02694	**Argillaceous**
Apathist ...	02695	The country is decomposed argillaceous schist
Apatico ...	02696	Argillaceous beds
Apatusco ...	02697	**Arm**
Apazote ...	02698	One arm broken
Apeadero ...	02699	Both arms broken
Apecula ...	02700	Arm injured but not broken
Apedazar ...	02701	**Around** (*See also* " About.")
Apedreado	02702	Around us
Apegar ...	02703	Around the property
Apelable ...	02704	**Arrange**
Apelacion ...	02705	Will arrange
Apelado ...	02706	To arrange
Apelambrar	02707	Arrange to
Apelante ...	02708	It is imperative that you (they) arrange at once
Apelativo ...	02709	Is it imperative for me (us) to arrange to
Apeligrado	02710	It is not imperative for me (us) to arrange
Apeliota ...	02711	It is imperative that I (we) should arrange the matter at once
Apella ...	02712	Arrange as soon as possible to (with)
Apellidar ...	02713	Arrange as soon as possible for
Apellido ..	02714	Ask —— to assist you to arrange matters
Apelmacar	02715	Can you arrange to
Apenas ...	02716	Can you arrange with
Apendencia	02717	Cannot possibly arrange matters amicably
Apendice ...	02718	Endeavour to arrange matters amicably
Apennino ...	02719	Useless to endeavour to arrange amicably
Apeonar ...	02720	I (we) cannot arrange to
Apepsia ...	02721	I (we) cannot arrange with
Aperador ...	02722	I (we) hope to arrange for a trial crushing of ore
Apercevoir	02723	I (we) hope to arrange for a trial with the
Apercibido	02724	If you (they) can arrange to (with) —— do so
Apercion ...	02725	In case you cannot arrange
Apercollar...	02726	To enable me (us) to arrange
Apercu ...	02727	Shall try and arrange matters
Aperdigado	02728	Should like to arrange to (with)
Aperiantur	02729	Within what time shall you be able to arrange
Aperiendus	02730	Shall I (we) arrange
Aperient ...	02731	Better arrange as soon as possible
Aperitivo ...	02732	Have only been able to arrange for
Apernador	02733	There was not sufficient time to arrange anything definite
Apernar ...	02734	Who will arrange for
Aperreado	02735	Arrange as you deem best
Apersonado	02736	Why do (did) you not arrange [report on
Apert ...	02737	Can you arrange with the following experts to examine and
Apertaro ...	02738	**Arranged**
Apertness ...	02739	Have you (they) arranged (for)
Apertura ...	02740	Has (have) arranged to take everything as they stand
Apestado ...	02741	Cannot the difference be arranged
Apetalous...	02742	Has (have) arranged to (with)
Apetecedor	02743	Has (have) not arranged to (with)
Apetecible	02744	Has (have) arranged not to
Apetencia ...	02745	What has been arranged respecting
Apetite ...	02746	Pending something more definite being arranged
Apetitoso ...	02747	Why have you not already arranged
Apexabonem	02748	Everything has been arranged most satisfactorily
Apezunar ...	02749	As arranged before you (——) left
Apfel ...	02750	As arranged with vendors
Apfelregal	02751	As arranged with lessees

Apfelsine ...	02752	As soon as everything is arranged telegraph
Aphaeremam	02753	Everything now satisfactorily arranged
Aphanite ...	02754	I (we) have arranged to leave for —— on ——
Aphidian ...	02755	Nothing yet finally arranged
Aphorism	02756	So far nothing has been arranged
Aphrodite	02757	Telegraph when all has been arranged
Aphthe ...	02758	To be arranged later
Aphthong	02759	Is it definitely arranged
Apiadador	02760	It is definitely arranged
Apiadarse...	02761	It is not definitely arranged
Apiary ...	02762	Must be arranged at once
Apiastris ...	02763	Left to be arranged by
Apicarado	**02764**	**Arrangement**
Apicatus ...	02765	Have made the following arrangement
Apicolo ...	02766	It will be necessary to alter arrangement
Apiculture	02767	. The final arrangement was to
Apilador ...	02768	Cable outline of arrangement
Apilascus ..	02769	There is no chance of making any arrangement
Apinado ...	02770	Refuse(s) to enter into any arrangement
Apiolar ...	02771	Has (have) made an arrangement on a basis of
Apirexia ...	02772	Can you make arrangements (for)
Apiro ...	02773	As a temporary arrangement
Apiscendi ...	02774	Endeavour to make an arrangement by which
Apishly ...	02775	Consider it a makeshift arrangement
Apisonar ...	02776	✓ Have made arrangements for (to)
Aplacador...	02777	Has (have) made an arrangement by which
Aplaciente	02778	If you (they) approve of this arrangement, telegraph
Aplanchado	02779	I (we) have not been able to make any arrangement for the
Aplanes ...	02780	Let —— make all arrangements [use of
Aplastado...	02781	Make such arrangements as may be necessary
Aplastic ...	02782	No time to make other arrangements
Aplaudir ...	02783	—— refuse(s) to confirm arrangement
Aplauso ...	02784	Try to come to some arrangement with ——
Aplayar ...	02785	Try to come to some arrangement with regard to
Aplicado ...	02786	The arrangements consist of
Aplomado...	02787	Arrangement is very costly
Aplustrum	02788	Arrangement is an economical one
Apnea ...	02789	Arrangement is altogether in our favour
Apoca ...	02790	Arrangement is entirely against us
Apocalisse	02791	What are the arrangements with regard to
Apocalypse	02792	The arrangement is almost unheard of
Apocema ...	02793	Make suitable arrangements for ——
Apocharum	02794	Make some definite arrangement as soon as possible
Apocimo ...	02795	Cannot make any more definite arrangement at present
Apocltibus	02796	Gravitation arrangement
Apocopar ...	02797	Owing to defective arrangements for
Apocrifo ...	02798	Arrangement is most unfair [regards
Apocryphal	02799	Call upon —— before you make any definite arrangement
Apodador ...	02800	Any arrangement made must be subject to confirmation by
Apodencado	02801	Any arrangement that you may make must be subject to con-
Apodixis ...	02802	**Arrastra(s)** [firmation by shareholders at general meeting
Apodosis ...	02803	Cannot run arrastra for want of water
Apofise ...	02804	Continue to use arrastra until
Apogeo ...	02805	Could you arrange for a trial of —— tons in an arrastra
Apografo ...	02806	There is an arrastra only —— miles distant at which I shall
		test —— tons of vein stuff and will telegraph result
Apolectus...	02807	There is no stamp mill, only arrastras available
Apolillado	02808	We cleaned up the arrastra on —— last, with the following
		[result for a —— ton run
Apolinar ...	02809	Telegraph what it would cost to put up an arrastra

Apollineo ...	02810	Put up an arrastra as soon as possible
Apologatio	02811	Has (have) crushed —— tons in arrastra; yield —— ounces
Apologico	02812	**Arrear(s)**
Apologista	02813	Arrears of
Apologum	02814	Still in arrear
Apomazar...	02815	**Arrest**
Aponer ...	02816	Has (have) left to avoid arrest
Apophasim	02817	To arrest
Apoplegia...	02818	**Arrested**
Apopletico	02819	Has been arrested for
Apoplexy ...	02820	Has not yet been arrested
Aporcar ...	02821	Shall I (we) have —— (him) arrested
Aposentar...	02822	Have —— (him) arrested if you feel sure that he is guilty
Aposicion ...	02823	Have —— (him) arrested if you have reasonable ground for
Aposito ...	02824	Materials have been arrested for Customs dues [suspicion
Aposorbic	02825	Consignment of explosives has been arrested
Apospelo ...	02826	**Arrival**
Apostadero	02827	On arrival
Apostador	02828	Await arrival of
Apostasia ...	02829	On your arrival at
Apostata ..	02830	Pending ——'s arrival
Apostatize	02831	Before arrival of
Apostatrix	02832	After the arrival of
Apostelar ...	02833	Cable your arrival at
Apostemate	02834	On arrival of —— matter can be definitely settled
Apostemero	02835	Cannot leave before arrival of
Apostemoso	02836	The matter must remain in abeyance until arrival of ——
Apostheke	02837	Everything will be in readiness on the arrival of ——
Apostilla ...	02838	**Arrive**
Apostle ...	02839	To arrive
Apostolado	02840	When do you expect to arrive at
Apostolo ...	02841	When may I (we) expect —— to arrive
Apostrofe ...	02842	Advise —— as soon as you arrive
Apostura ...	02843	Cannot wait until you arrive.—Telegraph the conclusions you
Apote ...	02844	How did you (they) arrive at this result [have come to
Apotegma	02845	When is —— expected to arrive
Apotelesma	02846	Is (are) expected to arrive here about
Apoteosi ...	02847	Will settle when arrive London; leaving here on ——
Apothecary	02848	**Arrived**
Apothegm	02849	Not yet arrived
Apotheosis	02850	Arrived on
Apoticario	02851	Who arrived here
Apotome ...	02852	Which arrived here
Apoyadero	02853	You may expect that I (——) will arrive about
Apoyar ...	02854	Arrived here safely yesterday
Apoyatura	02855	Arrived here safely on ——
Apozemam	02856	Arrived here safely to-day
Appagabile	02857	Arrived here safely to-day; leave for —— on ——
Appagarsi	02858	Arrived too late
Appalidire	02859	Instructions arrived too late to be of use
Appaltare	02860	Inform —— as soon as —— has arrived
Appamondo	02861	Telegraph as soon as —— has arrived
Appangere	02862	Result was arrived at as follows
Appannare	02863	Was arrived at
Apparaitre	02864	Can be arrived at
Apparandus	02865	Could be arrived at
Apparatio	02866	Arrived here to-day and has (have) met ——
Apparatrix	02867	**Arseniate**
Apparebat	02868	**Arsenic(al)**

Apparel ...	02869	Arsenical pyrites
Apparendum	02870	Contains —— per cent. of arsenic
Apparerem	02871	Grey arsenic
Apparesco...	02872	Sublimed arsenic
Appariteur	02873	The market quotation for white arsenic is ——
Apparitura	02874	**Articles**
Apparsione	02875	Forward as soon as possible the following articles
Appartato...	02876	The following articles were missing
Appartenir	02877	According to our Articles of Association
Apparuit ...	02878	According to our Memorandum and Articles of Association
Appassare...	02879	Cannot on account of our Memorandum & Articles of Association
Appastarsi	02880	Have mailed a copy of our Memorandum & Articles of Association
Appauvrer	02881	Mail a copy of your Memorandum and Articles of Association
Appeler ...	02882	Should require to amend our Memorandum and Articles of [Association
Appellate ...	02883	See clause —— of Memorandum and Articles of Association
Appenato ...	02884	Draft Articles of Agreement (*See also* " Agreement.")
Appendage	02885	Articles of Agreement have been drawn up
Appendant	02886	Articles of Agreement will be signed on
Appendice	02887	**Artificial**
Appenso ...	02888	The demand is entirely artificial
Appesantir	02889	The market is entirely artificial
Appetence...	02890	The price is entirely artificial
Appetibile...	02891	**As**
Appetit ...	02892	As in
Appetitoso	02893	As for
Appiattato	02894	As to
Appiccarsi	02895	As per
Appingerit	02896	As far as
Appingo ...	02897	As soon as
Appiombo...	02898	As quickly as possible
Applaudere	02899	As near as
Applause ...	02900	As yet
Apples ...	02901	The same as when
Appletree ...	02902	The same as for
Applicatur	02903	As asked for
Applique ...	02904	**Asbestos**
Appodiare	02905	Asbestos packing
Appoggiato	02906	Asbestos wool
Apponersi...	02907	Large quantities of Asbestos
Apporter ...	02908	The market price of Asbestos is
Appositivo	02909	**Ascertain**
Appostare...	02910	To ascertain
Apprecatus	02911	Endeavour to ascertain
Appreciado	02912	Will endeavour to ascertain
Apprecier ...	02913	Cannot ascertain
Appregiare	02914	Ascertain privately whether
Apprendre	02915	Ascertain from —— what he (they) has (have) done
Apprensiva	02916	Ascertain immediately and telegraph
Apprentice	02917	Ascertain what is being done with regard to
Appresso ...	02918	Ascertain the facts
Apprestare	02919	Ascertain if report is true
Approbare	02920	Ascertain financial position of ——
Approbatif	02921	Ascertain if serious
Approchant	02922	Can you (they) (——) ascertain who is acting for
Approprier	02923	Can you (they) ascertain anything about the (it)
Appulcrare	02924	Endeavour to ascertain the lowest price
Appulse ...	02925	Can only ascertain that
Appuntato	02926	Try and ascertain if other parties are bidding
Appuyer ...	02927	Will ascertain as soon as I (we) can

Appuzzare	02928	Ascertain and inform me (us) (——) at once
Aprante ...	02929	Ascertain if —— is coming to
Aprariam	02930	Can you ascertain what is the matter in [to)
Aprehender	02931	Cannot ascertain anything regarding it (the matter you refer
Apremiador	02932	Can you ascertain whether he (——) is a man of standing
Apremiar ...	02933	**Ascertained**
Aprendero	02934	Has (have) ascertained nothing so far
Aprendiz ...	02935	Has (have) ascertained beyond doubt that report is false
Aprensador	02936	Has (have) ascertained that no one else is bidding
Aprestar ...	02937	So far as I have ascertained the following are the facts
Apresto ...	02938	**Ash(es)**
Apresurado	02939	The coal contains —— per cent. of ash
Apresurar...	02940	Owing to the large amount of ash contained in the coal
Apretadera	02941	Coal should not contain more than —— per cent. of ash
Apretadizo	02942	The coke contains —— per cent. of ash
Apretado ...	02943	Owing to the large amount of ash contained in the coke
Apreton ...	02944	Coke should not contain more than —— per cent. of ash
Apretura ...	02945	**Aside**
Apricans ...	02946	Put aside
Apricatio ...	02947	Put aside for the present
Apricitas ...	02948	**Ask** (See also "Apply," "Ascertain," " Request.")
Apricots ...	02949	Ask for ——
Apriculos ...	02950	Ask respecting
Apriessa ...	02951	I (we) shall ask
Aprieto ...	02952	Ask —— if he (they) will
Aprikose ...	02953	Ask him
Aprimento	02954	Ask on my (our) account for it (this)
Aprimere ...	02955	Please ask —— point blank if
Aprinus ...	02956	I (we) shall probably ask you
Apriporta...	02957	**Asked**
Aprisco ...	02958	It is useless asking with regard to ——
Aprisionar	02959	Has (have) asked respecting
Apritore ...	02960	When I (we) asked respecting
Aproar ...	02961	**Aspect**
Aprobacion	02962	In my (our) opinion the present aspect
Aprobador	02963	Aspect is encouraging
Aprobante	02964	Aspect is discouraging
Aprobar ...	02965	The future aspect is most unpromising
Aprobativo	02966	Telegraph what is the present aspect of affairs
Aproches ...	02967	Telegraph what is the general aspect of the mine
Apron ...	02968	What is the present aspect of affairs ? Write fully
Aprontar ...	02969	What is the present aspect of the mine ? Write fully
Apropiado	02970	**Asphalt**
Apropiar ...	02971	**Assay(s)** (See also "Average," "Gold," "Ounces," " Per
Aproscimar	02972	List of assays [cent.," " Sample," " Silver," " Test.", &c.)
Aprovecer...	02973	Dry assay
Aprugnus ...	02974	Wet assay
Apsyctos ...	02975	Assays made by blowpipe give
Apsynthium	02976	Assay gave —— per cent. copper
Aptabamur	02977	Assay gave —— per cent. lead
Aptamus ...	02978	Assay gave —— per cent. zinc
Apteral ...	02979	Assay results very satisfactory
Apterous ...	02980	Assay results altogether unsatisfactory
Aptidao ...	02981	Assays average —— per ton of 2,240 lbs.
Aptitud ...	02982	Assays average $—— per ton of 2,000 lbs.
Aptness ...	02983	Assays of sample from fore breast —— feet level give
Aptoton ...	02984	Assay balance for fine work is required
Apud ...	02985	Complete set of assaying appliances should be sent
Apuesta ...	02986	Complete set of assaying appliances should be sent, including
Apulgarar...	02987	A fair assay office is available [fluxes and ordinary reagents

Apunchar...	02988	No assay office is available
Apuntado...	02989	From the assay results
Apuntalar	02990	Vein matter assays
Apunto ...	02991	The outcrop assays
Apuracion	02992	The ore streak assays
Apuradero	02993	The drill core(s) assay(s) [telegraph results
Apurativo ..	02994	Send duplicate samples to nearest government assay office, and
Apurement	02995	From the assay it looks as if sample(s) has (have) been salted
Apurrir ...	02996	The following are the assay results of the duplicate samples
Apyrexia ...	02997	Pulp assays at mill average
Aquagium	02998	Pulp assays at —— mill average per ton
Aquarelle ...	02999	Tailing assays average —— per ton
Aquarium...	03000	Control assay
Aquatico	**03001**	Have made control assay which gives
Aquatique	03002	Wait for cable giving results of assays
Aquatoris...	03003	Better wait for results of assays
Aquejar ...	03004	Assay of samples from —— to-day gives
Aquel ...	03005	Assays for the week do not show any improvement
Aquende ...	03006	I (we) believe the ore will assay at least —— ozs. to the ton
Aquestar ...	03007	Why do you not report assays
Aquidoccio	03008	What is the assay value
Aquiducum	03009	What is the assay value for silver per ton of ore
Aquietar ...	03010	What is the assay value for gold per ton of ore
Aquifolia ...	03011	Assay value —— per ton
Aquilatar ...	03012	Assay value for gold per ton
Aquilea ...	03013	Assay value for silver per ton
Aquilentam	03014	Telegraph the result of assays from
Aquilifero	03015	Are the assays absolutely reliable
Aquilino ...	03016	Assays are absolutely reliable
Aquilonal...	03017	Sample assays gold ——, silver —— per ton of 2,240 lbs.
Aquilotto ...	03018	Sample assays gold ——, silver —— per ton of 2,000 lbs.
Aquitibi ...	03019	Sample assays silver —— ozs., lead —— per cent., copper ——
Arabescato	03020	Sample(s) to be assayed for [per cent.
Arabesco ...	03021	Has (have) forwarded duplicates of samples for assay
Arabesque	03022	Average assay of ore milled last month is gold ——, silver ——
Arabian ...	03023	Average assay of ore milled for month of —— is gold ——, silver—
Arabiga ...	03024	—— Carload assays silver —— ozs. per ton, copper —— per
Arachidnam	03025	Cable assay results of stuff from [cent., lead —— per cent.
Arador ...	03026	Results of assays will follow ; have not yet received
Aradorcico	03027	Average assay of ore is
Aradura...	03028	Average assay value of the ore in the mine is ——
Aragnoides	03029	Average assays for last month are
Aragonesa	03030	Average assays for last week are
Araignee ...	03031	**Assayed**
Arambel ...	03032	Not yet assayed ——
Aramento...	03033	Some of it assayed as much as
Aranata ...	03034	**Assayer**
Arancel ...	03035	Employ as assayer ——
Aranciato ...	03036	Competent assayer should be sent out as soon as possible
Arandano ...	03037	Can you secure services of reliable and competent assayer
Arandela ...	03038	Send duplicate samples to nearest reliable assayer, and tele-
Araneas ...	03039	**Assent** [graph results
Araniego ...	03040	Shall I (we) assent
Arapende ...	03041	To assent
Aratoire ...	03042	Do you (they) assent
Aratura ...	03043	Do not assent
Arazzeria ...	03044	You have my (our) assent
Arbalete ...	03045	Cannot give my (our) assent
Arbeiten ...	03046	Cannot obtain ——'s assent
Arbeitsam	03047	Has (have) obtained ——'s assent

Arbeitslos...	03048	Pending receipt of assent
Arbelo	03049	Provided that you (they) assent
Arbinto ...	03050	Advise you strongly not to assent
Arbitrable	03051	As soon as you (they) assent
Arbitrador	03052	Cannot you assent now
Arbitraire...	03053	Do not assent unless
Arbitram...	03054	Give your assent as soon as you are satisfied everything **is in**
Arbitrante	03055	**Assert** [order
Arbitrio ...	03056	To assert
Arbitrista...	03057	In order that I (we) may be able to assert
Arbolado ...	03058	Strongly assert
Arboladura	03059	Again assert
Arbolario ...	03060	Useless to assert
Arbolecico	03061	**Asserted**
Arbolista ...	03062	It has been asserted that
Arbollon ...	03063	Cable what was actually asserted
Arborator...	03064	It was never really asserted
Arboreo ...	03065	**Assertion**
Arborise ...	03066	Contradict the assertion totally
Arborizado	03067	Assertion is undoubtedly false
Arboscello	03068	Assertion is practically true
Arbotante...	03069	Assertion would be very difficult to prove
Arbours ...	03070	Assertion would not be difficult to prove if you wish it
Arbrisseau	03071	Pending further proofs being forthcoming as to assertion
Arbusculas	03072	**Assessed**
Arbusteno	03073	Damage(s) has (have) been assessed at
Arbustillo...	03074	What have the damages been assessed at
Arbutorum	03075	Value may be assessed at
Arcabucear	03076	Value has been assessed at
Arcabuz ...	03077	**Assessment**
Arcabuzazo	03078	Assessment still owing
Arcaccia ..	03079	Assessment paid to-day
Arcacil ...	03080	All stock and supplies sold for assessment
Arcade ...	03081	All the shares have been assessed with a liability of —— per
Arcadore ...	03082	Am (are) now occupied with the assessment [share
Arcaduzar	03083	It is intended to levy assessment on
Arcagnolo...	03084	Only the requisite assessment work has been done
Arcaismo ...	03085	Only the requisite assessment is necessary to retain the claim
Arcam ...	03086	Take care that the necessary assessment work is done
Arcangel ...	03087	The necessary assessment work has not been done
Arcanidad	03088	I (we) have contracted for all the assessment work
Arcanna ...	03089	**Assets**
Arcanum ...	03090	Assets nil
Arcarius ...	03091	Assets large
Arcavola ...	03092	Assets not yet ascertained [be satisfactory
Arcazon ...	03093	If realization of assets be deferred, the result will undoubtedly
Arceatis ...	03094	Whole assets if sold at present prices would realize practically
Arcediano...	03095	Available assets consist of [nothing
Arcellam ...	03096	Assets are said to be about
Archaism ...	03097	Please forward statement showing assets and liabilities
Archbishop	03098	Assets will be sufficient to pay —— in the £1
Archdeacon	03099	Total assets amount to
Archduke...	03100	What do the total assets amount to
Archeology	03101	The whole of the assets including —— amount to ——
Archeotae...	03102	What are the estimated assets
Archera ...	03103	The amount of assets
Archet ...	03104	What is the balance of assets
Archetipo ..	03105	The balance of assets is
Archetto ...	03106	**Assign**
Archetype...	03107	You should assign your interest in —— to ——

Archeveche	03108	**Assist**
Archicello	03109	To assist
Archiducal	03110	Can you (they) assist me (us) with regard to
Archilaud...	03111	Regret unable to assist
Archiluito	03112	Will assist you (them) as much as I (we) can
Archiluth ...	03113	Will assist
Archimiare	03114	Will not assist
Archimista	03115	To assist you personally
Architecta	03116	To assist if possible
Architrave	03117	Can I (we) assist you
Archivar ...	03118	Cannot assist
Archivero...	03119	Assist —— in my (our) interest
Archiviato	03120	Do not go out of your way to assist —— (him)
Archiviole...	03121	To assist me to make examination at ——
Archiviste	03122	Do you know anyone who could assist
Archivos ...	03123	**Assistance**
Archness ...	03124	Would be no assistance
Archpoet ...	03125	Apply to —— for his (their) assistance
Arcibello ...	03126	Require assistance at once; please send
Arciduca ...	03127	You may apply to —— for assistance
Arcignezza	03128	Will be a great assistance
Arcilloso ...	03129	Shall you want assistance
Arcimastro	03130	Shall want assistance
Arcionato...	03131	Shall not want any assistance
Arciplago ...	03132	Telegraph if you (they) require immediate assistance
Arcipoeta...	03133	Telegraph if you require assistance
Arcipresso	03134	Would be of great assistance
Arcipreste	03135	Would be of no assistance
Arcitenens	03136	What would be the cost of obtaining assistance
Arcobaleno	03137	Will act as your assistant
Arcobugio	03138	With the assistance of
Arcola ...	03139	With a little assistance
Arconcello	03140	Write fully as to assistance required
Arcontado	03141	Send assistance
Arconte ...	03142	Examination will take until —— unless I (we) can have [assistance with the under-ground survey
Arctico ...	03143	Should you want assistance
Arctique ...	03144	Accept no assistance
Arcumbamur	03145	No assistance to be had
Arcuado ...	03146	**Associated**
Arcuccio ...	03147	Do not get associated with
Ardaleado...	03148	Do you know who is associated with
Ardasinas ..	03149	—— has associated himself with —— in this matter
Ardedor ...	03150	—— is associated with
Ardelionem	03151	The gold is associated with
Ardemment	03152	The ore occurs associated with
Ardency ...	03153	**Assorted**
Ardentia ...	03154	Assorted samples assay
Ardeola ...	03155	Ore as raised averages only —— but is readily sorted
Arderit ...	03156	Assorted ore assays as high as ——
Ardescens...	03157	We have now —— tons of assorted ore
Ardida ...	03158	**Assortment**
Ardiglione	03159	Send a complete assortment of
Ardimiento	03160	Send a small assortment of
Ardinculo...	03161	Should bring a small assortment of —— with him
Arditaggio	03162	Forward a good assortment of
Arditanza...	03163	Will bring an assortment of
Ardite ...	03164	**Assume(d)**
Arditezza...	03165	We assume these figures to be correct
Ardoise ...	03166	The figures are assumed

Ardoroso ...	03167	Figures may be assumed to be approximately correct
Arduamente	03168	**Assurance** (*See also* "Insurance.")
Arduatis ...	03169	Fire assurance effected at an(y) average of —— per cent.
Arduidad ...	03170	Have you effected fire assurance on the buildings and plant ?
Arduitate ...	03171	Has the fire assurance lapsed [if not, do so at once
Arduously	03172	Renew fire assurance with
Areca ...	03173	Renew fire assurance ; —— company preferred
Arefaccion	03174	**Assure**
Arelar ...	03175	Do all that you can to assure
Arenaceo ...	03176	Have done all that I (we) could to assure
Arenal ...	03177	—— has assured me (us)
Arenalejo ...	03178	I (we) can assure you that
Arencar ...	03179	**Assuredly**
Arengador	03180	Will assuredly be
Arenica ...	03181	Will assuredly go to
Arenillas ...	03182	**At**
Arenisco ...	03183	At a
Arenosita ..	03184	At a loss
Arenquera	03185	At a profit
Areola ...	03186	At a profit of
Areometro	03187	At about
Areopagita	03188	At least
Areopago ...	03189	At once
Arepennis ..	03190	At or about
Arestin ...	03191	At or about the limit of
Arestinado	03192	At present
Arestinian	03193	At the
Aretalogus	03194	**Atmosphere**
Aretology...	03195	Owing to atmospheric effects
Arfada ...	03196	On account of the rarefied state of the atmosphere
Arfil ...	03197	**Attach**
Argallera ...	03198	To attach
Argamandel	03199	Is there anything to attach
Argamason	03200	Could attach
Argamula	03201	There is really nothing to attach
Argana ...	03202	Attach anything that you can
Arganel ...	03203	Better attach the whole of the property
Argema ...	03204	**Attached**
Argemone	03205	Shall require ——, otherwise the property will be attached
Argentador	03206	Mine has been attached for
Argentatus	03207	Bullion has been attached for
Argenteria	03208	**Attachment**
Argentiere	03209	Get attachment removed as soon as possible
Argentina...	03210	Endeavour to get the attachment removed
Argentosum	03211	Fear an attachment will be levied
Argiglia ...	03212	Has (have) levied an attachment
Argiglioso	03213	Levy an attachment
Argileux ...	03214	No use to levy an attachment
Argiliere ...	03215	Unable to levy an attachment
Argillosum	03216	Will get attachment removed as soon as possible
Arginare ...	03217	An attachment has been levied
Arginetto...	03218	Attachment will be levied forthwith
Arginoso ...	03219	Several attachments have been levied on the property
Argiritas ...	03220	**Attack**
Arglistig ...	03221	Attack of
Argnone ...	03222	Only a slight attack
Argolleta ...	03223	A very serious attack
Argollon ...	03224	Has not yet recovered from attack of (fever)
Argomal ...	03225	Has fully recovered from attack of (fever)
Argonautas	03226	Shewing intended points of attack

Argosy ...	03227	**Attempt**
Argoudan...	03228	Do not care to attempt
Arguajaque	03229	No practical attempt
Arguoia ...	03230	Should you (——) like to attempt
Arguebat ...	03231	Shall I (we) attempt
Arguello ...	03232	Telegraph the result of your (——'s) attempt
Arguenas ...	03233	Useless to attempt to
Arguma ...	03234	Attempts so far fruitless
Argumentar	03235	Am (are) convinced it is useless for you to attempt
Argutatio ...	03236	Make a determined attempt to
Argutezza...	03237	A further attempt has been made to
Argutie ...	03238	Pending a final attempt being made to
Arguyente	03239	Strongly advise you not to attempt it
Arguxia ...	03240	Am (are) convinced that it would be useless to attempt
Argwohn ...	03241	**Attend**
Argyrosis ..	03242	To attend
Ariaccia ...	03243	Please attend to this
Aribar ...	03244	Cannot attend to —— before
Aridity ...	03245	Kindly attend to this matter as early as possible
Arientato ...	03246	Must attend first to
Arienzo ...	03247	When can you (they) attend to
Ariettina ...	03248	When can you attend to it (this)
Arillatore ...	03249	Will attend to it (this) at once
Arindajo ...	03250	**Attended**
Aringatore	03251	Which part is to be attended to first
Aringheria	03252	**Attention**
Arisaro ...	03253	Confine your attention to
Arisnegoo...	03254	Demands my (our) closest attention
Arista ...	03255	Demands your closest attention
Aristarco ...	03256	Pay great attention to
Aristocrat...	03257	Please give this matter your immediate attention
Aristoso ...	03258	Will give the matter attention immediately
Aristula ...	03259	Will give every care and attention to
Arithmum	03260	You need pay little or no attention to
Aritmancia	03261	Will give attention to
Aritmetico	03262	Cannot give much attention to —— for the present
Arlecchino	03263	Think it is well worth your attention
Arlequin ...	03264	Think it is hardly worth your attention
Arlet ...	03265	Particular attention should be paid to —— (him)
Arlienanse	03266	Direct ——'s attention to
Arlota ...	03267	At present my (our) attention is directed to
Arlotto ...	03268	Would suggest for the present you direct attention to
Armaccia ...	03269	Better confine your attention simply to
Armacollo...	03270	When this is completed will turn my (our) attention to
Armadilla...	03271	Shall I (we) have to give my (our) undivided attention
Armadino...	03272	Would require that you should give your undivided attention
Armador ...	03273	Am (are) willing to give my (our) undivided attention
Armajara ...	03274	Would beg you to direct attention to
Armajuolo	03275	**Attested**
Armamento	03276	Should be legally attested
Armario ...	03277	All documents sent are duly attested
Armatetta...	03278	Send attested copy(ies)
Armatoste	03279	Documents must be legally attested
Armatura ...	03280	Copies must be notarially attested
Armavit ...	03281	Has (have) the statement(s) been properly attested
Armband ...	03282	Statement(s) has (have) been properly attested
Armbone ...	03283	**Attle** (*See also* "Dump.")
Armbrust...	03284	Attle heap
Armecella...	03285	Full of attle
Armeggiare	03286	Examine old attle heap(s) for

[55]

Armelina ...	03287	Average sample of attle heap(s)
Armellino...	03288	Attle heap(s) indicate(s)
Armelluela	03289	As shown by attle heap(s)
Armengeld	03290	**Attorney**
Armenhaus	03291	Direct attorney to
Armeniaca	03292	Deliver to attorney
Armenrecht	03293	Employ as attorney
Armentario	03294	Your attorney is
Armentine	03295	Our attorney at
Armentorum	03296	Who have you secured as attorney
Armentose	03297	Have secured —— as my (our) attorney
Armerias ...	03298	Is attorney for
Armfull ...	03299	**Power of attorney**
Armhole ...	03300	Power of attorney mailed giving you power to sign agreement
Armigero ...	03301	Cannot send Power of attorney
Armilar ...	03302	Impossible to act without Power of attorney
Armillaire...	03303	Have cancelled Power of attorney held by
Arminado...	03304	—— holds my (our) Power of attorney
Arminian ...	03305	Must be provided with a Power of attorney
Armisonum	03306	Power of attorney unnecessary
Armisticio	03307	Power of attorney should provide for ——
Armlet ...	03308	Power of attorney miscarried; mail duplicate without delay
Armoiries ...	03309	**Attribute(d)**
Armoisin ...	03310	Attributed mainly to
Armonioso	03311	What do you (they) attribute this to
Armonista	03312	**Auction**
Armoraccio	03313	Auction will be held on or about ——
Armorial ...	03314	Auction to be held on ——
Armour ...	03315	Sell by auction
Armpit ...	03316	Sell by auction under
Armselig ...	03317	When will auction be held
Armsessel...	03318	Sell all effects by auction for what they will fetch
Armuelle ...	03319	What would the effects be likely to realize at an auction
Armurier ...	03320	Effects if sold at an auction would probably realize
Arnacho ...	03321	Effects sold by auction have realized ——
Arnessato...	03322	If sold by auction would probably not realize more than
Arnione ...	03323	Sell by private treaty or auction, as you think best
Aroma ...	03324	To be sold by auction on
Aromatario	03325	**Audit(ed)**
Aromatico	03326	Audited by
Aromatique	03327	Have been audited and found correct
Aromatizar	03328	Have been audited, but require the following corrections
Arouser ...	03329	**Auditor(s)**
Arpadura ...	03330	Particulars required by auditor(s)
Arpagone...	03331	Auditor(s) to
Arpanetta...	03332	**Augitic**
Arpar ...	03333	**August**
Arpeggiato	03334	August expenses amount to
Arpeggio ...	03335	August shipments amount to
Arpella ...	03336	At the beginning of August
Arpentage	03337	About the middle of August
Arpese ...	03338	During the entire month of August
Arpicare ...	03339	For the entire month of August
Arpicordo...	03340	Last August
Arpillera ...	03341	Next August
Arponado ...	03342	Near the end of August
Arquatus ...	03343	1st day of August
Arqueage ...	03344	2nd day of August
Arquebuse	03345	3rd day of August
Arqueo ...	03346	4th day of August

Arqueria ...	03347	5th day of August
Arquetipo...	03348	6th day of August
Arqueton ...	03349	7th day of August
Arquibanco	03350	8th day of August
Arquilla ...	03351	9th day of August
Arquimagia	03352	10th day of August
Arquimesa	03353	11th day of August
Arquitecto	03354	12th day of August
Arquitrabe	03355	13th day of August
Arrabal ...	03356	14th day of August
Arrabalero	03357	15th day of August
Arrabiare ...	03358	16th day of August
Arrabio ...	03359	17th day of August
Arrachage	03360	18th day of August
Arracheur	03361	19th day of August
Arracife ...	03362	20th day of August
Arracimado	03363	21st day of August
Arrack ...	03364	22nd day of August
Arraclan ...	03365	23rd day of August
Arraez ...	03366	24th day of August
Arraffato ...	03367	25th day of August
Arraigadas	03368	26th day of August
Arraigar ...	03369	27th day of August
Arraigned...	03370	28th day of August
Arralar ...	03371	29th day of August
Arramatare	03372	30th day of August
Arramblar	03373	31st day of August

Arrancada 03374 **Auriferous** (*See also* " Gold.")
Arrancato 03375 The country is undoubtedly auriferous
Arranger ... 03376 The country is highly auriferous
Arrangiren 03377 The pyrites is auriferous
Arranque .. 03378 **Auro-Argentiferous**
Arrapiezo .. 03379 **Authentic**
Arrapinato 03380 Not authentic
Arrasadura 03381 Quite authentic
Arraspare... 03382 **Authenticated**   [(——)
Arrastrado· 03383 Have everything properly authenticated under seal of company
Arrate .. 03384 Not properly authenticated
Arrayanal... 03385 **Authorities** (*See also* " Authority.")
Arreador ... 03386 Customs authorities require
Arrebanar... 03387 Land office authorities require
Arrebatado 03388 In case authorities require same
Arrebatina 03389 You must endeavour to work harmoniously with the authorities
Arrebol ... 03390 Is said to be supported by the authorities
Arrebolar ... 03391 Has the secret support of the authorities
Arrebolero 03392 **Authority**
Arrebozado 03393 An authority
Arrebozo ... 03394 By what authority
Arrebujar ... 03395 By authority of
Arrecafe ... 03396 Authority received ; shall act at once
Arrecarsi ... 03397 Authority came too late
Arrecatore 03398 Please give him (——) necessary authority
Arreciar ... 03399 Must have legally drawn authority
Arrecil ... 03400 Cannot give you authority pending meeting of directors
Arrectary ... 03401 Meeting of directors held —— ; you have full authority to act
Arredare ... 03402 Consider authority given on —— as withdrawn
Arredondar 03403 Is authority given on —— withdrawn
Arredro ... 03404 Authority given on —— still holds good
Arregazado 03405 Authority not necessary
Arreglado ... 03406 Do the Board give me (us) authority

Arreglo ...	08407	Full authority necessary
Arrehen ..	08408	Full authority will be given (sent) to you to decide
Arrejacar ...	03409	Have I (we) complete authority
Arrejada ...	03410	Full authority is given (sent) to you to
Arrel	03411	Have given —— full authority to (for)
Arremangar	03412	I am (we are) acting under full authority from
Arrembare	08413	Full authority has been given to —— for the purpose of
Arremeter...	03414	My (our) authority is full and complete
Arremetida	03415	No authority has been given to ——
Arrempujar	03416	On what (whose) authority
Arremueco	08417	To be successful must have full authority without delay
Arrendable	03418	Telegraph full authority
Arrendador	03419	Under what (whose) authority do you act
Arrendajo ..	03420	Written authority necessary; send immediately
Arrendante	08421	A competent authority states
Arrendersi	03422	You have my (our) full authority to
Arrenicus ...	03423	Cannot give you authority to pay
Arrenter ...	03424	On unimpeachable authority
Arrepapalo	08425	**Authorize(d)**
Arrepasate	03426	I am (we are) not authorized
Arrepimus	08427	Was (were) not authorized
Arrepistar	03428	The directors authorize you
Arrepit ...	03429	Unable to authorize you
Arrepticio...	03430	You had better not authorize
Arrequiare	03431	You are authorized by me (us)
Arrequife ...	03432	You are authorized by the Board of Directors
Arrequives	03433	You are fully authorized to do this
Arrerager ...	03434	Fully authorized to
Arrestarem	03435	Did you authorize
Arreticato...	08436	**Authorizing**
Arretin ...	08437	Authorizing you to
Arretranca	08438	Authorizing me (us) to
Arrezafe ...	08439	Authorizing him (them) to
Arrhes ...	08440	Authorizing —— to
Arrihabo ...	03441	**Autumn**
Arrianismo	08442	About last autumn
Arriano ...	08443	During the present autumn
Arribage ...	08444	In the autumn of this year
Arricchire ..	03445	Next autumn
Arricete ...	08446	**Available**
Arricises ...	03447	Available for working purposes
Arridebat ...	03448	Is (are) available
Arrideor ...	03449	—— is (are) not available
Arriendo ...	08450	Has (have) now available
Arrierico ...	08451	Only available in case of
Arriere ...	08452	In —— months shall have available
Arriesgado	03453	Amount of ore available is —— tons
Arrimadero	03454	Will be available
Arrimar ...	03455	When will —— be available
Arrimon ...	03456	When will same be available
Arrincado	08457	What funds have you available for remitting
Arrinconar	03458	**Average** (*See also* "Assay," "Ore," "Sample.")
Arringante	03459	Average standard
Arripiens ...	03460	Average produce
Arripuisse	03461	The average
Arripuit ...	03462	Average of —— assays is
Arriscarse	08463	Above the average
Arrisicato...	03464	Below the average
Arrisionem	03465	Is (are) considerably below the average
Arrisoris ...	03466	Is (are) considerably above the average

Arrivage ...	03467	Is (are) equal to the average
Arrizar ...	03468	Is equal to an average of
Arrobador	03469	Has (have) sent an average sample for assay
Arrobar ...	03470	Is below a general average of
Arrobero ...	03471	Send an average sample about —— lbs. for assay
Arrobiare ...	03472	Average may be taken as
Arrocinado	03473	Average value of the ore now in sight is
Arrodelado	03474	Average value of the ore now in reserve, say —— tons, is ——
Arrodeo ...	03475	Ore will certainly average
Arrodillar...	03476	The result of average sample is
Arrodrigar	03477	The whole must be a fair average
Arrogacion	03478	Taking the average at
Arrogancia	03479	Yield is above the average
Arrogante...	03480	Ore from the mine averaged for the last seven days ——
Arrogar ...	03481	True average sample arrived at by taking proportional quantities
Arrogasse...	03482	What is the average
Arrogetem	03483	Will average at least
Arrojadizo	03484	Will not average more than
Arrojador ...	03485	What are the average dimensions
Arrolarsi ...	03486	Average dimensions are —— ft. by ——
Arromanzar	03487	What is the average length
Arromper ...	03488	Average length is
Arrompido	03489	What is the average width
Arrondir ...	03490	Average width is
Arronzar ...	03491	What is the average depth
Arropado ...	03492	Average depth is
Arrope ..	03493	What is the average height
Arropera ...	03494	Average height is
Arropiero...	03495	What is the average weight
Arrosage ..	03496	Average weight is
Arrosement	03497	Will be above the average
Arrosoir ...	03498	Will be below the average
Arrosorem	03499	Was it a fair average
Arrostito ..	03500	Was undoubtedly a fair average
Arrotatore	03501	Was not a fair average
Arrovescio	03502	Average assay of ore is
Arrowy ...	03503	Ore will probably average
Arroyada ...	03504	Will only average about —— per ton
Arroyar ...	03505	**Avoid**
Arroyuela...	03506	Wish to avoid
Arroz ...	03507	Cannot avoid
Arrozero ...	03508	If I am (we are) to avoid
Arrozzire ...	03509	To avoid
Arruar ...	03510	Avoid the party named
Arrubinare	03511	Will avoid the party named
Arrufado ...	03512	Avoid any chance of mishap
Arrufadura	03513	Avoid any chance of
Arruffarsi ..	03514	Avoid all possible delay
Arrufo ...	03515	Avoid all possible delay and expense
Arrugiarum	03516	Avoid all unnecessary expense
Arrugias ...	03517	Avoid any communication with ——
Arrugon ...	03518	Do all in your power to avoid
Arruinador	03519	I (we) believe —— is trying to avoid
Arruinar ..	03520	I (we) know that —— is trying to avoid payment
Arrullo ...	03521	Is it possible to avoid
Arrumaco ..	03522	Have not been able to avoid
Arrumage...	03523	Shall endeavour to avoid
Arrumazon	03524	You must avoid
Arrumbadas	03525	Try to avoid
Arrumbar	03526	Unable to avoid

Arruotare ...	03527	Would this avoid
Arruvidare	03528	Was (were) not able altogether to avoid
Arsafraga ...	03529	This will avoid
Arsenal ...	03530	**Avoided**
Arseniato ...	03531	Can it (this) be avoided
Arsenico ...	03532	Cannot be avoided
Arsibile ...	03533	Could not be avoided
Arsicciato...	03534	Have avoided all possible expense
Arsinibus ...	03535	Have avoided all possible delay
Artabis ...	03536	In case it can be avoided
Artalejo ...	03537	Litigation must be avoided
Artalete ...	03538	Should have been avoided
Artamisa ...	03539	This must be avoided for the future
Artantis ...	03540	This shall be avoided for the future
Artecillo ...	03541	Could you not have avoided
Artefatto ...	03542	Could not have avoided
Artefice ...	03543	Could have avoided had I (we) known earlier
Arteggiare	03544	**Avoirdupois** (*See also* " Pound," " Ton," &c.)
Artejo ...	03545	**Awaiting**
Artemonis	03546	Where you will find letters awaiting you
Arterial ...	03547	Awaiting answer to
Arteriola ...	03548	Awaiting your (——'s) coming
Arteriuzza	03549	**Award**
Artesano ...	03550	The award amounts practically to
Artesilla ...	03551	No award has yet been made
Artesonado	03552	As soon as award is known
Artesuela ...	03553	Award may be expected on
Artetica ...	03554	What do the damages awarded amount to
Artful ...	03555	**Awarded**
Artfulness	03556	Damages to the extent of —— have been awarded
Arthritis ...	03557	Award is ——
Artiatis ...	03558	Award is only slightly against us
Articella ...	03559	Award is against us on every point
Artichaut...	03560	We have been awarded
Artichoke...	03561	What has been awarded
Articolare...	03562	**Aware**
Articoloso...	03563	Aware of
Articuler ...	03564	Is (are) —— aware of your plan
Articulus ...	03565	Fully aware
Artifex ...	03566	Not aware at all
Artificio ...	03567	Has (have) been aware since —— that
Artiga ...	03568	**Away**
Artigiano ...	03569	Is at present away
Artigkeit ...	03570	Will be away —— days
Artigliere ...	03571	When do you expect to get away
Artillar ...	03572	Expect to get away about
Artilleria ...	03573	Cannot get away before
Artilleur ...	03574	Get away as soon as you can
Artimana ..	03575	How long will you be away
Artimon ...	03576	Expect to be away until
Artista ...	03577	Whilst I am (we are) away
Artistique...	03578	Away from
Artiverat ...	03579	Away altogether from
Artizado ...	03580	Has (have) already sent away ——
Artless ...	03581	How many car loads of ore have you sent away since ——
Artolas ...	03582	How many car loads of ore have you sent away since —— ; and
Artolitos ...	03583	Going away from [what is about value
Artritico ...	03584	Is it going away from
Artrodia ...	03585	It is going away from
Artuna ...	03586	It is not going away from

Arunazo ...	03587	I (we) have sent away —— car loads, value about
Arunon ...	03588	It was (they were) sent away on
Arurarum...	03589	I shall be away from here at least —— days
Aruspex ...	03590	Has (have) shipped away
Aruspice ...	03591	**Axis**
Arveja ...	03592	Axis of
Arvejon ...	03593	Axis passes through
Arvigatis ..	03594	Near the axis
Arvum ...	03595	At some distance from the axis
Arzenei ...	03596	—— away from the axis
Arzigogolo	03597	**Azoic**
Arzobispal	03598	**B**
Arzobispo...	03599	**Back**
Asadero ...	03600	Back from
Asadorazo	03601	Back from —— again on
Asadura ...	03602	When will you (they) (——) be back from
Asadurilla	03603	Will be back from —— about
Asaeteador	03604	Back from there
Asaetinado	03605	Back out
Asalariar ...	03606	Unable to get back
Asalir ...	03607	So as to get back
Asalmonado	03608	To —— and back again
Asaltador ...	03609	When do you expect —— back
Asamblea ...	03610	Expect —— (him) back about
Asargado ...	03611	We shall then have —— feet of " Backs "
Asarma ...	03612	We have now —— feet of " Backs "
Asarotum ...	03613	Cable how many feet of " Backs " you have above adit
Asativo ...	03614	Cable how many feet of " Backs " the proposed deep adit will give
Asbest ...	03615	Cable how many feet of " Backs " you have above —— [you
Asbestino ..	03616	" Backs " will furnish —— tons of ore worth at least ——
Ascalonia ...	03617	Hold back
Ascalpet ...	03618	How much can you (they) hold back
Ascarides ...	03619	How long can you (they) hold back for
Ascaulibus	03620	I (we) can hold back for at least —— days
Ascella ...	03621	I (we) can hold back a matter of [information
Ascendatur	03622	I (we) believe —— is (they are) holding back important
Ascendente	03623	I (we) do not believe that —— is (are) holding back any
Ascender ...	03624	I (we) believe —— is backed up by [information
Ascension	03625	My (our) attempt to get back a portion has been unsuccessful
Ascenso ...	03626	Who is backing him up
Ascensuum	03627	Who is backing —— up
Asceteriam	03628	I (we) hope to get back at least
Ascetic ...	03629	—— would like to get back
Aschen ...	03630	Back of the level
Aschenfall	03631	Back of the stope
Aschensalz	03632	Back of the lode
Aschgrau ...	03633	**Backed**
Aschiancio	03634	Backed out
Aschig ...	03635	Backed up
Aschioso ...	03636	**Backward**
Asciare ...	03637	Very backward
Asciolto ...	03638	Somewhat backward
Asciolvere	03639	**Bad**
Ascion ...	03640	Not as bad as was thought
Asciro ...	03641	Quite as bad as was expected
Ascitico ...	03642	Will be as bad if not worse
Asciugante	03643	Very bad indeed
Asciugato...	03644	Is (are) not nearly so bad
Asciutto ...	03645	Is (are) in a bad way
Ascivimus	03646	**Badly**

Ascivitis ...	03647	Has (have) been badly managed
Asclepiada	03648	Has (have) been badly built
Ascoltare ...	03649	Badly supplied with
Ascondersi	03650	Has been very badly worked
Ascondito...	03651	Badly equipped as regards
Ascondrijo	03652	**Baggage**
Ascosaglia	03653	You can forward your baggage on in front
Ascription	03654	Have forwarded baggage to
Ascritto ...	03655	Was lost with baggage
Ascrivere ...	03656	**Bags**
Ascuas ...	03657	Double bags
Asechador	03658	Bags of ore
Asechar ...	03659	—— bags of samples left on ——
Asechoso ...	03660	—— bags of ore shipped on ——
Asecla ...	03661	How many bags can you ship
Asecucion...	03662	**Bail**
Asedado ...	03663	Accept the bail offered by
Asediador...	03664	Shall I (we) accept bail offered by
Asegundar	03665	Will not accept bail
Asegurador	03666	What is the sum required for bail
Asegurar ...	03667	**Bal**
Asemejar ...	03668	**Balance** (*See also* "Accounts.")
Asemplo ...	03669	Have forwarded balance to
Asenderear	03670	Balance remaining unpaid is
Asentada ...	03671	Balance of
Asentir ...	03672	Balance is correct
Asentista ...	03673	Balance is not correct
Asequi ...	03674	Balances all right
Asequible...	03675	What balance will there be
Aserradero	03676	Balance remaining will amount to
Aserrar ...	03677	Cable the balance you will have in hand after
Asertorio ...	03678	Cannot remit balance before ——
Asesinar ...	03679	Cable balance after all liabilities are discharged
Asesinato ...	03680	Shall ship balance about
Asesino ...	03681	This leaves a balance of only
Asesorarse	03682	Transfer the balance to
Asesoria ...	03683	Balance will amount to
Asestador...	03684	Balance will be (is) trifling
Aseverar ...	03685	Balance will be (is) enough for ——
Asfalto ...	03686	Will the balance be enough for ——
Asfixia ...	03687	What do you make the balance still owing
Asfodelo ...	03688	The balance owing is
Asgo ...	03689	Hold balance to disposal of
Ashlars ...	03690	Please pay balance to my credit with
Ashpan ...	03691	Pay balance to credit of ——
Ashpits ...	03692	Balance on debit side amounts to
Asiaticism	03693	Balance on credit side amounts to
Asidilla ...	03694	Balance is on the debit side
Asiduidad	03695	Balance is on the credit side
Asignado ...	03696	I (we) hold the balance at your disposal
Asignatura	03697	Please correct balance shown in last statement to
Asima ...	03698	There will be a large balance
Asimesmo	03699	There will be a small balance [end of the bond
Asimetria...	03700	Deposit required is —— per cent. Balance to be paid at the
Asimiento...	03701	Balance to be paid at the end of the bond [balance to you
Asimplado	03702	I (we) have cabled the bank (of) (at) —— to transfer the
Asinaccio ...	03703	I (we) have cabled the bank (of) (at) —— to transfer the
Asinaggine	03704	Our books show a balance to your credit of [balance to ——
Asinarias ...	03705	Our books show a balance to your debit of
Asinary ...	03706	Please instruct —— to transfer balance to me

Asine	...	03707	Please instruct —— to transfer balance to ——
Asinella	...	03708	**Balance sheet**
Asinitade	...	03709	Mail copy of balance sheet
Asinone	...	03710	Balance sheet was mailed on ——
Asisia	...	03711	Balance sheet must be certified to (by)
Asistencia	...	03712	Following particulars required for balance sheet
Asistenta	...	03713	Send duplicate balance sheet
Asistir	...	03714	**Ballast**
Askance	...	03715	Could be shipped as ballast
Aslant	...	03716	Could be used as ballast
Aslope	...	03717	Is used for ballasting the roads
Asmar	...	03718	**Banded**
Asmatico	...	03719	Banded structure
Asmoso	...	03720	**Bank** (*See also* " Credit.")
Asnada	...	03721	Bank draft
Asnales	...	03722	Bank has refused
Asnalmente		03723	What is the balance in the bank
Asnazo	...	03724	Bank balance is
Asnerizo	...	03725	Bank agrees
Asobarcado		03726	Bank refuses to cash bill
Asobiar	...	03727	Bank will guarantee
Asobinarse		03728	Bank refuses further advances
Asobio	...	03729	Bank draft for £ —— mailed ——
Asociado	...	03730	Cannot arrange with bank
Asociar	...	03731	Can make arrangements with the bank of —— to
Asolacion	...	03732	Cable terms upon which you can arrange with bank for an [overdraft of ——
Asolador	...	03733	Endeavour to arrange with bank for an overdraft of ——
Asolanar	...	03734	Express bullion to bank of —— at —— [terms
Asolvarse	...	03735	Have arranged with bank for an overdraft on —— following
Asombrador		03736	Have made arrangements with the bank of —— to ——
Asombrar	...	03737	Please give me a credit with bank of ——
Asombroso		03738	Please give me a credit of £ ——
Asonadia	...	03739	Money to be deposited with the bank of
Asonancia	...	03740	Bank has no agent at
Asonantar		03741	Bank rate is now
Asonante	...	03742	Bank rate is likely to be raised
Asosegarse		03743	Bank rate is likely to be easier
Aspado	...	03744	With the cashier of the bank (of)
Aspalato	...	03745	You can draw upon us through the bank of —— for ——
Aspamiento		03746	The only bank having an agent here is ——
Asparagus		03747	The banks here are closed
Aspecto	...	03748	The height of the banks varies from —— to —— (*See also*
Aspellito	...	03749	What is the height of the banks ["Alluvial.")
Asperear	...	03750	Shall commence sluicing the banks
Asperete	...	03751	**Banker(s)**
Aspergerie		03752	Banker(s) at
Aspergor	...	03753	Who is your banker
Asperiego	...	03754	Who is his (their) banker
Asperilla	...	03755	**Banket**
Asperiorem		03756	Banket has now been proved to extend
Asperitas	...	03757	Banket formation
Asperitudo		03758	Auriferous banket
Asperity	...	03759	Has (have) discovered auriferous banket
Aspernans		03760	Cable particulars, dimensions and value of auriferous banket
Aspernatio		03761	Auriferous banket is alleged to exist on the property
Asperon	...	03762	Have not discovered any auriferous banket of value
Aspersion	...	03763	Have struck banket at a depth of —— feet from surface
Aspersorio		03764	Have struck banket in —— level
Aspersus	...	03765	Have proved banket to extend a depth of —— ft.

Asphyxier...	03766	Have proved banket to extend for a length of —— ft.
Asphyxy ...	03767	Cable assays of banket
Aspic ...	03768	Send samples of banket to London
Aspiciens ...	03769	Send samples of banket to reliable assayer and cable result
Aspicior ...	03770	A bed of banket
Aspidam ...	03771	A bed of banket —— ft. thick
Aspilates ...	03772	The banket dips at an angle of
Aspiracion	03773	**Bankrupt**
Aspirante ...	03774	Has (have) become bankrupt
Aspirare ...	03775	Concern is practically bankrupt
Aspirating	03776	Company is practically bankrupt
Asplenon ...	03777	Owner(s) practically bankrupt
Asportare...	03778	Owner(s) became bankrupt on
Asportatio	03779	Is (are) not bankrupt
Asportavis	03780	Is (are) far removed from bankruptcy
Aspratilem	03781	There is a report that —— is (are) bankrupt
Aspredo ...	03782	**Bankruptcy**
Aspretum...	03783	Pending bankruptcy proceedings
Asprezza ...	03784	**Bar(s)** (*See also* " Bullion.")
Asprigno ...	03785	It will bar me (us)
Asquear ...	03786	It will not bar me (us) from
Asqueroso	03787	Will it (this) bar us from
Asquia ...	03788	This is likely to bar us
Asquint ...	03789	It will not bar us
Assabamur	03790	Have shipped —— bars of bullion by express
Assaberit ...	03791	—— bars of silver, weighing ——
Assaccia ...	03792	—— bars of gold, weighing ——
Assaggiato	03793	Bars of bullion
Assaillir ...	03794	Shall ship —— bars of bullion on
Assaissimo	03795	Shipments for week ending to-day (——) are —— bars
Assalire ...	03796	Our shipments for last four weeks to date are —— bars
Assalitore...	03797	Have you shipped any bars
Assannare	03798	Have you shipped any bars and of what value since
Assapere ...	03799	When are you likely to ship next and to what value
Assaporato	03800	The assay of bar is gold —— silver ——
Assarius ...	03801	Have shipped regularly —— bars per ——
Assassiner	03802	Bar of ground 　　[now at the rate of —— feet per week
Assatura ...	03803	A bar of hard ground has come in at the ——. 　Our speed is
Assavendum	03804	A bar of hard ground has come in in sinking shaft. 　Our speed [is now at the rate of —— feet per week
Assecla ...	03805	A bar of hard ground has come in, and will require blasting [before we can continue hydraulicing
Assectatio	03806	Send two spiral-cut turning bars (*See also* " Drills.")
Assector ...	03807	**Bar gold**
Assecurare	03808	**Bar silver**
Assecutus...	03809	**Bargain(s)**
Assedersi ...	03810	A good bargain
Assediante	03811	A bad bargain
Asseguire ...	03812	Cannot you make a better bargain
Assekuranz	03813	I (we) consider it a very good bargain for you
Assembiare	03814	Make the best bargain you can
Assemblage	03815	Best bargain I (we) can make is ——
Assembrato	03816	Bargain is very one-sided
Assemsmi...	03817	Cannot make a better bargain
Assennato ..	03818	If you cannot make any better bargain
Assentans...	03819	**Barge(s)**
Assentire ...	03820	A barge will cost
Asseoir ...	03821	Can you secure a river barge and what cost
Asserarsi ...	03822	Hire of a suitable barge amounts to
Asserella ...	03823	Will have to be transhipped in river barge

Asserenare	03824	**Barren** (*See also* " Lode," " Quartz," " Vein.")
Asserturus	03825	Barren-looking quartz
Asservir ...	03826	Vein has become barren
Assesseur ...	03827	Vein stuff is barren
Assevare ...	03828	The barren portion of the vein extends —— feet
Assibilare ...	03829	The quartz crushed is mixed with much barren rock
Assicella ...	03830	Entirely through barren country
Assiculo ...	03831	We are now in barren ground
Assidenza...	03832	We have intersected the lode, but it is barren
Assiderato	03833	You should take care that no barren quartz is milled
Assiduita ...	03834	For the last —— ft. the drivage has been barren
Assiegeant	03835	The proportion of barren to mineralized stone is as one to ——
Assiepare ...	03836	Quite barren
Assiette ...	03837	Not quite barren
Assillito ...	03838	Barren ground
Assimiler ...	03839	Barren rock
Assiuolo ...	03840	**Basalt(ic)**
Associare ...	03841	We are now in a bar of basaltic rock
Assolatio ...	03842	Is cut off by basalt
Assolement	03843	The basalt has come in again
Assolidare	03844	**Base**
Assoluto ...	03845	Base bullion
Assombrir	03846	At the base of the hill
Assomiglio	03847	From the base
Assommare	03848	Runs along the base of the
Assommer...	03849	Ore is very base
Assonante...	03850	Base of operations is at
Assonanza	03851	To the base
Assonnare...	03852	**Basic**
Assorbente	03853	**Basis**
Assordato ...	03854	In order to have a firm basis
Assortir ...	03855	Will only act on a basis of
Assouplir ...	03856	As a basis for negotiations
Assuefare ...	03857	Starting from a basis of
Assujettir...	03858	**Battery(ies)** (*See also* " Mill," " Stamps.")
Assumente	03859	Cable average assay of stuff before it enters battery
Assurdita ...	03860	What is average assay of pulp after it leaves battery
Assureur ...	03861	What is average assay of stuff sent to battery for last —— days
Assurgere ...	03862	Average assay of stuff before it enters battery is ——
Astaco ...	03863	Average assay of pulp after it leaves battery is ——
Astallare ...	03864	Average assay of stuff sent to battery for last —— days is ——
Astegnente	03865	A 5-head battery complete with engine, boiler, gearing and [amalgamated copper plates
Astenico ...	03866	A 10-head battery complete with engine, boiler, gearing and [amalgamated copper plates
Asterisco ...	03867	A 15-head battery complete with engine, boiler, gearing and [amalgamated copper plates
Asterism ...	03868	A —— head battery complete with engine, boiler, gearing and [amalgamated copper plates
Asterisque	03869	We require —— new iron shoes for battery
Asteroid ...	03870	We require —— new steel shoes for battery
Astersione	03871	We require —— new iron dies for battery
Astetta ...	03872	We require —— new steel dies for battery
Asticoter ...	03873	We require —— new tappets for battery
Astilejos ...	03874	We require —— new cams for battery
Astilico ...	03875	We require —— new lifters for battery
Astillazo ...	03876	We require a set of shoes and dies of iron for battery
Astillero ...	03877	We require a set of shoes and dies of steel for battery
Astillica ...	03878	We require shoes and dies of steel
Astinenza...	03879	We require shoes and dies of iron

Astipulatu	03880	Screens are required for battery
Astipulor ...	03881	The loss in the battery amounts to
Astiquer ...	03882	Can purchase a —— head battery complete for ——
Astloch ...	03883	Condition of the battery is very good
Astraere ...	03884	Condition of the battery is satisfactory
Astragalo...	03885	Condition of the battery is very defective
Astral ...	03886	Battery will crush —— tons of our stone per day of 24 hours
Astrancia ...	03887	Should suggest you advertise for —— head battery
Astrea	03888	**Be**
Astreindre	03889	Be at
Astriccton	03890	Shall be about
Astrictivo...	03891	When will you be at
Astricto ...	03892	Will be at —— on
Astride ...	03893	Be on the look-out for
Astrifero ...	03894	Be cautious as regards
Astringe ...	03895	Be sure that you are correct
Astringir ...	03896	Be sure and
Astroite ...	03897	Can you be there
Astrolabio	03898	Cannot be
Astrolatry	03899	I (we) can be there on
Astrologer	03900	I (we) can be there at
Astrologia	03901	I (we) cannot be there before
Astrologo ...	03902	To be applied at
Astronomia	03903	To be
Astroso ...	03904	Must not be
Astructus...	03905	Must not be allowed
Astucia ...	03906	Should be
Astucieux...	03907	Should not be
Asturion ...	03908	Will be
Astutaccio	03909	Will be at least
Astutezza...	03910	**Bear(s)**
Astuto ...	03911	A "bear" attack
Asubiar ...	03912	If we are to defeat the "bears"
Asueto ...	03913	Is (are) threatened with a "bear" attack
Asumir ...	03914	It is rumoured that a "bear" attack is in process of [formation
Asurarso ...	03915	Owing to "bear" operations
Asurcar ...	03916	Depression is due to a "bear" movement
Asuso ...	03917	To minimise "bear" operations
Asustadizo	03918	It will be necessary to bear in mind
Asustar ...	03919	**Bearer(s)**
Asustilar ...	03920	Should be payable "to bearer"
Atabaca ...	03921	Has been made out payable "to bearer"
Atabal ..	03922	Bearers for
Atabalear ...	03923	Fixing bearers for
Atabalejo ...	03924	Have fixed bearers for
Atabanado	03925	**Bearing** (*See also* "Lode," "Vein.")
Atabernado	03926	The general bearing of the lode is —— degrees east of north
Atabillar ...	03927	The general bearing of the lode is —— degrees west of north
Atabladera	03928	What is the true normal bearing of the lode
Atablar ...	03929	**Because**
Atacadera...	03930	Because of
Atacado ...	03931	**Become**
Atacar ...	03932	Do not let it (this) become
Atachonado	03933	It need never become
Atacola ...	03934	Has (have) become
Ataderas ...	03935	Has (have) become very
Atadijo ...	03936	This (it) may become
Atador ...	03937	Do you know what has become of
Atadura ...	03938	Do not know what has become of
Atafagar ...	03939	Endeavour to learn what has become of

Ataharre ...	03940	**Bed(s)**
Atahorma...	03941	Bed of the creek
Ataifor ...	03942	Bed of the river
Ataire ...	03943	Engine bed
Atajadizo ...	03944	There are enormous beds of ore exposed
Atajador ...	03945	**Bedded structure**
Atajar ...	03946	**Bedrock**
Atajea ...	03947	At bedrock price
Ataladrar ...	03948	The bedrock price is
Atalantar ...	03949	What is the bedrock price
Atalaya ...	03950	Above the bedrock (*See also* "Alluvial.")
Atalvina ...	03951	Immediately above the bedrock
Atamiento	03952	The bedrock came in at —— feet
Atanasia ...	03953	**Been**
Ataque ...	03954	I (we) have been
Ataquiza ...	03955	I (we) have not been
Ataracea ...	03956	Is —— likely to have been
Atarantado	03957	Has (have) been
Ataraxia ...	03958	Has (have) not been
Atarazana	03959	Has (have) not been yet
Atareado ...	03960	Might have been avoided
Atarfe ...	03961	This (which) should have been
Atarquinar	03962	**Before**
Atarraga ...	03963	Before he (they) will proceed
Atarrajar ...	03964	Just before
Atarugado	03965	Must be paid on or before ——
Atasajado...	03966	On or before the —— next
Atascadero	03967	**Beforehand**
Atascar ...	03968	Be beforehand with —— if possible
Ataud ...	03969	If I am (we are) to be beforehand with
Ataudado ...	03970	Have everything ready beforehand
Ataviado ...	03971	To enable me to be beforehand with
Atavio ...	03972	Everything will be ready beforehand
Ataxia ...	03973	Endeavour to be beforehand
Ateismo ...	03974	Had been there beforehand
Ateista ...	03975	**Begin**
Atelier ...	03976	To begin
Atemorizar	03977	Refuse(s) to begin
Atempa ...	03978	Consent(s) to begin if
Atemporado	03979	Before you (they) begin
Atencion ...	03980	To enable me (us) to begin
Atender ...	03981	When shall you begin
Atentar ...	03982	Expect to begin about
Atenuacion	03983	Shall begin this work on
Ateramnos	03984	When shall you begin to sink
Atericia ...	03985	Shall begin sinking on
Aterido ...	03986	When shall you begin to drift
Atermoyer	03987	Shall begin drifting on
Aternerado	03988	Begin(s) at
Ateroma ...	03989	Shall begin at
Aterrar ...	03990	When will you require me (us) to begin
Aterronar...	03991	**Begun**
Atesar ...	03992	Was (were) begun on
Atesorador	03993	Had been begun before your advice reached
Atesorar ...	03994	Has (have) begun very well
Atestacion	03995	Has (have) been recently begun
Atestadura	03996	**Behalf**
Atestiquar	03997	On behalf of
Atetado ...	03998	On my (our) behalf
Atetillar ...	03999	On whose behalf

Athanasian	04000	Who is to appear on our behalf
Atheism ...	**04001**	Can you arrange for —— to appear on our behalf
Athemholen	04002	Have arranged for —— to appear on my (our) behalf
Athemzug	04003	Will act on your behalf
Athenaeum	04004	Acting on behalf of vendors
Athetic ...	04005	Is not acting on behalf of anyone
Athlete ...	04006	—— is acting on behalf of
Athletique	04007	Will you act on behalf of ——
Atiborrar ...	04008	Arrange to take charge on behalf of
Aticismo ...	04009	On behalf of all concerned
Atico ...	04010	On behalf of the owners
Aticurga ...	04011	**Behind**
Atiesar ...	04012	Is (are) behind the
Atifle ...	04013	Is (are) behind with
Atildadura	04014	Is (are) behind time
Atirantir ...	04015	**Being**
Atisbadero	04016	Points to the value being principally in the
Atisbador...	04017	**Belief**
Atisbar ...	04018	Unworthy of belief
Atisuado ...	04019	**Believe**
Atizadero ...	04020	To believe
Atizador ...	04021	Who (which) are we to believe
Atizonar ...	04022	Do not believe
Atlante ...	04023	I (we) do not believe him (it)
Atlantico ...	04024	I have reason to believe
Atlas ...	04025	How much can I (we) believe
Atleta ...	04026	Should not believe what —— says
Atmosfera	04027	There is reason to believe
Atoage ...	04028	There is no reason to believe
Atobar ...	04029	You can implicitly believe
Atochado ...	04030	There is every reason to believe it will continue
Atochal ...	04031	**Believed**
Atocinado	04032	It is believed here that
Atolladero	04033	Not believed here in the slightest
Atollar ...	04034	Is not believed
Atolondrar	04035	**Belong(s)**
Atometto ...	04036	Belongs to
Atomism ...	04037	Does not belong
Atomista ...	04038	All that belongs to
Atomistico	04039	The whole belongs to
Atondar ...	04040	**Below** (*See also* "Under.")
Atonement	04041	Below the adit
Atonito ...	04042	Below the —— level
Atontado ...	04043	Mine has not been worked below
Atora ...	04044	**Belting**
Atorarse ...	04045	Rubber Belting
Atormentar	04046	Cotton belting, 3-ply
Atortolar ...	04047	Cotton belting, 4-ply
Atortujar...	04048	Cotton belting, 5-ply
Atosigador	04049	Cotton belting, 6-ply
Atosigar ...	04050	Leather belting, single
Atrabancar	04051	Leather belting, double
Atrabile ...	04052	Link belting
Atrabilis ...	04053	Require —— feet belting, width —— inches
Atracadero	04054	Send at once necessary belting to transmit —— h.p. width [of pulley —— inches; speed in feet per second is ——
Atracar ...	04055	**Bend**
Atractiz ...	04056	To bend
Atraer ...	04057	Must not be allowed to bend
Atrafagado	04058	Should not bend

Atraillar ...	04059	Will have either to bend or break
Atramental	04060	**Bending**
Atramparse	04061	Bending away from
Atramuz ...	04062	Bending towards
Atrancar ...	04063	By slightly bending
Atrapar ...	04064	Owing to a slight bending of
Atrasado ...	04065	**Benefit**
Atrasmano	04066	In order to benefit by
Atravesado	04067	Would it (this) be any benefit (if)
Atrayente	04068	If this would be any benefit
Atrascalar	04069	It would greatly benefit
Atreguado	04070	There would be no benefit
Atresnalar	04071	What benefit would you derive from —— (it)
Atreverse ...	04072	In order to derive the greatest benefit from
Atrevido ...	04073	**Besides**
Atriaquero	04074	Is there anything besides
Atribucion	04075	The only thing besides is
Atribuir ...	04076	There is nothing besides
Atribular ...	04077	Besides which
Atributivo	04078	**Best**
Atributo ..	04079	The best
Atriceses ...	04080	The best plan would appear to be
Atricion ...	04081	The best thing will be to
Atril ...	04082	What do you consider the best
Atrilera ...	04083	Select the best
Atristar ...	04084	Select the best points
Atrito ...	04085	Do the best you are able
Atrocement	04086	Advise —— (him) as best you can
Atrochar ...	04087	It is decidedly the best that can be done
Atrocidad...	04088	What do you consider the best thing to be done
Atrociter ...	04089	I (we) consider that the best thing would be to
Atrofia ...	04090	Provided that you think this the best thing to do
Atrofico ...	04091	Make the best of it
Atronado ...	04092	**At Best**
Atronadura	04093	Complete purchase at best
Atronar ...	04094	Shall I (we) complete at best
Atronerar...	04095	**Better**
Atropellar	04096	Expect to do better a little later
Atrophy ...	04097	If anything better
Atrozmente	04098	Will probably be slightly better
Atruhanado	04099	Think it would be better if
Attacca ...	04100	Cannot you get better terms
Attaccarla	04101	I (we) can suggest nothing better
Attachant...	04102	In case you (they) cannot do better
Attainture	04103	In case nothing better
Attapinato	04104	I am in much better health
Attaquants	04105	Under better circumstances
Attaquer ...	04106	What had better be done
Attardarsi	04107	Vendors will not give better terms
Attarder ...	04108	You had better
Attastare ...	04109	Had I (we) not better
Attecchire	04110	You had better return home
Atteindre ...	04111	Better remain a few days longer
Attelage ...	04112	Better not insist upon
Attempato	04113	Better decline
Attemper ...	04114	Is slightly better
Attendere...	04115	**Between**
Attendrir ...	04116	Between the dates mentioned
Attentarsi...	04117	Between now and ——
Attentat ...	04118	Between us

Attenuant	04119	Between you and ——
Attenuer ...	04120	Between ourselves
Atterrito ...	04121	You must settle it between yourselves
Attesoche ...	04122	Ranging between —— and ——
Attestans ...	04123	**Beware**
Atticciato	04124	I (we) advise you to beware of ——
Atticism ...	04125	**Beyond**
Atlifement	04126	Do not let it get beyond
Attignere ...	04127	The property lies beyond
Attinenza...	04128	Affair is beyond my (our) control
Attique ...	04129	**Bid**
Attiraglio ...	04130	Shall I bid
Attirail ...	04131	What shall I bid
Attitudine	04132	Bid for
Attivita ...	04133	Will bid against us
Attollent ...	04134	Bid has been accepted
Attoscato ...	04135	Bid has been declined
Attrahent...	04136	Bid accepted provided that
Attraper ...	04137	Do not bid, but wait until offered
Attrappare	04138	**Bill(s)**
Attrattiva...	04139	By bills of
Attrayant ..	04140	Bill(s) protested
Attribuer ...	04141	Bills are not protested
Attrice ...	04142	Can you renew bill
Attristant...	04143	Can you renew bill due —— for three months
Attrizione..	04144	Cannot renew the bill(s)
Attrouper...	04145	Do not present bill(s)
Attruppato	04146	Have arranged with —— to meet the bills
Attuariato	04147	Must renew the bill(s)
Attuffarsi ...	04148	The next bill is due —— prompt date
Attujare ...	04149	The bill for —— has been paid
Attune ...	04150	The bill should be presented and noted
Atucia ...	04151	Am (are) offered —— cash. Bill at —— months for balance.
Atufar ...	04152	When is the next bill due [Shall I (we) accept
Atunara ...	04153	Will you renew bill
Atunero ...	04154	Will —— renew bill for a commission of ——
Aturdido ...	04155	Will you accept bill for balance of ——
Aturdir ...	04156	I (we) will take bill at three months for £——
Aturrullar	04157	Unable to meet bills without a remittance from you of ——
Atusador ...	04158	Bill must be drawn by the Directors on their personal
Aubade ...	04159	Your bill on —— protested [guarantee
Aubepine ...	04160	Your bill on —— dishonoured ; instructions required
Auberge ...	04161	Bills are at seven days' sight
Aubergiste	04162	By bill(s) at seven days' sight
Aubertico ...	04163	The bills are at ten days' sight
Auburn ...	04164	The bills are at thirty days' sight
Aucchiare...	04165	The bills are at —— days' sight
Auceps ...	04166	By bill(s) at ten days
Aucunement	04167	By bill(s) at thirty days
Audace ...	04168	By bill(s) at —— days
Audacieux	04169	Have bills been protested
Audaculus	04170	Get bill protested
Audible ...	04171	Get bill renewed
Audiencia...	04172	Get holders to retain bill(s)
Audienza ...	04173	Has (have) left bills unpaid amounting to
Auditivo ...	04174	When bill is presented
Auditorato	04175	Has (have) the bill(s) been presented
Auditorio ...	04176	Bill(s) presented already
Auerhahn	04177	Bill(s) not yet presented
Auerochs ...	04178	Bill has not been paid

Aufackern	04179	Bill will be paid
Aufathmen	04180	Bill will not be paid
Aufbahren	04181	**Bills of Lading**
Aufbeissen	04182	Bills of lading posted on
Aufbersten	04183	Bills of lading should be to the order of
Aufblasen ...	04184	Have you received bill of lading
Aufblicken	04185	Goods detained : they are not as per bill of lading
Aufbrennen	04186	Mail duplicate bill of lading
Aufburdung	04187	No bill of lading received
Aufdichten	04188	—— arrived, but no bill of lading
Aufdrangen	04189	Refuse(s) to give up bill of lading without consent of ——
Aufeisen ...	04190	Have you mailed bills of lading
Aufenthalt	04191	Has drawn upon me with bill of lading attached
Auferlegen	04192	Has drawn upon me, but no bill of lading attached
Auffallend	04193	**Bill of Sale**
Auffallig ...	04194	Has (have) given a bill of sale on
Auffassung	04195	Shall have to take up bill of sale amounting to
Auffliegen ...	04196	Have taken up bill of sale
Auffordern	04197	**Bind**
Auffressen	04198	To bind
Auffuhrung	04199	So as to bind
Auffuttern	04200	Declines to bind himself
Aufgabeln	04201	Consents to bind himself
Aufgebot ...	04202	Consider it binds me (——) but not ——
Aufgeklart	04203	It will not bind you
Aufgeld ...	04204	It will only bind you to
Aufgelegt ...	04205	What will this bind me (us) to
Aufgeraumt	04206	Will this bind me (us) to
Aufgeweckt	04207	You must take care to bind ——
Aufgreifen	04208	**Binding**
Aufhakeln	04209	Will it be binding upon
Aufhalten ...	04210	Will be binding upon
Aufhaschen	04211	Not sufficiently binding
Aufhaufung	04212	**Bismuth**
Aufhebung	04213	Bismuth ore
Aufheitern	04214	Bismuth native or oxide
Aufhocken	04215	Sulphide of bismuth
Aufjagen ...	04216	The ore contains —— per cent. of bismuth
Aufkaufer ...	04217	The market price for bismuth is
Aufklaffen	04218	**Bit(s)**
Aufklauben	04219	Bits for
Aufklimmen	04220	A supply of bits
Aufklopfen	04221	For sharpening bits
Aufkrampen	04222	Blunts the bits almost at once
Auflage ...	04223	Owing to breakage of bits
Auflauerer	04224	A bit of
Auflehnen ...	04225	**Bitumen** (*See also* " Coal," " Fuel.")
Auflockern	04226	**Bituminous**
Auflosbar ...	04227	Bituminous beds
Auflosung ..	04228	Bituminous coal
Aufmarsch	04229	Non-bituminous
Aufmauern	04230	Good bituminous coal
Aufmerksam	04231	**Black**
Aufmuntern	04232	Black jack
Aufnahme	04233	Black tin
Aufopfern ...	04234	**Blackmail**
Aufpasser ...	04235	Trying to blackmail me (us)
Aufpfeifen	04236	In undoubtedly an attempt to levy blackmail
Aufpflugen	04237	Am (are) compelled to pay blackmail to the extent of
Aufprallen	04238	**Blackmailing**

Aufprotzen	04239	In order to defeat blackmailing attempts
Aufpumpen	04240	Do not submit to any blackmailing attempts
Aufquellen	04241	Shall not submit to any blackmailing attempts
Aufraumen	04242	**Blacksmith**
Aufrecht ...	04243	Good mine blacksmith should be sent out at once
Aufreizung	04244	**Blame**
Aufrichtig	04245	Who do you consider is to blame
Aufriss ...	04246	Do you consider —— (he) is to blame
Aufrutteln	04247	No one is really to blame
Aufsatzig...	04248	Is (are) probably to blame
Aufschauen	04249	Discover if possible who is to blame
Aufschlag...	04250	Do not blame me
Aufschluss	04251	**Blank(s)**
Aufschrift	04252	What is the order for filling in the blanks
Aufschwung	04253	Are the blanks to be filled up in consecutive order
Aufsein ...	04254	The blanks are to be filled up in consecutive order
Aufsieden...	04255	The blanks are to be filled up in the following order, viz. :—
Aufsingen	04256	The foregoing blank remains vacant
Aufspannen	04257	To be left blank
Aufsperren	04258	To be left blank until
Aufspielen	04259	Must not be left blank
Aufstand ...	04260	Cannot be left blank
Aufstobern	04261	Can remain blank until
Aufstossen	04262	**Blankets** (*See also* " Concentrates," " Stamps.")
Aufstreuen	04263	Our stock of blanket sand is now
Aufs'richt	04264	Stuff caught on the blankets assays gold —— per ton of 2240
Autstulpen	04265	I (we) require —— yards of good blanketing [lbs.
Auftakeln	04266	What blanket sand have you accumulated
Auftakt ...	04267	**Blast**
Auftauchen	04268	Shall require to blast
Aufthauen	04269	In order to blast
Aufthurman	04270	Duration of blast
Auftischen	04271	Blast holes
Auftrennen	04272	It will be necessary to blast
Auftritt ...	04273	**Blast furnace** (*See also* " Furnaces.")
Aufwachsen	04274	**Blasting** (*See also* " Boring.")
Aufwallung	04275	Accident occurred when blasting at ——
Aufwarten	04276	Accident occurred on —— when blasting. Killed —— men
Aufwechsel	04277	Continuous blasting is necessary
Aufwickeln	04278	Little or no blasting is required
Aufwiegler	04279	Ground is now harder but better for blasting
Aufwuhlen	04280	Forward promptly low tension electric blasting machine suffi-[ciently powerful to fire —— holes
Aufzehrung	04281	Forward promptly high tension electric blasting machine suffi-
Augapfel ...	04282	Blasting & clearing away stuff [ciently powerful to fire —— holes
Augelot ...	04283	**Blasting Gelatine** (*See also* " Dynamite," " Detonators," " Explosives.") [tine ¼ inch diameter
Augenblick	04284	Forward promptly —— cases (50 lbs. each) of blasting gela-[tine ½ inch diameter
Augenbraue	04285	Forward promptly —— cases (50 lbs. each) of blasting gela-
Augenglas	04286	Forward promptly —— cases (50 lbs. each) of blasting gela-[tine 1 inch diameter
Augenhohle	04287	Forward promptly —— cases (50 lbs. each) of blasting gela-
Augenlid...	04288	**Blende** (*See also* " Zinc.") [tine 1¼ inch diameter
Augenstern	04289	**Blocks**
Augenzeuge	04290	Pulley blocks for lifting —— must be sent, also snatch block
Augetto ...	04291	Pulley blocks for lifting will be sent
Auggiare ...	04292	I (we) require pulley block for lifting
Augmentar	04293	Three sheave blocks required for rope —— inches circumference
Auguralis...	04294	**Blower**

Augurante	04295	A Baker blower
Auguratore	04296	A Roots blower
Augurio ...	04297	**Blowing engine**
Augustales	04298	Shall require to stop for repairs to blowing engine
Augustin ...	04299	Blowing engines can only maintain a pressure of —— inches
Augustness	04300	**Blue ground** (*See also* "Diamonds.")
Aulaga ...	04301	Blue ground hauled —— loads (each 16 cubic feet)
Auledo ...	04302	Blue ground washed —— loads (each 16 cubic feet) yield ——
Aulico ...	04303	Loads of blue ground on floors [carats, approximate value £ ——
Aullador ...	04304	—— loads of blue ground hauled
Aullido ...	04305	—— loads of "reef" hauled
Aumentado	04306	**Blue stone**
Aumento ...	04307	Price of blue stone is —— per pound
Aumettare	04308	What are you paying for blue stone
Aumiliare...	04309	Our stock of blue stone amounts to
Aumonerie	04310	Have contracted for a supply of blue stone
Aunamiento	04311	**Board of Directors** (*See also* "Authorized," "Directors.")
Aunar ...	04312	Is now under consideration of the Board of Directors
Auncicare	04313	Board of Directors are most anxious
Aunque ...	04314	Board of Directors suggest that
Auparavant	04315	Local Board of Directors
Aurated ...	04316	Board of Directors will consist of
Aurelia ...	04317	Board of Directors to consist of the following
Aureola ...	04318	Would join the Board of Directors
Auricalco ...	04319	Will —— join the Board of Directors [instructions sent you
Auricolare	04320	Will be considered by the Board of Directors on —— and cable
Auricome...	04321	There has been no Board meeting to-day
Auricula ...	04322	There will be no Board meeting until
Aurifodina	04323	No Board could be held; absence of quorum
Auriga ...	04324	A quorum of the Board of Directors
Aurista ...	04325	Board of Directors have resolved that
Aurizzare...	04326	Board of Directors approve
Aurosus ...	04327	Board of Directors do not approve
Aurraugado	04328	A number of the Board
Auruspice	04329	Board meeting on ——
Ausartung	04330	By resolution of the Board
Ausathmen	04331	Cable for the information of the Board
Ausbacken	04332	Board have resolved that in future
Ausbeute ...	04333	Board have decided not to
Ausbilden...	04334	Board awaits further advices before decision
Ausbleiben	04335	Board have not decided to
Ausborgen	04336	The matter must remain in abeyance until the Board meeting
Ausbrechen	04337	Was before the Board, who have resolved [on ——
Ausbrugeln	04338	Will only become a member of the Board on condition that
Ausbursten	04339	Will the Board agree that (to)
Auscultate	04340	The Board met on ——
Ausdampfen	04341	To lay before the Board of Directors
Ausdauern	04342	Places the Board of Directors in a very satisfactory position
Ausdehnbar	04343	Places the Board of Directors in an unsatisfactory position
Ausdeutung	04344	Places the Board of Directors in a compromising position
Ausdienen	04345	The Board of Directors authorise you to
Ausdorren	04346	Has been laid before the Board of Directors
Ausdunsten	04347	**Board(s)** (*See also* "Timber.")
Ausencia ...	04348	Am (are) engaged in cutting boards for sluices, &c.
Ausentarse	04349	Shall require —— boards for sluices
Ausente ...	04350	There is plenty of timber available for boards
Auserkoren	04351	Is (are) delayed, pending delivery of timber for boards
Auserlesen	04352	**Boarding-house(s)**
Ausfahren	04353	Boarding-houses are much in need of repair
Ausfechten	04354	New boarding-houses will be required at ——, at a cost of ——

Ausfindig ...	04355	Boarding-house supplies [property
Ausfordern	04356	There is boarding-house accommodation for —— men on the
Ausfransen	04357	The boarding-house(s) is (are) in good repair
Ausfuhrung	04358	Men are boarded on contract free of cost to proprietors
Ausfullung	04359	Annual profit on the boarding-house amounts to £——
Ausgabe ...	04360	**Boat**
Ausgattern	04361	In order to catch boat at ——
Ausgeberin	04362	Boat for —— leaves on
Ausgeburt	04363	A boat runs between —— and ——
Ausgedient	04364	**Bob**
Ausgegeben	04365	Engine bob
Ausgemacht	04366	Angle bob (*See also* " Angle.")
Ausgiessen	04367	Breakage of bob
Ausglatten	04368	**Boiler(s)**
Ausguss ...	04369	Boiler arrangement
Aushaaren	04370	Shall arrange boiler(s) so as to
Aushalten...	04371	Boiler fittings
Aushebung	04372	Boiler tube(s)
Aushohlung	04373	Boiler flue(s)
Aushorchen	04374	Cornish boiler
Aushulfe ...	04375	Cornish boiler, with Galloway tubes
Aushungern	04376	Elephant boiler
Ausiliario	04377	Lancashire boiler
Ausjochen	04378	Locomobile boiler
Auskammen	04379	Portable boiler
Auskernen	04380	Portable engine and boiler
Ausklingen	04381	Require a new boiler at ——
Ausklugeln	04382	Require a new boiler for ——
Auskratzen	04383	Shall require a new boiler by ——
Auskunft ...	04384	Have you boiler power for
Auslander...	04385	Our boiler power is only just sufficient for present needs
Auslauten	04386	Our boiler power is only sufficient for
Ausleerung	04387	Cannot get adequate boiler power for
Auslichten	04388	Boiler explosion
Ausmergeln	04389	Boiler leaks
Ausmitteln	04390	Boilers should be thoroughly over-hauled
Ausmustern	04391	Shall require new boiler before we begin to repair present one
Ausonico ...	04392	Shall have to rely on present boiler power
Auspicato	04393	Require —— new boiler(s)
Auspichen	04394	Boiler power will have to be increased to
Auspicis ...	04395	Boiler(s) altogether defective
Auspoliren	04396	Boiler(s) need(s) slight repairs
Auspragen	04397	Boilers are too far gone to be worth repairing
Ausputzer	04398	Boiler(s) give(s) complete satisfaction
Ausradiren	04399	Boiler(s) do(es) not give satisfaction
Ausrauchen	04400	Boiler(s) is (are) erected
Ausrechnen	04401	Boiler house(s) is (are) now near completion
Ausreden ...	04402	Boiler(s) has (have) already arrived on the property
Ausrenkung	04403	Has (have) obtained estimate(s) for boiler(s)
Ausrotten...	04404	Boiler(s) is (are) already set
Ausrufung	04405	Owing to the boiler being out of repair
Ausschalen	04406	Continuous stoppage of boilers necessary
Ausschank	04407	Has (have) completed erection of boiler
Ausschlag	04408	Boiler is becoming much corroded; will you send surface con-
Ausschnitt	04409	We have only a surplus of —— h.p. [denser & connections
Aussenwerk	04410	Tubular boiler —— feet long by —— feet diameter
Ausserdem	04411	Boiler power should be ample for
Ausserhalb	04412	Should have boiler power for
Aussingen	04413	Owing to insufficient boiler power
Aussitot ...	04414	Forward promptly —— h.p. locomobile boiler

Ausspahen	04415	Forward promptly —— h.p. Cornish boiler
Ausstecken	04416	Forward promptly —— h.p. Cornish boiler with Galloway
Aussteller...	04417	Forward promptly —— h.p. tubular boiler · [tubes
Ausstopfen	04418	Forward promptly —— h.p. elephant boiler
Austausch	04419	Forward promptly —— h.p. Lancashire boiler
Austerior ...	04420	To connect boiler(s) to
Austerity ...	04421	Steam pipes
Austero ...	04422	Send complete specification of —— h.p. —— boiler with [time of delivery and cost F.O.B.
Austilgen ...	04423	Pending arrival of new boiler(s)
Austonen ...	04424	Boiler(s) arrived ; now being placed in position
Austral ...	04425	Forward new fire bars for boiler(s)
Austrifera	04426	Forward new tubes for boiler(s)
Austrinken	04427	Forward new pressure gauge for boiler(s)
Ausubung	04428	Forward new safety valve(s) for boiler(s)
Ausverkauf	04429	Forward donkey-feed pump for boiler(s)
Auswandern	04430	Obtain new boiler as soon as possible
Auswartig	04431	Have you boiler power for pump(s)
Ausweiden	04432	I (we) have boiler power for pumps
Ausweisung	04433	I (we) have not boiler power for pumps
Auswendig	04434	What is the power and condition of boiler
Auswuchs...	04435	Owing to limited boiler power
Auswurf ...	04436	Size of boiler —— nominal h.p.
Auszahler...	04437	Size of boiler —— actual h.p.
Auszehrend	04438	**Bonanza**
Auszirkeln	04439	Is a bonanza mine
Auszug ...,	04440	Have struck a bonanza
Auszupfen	04441	Drift has opened up a bonanza
Autenticar	04442	**Bond**
Autentico ...	04443	Get bond
Authentam	04444	Get bond for
Authoritas	04445	Get bond on
Autillo ...	04446	To bond
Autocefalo	04447	Did you bond
Autocracy...	04448	Did not bond
Autocrat ...	04449	Did they (——) bond
Autographe	04450	This will make it necessary to renew bond
Automata...	04451	Bond must be extended for —— months
Autonatico	04452	A bond on
Autonomia	04453	When does bond expire
Autopsia ...	04454	Since bond expired on
Autopyrus	04455	Bond can be renewed for —— month(s)
Autora ...	04456	Bond can be renewed on payment of
Autorcillo...	04457	Bond will certainly not be renewed
Autorevele	04458	You must secure bond
Autoridad...	04459	Working bond
Autorizar ...	04460	Will only renew bond on condition that
Autrefois ...	04461	Bond can only be obtained on following terms and conditions
Autrement	04462	Can you (——) obtain bond
Autruche ...	04463	Can get a working bond for —— months
Autumaris	04464	Can obtain a bond on —— for —— months for ——
Autunno ...	04465	Endeavour to obtain a bond
Auvent ...	04466	Has (have) secured bond for —— months
Auxiliador	04467	Owners will not give bond [satisfactory
Auxilio ...	04468	Obtain bond subject to inspection of property and report being
Auxiliorum	04469	Payable —— in six months and —— at expiry of bond
Avacado ...	04470	Renewal of bond amounts to a fine of ——
Avaccevole	04471	Bond provides
Avaccezza...	04472	Bond must be for —— months
Avacciato ...	04473	Bond must be for ——

Avachir	04474	Bond must be for —— days
Avadarse	04475	Bond will become forfeited
Avalanche	04476	So as to renew bond
Avalentado	04477	Unable to secure bond
Avaliar	04478	Unable to renew bond
Avaloire	04479	The main conditions of the bond are
Avalote	04480	What are the main clauses of the bond
Avambrazo	04481	Can you get bond extended
Avampies	04482	Bond has been extended to
Avancage	04483	On condition that bond is extended
Avance	04484	Cannot get bond extended
Avanotto	04485	Will not extend bond another day
Avantal	04486	New bond secured
Avanthier	04487	Very doubtful if can secure new bond
Avantiche	04488	Unless you get new bond before
Avantport	04489	To get new bond
Avantren	04490	Could not bond
Avantscene	04491	At what price could I (we) bond
Avanzare	04492	At what price can you (——) bond
Avanzatile	04493	In accordance with terms of bond
Avanzette	04494	Has (have) asked for extension of bond for —— months
Avanzuglio	04495	Ask for extension of bond for —— months
Avaraccio	04496	Will agree to extension of bond for —— months
Avaramente	04497	Will agree to —— months' extension if
Avaretto	04498	Accept work agreed to in the bond
Avariciar	04499	What is date of bond
Avaricieux	04500	—— originally held bond
Avaricioso	04501	Cable whether purchase completed or bond renewed
Avariento	04502	Bond on the property extended —— days
Avarissime	04503	Has (have) promised to extend the bond —— days
Avaritias	04504	Owners will not extend bond
Avarizia	04505	Owners will extend bond for —— months on payment of —— [cash
Avarone	04506	I will let bond expire
Avasallar	04507	I will not let bond expire
Avaunt	04508	Be careful not to let bond expire
Avechucho	04509	Will give a bond
Avecica	04510	It would be too great a risk to let bond expire
Avecinar	04511	It would be best to let bond expire
Avectos	04512	It would not be well to let bond expir
Avejentado	04513	Renew bond
Avejigar	04514	Had I (we) not better bond
Avelenare	04515	Please bond with (at)
Avelinier	04516	**Bonded**
Avellamus	04517	Not bonded
Avellana	04518	Has (have) bonded the mine for —— months
Avelluntur	04519	Is the property bonded
Avenado	04520	Not yet bonded
Avenarius	04521	Cannot get it bonded
Avenate	04522	Can you get the property bonded
Avenencia	04523	Can you get the property bonded with guarantee as to
Aveneteza	04524	Can you get the property bonded with guarantee, and for how long
Avengement	04525	**Bonus**
Aveniceo	04526	A bonus of
Aventadero	04527	Shall distribute as a bonus
Aventajado	04528	Bonus required
Aventura	04529	Ask(s) a bonus of
Aventurero	04530	Has (have) declared a bonus of —— per share
Avenue	04531	**Books**
Averamia	04532	Books and papers
Avergonzar	04533	Has (have) forwarded books of accounts

Averiada ...	04534	Book keeper (*See also* " Accountant.")
Averiarse ...	04535	During absence of book keeper
Averiguar...	04536	Close books on
Averment...	04537	Transfer books closed
Averno ...	04538	Transfer books closed on
Aversatio ...	04539	**Borax**
Aversiere ...	04540	**Border(s)**
Aversion ...	04541	Borders upon
Avertant ...	04542	On the border of
Avertebat ..	04543	**Borehole(s)** (*See also* " Diamond.")
Avertere ...	04544	A borehole just completed indicates that the " lead " is coming
Avertisse ...	04545	Borehole is now being put down [in our direction
Avestruz ...	04546	Do you advise a borehole
Aveugler ...	04547	Present depth of borehole —— feet
Aviador ...	04548	What would be the cost of a borehole
Aviarium ...	04549	Send particulars as to present depth of borehole(s)
Aviary ...	04550	Send tracing showing location of each borehole
Avibus ...	04551	**Borer** (*See also* " Drills.")
Aviciar ...	04552	**Boring(s)** (*See also* " Drills.")
Avidezza ...	04553	From —— boring(s) in face of drift
Avidious ..	04554	From —— boring(s) in
Aviditatem	04555	From —— boring(s) in floor of level
Avidity ...	04556	When boring for
Aviejarse ...	04557	**Borrow**
Aviesas ...	04558	To borrow
Avigorar ...	04559	Unable to borrow
Avihar ..,	04560	Can you not borrow —— to go on with
Avilantez ...	04561	I (we) can borrow enough to go on with
Avillanado	04562	Shall try and borrow from one of the adjoining mines
Avillir ...	04563	**Boss**
Avinagrado	04564	As mine boss
Aviolado ...	04565	To act as mine boss
Avion ...	04566	Will act as mine boss
Avipedes ...	04567	**Both**
Avironato...	04568	Both places
Avisames ...	04569	Both suggestions
Avispado ...	04570	Both together
Avispero ...	04571	Both in hand
Avispon ...	04572	Both are considered here
Avitailler ...	04573	Has (have) seen both
Avitium ...	04574	**Botryoidal**
Avituallar	04575	**Bottom**
Avivador ...	04576	At the bottom of
Avivas ...	04577	Cannot examine bottom working(s)
Avizorar ...	04578	Cannot get to bottom of mine
Avocable ...	04579	The bottom level
Avocar ...	04580	The bottom of mine
Avocasser ...	04581	In the bottom of drift
Avocation...	04582	In the bottom of sump
Avocatorem	04583	In the bottom of winze
Avogalla ...	04584	Bottom workings are looking exceedingly well
Avoisiner ...	04585	**Bought**
Avolabam...	04586	Was (were) bought on the understanding that
Avortement	04587	Have you (they) (——) bought
Avorton ...	04588	Has (have) not bought
Avouched ..	04589	I (we) have bought
Avowing ...	04590	I (we) have bought as per your instructions
Avucasta ..	04591	For whom have you (they) (——) bought
Avuguero...	04592	Has (have) bought on your account
Avugues ...	04593	Cannot be bought at your limit(s)

Avulsio ...	04594	Cannot be bought at less than
Avunculi ...	04595	Has (have) bought at limit given
Avutarda ...	04596	At what price have you bought
Avvallare ...	04597	Has (have) bought up all available supply(ies)
Avvampante	04598	Have bought —— shares
Avveduto ...	04599	„ „ 5 „
Avventizio	04600	„ „ 10 „
Avverdire ...	04601	„ „ 15 „
Avvicinare	04602	„ „ 20 „
Avvisaglia	04603	„ „ 25 „
Avvoltura...	04604	„ „ 30 „
Awakened	04605	„ „ 35 „
Awakening	04606	„ „ 40 „
Aweless ...	04607	„ „ 45 „
Awestruck	04608	„ „ 50 „
Awfulness	04609	„ „ 55 „
Awkwardly	04610	„ „ 60 „
Awnings ...	04611	„ „ 65 „
Axamenta...	04612	„ „ 70 „
Axeheads ...	04613	„ „ 75 „
Axiculus ...	04614	„ „ 80 „
Axiform ...	04615	„ „ 85 „
Axilar ...	04616	„ „ 90 „
Axillaris ...	04617	„ „ 95 „
Axioma ...	04618	„ „ 100 „
Axiomatis...	04619	„ „ 200 „
Axiometro	04620	„ „ 300 „
Axitiosus ...	04621	„ „ 400 „
Axletree ...	04622	„ „ 500 „
Axorcas ...	04623	„ „ 600 „
Axungia ...	04624	„ „ 700 „
Axungiarum	04625	„ „ 800 „
Ayanque ...	04626	„ „ 900 „
Ayme ...	04627	„ „ 1000 „
Ayontar ...	04628	**Boulder(s)**
Ayudador...	04629	Boulders of
Ayudante...	04630	Erratic boulders only
Ayunas ...	04631	**Bound(s)**
Ayuste ...	04632	Am (are) not bound to
Azabache ...	04633	I (we) do not consider that I (we) am (are) bound to
Azabara ...	04634	You are bound to
Azacaya ...	04635	They are (—— is) consequently bound to
Azadica ...	04636	**Boundary(ies)**
Azadon ...	04637	Near the —— boundary
Azadonado	04638	Boundary stones
Azafata ...	04639	Boundary marks
Azafran ...	04640	Have boundaries defined by Government surveyor
Azafranado	04641	On the northern boundary
Azahar ...	04642	On the southern boundary
Azaleas ...	04643	On the eastern boundary
Azamboa ...	04644	On the western boundary
Azanoriate	04645	Boundary marks should be well defined
Azarbe ...	04646	Boundary marks are perfectly well defined
Azarcon ...	04647	There is a dispute as to our —— boundary
Azarnefe ...	04648	**Box(es)**
Azarolla ...	04649	In —— pound boxes
Azaroso ...	04650	Packed in boxes
Azedeiras ...	04651	**Brace**
Azimuth ...	04652	Shaft brace
Azione ...	04653	At the brace of

Azofaifa ...	04654	At the brace of winze
Azofar ...	04655	Tackle at the brace of
Azogue ...	04656	**Brake**
Azogueria...	04657	Foot brake
Azolvar ...	04658	Owing to failure in action of brake
Azorado ...	04659	Should be fitted with steam brake
Azorrarse ...	04660	**Branch**
Azotador ...	04661	Right hand branch of
Azotaina ...	04662	Left hand branch of
Azotate ...	04663	A branch of
Azotea ...	04664	Believe it is a branch and not the main vein
Azucar ...	04665	The (this) branch is now —— wide
Azucarado	04666	There are several branches of quartz in the shaft
Azucarillo...	04667	**Brand**
Azucena ...	04668	Which is the best brand to employ
Azuela ...	04669	Best brand is
Azufrado ...	04670	Which brand
Azufroso ...	04671	Any brand will do
Azulaque ...	04672	Take the best brand you can obtain
Azular ...	04673	Must secure —— brand ; no other is any good
Azulejado...	04674	**Brass(es)**
Azulino ...	04675	The main brasses are much worn
Azumbar ...	04676	Spare brasses
Azuquero ...	04677	Brasses for
Azure ...	04678	**Breadth**
Azymous ...	04679	Cable present breadth
Aszalino ...	04680	What is the total breadth of
Azzampato	04681	The total breadth is —— ft.
Azzardare...	04682	Vary(ies) in breadth from —— to ——
Azzeruolo...	04683	Vary(ies) considerably in breadth
Azzicarse ...	04684	In breadth
Azzicatore	04685	At its maximum breadth
Azzimella	04686	Present breadth of —— is
Azzimina ...	04687	Breadth of the tunnel is
Azzimo ...	04688	Breadth of the drive is
Azzimutto	04689	Must not exceed —— ft. in breadth
Azzittarsi...	04690	Can I (we) increase the breadth to ——
Azzollare ...	04691	Do not increase the breadth
Azzoppato	04692	Can increase the breadth to ——
Azzuffarsi...	04693	Constantly vary(ies) in breadth
Azzurrigno	04694	From the breadth
Azzurro ...	04695	Judging from the breadth
Baazas ...	04696	For the whole breadth of the ——
Bababui ...	04697	—— ft. in breadth by —— ft. long
Babadero ...	04698	What is the average breadth and value of
Babanca ...	04699	For the last —— ft. the average breadth has been
Babazorro	04700	Average breadth is ——, the average value is ——
Babbaccio...	04701	What is the average breadth of
Babbler ...	04702	The average breadth is
Babbling ...	04703	Give breadth in inches (of)
Babbuasso	04704	Give breadth in feet
Babbusco...	04705	The breadth in inches is
Babear ...	04706	The breadth in feet is
Babeo ...	04707	**Break**
Babera ...	04708	Owing to a break in the ——
Baberol ...	04709	Ore break (See also " Ore.")
Babeurre ...	04710	The ore continues through the break
Babia ...	04711	**Break-down**
Babieca ...	04712	Cable the extent of delay caused by break-down
Babies ...	04713	Owing to break-down in the air compressor

Babillage ...	04714	Owing to break-down in the machinery
Babilonia ...	04715	Owing to break-down in the mill
Babiole ...	04716	Owing to a break-down at
Baboon ...	04717	Have you had a break-down
Babor ...	04718	There has been no break-down
Babordais ..	04719	Break-down will cause serious delay
Babosear ...	04720	Break-down is of no importance ; only caused slight delay
Babosilla ...	04721	Break-down serious ; will entail considerable cost
Babouches	04722	Break-down reported at ——; is this true
Babouin ...	04723	No break-down whatever
Babucha ...	04724	**Breast** (*See also* " Drift," "Level.")
Babuino ...	04725	Forebreast now is ore
Baburrum	04726	In the forebreast of the level
Babyhood...	04727	In the forebreast of the —— level
Babyishly...	04728	The ore in the forebreast assays
Babyism ...	04729	There is very little water in the breast
Babylonian	04730	**Brecciated**
Bacada ...	04731	Brecciated structure
Bacaleria ...	04732	**Breezes**
Bacalias ...	04733	At present employing breezes
Bacallao ...	04734	There is an ample supply of breezes suitable for the purpose
Bacalusia ...	04735	Coke breeze
Bacanales ..	04736	**Brick(s)**
Bacante ...	04737	Fire bricks [will be sent
Bacarozzo...	04738	—— thousand first quality fire bricks and supply of fire-clay
Baccalauro	04739	Send —— thousand fire bricks and —— tons fire-clay (Stour-
Baccanella	04740	**Bridge** [bridge)
Baccaris ...	04741	It has been necessary to repair bridge over the river ——
Baccate ...	04742	Owing to break-down of bridge over the river (at ——)
Baccellone	04743	To bridge over
Bacchanal...	04744	**Broad** (*See also* " Wide.")
Baccharim	04745	**Broken**
Bacchetta...	04746	Was (were) broken
Bacchiare...	04747	Arrived broken
Bacchicus	04748	Entirely broken up
Bacchilone	04749	Broken out in a fresh place
Bacchitero	04750	Broken in transit—Recover from agent(s)
Baccifer ...	04751	Broken down in health
Baccinam ...	04752	Negotiations have broken down
Bacciocolo	04753	Pumping engine has broken down
Baccula ...	04754	Mill has broken down
Baceolus ...	04755	—— has (have) broken his (their) promise
Bacera ...	04756	Scheme has broken down
Bacharel ...	04757	What is the estimated tonnage and value of the ore broken (*See*
Bachelor ...	04758	**Broker(s)** [*also* "Ore.")
Bacherozzo	04759	Who do you employ as broker(s)
Bachiller ...	04760	Generally employ —— as broker(s)
Bachique ...	04761	Can you recommend a good broker
Bachot ...	04762	Suggest you employ —— to act as broker
Bachoteur	04763	Employ some other broker to
Baciabasso	04764	**Brokerage**
Baciamano	04765	By way of brokerage
Baciamenta	04766	Charge —— per cent. brokerage
Bacianne ...	04767	Exclusive of brokerage
Baciapile ...	04768	Inclusive of brokerage
Baciarsi ...	04769	The brokerage is
Baciatore ...	04770	What is the usual charge for brokerage
Baciatrice...	04771	Who is to pay the brokerage
Bacillum ...	04772	Must pay the brokerage
Bacinada ...	04773	Brokerage to be divided between —— and ——

Bacinero ...	04774	Would allow you —— as brokerage
Bacinetto ...	04775	Cannot allow you any brokerage
Bacinicam	04776	Cannot allow —— any brokerage
Baciocco ...	04777	**Bromination**
Baciuccare	04778	Bromination experiment
Backbiter ...	04779	Suggest that a bromination experiment be tried
Backbiting	04780	Bromination of ore
Backboard	04781	The ore is suited for bromination
Backbone...	04782	By a bromination process
Backdoor ...	04783	Cost of bromination per ton would be
Backenbart	04784	What is your estimate for cost of bromination per ton
Backenzahm	04785	Bromination plant
Backerei ...	04786	Cost of erecting bromination plant would be about
Backfish ...	04787	Bromination plant capable of dealing with —— tons per day
Backfriend	04788	**Brought** [of 24 hours
Backgammon	04789	Can only be brought
Backhanded	04790	Has to be brought by steam from
Backobst ...	04791	Must be brought in before
Backofen ...	04792	Must be brought in from
Backpiece...	04793	Requires to be brought from ——, a distance of —— miles
Backslider	04794	**Bucket**
Backstays...	04795	Bucket pump (*See also* " Pumps.")
Backstelze	04796	Bucket pump for
Backstube	04797	Bucket pump at
Backtrog ...	04798	Bucket lift
Backwards	04799	Bucket rods
Backwerk...	04800	Owing to failure of bucket lift
Backwoods	04801	**Bucking**
Bacon ...	04802	Bucking hammers
Baculo ...	04803	Bruised down by bucking hammers
Baculum ...	04804	Bucking plate
Badaggio ...	04805	**Buddle** (*See also* " Dressing.")
Badajada ...	04806	To buddle
Badajear ...	04807	Ore would buddle
Badajuela...	04808	Ore would buddle very well
Badalichio	04809	Ore would not buddle without considerable loss of value
Badalona ...	04810	**Buddled**
Badalucco ..	04811	Buddled ore
Badaride ...	04812	How much ore have you buddled
Badean ...	04813	We have —— tons of buddled ore
Badegast ...	04814	**Buddles**
Badehaus...	04815	Round buddles
Badekur ...	04816	Centre-head buddles
Badereise...	04817	We have now —— buddles employed on this ore
Baderla ...	04818	We could employ —— more buddles
Badewanna	04819	Buddles are being erected
Badezeit ...	04820	Shall complete erection of buddles within next —— days
Badgeless ...	04821	As soon as the erection of buddles is completed
Badger ...	04822	Buddles are working satisfactorily
Badigeon ..	04823	Buddles are not working very satisfactorily as yet
Badigliaro	04824	**Buddling**
Badil ...	04825	**Build** (*See also* " Erect.")
Badilazo ...	04826	To build
Badinage ...	04827	When shall you commence to build
Badiorum...	04828	Shall commence to build about
Badissairt...	04829	Shall commence to build as soon as I (we) can obtain
Badisso ...	04830	It will be necessary to build
Baditidem	04831	What will it cost to build
Badius ...	04832	Will cost about —— to build
Badiuzza ...	04833	**Building(s)**

Badomia	...	04834	Am (are) now building
Badulaque		04835	Expect to finish building —— by ——
Baericoso	...	04836	Buildings must all be insured
Baetigenam		04837	Buildings are not insured; may be valued at ——
Bafaneria	...	04838	Buildings are as follows
Baffetini	...	04839	Buildings are all out of repair
Baffling	...	04840	Buildings are all old but could be repaired
Bafoner	...	04841	Buildings are all in a satisfactory condition (except)
Bafreur	...	04842	Building(s) is (are) nearly completed
Bagagero	...	04843	Buildings are completed and ready for machinery
Bagaglio	...	04844	Have completed foundation of building(s)
Bagaras	...	04845	Buildings are all very much dilapidated
Bagasa	...	04846	I (we) have let a contract for building —— (at)
Bagascia	...	04847	I (we) have let a contract for building mill (at)
Bagatelle	...	04848	**Bull** (*See also* "Bear.")
Bagattino	..	04849	There is reported to be a "bull" movement
Bagaso	...	04850	**Bullion** (*See also* "Bars," "Gold," &c.)
Baggage	...	04851	What is the value of the bullion
Baggianata		04852	Net value of the bullion is
Baggiolare		04853	Send the bullion
Baggiolo	...	04854	Bullion produced on cleaning up —— ozs.
Bagliore	...	04855	Have forwarded bullion to —— for transmission ; weight
Bagmen	...	04856	Shipment of bullion [—— ozs.
Bagnajuolo		04857	Shall make —— shipment of bullion on
Bagnamento		04858	Value of bullion shipped is
Bagnante	...	04859	Suggest you ship all available bullion before
Bagnarsi	...	04860	Bullion on hand amounts to
Bagnasco	...	04861	Make no further bullion shipment until further instructions
Bagnatore	...	04862	Have shipped —— bars of bullion worth
Bagnatrice		04863	The —— shipment of bullion has realized
Bagno	...	04864	The —— shipment of bullion realized —— ; shall remit ——
Bagnuolo	...	04865	Bullion in stock
Bagordare		04866	Bullion is shipped to the mint at
Bagout	...	04867	Bullion realizes —— per ounce
Bagpipes	...	04868	Can you attach bullion
Bagrada	...	04869	Can attach bullion if you authorize
Bagre	.	04870	Bullion has been attached by
Baguenaude		04871	In order to prevent bullion being attached
Baguettes	...	04872	Base bullion
Baguier	...	04873	No bullion operations to report
Bahari	...	04874	The following bullion operations
Bahian	...	04875	**Bunch(y)** (*See also* "Ore.")
Bahnhof	...	04876	A bunch of ore
Bahnlos	...	04877	Ore is very bunchy
Bahntuch	.	04878	It is alleged that the ore occurrence is very bunchy
Bahnwarter		04879	**Burden** (*See also* "Overburden.")
Bahuno	...	04880	A burden of
Baigner	...	04881	**Burning-house** (*See also* "Calciner," &c.)
Baignoire	...	04882	New burning-house
Baila	...	04883	Old burning-house
Bailador	...	04884	Location of burning-house
Bailarin	...	04885	Samples from burning-house
Bailbond	...	04886	Flues from burning-house
Bailete	...	04887	**Burnt** (*See also* "Damages.")
Bailiage	...	04888	Badly burnt
Bailiwick	...	04889	Partly burnt
Bailleur	...	04890	Wholly burnt
Baillonner		04891	Is (are) practically all burnt
Bailment	...	04892	Stamp mill was burnt down on —— [amounts to ——
Bailoteais	...	04893	The —— house was burnt down on —— ; the damage

Bailoteo ...	04894	Which has burnt down
Bailpiece ...	04895	Was (were) burnt
Bainmarie	04896	Everything has been burnt
Bairns ...	04897	Plant and machinery all burnt
Baisemain	04898	Nothing of value was burnt
Baisement	04899	The value burnt amounts to
Baisotter ...	04900	Fortunately no one was burnt
Baissiere ...	04901	Books and papers all burnt
Baisure ...	04902	Fortunately no books and papers were burnt
Baiting ...	04903	Engine-house burnt down, but damage to machinery slight
Baivel ...	04904	Engine-house burnt down ; damage to machinery very serious
Baixamaras	04905	**Burrow(s)** (*See also* " Attle," " Dump.")
Baixotes ...	04906	**Burst**
Bajada ...	04907	Burst on
Bajamar ...	04908	Ditch burst
Bajamente	04909	Flumes burst
Bajeccia ...	04910	Dam burst on ——; damage very serious
Bajelero ...	04911	Dam burst on ——; damage can be repaired by ——
Bajetta ...	04912	**Business**
Bajillo ...	04913	Leave the business as it stands
Bajocco ...	04914	Leave —— in charge of the business
Bajon ...	04915	In case business should occur again
Bajonaccio	04916	A large business is now being done in
Bajoncillo...	04917	Are you able to do business
Bajonetta...	04918	Am obliged to decline business
Bajonnet ...	04919	Business in —— shares dull
Bajucola ...	04920	Business in —— shares reviving
Bajulans ...	04921	Business in —— shares very lively
Bajulavis ...	04922	Can do the business
Bajulus ...	04923	Consider the business perfectly safe
Bakehouse	04924	Do not think the business at all safe
Bakery ...	04925	Decline(s) the business
Balada ...	04926	I (we) believe business would result if price reduced
Baladron ...	04927	It might lead to much business
Baladronea	04928	Is this business in your way
Balafrer ...	04929	Is there any prospect of doing business
Balaguero...	04930	There is no prospect at present of doing business
Balanatam	04931	There is every prospect that business will result
Balanatus...	04932	Will you undertake this business
Balancero...	04933	Shall be pleased to undertake the business
Balancia ...	04934	Am (are) compelled to decline business as my hands are full
Balancing...	04935	If it leads to business
Balancoise	04936	Cable if it is likely to lead to business
Balandra ...	04937	Seems likely to lead to business
Balangorum	04938	Does not promise well as regards ultimate business
Balangum	04939	Rather than lose the business
Balaninus...	04940	You can leave this business in my hands
Balanites ...	04941	No business, owing to
Balante ...	04942	No business, owing to holidays
Balanzario	04943	Has (have) no business to
Balanzon ...	04944	**But**
Balascio ...	04945	Nothing but
Balatro ...	04946	But not
Balatronem	04947	But if
Balaustium	04948	But only
Balaustra ...	04949	But in such case
Balayage ...	04950	**Buy**
Balayures...	04951	Buy freely
Balbettare	04952	Did you buy
Balbotire ...	04953	Difficult to buy

Balbussare	04954	Did not buy
Balbutier ...	04955	Did they buy
Balbuzie ...	04956	At what figure can you buy
Balconage ..	04957	Buy at once
Balconazo ..	04958	Buy for this account
Balcony ...	04959	Buy for next account
Balda ...	04960	Buy for meeting
Baldachin ..	04961	Buy back all you have sold
Baldamente	04962	Buy back —— of what you have sold
Baldanza ...	04963	Buy for our joint account
Baldaqui ...	04964	Buy as many as you can below
Baldear ...	04965	Buy on my account and hold to my order
Baldes ...	04966	Cannot buy more
Baldezza ...	04967	Cable immediately if you want to buy
Baldiges ...	04968	If you want to buy, telegraph at once how many and **top limit**
Baldness ...	04969	Do you still advise me (us) to buy
Baldonar ...	04970	Advise you strongly to buy
Baldonzoso	04971	Do not now advise you to buy
Baldosa ...	04972	Unable to buy
Baldracca...	04973	Could not buy at your limit, so have bought —— at
Baldrian ...	04974	Cannot buy at your limit, price is now
Baldrick ...	04975	Cancel my order to buy (of ——)
Balefire ...	04976	Cable if I am (we are) to buy
Balefully ...	04977	Could you buy
Baleine ...	04978	Can buy for cash
Baleiniere...	04979	Can buy —— share(s) at
Baleria ...	04980	Unable to buy more than
Balestrajo...	04981	Unable to buy at your limit
Balestrone	04982	In the event of your finally deciding to buy
Baleta ...	04983	Can buy cheaper at —— than here
Baliaggio ...	04984	Can buy cheaper here than at ——
Balido ...	04985	Can you buy —— shares below ——? If so will take ——
Balijero ...	04986	If you wish to buy, cable number and top limit
Balijon ...	04987	Immediate rise probable in ——; buy for my account
Balineum ...	04988	Immediate rise probable in ——; shall I (we) buy
Baliolus ...	04989	Immediate rise probable in ——; you had better buy
Balioso ...	04990	Had I (we) not better buy
Balisage ...	04991	Buy —— shares
Balista ...	04992	„ 5 „
Balistique...	04993	„ 10 „
Balitadera	04994	„ 15 „
Balivean ...	04995	„ 20 „
Baliverner	04996	„ 25 „
Balivus ...	04997	„ 30 „
Balker ...	04998	„ 35 „
Ballabile ...	04999	„ 40 „
Ballaccia ...	05000	„ 45 „
Ballades ... **05001**		„ 50 „
Ballar ...	05002	„ 55 „
Ballatella ...	05003	„ 60 „
Ballatina ...	05004	„ 65 „
Ballatojo ...	05005	„ 70 „
Ballatore ...	05006	„ 75 „
Ballatrice ...	05007	„ 80 „
Ballenato ...	05008	„ 85 „
Ballener ...	05009	„ 90 „
Ballerino ...	05010	„ 95 „
Ballesta ...	05011	„ 100 „
Ballestazo...	05012	„ 200 „
Ballestear...	05013	„ 300 „

Balleston ...	05014	Buy 400 shares
Ballette ...	05015	„ 500 „
Ballhaus ...	05016	„ 600 „
Ballholz ...	05017	„ 700 „
Ballico ...	05018	„ 800 „
Ballkleid ...	05019	„ 900 „
Ballonchio	05020	„ 1000 „

Buyer(s)

Ballonner ...	05021	
Ballonzare	05022	Is (are) said to be buyer(s)
Balloon ...	05023	Few buyers
Ballotta ...	05024	Plenty of buyers, but no sellers
Ballspiel ...	05025	No buyers; all sellers
Balluccia ...	05026	Buyers reserved
Ballucis ...	05027	Buyers plentiful
Balm ...	05028	Is —— a buyer of
Balmeal ...	05029	Are you a buyer of
Balnearium	05030	Am (is) a buyer of
Balneator ...	05031	Not a buyer of
Balneatrix	05032	No buyers

Buying

Balneolum	05033	
Baloardo ...	05034	Can you continue buying at same price
Baloccone ...	05035	Can you find out who is (are) buying
Baloncita ...	05036	Estimate buying outright for ——
Balotada ...	05037	Commence buying at
Balotar ...	05038	Do you (does ——) advise buying
Balourdise	05039	Do you (does ——) recommend buying at
Balsadera ...	05040	I (——) advise(s) prompt buying
Balsalm ...	05041	I am (we are) buying
Balsamico...	05042	Stop buying
Balsamina	05043	Wait further instructions before buying
Balsamique	05044	—— are reported to be buying largely
Balsamiren	05045	——'s clique are buying
Balsamorum	05046	People are buying
Balsamum	05047	Shall I (we) continue buying at same price
Balsear ...	05048	There is a sudden buying of shares

By

Balsimare	05049	
Balsopeto ...	05050	By the
Balteo ...	05051	By no means
Balteolus ...	05052	By means of
Baluarte ...	05053	—— × ——
Balucarum	05054	—— × —— × ——
Balucis ...	05055	

C

Balumba ...	05056	**Cable** (*See also* " Telegraph.")
Balusa ...	05057	To cable
Baluster ...	05058	By cable
Balustrade	05059	Recent cables
Balvano ...	05060	Based upon your cable of
Balzante ...	05061	With reference to (my) our cable dated ——
Balzellare...	05062	Why do you (does ——) not answer cable(s) sent
Bambagello	05063	Remit by cable
Bambagioso	05064	Cable not later than
Bambalina	05065	Cable advices from
Bambanca	05066	Will cable from
Bambarria	05067	Unless you cable
Bambinesco	05068	Pending receipt of cable
Bambino ...	05069	—— cable(s) as follows
Bamboccio	05070	Advise me (us) by cable as to course to be pursued
Bambochada	05071	We have received no reply to our last cable sent ——
Bambocheur	05072	Will duly advise you by cable as regards
Bamboleo...	05073	Do not hesitate to cable freely

Bambolla ...	05074	Shall not hesitate to cable freely
Bambolone	05075	There is no necessity for cabling so freely
Bamboo ...	05076	This cable contains —— words
Bamboozled	05077	Cable from —— this morning
Banadero ...	05078	In reply to your cable received ——
Banado ...	05079	Have remitted by cable to-day —— through ——
Banalite ...	05080	Cable all needful particulars for preparing report for public
Bananier ...	05081	Cable all needful particulars respecting this : wish to issue [circular to shareholders
Banasta ...	05082	Your (——'s) cable dated —— received
Banastillo...	05083	Shall cable for you to return
Banausus ...	05084	You must cable at once to catch me before I leave
Bancalero ..	05085	Cable is incorrect ; repeat from —— to ——
Bancaria ...	05086	Please acknowledge receipt of this cable
Bancaza ...	05087	Your cable has arrived mutilated
Banchetto...	05088	Cable received to-day unintelligible ; cable using other words
Banchidis	05089	Cable immediately whether —— or ——
Banchiere	05090	You had better cable to —— to get
Banchinae	05091	Have cabled to —— to get
Bandaging	05092	Have just received cable from —— to the effect that
Bandagiste	05093	Also cable
Bandana ...	05094	Have you received our cable dispatched on ——
Bandbox ...	05095	Have you received cable from ——
Bandear ...	05096	Cable which you advise
Bandeisen...	05097	As soon as your cable was received
Bandeja ...	05098	Your cable is not sufficiently clear
Bandelette	05099	With reference to our cable dated
Bandelier ...	05100	With reference to ——'s cable of
Bandella ...	05101	Cable without delay
Banderajo	05102	Send instructions by cable
Bandereta	05103	Cable who has won the case
Banderica...	05104	Have been unable to see —— ; hope to cable to-morrow
Banderizar	05105	Please arrange by cable with ——
Banderolas	05106	My last cable to you left here on ——
Bandido ...	05107	Confer with —— and cable your joint advice with regard to
Bandiera ...	05108	Waiting for a reply to my (our) cable of
Bandigen ...	05109	I (we) await reply to my (our) cable sent to
Bandigung	05110	Company adheres to cable sent on ——
Bandin ...	05111	Get —— to cable
Bandinella	05112	We have not received your cable of
Bandita ...	05113	Send a second cable
Banditore ...	05114	Send reply to our last cable
Bandogs ...	05115	Send copy of this cable after you have translated it to ——
Bandoliera	05116	Please cable payment
Bandore ...	05117	Do not go elsewhere before you cable
Bandosidad	05118	Cable number of last car shipped
Bandrol ...	05119	A portion of this cable is in cipher
Bandujo ...	05120	Your cable stating —— indicates there is an error somewhere
Bandullo ...	05121	**Cage**
Bandurria	05122	Whim cage
Bandwaaren	05123	Cage is a single one
Bandwurm	05124	Cage is a double one
Bandying ...	05125	See that cage is quite safe
Bandylegs	05126	The rope attached to the cage is
Banefully ...	05127	With present cage could draw —— tons per day of 12 hours
Bange ...	05128	What is the weight of the cage
Bangigkeit	05129	What is the weight of the cage and rope together
Banging ...	05130	Weight of the cage is —— lbs.
Banglich ...	05131	Weight of both cage and rope is —— lbs.
Banho ...	05132	**Cainozoic**

CALCAREOUS. Ban—Bar

Banianos ...	05133	**Calcareous**
Banishing...	05134	Calcareous matter
Banista ...	05135	—— per cent. of calcareous matter
Bankactie ..	05136	**Calcination**
Bankbruch	05137	Calcination plant
Bankerott...	05138	Calcination ground
Bankhalter	05139	**Calcine** (*See also* "Roast.")
Bankherr ...	05140	Calciner(s)
Banlieue ...	05141	The ore is roasted in calciners
Bannalis ...	05142	**Calcite**
Bannanican	05143	Associated with calcite
Banner ...	05144	**Calcspar**
Bannfluch...	05145	Veinstone is chiefly calcspar
Banniere ...	05146	**Calculate(ion)(s)**
Bannisso ...	05147	Safely calculate
Bannock ...	05148	According to the usual calculations
Banquera ...	05149	Calculating upon
Banquete ...	05150	I (we) calculate that
Banquier ...	05151	Do not calculate upon
Banquillo...	05152	The basis for my (our) calculation(s) was
Bantams ...	05153	Upon what have you (has ——) based your (his) calculations
Bantling ...	05154	Your calculation is too high for ——.
Bannelo ...	05155	You may calculate upon
Banyan ...	05156	Has altogether upset my (our) calculations
Baobab ...	05157	Cannot calculate with any degree of certainty
Baphia ...	05158	Can you calculate upon
Baptarum...	05159	Can calculate upon
Bapteme ...	05160	Cannot calculate upon
Baptism ...	05161	What can we calculate upon safely
Baptismal...	05162	**Calculated**
Baptistery	05163	How have you calculated
Baptisatio	05164	Is calculated upon the
Baque ...	05165	I calculated that
Baquetazo	05166	What have you calculated for
Baquetear...	05167	Have calculated for —— at the rate of
Baquico ...	05168	**Call**
Barabuffa	05169	Give you first call
Baraccando	05170	A first call of
Baraccuzza	05171	A second call of
Baragouin	05172	A —— call of
Baraja ...	05173	To call
Barandado	05174	Call(s) for no reply
Barandal ...	05175	Pending additional call being made
Barangay ..	05176	Is there any call liability on the shares
Barar ...	05177	There is no liability in respect of calls on the shares
Barasettes...	05178	There is a call liability of —— per share
Baratador	05179	Call for letters at
Baratas ...	05180	Call for letters at the post office at
Baratear ...	05181	Will call for letters at the post office at
Barathrum	05182	Please deduct call of —— on —— shares
Baratijas ...	05183	Please pay call of —— on —— shares
Baratillo ...	05184	Shall I (we) pay the call on your —— shares
Baratista ...	05185	Shall have to make a call of —— per share
Baratro ...	05186	Shall have to make further call of —— per share
Barattato ..	05187	The calls unpaid amount to ——
Baratteria...	05188	Unadvisable to make call at this moment
Barba ...	05189	A call of —— per share is payable on ——
Barbacana	05190	A call of —— per share has been made
Barbadillo	05191	No further calls will be made
Barbajove...	05192	No further calls can be made

[87]

Barbara ...	05193	**Call upon**
Barbaresco	05194	Call upon —— if possible at
Barbarian...	05195	Did you call upon ——
Barbaricum	05196	Call immediately upon ——
Barbaridad	05197	Call upon me as soon as you reach here
Barbarie ...	05198	Will call upon you as soon as arrive
Barbarismo	05199	Call upon —— (him) before you see ——
Barbarity ...	05200	**Called**
Barbarizar	05201	Has (have) called
Barbarossa	05202	Have not called
Barbarote...	05203	Have you called
Barbassimo	05204	Called upon ——
Barbato ...	05205	**Cam** (*See also* " Battery," " Stamps.")
Barbatulum	05206	Cam shaft
Barbazzale	05207	Cam shaft gearing
Barbear ...	05208	Cam shaft bearings
Barbechar...	05209	Pulley on cam shaft
Barbecho	05210	Spur wheel on cam shaft
Barbecue ...	05211	Send cams without key ways
Barbeissig...	05212	Send templet for key ways in cams
Barbertado	05213	**Cambrian**
Barberia ...	05214	**Camp**
Barberito ...	05215	**Camping**
Barbers ..	05216	**Can**
Barbescent	05217	Can be
Barbetteno	05218	Can I (we)
Barbica ...	05219	You can
Barbicano...	05220	Can you
Barbicella...	05221	Can we (they)
Barbichon...	05222	I (we) can
Barbieria ...	05223	If I (we) can
Barbifier ...	05224	If you can
Barbiger ...	05225	If we (they) can
Barbigorum	05226	I can go
Barbihecho	05227	—— (they) can
Barbilla ...	05228	Can not
Barbillera...	05229	**Canal(s)** (*See also* " Ditches.")
Barbinegro	05230	**Cancel** (*See also* " Annul.")
Barbiquejo	05231	To cancel
Barbiruccio	05232	Cancel at once (unless)
Barbitier ...	05233	Do not cancel
Barbiton ...	05234	Advise you to cancel
Barbogio ...	05235	Cancel agreement
Barbolina ...	05236	Cancel letter dated ——
Barbon ...	05237	Cancel my telegram of ——
Barboteur...	05238	Cancel instructions contained in letter dated ——
Barbucino...	05239	Has (have) threatened to cancel
Barbudo ...	05240	I (we) will cancel
Barbullon	05241	I (we) can cancel
Barcaccia ...	05242	I (we) cannot cancel
Barcage ...	05243	Please cancel my (our) order of ——
Barcajuolo	05244	Please cancel my (our) order to ——
Barcarola ...	05245	Are you able to cancel
Barcazo ...	05246	Should you not be able to cancel
Barceo ...	05247	Provided that —— is willing to cancel
Barchent ...	05248	Provided that —— declines to cancel
Barchetto ...	05249	Consent(s) to cancel
Barchilla ...	05250	Refuse(s) to cancel
Barcinar ...	05251	Do you mean me (us) to cancel
Barcino ...	05252	Expressly wish you (——) to cancel

Barcollato...	05253	Do not mean you (——) to cancel
Barcolongo	05254	Upon what terms can you (will ——) cancel
Bardado ...	05255	Willing to cancel on following terms
Bardaguera	05256	With an option to cancel
Bardaje ...	05257	Is there any option to cancel in the event of
Bardatura...	05258	There is an option to cancel
Bardellone	05259	There is no option to cancel
Bardeur ...	05260	We have no option except to cancel
Bardilla ...	05261	Give formal notice to cancel
Bardiorem	05262	Your instructions to cancel received
Bardioris ...	05263	Your instructions to cancel arrived too late to be acted upon
Bardist ...	05264	**Cancelled**
Bardoma ...	05265	Cancelled on account of
Bardomera	05266	Have cancelled the reference to ——.
Bareface ...	05267	Have cancelled clause ——
Barefoot ...	05268	Has (have) cancelled
Barelegs ...	05269	Has (have) not been cancelled
Barella ...	05270	Has (have) been cancelled
Barfol ...	05271	Is hereby cancelled
Barfrost ...	05272	Should be cancelled at once
Barfusz ...	05273	Will be cancelled immediately
Bargagnare	05274	Already cancelled
Barguigner	05275	Cancelled in error
Bariga ...	05276	Has (have) not cancelled
Bariglione	05277	If payment is not made before —— bond will be cancelled
Bariletta ...	05278	It was a violation of clause No. —— and —— has (have) [cancelled
Barillet ...	05279	Must be cancelled
Barilozzo ...	05280	Insist that clause No. —— is cancelled
Bario ...	05281	In consequent of non-payment bond is cancelled
Bariolage ...	05282	Will not sign agreement unless clause No. —— is cancelled
Baripto ...	05283	Will be cancelled except
Baritibus ...	05284	**Candidate** (*See also* "Applicant.")
Baritico ...	05285	Would you care to be a candidate for
Baritono ...	05286	Should not care to be a candidate for
Baritorum	05287	**Candles**
Barjuleta ...	05288	Cost of candles
Barkbed ...	05289	Candles suitable for
Barking ...	05290	Send supply of candles
Barleycorn	05291	**Cannot**
Barloar ...	05292	Cannot be
Barlovento	05293	If you cannot
Barmaiden	05294	If I (——) cannot
Barmecide	05295	If we (they) cannot
Barmherzig	05296	I (we) cannot
Barnabita...	05297	I cannot go before
Barnacles ...	05298	We (——) cannot
Barniz ...	05299	You cannot
Barocco ...	05300	**Canvas**
Barographs	05301	Canvas for
Barometro	05302	Suitable roofing canvas
Baronaccio	05303	**Cap**
Baronage ...	05304	The cap of
Baronal ...	05305	On the cap of the hill
Barone ...	05306	The entire cap of the hill is composed of
Baronesa ...	05307	**Cap of vein** (*See also* "Outcrop.")
Baronetage	05308	**Capability(ies)**
Baronevole	05309	Existing capabilities are poor as regards
Baronia ...	05310	What are the existing capabilities for
Baronnet ..	05311	Existing capabilities are satisfactory for
Baroscope	05312	Existing capabilities are excellent for

Barosum ...	05313	**Capable**
Barouche ...	05314	Is (are) capable of
Barquarde	05315	Is (are) not capable of
Barque ...	05316	Do you think —— (he) would be a capable man for the post
Barquear ...	05317	A very capable man for
Barquero ...	05318	Capable of great developments
Barquilla ...	05319	Do you know a capable man for the post
Barquin ...	05320	In the hands of a capable man
Barquinazo	05321	Property is capable of
Barquinero	05322	Mine(s) is (are) capable of
Barra ...	05323	Consider —— (him) quite capable of (for)
Barrachel ...	05324	**Capably**
Barragan ...	05325	If capably developed
Barragania	05326	Has been capably handled
Barrageant	05327	Has not been capably handled
Barranco ...	05328	**Capacity**
Barraque ...	05329	The capacity is —— tons per 24 hours
Barraquear	05330	**Capel**
Barrate ...	05331	Hard capels
Barrator ...	05332	**Capital** (*See also* " Amount," " Company," " Shares," &c.)
Barrear ...	05333	Additional capital
Barrederas	05334	Share capital
Barredura...	05335	Debenture capital
Barreled ...	05336	By means of debenture capital
Barrena ...	05337	Unallotted capital
Barrenado	05338	Issued capital
Barrendero	05339	Unissued capital
Barrenness	05340	Authorized capital
Barrenon ...	05341	What is the amount of unissued capital
Barrenwort	05342	The amount of unissued capital is
Barretear ...	05343	On a less capital
Barretero ...	05344	The total capital
Barrevoet ...	05345	What is the total capital
Barriada ...	05346	Working capital
Barricata	05347	Working capital should be
Barriers ..	05348	What is the working capital
Barrigon ...	05349	Cable amount of working and total capital respectively
Barril ...	05350	For working capital
Barrilame...	05351	Will leave —— for working capital
Barrilejo ...	05352	This would leave —— for working capital
Barrilla ...	05353	The working capital provided should be at least ——
Barriniore ..	05354	The working capital is ——
Barriquaut	05355	Total capital is ——
Barriscar ...	05356	What is the required capital
Barriscono	05357	Required capital is
Barriuntur	05358	Paid-up capital
Barrizal ...	05359	What is the amount of paid-up capital
Barrotines	05360	Amount of paid-up capital is
Barrueco ...	05361	The total capital is paid up
Barruntar	05362	How much of the capital can you arrange to get subscribed
Barrunto ...	05363	Can arrange to get —— of the capital subscribed
Barschaft ...	05364	In order to induce capital
Bartavelle...	05365	If not too heavily loaded with capital
Barterer ...	05366	Too heavily loaded with capital
Bartering ...	05367	Was very heavily loaded with capital
Barthaar ...	05368	Must not be loaded with too much capital
Bartulos ...	05369	Consider it has been too heavily loaded with capital
Baruca ...	05370	Total capital of company ought not to exceed
Barule ...	05371	Capital of company not to exceed
Barullare ...	05372	Capital may not exceed

Barullasti...	05373	Equal to —— per cent. on the entire capital
Baryterdo	05374	Believe would justify expenditure of —— additional capital
Barytone ...	05375	In order to return a minimum of —— per cent. on the capital
Barzon ...	05376	On a capital of [(on ——)
Barzonear	05377	Can you pay a dividend on the total capital of ——
Basalischo	05378	Owner(s) has (have) exhausted his (their) capital
Basaltibus	05379	What is the proposed capital
Basamento	05380	Capital of the company is fixed at
Basca ...	05381	Total capital of the company is to be
Bascauda ...	05382	Capital is too great
Basciare ...	05383	Capital is not sufficient
Bascula ...	05384	Capital should be increased by
Baseborn ...	05385	Capital should be decreased by
Basellam ...	05386	What amount of capital has been subscribed
Basettino ...	05387	Whole of the capital has been subscribed
Basfond ...	05388	All the capital has been underwritten
Bashed ...	05389	—— of the capital is already underwritten
Bashfull ...	05390	Only —— of the capital has been subscribed
Basiabamur	05391	The capital subscribed is sufficient for
Basiatis ...	05392	The capital subscribed is not sufficient for
Basiaverit...	05393	Otherwise shall be short of capital
Basiavisse...	05394	As sufficient working capital
Basilary ...	05395	**Capital Account**
Basilica ...	05396	To be charged to capital account
Basilicior ...	05397	Expenditure on capital account
Basilicon ...	05398	Expenditure on capital account must be kept distinct
Basilique ...	05399	Send statement showing your expenditure on capital account
Basilisko ...	05400	What is the balance of capital account [to date
Basisolute...	05401	The balance of capital account is
Basketing ...	05402	Which leaves —— as balance of capital account
Baskets ...	05403	Should this be charged to capital account
Basquear ...	05404	Should be charged to capital account
Basquina ...	05405	Has been charged to capital account meanwhile
Basrelief ...	05406	We have expended in addition on capital account
Bassecour...	05407	Mail statement showing expenditure on capital account since
Bassefosse	05408	Amount you have expended on capital account
Bassetto ...	05409	Approximate expense on capital account
Bassgeige...	05410	**Capitalist(s)**
Bassiner ...	05411	Strong syndicate of capitalists
Bassinoire	05412	**Capitalization**
Bassoon ...	05413	In a company of —— capitalization
Basspfeife...	05414	What is the proposed capitalization
Basstuba ...	05415	**Capitalize**
Bassviol ...	05416	Propose to capitalize at
Bastagarum	05417	Cannot capitalize beyond
Bastage ...	05418	**Capitalized**
Bastalena ...	05419	Capitalized at
Bastante ...	05420	Capitalized much too high
Bastarda ...	05421	**Capped**
Bastardelo	05422	Capped by
Bastardume	05423	This is capped by
Bastear ...	05424	**Capping .**
Basterna ...	05425	A rock capping
Bastevole ...	05426	A capping of
Bastida ...	05427	**Captain**
Bastilla ...	05428	Underground captain
Bastimento	05429	Mine captain
Bastinado...	05430	Dressing captain
Basting ...	05431	As captain of
Bastingage	05432	A good Cornish captain

Bastinguer	05433	**Car**
Bastions ...	05434	Car number
Bastista ...	05435	What is the number of car, up to ——
Bastmatte...	05436	**Carbonate (of)**
Bastonada	05437	Carbonate ore
Bastonear...	05438	**Carboniferous**
Bastracone	05439	Carboniferous limestone
Bastringue	05440	**Carbons** (*See also* " Diamonds.")
Basura ...	05441	**Care**
Batable ...	05442	Should you care
Batacazo ...	05443	Would —— care
Batacchia ..	05444	Would you care to accept
Bataclan ...	05445	Do not care to
Bataille ...	05446	Every care must be taken
Batalarius	05447	Every care was taken
Batalhao ...	05448	Every care will be taken
Batalla ...	05449	Great want of care
Batallador	05450	No care was taken
Batallon ...	05451	Take care (that)
Batalloso ..	05452	Take care in
Batanado ...	05453	Take care of
Batanar ...	05454	Take care to
Batanero ...	05455	Great care will have to be exercised
Batardeau...	05456	Great care in working
Batatin ...	05457	Who will take care of
Bateau ...	05458	—— will take care of
Batelejo ...	05459	Have not yet decided who will take care of
Bateolus ...	05460	Do (does) not care about it
Bathing ...	05461	The greatest care will be necessary
Bathymetry	05462	The greatest want of care is evident
Batiacam ...	05463	I (we) rely upon your care
Baticola ...	05464	Very great care should be taken
Batidera ...	05465	With extreme care
Batiente ...	05466	Exercise the greatest care as regards expenditure
Batifoler ...	05467	Exercise the greatest care in your dealings with
Batihoja ...	05468	Great care has been exercised (in working)
Batillorum	05469	Provided that sufficient care is taken to
Bationdeo...	05470	Take particular care not to
Batisseur ...	05471	Care must be used in
Batista ...	05472	Owing to insufficient care being exercised
Batocchio ...	05473	Are you satisfied that sufficient care was exercised
Batojar ...	05474	Only meant you to take care as regards
Batologia ...	05475	Take care that —— does not meet with ——
Batonic ...	05476	Take care that this information does not fall into ——'s hands
Batonnier ...	05477	Take every possible care to check
Batrach ...	05478	Take care that the quality is satisfactory
Battaglia ...	05479	**Careful**
Battailous	05480	Be careful
Battement	05481	Be careful to comply with all legal requirements
Batteria ...	05482	To be careful
Battering...	05483	Be careful about
Battesimo...	05484	Make careful enquiries
Batticuore	05485	Careful enquiries
Battifole ...	05486	Careful enquiries as to title
Battifredo	05487	Will be careful
Battifuoco	05488	Not sufficiently careful
Batting ...	05489	**Carefully**
Battiporto	05490	Carefully examine
Battitura ...	05491	After carefully examining the present workings my advice is to
Battleaxe ...	05492	After carefully examining the present workings my conclusions
		[are

Battledoor	05493	Have overhauled everything most carefully
Battlement	05494	Most carefully
Battoir ...	05495	**Car-load** (*See also* "Away," "Car.")
Battuamus	05496	How many car-loads
Battuaria ...	05497	This makes —— car-loads
Battuebas .	05498	What is the total number of car-loads for month
Battuendi ...	05499	What is the total number of car-loads since
Battuerit ...	05500	**Carpenter(s)**
Battuta ...	05501	A good mine carpenter
Batucar ...	05502	Carpenters are now employed at (with)
Batuda ...	05503	**Carriage** (*See also* "Freight.")
Batuffo ...	05504	Land carriage
Bauamt ...	05505	Water carriage
Baubabor ...	05506	Add —— for carriage
Baubantur	05507	Carriage costs —— per ton of 2240 lbs. [per ton of 2240 lbs.
Baubatus ...	05508	Carriage depends upon season of year. At present it is ——
Baubedarf	05509	Carriage from nearest railway station to mine is —— per ton
Bauchig ...	05510	What shall we add for carriage
Bauchweh	05511	Estimate should include carriage to ——
Baudet ...	05512	Shall the estimate include carriage to ——
Baudienst ..	05513	Carriage is by mules, no package should exceed —— lbs.
Baudrier ...	05514	**Carried** (*See also* "Carry.")
Bauerfrau..	05515	Carried by
Bauergut ...	05516	Carried off
Bauerhof ...	05517	Carried on
Bauerhutte	05518	Carried out
Bauerin ...	05519	Carried over
Bauerisch...	05520	Carried away
Baufallig ...	05521	Carried to
Baugerust...	05522	Carried through
Bauherr ...	05523	Can be carried out
Baukolz ...	05524	Cannot be carried out
Baukunde...	05525	Has (have) been carried out
Baul	05526	Is carried on for
Bauletto ...	05527	Should be carried through if possible
Baulente ...	05528	Should be carried on simultaneously (with)
Baulustig ...	05529	Will require to be carried
Baumartig	05530	Will require to be carried on
Baume ...	05531	**Carry(ies)**
Baumeister	05532	To carry
Baumgang	05533	To carry on
Baumgarten	05534	Will carry
Baumhoch	05535	How much will —— carry
Baumrinde	05536	Will safely carry ——
Baumsage...	05537	Carries about —— tons
Baumschlag	05538	Have not been able to carry through
Baumschule	05539	To carry into effect
Baumstam	05540	In order to carry into effect
Baumstark	05541	Shall proceed to carry this into effect immediately
Baumstein	05542	In order to carry it (this) through
Baumwolle	05543	Can you carry —— for —— days
Baupres ...	05544	Will carry —— for —— days
Baurath ...	05545	Will endeavour to carry out your (——'s) views
Bauriss ...	05546	Do not see how I (we) can carry out your (——'s) views
Bausbackig	05547	Have no doubt but that I (we) shall be able to carry out your
Bauschen ...	05548	**Carrying** [(——'s) views
Baustelle ...	05549	Capable of carrying up to
Bauwesen ...	05550	Not capable of carrying more than
Bauzador ...	05551	Carrying a heavy load
Bavaglino...	05552	Carrying all I (we) can

Bavalisco ...	05558	Carrying all he (they) can
Bavardage	05554	**Cartridge** (*See also* "Dynamite," "Gelatine," "Powder," &c.)
Bavarderie	05555	Dynamite cartridge
Baviera ...	05556	**Case(s)**
Bavolet ...	05557	Case of
Bawdricks	05558	It is a case for
Bayeton ...	05559	Please give size of cases
Bayoco ...	05560	Cases measure —— × —— × ——
Bayrum ...	05561	A case in point
Bazo ...	05562	Appeal case
Bazucar ...	05563	Entirely alters the case
Bazzarato ...	05564	Have no case against
Bazzecole ...	05565	In case delay occurs
Beabant ...	05566	It is not the case
Beach ...	05567	In any case
Beachten ...	05568	In which case
Beadle ...	05569	In no case
Beadleship	05570	In each case
Beadroll ...	05571	In every case
Beadsman...	05572	In case they (——) refuse(s)
Beagles ...	05573	In case I (we) should refuse
Beaming ...	05574	In such a case
Beandum ...	05575	In case you are convinced that
Beantragen	05576	In case of need
Bearbeiten	05577	The facts of the case are
Beard ...	05578	The facts of the case were
Beardless ...	05579	The case is a very strong one
Beastly ...	05580	They have a strong case against us
Beatanza ...	05581	Take legal opinion if —— has (have) any case
Beatico ...	05582	What are the facts of the case
Beatificar ...	05583	We (you) have a strong case against them
Beatitude ...	05584	They intend to carry the case to
Beaton ...	05585	Case has assumed a serious aspect
Beatorum ...	05586	Has (have) won the case
Beaturus ...	05587	Has (have) lost the case
Beaucoup ...	05588	**Cash** (*See also* "Amount," "Balance," "Bank.")
Beaumonde	05589	To cash
Beaupre ...	05590	Cash only
Beautifier...	05591	Cash down
Beautify ...	05592	Cash equal to
Beauty ...	05593	An equal amount in cash
Beautyspot	05594	Cash in
Beavers ...	05595	Have you obtained the cash
Beavisti ...	05596	Have not obtained the cash
Bebauen ...	05597	Have obtained —— in cash
Bebedero ...	05598	How is cash to be paid
Bebedizo ..	05599	Cash on ——
Bebedo ...	05600	Immediate cash must be paid
Bebende ...	05601	Cash in exchange for
Beber ...	05602	No cash whatever
Beberrao ...	05603	Cable amount of cash in bank
Bebida ...	05604	To give —— in cash
Bebistrajo	05605	Cash on signing agreement
Bebrage ...	05606	Cash in exchange for the following, viz:—
Beca ...	05607	Cash in one month
Becabunga	05608	Cash in two months
Becafigo ...	05609	Cash in three months
Becalmed ...	05610	Cash in four months
Becardon ...	05611	Cash in five months
Becasseau ...	05612	Cash in six months

Becassine ...	05613	Cash in nine months
Beccaccino	05614	Cash now in treasury amounts to
Beccafiche...	05615	Cash will be sent on
Beccajo ...	05616	Cash sent is at disposal of ——
Beccamorti	05617	Cash sent on (by)
Beccarello...	05618	The lowest cash price is
Beccatina ...	05619	Cash less —— per cent.
Becchetto ...	05620	Cash on delivery
Beccuccio ...	05621	Cash in hand
Becerrillo ...	05622	Telegraph cash in hand
Becfigue ...	05623	Cash at bankers
Bechamel ...	05624	Cash payable in —— equal instalments
Bechern ...	05625	Cash must be placed to my (our) credit before ——
Beckening	05626	Cash must be placed to credit of —— at Bank (of)
Beclouded...	05627	Cash in exchange for documents
Becoquin ...	05628	Bank —— has refused to cash bill
Becqueter	05629	Only —— cash required
Becuadro ...	05630	Payable —— in cash Balance in deferred shares
Bedabbled	05631	Payable —— in cash Balance in fully paid shares
Bedashed ...	05632	First payment of —— must be paid to my credit at bank of ——
Bedaubed .	05633	Net cash
Bedchamber	05634	Should have cash before
Bedclothes	05635	The amount payable in cash is
Bedding ...	05636	The whole to be payable in cash
Bedecked ...	05637	The amount of cash advanced is
Bedecking	05638	What is the amount of cash advanced
Bedel ...	05639	**Cashed**
Bedelin ...	05640	Cashed by
Bedenken ...	05641	Not yet cashed
Bedenklich	05642	**Cashier**
Bedenkzeit	05643	Cashier to
Bedeulend	05644	Would act both as cashier and
Bedeutsam	05645	Require to have a good cashier
Bedewing ...	05646	With the cashier of the bank at (of)
Bedfellow	05647	**Casing**
Bedienen ...	05648	A casing of
Bedija ...	05649	Through the casing
Bedlam ...	05650	The casing of the reef
Bedquilt ...	05651	Casing between
Bedrangen	05652	Broke through the casing
Bedriden ...	05653	Destroyed the casing between
Bedrohlich	05654	Did no damage to the casing
Bedrohnng	05655	**Cask(s)** (*See also* "Safety Fuse.")
Bedruckung	05656	Casks of safety fuse
Bedstead ...	05657	**Cassiterite** (*See also* "Tin.")
Bedstraw ...	05658	Averaging —— per cent. of cassiterite (black tin)
Bedtime ...	05659	The cassiterite (black or oxide of tin) occurs in
Bedurfniss	05660	**Castings**
Bedusten ...	05661	Castings received
Bedwarf ..	05662	Castings shipped on
Beebread ...	05663	Castings not yet received
Beefeater ...	05664	When may I (we) expect to receive castings
Beehive ...	05665	Castings will be forwarded not later than
Beehren ...	05666	Hope to receive this casting not later than
Beeidigen ..	05667	**Catch**
Beeifern ...	05668	To catch
Beenden ...	05669	Failed to catch
Beendigung	05670	**Caught**
Beemte ...	05671	Has (have) been caught
Beetling ...	05672	Has (have) not been caught

Befabemi ...	05673	**Caunter** (*See also* "Lode.")
Befahigen	05674	Caunter lode
Befahrbar...	05675	Through caunter lode
Befahren ...	05676	At junction of caunter lode with
Befanaccia	05677	**Cause(s)**
Befehlen ...	05678	Cause of
Befestigen	05679	There is no cause for alarm
Befeuchten	05680	Cable the cause of
Befeuern ...	05681	Cause not known
Beffardo ...	05682	Cause beyond my (our) control
Beffatore ...	05683	To cause
Beffevole ...	05684	This may cause
Beffroi ...	05685	This should not cause
Befinden ...	05686	The cause of
Befindlich...	05687	Which will not cause
Befleckung	05688	What is the cause of delay
Befleissen...	05689	**Caused**
Beflugeln ...	05690	Was caused by
Beforderer	05691	This has caused an advance
Befrachten	05692	How was it (this) caused
Befragen ...	05693	To be caused
Befreien ...	05694	This (which) might have caused
Befreinden	05695	This (which) must have caused
Befringe ...	05696	Delay caused on account of
Befugniss...	05697	Delay caused from want of
Befund ..	05698	—— days' delay will be caused
Befurchten	05699	**Causing**
Begabung...	05700	Causing further delay
Begaffen ...	05701	Causing further delay and expense
Begaiement	05702	**Caution**
Begangniss	05703	Am (are) acting with every caution
Begardo ...	05704	Can you caution —— with regard to ——
Begattung	05705	Exercise the greatest caution
Begayer ...	05706	Has (have) acted with every caution
Begegnen ...	05707	Have you cautioned —— with regard to
Begegniss ..	05708	May depend upon my (our) acting with caution
Begehrlich	05709	Notwithstanding the caution contained in
Begetting...	05710	**Cautious**
Beggars ...	05711	Be very cautious in your report
Begging ...	05712	Is a very cautious man
Beghino ...	05713	Is too cautious if anything
Begierig ...	05714	Is not sufficiently cautious
Begiessen...	05715	Has the reputation of being cautious
Beginnen ...	05716	You will need to be cautious
Begirded ...	05717	Be very cautious
Beglaubigt	05718	Will be very cautious how I (we) proceed
Begleiten ...	05719	Impossible to be too cautious
Beglucken	05720	Was (were) not sufficiently cautious
Begnadigen	05721	Has (have) not been sufficiently cautious
Begnugen...	05722	**Cautiously**
Begole ...	05723	Very cautiously
Begrabniss	05724	If cautiously done
Begranzen	05725	Not too cautiously
Begriff ...	05726	**Cave(d)** (*See also* "Ground.")
Begrime ...	05727	To cave
Begrudge...	05728	Cave in
Begrunden	05729	Cave struck
Begrussung	05730	Cave formation
Beguer ...	05731	Might cave in at any moment
Begueule ...	05732	Adit (tunnel) has caved in

Beguiling ...	05733	Caved in
Beguino ...	05734	Ground is all caved in
Begutert ...	05735	Examination impossible; adit caved in
Begutigen ...	05736	Examination impossible; shaft caved in
Behaart ...	05737	Examination impossible; workings caved in
Behaftet ...	05738	Examination impossible; tunnel caved in
Behaglich ...	05739	Cave-in of shaft; serious damage to pitwork
Behaltbar ...	05740	Seem(s) likely to cave in
Behaltniss ..	05741	Serious cave in occurred on
Behaltsam...	05742	Shaft has caved in
Behandeln...	05743	Tunnel entrance has caved in
Behandlung	05744	Workings have caved in
Beharren ...	05745	Opponents have caved in
Beharrlich ...	05746	**Caving**
Behaupten	05747	Caving badly
Behausung	05748	Impossible to prevent caving
Behaviour ...	05749	Lower workings are caving in
Behead ...	05750	There is considerable danger of the mine caving
Beheading...	05751	**Cease** (*See also* "Stop.")
Behelfen ...	05752	To cease
Behelligen ..	05753	Cease to
Behemoth ...	05754	As soon as I (we) cease to
Behenic ...	05755	Will enable me (us) to cease
Behetria ...	05756	Will it enable you (——) to cease
Behilflich ...	05757	Will not enable me (us) (——) to cease
Beholder ...	05758	Cease further proceedings
Behoove ...	05759	Cease for the present
Behorchen ...	05760	Cease all work
Behorde ...	05761	Cease buying
Behuft ...	05762	Cease all endeavours
Behutsam ...	05763	Do not cease before
Beiblatt ...	05764	Do not on any account cease your endeavours (to)
Beibringen	05765	Have not ceased
Beichten ...	05766	Have ceased buying
Beichtkind	05767	Shall not cease until
Beiderlei ...	05768	Shall only cease when
Beidlebig ...	05769	Will not cease
Beifallen ...	05770	Shall not cease my (our) endeavours to
Beifolgend	05771	**Cellular**
Beifugung...	05772	**Cement** (*See also* "Bricks," "Clay.")
Beignet ...	05773	Sufficient cement should be sent for
Beihilfe ...	05774	How much cement will you require
Beikommen	05775	Will require —— tons of cement
Beilaufig ...	05776	Cement works
Beilegung ...	05777	**Censure**
Beiliegen ...	05778	Is open to censure
Beimessen...	05779	Did not censure
Beimischen	05780	Unless open to actual censure
Beiname ...	05781	**Censured**
Beinbruch...	05782	Has (have) been severely censured
Beinern ...	05783	Was not even censured
Beinfaule ...	05784	**Cent(s)** (*See also* "Per Cent.," "Numbers," &c.)
Beinhaus ...	05785	**Centigrade**
Beinlos ...	05786	Degrees centigrade
Beiordnen ...	05787	Between —— and —— degrees centigrade
Beipferd ...	05788	**Centner**
Beisammen	05789	Per centner of 100 lbs. avoirdupois
Beischiff ...	05790	Per centner of —— lbs. avoirdupois
Beischluss...	05791	**Central**
Beiseit ...	05792	In a central

Beisetzen ...	05793	Is very central
Beispiel ...	05794	Is in a most central position as regards
Beissig ...	05795	As a central position for
Beisskorb ...	05796	**Centre**
Beisszange	05797	Working from —— as a centre
Beistand ...	05798	Working from this point as a centre
Beistehen ...	05799	About the centre of
Beisteuern	05800	Cable measurements from centre to centre
Beistimmen	05801	From centre to centre
Beistrich ...	05802	In the centre of
Beitragen ...	05803	Distance between the two centres is
Beitreiben ...	05804	Distance from centre of —— to centre of —— is
Beitritt ...	05805	**Centrifugal**
Beiwagen ...	05806	Centrifugal pump
Beiwerk ...	05807	Through centrifugal force
Beiwohnen	05808	**Certain**
Beiwort ...	05809	Are you (is ——) certain
Beizahlen ...	05810	If you are certain
Beizeiten ...	05811	Should you not be quite certain
Bejahend ...	05812	I am (we are) certain
Bejahung ...	05813	I am (we are) not certain
Bejammern	05814	I am (we are) quite certain to
Bejaune ...	05815	I am (we are) not quite certain
Bejinero ...	05816	It is quite certain that
Bejucal ...	05817	It is by no means certain
Bejuco ...	05818	—— (it) is quite certain
Bejuguillo...	05819	It is not possible for me to be certain
Bekampfen	05820	Not certain
Bekannte ...	05821	Nearly certain
Bekehrbar ..	05822	Quite certain
Bekehren ...	05823	You should be certain as regards
Beklecksen	05824	Be certain
Bekleiden ...	05825	Unless you are perfectly certain
Beklemmuno	05826	By no means unless you are certain
Beklunkern	05827	**Certainly**
Beknabbern	05828	Yes, certainly
Bekranzen...	05829	Certainly not
Bekritteln ..	05830	**Certainty**
Bekummert	05831	Every certainty
Belaboured	05832	Is there any certainty
Belace ...	05833	Little or no certainty
Belacheln ...	05834	The only certainty is
Belagerer ...	05835	There is no certainty
Belagerung	05836	With some degree of certainty
Belandre ...	05837	What degree of certainty is there (that)
Belangung	05838	**Certificate(s)**
Belassen ...	05839	Assay certificate
Belastigen...	05840	Analytical certificate
Belauben ...	05841	Consul's certificate
Belauf ...	05842	Certificate filed
Belauschen	05843	Certificate No. ——
Belcho ...	05844	Certificate(s) not properly drawn
Beleaquer ...	05845	Certificate(s) not yet received
Beledern ...	05846	Certificate(s) sent for record to
Beledin ...	05847	Certificate(s) will be filed on
Belehnung...	05848	Hope to send certificate for record not later than
Beleibt ...	05849	Can you obtain a certificate to the effect that
Beleidiger ...	05850	Have mailed certificate as desired
Belement ...	05851	Cannot obtain any such certificate as you wish
Belemnita...	05852	Certificate received

Belenito ...	05853	Has certificate been filed
Belerico ...	05854	Has certificate of incorporation been filed
Belesprit ...	05855	Has certificate of location been filed [—— shares
Belette ...	05856	Have mailed letter containing —— certificates representing
Belfern ...	05857	Have you received letter mailed on —— containing —— share [certificates
Belfry ...	05858	Have received letter dated —— containing certificates as stated
Belgivino ...	05859	Have received letter dated —— but it only contains —— certi- [ficates representing —— shares
Belhez ...	05860	Have received letter dated —— containing the following certi-
Belico ...	05861	Want certificate(s) for —— shares [ficates
Belicoso ...	05862	Have mailed letter containing —— transfers and —— share
Beliere ...	05863	Share certificate(s) [certificates
Bellabat ...	05864	As soon as share certificate(s) is (are) ready
Bellacada ...	05865	Share certificate(s) mailed you to-day
Bellaco ...	05866	Mail share certificate(s) as soon as possible
Bellacuelo...	05867	Share certificate(s) will be mailed as soon as it (they) can be
Belladama	05868	Certificate(s) will be mailed on [prepared
Bellamente	05869	Certificate(s) not yet mailed
Bellaquear	05870	Certificate(s) required for
Bellatrix ...	05871	Certificate(s) not yet passed by Board of Directors
Bellavi ...	05872	Certificate(s) not yet received; cable when mailed
Bellavisse ...	05873	Certificate(s) lost; please send letter of indemnity
Bellefille ...	05874	Has (have) share certificate(s) been mailed
Bellemere ...	05875	Mail as quickly as possible certificate(s) for
Bellemus ...	05876	Proper certificate(s)
Belleza ...	05877	Retain certificate(s) pending my (our) instructions
Bellicato ...	05878	Retain certificate(s) to my order
Belliqueux	05879	Transfer cannot be passed without —— certificate
Bellirico ...	05880	You (——) must produce certificate
Bellman ...	05881	What is (are) the number(s) of certificate(s)
Bello ...	05882	Number(s) of certificate(s) is (are)
Bellorio ...	05883	**Certified** (See also " Attested.")
Bellorita ...	05884	A certified transfer for —— shares mailed on
Bellote ...	05885	All the documents must be certified
Bellotica ...	05886	Certified abstract(s) of title mailed on
Bellowing...	05887	Mail certified abstract of title
Bellpull ...	05888	Mail a certified transfer for —— shares for me (——) to sign
Bellringer...	05889	Title must be duly certified
Bellwether	05890	Unless certified
Belobung ...	05891	Must be legally certified
Belohnen ...	05892	Has (have) been legally certified
Belongings	05893	Will be legally certified
Belorta ...	05894	Certified by ——
Beltate ...	05895	Certified by —— to be in order legally
Beluatiore	05896	**Certify**
Beluatus ...	05897	To certify
Belustigen	05898	Can certify
Belvedere ...	05899	—— refuse(s) to certify
Belvicida ...	05900	Can —— certify
Bemannen	05901	—— cannot certify
Bemeistern	05902	Can you certify if necessary as to
Bemerkbar	05903	I (we) can certify if necessary as to
Bemerklich	05904	I (we) cannot certify as to
Bemittelt ...	05905	I (we) should not care to certify
Bemmione	05906	Is there anyone who can certify
Bemol ...	05907	No one can certify here
Bemolado ...	05908	**Chain** (See also "Rope.")
Bemoliser...	05909	Shall you require any chain for
Bemoost ...	05910	Shall require —— feet of chain for

Bemuhung	05911	Send —— feet of suitable chain for
Bemused ...	05912	Extra chain
Benachbart	05913	Owing to a breakage of the chain
Benaffetto	05914	Chain will be required to lift —— actual weight
Benagurato	05915	Chain must be sufficiently strong for
Benalaque	05916	Caused by stretching of the chain
Benamset ..	05917	**Chalk** (*See also* " Cretaceous.")
Benandata	05918	**Chance(s)**
Benarriza ...	05919	The first chance you have
Benaschen	05920	Give you (——) the first chance
Bendatura	05921	What are the chances
Bendecir ...	05922	Chances are bad
Benderella	05923	Chances are good
Bendicion ...	05924	Chances indifferent
Bendito ...	05925	Is there any chance of
Benduccio	05926	I (we) have had no chance yet
Benebeln ...	05927	Do not leave anything to chance
Benedicite	05928	Can you see any chance of improvement
Benedicta ...	05929	Should you see any chance of immediate improvement
Benefactor	05930	Cannot see any chance of improvement
Benemerito	05931	The only chance of improvement is as regards
Benennung	05932	**Change**
Beneplacet	05933	To change
Benevivere	05934	Change to
Benevolent	05935	Change of
Benevolo ...	05936	Shall change
Bengala ...	05937	Cannot change
Bengelhaft	05938	Change not worth reporting
Beniesen ...	05939	Do not consider change worth reporting
Benighted	05940	Change the clause
Benignitam	05941	Any change
Benignity ...	05942	Change of address
Benigno ...	05943	Cable should any change occur
Beninanza	05944	Better have complete change of management
Beninteso ...	05945	Better change present system of
Benitier ...	05946	Is there any change of
Benjui ...	05947	No material change
Benmontato	05948	There is a very favourable change in (at)
Bennarium	05949	To make some change in
Benothigen	05950	I (we) consider it a change for the better
Benplacito	05951	I (we) consider it a change for the worse
Bentipiaci	05952	Is there any change respecting
Bentornato	05953	Is there any change in
Benumbed	05954	It will be necessary to change the
Benumbment	05955	It is not necessary to change the
Benutzen ...	05956	No change as regards
Benvisto ...	05957	There is a great change (for the)
Benvolere ...	05958	There is practically no change to report
Benzene ...	05959	There is a marked change in
Benzoate ...	05960	There is no change in the character of the rock
Benzoin ...	05961	The change is a great improvement
Benzole ...	05962	There is no change to report at this point
Beobachter	05963	There is no change of any importance
Beodez ...	05964	No change to report here
Beordern ...	05965	No change to report at
Beori ...	05966	There is (are) no material change(s) at the (this) (these)
Bepacken ...	05967	There is little or no change since [point(s)
Bepflanzen	05968	There is no change to mention
Bepinched	05969	There has been no change in prices
Beque ...	05970	There have been the following changes in prices

Bequeath ...	05971	Has there been any change in prices
Bequemen	05972	**Changed**
Bequillard	05973	The rock has changed
Bequille ...	05974	The rock has changed and become much harder
Beram ...	05975	The rock has changed and become much softer
Berathen ...	05976	Affairs are altogether changed
Beraubung	05977	Have changed my opinion
Berauscht	05978	Practically unchanged
Berbena ...	05979	Changed for the better
Berberis ...	05980	Changed for the worse
Berberry ...	05981	Has changed to
Berbicem ...	05982	Have changed
Bercail ...	05983	Have not changed
Bercebu ...	05984	**Character**
Berceria ...	05985	The character of
Berceuse ...	05986	The character of the rock
Bereave ...	05987	What is the character of
Berechnen	05988	Shall want reliable character
Bereich ...	05989	**Charcoal** (*See also* " Coal," " Fuel," &c.)
Bereichern	05990	**Charge(s)**
Bereiter ...	05991	In charge
Bereitung ...	05992	To charge
Berengena	05993	To take charge
Bergamotta	05994	Charge to the debit of
Bergantin...	05995	Charge to our account
Bergbau ...	05996	Charge to our account and mail to
Bergerie ...	05997	Charge to our account and pay to
Berggegend	05998	Charge to our account and cable to
Berggeist ...	05999	Who was in charge
Berghohle...	06000	—— was in charge
Bergkette...	**06001**	—— is now in charge of underground works
Bergknappe	06002	—— is now in complete charge
Bergleder ...	06003	Charges are now about
Bergleute ...	06004	Dead or development charges
Bergmann	06005	Extra charge(s)
Bergolo ...	06006	What will the total charges amount to
Bergrath ...	06007	Total charges will probably amount to
Bergrecht...	06008	Charges are considered heavy
Bergrucken	06009	Charges are reasonable
Bergsturz ...	06010	Charges are really too heavy
Bergwerk ...	06011	Charges are comparatively low
Bergwesen	06012	All charges will be paid by
Bergwohner	06013	Can you not reduce the charge to
Berhyme ...	06014	Do not incur any charges on account of
Berichten ...	06015	Debit the charges to
Berlanga ...	06016	Extra charge owing to
Berlina ...	06017	I think —— might be left in charge
Berlingare	06018	Require a competent man to take charge of
Bermejear	06019	Should advise you to charge
Bermejizo	06020	Send an itemised account of charges
Bermejo ...	06021	The charge is that he (——)
Bermejura	06022	Will pay charges
Bermellon...	06023	Who will pay the extra charge(s)
Bernachos...	06024	Who shall I (we) debit the charges to
Bernardo ...	06025	What would you advise me to charge
Bernegal ...	06026	What would you charge for
Bernicla ...	06027	Who was in charge of —— at the time
Berniesco ...	06028	—— was supposed to be in charge
Bernique ...	06029	Who will take charge
Berniz ...	06030	If —— returns home who would you place in charge

Bernocchio	06031	Would suggest that —— is left in charge
Bernstein ...	06032	I know a good man who would take charge
Berraza ...	06033	Let —— remain in charge of property until further notice
Berrear ...	06034	Less freight and smelting charges
Berrenchin	06035	**Charged**
Berrendo ...	06036	I (we) have only charged for
Berrettajo...	06037	I (we) have not charged anything for
Berrido ,..	06038	Should have been charged to
Berrinche ...	06039	What have you charged for
Berrizal ...	06040	**Charter**
Berrocal ...	06041	To charter
Berroquena	06042	Can you charter
Berroviere	06043	Cannot charter
Berrueco ...	06044	Shall endeavour to charter if possible
Berrugoso...	06045	Send complete copy of charter
Bersaglio ...	06046	Within what time and at what rate can you charter
Bertescone	06047	Can charter immediately for a sum of
Bertolotto...	06048	Can charter within —— days for a sum of
Bertovello...	06049	**Chartered**
Bertuccino	06050	Have chartered
Bertuzzo ...	06051	Have not chartered
Berufung ...	06052	Have you chartered
Beruhigen	06053	Cannot be chartered under
Beruhrung	06054	Have chartered subject to your confirmation by cable (——)
Berulam ...	06055	**Cheap**
Berussen ...	06056	Cheap at
Beryllum ...	06057	Do you think it cheap
Besador ...	06058	Consider it cheap at the price named
Besagt ...	06059	Should consider it cheap at ——
Besaigre ...	06060	Are the conditions those of cheap working
Besaiten ...	06061	I (we) should not consider it cheap
Besaufen ...	06062	May be considered very cheap
Beschaben	06063	Property is very cheap at the figure named
Beschaler ...	06064	**Cheapen**
Beschamung	06065	Will cheapen extraction by —— per ton
Beschatzen	06066	**Cheaper**
Bescheid ...	06067	Would expect —— to be cheaper before very long
Bescheinen	06068	It is cheaper to use
Beschenken	06069	Would it not be cheaper to use
Beschiffen	06070	Is (are) cheaper
Beschirmen	06071	Is (are) not cheaper
Beschlafen	06072	If can get cheaper
Beschlag ...	06073	Cannot obtain cheaper
Beschluss ...	06074	Cannot you obtain —— cheaper
Beschneien	06075	Cannot you obtain it (them) cheaper
Beschuhen	06076	It would not be cheaper
Beschutzer	06077	Will be cheaper
Beschwerde	06078	Will not be cheaper
Beschworen	06079	Would it be cheaper to
Beseelen ...	06080	Do you think it will be any cheaper to
Beseligen ...	06081	I (we) think it would be cheaper to
Besenstiel	06082	I (we) do not think it would be cheaper to
Besessen ...	06083	Rather cheaper if anything
Beseufzen...	06084	**Cheapest**
Beshrew ...	06085	By cheapest route
Besicles ...	06086	Cheapest way
Besico ...	06087	Cheapest possible means
Besiegeln ...	06088	**Cheaply**
Besieger ...	06089	Property can be purchased cheaply
Besieging ...	06090	From the general conditions the mine can be worked cheaply

Besingen ...	06091	Cheaply and economically
Besinnung	06092	General conditions do not permit of working cheaply
Besitz ...	06093	Mill can be run cheaply
Besitzthum	06094	Works can be cheaply carried on
Besitzung...	06095	—— can be brought to the mine cheaply
Besogne ...	06096	**Check**
Besoigneux	06097	Check assay
Besolden ...	06098	Check samples
Besonder ...	06099	Check incomplete
Besonnen ...	06100	Cable the result of check
Besorgniss	06101	It will be necessary to check
Besorgt ...	06102	Practically there is no check
Bespangle...	06103	Practically there has been no check
Bespeien ...	06104	Should check
Bespiegeln	06105	**Checked**
Bespotteln	06106	I (we) have checked
Besprechen	06107	Should be checked
Bespringen	06108	Should have been checked
Bespritzen	06109	**Chemical(s)** (*See also* " Assay.")
Bespucken	06110	Adjacent chemical works
Bessaggine	06111	Chemico-metallurgical process
Bessalarum	06112	Is a chemical process
Bessalis ...	06113	Is a chemical process required
Bestallen ...	06114	No chemicals required
Bestandig...	06115	Stock of chemicals
Bestandlos	06116	The cost of chemicals per ton ——
Bestarkung	06117	What would be the cost of chemicals per ton
Bestatigen	06118	**Chemist**
Bestattung	06119	He is a sound reliable chemist
Bestauben	06120	Is he a sound and reliable chemist
Bestechen...	06121	Should be a good chemist and assayer
Besteck ...	06122	Should be a good chemist
Bestehlung	06123	**Cheque** (*See also* " Bearer.")
Besteigen...	06124	Cheque dishonoured
Besteiro ...	06125	Cheque for ——
Bestemmia	06126	Cheque for —— has been lost; stop payment
Besternt ...	06127	Do not pay cheque
Besteuern...	06128	Has cheque been presented
Bestezuela	06129	Cheque has been presented and paid
Bestia ...	06130	Cheque has not yet been presented
Bestiaccia...	06131	Defer presentation of cheque until
Bestiage ...	06132	Have posted cheque for
Bestiaire ...	06133	Please remit cheque for —— as soon as possible
Bestialis ...	06134	Please remit cheque in payment of —— account
Bestiarius...	06135	Payment of cheque stopped
Bestiaza ...	06136	Present cheque again on ——
Bestielen ...	06137	Telegraph if you have received cheque mailed on ——
Bestievole...	06138	Will mail cheque for amount on ——
Bestimmen	06139	Your cheque was presented on ——
Bestiolina...	06140	**Chert**
Bestion ...	06141	Hard bar of black chert
Bestiuola ...	06142	Cherty limestone
Bestola ...	06143	**Chief**
Bestrafung	06144	The chief points are
Bestreiten...	06145	What are the chief points
Bestricken	06146	The chief consideration is
Bestud ...	06147	**Chiefly**
Besturmen	06148	Owing chiefly to
Besturzung	06149	Chiefly from
Besucar ...	06150	Chiefly from want of

Besucon	06151	**Chimney** (*See also* "Chute," "Ore Chute," &c.)
Besudeln	06152	Send iron chimney complete for
Besugada	06153	Chimney for
Besugo	06154	Chimney formation
Besuguera	06155	Chimney of ore
Beta	06156	Struck chimney of ore
Betaorcin	06157	Is it a new chimney of ore
Betarraga	06158	Believe it to be a new chimney of ore
Betasten	06159	Do not think that it is a new chimney of ore
Betbruder	06160	Ore chimney is narrowing; present dimensions —— ft. × ——
Bethatigen	06161	Ore chimney is widening; present dimensions —— ft. × ——
Bethauen	06162	Ore chimney maintains its former dimensions
Betheuern	06163	What is the present depth of the ore chimney
Bethorung	06164	Main ore chimney
Betiteln	06165	When do you expect to cut the ore chimney at
Betokening	06166	May cut ore chimney any day
Betonen	06167	We are not likely to cut the ore chimney for next —— feet
Betonica	06168	Expect to strike ore chimney within the next —— feet
Betracht	06169	**Chloride**
Betraufeln	06170	Chloride ores
Betreffend	06171	Chloride of
Betreiben	06172	Chloride of gold
Betriebsam	06173	Chloride of silver
Betroffen	06174	**Chloridization**
Betrothed	06175	The ore will require a preliminary roasting before chloridization
Betrubniss	06176	No preliminary roasting will be needful before chloridization
Betruglich	06177	Chloridization will cost —— per ton
Bettdecke	06178	Chloridization is necessary
Bettelhaft	06179	Chloridization is not necessary
Bettelmann	06180	When chloridization will become necessary
Bettelvogt	06181	**Chlorination**
Betterave	06182	Chlorination experiment
Bettlerin	06183	Chlorination of ore
Bettoletta	06184	The ore is well suited for chlorination
Bettoliere	06185	Chlorination plant capable of dealing with —— tons per day
Bettstelle	06186	By a chlorination process [of 24 hours
Bettwasche	06187	Cost of chlorination per ton would be
Bettzeug	06188	Cost of erecting a chlorination works would amount to
Betunar	06189	What would be the cost of a plant to chlorinate say —— tons [per day of 24 hours
Betwoche	06190	Suggest that a chlorination experiment be made
Beuglement	06191	**Chloritic**
Beugung	06192	**Choice**
Beul	06193	Your choice is certainly
Beuna	06194	Your choice should be based upon
Beurlauben	06195	Your choice is quite approved
Beurre	06196	Your choice is not altogether approved
Beurrier	06197	Is there any choice in the matter
Beuteln	06198	There is no choice in the matter
Bevanda	06199	Should there be any choice in the matter
Beveratojo	06200	Defer making any choice for the present
Bevibile	06201	**Chokedamp** (*See also* "Afterdamp.")
Bevigione	06202	**Choose**
Bevilacqua	06203	To choose
Bevitrice	06204	Which have you decided to choose
Bevitura	06205	Should you choose to do so
Bevolkern	06206	Choose a good opportunity
Bevorzugen	06207	Do as you choose
Bewachen	06208	**Chosen**
Bewaffnen	06209	Chosen on account of

Bewahren	06210	Chosen by
Bewailment	06211	**Chrome**
Bewassern	06212	Chrome iron ore [and —— per cent. of ferric oxide
Bewegbar ...	06213	Chrome iron ore containing —— per cent. of chromium oxide
Beweggrund	06214	Large quantities of chrome iron ore
Beweglich	06215	The sample you sent consists of chrome iron ore
Beweibt ...	06216	Has no value as chrome iron ore
Beweisen ...	06217	**Chute** (*See also* "Chimney," "Ore Chute," &c.)
Beweislich	06218	Chute of ore
Bewerbung	06219	Upon chute of —— ore
Bewilligen	06220	An entirely new chute of ore
Bewirthen	06221	Have struck ore chute assays (at)
Bewitzeln ...	06222	Ore chute is dipping
Bewohnbar	06223	Rich chute of ore
Bewolken ...	06224	Poor chute of ore
Bewunderer	06225	When we expect to strike chute of ore
Bewusstlos	06226	Ore chute is narrowing; present dimensions —— ft. × ——
Bexiga ...	06227	Ore chute has petered out
Bezaartico	06228	Ore chute is widening; present dimensions —— ft. × ——
Bezahlung	06229	Ore chute maintains its former dimensions
Bezante ...	06230	Ore chute is dipping at an angle of —— with the horizon
Bezaubern	06231	What is the present dip of the ore chute
Bezazas ...	06232	What are the present dimensions of the ore chute
Bezeichnen	06233	The dimensions of the ore chute are
Bezel... ...	06234	Pay chute
Bezeugen ...	06235	Have you done any stoping on pay chute
Beziehung	06236	Cable particulars of new ore chute, length, width and assay
Beziffern ...	06237	Cable particulars of the ore chute struck in the —— level
Bezo ...	06238	Have cut ore chute in the —— level
Bezoardico	06239	There is a rumour that a new ore chute has been cut, is it true
Bezote ...	06240	We have still to drive —— ft. before we can expect to cut pay
Bezudo ...	06241	—— tons from pay chute averages [chute
Bezuglich...	06242	**Cinnabar** (*See also* "Mercury.")
Bezugnahme	06243	Cinnabar ore assaying —— per cent. mercury
Bezwecken	06244	Cinnabar vein
Bezweifeln	06245	Cinnabar mine
Bezzicante	06246	Cinnabar property
Bezzicato ...	06247	Rock is more or less impregnated with cinnabar
Biadajuolo	06248	**Cipher** (*See also* "Code.")
Biadetto ...	06249	Cipher word
Biaiseur ...	06250	What is the new code cipher
Biambonas	06251	Cipher number
Biancheria	06252	This cable is all in cipher
Biancicare	06253	This cable is not all in cipher
Biancolina	06254	Cable in plain words, not in cipher
Biangular...	06255	Change our cipher number to ——
Biarchorum	06256	Change our cipher number and advise me (us) by mail
Biarchus ...	06257	Permit our cipher to be used by
Biasa ...	06258	Do not permit our cipher to be used
Biasciare ...	06259	Explain our cipher to
Biasimato...	06260	What is the cipher word for ——
Biastemare	06261	**Circular**
Bibaro ...	06262	Issue a circular
Bibebatis ...	06263	Official circular
Bibelfest ...	06264	A circular has been issued stating that
Bibelot ...	06265	Contradict by circular
Bibemus ...	06266	Do not on any account issue a circular
Bibendum	06267	We require this information for a circular to the shareholders
Bibens ...	06268	We propose to issue a circular forthwith, do not fail to cable
Bibentes ...	06269	We propose to issue a circular to-morrow [immediately

Biberam ...	06270	We propose to issue a circular at once
Bibergeil ..	06271	We propose to issue a circular on ——
Biberhut ...	06272	We published in an official circular that
Biberint ...	06273	In our official circular dated —— it was stated that
Bibesia ...	06274	In your official circular dated —— you stated that
Bibissent ...	06275	The information is required for circular to shareholders
Bibitote ...	06276	Suggest(s) that we issue a circular to the effect that
Bibitur ...	06277	As we wish to issue a circular

Circulate

Biblia ...	06278	
Biblico ...	06279	To circulate
Bibliofilo ...	06280	Propose to circulate
Bibliomane	06281	Circulate the report that
Bibliopole...	06282	I (we) believe —— is about to circulate a report

Circulated

Bibliotafo...	06283	
Biblioteca...	06284	Circulated by
Bibliothek	06285	Widely circulated
Biblique ...	06286	Can you trace who circulated the report that
Biblisch ...	06287	Do not let report be circulated that
Biblus ...	06288	I (we) believe —— circulated the report
Bibosus ...	06289	The report is circulated that

Circulation

Bibractem	06290	
Bibulous ...	06291	In circulation
Bibunto ...	06292	Not in circulation
Bicapsular	06293	Out of circulation
Bicchiere ...	06294	This is for your private use, not for circulation

Circumstance(s)

Bicepso ...	06295	
Bicessibus	06296	Circumstances changed
Bicessis ...	06297	Owing to change of circumstances
Bichero ...	06298	Circumstances beyond my control compel me to
Biahette ..	06299	Owing to circumstances beyond my (our) control
Bichonner	06300	Circumstances over which I had (have) no control
Bicipite ...	06301	The circumstances are
Bickering...	06302	What are the precise circumstances
Biclinium	06303	Under what circumstances
Bicoca ...	06304	After considering the whole of the circumstances
Bicolorem...	06305	The circumstances are peculiar
Bicoquete	06306	At once, if circumstances will permit
Bicoquin ...	06307	Considering the whole of the circumstances I (we) would [advise that
Bicornia ...	06308	Under these circumstances
Bicorniger	06309	Not under any circumstances
Bicorporeo	06310	Am (are) very anxious as soon as circumstances will permit
Bicos... ...	06311	Am (are) not clear as to circumstances; write fully
Bidental ...	06312	Am (are) not clear as to circumstances; cable fully
Biduum ...	06313	Cable the exact circumstances
Bieder ...	06314	Entirely depends on circumstances
Biederkeit	06315	In case circumstances justify
Biedermann	06316	May I (we) under the circumstances
Bieldar ...	06317	On account of the altered circumstances
Bienal ...	06318	If circumstances permit
Bienamado	06319	Should any unforeseen circumstance happen
Biendire ...	06320	Under these circumstances I (we) consider
Bienembrod	06321	Under any circumstances
Bienenhaus	06322	Under no circumstances whatever
Bienenkorb	06323	Under the present circumstances
Bienenmann	06324	Under the following circumstances
Bienenwolf	06325	Under such circumstances you may
Bienestar ...	06326	Considering all the circumstances
Bienfait ...	06327	Entirely depends on circumstances
Bienfonds...	06328	Under the circumstances it will be wise for you to
Bienhecho	06329	Under the circumstances what is the wisest thing for me to do

Bienio ...	06330	**Cistern(s)**
Biennial ...	06331	Which cistern
Bienquisto	06332	Cistern at
Bienseant ...	06333	The building over cistern is now nearly finished
Bienvenida	06334	Cistern has been fixed at
Bienvenue	06335	What is capacity of cistern
Bienvista ...	06336	Capacity of cistern is
Bierbank ...	06337	**Clack** (*See also* " Pumps.")
Bierfass ...	06338	Clack piece
Bierkanne...	06339	Clack door
Bierkneipe	06340	Failure of clack
Bierkrug ...	06341	Through clack getting trigged up
Bierschank	06342	**Claim(s)** (*See also* " Assessment.")
Bierwage ...	06343	To claim
Bierwarth...	06344	Claim compensation for
Biestings ...	06345	Claim sufficient compensation to cover
Bietolone ...	06346	Claim repudiated
Bifariam ...	06347	Claim cannot be allowed
Bifarious ...	06348	Claim extra compensation for
Biflorous ...	06349	What is the amount of claim
Bifolca	06350	Amount of claim is
Bifold ...	06351	Claim has been made
Biforibus ...	06352	What does —— (do they) claim
Biforme ...	06353	Who make(s) the claim
Bifronte ...	06354	Claim is made by
Bifteck ...	06355	Claim is made for
Bifurcarum	06356	Persist(s) in claim
Bifurcate ...	06357	Claim is withdrawn
Bifurquer...	06358	Claim was fraudulent
Bigamist ...	06359	Shall I (we) try to compromise claim
Bigamo ...	06360	Compromise claim if possible
Bigardear...	06361	Means to compromise claim
Bigardia ...	06362	Have compromised claim
Bigarrado...	06363	Willing to compromise claim against
Bigarreau...	06364	Can you compromise ——'s claim
Bigato ...	06365	Make a claim of
Bigatorum	06366	Settle claim so as to avoid delay
Bighellone	06367	Settle claim so as to avoid further cost
Bigherajo	06368	Settle claim under protest
Bights ...	06369	You must do sufficient work to hold all the claims
Bigiccio ...	06370	Have done sufficient work to hold all the claims
Bigliardo ...	06371	Will undertake to do sufficient work to hold all claims
Bignonia ...	06372	Refuse(s) to admit claim
Bigoncina...	06373	Is willing to admit claim if
Bigorda ...	06374	Timber claim
Bigorneta	06375	The claims all join
Bigot ...	06376	None of the claims join
Bigotazo ...	06377	Upper part of claim
Bigotera ...	06378	——'s claim should be settled
Bigotry ...	06379	It is advisable to acquire the —— claim
Bijou ...	06380	Has he (have they) any legal claim
Bijouterie...	06381	Make a claim for
Bijugorum	06382	Make a claim on account of
Bilancetto...	06383	Send particulars of claim(s)
Bilanciajo...	06384	Send plan showing claim(s)
Bilboes ...	06385	See that boundaries of claim are clearly defined
Bilboquet...	06386	Strongly urge you to acquire the —— claim : vein dips into it
Bildarbeit...	06387	Repudiate all claims
Bilden ...	06388	Take care not to admit any claim
Bilderbuch	06389	Dimensions of each claim are

Bildhauer	06390	Patented claim
Bildlich ...	06391	Mining claim
Bildniss ...	06392	Unpatented claim
Bildsam ...	06393	Your claim is now before
Bildsaule ...	06394	Length of claim —— ft. by —— ft. wide
Bildschon...	06395	The dimensions of the claim(s) is (are)
Bildseite ...	06396	Claim and mill site
Bildwerk ...	06397	Certain claims in outlying districts
Bilgewater	06398	Get in all outstanding claims
Bilharda ...	06399	At which claim
Biliario ...	06400	The property comprises —— claims
Bilibralem	06401	The adjacent claim(s)
Bilieux ...	06402	The claim is really only a location
Bilingue ...	06403	The following claims are protected by U.S. patents
Bilinguous	06404	U.S. patents have been obtained for all claims
Biliorsa ...	06405	Have U.S. patents been obtained for all claims
Bilioso ...	06406	U.S. patents are being obtained for the remaining claims
Biliottato ...	06407	They practically claim that
Billalda ...	06408	Their claim is for
Billebande	06409	He (they) has (have) no legal claim whatever
Billetdoux	06410	Seem to have a reasonable claim
Billete ...	06411	Claim has no value except for dumping purposes
Billetico ...	06412	Has (have) no facts to support his (their) claim(s)
Billevesee ..	06413	**Clamp** (See also "Drills.")
Billiards ...	06414	Forward promptly clamp to fit stretcher bar —— inches diameter; boss on cradle of boring machine is —— inches [diameter
Billigen ...	06415	Clamps for
Billigkeit ...	06416	**Class**
Billon ...	06417	First-class
Billows ...	06418	Second-class
Bilmador ...	06419	Third-class
Bilorta ...	06420	—— class
Biltrotear ...	06421	Same class as before
Bilustrem	06422	Better class than hitherto
Bimaes ...	06423	**Classed**
Bimanous...	06424	Classed at
Bimaribus	06425	Is classed
Bimatorum	06426	Is not classed
Bimbam ...	06427	**Classify(ied)**
Bimembre	06428	Classify under the following heads
Bimestre ...	06429	Ore is classified into the following grades
Bimmolle ...	06430	Should suggest you employ a classifier
Bimulum ...	06431	**Clause** (See also "Cancelled.")
Binadera ...	06432	What is the meaning of clause No. ——
Binario ...	06433	The precise meaning of clause No. —— is ——
Binary ...	06434	Object to clause No. ——
Binascenza	06435	Do (does) not object now to clause No. ——
Binateras ...	06436	Clause now modified
Bindekalk	06437	Cannot get clause modified
Bindella ...	06438	Will not modify clause
Binderlohn	06439	Modify clause
Bindewort	06440	Clause modified as follows
Bindfaben	06441	Clause must be modified so as to read
Binding ...	06442	Clause inserted
Bindoleria	06443	Has (have) inserted a clause which will
Bindolone...	06444	Clause is prohibitive
Binnacle ...	06445	Clause requires considerable modification
Binnensee...	06446	Strike out clause No. —— (relating to)
Binoctibus	06447	Have struck out clause
Binocular ...	06448	Customary clause

Binomia ...	06449	Clause must be left out
Binominis...	06450	Add a clause giving us the power to
Biografia ...	06451	By clause —— we shall be protected
Biographer	06452	By clause —— we are protected
Biology ...	06453	Do not consider clause No. —— necessary
Biombo ...	06454	Do (does) not consent to insertion of clause
Bioneus ...	06455	Clause is necessary
Biordare ...	06456	Clause must be omitted unless
Bipalme ...	06457	Have omitted —— clause
Biparous ...	06458	If you consent to clause —— cable
Bipartamur	06459	If you cannot consent to clause —— cable
Bipartido ...	06460	In violation of clause
Bipatentis	06461	Insert the following clause
Bipedal ...	06462	Modify the clause respecting
Bipedaneus	06463	No clause relating to —— will be
Bipemate ...	06464	Protest against clause relating to
Bipetalo ...	06465	Clauses relating to —— are too stringent
Biprorum ...	06466	Will this constitute a violation of clause
Biquadrate	06467	Enforce clause relating to
Biquet ...	06468	**Clay(ey)** (*See also* "Bricks.")
Biracchio ...	06469	Clay slate
Birada ...	06470	Clay seam
Birar ...	06471	Clay selvage
Birazones ...	06472	Fire clay
Birbantare	06473	In clay
Birboneria	06474	Send necessary fire clay
Birdlime ...	06475	**Clean**
Birds ...	06476	Clean ore
Birdseye ...	06477	**Clean up** (*See also* "Arrastra," "Hydraulicing," "Stamps," &c.)
Biremem ...	06478	Clean up amounts to
Biribara ...	06479	Clean up after
Biribis ...	06480	Now cleaning up; will report result as soon as possible
Biricu ...	06481	Clean up for the month of ——
Birilla ..	06482	Clean up from —— tons gave
Birkensaft	06483	Clean up resulted in only —— on account of
Birkhuhn ...	06484	Clean up from —— pans gave
Birlador ...	06485	Clean up after campaign No. ——, Tons crushed ——. Labour cost ——. Materials cost ——. General expenses ——. Yield ——. Net profit here ——.
Birlocha ...	06486	Could you have a clean up before
Birlon ...	06487	Cable result of last clean up
Birlonga ...	06488	Cable result of clean up not later than
Birnbaum...	06489	No good to have a clean up earlier than
Birnformig	06490	Our next clean up will be about
Biroccino ...	06491	Result of last clean up poor
Birota ...	06492	Result of last clean up misleading
Birracchio...	06493	Result of last clean up was —— ounces
Birrajo ...	06494	The clean up was from a fair average sample of stuff
Birresco ...	06495	We clean up every —— days
Birreta ...	06496	Will clean up on ——
Birretina ...	06497	When will the next clean up be
Birth ...	06498	We have cleaned up after a run of —— hours
Birthday ...	06499	**Clear(ed)**
Birthplace	06500	Are you (is ——) quite clear as to
Birthright	06501	Endeavour to clear up
Birthwort	06502	Is not at all clear
Bisabuela ...	06503	Is quite clear
Bisagra ...	06504	Is it quite clear that
Bisamkatze	06505	Must be cleared up before
Bisamthier	06506	Will endeavour to clear up

Bisannuel ...	06507	Have now sufficient ground clear to
Bisanteo ...	06508	Shall commence to clear up
Bisanuo ...	06509	Shall commence to clear out rubbish
Bisarma ...	06510	**Clearance**
Bisbetico ..	06511	Clearance space
Bisbille ...	06512	In order to effect a clearance
Bisbis ...	06513	Allow a clearance of —— between
Biscaien ...	06514	Allow a clearance of
Biscajuolo	06515	**Clearing**
Biscantare	06516	Preliminary cutting and clearing
Bischero ...	06517	In clearing out and re-timbering
Bischetto ...	06518	Have contracted for clearing —— square yards at ——
Bischof ..	06519	**Clerk** (*See also* "Books.")
Bisciuola ...	06520	As clerk and accountant
Biscornu ...	06521	**Cliff**
Biscottare ..	06522	**Climate** (*See also* "Altitude.")
Biscotte ...	06523	Climate good
Biscrome ...	06524	Climate exceedingly good
Biscuits ...	06525	Climate fairly good
Biseau ...	06526	Climate considered healthy
Biseccion ...	06527	On account of the severe climate
Bisegolo ...	06528	Winter climate very severe
Bisestare ...	06529	Climate unhealthy
Bisgonero ...	06530	Climate healthy except during the months of
Bishop ...	06531	**Climbing-way** (*See also* "Shaft," &c.)
Bishopric ...	06532	The climbing-way in shaft will require considerable repair
Bisiesto ...	06533	Will leave —— in. by —— in. for a climbing-way
Bisilabo ...	06534	**Close** (*See also* "Shut down," &c.)
Bislaccone	06535	Close to
Bislessare ...	06536	To close
Bislierig ...	06537	Shall I (we) close
Bislingua ...	06538	I (we) shall close
Bismuto ...	06539	May I (we) close on this basis
Bisnieto ...	06540	When do you expect to close
Bisnipote ...	06541	Expect to close almost immediately
Bisognoso...	06542	Do not expect to close before
Bisojo ...	06543	After the close of
Bisoneria ...	06544	Strongly advise you to close on terms offered
Bisonte ...	06545	Close down all operations
Bispon ...	06546	Close on the best terms you can obtain
Bisschen ...	06547	Advise you to close promptly
Bissextile ...	06548	Close immediately with
Bistentare	06549	Close the mine to all but employées
Bistola ...	06550	Figure as closely as you can
Bistorta ...	06551	Figures sent are as close as possible
Bistourner	06552	Am (are) unable to close owing to
Bistreux ...	06553	Close if you cannot obtain better terms
Bisturi ...	06554	Close at once with offer
Bisulco ...	06555	Can I (we) close with this offer
Bisulcorum	06556	Could you close if
Bisunto ...	06557	Do you advise me (us) to close
Bisurcado	06558	Do you authorize me (us) to close
Bisweilen ...	06559	I (we) advise you to close at once
Bitacora ...	06560	I (we) authorize you to close
Bitadura ...	06561	I could close if
Bitas ...	06562	No communication from ——; shall I (we) close
Bitmouth ...	06563	There is no chance of being able to close on such terms
Bitones ...	06564	Wait until you hear from —— before you close
Bitoque ...	06565	Why did you not close
Bitterbosc...	06566	You have the full authority of the directors to close

Bitterede ...	06567	Close timbered
Bitterish ...	06568	**Closed**
Bitterkeit ...	06569	Closed about
Bitterklee ...	06570	Closed at
Bitterlich ...	06571	Closed down
Bitterness ...	06572	Contract closed
Bittersalz ...	06573	Could not be closed
Bittersuss...	06574	Has (have) been closed
Bittweise ...	06575	Closed until
Biturro ...	06576	Has (have) closed
Bivalvo ...	06577	Have you closed with
Bivaquer ...	06578	I (we) have closed
Biverio ...	06579	I (we) have not closed
Biverticem	06580	Provided that you have not already closed
Bivio ...	06581	Cable as soon as you have closed
Bivouac ...	06582	Entirely closed up
Biza ...	06583	Have you closed all expenditure
Bizarrear ...	06584	Have closed down all expenditure
Bizarrerie...	06585	**Clue**
Bizarria ...	06586	Is there any clue as to
Bizazas ...	06587	Suggest as a clue
Bizcar ...	06588	The only clue I (we) have is
Bizma ...	06589	There is not the slightest clue
Biznaga ...	06590	Follow up the (this) clue
Biznieta ...	06591	Will follow up clue suggested
Bizquear ...	06592	**Coal** (*See also* "Anthracite," "Bitumen," "Coke," "Colliery,"
Blabbing ...	06593	Anthracite coal ["Fuel," &c.)
Blachfeld ...	06594	Brown coal
Blackamoor	06595	Coal seams ——
Blackart ...	06596	Coal seams discovered
Blackball ...	06597	Coal is found at a depth of ——
Blackberry	06598	Coal outcrops within —— miles of the property
Blackbird...	06599	Coal measures
Blackboard	06600	Coal seam —— feet thick
Blackeyed...	06601	Coal discovered
Blacking ...	06602	Coal is met with at a depth of —— feet between beds of
Blackish ...	06603	Coal is cheaper than wood
Blackleg ...	06604	Coal can be brought to the mill at
Bladed ...	06605	Fair caking coal
Blaesarum	06606	Fair coal
Blafard ...	06607	Good anthracite coal
Blagueur ...	06608	Good caking coal
Blahend ...	06609	Good bituminous coal
Blain ...	06610	Good coal can be obtained here at a cost of —— per ton
Blaireau ...	06611	Newcastle coal
Blamefully	06612	Welsh coal
Blamiren ...	06613	Poor coal
Blancazo ...	06614	Steam coal
Blancbec ...	06615	Ship —— tons of coal
Blanchatre	06616	Coal has been proved over an area of —— acres
Blanches ...	06617	Wood is cheaper here than coal
Blancheur	06618	Coal cannot be obtained here
Blancmange	06619	Coal is very unsatisfactory
Blanco ...	06620	Coal is satisfactory
Blandeador	06621	We shall need to get in a supply of coal for the coming winter
Blandiamur	06622	Get coal required for ——
Blandiente	06623	Get coal required; have arranged payment
Blandillo ...	06624	True coal measures
Blandir ...	06625	Doubtful if we have true coal measures [—— miles
Blandish ...	06626	True coal measures have been proved at —— a distance of

Blanditur...	06627	**Cob**
Blandizia ...	06628	To Cob
Blandness...	06629	**Cobalt**
Blandon ...	06630	Cobalt ores
Blanducho	06631	—— per cent. of cobalt
Blandura ...	06632	—— per cent. of cobalt by dry assay.
Blanketed...	06633	—— per cent. of cobalt by wet assay
Blankverse	06634	Arsenide of cobalt
Blanquecer	06635	Cobalt speise
Blanqueo ...	06636	What is the present price of cobalt
Blanquizal	06637	Market value of cobalt is
Blanquizco	06638	Cobalt as determined by electrolysis
Blao ...	06639	**Cobbed**
Blarney ...	06640	Cobbed ore
Blasebalg ...	06641	—— tons of cobbed ore
Blasehorn...	06642	Assay of cobbed ore is
Blasemusik	06643	**Cobbing**
Blaserohr...	06644	Cobbing hammers
Blasfemar...	06645	**Code** (*See also* "Cipher.")
Blasfemo ...	06646	Send copy of code to
Blason ...	06647	Code not intelligible
Blasonador	06648	By mining code
Blasonare...	06649	By private code
Blasonner...	06650	Send copy of McNeill's code
Blasphemed	06651	Reply according to McNeill's code
Blaterabit...	06652	What code do you use
Blateramus	06653	Using —— code
Blaterandi	06654	Please forward copy of code
Blateravi ...	06655	Send —— our private code
Blateretis...	06656	This code is employed by
Blattam ...	06657	This code is not employed by
Blattarum	06658	**Coin**
Blattchen ...	06659	Require(s) to be paid in coin
Blatteim ...	06660	**Coincide(s)**
Blattgold ...	06661	To coincide
Blatthaus...	06662	Do you coincide with this
Blattseite ...	06663	Do not coincide with
Blattstiel ...	06664	Entirely coincide with
Blaugrau ...	06665	Provided that —— coincides with you
Blauholz ...	06666	Should you not coincide with ——
Blaukohl ...	06667	**Coined**
Blaulich ...	06668	**Coke**
Blausaure...	06669	Cost of coke
Blaustein ...	06670	Can obtain coke at
Blavo ...	06671	Must have coke
Blazonry ...	06672	Prefer to use coke
Bleached ...	06673	**Coke oven(s)**
Bleachery...	06674	Shall require plans for erection of coke ovens
Bleakley ...	06675	Have commenced erection of coke ovens
Bleakness...	06676	Coke ovens are now in operation
Blear ...	06677	Shall require to erect coke ovens
Bleareyed...	06678	**Collapse**
Bleating ...	06679	To collapse
Blebs ...	06680	Fear a collapse
Blechern ...	06681	Endeavour to prevent collapse
Blechwaare	06682	If I am (we are) to prevent collapse
Blecken ...	06683	Likely to collapse
Bledo ...	06684	Owing to collapse of
Bleidach ...	06685	**Collapsed**
Bleierz ...	06686	Has (have) collapsed

Bleifarben	06687	Has (have) not collapsed
Bleifeder ...	06688	Practically the whole thing has collapsed
Bleigelb ...	06689	Should scheme have collapsed you had better
Bleiglanz ...	06690	Has (have) entirely collapsed
Bleiglatte ...	06691	Cable if —— has (have) entirely collapsed
Bleihutte ...	06692	Business has entirely collapsed
Bleischnur	06693	**Collar**
Bleisstift ...	06694	Collar of shaft
Bleiwage ...	06695	Depth from collar of shaft to —— is —— feet
Bleiweiss ...	06696	Collar launder
Bleizucker	06697	**Collect**
Blemish ...	06698	To collect
Blendling...	06699	Continue to collect
Blendung ...	06700	Provided that you can collect sufficient for
Blendwerk	06701	As soon as I (we) can collect sufficient for
Blennorrea	06702	Let the —— collect in the meanwhile
Blessing ...	06703	Collect until you have a stock of
Blessiren ...	06704	**Collected**
Blessure ...	06705	Have you collected
Bleuatre ...	06706	What quantity of —— have you collected
Blighted ...	06707	Have now collected —— tons
Blighting ...	06708	Have not yet collected sufficient for
Blindage ...	06709	**Collection**
Blindas ...	06710	Collection had better be made promptly
Blindekuh	06711	Collection cannot be made
Blindfold ...	06712	Collection has already been made
Blindheit ...	06713	**Colliery(ies)**
Blindingly	06714	There are extensive collieries at ——
Blindness...	06715	Are you disposed to negotiate for purchase of colliery
Blindside ...	06716	Embraces a colliery at ——: daily output —— tons
Blindworm	06717	Coal at the colliery costs —— per ton
Blinkard ...	06718	**Colour** (*See also* " Alluvial," " Gold," " Hydraulic.")
Blinkers ...	06719	What is the colour of
Blinking ...	06720	Not a single colour
Blinzaugig	06721	—— colours per dish
Blinzeln ...	06722	**Coloured**
Blissful ...	06723	**Combination**
Blistery ...	06724	Are believed to have formed a combination
Blithely ...	06725	Have formed a combination
Blitheness	06726	Combination already formed
Blitorum ...	06727	Combination has broken up
Blitos ...	06728	Have formed a combination in order to
Blitzblau ...	06729	**Combine**
Blixter ...	06730	To combine
Bloated ...	06731	Can you combine with
Bloating ...	06732	Will endeavour to combine with
Bloccatura	06733	Will he (they) combine with
Blockade ...	06734	Are anxious to combine with us on account of
Blockhead	06735	Do not on any account combine with
Blockhouse	06736	Endeavour to combine
Blodigkeit	06737	Have agreed to combine
Blodsinn ...	06738	If needful combine
Blondina ...	06739	It is useless to combine
Blooded ...	06740	If —— will make a firm offer to combine, accept
Bloodguilt	06741	Offer(s) to combine
Bloodheat...	06742	Owing to —— having agreed to combine
Bloodshed	06743	This will combine
Bloodshot...	06744	Unless agree to combine
Bloodstone	06745	—— will not combine
Bloomary ...	06746	—— will not combine with us because of

H

Blooming	06747	**Combined**
Bloquear ...	06748	Combined together
Bloqueo ...	06749	Either alone or combined with
Blossomed	06750	Chemically combined
Blossoms ...	06751	Has (have) combined to
Blotches ...	06752	Has (have) combined with
Blotters ...	06753	Has (have) combined for the sake of
Blotting ...	06754	Has (have) combined on account of
Blouse ...	06755	Has (have) combined forces with
Bloweth ...	06756	Has (have) not combined
Blowing ...	06757	If combined together
Blubber ...	06758	**Come**
Blubbering	06759	To come
Bludgeon ...	06760	Come up
Bluebells ...	06761	Come down
Blueblood...	06762	Come here
Bluebottle	06763	Come at any rate
Blueeyed ...	06764	Do not come
Bluelight ...	06765	Do not come here on any account
Bluemantle	06766	Do not come until I (we) cable again
Blumenbeet	06767	Will probably come by
Blumenflor	06768	Provided I (we) can come to terms
Blumenkohl	06769	Instruct —— (him) to come here
Blumenlese	06770	Instruct —— (him) to come to
Blunderbus	06771	Instruct —— (him) not to come
Blundering	06772	Come or send —— at once
Blunting ...	06773	Should it come to anything I (we) will cable you
Bluntness...	06774	By all means come
Blurtingly	06775	Can I (we) come
Blushfully	06776	Can —— come
Blushing ...	06777	Can you come
Blushless ...	06778	Come the moment you are able
Blustering	06779	Come home at once
Blustrous...	06780	Come here as quickly as possible; matter urgent
Blutador ...	06781	Cable when you expect to come
Blutbad ...	06782	Cable when you expect —— to come
Blutdurst ..	06783	Cable me instructions in case —— does not come
Blutegel ...	06784	Give —— instructions how to come here
Bluterie ...	06785	I cannot come until
Blutfluss ...	06786	I can come as soon as —— returns
Blutgefass	06787	I expect to come on
Blutgerust	06788	I expect —— (him) to come on (about) ——
Blutgierig	06789	If you —— can come
Bluthe ...	06790	It is useless for you to come
Bluthezeit	06791	It is useless for —— to come
Bluthund...	06792	It is useless for you to come until
Blutig ...	06793	In case you cannot come
Blutlauf ...	06794	Should not come
Blutleer ...	06795	When do you expect you can come
Blutlos ...	06796	Has not come to anything
Blutrache...	06797	Is it likely to come to anything
Blutreich ...	06798	Is not likely to come to anything
Blutroth ...	06799	**Coming**
Blutsauger	06800	Coming in
Blutschuld	06801	Are now coming in
Blutspeien	06802	Coming forward
Blutsturz ...	06803	Coming forward in considerable quantities
Blutthat ...	06804	Not coming forward to any extent
Blutumlauf	06805	**Command(s)**
Blutwarm...	06806	Command fair prices

Blutwasser	06807	Command high prices
Blutwenig	06808	I (we) place myself (ourselves) at your command
Blutzeuge...	06809	Should you have any commands
Boalage ...	06810	Have no commands at this moment
Boarhound	06811	**Commence**
Boarish ...	06812	To commence
Boarium ...	06813	Commence crushing ore
Boarrete ...	06814	Commence breaking ore
Boars	06815	Commence at once
Boastfully	06816	Commence action at once
Boatable ...	06817	Commence as soon as possible
Boathook ...	06818	Shall commence immediately (to)
Boating	06819	When will you commence
Boatshaped	06820	When can —— commence
Boatswain...	06821	When can you commence to
Bobaba ...	06822	I (we) shall be in a position to commence
Bobalias ...	06823	I am (we are) now making preparations to commence
Bobalicon...	06824	Mill will commence running about
Bobarron ...	06825	Commence work at
Bobatel ...	06826	Commence work at once
Bobatico .	06827	Cannot commence owing to
Bobazo ...	06828	Cannot commence for want of ——
Bobbins ...	06829	Cannot commence on account of ——
Bobear ...	06830	Cannot commence before
Bobeche ...	06831	Cannot commence until
Boberia ...	06832	Expect to commence about
Bobibation	06833	Why do you not commence
Bobilis ...	06834	When will you commence the erection of machinery
Bobillo ...	06835	When do you expect to commence milling
Bobinas ...	06836	When do (did) you commence
Bobolco ...	06837	When did you commence milling (washing)
Bobote ...	06838	Expect to commence not later than
Bobstays ...	06839	**Commenced**
Bobtail ...	06840	Just commenced
Bocacalle ...	06841	Has (have) commenced to
Bocacaz ...	06842	Has (have) already commenced
Bocadear ...	06843	Has (have) not yet commenced to
Bocadico ...	06844	Provided that you have not already commenced
Bocadillo ...	06845	Mill commenced running on ——
Bocage ...	06846	Cable why you have not commenced
Bocal ...	06847	Drift on new discovery commenced
Bocamanga	06848	Winze on new discovery commenced
Bocanada ...	06849	Experiments already commenced
Bocaran ...	06850	Have commenced
Bocardasse	06851	Have you commenced
Bocarder ...	06852	In case you have already commenced
Bocateja ...	06853	In case you have not already commenced
Bocaza ...	06854	Not yet commenced
Boccetta ...	06855	Rainy season has commenced
Bocchiduro	06856	Necessary grading already commenced
Boccioloso	06857	Erection of the machinery already commenced
Bocciuola ...	06858	Was commenced on ——
Boccolica ...	06859	Work was commenced on ——
Boccuccia ...	06860	Drivage on the vein was commenced on
Boccuzza ...	06861	Sinking on the vein was commenced on
Bocelete ...	06862	Drifting to —— was commenced on
Bocera ...	06863	Shaft was commenced on
Bocezar ...	06864	Have already commenced to
Bochazo ...	06865	Negotiations already commenced [If not, do so immediately
Bochin ...	06866	Referring to your letter of —— have you commenced ——?

Bochista ...	06867	**Commencement**
Bochorno ...	06868	The distance from commencement of —— is
Bocinero ...	06869	What is the distance from commencement
Bockchen ...	06870	Date of commencement
Bockfell ...	06871	**Commencing**
Bockgeruch	06872	Commencing at
Bocking ...	06873	Not commencing at —— but at ——
Bockleder ...	06874	Commencing with the words
Bockshorn	06875	**Commercial**
Boculorum	06876	What is the commercial value of
Bodegon ...	06877	Has it any commercial value
Bodegonero	06878	Has no commercial value
Bodeguero	06879	Present commercial value is
Bodeguilla	06880	**Commission(s)**
Bodenlos ...	06881	Expect no commission
Bodensatz	06882	Full commission
Bodenthur	06883	Will return —— all the commission
Bodian ...	06884	To pay a commission of
Bodices ...	06885	What does (do) the commission(s) amount to
Bodigo ...	06886	Commission(s) is (are)
Bodkins ...	06887	Commission(s) will be
Bodmerei ...	06888	In lieu of commission
Bodocal ...	06889	Am (is) entitled to charge a commission of —— per cent.
Bodocazo ...	06890	Agree to pay —— per cent. commission
Bodollo ...	06891	A Commissioner has been appointed
Bodoque ...	06892	Commission to be paid
Bodoquera	06893	Do you commission me to
Bodoquillo	06894	Forego(es) any commission
Bodorrio ...	06895	Has (have) arranged to get a commission in case business
Bodriere ...	06896	Has (have) arranged for a commission from vendors [results
Boeoticos ...	06897	Have to share commission with
Boezuelo ...	06898	Including —— per cent. commission to
Bofeta ...	06899	My (our) (——'s) commission amounts to
Bogada ...	06900	Must have a commission of —— per cent.
Bogar ...	06901	No commission
Bogavante	06902	—— per cent. commission
Bogengang	06903	—— per cent. commission to
Bogensenne	06904	Commission amounting to —— to be paid on
Bogenweise	06905	Are you including any commission
Bogenzahl	06906	This includes —— per cent. commission (for)
Boggled ...	06907	No commission is included
Bogliente ...	06908	What commission will have to be paid
Bohemian...	06909	What commission does this include
Bohemio ...	06910	What commission will you (they) pay if business results
Bohonero ...	06911	Will allow you —— per cent. by way of commission if business
Bohordar ...	06912	You must arrange for your commission from [results
Bohrloch ...	06913	No commission can be paid
Bohrspane	06914	Will you pay commission of
Boiling ...	06915	Will divide commission with you
Boiserie ...	06916	Will you divide commission with me
Boisselier ...	06917	**Commissioned**
Boisson ...	06918	I am (we are) commissioned by
Boisterous	06919	I am (we are) commissioned to
Boiteux ...	06920	Who are you commissioned by
Boitrino ...	06921	**Committee**
Bojedal ...	06922	Committee of investigation
Bojeo ...	06923	As one of a committee of investigation
Bolan ...	06924	A committee of management has been appointed with power
Bolantin ...	06925	By order of the committee of management [to
Bolazo ...	06926	Committee of management

Bolchaca ...	06927	Committee meeting held to-day (on ——)
Boldronajo	06928	**Common**
Boletin ...	06929	Common quality
Boletorum	06930	Very common
Bolichada...	06931	Not at all common
Boliche ...	06932	**Communicate**
Bolichero ...	06933	To communicate
Bolilla ...	06934	Communicate the cable to
Bolina ...	06935	Communicate the following to
Bolinear ...	06936	Communicate with me (us) at once
Bolingrin ...	06937	After —— communicate direct with
Bollario ...	06938	Anything you have to communicate to be sent direct to ——
Bollero ...	06939	Can you communicate with
Bollettino ...	06940	Communicate with
Bollicion ...	06941	Communicate anything important by cable
Bollido ...	06942	Communicate contents of letter dated —— to
Bollimento	06943	I (we) can communicate with
Bollizione...	06944	I am unable to communicate with —— owing to
Bollomino...	06945	In case you cannot communicate with
Bollon ...	06946	Please communicate with me, care of
Bollomazo ...	06947	Will communicate to
Bolluelo ...	06948	Will communicate with
Bollwerk ...	06949	With whom am I (are we) to communicate
Bolones ...	06950	Why do you not communicate with me (us)
Bolonio ...	06951	**Communicated**
Bolota ...	06952	Communicated with
Bolsa ...	06953	Communicated by
Bolsaggine	06954	Have you (has ——) communicated with
Bolsear ...	06955	Have communicated with
Bolseria ...	06956	Has (have) not communicated with
Bolsica ...	06957	**Communication(s)** (*See also* "Address," "Confidential,"
Bolsillo ...	06958	All communications to be sent to ["Letters," &c.)
Bolstered ...	06959	Have you any communication to make as to
Bolters ...	06960	No communication yet to hand
Bolula ...	06961	No postal communication
Bolus ...	06962	Put yourself into communication with
Bolzonato	06963	Postal communication every —— day(s)
Bomba ...	06964	The means of communication consists of
Bombance	06965	This communication is strictly private and confidential
Bombardier	06966	Telegraphic communication only reaches to ——, distant ——
Bombarding	06967	With whom shall I put myself in communication [miles
Bombasi ...	06968	Your promised communication not yet to hand
Bombastic	06969	Your last communication was dated ——; cable when we
Bombazine	06970	Direct all communications to [may expect next
Bombear ...	06971	Direct all communications addressed to myself, care of
Bombement	06972	Cannot understand your last communication
Bombenfest	06973	Communication has been made between —— and ——
Bomberie ...	06974	Use your own discretion as to making any communication to
Bombilo ...	06975	**Compact**
Bombileram	06976	**Company** (*See also* "Agree," "Allotment," "Capital,"
Bombketch	06977	Company will not be responsible for ["Shares," &c.)
Bomboletta	06978	Company adhere to telegram of ——
Bombship...	06979	Company have paid dividends amounting to ——
Bombyx ...	06980	Company have declared dividend of ——
Bomicare ...	06981	Company has never paid a dividend
Bonacciare	06982	Company is about to be re-constructed
Bonamente	06983	Company is now in liquidation
Bonanchon	06984	Company is much involved in litigation
Bonancible	06985	Company's solicitors require
Bonarieta ...	06986	Company has spent all its capital

[117]

Bonarobas	06987	Present company is now in debt to the extent of ——
Bonaso ...	06988	As soon as the company is registered
Bonbons ...	06989	Company was registered on ——, capital is ——
Boncinello	06990	Company's registered office is situated at
Bondage ..	06991	Can you not prevail on company to
Bondmaid...	06992	A company is now being arranged for
Bondman ...	06993	Preliminary work of organising company is now completed
Bondonner	06994	Dividend paying company
Bondslave...	06995	Non-dividend paying company
Bondwoman	06996	Can you form a company
Boneache ...	06997	Can you join board of company to work the affair
Boneggio ...	06998	Company formed to acquire
Bonelace ...	06999	Company formed with a capital of
Bonesetter	07000	Proposed company should have a total capital of not less than
Bonetas ...	**07001**	What is the proposed capital of company
Boneteria ...	07002	Capital of the company is ——
Bonetillo ...	07003	Capital of the company to be ——
Bonfire ...	07004	I am (we are) not now in service of company
Bonheur ...	07005	I am (——— is) now in service of —— company
Bonhomme	07006	On company's account
Bonico ...	07007	What will expenditure on company's account amount to for
Bonifatum	07008	Wishes to promote a company for [month(s) of
Bonificar ...	07009	Could you promote a company for
Bonina ...	07010	Will do my (our) best to promote a company for
Bonitalo ...	07011	On behalf of independent company
Bonjour ...	07012	On behalf of independent but friendly company
Bonneterie	07013	On behalf of independent and hostile company
Bonnets ...	07014	To form independent company
Bonsoir ...	07015	Net value to company
Bontadioso	07016	What will it net the company
Bonusculam	07017	—— company, Limited
Bonvaron ...	07018	**Compare**
Booby ...	07019	To compare
Booendi ...	07020	Compare my letter of
Bookbinder	07021	Better compare notes with
Bookcases...	07022	Will compare notes with
Bookcover	07023	Compare carefully with original
Bookshelf	07024	Will compare carefully with original
Bookworm	07025	**Compared**
Boopibus ...	07026	Have compared notes with
Boorishly ...	07027	Compared to
Bootes ...	07028	Compared with which
Bootjack ...	07029	**Compartment**
Bootstau ...	07030	Size of each compartment is —— × ——
Boottree ...	07031	**Compel**
Boqueada...	07032	To compel
Boquera ..	07033	Cannot compel
Boqueron ...	07034	Can you compel —— to
Boquiduro	07035	Endeavour to compel —— to
Boquilla ...	07036	Cannot compel —— to
Boquin ...	07037	**Compelled**
Boquinegro	07038	Do not do it unless compelled
Boquiroto...	07039	Almost afraid shall be compelled to
Boquiseco...	07040	**Compensate**
Boquita ...	07041	Would not compensate for the work involved
Boracico ...	07042	**Compensated**
Boracique...	07043	Has (have) been compensated
Borbollar ...	07044	Has (have) not been compensated
Borborigmo	07045	Will be compensated
Borbotar ...	07046	Will not be compensated

Borbottone	07047	Who compensated —— (them) for

Compensation

Borcegui ...	07048	
Borcellar ...	07049	By way of compensation
Borchiajo ...	07050	Claim(s) heavy compensation
Bordadillo	07051	Claim(s) slight compensation
Bordado ...	07052	Claim compensation enough to cover damage
Bordadura	07053	Compensation offered too small
Bordaglia ...	07054	Do not accept any compensation
Bordare ...	07055	Has claimed compensation amounting to ——
Bordelais ...	07056	Offer —— by way of compensation
Bordellare	07057	Shall I (we) accept compensation offered
Bordereau	07058	Compensation offered amounts to
Bordon ...	07059	Will be satisfied with a small compensation
Bordonero	07060	Will not accept compensation offered; demands at least ——
Bordura ...	07061	What compensation has he (have they) claimed
Boreal	07062	Who will give me (us) compensation
Boreotidem	07063	Compensation will be paid (for)
Borghese ...	07064	No compensation will be paid (for)
Borgnesse...	07065	Some compensation must be paid (for)
Borgolino ...	07066	Ample compensation will have to be made

Compete

Borgona ...	07067	
Boriosita ...	07068	If I am (we are) to compete
Boriptes ...	07069	In order to compete with
Borla ...	07070	As I (we) have to compete against
Borlica ...	07071	Do not forget who I (we) have to compete with

Competent

Borneadizo	07072	
Bornera ...	07073	I (we) do not consider him competent
Borniola ...	07074	Is he competent
Bornouse ...	07075	Is not competent
Bornoyer ...	07076	Is perfectly competent
Borough ...	07077	Not a competent authority
Borraccio ...	07078	Will send a competent man

Complain

Borraco ...	07079	
Borracha ...	07080	To complain
Borrachez...	07081	What does he (do they) complain about
Borrachon	07082	Complain(s) that

Complaining

Borrador ...	07083	
Borragear...	07084	Complaining about
Borragine...	07085	Not complaining

Complaint(s)

Borrajo ...	07086	
Borrar ...	07087	What ground is there for complaint
Borrasca ...	07088	There is ample ground for complaint
Borrascoso	07089	The ground of complaint is
Borratello...	07090	All ground of complaint removed
Borrego ...	07091	No cause for complaint
Borreguero	07092	Great cause for complaint
Borrellina...	07093	Remove as quickly as possible all grounds for complaint
Borren ...	07094	The complaint is that
Borriba ...	07095	What is the complaint
Borricada ...	07096	You had better formulate your complaint in writing
Borricon ...	07097	Has he (have they) any ground for complaint
Borriebat ...	07098	He has (they have) no ground for complaint
Borriquete	07099	Formal complaint

Complete

Borronazo...	07100	
Borrumbada	07101	To complete
Borsajuolo	07102	Complete this work on
Borstbesen	07103	Complete negotiations
Borstig ...	07104	Is everything now complete for
Borstwisch	07105	Everything is now complete for
Borujo ...	07106	By which date expect will be complete

Bosalage ...	07107	A most complete plant
Bosar ...	07108	Complete with all details
Bosartig ...	07109	Full and complete
Boscaglia ...	07110	Hope to complete within
Boschetto ...	07111	Erected complete
Boschung ...	07112	Mail complete statement
Bosewicht...	07113	Shall complete examination in —— days
Bosforo ...	07114	So as to complete
Boshaft ...	07115	Shall be able to complete
Bosheit ...	07116	Quite ready to complete
Bosladura...	07117	Will be ready to complete
Bosquejar...	07118	When will you mail complete report
Bosquete ...	07119	When will you be able to complete examination
Bosselage ...	07120	Within what time can you complete
Bosselbahn	07121	When can you complete
Bosselerai...	07122	Hope to complete all by
Bosseln ...	07123	I (we) shall complete this during the next week
Bossetier ...	07124	Is it necessary to first complete
Bossolajo ...	07125	It is not necessary to first complete
Bossoletto	07126	It is expected that this will be sufficient to complete
Bossuer ...	07127	**Completed**
Bostar ...	07128	Before purchase can be completed
Bostezante	07129	Completed report mailed
Bostezar ...	07130	Completed statement mailed
Bostezo ...	07131	Has (have) been completed
Bostrenum	07132	Has (have) not been completed
Boswillig ...	07133	If purchase is not completed within
Botabala ...	07134	Is purchase likely to be completed
Botafuego...	07135	Purchase should be completed
Botaguena	07136	Will be completed
Botalon ...	07137	Will not be completed
Botamen ...	07138	Purchase to be completed within
Botana ...	07139	When will you (they) be ready to have purchase completed
Botanico ...	07140	When you have completed
Botaniker...	07141	Has (have) almost completed the
Botanismum	07142	When it (this) is completed
Botanists ...	07143	Will be completed within next few days
Botantes ...	07144	Will be completed within —— days
Botarate ...	07145	**Completion**
Botarel ...	07146	Completion cannot be deferred after
Botasela ...	07147	Completion deferred
Botavante...	07148	Why is completion deferred
Botavara ...	07149	Completion deferred through
Botecico ...	07150	Until completion of
Botenlohn	07151	Pending the completion of some definite arrangement
Boteria ...	07152	**Compliance**
Bothering...	07153	In compliance with
Botica ...	07154	Not in compliance with
Boticage ...	07155	Should be in compliance with
Boticario ...	07156	You must take care only to act in compliance with
Botiguero...	07157	Is this in compliance with
Botijon ...	07158	It is in compliance with
Botilla ...	07159	It is not in compliance with
Botillero ...	07160	**Complication(s)**
Botin ...	07161	Serious complications have arisen
Botinero ...	07162	Is there any complication
Botiqueria	07163	There is no complication whatever
Botivoleo ...	07164	Should no complication arise
Botonadura	07165	Unless further complications should arise
Botonazo ...	07166	**Comply**

Botoneria ...	07167	To comply
Botriolite ...	07168	In order to comply
Botrites ...	07169	Cannot comply with your request
Botschaft ...	07170	If you cannot comply with
Bottaccino	07171	Decline(s) to comply with
Bottarga ...	07172	—— has (have) refused to comply with your cable
Bottcher ...	07173	Consent(s) to comply with
Bottegajo	07174	Better comply with demands
Botteghino	07175	Will comply with terms stated
Botticella ...	07176	Comply with terms stated
Bottiglia ...	07177	**Component** (See also "Analysis," "Assay.")
Bottling ...	07178	The component parts consist of
Bottomless	07179	What are the component parts
Bottonajo ...	07180	**Composed**
Bottone ...	07181	Composed of
Botularum	07182	**Composition** (See also "Bankrupt," "Liquidation," &c.)
Boucan ...	07183	Of the following composition
Boucanier ...	07184	Of inferior composition
Bouchonner	07185	A composition of —— in the pound
Bouclier ...	07186	What is the composition likely to amount to
Bouderie ...	07187	**Comprehend** (See also "Understand.")
Boudinage	07188	Clearly comprehend
Boudoir ...	07189	Unless you clearly comprehend
Bouffant ...	07190	Do(es) not clearly comprehend
Bouffarde ...	07191	**Comprehensive**
Bouffette ...	07192	Cable details and mail comprehensive report
Bougenais	07193	Mail comprehensive report
Bougeoir ...	07194	Not comprehensive enough, require further details as to
Bougran ...	07195	**Compressor** (See also "Air," "Breakdown," "Drills," &c.)
Bouilloire ...	07196	Erection of the air compressor
Bouillon ...	07197	Compressor cylinder
Boulevard	07198	Compressor piston
Boulevue ...	07199	Compressor valve(s)
Boulinger	07200	Air compressor and boiler to run —— drills
Boulingrin	07201	Air receiver
Bouncer ...	07202	Air cylinder —— in. diameter, steam cylinder —— in. diameter, [stroke —— ft.
Bouncing ...	07203	**Comprise(s)**
Bounteous	07204	Comprise(s) the following
Bouquet ...	07205	Do documents as mailed comprise —— (if not)
Bouquiner	07206	Figures given should comprise
Bouracan ...	07207	Letter (report) does not comprise
Bourbeux ...	07208	Letter(s) mailed (on ——) comprise(s) full information
Bourdaine	07209	Report should comprise
Bourdonner	07210	What does it comprise
Bourgade ...	07211	**Compromise**
Bourgeois ...	07212	Propose a compromise
Bourgogne	07213	Endeavour to compromise
Bourrache	07214	Try and effect a compromise
Bourrasque	07215	To compromise
Bourree ...	07216	Offer(s) to compromise
Bourrelet ...	07217	Do (does) not seem at all likely to compromise
Bourriquet	07218	Upon what basis could a compromise be effected
Boursicant	07219	Compromise effected
Bousculer	07220	Am (are) unable to compromise
Bousillage	07221	Compromise documents mailed
Bousilleur	07222	Cannot compromise
Boussole ...	07223	Do you advise me (us) to compromise with
Boutade ...	07224	I (we) strongly advise you to compromise with
Bouteille ...	07225	In case you cannot compromise
Boutique ...	07226	In case you can compromise

Bouton ...	07227	Is (are) making overtures for a compromise
Boutonnier	07228	Is (are) willing to compromise
Bovantibus	07229	—— is willing to compromise on the following basis. **Cable**
Bovatim ...	07230	Shall I (we) compromise [if acceptable
Bovedilla ...	07231	Try and effect compromise, or cable alternative proposition
Bovicida ...	07232	Try and effect compromise with ——; offer him (them)
Bovillarum	07233	You must not compromise
Bovillibus...	07234	Willing to compromise on a basis of
Bovino ...	07235	Compromise on best terms you can obtain
Bowable ...	07236	Compromise on no account whatever
Bowery ...	07237	Compromise satisfactory
Bowhand ...	07238	Compromise very unsatisfactory
Bowieknife	07239	Efforts to compromise have been successful
Bowlegged	07240	Efforts to compromise up to present time have **not been**
Bowline ...	07241	**Compromised** [successful
Bowman ...	07242	Has (have) compromised
Bowsprit ...	07243	Has (have) not compromised
Bowstring	07244	Has (have) —— compromised
Bowyer ...	07245	Is (are) decidedly compromised
Boxing ...	07246	Subsequently compromised
Boyada ...	07247	**Conceal**
Boyandier	07248	To conceal
Boyante ...	07249	Better conceal your connection with
Boyazo ...	07250	Conceal my connection with
Boyera ...	07251	Can you conceal
Boyezuelo ..	07252	Cannot conceal
Boyhood ...	07253	Conceal your plan(s)
Boyishly ...	07254	Conceal the fact
Boyishness	07255	Conceal the true state of affairs
Boyuna ...	07256	Shall I (we) conceal
Bozal ...	07257	Shall not be able to conceal
Bozalejo ...	07258	Conceal proposed plan of operations
Bozzacchio	07259	Do not conceal anything from
Bozzolare ...	07260	Has there been any attempt to conceal
Brabante ...	07261	There has not been the slightest attempt to conceal
Brabera ...	07262	No doubt there has been an attempt made to conceal
Brabeutam	07263	There is really nothing to conceal
Brabio ...	07264	**Concealed**
Bracalone ...	07265	No need to keep anything concealed from ——
Bracate ...	07266	It is said to have been concealed
Bracciere ...	07267	Must be kept concealed
Braceada ...	07268	Was concealed
Braceage ...	07269	**Concealing**
Bracear ...	07270	Concealing nothing
Bracelet ...	07271	Suspect —— of concealing
Braceral ...	07272	**Concede**
Bracete ...	07273	Do not concede
Brachesse	07274	If —— will not concede
Brachial ...	07275	Only concede
Brachiolum	07276	Will concede
Brachmonal	07277	Will not concede
Brackgut ...	07278	Will —— concede
Bracman ...	07279	**Concentrate** (*See also* "Blankets," "Dressed," "Ore," &c.)
Braco ...	07280	Concentrate all your efforts to (at)
Braconnage	07281	It is not economical to concentrate beyond
Braconnier	07282	Ore will readily concentrate
Bracteale ...	07283	Ore will not concentrate
Bracteolam	07284	Otherwise we cannot concentrate
Brafonera	07285	So as to concentrate
Braga ...	07286	This will enable us to concentrate

Bragado ...	07287	Why do you not concentrate
Bragadura	07288	Will not concentrate beyond
Bragazas ...	07289	Will concentrate up to
Braggart ...	07290	**Concentrates**
Braguero .	07291	Assay of concentrates is
Bragueta ...	07292	Concentrates shipped have realized
Bragueton	07293	Carriage on concentrates
Braguillas	07294	Concentrates are in the proportion of —— to —— of original
Brahmin ...	07295	Concentrates average [ore
Brahonera	07296	Stock of concentrates is say —— tons, worth say ——
Braiding ...	07297	Have shipped —— tons of concentrates
Braillard ...	07298	Concentrates are worked raw in pans
Brailleur ...	07299	Concentrates are roasted and then panned
Braiment ...	07300	Shall ship —— tons of concentrates about
Brained ...	07301	When will your next shipment of concentrates take place
Brainless ...	07302	What stock of concentrates have you, and what is the [approximate value
Brainpan ...	07303	What is the probable tonnage of "concentrate" ore available
Braiserie ...	07304	There is practically no "concentrate" ore [in upper levels
Bramadera	07305	We have —— tons of ore that would (will) concentrate
Bramador...	07306	How many tons of original stuff would give you one ton of [concentrates
Bramante...	07307	Would expect to get one ton of concentrates from —— tons of [stuff
Bramarbas	07308	Think "concentrate plant" should be decided upon immediately
Brambles ...	07309	Will send estimate for "concentrate plant" [mediately
Brameggio	07310	**Concentration**
Bramido ...	07311	Further concentration
Bramil ...	07312	Concentration works
Bramona ...	07313	Concentration stopped
Bramsegel	07314	Concentration has not been attempted
Branca ...	07315	Concentration plant to treat
Brancard ...	07316	Site for concentration works
Branchage	07317	Water for concentration purposes
Branchetto	07318	Without concentration
Branchias...	07319	Without considerable concentration
Branching	07320	What is your (——'s) opinion as to concentration
Branchless	07321	In my (——'s) opinion concentration is essential
Branciare ...	07322	**Concern**
Brancicone	07323	Quite a private concern
Brancolato	07324	Entirely a new concern
Brandbrief	07325	Does this concern you (——)
Brandecer ..	07326	It does not concern me (us) at all
Brandevin	07327	It only concerns me (us) to the extent of
Brandfleck	07328	Does not concern you in any way
Brandfuchs	07329	I believe it may become a good paying concern
Brandicht ..	07330	Is it a good paying concern
Brandiller	07331	Will be a good paying concern
Brandling...	07332	**Concerning**
Brandmauer	07333	Write to —— concerning
Brandon ...	07334	**Concession(s)**
Brandopfer	07335	Will not make any further concession(s)
Branlant ...	07336	Has (have) made further concession(s)
Branlement	07337	Must make further concession of
Branntwein	07338	Refuse(s) to make any further concession
Brano ...	07339	Consent(s) to make a concession of
Branque ...	07340	A concession will be needful as
Bransle ...	07341	Concession worthless
Braquial ...	07342	Concession valuable
Braquillo ...	07343	Government has granted a concession

Braserico ...	07344	Try and get a concession
Brasil ...	07345	Concession(s) comprise(s)
Brasilado ...	07346	The only concession
Brassando	07347	The entire concession
Brassard ...	07348	Unable to get a concession
Brasseur ..	07349	Will grant a concession
Brassey ...	07350	Will endeavour to get a concession
Brassiage ...	07351	Who is the concession granted by
Brassical ...	07352	Has (have) obtained the following concession from **vendors**
Bratbock ...	07353	Cannot obtain any concession from vendors [(——)
Bratenfett	07354	Will have a very valuable concession .
Bratfisch ...	07355	**Concessionaires**
Bratrohre...	07356	**Conclusion(s)**
Bratrost ...	07357	Cable conclusion(s) arrived at
Bratsche ...	07358	Cable as soon as you arrive at any conclusion
Bratspiess	07359	My (their) conclusions are
Bratwurst	07360	Shall not be able to arrive at any conclusion until
Brauchbar	07361	What are your conclusions respecting
Brauchen ...	07362	I (we) have come to the following conclusion
Braukessel	07363	Necessary to come to an immediate conclusion respecting
Brauknecht	07364	Hope to arrive at definite conclusion shortly
Braulis ...	07365	No conclusion possible at present
Braunkohle	07366	What conclusion have you come to respecting
Braunlich...'	07367	Conclusion I (we) have arrived at is
Braunroth	07368	Have not arrived at any conclusion
Braunstein	07369	Have come to the following conclusion
Braupfanne	07370	**Concur**
Brausekopf	07371	To concur
Brautbett ...	07372	Do you concur
Brautigam	07373	Do not concur
Brautkranz	07374	—— concurs with me (us) that
Brautlesse	07375	Do not concur with your views
Brautlied ...	07376	Do not concur with —— views
Brautnacht	07377	**Condemn(s)**
Brautpaar	07378	Condemn(s) the affair as worthless
Brautstand	07379	Strongly condemn the action of
Brautweber	07380	Which condemn(s)
Bravaccio ...	07381	Do not condemn —— (him) meanwhile
Bravache ...	07382	**Condemned**
Bravamente	07383	Has (have) been condemned
Bravato ...	07384	Supplies condemned as useless
Bravatorio	07385	Totally condemned
Braveador	07386	Was (were) condemned by
Bravear ...	07387	Will be condemned unless
Bravement	07388	Has (have) been condemned and sentenced to
Braveza ...	07389	**Condition**
Bravheit ...	07390	Amended conditions
Bruviabais	07391	Authorise you to accept on conditions named
Bravissimo	07392	Condition of mine
Bravo ...	07393	Condition of buildings
Bravonel ...	07394	Condition of machinery very defective
Bravoure ...	07395	Conditions generally improved
Bravura ...	07396	Conditions are too
Brawlers ...	07397	Conditions do not permit of
Brawling ...	07398	Conditions very favourable for economic mining
Brawney ...	07399	Conditions opposed to economic mining
Brazado ...	07400	Cannot accept conditions
Brazage ...	07401	Cannot authorize you to accept conditions until (before)
Brazalete ...	07402	Cable final conditions
Brazenface	07403	General conditions unsatisfactory

Brazening...	07404	If conditions favourable accept
Brasenness	07405	What is the condition of
Brazilnut ...	07406	Condition unchanged
Brazolas ...	07407	General condition of things better
Brazuelo ...	07408	General condition of things worse
Breached ...	07409	Condition of —— better than anticipated
Breastknot	07410	Condition of —— worse than anticipated
Breastwork	07411	Dilapidated condition
Breathable	07412	Do you advise me (us) to agree to conditions
Breathing...	07413	Do you agree to these conditions
Brebage ...	07414	In bad condition
Brecha ...	07415	In satisfactory condition for
Brecheisen	07416	In good condition
Brechnuss...	07417	In very good condition
Brechruhr	07418	In the present condition of
Brechwurz	07419	Condition(s) can be relied upon
Brecol ...	07420	Condition(s) cannot be relied upon
Bredo ...	07421	Are trying to impose absurd conditions
Breezy ...	07422	Conditions are as per my letter of ——
Bregar ...	07423	Conditions are as per my telegram of ——
Bregmarum	07424	Under the present conditions
Breloque ...	07425	Under more favourable conditions
Brenal ...	07426	Unless can secure more favourable conditions
Brennbar ...	07427	Do not agree with the conditions
Brennglas...	07428	Insist(s) upon the following conditions ——
Brennholz...	07429	General condition unsatisfactory
Brennofen	07430	Necessary condition(s) is (are)
Brennpunkt	07431	On condition
Brenoso ...	07432	Owing to the condition of the
Brenzlich ...	07433	Only upon condition that
Breque ...	07434	Strongly advise(s) me (us) to accept conditions named
Brescado ...	07435	Conditions are
Bresillet ...	07436	The condition of the —— could not be worse
Bresthaft ...	07437	The main conditions of the lease are
Bretador ...	07438	Upon the following conditions
Bretailler ...	07439	What are the conditions insisted upon
Bretana ...	07440	Will you authorize me (us) to accept these conditions
Bretauder	07441	Original conditions
Brete... ...	07442	Subject to the following conditions
Bretelle ...	07443	The whole is in very bad condition
Breterwand	07444	Has (have) been kept in good condition
Bretgeige ...	07445	Prosperous condition
Bretmuhle	07446	Conditions very favourable for cheap working
Bretonne ...	07447	Get permission to report on condition of
Bretsage ...	07448	What is (are) the condition(s) of
Bretspiel ...	07449	**Conditional**
Bretteur ...	07450	Conditional upon
Breuvage ...	07451	Acceptance conditional
Breval ...	07452	Is conditional upon
Brevecico ...	07453	This offer is conditional
Brevedad ...	07454	**Conduct**
Breviario ...	07455	The conduct of
Brevibus ...	07456	Consider such conduct
Brevicello...	07457	In consequence of bad conduct
Brevier ...	07458	**Confer**
Brevitate	07459	To confer
Brewage ...	07460	Confer with —— and cable what you agree upon
Brewhouse	07461	Confer with —— before proceeding further
Brezalle ...	07462	Confer with —— before acting
Brezzolone	07463	Confer personally with

Briarrose ...	07464	Will confer personally with you
Bribia ...	07465	Should like to confer with
Bribonada	07466	Think you had better confer with
Bribonear...	07467	Would you like to confer with
Briboneria	07468	With whom do you advise me to confer
Briccolare...	07469	Should like to confer with —— about
Bricho ...	07470	**Conferred**
Briciolino...	07471	Have you conferred
Brickbat ...	07472	Have conferred
Bricklayer	07473	Have not conferred
Bricole ...	07474	As soon as you have conferred with
Bridar ...	07475	Have conferred with ——; our joint decision is
Bridecake...	07476	Have conferred with ——, but cannot arrive at a joint decision
Bridegroom	07477	**Confidence** (*See also* " Communication.")
Bridemaid	07478	I (we) have every confidence
Bridewell ...	07479	Have you every confidence that
Bridling ...	07480	I (we) have no confidence
Bridon ...	07481	Do not put any confidence in him (——)
Briefadel ...	07482	You will find him (——) worthy of every confidence
Briefbuch...	07483	Do not treat him (——) with too great confidence
Briefchen ...	07484	Can I (we) treat —— with confidence
Briefform ...	07485	Do not place any confidence in ——
Brieflich ...	07486	Have always found —— worthy of all confidence
Briefpost ...	07487	In strict confidence
Brieftaube	07488	Must be treated with strictest confidence
Briefwage...	07489	Is well worthy of every confidence
Briffalda ...	07490	Shall be treated with confidence
Brigada ...	07491	Should not advise you to place any confidence in him
Brigadier ...	07492	You may place every confidence in him
Brigandage	07493	Your communication shall be treated with confidence
Brigantine	07494	You cannot safely treat him (——) with any confidence
Brigatella	07495	I (we) thank you for the confidence shown
Brightness	07496	In order to increase confidence
Brigliajo ...	07497	Have no confidence whatever in
Briglione ...	07498	Unworthy of confidence
Brigola ...	07499	So as to restore confidence
Briguer ...	07500	This is necessary in order to restore confidence
Brigueront	07501	**Confident**
Brillador ...	07502	Confident of
Brilladura	07503	Am (are) confident
Brillante ...	07504	Am (are) not at all confident
Brillar ...	07505	Feel confident of ultimate success
Brillatojo ...	07506	**Confidential**
Brillo ...	07507	This is confidential and for your personal guidance
Brimbaler...	07508	Confidential communication
Brimborion	07509	This message is absolutely private and confidential
Brin ...	07510	**Confine**
Brincador...	07511	To confine
Brincho ...	07512	Confine your energies to
Brindille ...	07513	Confine yourself for the present entirely to
Brindis ...	07514	Shall confine myself (ourselves) for the present to
Bringabala	07515	Confine your attention to
Brinquillo	07516	Confine attention for the present to
Briolin ...	07517	Confine all cost to
Brionia ...	07518	Shall confine myself for the present to
Brioso ...	07519	Will confine all cost for the present to
Brique ...	07520	**Confirm**
Briquetage	07521	To confirm
Briquetier	07522	Do you confirm
Briscado ...	07523	Can you confirm

Briscar	07524	Please confirm
Briseglace...	07525	Confirm purchase
Briselames	07526	Only partially confirm
Brisement...	07527	Confirm report
Brisetout ...	07528	Confirm sale
Brisevent ...	07529	Do not confirm the agreement
Brisket	07530	Do not confirm the report
Bristles	07531	Can you confirm ——'s statements
Bristling ...	07532	Confirm ——'s statement as regards
Brisure	07533	Cannot confirm ——'s statement with regard to
Britanica ...	07534	Cable if you confirm ——'s report or otherwise
Brittanno...	07535	Confirm ——'s statement as regards
Brixianum	07536	I (we) can fully confirm ——'s statement and figures
Brizatte ...	07537	I (we) cannot confirm ——'s statement or figures
Briznoso ...	07538	It is necessary for you to confirm ——'s report
Brizzolato	07539	Investigation does not confirm
Broadaxe ...	07540	Do you confirm ——'s statement and figures
Broadcast...	07541	**Confirmation**
Broadcloth	07542	Requires further confirmation
Broadside...	07543	If you consider additional confirmation necessary [——
Broadsword	07544	Cable in confirmation of ——'s report has been received from
Brobbioso...	07545	Is there any confirmation of the report
Brobbrio ...	07546	It is necessary that confirmation of report be forthcoming
Brocadel ...	07547	I cabled on —— confirmation of ——'s report, and am still
Brocadillo...	07548	Must wait for confirmation [here waiting instructions
Brocado ...	07549	Subject to the confirmation of ——'s report
Brocadura	07550	**Confirmed**
Brocanter ...	07551	Has (have) been confirmed
Brocardico	07552	Must be confirmed
Broccare ...	07553	Can be confirmed
Brocchiere	07554	Cannot be confirmed
Broccoluto	07555	Confirmed by
Brochage ...	07556	Will no doubt be confirmed
Broche	07557	**Confirming**
Brocheta ...	07558	**Conflict(ing)**
Brochon ...	07559	Conflicting accounts
Brochura ...	07560	Management in conflict
Brockelig ...	07561	Owing to conflicting interests
Brocula	07562	Report altogether conflicting
Brodequin	07563	**Conform**
Broderies ...	07564	Conform to
Brodettato	07565	Do (does) not conform to (with)
Brodiglia ...	07566	**Conformable**
Brodio	07567	Conformable to
Brodista ...	07568	Not conformable to
Brogan	07569	**Confusion**
Brogliare ...	07570	Confusion unavoidable
Brogue	07571	Accounts in confusion
Bromado ...	07572	Matters altogether in confusion
Bromate ...	07573	Owing to confusion
Bromaticem	07574	Intentional confusion
Brombeere	07575	To avoid all chance of confusion
Bromear ...	07576	Consequent on confusion caused by
Bromo	07577	**Conglomerate**
Bromosior	07578	Conglomerate with quartz pebbles
Bronce	07579	A conglomerate composed of
Bronceado	07580	**Connect**
Bronceria ...	07581	To connect
Broncha ...	07582	Connect with
Bronchial...	07583	Unable to connect by means of

Broncista ...	07584	Impossible to connect
Broncone ...	07585	So as to connect
Bronquial...	07586	So as to connect —— level and ——
Bronquios	07587	So as to connect the mill with shaft
Bronteam...	07588	So as to connect the works with
Brontolare	07589	So as to connect the —— shaft with
Bronzage ...	07590	So as to connect with the —— shaft
Bronzino ...	07591	To enable us to connect
Bronziren...	07592	Unable to connect
Broom ...	07593	Has (have) failed to connect
Broomstick	07594	Through having failed to connect
Broquelazo	07595	**Connected**
Broquelero	07596	Not connected
Broquelete	07597	Not connected in the slightest degree
Broqueta ...	07598	Are you (is ——) connected with
Brosame ...	07599	Am (is) (are) not connected with
Broschiert	07600	Connected by
Broschure	07601	Connected for
Brosquil ...	07602	Connected to
Brota ...	07603	Connected with
Brotadura	07604	Can you suggest how —— and —— can be connected
Brotano ...	07605	Has never been connected
Brotbacker	07606	Was formerly connected
Brotdieb ...	07607	**Connecting**
Broterwerb	07608	Connecting rods
Brotherly ...	07609	Connecting —— and ——
Brotkorb ...	07610	Connecting link between
Brotkrume	07611	**Connection**
Brotmesser	07612	Connection between
Brotneid ...	07613	Connection of
Broton ...	07614	By means of a connection between —— and ——
Brotrinde...	07615	Connection has been made with
Brotsuppe	07616	Avoid all connection with
Brouette ...	07617	Connection is necessary on account of
Brouiller ...	07618	Connection between —— and —— was made on
Brouissure	07619	In order to make connection with
Broussin ...	07620	My connection with —— ceased ——
Browless ...	07621	The only connection
Brownie ...	07622	There is no connection between
Broyeur ...	07623	This would afford a connection with
Brozar ...	07624	The value of this connection would be
Brozoso ...	07625	Avoid all connection with —— meanwhile
Brucasse ...	07626	Avoid a connection if possible
Brucero ...	07627	We have made a connection between —— and ——
Bruchstein	07628	Endeavour to establish connection between
Bruchstuck	07629	Said to be acting in connection with
Bruciatajo	07630	**Consent**
Brucine ...	07631	To consent
Bruciolato	07632	Do not consent
Bruckenbau	07633	Cable whether you consent to this
Bruderlich	07634	Consent was given on
Brudermord	07635	Should you not consent
Brueta ...	07636	You have the full consent of all
Brugidor ...	07637	Have obtained the consent of all parties interested
Brugir ...	07638	Cannot obtain consent
Brugnon ...	07639	Must obtain consent
Bruhheiss...	07640	When I (we) shall obtain consent
Brujear ...	07641	Only require to obtain the consent of
Brujeria ...	07642	The moment I (we) obtain ——'s consent
Brujuleo ...	07643	First obtain ——'s consent

Brulicame...	07644	—— has (have) refused consent. What do you advise
Brulote ...	07645	Without waiting for ——'s consent
Brulotto ...	07646	If —— persist(s) in refusing his (their) consent, you had better
Brulure ...	07647	Understood —— had given a tacit consent
Brumador...	07648	**Consenting**
Brumal ...	07649	In the event of your consenting
Brumalibus	07650	Consenting party(ies)
Brumario ...	07651	**Consequence(s)**
Brumazon...	07652	In consequence of
Brumeux ...	07653	Consequent upon
Brummbar	07654	Of no consequence
Brummeisen	07655	Of little consequence
Brumoso ...	07656	Of great consequence
Brunatre ...	07657	Of great consequence, owing to
Brunette ...	07658	In order to avoid consequence(s)
Brunften ...	07659	Do it (this) without regard to consequences
Brunido ...	07660	Must hold —— liable for consequences
Brunir ...	07661	No serious consequences need be apprehended
Brunissage	07662	Must take the consequences
Brunissoir	07663	Serious consequences
Brunitojo ...	07664	Shall hold you liable for consequences
Brunitura ..	07665	Shall be held liable for consequences
Brunnenkur	07666	The consequence(s) is (are)
Brunstig ...	07667	Very serious consequences are to be anticipated
Bruscate ...	07668	What are the probable consequences
Bruschetto	07669	**Consider**
Bruscolina	07670	To consider
Brusela ...	07671	Do you consider that
Bruseles ...	07672	Do not consider
Brusque ...	07673	In your estimation do you consider that —— is
Brusquerie	07674	I (we) consider it is undervalued
Brustbein...	07675	Do you still consider
Brustbild ...	07676	Still consider
Brustlatz ...	07677	Do not now consider
Brustthee...	07678	Consider and report by telegraph
Brustung ...	07679	**Considerable**
Brustwarze	07680	Very considerable
Brutal ...	07681	By no means considerable
Brutaliser...	07682	If considerable
Brutescent	07683	Unless considerable
Brutesco ...	07684	Cable if considerable
Bruthenne	07685	**Considerably**
Brutiani ...	07686	This will add considerably to
Brutify ...	07687	**Consideration**
Brutism ...	07688	Without consideration
Bruto ...	07689	Consideration of
Brutofen ...	07690	After further consideration
Bruttare ...	07691	Consideration deferred
Brutzeit ...	07692	Consideration must be deferred, pending result of
Bruyere ...	07693	Consideration must be deferred for full Board of Directors
Bruzador ...	07694	For a consideration of
Bruszaglia	07695	For the consideration of the Directors
Bryoniam...	07696	In consideration of
Bryoniarum	07697	Leaving out of consideration
Buanderie ..	07698	Must be taken into consideration
Buarda ...	07699	Not worth further consideration
Buba ...	07700	The only consideration
Bubalino ...	07701	Taking into consideration
Bubalo ...	07702	You must take into consideration
Bubastem...	07703	Will take it (them) into consideration

Bubbolare	07704	For further consideration
Bubilla ...	07705	Was not taken into consideration
Bubinavi ...	07706	Throw aside every consideration except
Bubon ...	07707	Subject to further consideration
Buboso ...	07708	**Considered**
Bubucia ...	07709	Will be considered
Bubulcata	07710	Considered perfectly safe
Bubulcorum	07711	Not considered safe on account of
Bucaldam ..	07712	Not considered safe
Bucarito ...	07713	Is (are) not to be considered as part of
Bucaro ...	07714	Is (are) to be considered as part of
Bucatino ..	07715	Is this (are they) considered as part of
Buccaneer...	07716	Cannot be considered
Buccellas ...	07717	Cannot be considered satisfactory
Bucchio ...	07718	Has (have) been considered
Buccia ...	07719	Has (have) not been considered
Bucciere ...	07720	Has (have) been most carefully considered
Bucciolina	07721	Is (are) considered quite satisfactory
Buccolico ...	07722	It is considered here
Bucear ...	07723	It is considered by me (us) that
Bucelario ..	07724	Must be most carefully considered
Bucentorio	07725	Will be considered by —— on
Buceo ..	07726	**Considering**
Bucerium ...	07727	Considering the whole of the circumstances
Buchar ...	07728	**Consign**
Bucherame	07729	To consign
Bucherbret	07730	Consign to
Bucherdieb	07731	Consign to my (our) agent at
Bucherello	07732	To whom shall we consign
Buchernarr	07733	**Consigned**
Bucheron ...	07734	Consigned to your agent at
Buchete ...	07735	Consigned to your order
Buchfuhrer	07736	To be consigned to
Buchhalter	07737	To be consigned to the order of
Buchsbaum	07738	Has (have) been consigned to
Buchschuld	07739	**Consignee(s)**
Buchstabe	07740	At consignees' risk
Buchweizen	07741	**Consignor(s)**
Buciacchio	07742	Who are the consignors
Bucinador	07743	**Consist(s)**
Bucinar ...	07744	Consists of
Bucinentor	07745	Now consists of
Buckbasket	07746	Consist(s) principally of the following, viz. :—
Buckbean...	07747	Consist(s) practically of
Buckish ...	07748	Do (does) not consist of —— at all
Buckles ...	07749	Formerly did consist of
Buckram ...	07750	What does it (do they) consist of
Buckskin ...	07751	**Consolidate**
Buckthorn	07752	To consolidate
Buckwheat	07753	Consolidate with
Bucolica ...	07754	To consolidate the claims
Bucolique...	07755	So as to consolidate the whole of the affair
Bucosidad	07756	So as to consolidate the whole of the property
Buddhism	07757	Consolidate interests
Budding ...	07758	**Consolidated**
Budellame	07759	Since consolidated with
Budgero ...	07760	Have just consolidated with
Budial ...	07761	The consolidated claims
Budlets ...	07762	Forming one consolidated property
Buega ...	07763	**Consolidation**

Buenabonya	07764	Consolidation of interests
Buenamente	07765	Consolidation most desirable
Buenpasar	07766	Consolidation inimical to our (your) interests
Buessa ...	07767	Consolidation has been effected
Bueyazo ...	07768	Consolidation is not possible
Bueyecillo...	07769	The benefit of the consolidation would be that
Bueyuno ...	07770	Try and effect consolidation
Bufala ...	07771	**Constantly**
Bufalino ...	07772	Constantly on the go
Bufetillo ...	07773	**Construction**
Buffeted ...	07774	A correct construction
Buffettare...	07775	An incorrect construction
Buffetto ...	07776	Necessary construction
Buffletin ...	07777	Owing to method of construction
Buffonare...	07778	What is the right construction
Buffoncino	07779	Your (——'s) construction is correct
Buffoon ...	07780	Your (——'s) construction is erroneous
Buffoonery	07781	What is the estimated cost of construction
Bufido ...	07782	Total estimated cost of construction amounts to
Bufolaccio...	07783	Owing to defective construction
Bufonada ...	07784	**Consul**
Bufonazo ...	07785	Certified by U.S. consul
Bufonem ...	07786	Certified by notary and consul
Bufoneria...	07787	Certified by consul at ——
Bufonibus...	07788	In consul's office
Bugaceta ...	07789	**Consular**
Bugalla ...	07790	Consular invoice
Buganker ...	07791	Owing to consular regulations
Bugbear ...	07792	**Consult** (*See also* "Confer.")
Bugeleisen	07793	To consult
Bugellada...	07794	Consult with
Bugeln ...	07795	Consult with —— promptly
Bugia ...	07796	Consult —— before you proceed further
Bugiardo ...	07797	Suggest that you should consult
Bugier ...	07798	**Consultation**
Bugigatto...	07799	After consultation with —— have decided
Bugillonem	07800	Cable result of your (——'s) consultation with
Bugiuzza ...	07801	Do not do anything without consultation with
Buglehorn	07802	Shall not act before consultation with
Bugler ...	07803	The result of my (our) (——'s) consultation with —— is
Bugling ...	07804	**Consulted**
Buglosa ...	07805	Has (have) you (has ——) consulted
Bugnoletta	07806	Has (have) consulted
Bugnolone	07807	Has (have) not consulted
Bugonis ...	07808	Consulted with
Bugsiren ...	07809	Consulted with —— (him) before proceeding
Bugspriet...	07810	Have you consulted with
Buharda ...	07811	I (we) have not yet consulted with
Buhardilla	07812	**Consulting**
Buharro ...	07813	Consulting engineer
Buhedal ...	07814	Is the consulting engineer of company
Buhera ...	07815	Consulting chemist
Buhldirne...	07816	**Consumption**
Buhlschaft	07817	On account of the large consumption
Buhoneria...	07818	What is the present consumption
Buhrstone	07819	Consumption is very large
Buitre ...	07820	Consumption is considerable
Buitrero ...	07821	Consumption is small
Bujaccio ...	07822	This means a consumption of
Bujarasol ...	07823	Consumption of stores

Bujarron ...	07824	Consumption per day of 24 hours
Bujeda ...	07825	What is the coal consumption per day
Bulario ...	07826	This will increase the consumption to
Bulbaceum	07827	This will decrease the consumption to
Bulbettino	07828	The consumption of —— amounts to ——: costing ——
Bulboso ...	07829	Consumption of —— excessive
Buldriana...	07830	Consumption will probably amount to
Bulero ...	07831	What does the consumption amount to
Buleutam ...	07832	Consumption will most likely increase
Bulganak ...	07833	Consumption is not likely to materially alter
Bulimia ...	07834	**Contact**
Bulkhead ...	07835	Is a contact fissure
Bulkiness ...	07836	Is not a contact vein
Bullage ...	07837	Has (have) made contact with
Bullar ...	07838	Has (have) made contact with —— at a depth of —— ft.
Bulldog ..	07839	A contact lode (vein)
Bullebulle...	07840	At the contact of —— with ——
Bullescent...	07841	Am (are) not likely to come into contact
Bullets ...	07842	Do not come in contact
Bulletta ...	07843	In contact with
Bullfight ...	07844	In immediate contact with
Bullfinch ...	07845	**Contain(s)**
Bullfrog ...	07846	It contains only
Bullicio ..	07847	It does not contain
Bullidor ...	07848	The lode contains
Bulliemus...	07849	The ore contains
Bulliendo ...	07850	The pipe contains
Bulliturus...	07851	The quartz contains
Bulliunt ...	07852	The chute contains
Bulliviati ...	07853	What does it contain
Bullocks ...	07854	**Contango(es)**
Bullrush ...	07855	Contango rates
Bullseye ...	07856	What is the contango on
Bultico ...	07857	Contango is
Bulto ...	07858	Contango will be
Bululu ...	07859	Contango(es) light
Bulwark ...	07860	Contango(es) heavy
Bumastorum	07861	Contango(es) excessive
Bumblebee	07862	Contango(es) will be light
Bumeliam...	07863	Contango(es) will be heavy
Bumpers ...	07864	Contango(es) will be excessive
Bumping ...	07865	Contango(es) moderate
Bumpkin ...	07866	**Contents**
Bundeslade	07867	Contents of
Bundestag	07868	Cable main contents
Bundniss ...	07869	—— per cent. of gold and silver contents [treatment charges
Bundweise	07870	—— per cent. of gold and silver contents, less ——per ton
Bunion ...	07871	—— per cent. of gold and silver contents, less —— per ton treatment charges, also less —— per unit for copper contents
Bunitiores	07872	—— per cent. of gold and silver contents, less —— per ton treatment charges, also less —— per unit for lead contents
Bunolero ...	07873	—— per cent. of gold and silver contents, less —— per ton treatment charges, also less —— per unit for zinc contents.
Buntdruck	07874	Pay nothing for copper contents
Buntfarbig	07875	Pay nothing for lead contents
Bunuelo ...	07876	Pay nothing for zinc contents
Buonaccio...	07877	Pay —— per unit for copper contents
Buondato...	07878	Pay —— per unit for lead contents
Buonfatto...	07879	Pay —— per unit for zinc contents [an ounce gold
Buontempo	07880	Pay for gold contents if assay shows more than one-tenth of

Burujon	...	07937	I (we) shall be unable to continue
Busardas	...	07938	Are we obliged to continue
Busaun	...	07939	Continue work
Busbacare		07940	Continue driving
Busberie	..	07941	Continue sinking
Buscador	...	07942	Continue upraise
Buscalfana		07943	Continue to report regularly every —— days
Buscapie	...	07944	Continue to report by cable regularly
Buscatore	...	07945	How long shall you continue
Buscavidas		07946	How long may I (we) continue
Buschetta	.	07947	How long will the expense of —— continue
Buschig	...	07948	In order to continue the
Busecchia	.	07949	In the event of my (our) declining to continue
Busennadel		07950	Shall continue until
Busilis	...	07951	Shall continue unless
Buskins	...	07952	Should suggest that the —— be continued
Busquer	...	07953	What will it cost to continue
Busquillo	...	07954	Will undertake to continue
Bussatrice		07955	You had better continue
Bussetto	..	07956	You cannot decline to continue
Bussfertig		07957	This will oblige me (us) to continue
Bussola	...	07958	Has been continued steadily
Busspsalm		07959	Shall I (we) continue to ——
Busstag	..	07960	I (we) should have liked to continue
Bussubung		07961	Should this favourable nature continue
Bustaccio	...	07962	It is of the greatest importance that you continue
Bustirapum		07963	**Continues**
Busto	...	07964	Continues to look
Bustualem		07965	Continues to look exceedingly well
Busybody	...	07966	Continues to improve
Butcher	...	07967	Continues to become poorer
Buthysiam		07968	**Continuing**
Butifarra	...	07969	Do you advise continuing
Butiner	...	07970	Do not advise continuing
Butiro	...	07971	Strongly advise continuing
Butlerage	...	07972	**Continuity**
Butlership		07973	Continuity of
Butment	...	07974	Continuity of ore body
Butoria	...	07975	Continuity of pay streak
Butrino	...	07976	In continuity with
Buttagra	...	07977	Are the workings in continuity with
Buttend	..	07978	The workings are in continuity with
Butterato	...	07979	Is (are) in continuity with
Butterbrod		07980	Is (are) not in continuity with
Buttercup	...	07981	Is the vein in continuity with
Butterfass		07982	**Continuous**
Butterfly	...	07983	Work has been continuous since
Buttericht		07984	**Continuously**
Buttermilk		07985	Continuously for —— days
Butterteig		07986	Continuously for —— ft.
Buttertree		07987	**Contortion**
Butterwort		07988	**Contract**
Buttner	...	07989	Contract with
Button	...	07990	Can contract
Buttonhole		07991	Cannot contract
Buttoning	...	07992	Can you contract
Buttress	...	07993	Contract for
Buttressed		07994	On contract
Butyl	...	07995	Let on contract
Butylene	...	07996	Contract accepted

Butyrate ...	07997	Contract declined
Buvable ...	07998	Private contract
Buvotter ...	07999	In violation of contract
Buxiferum	08000	Contract promptly for
Buxomly ...	**08001**	Make a new contract
Buxomness	08002	Contract fallen through
Buxorum ...	08003	Throw up contract
Buzano ...	08004	Contract thrown up
Buzardas ...	08005	Is (are) the contract(s) signed
Buzonera ...	08006	Contract(s) is (are) signed
Buzzard ...	08007	Contracts are running out
Buzzicare ...	08008	Contract(s) expired on
Buzzichio...	08009	Cannot obtain contract
Buzzing ...	08010	Are you bound by contract to
Byblow ...	08011	Are they bound by contract to
Bylane ...	08012	Accept contract if —— clause cancelled
Byplay ...	08013	Can you obtain new contract
Byroad ...	08014	Contract for as much of the work as possible
Byssine ..	08015	Cable main conditions of contract
Bystander	08016	Completion of contract delayed on account of
Byword ...	08017	Do not close the contract
Byzantine...	08018	Does the contract provide for
Cabaco ...	08019	Contract provides for
Cabalgador	08020	Contract does not provide for
Cabalgata...	08021	Contract entered into by myself personally
Cabalistic ...	08022	Can you sign contract in your own name
Caballage ...	08023	Do not sign contract unless
Caballarum	08024	Do not sign contract until
Caballeria	08025	Endeavour to negotiate for contract
Caballico ...	08026	Have made a contract with ——
Caballine ...	08027	Have made a contract for ——
Caballisch	08028	I (we) can obtain a new contract
Caballo ...	08029	I am (we are) personally liable for the fulfilment of contract
Caballona...	08030	If you can contract
Caballote ...	08031	Insist upon fulfilment of contract
Caballuelo	08032	In accordance with the terms of the contract
Cabalmente	08033	Is not in accordance with the terms of the contract
Cabanil ...	08034	Impossible to negotiate for contract
Cabanuela	08035	Impossible to obtain a new contract
Cabaret ...	08036	Most of the work is done on contract
Cabaretier	08037	Must be provided with P/A so that I may sign contract
Cabbage ...	08038	Mail proposed contract as quickly as possible
Cabbaging	08039	Negotiations for contract at an end
Cabeceo ...	08040	No contract exists
Cabecequia	08041	On completion of contract
Cabecera ...	08042	On account of prior contract
Cabecica ...	08043	On account of contract between —— and ——
Cabestan ...	08044	Terms of contract unsuitable
Cabestrage	08045	The work is all done on contract
Cabestrar ...	08046	Can contract for the sum of
Cabestrero	08047	Can contract at the rate of
Cabezador	08048	Sold by private contract
Cabezage ...	08049	Bought by private contract
Cabezal ...	08050	I (we) have let contract for whole of work at
Cabezorro...	08051	The following contracts have been let
Cabezota ...	08052	Shall let contract(s) on following terms
Cabezudo ...	08053	What contracts have you now running
Cabezuela...	08054	Have the following contracts now running
Cabildada ...	08055	Let on contract at —— per foot
Cabildante	08056	Obtain firm contract for

Cabildear ...	08057	This contract should be distinct from
Cabildero ...	08058	On contract for
Cabildo ...	08059	At what rate can you contract for
Cabillaud ...	08060	At what rate shall I (we) contract for
Cabimiento	08061	For breach of contract
Cabindoor	08062	Have let the following work on contract
Cabinroof...	08063	The terms of the contract were
Cabizbajo ...	08064	Act strictly in accordance with contract
Cabizcaido	08065	Do nothing to invalidate contract
Caboche ...	08066	The contract was signed on ——
Caboose ...	08067	The contract will be ready for signature on
Cabotin ...	08068	The contract is not yet signed
Cabrahigal	08069	Useless to insist upon fulfilment of contract
Cabrahigo ..	08070	When will the contract be signed
Cabreia ...	08071	What is the reason for delay in signing contract
Cabrero ...	08072	—— will not sign contract (because)
Cabrial ...	08073	I (we) ought to contract immediately for
Cabrilla ...	08074	You had better contract for
Cabrillear	08075	I have let a contract for
Cabrina ...	08076	„ „ „ „ „ „ the transportation
Cabriolet ...	08077	„ „ „ „ „ „ making tramway at
Cabrioleur	08078	„ „ „ „ „ „ sinking shaft —— ft. (at)
Cabritero ...	08079	„ „ „ „ „ „ sinking winze (at)
Cabritillo ...	08080	„ „ „ „ „ „ driving level (at)
Cabrituno	08081	„ „ „ „ „ „ driving tunnel (at)
Cabron ...	08082	„ „ „ „ „ „ driving crosscut (at)
Cabronada	08083	„ „ „ „ „ „ all surface work (at)
Cabronazo	08084	„ „ „ „ „ „ making —— ft. of ditch (at)
Cabujon ...	08085	„ „ „ „ „ „ completing —— ft. of flume (at)
Cabuya ...	08086	„ „ „ „ „ „ cutting No. —— section (at)
Cacabati ...	08087	„ „ „ „ „ „ cutting wood (at)
Cacacciano	08088	Fill in the contract as follows
Cacafretta	08089	Make contract very precise
Cacahuate	08090	Draw up contract in very precise terms, with penalties for non-
Cacajuola...	08091	**Contracted** [fulfilment of each clause
Cacalia ...	08092	Contracted by
Cacamini ...	08093	Have contracted for
Cacandi ...	08094	I (we) have contracted for
Cacaoyer ...	08095	„ „ „ „ „ all supplies
Cacareador	08096	„ „ „ „ „ complete survey
Cacarear ...	08097	„ „ „ „ „ supply of
Cacareo ...	08098	„ „ „ „ „ supply of wood
Cacasangue	08099	„ „ „ „ „ supply of mine timber
Cacasedo ...	08100	Have contracted for delivery of ——
Cacatessa ...	08101	Have contracted for erection of ——
Cacatojo ...	08102	Have contracted for the carriage of ——
Cacatura ...	08103	**Contraction**
Cacavisse ...	08104	**Contractor(s)**
Cacchione	08105	Contractors have
Cacciante ...	08106	Contractors will
Cacciatoja	08107	Contractor(s) refuse(s) to
Cacear ...	08108	Contractor(s) decline(s) to
Caceria ...	08109	Contractor(s) consent(s)
Cacerola ...	08110	Contractor(s) is (are)
Caceta ...	08111	Contractor(s) is (are) liable
Cachada ...	08112	Contractor(s) is (are) not liable
Cachalote...	08113	Contractor(s) is (are) waiting to begin
Cacharado	08114	Contractor(s) is (are) hindered by
Cacharro ..	08115	Contractor(s) has (have) thrown up contract
Cachazudo	08116	Contractor(s) cannot work for want of water

Cachecache	08117	Contractor(s) is (are) driven out of works by water
Cachemira	08118	Contractor(s) is (are) to furnish all stores
Cacherello	08119	Contractor(s) is (are) surprised to hear
Cachessia ...	08120	Contractors have driven since —— a further distance of ——
Cachetas ...	08121	Contractors are at work night and day [feet
Cachetero ...	08122	Do not inform contractor(s)
Cachettico	08123	Will not inform contractor(s)
Cachetudo	08124	Has (have) been obliged to inform contractor(s) ...
Cachexy ...	08125	On behalf of the contractor(s)
Cachican ...	08126	On what terms will contractor(s)
Cachillada	08127	**Contradict**
Cachinnant	08128	To contradict
Cachinnavi	08129	To enable me (us) to contradict the report
Cachinno ...	08130	Contradict the report
Cachipolla	08131	Can you (we) contradict the report
Cacholas ...	08132	Contradict the report at once on my (our) behalf
Cachonda ...	08133	I (we) require this information in order to contradict the
Cachondez	08134	**Contradicted** [report
Cachones ...	08135	Contradicted by authority of
Cachopice	08136	Contradicted by ——
Cachopo ...	08137	Has (have) contradicted the report
Cachorro ...	08138	The —— has been already contradicted
Cachucho ...	08139	**Contrary**
Cachuela ...	08140	Contrary to
Cachulera...	08141	To the contrary
Cachumbo	08142	Quite contrary to my (our) orders
Cachunde...	08143	Quite contrary to my (our) wishes
Cachupin ...	08144	Contrary to all anticipations
Cacillo ...	08145	—— acted contrary to instructions
Cacinola ...	08146	Contrary to written instructions
Caciolino ...	08147	Contrary to cable instructions
Cacique ...	08148	Except I (we) cable to the contrary before ——
Cackle ...	08149	Except you cable to the contrary before ——
Cackling ...	08150	Entirely contrary to
Cacodyle ...	08151	No instruction having been received to the contrary
Cacoethes ...	08152	On the contrary
Cacofonia ...	08153	Quite on the contrary
Cacography	08154	Unless I (we) hear to the contrary
Cacolet ...	08155	**Control(s)** (*See also* " Beyond.")
Cacology ...	08156	To control
Cacometer	08157	Absolute control
Cacophony	08158	Controls the stock
Cacoquimia	08159	Can you get —— under your control
Cacoxene ...	08160	Exercise greater control over ——
Cactuses ...	08161	Has (have) acquired control
Caculam ...	08162	Has (have) complete control of
Cacuminabo	08163	Has (have) no longer any control over
Cacuminant	08164	Is said to have control over
Cacuminate	08165	It is absolutely necessary that we should have control
Cacuminem	08166	So as to control
Cadalecho...	08167	So as to control the stock
Cadalso ...	08168	Entirely beyond my (our) control
Cadanal ...	08169	Within my absolute control
Cadanero ...	08170	Get control
Cadarzo ...	08171	Can you get control
Cadastre ...	08172	Get control at any cost
Cadaver ...	08173	Or any other cause beyond his (——'s) control
Cadavereux	08174	Or any other cause beyond our (your) control
Cadaverico	08175	**Controlled**
Caddisworm	08176	Formerly controlled by

Caddy	...	08177	Practically controlled by

Convenient(ce)

Cadebat	...	08178	
Cadeira	...	08179	At your convenience
Cadejo	...	08180	If altogether convenient
Cadella	...	08181	In case it is convenient
Cadenado	...	08182	In case it is not convenient
Cadenasser		08183	Is this convenient
Cadencia	...	08184	It is convenient
Cadeneta	...	08185	It is not convenient
Cadenilla	...	08186	It will not be convenient
Caderent	...	08187	When will it be convenient (to)
Caderillas	...	08188	Would it be convenient (to)
Cadetto	...	08189	It would be much more convenient (to)
Cadi	...	08190	It will not be at all convenient

Conveyance

Cadillar	...	08191	
Cadillero	...	08192	Deed of conveyance
Cadimento		08193	What means of conveyance exist
Caditoje	...	08194	There is no means of conveyance
Cadivus	...	08195	There are good facilities as regards conveyance

Convince

Cadmites	...	08196	
Cadoce		08197	To convince
Cadoso	...	08198	Convince —— if possible that

Convinced

Cadran	..	08199	
Caducante		08200	Convinced by
Caducar	..	08201	Convinced of

Co-operate

Caduceador		08202	
Caduceo	...	08203	To co-operate
Caduceous		08204	Co-operate with
Caducifer	...	08205	If you can co-operate with
Caducity	...	08206	It is impossible to co-operate with

Co-operation

Cadunt	...	08207	
Caduquez	...	08208	Secure ——'s co-operation
Cadurabus		08209	Cannot secure ——'s co-operation
Caduta	...	08210	Have secured ——'s co-operation

Copper

Cadytis	...	08211	
Caecilius	...	08212	Copper glance
Caecitatem		08213	Copper ore
Caecubarum		08214	Copper plates
Caecubis	...	08215	Copper wire
Caedebamus		08216	Copper chloride
Caedizo	...	08217	Copper matte
Caedura	...	08218	Copper matte assaying
Caelamen	...	08219	Copper mine
Caelatoris	...	08220	Copper property
Caelaturam		08221	Copper pyrites
Caelestis	...	08222	Copper vein
Caelibatus		08223	Copper ore carrying gold ——, silver —— per ton
Caelibis	...	08224	Black copper
Caelicolam		08225	Black oxide of copper
Caelifera	...	08226	Carbonate of copper
Caementum		08227	Blue and green carbonates of copper
Caenosibus		08228	Grey copper
Caeparum	...	08229	Grey copper carrying —— ozs. of silver per ton of ore
Caerimonia		08230	Metallic copper
Caeruleum		08231	Ore assays (dry) —— per cent. of copper
Caesariati		08232	Ore assays (wet) —— per cent. of copper
Cafarderie		08233	Yellow copper [inches long
Cafareo	...	08234	Copper plate —— of an inch thick —— inches wide by ——
Cafeiere	...	08235	Electro silvered copper plate —— ozs. of silver to square foot
Cafetal	...	08236	Copper plate for liners —— inches thick by —— inches long

[by —— inches wide (*See also* " Amalgamation.")

Cafetera	...	08237	**Copperas** (*Green Vitriol*)
Caffeista	...	08238	**Copy** (*See also* "Duplicate.")
Cafila	...	08239	A copy of
Cafura	...	08240	Copy of contract
Cagachin	...	08241	Copy of instructions
Cagada	...	08242	Copy mailed on ——
Cagadillo	...	08243	Copy of report
Cagafierro		08244	Cannot send copy
Cagalaolla		08245	Mail copy of report as soon as possible
Cagalera	...	08246	Mail copy of —— on ——
Cagamelos		08247	Please forward copy of
Cagaropa	...	08248	Instruct —— to send copy(ies) of
Cagarrache		08249	Have —— copies made
Cagarria	...	08250	Have —— copies type-written and sent to
Cagarruta	...	08251	Request —— (him) to send you a copy
Cagatinta	...	08252	**Cords**
Cagatorio	...	08253	Cords of
Caggente	...	08254	Cord of wood
Caggiamo	...	08255	—— per cord
Cagionante		08256	Have contracted for a supply of —— cords of wood [in
Cagionato	...	08257	Have contracted for a supply of —— cords before winter sets
Cagionuzza		08258	Have contracted for a supply of —— cords before rainy
Cagliare	...	08259	Our consumption is —— cords per week [season
Cagnaccio	...	08260	We have —— cords stacked
Cagnard	...	08261	Wood for fuel costs —— per cord
Cagnardise		08262	**Core** (*See also* "Assay," "Diamond Drill," &c.)
Cagnesco	...	08263	Forenoon core (6 a.m. to 12 noon)
Cagneux	...	08264	Afternoon core (12 noon to 6 p.m.)
Cagnoletto		08265	First core by night (6 p.m. to 12 midnight)
Cagon	...	08266	Last core by night (12 midnight to 6 a.m.)
Cagoterie	...	08267	What is the diameter of the diamond drill core
Cagotisme		08268	The diameter of the diamond drill core is
Cague	...	08269	Sample of diamond drill core
Cahoter	...	08270	**Corner**
Caidos	...	08271	Owing to corner operations
Caillelait	...	08272	Will endeavour to corner you
Cailleront	...	08273	Is (are) endeavouring to corner you (us)
Cailletage	..	08274	**Cornering**
Cailleteau	...	08275	Should they succeed in cornering you (us)
Caillon	...	08276	**Cornish** (*See also* "Miners," "Pump.")
Caillouter	...	08277	Permanent Cornish pump
Caiman	...	08278	I (we) have contracted for Cornish plunger pump at
Caimicnto	..	08279	**Correct**
Caique	...	08280	Please correct mistake
Cairel	...	08281	Cable which is correct
Cairelado	...	08282	Cable if this is correct
Cairelar	...	08283	The —— is correct
Cairnstone		08284	It is quite correct
Caisse	...	08285	Account(s) quite correct
Caitiff	...	08286	Account(s) not correct
Caixa	...	08287	Correct when necessary
Cajero	...	08288	Correct by cable if necessary
Cajetin	...	08289	Correct as stated
Cajilla	...	08290	Cannot make this come correct
Cajista	...	08291	The following is correct
Cajolery	...	08292	Do(es) not appear to be correct
Cajoncito	...	08293	Everything appears to be correct
Calabacero		08294	If this is not correct cable
Calabacica		08295	Is this reading correct
Calabacin	...	08296	Is this result correct

Calabash ...	08297	Is it correct that
Calabazada	08298	It is correct that
Calabazar ...	08299	Is it correct
Calabazate	08300	It is correct
Calabazon ..	08301	It is not correct
Calabobos .	08302	In case this is correct you should at once
Calabozage	08303	Result as you give it is correct
Calabozo ...	08304	The correct figure(s) is (are)
Calabriada	08305	The correct reading is
Calabricem	08306	Your reading is correct
Calabrino...	08307	The correct word(s) is (are)
Calabrote ...	08308	——'s statement not correct
Calacanto ...	08309	——'s statement quite correct
Caladre ...	08310	——, was not correct as to [be found correct
Calafate ...	08311	It is probable that the statements and estimates generally will
Calafatear	08312	It is probable that the statements will not be found correct
Calafeteo ...	08313	Statement as to width of vein is correct
Calafetin ...	08314	**Correction**
Calagoso	08315	For further correction
Calagrana ..	08316	Further correction necessary
Calaison ...	08317	**Correspond(s)**
Calaluz ...	08318	Corresponds with
Calamajo ...	08319	Entirely corresponds to
Calamar ...	08320	What depth does this correspond to (at)
Calambac...	08321	Correspond to a depth of —— (at)
Calambre ...	08322	Do (does) not correspond with
Calambuco	08323	**Corroborate**
Calamento	08324	To corroborate
Calametum	08325	To corroborate his statement
Calamidad	08326	Fully corroborate(s)
Calamistro	08327	Can fully corroborate
Calamita ...	08328	Do(es) not in any way corroborate
Calamiteux	08329	Cable whether you can corroborate
Calamities	08330	**Corrosion**
Calamitoso	08331	Corrosion extended to
Calamo ...	08332	On accounts of corrosion of
Calamocano	08333	Stoppage due to corrosion of boiler tubes
Calandrajo	08334	**Cost** (*See also* " Construction," " Price," " Value.")
Calandreur	08335	Cost of
Calandria...	08336	Cost of production is
Calangue ...	08337	Please estimate cost of
Calanticam	08338	Estimated cost
Calappio ...	08339	Estimated cost here
Calatoris ...	08340	Estimated cost of improvement(s) will amount to
Calautica ...	08341	Cannot estimate cost
Calavera ...	08342	Cost of stoping is
Calaverear	08343	Cost of stripping, per yard, is
Calbote ...	08344	Cost of sinking, per foot, is
Calcabile ...	08345	Cost of repairs will amount to
Calcagnare	08346	Cost of treatment (is)
Calcagno ...	08347	Cost of working (is)
Calcanal ...	08348	Cost per fathom (is)
Calcaneo ...	08349	Cost per foot (is)
Calcanhar...	08350	Cost per mile (is)
Calcanuelo	08351	What will be the cost of
Calcatrice ...	08352	Cost will be
Calcatura ...	08353	Is all cost stopped
Calceabat ...	08354	All cost is stopped
Calceanto ...	08355	Cost free on board
Calceatum	08356	Cost, freight and insurance

Calcedoine	08357	Owing to the cost of
Calcedonia	08358	Cost per ton for breaking and raising
Calceolum...	08359	„ „ fixed charges
Calceta ...	08360	„ „ for concentration
Calcetero ...	08361	„ „ „ crushing
Calcetilla ...	08362	„ „ „ development
Calceton ...	08363	„ „ „ dressing
Calcified ...	08364	„ „ „ extraction
Calciform ...	08365	„ „ „ freight
Calcifraga...	08366	„ „ „ hauling
Calcify ...	08367	„ „ „ levelling
Calcinante	08368	„ „ „ matting
Calcitrare ...	08369	„ „ „ milling
Calcitros ...	08370	„ „ „ mining
Calcografo	08371	„ „ „ packing
Calcolare ...	08372	„ „ „ pumping
Calcoleria ...	08373	„ „ „ reduction
Calculable...	08374	„ „ „ refining
Calculador	08375	„ „ „ roasting
Calcular ...	08376	„ „ „ sampling
Calculoso ...	08377	„ „ „ shipping
Calculus ...	08378	„ „ „ sinking
Caldaccio ...	08379	„ „ „ smelting
Caldaja ...	08380	„ „ „ sorting
Caldajone	08381	„ „ „ stamping
Caldajuolo	08382	„ „ „ stoping
Caldam ...	08383	„ „ „ treatment
Caldanino...	08384	Cost of stoping, per fathom, is
Caldanuzzo	08385	Cost of driving, per foot, is
Caldaria ...	08386	Costs amount to
Calderada ..	08387	Cost of treating ore excessive on account of
Calderero ...	08388	Can be operated at small cost [of ——
Caldereta ...	08389	Estimate does not include cost of ——; add a further amount
Calderico ...	08390	I (we) estimate the cost of additional machinery at ——
Calderilla ...	08391	I (we) estimate the cost of necessary machinery at ——
Calderuela	08392	I (we) estimate the cost of necessary exploratory works at ——
Calderugio	08393	Impossible to send close estimate of costs
Caldillo ...	08394	How much will the probable cost amount to
Calebasse ..	08395	Estimated cost delivered at the mine
Calebinini	08396	What is the amount of cost incurred to date (on)
Calecer ...	08397	The amount of cost incurred to date (on)
Calecico ...	08398	Any further cost on your side
Calefacit ...	08399	Cost of a complete underground survey
Calefatare...	08400	Cost of a surface survey
Calefato ...	08401	Cost of timbering, per foot
Calencas ...	08402	Cost per ton for ore concentration may be (is) taken at
Calenda ...	08403	The cost of
Calendario	08404	Telegraph cost of
Calendata	08405	What do you estimate the cost for —— at
Calendrier	08406	What is the estimated cost
Calendula...	08407	Our monthly cost has been heavy owing to
Calentador	08408	Our present cost amounts to —— per month
Calentar ...	08409	What do you estimate it has cost up to the present time on
Calentibus	08410	What is your estimate of cost to —— exclusive of
Calentito ...	08411	Estimated cost —— to ——
Calentura ...	08412	Total cost(s) per ton
Calepino ...	08413	What is the cost of —— per ton
Calerunt ...	08414	What is the cost of mining, per ton
Calescent ...	08415	What is the cost of milling, per ton
Calesero ...	08416	What is the cost of smelting, per ton

Calesin	...	08417	Total cost not to exceed
Calesse	...	08418	Total cost will not exceed
Caletre	...	08419	Is all cost at the —— stopped
Calfatage	...	08420	For all costs incurred at
Calfeutrer	...	08421	This is not likely to cost
Calibat	...	08422	At what cost per ton
Calibeado	...	08423	I have closed all costs and have mailed accounts
Calibita	...	08424	Limit your cost as nearly as possible to —— per month
Calibrar	...	08425	What would be the cost and time required for
Calicanto	...	08426	The cost would probably amount to ——
Calicetto	...	08427	State dimensions and approximate cost of
Caliche	...	08428	Telegraph your probable cost for month of January
Calicione	...	08429	Telegraph your probable cost for month of February
Calicud	...	08430	Telegraph your probable cost for month of March
Calidarum	...	08431	Telegraph your probable cost for month of April
Calidez	...	08432	Telegraph your probable cost for month of May
Calidity	...	08433	Telegraph your probable cost for month of June
Caliductos	...	08434	Telegraph your probable cost for month of July
Caliendri	...	08435	Telegraph your probable cost for month of August
Caliente	...	08436	Telegraph your probable cost for month of September
Calieta	..	08437	Telegraph your probable cost for month of October
Calificado	...	08438	Telegraph your probable cost for month of November
Calificar	...	08439	Telegraph your probable cost for month of December
Caliga	...	08440	Incur no cost whatever in connection with
Caligabunt		08441	Incur as little cost as possible in connection with
Caliginis	...	08442	Cost book
Caliginoso		08443	Cost book system

Cost sheet(s) (*See also* "Pay Roll.")

Caligrafia	...	08444	
Caligulam	...	08445	Cost sheets should show in detail cost of
Calilla	...	08446	Mail abstract of cost sheets for last —— month(s)
Calinerie	...	08447	Mail duplicate cost sheet
Calipedes	...	08448	Send by next mail a duplicate of cost sheet for month of ——
Caliphate	...	08449	Will mail cost sheet(s)

Costean

Calitriche	...	08450	
Calizo	...	08451	Costean pits
Calkerize	...	08452	Costean trenches
Calking	...	08453	By means of costean pits and trenches
Calladaris	...	08454	Busy prospecting by means of costean pits and trenches
Callado	...	08455	Workings only consist of costean pits and trenches

Costeaning

Callajetta	...	08456	
Callandico		08457	Shall commence costeaning almost at once
Callboy	...	08458	Cost of costeaning
Callejear	...	08459	Shall suspend costeaning
Callejon	...	08460	Have suspended costeaning
Callejuela	...	08461	Costeaning operations

Could

Callialto	...	08462	
Calligonum		08463	Could not
Callipers	...	08464	Could not have
Calliscere	...	08465	Could have
Calloria	...	08466	Could you (——)
Callosidad		08467	Could you (——) not
Callosity	...	08468	Could probably
Calloso	...	08469	I (we) could not
Callously	...	08470	Could you (——) if necessary
Calmeria	...	08471	Could not be accomplished
Calmness	...	08472	Could not accomplish it

Counsel

Calocha	...	08473	
Calofriado	...	08474	Who is the counsel on our side
Calofrio	...	08475	Who is counsel against us
Calognare	...	08476	Have you engaged counsel

Calognoso	08477	Have engaged counsel
Caloma ...	08478	Take counsel's opinion at once
Calomel ...	08479	Shall I (we) take counsel's opinion
Calomnier...	08480	Will obtain counsel's opinion
Calongia ...	08481	When do you expect to have counsel's opinion
Caloniar ...	08482	Expect to have counsel's opinion on
Calorico ...	08483	What is counsel's opinion
Calorifere...	08484	Counsel's opinion is ——
Calorific ...	08485	Counsel's opinion is that I (we) have a strong case
Calorique ...	08486	Counsel's opinion is that I (we) have a weak case

Count

Caloruccio	08487	To count
Calostro ...	08488	Shall count upon you
Calotter ...	08489	You may count upon me (us)
Calotype ...	08490	Do not count upon me (us)
Calotyping	08491	

Counted

Calpestare	08492	You should not have counted upon me (us)
Calpesto ...	08493	Counted upon you(r)
Calquer ...	08494	

Countermand

Calseco ...	08495	Obliged to countermand
Calterire ...	08496	Shall I (we) countermand
Caltharum	08497	Do(es) not countermand
Calthas ...	08498	Do you (does ——) countermand
Caluggine...	08499	I (we) countermand
Caluisti ...	08500	

Countermanded

Calumere ...	08501	Please consider my (our) order(s) countermanded
Calumet ...	08502	Must be countermanded
Calumiare...	08503	Better be countermanded at once
Calumnia ...	08504	Has (have) countermanded
Calvanist ...	08505	Am I (are we) to consider order(s) countermanded
Calvario ...	08506	Do not consider order(s) countermanded unless
Calvaza ...	08507	

Country (*See also* "Barren.")

Calvebant...	08508	Comprises a large tract of country
Calvello ...	08509	Country rock
Calvendum	08510	Horse of country rock
Calventis ...	08511	Owing to the hardness of country rock
Calvernus...	08512	Owing to the —— of country rock
Calvete ...	08513	What is the country rock
Calvinista	08514	The country rock is
Calvitie ...	08515	The country rock passed through
Calyx ...	08516	The country looks exceedingly well for
Calzada ...	08517	The bottom of the shaft is in country rock
Calzador ...	08518	The end of —— level is in country rock
Calzaretto...	08519	The country rock changes to
Calzerone ...	08520	The entire country is composed of
Calzettajo...	08521	The country rock is decomposed to a depth of
Calzolaro ...	08522	

County

Calzon ...	08523	In the county of
Calzonazo...	08524	County court
Camafeo ...	08525	County surveyor
Camaglio ...	08526	County attorney
Camalachar	08527	County clerk
Camaleon ...	08528	County commissioner
Camamila...	08529	

Coupon(s)

Camandula	08530	When will the coupons be due
Camangiare	08531	Coupons are due on
Camanonca	08532	Coupons mailed
Camarage	08533	No coupons enclosed
Camareria...	08534	

Course

Camareta ...	08535	In due course
Camariento	08536	

Camarilla ...	08537	In the course of
Camarin ...	08538	In course of the next ten days
Camarista...	08539	In course of the next —— days
Camarlengo	08540	The only course is
Camaronero	08541	Do not think course suggested a good one
Camarote ...	08542	An uniform course of
Camarroya	08543	On the course of the
Camastro ...	08544	On the course of the vein (lode)
Camatones	08545	On the course of the lead
Camauro ...	08546	The course of the vein is towards
Cambalache	08547	The course of the vein (lode) is
Cambales ...	08548	The course of the vein is in our favour
Cambanear	08549	The course or dip of the shoot is
Cambayas...	08550	The course of the ledge is
Cambered...	08551	This course
Cambiabile	08552	Suggest that you adopt the same course
Cambiador	08553	As a matter of course
Cambiar ...	08554	Ascertain and telegraph what course he (they) intend to take
Cambiatura	08555	By a drivage on the course of the vein
Cambija ...	08556	Is now in course of construction
Cambistry	08557	During the course of the next few days
Cambitatem	08558	Shaft sunk on the course of the vein
Cambouis...	08559	The course of the vein can be traced for
Cambrayon	08560	The course of the vein is —— degrees —— of —— and [dips —— at an angle of —— degrees
Cambretuch	08561	The only course appears to me (us) to be
Cambron ...	08562	What course do you advise
Cambronal	08563	Take the course you think best
Cambrure...	08564	Would it not be well to adopt a different course
Cambusier	08565	True course of
Cambuy ...	08566	What is the true course of
Camedafne	08567	The true course is
Camedrio ...	08568	There is no middle course
Camelea ...	08569	Is there no middle course
Camelete ...	08570	The only middle course is
Cameleuca	08571	**Court** [Company to pay costs
Camelina ...	08572	The court has granted a winding up order as petitioned for.
Camellarum	08573	The court has granted a winding up order, each party to pay [their own costs
Camellejo...	08574	The court has granted a winding up order, but company [allowed to liquidate itself
Camelleria	08575	The court has granted a winding up order, but subject to an [account being rendered to the court
Camellon ...	08576	The court has granted a further time before determining [whether to make liquidation compulsory or not
Camelopard	08577	The court has ordered another meeting of shareholders to be [called, so as to obtain the decided opinion of the [majority as to which course they prefer adopted
Camelotado	08578	The court has granted a winding up order. Company to be [wound up under an official liquidator
Camels ...	08579	**Courtesy**
Camemoro	08580	As an act of courtesy only
Cameo ...	08581	Extend every courtesy to
Camepitios	08582	**Cover**
Cameraccia	08583	To cover
Cameral ...	08584	Take care to cover
Camerated	08585	Cover up
Camerella...	08586	**Covered**
Cameribus	08587	Have covered up all trace of
Cameriere	08588	Are you (is ——) covered against
Camerino ...	08589	Only partly covered

Cameriste ...	08590	Completely covered against
Camerlingo	08591	When I (we) should be covered against all
Camerotto	08592	I am (we are) fully covered
Camicetta ...	08593	Covered by
Camicia ...	08594	Entirely covered by prior locations
Camicinola	08595	Covered by other claims
Camillas ...	08596	**Covering**
Caminada...	08597	Covering a large extent of
Caminante	08598	Covering a considerable part of
Caminar ...	08599	**Cracked**
Camionneur	08600	Bed plate cracked
Camisardo	08601	Boss cracked
Camiseta ...	08602	Owing to —— being cracked
Camisola ...	08603	Rim cracked
Camison ...	08604	—— was cracked in transport
Camlet ...	08605	**Cradle** (See also " Alluvial," " Drills," " Hydraulic.")
Cammarum	08606	Washing cradle
Cammellico	08607	Send two boring machine cradles
Camminare	08608	**Crank**
Cammino ...	08609	Crank shaft
Cammionage	08610	Crank bearings
Camojardo	08611	**Credit** (See also " Bank.")
Camomile ...	08612	Credit of
Camorra ...	08613	What amount is there to my (our) credit
Camosciare	08614	There is now a credit of
Camoscino	08615	Credit is nearly exhausted
Camote ...	08616	To my (our) credit
Camouflet...	08617	How much has been placed to my (our) credit
Campagna	08618	Has (have) placed —— to your credit
Campajuolo	08619	Has (have) bad credit
Campal ...	08620	Has (have) good credit
Campamento	08621	Has (have) fair credit
Campanario	08622	Has (have) overdrawn his (their) credit
Campanear	08623	Letter of credit
Campaneta	08624	Letter of credit to hand
Campanil ...	08625	Have not received letter of credit advised on
Campanino	08626	Letter of credit mailed on
Campanudo	08627	Have you received letter of credit mailed on
Campanuzzo	08628	Letter of credit not enclosed
Campbed ...	08629	Mail letter of credit for
Campchair	08630	Balance to your credit of
Campeador	08631	Leaving a credit balance of
Campeche...	08632	What is the credit balance
Campeggio	08633	The credit balance is
Campeon ...	08634	There is no balance to credit, but instead a debit of
Camperello	08635	Cannot arrange for a credit until after meeting on
Campero ...	08636	Cannot arrange for a credit before
Campesmo	08637	Is —— (he) worthy of credit
Campestre	08638	Enquire as to the credit of —— and cable
Campestris	08639	Have placed —— to your credit with
Camphene	08640	Have placed —— to the joint credit account of —— and ——
Camphorate	08641	Have cancelled credit
Camphoric	08642	Is worthy of credit
Camphre ...	08643	Is not worthy of any credit
Camphrier	08644	Please telegraph me a credit of
Campillo ...	08645	Please open a credit of
Campina ...	08646	Please cancel credit
Campiren ...	08647	——'s credit very good
Camposanto	08648	——'s credit bad
Campstool	08649	——'s credit good to the extent of ——

Camueso ...	08650	Cable me (us) a credit of
Camuffare	08651	I (we) have placed to your credit ——
Camunas ...	08652	I (we) have placed —— to your credit with
Canaballa...	08653	What sum has been placed to my (our) credit
Canagliume	08654	Have paid to your credit at the bank of —— the sum of
Canaille ...	08655	**Crediting**
Canalado ...	08656	Am I (are we) safe in crediting —— to the extent of ——
Canaleja ...	08657	**Creditor(s)**
Canaliser ...	08658	Creditors have commenced action
Canalita ...	08659	Meeting of creditors
Canalizo ...	08660	Decision arrived at, at meeting of creditors
Canalon ...	08661	Creditors are pressing for payment of account
Canamo ...	08662	Creditors becoming impatient
Canapajo ...	08663	Have arranged with principal creditors to
Canape ...	08664	The only creditors are
Canapiglia	08665	The principal creditors are
Canapuccia	08666	The largest creditor is
Canardeau*	08667	There are creditors against the mine to the extent of ——
Canarder ...	08668	There are creditors against the estate amounting to ——
Canario ...	08669	**Creek** (See also "Alluvial," "Bed," "Hydraulic," "Miners' [Inches.")**
Canarroya	08670	By diverting the —— creek
Canastilla...	08671	From the —— creek
Canatteria	08672	In the bed of the creek
Canavaccio	08673	There is no water in the creek
Cancabuz ...	08674	There has been no water in the creek since
Cancamos...	08675	The creek is nearly dry
Cancana ...	08676	The water in the creek amounts to —— miners' inches
Cancanier...	08677	There is only —— miners' inches in creek
Cancelar ...	08678	**Creep**
Cancellato	08679	**Creeper**
Cancelli ...	08680	**Cretaceous**
Cancellone	08681	Cretaceous formation
Cancer ...	08682	**Crisis**
Cancerate...	08683	Expect crisis on
Cancereux**	08684	Crisis was on
Canceroso...	08685	Crisis is now passed
Cancion ...	08686	So as to surmount the crisis
Cancrenare	08687	This will mean a crisis
Cancro ...	08688	There is likely to be a crisis
Cancroma...	08689	**Critical**
Candado ...	08690	Is in a very critical position
Candaliza...	08691	It is a very critical time
Candara ...	08692	When matters are not critical
Candeal ...	08693	**Crop**
Candefeci ...	08694	**Crop ore**
Candelabro	08695	**Cropped**
Candelaria	08696	Samples consisting of cropped ore
Candelero...	08697	Average samples not cropped ore
Candeletta	08698	**Croppings** (See also "Outcrop.")
Candelica ...	08699	Croppings extend for a distance of
Candellaja	08700	The croppings show up very well
Candente ...	08701	**Cross**
Canderent...	08702	Cross cutting
Candesco ...	08703	To cross
Candesemur	08704	So as to cross
Candesitor	08705	Should cross
Candicant...	08706	Will cross
Candidato	08707	Will not cross
Candidezza	08708	If it (this) does not cross
Candidness	08709	Cross vein (See also "Lode," "Vein.")

* To smelt "Commandeau" in Edition I.   ** To smelt "Cancereux" in Edition I.

Candidulus	08710	**Cross-course**
Candied ...	08711	By a cross-course
Candilada...	08712	The lode is disordered by a cross-course
Candirung	08713	**Crosscut** (*See also* "Drift," "Level," &c.)
Candlemas	08714	Crosscut No.
Candonga...	08715	Crosscut from
Canduisse	08716	Crosscut every —— feet
Canebrake	08717	Crosscut is in very tight ground
Canecillo ...	08718	Crosscut requires timbering
Canendus ...	08719	Have driven in the crosscut during the past —— days —— feet.
Canephora	08720	Have cut a —— lode in crosscut
Canescere...	08721	Have cut a lode in crosscut carrying
Canestalk...	08722	Have cut a reef in crosscut carrying
Canestro ...	08723	In No. —— crosscut
Canez ...	08724	Long crosscut
Canforato...	08725	Shall drive crosscut with rock drills
Cangear ...	08726	Suggest your driving a crosscut so as to
Cangiabile	08727	Struck vein in crosscut
Cangiato ...	08728	Struck body of ore by crosscut; will assay
Cangreja ...	08729	What is the distance driven in crosscut since
Cangrenoso	08730	Distance driven in crosscut since —— is —— feet
Cangroso ...	08731	Developed by a crosscut for a length of —— feet
Canibal ...	08732	Crosscut is laid with a double track
Canicidio ...	08733	Crosscut has been driven during the past month —— feet
Canicula ...	08734	Crosscut is still in country rock
Caniforme	08735	Crosscut is in —— feet
Canillera ...	08736	Length of No. —— crosscut is —— feet
Caninez ...	08737	The eastern crosscut
Caniqui ...	08738	The western crosscut
Canister ...	08739	Telegraph the present length of crosscut
Canistrum	08740	Telegraph estimated length of crosscut required (to)
Canitote ...	08741	Telegraph estimated length of crosscut to intersect vein
Caniveau ...	08742	To crosscut to the vein
Canixie ...	08743	Crosscut to the north
Cankered ...	08744	Crosscut to the east
Cankering	08745	Crosscut to the south
Cankerworm	08746	Crosscut to the west
Canna ...	08747	The crosscut from the winze
Cannabinus	08748	Crosscut has just intersected vein
Cannamele	08749	Continue crosscut to
Cannellino	08750	Have started to crosscut for [shall begin to crosscut
Cannelure...	08751	If we do not discover anything within the next —— feet we
Cannonata	08752	What are the dimensions of crosscut
Cannoneer	08753	Dimensions of the crosscut are
Cannoniera	08754	Crosscut has been abandoned owing to
Cannoning	08755	On which side are you crosscutting
Cannons ...	08756	Stop crosscut south
Cannonshot	08757	Stop crosscut north
Canocchia...	08758	Stop crosscut east
Canoeing ...	08759	Stop crosscut west
Canoero ...	08760	Crosscut making good progress
Canonesa ...	08761	Above the level of intersection of crosscut
Canonge ...	08762	Proposed crosscut should intersect the vein at
Canongible	08763	Crosscut is in granite
Canonical...	08764	" " limestone
Canonicita	08765	" " country rock
Canonico ...	08766	" " mineral
Canonista...	08767	" " pay ore
Canonizar...	08768	" " porphyry
Canopied ...	08769	" " quartz

Canopy ...	08770	Crosscut is in trachyte
Canororum	08771	„ „ vein matter, but carries no payable quartz
Canorous ...	08772	**Crossed**
Canoscenza	08773	Since crossed
Canovaccio	08774	Have crossed
Cansancio...	08775	Have not crossed
Cansar ...	08776	**Cross-head**
Cansatojo...	08777	Breakage of cross-head
Cansera ...	08778	**Crowd**
Cantabant	08779	Crowd the work all you can
Cantable ...	08780	Shall crowd this work as much as possible
Cantabris...	08781	Crowd developments day and night
Cantada ...	08782	Crowd output to the greatest extent possible
Cantafera...	08783	**Crucibles** (See also "Appliances," "Assay.")
Cantajuolo	08784	Crucibles for fluxing
Cantaloup	08785	Crucibles, round clay
Cantaminem	08786	Crucibles, plumbago No. ——
Cantante ...	08787	Crucibles, salamander [for melting gold
Cantaral ...	08788	Send as soon as possible —— salamander crucibles, No. ——
Cantarera...	08789	**Crush** (See also "Arrastra," "Mill," "Stamps.")
Cantarin ...	08790	To crush
Cantatore...	08791	Crush and sample
Cantatrice	08792	In order to crush
Cantatum...	08793	Shall commence to crush
Cantaverim	08794	Shall be able to crush —— tons per week
Cantazo ...	08795	When will you commence to crush
Canteens ...	08796	I (we) can commence to crush as soon as you instruct
Canteles ...	08797	I (we) cannot crush more than
Canterella...	08798	**Crushed** (See also "Milled," "Stamped.")
Canterito ...	08799	—— tons were crushed in —— months
Canteron ...	08800	No record has been kept of the total amount crushed
Cantharide	08801	Total amount crushed is at least
Canthos ...	08802	This yield is from —— tons crushed during —— days
Canticar ...	08803	—— tons were crushed during the month ending
Canticio ...	08804	Cable number of tons crushed
Canticorum	08805	Total amount crushed
Cantiga ...	08806	Total amount crushed —— tons (dry weight)
Cantilate ...	08807	**Crusher** (See also "Rolls," "Stonebreaker.")
Cantilever	08808	Crusher rolls
Cantina ...	08809	Blake's crusher
Cantinela...	08810	Krom's crusher
Cantinero...	08811	Crusher jaws
Cantingly...	08812	Bed plate of crusher
Cantitavi ...	08813	Foundation(s) of crusher
Cantizal ...	08814	**Crushing** (See also "Commence," "Mill," "Stamps.")
Cantocello	08815	Trial crushing
Cantonar ...	08816	A trial crushing of —— tons has yielded
Cantonment	08817	High speed crushing rolls
Cantonnier	08818	Our crushing is at the rate of —— tons per day
Cantonuto	08819	Steel shells for crushing rolls
Cantopean	08820	Telegraph result of crushing
Cantoria ...	08821	This will increase our crushing power to —— tons per day
Cantorral...	08822	We are now crushing —— tons per 24 hours
Cantrix ...	08823	Decrease in crushing is due to
Cantuccino	08824	**Crystalline**
Cantueso ...	08825	**Cube**
Cantusar ...	08826	**Cubic** (See also "Alluvial," "Gravel.")
Canuisti ...	08827	Cubic inches
Canuler ...	08828	Cubic feet
Canusina ...	08829	Cubic yards

Canutazo ...	08830	Cubic yards of gravel
Canutezza	08831	—— cubic yards washed
Canutiglia	08832	How many cubic yards have you washed in the last campaign
Canutillo ...	08833	**Currency**
Canvassed	08834	British currency
Canvassing	08835	American currency
Canzoncino	08836	French currency
Canzone ...	08837	Spanish currency
Canzonetta	08838	German currency
Canzoniere	08839	In what currency
Caoup ...	08840	**Custody**
Caozinha ...	08841	In safe custody
Capacatis ...	08842	**Custom**
Capaccio ...	08843	Customs ores
Capacete ...	08844	Say it is not according to custom
Capachero	08845	According to usual custom
Capacidad	08846	It has never been the custom to
Capaciorem	08847	Custom hitherto has been to
Capacitare	08848	What is the custom
Capador ...	08849	What is the usual custom in such cases
Capadura ..	08850	The custom here is to
Capanna ...	08851	**Custom House**
Capannello	08852	Custom house authorities will allow
Capannone	08853	Custom house authorities will not allow
Capannuola	08854	Will the custom house authorities allow
Capapie ...	08855	Custom house authorities have seized
Caparazon	08856	Custom house authorities will seize
Caparbieta	08857	Endeavour to get released from custom house authorities
Caparrare ...	08858	The custom house authorities refuse
Caparron ...	08859	**Cut** (*See also* " Cross-cut," " Ore," " Vein.")
Capassone	08860	Cut down all expenses possible
Capataz ...	08861	So as to cut down expenses
Capazon ...	08862	Do not expect to cut vein (ore) (lode) (reef) before
Capecchio...	08863	Expect to cut vein (ore) (lode) (reef) within the next —— ft.
Capegli ...	08864	Have cut vein (or ——)
Capellada ...	08865	Have cut a body of rich ore
Capellan ...	08866	Have cut a body of ore assaying
Capellarum	08867	Have cut pay chute [left
Capelluto ...	08868	Vein, where we have cut it, is barren ; shall drive on it right and
Capeon ...	08869	Telegraph as soon as you cut the ore in No. —— level
Caperant ...	08870	Telegraph as soon as you cut the vein [pumps
Caperatus...	08871	We shall have to cut down the shaft —— ft. to admit of ——
Capered ...	08872	When do you expect to cut vein (reef)
Capering ...	08873	We have still to drive —— ft. before we expect to cut
Capero ...	08874	**Cutting** [vein (or ——)
Caperoles ...	08875	Cutting into
Caperuceta	08876	Cutting at surface
Caperuza ...	08877	Ore from cutting assays
Capessent...	08878	——'s cutting
Capialzado	08879	**Cwt.** (*See also* " Pound," " Hundredweight," " Tons.")
Capicerio ...	08880	**Cyanide**
Capichola ...	08881	Cyanide process
Capidoglia	08882	**Cylinder**
Capiello ...	08883	Cylinder of
Capiendi ...	08884	End of cylinder
Capigliara	08885	Air cylinder
Capigorron	08886	Steam cylinder
Capilar ...	08887	Water cylinder
Capillaire ...	08888	**Cylindrical**

Capillatum	08889	**D**
Capillejo ...	08890	**Daily**
Capiller ...	08891	Daily reports
Capilludo ...	08892	Daily expected
Capilotade	08893	Daily expected to come
Capimento	08894	Daily expected to leave
Capingot ...	08895	Daily shipments
Capiparte	08896	Cable daily
Capiron ...	08897	Keep a daily record
Capirotada	08898	Will keep a daily record
Capirote ...	08899	Report daily until you have cable (telegram) ...
Capirotero	08900	Telegraph daily to —— respecting
Capisayo ...	08901	**Dam** (*See also* " Burst," " Hydraulic.")
Capisoldo ...	08902	Coffer dam
Capistrare	08903	Dam at —— swept away
Capistrem...	08904	Stability of the dam is very doubtful
Capita ...	08905	Dam must be repaired without delay ; will cost about
Capitacion	08906	Telegraph estimated cost of erecting dam and time required
Capitalem...	08907	Estimated cost of erecting dam —— ft. high and —— ft. [wide would be ——; time required ——
Capitana ...	08908	We could erect a dam that would give —— ft. fall
Capitanear	08909	Would suggest that a dam be erected across the —— at ——
Capitello ...	08910	By means of a dam
Capiteux ...	08911	**Damage(s)** (*See also* " Assessed," " Awarded.")
Capitolaro	08912	Action for damages
Capitolino	08913	Has (have) commenced action for damages
Capitoso ...	08914	Cable (telegraph) the cause of damage to ——
Capitozza ...	08915	Cable (telegraph) approximate cost of damage done and time
Capitudini	08916	Has (have) caused great damage to —— [required to repair
Capitulate	08917	Damage not very serious
Capitulero	08918	Repair damage as speedily as possible
Capiundus	08919	Damage is covered by insurance
Capnites ...	08920	Damage not covered by insurance
Capnomante	08921	Damage means an actual money loss of ——; the loss of time
Capnos ...	08922	Damage(s) was (were) covered by [will be ——
Capoc ...	08923	No damage was caused
Capocaccia	08924	Damage was caused by defect in
Capocenso	08925	Damage caused by fire amounts to
Capocollo ...	08926	Damage caused by water amounts to
Capocuoco	08927	Damage caused by the snow amounts to
Capofila ...	08928	Damage caused by the lightning amounts to
Capogatto	08929	Damage occasioned by snow slide
Capogirlo ...	08930	How long will it take to repair damage
Capolado ...	08931	Damage already repaired
Capoletto ...	08932	Damage now being repaired
Capolevare	08933	Will take —— days to repair damage
Capona ...	08934	As soon as the damage has been repaired
Caponcello	08935	Actual damage not yet ascertained
Caponized	08936	Please cable particulars of damage done
Capopiede	08937	Shall have all damage repaired by
Caporal ...	08938	How long will it take to replace damaged portion
Caporiccio	08939	Damage cannot be repaired
Caporione...	08940	You (——) will be held responsible for damage
Caposcuola	08941	Decline(s) all responsibility in case of damage
Capotasto ...	08942	Repudiate any claim for damage
Capotillo ...	08943	Damage has been very serious
Capoton ...	08944	The only serious damage is
Capotrupa	08945	Damage is alleged to be very serious
Capotudo ...	08946	Damage is alleged to be comparatively trifling
Capouch ...	08947	Actual amount of damage done cannot be ascertained before

Capoverso...	08948	Very serious damages
Capovolto...	08949	Causing (doing) considerable damage to ——
Cappare ...	08950	Damages awarded
Cappellata	08951	Might cause considerable damage to ——
Cappello ...	08952	Will damage me (us)
Capperone	08953	Cannot damage me (us) in any way
Cappietto ...	08954	Will do all he (they) can to damage me (us)
Capponaja	08955	It will considerably damage the project
Capponiera	08956	To damage
Cappucino	08957	**Damaged**
Capraria ...	08958	Has (have) damaged
Capreolus...	08959	Damaged by
Capretto ...	08960	Damaged to the extent of
Capricho ...	08961	Was (were) not damaged
Caprichudo	08962	Arrived in a damaged condition
Capricorn ...	08963	Only slightly damaged
Caprifico ...	08964	Very seriously damaged
Caprigena	08965	Is (are) practically all more or less damaged
Caprimulga	08966	**Danger**
Caprino ...	08967	Danger to
Capriolare	08968	In danger of
Capripede...	08969	What danger do you (does ——) apprehend
Capriuola ...	08970	Apprehend danger from
Caprone ...	08971	Do(es) not apprehend any danger
Caproyle ...	08972	Avoid any danger of ——
Caprylic ...	08973	Considerable danger
Capsario ...	08974	Danger to life and limb
Capsicam ...	08975	Danger might arise from
Capsis ...	08976	The only danger is
Capsized ...	08977	There is no danger at all
Capsizing...	08978	There will be no danger (if)
Capstan ...	08979	There will be some danger that
Capsular ...	08980	To continue means involving considerable danger
Captador ...	08981	What danger is there as regards
Captandus	08982	**Dangerous**
Captatio ...	08983	Any delay is dangerous
Captatorem	08984	I (we) consider it very dangerous
Captatrix...	08985	On account of the dangerous state of
Captiosum	08986	Owing to the dangerous state of the ground
Captious ...	08987	It would be too dangerous
Captivar ...	08988	Would it be dangerous
Captivatis	08989	They are a dangerous lot
Captivity ...	08990	It is very dangerous to work owing to
Capuccio ...	08991	Shaft is becoming very dangerous
Capuchina	08992	**Data**
Capucho ...	08993	Are ——'s data reliable
Capucinade	08994	Data given by —— quite reliable
Capucine ...	08995	Data given by —— altogether unreliable
Capulator...	08996	My (our) data were derived from
Capulin ...	08997	What reliable data have you (has ——)
Capullo ...	08998	Reliable data altogether wanting
Capulum ...	08999	**Date(d)**
Capumpeba	09000	On date of departure
Caput ...	09001	On date of arrival
Capuzar ...	09002	On date of delivery
Capzioso ...	09003	Date of contract ——
Caquage ...	09004	Can you name a date
Caquetage	09005	When I (we) hope to name the date of
Caqueteur	09006	Can you extend date of completion until
Caquetico...	09007	Cable (telegraph) the date you expect to

Caquexia ...	09008	On what date shall you (will ——) be free
Caquimia ...	09009	Have you received my letter dated
Carabina ...	09010	Dated as follows
Carabinero	09011	Please decide date
Caracal ...	09012	Date not yet fixed
Carache ...	09013	Must adhere to date already fixed
Caracoa ...	09014	Probable date will be about
Caracolear	09015	What is the probable date of
Caracolito...	09016	Date at present uncertain
Caracucho	09017	What is the earliest date
Caraffe ...	09018	Cable earliest possible date
Caraffino ...	09019	Earliest date possible
Carafon ...	09020	You must name an earlier date
Caragogum	09021	You must name a later date
Caralitana	09022	What is the latest date
Carambano	09023	Latest date is
Carambola	09024	What is the earliest date you can do it (this)
Caramelo ...	09025	At what date
Caramente	09026	At an earlier date
Caramillar	09027	At a later date
Caramogio	09028	Unable to fix any date until
Caramuyo	09029	What is the earliest date that you can (will)
Caramuzal	09030	What date has been fixed for
Carantona	09031	What is the date of ——
Carapacho	09032	What is the date of your last letter
Caraque ...	09033	Your letter dated —— received
Caratare ...	09034	Your cable dated —— received
Carato ...	09035	Prior date
Carattere ...	09036	Send date of letter to which you refer
Caratula ...	09037	What is the date fixed for
Caratulero	09038	Date fixed is
Caranz* ..	09039	To date
Caravan ...	09040	To date from
Caravero ...	09041	Will date from
Caray ...	09042	Not dated
Carbaseum	09043	**Day(s)** (*See also* "Hours," "Night.")
Carbaso ...	09044	To-day
Carbasorum	09045	Every day
Carbatinus	09046	Day shift
Carbide ...	09047	By day's work
Carbinier ...	09048	Three shifts per day of 24 hours
Carbinol ...	09049	Allowing —— working days per ——
Carbolic ...	09050	Any day
Carbonaria	09051	Day by day
Carbonchio	09052	Day before yesterday
Carbonero	09053	Day after to-morrow
Carbonizar	09054	Days per week
Carboys ...	09055	Days per month
Carbuncle...	09056	Days per year
Carbuncula	09057	Daily for the next —— days
Carbureto...	09058	During the day shift
Carcajada...	09059	During the night shift
Carcamal ...	09060	—— days are required to get from —— to ——
Carcanet ...	09061	How many days are required to get from —— to ——
Carcapuli ...	09062	How many days are required to get to ——
Carcasses ...	09063	It requires —— days
Carcavado	09064	It only requires —— days if
Carcavera...	09065	It will be several days before
Carcavina...	09066	Mailed to-day
Carcax ...	09067	Per day of 12 hours

's spelt "Caraus" in Edition I.

Carcel ...	09068	Per day of 24 hours
Carcelage ...	09069	Telegraphed (cabled) to day
Carcelero ...	09070	Experiment should be continued —— days
Carcerar ...	09071	Stoppage would last for —— days
Carcinoma	09072	Least stoppage would be for —— days
Carciofala...	09073	What number of days
Carciofino...	09074	Within the next —— days
Carciruela...	09075	Will reply within the next seven days
Carcomer ...	09076	Will reply within the next —— days
Carcomido	09077	You will require to be absent —— days
Cardada ...	09078	You will not be absent more than —— days
Cardamino	09079	On an earlier day
Cardatore...	09080	Sunday
Cardboard	09081	Monday
Cardelina ...	09082	Tuesday
Cardencha	09083	Wednesday
Cardenillo	09084	Thursday
Cardeno ...	09085	Friday
Cardiaca ...	09086	Saturday
Cardial ...	09087	Only for a few days
Cardinale ...	09088	It will take several days to
Cardita ...	09089	How many days will it take to
Cardosanto	09090	How many days are likely to be required for
Cardtable ...	09091	Will probably require —— days
Carduetum	09092	One day
Cardume ...	09093	Two days
Carduzador	09094	Three days
Carduzal ...	09095	Four days
Carecer ...	09096	Five days
Carectum ...	09097	Six days
Careened ...	09098	Seven days
Careering...	09099	Eight days
Caremini ...	09100	Nine days
Carenar ...	09101	Ten days
Carencia ...	09102	Eleven days
Carenum ...	09103	Twelve days
Careoribus	09104	Thirteen days
Caresser ...	09105	Fourteen days
Caressing ...	09106	Fifteen days
Carestia ...	09107	Sixteen days
Carestoso ...	09108	Seventeen days
Caretta ...	09109	Eighteen days
Careworn ...	09110	Nineteen days
Carezzante	09111	Twenty days
Carezzato ...	09112	Twenty-one days
Carezzina...	09113	Twenty-two days
Cargadas ...	09114	Twenty-three days
Cargadera	09115	Twenty-four days
Cargador ...	09116	Twenty-five days
Cargaison...	09117	Twenty-six days
Cargamento	09118	Twenty-seven days
Cargazon ...	09119	Twenty-eight days
Carguero ...	09120	Twenty-nine days
Carguica ...	09121	Thirty days
Cariacedo ...	09122	Thirty-one days
Cariado ...	09123	Thirty-two days
Carialegre...	09124	Thirty-three days
Cariancho...	09125	Thirty-four days
Cariante ...	09126	Thirty-five days
Cariarse ...	09127	Thirty-six days

Cariatide ...	09128	Thirty-seven days
Caribe ...	09129	Thirty-eight days
Caribito ...	09130	Thirty-nine days
Caribobo ...	09131	Forty days
Caricante ...	09132	Forty-one days
Caricare ...	09133	Forty-two days
Caricatura	09134	Forty-three days
Caricioso ...	09135	Forty-four days
Caridoso ...	09136	Forty-five days
Carigordo ...	09137	Forty-six days
Carilargo ...	09138	Forty-seven days
Carilleno ...	09139	Forty-eight days
Carilludo ...	09140	Forty-nine days
Carilucio ...	09141	Fifty days
Carinabat ...	09142	Fifty-one days
Carinantes	09143	Fifty-two days
Carinated ...	09144	Fifty-three days
Carinatus ...	09145	Fifty-four days
Carinegro ...	09146	Fifty-five days
Carinfo ...	09147	Fifty-six days
Cariosus ...	09148	Fifty-seven days
Cariota ...	09149	Fifty-eight days
Caripando ...	09150	Fifty-nine days
Cariparejo	09151	Sixty days
Cariraido ...	09152	Sixty-one days
Carisea ...	09153	Sixty-two days
Caritativo ...	09154	Sixty-three days
Caritevole ...	09155	Sixty-four days
Cariturus ...	09156	Sixty-five days
Carlan ...	09157	Sixty-six days
Carlancon ...	09158	Sixty-seven days
Carleabait ...	09159	Sixty-eight days
Carlear ...	09160	Sixty-nine days
Carlina ...	09161	Seventy days
Carmelita ...	09162	Seventy-one days
Carmenado	09163	Seventy-two days
Carmenar ...	09164	Seventy-three days
Carmesi ...	09165	Seventy-four days
Carmesiren	09166	Seventy-five days
Carminatio	09167	Seventy-six days
Carminavit	09168	Seventy-seven days
Carmino ...	09169	Seventy-eight days
Carnaccia ...	09170	Seventy-nine days
Carnagione	09171	Eighty days
Carnajuolo	09172	Eighty-one days
Carnalidad	09173	Eighty-two days
Carnalism ...	09174	Eighty-three days
†Carname ...	09175	Eighty-four days
Carnariam	09176	Eighty-five days
Carnassier	09177	Eighty-six days
Carnasso ...	09178	Eighty-seven days
Carne ...	09179	Eighty-eight days
Carnecilla ...	09180	Eighty-nine days
Carnefice ...	09181	Ninety days
Carnelian ...	09182	Ninety-one days
Carnerada ...	09183	Ninety-two days
Carnerage ...	09184	Ninety-three days
Carnerear ...	09185	Ninety-four days
Carneril ...	09186	Ninety-five days
Carneruno	09187	Ninety-six days

For "Carnardeau" see "Canardeau" (page 146).

Carnicero ...	09188	Ninety-seven days
Carnicol ...	09189	Ninety-eight days
Carnier ...	09190	Ninety-nine days
Carnifex ...	09191	One hundred days
Carnificis ...	09192	**Dead**
Carnival ...	09193	Is dead
Carnivora ...	09194	Dead charges
Carniza ...	09195	Dead charges amount to
Carnoc ...	09196	Dead ground
Carnosetto	09197	Dead work
Carnosita ...	09198	Is all dead work
Carochar ...	09199	Is dead ground
Carogna ...	09200	Is entirely in dead ground
Carolare ...	09201	No dead work has been done
Caroletta ...	09202	Cost for dead work amounts to
Caromomia	09203	**Deads**
Caronium ...	09204	Sample of deads
Carosiera ...	09205	**Deal**
Carotaccia	09206	Is there a great deal of
Carotajo ...	09207	There is a great deal of
Carotas ...	09208	Dissatisfied with the deal
Carotida ...	09209	Do not let anyone know of the deal
Caroubier ...	09210	Aware of the proposed deal
Carouser ...	09211	Explain our deal to
Carousing...	09212	Would you join in the deal
Carpacco ...	09213	Do not join —— (him) in any deal
Carpanel ...	09214	**Dealers**
Carpeau ...	09215	Dealers are
Carpebamur	09216	Dealers are not
Carpedal ...	09217	Dealers are ready to contract
Carpentry...	09218	Dealers are not ready to contract
Carpeta ...	09219	**Dealings**
Carpeting ...	09220	Is (are) most honourable in all his (their) dealings
Carpiccio ...	09221	Have no dealings with
Carpimini	09222	Do not have any dealings with —— (him)
Carpingly...	09223	Be very cautious in your dealings with
Carpintero	09224	Have no dealings with —— (him) if you can avoid
Carpinus ...	09225	Have no dealings with ——
Carpir ...	09226	**Dealt**
Carpitella...	09227	Will be dealt with
Carpofago	09228	Will be dealt with by letter
Carpone ...	09229	**Dear**
Carpsi ...	09230	Too dear
Carptim ...	09231	Price too dear
Carptura ...	09232	I (we) do not consider the price at all dear
Carqueja ...	09233	Is altogether too dear
Carquois ...	09234	Price is undoubtedly dear
Carradore	09235	Would be a very dear purchase
Carraleja ...	09236	**Death**
Carranclo ...	09237	Accidental death
Carranque	09238	What was the cause of death
Carrascal ...	09239	Was the cause of death accidental
Carraspada	09240	Cause of death was accidental
Carratello...	09241	Cause of death was not accidental
Carraway ..	09242	Death was actually caused by
Carrefour ...	09243	**Debenture(s)** (*See also* "Capital," "Certificates," "Shares.")
Carreler ...	09244	Debentures for
Carrelure ...	09245	Debentures secured by
Carreton ...	09246	Debentures have been issued to the extent of
Carrick ...	09247	Will subscribe for —— debentures

Carricoche	09248	Are proposing to issue debentures to the amount of
Carricola ...	09249	—— debentures subscribed for
Carriego ...	09250	Only way is to issue debentures
Carrillar ...	09251	Telegraph what amount of debentures you will subscribe for
Carriola ...	09252	Will you subscribe for —— of the debentures
Carrizal ...	09253	Meeting of debenture holders was held on —— with the
Carrocha ...	09254	**Debit** (*See also* "Balance," "Credit.")　[following result
Carrocin ...	09255	Debit all charges to ——
Carronar ...	09256	Debited in error
Carrono ...	09257	Debit as little as you can to —— account
Carrosse ...	09258	Debit all you can to —— account
Carrot ...	09259	Must be debited to
Carroza ...	09260	Should have been debited to
Carrozzino	09261	You can debit me (us) with
Carrubio ...	09262	What is the sum to our debit
Carrucarum	09263	**Debris** (*See also* "Level," "Stope.")
Carrujado...	09264	Are filled up with debris
Carrure ...	09265	Owing to accumulation of debris
Carsaya ...	09266	Removal of the debris will take
Cartabello	09267	Debris will require to be first removed, which will take ——
Cartabon ...	09268	Covered over with debris　[days
Cartaccia ...	09269	**Debt(s)** (*See also* "Bankrupt," "Discharged.")
Cartallum	09270	What do the debts amount to
Cartamo ...	09271	Debts amount to
Cartapacio	09272	There are no debts whatever
Cartapel ...	09273	All the debts can be liquidated by
Cartapesta	09274	Said to be heavily in debt
Cartazo ...	09275	Can you ascertain amount of debts
Cartellare...	09276	Will ascertain amount of debts and let you know later
Cartero ...	09277	Contracted debts to the amount of
Cartesiano	09278	In order to pay off outstanding debts
Cartibanas	09279	No debts must be allowed to accumulate
Cartilage ...	09280	It is absolutely necessary that we should pay debts amounting
Cartilla ...	09281	**Debtor(s)**　[to
Cartoccino	09282	**Deceit**
Cartonnage	09283	The deceit was (that)
Cartonneur	09284	There has been no deceit
Cartonpate	09285	**Deceive(d)** (*See also* "Mislead.")
Cartoon ...	09286	Has deceived me (us)
Cartooning	09287	May have allowed himself to be deceived
Cartouch ...	09288	Was undoubtedly deceived
Cartuccia ...	09289	**December**
Cartuchera	09290	At the beginning of December
Cartujano...	09291	About the middle of December
Cartujo ...	09292	During the entire month of December
Cartulario	09293	For the entire month of December
Cartulina ...	09294	Last December
Cartways ...	09295	Next December
Caruncula	09296	Near the end of December
Carvallo ...	09297	First day of December
Carvi ...	09298	Second day of December
Caryatides	09299	Third day of December
Carysteum	09300	Fourth day of December
Casabe ...	09301	Fifth day of December
Casabundum	09302	Sixth day of December
Casaccio ...	09303	Seventh day of December
Casalero ...	09304	Eighth day of December
Casalingo...	09305	Ninth day of December
Casalone ...	09306	Tenth day of December
Casamata ...	09307	Eleventh day of December

Casamuro...	09308	Twelfth day of December
Casanier ...	09309	Thirteenth day of December
Casaquilla	09310	Fourteenth day of December
Casaquin ...	09311	Fifteenth day of December
Casatella ...	09312	Sixteenth day of December
Casazo	09313	Seventeenth day of December
Cascabel ...	09314	Eighteenth day of December
Cascabillo...	09315	Nineteenth day of December
Cascade ...	09316	Twentieth day of December
Cascadura	09317	Twenty-first day of December
Cascaggine	09318	Twenty-second day of December
Cascajal ...	09319	Twenty-third day of December
Cascajoso ...	09320	Twenty-fourth day of December
Cascamajar	09321	Twenty-fifth day of December
Cascamorto	09322	Twenty-sixth day of December
Cascante ..	09323	Twenty-seventh day of December
Cascaras ...	09324	Twenty-eighth day of December
Cascarela ...	09325	Twenty-ninth day of December
Cascaroja ...	09326	Thirtieth day of December
Cascaron ...	09327	Thirty-first day of December
Cascarria ...	09328	December expenses amount to
Cascarudo	09329	December shipments amount to
Cascatelle...	09330	**Deception**
Caschetto ...	09331	The deception practised was
Cascissimo	09332	There has been no deception
Cascote ...	09333	**Decide**
Cascudo ...	09334	To decide
Caseharden	09335	You (——) must decide promptly
Casein ...	09336	You (——) must decide at once; cannot wait after ——
Casellina ...	09337	Cannot decide before
Casellulam	09338	In order that I (we) may be able to decide
Casemate ...	09339	In case —— should decide (to)
Caseolum ...	09340	In case —— should decide not (to)
Casera ...	09341	Let —— decide the best course to pursue
Casereccio	09342	As soon as you (——) decide(s)
Caserio ...	09343	Shall not be able to decide before
Caserne ...	09344	When will you (——) be able to decide
Cashmeer...	09345	Will not decide
Casiere ...	09346	Will decide
Casignete ...	09347	You (we) must decide quickly what you (we) are going to do
Casimbas ...	09348	Which (this) will enable us to decide which is best
Casimiro ...	09349	**Decided**
Casipola ...	09350	Decided in our favour
Casista ...	09351	Decided against us
Casitetur ...	09352	Have you decided on any plan
Casolare ...	09353	Cable (telegraph) what has been decided
Casotto ...	09354	I (we) have decided at once to
Casquetazo	09355	I (we) have decided that
Casquete ...	09356	Have decided to commence
Cassamadia	09357	—— has (have) decided to
Cassamento	09358	—— has (have) not decided to
Cassant ...	09359	It has been decided that
Cassapanca	09360	Has been finally decided to (that)
Cassatura...	09361	Not yet decided which is
Cassava ...	09362	It has not yet been decided
Casseretto...	09363	Nothing decided
Casserole ...	09364	What has —— decided
Cassesucre	09365	What has been decided
Cassetete ...	09366	What has (have) —— decided to do
Cassettino	09367	As soon as you have decided

Casseur	...	09368	Expect it will be decided on
Cassidis	...	09369	It has been decided to acquaint you with the following facts
Cassinere	...	09370	Should you (——) not already have decided
Cassiren	...	09371	Already decided
Cassolette	...	09372	Nothing decided up to the present
Cassoncino		09373	Has (have) decided to put in
Cassoner	...	09374	As soon as you have decided what to put in
Cassorum	...	09375	**Decidedly**
Castagno	...	09376	Yes, decidedly
Castalio	...	09377	Decidedly not
Castanal	...	09378	Is decidedly wrong
Castanazo	...	09379	Is decidedly right
Castaneteo		09380	Was decidedly wrong
Castellan	...	09381	**Decipher** (*See also* "Cable," "Code," "Telegram.")
Casteriam	...	09382	Cannot decipher your telegram; please repeat from —— to ——
Castificar	...	09383	Decipher this telegram and send translation to ——
Castigador		09384	Request —— to decipher
Castigar	...	09385	**Decision**
Castigated		09386	As soon as your decision is to hand
Castigavit	...	09387	Decision urgent
Castigetur		09388	Decision satisfactory
Castigo	...	09389	Decision unsatisfactory
Castillejo	...	09390	Decision in our favour
Castimonia		09391	Decision against us
Castitatis	...	09392	Refuse(s) to alter decision
Castle	...	09393	Endeavour to induce —— to alter his (their) decision
Castor	...	09394	For immediate decision
Castoreo	...	09395	What is ——'s decision
Castras	...	09396	What decision have you arrived at
Castracion		09397	How long will it be before decision is arrived at
Castrador	...	09398	Decision expected any moment
Castrafica	...	09399	Should be left to the decision of
Castrazon	...	09400	Cannot be left to the decision of
Castrense	...	09401	In spite of decision
Casuccina	..	09402	Leave decision to
Casucha	...	09403	Leave decision to you
Casuistic	...	09404	Pending decision
Casularum		09405	It will be necessary to arrive at a decision promptly if
Casulla	...	09406	Immediate decision necessary if I am (we are) to
Casullero	...	09407	No such decision was come to
Casupola	...	09408	No such decision is at all likely
Catabre	...	09409	The decision arrived at is
Catabulo	...	09410	Telegraph decision arrived at
Catacaldos		09411	Why was decision arrived at
Cataclism	...	09412	When do you expect final decision
Catacomb	...	09413	Refuse(s) to abide by decision
Catacresis	...	09414	Refuse(s) to alter decision unless you —— will undertake
Catacumbas		09415	Has (have) consented to abide by decision
Catadromo		09416	Is willing to alter decision if
Catadupa	...	09417	Cable decision
Catafalco	...	09418	Will cable decision
Catafalque		09419	——'s decision is adverse
Catafratta		09420	Decision has been given against ——
Catagrapho		09421	**Decisive**
Catalepsis	...	09422	Your answer must be decisive
Catalepsy	...	09423	Give decisive opinion as to
Catalessia	...	09424	As soon as anything decisive is known
Catalicon	...	09425	My decisive opinion is that
Catalogue	...	09426	Not sufficiently decisive
Catalufa	...	09427	Quite decisive enough

Catamount	09428	Telegraph as soon as you can give a decisive opinion
Catanance...	09429	**Declaration**
Cataplasma	09430	Make formal declaration of
Cataplis ...	09431	Have you filed formal declaration
Catapucia...	09432	Have filed formal declaration
Catapulta ...	09433	Have not filed formal declaration
Catarata ...	09434	When was formal declaration filed
Cataribera	09435	Formal declaration was filed on ——
Catarral ...	09436	Make formal declaration before a notary
Catarro ...	09437	**Declare(s)**
Catartico ...	09438	To declare
Catastare ...	09439	Must declare one way or the other
Catastarum	09440	Can you (they) emphatically declare (that)
Catastro ...	09441	Can I (we) emphatically declare (that)
Catauno ...	09442	It will be necessary to declare
Catavino ...	09443	You —— must be able to declare that
Catcall ...	09444	**Declared**
Catchable...	09445	Has (have) declared that
Catchup ...	09446	Has (have) not declared that
Catechiser...	09447	It has been officially declared that
Catecismo...	09448	How were the goods declared
Catecumeno	09449	Goods were declared as
Catedral ...	09450	**Decline(s)**
Catedrilla...	09451	Must decline business
Categorico ...	09452	To decline
Catellino ...	09453	Decline(s) to
Catenaccio	09454	Decline(s) the (it)
Catenarius	09455	At a decline of
Catenate ...	09456	Am (are) obliged to decline
Catenone ...	09457	Cannot decline without giving good reason for
Catequismo	09458	Decline(s) proposal
Catequista	09459	Decline(s) to compromise
Catequizar	09460	Decline(s) to reduce
Cateratta ...	09461	Decline(s) further correspondence
Caterer ...	09462	Expect to decline
Cateretico ...	09463	Decline offer
Caterva ...	09464	Decline the proposal made by
Caterwaul...	09465	Decline my (our) proposal
Cathartic ...	09466	Decline your proposal
Catheter ...	09467	Do you advise me (us) to decline
Catholic ...	09468	Do not decline until
Caticiego ...	09469	Every prospect of a decline
Catillorum	09470	What is the cause assigned for the decline (in)
Catimaron	09471	Must decline
Catinetto ...	09472	Must therefore decline
Catinorum	09473	No prospect of any decline
Catissage ...	09474	In case —— decline(s)
Cativacion	09475	In case —— should decline can you suggest any one else
Catocham ...	09476	I (we) must decline
Catolico ...	09477	I (we) decline [(without)
Catonium ...	09478	I (we) advise you to decline to proceed any further unless
Catoptrica	09479	I (we) advise you to decline all correspondence
Catorceno ...	09480	**Declined**
Catorcio ...	09481	Declined by
Catrafosso	09482	Declined on account of
Catribriga	09483	Declined with thanks
Catricofre...	09484	Absolutely declined
Catrioso ...	09485	Why have you declined
Cattam ...	09486	Why has —— declined
Cattaneo ...	09487	Declined already

Cattivanza	09488	Declined because of
Cattivare ...	09489	—— declined offer because of
Cattivello ...	09490	I (we) have declined
Cattiveria...	09491	Have not declined
Cattivita ...	09492	Has (have) not actually declined as yet
Cattivusso	09493	Will only be declined
Catturare ...	09494	Should not be declined unless
Catuba ...	09495	**Declining**
Catulinum	09496	Price is steadily declining
Catures	09497	What reason have you (has ——) for declining
Caucalide ...	09498	My (——'s) reason for declining was
Caucera ...	09499	Had —— any reason for declining besides ——
Cauchemar	09500	Cannot ascertain ——'s reason for declining
Cauchil ...	09501	As soon as can ascertain ——'s reason for declining will
Caucionero	09502	**Decompose** [inform you
Caudal ...	09503	Likely to decompose
Caudatario	09504	Not likely to decompose
Caudato ...	09505	**Decomposed**
Caudicalem	09506	Altogether decomposed
Caudicis ...	09507	Associated with decomposed
Caudillo ...	09508	Consists of decomposed
Caulicolo ...	09509	Has decomposed into
Cauline ...	09510	Is found decomposed to a depth of
Caulodem...	09511	Not at all decomposed
Cauponis ...	09512	Occurs in decomposed
Cauponulam	09513	Found in the decomposed
Causador ...	09514	**Decrease(d)**
Causalidad	09515	Cost will be decreased
Causalis ...	09516	Endeavour to decrease
Causarius ...	09517	Has (have) decreased
Causativo...	09518	This means a decrease of
Causeless ...	09519	This will mean a decrease in
Causerie ...	09520	Why have you decreased
Causeway...	09521	What is the reason for the decrease
Causidico ...	09522	Will endeavour to decrease
Caustical ...	09523	You must not expect any considerable decrease of —— before
Causticity...	09524	You need not fear any decrease as regards
Caustique ...	09525	You must not decrease your efforts to
Cautelam ...	09526	What is your explanation of the decrease of returns
Cauteleux ..	09527	Endeavour to decrease —— as much as possible
Cauteloso ...	09528	**Deduct**
Cauterio ...	09529	To deduct
Cauterize ...	09530	Will deduct
Cautionary	09531	Do not deduct
Cautionner	09532	Shall I (we) deduct
Cautiverio	09533	Cannot deduct
Cautoris ...	09534	If necessary deduct
Cavadenti ..	09535	Unless you deduct
Cavadiza ...	09536	Deduct all charges
Cavaedium	09537	Deduct commission of
Cavalcade...	09538	Shall I (we) deduct commission
Cavalcavia	09539	Do not deduct any commission
Cavalciare...	09540	**Deduction**
Cavaliera ...	09541	After making deduction of
Cavallaro ...	09542	Can make a deduction of
Cavalletta ..	09543	In order to compensate for this (such) deduction
Cavaliillo ...	09544	Making no deduction
Cavalry ...	09545	No deduction whatever
Cavamento	09546	Making the usual deduction for
Cavata ...	09547	We shall have to make a deduction of (for)

Cavatore ...	09548	You must make a deduction of
Cavedine ...	09549	You might continue negotiations on the basis of a deduction of
Cavefacit ..	09550	Allowing for all necessary deductions
Cavelike ...	09551	No further deductions can be allowed
Cavemen ...	09552	**Deed(s)** (*See also* " Conveyance," " Deposited," " Transfer.")
Cavemus ...	09553	Transfer deed(s)
Cavendum	09554	Draft of proposed deed
Cavernae ...	09555	Deposit deed(s) with
Caverneux	09556	Deed(s) received
Cavernilla	09557	Is (are) deed(s) in order
Cavernoso	09558	Have not yet received deed(s)
Cavernuzza	09559	When may I (we) expect to receive deed(s)
Cavezzina...	09560	Have you received the deed(s) yet
Cavezzuola	09561	Forward deed(s) as soon as possible
Caviare ...	09562	Deed(s) is (are) all in order ; title perfect
Cavicchio ...	09563	Who is (are) the deed(s) in favour of
Cavidoso ...	09564	Deed(s) is (are) in favour of ——
Caviglio ...	09565	Is (are) the deed(s) signed
Cavilacion	09566	Deed(s) is (are) not signed
Cavillador	09567	Deed(s) is (are) signed
Cavillarum	09568	Deed(s) will be signed on
Cavillita ...	09569	Deed(s) is (are) in possession of
Caviloso ...	09570	Is (are) deed(s) in your possession
Cavolesco...	09571	Deed(s) is (are) in my possession
Cavolino ...	09572	Deed(s) is (are) at
Cavolo ...	09573	All deeds ready for signature, only now await
Cavretto ...	09574	Owing to deeds not being in order
Cavriola ...	09575	All the deeds have been duly completed and recorded
Cavueram...	09576	As soon as the deed(s) has (have) been recorded the same [shall be mailed to you
Cavuisset ...	09577	It is merely a formal matter to amend deed(s)
Cayadilla ...	09578	Cannot complete deed(s) sent. You had better execute an
Cayanto ...	09579	Get deed(s) for [assignment to ——
Cayelao ...	09580	Make deed
Cayenne ...	09581	Make deed over to
Cayeput ...	09582	Make deed out in the name of
Cayuco ...	09583	Warranty deed
Cazabe ...	09584	Deed(s) mailed to company's attorney
Cazadero ...	09585	Deed(s) deposited " in escrow "
Cazador ...	09586	Deed(s) deposited " in escrow " with the bank of
Cazamoscas	09587	Deed(s) must be deposited " in escrow " with
Cazcalear ...	09588	Deed(s) has (have) been duly completed
Cazcarria ...	09589	Everything necessary has been done and the deed(s) mailed to
Cazioso ...	09590	Have possession of the deed(s) [you
Cazoleja ...	09591	Refuse to part with deed(s)
Cazolero ...	09592	Refuse(s) to part with deed(s) before payment of
Cazolillo ...	09593	Deed provides in effect that
Cazolon ...	09594	**Deep** (*See also* " Depth.")
Cazonal ...	09595	Deep workings
Cazudo ...	09596	How deep is
Cazuela ...	09597	Is (are) —— ft. deep
Cazumbrar	09598	—— ft. deep
Cazumbre...	09599	As soon as sufficiently deep for
Cazurro ...	09600	Not sufficiently deep
Cazzatello...	09601	Ought to be —— feet deep
Cazzottare	09602	Quite deep enough
Cazzuola ...	09603	The winze is now —— feet deep
Ceaseless ...	09604	Propose to drive deep adit —— feet below our present one
Ceatica ...	09605	Explorations to the deep
Ceavestis ...	09606	Not as deep as

Cebadazo ...	09607	**Deeper**
Cebadera ...	09608	Cannot work deeper
Cebadilla ...	09609	Cannot sink deeper (until)
Cebellina ...	09610	In order to sink deeper we shall require
Cebica ...	09611	Workings are ———- feet deeper than ours
Cebollana ...	09612	If anything deeper
Cebollero ...	09613	**Deepest**
Cebollon ...	09614	What is the deepest working at present
Ceboncillo	09615	Deepest workings are ——— feet from surface
Cebratana...	09616	Deepest workings are ——— feet below adit
Ceburro ...	09617	**Defeat(ed)**
Cecaggine...	09618	Can you make any suggestion to defeat
Cecato ...	09619	Have so far been defeated
Ceceoso ...	09620	Have so far defeated all attempts
Cecha ...	09621	In order to defeat
Cechezza ...	09622	Unless I (we) can defeat
Cecial ...	09623	**Defect(s)**
Cecidisse ...	09624	What is the defect in
Cecolina ...	09625	Believe defect is
Cedaceria ...	09626	Cannot discover any defect in
Cedacero ...	09627	Can make good defects here
Cedacillo ...	09628	Cannot make good defects
Cedars ...	09629	Can you make good defects
Cedarwood	09630	Defect(s) is (are) very slight
Cedazo ...	09631	Defect(s) is (are) very serious
Cedazuelo ..	09632	The most serious defect is
Cedebant ...	09633	**Defective**
Cedern ...	09634	Appliances are generally defective
Cedernholz	09635	Appears somewhat defective
Cedevole ...	09636	Is (are) defective
Cediza ...	09637	Is (are) becoming defective
Cedizione ...	09638	Is only defective as regards
Cedolone ...	09639	Not at all defective
Cedornella	09640	Unless otherwise defective
Cedrangola	09641	Ventilation very defective
Cedrato ...	09642	**Defence**
Cedrelatis ...	09643	Cannot make any defence
Cedride ...	09644	———'s only defence is
Cedrorum...	09645	Has (have) really no defence whatever
Cedulage ...	09646	**Defend** (*See also* " Action.")
Cedulon ...	09647	To defend
Cefalalgia...	09648	Must defend
Cefalica ...	09649	Cannot defend
Cefalo ...	09650	Do not defend
Ceffare ...	09651	Must certainly defend
Ceffatella ...	09652	Unless he can defend himself
Ceffatone ...	09653	**Defer**
Ceffautto ...	09654	Do not defer
Cefiro ...	09655	To defer
Cegajez ...	09656	Will defer
Cegajo ...	09657	Will not defer
Cegarrita ...	09658	Better defer
Cegatoso ...	09659	Better not defer
Ceguedad ...	09660	Unless you can safely defer
Ceguera ...	09661	Should you not be able safely to defer
Cegueries ...	09662	Cannot safely defer
Ceguta ...	09663	Cannot defer giving an answer beyond
Ceiba ...	09664	**Deferred** (*See also* " Completion.")
Ceilings ...	09665	By deferred payments
Ceindre ...	09666	By deferred payments as follows

Ceinture ...	09667	What is the amount of deferred payments
Cejadero ..	09668	Deferred payments amount to
Cejijunto ...	09669	Proceedings cannot be deferred much longer
Cejuela ...	09670	Should not be deferred any longer
Celabro ...	09671	Cannot be deferred any longer
Celada ...	09672	Has (have) deferred making an answer until
Celadilla..	09673	Report deferred
Celadon ...	09674	The matter must be deferred until
Celage ...	09675	Unless matter can be deferred
Celarsi ...	09676	Visit deferred on account of
Celatone ...	09677	Why have you deferred so long
Celavisti ...	09678	**Deficient**
Celebrador	09679	Altogether deficient as regards
Celebrante	09680	Is anything deficient
Celebrar ...	09681	Let nothing be deficient
Celebratio...	09682	Nothing deficient
Celebridad	09683	Following are still deficient
Celebrillo	09684	What is still deficient
Celebritas...	09685	**Deficit**
Celebrity ...	09686	There will be a considerable deficit
Celemin ...	09687	The deficit will be very slight
Celeminero	09688	What will the deficit amount to
Celemnam	09689	Deficit is already
Celerado ...	09690	Deficit will probably not be less than
Celerario ...	09691	**Define**
Celeribus ...	09692	To define
Celeridad ...	09693	This will define
Celerifere ...	09694	Did not define
Celeripes ...	09695	In order to define
Celerrime ...	09696	**Defined** (*See also* " Hanging wall," " Footwall.")
Celery ...	09697	Must be more clearly defined
Celeste ...	09698	Not sufficiently defined
Celestial ...	09699	Unless difference can be more clearly defined
Celestino ...	09700	Both walls are well defined
Celetur ...	09701	Both walls are well defined with a clay selvage
Celiaccia ...	09702	Is the vein (lode) (reef) well defined
Celiarca ...	09703	Not at all well defined
Celiatore ...	09704	The footwall is well defined
Celibacy ...	09705	The hanging wall is well defined
Celibatist ...	09706	The vein (lode) (reef) is well defined
Celibe ...	09707	There is no well-defined foot or hanging wall
Celicola ...	09708	We have driven —— feet along a well-defined wall
Celindrate	09709	**Definite**
Cellar ...	09710	Cannot get anything definite from
Cellarage ...	09711	Can say nothing definite at present (before)
Cellaring ...	09712	Have you arrived at any definite understanding as to ——
Cellarius ...	09713	Hope to be able to cable something definite by .
Cellenca ...	09714	Must have something more definite
Celleraria...	09715	Must have more definite proposal
Cellerier ...	09716	Nothing definite
Cellisca ...	09717	Not definite enough
Cellulaire ..	09718	Nothing definite is known yet
Cellule ...	09719	Require definite instructions as to
Cellulose ...	09720	Telegraph definite instructions immediately
Celocem ...	09721	Must have a definite answer to-day
Celonajo ...	09722	May be able to say something more definite by
Celonium ...	09723	**Definitely**
Celosia ...	09724	Do not definitely decide until
Celsiores ...	09725	Have you (has ——) definitely decided
Celsitude ...	09726	Has (have) definitely settled that

Celsos	...	09727	In case you cannot definitely decide
Celtiberia	...	09728	I (we) have definitely decided to (that)
Celtic		09729	It has been definitely decided to (that)
Celticismo		09730	Nothing definitely settled with (as to)
Cembalo	..	09731	Something must be definitely settled respecting~
Cembellina		09732	When do you expect to decide definitely
Cembolismo		09733	**Defray**
Cembolone		09734	Who will defray cost of
Cementar	...	09735	I (we) will defray cost of
Cementato		09736	—— will defray cost of
Cementerio		09737	What money will you require to defray all liabilities
Cementing		09738	**Degree(s)**
Cemetery	...	09739	Degrees below zero
Cemmanella		09740	Degrees Centigrade
Cempennare		09741	Degrees Fahrenheit
Cenacho	...	09742	At an angle of —— degrees
Cenacole	...	09743	In a less degree
Cenaculo	...	09744	**Delay(s)** (*See also* " Caused," " Delivery," " Departure.")
Cenadero	...	09745	Any delay
Cenagal	...	09746	No delay
Cenante	...	09747	Do not delay
Cenaticum		09748	Still delays
Cenationem		09749	Owing to delay through
Cenaturiam		09750	Delay caused by
Cenceno	...	09751	Delay entirely caused by
Cencerello	...	09752	Delay partly owing to
Cenceria	...	09753	How long will delay continue
Cencerril	...	09754	There is no real delay
Cencerron	...	09755	After —— days' delay
Cenchritis		09756	Delay arising from any cause whatever
Cenchrum		09757	Delay if you think better
Cenciaccio		09758	Delay as long as you possibly can
Cenciaja	...	09759	Prolong delay as much as possible
Cencido	...	09760	Must avoid delay
Cencioso	...	09761	Delay cannot be avoided
Cencris	...	09762	A delay that cannot be avoided
Cendal	...	09763	A delay that must be avoided in future
Cendolilla	...	09764	Prevent delay as much as possible
Cendreux	...	09765	Delay matter until you hear from
Cendrier	...	09766	There will be no delay on my (our) part
Cenefa	...	09767	This delay is unavoidable
Cenelle	...	09768	Advise you not to delay
Cenerella	...	09769	Anticipate any delays
Cenerino	...	09770	Delay will be about —— days
Ceniciento		09771	Delay will be about —— months
Cenitabam		09772	How long will the delay continue
Cenitandum		09773	In order to avoid delay
Cenitatis	...	09774	In order to avoid delay it will be necessary to (that)
Ceniza	...	09775	Causing a delay of ——
Cenizoso	...	09776	The want of —— has already caused great delay
Cennamella		09777	Would delay be injurious
Cennato	...	09778	Delay would not be injurious
Cennovanta		09779	Any delay would be most injurious
Cenobio	...	09780	Advise you that delay is injurious
Cenobita	...	09781	Owing to unavoidable delay
Cenobitico		09782	Expect several unavoidable delays
Cenogamist		09783	In consequence of unforeseen delay
Cenogil	...	09784	Shorten delay as much as possible
Cenoria	...	09785	Some little delay
Cenotafio	...	09786	There must be no delay

Cenotaph ...	09787	Unable to avoid delay
Censalista...	09788	Will avoid any delay
Censalito ...	09789	Will endeavour to delay
Censatario	09790	Will endeavour to prolong delay
Censeur ...	09791	Will endeavour to shorten delay
Censionis	09792	Cannot —— be induced to delay
Censitaire...	09793	What delay will be caused
Censitor ...	09794	What occasions delay
Censorare...	09795	Has (have) caused great delay
Censorino...	09796	The delay was caused by
Censuario...	09797	Has caused long delay
Censuisse ...	09798	This (it) has given us much trouble and caused·considerable [delay
Censurador	09799	Delay is causing great personal anxiety
Censuram	09800	Cannot delay after ——; must leave
Censurante	09801	Delay arose through your cable requiring repetition
Censurato	09802	Sick of the delay
Centaine ...	09803	For any delay or detention
Centaura ...	09804	**Delayed**
Centelleo ...	09805	Delayed through
Centenadas	09806	Delayed by
Centenam...	09807	Delayed until
Centenario	09808	Have not actually been delayed at all
Centenazo...	09809	Has (have) delayed
Centenier ...	09810	Has (have) been delayed through (by)
Centennial	09811	Shall be delayed
Centenoso...	09812	Unavoidably delayed
Centesimo	09813	Was (were) delayed at
Centifidus...	09814	**Delaying**
Centifolia...	09815	Why are you (is ——) delaying
Centilonia	09816	Delaying matters in your interest
Centimano	09817	Delaying matters in interest of
Centimo ...	09818	**Deliver**
Centinajo ...	09819	To deliver
Centinodia	09820	Deliver to
Centipede	09821	Can deliver
Centogambe	09822	Cannot deliver
Centola ...	09823	Do not deliver
Centonchio	09824	Deliver everything to
Centonodi...	09825	In order to deliver
Centrado ...	09826	In case you (——) can deliver
Centrico ...	09827	Shall deliver
Centrifugo	09828	Shall I (we) deliver
Centrines ...	09829	Will not deliver over
Centro ...	09830	Within what time could you deliver
Centumviri	09831	You may deliver
Centuplex...	09832	Deliver possession to
Centuplo ...	09833	Undertake to deliver within —— weeks
Centurion...	09834	Will undertake to deliver to
Centussim	09835	Will not undertake to deliver to
Centuzza ...	09836	In case will not undertake to deliver to
Cenzalo ...	09837	Instruct —— to deliver —— to us
Cepadgo ...	09838	Refuse(s) to deliver without your instructions
Cepejon ...	09839	Expect to deliver (on)
Cependant	09840	**Delivered**
Cephalic ...	09841	Partly delivered
Cepillar ...	09842	Already delivered
Cepillo ...	09843	Delivered to
Cepolindre	09844	Is (are) delivered to
Cepon ...	09845	Not yet delivered
Ceporro ...	09846	Delivered in good condition

Ceppaja ...	09847	Delivered in bad condition
Ceppatello	09848	Delivered to railway station at
Cequi ...	09849	Have you delivered —— to
Cerabam ...	09850	Has (have) delivered to
Ceraceous ..	09851	Has (have) not delivered to
Cerachates	09852	To be delivered to
Cerafolio ...	09853	**Delivering**
Cerajuolo ...	09854	Cease delivering for the present
Ceralacca ..	09855	Has (have) ceased delivering for the present
Ceramalla	09856	**Delivery**
Ceramic ...	09857	Delivery after
Cerapez ...	09858	Delivery before
Cerasina ...	09859	Delivery to commence
Ceraunio ...	09860	Delivery to be completed by
Ceraverim...	09861	Against delivery
Cerbere ...	09862	Delivery during —— month
Cerbiatto ...	09863	Delivery within
Cerboneca...	09864	Delivery to be completed within next —— days
Cerbottana	09865	Delivery to be completed within next —— weeks
Cercado ...	09866	Delivery to be completed within next —— months
Cercante ...	09867	For immediate delivery
Cercatrice	09868	Guarantee delivery not later than
Cercatura ...	09869	On making delivery of
Cerchiajo ...	09870	Wanting delivery of
Cerchiello...	09871	When will you (——) guarantee delivery
Cercueil ...	09872	When will you (——) make delivery
Cercuto ...	09873	Delay has been caused by non-delivery of
Cerdana ...	09874	I am (we are) waiting delivery of
Cerdear ...	09875	For future delivery
Cerdonem...	09876	What is the latest date for delivery
Cerdoso ...	09877	Payable on delivery
Cerebelo ..	09878	**Demand(s)**
Cerebral ...	09879	To demand
Cerecita ...	09880	Demand(s) to
Cerement ...	09881	Now demand(s)
Ceremonial	09882	Do not demand
Cerevisia ...	09883	Demand immediate
Cereza ...	09884	Demand immediate payment in full
Cerfoglio ...	09885	What demand is there for
Cerfoolant	09886	Strong demand for
Cergazo ...	09887	Weak demand for
Ceribon ...	09888	There is no demand for
Ceriferous...	09889	There is a steady demand for
Ceriflor ...	09890	There is no steady demand at all
Cerilla ...	09891	Great demand for ——
Cerintha ...	09892	——'s demands are unreasonable
Cerisaie ...	09893	Do you consider ——'s demands reasonable
Cerisier ...	09894	Demand is reasonable
Cerites ...	09895	Demand is not reasonable
Cermatore	09896	Consider ——'s demands extortionate
Cermena ...	09897	Require —— in order to meet immediate demands
Cernebant	09898	Able to meet immediate demands
Cernecchio	09899	Demand immediate cash payment
Cernedor ...	09900	Demand immediate settlement of claim
Cerneja ...	09901	Demand continues good
Cerner ...	09902	Demand seems likely to increase
Cernicalo ...	09903	Demand is likely to diminish
Cernidillo...	09904	Has (have) made no demand up to present
Cernido ...	09905	Have you made your demand
Cernidura	09906	I (we) have not made any demands

Cerniera	09907	I (we) do not intend to make any demand
Cernitore	09908	I did not intend to make any such demand
Cernualiam	09909	Is demand likely to increase or diminish
Cerography	09910	In case —— should demand
Cerollo	09911	Shall I (we) demand
Cerotero	09912	He (they) demand(s) practically that
Cerotine	09913	He (they) demand(s) an immediate cash payment of
Cerotum	09914	He (they) demand(s) immediate settlement of all claims
Ceroya	09915	Useless to demand
Cerpellone	09916	Unable to meet immediate demands
Cerquillo	09917	What do their (his) demands consist of
Cerquita	09918	When did you make your formal demand
Cerrada	09919	What is your demand
Cerrajeria	09920	You must demand
Cerrar	09921	Resist any such demand
Cerrero	09922	**Demanded**
Cerretano	09923	Demanded by
Cerrinus	09924	Has demanded immediate payment
Cerrion	09925	Have demanded immediate settlement
Cerrojillo	09926	Imperatively demanded under present circumstances
Cerruma	09927	**Demoralized**
Cerrumado	09928	Much demoralized
Certabunt	09929	Not nearly so demoralized as was stated
Certamente	09930	**Demurrage**
Certatim	09931	Claim —— for demurrage
Certatore	09932	Not liable for demurrage
Certeza	09933	Pay demurrage
Certidao	09934	Refuse(s) to pay demurrage
Certificar	09935	Shall I (we) pay demurrage
Certinidad	09936	**Dendritic**
Certiores	09937	**Denies**
Certissimo	09938	Denies all knowledge of
Certitude	09939	**Deny**
Certosino	09940	Can deny
Ceruchos	09941	Cannot deny
Cerulean	09942	Deny most emphatically
Cervaison	09943	**Depart**
Cerval	09944	Depart to
Cervarius	09945	Depart at once for
Cervatica	09946	**Departure**
Cervato	09947	Immediately after my (our) departure
Cerveceria	09948	Immediately after the departure of
Cervelet	09949	Hasten departure as much as possible
Cervellino	09950	Postpone departure until
Cervicabra	09951	Time of departure not yet fixed
Cervical	09952	Delay departure of
Cerviculam	09953	Delay departure if you consider it well to do so
Cervietto	09954	Delay departure until you hear from ——
Cervigudo	09955	**Depend(s)**
Cervillo	09956	To depend
Cerviolas	09957	Depend(s) upon
Cervisias	09958	Depends upon circumstances
Cerviz	09959	Depend upon it that
Cervogio	09960	Can depend upon
Cervulam	09961	Cannot depend upon
Cerziorare	09962	Do not depend upon
Cesante	09963	Entirely depends on
Cesareo	09964	Do (does) not entirely depend on
Cesation	09965	Depend(s) more upon
Cesellare	09966	You (——) can depend upon

Ceselletto ...	09967	You (——) should not depend upon
Cesible ...	09968	I (we) depend upon you to (fix)
Cesionario	09969	Cannot depend upon machinery
Cesped ...	09970	Cannot depend on pumps
Cespedera...	09971	Can depend on machinery
Cespicare ...	09972	Can depend on pumps
Cespitator	09973	Am (are) obliged to depend upon
Cespitoso ...	09974	Am (are) depending mainly upon
Cespuglio ...	09975	Obliged to depend upon
Cessabant...	09976	Can you thoroughly depend upon
Cessaturus	09977	Do not depend upon
Cessitur ...	09978	It (they) will mainly depend upon
Cesspool ...	09979	In case you can depend upon
Cestaccia ...	09980	In case you cannot depend upon
Cestarolo ...	09981	Depend upon you to (for)
Cestello ...	09982	Depend for —— upon
Cesteria ...	09983	Useless to depend upon
Cestica ...	09984	Was obliged to depend upon
Cestonada	09985	What remittances may I (we) depend upon up to
Cestro ...	09986	Can depend upon receiving at least —— (before ——)
Cestuto ...	09987	You may depend upon it I (we) shall do all I (we) can (to)
Cesural ...	09988	You can thoroughly depend upon —— (him)
Cetacea ...	09989	Have you anyone you can depend upon to
Cetarius ...	09990	**Depended**
Cetene ...	09991	Can be depended upon
Ceterare ...	09992	Cannot be depended upon
Ceteratore...	09993	Cannot be depended upon after
Ceteroquin	09994	Cannot be depended upon for more than
Cetis ...	09995	**Deposit**
Cetrifero ...	09996	Deposit has been paid
Cetrino ..	09997	Deposit has not been paid
Cetylic ...	09998	Have you paid the deposit(s)
Ceuma ...	09999	Have paid the deposit(s)
Chabacana	10000	Have not paid the deposit(s)
Chabeta ...	**10001**	A valuable deposit of
Chaborra ...	10002	A valuable gold-bearing deposit
Chabraque	10003	A cap deposit
Chacal ...	10004	Splendid deposit of ——
Chachara ...	10005	What is the area of deposit
Chacharero	10006	The area of the deposit is
Chacho ...	10007	Cement deposit
Chacina ...	10008	May be only a superficial deposit
Chacoli ...	10009	Proved to be only a superficial deposit
Chacotear ..	10010	Deposit proved to have an average depth of —— feet
Chacra ...	10011	Deposit document(s) with
Chacuaco ..	10012	Insist upon having a deposit
Chafallar ...	10013	In case —— refuse(s) to make a deposit
Chafarote...	10014	Require a deposit of ——
Chaferrer ...	10015	Require a deposit of —— per cent.
Chaffinch ...	10016	Require a deposit sufficient to cover expert's fee and travelling
Chaflan ...	10017	—— refuse(s) to make a deposit [expenses
Chafouin ...	10018	Must deposit
Chagrinant	10019	Must deposit amount of first payment
Chagrined...	10020	Must deposit —— to cover preliminary expenses
Chainon ...	10021	Must deposit sufficient to cover contingencies
Chalancar ..	10022	What amount of deposit is required
Chaland ...	10023	Would it not be well to pay deposit at once
Chalaneria	10024	**Deposited**
Chalazias ...	10025	Deed(s) to be deposited with
Chalcitis ...	10026	Have deposited

Chaldron ...	10027	Must be deposited
Chaleco ...	10028	To be deposited
Chaleur ...	10029	To be deposited with
Chalkiness	10030	Deposited with
Chalkpits ...	10031	Papers deposited with
Chaloreux	10032	Must be deposited with
Chalote ...	10033	Deposited to your credit with
Chalumeau	10034	**Deprecate**
Chalupa ...	10035	Strongly deprecate any such conduct
Chalybidis	10036	Board strongly deprecates
Chamarasca	10037	**Depreciate(d)**
Chamaraz ...	10038	Considerably depreciated
Chamaron...	10039	Has very much depreciated since
Chamarrer	10040	Has depreciated the value considerably
Chambellan	10041	**Depreciation**
Chamberga	10042	Allow(ance) for depreciation
Chambon ...	10043	Has (have) caused great depreciation of the value
Chambranle	10044	Will cause great depreciation of the value
Chambrette	10045	What is the proper allowance for depreciation
Chameleon	10046	**Depress**
Chamelier	10047	**Depressed**
Chamelote	10048	Not at all depressed
Chamerluco	10049	Very much depressed
Chamfer ...	10050	A little depressed
Chamicera	10051	Much depressed on account of
Chamiza ...	10052	**Depressing**
Chamma ...	10053	Depressing effect
Chamois ...	10054	Has not had any depressing effect whatever
Chamoiseur	10055	Has (have) a depressing effect on
Chamorrar	10056	Has (have) had a depressing effect on
Champada	10057	Has (have) not had a depressing effect on
Champagne	10058	**Depth** (*See also* " Deep.")
Champan ...	10059	Depth of
Champetre	10060	At a depth of
Champignon	10061	At a depth of —— ft
Chamuscado	10062	At this depth
Chamuscar	10063	Depth attained
Chancear ...	10064	Is stated to have failed in depth
Chancero ...	10065	In depth
Chancica ...	10066	Any depth [drive another level
Chancleta...	10067	As soon as we reach a depth of —— ft. shall commence to
Chanclo ...	10068	As soon as we reach a depth of —— ft. shall drive a cross-cut
Chandeleur	10069	Considerable depth [to lode
Chandelle...	10070	Considerable depth below surface
Chandlery	10071	Depth on the vein of —— ft.
Chanfaina	10072	Ore entirely worked out to a depth of
Chanflon ...	10073	Ore increases in value with depth
Changeant	10074	Ore diminishes in value with depth
Changeful	10075	Our present plant will only carry us down another —— ft. in
Changement	10076	Present depth is [depth
Changote ...	10077	This will mean a depth of
Chanoine ...	10078	This will give a depth of —— ft. on the vein
Chantar ...	10079	The depth on the vein is
Chantrerie	10080	At what depth do you intend
Chanza ...	10081	At a greater depth
Chansoneta	10082	At what depth am I (are we) to
Chaonides	10083	In order to prove whether it is persistent in depth
Chaos ...	10084	Depth of the shaft is
Chaotisch...	10085	Depth of the winze is
Chapadanza	10086	Depth of the winze below the level is

Chapado ...	10087	Depth sunk during the past week is —— ft.
Chapaleta	10088	Present workings only extend to a depth of —— ft.
Chapear ...	10089	To a depth of
Chapeliere	10090	To a total depth of —— ft.
Chapelina	10091	Sinking must be continued to a depth of at least —— ft.
Chapelo ...	10092	What is the depth sunk during the past —— days
Chapeta ...	10093	What is the depth of
Chapinazo	10094	What is the depth on the vein
Chapineria	10095	What is the depth of —— shaft
Chapinito ...	10096	What is the depth of winze
Chaplaincy	10097	What is the depth of winze below the —— level
Chaple ...	10098	Vertical depth
Chapman ...	10099	What is the average depth
Chapodar ...	10100	The average depth is
Chaponneau	10101	**Derrick**
Chapotear...	10102	**Describe**
Chapuceria	10103	To describe
Chapurrar	10104	Describe situation to
Chapuz ...	10105	Briefly describe
Chapuzar ...	10106	**Description**
Chaqueta ...	10107	Require more precise description
Chaquira ...	10108	Description misleading
Charabanc	10109	Description untrue
Characatus	10110	If according to description, very valuable
Charadrio ...	10111	Include short description of —— in your report
Charanchas	10112	Full description mailed
Charancon	10113	Of similar description to last
Charaxavi	10114	Of better description than the last
Charbonne	10115	Cable short description of
Charca ...	10116	Send full description and particulars of
Charcanas	10117	**Descriptive**
Charcoso ...	10118	Descriptive report
Charcutier	10119	**Desert**
Chariftia ...	10120	An alkali desert
Chariot ...	10121	Surrounding country is practically a desert
Charioteer	10122	**Desirable**
Charitable	10123	Very desirable
Charivari ...	10124	Is it desirable to
Charlador	10125	Not at all desirable at present
Charlante...	10126	By no means desirable
Charlantin	10127	Do you think it desirable to
Charlar ...	10128	It is very desirable that (to)
Charlatan...	10129	It is very desirable that no time be lost
Charleria ...	10130	In case this is not desirable, please suggest alternative(s)
Charmilla...	10131	Why do you think it is not desirable
Charming...	10132	**Desire**
Charnecal...	10133	What do you desire
Charnela ...	10134	What does —— desire
Charnure ...	10135	My (our) desire is
Charogne ...	10136	——'s desire is
Charol ...	10137	At the express desire of
Charolista...	10138	**Desired**
Charquillo	10139	Leaves nothing to be desired
Charrada ...	10140	Leaves much to be desired
Charretera	10141	Very much desired by
Charrette ...	10142	**Desirous**
Charroyer	10143	Seems very desirous
Chartarum	10144	Does not seem at all desirous
Chartist ...	10145	Suspect —— is desirous of
Chartreuse	10146	Do not suspect —— is at all desirous of

Chartulam	10147	**Despatch(es)** (*See also* "Letters," "Reports.")
Charwoche	10148	Despatch necessary
Chasquido	10149	Despatch in
Chasquista	10150	In a despatch from
Chassieux...	10151	In an official despatch
Chassoir ...	10152	Pending receipt of further despatches
Chastening	10153	In a confidential despatch from
Chastity ...	10154	Despatch received
Chataigne...	10155	Despatch not received
Chateau ...	10156	To despatch
Chatelaine	10157	Do not despatch unless
Chatiment	10158	There must be no uncertainty with regard to despatch of
Chaton ...	10159	Cannot despatch before
Chatoyant...	10160	Can despatch within next —— days
Chattemite	10161	Despatch (——) immediately (to ——)
Chatterie ...	10162	Hope to despatch at least —— tons this month
Chaudiere...	10163	Hope to despatch at least —— tons during —— month
Chauffage...	10164	Within what time could you despatch
Chauffeuse	10165	With the utmost despatch
Chauffoir ...	10166	You had better not despatch before
Chaulage ...	10167	**Despatched** (*See also* "Mailed.")
Chaussee ...	10168	Already despatched
Chaussette	10169	Not yet despatched
Chaveta ...	10170	Should be despatched not later than
Chavirer ...	10171	Cannot be despatched before
Chavonis ...	10172	Despatched before
Chazador ...	10173	Despatched to-day
Cheating ...	10174	Despatched on
Checkmate	10175	Despatched yesterday
Cheekbone	10176	Will be despatched to-morrow
Cheerfully	10177	**Destination**
Cheerless ...	10178	What is the next destination of
Cheese ...	10179	Destination is believed to be
Cheeserind	10180	Destination uncertain
Cheles ...	10181	Destination must be kept secret
Chelidonia	10182	Has (have) not arrived at destination
Chelidro ...	10183	My next destination will be
Chelin ...	10184	Reached destination quite well
Chelonite ...	10185	Telegraph destination as soon as possible
Chemiker ...	10186	What is your next destination
Chemisette	10187	**Destroy(ed)** (*See also* "Burnt," "Damages.")
Chemisier...	10188	Destroyed by tempest
Chenapan	10189	—— destroyed, but no lives lost
Cheneviere	10190	—— destroyed and —— lives lost
Chentunque	10191	Everything destroyed
Cheppia ...	10192	Have been destroyed by
Cheramites	10193	How was it (were they) destroyed
Chercheur	10194	Destroyed by fire
Chercuto ...	10195	Was (were) not totally destroyed
Cheremia ...	10196	Accidentally destroyed
Cherica ...	10197	Which has destroyed the greater part of
Chericile ...	10198	Nothing destroyed
Chericuzzo	10199	Practically destroyed
Cherisher ...	10200	Quite destroyed
Cherminale	10201	Quite destroyed through (from)
Chermisino	10202	The value destroyed amounts to
Cherry ...	10203	What is the value destroyed
Chersoneso	10204	Entirely destroyed by —— on ——
Cherubin ...	10205	**Details** (*See also* "Complete.")
Chessboard	10206	Further details required

Chestnut ...	10207	Further details will follow
Chetamente	10208	Cable full details
Chetare ...	10209	Should you require more details
Chetiche ...	10210	Do you (does ——) require more details
Chetone ...	10211	Do(es) not require more details
Cheunque	10212	When can you mail further details as to
Cheurron ...	10213	Mail further details respecting
Chevalerie	10214	Apply to —— for all details
Chevaline ...	10215	Full details already mailed
Chevaucher	10216	Full details will be sent by next mail
Cheveaux ...	10217	Full details will be mailed within —— days
Chevelure...	10218	It will be necessary to send full details as to
Chevreau ...	10219	You had better examine promptly into all details
Chevreuil ...	10220	Have gone minutely into all the details of
Chevronado	10221	Send particulars, giving details and cost
Chevrotant	10222	Have had no time to go minutely into details
Chevrotine	10223	Full details are contained in
Chiabello ...	10224	Details will be sent later
Chiaito ...	10225	**Detain**
Chiamante	10226	To detain
Chiamarsi...	10227	Detain only
Chiamatore	10228	Shall I (we) detain
Chiantare ...	10229	Detain if you consider proper to do so
Chiappato...	10230	You may detain —— (him)
Chiappola ..	10231	Can I (we) detain —— until
Chiar ...	10232	Is this (it) likely to detain you
Chiarata ...	10233	Must not detain
Chiarella ...	10234	This may detain me (us)
Chiarezza ...	10235	This will not detain me (us)
Chiarino ...	10236	This will detain me (us)
Chiarore ...	10237	Threaten(s) to detain
Chiassata ...	10238	Why does —— detain the documents
Chiasse ...	10239	**Detained**
Chiatto ...	10240	Detained by sickness
Chiavaccia	10241	Detained by —— ; will write
Chiavarda	10242	Detained by
Chiavello ...	10243	Am (are) only detained through
Chiaverina	10244	Am (are) detained in consequence of
Chiavicone	10245	Am (is) still detained
Chibalete ...	10246	Not detained
Chibato ...	10247	Has (have) been detained —— days through (by)
Chibetero ...	10248	Has (have) been detained
Chicada ...	10249	How much longer are you likely to be detained
Chicalote ...	10250	Shall be detained a further —— days
Chicanerie	10251	Which (this) has detained
Chicaniren	10252	Will probably be detained —— days
Chicarrero	10253	Shall be detained here —— days owing to
Chiccheria	10254	Detained by quarantine regulations
Chicha ...	10255	**Detention**
Chicharra...	10256	Cause of detention is
Chichisveo	10257	Cause of detention unknown
Chichon ...	10258	Detention is caused by
Chichonera	10259	What is causing detention
Chichota ...	10260	Detention may last until
Chicken ...	10261	Anticipate detention will last until
Chickweed	10262	Do not anticipate any detention
Chicolear ...	10263	Endeavour to prevent any chance of detention
Chicoria ...	10264	Is there any chance of detention
Chicuelo ...	10265	There is no chance of detention
...lere ...	10266	In case of detention

Chiedibile...	10267	Reason of detention is
Chieditore	10268	Will endeavour to prevent any chance of detention

Determine

Chieftain ...	10269	
Chieggia ...	10270	To determine
Chien ...	10271	How long will it be before you determine
Chiendent...	10272	Shall be able to determine within the next —— days
Chieresia ...	10273	As soon as I (we) can determine
Chiericale ...	10274	As soon as you (they) are able to determine
Chierico ...	10275	Please determine whether
Chiesino ...	10276	You should determine which is the best course to pursue
Chiesuccia	10277	How long will it take you to determine
Chiffonner	10278	In order to determine

Determined

Chiffreur ...	10279	
Chifla ...	10280	Must be speedily determined
Chifladera	10281	Shall be determined
Chiflete ...	10282	Now that I (we) have determined
Chiflido ...	10283	Have unanimously determined to
Chiglia ...	10284	Will be determined within the next —— days
Chignon ...	10285	Cannot be determined at present

Detonators

Chilblain ...	10286	
Childbirth	10287	Box(es) of detonators
Childhood	10288	Detonators suitable for
Childless ...	10289	Electric detonators
Chiliade ...	10290	Have you shipped the detonators
Chilidro ...	10291	Detonators not yet shipped
Chillado ...	10292	Detonators were shipped on
Chilleras ...	10293	Detonators will be shipped on
Chilliness ...	10294	Send treble detonators
Chiloso ...	10295	Send quadruple detonators
Chimaera ...	10296	Send quintuple detonators
Chimenea...	10297	Send sextuple detonators
Chimerical	10298	Forward promptly —— detonators for firing dynamite
Chimerique	10299	Forward promptly —— detonators strong enough to fire [gelatine dynamite
Chimico ...	10300	Forward promptly —— detonators strong enough to fire [blasting gelatine
Chimneypot	10301	Forward promptly —— single force high-tension electric [detonators with insulated wires; latter —— feet long
Chinarinde	10302	Forward promptly —— double force high-tension electric [detonators with insulated wires; latter —— feet long
Chinarro ...	10303	Forward promptly —— treble force high-tension electric [detonators with insulated wires; latter —— feet long
Chinateado	10304	Forward promptly —— single force low-tension electric [detonators with each wire —— feet long
Chinaware	10305	Forward promptly —— double force low-tension electric [detonators with each wire —— feet long
Chinche ...	10306	Forward promptly —— treble force low-tension electric [detonators with each wire —— feet long
Chinchilla	10307	Forward promptly —— electric detonators suitable for blasting [in very wet ground, preferably low-tension, with insulated [wires —— feet long
Chinchoso	10308	Forward promptly —— feet fine insulated wire for connecting [detonators

Detrimental

Chinela ...	10309	
Chinevole...	10310	Examination would be detrimental
Chinless ...	10311	Decidedly detrimental
Chintuft ...	10312	By no means detrimental

Detritus

Chioccare ...	10313	

Develop

Chioccia ...	10314	
Chiocciola ..	10315	To develop
Chiodato ...	10316	Develop vigorously

Chioderia ...	10317	It is no use to develop
Chiodetto ...	10318	So as to develop
Chiosare ...	10319	So as to develop ore body
Chiosatore	10320	Seems likely to develop into a very valuable property
Chiostra ...	10321	This will enable us to develop
Chiostrino	10322	Would suggest that you develop
Chiotto ...	10323	An outlay of —— would develop sufficient ore to supply the
Chiourme ...	10324	Develop as quickly as possible [mill to its full capacity

Developed (*See also* " Capable.")

Chiovatura	10325	
Chiovello ...	10326	Developed by
Chipoter ...	10327	Is a well-developed property
Chiquero ...	10328	Developed well
Chiragrato	10329	Developed poorly
Chiragre ...	10330	Can only be developed
Chiragrice	10331	Could be easily and cheaply developed by
Chiribitil ...	10332	Is developed sufficiently to justify
Chirigaita...	10333	Now being developed
Chirimia ...	10334	To be developed at your cost
Chirimoya	10335	Mine is practically undeveloped
Chirinola ...	10336	Cannot be satisfactorily developed from present shaft

Development(s)

Chirintana	10337	
Chiripa ...	10338	What is your general plan for future development
Chirografo	10339	Plan of development
Chirology ...	10340	Development of the mine
Chiromante	10341	More development work must be done
Chirrido ...	10342	Developments have disclosed
Chirurgie ...	10343	Ought to provide at least —— for the development of the pro- [perty
Chischas ...	10344	Cost of development
Chisciare ..	10345	The development(s) consist(s) of
Chiselling...	10346	The only development(s) is (are)
Chisguete...	10347	Recent developments
Chismar ...	10348	Will undertake to spend —— per month on developments
Chismeador	10349	Must undertake to spend —— per month on developments
Chismoso ...	10350	Owing to new developments
Chispear ...	10351	From our new development
Chispero ...	10352	All development works were stopped for want of funds
Chistera ...	10353	Developments on the lode
Chita ...	10354	Developments unsatisfactory
Chitarra ...	10355	Developments do not justify present rate of extraction
Chiticalla ...	10356	In order to continue developments
Chitinous ...	10357	Present developments justify further advance in shares
Chiudenda	10358	Present developments do not justify present price
Chiudere ...	10359	Present developments fully justify
Chiunque ...	10360	Recent developments mean an increase of —— tons of ore in [reserve
Chiurlare ...	10361	Recent developments increase our reserve by —— tons, approxi-
Chiurlo ...	10362	Recent developments justify our increasing [mate value ——
Chiusino ...	10363	Developments fully justify
Chiusura ...	10364	Developments do not justify
Chivalrous	10365	Developments do not justify the price asked
Chlamydata	10366	Recent developments have not added to value of property
Chlamydis	10367	Developments do not justify you in expecting immediate [dividends
Chloral ...	10368	Developments justify price asked
Chloreum....	10369	Important developments expected daily
Chlorion ...	10370	Developments have not justified anticipations
Chlorkalk	10371	There is no improvement in any of our developments
Chlorodyne	10372	I (we) have not made any critical examination of developments
Chloroform	10373	Do present developments justify the erection of
Chlorose ...	10374	Present developments do not warrant
caspitem	10375	Developments fully warrant
ador ...	10376	If present developments should warrant

Chocallo ...	10377	There are not sufficient developments to justify
Chocante ...	10378	If offer is not accepted stop all developments
Chocarrear	10379	Have instructed —— to stop all developments
Chochera ...	10380	Report as soon as possible on latest developments
Chochin ...	10381	Systematic developments
Chocilla ...	10382	There is undoubtedly a considerable quantity of ore, but the [developments made do not admit of estimating reserves
Chocolate...	10383	From present developments done
Chode ...	10384	What is the (your) estimate for development works in order
Chofero ...	10385	**Devonian** [to supply the mill to its full capacity
Chofeta ...	10386	**Diagonal**
Chofista ...	10387	In a diagonal line
Choisir ...	10388	Draw a diagonal line from —— to ——
Choleric ...	10389	On the north side of a diagonal line connecting —— and ——
Cholerique	10390	On the south side of a diagonal line connecting —— and ——
Choncar ...	10391	On the east side of a diagonal line connecting —— and ——
Chondros ...	10392	On the west side of a diagonal line connecting —— and ——
Chopine ...	10393	**Diagonally**
Choquant ...	10394	Drawn diagonally
Choque ...	10395	**Dial** (*See also* "Level," "Survey," "Theodolite.")
Choragorum	10396	To dial
Choraltar ...	10397	Must dial
Choramte ...	10398	Shall commence to dial
Choranles ...	10399	Must be competent to dial
Chorcha ...	10400	Is competent to dial
Chordam ...	10401	**Dialler** (*See also* "Surveyor.")
Chordienst	10402	Have engaged a dialler
Chorhemd	10403	Dialler's work incorrect
Choricero ...	10404	Dialler's work correct
Chorister ...	10405	**Dialling** (*See also* "Surveying.")
Choriza ...	10406	Result of dialling shows
Chorreado	10407	Entire absence of dialling
Chorrera ...	10408	Through want of proper dialling
Chorretada	10409	Now engaged dialling
Chorrillo ...	10410	As soon as the dialling is complete
Chorrock ...	10411	**Diameter**
Chotar ...	10412	The diameter is
Chotuno ...	10413	What is the diameter
Choucronte	10414	—— inches in diameter
Chouette ...	10415	—— feet diameter [" Drills," &c.)
Chowder ...	10416	**Diamond(s)** (*See also* "Blueground," "Carbons," "Core,"
Chozna ...	10417	Black diamonds or bort
Chozuela ...	10418	Diamonds sold have realized ——
Chretien ...	10419	Diamonds discovered at ——; weight —— carats; estimated
Christtag ...	10420	Parcel of diamonds [value ——
Chromatic	10421	The diamond market
Chromibus	10422	The diamonds occur along with
Chromotype	10423	There is a rumour that diamonds have been found at
Chronicle ...	10424	Loads of "blue" hauled ——; loads of "blue" washed ——; [value of diamonds produced ——
Chronique	10425	Loads of "blue" hauled ——; loads of reef hauled ——; loads [of "blue" washed ——. Revenue expenditure ——;
Chronology	10426	Diamond drill(s) [capital expenditure ——
Chrysalis ...	10427	Diamond drill-hole(s)
Chubarba...	10428	Diamond drill-plant
Chubasco ...	10429	Diamond drill-core(s)
Chucallo ...	10430	What is the depth of diamond drill-hole
Chuchero ...	10431	Present depth of diamond drill-hole No. —— is —— feet
Chuchoteur	10432	What diameter of core is given by diamond drill
Chuchumeco	10433	Diamond drill gives a core —— inches in diameter

Chuchurrar	10434	Diamond drill has located ore body
Chuecazo ...	10435	Have drilled with diamond drill —— feet ; no mineral disclosed
Chufar ...	10436	Have abandoned diamond drill hole No. —— (at ——)
Chufleta ...	10437	Prospect with diamond drill
Chufletero	10438	Prospecting with diamond drill
Chulada ...	10439	**Did**
Chuleria ...	10440	Did you
Chulillo ...	10441	Did I
Chulo ...	10442	Did I not
Chumacera	10443	Did he (they)
Chumbo ...	10444	Did he (they) say anything about
Chupadero	10445	I (we) did
Chupativo	10446	Did not
Chupetin ...	10447	I (we) did not
Chupona ...	10448	Why did you not
Church ...	10449	Why did you (they)
Churchyard	10450	When did you (they)
Churfurst ..	10451	What did he (you) (they) do
Churlish ...	10452	They did not
Churningly	10453	Certainly never did so
Churra ...	10454	It is asserted that you did
Churretada	10455	Did you do anything about
Churriento	10456	Did they do anything about
Churrupear	10457	Did you get there in time (to)
Churrus ...	10458	Did not get there in time (to)
Churrusco	10459	**Die** (*See also* " Dead," " Death.")
Churumo ...	10460	What did —— die of, and when
Churwurde	10461	**Died** (*See also* " Accident.")
Chuscada ...	10462	Died at
Chutney ...	10463	Died on —— of —— at ——
Chuzazo ...	10464	Died suddenly on —— of
Chuzon ..	10465	Died at —— of —— at —— ; telegraph (cable) instructions
Chyle ...	10466	Regret to tell you that —— died on —— of ——
Chylismam	10467	**Differ**
Ciabatta ...	10468	To differ
Ciaboya ...	10469	Should you differ
Ciaccona ...	10470	Do not differ
Ciaescurre	10471	Did not differ
Cialda ...	10472	Differ with
Cialdetta ...	10473	Differ with you
Cialdonajo	10474	How much do we (you) differ by
Cialtrone ...	10475	I (we) differ from you by
Ciambella...	10476	**Difference**
Ciampicare	10477	The difference is
Ciancetta ...	10478	There is no difference
Cianciare ...	10479	Is the difference in my favour
Ciancioso ...	10480	Difference in my favour
Cianciume	10481	Difference in your favour
Cianco ...	10482	The difference between
Cianfarda	10483	What is the difference between
Ciangolare	10484	What makes this difference
Cianquear	10485	A very material difference
Ciappola ...	10486	What does the difference actually amount to
Ciaramella	10487	Are you (they) willing to split the difference
Ciarlante ...	10488	Is —— (he) willing to split the difference
Ciarlatano	10489	Willing to split the difference
Ciarlatore	10490	Not willing to split the difference
Ciarleria ...	10491	Will split the difference with you (them)
Ciarlone ...	10492	Cannot consent to split the difference with you (them)
Ciarpame ...	10493	Endeavour to arrange the difference

Ciarpiere ...	10494	Difference as to assays
Ciascuno ...	10495	Difference as to weights
Cibaccio ..	10496	It will mean a difference of
Cibale ...	10497	Is there any difference between
Cibalita ...	10498	The difference to be paid by
Cibamento	10499	The difference to be divided between
Cibarsi ...	10500	There is a large difference
Cibatum ...	10501	Will there be any difference
Cibazione ...	10502	Will it (this) make any difference
Cibdeliore...	10503	**Different**
Cibdelum ...	10504	Altogether different
Cibeleo ...	10505	Not at all different
Cibera ...	10506	Details are different [of ——
Cibicon ...	10507	Actual state of affairs is altogether different to the report
Ciborio ...	10508	**Difficult**
Ciboulette	10509	Not at all difficult
Cicadas ...	10510	Very difficult
Cicalaccia...	10511	Would it be difficult to
Cicalante ...	10512	It would not be difficult to
Cicalatore...	10513	It would be difficult to
Cicaleria ...	10514	Question is difficult to answer by wire; am writing fully
Cicaliccio ...	10515	**Difficulty(ies)**
Cicalone ...	10516	Any difficulty
Cicatear ...	10517	Great difficulty
Cicatrice ...	10518	No difficulty with
Cicatrizal ...	10519	In case of any difficulty
Ciocantona	10520	In case of any difficulty apply to
Ciochera ...	10521	Difficulty removed entirely
Ciceon ...	10522	Do you anticipate any difficulty
Cicerbita ...	10523	If any difficulty as to (in)
Cicercha ...	10524	—— is (are) reported to be in difficulties
Cicerem ...	10525	Have you (has ——→) met with any difficulty(ies)
Ciceribus ...	10526	What is your difficulty
Cicerone ...	10527	My (our) difficulty is
Cichino ...	10528	Affair is beset with difficulties
Cichorie ...	10529	There is great difficulty in working the mine owing to
Cicigna ...	10530	Will have no difficulty
Cicilaon ...	10531	Will have some difficulty
Cicilendro...	10532	I (we) shall be able to get out of the difficulty
Cicisbeare...	10533	I (we) do not expect any difficulty with
Cicisbeo ...	10534	Can you devise any means of getting over the difficulty
Ciclamino	10535	Cannot devise any means at present of getting over the difficulty
Ciclan ...	10536	Cannot devise any other means of getting over the difficulty
Cicloide ...	10537	Presents an insurmountable difficulty
Ciclopes ...	10538	Endeavour to overcome difficulty at once
Cicognino...	10539	Will be the first difficulty to overcome
Ciconiarum	10540	What difficulties are there in the way
Ciconinos ...	10541	The only difficulties are
Cicotuda ...	10542	There are no special difficulties in the way
Cicurating	10543	Great difficulty with —— (him)
Cicuta ...	10544	**Dig**
Cicutaria ...	10545	To dig
Cidonium ...	10546	**Diggers** (*See also* "Prospectors.")
Cidral ...	10547	Gold diggers
Cidronela ...	10548	Diggers' licences
Ciechesco ...	10549	In order to induce diggers
Ciechita ...	10550	Diggers demand
Ciecolina ...	10551	There are now —— diggers prospecting
Ciegamente	10552	There are no diggers prospecting
Cieguecico	10553	Diggers have abandoned claims at

Cielo	10554	Diggers at —— have met with encouraging results
Cienaga	10555	Diggers very much discouraged
Cientanal	10556	Diggers refuse terms offered
Ciente	10557	What terms do diggers require
Cientifico	10558	Diggers will only work on the following terms
Cientopies	10559	**Diggings**
Cierertis	10560	Gold diggings
Cierna	10561	At the diggings
Cierto	10562	Diggings are deserted
Ciferista	10563	Diggings are flourishing
Cigarra	10564	**Dilapidated** (*See also* "Buildings," "Condition.")
Cigarrista	10565	The whole place is totally dilapidated
Cigatera	10566	**Diligence**
Ciglia	10567	Exercise the greatest diligence
Ciglione	10568	Has (have) exercised the greatest diligence
Cigliuto	10569	Did not exercise sufficient diligence
Cignatura	10570	Have you (has ——) exercised diligence
Cignere	10571	**Dimensions** (*See also* "By.")
Cigoglio	10572	Dimensions of
Cigolare	10573	Dimensions are
Cigonino	10574	What are the dimensions of
Cigonuela	10575	Cable external dimensions of
Ciguatera	10576	The external dimensions are
Ciguente	10577	Cable internal dimensions of
Cigulo	10578	The internal dimensions are
Cigzaque	10579	Dimensions are, long ——; wide ——; deep ——
Cilavegna	10580	Please cable dimensions of
Cilecca	10581	Please cable dimensions of largest piece
Ciliary	10582	Cannot send dimensions at present
Cilibantos	10583	Will send dimensions as soon as can ascertain
Ciliccino	10584	These dimensions must not be exceeded
Cilicio	10585	Cable dimensions in the clear of shaft and present depth
Ciliegia	10586	Dimensions of the shaft within timbers are —— × ——; the [present depth is —— ft.
Cilimonia	10587	**Diminish**
Cilindrico	10588	Endeavour to diminish expenses
Cillazgo	10589	You must diminish expenses
Cillement	10590	**Diorite**
Cillerero	10591	Diorite dyke
Cillibas	10592	Diorite country
Ciloma	10593	A bar of diorite
Cimacio	10594	**Dip(s)**
Cimare	10595	Dip of
Cimarron	10596	What is the dip of
Cimatore	10597	Dips into
Cimatura	10598	Dips to the
Cimbalaria	10599	Dips towards
Cimbalillo	10600	Following the dip
Cimbellare	10601	The dip of the strata
Cimberli	10602	The lode (vein) (reef) dips at an angle of —— degrees
Cimborio	10603	Do dip and direction agree with
Cimbottolo	10604	Dip and direction
Cimbrado	10605	Incline shaft dips at an angle of —— degrees with the horizon
Cimbreno	10606	Shaft dips at an angle of —— degrees from the perpendicular
Cimbronazo	10607	**Dipping**
Cimentador	10608	Is dipping out
Cimentarsi	10609	Is dipping into
Cimentiere	10610	Is dipping out of the shaft
Cimento	10611	Is dipping into the shaft
Cimerio	10612	**Direct** (*See also* "Address.")
Cimeter	10613	Direct to

Cimice ...	10614	Direct from
Cimicione ..	10615	Direct acting
Cimitarra ...	10616	Please direct that
Cimiterio ...	10617	Cannot go direct to —— op account of
Cimitic ...	10618	Come direct to —— at earliest moment possible
Cimmerian	10619	Proceed direct to —— at earliest possible moment
Cimmurro	10620	Direct all letters to the care of —— at ——
Cimorra ...	10621	Direct all letters to the —— hotel at ——
Cinabrese ...	10622	Direct all telegrams to the care of —— at ——
Cinamomina	10623	Direct all telegrams to the hotel —— at ——
Cincelador	10624	Intend to proceed direct to ——
Cincelito ...	10625	You had better direct —— to
Cinchadura	10626	**Directed**
Cinchera ...	10627	Was (were) directed to
Cinchona ...	10628	Directed to
Cinchuela..	10629	Will act as directed
Cinciglio ...	10630	**Direction(s)**
Cincinno ...	10631	What directions have you given as regards
Cincischio ...	10632	Have given the following directions
Cincoañal...	10633	Have not given any directions
Cinctorem	10634	In each direction
Cincuenta...	10635	What is the direction of
Cincuesma	10636	The direction of the vein is
Cinder ...	10637	In the same direction
Cinderpath	10638	It is not in the same direction as
Cineraire ...	10639	Is it in the same direction as
Cinereo ...	10640	Send immediately tracing showing direction of lode
Cinerizio ...	10641	**Directors** (*See also* "Board of Directors.")
Cingebant...	10642	Directors consider it vital
Cinghio ...	10643	Directors are opposed to
Cingladura	10644	By order of the directors
Cinhiaja ...	10645	At a directors' meeting
Cinife ...	10646	At a directors' meeting held on —— it was resolved as follows
Ciniglia ...	10647	At a directors' meeting held to day it was decided to
Cinismo ...	10648	Directors decline
Cinnamon...	10649	Advise the directors to acquire
Cinocefalo	10650	Do you advise the directors to acquire
Cinoglosa ...	10651	The directors suggest that
Cinosura ...	10652	Directors adhere to telegram of
Cinquante	10653	Directors will not be responsible
Cinquedea	10654	**Dirt.** (*See also* "Alluvial," "Hydraulic.")
Cinquefoil	10655	Wash dirt
Cinquemila	10656	Pay dirt
Cinquieme	10657	Now washing —— tons of pay dirt per day
Cintadero ...	10658	Now raising —— tons of pay dirt per day
Cintagorda	10659	**Disabled**
Cintajos ...	10660	Disabled through (by)
Cintarazo ...	10661	—— of the staff are disabled by
Cinteado ...	10662	Quite disabled
Cintolino ...	10663	Will be disabled at least ——
Cintonchio	10664	**Disappoint**
Cintrel ...	10665	To disappoint
Cinturero ...	10666	Do not disappoint
Cinturetta	10667	Will not disappoint
Cinzas ...	10668	Try not to disappoint me (us)
Ciocchetta	10669	**Disappointed**
Cioccolato...	10670	Much disappointed that
Cioccuto ...	10671	Am (are) much disappointed at (with)
Ciomperia	10672	Disappointed at slowness
Cioncare ...	10673	Disappointed that you have (—— has) not done more

Ciondolare	10674	**Disappointing**
Cioppetta ...	10675	Result is very disappointing
Ciotolone ...	10676	Trial is very disappointing
Ciottare ...	10677	Yield is very disappointing
Ciottolato ...	10678	Figures are very disappointing
Ciovetta ...	10679	**Disappointment**
Cipigliare...	10680	Has (have) caused great disappointment
Cipiglioso...	10681	Suffering from very severe disappointment
Cipion	10682	**Disburse** (*See also* " Expenses," " Pay.")
Cipolla ...	10683	To disburse
Cipolletta ...	10684	Refuses to disburse
Cipollino ...	10685	**Disbursement(s)**
Cipresal ...	10686	Disbursements to date
Cipressino...	10687	Disbursements are heavy
Ciprigna ...	10688	Disbursements are light
Ciragra ...	10689	Disbursements are too heavy
Circense ...	10690	Disbursements this month amount to
Circoletto ...	10691	Disbursements last month amounted to
Circolo ...	10692	Draw on account of disbursements up to ——
Circoncire...	10693	Draw upon me at seven days' sight for any disbursements
Circondato	10694	Draw upon me at —— days' sight for any disbursements
Circonfuso	10695	Will repay any disbursements
Circuitous	10696	What have been your (——'s) disbursements for
Circulaire...	10697	What have been your (——'s) total disbursements since
Circulante	10698	What have been your (——'s) disbursements on account of
Circulato ...	10699	To repay disbursements
Circumdar	10700	**Discharge**
Circumflex	10701	To discharge
Circumvent	10702	Notice to discharge
Ciregeto ...	10703	Do not discharge
Cirial ...	10704	Discharge entire force
Cirindone...	10705	Cannot discharge men before
Ciromanzia	10706	Cannot discharge the workmen until wages are paid
Cirque ...	10707	Discharge as quickly as possible
Cirroso ...	10708	Discharge all the hands not absolutely needed
Cirugico ...	10709	Give all hands immediate notice of discharge except ——
Cirujano ...	10710	Do not discharge —— until arrival of ——
Cirurgia ...	10711	Do not discharge —— until you have received our letter dated
Cisaille ...	10712	Have been obliged to discharge —— for [——
Cisalpine ...	10713	Shall gradually discharge
Ciscranna..	10714	You may discharge or retain —— (him) ; whichever you think
Ciseleur ...	10715	**Discharged** [best
Cismatico ...	10716	Discharged on
Cismontano	10717	Discharged by
Cispardo ...	10718	Has (have) been discharged for
Cisposita ...	10719	Was (were) discharged for
Cissidem ...	10720	Are all the hands paid and discharged
Cistam ...	10721	All unnecessary hands were paid and discharged on
Cistarum ...	10722	What number of hands have you discharged
Cistel ...	10723	Have discharged —— hands
Cistellula ...	10724	All debts discharged
Cisternica...	10725	What amount of debts have you discharged
Cistifera ...	10726	**Discharging**
Cistotomia	10727	Whilst discharging
Cistulae ...	10728	Discharging force
Citacion ...	10729	Now discharging cargo at
Citadel ...	10730	As soon as finished discharging
Citadine ...	10731	**Disclose**
Citaredo ...	10732	To disclose
Citarista ...	10733	Do not disclose

Citateur ...	10734	Shall I (we) disclose
Citatibus ...	10785	**Disconnect**
Citatorio ...	10736	To disconnect
Citerieur ...	10737	**Disconnected**
Citharas ...	10738	Entirely disconnected
Citharista...	10739	Has (have) been disconnected
Citharizam	10740	Said to be disconnected
Citissime ...	10741	**Discontinue**
Citizen ...	10742	To discontinue
Citolero ...	10743	When did you (——) discontinue the (it) (this)
Citoribus ...	10744	Discontinue sinking
Citoyen ...	10745	**Discontinued**
Citracca ...	10746	Discontinued on
Citraggine	10747	Has (have) been discontinued since ——
Citrate ...	10748	Must be discontinued
Citrine ...	10749	Now discontinued
Citrinezza...	10750	Why have you (has ——) discontinued
Citriuolo ...	10751	Was (were) discontinued owing to
Citronnal ..	10752	Should be discontinued
Citronnier...	10753	Discontinue work on
Citrouille ...	10754	I (we) have discontinued it (this)
Cittadella ...	10755	I (we) have discontinued the following points
Cittadino ...	10756	**Discount**
Cittadone ...	10757	Discount the
Cittola ...	10758	Can discount
Ciudad ...	10759	Cannot discount
Ciudadano	10760	Do not (will not) allow any discount
Ciuffagno ...	10761	Have been discounted at a cost of
Ciuffetto ...	10762	No discount allowed
Ciuffole ...	10763	—— per cent. discount allowed for cash
Ciurmadore	10764	Rate of discount
Ciurmaglia	10765	Shares can now be obtained at a discount (of)
Ciurmante	10766	Will you discount
Ciurmato ...	10767	**Discounted**
Ciurmeria...	10768	Have you (has ——) discounted
Ciuschero ...	10769	Has (have) discounted
Civanzare...	10770	Has (have) not discounted
Civanzo ...	10771	**Discourage**
Civetta ...	10772	To discourage
Civetteria ...	10773	Do not discourage
Civettino ...	10774	Discourage all efforts to
Civettuola	10775	**Discouraged**
Civilibus ...	10776	Not at all discouraged
Civilista ...	10777	Discouraged by
Civility ...	10778	Do not be discouraged
Civilizer ...	10779	**Discouraging** (*See also* "Appearance," "Aspect.")
Civilmente	10780	Report is very discouraging
Civismo ...	10781	Letter(s) to hand is (are) very discouraging
Civitatem	10782	Results are very discouraging
Civorio ...	10783	Present condition of affairs is very discouraging
Cizalla ...	10784	**Discover**
Clabandage	10785	To discover
Clabaudeur	10786	Hope(s) to discover
Clairement	10787	Has (have) been unable to discover anything up to the present
Clairiere ...	10788	In case you are (—— is) unable to discover anything
Clamabamur	10789	Try to discover why
Clamador ...	10790	Try and discover what
Clamandum	10791	Should I (we) fail to discover
Clamare ...	10792	**Discovered**
Clamatorem	10793	Discovered by

Clamazione	10794	Discovered on
Clamide ...	10795	Has (have) discovered nothing
Clamitavo...	10796	Have discovered something I believe good
Clamminess	10797	Has (have) recently discovered that
Clamorear...	10798	From what I (we) have discovered
Clamoso ...	10799	Has (have) discovered the
Clampiner ..	10800	Has (have) discovered why
Clams ...	10801	Have you discovered
Clanculum	10802	Has (have) discovered
Clangore ...	10803	Has (have) not yet discovered
Claostra ...	10804	Have you (has ——) discovered anything from
Clapotage...	10805	Has (have) not discovered anything from
Clapoteux ...	10806	Has (have) discovered from —— that
Claquement	10807	Which still remains to be discovered
Claraboya	10808	Has anything been discovered
Claramente	10809	**Discovery(ies)**
Clarear ...	10810	Any discovery
Clarescebo	10811	Is there any discovery of ore
Clarescet ...	10812	New discovery : prospects excellent
Claret ...	10813	Have made a new discovery
Claretcup ...	10814	Have made a new discovery, but prospects as yet uncertain
Claridad ...	10815	Send full particulars as to new discovery
Clarificar ...	10816	Will cable later as to new discovery
Clarify	10817	There is a rumour here of an important discovery (at)
Clarigare ...	10818	It is again rumoured that there is an important discovery (at)
Clarigati ...	10819	Report fully whether you have made any fresh discoveries at
Clarilla ...	10820	It may be premature to attach any considerable importance to
Clarinado ...	10821	**Discrepancy(ies)** [this discovery
Clarinette...	10822	Owing to the discrepancy between —— and ——
Clarionet	10823	What is your (——'s) explanation of the (this) discrepancy
Clarisa ...	10824	Discrepancy is due to
Clarisico ...	10825	Discrepancy is not due to
Clarisona ...	10826	Is discrepancy due to
Clarisonus	10827	There is no discrepancy whatever
Claritas ...	10828	Discrepancy was caused by
Claritatis ...	10829	There must be no discrepancy between —— and ——
Claritudo ...	10830	Should there be any discrepancy
Clarol	10831	Serious discrepancy
Classibus ...	10832	Slight discrepancy
Classical ...	10833	Unless discrepancy is a serious one
Classique ...	10834	**Discretion**
Clathratus	10835	At your (——'s) discretion
Clatrabam	10836	Cannot give discretion
Clatravi ...	10837	At your absolute discretion
Claudastri...	10838	At my (our) absolute discretion
Claudebar	10839	At the discretion of
Claudemus	10840	At my (——'s) discretion
Claudere ...	10841	I (we) have no discretion respecting
Claudicar ...	10842	I (we) leave it entirely to your discretion
Claudicavi	10843	Cannot give requested discretion
Clausola ...	10844	Is there any discretion allowed as to
Claustrum	10845	Left entirely to ——'s (his) discretion
Clausular ...	10846	**Discretionary**
Clausurus...	10847	Discretionary powers
Clavado ...	10848	Require discretionary powers
Clavarium	10849	Give you full discretionary powers
Clavatoris...	10850	Let —— (him) have full discretionary powers
Clavecin ...	10851	**Discriminate**
Clavelina ...	10852	Cannot discriminate
Claveque ...	10853	To discriminate

Clavetear ...	10854	So as to discriminate
Claviatur ...	10855	You must discriminate between
Clavichord	10856	Will discriminate
Clavicle ...	10857	**Disengage(d)**
Clavigero ...	10858	As soon as I am (we are) disengaged
Clawing ...	10859	When will you (——) probably be disengaged
Clayonnage	10860	Expect(s) to be disengaged on or about
Cleaver ...	10861	Not likely to be disengaged before
Cleft ...	10862	**Dish** (See also "Alluvial," "Colour," "Gold," "Hydraulic," &c.)
Clematis ...	10863	Washing dish
Clemencia...	10864	By means of the dish
Clemens ...	10865	A dish of dirt (—— pounds) gives —— grains gold
Clementina	10866	**Dishonest(ly)**
Clemesi ...	10867	Is said to have acted dishonestly
Clepsatis ...	10868	Was proved to have acted dishonestly
Clepseram	10869	Is (are) suspected to have acted dishonestly
Clepsidra ...	10870	Has (have) never been proved to have acted dishonestly
Clepsisti ...	10871	Was accused of having acted dishonestly
Clepturus...	10872	**Disintegration**
Clergyman	10873	**Dislocation**
Clerical ...	10874	**Dismiss** (See also "Discharge.")
Clerigo ...	10875	To dismiss
Clerizonte...	10876	Do not dismiss (——) him
Cleverness	10877	Should you be compelled to dismiss
Clibanario	10878	Was (were) compelled to dismiss —— (him) because of
Clichage ...	10879	Have you decided to dismiss
Clicheur ...	10880	Have decided to dismiss —— (him)
Clientela ...	10881	Have decided not to dismiss —— (him)
Clientship	10882	In case you should decide to dismiss
Clientulo ...	10883	**Dismissed** (See also "Discharged.")
Clignement	10884	Has (have) been dismissed
Clignoter ...	10885	Has (have) not been dismissed
Climatco ...	10886	Was dismissed for ——
Clisaminis	10887	**Dispense(d)**
Clinical ...	10888	To dispense
Clinique ...	10889	Can you dispense with
Clinopodio	10890	Cannot dispense with
Clinquant...	10891	Can be dispensed with
Clipeato ...	10892	Cannot be dispensed with
Cliqueter ...	10893	Has (have) been dispensed with
Cliquettes...	10894	Must be dispensed with
Clistelera ...	10895	Might be able to dispense with —— (it) (if)
Clistere ...	10896	Will be dispensed with for the future
Clitellam ...	10897	**Disposal** (See also "Auction," "Sale.")
Clivosum ...	10898	For disposal
Cloaca ...	10899	Is (are) quite at your (——'s) disposal
Cloacinam	10900	Please hold to my disposal
Cloaking ...	10901	Please hold to disposal of
Cloaque ...	10902	Will be placed at your (——'s) disposal on
Clochel ...	10903	**Dispose**
Clocheton...	10904	So as to dispose of
Clogdance...	10905	This will dispose of
Clogs ...	10906	Dispose of on the best terms you can obtain
Cloitrier ...	10907	Will not dispose of
Cloporte ...	10908	By all means dispose of
Cloquear ...	10909	Better dispose of for the present
Cloris ...	10910	Could you dispose quickly of same
Clothier ...	10911	Endeavour if you can to dispose of it quickly [it (this)
Cloturer ...	10912	Is there any probability of your (——) being able to dispose of
Clouding ...	10913	You have full authority to dispose of the whole

Cloudless ...	10914	Within what time could you (——) dispose of
Clouterie ...	10915	Could dispose of the whole within —— weeks
Clubfeet ...	10916	There is no chance of my (our) being able to dispose of it (them)
Clubiste ...	10917	**Dispute** (*See also* "Action," "Case.") [to advantage
Cluemini ...	10918	The dispute is
Clunibus ...	10919	The dispute was
Clunis ...	10920	Is (are) not in dispute
Clupeas ...	10921	Avoid dispute if possible
Clustery ...	10922	Dispute should be settled before you leave
Clypeate ...	10923	Dispute has been settled
Clysmos ...	10924	Dispute is (has been) settled as to
Clysterem ...	10925	Dispute has arisen with —— as to ——
Coabitare ...	10926	Dispute has arisen between —— and ——
Coaccion ...	10927	Cable (telegraph) what is the dispute
Coaccuse ...	10928	In case of any dispute refer to ——
Coacervare ...	10929	No settlement has as yet been arrived at respecting dispute
Coachman	10930	Settle dispute if possible
Coactoris ...	10931	Unable to settle dispute
Coacusado	10932	What is the precise matter in dispute
Coadjutor ...	10933	Dispute will require to be settled legally
Coadjuvato	10934	What is the prospect of dispute being settled
Coadorabam	10935	There is every prospect the dispute will be settled soon
Coadunar ...	10936	There is no prospect at present of the dispute being settled
Coaedifico...	10937	**Disputed**
Coaeguat ...	10938	Disputed ground
Coaeguavis	10939	Not disputed
Coagente ...	10940	**Dissatisfied**
Coagmento	10941	Am (are) dissatisfied with
Coagolare...	10942	Directors are dissatisfied with
Coagulate...	10943	Is (are) much dissatisfied
Coagulem ...	10944	Shareholders becoming dissatisfied
Coagulo ...	10945	**Disseminated**
Coalabar ...	10946	**Distance**
Coalbox ...	10947	Distance from
Coalition ...	10948	Distance to
Coalnuts ...	10949	Distance off
Coamante...	10950	For a distance of
Coangustas	10951	No great distance
Coapostol ...	10952	Too great a distance
Coaptar ...	10953	Has been extended a further distance of —— feet
Coartabam	10954	What is the distance from
Coartare ...	10955	What is the distance to
Coartativo	10956	What is the distance now driven at
Coassocie ...	10957	What will the distance to be driven approximately be
Coasting ...	10958	The distance to be driven will be
Coattivo ...	10959	Distance from the shaft to
Coaxandum	10960	Distance is no object
Coaxarem ...	10961	At a distance of —— feet
Coaxaturus	10962	At a distance of
Coaxavero	10963	Situated at a distance of
Coazione ...	10964	Distance —— miles from ——
Cobanillo ...	10965	The distance between —— and —— is ——
Cobardear	10966	At what do you estimate distance between —— and ——
Cobbola ...	10967	Estimate the distance at —— feet
Cobdicia ...	10968	The distance is ——
Cobegera ...	10969	What is the distance between
Cobertor ...	10970	The distance between the two points is about —— feet
Cobil ...	10971	For a long distance
Cobranza ...	10972	What is the distance from mine to smelters
Cobreno ...	10973	Distance of mine from smelters is

Cobrir ...	10974	I (we) think it will continue like it is at present some con- [siderable distance further
Cobwebs ...	10975	Within what distance do you expect to reach
Cocarar ...	10976	I (we) estimate the distance still to be driven at —— feet
Coccare ...	10977	I (we) estimate the distance at
Cocchetta ...	10978	What is the distance from —— to intersect ——
Cocchiere ...	10979	What is the distance you have advanced with
Cocchiglia	10980	**Distant**
Cocchina ...	10981	Distant from
Cocchione...	10982	Not the most distant
Cocchuime	10983	To the most distant
Coccinatum	10984	Which (what) is the most distant
Coccinelle...	10985	**Distinct**
Cocciuola ...	10986	Cable (telegraph) distinct instructions
Coccolone ...	10987	Give —— distinct instructions
Coceador ..	10988	Is (are) not sufficiently distinct
Cocedero ...	10989	Quite distinct
Cochambre	10990	The foregoing must be kept quite distinct
Cochenille	10991	**Distinction**
Cocherillo	10992	Draw a sharp distinction between the two
Cochero ...	10993	Draw a sharp distinction between the foregoing
Cochinata...	10994	Draw a sharp distinction between —— and ——
Cochineal ...	10995	**District**
Cochineria	10996	District court
Cochiquera	10997	District rules
Cochlidem	10998	Over the entire district
Cochura ...	10999	Not uncommon in this district
Cocimiento	11000	Situated in the district of
Cocinera ...	**11001**	District contains a plentiful supply of
Cociore ...	11002	District is practically denuded of
Cocitojo ...	11003	**Disturbance(s)**
Cockade ...	11004	There is a serious disturbance here owing to
Cockatoo ...	11005	Do you (does ——) apprehend any disturbance
Cockfight ...	11006	Do(es) not apprehend any disturbance
Cockroach	11007	Serious disturbances are anticipated
Cockscomb	11008	Disturbance not nearly so serious as was anticipated
Cockswain	11009	Disturbance(s) has (have) practically ceased
Cocktail ...	11010	Disturbance(s) has (have) been renewed
Coclearia ...	11011	There is no disturbance at all
Cocobolo ...	11012	Has there been any disturbance
Cocodrilo ...	11013	There has not been any disturbance
Cocoliste ...	11014	There has been a slight disturbance through
Cocollato ...	11015	**Ditch(es)** (See also " Burst," " Canal.")
Cocomerajo	11016	As soon as the necessary ditch(es) is (are) completed
Cocoonery...	11017	Until the necessary ditch(es) has (have) been constructed
Cocosbaum	11018	We have now —— feet of ditches
Cocosnusz	11019	Ditches are much in need of repair
Cocotier ...	11020	Ditches are beyond repairing
Cocotriz ...	11021	How much do you apportion for repair of ditches
Coctanam...	11022	Apportion —— for the repair of ditches
Cocuyo ...	11023	There are —— yards of ditches on the property
Cocuzzelo ...	11024	We could bring in water from —— to the property by means
Codadura ...	11025	Cost of ditch and flumes will amount to [of a ditch
Codardo ..	11026	Owing to the sides of the ditch having given way
Codaste ...	11027	Have commenced to repair breach in the side of the ditch
Codecillar...	11028	Have completed repairs to ditch
Codera ...	11029	When do you expect to finish repairs to ditch
Coderino ...	11030	Hope to finish repairs to ditch within the next —— days
Codiatore ...	11031	Have had to postpone repairs to ditch on account of
Codiciable...	11032	**Ditto**

Codicil ...	11033	**Divide**
Codicioso ...	11034	Divide into equal portions
Codilungo .	11035	To divide
Codimozzo	11036	Do you (does ——) agree to divide equally
Codione ...	11037	Suggest that you divide
Codorniz ...	11038	Will divide any commission
Coeficacia ...	11039	Will you divide
Coefizuela...	11040	Refuse(s) to divide
Coeguale ...	11041	Consent(s) to divide
Coercion ...	11042	Shall I (we) divide
Coercitivo ..	11043	Cannot divide
Coesencia ...	11044	**Divided**
Coesistere...	11045	How do you mean it (this) to be divided
Coestate ...	11046	Divided between
Coetaneo ...	11047	Divided into equal proportions
Coeternida	11048	Divided into
Coeterno ...	11049	Not divided at all
Coexistir ...	11050	Not yet divided
Cofaccia ...	11051	When it is divided
Cofanetto ...	11052	Had better be divided at once
Coffeemill	11053	**Dividend** (*See also* "Bonus.")
Coffeepot ...	11054	Dividend warrant(s)
Coffretier ...	11055	Do not declare too high a dividend
Cofina	11056	Dividend is expected to be at least ——
Cofrade ...	11057	Dividend declared —— per share payable on
Cofrecico ...	11058	Dividend declared of —— free of income tax payable on ——
Cofrero ...	11059	Do you think you (we) are justified in paying a dividend of
Cofundador	11060	Have declared usual dividend [more than ——
Cogedero ...	11061	Not sufficient to pay a dividend
Cogermano	11062	No dividend has been paid since
Cogimiento	11063	Dividend is likely to exceed the last
Cogitable ...	11064	Dividend is not likely to exceed ——
Cogitativo	11065	What dividend is likely to be paid
Coglitore ...	11066	What is the dividend declared
Cognado ...	11067	Expect a dividend of
Cognassier	11068	In order to provide cash for dividend
Cognation	11069	Final dividend for the year
Cognatus ...	11070	Cannot pay any dividend
Cogniac ...	11071	Dividend can be paid on
Cognitio ...	11072	Propose to declare a dividend of
Cogno ...	11073	We want to declare dividend of
Cognombre	11074	Dividend will be declared of
Cognominar	11075	Dividend has been declared of
Cognoscer...	11076	Dividends have been declared amounting to
Cogolaria ...	11077	Dividend has not been earned
Cogollico ...	11078	Have declared a dividend of —— per share payable on
Cogolmar ...	11079	For dividend purposes
Cogotera ...	11080	Cannot declare any dividend this year
Cogujonero	11081	Shall not pay a dividend
Cogulla ...	11082	**Do**
Cogwheel ...	11083	To do
Cohabit ...	11084	Do it
Cohechador	11085	Do not
Coheiress ...	11086	Propose to do this at once
Coheredera	11087	Do better
Coherent ...	11088	Do this if possible
Coheritier...	11089	Will not do at all for
Cohermano	11090	Will do very well for
Cohesion ...	11091	Are you (is ——) likely to do anything with it
Coheteria ...	11092	Can you do anything towards

Cohibir	...	11093	Can you do it (this)
Cohobacion		11094	Can you suggest anything that I (we) can do
Cohombral		11095	Do all you can
Cohonestar		11096	Do as I suggest
Cohorte	...	11097	Do this (it) at once
Coidar		11098	Do this (it) quietly
Coiffeur	...	11099	Do nothing at present
Coincidir	...	11100	Do nothing until (before)
Coitarse	...	11101	Do not do so
Coitoso	...	11102	Suggest that you do nothing at present
Cojaccio	...	11103	Could not make it do
Cojinete	...	11104	Would it be legitimate to do so
Cojitranco		11105	It would not be legitimate to do so
Cojudo	...	11106	What do you advise me to do
Cojugalem		11107	—— will advise you what to do
Colachon	...	11108	What (which) would you like to do
Colactaneo		11109	What more do you want
Coladero	...	11110	I (we) cannot do more than this
Colaggiu	...	11111	Can do nothing more
Colaire	...	11112	Would probably do
Colamento		11113	Would probably do if
Colander	...	11114	**Document(s)** *(See also* " Attested," " Detain," " Executed.")*
Colanilla	...	11115	Tender all documents
Colapez	...	11116	Do not tender the documents
Colascione		11117	Deliver documents
Colateral	...	11118	Deliver documents against
Colation	...	11119	Deliver documents to
Colatojo	...	11120	Deliver the documents to —— if —— concurs
Colatura	...	11121	Do not deliver the documents until (unless)
Colback	...	11122	Documents sent out
Colbertinc		11123	All necessary documents mailed to ——
Colcarsi	...	11124	Have mailed all the necessary documents
Colcedra	...	11125	All documents were forwarded by mail on ——
Colchadura		11126	All copies of documents should be legally certified
Colchero	...	11127	Apply to —— for all necessary documents
Colchonero		11128	Cable (telegraph) whether you have received the documents
Colcotar	...	11129	Documents are all in order
Coldishly	...	11130	Documents are not in order
Colectar	...	11131	Documents received on
Colection	...	11132	Documents not yet received
Colega	...	11133	Endeavour to obtain documents
Colegiado	...	11134	Forward documents at earliest possible date
Coleoptera		11135	What documents do you (does ——) want
Coletaneo	...	11136	Want(s) the following documents
Colewort	...	11137	Following documents necessary in order to prove
Colgadero	...	11138	Document(s) sent not in proper form
Colgajo	...	11139	Send duplicate copies of all documents
Colheita	...	11140	Refuse(s) to deliver documents
Colibeto	...	11141	Send attested copies of documents
Colicano	...	11142	Send me (us) the necessary documents
Colicky	...	11143	Have you received documents
Colicuable		11144	Documents must be returned to
Colicuar	...	11145	Documents to be delivered to
Colicuecer	..	11146	Do not deliver documents
Colidir	...	11147	Documents to be held as security for
Colifero	...	11148	Documents are held subject to
Colifichet	...	11149	Documents to be held subject to
Coligarse	...	11150	Documents will be forwarded by mail on
Colimacon		11151	Documents will follow as soon as possible
Colinabo	...	11152	When will you forward the documents

Colique	...	11153	Who has the necessary documents
Coliseo	...	11154	I (we) have delivered up the documents
Collada	...	11155	—— has (have) delivered up the documents
Collanone	...	11156	—— has (have) not delivered up the documents
Collapsing		11157	—— has (have) all necessary documents
Collarbone		11158	Forward all documents as soon as complete
Collaretto	...	11159	Endeavour to obtain documents
Collarin	...	11160	Get —— to certify officially to the proper execution of docu-
Collarstud		11161	Has (have) drawn upon me and attached documents [ments
Collatable		11162	Has (have) drawn upon me, but has not attached documents
Collatore	...	11163	Proper documents must be attached to
Collegial	...	11164	Proper documents should be sent with transfer
Collegiun	...	11165	Payable on delivery of documents
Collegue	..	11166	**Does**
Colleter	...	11167	Does it
Collettivo	...	11168	Does he
Collettore	...	11169	It does
Collevabat		11170	He does not
Collibravi	...	11171	He does
Collicello	...	11172	**Doing**
Colligrano		11173	Doing nothing
Collilungo		11174	Nothing doing
Collimare	...	11175	Doing something
Collimator		11176	Doing no good
Collinetto	...	11177	Cable (telegraph) what is doing in
Colliquare		11178	If you (——) can by so doing
Collocate	...	11179	I (we) are doing everything possible
Collodion	...	11180	Will doing this (it) assist you
Colloneria		11181	What do you suggest doing
Colloquer	...	11182	What are you doing
Colloquist	..	11183	**Dolerite**
Colloroso	...	11184	**Dollars** (*See also* "Cents," and Tables at end.)
Collotorto		11185	At an exchange of —— dollars to one pound sterling
Collottola	...	11186	Dollars per ton of 2000lbs
Colludere	...	11187	Dollars per
Collusoire	...	11188	Dollars per share
Collyrium		11189	Dollars per foot
Colmado	...	11190	Dollars per fathom
Colmatrice		11191	Dollars per day
Colmenilla		11192	Dollars per week
Colmetto	...	11193	Dollars per month
Colmigno	...	11194	Dollars per year
Colmillar		11195	Dollars per pound
Colmo	...	11196	Dollars per ton
Colocasia	...	11197	Dollars per hundred
Colocutor	...	11198	Dollars per thousand
Colodra	...	11199	**Dolomite**
Colodrillo	...	11200	Dolomite limestone
Colofonia	...	11201	**Done**
Colombajo		11202	Can this (it) be done
Colombella		11203	Has (have) not yet been done
Colombier	...	11204	Has (have) been done since
Colombrono		11205	It can be done (if)
Colonario	...	11206	It cannot be done (if) (unless)
Colonas		11207	In case it can be done at small cost
Colonelcy	...	11208	Must be done
Coloniale	...	11209	Not to be done
Colonicum		11210	Nothing can be done on account of
Colonise	...	11211	Should not be done
Colonnade		11212	To be done

Colophane	11213	Cable when done
Colophony	11214	Done as directed
Coloquinte	11215	Very little work has been done
Coloquio ...	11216	Will try to get this (it) done at once
Colorabile...	11217	Will be done almost immediately
Coloraccio	11218	What has been done
Colorandum	11219	What has been done respecting
Colorant ...	11220	When will this (it) be done
Colorarem...	11221	Why has this not been done
Colorativo	11222	Has not been done yet because of
Coloratote	11223	If it can be done at once
Coloratura	11224	Will be done within next —— days
Coloravero	11225	In case this (it) has not been done
Colorete ...	11226	Nothing practically can be done so long as
Coloritore...	11227	A considerable amount of work has been done (to)
Colossal ...	11228	Cannot be done before (until)
Colosseus ...	11229	Cannot be done owing to
Colossica ...	11230	If not, it (this) should be done at once
Colostras ...	11231	Should you not have done so
Colourable	11232	All that can be done at the present time is to
Colourific ...	11233	This has been done advisedly
Colourless...	11234	This (it) has been done already
Colperta ...	11235	**Double**
Colpettino	11236	Double the quantity
Colpevole ...	11237	Would enable me (us) to double the quantity
Colportage	11238	With double force
Colporteur	11239	Double your force
Colposo ...	11240	Could double output if
Coltella ...	11241	Double output if possible
Coltellino ...	11242	**Doubled**
Coltivare ...	11243	Has (have) doubled since
Coltivo ...	11244	**Doubt**
Coltra ...	11245	I (we) have not the slightest doubt that
Coltrice ...	11246	Why do you doubt
Colubrifer	11247	I (we) have no doubts at all
Colubrina...	11248	I (we) have scarcely a doubt that
Colubrorum	11249	Have you (has ——) any doubt
Columbaria	11250	Has (have) no doubt about
Columbio ...	11251	Has (have) grave doubts whether
Columbulus	11252	In case you have the least doubt do not hesitate to say so
Columellam	11253	Is there any doubt about it (this)
Columnari	11254	Pleased that there is no doubt as to
Columpiar	11255	Regret that there should be any doubt about
Colunica ...	11256	There is no doubt whether
Colurion ...	11257	There is some doubt whether
Colurnorum	11258	There must be no doubt about it
Colurnus ...	11259	Leaves no doubt at all
Colusorio ...	11260	Am (are) still in doubt as to
Comacum...	11261	**Doubtful**
Comadre ...	11262	Not at all doubtful
Comandant	11263	Somewhat doubtful
Comandigia	11264	Just a little doubtful (whether)
Comarcano	11265	It is very doubtful (whether)
Comarchus	11266	Is it at all doubtful
Comarina ...	11267	I (we) do not consider it at all doubtful
Comarum ...	11268	**Down**
Comatose ...	11269	Down in
Comatulos	11270	Coming down
Combaciare	11271	Down from
Combadum	11272	Down to

Combatant	11273	Down to the —— level
Combatible	11274	Down to the water level
Combatir ...	11275	Have gone down a depth of —— ft. (without)
Combattuto	11276	Have only gone down —— ft.
Combes ...	11277	Has (have) not gone down
Combiatare	11278	Manifest a tendency to go down
Combibbia	11279	As far as we have gone down
Combibebat	11280	**Downward(s)**
Combibent	11281	Downwards from
Combibisse	11282	Still downwards
Combibo ...	11283	**Draft(s)** (See also "Draw.")
Combibonem	11284	Draft received
Combinar ...	11285	Draft advised by cable not yet received
Combiniren	11286	Draft advised by letter dated —— not received
Comblezado	11287	Draft protected
Comblezo ...	11288	Draft protested
Comburebam	11289	Draft dishonoured
Comburemus	11290	Draft retained
Comburo ...	11291	Draft returned
Combussero	11292	Draft should not exceed
Combustion	11293	Draft for —— mailed on ——
Combutta...	11294	Draft must not exceed
Comecche...	11295	Draft at —— days' sight
Comedendum	11296	Draft advised in your letter of —— not enclosed
Comedero ...	11297	Draft dishonoured; drawer(s) without authority to draw
Comediante	11298	Draft dishonoured; drawer(s) exceeded his (their) authority to
Comediar ...	11299	Draft enclosed in your letter dated —— received [draw
Comedonem	11300	Duplicate draft enclosed in letter mailed
Comeliness	11301	Have honoured your draft
Comendable	11302	Have sent draft upon ——
Comendar...	11303	What is the amount of draft
Comentario	11304	In order to provide for draft due on ——
Comentual	11305	Please provide for draft due on
Comestible	11306	For recognition of drafts
Cometaccia	11307	Has draft been honoured
Cometary ...	11308	Draft has been duly protested
Comezon ...	11309	Draft refused by ——; cable amount
Comfiture ...	11310	Has draft been paid
Comfort ...	11311	Please pay draft
Comiato ...	11312	Send me (us) draft upon
Comically...	11313	Will send you draft upon
Comicios ...	11314	Will you honour draft for —— at —— days' sight
Comienzo ...	11315	Will honour draft as desired
Comignolo	11316	Will honour draft for
Comiliton ...	11317	Your draft for —— has been dishonoured at ——
Cominciato	11318	Your draft has been duly honoured
Comissor ...	11319	Has (have) accepted draft
Comistrajo	11320	Has (have) not accepted draft
Comisura ...	11321	Has (have) —— accepted draft
Comitativa	11322	**Drain**
Comitato ...	11323	Do you anticipate any difficulty in being able to drain the mine
Comiter ...	11324	So as to drain
Comitialio	11325	To drain
Commaculo	11326	There is no doubt that this will drain the mine
Commandery	11327	This will drain the mine to a depth of
Commandite	11328	Will effectually drain the mine
Commedia	11329	Does not drain workings
Commeditor	11330	**Drained**
Commemini	11331	Drained by
Commencant	11332	Will be drained

Commensus	11333	Not drained
Commenthur	11334	Now being drained
Commentors	11335	**Draining**
Commerebat	11336	Gradually draining the —— workings
Commerzio	11337	Is not draining
Commessa	11338	Is draining
Commettere	11339	Is the tunnel draining the upper workings
Commigrare	11340	**Draw**
Commigrent	11341	You must not draw at all
Commilite...	11342	Can I (we) draw for
Commiltone	11343	You can draw for
Comminabar	11344	You cannot draw for more than
Comminato	11345	You must not draw so long as
Commingle	11346	You can draw what money you want from
Comminutam	11347	Draw and attach bill of lading
Commiscent	11348	Defer to draw as long as possible
Commisto...	11349	Draw upon me (us) in any way you think proper
Commisura	11350	Draw with all documents attached
Commodezza	11351	Draw at
Commodity	11352	Draw on
Commodo...	11353	Draw on me through
Commolior	11354	Authorize you and —— to draw upon
Commonage	11355	Do not draw
Commonitum	11356	Do not draw upon me (us)
Commonweal	11357	Will not draw upon you until I receive formal permission
Commotivo	11358	You may draw upon me (us) to the extent of ——. I (we)
Commozione	11359	You can draw on us for [will protect the draft
Communire	11360	You may draw upon us, but not ——
Communitas	11361	Arrange to draw upon
Commuovere	11362	At how many days' sight shall I (we) draw
Commutable	11363	Draw at sight
Commutual	11364	Draw at —— days' sight
Comodatore	11365	Draw at 3 days' sight
Comodezza	11366	Draw at 5 days' sight
Comodidad	11367	Draw at 7 days' sight
Compacting	11368	Draw at 10 days' sight
Compacto...	11369	Draw at 15 days' sight
Compadrar	11370	Draw at 20 days' sight
Compadrone	11371	Draw at 30 days' sight
Compaginar	11372	Draw at 40 days' sight
Compagnie	11373	Draw at 50 days' sight
Companiero	11374	Draw at 60 days' sight
Companions	11375	Draw at 90 days' sight
Companuela	11376	Draw at —— months' sight
Comparecer	11377	Cannot draw out
Comparsa...	11378	Cannot permit —— to draw out
Compartire	11379	Have been obliged to draw for —— in order to keep works
Compascuo	11380	Has (have) no authority to draw [going
Compassato	11381	On whom shall I (we) draw
Compassion	11382	Please draw up a statement respecting
Compatia...	11383	May I (we) draw upon
Compatriot	11384	In what extent may I (we) draw upon
Compedivo	11385	You may draw upon me (us) for —— at —— days' sight
Compeler ..	11386	You may draw upon —— for —— at —— days' sight
Compellavi	11387	You (they) are authorized to draw
Compendium	11388	You may draw conjointly with
Compensar	11389	Must give full receipt for whatever amount you may draw
Compero ...	11390	**Drawback(s)**
Compescor	11391	It (this) will be a great drawback
Competence	11392	Are there any drawbacks

Competidor	11393	Can you recover the drawback
Compianto	11394	Is a most serious drawback
Compiegato	11395	The only drawback(s) is (are)
Compieta ...	11396	There are no serious drawbacks
Compiglio...	11397	The drawback can be recovered
Compilador	11398	The drawback cannot be recovered
Compiler ...	11399	What is the drawback allowed
Compimento	11400	**Drawer(s)**
Compinche	11401	Drawer(s) has (have)
Compitezza	11402	What is the name of drawer
Compitura	11403	Drawer unknown
Compiuto	11404	Drawer unknown to me
Complacent	11405	Name of drawer is ——
Complaudit	11406	**Drawing(s)**
Complesso	11407	Foundation drawing(s)
Completivo	11408	General drawing(s)
Complexion	11409	Drawing of general arrangement
Complicado	11410	Send drawings
Complice ...	11411	Stopped for want of drawings
Complicity	11412	Set of drawings mailed on
Compliquer	11413	**Drawn**
Complott ...	11414	Drawn on you by
Componer	11415	Drawn on ——
Componible	11416	Drawn by
Componist	11417	Drawn by —— on ——
Comportare	11418	Has (have) drawn upon
Composedly	11419	Has (have) drawn upon you for —— at —— days' sight
Compositor	11420	I have drawn upon you as authorized
Composteur	11421	To what extent have you drawn
Compostus	11422	Have drawn upon you for ——; please protect draft
Composure	11423	Has (have) drawn upon me (us) for
Compotera	11424	Has (have) drawn upon us, please cable instructions
Comprable	11425	Has (have) drawn at sight
Comprador	11426	Has (have) drawn at —— days' sight
Compremir	11427	**Dress** (*See also* " Buddle," " Concentrate.")
Comprender	11428	To dress [up to one ton of marketable ore
Comprimere	11429	By practical trial I find it will take —— tons of ore to dress
Comprisal...	11430	**Dressed** (*See also* " Concentration," &c.)
Comprobor	11431	Ore broken but not dressed
Compte ...	11432	Ore can readily be dressed
Comptoir ...	11433	—— tons of dressed ore
Comptulam	11434	**Dressing** (*See also* " Buddling," " Jigging," &c.)
Compuerta	11435	Ore dressing
Compugnere	11436	Ore dressing works
Compulsar	11437	Dressing floors
Compuncion	11438	**Drift** (*See also* " Begin," " Contract," " Cost," " Drive,"
Compuntivo	11439	Arrange to drift continuously [" Level," &c.)
Computable	11440	Bottom drift is ——
Computato	11441	South drift of level No. ——
Computista	11442	North drift of level No. ——
Comtistic ...	11443	Drift from the
Comulacion	11444	Drift from the incline shaft is in —— feet
Comulgar...	11445	Drift from the shaft is in —— feet
Comuna ...	11446	Drift is now in —— feet
Comunalta	11447	Expect soon to cut ore in the bottom drift
Comunche	11448	How far is the drift in
Comunicare	11449	Drift has advanced —— feet since
Comunidad	11450	Drift has advanced —— feet since passing clear of shaft
Comunione	11451	Breast of the drift is now less than —— feet from ——
Comunmente	11452	How is the drift looking

Comunque	11453	Drift at —— promises well
Conaviero ...	11454	What news have you as regards the drift
Concacetur	11455	Drift does not promise at all well
Concambio	11456	Shall probably abandon the drift (at)
Concaptivo	11457	Have driven to —— in the drift —— ft.
Concasseur	11458	Drift from the station is now in —— ft.
Concatenar	11459	Drift from the tunnel is now in —— ft.
Concavity ...	11460	Drift has tapped a flood of water
Concebidor	11461	Have stopped drift on account of
Concedente	11462	Have withdrawn men from drift until water slackens
Concedido...	11463	No. —— drift
Concenar ...	11464	No. —— drift north
Concentric	11465	No. —— drift south
Concepire ...	11466	No. —— drift east
Conception	11467	No. —— drift west
Concernir ...	11468	No work is being done on drift(s) ——
Concertant	11469	What is the cost of drifting per foot
Concertina	11470	The cost of drifting per foot is
Concestoro	11471	Ore in drift is poor
Concettare	11472	Drift is looking well
Concevoir ...	11473	Drift is looking exceedingly well
Concha ...	11474	Stone in the drift is barren
Conchabar	11475	Ground in the drift is ——
Concharum	11476	Drift is entirely in ore
Conchetta ...	11477	Ore in the drift assays
Conchiglia	11478	Ore in the drift has an average assay of ——
Conchilla ...	11479	Ore has come to an end in No. —— drift; it is not yet cut
Conchiuso...	11480	The forebreast of the drift [in ——
Conchoidal	11481	From present forebreast of drift
Conchology	11482	There is no ore in the bottom drift
Conciatura	11483	We have cut ore in the drift
Concidere ...	11484	We are continuing No. —— drift with a full force of men
Conciencia	11485	Why have you stopped the drift
Concierto ...	11486	What is the total length of the —— drift
Conciliar ...	11487	Total length of the north drift on the —— ft. level is
Concilium...	11488	Total length of the south drift on the —— ft. level is
Concimato	11489	Total length of the east drift in the —— ft. level is
Concime ...	11490	Total length of the west drift in the —— ft. level is
Concinidad	11491	Drift is let on contract to —— men
Concinnita	11492	Developed by drifts for a total aggregate length of —— ft.
Concionare	11493	Shall we stop prospecting drifts
Concision ...	11494	All drifts, shafts, winzes, &c., to be kept accessible
Concitador	11495	Drift is in granite
Concitoyen	11496	,, ,, ,, limestone
Conclave ...	11497	,, ,, ,, country rock
Concludere	11498	,, ,, ,, mineral
Concluir ...	11499	,, ,, ,, pay ore
Concluso ...	11500	,, ,, ,, porphyry
Concoction	11501	,, ,, ,, quartz
Concoide ...	11502	,, ,, ,, slate
Concolore ...	11503	,, ,, ,, trachyte
Concombre	11504	,, ,, ,, vein matter, but carries no payable ore
Concomerse	11505	**Drifted**
Concomitar	11506	Drifted —— feet
Concopulit	11507	When we have drifted a further —— feet
Concordar	11508	When you have drifted a further —— feet
Concordeth	11509	**Drifting** (*See also* "Commenced.")
Concorso ...	11510	Commence drifting
Concourir ...	11511	On which side are you drifting
Concozione	11512	Stop drifting

Concrecion	11513	If no improvement, stop drifting
Concresco ...	11514	If no improvement within —— feet shall stop drifting
Concretive	11515	Has (have) stopped drifting
Concubina	11516	**Drill(s)** (*See also* "Bars," "Bits," "Cradle," "Diamond," &c.)
Conculcar	11517	Without machine drills
Concunado	11518	Hope to start rock drills within present week
Concupire...	11519	When shall you commence with rock drills
Concupisco	11520	We have commenced with rock drills at
Concurrir ...	11521	Men not accustomed to use rock drills
Concurso ...	11522	Supply rock drills at
Concussive	11523	Would you advise employment of rock drills
Condalios ...	11524	Have you considered the question of rock drills
Condamner	11525	Why not use rock drills
Condannato	11526	Send a couple of cooks for rock drills
Condecabo	11527	—— additional men required to run rock drills
Condecente	11528	Now using machine drills
Condecoram	11529	Column to support rock drills
Condegnade	11530	Diamond drill will commence on
Condegnita	11531	Diamond drill plant has been delivered
Condenador	11532	Obtain estimate for diamond drill plant
Condennare	11533	Report rate of speed with diamond drill
Condensa ...	11534	Our present rate of speed with diamond drill for the last 24
Condesica...	11535	**Drilled** [hours has been —— inches per hour
Condezmero	11536	—— holes drilled in —— minutes
Condicere ...	11537	—— holes drilled in the face
Condignly	11538	**Drilling**
Condiment	11539	We are now drilling —— ft. per day
Conditrix ...	11540	What is the present drilling speed
Conditura...	11541	**Drivage(s)** (*See also* "Commenced," "Drift," "Level," &c.)
Condivisse	11542	Stop drivage
Condizione	11543	Recommence drivage
Condolence	11544	Report on drivages at
Condolersi	11545	Have stopped the drivage north
Condominio	11546	Have stopped the drivage south
Condonare	11547	We shall continue this drivage in the same direction
Condoneth	11548	Cable progress made with main drivage(s)
Condotta ...	11549	This drivage should come under the ore body within the next [—— ft.
Condrila ...	11550	**Drive(s)** (*See also* "Drift," "Level," "Tunnel," &c.)
Conduccion	11551	To drive
Conducible	11552	Commenced to drive on ——
Conductora	11553	Have you commenced to drive
Condumio...	11554	Have commenced to drive on the lode (vein)
Condurre ...	11555	Have discontinued drive on account of
Conduttura	11556	Ore from the drive is
Condyle ...	11557	We shall commence to drive —— on ——
Conejal ...	11558	We ought to drive at least
Conejillo ...	11559	To drive in order to
Conejuna ...	11560	How far is there yet to drive
Conesso ...	11561	I (we) estimate that we have still —— feet more to drive to reach
Confabular	11562	As soon as we reach a further depth of —— ft. we shall
Confacenza	11563	We have commenced to drive to the vein [commence to drive
Confaciunt	11564	I (we) estimate shall have to drive a further —— ft. before [cutting ore body
Confalon ...	11565	As soon as communication is effected with —— we shall
Confarrare	11566	**Driven** [commence to drive
Confarsi ...	11567	What distance, in feet have you driven since ——
Confection	11568	We have driven during the past month —— feet
Confederar	11569	Driven on ——
Confermato	11570	As soon as we have driven an additional —— feet
Conferva ...	11571	Have driven —— feet on lode since

Confesante	11572	Have driven —— feet in adit (tunnel) since
Confession	11573	Have driven —— feet in level since
Confiable ...	11574	Have driven upon the vein a distance of —— feet
Confiador ...	11575	Have driven —— feet in barren country rock
Confianza...	11576	**Driving**
Conficiens...	11577	I (we) propose driving on the average bearing of
Confictus ...	11578	We are now driving —— feet per day
Confidarsi...	11579	Have let contract at —— per foot for driving —— feet
Confidele ...	11580	When do you commence driving on (at)
Configgere	11581	Have you recommenced driving
Configurar	11582	Have recommenced driving
Confinante	11583	Have not recommenced driving
Confinar ...	11584	Are you driving north and south on the vein
Confiscado	11585	Shall start driving north and south after sinking (driving) a [further —— feet
Confiserie ...	11586	**Drop**
Confisquer	11587	To drop
Conflacion	11588	Better let the matter drop
Conflatil ...	11589	Advise you to drop the subject
Conflitto ...	11590	Will probably drop into
Confluence	11591	**Dropper**
Confluir ...	11592	Is a mere dropper from the main lode
Confondre	11593	Through the coming in of a dropper
Conformar	11594	**Drowned**
Conformita	11595	Drowned out of workings
Confornico	11596	Was drowned by ——
Confrate ...	11597	Was drowned on ——; the body has been recovered
Confricar ...	11598	Was drowned on ——; the body has not yet been recovered
Confronter	11599	**Drum** (See also "Hoist," "Winding engine," &c.)
Confugio ...	11600	Winding drum
Confuisti ...	11601	Gear for winding drum
Confusetto	11602	What is the diameter of the drum
Confuso ...	11603	Diameter of drum is
Confutare...	11604	**Dry** (See also "Stamps.")
Congaudere	11605	Dry weight
Congeal ...	11606	Dry weather
Congedier...	11607	Dry weather still continues
Congegnare	11608	Mine is now practically dry
Congelar ...	11609	**Dryer**
Congeneric	11610	Shall proceed to erect dryer
Congenial...	11611	Capacity of dryer —— tons per 24 hours
Congenitos	11612	What is the capacity of dryer
Congeries ...	11613	**Due**
Congestion	11614	When is it (this) due
Congiario ...	11615	Due on
Congiugare	11616	Is (was) due on
Congiunta	11617	Has been overdue since ——
Congiurato	11618	Will be due on (next)
Conglobant	11619	Was due on ——, but is not yet received
Conglobar	11620	Is now more than due
Congraciar	11621	Has (have) been due since
Congreso ...	11622	With all due deference
Congricis ...	11623	With due regard to
Congruence	11624	Having due regard to economy
Congruidad	11625	**Dump** (See also "Attle," "Burrows.")
Congruous	11626	Assays of dump heap
Conguaglio	11627	Ore on dump
Congylis ...	11628	With privilege to dump [will assay
Coniare ...	11629	I (we) estimate there are —— tons of ore on the dump that [will mill
Coniatore ...	11630	I (we) estimate there are —— tons of ore on the dump that

Conigliera...	11631	I (we) estimate there are —— tons of ore on the dump that
Conigliolo...	11632	The old dumps　　　　　　　　　　　　[will pay to
Conique ...	11633	Ore on the dumps is worthless
Coniza	11634	Ore on the dumps averages
Conjetura...	11635	The dumps show that
Conjoindre	11636	There is very little ore on the dump
Conjuez ...	11637	Have secured ample ground for dump
Conjugate	11638	The estimate that there are —— tons of —— class ore on dump
		[I (we) consider to be erroneous
Conjuguer	11639	**Duplicate(s)** (*See also* "Copy.")
Conjugulum	11640	Duplicates of documents shall be furnished as soon as possible
Conjuncion	11641	Mail duplicate(s) of
Conjunget	11642	Duplicate copy will be mailed on ——
Conjuntar...	11643	Duplicate copy was mailed on ——
Conjurador	11644	Mail duplicate copy of —— as soon as possible
Conjurante	11645	Duplicates must all be legally attested
Conjurer ...	11646	Will send you a duplicate copy
Conloar ...	11647	Mail duplicate of agreement
Conmensal	11648	Duplicate of agreement will be mailed on ——
Conmiliton	11649	Send duplicate of bill of lading
Conminar...	11650	Cannot send duplicate
Conmistion	11651	Duplicate documents will be forwarded on ——
Conmover...	11652	Shall I (we) send duplicates
Connaitre...	11653	**During**
Connascor...	11654	During the
Connate ...	11655	During it
Connatural	11656	**Dust** (*See also* "Gold.")
Connessita	11657	**Duty(ies)** (*See also* "Engine.")
Connetable	11658	Cost of duty
Connettere	11659	What are the duties
Connivance	11660	The duties are
Connombrar	11661	Arrange with —— to pay duty
Connotado	11662	*Ad valorem* duty
Connovicio	11663	Duty amounts to ——
Connubial	11664	Duty would probably be
Connudatos	11665	There is no duty on
Connuico ...	11666	Duty free
Conocchia...	11667	—— totally neglects his duty
Conocer ...	11668	—— attends to ——'s (his) duties
Conociblo ...	11669	—— is unable to attend to his duty
Conoidical	11670	—— returned to his duty on
Conopeos ...	11671	**Dwelling House** (*See also* "Boarding House.")
Conoscensi	11672	Erection of dwelling house completed　　[about ——
Conoscrito	11673	Shall have to erect a dwelling house, the cost of which will be
Conquadro	11674	Send supply of corrugated iron sheet for dwelling house
Conquerant	11675	There is no dwelling house at all
Conquest ...	11676	There is a good dwelling house at ——, —— rooms
Conquidere	11677	**Dyas (or Permian)**
Conquiesco	11678	**Dyke**
Conquista...	11679	A porphyry dyke
Conrear ...	11680	North of the dyke
Conreinar ...	11681	South of the dyke
Consaber ...	11682	East of the dyke
Consabidor	11683	West of the dyke
Consacrer ...	11684	A dyke of
Consagrado	11685	Outside the dyke
Consanabat	11686	**Dynamite** (*See also* "Blasting Gelatine," "Detonators,"
		["Explosives," "Powder," &c.)
˥nguin	11687	Forward promptly —— cases (50 lbs. each) of dynamite, ¾ in.
		[diameter

Consatum...	11688	Forward promptly —— cases (50 lbs. each) of dynamite, ¾ in. [diameter
Conscenza	11689	Forward promptly —— cases (50 lbs. each) of dynamite, 1 in. [diameter
Conscience	11690	Forward promptly —— cases (50 lbs. each) of dynamite, 1¼ in. [diameter
Conscript ...	11691	Forward promptly —— cases (50 lbs. each) of gelatine dyna- [mite, ¾ in. diameter
Conscritto	11692	Forward promptly —— cases (50 lbs. each) of gelatine dyna- [mite, ¾ in. diameter
Consecrate	11693	Forward promptly —— cases (50 lbs. each) of gelatine dyna- [mite, 1 in. diameter
Consecro ...	11694	Forward promptly —— cases (50 lbs. each) of gelatine dyna- [mite, 1¼ in. diameter
Consedonem	11695	**Dynamo** (*See also* " Electric," " Motor," " Volts," &c.)
Conseguir...	11696	Alternate current dynamo
Conseiller...	11697	Series wound dynamo
Consejador	11698	Shunt wound dynamo
Consejo ...	11699	Compound wound dynamo
Consejuela	11700	Causing a stoppage of dynamo
Consentios	11701	Send spare armature for dynamo
Consentir ...	11702	Send spare commutator for dynamo
Consepolto	11703	What is the E.M.F. required
Conserbare	11704	Dynamo should be capable of
Cònserge ...	11705	Dynamo is only capable of
Conservans	11706	Dynamo running continuously
Conservare	11707	**Dynamometer**
Consesso ...	11708	Dynamometer test
Considerar	11709	**E**
Consiervo ...	11710	**Each**
Consiglio ...	11711	From each one
Consigna ...	11712	To each one
Consignore	11713	Each claim
Consilium...	11714	In each end
Consimile ...	11715	In each instance
Consiroso ...	11716	Keep the details of each trial separate
Consistory	11717	Reply distinctly to each question
Consobrino	11718	Treat each separately and distinctly
Consociate	11719	**Eager(ly)**
Consolable	11720	Am (is) most eager to
Consolador	11721	Am (is) not at all eager to
Consolante	11722	Do you think that —— is at all eager
Consolatus	11723	Does not appear at all eager
Consoletur	11724	Not sufficiently eager
Consolida ...	11725	Too eager
Consoling...	11726	**Earlier**
Consolone...	11727	Earlier if possible
Consols ...	11728	Impossible to be earlier
Consommer	11729	**Earliest**
Consonante	11730	At the earliest possible date
Consonar ...	11731	Take the earliest opportunity to
Consopito ...	11732	Will take the earliest opportunity to
Consorte ...	11733	**Early**
Consorting	11734	Early to-morrow
Consorzia...	11735	Early in the season
Consoude ...	11736	As early as possible
Conspetto ...	11737	Expect to get to work early in ——
Conspexit	11738	It is too early yet to report anything
Conspicere	11739	Must have an early reply
Conspicuo...	11740	Not sufficiently early

Conspirado	11741	Too early
Conspuer ...	11742	**Earn** (*See also* "Earnings," "Men," "Miners," "Wages," &c.)
Constable ...	11743	Can earn from —— to —— per day
Constabunt	11744	What do the miners earn per day
Constancia	11745	What do the —— earn per day
Constater ...	11746	**Earnest**
Consternar	11747	As an earnest of my (his) intentions
Constituir...	11748	As an earnest
Constraint	11749	Can you find out if —— is in earnest
Constrenir	11750	Doubtful if in earnest
Constretto	11751	Is not in earnest
Constringe	11752	Is thoroughly in earnest
Construire	11753	I do not think that —— can be in earnest
Construpar	11754	Should —— be in earnest
Construxi ...	11755	**Earnestly**
Consubrino	11756	Earnestly request you to stop
Consuebat	11757	Earnestly request you to return
Consuegrar	11758	Earnestly ask you to
Consuelda	11759	**Earnings**
Consuesco...	11760	Present earnings are —— per day
Consuetare	11761	Net earnings for the period ending
Consuetud	11762	Net earnings since
Consulaire	11763	Average earnings per man about —— per month
Consulate...	11764	Average earnings amount to
Consulship	11765	What are the average earnings
Consulta ...	11766	**Earthquake**
Consultivo	11767	Have had earthquake shock; caused following damage
Consumado	11768	Earthquake occurred on ——; will cost —— to repair damage
Consumanza	11769	Have had severe earthquake; details later
Consumens	11770	Have had severe earthquake; considerable damage
Consumible	11771	Have had earthquake shock; no damage done
Consumir ...	11772	Have had earthquake shock; caused great damage
Consuno ...	11773	The country is subject to earthquakes
Consuonare	11774	**Easily**
Consurgere	11775	Can easily
Contacto ...	11776	Cannot very easily before (unless)
Contadino...	11777	Cannot very easily
Contaduria	11778	Could you easily do this (it)
Contage ...	11779	This could easily be done
Contagieux	11780	**East**
Contagioso	11781	Now going east
Contagium	11782	Drivage east
Contamento	11783	On the east of
Contaminar	11784	East line
Contante ...	11785	East corner
Contanza ...	11786	East end line
Contarios ...	11787	East side line
Contatore...	11788	East ledge
Contatrice	11789	East mine
Contatto ...	11790	Due east and west
Contectum	11791	In the east end
Contegnoso	11792	East winze
Contemplar	11793	East north east
Contenance	11794	East crosscut
Contender	11795	East vein (lode) (reef)
Contending	11796	Going to the east
Contenenza	11797	—— degrees east of north
Contenersi	11798	East of ——
Contenido...	11799	To the east of
Contentato	11800	The east drift

Contera ...	11801	East shaft
Conterebro	11802	East part of the mine (property)
Contessere	11803	Turns a little to the east
Contessina	11804	Coming in from the east
Contestar ...	11805	Dipping east
Contexture	11806	East wall
Conticinio	11807	East working(s)
Contienda...	11808	**Easterly**
Contigiato	11809	Run(s) easterly
Continent...	11810	In an easterly direction
Continenza	11811	Has an easterly trend
Contingere	11812	The most easterly of
Contino ...	11813	**Eastern**
Continuar...	11814	In the eastern portion
Continuita	11815	Eastern parts of
Continuvo	11816	**Easy**
Contironem	11817	You may rest perfectly easy
Contogatum	11818	Do not feel at all easy
Contondant	11819	To rest easy
Contoneo ...	11820	**Economical(ly)**
Contorcere	11821	Be as economical as possible
Contornato	11822	Be as economical as is prudent
Contorqueo	11823	Can you make any economical arrangement whereby
Contourner	11824	Is not at all economical
Contraband	11825	It would be more economical to (if)
Contrabios	11826	It will be more economical
Contractus	11827	This will be more economical
Contradizo	11828	Has the reputation of being an economical manager
Contraer ...	11829	**Economy**
Contrafoso	11830	Can you suggest any further economy
Contrafuga	11831	No economy is practised with money or labour
Contrahaz	11832	Overhaul all charges in the direction of economy
Contrahunt	11833	The greatest economy is being practised
Contraire ...	11834	The greatest economy is necessary
Contralar ...	11835	This will mean an economy of
Contralto ...	11836	There is a great want of economy
Contramina	11837	With economy
Contrapaso	11838	Do not study too much economy
Contrarsi ...	11839	There would really be no actual economy
Contrasena	11840	Every economy must be used
Contrata ...	11841	Every economy will be used
Contratela	11842	Every economy has been used
Contravato	11843	**Effect**
Contravene	11844	In effect
Contrayugo	11845	To effect
Contrebass	11846	Any effect
Contrecho...	11847	Effect a compromise
Contrecoup	11848	Effect a settlement
Contrefort	11849	Do not know what the effect might be
Contrepied	11850	Has had the desired effect
Contrepoil	11851	Has not had the desired effect
Contrerail...	11852	Has had the effect
Contrevent	11853	This has had a bad effect
Contribuir	11854	This has had a good effect
Contritare	11855	What effect has it had
Contrition	11856	Have been unable to effect
Controlant	11857	Hope to effect considerable improvement as regards
Controleur	11858	How will this effect us (it)
Contuendo	11859	In order to effect this
Contumacy	11860	In order to effect this it will be necessary to

Contumaz...	11861	May have some little effect
Contumelia	11862	To this effect
Contundir	11863	To effect this we should
Conturbado	11864	To take effect not later than
Conturbare	11865	Is practically to the same effect
Conturgeo	11866	The effect will probably be (that)
Contusion...	11867	This will have the following effect
Contutor ...	11868	What will be the effect (of)
Conuegno...	11869	When will it (this) come into effect
Convaincre	11870	Will come into effect on
Convalecer	11871	Has had a depressing effect on
Convecino	11872	Will do my (our) best to effect this object
Convelerse	11873	Do your best to effect this object
Convencido	11874	**Effective**
Convenible	11875	How many effective horse-power
Convenio ...	11876	Effective horse-power
Convention	11877	Effective work
Converger...	11878	Take effective means of proving
Conversion	11879	Have taken effective means of proving
Convertido	11880	**Effectual**
Convesco ...	11881	Am (are) afraid will not be effectual
Convessita	11882	But was not effectual
Convexity...	11883	Has been quite effectual
Conviccion	11884	This will be effectual
Convicians	11885	Will this be effectual
Convicium	11886	**Efficient**
Convictor ...	11887	Can only be made efficient at a cost of
Convidado	11888	How much will it cost to make it (this) efficient
Convincere	11889	Has rendered very efficient services
Convite ...	11890	Do you consider it (this) efficient
Convitigia	11891	Sufficiently efficient for my (our) purpose
Convittore	11892	Not nearly as efficient as I (we) would wish
Convivente	11893	**Effort(s)**
Convivial ...	11894	Wish every success to your efforts
Conviziare	11895	In spite of best efforts to hurry same
Convizioso	11896	All efforts so far unsuccessful
Convocador	11897	An effort will be made to
Convocate...	11898	Can you get —— to make additional effort
Convoglio...	11899	Efforts beginning to tell
Convoiter ...	11900	Every effort must be made so as to
Convoitise	11901	In order to induce extra effort you may
Convolgere	11902	No effort will be spared to
Convolnero	11903	Spare no effort to
Convolute...	11904	—— has so far made no effort
Convolve ...	11905	Every effort will be made to
Convolvulo	11906	Every effort has been made
Convoquer	11907	Great efforts are being made here to
Convoy ...	11908	**Either**
Convoying	11909	Do you know either —— or ——
Convulsed	11910	Either will do
Convulsion	11911	Either —— or ——
Conyzam	11912	Either might do; prefer latter
Conyzis ...	11913	Either might do; prefer former
Cookery ...	11914	Should avoid either
Coolescere	11915	Either direct, or by way of
Coonestare	11916	Either one or the other
Cooper ...	11917	**Elect**
Cooperante	11918	To elect
Cooperario	11919	Must elect on
Coopering	11920	**Elected**

Cooptabat...	11921	Not elected
Cooptation	11922	Unanimously elected
Cooptavit ...	11923	Has (have) elected to
Coordinare	11924	Has (have) not elected
Coordonner	11925	You cannot consider yourself elected until
Coortare ...	11926	You may consider yourself practically elected
Coortarum	11927	**Electric** (*See also* " Dynamo," "Motor," &c.)
Copaiba ...	11928	Electric battery
Copaljocol	11929	Electric arc lamps
Copanete ...	11930	Electric incandescent lamps
Coparceny	11931	Electric light plant
Copazo ...	11932	What would electric light installation include
Copelacion	11933	Electric light installation includes
Copelar ...	11934	Estimated cost of electric light installation is ——
Coperchino	11935	Electric motor
Coperillo ...	11936	Electric motor to transmit —— horse power
Coperta ...	11937	Later on electric power might be employed
Copetudo ...	11938	Bornhardt machine, double plate (*See also* "Blasting.")
Cophinorum	11939	Bornhardt high-tension electric machine, with a supply of fuses
Cophinus ...	11940	Send a low-tension electric firing machine, with suitable fuses
Copiador ...	11941	I have contracted for electric light plant
Copico ...	11942	I have contracted for electric transmission plant
Copieux ...	11943	**Electrician**
Copiglio ...	11944	Shall require competent electrician
Copilador...	11945	Shall not require electrician
Copiosita ...	11946	**Elevation** (*See also* "Plan.")
Copiosorum	11947	At an elevation of
Copista ...	11948	At this elevation
Copleador...	11949	Can you get sufficient elevation
Coplearo ...	11950	Send plan and elevation of —— (shewing)
Coplon ...	11951	Side elevation
Copparosa...	11952	**Elevator**
Coppettone	11953	Elevator chain
Coppice ...	11954	Elevator bucket, capacity —— lbs.
Coppietta ...	11955	Owing to breakdown of elevator
Copponi ...	11956	**Else**
Coprente ...	11957	**Elsewhere**
Coprirsi ...	11958	Would it be any use to try elsewhere
Copritura ...	11959	It would not be any use to try elsewhere
Coprolites...	11960	Shall try elsewhere unless
Copros ...	11961	Cannot apply elsewhere
Copulabat...	11962	Can you suggest elsewhere
Copulandum	11963	Please apply elsewhere
Copular ...	11964	Try elsewhere
Copulativo	11965	Useless to apply elsewhere
Copulatus...	11966	Will send elsewhere
Copulentur	11967	**Elude**
Copybook...	11968	To elude
Copyhold ..	11969	Should —— (he) elude
Copyright...	11970	Is (are) hoping to elude
Coquelicot	11971	Will try to elude
Coqueluche	11972	**Elvan**
Coquemar...	11973	An elvan course
Coqueteria	11974	Lode has been thrown by an elvan course
Coquetier ...	11975	**Emanate(d)**
Coquillage	11976	Can you find out whence this news emanated
Coquillo ...	11977	Could only have emanated from
Coquinabo	11978	Could not have emanated from
Coquinam...	11979	Is believed to have emanated from
Coquinario	11980	May have emanated from

Coquinus ...	11981	News emanated from
Coracero ..	11982	Rumour is said to have emanated from
Corachin ...	11983	**Emerald**
Coracilla ...	11984	Emerald mines
Coracna ...	11985	Emeralds found
Corage ...	11986	**Emergency**
Coraggine...	11987	In the present emergency
Coraggioso	11988	There is no emergency at present
Corailleur...	11989	In case of emergency
Corajoso ...	11990	Against any emergencies
Coralero ...	11991	**Emery**
Coralillo ...	11992	Emery stone
Corallina ...	11993	Emery wheel
Corallo ...	11994	**Employ**
Corallume...	11995	To employ
Coralmente	11996	Employ as
Coralreef ...	11997	Employ all your force
Corambre ...	11998	Employ only
Coramvobis	11999	Do not employ
Corascora...	12000	Employ other means if possible
Coratella ...	**12001**	Cannot employ other means
Coraznada	12002	Employ someone else to
Corazon ...	12003	Can you employ
Corazzina...	12004	Cannot employ more
Corbachada	12005	Employ all possible means in order to
Corbacho ...	12006	It will be necessary to employ at least
Corbatin ...	12007	In case you cannot employ
Corbeille ...	12008	May I (we) employ
Corbezzola	12009	Why do you not employ
Corbicino ...	12010	Suggest that you employ some other
Corbicula ...	12011	Suggest that you employ someone to
Corbillard...	12012	Shall then be able to employ
Corbillon ...	12013	Company employs a total of —— men
Corbularum	12014	Company employs —— miners
Corbulas ...	12015	What number of men do you consider it necessary to employ
Corcarsi ...	12016	As soon as I am (we are) able to employ
Corcesca ...	12017	Estimate(s) I (we) can employ —— men immediately
Corchabait	12018	**Employed**
Corchar ...	12019	Employed by
Corcheta ...	12020	Employed as
Corchoro .	12021	Was not employed as
Corcovado...	12022	Must not be employed
Corcovilla...	12023	Cannot safely be employed
Corcusido...	12024	Am (are) now employed in (with)
Cordacem...	12025	Has (have) not been employed
Cordacismo	12026	Has (have) employed
Cordaggio...	12027	Has (have) not yet employed
Cordatus ...	12028	Have been employed since —— with —— [regulations
Cordel ...	12029	How many men must be employed to comply with government
Cordelado...	12030	—— men must be employed to comply with government regu- [lations
Cordelaria...	12031	Must not be employed unless
Cordelette...	12032	Have not employed because of
Cordelico ...	12033	Why have you not employed
Cordeliere...	12034	Cable number of hands employed
Cordellate...	12035	Total number of men employed at the mines and dressing [floors is
Corderillo ...	12036	Have now —— men employed
Corderino...	12037	Shall be able to reduce number of men employed as soon as we [have finished erection of
Corderuela	12038	**Employés** (*See also* "Employ," "Hands," &c.)
Cordeta ...	12089	What is the total number of employés

| Cordiaco ... | 12040 | How many employés have the Company |
| Cordial ... | 12041 | A total number of —— employés |

Employers (*See also* "Lock-out," "Strike," &c.)

Cordialita...	12042	
Cordicella ..	12043	Employers are prepared to re-open works
Cordicina ...	12044	Employers have given notice to
Cordidalio	12045	Employers have given notice of reduction of wages
Cordiero ...	12046	Employers refuse to give in
Cordiglio ...	12047	Employers have given in
Cordoban ...	12048	There is no prospect of employers giving in
Cordojo ...	12049	Employers have agreed to shorten the hours
Cordolium	12050	Employers have agreed to allow men's demands

Employing

Cordonato ..	12051	
Cordoncico	12052	Now employing
Cordoneria	12053	Only employing
Cordonner	12054	Employing —— men
Cordovano	12055	Employing —— miners

Empower(ed)

Cordoyoso	12056	
Corduan ...	12057	Should have empowered —— to act
Corduroys	12058	Have empowered —— to act on my (our) behalf
Cordwainer	12059	Is empowered to act on my (our) behalf
Cordylam ...	12060	Is not empowered to act on my (our) behalf
Corecico ...	12061	Until you (——) are duly empowered to act

Empty

Coreggiajo	12062	
Coreggina...	12063	Are now empty
Coregrafia...	12064	Is at present quite empty
Corezuelo ...	12065	Will then be empty

Enable (*See also* "Able.")

Coriaceous	12066	
Coriaginem	12067	In order to enable
Coriambico	12068	In order to enable me (us) to do so, the following will be
Coriandro...	12069	Possibly this will enable me (us) [required
Coriarius ...	12070	So as to enable me (us) to
Coribante ...	12071	This will enable me (us) to determine
Corifeo ...	12072	What do you require to enable you to act
Corilato ...	12073	Shall require —— to enable me (us) to act
Corimbo ..	12074	Shall require —— to enable me (us) to proceed
Corinthian	12075	This will enable you (them) to determine
Corintico ...	12076	Will this enable you (them)
Coriorum ...	12077	To enable me (us) to prepare
Corista ...	12078	To enable me (us) to

Enclosing

Corkage ...	12079	
Corkbark ...	12080	Enclosing remittance of
Corkscrew...	12081	Enclosing the following

Enclosure

Corladura...	12082	
Corlaja ...	12083	Enclosure referred to in your letter not received
Cormano ...	12084	Enclosure referred to in my letter dated —— has been omitted. [will be forwarded on ——
Cormier ...	12085	Have received enclosure referred to in your letter dated ——

Encountered

Cormorant	12086	
Cornacchia	12087	Which we encountered on
Cornamenta	12088	Have encountered
Cornamusa	12089	Have not encountered
Cornatore...	12090	Have you (——) encountered

Encourage (*See also* "Appearance," "Aspect.")

Cornbrash	12091	
Cornbread	12092	Do nothing to encourage
Corneado ...	12093	Have you (has ——) done anything to encourage
Corneille ...	12094	I (we) have done nothing to encourage
Corneja ...	12095	I (we) shall do nothing to encourage
Cornemuse	12096	I (we) cannot encourage
Corneous ...	12097	I (we) will not encourage
Cornerina...	12098	I (we) cannot encourage the proposition

Cornety ...	12099	To encourage
Cornezuelo	12100	**Encouraged**
Cornflour ...	12101	Much encouraged
Cornicabra	12102	Not at all encouraged
Cornicello...	12103	**Encouragement**
Corniche ...	12104	For want of a little encouragement
Cornicione	12105	Shall stop this work unless we meet with some encouragement
Corniforme	12106	Can you hold out any encouragement
Cornigero ...	12107	Do (does) not hold out any encouragement
Corniola ...	12108	I (we) cannot hold out any encouragement
Cornipedem	12109	There is every encouragement to pursue
Cornisica ...	12110	—— holds out every encouragement
Cornison ...	12111	**Encouraging**
Cornix ...	12112	Looking very encouraging
Cornlaws ...	12113	Are present appearances encouraging
Cornoville...	12114	Most encouraging
Cornpoppy	12115	Present appearances most encouraging
Cornucopia	12116	Present appearances not at all encouraging
Cornudazo	12117	Present discoveries most encouraging
Cornuderia	12118	Which is very encouraging for the future
Cornudico...	12119	I (we) regard present outlook as decidedly encouraging
Cornupeta	12120	If results not more encouraging than last, should prepare to [shut down
Cornuta ...	12121	**Encroach**
Corolario ...	12122	Are they (is ——) attempting to encroach
Corolla ...	12123	Is (are) attempting to encroach
Corollaire ...	12124	Is (are) likely to encroach
Corollarum	12125	Claim that we have encroached
Coronado ...	12126	Do not permit any attempt to encroach
Coronarius	12127	Has (have) not attempted to encroach
Coronation	12128	Has (have) not really encroached, but seem likely to attempt
Coroncione	12129	Prevent if possible any attempt to encroach
Corondel ...	12130	To encroach upon
Coronet ...	12131	**Encroachment**
Coronica ...	12132	Give formal notice of encroachment
Coronidem	12133	Have given formal notice of encroachment
Corpaccio ...	12134	So as to stop any encroachment
Corpanchon	12135	So as to end any further encroachment
Corpecico ...	12136	Take legal steps to prevent encroachment
Corpettino	12137	**End**
Corpicello...	12138	Before the end of
Corpicino ..	12139	Has practically come to an end
Corporeity	12140	To the end of
Corporem ...	12141	End of
Corporosa...	12142	At an end
Corpudo ...	12143	At the end of
Corpulence	12144	In the end
Corpusculo	12145	In order to end
Corpuzzo ...	12146	Is now at an end
Corragero...	12147	Must now be considered at an end
Corralillo ...	12148	This will end further action
Corraliza ...	12149	Will this end
Corralon ...	12150	—— ft. from the end
Corrasum ...	12151	Have got to the end of
Correage ...	12152	The ends generally have increased in value
Correcteur	12153	This end is being extended by three shifts of eight hours each
Correcto ...	12154	All the ends continue poor
Corredato...	12155	The (this) end has not been driven since
Correduria	12156	**Endeavour**
Corregel ...	12157	To endeavour
'rreggere	12158	Endeavour to

Corregíble	12159	Endeavour to compromise claim
Correguela	12160	Endeavour to compromise
Correlate ...	12161	In spite of my (our) best endeavours
Correntiar	12162	Their endeavour has been
Correon ...	12163	Endeavour to get it (this) returned
Correptor ...	12164	What is their endeavour
Corretage ...	12165	Our endeavour should be
Corretera ...	12166	Endeavour to induce —— to consent
Correttore...	12167	It is useless to endeavour
Corridita ...	12168	Shall now endeavour
Corridor ...	12169	Use your best endeavours to
Corrigenda	12170	Endeavour to withdraw
Corrigens ...	12171	**Endeavoured**
Corrigiren...	12172	Have you (has ——) endeavoured to
Corrillero ...	12173	I (we) have endeavoured since —— to
Corrimacam	12174	I (we) have endeavoured
Corrimento	12175	—— has strongly endeavoured to
Corrincho ...	12176	**Endeavouring**
Corritrice ...	12177	Endeavouring to
Corrivent ...	12178	Has (have) been endeavouring since
Corroborar	12179	**Ended**
Corrodent...	12180	Not ended
Corroer ...	12181	Will be ended on
Corrogavit	12182	Should be ended by
Corromper	12183	**Ending**
Corrosible	12184	Now ending
Corrosivo ...	12185	**Endline**
Corrotto ...	12186	From our endline
Corrotundo	12187	Breast of drift is undoubtedly beyond our endline
Corroyente	12188	Breast of drift is close to our endline
Corrugar ...	12189	Should not on any account pass our endline
Corruisse ...	12190	**Endorse**
Corruptive	12191	Can you endorse
Corruptor ...	12192	Cannot endorse
Corruptrix	12193	Can certainly endorse
Corruscare	12194	**Endorsed**
Corrusco ...	12195	Endorsed by
Corruttela	12196	Was endorsed by
Corsair ...	12197	Was not endorsed by
Corsaletto...	12198	Will require to be endorsed by
Corselet ...	12199	**Endorsement**
Corsescata	12200	Refuse(s) to pay without proper endorsement
Corsiere ...	12201	**Enforce**
Corsoides ...	12202	To enforce
Cortadoras	12203	Must enforce
Cortafrio ...	12204	Do not enforce
Cortafuego	12205	Do not enforce the claim
Cortamente	12206	Do not enforce the payment
Cortante ...	12207	Cannot enforce owing to
Cortapicos	12208	Can you see your way clear to enforce
Corteare ...	12209	Do you (they) intend to enforce
Cortecica ...	12210	Do not consider it prudent to enforce
Cortedad ...	12211	Do not consider it worth while to enforce
Corteggio ...	12212	Enforce the claim at all cost
Cortejador	12213	Has (have) commenced to enforce
Cortejo ...	12214	Is it worth while to attempt to enforce
Cortesania...	12215	If there is any chance of succeeding, enforce the claim at once
Cortesuela ..	12216	May be expected to enforce
Cortical ...	12217	There is no need to enforce
Corticatus...	12218	Will certainly enforce

Corticella ...	12219	**Enforced**
Corticibus	12220	Cannot be enforced owing to
Corticosum	12221	Have you (has ——) enforced
Cortigiana	12222	Has (have) been enforced
Cortiletto ...	12223	Must be enforced
Cortinage ...	12224	Ought to be enforced
Cortinarum	12225	Will not be enforced
Cortinon ...	12226	Orders must be strictly enforced
Cortulla ...	12227	Regulations of Board of Directors must be strictly enforced
Coruscant	12228	**Engage**
Coruscis ...	12229	To engage
Coruscorum	12230	Do not engage
Corvadura	12231	Engage services of
Corval ...	12232	Engage to
Corvecito ...	12233	Engage for
Corvedad ...	12234	Engage by
Corvette ...	12235	Do you mean me (us) to engage
Corvillo ...	12236	Can you not engage someone else in place of
Corvina ...	12237	At what rate do you wish me (us) to engage
Corybantes	12238	Can you engage at once
Corycian ...	12239	Cannot engage before
Corycos ...	12240	May I (we) positively engage
Corydalum	12241	Please engage at once
Corylaceae	12242	Please engage at —— per man, per month
Coryleti ...	12243	Will engage as desired
Corylorum	12244	Will undertake to engage that
Corymbus...	12245	You may engage for —— months
Coryphee ...	12246	You may engage
Corzuelo ...	12247	**Engaged**
Cosacchi ...	12248	Has (have) engaged
Cosario ...	12249	Has (have) not engaged
Coscarana...	12250	Fully engaged until
Coscendere	12251	Was specially engaged to
Coscinetto	12252	Am (are) too much engaged
Coscoja ...	12253	Has (have) engaged to leave immediately
Coscorron...	12254	Has (have) engaged to
Cosecante...	12255	Has (have) not yet engaged to
Cosecha ...	12256	Might be engaged in the meantime
Cosechero	12257	Regret am (are) already engaged
Cosedizo ...	12258	Should not be engaged until
Coseno ...	12259	**Engagement**
Cosentient	12260	As a temporary engagement
Cosetada ...	12261	Am (are) under an engagement to
Cosible ...	12262	Cannot fulfil their engagements
Cosicosa ...	12263	Do not make any engagements
Cosmetarum	12264	Has (have) accepted engagement
Cosmetas ...	12265	No such engagement was made
Cosmetico...	12266	No such engagement has been made
Cosmetique	12267	No positive engagement was made
Cosmicos ...	12268	Has (have) made a positive engagement to
Cosmogony	12269	Refuse(s) to fulfil his (their) engagements
Cosmografo	12270	Cannot fulfil his (their) engagements
Cosmology	12271	The only engagement was that (to)
Cosmorama	12272	Will not enter into any such engagement
Cospargere	12273	What are the terms of the engagement
Cosparso ...	12274	What engagements have you made
Cospettone	12275	**Engine** (See also " Bob," " Boiler," " Broken," " Machinery," [" Plant."])
Cospiciuta	12276	Combined winding and pumping engine —— h.p. (indicated)
Cospirante	12277	Combined winding and pumping engine
Cospirato ...	12278	Can purchase a suitable engine for ——

Cosquillas...	12279	Air pump of engine
Costado ...	12280	Condenser of engine
Costaggiu...	12281	Crankshaft of engine.
Costalada ...	12282	Bedplate of engine
Costaleira ...	12283	Engine is in good repair
Costamoma	12284	Engine is in fair condition
Costaneras	12285	Engine is badly worn
Costeador...	12286	Engine broken down
Costellato ...	12287	Engine in excellent order, practically new
Costeno ...	12288	Estimate for repairs to engine
Costernato	12289	Hoisting engine (*See also* " Hoist.")
Costezuela	12290	Have started engine(s)
Costiere ...	12291	Ought to have a —— h.p. engine
Costillica ...	12292	Owing to repairs required to engine
Costilludo...	12293	Must have new engine
Costively ...	12294	Piston rod of engine
Costliness...	12295	Portable engine and boiler
Costola ...	12296	Engine of air compressor
Costoliere...	12297	Pumping engine
Costoso ...	12298	Mill engine
Costrada ...	12299	Slide valve of engine
Costribar ...	12300	This engine was formerly at ——
Costrilla ...	12301	Repairs to the engine will cost —— and require —— weeks' time
Costringir...	12302	Cost of transport and erection of engine may be estimated
Costrivo ...	12303	Cost of transporting engine will be [at ——
Costumado	12304	Full load of the engine is
Costumbre	12305	Shall require to have new engine for
Costumes ...	12306	Winding engine
Costumier...	12307	A winding engine of —— h.p. (indicated)
Costurera ...	12308	Mill engine of —— h.p. (indicated)
Costuron ...	12309	What power could the engine develop
Cosuccia ...	12310	We ought to be able to develop at least —— h.n
Cotalche ...	12311	Loading of engine
Cotangent	12312	Owing to loading of engine having given way
Cotanhilo...	12313	Complete breakdown of engine
Cotarrera ...	12314	Shall require a separate engine for this purpose
Cotear ...	12315	Indicate the pumping engine
Cotelette ...	12316	Indicate the winding engine
Cotenancy	12317	Indicate the air compressor engine
Cotennone	12318	Mail indicator diagrams of engine (at)
Coterie ...	12319	What is the power and condition of engine
Cotestoro ...	12320	Engine runs very satisfactorily
Cothurn ...	12321	Engine does not run altogether satisfactorily
Cothurnata	12322	Does engine run satisfactorily
Cothurnos	12323	Engine shaft (*See also* " Shaft.")
Coticulas ...	12324	**Engineer** (*See also* " Mining Engineer.")
Cotidiano ...	12325	Require a competent engineer for
Cotillero ...	12326	Send competent engineer at once
Cotillion ...	12327	Should be a reliable and competent engineer
Cotisames...	12328	Should be placed in charge of a competent engineer
Cotiza ...	12329	Will engage local man as engineer till
Cotofre ...	12330	Would require to take charge of engines and all machinery at
Cotogna ...	12331	Engineer cannot be sent for —— weeks [surface
Cotonada ...	12332	Engineer unable to attend
Cotoncillo...	12333	Engineer has stated emphatically that
Cotonearum	12334	Shall require assistant engineer
Cotoness ...	12335	Owing to death of engineer
Cotoniella...	12336	Engineer not competent for
Cotonnade	12337	Must be competent engineer
Cotonnerie	12338	Chief engineer to take charge of entire machinery

Cotonnine...	12339	Engineer to take charge of
Cotornice ...	12340	Engineer refuses to work
Cotorra ...	12341	Engineers have gone out on strike
Cotorreria...	12342	What is the opinion of engineer
Cotovelo ...	12343	Engineer's opinion is
Cotral ...	12344	Employ as engineer
Cottaborum	12345	**Engine-man** (*See also* " Fitter," " Mechanic.")
Cottabos ...	12346	A good engine-man
Cottager ...	12347	**English**
Cottardita...	12348	Of English make
Cotticcio ...	12349	In the English market
Cotton ...	12350	The English public
Cottonning	12351	**Enough**
Cotufero ...	12352	Barely enough for
Coturnato...	12353	Shall have barely enough for
Cotuteur ...	12354	Have you enough to
Cotyledon...	12355	I (we) have enough
Couchant ...	12356	I (we) have only enough for
Couchette...	12357	Is there enough
Coudoyer ...	12358	There is enough
Coudraie ...	12359	There is not enough
Coughdrop	12360	Have you (has ——) enough time
Coughing ...	12361	There is not enough time
Coulage ...	12362	There will be barely enough time to
Coulamment	12363	Have you enough to go on with
Couleur ...	12364	Have not enough to go on with
Counters ...	12365	Have enough to last until
Coupable ...	12366	Not enough to complete
Coupeller ...	12367	**Enquire** (*See also* " Inquire.")
Couperose...	12368	**Enter**
Coupure ...	12369	Do not enter into any such agreement
Courbature	12370	Has (have) attempted to enter
Courbure ...	12371	Is —— willing to enter
Coureuse ..	12372	In case —— is not willing to enter
Couronne ...	12373	Refuse(s) to enter
Courroux ...	12374	Should not be allowed to enter
Coursiren ...	12375	Should not advise you to enter
Courtant ...	12376	To enter
Courtisan ...	12377	To enter into
Courtoisie...	12378	**Entered**
Courtship...	12379	Is (are) said to have entered
Cousinage ..	12380	Have been entered
Cousinhood	12381	Has (have) not yet entered
Coussinet ...	12382	**Enterprise**
Couteau ...	12383	A speculative enterprise
Coutelina ...	12384	Enterprise is a very speculative one
Couteux ...	12385	Enterprise is devoid of all speculation
Couturiere	12386	Enterprise could only succeed in the event that
Couvercle ...	12387	Enterprise is one to be avoided
Couverture	12388	**Entertain(ed)**
Couvreur ...	12389	Will not entertain
Covacha ...	12390	Will entertain if
Covachuela	12391	Would you entertain the following proposition
Covaticcio...	12392	Should you entertain the proposal
Covazione...	12393	Should you not entertain the proposal
Coverlet ...	12394	Refuse(s) to entertain the idea
Covertato ...	12395	Cannot entertain any such proposition
Covertly ...	12396	Can you say if the (this) proposal is likely to be entertained
Covertness	12397	Do(es) not seem at all likely to entertain
ˇovertus ...	12398	In case you entertain

Covezuela...	12399	In case you do not entertain
Covidiglia ..	12400	Is (are) not at all likely to entertain
Coviglio ...	12401	Seem likely to entertain
Covinos ...	12402	Might entertain
Covoncello	12403	Might be inclined to entertain
Covrimento	12404	Refuse(s) to entertain any such proposal
Coward ...	12405	Refuse(s) to entertain any such proposition unless it is agreed [to
Cowherd ...	12406	**Entire(ly)**
Cowlick ...	12407	Is it entirely
Cowslips ...	12408	It is entirely
Coxam ...	12409	Is now entirely
Coxarum ...	12410	Is entirely out of the question
Coxcojilla...	12411	May be taken as entirely correct
Coxcomb ...	12412	Will be entirely
Coxendicem	12413	Entirely alters situation
Coyness ...	12414	Entirely on account of
Coyunda ...	12415	Entirely useless
Coyundilla	12416	Entirely worthless
Coyuntura	12417	Depends entirely on
Cozzone ...	12418	Depends entirely on yourself
Crab ...	12419	**Entitle**
Crablike ...	12420	To entitle
Crabron ...	12421	This payment will entitle me (us) to -
Crabronem	12422	This does not entitle
Crachat ...	12423	This will not entitle
Cracheur ...	12424	This (it) will entitle
Crachoter...	12425	Will (it) this entitle
Cracknels...	12426	What does this entitle me (us) to
Cradle ...	12427	What does it entitle you to
Craftiness...	12428	**Entitled**
Craftsman	12429	Entitled to full consideration
Cragginess	12430	Entitled to
Craindre ...	12431	Fully entitled
Cralo ...	12432	Is (are) entitled to (it)
Crambes ...	12433	Is (are) not entitled to (it)
Cramming	12434	Ought to be entitled to
Crampfish	12435	To be entitled to
Cramponner	12436	I (we) shall then be entitled to
Cranberry...	12437	Claim(s) that he is (they are) entitled to
Craniology	12438	Do not consider that we are entitled to
Cranium ...	12439	What do you think I am (we are) entitled to
Crapaudine	12440	Entitled to at least
Crapoussin	12441	Consider(s) that he is (they are) entitled to -
Crapulam ...	12442	Do you consider that he is (they are) entitled to
Crapuleux	12443	I consider that he is (they are) entitled to
Crapulone	12444	I do not consider that he is (they are) entitled to
Craquelin...	12445	He is (they are) certainly not entitled to
Craqueter...	12446	**Eocene**
Crasamente	12447	Eocene formation
Crascitar ...	12448	**Epidemic**
Crasedad ...	12449	Epidemic of —— broken out at ——
Crashing ...	12450	Epidemic increasing
Crasiento ...	12451	Epidemic diminishing
Crassamen	12452	Epidemic apparently at an end
Crassezza ...	12453	Men leaving on account of —— epidemic
Crassitudo	12454	**Equal**
Crateram ...	12455	To equal
Crateris ...	12456	Equal to
Craticula ...	12457	Equal to sample marked
Cravache ...	12458	Equal to a per centage of

Cravat ...	12459	Do you consider it equal
Cravatted...	12460	Do you consider they are equal
Crayeux ...	12461	Equal quantities by weight
Crayiness...	12462	Equivalent quantities according to assay
Crayons ...	12463	Fully equal
Creable ...	12464	Is (are) not equal to
Creador ...	12465	Is (are) equal to
Creagras ...	12466	It is certainly equal
Creaking ...	12467	Not at all equal
Creamlaid...	12468	Should have at least an equal amount
Creamy ...	12469	This is equal to
Creancier ..	12470	They are certainly equal
Creanza ...	12471	Facts are not at all equal to the statements made
Createth ...	12472	**Equally**
Creativo ...	12473	Pretty equally divided
Creatricem	12474	Not at all equally divided
Creatrix ...	12475	**Equipment(s)**
Creaturus...	12476	Full and complete equipment
Crebantar...	12477	Equipment of
Crebresco ...	12478	**Erect** (*See also* " Build.")
Crebritas ...	12479	To erect
Crecedero ...	12480	How long will it take to erect
Crecerelle ...	12481	Will take —— weeks to erect
Crecida ...	12482	Before I (we) can begin to erect
Creciente ...	12483	It will be necessary to erect
Credencia...	12484	Shall begin to erect at once
Credendum	12485	When will you begin to erect
Credente ...	12486	What will it cost to erect
Credibile ...	12487	Will cost to erect about
Creditojo ...	12488	**Erected**
Creditrice...	12489	Machinery erected ready for work
Credulita ...	12490	As soon as erected
Credulous...	12491	Erected complete
Creduto ...	12492	Not yet erected
Creguela ...	12493	**Erecting**
Crelia ...	12494	Have received the following tenders for erecting the
Cremabant	12495	Have let the contract for erecting the —— at
Cremaillon	12496	I have contracted for erecting necessary plant
Crematos ...	12497	Contract for erecting
Cremaveram	12498	The erecting alone
Cremavisse	12499	**Erection**
Cremesin ...	12500	Contract for erection amounts to
Cremiere ...	12501	Erection cannot be deferred after ——
Cremisino...	12502	Estimated cost of erection
Cremor ...	12503	I (we) advise immediate erection
Crencha ...	12504	I (we) advise that erection be deferred pending
Crenelure ...	12505	Is (are) now in course of erection
Crenulated	12506	Push on with all grading prior to erection
Creosote ...	12507	The erection of
Crepaccio ...	12508	The actual erection will only occupy —— days
Crepacuore	12509	Telegraph (cable) whether you advise immediate erection of
Crepatura...	12510	For cost of transport and erection on mine add
Crepitate ...	12511	Erection of which will be completed on
Crepolare ...	12512	Erection of which was completed on
Crepone ...	12513	The erection of this (it) will shortly be completed
Crepunde ...	12514	Erection of all machinery is being vigorously pushed
Crepuscolo	12515	As soon as I (we) have finished the erection of
Crescentar	12516	**Erosion**
Crescere ...	12517	**Erratic**
Crescevole...	12518	**Erroneous**

Crescione ...	12519	Price erroneous
Crescitore	12520	Conclusion erroneous
Cresciuto ...	12521	Altogether erroneous
Cresentina	12522	Not so erroneous as was at first thought
Cresimante	12523	Is it (this) erroneous
Cresimato...	12524	Is erroneous
Crespar ...	12525	Is not erroneous
Crespilla ...	12526	**Error**
Cress ...	12527	Advised in error
Cresylic ...	12528	Cancelled in error
Cretam ...	12529	Is this not an error
Cretarium...	12530	Ordered in error
Cretatus ...	12531	Omitted in error
Creteler ...	12532	Are you sure there is no error
Crethmorum	12533	There is no error whatever
Cretinism...	12534	There is an error in clause —— of my letter dated
Cretona ...	12535	There would appear to be a considerable error
Creuser ...	12536	The only error is
Crevasser ...	12537	Error may be disregarded
Crevisset ...	12538	Owing to error on my part
Creyente ...	12539	Owing to error on your part
Crezneja ...	12540	Owing to error on part of ——
Criacao ...	12541	Was written in error, it should read
Criacion ...	12542	Please correct error
Criadero ...	12543	Cannot correct error until [mail
Criadilla ...	12544	Error of —— in accounts; please trace it and correct by first
Criaduela ...	12545	Cannot trace error; have gone systematically through the
Criailleur ...	12546	Has (have) discovered error; will mail correction [accounts
Criarde ...	12547	**Eruptive**
Criaturica...	12548	Eruptive rock
Criazon ...	12549	Eruptive series
Cribador ...	12550	**Escape**
Cribbage ...	12551	Escape if you can
Cribillo ...	12552	Too late to escape
Criblure ...	12553	Escape is practical so far
Criborum ...	12554	A very narrow escape
Cribos ...	12555	In order to escape consequences
Cribrandum	12556	**Escaped**
Cribrare ...	12557	Has (have) escaped
Cricchio ...	12558	All the men escaped unhurt
Cricket ...	12559	Only —— men escaped
Cricketing	12560	**Escarpment**
Crimenlese	12561	**Escrow** (*See also* " Deeds.")
Criminal ...	12562	We hold " in escrow "
Criminem...	12563	We hold " in escrow " deed on
Criminoso	12564	Do you hold " in escrow "
Crimple ...	12565	Do not hold " in escrow "
Crimson ...	12566	Placed " in escrow "
Crimsoned	12567	To be placed " in escrow " with
Crimsoning	12568	**Essential**
Crinado ...	12569	Essential to
Cringed ...	12570	Do you (does ——) consider it essential
Cringeling	12571	I (we) do not consider it essential
Crinibus ...	12572	I (we) consider it essential
Criniera ...	12573	Is it essential that I (we)
Criobolium	12574	It is essential that I (we) should control
Criocca ...	12575	It is absolutely essential that (to)
Criollo ...	12576	It is not at all essential that (to)
Crippled ...	12577	To be essential
Crisalida ...	12578	The essential difference is

Crisantemo	12579	What is the essential difference between
Crisma ...	12580	Would then become essential
Crismera ...	12581	**Establish**
Crisocola ...	12582	To establish
Crisolada ...	12583	Endeavour to establish it (this) to ——'s satisfaction
Crisolito ...	12584	Establish if possible whether
Crisopasso	12585	Has (have) tried to establish but failed
Crisopeya ...	12586	Might establish
Crispation	12587	To fully establish would cost
Crispatura	12588	Unable to establish
Crispula ...	12589	**Established**
Cristal ...	12590	Has (have) fully established (that)
Cristalino ...	12591	Established beyond doubt (that)
Cristianar...	12592	Has (have) been established
Cristiere ...	12593	Might be established at ——
Cristifero ...	12594	**Establishment**
Criterion ...	12595	Entire establishment is
Crith	12596	Establishment was very extravagant
Criticable...	12597	Entire establishment was demoralized
Criticar ...	12598	Establishment was very economical
Criticised ...	12599	**Estate** (*See also* "Property.")
Critique ...	12600	What does the estate consist of
Crivellajo...	12601	Estate consists of
Croajar ...	12602	Estate covers an area of
Croasser ...	12603	Estate is valued at
Crocchetto	12604	What is the approximate value of the estate
Crocchiere	12605	In real estate
Crocchione	12606	Will require to come out of the estate
Crocellino...	12607	Should the estate not realize more than
Croceous ...	12608	**Estimate(s)** (*See also* "Excess.")
Crocevia ...	12609	To estimate
Crochel	12610	Estimate to
Crocheter ...	12611	Estimate of
Crocicchio	12612	Estimate is for
Crocifisso ...	12613	Estimate altogether exaggerated
Crocione ...	12614	Estimate altogether incorrect
Crocitar ...	12615	Is (are) included in the estimate
Crockery ...	12616	At what do you estimate
Crocodile ...	12617	At what do you estimate cost for next four weeks
Crocomagna	12618	My (our) estimate of cost for next four weeks is
Crocotam ...	12619	At what do you estimate the returns for the next four weeks
Crocuses ...	12620	My (our) estimate of returns for the next four weeks is
Crogiuolo ...	12621	Cannot form any reliable estimate as to
Croisement	12622	Cannot estimate the value of
Croisillon ...	12623	Can you estimate how long it will take to complete
Croissant ...	12624	Not possible to estimate
Croix ...	12625	Estimate(s) mailed on ——
Crollante ...	12626	Estimate(s) will be mailed within —— days
Cromhorn	12627	Estimate(s) accepted
Cromorna...	12628	Estimate(s) not accepted
Cronea ...	12629	I (we) estimate the value of the ore actually in reserve at ——
Cronicon ...	12630	I (we) estimate the quantity of ore actually in reserve at ——
Cronista ...	12631	I (we) estimate the total expenses at
Cronografo	12632	I (we) cannot estimate
Cronologia	12633	Please mail detailed estimate for
Cronometro	12634	What do you estimate your expenditure at for the month(s) of
Crookedly...	12635	Please cable rough estimate of time required
Crooks ...	12636	Please cable rough estimate of cost required
Croquant ...	12637	This is a conservative estimate
Croqueur ...	12638	Following are not included in my (our) estimate

Crosazzo ...	12639	In your estimate have you included ——
Crosier ...	12640	When do you estimate
Crosmis ...	12641	Do(es) your estimate(s) include
Crossbow ...	12642	Estimate(s) do(es) include
Crossroad...	12643	Mail estimate for complete equipment of hoisting and pump-
Crosswise...	12644	Get estimate(s) in for [ing machinery at shaft
Crostata ...	12645	**Estimated**
Crotalorum	12646	Estimated at
Crotalos ...	12647	Estimated at about
Crotchet ...	12648	Was then estimated at
Crotorar ...	12649	Estimated cost
Croulement	12650	What is the estimated cost of
Croupier ...	12651	The estimated cost is
Croustade...	12652	What is the estimated delay
Croustille...	12653	Estimated delay will be —— days
Crowle ...	12654	Estimated higher by ——
Crowning...	12655	Estimated lower by ——
Croyable ...	12656	What is the estimated value
Croyance ...	12657	What is the estimated value and tonnage of
Cruaute ...	12658	The estimated value is
Cruccevole	12659	The estimated tonnage is ——
Crucciare ...	12660	Estimated at —— tons, approximate value ——
Cruccioso ...	12661	May be estimated loosely at
Crucera ...	12662	Estimated expenses of the trip would amount to ——
Crucetas ...	12663	Value of plant, stores and machinery is estimated at ——
Cruche ...	12664	Value of mines alone is estimated at ——
Cruciando...	12665	Value of buildings is estimated at ——
Cruciate ...	12666	The total value of mines, plant, movables and immovables is
Crucifero ...	12667	What is the estimated time [estimated at ——
Crucificar...	12668	The estimated time is —— days
Crucifixor...	12669	What is your estimated expenditure next three months
Cruciform	12670	Estimated expenditure next three months will be at the rate
Crucigero ...	12671	**Estimation** [of —— per month
Crucillo ...	12672	What is your estimation of
Crudamente	12673	Formed a very different estimation
Crudariam	12674	In my (our) estimation
Crudeletto	12675	**Et cetera**
Crudelibus	12676	**Even**
Crudelta ...	12677	Even money
Crudity ...	12678	Even figures
Crudivoro...	12679	Even if
Crueldad ...	12680	Even if you could
Cruelty ...	12681	Even if you can insure
Cruentabo	12682	Even if I (we) were able
Cruentar ...	12683	**Evening**
Cruet ...	12684	Arrived on the evening of the ——
Cruetstand	12685	On the evening of the ——
Crujido ...	12686	Last evening
Crumble ...	12687	This evening
Crument ...	12688	To-morrow evening
Crumillas...	12689	Each evening
Crunching	12690	Shall start on the evening of the ——
Crupper ...	12691	**Event**
Crusader ...	12692	In any event
Cruscajo ...	12693	In such an event
Cruschello	12694	In this event you had better
Cruscone ...	12695	Only in such an event shall I (we)
Crust ...	12696	Except in the event of
Crustaceo...	12697	In the event of
Crustily ...	12698	**Ever**

Crustulum	12699	If ever
Cruzada ...	12700	**Every**
Cruzamen...	12701	Every minute is of importance
Crying ...	12702	Every allowance will be made
Cryptarum	12703	Every prospect of
Cryptas ...	12704	Every prospect of getting
Cryptic ...	12705	Every opportunity
Cryptogam	12706	**Everybody**
Cuacaro ...	12707	Everybody safe
Cuaderna ...	12708	Everybody here
Cuaderviz...	12709	**Everyone**
Cuadrantal	12710	Is everyone
Cuadratin...	12711	**Everything**
Cuadrete ...	12712	Everything arranged
Cuadricula	12713	Everything is
Cuadrienal	12714	Is everything
Cuadriga ...	12715	Everything to
Cuadrilla ...	12716	Everything to be
Cuadrivio...	12717	Everything will be
Cuajada ...	12718	Is everything to be.
Cuajadillo	12719	Everything arranged for speed
Cuajaleche	12720	Everything will be arranged for
Cuajarejo ...	12721	As soon as everything is satisfactorily arranged
Cuajaron ...	12722	Everything continues satisfactory
Cualidad ...	12723	Everything is very satisfactory
Cualque ...	12724	Do everything you can
Cualquiera	12725	As soon as everything
Cuamano ...	12726	Do everything possible to prevent
Cuantimas	12727	Everything will soon be put right
Cuarango ...	12728	Everything is now on the property
Cuarentena	12729	Everything was delivered except
Cuaresma ...	12730	Everything will be ready to begin
Cuartago ...	12731	Everything possible will be done
Cuartal ...	12732	Everything possible has been done
Cuartanal...	12733	Forward everything in good order
Cuartear ...	12734	I (we) have contracted for everything necessary
Cuartilla ...	12735	**Evidence(s)**
Cuasimodo	12736	Evidence is not to be depended upon
Cuatequil ...	12737	Evidence can be depended upon
Cuatorce ...	12738	Get evidence of —— (as to)
Cuatralbo...	12739	If you consider you have sufficient evidence
Cuatrero ...	12740	Arrived too late to give evidence
Cuatrin ...	12741	Can you obtain any evidence as to
Cuatrodial	12742	Evidence is distinctly in favour of
Cuatropea...	12743	Get all the evidence you can to prove
Cubantem	12744	Get all the favourable evidence you can collect
Cubantibus	12745	The only favourable evidence is
Cubatto ...	12746	Withhold any evidence (as to)
Cubature ...	12747	**Evidently**
Cubeba ...	12748	Is evidently
Cubertado	12749	Evidently not
Cubetilla ...	12750	Evidently for effect
Cubetis ...	12751	Evidently *bonâ fide*
Cubicacion	12752	**Exact**
Cubichete...	12753	As nearly exact as possible
Cubiculare	12754	As nearly exact as I (we) can
Cubicule ...	12755	The exact quantity
Cubierta ...	12756	What is the exact quantity
Cubijadera	12757	Cannot tell the exact quantity
Cubijar ...	12758	Need not be very exact

Cubilete	...	12759	**Exactly**
Cubillo	...	12760	Exactly as
Cubitalis	...	12761	Wish(es) to know exactly
Cubitoso	...	12762	Was not exactly so
Cuboidal	...	12763	Was exactly as stated
Cubrepan	...	12764	Is (are) not exactly what was (were) wanted
Cubriente	...	12765	Is (are) exactly what was (were) wanted
Cucaracha		12766	Act exactly as requested
Cucarda	...	12767	**Exaggerated**
Cuccagna	...	12768	Has been grossly exaggerated
Cucchiaino		12769	Has not been exaggerated to any extent
Cucchiaja	...	12770	Is altogether exaggerated
Cucciolino		12771	Not in any way exaggerated
Cuccuma	...	12772	**Examination** (*See also* "Assistance," "Caved," "Exonerates,"
Cuchar	...	12773	Examination will ["Inspection," "Report," &c.)
Cucharazo		12774	Examination will not
Cuchicheo		12775	Will examination
Cuchilla	...	12776	Examination can be made at once
Cuchillazo		12777	Examination can be deferred until
Cuchitril	...	12778	Examination completed
Cuchufleta		12779	When will examination be completed
Cucimento		12780	Examination will be completed by
Cucinajo	...	12781	Examination nearly finished
Cucinetta	...	12782	Examination will be made by
Cuciniera	...	12783	Examination satisfactory
Cucieso	...	12784	Examination not at all satisfactory
Cucitore	...	12785	Examination altogether unsatisfactory
Cucitrice	...	12786	If examination is not satisfactory
Cuclillas	...	12787	If examination is satisfactory
Cucufa	...	12788	Examination finished and report mailed
Cuculiare	...	12789	You will have every facility for examination
Cucullato	...	12790	After making a most thorough examination my (our) opinion is
Cuculo	...	12791	Examination impossible owing to
Cucumber		12792	Examination has disclosed
Cucurbit	...	12793	How long is examination expected to take
Cucurucho		12794	Examination would probably take
Cucuzza	...	12795	Examination fee, exclusive of travelling expenses
Cucuzzolo	...	12796	Examination fee, inclusive of travelling expenses
Cudbear	...	12797	Make a thorough examination
Cudgeled	...	12798	Examination should be most severe
Cudiciar	...	12799	Make an examination of —— mine, and cable opinion
Cudonem	...	12800	Make examination of —— mine, and cable abstract report as
Cudweed	...	12801	Subject to examination and report [quickly as possible
Cuebano	...	12802	Will you undertake examination and report of mine in (at) ——
Cueillette	...	12803	What would be your fee for examination of mine within ——
			[days' journey of ——
Cueilloir	...	12804	What would be your fee for examination of —— mine
Cuelga	...	12805	Will not admit of close examination
Cuembas	...	12806	When can you commence examination
Cuentero	...	12807	Could commence examination about ——
Cuentista	...	12808	When can you leave to examine —— mine
Cuerdecito		12809	The cost of examination will amount to ——
Cuerezuelo		12810	My opinion is confirmed by the examination of adjoining mines
Cuerpecico		12811	Can you suggest reliable expert for examination of —— mine
Cuesco	...	12812	I (we) cannot recommend —— mine after my (our) examination
Cuesquillo		12813	I (we) can strongly recommend —— mine after my (our)
Cuestecica		12814	I (we) find on closer examination that [examination
Cuestura	...	12815	Since my last examination
Cuetzale	...	12816	Everything should be submitted to the most rigid examination
Cuevero	...	12817	In case special examination should cause you to alter your opinion

Cuferionem	12818	Special examination has not altered my opinion
Cuffia ...	12819	Special examination has shown [ficial
Cuffiaccia ...	12820	Was only on the property —— days ; examination most super-
Cuffiare ...	12821	Surface examination could not be made on account of snow
Cuffietta ...	12822	Have arranged for examination of mine
Cuffione ...	12823	Have you arranged for examination of mine
Cufflotto ...	12824	Have not arranged for examination of mine
Cuginomo	12825	Will probably arrange for examination of mine within next few
Cuguiada ...	12826	How long would examination occupy [days
Cugulla ...	12827	Examination would occupy —— days
Cuidado ...	12828	Examination would occupy —— weeks
Cuirassier...	12829	Examination of property
Cuisine ...	12830	Examination of mine
Cuitades ...	12831	Of examination
Cuitar ...	12832	To complete the examination will take another —— week(s)
Cuivreux ...	12833	Proceed without delay to make an examination of property ; [cable opinion and mail report
Cujusmodi	12834	Have made a more careful examination of the ground
Cujusso ...	12835	**Examine** (See also "Report.")
Culaccino...	12836	To examine
Culajo ...	12837	Examine carefully
Culatazo ...	12838	Examine and report
Culattario...	12839	Examine carefully and be on the look out for
Culbuter ...	12840	Can you examine property immediately
Culcitas ...	12841	Can you proceed immediately to examine —— mine
Culcusido ...	12842	To examine mining property
Culebrazo...	12843	To examine and report upon
Culebrica ...	12844	Arrange to leave as soon as possible to examine
Culebron ...	12845	I could leave to examine the property you mention on —— ; [will do so on receipt of your written or cabled instructions
Culeggiare	12846	**Examined**
Culetta ...	12847	Have examined as requested
Culignam...	12848	When you have examined, send account to
Culinary ...	12849	When you have examined, send report to
Cullare ...	12850	To be examined
Cullendor...	12851	Previously to being examined
Cullidor ...	12852	Have you previously examined the ——
Culmifero...	12853	Have examined
Culminare	12854	Is said to have been examined by ——
Culmine ...	12855	Must be most minutely examined
Culmosas ...	12856	The property has already been examined by ——, who ——
Culon ...	12857	Examined by ——, whose report was favourable
Culottier ...	12858	Examined by ——, whose report was distinctly unfavourable
Culpable ...	12859	Examined by
Culpacion...	12860	Never examined by
Culpavit ...	12861	**Examining** (See also "Carefully.")
Culprits ...	12862	Now examining
Cultamente	12863	Since examining
Cultedad ...	12864	**Exceed(s)**
Culterano...	12865	Will exceed
Culticulam	12866	Will not exceed
Cultiello ...	12867	Will it exceed
Cultiparlo...	12868	Exceed(s) the estimates by
Cultivable...	12869	Is said to exceed
Cultivar ...	12870	Must not exceed
Cultivated	12871	Must not be allowed to exceed
Cultore ...	12872	Not to exceed —— lbs. in weight
Cultoribus	12873	You may exceed
Cultro ...	12874	Do (does) not exceed
Culturar ...	12875	**Exceeded**

Cultus ...	12876	Has (have) already exceeded
Culvertail	12877	Has (have) not yet exceeded
Cumatile ...	12878	Has (have) exceeded
Cumbrous	12879	Must not be exceeded
Cuminic ...	12880	Have you exceeded
Cumplidero	12881	**Exceeding**
Cumplir ...	12882	If exceeding
Cumque ...	12883	If not exceeding
Cumulabant	12884	Not exceeding
Cumular ...	12885	Exceeding —— but not ——
Cumulativo	12886	**Exceedingly**
Cumylic ...	12887	Exceedingly profitable
Cunadia ...	12888	I regard it as likely to be exceedingly
Cundido ...	12889	Of exceedingly rich ore
Cunera	12890	Exceedingly glad
Cunningly	12891	**Excellent**
Cunziera ...	12892	Believed to be excellent
Cuociore ...	12893	Excellent accounts from
Cuocitura...	12894	**Except**
Cuodlibeto	12895	Except to
Cuoprire ...	12896	Except for
Cuoricino ..	12897	Except that
Cupboard...	12898	Except only
Cupidezza	12899	Except you are (—— is) able
Cupidigia ...	12900	Do not agree except
Cupiditam	12901	Will not agree except
Cupidity ...	12902	Will not go except
Cupivere ...	12903	Will go except prevented by
Cuplarum	12904	**Excepted**
Cupoletta ...	12905	Was (were) excepted
Cuppedias	12906	Was (were) not excepted
Cupping ...	12907	Excepted only
Cupressina	12908	**Exception(s)**
Cupulino ...	12909	No exception should be made
Curador ...	12910	No exception can be allowed
Curagione...	12911	With no exception whatever
Curalle ...	12912	The only exception is (was)
Curandajo	12913	Without exception
Curandero	12914	With the exception of
Curandibus	12915	With few exceptions
Curante ...	12916	With the following exceptions
Curates ...	12917	**Excess**
Curative ...	12918	If any excess
Curatore ...	12919	Any excess to be paid for
Curatrice .	12920	Any excess would be devoted to
Curattiere ..	12921	Do you anticipate any excess
†Curazgo ...	12922	Do not anticipate there will be any excess
Curazione	12923	Is largely in excess of
Curdling ...	12924	In case there is any excess
Cureless ...	12925	In excess of original estimate
Curement...	12926	There is no excess
Cureria ...	12927	There will be no excess
Curesca ...	12928	There will be a slight excess
Curfew ...	12929	**Excessive**
Curfewbell	12930	Excessive valuation
Curialita ...	12931	Is not the charge for —— excessive
Curiandolo	12932	An excessive demand
Curicciare	12933	Can you induce —— to reduce figure ; price excessive
Curile ...	12934	Price asked is excessive
Curiosetto...	12935	**Exchange** (*See also* " Stock Exchange.")

Curiosidad	12936	Exchange on
Curioso ...	12937	Exchange on London
Curliness ...	12938	Exchange on New York
Curmudgeon	12939	Exchange is rising
Curruca ...	12940	Exchange is falling
Currycomb	12941	Exchange on —— is ——
Cursado ...	12942	Exchange is likely to be
Cursante ...	12943	At what rate of exchange
Cursarily ...	12944	At current rate of exchange
Cursillo ...	12945	Calculated at an exchange of
Cursor ...	12946	In exchange for
Curtacion ...	12947	If the exchange is favourable
Curtaribus	12948	Rate of exchange is
Curtidero ...	12949	What is the present rate of exchange
Curvated ...	12950	**Exchanged**
Curvatura...	12951	Are to be exchanged on
Curvescent	12952	Was (were) exchanged at (on)
Curvetto ...	12953	Now ready to be exchanged
Curviligne	12954	**Exchequer**
Curvilineo	12955	Exchequer exhausted
Curvitate ...	12956	In the exchequer
Cusarsi ...	12957	**Excite**
Cuscitore ...	12958	To excite
Cuscitrice...	12959	Do not excite
Cuscolios ...	12960	Must on no account excite
Cusculia ...	12961	Will it excite
Cusoliere ...	12962	It will excite
Cuspidal ...	12963	It will not excite
Cuspidibus	12964	Take care not to excite any suspicion
Custodiens	12965	**Excitement**
Custodire ...	12966	Excitement increasing
Custoditio	12967	Much excitement prevails as to
Customary	12968	Might take advantage of excitement to
Custos ...	12969	There is considerable excitement
Cutaneous	12970	There is no excitement at all
Cuterzola ...	12971	Excitement is diminishing
Cutiano ...	12972	Has the excitement about —— subsided
Cuticagna	12973	The excitement has subsided
Cuticola ...	12974	**Exclusive**
Cutidero ...	12975	Exclusive of foregoing
Cutis ...	12976	Exclusive of following
Cutlasses ...	12977	Exclusive of above
Cutretta ...	12978	Is this exclusive of
Cuvelage ...	12979	This is not exclusive of
Cuvidoso ...	12980	This should be exclusive of
Cyamelide	12981	This is exclusive of
Cyanogen...	12982	Exclusive of travelling expenses
Cyanurate	12983	Exclusive of
Cyceonem	12984	**Exclusively**
Cycloidal ...	12985	Exclusively derived from
Cyclometry	12986	It has been exclusively shown that
Cyclopean	12987	**Execute**
Cydoniam...	12988	Execute promptly
Cygnet ...	12989	Refuse(s) to execute
Cylindrage	12990	Consent(s) to execute
Cylindrum	12991	To execute
Cymam ...	12992	**Executed**
Cymbals ...	12993	Executed by
Cymiferous	12994	Cannot be executed before
Cymol ...	12995	Have the documents been executed

Cynanchis	12996	To be executed on
Cynicism ...	12997	Documents will be executed on
Cynique ...	12998	Documents were executed on
Cynography	12999	Was (were) executed
Cynomyias	13000	Was (were) executed to-day
Cynopis ...	**13001**	When will the documents be executed
Cynosure ...	13002	Has (have) been very well executed
Cyperidum	13003	Has (have) been badly executed
Cypresse ...	13004	**Exercise** (*See also* " Care," " Diligence.")
Cyprinos ...	13005	Exercise yourself meanwhile
Cytherean	13006	Must exercise a little patience
Dabbene ...	13007	**Exertion(s)**
Dabovis ...	13008	Will require my (our) utmost exertions
Dabster ...	13009	No exertion on my part shall be wanting
Dachdecker	13010	In spite of every exertion
Dachfahne	13011	Suggest further exertions on your part to induce
Dachkammer	13012	Use every exertion possible
Dachrinne	13013	Utmost exertion
Dachstuhl	13014	**Exist(s)**
Dachtraufe	13015	To exist
Dachziegel	13016	Alleged to exist
Dacion ...	13017	Ceased to exist (when)
Dactilo ...	13018	Do they still exist
Dactylion ...	13019	Profitable conditions do not exist
Dactylique	13020	Do not now exist
Dactylotum	13021	**Existed**
Dactylus ...	13022	Could not have existed
Daddevero	13023	Only existed until
Daddy ...	13024	**Existence**
Dadero ...	13025	In order to prove existence of
Dadivado ...	13026	This will prove existence of
Dadoxylon	13027	**Existing**
Dadurch ...	13028	My (our) existing contract
Daedalum	13029	My (our) existing agreement
Daemonos	13030	If now existing
Daente ...	13031	I should suggest under existing circumstances that
Dafern ...	13032	Under existing circumstances
Daffodil ...	13033	What do you suggest under existing circumstances
Daftish ...	13034	Is (are) at present existing
Dagegen ...	13035	As at present existing
Daggers ...	13036	**Exonerate(s)**
Daggled ...	13037	Examination completely exonerates
Daggling ...	13038	Examination does not altogether exonerate ——
Daghetta ...	13039	Board exonerates —— fully
Dagorne ...	13040	Verdict fully exonerates
Daguilla ...	13041	**Expect**
Daheim ...	13042	To expect
Dahier ...	13043	Expect to
Dahingeben	13044	Expect to be
Dahinten ...	13045	Expect to be in —— about
Dahlia ...	13046	Expect to be with
Dainos ...	13047	Within what length do you expect
Daintiness	13048	Within what time do you expect
Dainty ...	13049	Do you expect
Daire ...	13050	Do not expect
Dairying ...	13051	Expect will be about
Dairyman	13052	Expect to be able to cable definitely about
Daisies ...	13053	How many (much) do you expect
Dalesmen ...	13054	I (we) expect
Dalfino ...	13055	I (we) do not expect

Dallador ...	13056	You can expect me soon
Dallage ...	13057	+ You can expect me (——) on
Dallato ...	13058	What do you expect profit will be
Dalliance ...	13059	Expect profit to be at least
Dallied ...	13060	I (we) expect —— will refuse
Dalmatian	13061	+ Expect(s) to see you about
Dalmatique	13062	When do you expect
Daltonism	13063	When do you expect to know results
Damaceno	13064	When do you expect that (to)
Damaggio	13065	When may I (we) expect to hear from you
Damajuana	13066	You may expect
Damalig ...	13067	**Expected**
Damalionem	13068	Expected to be ready not later than
Damasanio	13069	Expected to be about
Damascado	13070	Better than expected
Damascened	13071	Can be expected at any moment
Damaschino	13072	Expected to arrive
Damasco ...	13073	Expected to leave
Damasina...	13074	Is expected to
Damask ...	13075	Is not expected before
Damasqueta	13076	Was not altogether expected
Damasseur	13077	Is as I (we) expected
Damasten	13078	Improvement may be expected
Damaza ...	13079	Not so good as expected
Dameggiare	13080	More than I (we) expected
Damenbret	13081	**Expedient**
Damenhut	13082	Not expedient
Damenspiel	13083	Not expedient just now
Damenwelt	13084	If expedient
Damhirsch	13085	As may be deemed expedient
Damiento...	13086	If this should be deemed expedient
Damigella	13087	If I (we) should deem it expedient
Damigiana	13088	Very expedient
Damisela ...	13089	**Expedite**
Dammara...	13090	Would expedite
Dammerig	13091	Would not expedite
Dammerung	13092	Expedite matters
Dammulas	13093	Would it expedite matters if
Damnabat	13094	It would expedite matters if
Damnandi	13095	Can you suggest anything to expedite matters
Damnar ...	13096	Expedite the matter all you can
Damnation	13097	Can you not expedite this business
Damnatory	13098	In order to expedite
Damnetur	13099	**Expedited**
Damnificar	13100	Since expedited
Damoiseau	13101	Was (were) very much expedited
Damoiselle	13102	**Expedition**
Damonia ...	13103	Expedition is to start on
Damonisch	13104	Expedition started on
Damourite	13105	Expedition should be equipped with
Dampers ...	13106	Expedition will consist of
Dampfbad	13107	Members of expedition are all in good health
Dampfboot	13108	Cost of fitting out expedition will amount to
Dampfen ...	13109	Cost of fitting out expedition amounted to
Dampfkraft	13110	While the expedition is on the road
Dampfrohre	13111	Expedition will be absent at least —— weeks
Dampfwagen	13112	Has seriously crippled expedition
Damping ...	13113	All communications for expedition can be directed to
Dampishly	13114	**Expended**
Dampness	13115	To be expended upon

Damsels ...	13116	Twice expended
Damsons ...	13117	What has been expended since
Damularum	13118	Already expended
Danador ...	13119	**Expenditure** (*See also* " Care," " Cost.")
Danajaccio	13120	Telegraph at what you estimate monthly expenditure
Danajale ...	13121	Cable present total monthly expenditure
Danajoso ...	13122	Authorize expenditure of —— monthly
Danajuolo	13123	All expenditure on —— must be kept distinct from
Danaresco	13124	By a limited expenditure of say
Danaruzzo	13125	By a judicious expenditure of
Danced ...	13126	Can you achieve success by a further expenditure of
Danchado...	13127	Do the prospects justify any further expenditure
Dancing ...	13128	Present prospects do not justify any further expenditure
Dancingly	13129	Expenditure must be reduced to [whatever
Dandelion	13130	Expenditure on Capital account
Dandiner ...	13131	Expenditure on Revenue account
Dandruff ...	13132	I believe a further expenditure of —— would be amply
Dandyism	13133	The expenditure of [justified
Daneben ...	13134	The expenditure has been mainly on account of
Dangereux	13135	Expenditure has undoubtedly been extravagant
Dangiero ...	13136	Expenditure has been very economical
Danieder ...	13137	To reduce expenditure at this moment would I (we) think be
Danino ...	13138	This will mean an expenditure of [unwise
Danistarum	13139	Suggest you limit your expenditure to
Dankbar ...	13140	Keep your expenditure as low as possible
Dankfest ...	13141	The expenditure on improvements will amount to ——
Dankleid ...	13142	I (we) believe would well repay expenditure of ——
Dankopfer	13143	Cannot recommend any additional expenditure
Danksagung	13144	Would strongly recommend an additional expenditure of ——
Dannabile...	13145	Stop all further expenditure
Dannaggio	13146	Before I (we) order further expenditure
Dannagione	13147	Expenditure has been mainly on capital account [mailed
Dannevole	13148	We understand that all expenditure is stopped and accounts
Dannoso ...	13149	Close all expenditure and mail accounts as quickly as possible
Danoja ...	13150	Secretary of —— instructs that all expenditure be stopped
Dansant ...	13151	Have telegraphed —— to stop all further cash expenditure
Danseries ...	13152	Stoppage of all expenditure ordered
Danseuse ...	13153	Stop all further cash expenditure forthwith
Danta ...	13154	—— has ordered stoppage of all cash expenditure
Dantelado	13155	Further expenditure for the present
Dantesco ...	13156	Estimated Revenue expenditure for the month of
Dantesque	13157	Estimated Capital expenditure for the month of
Dantista ...	13158	**Expense(s)** (*See also* " Estimate.")
Danzador ...	13159	Expenses to be divided between
Danzante ...	13160	Will —— agree to divide expenses
Danzarin ...	13161	Expenses exceed estimate by ——
Danzatrice	13162	Expenses must not exceed
Danzetta ...	13163	Expenses per ton of 2,240 lbs.
Daonella ...	13164	Expenses per ton of 2,000 lbs.
Daphnias ...	13165	For expenses
Daphnonis	13166	Expenses will be about
Dapibus ...	13167	Expenses will be at least
Dapifex ...	13168	Expenses will be allowed
Dapificem...	13169	Expenses will not be allowed
Dapperling	13170	Attendant expenses make it not worth while
Dappiede ...	13171	Current expenses
Dappled ...	13172	Cut down expenses
Dappoco ...	13173	Cannot lessen expenses
Dappoiche	13174	To lessen expenses
Dappresso	13175	Week's expenses

Darbringen	13176	Fortnight's expenses
Dardabasi	13177	Month's expenses
Dardetto ...	13178	All expenses should be paid by ——
Dardiero ...	13179	All expenses to be paid by ——
Daricus ...	13180	Cable total expenses for month ending ——
Daringly ...	13181	Total expenses for month ending —— are
Dariole ...	13182	Does —— include fee and travelling expenses
Darkened...	13183	Future expenses will be less
Darkening	13184	Do not spare any reasonable expense of time or money
Darksome...	13185	No reasonable expense(s) will be spared
Darlegung	13186	At whose expense
Darleihen...	13187	Total working expenses
Darmgicht	13188	Out of pocket expenses
Darmsaite	13189	Do not incur any serious expense until authorized
Darnach ...	13190	—— will have to bear the expense
Darning ...	13191	Expenses must be limited to
Darreichen	13192	Expenses to be charged to ——
Darsena ...	13193	Must limit expenses to —— for the present
Darsteller...	13194	Expense is an object
Darthun ...	13195	Expense is not of much object provided we get the right man
Dartreux ...	13196	Absolute expenses will necessitate a cash outlay of ——
Daruber ...	13197	To meet current expenses
Darwinism	13198	Shall require —— to meet current expenses
Daseas ...	13199	Expenses exceed returns by ——
Daselbst ...	13200	Returns exceed expenses by ——
Dasornis ...	13201	Expenses will probably not exceed
Dassajezza	13202	For general expenses
Dassezzo ...	13203	If expenses do not exceed
Dasyceps ...	13204	Have paid —— on account of expenses
Dataria ...	13205	What do the legal expenses amount to
Datilado ...	13206	Legal expenses amount to ——
Datilillo ...	13207	Legal expenses will probably amount to ——
Datiren ...	13208	Expenses —— amount to
Datisceal ...	13209	What will be the additional expense
Dativo ...	13210	Additional expense will amount to ——
Datore ...	13211	Keep expenses quite distinct
Datrice ...	13212	This will avoid the extra expense of ——
Dattelbaum	13213	No further expenses must be incurred on my (our) a/c
Dattilogia	13214	Our funds are insufficient to meet extra expenses by ——
Dattorno ...	13215	Our monthly expenses will in future be diminished
Daubiere ...	13216	Regardless of expense
Daubing ...	13217	To cover expenses
Daucorum	13218	—— refuse(s) to pay expenses
Dauerhaft	13219	Specify each item of expense
Daughters	13220	So as to avoid unnecessary expense
Daumling...	13221	Will travelling expenses be allowed
Dauntless...	13222	Inclusive of travelling expenses
Dauphine...	13223	Exclusive of travelling expenses
Davanzale	13224	Will pay travelling expenses and fee of
Davidico ...	13225	Travelling expenses will be allowed
Dawider ...	13226	Travelling expenses will not be allowed
Dazwischen	13227	The expense is too great
Deaconship	13228	The only expense will be ——
Deadlight...	13229	The expense will be between —— and ——
Deadliness	13230	To meet necessary expense
Deafmute...	13231	To meet the expense of this (it)
Dealbamus	13232	Total expenses for
Dealbavi ...	13233	What will be about the expense
Deamavisse	13234	We have only sufficient in hand to meet one month's expenses
Deanery ...	13235	What will the extra expense amount to

Deartuare...	13236	The extra expense will amount to ——
Deathbed ...	13237	Who shall I (we) look to to pay expenses
Deathlike...	13238	You must look to —— for your expenses
Deathscene	13239	Total monthly expense ——
Debaccare...	13240	Total expense for the month of ——
Debacher ...	13241	Telegraph me —— for travelling expenses
Debajo ...	13242	Have you closed all expense as regards
Debandar ...	13243	Do not incur any serious expense
Debaptiser	13244	Limit all expenses as much as possible
Debardeur	13245	Shall curtail all expenses when such can be done properly
Debasingly	13246	Stop all expenses meanwhile
Debatir ...	13247	Witnesses expenses must be guaranteed
Debattiren	13248	**Expensive**
Debatuit ...	13249	Is an expensive man
Debauchery	13250	A very expensive arrangement
Debeacion...	13251	Not at all expensive
Debelar ...	13252	Considered expensive
Debellare ...	13253	**Experience**
Debelletur	13254	Has had considerable experience with
Debilezza ...	13255	Has not had much experience with
Debilidad ...	13256	Will tell by experience
Debilitare ...	13257	Judging from past experience
Debility ...	13258	Judging from past experience I (we) think not
Debilmente	13259	**Experiment**
Debiteur ...	13260	Experiment most successful
Debito ...	13261	Experiment fairly successful
Debitricem	13262	Experiment total failure
Debitrix ...	13263	What has been result of experiment
Debitaolo...	13264	Experiment on the whole favourable
Deblaterer	13265	Pending result of further experiment
Deblayer ...	13266	Is experiment satisfactory
Debloquer	13267	As an experiment only
Deboiter ...	13268	By no means an experiment
Debole ...	13269	**Expert**
Deboletto ...	13270	When may I (we) expect arrival of expert
Debolita ...	13271	Expect arrival of expert on
Debonnaire	13272	Expert will only report in interest of
Debouch ...	13273	Expert can be depended upon
Deboucler...	13274	Expert cannot be depended upon
Debrider ...	13275	Expert should not see
Debrocar ...	13276	Am suspicious of expert
Debrutir ...	13277	Expert no good
Debut ...	13278	Expert considered most reliable
Debutant ...	13279	What is your opinion of expert
Decacordo	13280	Employ as expert
Decadenza	13281	Expert evidence
Decadere ...	13282	Expert is alleged to be
Decaer ...	13283	Expert's opinion favourable
Decagon ...	13284	Expert's report
Decagynia	13285	Expert's report favourable
Decaisser ...	13286	Expert's report very favourable
Decalescet	13287	Expert's report discouraging
Decalogue...	13288	Expert's report unreliable
Decalvare ...	13289	Expert's report very unfavourable
Decalvetur	13290	Expert's report may be expected on
Decamerone	13291	Expert's report mailed
Decampar...	13292	Expert's report not yet received
Decamping	13293	Expert's report will be mailed
Decampment	13294	Could you select a reliable expert to
Decanato ...	13295	A careful and reliable expert

Decandria...	13296	Cannot select an expert
Decangular	13297	Most reliable experts
Decani ...	13298	Experts cannot be sent for —— weeks
Decanting...	13299	Provide expert(s) with everything necessary
Decapitar ...	13300	Have provided expert(s) with everything necessary
Decapod ...	13301	**Expire(s)** (See also " Bond," " Time.")
Decarreler	13302	Will expire
Decasilabo	13303	When does the time expire
Decastilo ...	13304	Do not let the time expire
Decaying ...	13305	Time expires on
Decebir ...	13306	As soon as the time expires
Decelleram	13307	Bond will expire
Decemment	13308	Mine was bonded for ——; will expire on
Decempedal	13309	Has (have) allowed the time to expire
Decemplex	13310	**Expired**
Decemplice	13311	Has expired
Decemviro	13312	Has not expired
Decenal ...	13313	Will have expired
Decencia ...	13314	Will not have expired
Decennalis	13315	Must be completed before the time has expired
Decennium	13316	As soon as the time has expired
Deceptious	13317	As soon as the —— has expired
Decernama	13318	**Expiry**
Decerner ...	13319	Before the expiry of
Decertabat	13320	On the expiry of
Decevant ...	13321	**Explain**
Decevoir ...	13322	To explain
Dechado ...	13323	Explain to
Dechainer ..	13324	Explain fully
Dechargeur	13325	Explain fully what you mean by
Dechausse	13326	Please explain cost of
Decheance	13327	Cannot explain until
Decheveler	13328	Explain by cable
Dechiarare	13329	Explain by mail
Dechirage...	13330	Please explain in detail
Decidable...	13331	Please explain fully in your next letter
Decidement	13332	How do you explain
Decideras ...	13333	Will explain fully by mail
Decidero ...	13334	Please explain by cable the value of
Deciduim ...	13335	Will explain everything when I (we) meet
Deciduous	13336	**Explained**
Deciembre	13337	As explained to you (or to——)
Deciferare	13338	Must be explained
Decimabile	13339	As explained in my (our) letter dated
Decimare ...	13340	As explained in my (our) cable sent on
Decimated	13341	**Explanation(s)**
Decimation	13342	Explanation(s) is (are) all in order
Decimatore	13343	Ask —— to give full explanation
Decimino ...	13344	Explanation quite satisfactory
Decimole ...	13345	Explanation unsatisfactory
Decimonono	13346	Explanation not understood
Decinueve...	13347	—— refuses to give any explanation
Decipiunt...	13348	What explanation shall I make to —— (as regards)
Decipula ...	13349	What explanation can I (we) give
Deciseis ...	13350	Wait explanation by mail
Decisorio ...	13351	Wait explanation given in my (our) letter mailed on
Decitantis...	13352	—— will give full explanation
Deckbett ...	13353	Do not understand your (——'s) explanation
Deckblatt...	13354	Cable (telegraph) explanation (of)
Deckelglas	13355	Asking for explanation

EXPLICIT.   Dec

Deckfarbe...	13356	Cable on —— with explanation
Decking ...	13357	**Explicit(ly)**
Deckmantel	13358	Be very explicit
Deckpumps	13359	Be more explicit
Declamador	13360	Have requested —— to be more explicit
Declarado...	13361	Not sufficiently explicit
Declarante	13362	—— refuses to be more explicit
Declasser ...	13363	Unless you can be explicit
Declavo ...	13364	You can be quite explicit with
Declinable	13365	Must be most explicit as to
Declinante	13366	As explicit as possible
Declinibus	13367	**Exploder** (*See also* "Detonator.")
Declividad	13368	**Exploration(s)**
Declivity ...	13369	All explorations so far show that
Declivus ...	13370	An exploration level
Declouer ...	13371	Exploration works
Decoctas ...	13372	From former explorations
Decocted ...	13373	From present explorations
Decoctible...	13374	Now driving an exploration level
Decoctions	13375	Explorations have only been carried down to the water level
Decoiffer ...	13376	What would be the cost of necessary explorations
Decolacion	13377	Cost of necessary explorations would be
Decolavit ...	13378	Explorations to the deep
Decolgar ...	13379	**Explosion**
Decollate ...	13380	Powder explosion
Decolleter...	13381	Dynamite explosion
Decomisar	13382	Boiler explosion
Deconfire ...	13383	Explosion of ——
Deconvenue	13384	Serious explosion occurred on ——; lives lost ——
Decorator...	13385	Serious explosion occurred on ——; no lives lost
Decoroso ...	13386	**Explosive(s)** (*See also* "Blasting Gelatine," "Detonators,"
Decorously	13387	Ammonite ["Dynamite," "Fuse," &c.)
Decorticat...	13388	Ballistite
Decorum ...	13389	Bellite
Decoudre ...	13390	Blasting gelatine No. 1
Decoupeur	13391	Blasting gelatine No. 2
Decourager	13392	Camphorated gelatine
Decousure...	13393	Carboazotine
Decouvert...	13394	Carbodynamite
Decouvrir...	13395	Carbonite
Decoxivit ...	13396	Chilworth special powder
Decoybird...	13397	Cooppals powder
Decoyed ...	13398	Di-flamyr
Decrecer ...	13399	Dynamite No. 1
Decremento	13400	Dynamite No. 2
Decrepitar	13401	E. O. Powder
Decrescent	13402	Forcite
Decretal ...	13403	Fortis explosive
Decretista...	13404	Gathurst powder
Decretory...	13405	Gelatine Dynamite No. 1
Decriditer...	13406	Gelatine Dynamite No. 2
Decrire ...	13407	Guncotton
Decrocher...	13408	Gunpowder
Decrottoir...	13409	Lithofracteur
Decruer ...	13410	Nitrated guncotton
Decubito ...	13411	Picric acid
Decumana	13412	Potentite
Decumbence	13413	Rifle guncotton
Decuplo ...	13414	Roburite No. 1
Decurion ...	13415	Roburite No. 2

Decurrent...	13416	Sawdust and guncotton powder
Decursas ...	13417	Schultze blasting powder
Decussate...	13418	Schultze gunpowder
Dedaigner...	13419	Securite
Dedal ...	13420	Smokeless powder
Dedalera ...	13421	Stonite
Dedalisimo	13422	Tonite No. 1
Dedamnetur	13423	Tonite No. 2
Dedecoros...	13424	Tonite No. 3
Dedicandus	13425	**Export(s)**
Dedicante...	13426	Export duties
Dedicarsi ...	13427	Export orders for
Dedicated...	13428	For immediate export
Dedication	13429	**Exposed**
Dedicatory	13430	As exposed at
Dedicemur	13431	Now exposed
Dedignar ...	13432	Is (are) not at present exposed
Deditionem	13433	**Express**
Dedolento...	13434	Express to
Dedommager	13435	By express
Dedotto ...	13436	Forward by express (from)
Dedoubler...	13437	Express charges
Deduccion	13438	**Expressed**
Deducible...	13439	Has (have) expressed
Deducir ...	13440	Has (have) not expressed
Deductivo	13441	Should be strongly expressed
Deduire ...	13442	As expressed in
Deepening	13443	**Expressly**
Deessa ...	13444	Expressly stated
Defacement	13445	Was not expressly stated
Defacto ...	13446	Was it not expressly stated
Defaillant ..	13447	Was expressly stated
Defaite ...	13448	—— expressly stated that
Defalcare ...	13449	**Extend** (*See also* "Bond," "Time.")
Defalquer...	13450	To extend
Defamar ...	13451	Extend to
Defaveur ...	13452	Extend time
Defeasance	13453	Can you extend your stay until
Defeasible...	13454	Cannot extend stay beyond
Defecado ...	13455	Cannot extend time beyond
Defecated ...	13456	Not to extend beyond
Defectible ..	13457	Will extend
Defectillo ...	13458	Will not extend
Defectrix ...	13459	Will —— extend
Defectueux	13460	Cannot extend
Defectuoso	13461	I (we) can extend time —— days on a payment of ——
Defences ...	13462	Can you (——) extend time for
Defendedor	13463	**Extended**
Defender ...	13464	Extended to
Defending	13465	Extended by
Defendisse	13466	Is now extended (to)
Defensable	13467	Might be extended to
Defensas ...	13468	Has (have) only extended to
Defenseur...	13469	Has (have) been extended
Defension...	13470	Has (have) only been extended
Defensorio	13471	Since —— the level has been extended —— feet
Deferencia	13472	To be extended
Deferir ...	13473	Will require to be extended
Defesa ...	13474	**Extension(s)**
Defettivo ...	13475	Extension of

Defeuillir ...	13476	Extension asked until
Defiantly ...	13477	Extension granted until
Defianza ...	13478	Further extension
Deficiente...	13479	No further extension
Defidacion	13480	Further extension required
Defigurer ...	13481	Cannot grant extension
Defilement	13482	Cannot grant extension as other parties are wanting
Defiliren ...	13483	Must have extension of time
Defingit ...	13484	Can you obtain extension of time
Definibile ...	13485	Try to induce —— to grant extension of agreement
Definidor ...	13486	Will not grant any extension
Definire ...	13487	—— will grant extension
Definitivo...	13488	Extension on vein
Defixionem	13489	Will give a further extension on the vein of —— feet
Deflagrate	13490	Get extension of
Deflagro ...	13491	Get extension of time .
Deflecting...	13492	Extension(s) north
Defleurir ...	13493	„ south
Deflorare ...	13494	„ east
Defloresco...	13495	„ west
Deflusso ...	13496	**Extensive(ly)**
Defluvium	13497	Old workings are very extensive
Defoir ...	13498	Old workings are not extensive
Defoliate ...	13499	Extensively worked
Defoncer ...	13500	Alleged to have been extensively worked
Deforest ...	13501	Alleged extensive workings turn out to be
Deformador	13502	There are no extensive old workings, only natural caves
Deforme ...	13503	Extensive workings undoubtedly of human origin exist on the
Deformidad	13504	Workings are very extensive [property
Deformity	13505	The falls of ground are very extensive
Defraichir...	13506	Cover(s) an extensive area
Defraudar	13507	**Extent**
Defrenatum	13508	Extent altogether unknown
Defricheur	13509	Extent at present unknown
Defroque ...	13510	What is the extent of
Defrugavi	13511	Will share with you to the extent of
Defuera ...	13512	Covering a large extent of
Defulgurat	13513	An extent of
Defuncion	13514	To what extent
Defunto ...	13515	To the extent of
Degagement	13516	There is no extent (of) .
Degagna ...	13517	Not to any great extent
Degauchir	13518	There is a great extent of
Degendus...	13519	To the fullest extent possible
Degenerate	13520	**Extra** (*See also* " Expense.")
Degenere ...	13521	Extra expense
Degenstoss	13522	Owing to the extra expense
Degingande	13523	Extra expense will be less than
Deglucion	13524	Any extra expense must be paid by
Degnante ...	13525	Refuse(s) to pay any extra expense
Degnazione	13526	**Extract(s)**
Degnevole...	13527	Can only extract
Degobiller	13528	Cannot extract more than
Degollador	13529	So as to extract
Degonfler ...	13530	This will enable us to extract .
Degourdir...	13531	Please forward extract of
Degradato	13532	Will forward extract as soon as possible
Degraded ...	13533	**Extracted**
Degrading	13534	Easily and cheaply extracted
Degrafer ...	13535	**Extraction**

Degraisser	13536	What is the present rate of extraction
Degravatus	13537	Present rate of extraction is
Degressum	13538	Cost of extraction
Degrossir ...	13539	Minus cost of extraction
Deguello ...	13540	Plus cost of extraction
Deguenille	13541	Cost of extraction and reduction
Deguerpir...	13542	So as to increase our extraction
Degulavit ...	13543	The extraction now amounts to
Degustetur	13544	Our monthly extraction amounts to
Degustibus	13545	A better mode of extraction must be adopted
Dehanche ...	13546	**Extravagant** (*See also* "Expensive.")
Dehaurivi...	13547	Management has been very extravagant
Dehesar ...	13548	The price is an extravagant one
Dehesero ...	13549	**Extreme(s)**
Dehiscente	13550	If you are pushed to extremes you may
Dehnung ...	13551	At the extreme point
Dehonorant	13552	I (we) consider it extremely doubtful
Deichsel ...	13553	**F**
Deicida ...	13554	**Face**
Deicidio ...	13555	Face of
Deifero ...	13556	In face of
Deificare ...	13557	Face is not looking so well
Deinceps ...	13558	Face has changed to
Deinosaurs	13559	Face is improving in value
Deiparam ...	13560	Face of drift is in
Deiscere ...	13561	Face of drift looks
Deismo ...	13562	Face of cross-cut is in
Dejacion ...	13563	Face of cross-cut looks
Dejamiento	13564	Face of level is in
Dejativo ...	13565	Face of level looks
Dejectedly	13566	From the appearance of the face
Dejection ...	13567	The face is still in country rock
Dejectory ...	13568	Mineral still in face
Dejectus ...	13569	In face of ——'s decided opinion
Dejemplar	13570	Must face
Dejeravit ...	13571	If I am (we are) to face
Dejeuner ...	13572	**Facilitate**
Dejiciunt ...	13573	Do what you can to facilitate
Dejillo ...	13574	Do not hinder, but do not facilitate matters
Dejoindre...	13575	So as to facilitate matters
Dejucher ...	13576	Think it will considerably facilitate matters
Dejugar ...	13577	Will do my (our) best to facilitate
Deklamiren	13578	In order to facilitate
Delantera ...	13579	Will this (it) facilitate matters
Delapsion...	13580	Will facilitate matters
Delapsis ...	13581	Will not facilitate matters
Delationis...	13582	**Facility(ies)**
Delatrice ...	13583	Afford —— every facility in your power
Delayant ...	13584	Do not afford —— any facilities
Deleble ...	13585	Every facility exists for cheap and economic working
Delectable	13586	Every facility exists here for
Delecto ...	13587	Every facility will be given
Delegado ...	13588	Give every facility
Delegates ...	13589	What facilities have you
Deleguer ...	13590	Shall I (we) afford any facility for
Deleitante...	13591	There are no facilities at all for
Deleite ...	13592	What facility(ies) are there for
Deleitoso ...	13593	—— will afford every facility in his power
Delessite ...	13594	No facility(ies) exist here for
Delestage ...	13595	With more facility

Deletereo ...	13596	In the absence of the necessary facilities for
Deletrear ...	13597	Extend every facility to
Deletricis ...	13598	**Facing**
Delettare ...	13599	Immediately facing
Deleznable	13600	**Fact(s)**
Deleznar ...	13601	As a matter of fact
Delfiniera ...	13602	It is not a fact (that)
Delfinio ...	13603	It is a fact (that)
Delftware ...	13604	Is it a fact (that)
Delgacero ...	13605	Is an undoubted fact (that)
Delgadez ...	13606	In fact
Delgazar ...	13607	Cannot ascertain what are the real facts
Delibato ...	13608	Cable the actual facts respecting
Delibebor ...	13609	So far as I (we) can ascertain the real facts are
Deliberato	13610	The actual facts of the case are
Delibra ...	13611	You have been misled as to the facts
Delibuere ...	13612	Cannot hide the fact
Delicacy ...	13613	To hide the fact
Delicadez ...	13614	Do not try to hide the fact(s)
Delicadura	13615	Shall not try to hide the fact(s)
Delicieux ...	13616	Are you (is ——) acquainted with the fact
Deliciosum	13617	Let me (us) have a signed statement of the facts
Delightful	13618	Notwithstanding the fact that
Delimare ...	13619	**Fahrenheit**
Delimiter ...	13620	Degrees Fahrenheit
Delinquant	13621	Between —— and —— degrees Fahrenheit
Delinquere	13622	**Fail**
Delinquio ...	13623	I (we) will not fail
Delintar ...	13624	To fail
Deliquesce	13625	Will not fail to
Delirante ...	13626	Without fail
Deliratio ...	13627	You (they) must not fail
Delirio ...	13628	Do not fail to
Delirium ...	13629	Should I (we) fail
Deliziarsi ...	13630	**Failed**
Delongar ...	13631	Failed to arrive
Deloyante...	13632	Failed to send
Delphinus...	13633	Is (are) rumoured to have failed
Delphus ...	13634	Has (have) failed
Delubro ...	13635	Has (have) not failed
Deluditore	13636	So far we have failed to meet with any ore
Delumbe ...	13637	So far we have failed to meet
Delusively	13638	Hitherto it (this) has failed to work satisfactorily
Delusivo ...	13639	Has (have) never hitherto failed
Delusorio ...	13640	**Failing**
Delustrer ...	13641	Failing to
Delyn ...	13642	Failing this
Demadesco	13643	Failing this you had better
Demagogue	13644	Failing which I (we) shall
Demandable	13645	Failing anything better
Demandador	13646	**Failure** (*See also* " Experiment.")
Demandante	13647	Can you determine cause of failure
Demandeur	13648	Cannot yet determine cause of failure
Demanial ...	13649	Give full particulars of failure
Demantler	13650	Is a total failure
Demarcar ...	13651	Is so far a failure
Demarquer	13652	I (we) feel the failure is due to
Demarrarse	13653	Owing to the failure of
Demasia ...	13654	Owing to failure with
Demasiado	13655	Owing to a failure on the part of —— to

Demediar ...	13656	Prove(s) to be a failure
Demeloir ...	13657	What was the failure due to
Demembrer	13658	The failure is due to
Demenager	13659	The failure of
Demencia ...	13660	To avoid absolute failure
Dementio ...	13661	What has caused failure
Demergere	13662	Failure is said to be due to speculation
Demerit ...	13663	Was a complete failure until recently
Demerseram	13664	**Fair**
Demersion	13665	Perfectly fair
Demesure ...	13666	A fair supply of
Demeubler	13667	A very fair showing
Demeurant	13668	A very fair quality
Demeurer ...	13669	Has (have) not acted altogether fair by
Demias ...	13670	Do whatever is fair
Demiditone	13671	Consider the fair thing to do would be to
Demientra	13672	Perfectly fair and straight
Demigar ...	13673	I (we) consider it would be fair if
Demiguaver	13674	Fair allowance will be made
Demijeu ...	13675	No fair allowance was made for
Demimesure	13676	Prospects very fair
Demimonde	13677	**Fairly**
Demipause	13678	Am (are) willing to act fairly
Demiquart	13679	Everything progressing very fairly
Demisory ...	13680	Has (have) not behaved at all fairly
Demisoupir	13681	Has (have) behaved very fairly
Demnach ...	13682	Fairly balanced
Democracy	13683	**Faith**
Democrat ...	13684	You may place implicit faith in ——
Demodex ...	13685	Have no faith personally in
Demoiselle	13686	Faith in
Demoliren	13687	Have great faith in
Demolished	13688	Would give me (us) more faith in
Demolition	13689	Violation of good faith
Demolitor	13690	In good faith
Demonetize	13691	**Fall** (*See also* " Cave," " Price," " Shares.")
Demoniacal	13692	To fall
Demoniado	13693	A serious fall
Demoniaque	13694	Appear(s) likely to fall into
Demonism	13695	In the fall
Demontage	13696	Owing to fall of ground
Demonuelo	13697	May cause a fall
Demorar ...	13698	The fall will be rapid
Demostrar	13699	The fall will be gradual
Demotic ...	13700	Prices may be expected to fall
Demotique	13701	What fall is there for
Demudar ...	13702	What is the fall between
Demulcent	13703	The fall between —— and —— is —— feet
Demurely ...	13704	Report as to obtaining fall for power purposes
Demureness	13705	We can obtain —— feet of fall
Demuseler	13706	The ground falls away very rapidly from
Demuthig...	13707	What is the difference of fall
Denario ...	13708	The difference of fall is
Denatier ...	13709	Send section of country showing fall
Denaturer...	13710	Will give us —— feet of fall
Dendriform	13711	Require at least —— feet of fall
Dendrites ...	13712	There is ample water and fall for power purposes
Dendrodus	13713	The length of pipes required to obtain —— feet fall is ——
Dendrology	13714	**Fallen** [yards
Denegacion	13715	Fallen to

Denegare ...	13716	Has (have) fallen since my last
Denegatus	13717	Has (have) not fallen
Denegrecer	13718	Has fallen through
Denegrido	13719	Has not fallen through
Dengeln ...	13720	Should it (this) have fallen through
Dengoso ...	13721	**Falling**
Denguero ...	13722	How do you explain this (the) falling off in
Deniaise ...	13723	Prices all falling
Denicher ...	13724	Show signs of falling in
Denigratio	13725	Shows a considerable falling off
Denigreur...	13726	The falling off is due to ——
Denization	13727	What is the falling off due to
Denizens ...	13728	I regard the falling off in value as only temporary
Denkart ...	13729	I regard the falling off in value as likely to be permanent
Denkkraft	13730	Do you think the falling off in value is only temporary or will
Denklehre	13731	**False** [it be permanent
Denkmal ...	13732	Not altogether false
Denkmunze	13733	Perfectly false
Denkspruch	13734	An entirely false report
Denkstein...	13735	Owing to false statements
Denkwurdig	13736	**Far**
Denkzettel	13737	Do not go too far
Demnoch ...	13738	How far in is the ——
Denodado...	13739	As far as
Denominar	13740	As far as you can
Denommer	13741	By far the best
Denostador	13742	How far
Denostar ...	13743	How far off are you from
Demotandus	13744	How far have you still to drive in order to
Denotation	13745	How far do you intend to go (before)
Denotatus	13746	How far is it to
Denoting ...	13747	Not far from
Denouer ...	13748	Far from being satisfactory
Denoument	13749	Go as far as you can with safety
Densamente	13750	**Farther** (*See also* "Further.")
Densato ...	13751	Considerably farther
Denseness	13752	Have come up farther
Densezza ...	13753	Have gone farther down
Densidad ...	13754	No use to continue farther
Densissime	13755	Only a little farther
Densitate ...	13756	To bore farther
Density ...	13757	To drive farther
Densuno ...	13758	To sink farther
Dentaccio ...	13759	We have still —— feet farther to drive
Dentadura	13760	We have still —— feet farther to sink
Dentalma ...	13761	We have to continue —— feet farther
Dentame ...	13762	**Fast(er)**
Dentated ...	13763	As fast as possible
Dentecillo...	13764	Arrange for this to be done as fast as possible
Denteler ...	13765	Can you not push on faster
Dentellada	13766	Cannot push on faster owing to
Dentellear	13767	Shall then be able to push on faster
Dentellon ...	13768	Too fast
Dentera ...	13769	Think you might push on faster
Dentezuelo	13770	Will try to push on faster
Denticle ...	13771	Will do it (this) as fast as possible
Denticular	13772	**Fatal** (*See also* "Accident.")
Dentiems ...	13773	Fear will be fatal
Dentifrice...	13774	No need to fear fatal result
Dentilegus	13775	**Fathom(s)** (*See also* "Feet," "Yards" and Table at end.)

Dentine ...	13776	One fathom
Dentistry ...	13777	—— fathoms deep
Dentitio ...	13778	—— fathoms apart
Dentivano	13779	Is —— fathoms deep
Dentizione	13780	Since —— the shaft has been sunk —— fathoms
Dentoid ...	13781	**Fault(s)**
Dentrambos	13782	Great fault is being found with
Dentrifico ...	13783	Delay arising from any fault of mine
Dentudo ...	13784	Delay arising from any fault of yours
Denudandum	13785	Can any fault be attached to
Denudare ...	13786	Great fault has been found with
Denudatus	13787	There is a serious fault in
Denuesto ...	13788	Who was at fault
Denumero...	13789	Was (were) chiefly at fault
Denunciar...	13790	The main fault was
Denunzia ...	13791	Great fault attached to
Deodand ...	13792	There can be no fault attached to
Deodourise	13793	—— was not at fault
Deogracias	13794	A fault has come in
Deonerit ...	13795	Fault still continues
Deontology	13796	Owing to a fault in
Deoptavi ...	13797	Owing to a fault at
Deoptent ...	13798	Beyond the influence of the fault
Deoxidise ...	13799	Am inclined to think that a fault has occurred
Depalabat...	13800	Fault has thrown the lode
Depaqueter	13801	Fault has thrown the shoot
Deparar ...	13802	North of fault
Deparquer	13803	South of fault
Departager	13804	East of fault
Departidor	13805	West of fault
Departir ...	13806	**Faulted**
Depascent...	13807	Faulted by
Depauperar	13808	Not faulted
Depaverunt	13809	**Faulting**
Depayser ...	13810	By a faulting of
Depecement	13811	**Faulty**
Depeindre...	13812	Very faulty
Depenaille	13813	**Favour(s)**
Depesche ...	13814	As a personal favour
Depeupler	13815	In whose favour
Depicted ...	13816	Am (is) (are) not at all in favour of ——
Depilatory	13817	Can you favour me (us) with
Depinxero...	13818	Regret cannot favour you with
Depister ...	13819	Bill(s) is (are) drawn in favour of the
Deplaire ...	13820	In your favour
Deplaisant	13821	In favour of
Deplantoir	13822	In my (our) favour
Depleor ...	13823	May I comply as a favour
Depletion ...	13824	You may comply but only as a favour
Deplico ...	13825	Not in favour of
Deplisser ...	13826	Quite as a favour
Deplomber	13827	Accept no favours from
Deplorando	13828	**Favourable**
Deploratus	13829	Not at all favourable
Deploredly	13830	Most favourable
Deplumatio	13831	Presents a favourable appearance
Depolarise	13832	Prospects favourable
Deponente	13833	Is a favourable opportunity for
Deponer ...	13834	The general indications are favourable
Deportar ...	13835	Have you any favourable news

Deportiren	13836	As soon as I (we) have any favourable news
Deportment	13837	I (we) have no favourable news
Deportoso...	13838	Has made a favourable report
Deposable...	13839	On favourable terms
Deposante	13840	Verdict favourable
Depositare	13841	Verdict not at all favourable
Deposition	13842	A favourable opportunity will I think occur
Deposito ...	13843	Are conditions favourable for
Deposseder	13844	Conditions are not at all favourable
Depouille ...	13845	Do you consider it (this) a favourable opportunity to
Depourvoir	13846	This (it) is not a favourable opportunity
Depravador	13847	Everything looks most favourable
Depravar ...	13848	Everything favourable for
Depravity	13849	There is not a single favourable condition
Depredare	13850	**Favourably**
Deprehendo	13851	Proceeding favourably
Depremere	13852	Not proceeding so favourably
Depremuto	13853	Favourably inclined to
Deprander	13854	Not at all favourably inclined
Depresivo ...	13855	**Fear(s)**
Depresor ...	13856	To fear
Deprimir ...	13857	Fear cannot do any good
Depriving...	13858	I (we) fear that
Depulvero...	13859	Should you have any fear of
Depurate ...	13860	There is nothing to fear at this moment
Depuration	13861	—— fears that
Deputato ...	13862	Fear it is practically exhausted
Deputirter	13863	Fear the whole thing is played out
Deputised...	13864	Have you any fear as to results
Deraciner ...	13865	I (we) have no fear at all as to results
Deradendus	13866	I (we) fear very much as to results
Deraidir ...	13867	Is there any reason to fear
Derailler ...	13868	There is no reason to fear
Deraison ...	13869	There is reason to fear
Derecera ...	13870	The only cause for fear is
Derechez ...	13871	You need have no fear
Derechuelo	13872	**Feared**
Derechuria	13873	It is feared here that
Deregler ...	13874	Need no longer be feared
Dereinst ..	13875	**Fearing**
Derelict ...	13876	Fearing which
Derelinquo	13877	**Feasible**
Derelitto ...	13878	Hardly feasible
Deretano ...	13879	Do not consider this feasible
Dergestalt...	13880	Do you consider this (it) feasible
Deridere ...	13881	Is feasible
Deriditore...	13882	Is not feasible
Derisibile ...	13883	Is it feasible
Derisivo ..	13884	It is quite feasible (if)
Derisory ...	13885	It would be feasible (if)
Derivable ...	13886	**Feature(s)**
Derivante...	13887	Do not omit any important features
Derivar ...	13888	The most important feature is
Derivation	13889	What are the most important features
Derivatus...	13890	**February**
Derivieni ...	13891	At the beginning of February
Derjenige...	13892	About the middle of February
Dermal ...	13893	During the entire month of February
Dermassen	13894	For the entire month of February
Dermestes	13895	Last February

Derogabile	13896	Next February
Derogatio...	13897	Near the end of February
Derogavi ...	13898	First day of February
Derogent ...	13899	Second day of February
Deronchar	13900	Third day of February
Derouler ...	13901	Fourth day of February
Derraigar ...	13902	Fifth day of February
Derramador	13903	Sixth day of February
Derramar...	13904	Seventh day of February
Derrame ...	13905	Eighth day of February
Derraspado	13906	Ninth day of February
Derrata ...	13907	Tenth day of February
Derredor ...	13908	Eleventh day of February
Derrenegar	13909	Twelfth day of February
Derrengada	13910	Thirteenth day of February
Derrengo ...	13911	Fourteenth day of February
Derreria ...	13912	Fifteenth day of February
Derretido ...	13913	Sixteenth day of February
Derribado	13914	Seventeenth day of February
Derrocar ...	13915	Eighteenth day of February
Derromper	13916	Nineteenth day of February
Derrotero ...	13917	Twentieth day of February
Derrubiar ...	13918	Twenty-first day of February
Derruecar...	13919	Twenty-second day of February
Derruir ...	13920	Twenty-third day of February
Derrumbar	13921	Twenty-fourth day of February
Derselbe ...	13922	Twenty-fifth day of February
Deruisse ...	13923	Twenty-sixth day of February
Derumpo ...	13924	Twenty-seventh day of February
Deruncino	13925	Twenty-eighth day of February
Deruptum...	13926	Twenty-ninth day of February
Deruunto ...	13927	February expenses amount to
Dervis ...	13928	February shipments amount to
Derwisch ..	13929	**Fee(s)**
Desabatir ...	13930	What would be your (——'s) fee for
Desabido ...	13931	My fee would be
Desabille ...	13932	Fee for —— is ——
Desabollar	13933	——'s fee would be
Desabono ...	13934	Cable your fee for report on —— mine
Desaborido	13935	A fee of —— and travelling expenses
Desabrigar	13936	Cable fee. Report is for my private guidance, not for [publication
Desabrir ...	13937	Fees and expenses amount to ——
Desabuser...	13938	Please pay fee and expenses to my credit with ——
Desacatado	13939	Report mailed to —— bank, who will hand same to you on [payment of —— for fee and travelling expenses
Desaceitar	13940	Should advise you not to proceed unless at least half fee and [travelling expenses are paid on account
Desacerbar	13941	Cable name and fee required
Desacoplar	13942	Fee for examination and report
Desacorde...	13943	Fee not to exceed
Desacotar ..	13944	An inclusive fee for report and travelling expenses
Desacretur	13945	Fee for examination and report not to exceed
Desacro ...	13946	Fee for examination and report will not exceed
Desacuerdo	13947	Fee to include all expenses
Desadorno	13948	Fee does not include travelling expenses
Desafear ...	13949	**Feed** (*See also* " Boilers," " Pumps.")
Desafecto ...	13950	Feed water
Desafeitar...	13951	Automatic feed
Desafiador	13952	**Feeder**
Desafuero...	13953	Is a feeder of

Desagarrar	13954	**Feeling**
Desagravio	13955	What is the present feeling
Desaguador	13956	Feeling as regards
Desaguar ...	13957	Present feeling better
Desague ...	13958	Present feeling confident
Desahogado	13959	A strong feeling in favour of
Desahuciar	13960	A strong feeling against
Desainar ...	13961	Great feeling has been manifested in the locality against
Desairado ...	13962	My (our) feeling is that
Desaire ...	13963	I have (there is) much feeling against
Desajuntar	13964	I have (there is) a strong feeling in favour of
Desajuste...	13965	The feeling is one of great confidence
Desalabar ...	13966	The feeling is one of distrust
Desalar ...	13967	What is the (your) feeling as regards
Desalentar	13968	Feeling somewhat discouraged
Desalinnan	13969	The general feeling here is
Desalojar ...	13970	General feeling good
Desaltato ...	13971	General feeling is in favour of
Desalterar	13972	There is a good feeling here as regards
Desamable	13973	The feeling here is decidedly
Desamador	13974	Has (have) a feeling that
Desamigado	13975	Feeling of disquietude
Desamistad	13976	**Feet** (*See also* " Foot " and Table at end.)
Desamoldar	13977	Cubic feet
Desamor ...	13978	Lineal feet
Desamoroso	13979	Square feet
Desamparar	13980	Drift is now —— feet
Desancorar	13981	—— feet driven since ——
Desancre ...	13982	How many feet have you driven
Desandar ...	13983	How many feet have you sunk
Desanimar	13984	How many cubic feet have you washed
Desaparean	13985	—— feet driven this month
Desapiolar	13986	Have now —— feet of ore
Desapoyo ...	13987	Feet sunk since
Desaprecio	13988	Feet sunk this month
Desaprir ...	13989	Cubic feet washed since
Desaprobar	13990	Cubic feet washed this month
Desapuesto	13991	An area of —— square feet
Desapuntar	13992	Cubic feet per
Desarbolo...	13993	Cubic feet per minute
Desarenar...	13994	Drift has been advanced —— feet since ——
Desarmaban	13995	The distance of —— feet
Desarme ...	13996	How many feet
Desarraigo	13997	Feet square
Desarreglo	13998	Feet wide
Desarrimar	13999	Feet deep
Desarrollo	14000	Feet high
Desarropar	**14001**	Feet long
Desarrufar	14002	Over —— feet
Desasado ...	14003	Under —— feet
Desaseo ...	14004	—— feet distance
Desasesado	14005	—— feet of banks
Desasir ...	14006	—— feet of backs
Desasnar ...	14007	—— feet wide by —— feet long
Desastrado	14008	Is (are) about —— feet distant from
Desatadura	14009	Is now —— feet deep
Desatancar	14010	The claim is —— feet wide by —— feet long
Desatasque	14011	The distance between is —— feet
Desatavio...	14012	Tunnel has been extended —— feet since ——
Desatender	14013	Within the next —— feet

Desatento...	14014	What is the distance in feet
Desatollar	14015	Still short by —— feet
Desatracar	14016	For the first —— feet
Desaturdir	14017	Within a few feet
Desavahado	14018	**Felsitic**
Desavencar	14019	**Felspar**
Desaveu ...	14020	Chiefly felspar
Desavezar...	14021	**Felspathic** (*See also* "Minerals.")
Desaviar ...	14022	Foot wall is felspathic rock
Desavisado	14023	Hanging wall is felspathic rock
Desavouer	14024	Felspathic matrix
Desayudar	14025	**Ferruginous** (*See also* "Quartz.")
Desayuno ...	14026	Ferruginous stains
Desayustar	14027	**Fetch**
Desazogar	14028	What is it likely to fetch
Desazon ...	14029	Will fetch about
Desazonado	14030	Will not fetch more than
Desbagaba	14031	Has (have) gone to fetch
Desbalijar	14032	**Few**
Desbanado	14033	For a few days
Desbancar	14034	Could spare a few
Desbarate...	14035	Has (have) only a few
Desbaste ...	14036	Are a few any use
Desbeber ...	14037	Can obtain a few
Desbocado	14038	Endeavour to obtain a few
Desbombar	14039	Forward a few more
Desbordar	14040	Mail a few
Desboronar	14041	Only a few days' delay will be caused
Desbozar ...	14042	Very few to be obtained
Desbragado	14043	**Fiery**
Desbravar	14044	The mine is a fiery one
Desbrincar	14045	Owing to the fiery nature of the coal
Desbriznar	14046	**Figure(s)**
Desbruar ...	14047	The following figures
Desbuchar	14048	What are the exact figures
Desbulla ...	14049	The exact figures are
Descabezar	14050	Figure(s) too high
Descaccio ...	14051	Figure(s) too low
Descacilar...	14052	The foregoing is approximate; will send exact figures later
Descaderar	14053	Exact figures cannot be given at present
Descaecido	14054	Is there no mistake in your (——'s) figures
Descalabro	14055	Insert the following figures
Descalces ...	14056	I (we) have repeated calculations, cannot discover any error in
Descalzar ...	14057	There is an error in the figures relating to [figures
Descaminar	14058	The figures are not at all accurate
Descampado	14059	The figures are most accurate
Descansado	14060	Please revise figures
Descanso ...	14061	Are not your figures wrong
Descanteth	14062	Figures are not wrong
Descapan ...	14063	I strongly advise you to accept the figure named
Descapucho	14064	Figure named is very low but I (we) will accept it
Descarado	14065	Figure named is too low and I (we) cannot accept it
Descararse	14066	What figure is the gold sold at
Descargue	14067	What figure is the silver sold at
Descarino ...	14068	Figure gold at —— per ounce
Descarriar	14069	Figure silver at —— per ounce
Descasaban	14070	**Figured**
Descassio ...	14071	Need only be figured, not drawn to scale
Desceller ...	14072	Figured at
Descendant	14073	**Fill**

Descendere	14074	To fill
Descendida	14075	To fill in
Descension	14076	To fill up
Descensus	14077	Fill up
Descepar ...	14078	Fill up with
Descercado	14079	Fill up my order
Descerco ...	14080	Please fill in
Deschetto...	14081	How shall I (we) fill in
Descifrar ...	14082	You had better fill in
Descinchar	14083	**Filled**
Desciscunt	14084	Have filled your order
Descitum ...	14085	All the surface works were filled with snow
Desciverim	14086	Could not examine as it was (they were) completely filled in
Desclavar ...	14087	Filled up with [with)
Descobajar	14088	My time is completely filled ; regret cannot undertake
Descocer ...	14089	The shaft was filled with water to within —— feet of surface
Descocho ...	14090	**Filling**
Descolchar	14091	Filling in with
Descolorar	14092	Filling up with
Descombrar	14093	Filling up with water
Descompas	14094	Is (are) filling
Descomunal	14095	Is (are) not filling
Desconejar	14096	**Final** (*See also* " Condition.")
Desconfiar	14097	Not final
Descontar	14098	Is this your (——'s) final decision
Descordojo	14099	No final decision yet arrived at
Descornar	14100	The final decision is
Descortes ...	14101	Have you (——) come to any final decision respecting
Descosido...	14102	Will cable as soon as the final result is known
Descostrar	14103	Final result is
Descreer ...	14104	Final result not yet known
Descreido...	14105	What is the final result (of)
Descrestar	14106	Final payment of purchase-money
Descriarse	14107	No final payment
Describere	14108	Must come to some final understanding with regard to this (it)
Describing	14109	**Finally**
Describir ...	14110	Has (have) finally arranged that
Describunt	14111	Before deciding finally
Descripsit...	14112	Before deciding finally can you suggest anything to make the
Descripto ...	14113	**Finance** [property a paying investment
Descrismar	14114	The matter is one of finance
Descruzar	14115	Pending arrangements as to finance
Descry ...	14116	**Financial**
Descuajo ...	14117	Owing to unsatisfactory financial arrangements
Descubrir ...	14118	Pending completion of satisfactory financial arrangements
Descuello ...	14119	When will your financial arrangements be completed
Descuento...	14120	Financial arrangements not yet completed
Descuerno	14121	Hope to complete financial arrangements not later than
Descuidado	14122	Hope to complete financial arrangements within next —— days
Descular ...	14123	**Find**
Descumplir	14124	To find
Descura ...	14125	Find out
Desdar ...	14126	Find out about
Desdecir ...	14127	Endeavour to find
Desdel ...	14128	Endeavour to find out what is the matter with
Desdenable	14129	Can you find out who
Desdenador	14130	Can you find out whether this is true
Desdenanza	14131	If you find
Desdenoso	14132	If you do not find
Desdentado	14133	If you cannot find

Desderanar	14134	I (we) cannot find out
Desdichado	14135	I find on repeating trial that
Desdinerar	14136	This is all I (we) can find out
Desdoblar...	14137	Now find(s) that
Desdon ...	14138	Now find(s) that he was (they were) mistaken
Desdonado	14139	Use every means to find
Desdormido	14140	—— cannot find
Desdoro ...	14141	Can you (he) find someone to
Deseable ...	14142	Find out all you can
Deseador ...	14143	Will find out all I (we) can and cable
Desecante...	14144	You will find letter at
Desecativo	14145	You will find cable at
Desechado	14146	Where shall I (we) find
Desecho ...	14147	Will probably find —— at
Desecrate ...	14148	Endeavour to find him
Desectio ...	14149	Will endeavour to find him
Deseguida	14150	Have not yet been able to find him (it)
Deseguir ...	14151	**Fine**
Desembalar	14152	Excessively fine
Desembarco	14153	Very fine
Desembolso	14154	As fine as
Desembudar	14155	Not particularly fine
Desemejar	14156	Fine paid on
Desempacho	14157	Fine has not been paid
Desempegar	14158	Has (have) imposed a fine of
Desempeno	14159	Cable amount of fine
Desemplir...	14160	Can you get fine reduced or remitted
Desempulga	14161	Has (have) consented to reduce fine to
Desencanto	14162	May consent to reduce fine to
Desencoger	14163	I (we) shall be subject to a fine except
Desencolar	14164	The fine amounts to
Desencono	14165	The fine will be paid on
Desenfadar	14166	When will the fine be paid
Desenfiler...	14167	Has (have) a fine body of ore
Desenflure	14168	Has (have) a very fine showing
Desengano	14169	The shaft is now in fine ore
Desengruda	14170	**Fineness**
Desenivrer	14171	What is the fineness of the bullion
Desenlace ...	14172	The fineness of the bullion is
Desenlosar	14173	**Finest**
Desenlutar	14174	Of the finest quality
Desennuyer	14175	Of the finest water
Desenojoso	14176	**Finish**
Desenredar	14177	To finish
Desenredo...	14178	So as to finish
Desensebar	14179	Can finish
Desenteter	14180	Cannot finish
Desentolda	14181	When can you (——) finish
Desentono	14182	Finish —— before you commence (to)
Desentumir	14183	To finish the work on hand
Deseoso ...	14184	Will finish the (this) work as soon as I (we) can
Desepitis ...	14185	Hope to finish within the next few days
Desequido	14186	How soon will you be able to finish
Deserendus	14187	Finish as soon as possible
Deserpendi	14188	Cannot finish owing to
Deserpere ...	14189	Do not stop to finish
Deserpo ...	14190	Expect to finish about
Deserrado...	14191	,, ,, building on
Desertatus	14192	,, ,, order by
Deserter ...	14193	,, ,, drilling by

Desertiore...	14194	Expect to finish by
Desertiren	14195	Expect to finish
Desertless...	14196	Finish as speedily as possible
Deserturus	14197	If you can finish on
Deseruit ...	14198	If you cannot finish until
Deservedly	14199	I (we) expect to finish not later than
Deservicio...	14200	Shall finish on
Deservidor	14201	Shall finish to-day
Deserviens	14202	Shall finish to-morrow
Deserviret...	14203	I shall no doubt finish all that I have to do here by
Deserviunt	14204	Shall finish at the end of this week
Desersione	14205	Shall finish at the end of next week
Desesperar	14206	The work on hand will cost —— and require —— days to finish
Desespoir ...	14207	Will take me —— days more to finish everything
Desestero ...	14208	Will require —— days to finish work on hand
Desestima...	14209	When do you expect to finish
Desestivar	14210	Cannot finish it (this) if I (we)
Desfacedor	14211	**Finished**
Desfalcar ...	14212	To be finished (by)
Desfalls ...	14213	Will be finished
Desfavor ...	14214	If you have finished
Desfeita ...	14215	If you have not finished
Desferrar ...	14216	I (we) have finished
Desfilar ...	14217	I (we) have not finished
Desfiuxar ...	14218	If not yet finished
Desflecar ...	14219	Not quite finished
Desflorido	14220	Was (were) finished on
Desfogonar	14221	Cannot be finished before
Desfogue ...	14222	Have finished shipping to-day
Desformar	14223	Have finished shipping for this season
Desfradado	14224	Finished better
Desfrenar...	14225	Finished worse
Desfrutar ...	14226	Finished at former prices
Desfundar	14227	Finished at highest prices
Desgaire ...	14228	Cannot be finished
Desgalgado	14229	Cannot be finished owing to want of
Desgalgar...	14230	Everything completely finished
Desganar ...	14231	Hoped to have finished on ——; delayed owing to
Desganchar	14232	Get this work completely finished before you
Desgarban	14233	Get it (them) finished as speedily as possible
Desgaritar	14234	Get it finished smartly
Desgarrado	14235	Why have you not finished
Desglosar ...	14236	Was not finished owing to
Desglose ...	14237	When does —— expect to get finished
Desgonzar	14238	Expects to get finished within the next few days
Desgracia ...	14239	Will be finished within the time specified
Desgradar	14240	Will not be finished within the time specified
Desgrado ...	14241	Will this (it) be finished within the time specified
Desgramara	14242	Unless some unforeseen circumstance arises, this (it) should be [finished on (before)
Desguarnir	14243	I expect to have finished the whole not later than
Desguince...	14244	When I have finished at —— shall proceed to
Desguindar	14245	**Finishing**
Desguisado	14246	Now finishing
Deshabido	14247	Only requires finishing touches
Deshabitar	14248	Now finishing up
Deshacedor	14249	**Fire** (*See also* "Assurance," "Damage.")
Deshacer ...	14250	Owing to a fire underground
Deshalben	14251	Fire still raging underground [done
Deshaldo ...	14252	A fire broke out on —— fortunately but little damage was

Deshebrar...	14253	A fire occurred in mine; cannot ascertain damage as yet
Deshecha ...	14254	A fire occurred in the mine; damage done is ——
Deshechizo	14255	Fire has destroyed
Deshechura	14256	Fire will not retard operations
Deshelar ...	14257	Fire will retard operations —— weeks
Desherence	14258	Cause of fire ——
Desheriter	14259	Cause of fire not known yet
Deshielo ...	14260	Forest fires have almost ceased
Deshiladiz	14261	A forest fire has occurred at
Deshincar...	14262	Do not apprehend any further danger from forest fires
Deshojador	14263	Fire insurance policy
Deshonesto	14264	Fire has broken out again
Deshonneur	14265	Fire now completely extinguished
Deshonorar	14266	Several fires have occurred in the works lately
Deshora ...	14267	Serious fire occurred on ——
Deshornar	14268	Damage caused by fire and water will amount to
Deshospedo	14269	Was (were) totally destroyed by fire
Deshuesar...	14270	**Fire-Damp** (*See also* "After-damp.")
Deshumano	14271	Explosion of fire-damp
Desiabile ...	14272	Killed by fire-damp
Desiccate ...	14273	Owing to fire-damp
Desiderare	14274	**Firing-Cable** (*See also* "Blasting," "Detonators.")
Desiderio ...	14275	Firing-cable for
Desidiam ...	14276	Send —— feet of single firing-cable
Desidioso ...	14277	Send —— feet of double firing-cable
Desierto ...	14278	**Firm**
Desierunt ...	14279	Closed firm
Designabas	14280	Not at all firm
Designandi	14281	Quite firm
Designar ...	14282	Very firm
Designatus	14283	Not quite so firm
Designavit	14284	Firm offer of
Designed ...	14285	Be firm as regards
Desigual ...	14286	Make a firm offer of
Desinant ...	14287	Can you obtain a firm offer of property
Desinencia	14288	Do you know the following firm(s)
Desinimum	14289	Firm you name is not known to me (us)
Desinteres	14290	Have nothing to do with firm(s) you name
Desinviter...	14291	Firm(s) you name is (are) composed of
Desiosculo	14292	Firm(s) you name is (are) every way most respectable
Desirare ...	14293	Firm(s) you name is (are) very doubtful [spectable
Desireux ...	14294	Firm(s) you name has (have) a small capital but highly re-
Desiringly	14295	Firm(s) you name eminently respectable and sound financially
Desistente...	14296	A firm policy
Desistere ...	14297	**Firmly**
Desjarrete...	14298	You had better hold firmly
Desjugar ...	14299	I (we) shall hold firmly
Desjuntar...	14300	Shall I (we) hold firmly
Deslabonar	14301	Are you firmly of opinion
Deslamar ...	14302	Deal firmly with
Deslastrar...	14303	I am (we are) most firmly convinced that
Deslavado...	14304	I am (we are) firmly convinced that the property will become
Desleal ...	14305	**First** [a paying investment
Deslealtad	14306	At the first opportunity
Deslechar ...	14307	Do not be the first to
Desleidura	14308	For the first few days
Deslenguar	14309	From first to last
Desligar ...	14310	I (we) consider it first-class in every respect
Desliz ...	14311	Is (are) in first-class condition
Deslizable...	14312	Take the first chance you have to

Desloar ...	14313	Cable which I shall proceed to first
Deslucido...	14314	First-class work
Deslumbrar	14315	The first thing should be to
Deslustre ...	14316	The first thing will be to
Desmadejar	14317	Give(s) a first-rate account of
Desman ...	14318	Let me (us) know first what you think of
Desmanarse	14319	**Fissure** (*See also* "Lode," " Vein.")
Desmancho	14320	**Fitted**
Desmandado	14321	To be fitted with
Desmanear	14322	Fitted according to your instructions
Desmarojar	14323	Do you consider him (it) well fitted for
Desmatar ...	14324	Is (are) not at all fitted for
Desmayo ...	14325	Is (are) in every way well fitted for
Desmedido	14326	Is it being fitted with
Desmedirse	14327	I (we) have had it (them) fitted with
Desmedrar	14328	Not fitted according to specification
Desmelar ...	14329	Should have been fitted with
Desmembrar	14330	**Fitter**
Desmenguar	14331	Should be a good mechanic and fitter
Desmentida	14332	Is a thoroughly competent mechanic and fitter
Desmenuzar	14333	Has not much ability as a mechanic and fitter
Desmeollar	14334	Want a good mechanic and fitter
Desmerecer	14335	**Fix**
Desmesura	14336	Fix at your end
Desmigajar	14337	Fix at
Desminuir	14338	Do not fix until
Desmocar ...	14339	Fix on the best terms you can
Desmogue	14340	Can you fix an early date
Desmolado	14341	If you can fix
Desmolaret	14342	If you cannot fix
Desmontar	14343	Impossible to fix any date
Desmoronar	14344	The earliest date I can fix
Desmotador	14345	Endeavour to fix
Desmote ...	14346	Expect to fix
Desmuelo ...	14347	**Fixed**
Desmugerar	14348	Not yet fixed
Desmuir ...	14349	Unless already fixed
Desmurador	14350	According to fixed scale
Desnatural	14351	Cannot be fixed before
Desnegar ...	14352	Cable as soon as anything is fixed
Desnevado	14353	Has (have) fixed
Desnivel ...	14354	Has (have) not yet fixed
Desnoviar	14355	Is not yet fixed
Desnucar ...	14356	The trial is fixed for
Desnudez ...	14357	When will the date be fixed
Desobeir ...	14358	What date is the meeting fixed for
Desobligar	14359	The meeting is fixed for
Desoccupe	14360	As soon as you have fixed upon
Desocupado	14361	To be fixed at
Desoeuvre	14362	Now being fixed
Desojar ...	14363	**Flat**
Desolacion	14364	Flat vein
Desolandi...	14365	Flat lode
Desolarent	14366	The vein is very flat
Desolatote	14367	Not quite so flat
Desolateth	14368	By flat rods
Desolateur	14369	Breakage of flat rods
Desolatio ...	14370	Country is quite flat
Desoletis ...	14371	**Flatter**
Desollado ...	14372	Is becoming flatter

Desolvunt...	14373	**Flaw(s)**
Desomur ...	14374	Owing to a flaw in the
Desonce ...	14375	There is not the slightest sign of a flaw
Desonzar ...	14376	The flaw extends
Desopilar ...	14377	**Flint(y)**
Desoprimir	14378	Flinty beds
Desorejar ...	14379	On account of the very flinty nature of the bed
Desorillar...	14380	The flinty nature of the rock has entirely disappeared
Desormais	14381	Very hard flinty rock
Desortijar ..	14382	**Float** (*See also* " Company," " Ore.")
Desosado ...	14383	To float
Desosser ...	14384	Endeavour to float
Desove ...	14385	Would certainly float
Desovillar...	14386	Impossible to float
Despabilar	14387	**Floated** (*See also* " Company.")
Despachar	14388	Company was floated about
Despacio ...	14389	Almost as soon as was floated
Despagado	14390	Company was never actually floated
Despairing	14391	**Float-gold** (*See also* " Gold.")
Despaldar...	14392	Are losing at least —— of the float-gold
Despanado	14393	In order to save some of the float-gold
Desparcir ...	14394	Probably —— of the gold is " float "
Desparejar	14395	The gold is " rusty " and partly " float "
Desparpajo	14396	**Floating**
Despavorir	14397	Floating reef
Despeadura	14398	In floating company
Despear ...	14399	Has (have) succeeded in floating company
Despectans	14400	Has (have) not succeeded in floating company
Despecto ...	14401	**Flood(s)**
Despedazar	14402	Owing to floods
Despedida	14403	Floods decreasing
Despedrar	14404	Floods decreasing rapidly
Despegáble	14405	Flood increasing
Despegado	14406	Flood occurred on
Despeinar	14407	Flood(s) prevent(s)
Despelotar	14408	Little damage was done by the flood
Despeluzar	14409	Much damage was done by the flood which occurred on ——
Despensado	14410	Flood carried away
Desperabat	14411	What amount of damage has the flood caused
Desperanza	14412	Flood has done damage to the extent of ——
Desperatus	14413	**Floor(s)**
Desperavit	14414	Depositing floors
Desperteza	14415	Dressing floors
Despesar ...	14416	Drying floors
Despezonar	14417	Floor No. ——
Despiadado	14418	Sufficient area for dressing floors
Despicable	14419	Loads on the floors
Despicar ...	14420	**Flow** (*See also* " Water.")
Despidida...	14421	Have struck flow of water
Despierto ...	14422	Pumps cannot cope with flow of water
Despiezo ...	14423	To cope with present flow of water
Despilare ...	14424	What is the flow
Despinces...	14425	**Flowing**
Despintar	14426	Now flowing
Despiojar ...	14427	There is no water flowing at all
Despique ...	14428	Water flowing at present amounts to —— miners' inches
Despiting...	14429	**Flucan**
Desplacer...	14430	Flucan-course
Desplanaba	14431	Soft flucan
Desplantar	14432	**Fluctuate(ing)**

Desplate ...	14433	To fluctuate
Desplegar	14434	Continues to fluctuate
Desplomar	14435	Fluctuates between —— and ——
Despoblado	14436	**Fluctuation(s)**
Despoiler ...	14437	Owing to fluctuations in
Despoliare	14438	Owing to rapid fluctuations of
Despolio ...	14439	In spite of rapid fluctuations
Despolvar...	14440	Subject to market fluctuations
Desponerse	14441	What is the maximum fluctuation
Desposajas	14442	**Flume(s)** (*See also* "Alluvial," "Hydraulic.")
Desposeer...	14443	We are now vigorously engaged on the flumes
Desposoric	14444	Flume(s) is (are) in first-rate order
Despotic ...	14445	The flume(s) is (are) in fair order
Despotique	14446	The flume(s) is (are) altogether out of repair
Despotism	14447	The flume(s) has (have) been partially destroyed
Despreciar	14448	The flume(s) has (have) been completely destroyed
Desprivar...	14449	Will have to construct —— feet of flume
Desproveer	14450	**Fluorspar** (*See also* "Minerals.")
Despuebat	14451	**Flux(es)**
Despuemini*	14452	Can you obtain a suitable supply of flux(es)
Despuemus	14453	Fluxes for assaying
Despuente	14454	In order to obtain a suitable supply of flux(es)
Despues ...	14455	Suitable fluxes can be obtained within —— miles
Despuisse...	14456	There is an abundant supply of suitable fluxes, but no fuel
Despuitote	14457	There is an abundant supply of suitable fluxes and good fuel
Despulsar...	14458	Cost of flux(es), per ton
Despumatio	14459	**Flywheel**
Despuntar	14460	Accident to flywheel
Desquamare	14461	Requires a heavier flywheel
Desquejar...	14462	As soon as the new flywheel arrives
Desqueje ...	14463	Hope to fix flywheel on
Desquicar...	14464	**Foliated**
Desquierdo	14465	**Follow(s)**
Desrabar ...	14466	To follow
Desrabotar	14467	Follow the
Desraigar ...	14468	Follow me (at)
Desreglado	14469	I (we) will follow
Desrizar ...	14470	As follows
Desronar ...	14471	Do not follow
Desrostrar	14472	How do you propose to follow
Dessangler	14473	Follow this
Dessauer ...	14474	Follow this up
Desservant	14475	I (we) will follow this up
Dessiner ...	14476	I should follow this up by
Dessouder...	14477	Shall follow this up by
Dessus	14478	Follow instructions contained in
Destablar ...	14479	Follow ——'s instructions
Destacar ...	14480	Follow my (our) instructions
Destajador	14481	Refuse(s) to follow instructions
Destajero ...	14482	The only course open is to follow
Destallar ...	14483	Balance to follow
Destalonar	14484	Follow the market
Destamento	14485	Will follow by next mail
Destans ...	14486	Will follow on ——
Destapada	14487	Will follow within next —— days
Destapo ...	14488	**Followed**
Destechar...	14489	Has (have) followed
Destejer ...	14490	Has (have) not yet followed [—— (given by ——)
Destemplar	14491	Have you followed the instructions contained in letter dated
Destemple	14492	Is (are) being followed

* Is spelt "Dispuemini" in Edition I.

Destender	14493	To be followed by.
Destenir ...	14494	Should be followed by
Desterrado	14495	Useless unless followed by
Destertero	14496	Why have you (——) not followed
Destertuit...	14497	You (——) should have followed
Destetar ...	14498	You (——) should not have followed
Destiempo	14499	**Following** (*See also* "Exclusive.")
Destierro ...	14500	Following which
Destilador	14501	Following advance
Destillare ...	14502	The following
Destillent...	14503	Following articles wanted
Destino ...	14504	Following clause
Destituer ...	14505	Only by following
Destituido	14506	Substitute the following (for)
Destorcer ...	14507	Following from ——
Destoserce	14508	The following has (have) been saved
Destrabar...	14509	The following is absolutely private
Destral ...	14510	Am (are) now following
Destraleja...	14511	Is now following
Destrejar ...	14512	In accordance with the following instructions
Destrenzar	14513	**Foot** (*See also* "Feet," and Table at end.)
Destrezza ...	14514	From —— feet to —— feet
Destrinxit...	14515	One foot
Destripar ...	14516	The width varies from one foot to —— feet
Destronar...	14517	Inclination is —— per fathom
Destroyers	14518	**Footwall** (*See also* "Defined," "Hanging wall.")
Destroying	14519	Along the footwall
Destrozon...	14520	What is the footwall
Destructor	14521	Against the footwall
Destrueco ...	14522	On the footwall side of the vein
Destruible	14523	Strong footwall
Destruir ...	14524	We have a good footwall but have not discovered any hanging
Desturbar...	14525	We have so far not met with the footwall [wall
Desubito ...	14526	The footwall is well defined
Desubulavi	14527	Samples from footwall average
Desucacion	14528	On the footwall side
Desudent ...	14529	Close against the footwall
Desuefeci ...	14530	The footwall is
Desuetude	14531	Crosscut to the footwall
Desultorem	14532	No true footwall yet discovered
Desulturas	14533	On the footwall
Desumere...	14534	The distance to the footwall is —— feet
Desumpsit	14535	We are following the footwall
Desunar ...	14536	The mineral is mainly upon the footwall
Desuncir ...	14537	The footwall is becoming
Desuper ..	14538	**Footway**
Desurcar ...	14539	In the footway
Desurdir ...	14540	Footway shaft
Desusado ...	14541	Can convert into a footway shaft
Desuso ...	14542	Fell down the footway
Desvahar ...	14543	Found in the footway at
Desvainar...	14544	**For**
Desvalor ...	14545	For me (us)
Desvanecer	14546	For whom
Desvano ...	14547	For fear of
Desvariado	14548	Who is it (this) for
Desvedado	14549	What is it (this) for
Desvelar ...	14550	This is for
Desvendar	14551	For whom are you acting
Desviado ...	14552	For whom is —— acting

Desviare ...	14553	For whom are they acting
Desviejar ...	14554	For you
Desvirar ...	14555	For all charges
Desvirtuar	14556	For cash
Desvivirse	14557	For my personal benefit
Desvivo ...	14558	For sale at (by)
Deswegen...	14559	For some time past
Desydero ...	14560	For some time to come
Dessocar ...	14561	For further orders
Deszumar...	14562	For our joint account
Detachment	14563	**Forage**
Detalage ...	14564	Forage is
Detalingar	14565	Cost of forage is
Detallo ...	14566	Ample forage
Deteindre...	14567	**Forbidden**
Detenedor	14568	Not forbidden
Detenido ...	14569	Forbidden to
Detentador	14570	I (we) have not forbidden
Detention...	14571	Must be forbidden
Detentore...	14572	Why have you forbidden
Detergent...	14573	Strictly forbidden
Deterior ...	14574	Will be forbidden in the future
Determinar	14575	**Force** (*See also* "Hands," "Men," &c.)
Deterrendo	14576	To force
Detersion ...	14577	Do not attempt to force
Detersorio	14578	Has (have) attempted to force
Detestable	14579	Force the market
Detestando	14580	If necessary employ force
Detestar ...	14581	Do not employ force unless compelled
Detesting ...	14582	On no account employ force
Detexeram	14583	What is the total force
Detisser ...	14584	The total force employed at grass and underground is now
Detonacion	14585	Cut down force as much as possible [—— men
Detonar ...	14586	**Forebreast** (*See also* "Drift," "Level," &c.)
Detoniren...	14587	From forebreast
Detonner ...	14588	From our present forebreast to
Detortion ...	14589	**Foreclose** (*See also* "Mortgage.")
Detourner...	14590	**Forego(ing)** (*See also* "Exclusive.")
Detractar ...	14591	Is foregoing
Detraer ...	14592	Foregoing from ——
Detraggere	14593	Foregoing prices based on
Detraquer...	14594	Foregoing figures based on a monthly shipment of —— tons
Detras ...	14595	If foregoing is correct
Detraxisse	14596	If foregoing is not correct
Detrazione	14597	**Foreign**
Detrimento	14598	Foreign advices have had —— effect
Detrousser	14599	**Foreman**
Detruncate	14600	Foreman of
Dettatrice...	14601	As mine foreman
Dettatura...	14602	A good foreman
Deudilla ...	14603	Foreman of night shift
Deudor ...	14604	Foreman of day shift
Deuteln ...	14605	Can the foreman be relied upon as to
Deuteria ...	14606	Can you engage a good, able and reliable foreman at about ——
Deutlich ...	14607	Require a good, able and reliable foreman [per month
Deutoxide...	14608	Employ as foreman
Deutsche ...	14609	What is foreman's opinion
Deutzia ...	14610	**Foresee**
Deuxieme ...	14611	Do you foresee any difficulty as to
Devagare ...	14612	I (we) cannot foresee how any difficulty can arise

Devalar	...	14613	I (we) foresee distinctly that
Devaliser	...	14614	**Forest**
Devanadera		14615	An area of —— acres of forest is included in the property
Devanear	...	14616	The nearest forest is —— miles distant
Devanture		14617	There is no large forest timber
Devastador		14618	Timber for fuel and mine purposes can be cut from forest
Devehunt	...	14619	**Forfeit** [within —— miles of property
Devengar	...	14620	A forfeit of
Deventos	...	14621	Forfeit must be paid on
Devergonde		14622	Forfeit was paid on
Deversatum		14623	**Forfeited**
Devexisti	...	14624	To be forfeited
Devexus	...	14625	Will be forfeited
Deviato	...	14626	All the money already paid will be forfeited
Devidage	...	14627	Has (have) forfeited all rights (through)
Devideur	..	14628	Has (have) forfeited all claims (through)
Devilry	...	14629	Has (have) been forfeited
Devisa	...	14630	Has (have) not been forfeited
Devocabat		14631	From sale of forfeited shares
Devocion	...	14632	Will not agree to pay any deposit liable to be forfeited
Devoiement		14633	Will run considerable risk of being forfeited
Devolavit	...	14634	All ——'s (his) shares were forfeited
Devoluto	...	14635	Claims are all forfeited
Devolver	...	14636	**Forfeiture**
Devorante		14637	Under chance of forfeiture
Devoraz	...	14638	Must have forfeiture clause
Devotedly	..	14639	Have received formal notice of forfeiture
Devoting	...	14640	Forfeiture notice
Devoto	...	14641	**Forgery(ies)**
Devouring		14642	Is probably a forgery
Devoutly	...	14643	Will no doubt prove to be a forgery
Devozione		14644	Is a forgery
Dewdrops	...	14645	Is not a forgery
Dewpoint	...	14646	**Forget**
Dexter	...	14647	Do not forget
Dexterity	...	14648	To forget
Dexterous	...	14649	Did not forget
Dextinam	...	14650	In case —— should forget
Dextrabus		14651	**Forgotten**
Dezmar	...	14652	Not forgotten
Dezmatorio		14653	Has (have) forgotten to
Dezmeno	...	14654	Has (have) forgotten to take
Dezmeria	...	14655	Has (have) been forgotten
Diabetes	...	14656	It must not be forgotten that
Diablar	...	14657	Appears to have forgotten to (that)
Diablement		14658	**Fork**
Diablerie	...	14659	Water "in fork"
Diablillo	...	14660	In fork
Diablotin	...	14661	Mine will be "in fork" about
Diablura	...	14662	Mine is now "in fork"
Diabolico	...	14663	Expect mine will be "in fork" in —— days
Diacanato	...	14664	When do you expect the mine will be "in fork"
Diacano	...	14665	**Form(s)**
Diacciare	...	14666	To form
Diacciuolo		14667	To form a
Diacere	...	14668	To form a good
Diachisma		14669	To form a syndicate
Diachylon		14670	To form a small private syndicate
Diacitron	...	14671	Will send necessary form(s)
Diacitura	...	14672	Unable to form

Diacodion...	14673	Endeavour to form,
Diaconessa	14674	What form should it take
Diaconicon	14675	Might take the form of
Diacustica	14676	Send additional forms
Diadelphia	14677	Are you (is ——) able to form any idea as to
Diadem ...	14678	**Formation**
Diadoches	14679	Is a formation of
Diafanidad	14680	The formation is
Diafano ...	14681	The formation changes
Diafragma	14682	Formation of new company
Diagnosis...	14683	The formation has become considerably harder
Diagnostic	14684	Geological formation
Diagrafica	14685	Geological formation is similar
Diagrams ...	14686	Geological formation is not similar
Dialect ...	14687	What is the general formation
Dialectico...	14688	**Formed**
Dialettica...	14689	To be formed
Dialetto ...	14690	Formed to
Diallogite	14691	Formed of
Dialogal ...	14692	Cannot be formed until (unless)
Dialogismo	14693	Formed through
Dialogist ...	14694	Has (have) not been formed
Dialogizar	14695	Has (have) been formed
Dialoquer	14696	Have you (——) formed
Dialtea ...	14697	Might be formed
Dialysing ...	14698	Now being formed
Dialysis ...	14699	Have you formed any idea (whether)
Diamantado	14700	**Former**
Diamante...	14701	Former credit renewed
Diametral...	14702	In former communications
Diamoron	14703	**Forsake(n)**
Diapalma ...	14704	You must forsake
Diapasmam	14705	Will forsake
Diapason ...	14706	Will not forsake
Diapente ...	14707	Has (have) been forsaken
Diaphanous	14708	Not forsaken
Diaphonie	14709	**Fortnight(ly)** (See also "Days," "Weeks.")
Diaphragm	14710	For the last fortnight
Diaporesis	14711	For the next fortnight
Diapreado	14712	Will take at least a fortnight
Diarista ...	14713	Should not take more than a fortnight
Diarrhoea	14714	Within the next fortnight
Diaspero ...	14715	**Forward**
Diaspores...	14716	To forward
Diastema ...	14717	Forward to
Diastilo ...	14718	Forward the
Diastolik ...	14719	Forward account sales of
Diastrome	14720	Send forward to
Diatesaron	14721	Send forward all you can
Diathermic	14722	Forward as soon as possible
Diathyrae	14723	Send forward at once
Diatoms ...	14724	Do not forward until you hear from me (us)
Diatomic ...	14725	Is not yet sufficiently forward
Diatonique	14726	In case you cannot forward
Diatonisch	14727	Please forward as quickly as possible
Diatretum	14728	Push —— forward as much as you can
Diatribe ...	14729	When can you forward
Diavola ...	14730	When do you intend to forward
Diavoleria	14731	Will forward immediately
Diavolesco	14732	Everything is now well forward

Diavolico ...	14733	As soon as this work is sufficiently forward
Diavolone ...	14734	Request —— to forward to —— without delay
Dibaphum	14735	**Forwarded**
Dibarbare...	14736	Forwarded to
Dibassanza	14737	Will be forwarded to
Dibassare...	14738	Were forwarded on
Dibattere ...	14739	Forwarded by
Dibattuto...	14740	Forwarded by express
Diboscare...	14741	Has (have) been forwarded
Dibrancare	14742	To be forwarded
Dibrucare	14743	To be forwarded by special messenger
Dibucciato	14744	Were forwarded on
Dibujador	14745	Will be forwarded on
Dibujo ...	14746	Forwarded to-day
Dicabulas...	14747	Forwarded yesterday
Dicace ...	14748	Will be forwarded to-morrow
Dicacibus...	14749	Will be forwarded end of this month
Dicacidad	14750	Will be forwarded end of this week
Dicacitas ...	14751	Why have you not forwarded
Dicadenza	14752	**Forwarding**
Dicadere ...	14753	Cease forwarding for the present
Dicaduto ...	14754	Please instruct me (us) as to forwarding
Dicalvare ...	14755	**Fossiliferous**
Dicandum	14756	**Foul**
Dicapitato	14757	Very foul
Dicatote ...	14758	On account of foul air
Dicebox ...	14759	**Found**
Dicelie ...	14760	Not yet found
Dicembre ...	14761	Found out
Diceria ...	14762	Found out that
Diceriuzza	14763	Has (have) been found
Dicerto ...	14764	Has (have) not been found
Dicessare ...	14765	Found nothing so far
Dicevole ...	14766	As soon as found
Dicharacho	14767	To be found by
Dichiarire...	14768	Was found on
Dichido ...	14769	How have you found things generally
Dichinante	14770	Found things generally as represented
Dichinare...	14771	Found things not at all as represented
Dichobune	14772	Found things as represented except
Dichodon ...	14773	Have found everything so far satisfactory
Dichord ...	14774	Have found all the statements made satisfactory
Dichoreos	14775	Have found all the statements made fairly satisfactory
Dichoso ...	14776	Have found none of the statements made satisfactory
Dichroism	14777	When you have found the ore in (at) —— telegraph
Dichter ...	14778	Have found out nothing so far, despair of success
Dichtheit ...	14779	Have found out nothing so far, but am sanguine of ultimate [success
Dichtkunst	14780	**Foundation(s)**
Diciannove	14781	Without foundation
Dicibile ...	14782	All foundations completed and ready for machinery
Diciferare	14783	Foundations require repair
Dicimento	14784	Foundations very good and substantial
Dicioccare	14785	Have commenced foundations
Diciotto ...	14786	In order to obtain a secure foundation [immediately
Diciplina ...	14787	Shall commence to place the machinery on the foundations
Dicitore ...	14788	The foundations for machinery are being proceeded with
Dicitura ...	14789	Excavations for the foundations of —— are making progress
Dickkopf ...	14790	Should there be any foundation for this
Dickleibig	14791	Cannot discover any real foundation for
Dicklich ...	14792	**Foundery**

Dickwanst	14793	Have been delivered from the foundery
Diclinical ...	14794	From the foundery
Dicollare ...	14795	Send to the foundery for
Dicorso ...	14796	To be supplied by local foundery
Dicotomia	14797	**Fraction**
Dicozione ...	14798	As a fraction of a claim
Dicrescere	14799	What is the area of fraction
Dicreto ...	14800	To secure this fraction
Dicrinare ...	14801	A fraction which lies between the following claims
Dicroceras	14802	This fraction would give us the right to
Dicrudare...	14803	If you secure fraction you would shut out opponents
Dictadoe ...	14804	Must secure fraction if possible
Dictadura...	14805	Am offered fraction at
Dictamen ...	14806	Strongly advise you to secure fraction
Dictamnus	14807	Fraction has no value
Dictar ...	14808	Fraction has very considerable prospective value
Dictateur ...	14809	Cost of fraction
Dictation ...	14810	Decimal fraction
Dicterio ...	14811	**Fracture**
Dicuocere...	14812	A new fracture
Didactic ...	14813	An old fracture
Didelphys...	14814	A simple fracture of
Didotto ...	14815	A compound fracture of
Diducunt ...	14816	**Fractured**
Didynamia	14817	Arrived fractured
Diebisch ...	14818	Has (have) unfortunately been fractured
Diebsbande	14819	**Fragmental**
Diebstahl ...	14820	**Fragmentary**
Diecina ...	14821	**Fraud(s)**
Dienlich ...	14822	Can you discover if it is a fraud
Dienstag ...	14823	Has long been known as a complete fraud
Dienstbote	14824	Has (have) been charged with fraud
Dienstherr	14825	Is undoubtedly a fraud
Dienstlos ...	14826	Is suspected to be a fraud
Dienstmann	14827	Have no reason to suppose is a fraud
Dienstzeit...	14828	Frauds abound
Diente ...	14829	A big fraud
Dieresi ...	14830	**Free**
Dieronosi ...	14831	Free of expense
Diesfalls ...	14832	Free of water
Diesjahrig	14833	Free gold (See also " Gold.")
Diesseitig ...	14834	Free smelting ore
Diestra ...	14835	Free milling ore
Dietamente	14836	Are you free to
Dieterich ...	14837	Am quite free to
Dietetic ...	14838	Ascertain if or when ——— will be free to
Diesmal ...	14839	Consider yourself perfectly free to act
Diesmero ...	14840	Can I consider myself free to act as I think best
Diesmesino	14841	Cost free on board at
Diesnio ...	14842	Cost free on board plus cost of freight and insurance to
Difalcare ...	14843	When will you be free to
Difalta ...	14844	Shall be free about
Difamacion	14845	Free from all encumbrances
Difamador	14846	**Freehold**
Difendere...	14847	The property is freehold
Difensivo ...	14848	**Freely**
Diferencia	14849	As freely as possible
Diferente ...	14850	Has (have) been freely dealt in
Diferir ...	14851	Not so freely
Difettante	14852	**Freeze**

Difetto ...	14853	So as to freeze out
Difettuoso	14854	An attempt to freeze out
Diffalco ...	14855	**Freight** (*See also* " Carriage.")
Diffamant...	14856	Freight charges
Diffamato...	14857	Freight to
Differenza	14858	Freight of
Differire ...	14859	Engage freight
Differmare	14860	Freight to smelters
Difficolta ...	14861	Do not engage freight
Diffidante ..	14862	Have engaged freight at
Diffidato ...	14863	Inclusive of freight and smelters charges
Diffidenza...	14864	Exclusive of freight and smelters charges
Diffinito ...	14865	The rate of freight is
Difflugia ...	14866	The freight and charges amount to
Diffondere	14867	What is the rate of freight (between)
Difformare	14868	All freight to be charged forward
Difformato	14869	Cost here exclusive of freight is
Difformite	14870	Cost inclusive of freight amounts to
Diffusedly	14871	Freight to be paid at
Diffusible ...	14872	Freight to be paid as follows
Diffusion ...	14873	Cable when you are likely to get freight to
Diffusive ...	14874	What is the freight from —— to ——
Dificato ...	14875	Can deliver the mineral to —— at a cost per ton for freight
Dificile ...	14876	Freight to the mines from —— costs per 2,000 lbs. [of ——
Dificultad...	14877	Freight from the mines to —— costs per 2,000 lbs.
Difidacion...	14878	What is the best freight you can obtain for
Difidencia...	14879	Quote freight rates between —— and ——
Difilarsi ...	14880	Can quote freight rates between —— and —— at
Difinecer ...	14881	Would allow a rebate on freight of
Difinire ...	14882	**Freighter(s)**
Difrige ...	14883	Cable name of freighter(s)
Difugio ...	14884	Freighter(s) are
Difundido	14885	Are freighters
Difundir ...	14886	**Freighting**
Difunto ...	14887	Now freighting
Difuso ...	14888	Has (have) stopped freighting
Digamias ...	14889	**Frequent**
Digenerare	14890	Is a frequent occurrence
Digerir ...	14891	Now making frequent shipments
Digesteur ...	14892	Becoming more frequent
Digestible ...	14893	Not so frequent as formerly
Digestion ...	14894	**Frequently**
Digestivo ...	14895	Frequently met with
Digiogare...	14896	Occasionally, not frequently
Digital ...	14897	**Fresh**
Digitellus ...	14898	Cable as soon as anything fresh is known
Digitorium	14899	Nothing fresh
Digitus ...	14900	Nothing fresh need be expected until
Digiugnere	14901	The only fresh matter is
Digiunare...	14902	**Friday** (*See also* " Days.")
Digiunto ...	14903	About Friday week
Digladiar ...	14904	Every Friday
Dignabile ...	14905	Every alternate Friday
Dignacion...	14906	Last Friday
Dignamente	14907	Next Friday
Dignandus	14908	Next Friday week
Dignificar..	14909	On Friday
Dignified ...	14910	On Friday morning
Dignitade...	14911	On Friday afternoon
Dignitary ...	14912	On Friday night

Dignitoso ...	14913	During Friday
Digozzare...	14914	During Friday night
Digranare...	14915	—— Friday in each month
Digredire ...	14916	**Friend(s)**
Digressed ...	14917	Certainly no friend of yours
Digressing	14918	Is a friend of ——
Digression	14919	Is a friend of mine
Digrignare	14920	Was (were) never my friend(s)
Digrossare	14921	**Friendly**
Digrumato	14922	Quite friendly
Diguastare	14923	If friendly
Diguazzato	14924	Friendly at present
Digusciare	14925	Friendly so far as I am (we are) aware
Dihedron ...	14926	As a friendly action
Dijudicor ...	14927	**From**
Dijugator...	14928	From the
Dijunctio ...	14929	From whom (which)
Diktiren ...	14930	From the date of
Dilabens ...	14931	From date of notice
Dilabimur	14932	All from
Dilabilis ...	14933	From next
Dilaccarsi...	14934	From to-day
Dilacciare...	14935	Not any is (was) from
Dilacerate	14936	To and from
Dilaceror ...	14937	From what I (we) have discovered
Dilacrumo	14938	From how many tons
Dilagato ...	14939	From how many yards
Dilajare ...	14940	From what portion of
Dilamino ...	14941	From the shaft
Dilaniato ...	14942	From the drift
Dilanior ...	14943	From the crosscut
Dilapidans	14944	From the level
Dilapido ...	14945	From the winze
Dilargare ...	14946	From the stopes
Dilargior ...	14947	From whom did you learn
Dilargitus	14948	From whom did you get
Dilatable ...	14949	Has from —— to ——
Dilatador ...	14950	From —— to ——
Dilatante ...	14951	**Front**
Dilatar ...	14952	Should like to get in front of
Dilatation	14953	Try to get in front of
Dilatesco ...	14954	In front of
Dilatoria ...	14955	Will be placed in front of
Dilaturus ...	14956	**Frost** (See also "Weather," "Winter.")
Dilaudatio	14957	As soon as the frost is all gone
Dilaxant ...	14958	On account of severe frost
Dilazione ...	14959	Prevented by the frost
Dilection ...	14960	The frost is now all gone
Dilecto ...	14961	Frost is beginning to break up
Dileggiare	14962	**Frue Vanners**
Dileggino ...	14963	Frue vanners started
Dilegine ...	14964	Frue vanners doing good duty
Dileguo ...	14965	Frue vanners not suited to the ore
Dilemma ...	14966	Plant should include frue vanners
Diletant ...	14967	Plant includes —— frue vanners
Dileticoso...	14968	Concentrates from frue vanners
Dilettarsi ...	14969	Shall not treat at present the concentrates from frue vanners
Dilettato ...	14970	Have shipped —— tons of concentrates from frue vanners
Diletuare ...	14971	Proceeds of sale of —— tons of concentrates from frue
Dilezioso ...	14972	Cable cost of —— frue vanners delivered at [vanners

Diliberare...	14973	Cost of —— frue vanners delivered is ——
Dilibero ...	14974	**Fuel** (*See also* " Bitumen," " Coal," " Wood," &c.)
Dilibrarsi...	14975	An inferior coal is the only available fuel
Diligencia...	14976	Can you obtain a plentiful supply of good fuel
Diligenter	14977	Fuel is scarce and costly [the mine
Diligione ...	14978	Good wood fuel can be obtained, —— per cord delivered on
Dilimarsi ...	14979	Have let a fuel contract for —— cords at —— per cord
Diliscare ...	14980	Owing to the increased cost of fuel
Diliticare ...	14981	Should be arranged for burning wood fuel
Diliziano ...	14982	Should be arranged for burning —— fuel
Diloggiato	14983	There is a plentiful supply of —— fuel [costs ——
Dilogias ...	14984	The present daily consumption of fuel amounts to —— and
Dilombarsi	14985	The property contains a supply of fuel that will last —— years,
		[the cost of cutting and transport amounts to —— per cord
Dilontuno...	14986	There is practically no fuel to be obtained
Dilucidare	14987	This will reduce our fuel cost considerably
Dilucido ...	14988	Includes —— for candles and fuel
Diluculo ...	14989	Fuel account
Diludium ...	14990	**Fulfil**
Diluent ...	14991	To fulfil
Dilungarsi	14992	Must certainly fulfil
Dilungato...	14993	Ready to fulfil
Dilusive ...	14994	Refuse(s) to fulfil his (their) promises
Diluteth ...	14995	To fulfil promise made
Dilutium ...	14996	Take necessary steps to compel him (them) to fulfil
Diluviare ...	14997	They can compel us to fulfil or forfeit deposit paid
Diluvies ...	14998	Unable to fulfil
Diluvioso ...	14999	Unless I (we) fulfil
Dimachas ...	15000	Regret cannot fulfil
Dimadesco	**15001**	Will do my best to fulfil
Dimagrare	15002	Will fulfil
Dimanabat	15003	Will not fulfil
Dimanacion	15004	**Fulfilled**
Dimanante	15005	Has (have) been fulfilled
Dimanar ...	15006	Has (have) not been fulfilled
Dimanche...	15007	**Full**
Dimando ...	15008	Already full
Dimembrare	15009	Full up to
Dimenio ...	15010	Full up with
Dimeritare	15011	Full instructions mailed on
Dimessione	15012	Has (have) been full since
Dimesso ...	15013	I (we) sent full details by mail on ——
Dimettere...	15014	Now entirely full
Dimezzato	15015	Send full particulars by cable
Dimicantur	15016	Send full details by next mail
Dimicetis ...	15017	The —— is (are) full of water
Dimidiar ...	15018	The shaft is full of water
Diminuent	15019	Everything is full of
Diminuir ...	15020	Make full allowance for
Diminutive	15021	Will send full description to
Diminuto ...	15022	At present full of
Dimision ...	15023	Full of ore
Dimissoria	15024	Full of debris
Dimitir ...	15025	Full particulars published in
Dimojare ...	15026	**Fully**
Dimolto ...	15027	Fully answered on
Dimorante	15028	Fully expected that
Dimorphous	15029	Were fully protected
Dimorsare	15030	Are we fully protected
Dimostrare	15031	We are not fully protected

Dimostro ...	15082	I am (we are) fully protected
Dimotus ...	15033	**Fund(s)** (*See also* "Money.")
Dimunto ...	15034	Reserve fund
Dinanderie	15085	From reserve fund
Dinansi ...	15086	For want of funds
Dinasato ...	15087	What are the available funds
Dinascoso...	15088	Available funds amount to
Dinasty ...	15039	No funds at all
Dinatoire ...	15040	In order to raise necessary funds
Dinderlo ...	15041	Only sufficient funds in hand to
Dindonneau	15042	Limited funds at our disposal do not justify
Dinegato ...	15043	Shall be compelled to stop for want of funds
Dinegrare ...	15044	Funds at my (our) disposal are limited to
Dinerada ...	15045	What funds have you available
Dinerista ...	15046	What funds will you want up to
Dineroso ...	15047	What funds will you want to complete work in hand
Dineruelo...	15048	No reserve fund at all
Dinervave ..	15049	Place to reserve fund
Dinette ...	15050	Reserve fund is really represented by materials
Dingdong...	15051	Will supply all funds
Dinginess...	15052	Will you arrange to supply necessary funds
Dinglich ...	15053	What funds shall you have in hand after
Dinichthys	15054	Funds are exhausted
Diniego ...	15055	Funds are nearly run out
Dinners ...	15056	Funds must be furnished promptly
Dinobolus...	15057	Must have funds before
Dinoccare...	15058	Funds received only sufficient for
Dinominare	15059	Have no funds for this particular purpose
Dinornis ...	15060	Provided that you remit necessary funds
Dinosaurs...	15061	I have not sufficient funds in hand to enable me to carry on the
Dinoscent	15062	Practically bare of funds [work; cable remittance of ——
Dinotare ...	15063	What funds of mine (ours) shall you have in hand
Dintelar ...	15064	What funds will you have in hand after allowing for the
Dintorno ...	15065	**Furnace** (*See also* "Calciner," "Roaster.") [cost of
Dinudato ...	15066	Furnace assay
Dinumerare	15067	Bruckner calcining furnace
Dinunzia ...	15068	Blast furnace
Dinuptilam	15069	Calcining furnace
Dinvolo ...	15070	Drying furnace
Diocesano	15071	Reverberatory furnace
Diocesi ...	15072	Roasting furnace
Dioecia ...	15073	Water jacket furnace
Dionites ...	15074	What is the cost of furnace
Diopside ...	15075	Cost per furnace complete
Dioptase ...	15076	What is the capacity of the roasting furnace
Dioptra ...	15077	The roasting furnace can treat —— tons in 24 hours
Dioptrics ...	15078	Owing to the limited capacity of our roasting furnace(s)
Diorama ...	15079	Furnace(s) working splendidly
Diosecillo ...	15080	Furnace started on —— not working at all well
Diosecita ...	15081	Shall commence erection of furnace on ——
Diosma ...	15082	Shall complete furnace on
Diospyros ..	15083	Furnace blown out on
Diotas ...	15084	Furnace now running smoothly
Diottrica ...	15085	Furnace now turning out
Dioxia ...	15086	Furnace(s) will require to be modified
Diparere ...	15087	**Furnish**
Dipartenza	15088	To furnish
Dipartito ...	15089	Refuse(s) to furnish
Dipelato ...	15090	Do not volunteer to furnish
Dipellare ...	15091	Furnish all information possible

Diphonium	15092	Has (have) agreed to furnish the necessary funds
Diphtheria	15093	Has (have) agreed to furnish
Diphthong	15094	Not necessary to furnish
Dipingere...	15095	Please furnish all necessary documents
Dipintrice...	15096	Please furnish such particulars as will enable me (to)
Dipintura...	15097	Refuse(s) to furnish additional
Diploe	15098	Furnish estimates for
Diplomacy	15099	Furnish details of
Diploma	15100	**Furnished**
Diplomatic	15101	To be furnished by
Diplopora...	15102	To be furnished within the next —— days
Diplopus	15103	Get it furnished
Diportarsi	15104	Has (have) been furnished (by)
Dipositare	15105	Has (have) not yet been furnished
Dippings	15106	**Further** (*See also* " Farther.")
Dipressare	15107	Further steps
Dipsaceae...	15108	Further on
Dipsaco	15109	Further from
Dipsadibus	15110	For further orders
Dipterus	15111	Further information
Diptica	15112	Further information very desirable
Diptongar	15113	Further information will be sent by first mail
Diptotas...	15114	As soon as I (we) hear anything further of
Diputado...	15115	After further consideration
Diputar	15116	Cannot anything further be done (to)
Dipylos	15117	Do nothing until you hear further
Dique	15118	Do all you can to further ——'s (his) wishes
Diquecillo	15119	Do not go any further
Diradare...	15120	Will not go any further
Diradicato	15121	Cannot go any further
Diramato...	15122	Further information by cable later
Directive...	15123	Have you any further news respecting
Directora...	15124	Have remitted you ——; further amount(s) will follow
Directorio...	15125	Further amount will follow on ——
Directrice...	15126	Have you done anything further respecting
Direfull	15127	I (we) await your letter before taking further steps
Dirempsit...	15128	In case you hear anything further
Direpzione	15129	In case you hear nothing further you may conclude that
Diretano	15130	Nothing further has been done
Diretro	15131	Nothing further can be done with
Direttore	15132	Refuse(s) to further consider the matter
Diricciare...	15133	Shall await further instructions
Diridere	15134	Still await your further instructions at
Dirigar	15135	**Fuse** (*See also* "Blasting," "Detonators," &c.)
Dirigenza...	15136	Bickford Smith's safety fuse
Dirimpetto	15187	Coils of safety fuse
Diripuit	15138	German safety fuse
Dirisiare...	15139	Send some taped fuse suitable for sinking in very wet ground
Diritta	15140	Send fuse suitable for dry ground
Dirittezza...	15141	Forward promptly —— coils of safety fuse
Dirittura...	15142	—— casks of safety fuse shipped on ——
Dirivieni...	15143	Instantaneous fuses
Dirizzone...	15144	**Future**
Diroccato...	15145	Cost in future
Dirompere	15146	In future
Dirovinare	15147	The future
Diruendum	15148	I (we) shall be able in future
Diruir	15149	For future delivery
Dirupato...	15150	Future rates likely to be
Disabilita...	15151	Future shipment(s)

Disaccoso ...	15152	In future you must take care (to)
Disadatto	15153	In future I (we) will take care (to)
Disadorno	15154	Please note this for future reference
Disagevole	15155	Future prospects are very discouraging
Disagiare ...	15156	Future prospects are somewhat encouraging
Disamabile	15157	Future prospects are excellent
Disamato ...	15158	Will be continued for the future
Disamenita	15159	Will make a great change in our future prospects
Disaminato	15160	Without any thought of (for) the future

G

Disamoroso	15161	
Disanimare	15162	**Gad(s)** (*See also* "Picks.")
Disarming	15163	A supply of gads
Disarmonia	15164	Include six gads
Disarray ...	15165	**Gain(s)**
Disascoso ...	15166	To gain
Disasprire	15167	Expect to gain about
Disastrare	15168	Can gain very little information
Disastro ...	15169	What do I (we) stand to gain by it
Disattento	15170	By this (it) I (we) shall gain
Disavanzo	15171	—— gain(s) at least
Disbanded	15172	Has (have) nothing to gain personally
Disbandire	15173	It will be a decided gain to us
Disbarbato	15174	My (our) personal gain will be *nil*
Disbattere	15175	My (our) personal gain will amount to
Disboscare	15176	Renounce(s) all personal gain
Disbramato	15177	The gain will amount to —— per ton
Disbuffare	15178	The money gain is slight
Discaduto...	15179	The money gain alone amounts to
Discaggere	15180	What do you (does he) gain by the purchase
Discante ...	15181	Will gain nothing
Discapito ...	15182	We have everything to gain and practically nothing to lose
Discarchi ...	15183	Whether we gain or win we shall lose
Discavent...	15184	**Gained** (*See also* "Action.")
Discedere ...	15185	Have gained our case
Discensore	15186	—— has (have) gained
Discepola ...	15187	Has gained nothing so far
Disceptar ...	15188	Have you (has ——) gained
Discernent	15189	Have not gained
Discernir ...	15190	**Gaining**
Discernuto	15191	Gaining rapidly
Discettato	15192	Gaining —— daily
Disceum ...	15193	**Galena** (*See also* "Argentiferous," "Lead," "Ore.")
Discezione	15194	Galena ore
Dischiesta	15195	Vein carries a little galena
Dischiuso ...	15196	Argentiferous galena
Discignere	15197	Coarse grained galena
Disciple ...	15198	Fine grained galena
Discipline...	15199	Grey copper with galena
Discipulo ...	15200	Galena associated with blende
Discites ...	15201	Galena associated with blende and carries —— ounces of silver
Discobolum	15202	**Gallery(ies)** [per ton
Discoid ...	15203	Upper galleries of the mine
Discoletto...	15204	Lower galleries
Discolor ...	15205	**Gallons**
Discolpare	15206	Of a gallon
Discomfit ...	15207	American gallon(s)
Discomodo	15208	English gallon(s)
Disconcio ...	15209	Gallons per minute
Discoperto	15210	Gallons per hour
Discoprire	15211	**Gallows**

Discorato ...	15212	Gallows frame
Discord ...	15213	Erection of gallows frame completed
Discordant	15214	**Gangue**
Discordia ...	15215	Gangue matter is
Discorrere	15216	Gangue consists mainly of
Discorsivo	15217	Gangue, which was supposed to be worthless, contains
Discosceso	15218	What is the gangue
Discoureur	15219	**Garnet(s)** (*See also* "Minerals.")
Discous ...	15220	**Garnetiferous**
Discredito	15221	**Gas** (*See also* "Afterdamp.")
Discretear...	15222	Marsh gas
Discrimine	15223	Coal gas
Discritto ...	15224	Water gas
Disculpa ...	15225	**Gauge**
Discumbant	15226	What is the gauge of
Discuojare	15227	The gauge is
Discurrir ...	15228	Birmingham wire gauge
Discursive	15229	Same gauge as previously
Discurso ...	15230	Send exact gauge required
Discussion	15231	How did you gauge
Discutient	15232	**Gauged** (*See also* "Miners' Inches," "Water.")
Discutir ...	15233	Have you gauged
Disdainful	15234	As soon as you have gauged
Disdaining	15235	When was it gauged
Disdirsi ...	15236	Was gauged on
Disebriare	15237	Cannot be gauged until
Disegnare...	15238	Has not yet been gauged
Disegnetto	15239	As soon as it has been properly gauged
Diseguale ...	15240	Should be gauged for a considerable period
Disembark	15241	Gauged at intervals of —— days
Disembogue	15242	**Gave**
Diseminar	15243	Gave to
Disenchant	15244	Gave him (them) all necessary instructions
Disenfiare...	15245	Gave him (them) all necessary information
Disennato...	15246	Gave away everything
Disenrol ...	15247	Gave him (——) as much as possible
Disension ...	15248	Gave up everything
Disenteria	15249	**Gazette**
Disentir ...	15250	In the Gazette
Diseredare	15251	Official gazette
Diserede ...	15252	Must publish final notice in gazette
Diserrato ...	15253	Final notice has been published in gazette
Disertim ...	15254	Send draft for final notice in gazette
Disertore ...	15255	**Gear**
Diservigio	15256	Gear wheels
Diservire ...	15257	Hauling gear
Disesteem...	15258	In gear
Diseurs ...	15259	Out of gear
Disface ...	15260	Overhead gear
Disfamador	15261	Pumping gear
Disfamia ...	15262	Valve gear
Disfatto ...	15263	Gear for
Disfavored	15264	With all necessary gear
Disfazione	15265	**Gearing**
Disferrare...	15266	With necessary gearing to enable us
Disfidante	15267	**General** (*See also* "Condition.")
Disfigured	15268	In general
Disfingere...	15269	What is the general feeling
Disformar...	15270	The general feeling here is
Disfraz ...	15271	The general average is

Disfrenare	15272	What is the general average
Disfrodare	15273	According to general opinion
Disgannato	15274	What is the general opinion
Disgombare	15275	General opinion is favourable
Disgorged	15276	From the general outlook
Disgracier	15277	General contingency(ies)
Disgradato	15278	What are the general contingencies
Disgregant	15279	General contingencies are
Disguaglio	15280	**Generally**
Disguisato	15281	State generally
Disguising	15282	It is generally believed here that
Disgustado	15283	**Genuine**
Disgusting	15284	Not genuine
Disgustoso	15285	Perfectly genuine
Dishearten	15286	Do you consider this (it) genuine
Dished ...	15287	Is believed here to be thoroughly genuine
Dishevel ...	15288	I believe him (it) to be thoroughly genuine
Dishiasco ...	15289	A genuine offer of
Dishing ...	15290	Offer was not genuine
Disianza	15291	Offer was undoubtedly genuine when made
Disiato ...	15292	If you are convinced that this (it) is genuine
Disidencia	15293	**Geological** (*See also* "Mineral," "Rocks.")
Disideroso	15294	The main geological features
Disidir ...	15295	The geological formation
Disiguale ...	15296	What is the geological formation
Disilabo ...	15297	Geological report
Disimilar ..	15298	Geological survey
Disimpegno	15299	A geological map
Disimulado	15300	A geological section
Disimulo ...	15301	The general geological conditions are such that
Disinanza...	15302	From the geological formation I (we) would expect
Disinare ...	15303	**Geologist**
Disinfect ...	15304	Government geologist
Disinfinto...	15305	A geologist of repute
Disinganno	15306	A good field-geologist
Disinherit...	15307	**Geology**
Disinter ...	15308	The general geology of the district
Disinvolto	15309	Geology of the mine
Disioso ...	15310	Geology of the property (concession)
Disipable ...	15311	**Get**
Disipacion	15312	To get
Disipador...	15313	To get to
Disipula ...	15314	To get under
Disistima ...	15315	To get rid of
Disjected ...	15316	Unable to get away
Disjecting	15317	Can get
Disjicior ...	15318	Cannot get
Disjoindre	15319	I (we) will get
Disjunct ...	15320	Cannot get it (this)
Diskant ...	15321	Can you get away
Diskuriren	15322	Could only get
Dislate ...	15323	Did you get
Disleale ...	15324	Did not get it (them)
Dislegato ...	15325	Can you get anything out of —— respecting
Disliking ...	15326	Do not expect to get more unless
Dislodge ...	15327	Do not get more than
Disloquer...	15328	Get as much (many) as you can at —— or anything lower
Disloyal ...	15329	Get what you can at —— or about
Disluogare	15330	Get as much (many) as you can
Dismal ...	15331	How much (many) can you get

Dismalare...	15332	Get rid of
Dismantled	15333	You should get at least
Dismassed	15334	You should get
Dismasting	15335	Has all he can do in order to get along
Dismaying	15336	I (we) did not get
Dismentare	15337	Endeavour to get
Dismesso ...	15338	Get me (us)
Dismettere	15339	Get me some
Dismimur...	15340	Get me some of (from)
Dismisura...	15341	If you cannot get
Dismodato	15342	Get whatever you are really in need of
Dismounts	15343	Only get for the present
Dismuovere	15344	I (we) can get
Disnervare	15345	I (we) will get
Dismetto ...	15346	Get ready
Disnidarsi	15347	Get ready for
Disobeyed...	15348	Get his (their)
Disobeying	15349	Get order if possible
Disociar ...	15350	Get news
Disolatora	15351	Get abstract of
Disoluble ...	15352	Get details arranged promptly
Disolucion	15353	Get all details arranged and let me (us) know
Disoluto ...	15354	Get all assistance you possibly can
Disolver ...	15355	Get away
Disonancia	15356	Get away promptly
Disonante...	15357	Has (have) promised to get
Disonar ...	15358	Is it still possible to get an interest
Disonnarsi	15359	So as to get
Disonorare	15360	Shall be able to get out at least
Disorderly	15361	Get —— to advance
Disordine ...	15362	Get —— to advance necessary amount
Disottano...	15363	Get rid of shares at present price
Disovolato	15364	Get rid of shares at any price
Disowned ...	15365	Do not get mixed up in any affairs at
Disowning	15366	**Getting**
Dispaccare	15367	Am (are) getting ready for (to)
Dispalesco	15368	Are now getting
Dispansus	15369	Getting out of
Disparador	15370	How are you getting along
Disparate ...	15371	Getting along slowly
Disparidad	15372	Now getting along faster
Disparilis ...	15373	Getting along fast now
Disparked	15374	Has (have) been getting
Dispartire...	15375	—— is said to be getting rid of his holding
Dispendium	15376	Now getting enough to
Dispennato	15377	Only getting enough to
Dispensary	15378	The ore we are now getting
Dispensing	15379	We are gradually getting over it
Dispeople...	15380	**Give**
Dispepsia ..	15381	To give
Disperrare ...	15382	Give to
Disperging	15383	Give me (us)
Dispersive	15384	Can you (——) give
Disperso ...	15385	Can give
Dispettato	15386	Cannot give anything
Dispianato	15387	Can only give
Dispiegare	15388	Cannot give salary asked
Dispirited ..	15389	Give more
Displant ...	15390	Will you give me (us) leave to
Displanted	15391	Give you (——) full leave to

Displeased	15392	Cannot give you (——) leave to
Displode ...	15393	Give formal notice
Dispnea ...	15394	Give great attention
Disponedor	15395	Give —— written instructions to
Disponens	15396	Give me (us) as much information as you can about
Disponible	15397	Give more information about
Disported ...	15398	Give precise details as to
Disporting	15399	Give further details
Disposare ...	15400	No need to give any attention to
Dispotico ...	15401	Can you induce —— to give way
Dispraise ...	15402	Can only give way to the extent of
Dispregio ...	15403	Cannot give more than
Disprizeth	15404	Do not give beyond
Disprunare	15405	Decline(s) positively to give more
Dispuesto	15406	Give him (them) to understand
Dispumato	15407	Give for a call of
Disputa ...	15408	Give for a put of
Disputable	15409	Expect to give
Disputador	15410	Expect to see him (them) and give answer by
Disputeur...	15411	How long can you (——) give
Disputing...	15412	Cannot give longer time than
Disputiren	15413	Impossible to give longer time; other parties waiting
Disquieted	15414	You (——) must give longer time
Disragione	15415	I (we) should not give way
Disrated ...	15416	If I (we) give way
Disrelish ...	15417	To give way
Disrobed ...	15418	To give way would be very unadvisable
Disrompere	15419	Should advise you (him) (them) to give way
Disruption	15420	Must give
Disrupture	15421	Refuse(s) to give
Dissacrato	15422	Refuse(s) to give more
Dissagrare	15423	Refuse(s) to give up documents
Dissapito ...	15424	Instruct —— to give up documents
Dissecator	15425	Unless you can give
Disseccare	15426	Will enable me to give more attention to
Dissected ...	15427	What will you (——) give
Dissection	15428	What can I (we) give
Dissemble...	15429	You (——) may give
Disseminer	15430	Will not give more than
Dissennato	15431	Will give you (——) until
Dissenting	15432	Will you give anything towards
Dissequer ...	15433	Will give what is right
Disservice...	15434	Will give up (to)
Dissetare ...	15435	Will not give up (to)
Dissezione	15436	Will you give me (us)
Dissident ...	15437	Will you give me (us) all profits as from
Dissimilar	15438	**Given**
Dissimule...	15439	How much have you (has ——) actually given for it
Dissipato ...	15440	Have you given notice as to
Dissocial ...	15441	Have not yet given notice
Dissodare ...	15442	I (we) have given
Dissoluto ...	15443	I (we) have given up all hope of
Dissolvent	15444	I (we) have given up
Dissonance	15445	I (we) have not yet given up
Dissoniren	15446	Must be given up
Dissonner...	15447	Must be given up to
Dissuader...	15448	—— has not yet given up
Dissuasory	15449	It has been given out that
Dissuria ...	15450	Notice must be given not later than —— of my (our) inten-
Distacio ...	15451	Notice was given on [tion to

† For "Dispuemini" see "Despuemini" (page 243).

Distaffs ...	15452	When must notice be given
Distancia ...	15453	Within a given time
Distar ...	15454	Within the given time, namely

Glad

Distaste ...	15455	Glad
Distastful...	15456	Very glad to know it
Distemper	15457	I am (we are) very glad to inform you that
Distendere	15458	I (we) shall be glad to know that you are able (to)
Distention	15459	I (we) shall be glad to hear from you by cable (as to)
Distessere...	15460	I (we) shall be glad to learn that
Distico ...	15461	I (we) shall be glad to receive earliest news respecting

Gland(s)

Distillery ...	15462	Gland(s)
Distincion	15463	Gland of
Distinguir	15464	Gland requires re-packing
Distintivo ...	15465	Send dimensions of gland
Distinto ...	15466	Send sketch with figured dimensions of gland
Distique ...	15467	Packing for gland
Distirpare...	15468	Has injured gland

Gneiss(ic)

Distolto ...	15469	Gneiss(ic)
Distorcere	15470	Gneissic rock
Distorted ...	15471	Hanging wall is gneiss
Distorting	15472	Footwall is gneiss
Distracto ...	15473	The country rock is gneiss
Distraemos	15474	The gneiss is decomposed to a depth of —— feet
Distraer ...	15475	In decomposed gneiss

Go(es)

Distraido ...	15476	Go(es)
Distraint ...	15477	To go
Distrarre ...	15478	To go to
Distretta ...	15479	To go for
Distribuir...	15480	To go up
Distrigare...	15481	To go down
Distringor	15482	To go with
Disturbing	15483	Go ahead as hard as you can
Disuasion...	15484	Go ahead until you receive cable from
Disuasivo...	15485	Go ahead until I (we) cable to stop
Disudire ...	15486	Go slow
Disugguale	15487	Go at once (to)
Disumanare	15488	Go if you possibly can manage
Disunibile...	15489	You had better go as quickly as possible to —— and report
Disunion ...	15490	Will go as quickly as possible to —— and report [fully
Disunity ...	15491	I go as soon as possible to
Disusanza...	15492	Could you (——) go to —— on ——
Disusato ...	15493	Cannot go unless you cable me
Disutilita ...	15494	Can only go by steamer as far as
Disvalere ...	15495	Can only go by rail as far as
Disvariare	15496	Could go by way of
Disviarsi ...	15497	Could you go by way of
Disvolgere	15498	Could you go to ——? You would probably require to be away [——
Disyuncion	15499	Can go
Disyunta ...	15500	Do not go beyond
Disyuntivo	15501	Go as quickly as possible
Ditatorem...	15502	If —— can go, make necessary arrangements with him
Ditello ...	15503	If —— cannot go, can you suggest anyone else
Ditenere ...	15504	If —— cannot go
Ditheistic ...	15505	Must go to
Dithyrambe	15506	Must not go to
Ditirambo...	15507	Only in case you cannot go yourself
Ditissime ...	15508	Regret cannot go
Ditono ...	15509	Shall not be able to go before
Ditrappare	15510	Within what time could you go to ——
Dittato ...	15511	You may go

Dittatorio...	15512	You cannot go
Ditties ...	15513	You had better go at once to mine and make full report
Dittongo ...	15514	—— will go with you
Diturpare...	15515	—— and I shall go together
Diuresis ...	15516	—— unable to go
Diuretico ...	15517	The ore goes up
Diuturnal ..	15518	The ore goes down
Diuturnity	15519	Very likely to go
Divagante	15520	Did you go to
Divagar ...	15521	**Going**
Divagation	15522	Going to
Divaguer ...	15523	Not going to
Divalibus ...	15524	X Going up
Divampare	15525	Going down
Divaricate	15526	Going in
Divegliere...	15527	Going out
Divenire ...	15528	Going away
Diverbio ...	15529	Going forward
Divergente	15530	Going forward by —— on ——
Divergir ...	15531	Are you going
Diversare ...	15532	Do you know if —— is going
Diversify ...	15533	—— is not going
Diversions	15534	Going to run it up
Diversitas ..	15535	Going to run it up to
Diversorio	15536	Going to run it down to
Divertebam	15537	He is (they are) going to
Divertido ..	15538	I am (we are) going to
Divesture...	15539	I am (we are) not going to
Divexavi ...	15540	Not going for the present
Dividevole	15541	Going to —— till
Dividicula	15542	When are you going
Dividero	15543	When are you going and where
Dividir ...	15544	Everything going on all right
Dividitore...	15545	Everything is going on fairly
Dividuo ...	15546	Things are now going better
Diviesco ...	15547	The only thing that is going well is
Divigenam	15548	Everything seems to be going badly
Divimarsi...	15549	What are you going to do
Divinacion	15550	Owing to —— not going
Divinare ...	15551	If —— is going to
Divinatory	15552	If —— is not going to
Divinement	15553	**Gold** (*See also* "Auriferous," "Average," "Ounces," "Per
Diviniser ...	15554	Gold chloride [Cent.," "Sample," "Silver," "Test," &c.)
Divinitus ...	15555	Gold cyanide
Divinizado	15556	Gold bearing
Divino ...	15557	Gold dust
Divisero ...	15558	Gold nuggets
Divisible ...	15559	Gold free
Divisivo ...	15560	Gold has been found in bed of creek
Divisurus .	15561	Gold ore
Divizioso ...	15562	Gold was discovered at
Divorativo	15563	Gold has been discovered here
Divoratura	15564	Gold amalgam
Divorced ...	15565	The gold is " rusty "
Divorciar ...	15566	Alluvial gold
Divulgable	15567	The gold is very fine
Divulgar ...	15568	The gold is coarse
Divulgeter	15569	The gold is coarse and readily amalgamates
Divulsion ...	15570	Retorted gold
Dixieme ...	15571	Visible free gold

Dizain ...	15572	Can pan out gold
Dizionario	15573	—— gold from each pan
Dizziness ...	15574	Have made many pannings and have always found gold
Dobblone ...	15575	Value for gold and silver
Dobladilla	15576	Gold and silver
Doblado ...	15577	Gold, silver and copper
Dobladura	15578	Gold, silver and lead
Doblar ...	15579	Have saved —— per cent. of the gold
Doblegable	15580	Little or no gold present
Doblegar ...	15581	Must be paid in gold coin
Doblemente	15582	Pennyweights of gold per ton of 2,240 lbs.
Dobleria ...	15583	Prevents us recovering a fair proportion of the gold
Doblete ...	15584	On account of the gold being associated with
Doblonada	15585	I apprehend difficulty in treating the gold
Docciatura	15586	Gold is very fine and will present great difficulty in treatment
Docetur ...	15587	Gold is very rusty, and I (we) apprehend difficulty in treatment
Dochleas ...	15588	Gold extracted since the mine was commenced is valued at
Docht ...	15589	Gold and silver are in about equal proportions
Docidium ...	15590	What is the fineness of the gold
Docientos ..	15591	Gold is —— fine
Docilidad ...	15592	Gold is increasing in fineness
Docility ...	15593	The gold is associated with
Docilmente	15594	Gold is associated with iron pyrites
Docimastic	15595	Gold is associated with arsenical pyrites
Docketing	15596	The gold is associated with black iron sand
Dockyards	15597	Ore contains no visible gold
Doctificam	15598	Ore contains visible gold
Doctissime	15599	There is no visible gold
Doctorando	15600	Gold is very fine and most difficult to save
Doctorar ...	15601	Have found a nugget of gold weighing —— ozs.
Doctorate ...	15602	Owing to reputed find of nuggets of gold
Doctoribus	15603	Nuggets of gold are occasionally found
Doctress ...	15604	Washing for gold
Doctricem...	15605	Gold is mainly in the free state and coarse
Doctrinal ...	15606	The gold is mainly in the free state but very fine; apprehend [considerable difficulty in saving a fair proportion
Doctrinero	15607	The gold is entirely alluvial
Doctrino ...	15608	The gold occurs in
Documento	15609	The gold is very base
Dodder ...	15610	The gold contents is increasing
Doddering	15611	The gold contents is diminishing
Dodecaedro	15612	The gold contents has become practically *nil*
Dodecagon	15613	The yield amounts to —— ounces of retorted gold
Dodgingly	15614	An average assay for gold gave —— per ton of 2,240 lbs.
Dodicina ...	15615	An average assay for gold gave traces only
Dodliner ...	15616	An average sample assayed, gold *nil*
Dodrante ..	15617	The quartz carrying the gold is
Doffing ...	15618	The paystreak carrying the gold is
Dogana ...	15619	A paystreak —— inches wide, full of visible gold
Doganiere...	15620	Samples can be found showing free gold but the average is low
Dogaresse...	15621	We shall then materially increase the amount of gold saved
Dogcart ...	15622	There are plenty of indications of the existence of gold
Dogdays ..	15623	Ounces of gold
Dogfishes ...	15624	Bar of gold, total weight ——, has been shipped
Dogged ...	15625	What quantity of gold have you on hand
Doggerel ...	15626	Ship as much gold prior to —— as you can
Doghetto ...	15627	What quantity of gold have you shipped
Doglia ...	15628	Expect to ship balance of gold on ——
Doglianza...	15629	During the No. —— campaign we have crushed —— tons of [stone which has yielded —— ounces of gold, —— fineness

Doglietto ...	15630	A paystreak of ore rich in gold
Dogmatical	15631	A paystreak of ore carrying —— dwts. of gold per ton
Dogmatico	15632	As a gold mine has a great reputation for richness
Dogmatique	15633	Endeavour to get as large an average as possible of the gold [quartz crushed at the neighbouring mill
Dogmatist	15634	Expect to save —— per cent. of the gold
Dogmatizar	15635	Is there not enough gold to pay for its extraction
Dogsbane...	15636	**Gone**
Dogtooth ...	15637	Gone up
Dogtrot ...	15638	Gone down
Dogwood ...	15639	Can you discover where —— has gone
Doigter ...	15640	—— has gone to ——, is expected to be absent until ——
Doktorhut	15641	—— has gone to ——, will return about
Dolabamur	15642	—— has not gone. It is not at all certain if he will go
Dolabratus	15643	Have already gone forward
Doladera ...	15644	Nothing yet gone forward
Dolage ...	15645	Should have gone forward on
Dolamas ...	15646	Has (have) —— gone yet
Dolavisse ...	15647	Is supposed here to have gone
Dolcemente	15648	In case —— has gone to —— could you arrange
Dolcezza ...	15649	In case —— has not gone to —— could you arrange
Dolciano ...	15650	They have now all gone forward
Dolciore ...	15651	Where has it (this) all gone to
Dolcissimo	15652	**Good** (*See also* "Condition," "Expected.")
Dolde ...	15653	Fairly good
Doldrums...	15654	Very good
Doleance ...	15655	In good condition
Dolefully ...	15656	Good progress is being made with
Dolemment	15657	Good for
Dolencia ...	15658	Good for at least
Dolesome ...	15659	Good for any reasonable amount
Doletote ...	15660	Not sufficiently good
Dolichorum	15661	As good as
Doliente ...	15662	Do you (does ——) think it will be any good
Doliman ..	15663	Do(es) not think it would be good enough for you
Dolioso ...	15664	Good to hold
Dolitando...	15665	Good to sell
Dolitavi ...	15666	Good to sell short
Doliturus ...	15667	Good to buy
Dolobre ...	15668	I (we) do not think any good would result
Dolorato ...	15669	The only good that could result would be
Dolorcillo...	15670	In order to be of any good
Dolorido ...	15671	Is it good enough
Dolorific ...	15672	Little good, if any
Dolorous ...	15673	Much too good
Dolphin ...	15674	Not as good as
Doltishly ...	15675	Not good enough
Doluero ...	15676	No good at all
Doluistis ...	15677	Be good enough to
Dolzaino ...	15678	—— has (have) been good enough to
Domable ...	15679	Everything is in good shape
Domador ...	15680	**Goods**
Domandus	15681	The goods should be consigned to the order of
Domane ...	15682	All the goods have arrived in good condition
Domatio ...	15683	All goods now shipped
Domatriare	15684	Goods have all gone forward to the mine
Domatrice	15685	Goods as per your indent —— now being shipped
Domattina	15686	Goods will have to be sent
Domefacto	15687	Have the goods been shipped
Domeneddio	15688	Main portion of goods now shipped

Domenicale	15689	The damage to the goods amounts to
Domesticar	15690	Some of the goods are in course of transit
Domestics	15691	**Gossan**
Domestique	15692	Entirely gossan
Domevole...	15693	For a depth of —— feet in gossan
Domherr ...	15694	Samples of the gossan assay
Domicilio...	15695	**Got**
Dominador	15696	Got off
Dominant...	15697	Have you got possession
Dominateur	15698	Have not got possession
Dominativo	15699	As soon as I (we) have got possession
Dominatore	15700	Got clear away
Domineered	15701	**Government** (*See also* "Authorities," "Regulations.")
Dominguero	15702	Government taxes
Dominicus	15703	Government demand
Dominium	15704	Government inspector
Dominoes...	15705	Government surveyor
Dominotier	15706	Government enquiry
Domkapitel	15707	**Grade** (*See also* "Incline," "Ore.")
Domkirche	15708	Low grade
Dommage	15709	Low grade ore
Dommasco	15710	Is of lower grade
Domptable	15711	The ore is —— grade
Dompteur...	15712	About the same grade
Donadello...	15713	Am (are) working entirely on high grade ore
Donagione	15714	Am (are) working entirely on low grade ore
Donaire ...	15715	High grade
Donairoso...	15716	High grade ore
Donatario...	15717	The high grade ore carries gold —— silver —— per ton of [2,240 lbs.
Donateur ..	15718	The low grade ore carries gold —— silver —— per ton of
Donation ...	15719	Have discovered paystreak of high grade ore [2,240 lbs.
Donatista...	15720	There are —— tons of high grade ore actually in reserve
Donativum	15721	There is no high grade ore in reserve
Donatrix ...	15722	The high grade ore has been extracted
Doncellica	15723	The probabilities of finding high grade ore are remote
Doncellona	15724	There are —— tons of low grade ore
Dondeche...	15725	The supplies of low grade ore are enormous
Dondolare	15726	The ore is divided into —— grades
Dondolona	15727	What is the average value of the high grade ore
Dondunque	15728	What is the average value of the low grade ore
Donecillo ...	15729	What is the average value of the —— grade ore
Donillero ...	15730	The extraction of high grade ore is —— tons per month
Donjonne...	15731	The ore seems to be of better grade
Donkeys ...	15732	The grade of the ore shows considerable improvement
Donnaccia	15733	The grade of the ore is becoming lower
Donneare ...	15734	The grade of the ore remains very much the same
Donnern ...	15735	The grade is very steep between —— and ——
Donnerkeil	15736	The grade of the road is one in ——
Donnerstag	15737	**Graded**
Donnicina	15738	Have graded ground for
Donosidad	15739	**Gradient(s)**
Donosilla ...	15740	At a gradient of one in ——
Donosura...	15741	What is the gradient between —— and ——
Donuzzo ...	15742	What is the steepest gradient
Donzellone	15743	The gradient between —— and —— is
Doomsday	15744	The steepest gradient is
Doppelbier	15745	Route suggested contains several very steep gradients
Doppellant	15746	Route suggested contains no gradient above one in ——
Doppelsinn	15747	In order to overcome the gradient between —— and —— (at
Doppelt ...	15748	Can you escape gradient a —— [——)

Doppelthur	15749	Cannot escape gradient at ——
Doppiare ...	15750	Can only escape gradient at —— by
Doppiatura	15751	**Grading**
Doppiezza	15752	Preliminary grading
Dorada ...	15753	Grading is completed (for)
Doradilla ...	15754	Grading will be completed about ——
Doramento	15755	When will the grading be completed
Doratore ...	15756	**Gradually**
Doremal ...	15757	Gradually improving
Dorenavant	15758	Gradually becoming impoverished
Dorfchen ...	15759	Gradually lessening in width and value
Dorfjunker	15760	Gradually opening out
Dorfschaft	15761	Proceed gradually with
Dorian ...	15762	**Grain(s)** (*See also* Tables at end.)
Doricism ...	15763	Grain tin
Dorloter ...	15764	In separate grains
Dormancy	15765	**Granite**
Dormidera	15766	A boss of granite
Dormidos...	15767	A dyke of granite
Dormiendus	15768	Owing to the proximity of the granite
Dormiente	15769	The granite lies within
Dormilon ...	15770	The footwall is granite
Dormirlas...	15771	The hanging wall is granite
Dormitator	15772	**Granitic**
Dormitif ...	15773	**Granitoid**
Dormitory	15774	**Grant**
Dormitura	15775	A grant of
Dormouse...	15776	Government grant
Dornajo ...	15777	Refuse(s) to grant
Dornbusch	15778	To get a grant
Dornig ...	15779	Try and persuade —— to grant
Dorofago ...	15780	The area of the grant is
Doronico ...	15781	The grant is for —— years
Dorsal ...	15782	—— will grant
Dorther ...	15783	—— will grant request but on condition
Dorypyge...	15784	Cable particulars of grant
Dosanal ...	15785	**Granted**
Doscientos	15786	Has (have) not been granted
Doselera ...	15787	Has (have) been granted
Doselico ...	15788	Take nothing for granted
Dosines ...	15789	**Granular**
Dotador ...	15790	Granular structure
Dotingly ..	15791	Granular passing into compact
Dottaggio...	15792	Of a granular texture
Dottanza ...	15793	**Grass**
Dottorale...	15794	At grass
Dottorello	15795	Up to grass
Dottrina ...	15796	From the grass downwards
Douaire ...	15797	**Grate(s)** (*See also* "Stamps," "Screens.")
Douanier ...	15798	Stamps grates
Doublage ...	15799	A supply of stamps grates
Doubleness	15800	**Gratis**
Doublette...	15801	Would it (this) be gratis
Doubloons	15802	It (this) would be gratis
Doublure ...	15803	It (this) would not be gratis
Doubtingly	15804	Will act gratis
Doucement	15805	Will not act gratis
Doucereux	15806	Would —— act free gratis
Doucette ...	15807	Have put it in gratis
Douceur ...	15808	I think you might put it in gratis

Douillet ...	15809	Please accept this report gratis, but for your personal use only
Dousing ...	15810	Should you put it in gratis
Douzieme ..	15811	**Gravel** (*See also* " Alluvial," " Hydraulic.")
Dovecot ...	15812	In the gravel
Dovelage ...	15813	Through the gravel
Dovelike ...	15814	What is the average depth of the gravel
Doventare	15815	The average depth of the gravel is
Doveroso ...	15816	Gravel will not pay
Dovetail ...	15817	Gravel would pay if had sufficient water
Dovidere ...	15818	Gravel would undoubtedly pay
Dovizioso ...	15819	Cannot handle gravel
Dovunche...	15820	There is every indication that the gravel
Dowager ...	15821	Is the gravel rich enough to justify
Dowdyish...	15822	I believe the gravel would pay if we had an ample supply of water
Dowelpins	15823	With ample water would the gravel pay
Dowered ...	15824	The gravel would not pay even if we had ample water
Downstairs	15825	By hand washing I obtained —— dwts. of gold from —— cubic [yards of gravel. Value approximately per cubic yard ——
Doxology ...	15826	I believe the value of the gravel will increase as we go further [into the banks
Dozavado ...	15827	**Great**
Dozavo ...	15828	Very great
Dozzina ...	15829	A great deal of
Dozzinale...	15830	A great many
Dozzinante	15831	A great quantity of
Drabbe ...	15832	A great deal has yet to be done
Drachme ...	15833	A great deal has been done
Draconites	15834	My (our) great difficulty is
Dracontium	15835	To a great extent
Dracunculo	15836	The great evil is
Draffish ...	15837	Great quantity of —— now being offered
Draftsman	15838	**Greater**
Dragante ...	15839	Greater than anticipated
Drageoir ...	15840	Less rather than greater
Drageonner	15841	**Greatly**
Draggling	15842	Greatly thought of
Dragnet ...	15843	Greatly over-estimated
Dragoman	15844	**Greenstone**
Dragonazo	15845	The country is greenstone
Dragonfly...	15846	A boss of greenstone
Dragonish	15847	A dyke of greenstone
Dragonlike	15848	Lying upon greenstone
Dragontea	15849	Dies out entirely in the greenstone
Dragontino	15850	**Grievance**
Dragontree	15851	Endeavour to remove the grievance with
Drahtern ...	15852	Has he a bonâ fide grievance
Drahtpuppe	15853	The grievance is mainly as regards
Drahtsaite	15854	There is no real grievance but I would suggest that
Drahtstift...	15855	What is the grievance
Dramatic ...	15856	What is your (——'s) grievance
Dramatique	15857	**Grind** (*See also* " Crush," " Stamp.")
Dramatise	15858	Necessary to grind exceedingly fine
Dramaturg	15859	If we could grind finer
Drammatico	15860	**Grindstone(s)**
Drangsal ...	15861	Forward grindstone
Drapeau ...	15862	Grindstone lost in transit
Drapery ...	15863	**Groove(s)**
Drappella .	15864	Send exact pattern of groove
Drappiere .	15865	Grooves not properly cut
Drastic ...	15866	**Grooved**

Drastisch ...	15867	To be grooved
Draucus ...	15868	Not to be grooved
Draussen ...	15869	Is it (are they) to be grooved
Drawbridge	15870	To be grooved to fit
Drawwell ...	15871	**Gross**
Drayhorse	15872	Gross yield
Drayman ...	15873	Gross yield per ton
Dreamer ...	15874	Gross weight
Dreamingly	15875	Gross output
Dreamless	15876	Gross output for
Drearily ...	15877	Gross proceeds
Drechsela ..	15878	Gross proceeds amount to
Drechsler ...	15879	Cable gross
Dreckig ...	15880	Gross tonnage
Dredged ...	15881	Gross estimated value
Drehbank...	15882	Gross approximate value
Drehbaum	15883	Gross yield amounts to
Drehkreuz	15884	What is the gross and net weight of
Drehorgel	15885	What is the gross weight of
Drehstift ...	15886	What are the gross receipts
Drehstuhl...	15887	The gross receipts are
Drehwage...	15888	The gross weight is ——, the net weight is
Dreiangel ...	15889	The gross returns for the period ending
Dreichorig	15890	What do the gross returns for the period ending —— amount to
Dreieck ...	15891	**Ground** (*See also* "Bar," "Barren," "Cave," "Dangerous," ["Fall.")
Dreieinig ...	15892	Above ground
Dreifach ...	15893	Below ground
Dreifaltig ...	15894	Dumping ground
Dreifuss ...	15895	Has he (have they) any ground for
Dreigesang	15896	He has (they have) no ground for
Dreijahrig	15897	Have they any ground
Dreiklang	15898	Is there any ground for this
Dreiling ...	15899	No ground at all for
Dreimalig...	15900	Plenty of ground [discovery
Dreimaster	15901	So far as I can discover there is no ground at all for the reported
Dreireim ...	15902	The ground is practically worked out to a depth of —— feet
Dreiseitig	15903	Their grounds are
Dreisilbig	15904	They have no grounds
Dreispiel ...	15905	About the ground lying to the —— of us
Dreissig ...	15906	The ground lying —— higher up than ours
Dreitagig ...	15907	The adjacent ground
Dreito ...	15908	Upon what ground
Dreizack ...	15909	Ground is harder
Dreizehn ...	15910	Ground is harder than hitherto
Drenching	15911	The ground at this point continues very hard
Drepanis ..	15912	The ground is still very hard, likely to become more so
Dreschen ...	15913	The ground is now hard but will probably become softer
Dressiren ...	15914	The ground is softer than we have ever had it
Dressoir ...	15915	In softer ground
Driada ...	15916	Ground is becoming softer
Driblets ...	15917	Ground is very heavy
Dricoceras	15918	Ground is not so heavy
Drillich ...	15919	Ground continues about the same
Dringlich ...	15920	Ground is softer than hitherto
Dringolare	15921	What is the ground worth
Drino ...	15922	The ground is worth [encouraging
Dripstone...	15923	The ground through which we are now driving is somewhat
Drittezza ...	15924	Make quite sure of your ground before you proceed to
Dritthalb ...	15925	There is no ground for any uneasiness
Drittura ...	15926	Ground is highly mineralized

Driveller ...	15927	Ground is almost barren of any mineral
Drivelling...	15928	Ground presents a very broken and crushed appearance
Drizar ...	15929	The ground is become very disordered
Drizzly ...	15930	There is considerable ground between —— and —— as yet
Droghiere ...	15931	Here the ground is improving [unexplored
Drogueria...	15932	Here the ground is not so good
Droguete ...	15933	Separated by a belt of ground
Droguista..	15934	Am (are) of opinion that the ground is well worth attention
Drohne ...	15935	The ground in the bottom of shaft is becoming harder
Drohung ...	15936	To provide dumping ground
Droitement	15937	Divide the ground in dispute
Droiture ...	15938	The (this) level has been driven —— feet in barren **ground**
Drolesse ...	15939	The ground is covered with a dense mass of brushwood
Drollery ...	15940	I (we) have let a contract for clearing ground (at)
Dromedary	15941	Have been below ground at
Droopingly	15942	Was never below ground at
Dropacismo	15943	Prospect the ground thoroughly
Dropar ...	15944	**Group**
Dropscene	15945	A group of men
Dropsical ...	15946	Belongs to a group of miners
Droschke ...	15947	Is the richest of the group
Drosera ...	15948	Is it proposed to combine the group
Drowziness	15949	It is proposed to combine the group
Drucken ...	15950	None of the group have been remunerative
Druckprobe	15951	—— of the group have been remunerative
Druckpumpe	15952	The group of mines
Drudgery ...	15953	The entire group
Druidess ...	15954	Near the —— group
Druidical ...	15955	**Guarantee** (*See also* "Delivery.")
Druidism ...	15956	As per guarantee
Drumager...	15957	Against guarantee of ——
Drummer ...	15958	Against suitable guarantee
Drumslade	15959	Do not proceed without proper guarantee
Drumstick	15960	If —— will guarantee
Drupaceous	15961	I (we) cannot guarantee
Dryandra ...	15962	Insists upon guarantee
Drygoods ...	15963	Not possible to arrange guarantee
Dryness ...	15964	—— refuse(s) to give guarantee
Dryolestes	15965	Vendor will guarantee expense of examination
Dryshod ...	15966	Will vendor agree to guarantee expense of examination
Dualismo ...	15967	Will you guarantee
Dualita ...	15968	Will —— guarantee
Dubbiare ...	15969	Will guarantee
Dubbiezza	15970	Will guarantee you —— per cent. commission
Dubdanza...	15971	Will you guarantee expense of travelling and **examination, say**
Dubiedad ...	15972	Unless accompanied by guarantee [——
Dubious ...	15973	Will guarantee nothing
Dubitable...	15974	Has (have) given guarantee
Dubitation	15975	Guarantee offered quite satisfactory
Ducado ...	15976	Guarantee offered not satisfactory
Ducatris ...	15977	Unless will offer satisfactory guarantee
Ducenarius	15978	Require(s) more substantial guarantee
Ducendus	15979	**Guard**
Ducenties ...	15980	Guard as much as possible against
Duchesco ...	15981	Guard —— if you can against
Duchessina	15982	I am on my guard against
Ducientos...	15983	Is on his guard against
Duciffa ...	15984	Be on your guard against "salting
Ducklegged	15985	**Guidance**
Duckling ...	15986	For your guidance

Duckmauser	15987	For ——'s guidance
Duckmeat	15988	Have mailed full instructions for your guidance
Duckweed	15989	For general guidance
Ductabunt	15990	Send full instructions for my personal guidance
Ductandum	15991	Only act under legal guidance
Ductarius	15992	If so cable for my guidance
Ductatis ...	15993	Cable for guidance (of)
Ductavit ...	15994	For my guidance in buying
Ductil ...	15995	For my guidance in selling
Ductilidad	15996	For your guidance in buying
Ductility ...	15997	For your guidance in selling
Ductitatio...	15998	Cable for my personal guidance
Ductitius ...	15999	Have cabled for your personal guidance
Ductrix ...	16000	Have cabled for personal guidance of
Ducturus ...	**16001**	**Guide**
Dudable ...	16002	To guide
Dudail ...	16003	In order to guide
Dudeln ...	16004	So as to guide me (us)
Dudelsack	16005	As a guide for the future
Dudilla ...	16006	Take as your guide
Dudler ...	16007	Now fixing guides
Dudoso ...	16008	Stamp guides
Duelage ...	16009	Wooden guides
Duellante...	16010	**Guided**
Duellarius	16011	Do not let yourself be guided by ——
Duellatore	16012	You must be guided by
Duelliren ...	16013	You must be guided by circumstances
Duellist ...	16014	**Guilty**
Duemila ...	16015	Not guilty
Duenaza ...	16016	Cannot discover the guilty party
Duenesco ...	16017	Try and find the guilty party
Duerno ...	16018	Believe the guilty party(ies) to be
Duett ...	16019	**Gulch**
Duettino ...	16020	**Gully**
Duften ...	16021	**Gunny(ies)**
Dugongs ...	16022	Old gunnies
Dukaten ...	16023	**Gypsum**
Dukedom ...	16024	Beds of gypsum
Dulcamara	16025	**H**
Dulcano ...	16026	**Hacienda**
Dulcaynas	16027	Property includes an hacienda, but it is in a very dilapidated
Dulce ...	16028	Property includes a well-appointed hacienda [condition
Dulcecillo	16029	Property does not include an hacienda
Dulcemele	16030	Within what distance from the property is the nearest hacienda
Dulciana ...	16031	Nearest hacienda is situated at ——, a distance of —— miles
Dulcificar...	16032	Extensions to hacienda
Dulcified ...	16033	As soon as I (we) have completed the improvements to hacienda
Dulcimer ...	16034	Our ores are now being treated at the —— hacienda
Dulcinea ...	16035	At what do you value the hacienda
Dulciolam	16036	The hacienda is well placed for economic working
Dulcir ...	16037	The situation of the hacienda will not permit of economic
Dulcisono...	16038	**Had** [working
Duldsam ...	16039	Not to be had
Dulzazo ...	16040	To be had for
Dulzorar ...	16041	Can be had at the present time for
Dulzura ...	16042	Had left previous to
Dumbbells	16043	Had I (we) not better
Dumbshow	16044	You (——) had better at once
Dummheit	16045	The best thing that could be had
Dummkofp	16046	**Half**

Dumpfig	16047	Allow one half of
Dumpling	16048	Add one half more
Dunfish	16049	One half
Dungarras	16050	One half at the same rate
Dungeons	16051	Reduce by one half
Dunkelhaft	16052	Half way
Dunkeln	16053	Will meet you half way
Dunstkreis	16054	Will be responsible for one half of
Duntaxat	16055	Half cash balance on ——
Duodecimo	16056	Half in cash, balance in fully paid shares
Duodecuple	16057	Wants half per cent.
Duodenal	16058	Half the amount
Duodenum	16059	On half time
Duodramma	16060	Half of which
Duoliteral	16061	First half
Duomesino	16062	Second half
Dupable	16063	**Halvan(s)**
Duplares	16064	Old halvan heaps
Duplex	16065	Sample of halvans
Duplicado	16066	Assay of halvans
Duplicatus	16067	Halvans dressing floor
Duplice	16068	**Hand(s)** (*See also* " Employ," " Men.")
Duplicemus	16069	To hand
Duplicity	16070	Came to hand
Duplicor	16071	Hand to
Duplo	16072	In hand
Dupondius	16073	Not yet to hand
Duque	16074	On hand
Duquecito	16075	On the one hand
Duquesa	16076	On the other hand
Durabilis	16077	Shall you have sufficient in hand to
Duracinus	16078	Have still a large supply in hand
Duradero	16079	Hand over everything to
Duramater	16080	At present my (our) hands are full with
Duramente	16081	What number of hands do you employ
Duraminis	16082	Number of hands is generally
Durando	16083	Have you sufficient hands for
Durar	16084	Cannot obtain enough hands to enable me (us) to
Durateus	16085	Have given hands notice
Duratrix	16086	Shall keep on as many of the old hands as possible
Durasnito	16087	Hands have given notice
Durazno	16088	This is already put in hand
Durchbruch	16089	The balance in hand is now
Durchseilen	16090	The balance in hand after allowance for —— will be, say ——
Durchfahrt	16091	What will you have in hand after
Durchfall	16092	What funds have you in hand
Durchfluss	16093	Have already too many on hand
Durchfuhre	16094	After paying the foregoing what will you have in hand
Durchgang	16095	After allowing for this (it) what will you have in hand
Durchgehen	16096	Funds in hand are now £——; enough to last until
Durchhaus	16097	Together with what I (we) have in hand
Durchlesen	16098	**Handle(ing)**
Durchlugen	16099	To handle
Durchreise	16100	Cannot handle
Durchsein	16101	Difficult to handle
Durchsicht	16102	I (we) find —— very difficult to handle
Durchwaten	16103	This will enable us to handle
Durchweg	16104	At present cannot handle more than —— tons per day of 24 hours
Durescens	16105	This will enable us to handle comfortably —— tons per day of [24 hours

Durevole ...	16106	This will enable us to handle comfortably —— tons per day of [—— hours
Durezza ...	16107	What amount can you handle per day of —— hours
Durftig ...	16108	We can handle easily —— tons per day of —— hours
Duriagra ...	16109	So as to handle the stuff with greater facility
Duricorius	16110	**Handsomely**
Durillo ...	16111	Has (have) behaved very handsomely
Duritas ...	16112	Has (have) not behaved at all handsomely
Duriuscule	16113	**Handwriting**
Durmentes	16114	To be in your own handwriting
Durmiente	16115	**Hanging Wall** (*See also* "Defined," "Footwall.")
Durotto ...	16116	Against the hanging wall
Duselig ...	16117	What is the hanging wall
Dusideia ...	16118	The hanging wall is
Duskily ...	16119	Cross-cut to the hanging wall
Dustbrush	16120	No true hanging wall yet discovered
Dusterkeit	16121	On the hanging wall side
Dustiness ...	16122	On the hanging wall side of the vein
Dustpan ...	16123	The hanging wall is
Dutchen ...	16124	The distance to the hanging wall is —— feet
Duteously	16125	We are following the hanging wall
Dutifully ...	16126	The mineral is mainly upon the hanging wall
Duttilita ...	16127	On the hanging wall
Dutzbruder	16128	The hanging wall is well defined
Dutzend ...	16129	Along the hanging wall
Duumvirate	16130	Close against the hanging wall
Duunvir ...	16131	Strong hanging wall
Duunvirato	16132	We have so far not met with the hanging wall
Duveteux ...	16133	Samples from hanging wall average [footwall
Dwarfed ...	16134	We have a good hanging wall but have not discovered any
Dwarfish ...	16135	The hanging wall is becoming very insecure
Dynamics ...	16136	It has been necessary to put in timber to secure the hanging wall
Dynastique	16137	**Happen** (*See also* "Occur.")
Dysentery...	16138	To happen
Dyspeptic...	16139	When did it happen
Dystonic ...	16140	How did it happen
Dytiscus ...	16141	**Happened**
Earldom ...	16142	Happened on
Earless ...	16143	Happened through
Earpick ...	16144	What actually happened
Earring ...	16145	What actually happened was
Earthborn	16146	**Hard** (*See also* "Ground," "Rock.")
Earthbred ·	16147	Continues very hard
Earthling ...	16148	Has become more hard
Earthnut ...	16149	Not quite so hard
Earthworm	16150	Not nearly so hard
Easeless ...	16151	Progress slow owing to rock becoming harder
Eating ...	16152	Country is not so hard as to require employment of rock drills
Ebanificar	16153	The country is hard compact ——
Ebanista ...	16154	The rock is both hard and tough
Ebaucher ...	16155	The rock is hard but blasts well
Ebbrezza ...	16156	**Harder**
Ebbriaco	16157	Is it harder (than)
Ebbtide ...	16158	Is not harder
Ebenbild ...	16159	If anything harder
Ebenburtig	16160	**Hardness**
Ebenfalls ...	16161	Owing to the hardness
Ebenholz ...	16162	Is not entirely due to the hardness
Ebeniste ...	16163	**Harm**
Ebenmass...	16164	What harm do you anticipate

Ebetazione	16165	No actual harm has occurred
Ebiscos ...	16166	I (we) do not anticipate any harm
Eblouir ...	16167	Much harm has been caused by
Ebolimento	16168	**Harmed**
Ebony ...	16169	No one was harmed
Eborarius...	16170	Was anyone harmed
Eborgner ...	16171	**Haste**
Eboulement	16172	Great haste is necessary
Ebouriffer	16173	Is haste necessary
Ebraismo ...	16174	Haste is not necessary
Ebrancher	16175	**Hasten** (*See also* "Hurry.")
Ebriabamur	16176	To hasten
Ebriarsi ...	16177	Do not hasten
Ebriatore ...	16178	No need to hasten
Ebriatus ...	16179	Hasten the (this)
Ebriavero...	16180	Hasten the departure of
Ebriedad ...	16181	Hasten the completion of
Ebrietate ...	16182	Hasten the discharge of
Ebriety ...	16183	Hasten forwarding
Ebriola ...	16184	Do all you can to hasten it (him)
Ebriolatus	16185	Do all you can to hasten the completion of
Ebriositas...	16186	I am (we are) doing everything possible to hasten the work in [hand
Ebrioso ...	16187	I am (we are) doing everything possible to hasten this matter
Ebruiter ...	16188	Impossible to hasten further
Ebullio ...	16189	There is no need to hasten if you can reach —— by ——
Ebullition...	16190	**Hastened**
Ebulum ...	16191	Must be hastened
Eburatus ...	16192	No use unless can be hastened
Eburnean ...	16193	Should be hastened all you can
Eburneolus	16194	Shall be hastened
Eburneus ...	16195	Has (have) been hastened
Eburno ...	16196	Has (have) not been hastened
Ecacher ...	16197	Why have you not hastened
Ecailleux ...	16198	Negotiations should be hastened on account of
Ecarlate ...	16199	**Hastily**
Ecarteler ...	16200	Will not act hastily
Ecatombe...	16201	Do nothing hastily
Ecbasis ...	16202	**Hasty**
Eccellenza	16203	Hasty conclusion
Eccentrico	16204	Was (were) very hasty
Eccessivo ...	16205	Too hasty
Eccettare ...	16206	**Haul** (*See also* "Cage," "Hoist," "Wind.")
Eccitante ...	16207	How many tons can you haul per day of 24 hours
Eccitativo...	16208	Can haul —— tons per day
Ecclesia ...	16209	Can haul —— tons per 24 hours
Ecclissare	16210	Cannot haul more than —— tons owing to
Ecdicorum	16211	Cannot do more than haul the dirt from present drifts
Ecervele ...	16212	Cannot do more stoping as cannot haul the stuff
Ecetuar ...	16213	To haul
Ecfractico...	16214	This will enable us to haul —— tons per day
Echacantos	16215	How much can one team haul per day
Echada ...	16216	Can haul —— tons per day with one team
Echadero ...	16217	Teams cannot haul ore at present on account of severe weather
Echadillo ...	16218	**Haulage** (*See also* "Cost.")
Echafaud ...	16219	Haulage by
Echalasser	16220	Under the present system of haulage
Echalier ...	16221	Underground haulage
Echamiento	16222	Wire rope haulage
Echancrer...	16223	What system of haulage do you intend to employ
Echappade	16224	Shall have to rearrange the present haulage system

Echarper ...	16225	Can arrange to use water power for haulage
Echaudoir ...	16226	Electric haulage
Echazon ...	16227	**Hauled**
Echeniller ...	16228	—— tons were hauled in —— months
Echeveau ...	16229	Cable number of loads hauled up to
Echidnas ...	16230	Number of loads (each 16 cubic feet) hauled is
Echoing ...	16231	—— tons were hauled during the month ending
Echometre ...	16232	Cable number of tons hauled during the month of
Echouage ...	16233	**Hauling** (*See also* "Hoisting.")
Echtheit ...	16234	Not hauling
Eckhaus ...	16235	Hauling recommenced on ——
Eckstein ...	16236	We shall commence hauling on ——
Eclairage ...	16237	We hope to commence hauling on ——
Eclaireur ...	16238	Delay hauling until further orders
Eclatant ...	16239	Cable when you will commence hauling
Eclectic ...	16240	**Have**
Ecletique ...	16241	—— has (have)
Eclipsable ...	16242	—— has (have) not
Eclipsis ...	16243	As soon as you have (—— has)
Eclisses ...	16244	As soon as I (we) have
Eclittica ...	16245	Can I have
Eclogarum ...	16246	Have I (we)
Eclogue ...	16247	Have you
Ecloppe ...	16248	Have they
Eclosion ...	16249	Has he
Eclusier ...	16250	Has (have) not been
Ecobenes ...	16251	Has (have) been
Ecoeurer ...	16252	Have had
Ecoico ...	16253	Has (have) not had
Ecolier ...	16254	Have you had
Ecometria ...	16255	Have you not had
Economia ...	16256	I (we) have
Economique	16257	I (we) have not
Economista	16258	I (we) shall have
Economizar	16259	If I (we) have
Economo ...	16260	If you have
Econverso ...	16261	If they have
Ecorcherie ...	16262	If he has
Ecorchure...	16263	If I (we) have not
Ecornifler ...	16264	If you have not
Ecossaise ...	16265	If they have not
Ecoulement	16266	If he has not
Ecourter ...	16267	Let them have
Ecouteux ...	16268	Let me (us) have
Ecoutille ...	16269	Must have the foregoing not later than
Ecouvillon	16270	Unless have them before —— they will be useless
Ecquando...	16271	Should have at least
Ecrasant ...	16272	Should have had
Ecremer ...	16273	To have
Ecravisse ..	16274	To have to
Ecritoire ...	16275	They have not
Ecrivain ...	16276	When ought I to have
Ecrouelles	16277	When are you (is ——) likely to have
Ecrouter ...	16278	Will have
Ecstasy ...	16279	Will not have
Ectipo ...	16280	When I (we) have
Ecuable ...	16281	You can have
Ecuacion ...	16282	You cannot have
Ecuante ...	16283	You (they) shall not have
Ecuestre ...	16284	You have not

Ecumenical	16285	You have
Ecumeux ...	16286	They have
Ecumoire ...	16287	Expect(s) to have
Ecuoreo	16288	Have had no reliable information
Ecureuil ...	16289	Have you given instructions for
Ecussonner	16290	**Having**
Edacious ...	16291	Worth having
Edacity ...	16292	Not worth having
Edecan ...	16293	Having regard to
Edelknabe	16294	Upon having
Edelmuth ...	16295	Having this in view
Edelsinn ...	16296	**Heading** (*See also* " Drift," " Forebreast," " Level.")
Edelstein ..	16297	Heading advanced
Edema ...	16298	Heading is now in
Edematoso	16299	Heading has been advanced —— feet
Edentabat	16300	How is the heading looking
Edentavero	16301	**Health** (*See also* " Better," " Broken.")
Edenter ...	16302	Health of the camp is fairly good
Ederoso ...	16303	The health of the staff is excellent
Edgeless ...	16304	**Hear**
Edgewise ...	16305	Expect to hear
Edicolo ...	16306	Do not expect to hear
Edicto ...	16307	Expect to hear from
Edificador	16308	Expect to hear of
Edificante...	16309	Let me (us) hear frequently
Edificar ...	16310	You shall hear from me by the next mail
Edificio ...	16311	Do not do anything until you hear from ——
Edilidad ...	16312	I (we) shall not do anything until I (we) hear from ——
Edilitius ...	16313	If I (we) do not hear from you before ——, I (we) shall leave
Edisserto ...	16314	Do not act until you hear from me [at once for
Editore ...	16315	Do not act until you hear from
Editorial ...	16316	**Heard**
Edizione ...	16317	Has not been heard of since
Edredon ...	16318	All that I (we) heard was
Educando	16319	As soon as you have heard anything further please telegraph
Educare ...	16320	Have you heard anything yet (as to)
Educatore...	16321	Have not yet heard anything from you about
Educavit ...	16322	Expected to have heard from ——
Educazione	16323	I will send full particulars of what I have heard by mail
Educir ...	16324	I (we) have heard that
Eduction ...	16325	I (we) had hoped to have heard that (as to)
Edulcorer...	16326	Is said to have heard that
Edulio ...	16327	Have not heard as expected
Eduquer ...	16328	Have only just heard from —— (that)
Efaufiler ...	16329	Have you heard anything of this (it) (——)
Efectuar ...	16330	I have not heard anything at all
Efemera ...	16331	I have not heard anything further
Efemerides	16332	To have heard
Effable ...	16333	**Heat** (*See also* " Climate.")
Effection ...	16334	As soon as the heat permits
Effeminato	16335	Great heat has now set in here
Effeminer ...	16336	Owing to the great heat
Efferato ...	16337	Summer heats commence about —— and last until ——
Effervesco...	16338	The heat in summer is very great
Effettuale	16339	**Heave(d)** (*See also* " Fault.")
Effeuiller ...	16340	I consider there is a heave at this point
Efficacite ...	16341	The lode has been heaved
Efficienza	16342	**Heaviest**
Efficitur ...	16343	What is the weight of the heaviest piece
Effigiare ...	16344	The heaviest weight not to exceed

Effigiatus ...	16345	**Heavy**
Effiloche ...	16346	Very heavy
Effiloquer...	16347	Too heavy
Effingens ...	16348	Heavy spar
Effingor ...	16349	A heavy allowance for
Effinxisti ...	16350	Heavy compensation for
Efflagito ...	16351	Expenses will be too heavy
Efflaveram	16352	Expenses will not be heavy
Effloresco ...	16353	**Height**
Effluvio ...	16354	What is the height of
Effluvium...	16355	The height of —— is —— feet
Effondrer ...	16356	The height is —— feet
Efformato...	16357	Within what height
Effraction...	16358	What is the average height of
Effrayant ...	16359	The average height is
Effrenato ...	16360	**Held**
Effroyable	16361	Is (are) mostly held by
Effugemur	16362	Very few held by
Effulgence	16363	Some of the shares are held by
Eficacia ...	16364	The shares are principally held by
Eficaz ...	16365	None of the shares are held by
Eficiencia ...	16366	Held over for the present
Efigie ...	16367	**Help** (*See also* "Assist," "Assistance.")
Eflorecer ...	16368	To help
Efluencia ...	16369	Cannot help
Efluente ...	16370	Help me (us) to
Efugio ...	16371	Will help you as much as possible
Efundir ...	16372	Would be a great help if
Efusion ...	16373	**Helpless**
Egalement	16374	At present helpless
Egalite ...	16375	Shall be quite helpless unless
Egelatus ...	16376	**Here**
Egelidabit	16377	Be here
Egelidandi	16378	Come here
Egeno ...	16379	Come here as soon as you can
Egestad ...	16380	I (we) do not expect to be here after ——
Egestion ...	16381	I (we) must remain here until
Egida ...	16382	It is useless for you to come here before ——
Egidarmato	16383	Mail to be addressed to me here
Egignetis ...	16384	Mail to be addressed to me here, letters will be forwarded
Egignunt ...	16385	Not here
Egilope ...	16386	When may I (we) expect you (——) here
Egipciaco ...	16387	—— is not expected here till
Egiziano ...	16388	—— left here on ——
Eglantine ...	16389	—— intends to leave here on ——
Eglise ...	16390	Will return here
Egloga ...	16391	Shall leave here for —— on ——
Egoismo ...	16392	You should be here before
Egosiller ...	16393	You should arrange to stay here
Egotista ...	16394	I can do no good by remaining here
Egoutier ...	16395	**Hereafter**
Egouttage	16396	To avoid trouble hereafter
Egoutture...	16397	If we are to avoid trouble hereafter
Egrapper ...	16398	Cannot possibly cause trouble hereafter
Egratigner	16399	Is certain to cause trouble hereafter
Egregio ...	16400	Unless you can maintain hereafter
Egression ...	16401	Is it (this) likely to cause trouble hereafter
Egrette ...	16402	**Hereby**
Egrillard ...	16403	**Hesitate(s)**
Egrisador ...	16404	Do not hesitate now

Egrisar ...	16405	Cannot hesitate
Egritudine	16406	Do(es) not hesitate at anything
Egrugeoir...	16407	Do not hesitate to act if necessary
Eguagliare	16408	Why do(es) —— hesitate
Egualar ...	16409	Hesitate(s) because of
Egualezza...	16410	**Hide** (*See also* " Conceal.")
Egualitade	16411	To hide
Egualmente	16412	Hide from
Egueuler ...	16413	**High** (*See also* " Height.")
Egularum...	16414	Do(es) not look as if likely to go high
Egulas ...	16415	—— feet high
Egyptian ...	16416	How high is (are)
Ehanche ...	16417	High enough
Ehebett ...	16418	Not high enough
Ehebrechen	16419	Not high at all
Ehebruch ...	16420	Quite high enough
Ehefrau ...	16421	Too high
Ehegemahl	16422	Price asked is too high
Ehegestern	16423	Figure is too high
Eheleute ...	16424	The price is certainly high, but
Ehelichen...	16425	How high has the water to be pumped
Ehelos ...	16426	**Higher**
Ehemalig ...	16427	Cable your opinion whether they are likely to go higher
Ehepaar ...	16428	My (our) opinion is they will go higher
Ehepflicht	16429	My (our) opinion is they are not likely to go higher
Ehesegen ...	16430	Is there any immediate prospect of their going higher
Ehesteuer ...	16431	There is no immediate prospect of their going higher
Ehevertrag	16432	May perhaps go —— higher
Eheweib ...	16433	Not higher
Ehrbarkeit	16434	Higher or lower
Ehrbarlich	16435	Now ask a higher price
Ehrenamt...	16436	Please explain higher figures
Ehrenhaft	16437	The value is much higher
Ehrenlohn	16438	Price is already higher than your limit
Ehrenmann	16439	You should not go higher than
Ehrensache	16440	**Highest**
Ehrentitel	16441	The highest assay of the ore is
Ehrenwerth	16442	The highest yet reached
Ehrenwort	16443	The highest point is
Ehrfurcht...	16444	What is the highest point
Ehrgefuhl	16445	**Hill(s)(y)**
Ehrgeiz ...	16446	Am ordered to the hills to recruit
Ehrlich ...	16447	At the base of the hill
Ehrliebend	16448	Could carry a wire tramway down the hill
Ehrsam ...	16449	From the face of the hill
Ehrsucht ...	16450	In a gorge between two hills
Ehrwurden	16451	On the crest of the hill
Eichbaum...	16452	On the face of the hill
Eichel ...	16453	The vein may be traced right across the hill
Eichwald ...	16454	The hill slopes at an angle of
Eidbruchig	16455	The country consists of rolling hills
Eidechse ...	16456	**Him**
Eiderdown	16457	From him (——)
Eiderdunen	16458	To him (——)
Eidergans...	16459	By him (——)
Eidotter ...	16460	**Hindered**
Eidschwur	16461	Much hindered through
Eierkuchen	16462	Much hindered for want of
Eierschale...	16463	Have not been hindered by
Eierstock ...	16464	**Hire**

Eiferer ...	16465	Can you not hire until
Eifersucht	16466	Do not hire
Eifrig ...	16467	Either hire or purchase
Eigenheit ...	16468	Hire if you can
Eigenliebe	16469	Have you (has ——) been able to hire
Eigenlob ...	16470	Has (have) not been able to hire
Eigenname	16471	I have hired
Eigennutz	16472	I shall hire if I can
Eigensinn	16473	Have hired what I want from our neighbours
Eigenthum	16474	In case you cannot hire
Eigentlich	16475	To hire
Eigenwille	16476	Ask —— for the hire alone (without)
Eightfold ...	16477	**His**
Eigner ...	16478	What are his (——'s) views
Eilbote ...	16479	His (——'s) views are that
Eilfertig ...	16480	Cannot ascertain his (——'s) views
Eilmarsch...	16481	**Hoist** (*See also* " Cage," " Cost," " Haul.")
Eilpost ...	16482	To hoist
Eilzug ...	16483	To hoist up
Einander ...	16484	Hoist more if possible
Einarmig ...	16485	Cannot hoist before
Einaschern	16486	Can only hoist —— tons per day of 24 hours
Einathmen	16487	This will enable me (us) to hoist
Einatzen ...	16488	I (we) cannot hoist any gangue
Einaugig ...	16489	The hoist and pump are in full operation
Einband ...	16490	What is the capacity and condition of hoist
Einbildung	16491	Hoist is first rate condition
Einbinden	16492	Condition of hoist unsatisfactory
Einblasen...	16493	Shall require a new hoist
Einbrechen	16494	**Hoisted**
Einbringen	16495	Hoisted since
Einbrocken	16496	Cable number of tons hoisted since
Einburgern	16497	We hoisted —— tons for the period from —— to —— in- [clusive
Eindicken...	16498	**Hoister**
Eindorren...	16499	Hoister for
Eindrangen	16500	Hoister now erected
Eindruck ...	16501	Hoister broken down
Einernten...	16502	Hoister is doing excellent work
Einfacher ...	16503	**Hoisting** (*See also* "Boiler," "Machinery.")
Einfadeln ...	16504	Hoisting engine
Einfahrt ...	16505	Our hoisting capacity is limited to
Einfallen ...	16506	Have you hoisting tackle capable of lifting
Einfaltig ...	16507	Hoisting per day of —— hours
Einfangen	16508	Hoisting ore
Einfassung	16509	Hoisting water
Einflossen	16510	Hoisting works
Einfluss ...	16511	Have you boiler power for hoisting
Einfordern	16512	I (we) have boiler power for hoisting
Einformig ...	16513	I (we) have not sufficient boiler power for hoisting
Einfrieden	16514	I (we) have contracted for hoisting plant
Einfuhren	16515	Machinery broken down. Have had to stop hoisting
Eingang ...	16516	Unless we can increase our hoisting capacity
Eingeboren	16517	Our hoisting capacity is limited to —— per 24 hours
Eingebung	16518	Commence hoisting
Eingedenk	16519	Commence hoisting ore
Eingehen ...	16520	Commence hoisting again on
Eingeweide	16521	**Hold(s)**
Eingezogen	16522	To hold
Einglied ...	16523	To hold for
Eingraben	16524	To hold on

Eingreifen	16525	Hold the
Eingriff ...	16526	Hold for
Einhagen ...	16527	Hold until
Einhallig ...	16528	Have hold of
Einhalten...	16529	To hold to
Einhandeln	16530	To hold up
Einhandig	16531	Can you hold your ground
Einhauchen	16532	Will hold good until
Einheit ...	16533	Still holds good
Einhelfen ...	16534	Hold subject to
Einholen ...	16535	Hold subject to my (our) order
Einhorn ...	16536	Hold subject to ——'s order
Einhufig ...	16537	Holds out every encouragement
Einigem ...	16538	Can you hold out any encouragement
Einigkeit ...	16539	Can hold out every encouragement
Einigung ...	16540	Cannot conscientiously hold out any encouragement
Einimpfen	16541	Do you advise me (us) to hold
Einjahrig...	16542	Do not hold after
Einkaufen	16543	How much do you hold
Einkehr ...	16544	Hold as long as you can
Einklang ...	16545	How many does —— hold
Einkleiden	16546	I (we) advise you to hold
Einklingen	16547	If you can get hold of any, do so
Einkochen	16548	It would be worth your while to get hold of
Einladung	16549	Not safe to hold any number
Einlagern...	16550	Hold back for the present
Einlassen...	16551	Hold back till I (we) cable again
Einleitend...	16552	Will certainly pay you to hold
Einleitung	16553	Endeavour to get hold if you can
Einlernen...	16554	Not yet got hold of
Einliefern...	16555	**Holders**
Einlogiren	16556	Who are the principal holders
Einlosung	16557	The holders are
Einmachen	16558	The holders are mainly
Einmal ...	16559	The holders are very firm
Einmaleins	16560	Holders are anxious to
Einmalig ...	16561	Holders are willing to
Einmarsch	16562	There are but few firm holders
Einmaster	16563	There are no firm holders
Einmauern	16564	The present holders
Einmengen	16565	The present holders would accept
Einmiethen	16566	**Holding**
Einmuthig	16567	Holding off
Einnahmt...	16568	Holding up
Einnehmen	16569	Holding for
Einnicken...	16570	**Hole(d)** (*See also* "Diamond.")
Einode ...	16571	Cable as soon as you hole through
Einolen ...	16572	Expect to hole through
Einpacken	16573	Holed through
Einpaschen	16574	Holed through to the drift
Einpfarren	16575	Have holed through to former workings
Einpfundig	16576	The raise holed through to the winze
Einpokeln...	16577	At a depth of —— feet we lost —— diamonds, and had to
Einpragen	16578	**Holiday(s)** [abandon the hole
Einprugeln	16579	Native holidays
Einraffen ...	16580	Bank holiday
Einrahmen	16581	Holidays commence on
Einrechnen	16582	Holidays last until
Einreissen	16583	Is away on a holiday
Einrichten	16584	As soon as the holidays are over

Einruckung	16585	Cannot do anything until after the holidays
Einsalben...	16586	Must allow —— days per annum for holidays
Einsam ...	16587	General holiday(s)
Einsamkeit	16588	Previous to the holidays
Einsammeln	16589	We propose to bring out the company soon after the holidays
Einsauern...	16590	**Hollow**
Einschlag...	16591	Perfectly hollow
Einschluss	16592	Found to be perfectly hollow
Einschnitt	16593	Sufficiently hollow to admit of
Einsegnung	16594	Worn quite hollow
Einseifen ...	16595	**Home**
Einsender...	16596	Cable me how all are at home
Einsetzen...	16597	—— is not well, otherwise all are satisfactory at home
Einsichtig	16598	Can I do any good if I come home
Einsiedler ..	16599	Come home
Einsilbig ...	16600	Expect to be home on ——
Einspannen	16601	Is not at home
Einsperren	16602	Is not expected home before
Einsprache	16603	Return home as quickly as possible
Einstecken	16604	Return home immediately —— died on
Einstimmen	16605	Return home immediately —— is very seriously ill
Einstmals...	16606	Send —— home immediately
Einstossen	16607	Shall come home viâ —— address to me °/₀ —— at that place
Einstreuen	16608	Shall arrange to come home as soon as I receive your reply
Einsturz ...	16609	There is no urgent necessity for you to come home
Eintauchen	16610	You could not do any good if you were to come home
Eintheilen	16611	Cease all expenditure and come home
Eintonig ...	16612	Get —— home as soon as possible
Eintracht...	16613	**Home pay**
Eintreffen...	16614	—— per month to be taken as home pay
Eintretend	16615	For arrears of home pay
Eintritt ...	16616	No home pay
Eintunken	16617	Stop home pay
Einuben ...	16618	Increase home pay to
Einwand .	16619	Remit to —— on account of home pay
Einwandern	16620	Home pay to cease on and after
Einwarts ...	16621	**Honest(y)(ly)**
Einwassern	16622	Can you recommend him as being honest
Einweichen	16623	Do you regard him (them) as honest
Einwendung	16624	Gave an honest report
Einwickeln	16625	Has (have) certainly not been honest
Einwintern	16626	Has (have) no great reputation for honesty
Einwohner	16627	Has (have) a splendid reputation for honesty
Einwurf ...	16628	Is not much to look at but may be depended on for honesty
Einwurzeln	16629	May be relied upon for an honest report
Einzaunen	16630	What is his (their) reputation for honesty
Einziehen .	16631	Honestly worth
Eisberg ...	16632	Honestly speaking, not worth a cent
Eisbock ...	16633	**Honeycombed**
Eisenbleck	16634	The castings are very much honeycombed
Eisenfest ...	16635	Is (are) very much honeycombed
Eisenrost ...	16636	Examine and report as to whether the —— is (are) honey-
Eisenwaare	16637	No trace of being honeycombed [combed
Eisenwerk	16638	Are honeycombed sufficiently to account for breakage
Eisgrau ...	16639	**Honorarium**
Eisgrube ...	16640	As an honorarium
Eiskalt ...	16641	**Honourable**
Eismeer ...	16642	Is a most honourable man (firm) in every respect
Eiszapfen ...	16643	**Hook(s)**
Eitelkeit ...	16644	Hook handle(s)

Eiterig ...	16645	Self-detaching hook
Eiweiss ...	16646	Hook for

Hope(s) (ing)

Ejaculetur	16648	Hope soon to be making
Ejaculor ...	16649	Hope to receive not later than
Ejectant ...	16650	You may hope to receive
Ejectatote	16651	Have you (has ——) any hope of ultimate success
Ejectavit ...	16652	I (we) have no hope of ultimate success
Ejectionis ..	16653	I (we) have a little hope of ultimate success
Ejectment	16654	I have every hope of ultimate success
Ejecucion ...	16655	I (we) hope you will be able to
Ejecutable	16656	Have you any hope
Ejecutar ...	16657	I (we) have little or no hope
Ejecutivo ...	16658	I (we) have every hope
Ejecutoria	16659	Hope to be able to
Ejemplar ...	16660	My (our) only hope is that
Ejemplo ...	16661	There is really no hope
Ejercer ...	16662	—— still hope(s)
Ejercicio ...	16663	Has (have) been hoping to
Ejercitar ...	16664	Hope to be able to
Ejercito ...	16665	Hope to do better by waiting
Ejido ...	16666	Hope you will be able to secure something good

Horizontal(ly)

Ejulando ...	16667	
Ejulatio ...	16668	Is worked horizontally
Ejulatum ...	16669	Bed is pinching horizontally
Ejulazionc	16670	The horizontal distance is
Ejurabat ...	16671	What is the horizontal distance (between)

Hornblende(ic)

Ejuravisse	16672	
Ejusmodi ...	16673	Hornblendic gneiss

Horse

Ekelig ...	16674	
Elabilis ...	16675	Horse of country rock
Elaborato...	16676	Horse of —— is coming in
Elain ...	16677	Now driving through a horse of country rock
Elancement	16678	As soon as we get through to the other side of the horse
Elanguemus	16679	Horse of ground
Elanguendi	16680	For purchase of horse(s)
Elanguero	16681	Saddle horse(s)

Horsepower (See also "Boiler," "Engine.")

Elanguesco	16682	
Elanguetis	16683	Effective horsepower ——
Elanguit ...	16684	Engine of —— horsepower (indicated)
Elargir ...	16685	Nominal horsepower ——
Elasticita ...	16686	What is the horsepower required
Elastico ...	16687	Electrical horsepower ——

Horse whim(s)

Elastisch ...	16688	

Hose

Elaterio ...	16689	
Elation ...	16690	Suction hose
Eleborina ..	16691	India rubber hose
Eleboro ...	16692	Send two 20-foot lengths of India rubber hose

Hospital

Election ...	16693	
Electoral ...	16694	Now in hospital
Electrico ...	16695	Left hospital on

Hostile

Electrique ..	16696	
Electrizar .	16697	Will be decidedly hostile to me (us)
Electuary...	16698	Not at all hostile
Elefancia ...	16699	Is decidedly hostile to me (us)
Elefantino	16700	Am decidedly hostile to it
Elegamment	16701	Will be decidedly hostile
Elegance ...	16702	Decidedly hostile
Elegantly ...	16703	Decidedly hostile to
Eleganzia...	16704	To avoid property passing into hostile hands

Eleggibile...	1C705	If in hands of hostile parties would be very unfortunate
Elegia ...	16706	Must on no account get into hostile hands
Elegiacal ...	16707	Do you consider —— hostile
Elegiaque...	16708	Do not consider —— hostile.
Elegidium	16709	Cable if hostile or otherwise
Elegido ...	16710	Likely to become hostile
Elegist ...	16711	Not at all likely to become hostile
Eleleis ...	16712	**Hot**
Elembico ...	16713	How hot
Elementado	16714	Has been in hot water since
Elemental	16715	Very hot work
Elementary	16716	**Hotel**
Elementi ...	16717	At what hotel shall you stay in ——
Elemosina	16718	My hotel at —— is the ——
Elenchus ...	16719	Meet him —— at the —— hotel in ——
Elenco ...	16720	Hotel expenses
Elencticus	16721	**Hour(s)** (*See also* " Days.")
Elephantus	16722	Between —— and —— hours
Elettivo ...	16723	Within the next —— hours
Elettorale...	16724	Within —— hours of the mine
Elettore ...	16725	Will cause a delay of —— hours
Elettrice ...	16726	—— hours run
Elettuario...	16727	—— shifts per day of 24 hours
Eleusinian	16728	—— hour shifts
Eleutheria	16729	—— hours journey by rail
Elevar ...	16730	—— hours journey by coach
Elevateth ...	16731	—— hours journey by ——
Elevatezza	16732	Per day of 8 hours
Elevating ...	16733	Per day of 12 hours
Elevatus ...	16734	Per day of 24 hours
Elevazione	16735	One hour
Elezionare	16736	Two hours
Elezione ...	16737	Three hours
Elfchild ...	16738	Four hours
Elfenbein ...	16739	Five hours
Elfmal ...	16740	Six hours
Elftens ...	16741	Seven hours
Eliberatio...	16742	Eight hours
Elicere ...	16743	Nine hours
Eliciendus	16744	Ten hours
Elicior ...	16745	Eleven hours
Elicited ...	16746	Twelve hours
Elicitus ...	16747	Thirteen hours
Elicona ...	16748	Fourteen hours
Eligens ...	16749	Fifteen hours
Eliguritor	16750	Sixteen hours
Elijable ...	16751	Seventeen hours
Eliminatio	16752	Eighteen hours
Eliminer ...	16753	Nineteen hours
Eliminium	16754	Twenty hours
Eliotropia...	16755	Twenty one hours
Elipse ...	16756	Twenty two hours
Eliseos .	16757	Twenty three hours
Elixir ...	16758	Twenty four hours
Elizion .	16759	**House(ing)** (*See also* " Burnt," " Dwelling House.")
Ellebore ...	16760	Engine house
Ellenismo...	16761	House or houses for
Ellipais ...	16762	A suitable house for
Ellipsoid ...	16763	There is house accommodation for —— men
Elliptical ...	16764	**How**

Elmate ...	16765	How (is) are
Elocution ...	16766	How are you
Elogiador ...	16767	How are you getting on with
Elogietur ...	16768	How are you off as regards
Elogista ...	16769	How can
Elogium ...	16770	How do(es)
Elongacion	16771	How far
Elopement	16772	How far in
Eloquence	16773	How large
Eloquently	16774	How long
Eloquenzia	16775	For how long
Eloquio ...	16776	How long can
Elucidated	16777	How long will it take
Elucubrato	16778	How soon
Eludere ...	16779	How near
Eludible ...	16780	How many
Eluscabat...	16781	How much
Elusive ...	16782	How much more
Elusory ...	16783	How much more will it take to
Elutriate ...	16784	How much will it cost to
Elvezio ...	16785	How often
Elysian ...	16786	How shall I (we)
Emaciate ...	16787	How high
Emaculato	16788	How low
Emaculo ...	16789	How high is it (are they) likely to go
Emailler ...	16790	How low is it (are they) likely to go
Emanadero	16791	Advise me how I (we) ought to proceed
Emanante	16792	How many —— has ——
Emanar ...	16793	**Hundredweight** (*See also* "Pound," "Ton" and Table at
Emanation	16794	Per hundredweight [end.)
Emancipare	16795	At per hundredweight
Emargement	16796	Cost per hundredweight
Ematita ...	16797	How many hundredweights
Embachar	16798	The cost per hundredweight is
Embadurnar	16799	What is the cost per hundredweight
Embaidor...	16800	Twenty hundredweights per ton
Embair ...	16801	Twenty-one hundredweights are taken to the ton
Embajada	16802	About one hundredweight
Embaldosar	16803	About two hundredweight
Embalijar	16804	One hundredweight
Emballage	16805	Two hundredweights
Emballenar	16806	Three hundredweights
Emballeur	16807	Four hundredweights
Embalm ...	16808	Five hundredweights
Embalmers	16809	Six hundredweights
Embalsamar	16810	Seven hundredweights
Embanastar	16811	Eight hundredweights
Embarazada	16812	Nine hundredweights
Embarazo	16813	Ten hundredweights
Embarbecer	16814	Eleven hundredweights
Embarcador	16815	Twelve hundredweights
Embarco ...	16816	Thirteen hundredweights
Embargante	16817	Fourteen hundredweights
Embargar...	16818	Fifteen hundredweights
Embariller	16819	Sixteen hundredweights
Embarnizar	16820	Seventeen hundredweights
Embarque	16821	Eighteen hundredweights
Embarrass	16822	Nineteen hundredweights
Embastar ...	16823	Twenty hundredweights
Embate ...	16824	**Hunt**

Embattled	16825	To hunt
Embauchage	16826	Shall have to hunt for
Embauchoir	16827	Shall continue to hunt for it
Embaular...	16828	**Hunting**
Embaumer	16829	Hunting for
Embausonar	16830	**Hurricane**
Embasador	16831	Delay caused by damage to wires by hurricane
Embebecer	16832	Great damage done to out-buildings by hurricane
Embeber ...	16833	Will take —— days and cost —— to repair damage caused by
Embeguiner	16834	**Hurry** (*See also* "Hasten.") [hurricane
Embeleco ...	16835	To hurry
Embelenado	16836	Hurry up
Embelesar	16837	Hurry on with
Embeodar...	16838	Hurry off
Emberar ...	16839	Hurry to
Embermejar	16840	Hurry forward all you can
Embesogne	16841	Hurry delivery as much as you can
Embestida	16842	Everything is being done to hurry
Embestir ...	16843	In the hurry of
Embetunar	16844	Is there any hurry as regards
Embion ...	16845	Is there any real reason to hurry
Emblaver...	16846	Is important that you should hurry
Emblazonry	16847	There is no need to hurry
Emblema ...	16848	There is no need to hurry for the present
Emblematic	16849	Your only chance is to hurry
Emblemise	16850	There is no hurry
Embocadero	16851	Do not be in a hurry to
Embocinado	16852	There is no particular hurry for
Embodarse	16853	Will do all I (we) can to hurry
Embody ...	16854	Useless to attempt to hurry
Embodying	16855	Hurry things as much as possible
Emboiture	16856	**Hurt** (*See also* "Injured.")
Embolicus	16857	—— has (have) been seriously hurt
Embolios ...	16858	No one seriously hurt
Embolismal	16859	Was any one hurt
Embolismo	16860	No one hurt at all
Embolus ...	16861	The following have been hurt
Embonada	16862	Only —— was hurt, and he not at all seriously
Embonigar	16863	Only —— was seriously hurt
Embono ...	16864	**Hutch(es)**
Embonpoint	16865	Hutch work
Emboque ...	16866	Ore hutches
Emborder	16867	**Hydration** ["Washing," "Water."]
Embornal ..	16868	**Hydraulic(ing)** (*See also* "Dirt," "Gravel," "Tailings,"
Emborrazar	16869	Hydraulic mining
Emboscada	16870	Hydraulic machinery
Embossed	16871	Hydraulic engineer
Embossing	16872	To examine and report upon an hydraulic property situate near
		—— . You would require to be absent about —— days
Embossment	16873	Hydraulic mining property
Embotado	16874	Hydraulic operations will commence on
Embotadura	16875	When will you commence hydraulicing
Embotar ...	16876	Hydraulic washing has not been a fair average. I have reason
		[to believe the next will be materially improved
Embotellar	16877	There is not sufficient water to hydraulic steadily. Have had
		to stop running —— hours for want of water. There
		[is only enough when a freshet comes down
Emboticar	16878	Ditches gave way, hydraulicing stopped —— hours for repairs
Embouchure	16879	We have —— feet of ditch to make, requiring —— days
		[before we commence hydraulicing

Embouquer	16880	Tailings banked us in. Stopped on —— instant. Put in —— feet sluices. Will be —— days before hydraulicing [re-commenced
Embower ...	16881	Tailings banked us in on —— instant. We shall have to make —— feet of channelling which will take —— [hours before can re-commence hydraulicing
Embraced...	16882	Water supply insufficient to carry on steady hydraulicing
Embractum	16883	Run with one monitor —— hours. Have washed —— cubic yards of gravel. Have cleaned up —— feet sluices. Have obtained —— ounces retorted gold. Estimated [value ——
Embrancher	16884	Have only cleaned up —— feet of sluices this washing
Embrassade	16885	Cannot get rid of tailings they have banked up and will take [—— days to clear
Embrasure	16886	Everything complete ; water ready to be turned on
Embravecer	16887	Clean up after —— hours run with —— inches of water. Labour cost ——. Materials cost ——. General expenses [here ——. Net profit, ——
Embreadura	16888	On —— water was turned on, everything proceeding satisfac- [torily
Embrear ...	16889	Have now sufficient ground clear to commence hydraulicing
Embregarse	16890	**Hypothecate(d)**
Embriagado	16891	Do not hypothecate
Embriago	16892	Hypothecate the
Embriaguez	16893	Hypothecate the bonds
Embrice ...	16894	Hypothecate the ore
Embrochado	16895	Hypothecate —— if necessary to raise funds quickly
Embroider	16896	Property hypothecated for ——
Embrolla ..	16897	**I**
Embromado	16898	**Ice** (*See also* "Climate," "Weather.")
Embrowned	16899	Until prevented by ice
Embrume...	16900	Destroyed by the ice
Embrutecer	16901	There is no ice at present
Embryo ...	16902	Will be impossible as soon as the ice forms
Embryonem	16903	There is no traffic on account of the ice
Embryotic	16904	Ice is now —— ft. thick
Embuchado	16905	Cannot work on account of ice
Embuciar...	16906	Ice is beginning to break up
Embudar ...	16907	River is impassable from moving ice
Embudico...	16908	It will not be possible to do anything until the ice gives
Embudista	16909	We shall do this as soon as the ice has gone
Emburrion	16910	Ice has now entirely gone
Emburujar	16911	Expect that the ice will have entirely disappeared by
Embusquer	16912	This is an exceptionally severe season for ice
Embusteria	16913	**Idea** (*See also* "Form.")
Embustir ...	16914	What is your (——'s) idea of
Embutidera	16915	Have you formed any idea as to
Emelgar ...	16916	The only idea I (we) have formed is
Emendable	16917	Have not been able to form any idea
Emendacion	16918	The idea is absurd
Emendated	16919	Idea not so absurd as appears
Emendators	16920	The idea is an excellent one
Emendetur	16921	Can you form any idea as to
Emendevole	16922	Cannot form any idea as to
Emeraude...	16923	Can only form a loose idea as to
Emergencia	16924	**Identical**
Emergently	16925	Not identical
Emerito ...	16926	If identical
Emersed ...	16927	Identical with
Emersion ...	16928	**Identification**

Emeticarum	16929	Refuse(s) without proper identification
Emetico ...	16930	For the purposes of identification
Emetique ...	16931	Further identification absolutely necessary
Emeutier ...	16932	Further proof of identification impossible
Emienda ...	16933	Can you suggest any further means of identification
Emigracion	16934	Identification perfect
Emigrado	16935	Pending complete identification of
Emigrania	16936	So long as the identification is uncertain
Emigrar ...	16937	**Idle**
Emigrating	16938	Still idle
Emina ...	16939	Has (have) been idle since
Eminebit ...	16940	Has (have) remained idle for want of ——
Eminebunt	16941	Idle owing to
Eminencia	16942	Has (have) stood idle ever since
Eminente ...	16943	**If**
Eminuisti +16944		If so
Emisario ...	16945	If already
Emisferio...	16946	If any
Emissaries	16947	If any prospect
Emitir ...	16948	If it is quite clear
Emmancher	16949	If correct
Emmariner	16950	If not correct
Emmenager	16951	If done
Emmenotter	16952	If not already done
Emmieller	16953	If he can
Emoliente...	16954	If he cannot
Emollition	16955	If you can
Emolumento	16956	If you cannot
Emondage	16957	If I (we)
Emorragia	16958	If I (we) can
Emorroidi	16959	If I (we) cannot
Emotional	16960	If I do
Emouchet	16961	If I (we) do not
Emouchoir	16962	If I get
Empachado	16963	If I do not get
Empacho ...	16964	If I (we) have
Empadronar	16965	If I (we) do not have
Empaillage	16966	If I (we) must
Empalagar	16967	If it (this)
Empalar ...	16968	If it is not
Empaliada	16969	If it will not
Empalizar	16970	If not
Empalomar	16971	If safe
Empanacher	16972	If the
Empanadura	16973	If they
Empandar	16974	If you
Empanelled	16975	If you are
Empanicar	16976	If you are not
Empantanar	16977	If you do
Empapelar	16978	If you do not
Empaque ...	16979	**Igneous**
Empaquetar	16980	Caused by an irruption of igneous rock
Emparchar	16981	Dyke of igneous rock
Emparedado	16982	Until we have passed through the bar of igneous rock
Emparejar	16983	Igneous rock is coming in again in the breast of No. —— level
Emparentar	16984	**Ignorant(ly)**
Empark ...	16985	Am I (are we) to keep —— ignorant as to
Emparrado	16986	Endeavour to keep —— ignorant as to
Emparvar...	16987	Entirely ignorant
Empastador	16988	Have kept —— ignorant as to

Empaste ...	16989	I am (we are) quite ignorant respecting
Empatadera	16990	Not altogether ignorant
Empatement	16991	Was unable to keep —— ignorant as to ——
Empater ...	16992	**Ill**
Empavesada	16993	I am very ill, send competent advice
Empecatado	16994	I have (—— has) been ill, but am (is) now recovered
Empecible	16995	I have been ill with ——; have been forced to go to —— to [recruit
Empedernir	16996	Is —— dangerously ill
Empedrado	16997	—— is too ill to leave
Empegadura	16998	Inform —— that his —— is ill
Empeguntar	16999	Inform —— that his —— is dangerously ill
Empeine ...	17000	—— has been ill with ——; has been forced to go to —— to
Empelechar	**17001**	Your —— is dangerously ill [recruit
Empella ...	17002	Your —— is ill, will keep you advised
Empellejar	17003	Delay was caused through my being ill
Empeltre ...	17004	**Illegal** (*See also* "Lawyer," "Legal.")
Empentar...	17005	Illegal according to the local law
Emperatriz	17006	Not illegal in the slightest degree
Empereur	17007	Do not do anything that is illegal
Emperezar	17008	Transaction illegal
Empernado	17009	Obtain competent opinion whether it is not illegal
Emperrada	17010	**Imagine(d)**
Emperrarse	17011	Can you imagine
Empesador	17012	Cannot imagine why
Empetro ...	17013	Do not imagine
Empfangen	17014	I (we) should imagine that you had better
Empfehlen	17015	It is as bad as you can imagine
Empfehlung	17016	Not nearly so bad as you seem to imagine
Empfindbar	17017	To imagine
Empfindsam	17018	Unable to imagine
Empfindung	17019	**Immaterial**
Emphase ...	17020	Is it immaterial (whether)
Emphasibus	17021	It is quite immaterial (whether)
Emphatique	17022	Is by no means immaterial
Emphatisch	17023	Regard it as quite immaterial
Emphractus	17024	The only thing that is immaterial is the following
Emphragma	17025	**Immediate**
Emphyteuta	17026	For immediate delivery
Empiastro	17027	For immediate shipment
Empicotar	17028	Immediate action is essential
Empiedro...	17029	Immediate action is necessary if you wish for any good to [result
Empierrer...	17030	Immediate instructions required
Empilement	17031	Please give this matter immediate attention
Empimento	17032	The question is one for immediate settlement
Empinado	17033	Must have immediate answer
Empiolar ...	17034	Your (——'s) immediate attention is requested
Empireo ...	17035	Immediate examination most desirable
Empireuma	17036	Immediate attention necessary
Empiric ...	17037	Immediate assistance advisable
Empiricism	17038	For immediate reply
Empirique	17039	**Immediately**
Empirismo	17040	Immediately or not at all
Empitura...	17041	Cable reply immediately
Empizarrar	17042	Come immediately
Emplagia...	17043	Cannot act immediately owing to
Emplastar	17044	Prepare immediately (to)
Emplastrum	17045	Immediately renew
Emplatre ...	17046	Send immediately
Emplazador	17047	Should be done immediately if at all
Empleado...	17048	Should be done immediately

Emplecton	17049	Should be sent immediately
Empleita ...	17050	The following are immediately required
Emplomar	17051	Matter was attended to immediately on receipt of your [instructions
Emplumecer	17052	**Immense(ly)**
Empobrecer	17053	Immense quantities of
Empocher...	17054	Profits are alleged to have been immense
Empoigner	17055	Immense old workings
Empoisoned	17056	**Impatient(ly)**
Empollado	17057	Are you (is ——) not a little impatient
Empolvar...	17058	Becoming impatient
Emponzonar	17059	Is (are) becoming impatient
Emporcar...	17060	Impatient to know whether
Emporend	17061	Shareholders are becoming very impatient in the absence of all [news
Emporetico	17062	**Impeded**
Emporium	17063	The work has been impeded by
Emposta ...	17064	Have you (has ——) been at all impeded by
Empotrar...	17065	Has (have) been impeded by
Empourprer	17066	Has (have) not been impeded by
Emprender	17067	**Imperative**
Empresario	17068	This is imperative
Empresse ...	17069	If imperative
Emprestado	17070	Is it (this) imperative
Emprestito	17071	Not imperative
Emprimado	17072	**Imperfect**
Emprimerar	17073	Is (are) still in a very imperfect state
Empringar	17074	Is still imperfect as regards
Emprunt ...	17075	Owing to the imperfect state of
Emptionem	17076	The only thing that is grossly imperfect is (——)
Emptitatus	17077	**Imply(ies)**
Emptitius...	17078	Undoubtedly meant to imply
Emptoribus	17079	Do (does) not imply
Emptoris ...	17080	Undoubtedly implies
Emptricem	17081	Do (did) you mean to imply that
Empturiens	17082	I (we) do (did) not mean to imply anything of the sort
Empturio ...	17083	Am I (are we) to understand that you imply
Empuantir	17084	I (we) do not think he (——) meant to imply that
Empuchar	17085	State more clearly what you mean to imply
Empuesta ...	17086	—— mean(t) to imply that
Empulgar...	17087	What will the agreement imply as regards
Empunador	17088	**Import(s)** (*See also* "Export.")
Empunidura	17089	To import
Empunir ...	17090	Would require to import
Empuris ...	17091	Would only require to import
Empurple...	17092	It will be necessary to import
Empuyarse	17093	It will not be necessary to import anything
Empyema...	17094	Cable the full import of
Empyrean	17095	Do not understand import of
Empyrosis	17096	Send list of imports
Emsigkeit	17097	Send details of imports and value
Emucidus...	17098	Send details of imports showing
Emugnere	17099	List of imports mailed on
Emulador	17100	Awaiting particulars of imports
Emulante...	17101	Amongst list of imports you will find
Emulare ...	17102	Duty on imports
Emulation	17103	No duty on imports
Emulative	17104	No duty on imports for mining purposes
Emulatore	17105	What is the import duty on
Emulatrice	17106	**Importance**
Emulgatio	17107	Do you (does ——) regard it as of the utmost importance (that)
Emulgendus	17108	It is of the utmost importance

[287]

Emulgente	17109	It has no real importance
Emulgeo ...	17110	It is not of much importance
Emulous ...	17111	There is no immediate importance
Emulsion ...	17112	It would only be of importance in the event of
Emunctory	17113	The point of most importance is
Emundacion	17114	Would urge upon you the importance of
Enacerar ...	17115	If he (you) concur with the importance of
Enaciyar ...	17116	Not of the slightest importance

Important

Enagenable	17117	
Enagenar ...	17118	On important business
Enaguazar	17119	Most important
Enaguelar	17120	Has (have) mailed important information to
Enaguillas	17121	It is very important that you (——) should
Enalage ...	17122	It is very important that I (we) should
Enalbar ...	17123	I do not think it at all important
Enalforjar	17124	It is exceedingly important that
Enalmagrar	17125	If it is not exceedingly important, should suggest that
Enalmenar	17126	It is not important
Enamels ...	17127	Is (are) very important
Enamorado	17128	Could effect no important change
Enamorar...	17129	This is urgently important
Enangostar	17130	It is important that
Enanico ...	17131	Very important

Importation

Enante ...	17132	
Enardecer...	17133	Importation license (for)

Imported

Enarenar ...	17134	
Enargiarum	17135	Everything practically requires to be imported
Enargias ...	17136	The only things that need to be imported are

Importing

Enarmonar	17137	
Enarmonico	17138	Owing to the necessity of importing all the materials

Impossible

Enarrabit ...	17139	
Enarracion	17140	If this is impossible
Enarratum	17141	Impossible to
Enartrosis	17142	Impossible at present
Enatavero...	17143	Impossible to deal with
Enatieza ...	17144	Impossible to get through before
Encabalgar	17145	Impossible to get away before
Encabellar	17146	Impossible to discover
Encabezar	17147	Impossible to determine
Encablure	17148	Impossible to continue with
Encabriar...	17149	Impossible to supply you with money
Encabronar	17150	Impossible to obtain reliable information
Encadrer ...	17151	Condition(s) is (are) impossible
Encaisse ...	17152	Do you regard it as impossible to make the property pay
Encaja ...	17153	Is it impossible for you to
Encajera ...	17154	It is impossible
Encajonado	17155	Not at all impossible that
Encajonar...	17156	If it is not impossible
Encalada ...	17157	It will be impossible for me (us) to do so before
Encalar ...	17158	Impossible at present to form any reliable judgment
Encalmarse	17159	Impossible to comply with your request
Encalvecer	17160	Quite impossible as long as
Encamacion	17161	Quite impossible to say
Encambijar	17162	Should you (——) think it impossible to
Encambrar	17163	Execution impossible

Impracticable

Encaminar	17164	
Encamisada	17165	Quite impracticable
Encamp ...	17166	Impracticable so long as

Impress(ed)

Encampment	17167	
Encanalar...	17168	You must impress upon —— the necessity of

Encanarse	17169	Would endeavour to impress upon you (——) most earnestly
Encanastar	17170	Impress most earnestly on ... [that
Encandecer	17171	Not at all impressed with
Encandilar	17172	Much impressed with
Encantar ...	17173	**Impression(s)**
Encantorio	17174	Impression produced favourable
Encantusar	17175	Impression produced unfavourable
Encapazar	17176	Not made the slightest impression
Encapillar	17177	The impression here is that
Encapotar	17178	What is the prevailing impression
Encapuzado	17179	The prevailing impression is that
Encaquer ...	17180	What is your (——'s) impression respecting
Encarado ...	17181	My impression is that
Encaramar	17182	Is this impression correct
Encarar ...	17183	Your impression is correct
Encarbo ...	17184	Your impression is not correct
Encarcelar	17185	My (our) impression is very favourable
Encardia ...	17186	My (our) impression is distinctly favourable
Encarna ...	17187	My (our) impressions are on the whole favourable
Encarnizar	17188	My (our) impressions are the reverse of favourable
Encarporum	17189	My (our) only impression was one of
Encarronar	17190	Have you been able to form any impression respecting
Encartado	17191	Ascertain as soon as you can his (——'s) impressions respecting
Encascotar	17192	His (——'s) impressions are doubtful. I (we) do not think you
Encashed ...	17193	**Improper(ly)** [need regard them at all
Encastele ...	17194	He (——) has not acted at all improperly
Encaustice	17195	He (——) has certainly acted very improperly
Encaustus	17196	If he has really acted improperly
Encebadar	17197	It has been alleged that he (——) acted improperly
Encella ...	17198	The works in the first instance were improperly arranged
Encenagado	17199	**Improve(s)**
Encenagar	17200	To improve
Encender ...	17201	Will not improve as long as
Encendido	17202	Expect(s) to improve
Encenias ...	17203	Do(es) they (it) improve
Encenizar	17204	I (we) see my (our) way to much improve
Encenseur	17205	Can you (——) improve
Encensio ...	17206	Anticipate(s) being able to improve
Encentador	17207	Do you think matters will improve
Encepador	17208	I (we) have no hope that matters will improve
Encepar ...	17209	I (we) have strong reasons for believing that matters will im-
Encerado ...	17210	I (we) have no doubt we can improve upon this [prove
Encernadar	17211	To improve the rate of
Encerotar...	17212	To materially improve
Encerrona...	17213	**Improved**
Encespedar	17214	Have you improved the results
Enchainer	17215	Has (have) improved
Enchant ...	17216	Has (have) not improved
Enchanteur	17217	Would be improved if
Enchanting	17218	Not at all improved
Encharcada	17219	**Improvement(s)** (*See also* "Expected," "Expenditure.")
Encharetar	17220	Marked improvement in
Encherir ...	17221	Improvement reported at
Enchicar ...	17222	Considerable improvement
Enchiridio	17223	For improvement
Enchristas	17224	Is there any improvement
Enciclico ...	17225	On the whole there is a decided improvement
Enciensos ..	17226	On the whole there is no decided improvement whatever
Encierro ...	17227	The only improvement is as regards
Encima ...	17228	There is no improvement to report

T

Encimero ...	17229	Figures show considerable improvement
Encinal ...	17230	There is a slight but undoubted tendency to improvement
Encinilla ...	17231	Improvement in value [stop
Encinta ...	17232	In the absence of any decided improvement I (we) advise you to
Encircled ...	17233	Show(s) great improvement
Encircling	17234	Shows a marked improvement
Enciso ...	17235	Improvement(s) must be postponed [necessary
Enclavar ...	17236	Improvement(s) should not be postponed unless absolutely
Enclavijar	17237	Cost of improvement(s) will be ——, time required ——
Enclenque	17238	Unless some improvement should soon manifest itself, it will be
Enclitic ...	17239	There is a great improvement at (in) [necessary to stop
Encliticos ...	17240	There is a slight improvement generally
Encloclar ...	17241	There is a slight improvement at (in)
Enclosure ...	17242	There is no improvement at (in)
Enclouer ...	17243	There is a steady improvement in the value of the ore
Enclume ...	17244	There is at present no prospect of any improvement
Encobijar...	17245	I anticipate a marked improvement on
Encobrado	17246	Improvements announced do not really amount to anything
Encobrit ...	17247	The(se) improvements will cost
Encoclar ...	17248	Am (are) sanguine that increased depth will show improvement
Encoger ...	17249	Contemplated improvement(s) [in value
Encogido ...	17250	Cost of contemplated improvement(s)
Encohetar...	17251	Further expenditure on improvements
Encoignure	17252	What is your estimate of cost upon improvements for the next
Encoladura	17253	When improvement(s) is (are) completed [three months
Encollage ...	17254	Pending completion of improvements
Encolpiae ...	17255	**Improving**
Encolure ...	17256	Almost daily improving
Encomiador	17257	Still improving
Encomiast	17258	Is it (are they) still improving
Encomienda	17259	Not now improving
Encomio ...	17260	Anything but improving
Encomium	17261	Ceased improving on
Encompasar	17262	If should begin improving, cable
Enconado...	17263	Shows no signs of improving
Enconoso ...	17264	Shows considerable signs of improving
Enconrear	17265	Cable whether any signs of improving
Encontrado	17266	If anything improving
Encontron	17267	Unless improving
Encorar ...	17268	**Imprudent(ly)**
Encordelar	17269	Do not let him (——) do anything imprudently
Encordonar	17270	Very imprudently told
Encore ...	17271	Has (have) acted imprudently
Encornudar	17272	Has (have) not acted imprudently
Encorozar...	17273	**In**
Encorporar	17274	In a
Encorralar	17275	In a few days
Encorrer ...	17276	In a week
Encorvada	17277	In about
Encostarse	17278	In about —— days
Encostrar ...	17279	In about five days
Encrespar...	17280	In about ten days
Encrestado	17281	In about twenty days
Encrinado	17282	In about thirty days
Encrinites	17283	In any case
Encrouter...	17284	In each case
Encrudecer	17285	In each
Encubertar	17286	In both
Encubieto ...	17287	In case of
Encubridor	17288	In consequence of

Encubrir ...	17289	Is now in course of
Encuentro	17290	In the event of
Encuesta ...	17291	In my (our)
Enculatar...	17292	In my opinion
Enculpar ...	17293	In need of
Encumbrado	17294	In sight
Encyclical	17295	In such case
Encyclius...	17296	In (the) this
Encysted ...	17297	In your
Endanger...	17298	In different directions
Endearment	17299	In the name of
Endeble ...	17300	**Inaccessible** (*See also* " Situation.")
Endecagono	17301	Inaccessible from the month of —— to the month of ——,
Endechar ...	17302	Generally inaccessible [both inclusive
Endechoso	17303	**Inadequate(ly)**
Endelechia	17304	If this is considered inadequate, cable what you would [consider would be more in accordance with your wishes
Endelinado	17305	Quite inadequate
Endemas ...	17306	Quite inadequate to secure the object in view
Endemico...	17307	Funds are altogether inadequate
Endemique	17308	**Inadmissible**
Endemoniar	17309	Is (are) inadmissible
Endentado	17310	Evidence regarded —— was ruled to be inadmissible
Endentecer	17311	**Inadvisably**
Enderecera	17312	Do not act inadvisably
Enderezar...	17313	Has (have) not acted inadvisably
Enderezo ...	17314	**Incapable**
Endergue ...	17315	Has been quite incapable
Endetter ...	17316	—— has an attack of —— and will be quite incapable for the
Endiablada	17317	Is (are) incapable of [next —— days
Endibia ...	17318	I (we) regard —— as incapable of
Endigen ...	17319	While —— is incapable
Endilgador	17320	Which has rendered —— (him) quite incapable
Endiosar ...	17321	**Inch(es)** (*See also* " Feet," Table at end, &c.)
Endlich ...	17322	After which are —— inches of ——
Endoblado	17323	For each —— miners' inch(es)
Endodermic	17324	—— inches high
Endoitium	17325	—— inches long
Endolirir ...	17326	—— inches wide
Endommager	17327	Not a single inch
Endonar ·...	17328	Of an inch
Endormeur	17329	One inch
Endosador	17330	Two inches
Endoselar	17331	Three inches
Endospores	17332	Four inches
Endowment	17333	Five inches
Endpunkt	17334	Six inches
Endriago ...	17335	Seven inches
Endrina ...	17336	Eight inches
Endroit ...	17337	Nine inches
Endromidis	17338	Ten inches
Endromis...	17339	Eleven inches
Endschluss	17340	Twelve inches
Enducir ...	17341	One foot —— inches
Enduire ...	17342	Two feet —— inches
Endulzar ...	17343	Using a —— inch [" Miners' inches.")
Endurador	17344	Water may be obtained at —— per miners' inch (*See also*
Endurant ...	17345	**Incidental(ly)** (*See also* " Expenses.")
Endurecer	17346	Incidental to
Endurecido	17347	Unless incidental to

Endursache	17348	**Inclination** (*See also* "Foot.")
Endurtheil	17349	Inclination to
Endwise ...	17350	What is the (your) inclination
Endziel ...	17351	Ascertain his (——'s) inclination
Enebral ...	17352	His (——'s) inclination is to
Enebrina ...	17353	My inclination is for
Enebro ...	17354	The inclination is —— feet per fathom
Enecatrice	17355	At a depth on the inclination of the vein of ——
Enechado ...	17356	**Incline** (*See also* "Shaft.")
Enectam ...	17357	Incline winze
Enejar ...	17358	Incline is now down to
Eneldo ...	17359	Depth of incline
Enemiga ...	17360	An incline shaft on the vein
Enemigable	17361	Incline shaft is now down
Enemistad	17362	Intend to start an incline shaft on the vein
Energetice	17363	Do you (does ——) incline to the belief that
Energia ..,	17364	I (we) do not incline in the least to the belief
Energique	17365	I (we) incline to the
Energisch...	17366	Ground would permit of easy grade for incline
Energumeno	17367	When do you expect to get incline finished
Enermizar	17368	Expect to get incline finished and in working order by ——
Enervado ...	17369	Self-acting incline
Enervating	17370	**Inclined** (*See also* "Favourably.")
Enervatote	17371	Inclined to
Enervatus...	17372	To be inclined to
Enervetur...	17373	Not inclined to
Enervibus	17374	An inclined shoot
Enervor ...	17375	Are you (is ——) inclined to
Enfadadizo	17376	I do not feel at all inclined to
Enfadoso ...	17377	I am (we are) inclined to
Enfagione	17378	I am (we are) not at all inclined to
Enfaiter ...	17379	In such a case would you be inclined to
Enfaldador	17380	I am (we are) not inclined one way or the other
Enfangarse	17381	I am (we are) inclined to think that
Enfantin ...	17382	Is not at all inclined
Enfardelar	17383	Is (are) inclined to
Enfariner ...	17384	Not at all inclined to
Enfasis ...	17385	Not at all inclined at present
Enfastiar ...	17386	Seems somewhat inclined
Enfeeble ...	17387	**Include(s)**
Enfeebling	17388	Do(es) —— include
Enfeoff ...	17389	Do(es) not include
Enfermar ...	17390	This would not include
Enfermedad	17391	Specify what you include in this (it)
Enfermeria	17392	To include
Enfermizo	17393	What does this (it) include
Enferozar...	17394	Will this (it) include
Enfestar ...	17395	This (it) will include
Enfiamento	17396	You should include sufficient to cover
Enfiatello ...	17397	Include as much as possible
Enfiatura ...	17398	**Included**
Enfiazione	17399	It (this) must be included
Enfielar ...	17400	**Inclusive**
Enfilade ...	17401	Inclusive of
Enfilading	17402	Inclusive of all charges
Enfintoso ...	17403	This is inclusive of everything
Enfiteusis...	17404	Words inclusive
Enfiteuta ...	17405	Words inclusive of address
Enflammer	17406	For —— days inclusive
Enflautado	17407	Fee inclusive of travelling expenses

Enflautar ...	17408	Is —— inclusive of
Enfler ...	17409	Inclusive of the following
Enflure ...	17410	Is not inclusive of the following
Enfogar ...	17411	Must be inclusive of
Enfold ...	17412	These numbers are inclusive
Enfolding...	17413	Inclusive of —— but exclusive of ——
Enfoldment	17414	**Income** (*See also* " Profit.")
Enfoncure	17415	Income tax
Enfonsado	17416	Net income
Enforcing ...	17417	**Inconsistent**
Enfornar ...	17418	Altogether inconsistent
Enfortiran	17419	Not at all inconsistent
Enfourcher	17420	Is not this suggestion inconsistent with
Enfractico	17421	Facts are inconsistent with the statements made
Enfrailar ...	17422	This statement is inconsistent with
Enfrascar ...	17423	**Inconvenience**
Enfrenador	17424	Great inconvenience
Enfrenar ...	17425	No inconvenience
Enfriadera	17426	To avoid the inconvenience of
Enfriar ...	17427	**Inconvenient(ly)**
Enfundar ...	17428	Will it be inconvenient
Enfurcion ...	17429	It will not be at all inconvenient
Enfurecer...	17430	If it is inconvenient, cable
Enfurtir ...	17431	Unless this is inconvenient
Engabanado	17432	Would be very inconvenient. I (we) would suggest
Engace ...	17433	Has (have) come very inconveniently
Engafar ...	17434	**Incorporate(d)**
Engageant	17435	Incorporated on —— last
Engaitar ...	17436	Could incorporate with
Engalgar ...	17437	Could they not be incorporated together
Engallado...	17438	I (we) think might be very well incorporated
Enganadizo	17439	I (we) do not think this (they) should be incorporated
Enganador	17440	Is it suitable to be incorporated with
Enganchar	17441	Might be incorporated with
Engandujo	17442	Is the company really incorporated
Engangento	17443	The company has been duly incorporated
Enganifa ...	17444	The company duly incorporated ; everything in order
Enganoso ...	17445	**Incorporation**
Engarce ...	17446	Certificate of incorporation
Engargola	17447	Duplicate certificate of incorporation
Engarland	17448	**Incorrect**
Engarrafar	17449	Found to be incorrect
Engarzador	17450	Is it not incorrect
Engasajar...	17451	Now appears to have been incorrect
Engastador	17452	What is incorrect
Engastato ..	17453	The former was incorrect
Engatillar*	17454	Statement made by him (——) incorrect
Engbrustig	17455	Statement made in his (——'s) report incorrect
Engendrar	17456	If this should prove incorrect you (——) had better
Engenero ...	17457	So far nothing has been found to be incorrect
Engerber	17458	So far the only thing I have found incorrect is that ——
Engherzig	17459	**Increase**
Engibamos	17460	To increase
Engibar ...	17461	Can you increase
Engilmar ...	17462	Cannot increase
Engimelgar	17463	Increase quantity
Englanado	17464	Increase the price
Engleur ...	17465	Increase of rates
Englished...	17466	Will you have to increase (the)
Engloutir...	17467	Will have to increase (the)

Engolado ...	17468	To increase the
Engomadero	17469	Need not at present increase the
Engomar ...	17470	I (we) expect to increase this number (quantity) shortly
Engonasis	17471	An increase may be expected about
Engonata ...	17472	As soon as I (we) can increase
Engoncer ...	17473	Do not on any account increase
Engordador	17474	I (we) hope to increase
Engorged ...	17475	Why cannot you increase
Engorroso...	17476	I (we) cannot increase because (owing to)
Engouffrer	17477	I am (we are) not able to increase
Engourdir	17478	I (we) shall be able to increase
Engoznar ...	17479	It would be no use at present to increase
Engpass ...	17480	Increase if possible
Engrail ...	17481	Must increase
Engraisser	17482	This will mean an increase of ——
Engrandar	17483	The increase occurred ——
Engranerar	17484	What is the (this) large increase (of ——) due to
Engrapar ...	17485	The large increase is mainly due to
Engravedar	17486	Shall have to increase —— by the following amount (number)
Engredar ...	17487	**Increased**
Engreido ...	17488	Increased to
Engreir ...	17489	Has (have) not been increased
Engrenage	17490	Increased expenses must be paid by
Engrosar ...	17491	**Increasing**
Engrossed...	17492	Not increasing
Engrudador	17493	**Incur**
Engrudo ...	17494	Do not incur
Engrumeler	17495	Should you incur
Enguantado	17496	Incur no liability
Engueuler	17497	**Incurred**
Enguillar ...	17498	Cost incurred from
Enguinorum	17499	Any cost incurred from to-day (——)
Enguizgar	17500	Incurred to date
Engulfing...	17501	**Indebted(ness)**
Engullidor	17502	What is the present indebtedness
Enhacinar	17503	Indebtedness amounts to
Enhardir ...	17504	At the present time what is the (your) total indebtedness
Enharinar...	17505	At the present time my (our) indebtedness is
Enhastiar ...	17506	Exclusive of the foregoing what is your total indebtedness
Enhatijar ...	17507	Exclusive of —— what is your total indebtedness to ——
Enhebrar ...	17508	Could you raise —— to clear off present indebtedness
Enhenar ...	17509	Imperative to clear off present indebtedness amounting to ——
Enherbolar	17510	To enable you to clear off present indebtedness amounting to
Enhestador	17511	**Indefinite**
Enhestar ...	17512	Proposal too indefinite
Enhibir ...	17513	At present the matter is altogether indefinite
Enhielar ...	17514	Is (are) too indefinite
Enhiesto ...	17515	Proposal too indefinite, cable more precisely
Enhilado ...	17516	Report too indefinite as to ——, can you give further details
Enhoramala	17517	Terms of your letter too indefinite
Enhornar ...	17518	Instructions sent too indefinite, please supplement
Enhuecar ...	17519	**Indemnified**
Enhydridem	17520	If indemnified
Enhydrorum	17521	I (we) must be indemnified
Enhydros ...	17522	Unless indemnified
Enigma	17523	**Indemnify**
Enigmatico	17524	To indemnify
Enivremeat	17525	Will you (——) indemnify
Enjabonar	17526	Will indemnify
Enjaezar ...	17527	Will not indemnify

Enjaguar ...	17528	Must indemnify ...
Enjague ...	17529	Cannot indemnify
Enjalbegar	17530	Will you indemnify against litigation
Enjalmero	17531	Cannot indemnify against litigation
Enjalmos ...	17532	To indemnify me (us)
Enjambrar	17533	**Indemnity**
Enjarciar ...	17534	Will give full indemnity
Enjardinar	17535	Will you give full indemnity against
Enjaveler ...	17536	What indemnity do you (does ——) require
Enjebar ...	17537	Must have a letter of indemnity
Enjeno ...	17538	Will give you a letter of indemnity
Enjergar ...	17539	Will sign letter of indemnity if you will prepare and forward
Enjerido ...	17540	**Indent(s)** [same
Enjeridura	17541	Repeat indent
Enjerir ...	17542	Cancel indent
Enjertal ...	17543	Send revised indent
Enjoindre...	17544	Pass on indent to
Enjoining...	17545	Have ordered goods as per your indent dated
Enjoleur ...	17546	Delay execution of indent
Enjolivure	17547	Complete indent dated —— as quickly as possible
Enjoyable...	17548	When will indent be completed
Enjoyelado	17549	Indent will be completed on ——
Enjoying ...	17550	This completes indent dated
Enjoyment	17551	When will you ship goods forming indent
Enjugador	17552	Require(s) cash deposit of —— before commencing to ship in-
Enjugar ...	17553	Indent will be shipped by the —— sailing on [dent
Enjuiciar ...	17554	Hope to ship indent about
Enjullo ...	17555	**Independent(ly)**
Enjuncar ...	17556	Independently of
Enjundia ...	17557	If I am (we are) independent
Enjundioso	17558	I am (we are) quite independent
Enjunque...	17559	I am (we are) by no means independent
Enjutez ...	17560	If I was (we were) independent
Enkelin ...	17561	As soon as I am (we are) independent
Enkindle ...	17562	On behalf of independent
Enlabiar ...	17563	Would be perfectly independent
Enlablador	17564	**India Rubber** (See also "Belting.")
Enlace ...	17565	India rubber belting
Enlaider ...	17566	—— ft. of India rubber belting —— ft. wide —— ft. thick
Enlargues...	17567	India rubber for
Enlazable...	17568	India rubber packing
Enlazar ...	17569	India rubber hose
Enlevar ...	17570	India rubber sheet
Enlicador...	17571	**Indicate(s)**
Enlisted ...	17572	Can you indicate
Enllenar ...	17573	I (we) might indicate that
Enlodadura	17574	I (we) indicate this because
Enloquecer	17575	There is everything to indicate (that)
Enlucernar	17576	There is nothing to indicate (that)
Enlucidor...	17577	What would you indicate as proving
Enlucir ...	17578	Would suggest that you (——) indicate(s)
Enluminer	17579	It (this) indicates that
Enmaderar	17580	What does it (this) indicate
Enmagrecer	17581	This (it) would seem to indicate that
Enmalecer	17582	Do(es) not indicate
Enmantar...	17583	**Indication(s)**
Enmaridar	17584	Indications of
Enmascarar	17585	Surface indications are very misleading
Enmechar...	17586	Surface indications are confined to
Enmelar ...	17587	Indications are favourable

Enmerdar...	17588	Indications are not favourable
Enmiendo...	17589	Every indication of
Enmocecer	17590	Favourable indications have continued
Enmohecido	17591	There are no favourable indications whatever
Enmollecer	17592	The indications are favourable for good profits in the future
Enmondur	17593	Judging from indications it is my opinion that
Enmordazar	17594	There is no indication at present
Ennegrecer	17595	General indications are very promising
Ennobled ...	17596	There is every indication that
Ennobling	17597	From present indications I (we) have no doubt I (we) have
Ennoviar ...	17598	**Indorse**
Ennuyant...	17599	Can you indorse ——'s statement
Ennuyeux...	17600	Cannot indorse ——'s figures or statements
Enodacion	17601	Do you indorse this statement
Enojoso ...	17602	It will be necessary for you to indorse ——'s statements
Enojuelo ...	17603	Refuse(s) to indorse
Enoncer ...	17604	Unable to indorse
Enormement	17605	Will indorse
Enormezza	17606	—— will indorse the statements made
Enormidad	17607	**Indorsed**
Enormous...	17608	Indorsed by
Enotera ...	17609	Statements are indorsed (by)
Enquerir ...	17610	Statements are useless unless indorsed by
Enquistado	17611	**Induce**
Enraciner...	17612	To induce
Enraged ...	17613	Bring all the pressure you can to induce
Enraigonar	17614	Can you induce vendors
Enramada...	17615	Can you induce
Enrarecer...	17616	Useless to endeavour to induce
Enrasado ...	17617	Endeavour to induce
Enrastrar...	17618	Has (have) endeavoured to induce
Enravish ...	17619	Is there any chance of your being able to induce
Enrayure ...	17620	Should you be able to induce
Enredadera	17621	Unable to induce
Enredador	17622	**Induced**
Enredoso ...	17623	Induced by
Enrehojar...	17624	Might be induced
Enrejado ...	17625	If induced to
Enrevasado	17626	**Inducement**
Enrhumer	17627	Can you (——) offer any inducement
Enriador ...	17628	Cannot offer any further inducement
Enricher ...	17629	Except much inducement were offered
Enrichment	17630	In case sufficient inducement is offered
Enriqueno	17631	Inducement not sufficient
Enriscado...	17632	The only inducement would be that
Enristrar ...	17633	The only inducement I (we) could offer is
Enrizado ...	17634	There is no inducement whatever
Enrobe ...	17635	What do you consider sufficient inducement
Enrocar ...	17636	**Inference**
Enrodelado	17637	What inference would you (——) draw from
Enrolled ...	17638	My (our) (——'s) inference is that
Enrona ...	17639	What inference would you draw from ——'s report
Enrouler ...	17640	**Inferior**
Enrubescer	17641	An inferior quality
Enrubiador	17642	Not at all inferior
Enrubio ...	17643	**Influence**
Enruinecer	17644	To influence
Enrunar ...	17645	Influence can be obtained
Ensabanada	17646	——'s influence very desirable
Ensabler ...	17647	Can you secure ——'s influence

Ensacular...	17648	Cannot influence him (——)
Ensalada ...	17649	Have you any personal influence with
Ensaladera	17650	Have not sufficient personal influence
Ensalmo ...	17651	Has (have) considerable personal influence with
Ensalvajar	17652	Cannot influence
Ensalzar ...	17653	Can you exert your influence to
Ensanchar	17654	Could —— exert any influence
Ensanche ...	17655	—— might be able to exert considerable influence
Ensanguine	17656	Do not attempt to influence
Ensareyar...	17657	Do you think —— has any influence
Ensarnecer	17658	Little or no influence
Ensay ...	17659	Very great influence
Ensayador	17660	Exert all your influence to
Ensconced	17661	**Influenced**
Ensebar ...	17662	Influenced by
Enseigner	17663	Likely to be influenced by
Enselvado	17664	Not likely to be influenced by
Ensemble ...	17665	**Inform**
Ensemencer	17666	To inform
Ensenada ...	17667	Inform owner
Ensenadero	17668	Inform me of
Ensenador	17669	Inform —— immediately
Ensenorear	17670	Cannot inform you
Enserar ...	17671	Do not inform
Enserrinar	17672	It is most urgent that you inform me (us)
Enshrined	17673	Please inform me (us) by
Ensiculi ...	17674	Inform me (us) by letter
Ensiculos ...	17675	Inform me (us) by telegraph immediately
Ensiform ...	17676	Inform me (us) the moment you are able
Ensigerum	17677	Hope to inform you by
Ensigncy ...	17678	Please inform —— that
Ensilar ...	17679	Pleased to inform you that
Enslave ...	17680	Regret to inform you that
Eusogar ...	17681	When you inform me (us) as to
Ensolerar ...	17682	You may rely upon me (us) informing you the moment I am
Ensolvedor	17683	Have cabled —— to inform you direct [(we are) able
Ensolver ...	17684	Inform us immediately of any change in (at)
Ensotarse	17685	Inform me (us) at once that you agree to these terms
Ensuciador	17686	Inform me (us) at once if anything new happens
Ensueno ...	17687	Please inform me (us) of
Ensuivre ...	17688	Better inform him (——) at once that
Ensullo ...	17689	Write fully to —— and inform him (them) of all that has
Entablado	17690	**Informant** [passed
Entacher ...	17691	Who is (was) your informant
Entailed ...	17692	My (our) informant was
Entalamado	17693	Is your informant reliable
Entalamar	17694	My (our) informant is absolutely reliable
Entalegar	17695	My (our) informant is not altogether reliable
Entalingar	17696	Do(es) not regard your informant as reliable
Entallable	17697	**Information** (*See also* " Gain," " Have.")
Entalle ...	17698	Get information about
Entamure...	17699	Get information from
Entangling	17700	Get me (us) more information respecting
Entapizar ...	17701	Shall be glad to have some information about
Entarascar	17702	I (we) have reliable information that
Entarten ...	17703	According to the best of my information and belief
Entaussern	17704	This information is for
Entbehrung	17705	This information is not for
Entbieten...	17706	Is this (the) information for
Entbindung	17707	Latest information wanted

Entdecker	17708	For my personal information
Entdeckung	17709	Send particulars for my private information
Entecado ...	17710	This is for your private information only
Enteco ...	17711	Your answer will be for my private information
Entehrend	17712	The (this) information is important to myself
Enteilen ...	17713	For your personal information
Entelechia	17714	Decline(s) to give any information
Entelerido	17715	Get all the information you can about this and telegraph
Entenada ...	17716	The information you wish was mailed on
Entenallar	17717	Complete information will follow by mail
Entendedor	17718	Further information will follow by mail
Entendido	17719	Full information is given in letter mailed on
Enterbung	17720	Mail all the information you can get
Enterhaken	17721	Supply him (——) with all the information you can
Enterimer	17722	Send us the fullest and latest information
Enternecer	17723	— Detailed information required since
Enterprise	17724	All the information I (we) have obtained is very satisfactory
Enterrador	17725	Am (are) promised reliable information on
Entesar ...	17726	Can this information be depended upon
Entestado...	17727	Is there any truth in the information
Entfahren	17728	Can you obtain reliable information respecting
Entfernen	17729	Cannot obtain any reliable information
Entfernung	17730	I (we) do not consider the information reliable
Entflammen	17731	Please supplement your information by
Entfremden	17732	Can you supplement your information by details of
Entfuhrung	17733	Cannot supplement my information by details of
Entgegen ...	17734	Can you obtain any information as regards
Entgluhen	17735	Have you any information as regards
Enthalten	17736	Information not at all satisfactory
Enthaupten	17737	Have you any further information
Entheal ...	17738	I (we) have no further information
Enthecarum	17739	— Give earliest possible information
Enthecas ...	17740	For further information refer to
Entheos ...	17741	I am (we are) unable to obtain any information
Enthroned	17742	I (we) hope to obtain all necessary information
Enthusiasm	17743	I (we) have private information that
Entibador...	17744	Information has reached me (us) that
Entibiar ...	17745	Confirm the information given in
Enticingly	17746	Keep this information to yourself
Entidad ...	17747	Must I keep the (this) information to myself
Entierro ...	17748	There is no need to regard this information as confidential
Entimema	17749	Please regard this information as strictly confidential
Entintar ...	17750	Have you any more information
Entitular ...	17751	Can you send any more information
Entiznar ...	17752	You will be able to obtain all information from
Entkleiden	17753	Was able to obtain information from —— as to
Entkommen	17754	Was unable to obtain any information as to
Entkraften	17755	—— gave me the information
Entladen ...	17756	—— is believed to have given the information
Entlassung	17757	— Information is desperately needed
Entlehnen	17758	My information amounts to
Entlocken	17759	Many thanks for the information contained in
Entmannen	17760	No information has yet been received respecting
Entnerven	17761	No information can be obtained as to
Entoilage ...	17762	Refuse(s) to give any information
Entoldado	17763	The only information I (we) have is
Entomata...	17764	The information is not correct
Entombed	17765	The information is absolutely correct
Entombment	17766	The information is essentially correct
Entonacion	17767	Will cable any information I (we) may get

ntonador	17768	The only information I (we) have is to the effect that
ntonces ...	17769	Waiting for information as to
ntonelar	17770	Our information is (was) totally incorrect
ntonnoir	17771	Your information is totally incorrect
ntorchado	17772	I will wire you about —— as soon as I have positive information
ntorpecer	17773	Have not been able to see —— and cannot give any information
ntortille ...	17774	What is your information
ntosicaba	17775	Our information is
ntosigar	17776	Cable the earliest possible information regarding
ntournure	17777	What information have you respecting
ntrada ...	17778	Information required for Shareholders' Meeting
ntradero...	17779	We require this information for our Annual Report to Share-
ntrailles	17780	(And) latest information regarding [holders
ntrainer ...	17781	**Informed**
ntrambos	17782	Have not been kept informed lately as regards
ntrampait	17783	Has —— informed you that
ntrampar	17784	—— has informed me (us) that
ntranable	17785	—— has not informed me (us) that
ntrancing	17786	Is said to have been informed
ntranizar	17787	Is said to have been informed by —— that
ntrante ...	17788	Keep me (us) regularly informed
ntrapped	17789	Have been informed on reliable authority that
ntrathen	17790	Has (have) been incorrectly informed
ntratico ...	17791	Has (have) been correctly informed
ntratrice	17792	What is your (——'s) reason for keeping back information
ntratura...	17793	Will keep you better informed
ntreabrir	17794	**Infringement**
ntreacto ...	17795	Is an infringement of
ntreaties	17796	Is not an infringement of
ntreaty ...	17797	Should it prove to be an infringement
ntrecanal	17798	**Injunction**
ntrecava	17799	Injunction refused
ntrecerca	17800	Injunction granted
ntrechat...	17801	Injunction applied for
ntrecielo	17802	Shall I (we) apply for an injunction
ntreclaro	17803	Do not apply for an injunction
ntrecoger	17804	Apply for an injunction at once
ntrecoro ...	17805	Has (have) applied for an injunction
ntrecriar	17806	Court has granted an injunction
ntredecir	17807	Court has refused an injunction
ntredoble	17808	Please authorise me (us) to apply for an injunction
ntree ...	17809	**Injure(d)** (*See also* " Accident," " Death.")
ntreissen	17810	A few —— have been injured
ntrejerir...	17811	How are the injured
ntrelazar	17812	All the injured are doing well
ntreligne	17813	About —— are reported injured
ntrelucir	17814	Seriously injured
ntremeler	17815	Very much injured
ntremes ...	17816	No one injured
ntremorir	17817	—— man (men) injured
ntrenched	17818	Slightly injured
ntrepano	17819	—— of the injured have since died
ntrepelar	17820	**Injury** (*See also* " Damage.")
ntreponer	17821	Is it likely to cause me (us) any injury
ntrepot ...	17822	No injury whatever
ntresaca	17823	What injury has been done
ntrescuro	17824	But little injury has been done
ntresol ...	17825	No injury has been caused
ntresuelo	17826	Has already caused me (us) much injury
ntretalla	17827	Great injury has occurred (to)

Entretejar	17828	Resulting in an injury of
Entretenir	17829	Slight injury has been caused
Entretien ...	17830	The injury has caused a delay of
Entretoise	17831	Injury has been confined to
Entreuntar	17832	Injury might have been more serious
Entrevenir	17833	Will do me (us) much injury
Entrever ...	17834	To prevent any injury being done to (by)
Entrevista	17835	**Inquire**
Entrevoir ...	17836	To inquire
Entricar ...	17837	Inquire about
Entrichten	17838	Do not inquire
Entrincado	17839	Inquire again and let me (us) know
Entringen	17840	Inquire at —— for cables
Entripado	17841	Inquire at —— respecting
Entrojar ...	17842	**Inquiry(ies)**
Entromesso	17843	Inquiry is to be held on
Entronerar	17844	Inquiry will be held on
Entronizar	17845	Have an inquiry for
Entronque	17846	Have no inquiry for
Entruchada	17847	Have you any inquiry for
Entruchon	17848	Has (have) replied to my inquiry
Entrucken	17849	Inquiry now being made
Entrusting	17850	No reply yet to my (our) inquiry
Entsagung	17851	Now engaged on inquiry
Entschluss	17852	Make full inquiry
Entseelt ...	17853	On my making inquiry
Entsetzen	17854	Please make an inquiry respecting
Entsinnen	17855	What is the result of your inquiry
Entstehen	17856	The result of a very careful inquiry is
Entuerto ...	17857	Who is making the inquiry
Entumirse	17858	Please make inquiry and cable
Entupir ...	17859	This cable is in reply to your inquiry (of)
Enturbiar	17860	Make careful inquiries respecting
Entusiasmo	17861	Will make careful inquiries respecting
Entvolkern	17862	Have made careful inquiries respecting
Entwaffnen	17863	—— inquiry for
Entweder...	17864	No inquiry at all
Entweichen	17865	What inquiry is there for
Entwerthen	17866	**Insert**
Entwickeln	17867	To insert
Entwined ...	17868	Do not insert
Entwirren	17869	Insert in the
Entwisting	17870	Insert in local papers
Entwohnen	17871	Contract—Insert the following clause
Entwurf ...	17872	Deed—Insert the following clause
Entziehen...;	17873	Lease—Insert the following clause
Entziffern	17874	Insert the following in
Entzuckung	17875	In clause —— after the word —— insert
Entzundbar	17876	Insert the usual clause for
Enucleate...	17877	In my message of —— after the word —— insert the following
Enumerar...	17878	**Inserted**
Enunciar ...	17879	Should be inserted between —— and ——
Enuntiabit	17880	Cannot be inserted
Enuntianto	17881	Must be inserted
Enuntietis	17882	Do not sign unless a clause is inserted to the following effect
Enuptionem	17883	Has (have) had required clause inserted
Envainar ...	17884	In agreement a clause must be inserted
Envanecer	17885	In bond a clause should be inserted giving me (us) the option
Envaronar	17886	Is it essential that it should be inserted
Envasador	17887	It is not essential that —— should be inserted.

Invejecido	17888	**Inside**
Inveloped	17889	Inside of
Inveloping	17890	What are the inside figures
Invenenar	17891	Inside figures
Invenom ...	17892	Inside dimensions
Inverdir ...	17893	Inside the timbers
Invergure	17894	On the inside of
Inverques	17895	Inside my (our)
Inviable ...	17896	Inside our boundaries
Inviadizo...	17897	**Insiders**
Inviajado...	17898	Insiders must be kept in the dark
Invidia ...	17899	What are insiders doing
Invidiable	17900	Insiders are buying
Invidiador	17901	Insiders are selling
Invidioso...	17902	Insiders are holding
Invieux ...	17903	**Insist**
Invilecer ...	17904	To insist
Invinado ...	17905	Insist on
Invinagrar	17906	Insist for
Invion ...	17907	Can you insist
Inviously...	17908	Do not insist
Inviperado	17909	I (we) must insist
Invirar ...	17910	Insist upon our (your) rights
Invironner	17911	Is (are) beginning to insist
Invisager...	17912	If —— insists upon
Inviscar ...	17913	In case —— insist(s)
Inviudar ...	17914	Shall I (we) insist
Invoisiner	17915	You must insist upon
Involcarse	17916	You need not insist upon
Involtorio	17917	Useless to insist
Involturas	17918	Unless —— insist(s)
Invoyeur ...	17919	Vendor(s) insist(s) upon
Invoyship	17920	Will lose all if you (they) insist
Invuelto ...	17921	You had better insist immediately that
Inwrapped	17922	**Insolvent**
Inzarzado	17923	Am (are) likely to become insolvent
Inzurdecer	17924	Is (are) insolvent
Inzurronar	17925	Not at present insolvent
Eolico ...	17926	Not at all likely to become insolvent
Eolipile ...	17927	Reported to be insolvent
Eolique ...	17928	**Inspect** (*See also* " Examine," " Report.")
Epactarum	17929	To inspect
Epactas ...	17930	In order to inspect
Epactilla ...	17931	Inspect at once
Epagneul ...	17932	Could you (——) inspect —— at same visit
Epagontis	17933	Can you (——) proceed to —— to inspect
Epaisseur...	17934	Can you nominate anyone to inspect
Epamprer...	17935	Within what time could you (——) inspect
Epanaphora	17936	Will you inspect —— mine for my private information
Epanodos ...	17937	Could not inspect owing to the workings being full of water
Epanouir ...	17938	**Inspected** (*See also* " Mine," " Property.")
Epargner ...	17939	Has (have) been inspected
Eparoja ...	17940	Not yet inspected
Eparpiller	17941	Inspected by
Eparvin ...	17942	Mine cannot be inspected during winter, which lasts —— to ——
Epatico ...	17943	**Inspection**
Epaticorum	17944	Inspection cannot be made for —— weeks
Epattement	17945	Only made a superficial inspection
Epaulet ...	17946	From a superficial inspection
Epeautre ...	17947	It will take —— days longer to complete inspection

Epentesis ...	17948	Cable the general result of your inspection
Eperlano ...	17949	Can you arrange to inspect —— mine previous to your return
Eperonner	17950	Cannot arrange any further inspections
Epervier ...	17951	The general results of my inspection are very satisfactory
Ephedras ...	17952	The general results of my inspection are not at all satisfactory
Ephelidem	17953	What shall I (we) pay for the inspection
Ephemeral	17954	Who will pay for the inspection
Epicamente	17955	When may I (we) expect to learn the result of inspection
Epicedio ...	17956	Will cable before —— whether I (——) can arrange to under-
		[take inspection
Epiceno ...	17957	Regret engagements do not permit of making inspection
Epicerie ...	17958	Can undertake inspection, but cannot leave for —— weeks
Epicurean	17959	On my previous inspection
Epicurismo	17960	I (——) was obliged to hasten over the inspection
Epicycloid	17961	I (——) only made a cursory inspection

Instalment(s)

Epidemia ...	17962	
Epidemique	17963	Instalment of
Epidermis	17964	First instalment of purchase money
Epidimo ...	17965	Second instalment of purchase money
Epifania ...	17966	Third instalment of purchase money

Instance

Epifisis ...	17967	
Epifonema	17968	In this instance
Epigastris	17969	In the first instance you (——) had better

Instant *(See also "January," "February," &c., &c.)*

Epiglottis	17970	
Epigrafe ...	17971	On the —— instant

Instantly

Epigrama	17972	
Epilatoire...	17973	Must be done instantly
Epilectico	17974	Will be done instantly
Epilepsy ...	17975	Unless it can be done instantly

Instead

Epilessia ...	17976	
Epilogal ...	17977	Can you (——) suggest anything instead
Epilogismo	17978	The only thing I (——) would suggest instead is (to)
Epilogue ...	17979	Unless you can suggest anything instead
Epimenis ...	17980	I (we) cannot suggest anything instead
Epinards ...	17981	Could —— come instead
Epineux ...	17982	If —— cannot come, send —— instead
Epinglette	17983	Instead of
Epinglier ...	17984	I (we) would suggest instead that
Epinicio ...	17985	To be used instead

Instruct

Epinoche ...	17986	
Epipactide	17987	To instruct
Epiplexis ...	17988	Instruct agent for
Epiplocele	17989	Please instruct
Epiqueya ...	17990	Please instruct —— to proceed as originally arranged
Episcopacy	17991	Is there time to instruct
Episcopado	17992	There is still time to instruct
Episodico ...	17993	There is no time to instruct
Epistilo ...	17994	Would suggest that you at once instruct
Epistolar ...	17995	You had better instruct
Epistolero	17996	Provided that you instruct me (us) to do so

Instructed

Epistolize	17997	
Epitafio ...	17998	Instructed to
Epitalamio	17999	Instructed by
Epitaphe ...	18000	Instructed on account of
Epitasis ...	**18001**	Not unless instructed
Epitetic ...	18002	Unless instructed to the contrary
Epithalame	18003	Has (have) instructed
Epithete ...	18004	Has (have) not instructed
Epitima ...	18005	Am I (are we) instructed to
Epitomized	18006	Consider yourself as instructed to

Epizootia ...	18007	If so instructed
Epluchage	18008	**Instruction(s)** (*See also* "Give," "Have," "Immediate.")
Epluchoir...	18009	Do you confirm ——'s instructions (to)
Epluchure	18010	Have received instructions from —— to
Epodo ...	18011	Supply —— with all needful instructions
Epointer ...	18012	Did you strictly obey instructions sent on ——
Epopeya ...	18013	Cable specific instructions to ——
Epoumoner	18014	Cable full instructions
Epouseur ...	18015	Cable if you have any instructions before
Epoussette	18016	Cable any instructions to await me at
Epouvanter	18017	Cable instructions direct to
Epriendre...	18018	As per your instructions
Eprouver ...	18019	Apply to —— for instructions
Epuisable...	18020	According to instructions
Epuisement	18021	Am (are) still without instructions
Epulon ...	18022	Cancel instructions
Epuration...	18023	Instructions cancelled
Equabile ...	18024	Do not act unless you have written instructions
Equamente	18025	Do not act upon instructions as given in (on)
Equanimita	18026	Do not act without positive instructions from him (——)
Equarrir ...	18027	Do not proceed without precise instructions
Equated ...	18028	Full instructions were mailed on ——
Equator ...	18029	Give full instructions to —— to ——
Equazione	18030	Give (send) written instructions to (for)
Equerry ...	18031	Have you any instructions as regards
Equestre ...	18032	Have no instructions as regards
Equestrian	18033	Have cabled —— to telegraph instructions direct to you
Equiangulo	18034	Have mailed instructions and reports to care of —— at ——
Equicrure...	18035	You must obey instructions
Equidad ...	18036	Refuse(s) to obey instructions
Equidistar	18037	Do not obey instructions
Equiform ...	18038	The following instructions must be followed
Equilatero	18039	Will strictly follow your instructions
Equilibrar	18040	Your instructions have been strictly followed
Equimentum	18041	Am (are) only waiting for your instructions
Equimosis	18042	Awaiting instructions
Equino ...	18043	Cannot await instructions
Equinoccio	18044	According to my (our) instructions
Equinoxial	18045	Wait for further instructions before you act
Equinozio...	18046	Wait instructions
Equipage ...	18047	Wait instructions mailed on ——
Equipaggio	18048	Notify to —— change of instructions
Equiparar	18049	Telegraph instructions direct to —— that he (they)
Equipoise...	18050	Have you (has ——) any further instructions
Equisonant	18051	Has (have) received instructions to ——. Please confirm
Equitacion	18052	Has (have) given full instructions
Equitare ...	18053	Instructions insufficient
Equitativo	18054	Instructions not sufficiently clear
Equitium ...	18055	Instructions received; shall proceed at once (to)
Equivaler ...	18056	Instructions arrived, but too late to be of use
Equivocado	18057	Instructions arrived, but —— had already left
Equivoke ...	18058	In the event of no further instructions being received
Eradicare ...	18059	Instructions have already been given to
Eraflure ...	18060	Let me have full instructions
Erasement	18061	No such instruction(s) was (were) given
Erbaccia ...	18062	Proceed the moment your instructions arrive
Erbajuolo...	18063	Proceed without further instructions
Erbaluccia	18064	Please adhere to instructions given
Erbarmlich	18065	What are your instructions
Erbato ...	18066	Will cable instructions

Erbauer	...	18067	Will meet you at —— with full instructions
Erbeben	...	18068	What instructions have you given ——
Erbetta	...	18069	Your instructions are being carried out
Erbetteln	...	18070	Your instructions cannot be carried out
Erbfahig	...	18071	Your instructions had already been attended to
Erbfolge	...	18072	Shall remain here up to —— for instructions
Erbitten	...	18073	Give —— full instructions to act upon during your absence
Erbittlich	...	18074	—— has received instructions
Erblassen	...	18075	—— has not received instructions
Erblicken	...	18076	Leave full instructions with ——
Erbluhen	...	18077	Send full instructions as to
Erbolajo	...	18078	Unless I find instructions awaiting me
Erbolina	...	18079	This has been done under instructions from
Erborare	...	18080	Am (are) awaiting your instructions as to
Erborgen	...	18081	I (we) await your further instructions at
Erbosetto	...	18082	I await your instructions at
Erbprinz	...	18083	Cable what specific instructions you require
Erbritter	...	18084	Since your previous instructions
Erbstuck	...	18085	As soon as instructions are to hand
Erbtheil	...	18086	I advise you to telegraph me (us) instructions to
Erbvertrag		18087	When may I (we) expect instructions
Erdapfel	...	18088	Explicit instructions mailed on ——
Erdbeere	...	18089	Further instructions will be sent you
Erdboden	...	18090	Have received your letter of instructions, and leave on —— for
Erdenkbar		18091	Have you given necessary instructions for
Erdenklich		18092	Instructions have been given to shut down
Erdgurtel	...	18093	Instructions have been given to re-start
Erdichten	.	18094	Instructions have been given to
Erdkorper		18095	Instructions have been given to him (them)
Erdkreis	...	18096	For instructions apply to
Erdmesser		18097	Had bought before receipt of your instructions
Erdolchen	...	18098	Had sold before receipt of your instructions
Erdreisten		18099	Then cable for instructions
Erdrosseln		18100	I (we) shall then cable for instructions
Erdstrich	...	18101	**Insurance** (See also "Assurance," "Buildings," "Damages," ["Policy.")
Erecha		18102	Insurance office admits claim
Erectness	...	18103	Insurance office disputes claim
Erector	...	18104	Insurance policy
Ereditario	...	18105	Have received insurance policy
Ereifern	...	18106	The insurance premium is
Ereigniss	...	18107	Covered by insurance
Ereinter	...	18108	Fire insurance
Eremigat	...	18109	In a good insurance office, —— preferred
Eremita	...	18110	Has (have) been paid by the insurance office
Eremitique		18111	Only —— was covered by insurance
Ererben	...	18112	The whole damage was covered by insurance
Eresiarca	...	18113	The insurance office refuses to pay until
Eresipele		18114	Take care that the insurance policies do not lapse
Eretaggio	...	18115	**Insure**
Ereticale	...	18116	How much shall I (we) insure for
Erezione	...	18117	At what rate can you insure
Erfahrung		18118	Can insure at —— per cent.
Erfinder	...	18119	Shall I (we) insure
Erflehen	...	18120	You had better insure
Erfordern	...	18121	**Insured**
Erforscher		18122	Are the buildings and plant insured
Erfreulich	...	18123	The buildings and plant are insured
Erfullung	...	18124	The buildings and plant are not insured
Erganzend		18125	The buildings and plant were insured for
Ergastolo	...	18126	The buildings and plant were not insured

Ergiessen ...	18127	Had better be insured at once, if not already done
Erglanzen	18128	Now insured
Ergotear ...	18129	Not insured
Ergoterie ...	18130	**Intend(s)**
Ergotzen ...	18131	To intend
Ergotzlich	18132	Intend(s) to
Ergrauen ...	18133	Intend to have
Ergreifen ...	18134	Do(es) not intend to have
Ergrimmen	18135	Evidently intends not to
Ergrunden	18136	What do you intend to do with regard to
Erguir ...	18137	Do not intend
Erhaben ...	18138	Do you intend
Erhaltung	18139	Ascertain what —— intends to do
Erhangen	18140	Do(es) not intend to come
Erhaschen	18141	Do(es) not intend to go
Erheblich	18142	**Intendant**
Erhebung...	18143	**Intense(ly)**
Erheitern ...	18144	**Intention(s)**
Erhenken ...	18145	Has (have) no intention (to)
Erheucheln	18146	Have altered my first intention
Erhitzung	18147	Appear(s) to have abandoned the intention (of)
Eriazo ...	18148	Do you abandon your intention
Ericera ...	18149	Do not abandon your intention
Ericetum ...	18150	Has (have) certainly not abandoned the intention (of)
Erigamini	18151	I (we) have not the slightest intention to
Erigendum	18152	Is it still your intention
Erigenza ...	18153	My present intention is still to
Erigeron ...	18154	Try and discover what is ——'s intention
Erigimur ...	18155	——'s intention appears to be
Erigir ...	18156	Cannot discover what his (their) intentions are
Erimanto ...	18157	What is (are) your intention(s)
Eringio ...	18158	My (our) intention(s) is (are)
Erinnern ...	18159	My only intention was to
Eriphias ...	18160	My first intention was to
Eripuit ...	18161	Unless you have already altered your intention
Erisimo ...	18162	—— disclaim(s) any such intention
Erisipela ...	18163	What are your present intentions as regards
Erizado ...	18164	**Intercept**
Erkalten ...	18165	**Intercepted**
Erkauflich	18166	Am suspicious that letters and cables have been intercepted
Erkennbar	18167	No doubt it has (they have) been intercepted
Erkennung	18168	Intercepted by (at)
Erklarbar...	18169	Should letters have been intercepted
Erklarung	18170	Take care letters are not intercepted
Erklettern	18171	**Intercepting**
Erklimmen	18172	**Interception**
Erklingen	18173	**Intercession**
Erkranken	18174	**Interchangeable**
Erkundigen	18175	**Interest(s)** (*See also* " Conflict.")
Erkunsteln	18176	In the interest of
Erlahmen...	18177	In the interest of all parties
Erlasslich	18178	Interest to be charged at bank rate
Erlaubniss	18179	Interest to be charged at —— above bank rate
Erlaucht ..	18180	Have you any interest at all
Erlautern ...	18181	I have personally no interest whatever
Erledigung	18182	Has (have) no interest at all
Erlehren ...	18183	One-half interest
Erlernbar ...	18184	One-third interest
Erleuchten	18185	One-fourth interest
Erlogen ...	18186	One-eighth interest

Erloschen...	18187	Would this be in my (our) interest
Erlosung ...	18188	I do not think it would be in our interest
Ermador ...	18189	I consider it would be greatly to your interest to
Ermahung	18190	I do not think it would be at all to your interest
Ermangeln	18191	I (we) have no personal interest whatever in it
Ermassigen	18192	I (we) have a very large personal interest
Ermellino	18193	My personal interest amounts to
Ermessen ...	18194	Our interest is to
Ermesslich	18195	What interest have you
Erminites ...	18196	What interest has (have) ——
Ermita ...	18197	Is (are) trying to acquire an interest
Ermitano ...	18198	I would suggest in the interest of all (that)
Ermitteln	18199	I consider might then pay —— per cent. interest
Ermorden	18200	Is willing to sell one-half of his interest for
Ermudung	18201	Is willing to sell one-third of his interest for
Ermunio ...	18202	Is willing to sell —— of his interest for
Ermuntern	18203	Interest at the rate of
Ermuthigen	18204	Interest per annum
Ernahrer ...	18205	—— per cent. per annum interest.
Ernennung	18206	Interest per
Erneuerung	18207	Might remain at —— per cent. per annum interest
Erniaria ...	18208	May I ask you to exercise your interest on my behalf
Ernsthaft ...	18209	May I ask you to exercise your interest on ——'s behalf
Ernstlich ...	18210	Owing to conflicting interests
Erntemonat	18211	Purchase ——'s interest for
Erntezeit ...	18212	Have purchased ——'s interest for
Eroberer ..	18213	Will undoubtedly pay good interest
Eroberung	18214	Will retain —— interest
Erodio ...	18215	Will take shares for —— of his interest
Eroessa ...	18216	Would you be disposed to take any interest
Eroffnung	18217	——'s interest amounts to
Erogation	18218	My (our) interests are
Erogatorio	18219	My interest consists of a commission of
Erosion ...	18220	I have no longer any interest whatever in
Erotema ...	18221	—— will act in the interest of
Erotesis ...	18222	Would not suffice to pay more than —— per cent. interest
Erotique ...	18223	Your interests are fully protected
Erotismo ...	18224	You may rely that I shall do my best in your interests
Erotomania	18225	Your duty would consist mainly in watching our interests
Erotylum ...	18226	I will represent your interests
Erpicare ...	18227	—— intends to part with his interest in
Erpicatojo	18228	—— has already parted with his interest in
Erpicht ...	18229	—— has already agreed to part with his interest in
Erpressen...	18230	**Interested**
Erproben ...	18231	Is (are) interested
Erquicken	18232	Interested party(ies)
Errabit ...	18233	**Interesting**
Errabundo	18234	**Interfere(s)**
Erradizo ...	18235	To interfere
Erramento	18236	Decline(s) to interfere
Errante ...	18237	Will interfere (if)
Errarent ...	18238	Will not interfere with
Erratico ...	18239	Will not interfere unless
Errationis	18240	Interfere with
Erravisti ...	18241	Interfere if you think it necessary
Erregbar ...	18242	Allow nothing to interfere with
Erregung ...	18243	May I (we) interfere
Erreichen...	18244	Do(es) not interfere
Errements	18245	Shall I (we) interfere
Errettung...	18246	I (we) think it would be well for you to interfere

Errichten ...	18247	Do not let —— interfere with
Erroneo ...	18248	If this will not interfere with
Erroraccio	18249	If they (it) do(es) not interfere
Erroretto ...	18250	I should suggest that you do not interfere
Errorone ...	18251	Has —— been trying to interfere
Errothen ...	18252	Has (have) been attempting to interfere
Ersattlich...	18253	To interfere with
Ersatzmann	18254	Will interfere with
Ersaufen ..	18255	Do not allow —— to interfere in the matter
Erschaffen	18256	**Interference**
Erscheinen	18257	Avoid interference from
Erschlagen	18258	Avoid any interference with
Erschopfen	18259	**Interfering**
Erschweren	18260	Caution —— against interfering
Ersehnen ...	18261	If it can be done without interfering (with)
Ersetzung	18262	It cannot be done without interfering (with)
Ersinnlich	18263	Cannot it be done without interfering (with)
Erspahen ...	18264	If it cannot be done without interfering (with)
Erstarrung	18265	Without interfering with
Erstaunen	18266	**Interim**
Erstechen...	18267	In the interim
Ersteigen ...	18268	Shall devote the interim to
Ersterben...	18269	It (this) can be done in the interim
Erstgeburt	18270	There is not time in the interim to do (this)
Erstlich ...	18271	**Interim Dividend (for)** *(See also* "Dividend.")
Erstreben...	18272	**Interlocutory**
Ersturmen	18273	**Intermediate**
Ertappen ...	18274	An intermediate level
Ertonen ...	18275	Intermediate level No.
Ertragen ...	18276	**Intermittent(ly)**
Ertraglich	18277	**Interpolate(d)**
Erubescent	18278	**Interruption**
Erubrigen	18279	Without interruption
Eructacion	18280	Cable any interruption
Eructar ...	18281	Continue without any interruption (to)
Eruderata...	18282	**Intersect**
Erudiebat...	18283	To intersect
Erudimento	18284	So as to intersect it
Erudition...	18285	We are not likely to intersect before ——
Erudito ...	18286	At what distance do you expect to intersect
Erudituli ...	18287	To intersect —— lode
Erumnoso	18288	We hope to intersect within the next ,—— feet
Erumperunt	18289	We have already passed the point where we hoped to intersect
Eruptions ..	18290	**Intersected**
Ervato ...	18291	As intersected by the —— level shows
Ervellada ...	18292	Have intersected
Ervilla ...	18293	Not yet intersected
Erwachen...	18294	Was intersected to-day (on ——)
Erwagung	18295	Which we supposed we had intersected
Erwahlen ...	18296	Nothing has been intersected as yet
Erwahnung	18297	The vein has been intersected by the shaft at a depth of
Erweckung	18298	**Intersection**
Erweislich	18299	To the intersection of
Erweitert ...	18300	To its intersection by
Erwerben ...	18301	**Interval**
Erwischen	18302	In the interval (between)
Erwurgen...	18303	During this interval
Erythinum	18304	So as to fill up the interval
Erythrosis	18305	**Interview**
Erzahlend	18306	Anxious for an interview

Erzahler ...	18307	Try and avoid an interview
Erzbisthum	18308	Will grant an interview
Erzdieb ...	18309	What took place at your interview with
Erzengel ...	18310	I (——) will represent your interests at interview
Erzeugbar	18311	Could settle nothing at interview owing to (absence of)
Erzeugerin	18312	Should suggest that you interview
Erzeugniss	18313	Have not been able to interview
Erzhaltiz ...	18314	I had an interview with —— on ——
Erzherzog	18315	Result of interview very satisfactory
Erziehen ...	18316	Result of interview not at all satisfactory
Erzittern ...	18317	So far nothing has resulted from interview
Erzketzer ...	18318	Was unable to come to any conclusion from interview
Erzscheln...	18319	We are to have another interview on
Erzspieler...	18320	**Intimate**
Erzurnen ...	18321	Please intimate to
Erzvater ...	18322	Will intimate this (it) to —— the first chance I have
Erzwingen	18323	**Intimated**
Esacerbare	18324	Have you (——) intimated
Esacords ...	18325	Has (have) intimated
Esagitare ...	18326	Has (have) not intimated
Esagono ...	18327	**Intimation**
Esalabile ...	18328	**Intimidated**
Esalamento	18329	Do not be intimidated
Esalazione	18330	**Into**
Esaldire ...	18331	Into the
Esaltatore	18332	Cannot go into
Esametro ...	18333	Change(s) into
Esamina ...	18334	Owing to the change into
Esangue ...	18335	Not yet into
Esanimare	18336	To go into
Esaparino...	18337	Will go into the matter
Esasperare	18338	**Intolerable(ly)**
Esattore ...	18339	**Intractable(ly)**
Esaudevole	18340	**Intricate(ly)**
Esaudire ...	18341	**Introduce(d)**
Esauditore	18342	**Introducing**
Esauribile...	18343	**Intrusive**
Esausto ...	18344	Intrusive rock
Esbaforido	18345	**Intrust(ed)**
Esbelteza ...	18346	**Invalid(ate)**
Esbelto ...	18347	Will possibly invalidate
Esbirro ...	18348	Conduct proposed will invalidate
Esblandia ..	18349	Course suggested will invalidate
Esbrouffe ...	18350	——'s opinion is that it will invalidate
Escabeau ..	18351	——'s opinion is that it will not invalidate
Escabechar	18352	**Invalidated**
Escabioso ..	18353	**Invariable(ly)**
Escabro ...	18354	**Invention** (*See also* " Patent.")
Escacho ...	18355	**Inventory**
Escadrille...	18356	Mail inventory of
Escadron ...	18357	Make complete inventory giving value of all plant
Escalade ...	18358	Sale valuation of inventory
Escalading	18359	As soon as inventory is complete
Escalador...	18360	With complete inventory attached
Escalante...	18361	According to inventory
Escalar ...	18362	As soon as inventory is to hand
Escaldado	18363	Inventory does not appear to include
Escaldrido	18364	Inventory must include
Esculeno ...	18365	Which were omitted from inventory
Escalentar	18366	Inventory does not include

Escaleta ...	18367	Inventory dated —— does not apparently include ——; please
Escalfador	18368	Send inventory of buildings, plant and stores [explain
Escalfar ...	18369	Send complete inventory showing
Escalin ...	18370	**Invest**
Escalofrio...	18371	To invest
Escaluna ...	18372	Do not invest
Escamada...	18373	Do not invest more than
Escamadura	18374	Do not invest further
Escamel ...	18375	Am (is) about to invest
Escamocho	18376	Would you advise me (us) to invest in it
Escamonda	18377	Invest on my account at once
Escamoso...	18378	I (we) will invest on your account
Escamotage	18379	Shall I (we) invest on your account
Escamotur	18380	Would advise you not to invest
Escampado	18381	Would advise you to invest
Escampette	18382	Will invest subject to your advice
Escamujar	18383	How much do you (does ——) propose to invest
Escandalar	18384	**Invested**
Escandallo	18385	Have you invested as requested
Escandecer	18386	Have invested
Escandia ...	18387	Have not invested
Escanero ...	18388	Have invested on your account
Escanilla ...	18389	There can be no return for the money invested until
Escanuelo ..	18390	**Investigate**
Escaparate	18391	To investigate
Escapement	18392	To thoroughly investigate
Escaping ...	18393	Investigate promptly
Escapo ...	18394	Not yet been able to investigate
Escapula ...	18395	Can you suggest reliable man to investigate
Escaque ..	18396	I (we) think —— would be a reliable man to investigate
Escaqueado	18397	**Investigated**
Escarabajo	18398	About to be investigated
Escaramuza	18399	Now being investigated
Escarapela	18400	Investigated on behalf of
Escarbot ...	18401	**Investigation** (*See also* "Committee," "Examination.")
Escarios ...	18402	Pending further investigation
Escarotico	18403	What is the result of your investigation
Escarpin ...	18404	After a searching investigation my report is
Escatile ...	18405	Instruct —— to make a thorough investigation
Eschalots ...	18406	After a thorough investigation —— reports that
Eschararum	18407	Make a searching investigation
Escharas ...	18408	Could not make any real investigation owing to
Escharotic .	18409	Result of investigation is (to)
Eschetta ...	18410	Result of investigation has confirmed suspicion(s)
Eschewed...	18411	Close investigation
Eschewing	18412	The investigation proves
Esciame ...	18413	Careful investigation and experiment
Escient ...	18414	Well worthy of investigation
Escifera ...	18415	Not worthy of investigation
Escimento	18416	Trying to stop investigation
Esclamare	18417	Will do all he (they) can to stop investigation
Esclandre...	18418	Investigation will assuredly disclose
Esclavage	18419	**Investment**
Escludente	18420	Good investment
Esclusione	18421	Bad investment
Escobarder	18422	A sound and profitable investment
Escoda ...	18423	Can you suggest anything to make it a good paying investment
Escodadero	18424	Do not regard it as a good investment
Escofieta ...	18425	Do not regard it as a promising investment
Escofinar ...	18426	I believe that it will eventually be a good investment

Escogedor	18427	I believe it will prove a bad investment
Escoger ...	18428	It would be a good investment if capital does (did) not exceed
Escogido ...	18429	**Invisible**
Escogitare	18430	**Invite(d)**
Escogriffe...	18431	**Invoice(s)**
Escolarina	18432	Invoice at
Escoliador	18433	Bill(s) of lading with invoice(s)
Escolimado	18434	Must be accompanied by Consular invoice
Escolimoso	18435	Must be specified in the invoice
Escolio ...	18436	Consular invoice mailed on
Escolta ...	18437	Invoice value
Escombra...	18438	Invoice was omitted in letter dated ——; will be mailed on
Escomenzar	18439	Invoice will follow
Escomerse	18440	Invoice was omitted in your letter dated ——
Escompter	18441	**Involve(s)**
Esconce ...	18442	It is likely to involve us in legal proceedings
Esconder ...	18443	It is not likely to involve us in legal proceedings
Escondidas	18444	Will involve us in legal proceedings
Escondite...	18445	To what extent will it involve us
Escondrijo	18446	It will involve us to the extent of
Escontrete	18447	Take care not to involve yourself (us)
Escoperas...	18448	To involve
Escopetero	18449	It (this) will involve
Escopeton	18450	So as not to involve
Escopette ...	18451	**Involved**
Escopir ...	18452	**Iron**
Escoplear...	18453	Bar iron
Escoplillo	18454	Round iron
Escorar ...	18455	Cast iron
Escorbuto	18456	Wrought iron
Escorchar...	18457	Iron castings
Escordia ...	18458	Sheet iron
Escorial ...	18459	Galvanized iron
Escorrozo...	18460	Corrugated sheet iron
Escorted ...	18461	Iron screens
Escorting ...	18462	Assay(s) —— per cent. metallic iron
Escorvador	18463	Is valueless as a deposit of iron ore
Escorzon ...	18464	Iron ore occurs within —— miles
Escotado ...	18465	Iron pyrites
Escotera ...	18466	Arsenical iron pyrites
Escotilla ...	18467	Carbonate of iron
Escotines ...	18468	Iron ore chimney
Escotista ...	18469	Spathic iron ore
Escotomia	18470	Magnetic oxide of iron
Escouade ...	18471	Owing to the oxidation of the iron
Escoznete	18472	Splendid deposit of iron ore
Escrevente	18473	**Irreconcilable**
Escriba ...	18474	**Irregular**
Escribania	18475	Has (have) ceased to be irregular
Escribir ...	18476	Has (have) become very irregular
Escrino ...	18477	The labour supply has become very irregular
Escriptura	18478	The shipments will be very irregular during the winter
Escritoir ...	18479	The lode has become very irregular
Escritura ...	18480	The deposit has become very irregular
Escrocon ...	18481	The walls have become very irregular
Escrofula...	18482	**Irregularity(ies)**
Escroquer...	18483	**Irrespective**
Escroto ...	18484	Irrespective of
Escrudinar	18485	**Irrigate(ion)**
Escrupulo	18486	**Irritate(d)**

Escrutador	18487	**Irritation**
Escrutimo	18488	**Is**
Escuadrar...	18489	Is (are) the
Escuadreo	18490	Is (are) not
Escuadron	18491	How is (are)
Escualo ...	18492	Is it
Escuba ...	18493	Is it a
Escuderage	18494	Is this not
Escuderear	18495	Is (are) very considerable
Escuderia...	18496	Is (are) very small
Escudete ...	18497	Is (are) very low
Escudilla ...	18498	Is (are) very high
Escuditon...	18499	Is everything all right
Escueto ...	18500	Everything is all right
Escueznar	18501	Is there any
Esculapio...	18502	Is (are) fully
Esculcar ...	18503	Is (are) good
Esculento...	18504	Is (are) my
Escullador	18505	Is (are) here
Escullirse...	18506	Is (are) quite
Esculpidor	18507	Is (are) however
Esculpir ...	18508	Is (are) about
Escultura...	18509	Is (are) in
Escupidera	18510	Is (are) now in (at)
Escupido ...	18511	Is (are) not very
Escupita ...	18512	Is of (from)
Escurar ...	18513	Is it best to
Escurecer ...	18514	What is it (there)
Escurina ...	18515	**Issue**
Escurrida...	18516	To issue
Escurrir ...	18517	New issue
Escusavel...	18518	Can then issue
Escutas ...	18519	Do not see how to bring matters to a satisfactory issue
Escutcheon	18520	Have not succeeded in bringing matters to a satisfactory issue
Escuyer ...	18521	So as to bring matters to a satisfactory issue
Esdrujulo...	18522	Must issue a circular to the shareholders
Esecilla ...	18523	Do not issue any circular until you have received letter
Esecrare ...	18524	Prior to the issue [dated ——
Esecutore...	18525	Propose to issue
Eseguire ...	18526	Suggest that you issue
Eselsohr ...	18527	Will have to issue
Esempio ...	18528	When do you propose to issue
Esemplare	18529	**Issued**
Esemprario	18530	Since issued
Esencia ...	18531	As issued
Esentato ...	18532	Have all the shares been issued
Esequiale...	18533	All the shares have been issued
Esercere ...	18534	Only a part of the shares have been issued
Esercitare...	18535	Has (have) issued
Esfacelado	18536	Has (have) not issued
Esfacelo ...	18537	None of the shares were issued
Esfera ...	18538	Issued as —— per share paid
Esferista ...	18539	**Issuing**
Esferoidal...	18540	**It**
Esfinge ...	18541	It is
Esfinter ...	18542	It is not
Esforzador	18543	If it is
Esforzar ...	18544	If it is not
Esfriador ...	18545	It does not appear probable
Esfumado ..	18546	It cannot be

Esgambete	18547	It might be
Esgarro ...	18548	It should not be done
Esgrafiar ...	18549	It should be done
Esgrima ...	18550	It will be all right
Esgrimidor	18551	It will take at least
Esguardar	18552	It is generally known
Esguazable	18553	I know nothing about it
Esguazo ...	18554	It does
Esgucio ...	18555	It does not
Esguince ...	18556	It is too
Esguizaro...	18557	It will be
Esibire ...	18558	It will not be
Esibitore ...	18559	Will it be
Esibitrice ...	18560	It will not
Esigibile ...	18561	Will it not
Esilarare ...	18562	**Item(s)** (*See also* " Expense.")
Esistere ...	18563	Each item
Esitabatur	18564	Specify each item
Esitabitis ...	18565	The various items of expense
Esitabondo	18566	**Itself**
Esitabunt...	18567	**J**
Esitamento	18568	**January**
Esitumus ...	18569	At the beginning of January
Esitandi ...	18570	About the middle of January
Esitato ...	18571	During the entire month of January
Esitatura ...	18572	For the entire month of January
Esitavero ...	18573	Last January
Esitavisti ...	18574	Next January
Esitazione	18575	Near the end of January
Esitemini ...	18576	First day of January
Esiziale ...	18577	Second day of January
Eslabon ...	18578	Third day of January
Esleidor ...	18579	Fourth day of January
Eslinga ...	18580	Fifth day of January
Eslora ...	18581	Sixth day of January
Esmalequen	18582	Seventh day of January
Esmalte ...	18583	Eighth day of January
Esmaltin ...	18584	Ninth day of January
Esmarchazo	18585	Tenth day of January
Esmarido ...	18586	Eleventh day of January
Esmerar ...	18587	Twelfth day of January
Esmerejon	18588	Thirteenth day of January
Esmerie ...	18589	Fourteenth day of January
Esmerilazo	18590	Fifteenth day of January
Esmoladera	18591	Sixteenth day of January
Esofago ...	18592	Seventeenth day of January
Esondare ...	18593	Eighteenth day of January
Esophagus	18594	Nineteenth day of January
Esopico ...	18595	Twentieth day of January
Esopon ...	18596	Twenty-first day of January
Esordire ...	18597	Twenty-second day of January
Esoribus ...	18598	Twenty-third day of January
Esormarer	18599	Twenty-fourth day of January
Esortativo	18600	Twenty-fifth day of January
Esotericus	18601	Twenty-sixth day of January
Esoterie ...	18602	Twenty-seventh day of January
Esoterism...	18603	Twenty-eighth day of January
Espabilar ...	18604	Twenty-ninth day of January
Espacement	18605	Thirtieth day of January
Espacer ...	18606	Thirty-first day of January

Espaciar ...	18607	January expenses amount to
Espacico ...	18608	January shipments amount to
Espacioso...	18609	**Jealous(ly)**
Espadachin	18610	**Jeopardize**
Espadador	18611	**Jeopardy**
Espadanada	18612	**Jig(s)**
Espadar ...	18613	The ore would jig
Espaderia...	18614	The ore would jig very well
Espadilla ...	18615	The ore would not jig
Espadita ...	18616	**Jigged**
Espadrapo	18617	Jigged ore
Espagirica	18618	How much ore have you jigged
Espagnol ...	18619	We have —— tons of jigged ore
Espais ...	18620	**Jiggers**
Espalda ...	18621	We have now —— jiggers employed on this ore
Espaldaron	18622	We could employ —— more jiggers
Espaldear ..	18623	Jiggers are being erected
Espaldon ...	18624	Shall complete erection of jiggers within next —— days
Espaldudo	18625	As soon as the erection of jiggers is completed
Espalera ...	18626	The jiggers are working satisfactorily
Espalier ...	18627	The jiggers are not working satisfactorily as yet
Espalmar ...	18628	**Jigging** (*See also* "Dressing.")
Espalto ...	18629	**Join**
Espanasca	18630	To join
Espandere	18631	Join me (us)
Espanolado	18632	Cannot join you owing to
Espantable	18633	Could you get —— to join
Espantador	18634	Refuse(s) to join
Espantajo...	18635	Could you get friends to join
Espantoso	18636	Will join
Esparagon	18637	Will you join
Esparavel...	18638	Cannot join
Esparceta ...	18639	Cannot join you before
Esparcido ...	18640	Do not join
Esparganio	18641	If you will join
Esparsion	18642	In case you do not care to join
Espartal ...	18643	In order to join
Espartena	18644	Might join
Esparteria	18645	How would it be if you were to join
Espartizal	18646	Name the extent to which you would be disposed to join
Espasmo ...	18647	Would you join the Board
Espatula ...	18648	Will join the Board
Espaviento	18649	Will you join to the amount of
Espavorido	18650	I believe it will be a good thing—Do you care to join ?
Especeria ...	18651	Join forces with
Especia ...	18652	Will you join me (us) in the purchase of
Especifico...	18653	Why did you not join
Especioso ...	18654	Cannot join on terms named
Espectable	18655	Will join on terms named
Espectador	18656	Cannot join on terms named in your letter dated ——
Espectro ...	18657	Willing to join —— in anything
Especular...	18658	Will be pleased to join with you to
Espedazar	18659	I will join you by
Espedirse ...	18660	Join issue (with)
Espeditivo	18661	Can you join me at ——
Espejado ...	18662	Can —— join me at ——
Espejeria ...	18663	I will join —— at —— on ——
Espejuela ..	18664	Can you name anyone who would join
Espelta ...	18665	**Joined**
Espelteo ...	18666	As I have joined

Espelunca	18667	Could the two concerns be joined
Espeluzar...	18668	Have already joined
Esperable ...	18669	If these could be joined
Esperador...	18670	Has (have) joined
Esperanza	18671	Has (have) not joined
Esperdecem	18672	**Joint**
Esperezo ...	18673	Joint account
Espergurar	18674	Joint owners of
Esperide ...	18675	Joint shareholders of
Esperiego...	18676	In our joint names
Esperlan ...	18677	At our joint expense
Esperma ...	18678	For our joint account
Espernada	18679	Not on joint account
Espernible	18680	Suggest joint action with
Esperonte...	18681	Have commenced joint action
Esperriaca	18682	**Journey**
Espesar ...	18683	How long would the journey take
Espesativo	18684	The entire journey occupies —— days
Espesura ...	18685	—— days' journey by rail and coach
Espetera ...	18686	—— miles' journey by rail (and ——)
Espetibile...	18687	—— miles' journey by coach
Espeton ...	18688	—— will give you full instructions as to the journey
Espettante	18689	Hope to continue my journey on ——
Esphacelar	18690	Have been delayed on the journey owing to
Espiacion ...	18691	Is now away on a journey
Espiador ...	18692	Journey direct to
Espibio ...	18693	The journey is difficult owing to
Espichar ...	18694	What would be the cost of the journey
Espichon ...	18695	You could journey with —— as far as ——
Espicular ...	18696	A very heavy journey
Espiegle ...	18697	**Judge**
Espigadera	18698	District judge
Espigado ...	18699	I (we) can only judge by
Espigon ...	18700	Not able to judge
Espiguilla	18701	Quite competent to judge
Espilatore	18702	Can judge thereby
Espillador	18703	Shall be able to judge thereby
Espilocho...	18704	**Judging**
Espinadura	18705	Judging from
Espinazo ...	18706	I (we) have no means of judging
Espinela ...	18707	In judging
Espingarda	18708	Judging by past experience
Espingole...	18709	**Judgment** (*See also* "Impossible," "Verdict.")
Espinoso ...	18710	Will abide by your judgment
Espionage	18711	Can you form any judgment as to
Espionner...	18712	Could not form any judgment as to
Espiote ...	18713	Have you formed any judgment as to
Espirable ...	18714	As far as I can form any judgment
Espiradero	18715	It is difficult to form any judgment owing to
Espiral ...	18716	Cannot form any judgment until
Espirante ..	18717	Cannot form any judgment owing to
Espirativo	18718	In whose favour is judgment given
Espirea ...	18719	The judgment is practically in our favour
Espirenque	18720	When do you expect judgment will be given
Espiritado	18721	Altogether uncertain when judgment will be given
Espiritar ...	18722	Judgment postponed
Espiritu ...	18723	Judgment will be given (on)
Espivia ...	18724	Judgment has been given in my (our) favour
Espivicion	18725	Judgment has been given against you (us)
Esplanade	18726	Judgment has been given against —— for ——

Esplayer ...	18727	Is the judgment likely to be set aside
Esplender ..	18728	So as to form a reliable judgment
Esplendido	18729	You must use your own judgment
Esplenico ...	18730	Left entirely to your judgment
Espletivo ...	18731	**Judicious(ly)** (*See also* " Expenditure.")
Espliego ...	18732	Very judicious
Esplinque	18733	Not at all judicious
Espolazo ...	18734	Judicious to
Espoleta ...	18735	Seems judicious to
Espolinado	18736	Yes, if you believe it to be judicious
Espolinar ...	18737	No, unless you believe it would be more judicious to
Espolique ...	18738	Act as soon as you judiciously can
Espolista ...	18739	As soon as you think it judicious
Espolvoro...	18740	Do you think this (it) would be judicious
Espondaico	18741	I do not think it would be very judicious (unless) (until)
Espondeo ...	18742	Would it be judicious now to
Esponente	18743	What increase do you think would be judicious
Esponjado	18744	**July**
Esponjar ...	18745	At the beginning of July
Esponjilla	18746	About the middle of July
Esponjoso	18747	During the entire month of July
Esponsales	18748	For the entire month of July
Espontaneo	18749	Last July
Esporadico	18750	Next July
Esportear ...	18751	Near the end of July
Esportilla ...	18752	First day of July
Esportula ...	18753	Second day of July
Esposado ...	18754	Third day of July
Espositivo	18755	Fourth day of July
Espoused ...	18756	Fifth day of July
Espousing	18757	Sixth day of July
Espremedor	18758	Seventh day of July
Espressivo	18759	Eighth day of July
Esprimere...	18760	Ninth day of July
Esprobare...	18761	Tenth day of July
Espuela ...	18762	Eleventh day of July
Espuenda ...	18763	Twelfth day of July
Espuesto ...	18764	Thirteenth day of July
Espulgador	18765	Fourteenth day of July
Espulgo ...	18766	Fifteenth day of July
Espumadera	18767	Sixteenth day of July
Espumajo...	18768	Seventeenth day of July
Espumante	18769	Eighteenth day of July
Espumarajo	18770	Nineteenth day of July
Espumero...	18771	Twentieth day of July
Espumilla...	18772	Twenty-first day of July
Espumoso...	18773	Twenty-second day of July
Espundia ...	18774	Twenty-third day of July
Espungere	18775	Twenty-fourth day of July
Espuntoria	18776	Twenty-fifth day of July
Espurgato	18777	Twenty-sixth day of July
Espurio ...	18778	Twenty-seventh day of July
Espuristes	18779	Twenty-eighth day of July
Esqueje ...	18780	Twenty-ninth day of July
Esquena ...	18781	Thirtieth day of July
Esquenanto	18782	Thirty-first day of July
Esquerro ...	18783	July expenses amount to
Esquicier ...	18784	July shipments amount to
Esquifada...	18785	**Jump**
Esquife ...	18786	To jump

Esquila ...	18787	To jump the claim(s)
Esquilador	18788	So as to frustrate any attempt to jump
Esquilmar	18789	Will endeavour to jump
Esquilmo ...	18790	**Jumped**
Esquilon ...	18791	Were jumped
Esquinado	18792	Have not been jumped
Esquinante	18793	Liable to be jumped
Esquinco ...	18794	**Jumpers**
Esquinzar...	18795	Have entered action against jumpers
Esquipado	18796	Have succeeded in my (our) action against jumpers
Esquipot ...	18797	Have not succeeded in my (our) action against jumpers
Esquisar ...	18798	**Junction**
Esquisito ...	18799	At the junction of
Esquisser ...	18800	From the junction of —— and ——
Esquiveza	18801	At the junction of the lodes
Essaimer ...	18802	Will probably make a junction
Essartage...	18803	In order to effect a junction with
Essayeur ...	18804	Have effected a junction between —— and ——
Essayist ...	18805	Have not been able to effect a junction between —— and ——
Essedarius	18806	On the —— side of the junction
Essedorum	18807	Within —— feet of junction
Essence ...	18808	**Juncture**
Essencing	18809	**June**
Essenszeit	18810	At the beginning of June
Essenziale	18811	About the middle of June
Essequio ...	18812	During the entire month of June
Essercito ...	18813	For the entire month of June
Essgier ...	18814	Last June
Essicante ...	18815	Next June
Essiggurke	18816	Near the end of June
Essigsaure	18817	First day of June
Essloffel ...	18818	Second day of June
Essoriller ...	18819	Third day of June
Esstisch ...	18820	Fourth day of June
Esswaare ...	18821	Fifth day of June
Establear ...	18822	Sixth day of June
Establecer	18823	Seventh day of June
Establillo ...	18824	Eighth day of June
Estaca ...	18825	Ninth day of June
Estacion ...	18826	Tenth day of June
Estacte ...	18827	Eleventh day of June
Estadel ...	18828	Twelfth day of June
Estadista ...	18829	Thirteenth day of June
Estadizo ...	18830	Fourteenth day of June
Estadojo ...	18831	Fifteenth day of June
Estafermo	18832	Sixteenth day of June
Estafeta ...	18833	Seventeenth day of June
Estafetil ...	18834	Eighteenth day of June
Estafier ...	18835	Nineteenth day of June
Estafilea ..	18836	Twentieth day of June
Estafiloma	18837	Twenty-first day of June
Estajero ...	18838	Twenty-second day of June
Estalacion	18839	Twenty-third day of June
Estalage ...	18840	Twenty-fourth day of June
Estalingar	18841	Twenty-fifth day of June
Estallar ...	18842	Twenty-sixth day of June
Estallido ...	18843	Twenty-seventh day of June
Estambor ...	18844	Twenty-eighth day of June
Estambrado	18845	Twenty-ninth day of June
Estambre ...	18846	Thirtieth day of June

Estamena...	18847	June expenses amount to
Estamento	18848	June shipments amount to
Estamnete	18849	**Jurassic**
Estampador	18850	**Jurisdiction**
Estampar ...	18851	Comes under the jurisdiction of
Estampero	18852	Is not under the jurisdiction of
Estampida	18853	**Jury**
Estampilla	18854	Jury trial
Estancar ...	18855	Special jury
Estanciero	18856	Endeavour to get case tried by a jury
Estandarte	18857	The case will be tried by a jury
Estandista	18858	Endeavour to prevent case being tried by a jury
Estanque...	18859	The case will not be tried by a jury
Estanquito	18860	Jury have disagreed. Shall require to have a fresh trial which
Estante ...	18861	Owing to absence on a jury [will commence about
Estanterol	18862	The verdict of the jury is (was)
Estantigua	18863	**Just**
Estaquero	18864	Has (have) just
Estaquida	18865	Is certainly not just
Estarcido ...	18866	Just now
Estarna ...	18867	Just finished
Estaroste ...	18868	Just commenced
Estarostia	18869	Just arrived
Estatera ...	18870	Just complete
Estatico ...	18871	Just completed erection of
Estatuder...	18872	Just completed opening up
Estatura ...	18873	Just too late
Estatuto ...	18874	Just in time
Esteatomo	18875	Just to hand
Estebar ...	18876	Not just now
Esteemed ...	18877	Your cable just to hand
Esteeming	18878	Your instructions just to hand
Estegnosis	18879	Your —— just to hand
Estelaria ...	18880	Have just heard that
Estelifero ...	18881	**Justice**
Estelina ...	18882	In justice to all parties concerned
Estelion ...	18883	If justice is done to all parties concerned
Estemporal	18884	Doing justice to all parties concerned
Estendere...	18885	**Justification**
Estensivo ...	18886	**Justified** (*See also* "Expenditure.")
Estentorea	18887	Was (were) justified
Estenuare...	18888	Was (were) not justified
Estepilla ...	18889	Was —— justified
Estercolar...	18890	Do you think I am (we are) justified
Estercuelo	18891	I consider you are justified
Esterero ...	18892	I do not think you are justified
Esteriore ...	18893	I consider we are justified
Esterlin ...	18894	I do not think I am (we are) justified
Esterminio	18895	We should then be justified
Esterquero	18896	You are certainly justified
Estevado ...	18897	You would then be justified
Estezador...	18898	**Justify**
Esthetic ...	18899	In order to justify expenditure of
Estibia ...	18900	How do you propose to justify
Estigio ...	18901	If I am (we are) to justify
Estilito ...	18902	**K**
Estimably	18903	**Keen(ly)**
Estimador	18904	**Keep(ing)** (*See also* "Expenditure.")
Estimateur	18905	To keep
Estimativa	18906	To keep out

Estimular...	18907	Do not keep
Estincion ...	18908	Do not keep back
Estinguere	18909	Shall not keep
Estiomenar	18910	Keep cool
Estipendio	18911	Keep it (this)
Estipite ...	18912	Will keep it (this)
Estipticar...	18913	I (we) will keep you well informed
Estirajar ...	18914	Keep on as long as you can
Estiron ...	18915	Shall keep a few hands at
Estirpare ...	18916	Shall keep —— men at
Estirpe	18917	Keep —— with you
Estitivo ...	18918	Will it keep until
Estitiquez	18919	You had better keep it (this) to yourself for the present
Estiva ...	18920	Keep a sharp look-out for
Estivacion	18921	Keep a watch on
Estivale ...	18922	Will keep a watch on
Estocada ...	18923	Keep this (it) quiet if possible
Estocapris	18924	Keep all information from —— if possible
Estocar ...	18925	Do not keep anything back from
Estofador...	18926	Will not keep anything back from
Estoglia ...	18927	Will keep —— in the dark as much as I (we) can
Estogliere...	18928	Do your best to keep it down
Estoicismo	18929	Keep me (us) secure
Estoico ...	18930	Will keep you secure
Estolidez ...	18931	Keep within limits named
Estollenza	18932	Cannot keep within limits named
Estollere ...	18933	Will keep within limits named
Estolon ...	18934	Keep away from
Estomacal	18935	Will keep away from
Estomagazo	18936	Do not keep away from
Estomago	18937	There is no need to keep
Estomper ...	18938	Keep down cost as much as you can
Estopeno ...	18939	Will keep down cost as much as I (we) can
Estoperol ...	18940	Keep me (us) well posted up
Estopilla ...	18941	Will keep you well posted up
Estopin ...	18942	Keep me (us) well posted up of any change in the mine
Estoppels ...	18943	Will keep you well posted up of any change in the mine
Estopuer ...	18944	Keep me advised of changes in quotations
Estoraque...	18945	Will keep you advised of changes in quotations
Estorbador	18946	Keep me well informed as to prices
Estorcer ...	18947	Will keep you well informed as to prices
Estormente	18948	Keep this to yourself absolutely
Estornija ...	18949	Will keep information strictly private
Estornudar	18950	Keep up shipments as long as weather permits
Estorquere	18951	Will keep up shipments as long as weather permits
Estorta ...	18952	Keep me well informed as to your movements
Estotro ...	18953	Will keep you well informed as to my movements
Estrabismo	18954	Keep information out of papers as much as you can
Estrabo ...	18955	Will keep information out of papers as much as I (we) can
Estraccion	18956	Keep buying
Estracilla ...	18957	Keep on buying. Advise me daily how much (many) you have [bought
Estractar ...	18958	Keep selling
Estrada ...	18959	Keep on selling. Advise me daily how much (many) you have [sold
Estradiota	18960	Keep to the facts
Estragador	18961	Cannot keep water below
Estragar ...	18962	How long can you keep on at this rate
Estragon ...	18963	Cannot keep on
Estrambote	18964	I (we) hope to keep on for the present
Estramonio	18965	Cannot keep —— out
Estraneo ...	18966	Do your best to keep him (——) out

Estranging	18967	Do not keep offer open any longer
Estrangol ...	18968	Endeavour to keep good friends with
Estrapado...	18969	**Kept**
Estrategia	18970	Must be kept
Estratiote...	18971	To be kept
Estrave ...	18972	Will be kept
Estrechar ...	18973	Is (are) being kept
Estrecho ...	18974	Has (have) not been kept
Estrechura	18975	No accounts have been kept
Estrella	18976	The accounts as kept are useless
Estrellera...	18977	Has —— been kept in the dark
Estrellon ...	18978	—— has been kept in the dark
Estremecer	18979	Mean(s) —— to be kept entirely in the dark
Estremiche	18980	This information cannot be kept too private
Estremita	18981	Offer cannot be kept open after
Estrena ...	18982	Offer can be kept open until
Estrenido ...	18983	Have kept you well posted up
Estrenir ...	18984	Have kept —— (him) well posted up
Estrenque	18985	**Keuper**
Estrepito ...	18986	**Kibble**
Estriar ...	18987	Kibble filler(s)
Estribador	18988	What is the capacity of kibble
Estribera ...	18989	Ought to have a kibble of —— capacity
Estriberon	18990	The kibble has a capacity of —— pounds
Estribillo ...	18991	Have ordered a new kibble
Estribor ...	18992	Now lifting water with the kibble
Estricia ...	18993	Send outside dimensions of kibble
Estricibus...	18994	**Killas**
Estricote ...	18995	**Killed** (*See also* " Accident.")
Estricto ...	18996	No one killed
Estrige ...	18997	No one killed as far as I can ascertain
Estringer ...	18998	Cable names and particulars of men killed
Estrinseco	18999	The following persons were killed
Estrix ...	19000	Has any one been killed
Estrofa ..	**19001**	Is (are) said to have been killed ; cable whether true
Estropeado	19002	**Kiln(s)**
Estropeo ...	19003	**Kind(s)**
Estropiezo	19004	What kind do you (does ——) want
Estrovito ...	19005	What kind of —— will be needed
Estrovo ...	19006	Might send a few of each kind
Estrudere...	19007	—— know(s) exactly the kind required
Estruendo	19008	What kind of
Estruir ...	19009	Consists mainly of a kind of
Estrujar ...	19010	A kind of
Estrutto ...	19011	Is of a very poor kind
Estuacion	19012	First class kind
Estuante ...	19013	How many kinds
Estuaries ...	19014	There are all kinds of
Estuary ...	19015	The only kinds we have here are
Estucador...	19016	Exceedingly kind
Estuche ...	19017	Is (was) exceedingly kind
Estudiador	19018	Is it (this) the kind you want
Estudiante	19019	**Kindness(es)**
Estudiar ...	19020	**Knew**
Estudioso	19021	No one knew
Estufero ...	19022	Was the only one who knew
Estufilla ...	19023	**Know(ing)**
Estulticia...	19024	To know
Estulto ...	19025	Do you (does ——) know
Estuosidad	19026	As soon as you know

Estuoso ...	19027	As soon as I (we) know
Estupendo	19028	Do not know
Estupidez...	19029	Do you know that
Estupido ...	19030	I (we) know
Estuprador	19031	I (we) know all about it
Estuprar ...	19032	I (we) know nothing about it
Estuque ...	19033	You shall know about it
Esturion ...	19034	We know of parties here who are willing to
Esuberanza	19035	Let me (us) know
Esula ...	19036	Do not let —— know
Esulcerare	19037	Do not let anyone know of the business
Esuriatur ...	19038	Do you think —— would know anything
Esuriebant	19039	—— does not know anything
Esurietis ...	19040	Do not fail to let us know the moment you can
Esurimini...	19041	Must let me (us) know not later than
Esuriverat	19042	Do not expect to know before
Esurivisti ...	19043	Did not know anything about it
Etablage ...	19044	Let us know by wire
Etabliren ...	19045	You can let us know by mail
Etagere ...	19046	Let me (us) know the worst
Etalagiste...	19047	I (we) expect to know about
Etalier ...	19048	I (we) know for certain
Etalonnage	19049	Know(s) a good deal
Etalonner...	19050	Know(s) practically nothing
Etambot ...	19051	—— knows a good deal. Try to induce him to speak
Etamure ...	19052	Know(s) nothing of the suitability of
Etancher ...	19053	Professed not to know anything of it
Etanconner	19054	Really know(s)
Etayer ...	19055	All I (we) know is that
Etching ...	19056	The only thing I (we) know is that
Eteignoir ...	19057	When shall you know
Etendard ...	19058	Do you know whether
Etendre ...	19059	When can you manage to let us (——) know
Eternal ...	19060	You ought to know
Eternidad...	19061	Cannot know until
Eterniza ...	19062	When can I (we) know as to
Eternuer ...	19063	Expect to know
Eteroclito...	19064	Should know
Eterogeneo	19065	I do not know anything of him
Etesian ...	19066	I do not know anything of his suitability for
Ethereal ...	19067	I do not know anything of the value of
Ethique ...	19068	Do you know any reason why
Ethnical ...	19069	Do not know any reason why
Ethnicarum	19070	The only reason I know of, is
Ethnicas ...	19071	No one knows
Ethnico ...	19072	Know(s) nothing as yet
Ethnology	19073	Practically everyone knows
Ethologia ..	19074	Let me (us) know what has taken place in
Ethologos...	19075	Let me (us) know immediately
Etiamsi ...	19076	Let me (us) know as soon as you can
Etiamtum	19077	I (we) require to know
Etichetta ...	19078	Arrange to let me (us) know during your absence
Etimologia	19079	Do you know —— (him)
Etinceler ...	19080	Do you know sufficient of —— to make a report
Etiolate ...	19081	Do not know sufficient
Etiolement	19082	I know all about the former
Etiopeno ...	19083	I know all about the latter
Etiopide ..	19084	I know sufficient about the former to draw up a report
Etiqueta ...	19085	I know sufficient about the latter to draw up a report
Etiquetero	19086	**Knowledge**

Etites	19087	Has —— (he) a good knowledge of
Etliche	19088	—— has a good knowledge of
Etoffer	19089	Great practical knowledge and experience
Etonnement	19090	Is it within your knowledge that
Etopea	19091	Has (have) just come to my knowledge
Etouffade	19092	It has just come to my knowledge that
Etouffe	19093	Owing to this knowledge
Etouffoir	19094	Owing to this knowledge I (we) must
Etoupille	19095	Very little practical knowledge
Etourderie	19096	Has (have) not the slightest knowledge of
Etourneau	19097	Is it within your knowledge (that)
Etrangleur	19098	It is not within my knowledge
Etreinte	19099	Have you sufficient knowledge to (for)
Etrenner	19100	Have no personal knowledge of —— (him)
Etrique	19101	**Known**
Etriviere	19102	Has (have) been known to me (us) since
Etroit	19103	Is it known generally that
Etrurieno	19104	It is not known at all
Etudiant	19105	It is well known
Etuvement	19106	Is well known here
Etymology	19107	Is well known to me (us)
Etymon	19108	Is not well known to me (us)
Eubolia	19109	Nothing is known here
Eucalyptus	19110	Practically nothing is known yet
Eucharist	19111	Is (are) not known to me (us)
Euchlorine	19112	Do not let this be known
Eucologio	19113	Scarcely known yet
Eucrasia	19114	Very little is really known yet
Eucratico	19115	Not known by anybody
Eudiometry	19116	Known by everybody
Euerig	19117	—— is well known as a man of much ability [and character
Eufonia	19118	Is —— of —— favourably known to you for mining ability
Euforbio	19119	**L**
Eufrasia	19120	**Labour**
Eulogist	19121	What is (are) the labour cost(s)
Eunuco	19122	Labour cost alone is
Euonymus	19123	For labour alone
Eupatoria	19124	Labour is dear
Eupepsy	19125	Labour is scarce
Euphonique	19126	The labour is mainly
Euphony	19127	All white labour must be imported
Euphuism	19128	A plentiful supply of labour can be obtained on the spot
Euripo	19129	A plentiful supply of labour could be imported (from)
Euritmia	19130	In addition the labour is costly and supply poor
Eurythmy	19131	The labour is good and cheap
Euthanasy	19132	The labour is of a very poor class [labour
Eutimia	19133	The climate does not permit of the employment of much white
Eutiquiano	19134	White labour is plentiful and averages —— per week
Eutrapelia	19135	Supply of labour is limited [and stop all work
Evacuante	19136	Apply for extension of labour contracts for three to six months
Evacuar	19137	Shall I (we) apply for extension of labour covenants
Evacuativo	19138	**Labourers**
Evadingly	19139	Labourers at present on strike
Evadir	19140	Great dearth of labourers owing to
Evagacion	19141	**Lack(s)**
Evanescer	19142	Still lacks
Evangelio	19143	Lacks tact enough for
Evangile	19144	From lack of
Evanouir	19145	**Ladder(s)**
Evaporable	19146	Destroying the ladder way

Evaporar ...	19147	In order to repair the ladder ways
Evaporizar	19148	Owing to the ladder ways being destroyed
Evehente ...	19149	The ladder ways are good
Evellere ...	19150	The ladder ways are unsafe
Evensong ...	19151	**Laminated**
Eventaire ...	19152	**Land**
Eventilor ...	19153	Forest land
Eventrer ...	19154	Of farming land valued at —— per acre
Eventual ...	19155	Of grazing land valued at —— per acre
Evergreen...	19156	The total area of the land is —— acres
Evicting ...	19157	The land surrounding the mine
Eviction ...	19158	Can secure necessary land
Evidemment	19159	Land adjacent
Evidencia	19160	**Landed** (*See also* " Goods.")
Evigilatus	19161	I landed on
Evilassa ...	19162	Landed here at
Evincer ...	19163	Has (have) all been landed
Evirati ...	19164	Not yet been landed
Eviscerare	19165	Have been landed and passed through customs
Evitable ...	19166	Have been landed but are delayed by customs
Evitado ...	19167	Will be landed and forwarded to mine as quickly as possible
Evitation ...	19168	**Landing**
Evitatore ...	19169	Now engaged landing
Eviterno ...	19170	Shall have finished landing on
Evocar ...	19171	Shall commence landing on
Evocation...	19172	Have finished landing and shall commence transportation on
Evolution	19173	At the landing station No. —— level
Evoquer ...	19174	When do you expect to finish landing
Evulsion ...	19175	**Lapse(s)**
Ewigkeit ...	19176	About to lapse
Ewiglich ...	19177	Must not be allowed to lapse
Exaceratus	19178	Policy(ies) was (were) allowed to lapse
Exacteur ...	19179	Otherwise will lapse
Exaction ...	19180	Will lapse on
Exactitude	19181	**Large**
Exactness...	19182	How large
Exactor ...	19183	Is (are) large
Exagerador	19184	If not sufficiently large
Exagerar ...	19185	If too large
Exagogicus	19186	Large supply of
Exaltacion	19187	Large delivery(ies)
Exaltar ...	19188	Large shipment(s)
Exaltatus ...	19189	Large sales by
Exaltingly	19190	Anticipate large sales
Examen ...	19191	Do you think this large enough
Examinador	19192	Is (are) quite large enough
Examinatus	19193	Not large enough
Examiniren	19194	Too large altogether
Examitum	19195	Will this (it) be large enough
Examurco...	19196	As large as you can
Examussim	19197	Is not at all large
Exancillor	19198	Not so large as you think
Exanclo ...	19199	On a large scale
Exangulo ...	19200	Large body of good ore
Exanimalis	19201	Large body of ore but low grade
Exarar ...	19202	Large body of ore but will not pay to ship
Exarcado ...	19203	Large flood of water
Exasperado	19204	Large purchases are being made for
Exaucement	19205	Was a large producer in times gone by
Exaudible...	19206	Is at present time a large producer

Excantavi...	19207	**Largely**
Excavar ...	19208	Have been largely worked for
Excavillo ...	19209	Is largely composed of
Excedente	19210	The total is largely made up of
Exceder ...	19211	Very largely
Excelencia	19212	Will largely increase
Excelsior ...	19213	Has bought largely
Excelsitud	19214	Is buying largely
Excentrico	19215	**Larger**
Excepcion...	19216	Or larger if possible
Exceptar ...	19217	On no account larger
Exceptivo...	19218	A little larger would not matter
Excerta ...	19219	**Largest**
Excesivo ...	19220	**Last**
Exchequer	19221	To last
Excidio ...	19222	Will not last
Exciper ...	19223	Will last about
Excisa ...	19224	Last time
Excision ...	19225	Last report was
Excitable ...	19226	Last about
Excitar ...	19227	I (we) think will last about
Excitateur	19228	Can you make it (this) last until
Excitativo	19229	At present rate will last another —— days
Excitingly	19230	Cannot make it last beyond
Exclamator	19231	How long can you make it last
Excluir ...	19232	Will try and make it last
Exclusiva ...	19233	Cannot last very much longer
Exclusurus	19234	Estimate will last us about
Excogitans	19235	The last shipment of ore was
Excomulgar	19236	The last shipment of bullion was
Excomunion	19237	What was the number of the last car load shipped
Excrecion...	19238	Will probably be the last this season
Excremento	19239	**Late**
Excretar ...	19240	Of late
Excretoria	19241	Too late
Excrex ...	19242	Will be too late
Excusador	19243	Was (were) too late for
Excusar ...	19244	Cable whether this is (will be) too late
Execrador	19245	It is not too late
Execrando	19246	Is this (it) too late
Execrated...	19247	It is too late
Execration	19248	Before it is too late
Executant	19249	Otherwise will be too late
Exegesis ...	19250	**Lately**
Exegetical	19251	Just lately
Exegetico ...	19252	**Later**
Exemplaris	19253	Later in the season
Exempted...	19254	Later news is to the effect (that)
Exencion ...	19255	Later reports state
Exento ...	19256	Know(s) nothing later
Exequialis	19257	Can you give me (us) a later date than
Exequible...	19258	Cannot give you a later date than
Exequies ...	19259	Have nothing later to offer
Exercitium	19260	Later in the year
Exergo ...	19261	Not later than
Exfoliar ...	19262	Will be later than expected
Exhalable...	19263	Want something later
Exhalacion	19264	**Lateral**
Exhalador	19265	**Laterally**
Exhalaison	19266	Proceeding laterally

Exhausser	19267	**Latest**
Exhausto ...	19268	What is your latest news respecting
Exheredar	19269	The latest is
Exhibicion	19270	Is —— the latest you (——) can give
Exhibir ...	19271	And the latest
Exhortador	19272	At the latest
Exhortar ...	19273	The latest information
Exhumar ...	19274	The latest information is more favourable
Exicial ...	19275	The latest information is not so favourable
Exido ...	19276	**Law(s)**
Exigeant ...	19277	Avoid law if you possibly can
Exigencia...	19278	According to law
Exigidero...	19279	Contrary to law
Exiguidad	19280	In accordance with the mining laws of this State
Exiguo ...	19281	So as to comply with the laws
Eximicion...	19282	**Lawsuit**
Eximio ...	19283	Are determined to bring on a lawsuit
Exinanido...	19284	Endeavour to prevent a lawsuit if possible
Existencia	19285	Have commenced a lawsuit against me (us)
Existente ...	19286	Have commenced a lawsuit against
Existimar...	19287	Have no ground at all for a lawsuit
Existir ...	19288	To obtain a clear title will involve a lawsuit
Exodo ...	19289	**Lawyer(s)** (*See also* "Solicitor.")
Exonerar ...	19290	Can you recommend a reliable lawyer who would undertake
Exorable ...	19291	Is a (are) thoroughly competent lawyer(s)
Exorbitant	19292	As soon as you have had a lawyer's opinion on the title
Exorcism ...	19293	Lawyer(s) is (are) now examining titles
Exorcista ...	19294	Lawyers are quite satisfied with titles
Exorcizar ...	19295	Lawyers are not yet satisfied with titles
Exordial ...	19296	Do lawyers advise you (us) to
Exornacion	19297	Lawyers do not advise
Exornar ...	19298	What do(es) lawyer(s) advise
Exoticism...	19299	Lawyer(s) advise(s)
Exotique ...	19300	Employ a lawyer
Exotose ...	19301	Will employ a lawyer
Expalmado	19302	Is it necessary to employ a lawyer
Expansible	19303	It is very necessary to employ a lawyer
Expansion	19304	It is not necessary to employ a lawyer
Expatriar...	19305	I am (we are) employing a lawyer
Expavesco	19306	In the opinion of my (our) lawyer
Expectorar	19307	Consult a thoroughly competent lawyer
Expedicion	19308	See lawyer and make the best arrangement you can
Expedido ...	19309	Consult lawyer and commence action
Expedir ...	19310	See lawyer and be governed by his advice
Expediteur	19311	Matter is now in lawyer's hands
Expeditus...	19312	Who is the most eminent lawyer here
Expeler ...	19313	**Lay(s)**
Expeliente	19314	Which lay(s)
Expendedor	19315	This (it) lays
Expender ...	19316	Lay one over the other
Expending	19317	Lay one against the other
Expertise ...	19318	Lay somewhat inclined
Experto ...	19319	**Layer(s)**
Expiable ...	19320	An overlying layer of
Expiandus	19321	A layer of ——, —— feet thick
Expiativo ...	19322	Between layers of
Expiatory...	19323	Made up of layers of —— alternating with ——
Explanar ...	19324	To strip off the layer of overburden
Expletivus	19325	I am (we are) now sinking through a layer of
Expletus ...	19326	**Laying**

Explicar ...	19327	Laying over against
Explicatif	19328	**Lead**
Explicito ...	19329	Carbonate of lead
Expliquer ...	19330	Lead ore
Exploded ...	19331	Lead and zinc ore
Exploding	19332	Oxide and carbonate ores of lead
Exploiteur	19333	Of lead ore " dressed "
Explorador	19334	Carbonate of lead carrying —— ozs. of silver
Expolicion	19335	Argentiferous lead ore
Exposito ...	19336	Assaying —— per cent. of lead but has no value for silver
Exposure ...	19337	Assaying —— ozs. of silver
Expound ...	19338	Antimonial lead
Expremijo	19339	Soft pig lead [silver per ton of 2,000 lbs.
Expresar ...	19340	The lead ore assays —— per cent. of lead and —— ozs. of
Expresivo...	19341	The lead ore carries —— per cent. of copper and —— per cent.
Exprimable	19342	What is the market price for lead [of zinc
Exprimido	19343	The market price for lead is
Exproprier	19344	**Leads**
Expuens ...	19345	The lead has now been proved to extend for a distance of
Expugnable	19346	What is the actual known length and width of lead
Expugnador	19347	The lead has been proved for a length of —— average width—
Expugning	19348	The lead is reported to be entirely worked out
Expulsar ...	19349	**Leader(s)**
Expulsivo...	19350	A leader of
Expultriz ...	19351	**Leading**
Expungir ...	19352	Leading from
Exputaris ...	19353	Leading to
Exsiccant ...	19354	**Learn**
Extasis ...	19355	From whom did you (——) learn
Extatique...	19356	I (we) learn from a reliable source that
Extempore	19357	Endeavour to learn
Extendedor	19358	Can only learn
Extendeth	19359	If you learn anything
Extendido	19360	Expect(s) to learn
Extenuado	19361	From what I (we) can learn
Exterieur ...	19362	Learn as much as you can
Exterminar	19363	You will probably learn from ——
Externo ...	19364	You will probably learn a good deal from —— about
Exterritus	19365	From what I can learn there will soon be a move in
Extinctus ...	19366	From what I can learn I advise you to ——
Extinguir...	19367	**Learnt**
Extinto ...	19368	Have you (has ——) learnt
Extirpador	19369	Has (have) learnt
Extispex ...	19370	Has (have) not learnt
Extollens ...	19371	Have learnt the same thing from several people
Extolling ...	19372	**Lease** (*See also* " Condition.")
Extorreo ...	19373	To lease
Extorridus	19374	Extend lease on
Extorsion...	19375	Expect to lease
Extortus ...	19376	Get lease
Extractivo	19377	Get lease for
Extractus...	19378	Get lease on
Extradited	19379	Did you get lease
Extraente...	19380	Did not lease
Extraer ...	19381	Did they lease
Extranar ...	19382	Lease continues for
Extraneza...	19383	Secure lease
Extrangero	19384	Can you secure lease on
Extravaser	19385	Can secure lease on
Extraviar ...	19386	Cannot secure lease on

Extremadas	19387	Consent(s) to grant lease if
Extremar ...	19388	Decline(s) to grant lease on any terms
Extremidad	19389	What is the length of lease
Extremis ...	19390	Would he (they) be willing to extend lease
Extremoso	19391	Is (are) willing to extend lease for
Extrusion...	19392	Is (are) not willing to extend lease
Exuberante	19393	Are said to be only waiting for lease to expire
Exuberar ...	19394	Forfeiture of lease
Exudated ...	19395	Is a government lease [general terms
Exultacion	19396	Is willing to grant a lease for —— year(s) on the following
Exultant ...	19397	Is willing to renew lease for —— years on payment of
Exustion ...	19398	Owing to the lease having expired
Exutionem	19399	The agreement should contain a clause for renewal of lease
Exvoto ...	19400	Take good care that all the conditions of the lease are complied [with
Eyeball ...	19401	Will not renew lease
Eyebrow ...	19402	Will renew lease for same terms and conditions
Eyeglass ...	19403	When does ——'s lease expire
Eyeless ...	19404	Lease expires on
Eyesore ...	19405	Shall I (we) give notice in writing to terminate lease
Eyetooth ...	19406	Do you advise my (our) giving notice to terminate lease
Exiandio ...	19407	Have you given notice in writing to terminate lease
Ezquerdear	19408	Have not given notice to terminate lease
Fabacrasa...	19409	Have given notice to terminate lease
Fabataria...	19410	I gave notice to terminate lease on —— last
Fabbricare	19411	**Leased**
Fabbricato	19412	Leased until
Fabbricone	19413	Leased to
Fabbrile ...	19414	**Leasehold**
Fabelhaft...	19415	**Least**
Fabeln ...	19416	Which is the least
Fabled ...	19417	Is the least
Fablian ...	19418	The least of
Fabordon ...	19419	With the least delay
Fabricador	19420	On the least opportunity
Fabricante	19421	**Leat**
Fabriciren	19422	Water leat
Fabrics ...	19423	Breakage of leat
Fabriella ...	19424	**Leave(s)**
Fabrikat ...	19425	To leave
Fabrikherr	19426	Can leave to
Fabriliter ...	19427	Get leave of absence
Fabriquero	19428	What profit would it leave
Fabrum ...	19429	Would not leave any profit whatever
Fabueno ...	19430	Leaves a profit of
Fabulacion	19431	Leave(s) at first opportunity
Fabulador	19432	Take care to leave everything in good order
Fabulans ...	19433	Leave on receipt of cable (from)
Fabuleux ...	19434	Did not leave
Fabulilla ...	19435	Arrange to leave for —— not later than
Fabulist ...	19436	Before I leave for
Fabulizer ...	19437	Leave nothing to chance
Fabuloso ...	19438	Leaves nothing to be desired
Faburden...	19439	When did —— leave for
Facade ...	19440	When did he (——) leave mines
Faccella ...	19441	Cable when you intend to leave for
Faccellina...	19442	Competent engineer will leave for the property on [that place
Faccenda ...	19443	Leave as soon as you can for ——. Telegraph your arrival at
Facchino ...	19444	When can you leave
Facciata ...	19445	When do you expect to leave
Faccidanno	19446	I (we) expect to leave on

Faccion	19447	Shall leave on —— for
Faccioso	19448	When does —— expect to leave
Facciuola	19449	—— expects to leave on ,
Faceache	19450	You can leave it to me
Facedor	19451	I (we) leave it entirely to you
Facendiere	19452	Do not leave until (before)
Facendoso	19453	Cannot leave
Facessitur	19454	Must leave
Facetare	19455	Must not leave
Facetieux	19456	Will not leave before
Faceto	19457	You had better not leave —— until
Facetter	19458	Intend to leave here on —— for ——
Facezia	19459	—— Shall leave as soon as possible for
Fachada	19460	Shall leave to-day
Fachendear	19461	Shall leave to-morrow
Fachendon	19462	Shall not leave for —— until
Facherie	19463	Cable when you leave ——
Facheux	19464	—— Will not leave for —— until I (we) hear from you
Fachin	19465	Will leave immediately for
Fachwerk	19466	Can I (we) leave
Facial	19467	You can leave if
Faciens	19468	You can leave as soon as
Facilement	19469	Obtain leave of absence for the purpose of
Facilibus	19470	Have obtained leave
Facilidad	19471	Leave refused owing to
Facilillo	19472	Cannot leave in the absence of
Facilis	19473	Before I (we) leave
Faciliter	19474	Will cable before I (we) leave
Facimola	19475	Will leave early this month for —— (to)
Facinoroso	19476	Will leave towards the end of the month
Facistol	19477	Will leave early next month for
Facitojo	19478	Will leave towards the end of next month for
Facitore	19479	Should suggest your leaving as soon as possible
Facitrice	19480	I cannot leave here until you send funds
Facitura	19481	I could leave within the next —— days
Fackelzug	19482	Do not leave anything unsatisfactory
Facoltate	19483	Will not leave anything unsatisfactory
Facondioso	19484	Leaving by —— on —— for ——
Facondita	19485	Leaving by the mail steamer on —— for
Faconner	19486	Before you (they) leave
Factage	19487	Propose to leave —— in charge
Facteur	19488	Now ready to leave
Factible	19489	You had better leave it to me (us)
Facticio	19490	Be prepared to leave for —— on ——
Factionist	19491	Cannot leave unless you cable me
Factitabat	19492	Hope to leave
Factorage	19493	Could not leave on
Factorerie	19494	**Leavings**
Factorizar	19495	Burnt leavings
Factotum	19496	Leavings from
Facturer	19497	**Ledge**
Facultad	19498	Follow the ledge
Facultatif	19499	Expect to strike ledge within next —— f·
Facultoso	19500	Outside the ledge
Facundia	19501	Through a ledge of
Fadaise	19502	How wide is the ledge
Fadennackt	19503	The thickness of the ledge is —— ft.
Fadiga	19504	A well-defined ledge of
Fadingly	19505	As soon as we are through the ledge
Fadrin	19506	The ledge is improving in value

Faena	...	19507	The ledge is improving in width
Faenicicem		19508	Average width of the ledge is
Faeton	...	19509	The ledge is not so wide
Faggeto	...	19510	The ledge is —— ft. wide
Fagging	...	19511	**Left**
Fagiano	...	19512	Left arm
Faginada	...	19513	Left leg
Faginus	...	19514	Has (have) left
Fagiuolata		19515	Has (have) not left
Fagiuolo	...	19516	Left over
Fagnone	...	19517	Left entirely to
Fagotage	...	19518	Had to be left unfinished
Fagoteur	...	19519	—— left yesterday for
Fagott	...	19520	—— left mines on
Fagottino		19521	Who have you left in charge
Fagottista		19522	—— has been left in charge
Fahigkeit	...	19523	How much will you have left on (of)
Fahnrich	...	19524	What will you have left in hand
Fahrbar	...	19525	There will be nothing left in hand
Fahrbillet	...	19526	I shall have —— left in hand
Fahrend	...	19527	Must be left over until
Fahrgeld	...	19528	Cannot be left over until
Fahrlassig		19529	Might be very well left over
Fahrmann		19530	All that has been left is
Fahrpreis	...	19531	Has not yet left
Fahrwasser		19532	On the left-hand side
Fahrweg	...	19533	Both right and left
Faiblir	...	19534	Only on the left
Faiencerie		19535	Has (have) already left for ——
Faillite	...	19536	—— left —— on —— for ——
Faineant	...	19537	—— left for —— on
Faintingly		19538	**Leg**
Faintish	...	19539	Has (have) broken —— leg
Faintness	...	19540	Injury to leg not serious
Fairies	...	19541	Both legs
Fairplay	...	19542	**Legal** (*See also* " Guidance," " Expenses.")
Fairyland	...	19543	Legal opinion is
Faisable	...	19544	Legal position is doubtful
Faisan	...	19545	Contract is quite legal
Faisandeau		19546	Agreement is quite legal
Faisceau	...	19547	Legal tender
Faiseur	...	19548	Transfer is legal
Faithfully		19549	Transfer is not legal
Fajadura	...	19550	Take legal proceedings
Fajamiento		19551	Legal proceedings have been commenced against the Company
Fajardo	...	19552	In consequence of legal proceedings
Fajeddo	...	19553	Ascertain good legal opinion
Fajera	...	19554	Have obtained legal opinion to the effect that
Fajuela	...	19555	Will obtain legal opinion and cable
Faktum	...	19556	Only act under competent legal advice
Fakultat	...	19557	Legal rights comprise
Falacia	...	19558	What are the legal rights of
Falagar	...	19559	Have no legal rights
Falaiser	...	19560	What is our legal position
Falandum		19561	In order to establish our legal position
Falangia	...	19562	Has (have) no legal position whatever
Falangines		19563	Has (have) no legal redress
Falarica	...	19564	Give legal notice that you will hold —— (them) responsible
Falaride	...	19565	Give legal notice at once to [for all that happens
Falazmente		19566	Legal preliminaries require

Falbala ...	19567	Fulfilment of legal preliminaries required
Falcario ...	19568	Have threatened —— with legal action
Falcastro ...	19569	May bring legal action, but have no chance of success
Falcate ...	19570	There is no need to fear legal action
Falcatore ...	19571	Individual named has no legal status
Falcazar ...	19572	Individual named has full legal status
Falchetto ...	19573	Must resort to legal proceedings
Falchions ...	19574	Has (have) full legal status
Falciata ...	19575	Has (have) no legal status
Falcidia ...	19576	Have I (we) legal status
Falcifero ...	19577	We (you) have legal status
Falcinello...	19578	We (you) have no legal status
Falcione ...	19579	**Legally** (*See also* "Attested.")
Falciuola ...	19580	**Legislation**
Falcola ...	19581	Recent legislation
Falcolotto...	19582	The effect of legislation
Falconare...	19583	Legislation decidedly hostile
Falconeria	19584	Legislation is satisfactory from my (our) point of view
Falconete ...	19585	**Legislature**
Falconetto	19586	Now before the legislature
Falconiere	19587	**Legitimate(ly)**
Falconis ...	19588	Not legitimate
Falconry ...	19589	Do not consider it would be legitimate
Faldamento	19590	Would it be legitimate to (if)
Faldar ...	19591	Quite legitimate
Faldellato...	19592	**Lend**
Faldellin ...	19593	To lend
Falderillo...	19594	Could lend
Faldero ...	19595	Lend to
Faldetes ...	19596	Cannot lend
Faldicorto	19597	Will lend
Faldiglia ...	19598	Will one of your neighbours lend
Faldilla ...	19599	Refuse(s) to lend
Faldistoro	19600	Do not lend
Faldon ...	19601	Shall I lend
Faldstool ...	19602	Shall not lend
Faldulario	19603	Do not lend —— any assistance whatever
Falegname	19604	Lend as much assistance as you can
Falencia ...	19605	**Length** (*See also* "Distance.")
Falernian ...	19606	The length of
Falerno ...	19607	In length
Falimbello	19608	Extreme length
Falimiento	19609	Actual measured length
Falkenauge	19610	Length of claim
Fallabile ...	19611	Present length of drift
Fallace ...	19612	Length of lease
Fallacieux	19613	Length of time
Fallador ...	19614	What length is there still to drive in order to
Fallaggio ...	19615	What do you estimate the length of (at)
Fallanza ...	19616	The estimated length is —— feet
Fallbeil ...	19617	What do you estimate the length between
Fallbrucke	19618	I (we) cannot form any estimate of length
Falleba ...	19619	What is the total length
Fallecedor	19620	The total length is —— feet
Fallecer ...	19621	By increasing the length
Fallente ...	19622	Do not increase the length
Fallgatter...	19623	Can extend the length
Fallido ...	19624	Cannot extend the length
Falligione ..	19625	For a length of —— feet
Falliment...	19626	For a length of —— feet and a width of —— feet

Falliren ...	19627	Giving an additional length of ——— feet
Fallitore ...	19628	This will mean an increased length of
Fallschirm	19629	Owing to the error in estimation of length
Fallstrick...	19630	There is no error in the estimated length of ——— feet
Fallsucht ...	19631	Give length in feet of
Fallthur ...	19632	The length is ——— feet
Falolico ...	19633	What is the average length
Falordia ...	19634	The average length is
Falourde ...	19635	The entire length of the
Falsabraga	19636	What is the length of
Falsada ...	19637	What is the length of option
Falsamente	19638	**Lengthen**
Falsario ...	19639	To lengthen
Falsatore ...	19640	Can you not lengthen
Falschheit	19641	Can lengthen
Falschlich	19642	Cannot lengthen
Falseador...	19643	**Less**
Falsedad ...	19644	Less than
Falseface ...	19645	Much less
Falsehood	19646	If less than
Falsetto ...	19647	Is less than
Falsezza ...	19648	Less discount of
Falsidico ...	19649	Less usual discount
Falsificar ...	19650	Less difference of exchange
Falsilla ...	19651	Less exchange at
Falsitade ...	19652	Is this less cost of
Falsura ...	19653	Is less cost of
Faltare ...	19654	Is not less cost of
Falteln ...	19655	Less treatment cost
Faltenwurf	19656	Could you induce ——— to accept less
Faltered ...	19657	Will take ——— less
Faltrero ...	19658	Can you work at a less cost for
Faluner ...	19659	Cannot work at any less cost
Falzbein ...	19660	At a much less cost
Falzhobel...	19661	Has (have) been less owing to
Falzziegel	19662	Considerably less than I (we) expected
Famelico ...	19663	Is less than what was expected (by)
Famelique	19664	Less ——— per cent.
Famigerato	19665	The ——— for next six months will be less owing to
Famigliare	19666	Not less than
Famiglio ...	19667	Will not be less than
Famished...	19668	Will not take less
Famishing	19669	Will now cost much less
Famosita ...	19670	Less will not be satisfactory
Famoso ...	19671	Less will be of no use whatever
Famuccia ...	19672	**Lessee(s)**
Famulato ...	19673	Who is (are) the lessee(s)
Famulento	19674	The present lessee(s)
Famulo ...	19675	The present lessee(s) is (are)
Fanaison ...	19676	The present lessee(s) could not work at a profit
Fanatical ...	19677	The present lessees are anxious to sell because
Fanaticism	19678	The present lessee(s) have made considerable profit
Fanatico ...	19679	The present lessees are very successful
Fanatiker...	19680	The present lessees have had very little success
Fanatique...	19681	Lessee(s) has (have) cleared his (their) expenses
Fanatismo	19682	Lessees have made a profit of
Fanciulla ...	19683	On behalf of the lessees
Fandango...	19684	The former lessee(s) could not work at a profit
Fandonia ...	19685	The former lessees were very successful
Fanega ...	19686	The former lessees were not very successful

Fanegada	...	19687	**Lessor(s)**
Fanfaluca	...	19688	On behalf of the lessor(s)
Fanfare	...	19689	**Let**
Fanfarina		19690	To let
Fanfarria	...	19691	Let to
Fanfinot	...	19692	Shall I (we) let
Fangaccio	...	19693	Do not let
Fangal	...	19694	You might let
Fangball	...	19695	Advise you to let it alone
Fangeisen	...	19696	Shall let it alone
Fangeux	...	19697	Let it alone
Fanghiglia		19698	How would it be to let them (it) alone
Fangled	...	19699	Shall let them (it) alone meanwhile
Fangless	...	19700	Would let it alone for the present
Fangoso	...	19701	Better let things stand as they are
Fangzahn		19702	Let as much work as you can on contract
Fanlights	...	19703	Have let contracts for
Fanning	...	19704	Better let the matter rest
Fantaccino		19705	Let —— have
Fantaisie	...	19706	Let —— have as much —— as he (they) want(s)
Fantajo	...	19707	Let me know
Fantasear	...	19708	Let me (us) have ["Indefinite."]
Fantasia	...	19709	**Letter(s)** (*See also* "Call," "Dated," "Direct," "Find,"
Fantasioso		19710	My (our) letter dated
Fantasmon		19711	Anxiously awaiting letter from you respecting
Fantasque		19712	Letter was mailed on —— with full particulars; cable if it has
Fantastico		19713	Awaiting reply to my (our) letter dated [not reached you
Fantello	...	19714	Have not received the letter dated —— (referred to)
Fantesca	...	19715	Did not receive your letter until
Fanticella	...	19716	Have you received any letter from ——
Fantilita	...	19717	Have not received any letter from ——
Fantineria		19718	Have received your letter dated ——, and shall
Faonner	...	19719	Did you receive my letter dated
Faquin	...	19720	Received your letter dated
Farachar	...	19721	Have not received your letter dated
Farallon	...	19722	Direct my letters until —— to
Faramalla	...	19723	You will find letters awaiting you at ——
Farandole	...	19724	Letter was sent without enclosures
Farandula		19725	Do not understand what you mean in your letter of ..
Farante	...	19726	As soon as receive letter from
Farbeholz	...	19727	Can you obtain letter of introduction to
Farben	..	19728	Have given —— a letter of introduction to you
Farbenbret		19729	Cancel the following clauses contained in my (our) letter
Farblos	...	19730	Cable your reply to my (our) letter of [dated ——
Farbstoff	...	19731	Directors are fully satisfied with your letter
Farceur	...	19732	Directors are not altogether satisfied with your letter respecting
Farchetola		19733	Duplicate of enclosures contained in my (our) letter dated —— [mailed
Farcical	...	19734	Do not do anything until you receive my (our) letter dated
Farcimini	...	19735	Have received your letter dated —— with enclosures as stated
Farcinador	.	19736	Have received your letter dated —— but no enclosures [upon
Farcitote	...	19737	Have to-day received your letter dated ——. I will at once act
Farcivit	...	19738	Letter dated —— received, but cannot act upon same
Farctura	...	19739	Have addressed your letter(s) under cover to
Fardacho	...	19740	Have addressed your letter(s) to
Fardage	...	19741	Has (have) received letter from ——
Fardaggio	...	19742	Have not received your letter; am awaiting instructions
Fardel	...	19743	Have received your letter dated ——, but
Fardeleria	...	19744	Have not received any letter from you since ——
Fardelillo	...	19745	Immediately after receipt of your letter

Faretrato ...	19746	Immediately after the despatch of my (our) last letter
Farewell ...	19747	I (we) consider your letter dated —— most satisfactory
Farfadet ...	19748	I (we) consider your letter dated —— not at all satisfactory
Farfala ...	19749	In the absence of any letter from you
Farfallone	19750	Inform me (us) fully by letter
Farfalloso...	19751	Instructions contained in my (our) letter dated —— are
Farfante ...	19752	In future forward all letters to —— [subject to
Farfarello	19753	The post office for registered letters is at ——
Farfaria ...	19754	Your letter of —— received, but contains no reference to ——
Farfulla ...	19755	Letter mailed containing certificates of stock
Fargallon...	19756	Letter mailed containing following certificates of stock, namely
Faribole ...	19757	Cable date of last letter
Faricello ...	19758	My (our) last letter was dated
Farinaceo ...	19759	My (our) letter dated —— contains necessary information
Farinetas ...	19760	My (our) letter dated —— contains necessary instructions
Farineux ...	19761	Suspicious that my letters are intercepted
Faringe ...	19762	Referring to your letter dated
Fariniere ...	19763	Referring to remarks in my letter dated —— about ——
Farisaico ...	19764	Referring to remarks in your letter dated —— about ——
Farisaismo	19765	Forward me letter of credit [very careful what you do
Fariseo ...	19766	Have been obliged to give letter of introduction to ——. Be
Farmaco ...	19767	Give letter of recommendation to
Farming ...	19768	Give letter of introduction to
Farmlands	19769	Enclosures for your letter dated —— mailed in error to
Farmyard	19770	Enclosures mentioned in your letter of —— not received.
Farnero ...	19771	Letter of advice [Please mail duplicates
Farnetico ...	19772	Letter of credit
Farnkraut	19773	Letter of indemnity
Farol ...	19774	Letter of guarantee
Farolero ...	19775	Letter of introduction ——
Farolico ...	19776	Letter of identification
Farota ...	19777	Letter mailed gives full explanation
Farpado ...	19778	Please explain fully by letter
Farraceus...	19779	Letter with full details follows by mail
Farraggine	19780	Letter(s) for you was (were) mailed on ——
Farrata ...	19781	Mail duplicate of your letter dated ——
Farropea ...	19782	Mail arrived but no letter from you
Farsanta ...	19783	Must have a reply to my letter dated —— not later than ——
Farsar ...	19784	No letter to hand yet
Farsetajo ...	19785	My (our) last letter was mailed just prior to receipt of your
Farsettino	19786	No letter received from you. Cable if necessary [cable
Farsettone	19787	On referring to letter from ——
Farsuras ...	19788	Please send duplicate(s) of letter(s) referred to
Fasanerie ...	19789	Pending arrival of letter [——
Fascello ...	19790	Please supplement instructions contained in your letter dated
Fascetta ...	19791	Will cable address for letters
Faschine...	19792	Packet mailed —— contains instructions and letter(s) of in-
Fasciato ...	19793	Please refer to my (our) letter dated [troduction
Fascicular	19794	Please refer to your letter dated
Fascinador	19795	My letter of —— is still unanswered
Fascinante	19796	Received your letter; will answer as soon as possible
Fascinar ...	19797	Since my (our) last letter
Fascinola ...	19798	Sent you by registered letter on
Fascio ...	19799	Shall await arrival of letter from ——
Fasciuccio	19800	The following enclosures were contained in my (our) letter dated
Fasciume ...	19801	Your letter received, but it was too late to act upon
Faselarios	19802	Your letter received; will answer not later than
Faseln ...	19803	Your letter dated —— to hand
Faseole ...	19804	Letter forwarded in error to
Faserchen	19805	Your letter forwarded in error to

Faserig ...	19806	Upon receipt of my (our) letter dated
Faserstoff ...	19807	Until you receive my (our) letter [portance to report
Fashioned	19808	Unfortunately missed mail leaving yesterday. Nothing of im-
Fasoles ...	19809	In case you should receive a letter from ——
Fassbinder	19810	In case you have not received my (our) letter dated
Fassdaube	19811	Letters for you mailed on —— to
Fassalich ...	19812	Enclosures referred to in my letter dated —— will be mailed
Fastial ...	19813	Any letters should reach me not later than [to you on
Fastidiar ...	19814	Please refer to my last letter
Fastidieux	19815	In your letter dated
Fastidioso	19816	With reference to your letter dated
Fastidire ...	19817	With reference to your letter dated —— please note that
Fastidiume	19818	Send all letters addressed as follows
Fastigio ...	19819	Cable —— your address for letters
Fastnacht...	19820	Wish to post you a letter; cable correct address
Fastness ...	19821	Call for letter containing instructions at the post office at
Fasttag ...	19822	Letter addressed to
Fatagione...	19823	Contents of letter dated —— considered satisfactory
Fatalidad ...	19824	Contents of letter dated —— not considered satisfactory
Fatalista ...	19825	Correct by letter
Fatalmente	19826	Call for letters at the post office at ——; but if they have not [arrived do not wait
Fatappio ...	19827	Have sent letters addressed to you (——) to the post office at [——; wait until you receive them
Fatato ...	19828	On your arrival at —— call at post office for letters to you [(——). If they have not arrived telegraph for
Fatatura ...	19829	Have posted letters to address at —— [instructions
Fatherland	19830	Several letters have been forwarded to the following address(es)
Fathomless	19831	**Level** (See also " Adit," " Backs," " Landing," &c.)
Faticabile ...	19832	Level number one
Faticaccia...	19833	Level number two
Faticatore...	19834	Level number three
Fatidical ...	19835	Level number four
Fatidique ...	19836	Level number five
Fatiga ...	19837	Level number six
Fatigabunt	19838	Level number seven
Fatigador ...	19839	Level number eight
Fatigare ...	19840	Level number nine
Fatigoso ...	19841	Level number ten
Fatiguing...	19842	Level number ——
Fatoria ...	19843	100 foot level
Fattamente	19844	200 foot level
Fattening...	19845	300 foot level
Fattevole ...	19846	400 foot level
Fattibello...	19847	500 foot level
Fattibile ...	19848	600 foot level
Fatticcio ...	19849	700 foot level
Fattivo ...	19850	800 foot level
Fattojano ...	19851	900 foot level
Fattojo ...	19852	1,000 foot level
Fattorello...	19853	—— foot level
Fattoressa	19854	In the lower levels
Fattoruzzo	19855	In the upper levels
Fattosta ...	19856	At what level
Fatturato ...	19857	At a higher level
Fatty ...	19858	At a lower level
Fatuatis ...	19859	At the lowest level
Fatue ...	19860	At the deep level
Fatuidad ...	19861	By a proposed deep level
Fatuitate ...	19862	By means of a winze at the —— foot level

Fatuor ...	19863	Cable progress with level
Fatura ...	19864	Down to the —— foot level
Faubourg...	19865	To the —— foot level
Faubourien	19866	Day level(s)
Fauchage ...	19867	At a distance of —— feet from mouth of level
Fauchaison	19868	At the back of the stope in the —— foot level
Faucheur ...	19869	Above the —— foot level
Faucibus ...	19870	Crosscut on the —— foot level
Faucille ...	19871	From the —— foot level
Fauconnier	19872	To the —— foot level
Faufan ...	19873	From the —— foot level to surface
Faufleber ...	19874	Bottom level
Faullenzen	19875	Is at present our bottom level
Faulniss ...	19876	Level has at present a length of —— feet
Faulthier ...	19877	Prospect level
Faumele ...	19878	Since —— the —— foot level has been driven
Faussaire ...	19879	There is no ore practically above the —— foot level
Faussement	19880	This level should intersect
Fausset	19881	The level is in ore for a distance of ——
Faustling ...	19882	To connect the —— foot level with the level above
Fausto ...	19883	To connect the —— foot level with the level below
Faustrecht	19884	To connect with the —— foot level
Fauteuil ...	19885	Level north driven —— feet
Fautoria ...	19886	Level south driven —— feet
Fautrice ...	19887	At which point we propose to drive a level
Fauvette ...	19888	In the —— foot level the vein narrows down to —— inches
Favagello ...	19889	The vein in the —— level is small and narrow
Favebaris ...	19890	From floor of —— level
Favebunt ...	19891	From floor of first level
Favellare ...	19892	As the breast of the level is advanced
Favellio ...	19893	I consider the best thing will be to stop driving this level
Faventur ...	19894	As soon as the level communicates with the shaft
Faverella ...	19895	The level is at present running through
Favetote ...	19896	As soon as we are deep enough for another level
Faviforme...	19897	This level is being vigorously pushed forward
Favilla ...	19898	What are the dimensions of the level
Favillarum	19899	Owing to the water in this level
Favilletta ...	19900	About to the water level
Favolatore	19901	Down to the water level [line
Favolesca ...	19902	The present face of —— level is —— feet from the boundary
Favolone ...	19903	—— level has approximately —— feet to drive to reach the [apparent edge of ore bodies operated on in upper levels
Favonio ...	19904	The tonnage of —— class ore standing above —— level is approx- [imately —— tons of the approximate value of —— per ton
Favorabile	19905	A large portion (—— per cent.) of the lode exposed above —— [level is of such a character as not to pay for extraction [and treatment
Favorcillo...	19906	The ore in bottom of —— level averages —— inches wide, of [good quality ore for a length of —— feet
Favorecer ...	19907	**Levelling**
Favorito ...	19908	Am (are) now engaged levelling a site for ——
Fawning ...	19909	Am (are) now engaged levelling for railroad
Fayado ...	19910	By levelling
Fayanca ...	19911	Levelling staff and chain
Fazana ...	19912	**Levied**
Fazionario	19913	Have been levied on
Fazioso ...	19914	Was (were) levied on
Fazzoletto	19915	**Levy**
Fealdad ...	19916	Shall I levy judgment
Feamente ...	19917	Levy judgment

Fearless ...	19918	Do not levy judgment
Feastful ...	19919	Levy judgment as soon as
Feasting ...	19920	**Liability(ies)** (*See also* "Call," "Defray," "Incur.")
Featherbed	19921	Liabilities are
Feathering	19922	What are the gross liabilities
Feathers ...	19923	The gross liabilities are
Febbrajo ...	19924	Do not incur any further liability(ies)
Febbretta...	19925	Shall not incur any further liability(ies)
Febbricita	19926	What is (are) the liability(ies)
Febbrifero	19927	The liabilities amount to
Febbruzza	19928	Liabilities are estimated at
Febledad ...	19929	The liabilities are heavy
Febrera ...	19930	The liabilities are light
Febricitor...	19931	There is practically no liability
Febricula ...	19932	What liability is attached (to)
Febrido ...	19933	Absolutely no liability
Febriens ...	19934	No further liability beyond
Febrifuge...	19935	Cannot accept liability
Febrilis ...	19936	Will not accept liability
Februarius	19937	Liabilities must not exceed
Februatus	19938	Liabilities to cease with
Februum ...	19939	Will accept no liability for ——'s statement(s)
Feccioso ...	19940	You must repudiate any liability
Fechar ...	19941	I (we) repudiate any liability
Fechoria ...	19942	My liability must be limited to
Fechten ...	19943	I (we) shall incur liability to the extent of
Fechtkunst	19944	After meeting all our liabilities the amount to the credit of
Fechtplatz	19945	Discharge all liabilities [the Company in cash is
Fecial ...	19946	Discharge all liabilities, and inform me (us) of the amount by
Fecinium ...	19947	Have discharged all liabilities [cable
Feconder ...	19948	All the liabilities have been discharged on payment of
Feculencia	19949	Have discharged liabilities amounting to ——
Feculento...	19950	What is the balance of liabilities
Fecundatis	19951	The balance of liabilities is
Fecunde ...	19952	You should include in the liabilities
Fecundidad	19953	To meet the whole of our liabilities we require a further sum of
Fecundizar	19954	Telegraph the total amount of your cash liabilities
Fededegno	19955	Cable amount required to settle all liabilities
Fedelmente	19956	The only liabilities are
Federado ...	19957	What are the liabilities to end of present month
Federalist...	19958	The liabilities to end of present month are
Federation	19959	**Liable**
Federative	19960	Liable to
Federball ...	19961	Liable at any moment to
Federbett...	19962	Will render me (us) liable to
Federbusch	19963	Will not render me (us) liable in the slightest degree
Federharz...	19964	If it does not render me (us) liable
Federkiel ...	19965	Company will not be liable for any further outlay
Federkraft	19966	**Lias**
Federkrieg	19967	**Liassic**
Federvieh ...	19968	**Liberty**
Federweiss	19969	You have full liberty of action
Feditore ...	19970	Cannot give you any further liberty
Feebleness	19971	Do not allow —— any liberty
Feeding ...	19972	Without liberty of action
Feedwater	19973	You have full liberty to proceed
Feenhaft ...	19974	**License(s)** (*See also* "Diggers," "Prospectors.")
Feenwelt ...	19975	Prospector's license
Feerique ...	19976	Terms of license
Fegatella ...	19977	On license

Fegatoso	19978	On same terms for license as adjoining companies
Fegefeuer	19979	Company will grant license on following terms
Feggere	19980	**Lie(s)** (*See also* "Situated.")
Fehlbar	19981	**Lien(s)**
Fehlbitte	19982	Claim(s) has (have) a lien
Fehlerfrei	19983	Has (have) no lien at all
Fehlerhaft	19984	Have you any lien
Fehlgeburt	19985	Must have a lien
Fehlgehen	19986	Lien filed
Fehlgriff	19987	Lien removed
Fehltreten	19988	Lien amounts to
Fehltritt	19989	Lien discharged
Feierabend	19990	**Lift(s)** (*See also* "Pump.")
Feierlich	19991	To lift
Feiern	19992	In order to lift
Feiertag	19993	Should be able to lift
Feigenbaum	19994	Not strong enough to lift
Feigheit	19995	Quite strong enough to lift
Feigling	19996	Shall require to lift
Feilicht	19997	Standing lift
Feilschen	19998	Pump lift
Feilspane	19999	For another lift
Feindin	20000	Will require —— days to complete present lift
Feindlich	**20001**	**Lifter(s)**
Feindselig	20002	Stamps lifter (*See also* "Stamps.")
Feinsinnig	20003	**Lighter(age)**
Fejuguez	20004	Cost of lighterage to be paid by
Felandrio	20005	Demand(s) —— for lighterage
Felciata	20006	Arrange lighterage
Feldarbeit	20007	Have arranged lighterage
Feldbauer	20008	**Like** (*See also* "Prefer.")
Feldbett	20009	If you (——) like(s)
Feldbinde	20010	In case you (——) do(es) not like
Felddienst	20011	Or the like
Feldfrucht	20012	For a like period
Feldgerath	20013	For a like sum
Feldherr	20014	On like terms
Feldjager	20015	**Likely**
Feldkummel	20016	Likely to
Feldmark	20017	Likely to cost
Feldmesser	20018	Not in the least likely to cost
Feldmusik	20019	Likely to show considerable profit
Feldposten	20020	Do you know anyone likely to suit
Feldschutz	20021	Do not know anyone likely to suit
Feldsoldat	20022	Is there likely to be
Feldstuck	20023	There is not likely to be
Feldtisch	20024	There is likely to be
Feldtone	20025	Is not at all likely to be
Feldwache	20026	Not at all likely
Feldwebel	20027	Is it at all likely that
Feldweg	20028	It is not at all likely (that)
Felibote	20029	It is most likely (that)
Felice	20030	Would —— be likely to accept
Felicibus	20031	—— would be very likely to accept
Felicitar	20032	Most likely
Felicity	20033	Which (what) is likely to happen
Feligres	20034	As most likely to
Felineus	20035	How much are you (is ——) likely to want
Fellator	20036	How long is it likely to take
Felleisen	20037	**Lime**

Fellicabam	20038	Carbonate of lime
Fellicator ...	20039	Carbonate of lime and magnesia
Fellicavit ...	20040	Carbonate of lime heavily charged with
Felliduco ...	20041	**Limestone**
Fellowheir	20042	Beds of limestone
Felonesco ...	20043	Mainly consists of limestone
Felonia ...	20044	Dolomitic limestone
Felonious ...	20045	Black limestone
Felonque ...	20046	Cherty limestone
Felpado ...	20047	Brecciated limestone
Felpilla ...	20048	Carboniferous limestone
Felsenriff...	20049	Limestone lying upon
Felsenwand	20050	**Limit(s)** (*See also* "Higher.")
Faltrare ...	20051	Limit cancelled
Femella ...	20052	Limit advanced to
Femenino...	20053	Limit decreased to
Fementido	20054	Limit is
Femmelette	20055	What is your (——'s) limit
Femminale	20056	My (our) (——'s) limit is
Femminetta	20057	May I (we) increase limit
Femminiera	20058	Cannot increase limit
Femoral ...	20059	Cannot reduce limit
Fenaison ...	20060	May I (we) reduce limit
Fenchel ...	20061	Can increase limit to
Fencibles ...	20062	Can reduce limit to
Fendedura	20063	Could not operate within your limits
Fenderie ...	20064	Can do nothing at present limit
Fendiente	20065	Do not limit you at all
Fendiller ...	20066	Limit too small
Fenditojo ...	20067	Limit too high
Fenecer ...	20068	Limit too low
Fenedal ...	20069	Beyond my (our) limits
Feneratore	20070	Is this (are these) beyond your limit(s)
Fenestella...	20071	Not to exceed my (our) last limit(s)
Fenetrage...	20072	For the present limit your operations to
Fenianism	20073	Until I hear from you shall limit the work to ——
Feniciotto...	20074	No limit was given by you
Fenigeno ...	20075	What is the limit
Fenlands ...	20076	Within what limits
Fenogreco	20077	Within these limits
Fenomeno	20078	I believe they have reached their limit
Fenouil ...	20079	I do not think the limit has been reached yet
Feodalite ...	20080	**Limited** (*See also* "Company," "Expenditure.")
Feracidad	20081	Limited to
Feracius ...	20082	As a limited liability Company
Feralia ...	20083	Must be limited to
Feralmente	20084	Not limited
Feratrina ...	20085	On too limited a scale
Ferblanc ...	20086	Owing to the limited nature of
Ferchaud ...	20087	Our present —— capacity is limited to
Feretrius ...	20088	Should be limited to
Feretrum ...	20089	The liability is limited to
Feriante ...	20090	Your expenditure should be limited to
Feriatio ...	20091	**Line** (*See also* "Tramway," "Railway.")
Feridore ...	20092	A pipe line
Feriendus...	20093	Am (are) already beyond our boundary line
Ferino ...	20094	Beyond the line
Feriones ...	20095	Close to our boundary line
Feritas ...	20096	End line(s)
Feritoja ...	20097	In a line with

Fermaglio	20098	On the line of
Fermate ...	20099	Must be in line with
Fermement	20100	For a tram line
Fermentare	20101	Side line(s)
Fermented	20102	Line blocked up
Fermenting	20103	Line clear
Fermento ...	20104	**Lined**
Fermeture	20105	Lined with
Fermiere ...	20106	Not lined
Fermoir ..	20107	**Lining(s)**
Fernandina	20108	Lining(s) of
Fernerhin	20109	**Link** (*See also* " Connecting.")
Fernery ...	20110	**Liquidate(d)** (*See also* " Company.")
Fernglas ...	20111	**Liquidation**
Fernleaf ...	20112	Endeavour to avoid liquidation
Fernrohr ...	20113	Impossible to avoid liquidation
Fernwerk ...	20114	Liquidation will now be avoided
Feroce ...	20115	Liquidation would be avoided if
Ferociatis ..	20116	The only way to avoid liquidation is to
Ferociebat	20117	Has (have) filed a petition for liquidation
Ferociens ...	20118	Is now in liquidation
Ferocita ...	20119	Liquidation not yet closed
Feroculus...	20120	Liquidation cannot be closed pending
Ferozmente	20121	To put into liquidation
Ferraccia ...	20122	Will be put into liquidation
Ferragosto	20123	**Liquidator(s)**
Ferrajolo ...	20124	By order of the liquidator(s)
Ferramento	20125	Who has been appointed liquidator
Ferratilis ...	20126	—— has (have) been appointed liquidator(s)
Ferratore ..	20127	Due to the liquidator(s)
Ferreria ...	20128	Liquidator(s) refuse(s)
Ferreruelo	20129	Liquidator has consented
Ferrete ...	20130	I have been appointed liquidator
Ferreteado	20131	**List** (*See also* " Specification.")
Ferreum ...	20132	In the official list
Ferriterus...	20133	Before lists opened
Ferronnier	20134	Lists will open on
Ferropea ...	20135	Please send a complete list of
Ferrotype...	20136	A complete list was forwarded on ——
Ferrules ...	20137	A complete list will be forwarded on ——
Ferruzzo ...	20138	What does the list include
Ferrying ...	20139	Do(es) the list(s) include
Fertigen ...	20140	Should have been included in the list sent you
Fertigkeit	20141	The list is made up and includes
Fertilatis ...	20142	To what date is the list made up
Fertilezza...	20143	List of buildings, plant and machinery
Fertilidad	20144	**Listed**
Fertilizer ...	20145	Listed on
Feruggino	20146	Listed stocks
Ferulaceo .	20147	**Litigation** (*See also* " Company.")
Fervefacio	20148	Avoid litigation
Fervens ...	20149	Is it possible to prevent litigation
Fervently ...	20150	Litigation cannot be prevented
Fervesco ...	20151	Do not understand why I (we) should indemnify against liti-
Fervidly ...	20152	**Little** [gation
Fervidus ...	20153	Very little doing
Ferviente ...	20154	Little better
Fervor ...	20155	Little worse
Fervorizar	20156	As little as possible
Fervoroso...	20157	At a little distance from

Fesceninos	20158	But little work has been done
Fescera ...	20159	Do as little as possible pending
Fesseln ...	20160	Little if any
Fessitudo ...	20161	Little or nothing has been done to
Fessolino ...	20162	Of little or no value
Fessus ...	20163	Very little has been done since
Festanza ...	20164	Load(s) (*See also* "Carload," "Carrying.")
Festejador	20165	How many loads of
Festevole ...	20166	Have received —— loads
Festgesang	20167	Loads of 16 cubic feet each
Festichino	20168	Loads of —— cubic feet each
Festiglick ...	20169	To load
Festinare ...	20170	Too heavy a load
Festinatio...	20171	What is the total load
Festino ...	20172	The total load is
Festival ...	20173	**Loaded**
Festividad	20174	Too heavily loaded with capital
Festiviter ...	20175	**Loading**
Festkleid ...	20176	Now loading
Festland ...	20177	The loading of
Festlich ...	20178	Loading of foundation
Festoccia ...	20179	Loading up with
Festonear...	20180	**Loan**
Festoon ...	20181	Get loan
Festosetto...	20182	Get loan for
Festoyer ...	20183	Get loan from
Festsetzen	20184	Has (have) raised a loan on the property
Festtag ...	20185	At present on loan to
Festucago...	20186	Can you arrange for loan of —— until
Festucam ...	20187	Have been obliged to raise a loan
Festung ...	20188	On loan
Festzeit ...	20189	To repay loan
Fetiales ...	20190	Was (were) obliged to raise a loan
Fetichism...	20191	As security for loan
Fetidite ...	20192	What security for loan can you offer
Fetido ...	20193	**Loaned**
Fetlocks ...	20194	Loaned on
Fettig ...	20195	Loaned for
Feuchten ...	20196	Not loaned
Feudalism	20197	**Locality**
Feudatary	20198	Most of the mines in this locality are paying
Feudum ...	20199	None of the mines in the locality are paying
Feuerbock	20200	In the same locality
Feuerbrand	20201	Is in the locality of
Feuereifer	20202	Judging from the mines in the locality
Feueresse ...	20203	Nothing has previously been found in this locality
Feuerfest ...	20204	The whole locality
Feuerhaken	20205	The locality has long been famous for
Feuerheerd	20206	**Locate**
Feuerkugel	20207	To locate
Feuerkunst	20208	Endeavour to locate
Feuerlarm	20209	Where do you intend to locate
Feuermauer	20210	**Located**
Feuerprobe	20211	Located on
Feuerrohr...	20212	The mine was located in
Feuersnoth	20213	The mine was located again in
Feuerstein	20214	Have located
Feuerung ...	20215	Should be located at once
Feuerwache	20216	Was (were) located by
Feuerwerk	20217	Was originally located by

Feuillage ...	20218	**Location(s)**
Feuillet ...	20219	Location adjoining
Feuillure ...	20220	Claim and adjoining location(s)
Feurig ...	20221	Is it a suitable location
Feutrer ...	20222	Is the most suitable location
Feverish ...	20223	Is not at all a suitable location
Feverole ...	20224	A plan of the location
Fiable ...	20225	The following location(s)
Fiaccare ...	20226	Which is (are) the oldest location(s)
Fiaccaturn	20227	Claim as the oldest location(s)
Fiacchetto	20228	All location work has been done
Fiacker ...	20229	Location number
Fiador ...	20230	Location work
Fiambrar ...	20231	Location certificate
Fiambrero	20232	Necessary before filing location certificate
Fiammante	20233	Location certificate has been filed
Fiammella	20234	Location certificate is all in order
Fiammifero	20235	Location certificate is not in order
Fiammore...	20236	Location certificate will require to be amended
Fiancata ...	20237	Do necessary work to secure location certificate
Fiascaccio...	20238	All necessary work to secure location certificate has been done
Fiascajo ...	20239	I have contracted for location work
Fiaschatta	20240	**Lock-out** (*See also* "Strike.")
Fiascone ...	20241	A lock-out is threatened
Fiatamento	20242	Should a lock-out be determined upon
Fiatente ...	20243	Lock-out not likely to continue
Fiatolo ...	20244	Lock-out seems likely to continue for some time
Fibbiajo ...	20245	Lock-out decided upon
Fibbietta ...	20246	Lock-out still continues
Fibbing ...	20247	Owing to a lock-out
Fibretta ...	20248	Lock-out terminated on
Fibreux ...	20249	Impossible to avoid a lock-out
Fibriform	20250	**Lode** (*See also* "Barren," "Bearing," "Quartz," "Vein.")
Fibrilla ...	20251	Lode at
Fibrinus ...	20252	Lode in forebreast
Fibroso ...	20253	Lode in bottom of shaft
Fibularent	20254	Lode in top of stope
Fibulatio ...	20255	Lode in bottom of stope
Ficarius ...	20256	Lode in winze
Ficcabile ...	20257	Lode claim
Ficedula ...	20258	Lode in shaft improving
Ficetum ...	20259	The lode is full of sulphurets
Fichant ...	20260	My opinion is there has been a heave in the lode
Fichereto ...	20261	The lode has been thrown —— feet to the east
Ficitas ...	20262	The lode has been thrown —— feet to the west
Ficosecco ...	20263	The lode has been thrown —— feet to the north
Ficticio ...	20264	The lode has been thrown —— feet to the south
Fiction ...	20265	I consider the lode we have to be the hanging-wall side
Fictionist ...	20266	I consider the lode we have is the foot-wall side
Fictitius ...	20267	A very powerful lode
Fictrix ...	20268	A cross lode
Fictura ...	20269	An incline shaft on the lode
Ficulneum	20270	A vertical shaft could be sunk to intersect the lode at a depth [of —— feet
Fidanzato	20271	From the disordered state of the lode
Fiddling ...	20272	By means of an incline shaft on the lode [depth of ——
Fidedigno...	20273	By means of an adit driven to intersect the lode at a vertical
Fidefragus	20274	Lode could be unwatered by an adit at a vertical depth of
Fidejubeo	20275	Is supposed to be a continuation of the same lode
Fidejuffor...	20276	For cutting and exploring lode
Fidelidad ...	20277	When through the lode

Fidelisimo	20278	Have driven a cross-cut to the lode
Fidelity ...	20279	Lode continues hard and barren
Fidentia ...	20280	Have cut the lode, but it is barren
Fideos ...	20281	Owing to the lode having faulted
Fidgety ...	20282	The lode stuff consists of
Fidibus ...	20283	The hanging-wall of the lode is ——
Fidicen ...	20284	The foot-wall of the lode is ——
Fidicinal ...	20285	There is no lode at this point
Fidicinius...	20286	The lode has a clay selvage
Fiducia ...	20287	The lode in the end is composed of
Fidustus ...	20288	The lode here is worth by assay
Fieberhaft	20289	The lode has every appearance of being permanent in depth
Fiebolezza	20290	The lode carries a considerable quantity of water
Fiebre ...	20291	The lode runs
Fiedeln ...	20292	On the course of the lode
Fieditore ...	20293	The strike of the lode is east and west, and it underlies
Fiedler ...	20294	The lode is now the full width of the level (viz. ——)
Fielazgo ...	20295	The lode in the end is —— feet wide and carries
Fieldad ...	20296	The lode is beginning to pinch
Fieldbed ...	20297	The lode continues very low grade
Fieldbook	20298	Lode in shaft improving
Fieldmouse	20299	The lode improves with each foot sunk
Fieldpiece.,	20300	Above the level of intersection of lode
Fielmente...	20801	The lode is small
Fieltrar ...	20802	The lode is inclined
Fiendish ...	20803	What is the depth on the dip of the lode
Fierabras ...	20804	Lode number ——
Fierement...	20305	Is a parallel lode to
Fierro ...	20306	The lode does not yield sufficient value to pay for stoping
Fierucola ...	20807	The lode is getting more defined
Fievole ...	20808	This end (these ends) is (are) in barren rock
Fievolezza	20809	We should probably have met lode before this
Fievreux ...	20810	Expect to meet with lode within the next —— feet
Figliare ...	20811	The lode is well defined
Figliastro...	20812	The lode runs north and south
Figliatura...	20813	The lode runs east and west
Figlina ...	20814	The lode runs —— degrees east of north
Figlinetto...	20815	The lode runs —— degrees west of north
Figlioccia...	20816	The drive north on the lode is now in —— feet
Figliuono...	20817	The drive south on the lode is now in —— feet
Figmentum	20818	The drive —— on the lode is now in —— feet
Fignolare ...	20819	The apex of the lode
Figonero ...	20320	The outcrop of the lode can be traced for a distance of
Figtree ...	20821	The outcrop of the lode
Figueral ...	20822	The width of the lode is —— feet
Figuier ...	20823	What is the width of the lode
Figularis ...	20824	The lode is narrow and practically barren
Figulino ...	20825	The lode is narrow but well mineralized
Figurable...	20826	The lode is wide but barren as yet
Figurandus	20827	The lode is wide and carries much mineral
Figurante	20828	The lode is open
Figuranza	20829	The lode is very close
Figurativo	20830	The lode looks exceedingly promising
Figuratus	20831	The lode does not look very promising at present
Figureria ...	20832	The lode is pinching up
Figurilla ...	20833	The lode is widening out
Figurine ...	20834	The lode is very flat
Figurlich ...	20335	The lode inclines at an angle of —— degrees to the per-
Fijacion ...	20336	The lode dips [pendicular
Fijamente	20337	The lode is dipping out of our ground

Fijeza	20338	The lode is dipping into our ground [means of
Filaceous	20339	The lode has been proved for a vertical depth of —— feet by
Filaciga	20340	The lode has practically not yet been proved
Filacteria	20341	The lode stuff is very poor, and I have grave doubts if it will
Filadier	20342	Lode maintains its width and value [pay to mine
Filagramme	20343	The lode is very much broken up
Fjlalero	20344	The lode is becoming much more
Filaments	20345	The walls of the lode are composed of
Filandreux	20346	To drive on the lode itself
Filandria	20347	To sink on the lode itself
Filantropo	20348	To cross-cut to the lode
Filarete	20349	There is nothing to show we are yet near the lode
Filarium	20350	We believe we are near the lode [disordered
Filastica	20351	The lode in face of —— level is low grade, and at present much
Filaticcio	20352	The lode in the lower levels is not so regular and strong as in [the upper levels, it being more disordered and broken
Filatim	20353	The upper levels have been extended beyond the ore operated [on, in a disordered lode
Filatojo	20354	The lode in the bottom levels is much broken, a large portion [of it being very low grade
Filature	20355	The lode in face of drive is of a promising character, carrying [pay streak of ore —— inches wide
Filban	20356	The lode in face of drive is well defined and of a promising [nature, carrying ore —— inches wide of good quality
Filberts	20357	On account of a change in the inclination of the lode
Filerie	20358	Traversing the lode
Filetear	20359	The property is traversed by the following lodes
Filial	20360	Report, as soon as you can, assay from lode
Filibuster	20361	The assays from the lode average
Filicatus	20362	When shall you commence to drive on the lode
Filicetum	20363	Shall commence to drive on the lode on ——
Filicida	20364	Shall commence to stope on the lode
Filicula	20365	Anticipate cutting lode within next —— feet
Filiform	20366	Anticipate cutting lode within next —— days
Filiggine	20367	The mineral is pretty evenly distributed through the mass of
Filigrana	20368	**Log(s)** [the lode
Filigree	20369	Logs for mill timbers
Filipica	20370	Log huts
Filipichin	20371	There are one or two log huts on the property
Filisteo	20372	**Long**
Filius	20373	Too long
Fillette	20374	Not sufficiently long
Filleule	20375	For a long time to come
Fillibegs	20376	For a long time back
Filoche	20377	By means of a long
Filoduxo	20378	As long as
Filologia	20379	As long as I am (we are) able to
Filomena	20380	How long
Filopos	20381	—— feet long
Filoseda	20382	How long will it (they) take to
Filosofal	20383	It will not take long
Filotimin	20384	How long can I (we) have
Filouter	20385	How long can you give
Filtracion	20386	How long will you require for
Filtrated	20387	How long will it be (before)
Filugello	20388	I (we) hope before long to inform you
Filzhut	20389	Before long
Filzigkeit	20390	Cannot give so long
Filzlaus	20391	Cannot be away so long
Fimarium	20392	How long shall you be away

Fimbria ...	20393	Not long enough
Fimetum ...	20394	How long will —— give
Finado ...	20395	Have been too long already
Finalizar ...	20396	Should be as long as possible
Finalmente	20397	They are (it is) too long
Finanzen ...	20398	It was long ago
Finasserie...	20399	You must not be long
Finaud ...	20400	How long will it require to examine and report
Fincable ...	20401	About how long will be required
Findelhaus	20402	**Longer**
Findelkind	20403	Longer time
Findendus	20404	Not much longer
Finement ...	20405	Can I remain —— days longer
Finestrone	20406	You had better not remain longer than —— days
Fingente ...	20407	You had better not remain longer than
Fingered ...	20408	Not a day longer
Fingerhut...	20409	How much longer will it be before
Fingering...	20410	About —— weeks longer
Fingersatz	20411	About a month longer
Fingerzeig	20412	How many days longer
Fingido ...	20413	—— days longer
Fingitore ...	20414	A little longer
Finiestra ...	20415	Cannot give longer
Finimondo	20416	Cannot remain longer
Finiquito ...	20417	Do not stay longer
Finisseur ...	20418	Do not be longer than
Finito ..	20419	Longer than needful
Finiturus ...	20420	Longer than expected
Finocchino	20421	Must have longer
Finteria ...	20422	No use unless can have longer
Fintoed ...	20423	The longer the better
Finzione ...	20424	How much longer do you anticipate being idle
Fiocaggine	20425	Cannot do any good unless you can allow longer time
Fioccare ...	20426	**Longest**
Fiochetto ...	20427	What is the longest you (they) can give
Fiochezza...	20428	Is the longest I (we) can give
Fiociniere ..	20429	Is the longest —— will give
Fiondatore	20430	Which is the longest
Fioraja ...	20431	Longest of
Fioraliso ...	20432	At the longest
Fiorellino...	20433	**Look(s)**
Fioretti ...	20434	To look
Fiorista ...	20435	Look to
Fioritezza...	20436	Does it look
Fioriture ...	20437	Does it look as if
Fiorrancio	20438	It looks as if
Fiotola ...	20439	It does not look as if
Fippern ...	20440	Looks almost as if
Firearms ...	20441	Look out
Firelock ...	20442	Look out for
Fireplace ...	20443	Will look out for
Fireship ...	20444	Look out for collapse
Fireside ...	20445	Look out for substantial improvement
Fireworks...	20446	Look into previous history
Firlefanz ...	20447	Looks exceedingly like failure
Firmamento	20448	Could you look it through
Firmandus	20449	I will look it through
Firmator ...	20450	Had better look into the matter immediately
Firmaturus	20451	Shall look into the matter immediately
Firmeln ...	20452	Am very well pleased with the general look of

Firmeza ...	20453	Am (is) on the look out
Firmitas ...	20454	Does not look as well as I anticipated
Firmitudo	20455	Looks better than anticipated
Firniss ...	20456	I do not like the look of
Firstborn ...	20457	It will take —— to look into things properly
Firstfruit ...	20458	I shall continue on the look out for
Firstling ...	20459	Looks very discouraging
Fiscalia ...	20460	Looks the reverse of encouraging
Fiscalidad	20461	Looks as bad as possible
Fiscalizar ...	20462	Look after
Fiscella ...	20463	Look up
Fischangel	20464	Look into
Fischbein ...	20465	Have been too busy to look into
Fischblase	20466	Look into the matter the first opportunity
Fischbrut ...	20467	—— might look into
Fischen ...	20468	Shall not be able to look into
Fischfang	20469	The present look-out is very
Fischgrate	20470	When could you look at
Fischiare ...	20471	Could look at —— on ——
Fischkoder	20472	Look ahead as far as you can with a view to
Fischlaich	20473	Would require to look after
Fischotter	20474	Looks pretty much the same
Fischrogen	20475	Looks on the whole better
Fischthran	20476	Looks grand
Fischzug ...	20477	Looks most promising
Fiscus ...	20478	Looks as if something was decidedly wrong
Fiseter	20479	Do not look for any improvement yet
Fisgador ...	20480	Do not look for any change
Fisgon ...	20481	Everything looks bad
Fisgonear...	20482	Everything looks encouraging
Fisherman	20483	Everything looks well
Fishery ...	20484	**Looked**
Fishhook ...	20485	As soon as I (we) have looked round
Fishified ...	20486	After I (we) have looked into
Fishknives	20487	Could not have looked
Fishmarket	20488	Does not appear to have been properly looked after
Fishmonger	20489	As soon as you have looked through
Fishpond ...	20490	I have looked it through
Fisiciano ...	20491	Must be well looked into
Fisicoso ...	20492	This must be looked to at once
Fisiomante	20493	—— says that he (it) looked
Fisofolo ...	20494	**Looking**
Fisole ...	20495	How are things looking
Fisonomia	20496	Looking well
Fissazione	20497	Looking exceeding well
Fissiculo ...	20498	Looking grand
Fissility ...	20499	Am (are) looking for considerable improvement
Fissured ...	20500	Looking up all round
Fistiata ...	20501	How is (the) —— looking
Fistiatore ...	20502	Could not be looking better
Fisticuffs ...	20503	Not looking quite so well
Fistolado ...	20504	Looking rather worse if anything
Fistucatio...	20505	Looking rather better if anything
Fistulatim	20506	All the ends are looking poor
Fistulofus	20507	All the ends are looking well
Fistuloso ...	20508	I am (we are) looking after
Fithele ...	20509	I am (we are) looking after it (this) (until)
Fitonisa ...	20510	Is looking pretty much the same
Fitscheln ...	20511	Looking out
Fittajuolo...	20512	Looking into

Fittamente	20513	Looking poor
Fittich ...	20514	Not looking quite so bad
Fittizio ...	20515	Not looking at all well
Fittuario ...	20516	**Loosely**
Fiucia ...	20517	Very loosely
Fiumana ...	20518	The whole thing has been carried out loosely
Fiumatico...	20519	**Lose**
Fiumetto ...	20520	To lose
Fiuminale...	20521	Do not lose
Fixation ...	20522	Do not lose sight of
Fixiren ...	20523	I (we) will not lose sight of
Fixstern ...	20524	Do not lose a moment
Fixurus ...	20525	Do not lose any time as soon as you receive
Flabbiness	20526	Lose no time in
Flabellum...	20527	I shall not lose more time than I can help
Flabrum ...	20528	How much am I (are we) likely to lose
Flacamente	20529	We lose at least
Flacceo ...	20530	We do not lose more than
Flaccidity	20531	How much are you (is ——) likely to lose
Flaccidus ...	20532	We lose by the present method at least —— per cent.
Flachheit ...	20533	Stand(s) to lose nothing at all
Flachkopf...	20534	Only stand(s) to lose
Flachsgelb	20535	I (we) stand to lose
Flachshaar	20536	—— stand to lose at present price
Flacida ...	20537	He (they) will lose
Flackern ...	20538	Apparently loses sight altogether of
Flacura ...	20539	I think you would lose rather than gain
Fladen ...	20540	I think you will certainly lose
Flagelante	20541	If you do not wish to lose
Flagellor ...	20542	Lose no opportunity
Flageolet ...	20543	Unless you want to lose
Flagicio ...	20544	You will certainly lose unless
Flagitans ...	20545	**Losing**
Flagitatus	20546	What do you estimate you are at present losing
Flagitious...	20547	Probably losing —— per cent. of value
Flagizioso...	20548	Losing in the tailings
Flagmast ...	20549	Losing ground in every direction
Flagons ...	20550	Provided you are not losing more than
Flagorner...	20551	Is playing a losing game
Flagrar ...	20552	**Loss(es)**
Flagrifer ...	20553	What is the loss of time due to
Flagrum ...	20554	The loss of time is mainly owing to
Flagship ...	20555	What will be the total loss
Flagstaff ...	20556	Cannot estimate the total loss
Flagstone...	20557	What do you estimate the loss at
Flails ...	20558	Very heavy loss indeed
Flaireur ...	20559	What amount of loss
Flamante ...	20560	The total loss is
Flambeau...	20561	As to the loss that occurs
Flamboyer	20562	A loss of —— per cent.
Flamenco ...	20563	Am (are) at a loss to understand how (why)
Flamigero...	20564	A loss of
Flamingo ...	20565	At no great loss
Flaminium	20566	At a great loss
Flammandus	20567	A very severe loss
Flammator	20568	Cable as soon as you know the total loss
Flammeche	20569	Explain how you account for the loss
Flammentod	20570	How do you apportion the loss(es)
Flammeolum	20571	—— has (have) incurred severe loss
Flammeous	20572	—— has (have) sustained loss of

Flammig ...	20573	I do not think there will be any loss
Flamula ...	20574	I do not think the loss is more than
Flanco ...	20575	Loss by theft
Flandrin ...	20576	Owing to the loss of
Flanela ...	20577	The present loss is not less than
Flanerie ...	20578	The estimated loss may be taken at
Flanquear	20579	The present loss(es) may be attributed to
Flapjack ...	20580	The loss already incurred is
Flapping ...	20581	The loss will probably amount to
Flaquecer ...	20582	The loss will be great
Flaqueza ...	20583	The loss will be small
Flaquillo ...	20584	The loss will be trifling
Flasche ...	20585	The loss will be severe
Flaschner ...	20586	Sell if you can do so without loss
Flashily ...	20587	Sell if you can do so without a loss of more than ———
Flasket ...	20588	The loss(es) is (are) heavy
Flasque ...	20589	The loss(es) is (are) small
Flatilis ...	20590	What amount of loss is due to
Flatirons ...	20591	The working loss is
Flatoso ...	20592	The loss is mainly due to
Flatterer ...	20593	In order to avoid further loss
Flattering...	20594	Try to avoid any further loss
Flatteur ...	20595	To prevent any loss
Flatulence	20596	Will lessen the loss by
Flatuosite...	20597	Without loss of time
Flatuosus...	20598	Has resulted in a loss of
Flatus ...	20599	Consequent on the loss of
Flauheit ...	20600	Will counterbalance loss due to
Flaunted ...	20601	An aggregate loss
Flaunting...	20602	Provided loss does not exceed
Flautato ...	20603	**Lost**
Flautero ...	20604	The following has (have) been lost
Flautillo ...	20605	How much is lost
>Flautista....	20606	Entirely lost
Flavedo ...	20607	What per cent. is lost
Flavoured...	20608	All trace of ore entirely lost
Flavourous	20609	Has (have) lost
Flebile ...	20610	Has (have) not lost
Flebiliter ...	20611	Is (are) lost
Flebotomar	20612	Is (are) not lost
Flecha ...	20613	Must be lost until
Flechador...	20614	The remainder is lost
Flechastes	20615	Was lost
Flecheria ...	20616	Has (have) lost heavily
Flechsig ...	20617	Has (have) been lost. Please mail duplicate(s)
Flechten ...	20618	Supposed to have been lost
Flechtwerk	20619	**Lot(s)**
Flecker ...	20620	A great lot
Fledermaus	20621	A lot of
Fledged ...	20622	The whole lot
Fledgeling	20623	From the lot
Fleecy ...	20624	**Low**
Fleeting ...	20625	Very low owing to
Flegelei ..	20626	Low quality
Flegelhaft...	20627	Low grade
Flegma ...	20628	How low will it (they) go
Flegmon ...	20629	Very low
Fleischer ...	20630	As low as you can
Fleissig ...	20631	As soon as we are low enough
Flemmatico	20632	As soon as the water is low enough

Flembao	20633	Is (are) as low as it (they) will go
Flendus	20634	Is very low already
Flennen	20635	Not quite low enough
Fleshbrush	20636	Quite low enough
Fleshiness	20637	You can go as low as —— if you think business will result
Fleshlike	20638	**Lower(ing)**
Fleshpots	20639	Cannot lower
Flessible	20640	Lower limit
Fleasura	20641	So as to lower
Fletador	20642	In the lower level(s)
Fletamento	20643	In the lower working(s)
Fletar	20644	Can I (we) go any lower
Fletschen	20645	Cannot go lower
Flettere	20646	Do you think it advisable to go lower
Fleuraison	20647	I do not think it would do any good to go lower
Fleurette	20648	Cannot do anything unless you can go lower
Fleuron	20649	Do not go lower unless absolutely necessary
Flexanimus	20650	Is (are) bound to go lower
Flexibilis	20651	Is (are) not likely to go lower
Flexionem	20652	I do not think will go any lower
Flexipes	20653	I think the —— will go lower
Flexuous	20654	I (we) must have lower terms
Flexure	20655	Might go a little lower
Flicken	20656	Prevents me (us) going any lower
Flickered	20657	Refuse(s) to go any lower
Flickering	20658	What is your idea of a lower price
Flickwort	20659	**Lowest**
Flieder	20660	Ascertain lowest price of —— and cable
Fliedermus	20661	Lowest price for —— is
Fliessen	20662	What is the lowest he (——) is (they are) likely to take
Flimmern	20663	The lowest terms are
Flinched	20664	What is the lowest price for
Flinching	20665	Lowest price is
Flinflon	20666	What is the lowest price you (they) will take for the whole
Flinkheit	20667	What is the lowest price you (they) will take
Flippancy	20668	Is this your lowest figure
Flippantly	20669	At the lowest figure possible
Flirtation	20670	Telegraph lowest quotation for
Flirting	20671	In the lowest level(s)
Flitter	20672	Lowest level(s) very poor
Floccidus	20673	Lowest level(s) is (are) the best
Flocculus	20674	Ascertain the lowest rate
Flockbed	20675	The lowest rate is
Flockig	20676	**Luck(y)**
Flocks	20677	Decidedly in luck
Flockseide	20678	Exceedingly bad luck
Floconneux	20679	No luck at all
Floculent	20680	**Lumber**
Flogged	20681	Lumber yard
Flogging	20682	As soon as the lumber arrives
Flohstick	20683	Lumber costs
Flojamente	20684	Lumber is plentiful
Flojear	20685	Lumber is scarce
Flojedad	20686	Have contracted for a supply of lumber
Flojisto	20687	Shall arrange for a supply of lumber immediately
Flomis	20688	Lumber now costs —— per 1,000 feet
Floodgate	20689	What are you now paying for lumber
Floqueado	20690	The cost of lumber
Florales	20691	**M**
Florbinde	20692	**Machine**

Floreado ...	20693	Send a couple of machine forwarding screws
Florecer ...	20694	Machine for
Florecica ...	20695	Additional machine(s)
Florentina	20696	Have put machine at ["Depend," "Foundations."]
Floraro ...	20697	**Machinery** (*See also* "Breakdown," "Broken," "Condition,"
Floresco ...	20698	Owing to breakdown of machinery
Floresta ...	20699	How long will the repairs to the machinery take
Floretada ...	20700	Repairs to the machinery will take at least
Florete ...	20701	How much do you estimate repairs to the machinery will cost
Floretista...	20702	Repairs to machinery would (will) cost ——
Floridezza	20703	Shall you require skilled assistance for repairs to machinery
Floridly ...	20704	Shall require skilled assistance for repairs to machinery
Floridness	20705	Shall not require skilled assistance for repairs to machinery
Floridulus	20706	The repairs to the machinery would be, say ——, new would
Florifero ...	20707	The estimated cost of repairs to machinery will be [cost —,——
Florilegio ...	20708	Shall be glad to have your opinion as to the machinery ,
Florseide ...	20709	Machinery all right
Flortuch ...	20710	The machinery generally is in good order
Floscular ...	20711	The machinery generally is out of order
Flosculoso	20712	The machinery is in good order except
Floskel ...	20713	When are you likely to commence erection of the machinery
Flotadura...	20714	We shall commence erection of the machinery within the next
Flotante ...	20715	Send complete schedule of machinery [—— days
Flotilla ...	20716	Schedule of machinery mailed on ——
Flotsam ...	20717	Have finished erection of machinery
Flottable ...	20718	Exclusive of erection of machinery
Flottage ...	20719	Inclusive of erection of machinery
Flottement	20720	What is your estimate inclusive of erection of machinery
Flouncing	20721	What is your estimate exclusive of erection of machinery
Flourished	20722	A complete plant and machinery would mean an outlay of [—— exclusive of erection
Fluchten ...	20723	Causing much damage to the machinery
Fluchtling	20724	Damage to the machinery is very slight
Fluctifer ...	20725	Damage to the machinery is very great
Fluctigena	20726	The damage to the machinery is not very serious
Fluctuar ...	20727	Causing little damage to the machinery
Fluctuatim	20728	Expect to receive all the machinery within next —— weeks
Fluctuosus	20729	Including the whole of the machinery
Fluency ...	20730	Started the machinery on —— everything working well
Fluenter ...	20731	Started the machinery on —— but a few alterations are still
Flugblatt...	20732	The machinery runs [needed
Flugel ...	20733	The machinery should be left carefully protected from the
Flugelmann	20734	The machinery consists of [weather
Flugelthur	20735	There is no machinery at all
Flugge ...	20736	The machinery has been received with the exception of
Fluidez ...	20737	The whole of the machinery has now been shipped
Fluidity ...	20738	Machinery now being shipped
Fluir ...	20739	The whole of the machinery is now on the mine
Fluitans ...	20740	What machinery will be required
Flukes ...	20741	The mine is well equipped with machinery
Flumineus	20742	You will not require to incur any outlay for machinery
Flummery	20743	In consequence of an accident to the machinery we have had to stop
Flurschutz	20744	Should be competent to overhaul the whole of the machinery ,
Flushingly	20745	The machinery is not sufficiently adequate
Fluslera ...	20746	The general condition of machinery is
Flussbett ...	20747	The general condition of machinery is indifferent
Flussibile...	20748	What is the general condition of the machinery and plant
Flussig ...	20749	The general condition of the machinery and plant is good
Flussione ...	20750	The general condition of the machinery and plant is fair
Flusspferd	20751	The machinery and plant are almost new

Fluteur ...	20752	The machinery and plant have been much used
Fluthen ...	20753	The machinery and plant are altogether out of repair
Fluting ...	20754	All the machinery is in good working order
Fluttered ...	20755	Examine and report on condition of machinery
Fluttering	20756	Will take care that all the machinery and stores are safely housed
Fluttuan ...	20757	The machinery is now running
Fluttuoso...	20758	Machinery is in good condition considering
Fluvial ...	20759	Engine and boiler are in good condition
Fluviatus ...	20760	Machinery not in good condition
Fluxion ...	20761	Erect adequate machinery for
Fluxissime	20762	The machinery is now in course of erection
Flyblow ...	20763	Can you depend on machinery another —— months
Flyboat ...	20764	All machinery in good order and working well
Flyleaf ...	20765	Is new machinery on property
Flypaper ...	20766	New machinery is on property
Foaming ...	20767	New machinery is not on property
Fobpocket	20768	**Machinist(s)** (*See also* " Fitter.")
Focaneus ...	20769	Machinists for
Fochettolo	20770	General machinist's outfit
Focillabat...	20771	**Made**
Focillatus...	20772	Not made
Focilletur ...	20773	Am (are) now having the —— made
Focillor ...	20774	As made up to
Focino ...	20775	Cannot be made up
Fockmast ...	20776	Cannot be made up later than
Focolare ...	20777	Can be made here
Foculus ...	20778	Cannot be made here
Foderatore	20779	Cannot be made too heavy
Fodicatio ...	20780	Can only be made larger by
Fodiendus	20781	Has (have) not been made
Foedifraga	20782	Has (have) already been made
Fogaril ...	20783	Has (have) been made [instructions
Foggetta ...	20784	Has (have) been made and is (are) now awaiting forwarding
Foggiare ...	20785	Had to wait whilst it (they) was (were) being made
Fogliaceo ...	20786	How long would it take to have new made
Foglietta ...	20787	Get it (them) made locally if you can
Fogliolina...	20788	I am (we are) getting it (them) made
Fogonadura	20789	I expect it (they) will be made and delivered within next
Fogonazo ...	20790	If you can get it (them) made [—— days
Fogueacion	20791	If you cannot get it (them) made
Foguear ...	20792	It (they) could not be made out
Foguezuelo	20793	Is said to have made
Fohlen ...	20794	In consequence of the —— having to be made
Folaghetta	20795	Made and supplied by
Folcire ...	20796	Made up to date
Folganza ...	20797	Made up of
Folgericht	20798	Made up mainly of
Folgerung	20799	Must be made up to
Folgesatz ...	20800	Must be made immediately
Folgezeit ...	20801	Made by
Folgorante	20802	Not made by
Folgsam ...	20803	All made by
Foliaceous	20804	Must be made sufficiently heavy
Foliacion ...	20805	Return if not made in accordance with specification
Foliated ...	20806	Was (were) made too heavy
Foliatura ...	20807	Was (were) made not nearly heavy enough
Folichon ...	20808	Shall I (we) get it (them) made here
Foliculo ...	20809	To be made
Folijones ...	20810	What is it made up of mainly
Foliole ...	20811	Will have to be made

Follados ...	20812	Will have to be made larger by
Follastro ...	20813	Would —— undertake to get them made
Follement	20814	You had better have duplicate(s) made
Folletista ...	20815	You had better have —— made
Follicle ...	20816	Can —— (it) (they) be made at
Folliculus	20817	When will it (they) be made
Follitim ...	20818	Better have made at
Foltern ...	20819	Has (have) made good headway
Fomentador	20820	As soon as made
Fomented	20821	**Mail(s)(ed)**
Fomenting	20822	Explain fully by next mail
Fomentos ...	20823	Will explain fully by next mail
Fomite ...	20824	Write fully by next mail
Foncete ...	20825	Will write fully by next mail
Foncier ...	20826	Send full report by mail (on)
Fondable ...	20827	Send full report by earliest mail you can
Fondacajo	20828	My report will be sent by to-day's mail
Fondaccio...	20829	My report will be sent by mail leaving on ——
Fondado ...	20830	By the first mail
Fondatore	20831	By the last mail
Fondatrice	20832	By an early mail
Fondeadero	20833	By the next mail
Fondement	20834	Caused a delay in the mail
Fonderie ...	20835	Forwarded by mail of ——
Fondeza ...	20836	Mail has arrived but no letter from you
Fondillon ...	20837	Mail has arrived but no letter for you
Fondirse ...	20838	Mail arrived just after closing my report
Fondista ...	20839	Mails detained owing to an accident to
Fondle ...	20840	No dependence can be placed on the mails
Fondling ...	20841	Shall be glad to hear from you by next mail respecting
Fondness ...	20842	The mail only leaves here once in —— days
Fondrilles	20843	The last mail from you was received on ——
Fondura ...	20844	The mail leaves —— for —— on ——
Fonsadera	20845	The communication is by mail leaving every —— day(s)
Fonsario ...	20846	The next mail leaves on —— when I shall write fully
Fontainier	20847	Will deal with this matter by the next mail
Fontanal ...	20848	Was (were) forwarded by mail leaving here on
Fontanche	20849	My report will be sent by mail leaving on
Fontanelle	20850	Mail as quickly as possible
Fontaneria	20851	When was it mailed
Fontaniere	20852	Have mailed to-day
Fontezuela	20853	Please send by first mail schedule of
Fonticella	20854	Have sent full particulars by mail
Fonticulus	20855	By next mail full particulars will be sent
Foolery ...	20856	**Main**
Foolscap ...	20857	At a distance of —— feet from the main shaft
Footboy ...	20858	Cable progress sinking main shaft
Footman ...	20859	Cable progress driving main level
Footnote ...	20860	By a level driven from the main shaft
Footprint ...	20861	From the main shaft (to)
Footstep ...	20862	In the main shaft
Footstool ...	20863	It will be necessary to deepen the main shaft
Foppery ...	20864	In the main
Foppish ...	20865	In the main drift
Forabilis ...	20866	Main drift
Foradar ...	20867	Main engine shaft
Foraggiare	20868	Main tunnel
Foragido ...	20869	As a main engine and pumping shaft
Foraging ...	20870	Main drift is now in —— feet
Foramen ...	20871	Main shaft is now down —— feet

Forametto	20872	Suggest making this (it) our main shaft
Forandus ...	20873	Sunk at a distance of —— feet from the main shaft
Foraneo ...	20874	Main workings
Forasiepe ...	20875	The main workings are
Forasteria	20876	**Mainly**
Foraterra ...	20877	Mainly true
Foratojo ...	20878	Was mainly to the effect that
Forbannuto	20879	Mainly false
Forbicette...	20880	Mainly made up of
Forbiciaro	20881	**Maintain(s)(ing)**
Forbitezza	20882	To maintain
Forbitrice...	20883	If we are to maintain
Forbottare	20884	Shall you be able to maintain
Forcat ...	20885	Expect to be able to maintain
Forcatella...	20886	Do not expect to be able to maintain
Forcatura...	20887	Maintain if you possibly can
Forceful ...	20888	Can maintain
Forcejar ...	20889	Cannot maintain
Forcejudo...	20890	Unless you can maintain
Forcelluto*	20891	**Make(s)**
Forcemeat	20892	To make
Forchetta ...	20893	Make haste
Forchina ...	20894	Will make haste
Forcillo ...	20895	Make as much as you can out of
Forcuzza ...	20896	Make over to
Forderlich	20897	You will make
Forderung	20898	I (we) will make
Fordicidia	20899	Can make
Forearm ...	20900	Cannot make
Foreboded	20901	Can you (——) make any suggestion
Forecastle...	20902	The only suggestion I (——) can make is
Foreground	20903	What alterations would you suggest I should make
Forehead ...	20904	Cannot make any alteration
Foreigner...	20905	The only alteration I (we) can make
Foreland ...	20906	How long would it take to make
Foreleg ...	20907	Would take —— week(s) to make
Forelle ...	20908	Do not make (it)
Forellino ...	20909	It has been necessary to make
Forensic ...	20910	Make it your first business to
Forerank ...	20911	Unless you can make
Foreshadow	20912	Can you make arrangements for (to)
Foresight...	20913	You must make the best arrangement you can
Foresozza...	20914	—— wants to make me (us)
Forestall ...	20915	Is trying to make me (us)
Forestaria	20916	Can you not make
Forestier ...	20917	Cannot make me (us)
Foretaste ...	20918	You should endeavour to make —— (him)
Foretoken...	20919	What do you expect to make out of it
Foretop ...	20920	Expect to make at least —— out of it
Forfaire ...	20921	Make contract for
Forfatto ...	20922	Make a new contract
Forfattura	20923	Make counter offer
Forfecchia	20924	Make firm offer
Forficette ...	20925	Must make some concession
Forficiata ...	20926	What do you make it
Forfolas ...	20927	Make(s) a very material difference
Forgeron ...	20928	**Maker(s)**
Foricula ...	20929	Who are the best makers
Forinseco ...	20930	The best makers are
Forjadura	20931	Have —— a good reputation as makers

[351]

* Is spelt "Foscelluto" in Edition I.

Forkedness	20932	Has (have) a good reputation as maker(s)
Forlane ...	20933	Has (have) no reputation as maker(s)
Formable ...	20934	Has (have) a fair reputation as maker(s)
Formador ...	20935	The best local maker(s) is (are)
Formage ...	20936	**Making**
Formaggio	20937	Making a reasonable allowance for
Formalidad	20938	Make all the progress possible
Formalist...	20939	Making water rapidly
Formandus	20940	Making fair progress
Formativo	20941	**Man** (*See also* " Capable," " Expensive.")
Formatore	20942	Require a good steady man as
Formatriz...	20943	Was a very steady man
Formatura	20944	Was a good and reliable man
Formejar ...	20945	A very steady and reliable man
Formelbuch	20946	Select a good man capable of
Formeros ...	20947	He is an excellent man in every respect
Formic ...	20948	He is a man that personally I should avoid
Formicajo	20949	He is a good practical man but cannot write a report
Formicante	20950	The post requires a man of
Formicetum	20951	—— is (would be) a good man for
Formicinus	20952	Would —— be a good man for the post
Formicolio	20953	Would not be a good man for the post
Formidable	20954	Can you obtain a reliable man for the following work
Formidatus	20955	He is not a man to be relied upon in the slightest degree
Formidine	20956	He is a man in whom you can implicitly trust
Formidor ...	20957	He is a man of great reputation for
Formisura	20958	He is a man of great experience
Formless ...	20959	Is a sound reliable man
Formosello	20960	I have always found him most reliable
Formositas	20961	I do not know the man to whom you refer
Formosus...	20962	I cannot find out anything about the man to whom you refer
Formulary	20963	The man to whom you refer is known to me as
Formulista	20964	**Manage(s)**
Fornacalia	20965	Can you manage
Fornaceus	20966	Can manage
Fornaciajo	20967	Cannot manage
Fornalla ...	20968	Do you think you could manage it (this)
Fornecer ...	20969	Could manage if
Fornecino...	20970	Will you be able to manage this
Fornelo ...	20971	I hope to be able to manage it (this) within
Fornicador	20972	When are you likely to manage it
Fornicario	20973	Fear shall not be able to manage it before
Fornicatim	20974	Fear shall not be able to manage it without
Fornitura...	20975	Try and manage if you can
Forosetto ...	20976	I (we) can manage very well
Forpex ...	20977	Would you be able to manage if
Forquilla ...	20978	Shall hope to manage
Forrago ...	20979	What chance is there of your being able to manage
Forscher ...	20980	There is every chance shall be able to manage
Forschung	20981	There is no chance of my (our) being able to manage
Forseche ...	20982	Will you be able to manage to
Forsennare	20983	I am afraid shall not be able to manage
Forsitan ...	20984	Cannot say whether I shall be able to manage before
Forsooth ...	20985	Do you think —— could manage to
Forsterei ...	20986	Has (have) been able to manage
Forstrecht	20987	Has (have) not been able to manage
Forstregal	20988	If you could manage
Forstwesen	20989	If you cannot manage
Fortachon	20990	If you are unable to manage this (it)
Fortalecer...	20991	In the event of your being able to manage

Fortalesa ...	20992	I (we) cannot manage
Fortassean	20993	Matter is difficult to manage
Fortassis ...	20994	Not at all difficult to manage
Fortdauer...	20995	Very difficult to manage
Fortdurfen	20996	To manage
Forteilen ...	20997	**Managed**
Fortement	20998	Can be easily managed
Forteresse	20999	Could be managed if
Forteruzzo	21000	Has (have) not been managed at all well
Fortesco ...	**21001**	Everything managed all right
Fortezza ...	21002	Whilst there he (——) managed
Fortfahren	21003	**Management** (*See also* " Conflicting.")
Fortgang ...	21004	Management very poor
Fortgehen...	21005	Management excellent
Forthelfen	21006	Left entirely to your management
Forthward	21007	Exhibit(s) great want of care and management
Fortifiant ...	21008	I (we) have the management
Fortificar ...	21009	I am (we are) likely to have the management
Fortified ...	21010	I (we) have nothing to do with the management
Fortigno ...	21011	Leave the management entirely in your hands
Fortin ...	21012	Management might be left to
Fortissimo	21013	Management of the affair
Fortiter ...	21014	Owing partly to bad management
Fortitude ...	21015	The management is in the hands of
Fortjagen	21016	The management is under the control of
Fortkommen	21017	Without very careful management
Fortlassen	21018	With care and proper management
Fortleben ...	21019	Will require some little management
Fortmachen	21020	Would —— be disposed to take the management
Fortregnen	21021	Am (is) unable to accept offer of management
Fortsein ...	21022	Would you be disposed to take the management
Fortsetzen	21023	Will accept offer of management
Fortsingen	21024	—— is unable to accept offer of management
Forttonen...	21025	—— will take the entire management
Forttragen	21026	—— will take the management of the
Fortuitous	21027	Said to be on account of bad management
Fortuity ...	21028	The previous management is said to have been very bad
Fortunatus	21029	Demand(s) a change of management
Fortune ...	21030	Management not economical. Supplies exceed requirements
Fortunium	21031	Systematic management
Fortunoso	21032	Through want of systematic management
Fortwahren	21033	**Manager**
Fortwirken	21034	Manager of
Fortwollen	21035	Better appoint —— as manager
Fortziehen	21036	The appointment of manager is in the hands of
Forum ...	21037	Who is the manager of
Forviare ...	21038	Has (have) appointed —— as manager
Forvoglia...	21039	Who would you suggest as manager
Forzador ...	21040	There is no one I can suggest at this moment as manager
Forzamento	21041	Would you consider —— as suitable for manager
Forzando ...	21042	I believe —— would make an excellent manager
Forzevole ...	21043	Am (is) not responsible manager
Forziere ...	21044	Is at present manager of
Forzosa ...	21045	Was formerly manager of
Forzudo ...	21046	Manager should have special experience in
†Fosfato ...	21047	**Manganese**
Fosforico ...	21048	Black oxide of manganese
Fosico ...	21049	Black oxide of manganese containing —— per cent. of the metal
Fossabam ...	21050	**Manganiferous**
Fossaccia ...	21051	**Manifest(ly)**

Fossarius ...	21052	It is quite manifest that
Fossatella...	21053	It is not at all manifest
Fossatum ...	21054	It is becoming more and more manifest (that)
Fossavero ...	21055	Will become manifest very shortly
Fossavisti	21056	**Manipulate(d)**
Fossemus ...	21057	Said to be manipulated through
Fossentur	21058	Probably manipulated by
Fossette ...	21059	Manipulated in the interest of
Fossicina ...	21060	Appears to have been manipulated somehow
Fossile ...	21061	**Manner**
Fossoyage	21062	In what manner
Fossoyeur	21063	In the same manner as
Fostered ...	21064	In like manner
Fostering ...	21065	In some manner
Fottivento	21066	In the manner explained
Fouailler ...	21067	In the following manner
Fouetter ...	21068	Is rather hasty in manner
Fougasse ...	21069	Has a very pleasant manner
Fougeraie...	21070	Owing to the very unfavourable manner in which
Fouillis ...	21071	**Manufacture(rs)** (*See also* "Makers.")
Foulerie ...	21072	**Many** (*See also* "Great.")
Foulque ...	21073	How many
Foundling	21074	Many more
Fountains...	21075	Do you require many
Fourchette ...	21076	As many as possible
Fourchon ...	21077	How many do you require
Fourmilier	21078	I (we) do not want many
Fournaise...	21079	As many as you can get
Fourneau ...	21080	How many do you hope to
Fourniment	21081	How many will that leave
Fourriere ...	21082	I (we) shall want a great many
Fourscore...	21083	In many cases
Fourvoyer	21084	Not many additional
Foutelaie ...	21085	Owing to many difficulties
Fovendus...	21086	Not so many as
Fovila	21087	How many can you get at that price
Fowling ...	21088	How many days
Foxchase ...	21089	Buy as many as you can get at that price
Foxdog ...	21090	**Map(s)**
Foxglove ...	21091	Can you send a map showing the relative positions of ——
Foxhound...	21092	Have mailed the best map I can obtain [(and ——)
Fracassare	21093	According to the —— map
Fracesco ...	21094	As shown on the map attached to the lease (bond) (——)
Frachtgut...	21095	No government maps are yet published
Fracidare ...	21096	The map is altogether incorrect
Fracidume	21097	You will find it (——) marked on the map sent you on ——
Fractures ...	21098	Map of the surrounding country
Fradear ...	21099	Map of the property
Fragancia ..	21100	**March**
Fragante ...	21101	At the beginning of March
Fragaria ...	21102	About the middle of March
Fragellare	21103	During the entire month of March
Fragepunkt	21104	For the entire month of March
Frageweise	21105	Last March
Fragil ...	21106	Next March
Fragilatis ...	21107	Near the end of March
Fragility ...	21108	First day of March
Fraglich ...	21109	Second day of March
Fragment...	21110	Third day of March
Fragola ...	21111	Fourth day of March

Fragolino ...	21112	Fifth day of March
Fragose ...	21113	Sixth day of March
Fragosidad	21114	Seventh day of March
Fragrantly	21115	Eighth day of March
Fraguador	21116	Ninth day of March
Fraguar ...	21117	Tenth day of March
Fraîcheur ...	21118	Eleventh day of March
Frailada ...	21119	Twelfth day of March
Fraile ...	21120	Thirteenth day of March
Frailecico ...	21121	Fourteenth day of March
Frailengo ...	21122	Fifteenth day of March
Fraileria ...	21123	Sixteenth day of March
Frailesco ...	21124	Seventeenth day of March
Fraililllos ...	21125	Eighteenth day of March
Frailness ...	21126	Nineteenth day of March
Frailote ...	21127	Twentieth day of March
Fraisiere ...	21128	Twenty-first day of March
Framboise	21129	Twenty-second day of March
Frambuesa	21130	Twenty-third day of March
Framea ...	21131	Twenty-fourth day of March
Frammesso	21132	Twenty-fifth day of March
Francalete	21133	Twenty-sixth day of March
Francatura	21134	Twenty-seventh day of March
Franchigia	21135	Twenty-eighth day of March
Franchise ...	21136	Twenty-ninth day of March
Francioso ...	21187	Thirtieth day of March
Franciscan	21138	Thirty-first day of March
Franciser ...	21189	March expenses amount to
Francisque	21140	March shipments amount to
Francolin ...	21141	**Margin**
Franela ...	21142	What margin have you left for
Frangendus	21143	A margin of
Frangente	21144	Can you work with so narrow a margin
Frangersi ...	21145	A very narrow margin of profit
Frangiato ...	21146	Leaves no margin whatever
Frangible ...	21147	Margin not sufficient
Frangipane	21148	Margin quite sufficient
Frangollar	21149	Margin would be sufficient if
Frangote ...	21150	Should leave a good margin for
Franjar ...	21151	Swallowed up the entire margin of profit
Franjeado ...	21152	Should allow a margin of at least —— for ——
Franjuela ...	21153	Unless it (they) leave(s) a good margin
Franking ...	21154	Must have a margin for contingencies
Frankiren ...	21155	Which leaves no margin for contingencies
Frankness	21156	**Mark(s)** (*See also* "Boundary.").
Franquear	21157	What is (are) the marks
Franquicia	21158	The mark(s) is (are)
Fransig ...	21159	No marks at all
Franticly ...	21160	Marks and shipping instructions will be given by
Franzband	21161	**Marked**
Franzbrod	21162	How was it (were they) marked
Frappant ...	21163	Everything was marked in accordance with instructions
Frappatore	21164	Must be most carefully marked
Frappeur ...	21165	Were all properly marked
Frapposto ...	21166	To be marked ——
Fraque ...	21167	**Market** (*See also* "Force.")
Frascante ...	21168	Cable the state of the market
Fraschetto	21169	Market excited
Fraschiere	21170	Market dull
Frasco ...	21171	Market firm owing to

Frasconaja	21172	Market dull owing to
Frasista ...	21173	Market lifeless
Frasqueta...	21174	Market steady —— in demand
Frassineto	21175	The market is strong
Frastaglia	21176	The market is strong now. Do not think it will last
Frastenere	21177	The market is weak
Frastuolo ...	21178	The market is at present weak ; believe tendency is to become
Fratacar ...	21179	The market is flabby [——
Frateccio ...	21180	The market becoming much firmer
Fratellino...	21181	The market is steadily rising
Fratellus ...	21182	The market is over stocked
Fraterculo	21183	The market is very limited
Fraternal ...	21184	The market is steadily falling
Fraternity	21185	The market has hardened considerably
Fraticello ...	21186	The market is now ——
Fraticidio...	21187	The market exhibits tendency to panic
Fratricide...	21188	Cable what market there is for ——
Fratrissam	21189	There is no market at all
Fraudador	21190	The only market is at
Fraudandus	21191	There is a good market at
Fraudeur ...	21192	Cable if market becomes more favourable
Fraudevole	21193	Cable if any change in market
Frauduleux	21194	What should you advise with present market
Frauenhaft	21195	In the present state of the market I do not advise you to sell
Frauenhemd	21196	In the present state of the market I do not advise you to buy
Frauenhut	21197	Market declining. I should advise you to sell
Frauenvolk	21198	I should advise you with the present market to ——
Fraulein ...	21199	Consider the market
Fraustina...	21200	Keeps the market fairly lively
Fraxinela ...	21201	Keeps the market steady
Fraxinetum	21202	Keeps the market dull
Frazadilla	21203	The market closed strong
Freakish ...	21204	The market closed weak
Frecciare ...	21205	A strong upward movement in the market
Freckheit ...	21206	A strong downward tendency in the market
Freckled ...	21207	A very slight downward movement in the market
Frecuencia	21208	A very slight upward movement in the market
Frecuentar	21209	The market is depressed
Fredaine ...	21210	The market opened firm
Freddezza ..	21211	The market opened weak but closed firm
Freddiccio	21212	The market has been flooded with
Freddotto...	21213	Owing to fluctuations in the market
Fredonner	21214	Do not force the market
Freebooter	21215	From the tone of the market at present
Freeborn ...	21216	The present market price is
Freedom ...	21217	The circular (report) had a good effect on the market
Freeman ...	21218	The circular (report) has depressed the market
Freemasons	21219	Watch the market
Freeport ...	21220	Watch market carefully and cable if any change
Freestates...	21221	No movement in the market
Freewill ...	21222	**Marl**
Freezed ...	21223	**Massive**
Fregacion...	21224	**Match**
Fregadero...	21225	No match for
Fregajo ...	21226	To match
Fregarono...	21227	Must match
Fregatina...	21228	Can you match
Fregatriz ...	21229	Cannot match
Fregatte ...	21230	Can match
Fregiatura	21231	If you cannot match

Fregole ...	21232	If I (we) cannot match
Fregonil ...	21233	Match as nearly as possible
Freibeuter	21234	**Matching-piece**
Freibrief ...	21235	Matching-piece for
Freicorps ...	21236	Send matching-piece to go
Froidenker	21237	Have forwarded templet for matching-piece
Freidura ...	21238	Send particulars of matching-piece
Freifrau ...	21239	Send duplicate matching-piece
Freigebig ...	21240	**Mate's receipt**
Freigeist ...	21241	Who has mate's receipt
Freigut ...	21242	—— has mate's receipt
Freihafen ...	21243	Do not give up mate's receipt unless (until)
Freiherr ...	21244	In which case you can give up mate's receipt
Freilar ...	21245	In exchange for mate's receipt
Freilich ...	21246	Retain mate's receipt
Freimaurer	21247	**Material(s)** (*See also* "Stores.")
Freimuth ...	21248	If you consider this material
Freiria ...	21249	It is most material that
Freisass ...	21250	I (we) shall have to send to —— for materials
Freischule	21251	I (we) have had to send to —— for materials
Freisinn ...	21252	Materials for
Freistaat ...	21253	Materials for which can readily be obtained
Freistunde	21254	The materials necessary are all at hand
Freitreppe	21255	There are none of the necessary materials at hand
Freiwillig...	21256	**Matrix**
Frejol ...	21257	In a matrix of
Frelatage ...	21258	The matrix is
Frelaterie...	21259	What is the matrix
Freluquet...	21260	**Matte** (*See also* "Matting.")
Fremdartig	21261	What will matte average
Fremdling	21262	Matte will average —— for
Fremente ...	21263	The matte is worth —— per ton
Fremitare	21264	What is the output of matte
Fremitus ...	21265	Output of matte is
Frenchlike	21266	Matte ready for shipment
Frendiente	21267	What is the value of matte
Frenello ...	21268	What is the weight of matte
Freneria ...	21269	The value of the matte is
Frenetico ...	21270	The weight of the matte is ["Facilitate," "Immediate."]
Frenetique	21271	**Matter(s)** (*See also* "Deferred," "Delaying," "Expedite,"
Freniger ...	21272	Have brought the matter to a successful issue
Frenillar ...	21273	Hasten matter(s) if you can
Frental ...	21274	Am (are) doing all I (we) can to hasten matters
Frentaza ...	21275	Cannot hasten matter(s)
Frentecica	21276	Can you suggest anything to hasten matter(s)
Frentero ...	21277	Settle the matter as you suggest
Frescachon	21278	How do matters stand
Freschezza	21279	Matters generally are improved
Frescoccio	21280	What is the matter
Frescoes ...	21281	There is nothing the matter
Frescura ...	21282	When will the matter be settled
Fresera ...	21283	I (we) expect the whole matter will be settled on ——
Freshening	21284	You had better refer the matter to
Freshmen	21285	I have already referred the matter to
Freshness...	21286	Shall I refer the matter to
Fresneda ...	21287	What has been the matter
Fresnillo ...	21288	The real matter is that
Fresquista	21289	Have nothing to do with the matter
Fressend ...	21290	As soon as the matter is settled
Fressgier ...	21291	Is the matter settled yet

Fretalis ...	21292	The sooner the matter is settled the better
Fretfully ...	21293	This should settle the matter
Fretillant ...	21294	Until this matter is settled
Fretsaw ...	21295	I (we) leave you free to settle the matter
Frettevole...	21296	It does not matter
Frettoloso...	21297	If —— does so it will upset matters considerably
Fretwerk ...	21298	It is a matter of
Freuden ...	21299	It might be matter of
Freudentag	21300	Is still a matter of
Freundin ...	21301	It (which) might become a matter of importance
Freundlich	21302	It (which) is a matter of great importance to me (us)
Frevelhaft	21303	It is a matter of great importance
Freveln ...	21304	In the event of the matter becoming of more importance
Frevelthat	21305	I (we) will have nothing to do with the matter
Frevelwort	21306	You had better have nothing to do with the matter
Frezador ...	21307	No matter
Friabilita ...	21308	No matter what —— may say
Friable ...	21309	Matters generally very unsatisfactory
Frialdad ...	21310	Matters generally are unsettled
Friamente	21311	There is no improvement in matters
Friandise ...	21312	Shall go into the matter carefully
Friatico ...	21313	Shall go into the matter in detail by mail
Fribbling ...	21314	I find on examining into the matter that
Fricandean	21315	Please go into the matter
Fricando ...	21316	The only matter
Fricar ...	21317	The only matter you should concern yourself with is
Fricassee ...	21318	The matter is now out of my (our) hands
Fricatrix ...	21319	The matter is now in the hands of ——
Fricatura ...	21320	The matter of
Fricoter ...	21321	Has the matter been placed before
Friecillo ...	21322	The matter has been placed before
Friedhof ...	21323	The matter to which you refer
Friedlich ...	21324	The (this) matter to which you refer was told me in strict
Friega ...	21325	Looking at the matter impartially [confidence
Friendship	21326	As matters are now
Frieren ...	21327	How are matters looking
Frigates ...	21328	How do matters stand as regards
Frigefacio...	21329	Matters are progressing favourably
Frigerans ...	21330	Feel your way in the matter
Frigeratio...	21331	I (we) leave the matter entirely for you to arrange
Frigescens	21332	Should you do so the matter will be altogether upset
Frightful ...	21333	Do not close matter until you hear from me again
Frigidato ...	21334	The matter will be considered within the next few days
Frigidez ...	21335	Leave matters as they are for the present
Frigidity ...	21336	Leave matters exactly as they are
Frigidulus	21337	Will close up the matter at the earliest moment
Frigillam ...	21338	Will give the matter immediate attention
Frigultio ...	21339	Will give the matter immediate attention and cable you
Frilling ...	21340	Will give the matter immediate attention and write
Frimario ...	21341	**Matting** (See also " Matte.")
Frinnousse	21342	Is the ore suitable for matting
Frinfino ...	21343	The ore is suitable for matting
Fringilago	21344	The ore is not suitable for matting
Fringilla ...	21345	Matting process
Fringuello	21346	Matting furnace(s)
Fringuer ...	21347	Profit on matting process
Friolento ...	21348	What saving would there be per ton on matting the ore
Friolera ...	21349	Matting the ore would mean a saving of —— per ton
Friponner	21350	Cost of matting
~very ...	21351	**May** (See also " Might.")

Friritus ...	21352	May be able to
Frisadura...	21353	May not be able to
Friscello ...	21354	May go to
Frischling	21355	May do for
Friscur ...	21356	May he
Frisiren ...	21357	May I (we)
Friskiness	21358	May I (we) fix
Frisking ...	21359	I (we) may
Frisotter ...	21360	May you
Frisuelo ...	21361	How long may I expect
Fritada ...	21362	You may expect
Fritilaria ...	21363	How much may I (we) ask
Fritillas ...	21364	How much may I (we) take
Fritinnio ...	21365	If I (we) may
Frittatone	21366	You may
Frittered ...	21367	May he (they)
Frivolidad	21368	He (they) may
Frivolity ...	21369	In case —— may
Frivolo ...	21370	In case —— may not
Frixion ...	21371	When may I (we)
Frixorium	21372	You may require
Frizzante ...	21373	—— may require
Frizzled ...	21374	May probably go
Frizzling ...	21375	May probably go better
Frodatore ...	21376	May probably go worse
Frodolente	21377	May probably have to pay a little more
Frohlich ...	21378	**May**
Frohlocken	21379	At the beginning of May
Frohnfeste	21380	About the middle of May
Frohnvogt	21381	During the entire month of May
Frohsinn ...	21382	For the entire month of May
Froidement	21383	Last May
Froidure ...	21384	Next May
Frolicking	21385	Near the end of May
Fromager ...	21386	First day of May
Frombolare	21387	Second day of May
Fromental	21388	Third day of May
Frommeln	21389	Fourth day of May
Frommler...	21390	Fifth day of May
Frondator	21391	Sixth day of May
Frondesco...	21392	Seventh day of May ✓
Frondetta...	21393	Eighth day of May
Frondifero	21394	Ninth day of May
Frondoso ...	21395	Tenth day of May
Frontatus...	21396	Eleventh day of May
Fronted ...	21397	Twelfth day of May
Fronterizo	21398	Thirteenth day of May
Frontiere ...	21399	Fourteenth day of May
Frontlet ...	21400	Fifteenth day of May
Frontonem	21401	Sixteenth day of May
Frontudo ...	21402	Seventeenth day of May
Frostbeule	21403	Eighteenth day of May
Frostbites...	21404	Nineteenth day of May
Frostig ...	21405	Twentieth day of May
Frostwork	21406	Twenty-first day of May
Frothiness	21407	Twenty-second day of May
Frottage ...	21408	Twenty-third day of May
Frottelare...	21409	Twenty-fourth day of May
Frottoir ...	21410	Twenty-fifth day of May
Frouer ...	21411	Twenty-sixth day of May

Fruchtbar...	21412	Twenty-seventh day of May
Fruchten ...	21413	Twenty-eighth day of May
Fruchtlos ...	21414	Twenty-ninth day of May
Fructero ...	21415	Thirtieth day of May
Fructidor ...	21416	Thirty-first day of May
Fructifier ...	21417	May expenses amount to
Fructueux	21418	May shipments amount to
Fruendus ...	21419	**Meagre**
Frugal ...	21420	Very meagre
Frugatojo...	21421	Too meagre
Frugifero ...	21422	Very meagre news
Frugilegus	21423	Continue(s) to be meagre
Frugiperda	21424	**Mean(s)**
Frugivore...	21425	By no means
Frugnolare	21426	By this means
Frugnuolo	21427	What means have you for
Frugolino ...	21428	Do you mean that
Fruhgeburt	21429	Do you mean to infer that
Fruhjahr ...	21430	I (we) did not mean to infer
Fruhklug ...	21431	If you mean this
Fruhling ...	21432	I (we) did not mean
Fruhmette	21433	What do you mean by
Fruhobst ...	21434	What do you mean in
Fruhreif ...	21435	Where do you mean
Fruhstuck	21436	When do you mean
Fruitage ...	21437	As a means to an end
Fruiterer ...	21438	By what means
Fruition ...	21439	By all means
Fruiturus...	21440	Adopt such means as you think necessary
Frumentoso	21441	I am told that —— means to
Frumenty...	21442	I know that —— means to
Frumitor ...	21443	I mean to
Frummaire	21444	Is a man of means
Fruncidor...	21445	Is not a man of sufficient means
Fruncir ...	21446	Find out what —— means (to do)
Fruniscor...	21447	Prompt means must be adopted
Fruslera ...	21448	The only means I (we) have is to
Frusquin ...	21449	Take such means as you think best
Frustagno	21450	What means would you propose to adopt
Frustatim...	21451	Owing to the imperfect means employed
Frustatore	21452	What do (does) —— mean by
Frustatura	21453	Means well
Frustranco	21454	Means well but has no tact
Frustrar ...	21455	Have no means
Frustulum	21456	Have no means of knowing
Frutectum	21457	Have no means of sinking
Fruteria ...	21458	Take every means to
Frutetosus	21459	Take every possible means to accomplish it
Fruticans...	21460	Will take every possible means to
Frutice ..	21461	Take every possible means to bring forward
Fruticoso ...	21462	Will take every possible means to bring forward
Frutificar ...	21463	Take every legitimate means to suppress
Frutilla ...	21464	Will take every legitimate means to suppress
Fruttajolo	21465	**Meaning**
Fruttato ...	21466	Do you understand the meaning of
Fruttevole	21467	Explain by mail the meaning of
Fruttifero...	21468	Explain by telegram (cable) the meaning of
Fruttuare...	21469	Meaning not clear
Fruttuoso...	21470	**Meant**
Fryingpan	21471	I (we) meant

Fuchseisen	21472	Is what was meant
Fuchsias ...	21473	Meant to convey
Fuchsig ...	21474	Was certainly not meant
Fuchsroth	21475	Inform me what —— meant
Fuchteln ...	21476	All that was meant was
Fueiliere ...	21477	If this is what was meant
Fuellar	21478	Certainly meant
Fuellecico...	21479	Could not have been meant
Fuelling ...	21480	What I meant was
Fuente ...	21481	**Meanwhile**
Fueret	21482	Meanwhile do as much as possible in connection with
Fugacidad	21483	Meanwhile get as much —— ready as possible
Fugaciter ...	21484	**Measure(s)** (*See also* "Dimensions" and Table at end.)
Fugamento	21485	When shall you measure up
Fugandus...	21486	Prompt measures taken
Fugara ...	21487	What measures do you propose to adopt
Fugatore ...	21488	Propose to adopt the following measures
Fugaturus	21489	The measures are not arbitrary
Fuggevole	21490	Arbitrary measures
Fuggiasco	21491	Take measures accordingly
Fuggibile ...	21492	Measures —— from —— to ——
Fuggitrice	21493	What does it (do they) measure
Fughetta ...	21494	**Measured**
Fugido ...	21495	Will be measured up on
Fugiendos	21496	**Measurement(s)**
Fugitabat...	21497	All the measurements are up to
Fugitatio ...	21498	Superficial measurements
Fugitivo ...	21499	You should personally check all measurements made
Fugleman...	21500	Give details of measurements
Fuglich ...	21501	**Mechanic(s)** (*See also* "Engine-man.")
Fugsam ...	21502	**Mechanical(ly)**
Fuhlbar ...	21503	Very mechanical
Fuhlhorn ...	21504	Is it mechanically possible
Fuhllos ...	21505	It is possible mechanically
Fuhrknecht	21506	**Medium** (*See also* "Grade," "Quality.")
Fuhrmann	21507	As a medium course
Fuhrung ...	21508	Is there no medium course
Fuhrwerk...	21509	There is no medium course
Fuhrwesen	21510	The only medium course would be to
Fuimiento	21511	**Meet**
Fuina ...	21512	To meet
Fulanito +	21513	Meet me (——) at
Fulano ...	21514	Expect to meet
Fulcibilis ...	21515	Arrange to meet —— at —— on ——
Fulciendus	21516	When could you meet —— and where
Fulcire ...	21517	Could meet —— on —— at ——
Fulgecer ...	21518	Am proceeding to —— in absence of —— who failed to meet me
Fulgente ...	21519	Could meet at
Fulgetra ...	21520	Cannot meet you (until)
Fulgidezza	21521	Cannot meet you owing to
Fulgilatus	21522	Might meet me at
Fulgorato ...	21523	So as to meet
Fulgura ...	21524	Unless should soon meet with
Fulguritas	21525	Will help me (us) to meet
Fuligines ...	21526	Who promised to meet me on my arrival has not done so
Fuliginoso	21527 ✗	Try and arrange for —— to meet ——
Fulldress ...	21528	Shall I (we) meet ——. If so, where
Fullerazo ...	21529	Arrange to meet —— at —— on receipt of a telegram from
Fulleria ...	21530	**Meeting** (*See also* "Fixed," "Vote.") [him
Fullona ...	21531	Shareholders' meeting

Fullonicus	21532	Directors' meeting
Fullsel ...	21533	Call a meeting for —— o'clock on ——
Fulmentum	21534	Call a meeting on
Fulmicoton	21535	Call meeting of Company
Fulminado	21536	Call meeting of directors
Fulmineus	21537	Call meeting of creditors
Fulsome ...	21538	Call meeting of parties interested
Fulviana ...	21539	Call meeting of stockholders
Fumacchio	21540	Meetings are held half-yearly
Fumadero...	21541	Meetings are held annually
Fumajuolo	21542	Annual general meeting
Fumante ...	21543	Can you attend meeting
Fumaria ...	21544	Am sending you P/A to act at meeting
Fumbler ...	21545	Please attend meeting and telegraph the outcome
Fumbling ..	21546	Please attend meeting and watch our interests
Fumeron ...	21547	The result of the meeting is that
Fumeterre	21548	Meeting passed off very quietly ; things remain as they were
Fumeuse ...	21549	When will the next directors' meeting take place
Fumifero ...	21550	The next directors' meeting is on ——
Fumificus...	21551	No date has been fixed for meeting
Fumigador	21552	A meeting has been called for the purpose of
Fumigatio	21553	A meeting was held but nothing was resolved upon
Fuming ...	21554	At a meeting held on —— it was resolved to
Fumivore ...	21555	At the adjourned meeting [accepted (payable on ——)
Fummicare	21556	At a meeting of the creditors a composition of —— was
Fummosita	21557	Has been appointed for the meeting
Fumorolas	21558	Issue formal notice(s) for a meeting
Fumosidad	21559	Meeting of the committee
Fumosus ...	21560	Notices for meeting were issued on
Funambulo	21561	Require this information for shareholders' meeting
Fundador	21562	Shareholders' meeting is to be held on ——
Fundaturus	21563	Shareholders' extraordinary meeting
Fundendus	21564	When is shareholders' ordinary general meeting to be held
Funderia ...	21565	Statutory meeting [information not later than ——
Fundgrube	21566	Statutory meeting is to be held on ——. Telegraph latest
Fundibalum	21567	We are obliged to hold shareholders' meeting not later than
Fundible ...	21568	The annual meeting of shareholders is fixed for —— at ——
Fundir ...	21569	Will be laid before the next board meeting [o'clock
Funditatio	21570	We are meeting with
Funditore...	21571	**Member(s)**
Fundulus...	21572	Members of committee
Funebre ...	21573	Is (are) members of
Funebridad	21574	Is (are) not members of
Funeraire...	21575	Is (are) members of the firm of
Funerarius	21576	**Men**
Funereal ...	21577	Plenty of men
Funerepus	21578	How many men
Funestar ...	21579	Shall require at least —— men
Funestatio	21580	Cannot continue until arrival of more men
Funetum ...	21581	Is (are) short of men
Funfmalig	21582	Owing to being short of men
Funfseitig	21583	Short of men since
Funginus...	21584	Short of men this month
Fungofitas	21585	What number of men are to be employed
Fungous ...	21586	What number of men have been employed monthly
Funicella ...	21587	What number of men have you employed and what money is
Funicular...	21588	**Mention(s)** [required for supplies
Funkeln ...	21589	Do not omit to mention
Funzione ...	21590	Can I (we) mention it (this) to
Fuorche ...	21591	If you think fit you can mention this to

Fuormisura	21592	Was any mention made of
Fuoruscito	21593	No mention was made of
Fuorvoglia	21594	Better avoid any mention of
Furacar	21595	To mention
Furaciter ...	21596	**Mentioned**
Furatrice ...	21597	Has already been mentioned
Furbaccio ...	21598	Is not mentioned
Furbished	21599	Only in case it is mentioned
Furbishing	21600	Shall not be mentioned
Furbitte ...	21601	Should not be mentioned
Furchen ...	21602	Should not have been mentioned
Furchtsam	21603	The sooner it is mentioned the better
Furcilla ...	21604	Unless it is mentioned
Fureter ...	21605	Was not mentioned at all
Furfantare	21606	Was mentioned quite casually
Furialis ...	21607	You have not mentioned
Furialiter...	21608	**Merchant(s)**
Furiamini...	21609	Merchants' bills
Furibond ...	21610	Who is (are) leading merchants at
Furibundus	21611	Who is (are) the merchants
Furieux ...	21612	Was formerly a merchant at
Furinalia ...	21613	**Mercury** (*See also* "Amalgam," "Cinnabar," "Quicksilver."
Furioso	21614	Mercury riffles
Furlieb ...	21615	Bottle(s) of mercury
Furlongs ...	21616	**Merit(s)**
Furlough ...	21617	Has (have) great merit
Furnaceus	21618	Has (have) no actual merit
Furniture...	21619	Is of undoubted merit
Furoncello	21620	What merit has it (have they)
Furoncle ...	21621	**Mesozoic**
Furriela ...	21622	**Message** (*See also* "Insert.")
Furriers ...	21623	Cable message
Fursorge ...	21624	Send message in plain words
Fursprache	21625	A message was sent
Furstlich ...	21626	From message received we gather
Furtible ...	21627	Has (have) not sent any message since
Furtificus ...	21628	In accordance with your message
Furtively ...	21629	I (we) have not received the message referred to ; if necessary [repeat
Furtivo ...	21630	I (we) understand your message to mean
Furwahr ...	21631	I (we) do not think you understand the message
Furwort ...	21632	Last message received from you was dated
Furze ...	21633	My last message to you was sent on
Fusaggine	21634	Owing to your message being unintelligible
Fusajuolo...	21635	Repeat the message
Fuscar ...	21636	Send following message to ——
Fuscinulo ...	21637	—— has sent a message to the effect that
Fusella ...	21638	Please place this message in Code book opposite the word ——
Fusibilita ...	21639	How many words did your message received on the —— contain
Fusileer ...	21640	Message sent you on the —— contained —— words
Fusillade ...	21641	This message contains inclusive of address five words
Fusillos ...	21642	This message contains inclusive of address six words
Fusorium ...	21643	This message contains inclusive of address seven words
Fussbad ...	21644	This message contains inclusive of address eight words
Fussbiege ...	21645	This message contains inclusive of address nine words
Fussboden	21646	This message contains inclusive of address ten words
Fussfall ...	21647	This message contains inclusive of address eleven words
Fussganger	21648	This message contains inclusive of address twelve words
Fussgieht...	21649	This message contains inclusive of address thirteen words
Fussoldat...	21650	This message contains inclusive of address fourteen words
Fusston ...	21651	This message contains inclusive of address fifteen words

Fusstritt ...	21652	This message contains inclusive of address sixteen words
Fussvolk ...	21653	This message contains inclusive of address seventeen words
Fusswurzel	21654	This message contains inclusive of address eighteen words
Fustado ...	21655	This message contains inclusive of address nineteen words
Fustanero...	21656	This message contains inclusive of address twenty words
Fusternam	21657	This message contains inclusive of address twenty-one words
Fustete ...	21658	This message contains inclusive of address twenty-two words
Fustian ...	21659	This message contains inclusive of address twenty-three words
Fustibalus	21660	This message contains inclusive of address twenty-four words
Fusticello ...	21661	This message contains inclusive of address twenty-five words
Fustigatur	21662	This message contains inclusive of address twenty-six words
Fustigemus	21663	This message contains inclusive of address twenty-seven words
Fustiness ...	21664	This message contains inclusive of address twenty-eight words
Fustuario ...	21665	This message contains inclusive of address twenty-nine words
Fustuccia ...	21666	This message contains inclusive of address thirty words
Futaille ...	21667	This message contains inclusive of address —— words
Futainier ...	21668	**Met**
Futatim ...	21669	Have met with
Futilidad ...	21670	Has (have) not yet met
Futiliter ...	21671	Which we have met with at
Futteral ...	21672	Was (were) met with
Futterung	21673	Who was to have met me (us)
Futurario...	21674	Unless should soon be met with
Futurity ...	21675	Arrived here —— have met —— am leaving to-day (——) for
Fututrix ...	21676	**Metal(s)**
Fuyard ...	21677	The metal used in the castings
Gabacha ...	21678	To be made of best metal
Gabalium...	21679	Of gun metal
Gabamentos	21680	Of the precious metals
Gabanzo ...	21681	**Metallic**
Gabardina	21682	**Metalliferous**
Gabarier ...	21683	Distinctly metalliferous
Gabarrero	21684	**Metamorphic**
Gabbadeo...	21685	Metamorphic rock
Gabbamento	21686	Metamorphic slate
Gabbanella	21687	Overlaid by metamorphic schist
Gabbatha...	21688	The rock gradually becomes more metamorphic
Gabbatore	21689	**Method**
Gabbatrice	21690	By what method
Gabbevole	21691	By the following method
Gabbiajo ...	21692	By this method
Gabbiolina	21693	Visit —— and see their method of working (the)
Gabbiuola	21694	The method in which they work (the)
Gabela ...	21695	By the method hitherto employed
Gabellare ...	21696	What is the method hitherto employed for (at)
Gabelpferd	21697	Their previous method of working
Gabelroof...	21698	By this method I (we) should expect
Gabesina ...	21699	As the method that should be employed
Gabionner	21700	A new method for
Gaburones	21701	As the best method
Gacetero ...	21702	Is the only method
Gacetilla ...	21703	Is extracted by the following method
Gacetista ...	21704	The method employed is very defective
Gachas ...	21705	The method employed is the only one suitable
Gachoneria	21706	The method employed consists of
Gadder ...	21707	Present method not suitable
Gadfly ...	21708	Present method is the best hitherto devised
Gafedad ...	21709	The method of extraction employed is the best under present
Gagate ...	21710	**Mica** (*See also* " Mineral," " Rocks.")　　[circumstances
Gageur ...	21711	**Micaceous**

Gagiste ...	21712	Micaceous rock
Gagliarda ...	21713	Micaceous schist
Gaglioffo ...	21714	**Middle**
Gagnepain	21715	About the middle of
Gagnepetit	21716	In the middle of
Gagnolare	21717	Not later than the middle
Gagnolio ...	21718	Through the middle
Gaieties ...	21719	—— ft. beyond the middle
Gailie	21720	**Might** (*See also* "May.")
Gaiment ...	21721	Might be made
Gainful ...	21722	As soon as it might be possible
Gainless ...	21728	I (we) might be able to
Gainsayer ...	21724	It might not
Gainsaying	21725	It might be possible to do it
Gaitano ...	21726	It might
Gaiteria ...	21727	I (they) might
Gajacum ...	21728	Might be possible (if)
Gajamonto	21729	Might I (we)
Gajezza ...	21730	You might
Gajoso	21731	Might he (they)
Gajuza ...	21732	Might I (we) not
Galactite ...	21733	Might be
Galamero ...	21734	**Mile(s)** (*See also* "Foot," "Yards" and Table at end.)
Galammant	21735	—— miles from ——
Galancete ...	21736	How many miles are you from ——
Galanteria	21737	Only —— miles from
Galantine ...	21738	Can be traced for —— miles
Galanto ...	21739	Is —— miles across
Galantuomo	21740	Miles distant
Galapago ...	21741	Miles distant from
Galardon ...	21742	Nearly a mile
Galavanted	21743	Over a mile
Galavardo	21744	Total length is —— miles —— yards
Galaxia ...	21745	Within a distance of —— miles
Galbanado	21746	Miles from the frontier of
Galbanatus	21747	**Mill** (*See also* "Battery," "Breakdown," "Broken," "Com-
Galbanero	21748	Mill site [menced," "Connect," "Stamps.")
Galbanum	21749	As a mill site
Galbeorum	21750	A mill site of —— acres
Galbineus ...	21751	The mill is
Galdente ...	21752	Mill shut down owing to (for)
Galdres ...	21753	Will overhaul the mill
Galdrope ...	21754	The whole of the machinery for the mill is now on the ground
Galdrufa ...	21755	Chilian mill
Galeabimus	21756	Huntingdon mill
Galeantor ...	21757	Five stamp mill
Galeato ...	21758	Ten stamp mill
Galeazza ...	21759	Fifteen stamp mill
Galeere ...	21760	Twenty stamp mill
Galeffare ...	21761	Forty stamp mill
Galenum ...	21762	—— stamp mill
Galeon ...	21763	Mill —— tons as promptly as possible
Galeopsis ...	21764	What would it cost you to mill —— tons
Galeotta ...	21765	Could you arrange to mill
Galerada ...	21766	Am trying to arrange to mill
Galeratus ...	21767	Have arranged to mill —— tons
Galeria ...	21768	Have arranged to mill —— tons at a cost of
Galerilla ...	21769	Have you any reason to doubt mill results
Galerno ...	21770	Have no reason at all to doubt result of mill trial
Galetas ...	21771	Have reason to doubt result of mill trial

[365]

Galgana ...	21772	My reason for doubting mill trial is
Galgendieb	21773	The mill has been running since
Galgueno ...	21774	The mill(s) is (are) still standing idle
Galgulum...	21775	Cable number of tons you can mill per week
Galiambo ...	21776	Can mill —— tons per day of twenty-four hours
Galicado ...	21777	Mill only low-grade ore
Galicismo...	21778	Mill only high-grade ore [natural proportions
Galilla	21779	The mill has been running on high and low-grade ore in their
Galimatias	21780	We are now putting high-grade ore through the mill
Galipot ...	21781	You should mill as much high-grade ore as possible to provide
Galizabra ...	21782	We are now putting low-grade ore through the mill [for
Galladura...	21783	Mill the ore so as to maintain a regular result of
Gallantly ...	21784	Require full particulars as to mill site
Gallapfel ...	21785	Sundry mill repairs
Gallarda ...	21786	Has the mill erected at —— given full satisfaction
Gallardete	21787	I believe it will mill at least —— ozs. per ton
Gallaruza...	21788	We have now ready —— tons of quartz stacked ready for the
Gallegada...	21789	The mill is only adapted for wet crushing [mill
Gallego ...	21790	The mill is running very well
Gallerte ...	21791	The mill is running only fairly
Galliambus	21792	The mill is not running at all well
Gallicinio...	21793	Shall commence running the mill on
Gallinago	21794	There is a mechanical roaster as part of the mill
Gallineria...	21795	The mill does not include any mechanical roaster
Gallineta ...	21796	The mill has run —— days
Gallinoso ...	21797	After a mill run of —— hours
Gallinulam	21798	The mill will be run —— days before we clean up
Gallipavo ...	21799	The average run of the mill is —— days
Gallipollo...	21800	What is the average run of the mill
Gallito ...	21801	The mill was not working when I was there
Gallofear ...	21802	The mill is only running —— days per month
Gallonada...	21803	Cable mill result
Gallondero	21804	Mill closed in consequence of repairs
Galloper ...	21805	Continuous stoppage of mill necessary as
Galloping...	21806	I shall shut down the mill on
Gallsucht ...	21807	Mill shut down on —— for thorough repair
Galluzzare	21808	Mill will be shut down for —— days
Galonazo ...	21809	How long will the mill be shut down
Galopeado	21810	Mill shut down for —— days
Galoppare...	21811	Mill in working order
Galoppiren	21812	Mill running steadily
Galoube ...	21813	The mill was stopped —— hours
Galpito	21814	Cost of transport to mill
Galvanic ...	21815	Transport to mill
Galvanique	21816	There are no figures available as to mill trials of the quartz
Galvanised	21817	The latest mill returns are
Gamarra ...	21818	Mill test
Gambaccia	21819	Make a second mill test
Gambader	21820	The result of second mill test is
Gambalua	21821	Have you arranged for mill test
Gambaruolo	21822	Hope to arrange for mill test
Gamberello	21823	Shall start mill —— heads within next —— days
Gambetear	21824	Shall start the mill crushing on
Gambette...	21825	Mill crushing well
Gambiera...	21826	Have no ore that we can crush to a profit
Gambist ...	21827	Why have you stopped mill
Gambotes...	21828	Stoppage of mill due to (for)
Gambouge	21829	The present mill is capable of
Gambrel ...	21830	The present mill would cost —— to repair
Gambux ...	21831	Repairs to mill

Gamesome	21832	Mill has been running continuously —— hours —— ons
Gamester ...	21833	Foundations of mill [crushed, estimated yield —— oz.
Gamezuo ...	21834	Can only run mill —— hours out of the twenty-four owing to
Gammarus	21835	Would suggest immediate erection of mill
Gammautte	21836	Cannot recommend the erection of a mill until
Gammes ...	21837	A mill of —— heads would have to be erected
Gammoned	21838	A mill of —— heads should be erected as soon as possible
Gammoning	21839	What is the crushing capacity of the mill per 24 hours
Gammurra	21840	The mill can crush —— tons of 2,240 lbs. per 24 hours
Gamologia	21841	The mill is driven by water power
Gamoncillo	21842	The mill is driven by steam
Gamonito ...	21843	Dry crushing mill
Gamuno ...	21844	Wet stamping mill
Gamuzado	21845	Cannot run mill for want of water
Ganache ...	21846	Expect to have sufficient water to run mill on ——
Ganaderia	21847	When will you re-start the mill
Ganador ...	21848	Shall re-start mill on
Ganancia ...	21849	Mill trial very satisfactory
Ganancioso	21850	Mill trial fairly satisfactory
Ganapan ...	21851	Mill trial not at all satisfactory
Ganascione	21852	The present mill is practically worn out
Gancetto ...	21853	Shall at once invite tenders for new mill
Ganchero ...	21854	Shall start erection of mill at once
Ganchillo ...	21855	Will delay erection of mill
Ganchoso ...	21856	Mill(s) now crushing ore from
Gandalin ...	21857	Mill tests show
Gandujado	21858	A lot of —— tons put through the mill gave
Gandul ...	21859	As a mill result of —— tons
Ganeonem	21860	Calculations based on mill results from —— tons
Ganfanon ...	21861	Break-down at mill. Repairs will take —— days to complete
Ganforro ...	21862	Send further particulars of break-down at mill
Gangaba ...	21863	Mill stopped for ordinary repairs and clean up —— hours
Gangarilla	21864	Shut down the mill
Gangelband	21865	Shall shut down the mill unless (until)
Gangherato	21866	Do not shut down the mill unless (until)
Gangliform	21867	During —— the mill worked —— days, yield being as follows: bullion ——, concentrates realized ——, concentrates in process of realization ——, total ——. The working expenses for the month were ——. We have also spent on development work during the month ——
Ganglios ...	21868	Cable full particulars of estimated run for month: Working expenses, extraneous expenses, expenditure chargeable to capital, value of bullion and concentrates on hand and in transit, value of stores on hand, estimated total assets and liabilities, state of bank account, all approximate for end of month. State how much you will be able to remit on account of the month's profit. Give approximate tonnage and average value of ore reserves at end of month. We wish you to cable the above information on the ——
Ganguear ...	21869	The following are the particulars you require: Working expenses ——, extraneous expenses ——, expenditure chargeable to capital ——; value of bullion and concentrates on hand and in transit ——, value of stores on hand ——, estimated total assets ——, estimated liabilities ——, the bank balance amounts to ——. Shall be able to remit on account of the month's profit ——. There are —— tons of ore average value —— in reserve. All the foregoing figures are approximate
Ganguil ...	21870	**Milled** (*See also* "Stamped.")
Gangways	21871	Ore milled —— ozs. per ton

Ganniatur	21872	—— tons of ore milled —— stamps running —— days
Ganniebat	21873	**Milling** (*See also* "Commenced," "Free.")
Ganniendo	21874	What is your estimate of cost of milling on a basis of say ——
		[tons per 24 hours
Gannitus ...	21875	What is your estimate of cost of mining and milling with
		[present plant
Gannivero	21876	The cost of milling alone may be taken at —— per ton
Gansaron ...	21877	As a result of milling —— tons
Gansehaut	21878	Estimate the cost of mining at —— per ton and milling at ——
Gansekiel ...	21879	Milling ore [per ton with present plant
Ganseklein	21880	Of milling ore
Ganserich...	21881	The ore is milling better than I (we) anticipated
Ganterie ...	21882	Cost of hauling and milling [—— days
Ganze ...	21883	The cost of milling —— tons would be —— the time required
Ganzeton ...	21884	The whole of the ore extracted has been put through the mill
Ganzewerk	21885	There is an ample supply of water for milling purposes
Ganzheit ...	21886	The available water supply for milling is
Ganzlich ...	21887	The water supply would suffice for milling —— tons per 24
Ganzuar ...	21888	How many tons have you milled since —— [hours
Gaolbird ...	21889	For milling quartz
Garabatada	21890	Have sufficient water for milling purposes
Garabatear	21891	It will be necessary to supplement the milling plant with
Garabato ...	21892	**Millman** (*See also* "Amalgamator.")
Garagollo ...	21893	An excellent millman
Garambaina	21894	Secure —— as millman for
Garanciere	21895	Shall I secure —— as millman
Garantia ...	21896	**Mind**
Garapinera	21897	Bear in mind that
Garapito ...	21898	Will bear in mind
Garapullo	21899	Do you (does ——) mind
Garbage ...	21900	In case you do not mind
Garbancico	21901	Mind and
Garbanzal	21902	Was never in my mind
Garbatezza	21903	You need not mind
Garbatura	21904	As a thing to be borne in mind
Garbear ...	21905	It must be borne in mind that
Garberei ...	21906	No need to mind what is said
Garbestoff	21907	Mind your own business entirely
Garbias ...	21908	**Mine(s)** (*See also* "Appearance," "Aspect," "Bonded,"
		["Bottom," "Condition," "Developed," "Development," &c.)
Garbillar ...	21909	At the mine(s)
Garbled ...	21910	From the mine
Garboso ...	21911	To the mine
Garbuglio...	21912	On the mine
Garbullo ...	21913	In the mine
Garceta ...	21914	As soon as the mine is in fork
Gardebois...	21915	When do you expect the mine to be in fork
Gardecorps	21916	I strongly recommend the purchase of the —— mine
Gardefrein	21917	I cannot recommend the purchase of the —— mine
Gardenappe	21918	In my opinion the mine(s) is (are) not worth the sum asked
Gardener ...	21919	In my opinion the mine(s) is (are) worth the sum asked
Gardening	21920	In my opinion the mine is
Gardepeche	21921	In my opinion the —— mine(s) is (are) worth, say ——
Garderobe	21922	In my opinion the value of —— mine as it at present stands
Gardetemps	21923	Mine was closed down on [is ——
Gardianus	21924	Mine has been shut down since
Garduja ...	21925	Mine is producing a little rich ore
Gareggioso	21926	Mine is producing payable ore
Garennier...	21927	Mine is not producing any payable ore
Garfada ...	21928	Cable how is (are) the mine(s) looking generally

Garfio ...	21929	Mine(s) is (are) not looking at all well
Gargabero	21930	Mine(s) is (are) looking well
Gargajal ...	21931	Mine(s) is (are) looking well and promise(s) better
Gargajeada	21932	The mine continues to look
Gargajeo ...	21933	The mine does not look very encouraging at this moment
Garganchon	21934	The mine(s) look(s) splendid
Gargantear	21935	The mine does not look nearly so well as I was led to expect
Garganton	21936	The mine looks even better than I anticipated
Gargarismo	21937	The mine looks exceedingly well
Gargarizar	21938	Mine promises exceedingly well for the future
Gargling ...	21939	Mine has evidently been poorly managed
Gargola ...	21940	Mine has been anything but fairly managed
Gargotage	21941	Mine has been worked economically and well
Gargotero...	21942	Mine has not been worked with any view to economy
Gargouille	21943	Mine has been worked in a miner-like and systematic manner
Gargoyle ..	21944	The mine(s) lie(s)
Gariandro...	21945	The mine(s) is (are) situated within —— miles of
Gariofilea ...	21946	The distance between the mine and mill site is —— miles
Garishness	21947	The mine(s) is (are) situated —— feet above the sea-level
Garitear ...	21948	The mine(s) is (are) heavily watered
Garkuche...	21949	What will the mine cost for —— month(s) be
Garlador ...	21950	The profit from the mine(s) is —— per annum
Garlanded	21951	The mine(s) is (are) very limited in extent
Garlands ...	21952	The mine has been worked hitherto at a loss
Garlic ...	21953	The mine has been worked at the lowest cost possible
Garnato ...	21954	The mines are only valuable as prospects
Garnement	21955	The mine(s) promise(s) well but is (are) practically undeveloped
Garnered ...	21956	The mine is a dry one
Garnisaire	21957	It is a very wet mine
Garnished	21958	The mine(s) is (are) easily accessible (from)
Garnishing	21959	The mine(s) is (are) easily accessible by —— from ——
Garnissage	21960	The mines are situated a long distance from
Garniture ...	21961	The great drawback to the mine(s) is its (their) inaccessibility
Garnspule	21962	The mines are practically inaccessible from —— to ——
Garnwinde	21963	During the winter months the mine is completely cut off
Garofanare	21964	Has (have) been through mine
Garofano ...	21965	Old mine
Garontolo ...	21966	The mine(s) is (are) producing at the rate of —— tons per
Garosello ...	21967	The mine(s) is (are) producing —— tons per week
Garrafal ...	21968	The mine(s) is (are) producing high grade ore
Garrafinar	21969	The mine(s) is (are) producing low grade ore
Garrais ...	21970	The mine(s) produced for the past
Garrama ...	21971	Mine is not what it is stated to be in ——'s report
Garrancha	21972	The mine(s) is (are) situated at ——
Garrapata...	21973	The mines are situated in the near vicinity of
Garrevole ...	21974	The mines are situated in the mining district of
Garrideza ...	21975	The mine(s) is (are)
Garriebat ...	21976	Group of mines
Garriendo...	21977	The mine is really confined to
Garrimus ...	21978	The mine is alleged to
Garrire ...	21979	The mine has been worked simply for what it was worth
Garrison ...	21980	Is (are) the mine(s) well equipped with machinery
Garrissa ...	21981	The mine(s) is (are) poorly equipped with machinery
Garritore ...	21982	The mine(s) is (are) well equipped with machinery
Garritrice ...	21983	The mine(s) as it (they) at present stand(s) is (are)
Garritus ...	21984	The mine(s) is (are) at the present moment full of water
Garrobal ...	21985	The mines have not been worked since
Garrochear	21986	I think the sum altogether too large for the mine(s)
Garrochon	21987	Do you consider it is too large a sum for the mine(s)
Garrotazo ...	21988	I think the sum asked a very fair price for the mine(s)

▲▲

Garrote	...	21989	What do you think is about the value of the mine(s)
Garrotillo	.:.	21990	I estimate the value of the mine(s) at
Garrudo	..	21991	There is every indication to show that the mine is one of value
Garrulador		21992	I believe vendors would accept —— for the mine(s)
Garrular	...	21993	I do not think vendors would take less than —— for the
Garrulatis		21994	Mine superintendent [mine(s)
Garrulity	...	21995	Mine will be fairly opened up by
Garrulous	...	21996	Mine can be opened up within —— months
Garstig	...	21997	The mine(s) has (have) been working continuously since
Gartenbau		21998	Have arranged for a watchman at the mine
Gartenbeet		21999	The mine being free from water
Gartenhaus		22000	As soon as the mine(s) is (are) free from water
Gartnerei		**22001**	None of the mines of the district are being worked
Garzetto	...	22002	The only mine in the district that pays is
Garzolino	...	22003	The mine(s) has (have) only been partially worked
Garzonotto		22004	Could only partly examine the mine on account of
Garzota	...	22005	Have nothing to do with mine unless patented
Garzuolo	...	22006	A dividend paying mine
Gasalier	...	22007	The mine(s) is (are) dividend paying
Gasartig	...	22008	The mine(s) is (are) not dividend paying
Gasbags	...	22009	Has —— (have you) personally seen the mine
Gasbracket		22010	I have not personally seen the mine
Gasbrenner		22011	The mine(s) was (were) offered
Gasburner		22012	Mine and mill
Gasconade		22013	Believe the mine is well worthy of being further prospected
Gasconner		22014	The mines have often been
Gasengine		22015	Both mines should be owned by one company
Gaseous	...	22016	The mine(s) is (are) owned by
Gasfitters	...	22017	Mine(s) has (have) hitherto paid
Gasfitting	...	22018	What have the mines paid during the past five years
Gaskins	...	22019	The mine is practically a mere shell
Gaslaterne		22020	The mines were originally worked by
Gaslight	...	22021	What has been the output of the mine since
Gasometer		22022	The output of the mine since —— has been —— tons valued at
Gaspillage		22023	From other parts of the mine(s)
Gaspilleur		22024	Taken from all parts of the mine
Gasrohre	...	22025	Mainly from the lower workings of the mine
Gassenbube		22026	The mines can be worked without much outlay
Gasstoves	...	22027	The mines will need an outlay of at least
Gastable	...	22028	Is (are) offering the mine for
Gastadero	...	22029	What is the mine now offered for
Gastfrei	...	22030	Mine had to be abandoned owing to
Gastgeber	...	22031	Mine has been worked extensively by open cuts
Gasthaus	...	22032	What will be the cost of re-opening the mine
Gasthof	...	22033	I estimate the cost of re-opening the mine at probably
Gastiren	...	22034	The mines are practically cut off from all supplies during ——
			[months of the year
Gastmahl	...	22035	Occurs in many of the mines around
Gastrique	...	22036	Have you anything to report in connection with the mine(s)
Gastritis	...	22037	Nothing new to report in the mine(s)
Gastronome		22038	Ascertain what has occurred at the mine
Gaststube	...	22039	—— has occurred at the —— mine
Gastwirth	..	22040	Nothing has occurred at the —— mine
Gatafura	...	22041	The latest news from the mine is
Gateado	...	22042	What machinery is there on the mine
Gatemetier		22043	The machinery on the mine consists of
Gatesco	...	22044	At the present moment there is no pay ore in the mine
Gatetout	...	22045	Practically the eyes of the mine have been picked out
Gateway	...	22046	The improvement in the mine is most marked
Gathered	...	22047	There is no improvement whatever in the mine

Gaticida	22048	The only improvement in the mine is at —— where
Gatico	22049	There is a good prospect of improvement in the mine. [mine
Gatillazo	22050	There is little prospect of any immediate improvement in the
Gattuccio	22051	There is a manifest improvement in the mine
Gatunero	22052	It will be necessary to make an immediate expenditure of —— [on the equipment of the mine
Gatuperio	22053	The water is steadily rising in the mine
Gauchement	22054	If the mine(s) could be acquired for say —— I believe it [(they) would be an excellent investment
Gaucherie	22055	The working capital required for the mine will not be less [than ——
Gaucho	22056	What would be the working capital required for the mine
Gaudeamus	22057	I cannot confirm any of the statements contained in ——'s [report on the mine
Gaudebant	22058	When I shall have to close down the mine
Gaudente	22059	In this event you have full authority to close down the mine
Gaudialis	22060	Close down the mine if you are convinced that
Gaudieb	22061	Cable your distinct views as to policy of closing down the
Gaudiness	22062	The accounts for the mine are very misleading [mine pending
Gaudiolum	22063	Have examined the —— mine(s)
Gaudioso	22064	When shall you examine the —— mine(s)
Gaudriole	22065	Since I (——) examined the ——mine(s)
Gauffers	22066	Cable from time to time any change in the mine(s)...
Gaukelhaft	22067	Keep the mine(s)
Gaultheria	22068	Must re-timber mine
Gaunica	22069	In order to keep the mine free from water [following rumour
Gausapatus	22070	Respecting the —— mine(s) what truth is there in the
Gausapina	22071	There is no truth in the rumour that rich ore has been found [in the mine
Gavanza	22072	There is no truth in the rumour that any ore has been found [in the mine
Gavazzare	22073	I consider recent developments at the mine justify erection of [an additional —— heads of stamps
Gaveggiare	22074	There is no development at the mine to justify
Gaveggino	22075	Do recent developments at the mine justify
Gavilan	22076	Recent developments at the mine fully justify
Gavillero	22077	There is every indication at the mine to show
Gaviota	22078	There is no indication whatever at the mine to show
Gavisus	22079	Ascertain if anything has happened at the mine to justify an [advance of —— per share
Gavocciolo	22080	There is nothing at the mine to justify fall in price of shares
Gavonchio	22081	This (these) mine(s)
Gayety	22082	Quite justify(ies) advance in price of —— mine shares
Gaylussite	22083	In various parts of the mine
Gayomba	22084	From all available points in the mine
Gazafaton	22085	From the only available points in the mine
Gazapela	22086	When I was in the mine
Gazapico	22087	Since I was in the mine [request
Gazeful	22088	—— has requested to see over the mine; shall I accede to his
Gazetero	22089	Admit —— to see the mine [I learn
Gazetista	22090	Am refused admittance to —— mine, but from a reliable source
Gazetteer	22091	Am refused admittance to —— mine, so far cannot ascertain [anything
Gazmiar	22092	Do not admit anyone into the mine without written orders
Gazmol	22093	Do not admit anyone into the mine(s) [from me (——)
Gazmonada	22094	The value of the mine is entirely prospective
Gaznatada	22095	The value of the mine is exceedingly problematical
Gaznatico	22096	Have struck ore assaying —— in the mine
Gazogene	22097	Have struck vein at the —— mine; prospects promising
Gazophylax	22098	Have struck a side vein at the —— mine

Gazouiller	22099	Have just come up from the mine
Gazpachero	22100	Have just visited the —— mine; would advise you (to)
Gazzella ...	22101	There is really nothing in the mine
Gazzerotta	22102	The mine has paid not less than —— in dividends
Gazzettino	22103	I am glad to report favourably on the mine as a whole
Gazzolone...	22104	I am convinced the mine can be worked to a profit
Geachtete...	22105	I believe the mine to be a good sound investment
Geadert ...	22106	I believe the mine will develop into a good steady dividend
Gearwheel	22107	The mine has paid to date —— in dividends [payer
Gebarerin ...	22108	The mine(s) can be economically worked
Gebarhaus	22109	What is the elevation of the mine
Gebaude ...	22110	The mine(s) has (have) been worked on a considerable scale
Gebelfer ...	22111	The mine(s) has (have) not been worked to any extent
Geberden ...	22112	The mine was recently examined by
Gebieter ...	22113	As soon as the mine is free from water
Gebirgig ...	22114	Now that the mine is free from water
Geblase ...	22115	This mine has been famous for many years
Geborgen ...	22116	Has (have) forbidden the mine to be shown
Gebrauch ...	22117	The mine accounts are not correct
Gebrechen	22118	The mine accounts are quite correct
Gebruder ...	22119	Have just examined the workings of the —— mine and from [recent developments believe
Gebrull ...	22120	What are your views as to the future developments of the mine
Gebuhren...	22121	—— has (have) examined the mine(s). Ascertain what he [(they) think(s) of it (them)
Gebuhrlich	22122	Have arranged for you to examine —— mine(s) near ——
Gebunden...	22123	From my examination of the mine I should conclude that
Geburtsort	22124	I do not believe there is any payable ore in the mine
Geburtstag	22125	The payable ore in the mine is confined to
Gebusch ...	22126	Everyone who has visited the mine reports
Geckenhaft	22127	—— is said to have reported favourably on the mine
Gedanke ...	22128	What is your opinion as to the mine(s)
Gedeck ...	22129	Will examine the —— mine(s) and report fully
Gedeihen ...	22130	Obtain an estimate for proper equipment of mine with machinery
Gedeihlich	22131	What would it cost to equip the mine with proper machinery
Gedenkbuch	22132	The equipment of the mine, with pumping and hoisting gear, [would cost
Gedulgen ...	22133	The mine will undoubtedly become a very valuable property
Geduque ...	22134	Do you think the mine is of sufficient value
Gefahrlich	22135	The mine has become a very valuable one
Gefallig ...	22136	**Miner(s)** (*See also* " Men.")
Gefangniss	22137	Cornish miners
Gefecht ...	22138	On behalf of the miners
Gefiedert ...	22139	Miners are
Geflugel ...	22140	Miners accept
Gefluster ...	22141	Miners refuse
Gefolge ...	22142	But they are very poor miners
Gefrassig ...	22143	Good miners receive
Gefrierbar	22144	Good practical miner(s)
Gefrorenes	22145	Is —— a thoroughly capable, honest and reliable miner
Gefugig ...	22146	It will be necessary to have at least —— good white miners
Gefuhllos ...	22147	Miners generally work on contract
Gefuhlvoll	22148	Miners do not care to work on contract
Gegacker ...	22149	Miners require to be boarded
Gegenbild...	22150	Miners threaten to strike unless grant extra pay
Gegenfalls	22151	Miners have struck, demand —— per shift increase
Gegengift	22152	The miners here are a very rough lot
Gegengruss	22153	—— miners leave to-day
Gegenklage	22154	We are short of miners
Gegenlist ...	22155	There are no good miners to be had

Gegenmacht	22156	There are plenty of good miners to be had at ——					
Gegenmine	22157	Until the arrival of —— miners					
Gegenrede	22158	Who make excellent miners					
Gegensatz	22159	Good —— miners are necessary for this work					
Gegensinn	22160	Miners prevented from working by					
Gegenstand	22161	Miners cannot work on account of bad air					
Gegenstuck	22162	Miners cannot work on account of water					
Gegentheil	22163	Watch the miners so as to prevent					
Gegenuber	22164	Watch the miners					
Gegenwerth	22165	**Mineral(s)**					
Gegenzeuge	22166	Mineral salts					
Gegliedert	22167	Shows a little mineral					
Gegnerisch	22168	Follow the mineral					
Gegrundet	22169	Outside the mineral belt					
Gehaben ...	22170	The rock is absolutely barren of mineral					
Gehaltleer	22171	The breast of the drift shows some good mineral					
Gehassig ...	22172	Adularia	Gelbsucht...	22216	Borax		
Gehause ...	22173	Alabaster	Geldable ...	22217	Bornite		
Geheimniss	22174	Albite	Geldbusse	22218	Bournonite		
Geheiss ...	22175	Alum	Geldkasten	22219	Braunite		
Geheul ...	22176	Aluminite	Geldlos ...	22220	Bromite		
Gehilfin ...	22177	Alumstone	Geldposten	22221	Bronzite		
Gehlenite ...	22178	Amalgam	Geldstols ...	22222	Brown coal		
Gehorgang	22179	Amethyst	Geldstuck	22223	Brown-spar		
Gehorlos ...	22180	Amphibole	Geldsumme	22224	Calamine		
Gehorsinn	22181	Analcime	Geldwerth	22225	Calamite		
Geiferer ...	22182	Anhydrite	Gelecidio ...	22226	Calcedony		
Geigen ...	22183	Anorthite	Gelehrig ...	22227	Calcite		
Geigenhals	22184	Anthracite	Geleise ...	22228	Calc-spar		
Geigensteg	22185	Antimonite	Gelingen ...	22229	Calomel		
Geilheit ...	22186	Antimony ochre	Gelinotte ...	22230	Carnallite		
Geimbriel ...	22187	Apatite	Gelispel ...	22231	Cassiterite		
Geissbock...	22188	Argentite	Gellen ...	22232	Cassitero tantalite		
Geisseln ...	22189	Arragonite	Gellflote ...	22233	Celestine		
Geisselung	22190	Arsenic	Geloben ...	22234	Cerussite		
Geistlos ...	22191	Arsenical pyrites	Gelobniss...	22235	Chalcolite		
Geistreich...	22192	Arsenite	Gelesaccio	22236	Chalcopyrite		
Geizhals ...	22193	Asbestos	Gelsemium	22237	Chalk		
Gejauchse	22194	Asphaltum	Gelsomino	22238	Chalybite		
Geklapper	22195	Atacamite	Geltung ...	22239	Chert		
Geklimper	22196	Augite	Gelusten ...	22240	Chiastolite		
Geklingel...	22197	Avanturine	Gemachlich	22241	Chloanthite		
Gekluft ...	22198	Azurite	Gemachsam	22242	Chlorite		
Gekopert ...	22199	Barytes	Gemahlig ...	22243	Chromeochre		
Gekrache ...	22200	Baryto-calcite	Gemassheit	22244	Chromite		
Gekritzel ...	22201	Bell-metal ore	Gemassigt	22245	Chrysoberyl		
Gekrose ...	22202	Beryl	Gemauer ...	22246	Chrysocolla		
Gekunstelt	22203	Biotite	Gemeaux ...	22247	Cinnabar		
Gelabilis ...	22204	Bismuth	Gemebundus	22248	Clay		
Gelamento	22205	Bismuthine	Gemeinde...	22249	Claystone		
Gelangen ...	22206	Bismuthite	Gemeinheit	22250	Coal		
Gelascit ...	22207	Bismuth ochre	Gemeinsam	22251	„ brown		
Gelasino ...	22208	Bitter-spar	Gemellar ...	22252	„ cannel		
Gelatineux	22209	Bitumen	Gemelo ...	22253	„ common		
Gelatinous	22210	Blende	Gemetzel ...	22254	Cobalt		
Gelatus ...	22211	Blue iron	Gemidor ...	22255	Cobalt bloom		
Gelaufig ...	22212	Blue john	Geminator	22256	Cobaltine		
Gelaut ...	22213	Blue spar	Geminis ...	22257	Cobalt pyrites		
Gelbholz ...	22214	Bog-iron ore	Geminitudo	22258	Copper		
Gelblich ...	22215	Boracite	Gemmato ...	22259	„ black		

Gemmeous	22260	Copper blue		Genovino ...	22320	Iron ore	
Gemmiera...	22261	„ carbonate		Gentalla ...	22321	„ „ magnetic	
Gemmifer ...	22262	„ emerald		Gentame ...	22322	„ phosphate	
Gemmosus	22263	„ glance		Gentecilla...	22323	„ pyrites	
Gemmula ...	22264	„ gray		Genteelish	22324	„ sparry	
Gemonides	22265	„ green		Gentian ...	22325	„ specular	
Gemoso ...	22266	„ mica		Genticus ...	22326	„ sulphuret	
Gemsbock	22267	„ nickel		Gentilesco	22327	„ titanitic	
Gemshorn	22268	„ purple		Gentileza ...	22328	Jasper	
Gemulus ...	22269	„ pyrites		Gentilicio	22329	Jet	
Gemurmel	22270	„ salts		Gentiluomo	22330	Kaolin	
Gemuthlich	22271	„ red		Gentualla ...	22331	Kupfernickel	
Gemuthsart	22272	„ variegated		Genualia ...	22332	Lead	
Genaschig	22273	„ yellow		Genuflesso	22333	„ arseniate	
Genciana ...	22274	Copperas		Genugen ...	22334	„ carbonate	
Gencive ...	22275	Corundum		Genugsam	22335	„ chromate	
Gendarme	22276	Crocoisite		Genuino ...	22336	„ ochre	
Genealogia	22277	Cryolite		Geocentric	22337	„ phosphate	
Genearca ...	22278	Cube-ore		Geodesia ...	22338	„ sulphate	
Geneatico...	22279	Cuprite		Geodetic ...	22339	„ sulphide	
Genebro ...	22280	Cyanite		Geogony ...	22340	Leucopyrite	
Genehmigen	22281	Diallage		Geografia ...	22341	Lime	
Generable...	22282	Diallogite		Geography	22342	„ carbonate	
Generador	22283	Diamond		Geolage ...	22343	„ phosphate	
Generalato	22284	Diopside		Geolier ...	22344	„ sulphate	
Generalise	22285	Dioptase		Geomantia	22345	Limonite	
Generandus	22286	Discrasite		Geometra ...	22346	Lithia mica	
Generateur	22287	Disthene		Geometrico	22347	Magnesia	
Generatim	22288	Dolomite		Geoponics...	22348	„ borate	
Generatrix	22289	Electrum		Georgic ...	22349	„ carbonate	
Genereux ...	22290	Emerald		Geoscopia...	22350	„ sulphate	
Generique	22291	Emery		Geotico ...	22351	· Magnesite	
Generoso ...	22292	Enargite		Geplander	22352	Magnetic iron	
Genesung ...	22293	Enstatite		Geplarr ...	22353	„ „ py-	
Genethlia ...	22294	Epidote		Gepolter ...	22354	Magnetite [rites	
Genetivo ...	22295	Fahlore		Geprange ...	22355	Malachite	
Genetliaca	22296	Felspar		Geprassel ...	22356	Manganese	
Genetrix ...	22297	Flint		Geradheit ...	22357	„ carbonate	
Genevrier ...	22298	Fluorite		Geradlinig	22358	„ spar	
Gengibre ...	22299	Fluor spar		Geranites ...	22359	Manganite	
Gengiovo ...	22300	Franklinite		Geranium ...	22360	Marble	
Geniaccio ...	22301	Galena		Gerant ...	22361	Marcasite	
Genialidad	22302	Garnet		Gerapliega	22362	Mercury	
Genialis ...	22303	Gold		Gerarquia...	22363	„ chloride	
Genialiter ..	22304	Graphite		Gerasca ...	22364	„ sulphide	
Genialness	22305	Guanite		Geraumig...	22365	Mica	
Genick ...	22306	Gypsum		Gercure ...	22366	„ lithia	
Genickfang	22307	Hæmatite		Gerendus ...	22367	„ magnesia	
Geniculate	22308	Heavy spar		Gerfaut ...	22368	„ potash	
Geniculum	22309	Hepatite		Gerifaloo ...	22369	Millerite	
Geniessbar	22310	Hornblende		Gerigonza...	22370	Mispickel	
Genipi ...	22311	Horn-silver		Geringar ...	22371	Molybdenite	
Geniren ...	22312	Hornstone		Gerinnen ...	22372	Muscovite	
Genistilla...	22313	Hyacinth		Gerippe ...	22373	Naphtha	
Genitabile	22314	Idocrase		Germacion	22374	Natron	
Genital ...	22315	Ilmenite		Germandria	22375	Needle ore	
Genitive ...	22316	Iridium		Germanesco	22376	„ spar	
Genitura ...	22317	Iron		Germanis ...	22377	Nickel	
Genizaro ...	22318	„ carbonate		Germaniter	22378	„ antimonial	
Genoles ...	22319	„ chromate		Germinated	22379	„ arsenical	

Germoglio	22380	Nickel pyrites	Getose ...	22440	Silver chloride	
Germoir ...	22381	„ white	Getrampel	22441	„ fahlore	
Gerofante ...	22382	Nitre	Getrauen...	22442	„ horn	
Gerondif ...	22383	Ochre	Getreide ...	22443	„ iodic	
Gerricote ...	22384	Oligoclase	Getreulich	22444	„ ruby	
Gertibulum	22385	Onyx	Getrost ...	22445	„ sulphuret	
Geruchlos	22386	Opal	Gettamento	22446	Sinter	
Gerucht ...	22387	Orpiment	Gettarsi ...	22447	Slate	
Gerulator ...	22388	„ red	Gettatrice	22448	Smaltine	
Gerumpel ...	22389	Orthoclase	Gettone ...	22449	Soapstone	
Gerund ...	22390	Parafine	Getummel	22450	Soda	
Gerundiada	22391	Pearl mica	Gevatter ...	22451	„ carbonate	
Gerundium	22392	„ spar	Geviert ...	22452	„ nitrate	
Gesandte ...	22393	Peat	Gewachs ...	22453	„ sulphate	
Gesangduch	22394	Peridot	Gewalthat	22454	Sparry iron ore	
Gesausel ...	22395	Petroleum	Gewaltig ...	22455	Specular iron ore	
Geschaft ...	22396	Pitch-blende	Gewaltsam	22456	Sphene	
Geschehen	22397	Platina	Gewandt ...	22457	Spinel	
Gescheit ...	22398	Platiniridium	Gewartigen	22458	Spodumene	
Geschick ...	22399	Plumbago	Geweih ...	22459	Stannine	
Geschieden	22400	Polybasite	Gewerbe ...	22460	Steatite	
Geschlecht	22401	Proustite	Gewerblich	22461	Stibine	
Geschmack	22402	Pyrargyrite	Gewgaw ...	22462	Stiblite	
Geschmeide	22403	Pyrites	Gewichtig	22463	Stromeyerite	
Geschoss ...	22404	„ arsenical	Gewimmer	22464	Sulphur	
Geschutz ...	22405	„ cobalt	Gewiss ...	22465	Talc	
Geschwader	22406	„ copper	Gewissheit	22466	Tantalite	
Geschwind	22407	„ iron	Gewitter ...	22467	Tellurium	
Geschwulst	22408	„ magnetic	Gewohnen	22468	„ black	
Gesellen ...	22409	„ nickel	Gewohnlich	22469	„ foliated	
Gesetzbuch	22410	„ tin	Gewolbe ...	22470	„ graphic	
Gesetzlos ...	22411	„ white iron	Gewurm ...	22471	Tetradymite	
Gesichert ...	22412	Pyrolusite	Geysers ...	22472	Tetrahedrite	
Gesinge ...	22413	Pyromorphite	Gezelt ...	22473	Tin	
Gesittet ...	22414	Pyroxene	Geziefer ...	22474	„ oxide	
Gesolrent ...	22415	Quartz	Geziement	22475	„ pyrites	
Gespenst ...	22416	Quicksilver	Gezischel...	22476	„ sulphide	
Gespielin ...	22417	Realgar	Gezucht ...	22477	Titanite	
Gespott ...	22418	Red copper ore	Gezweig ...	22478	Topaz	
Gesprachig	22419	Redruthite	Gezwungen	22479	Tourmaline	
Gessato ...	22420	Rock crystal	Ghastliest	22480	Tufa	
Gestank ...	22421	„ salt	Gheggia ...	22481	Tungsten	
Gestatus ...	22422	Ruby	Gherbino	22482	Turquoise	
Gestehen ...	22423	„ oriental	Gherkin ...	22483	Uralite	
Gesticular	22424	„ spinel	Ghermire	22484	Uranite	
Gestiefelt ...	22425	Ruby-silver	Gherofano	22485	Vanadinite	
Gestielt ...	22426	Salt	Ghiaccesco	22486	Vitriol	
Gestober ...	22427	Saltpetre	Ghiacciaja	22487	„ blue	
Gestolper ...	22428	Sapphire	Ghiacere ...	22488	„ cobalt	
Gestossen...	22429	Schorl	Ghiacinto	22489	„ green	
Gestrauch ...	22430	Selenite	Ghiajoso ...	22490	„ iron	
Gestrenge	22431	Serpentine	Ghiandaja	22491	„ red	
Gestrupp ...	22432	Shale	Ghibellino	22492	„ white	
Gestuosus...	22433	Siderite	Ghignare...	22493	Vivianite	
Gestures ...	22434	Silica	Ghignatore	22494	Wad	
Gesturiens	22435	Silvanite	Ghignetto	22495	Witherite	
Gesturing	22436	Silver	Ghiribizzo	22496	Wolfram	
Gesundheit	22437	„ antimony	Ghirigoro	22497	Yttrocerite	
Getandel ...	22438	„ bismuthic	Ghirlanda	22498	Zeolite	
Gethyon ...	22439	„ bromic	Ghironda	22499	Zinc	

Ghostly ...	22500	Zinc blende
Giacchera...	22501	„ carbonate
Giaciglio ...	22502	„ red
Giacitura ...	22503	„ silicate
Giacuito ...	22504	„ sulphate
Giallamina	22505	„ sulphide
Gialletto ...	22506	Zircon
Giallogno ...	22507	**Minerlike**
Gialluccio	22508	In a minerlike manner
Giantess ...	22509	Not at all in a minerlike manner
Giantlike ...	22510	Must be worked in a minerlike manner
Giardinato	22511	Has not been worked in a minerlike manner
Giardoni ...	22512	In order to work the property in a minerlike manner
Giargone ...	22513	**Miners' Inches** (*See also* "Creek," "Water.")
Giattanza...	22514	—— miners' inches of water
Giavazzo ...	22515	The cost of water is —— per miners' inch
Gibado ...	22516	We require —— miners' inches of water additional
Gibberish...	22517	Can secure an additional supply of—— miners' inches at a cost of
Gibberosus	22518	What is the present supply in miners' inches of water
Gibbeted ...	22519	The present supply is —— miners' inches [out the year
Gibbeux ...	22520	What is the average supply of water in miners' inches through-
Gibbosity...	22521	The average supply of water throughout the year is ——
Gibbous ...	22522	An additional supply of —— miners' inches [miners' inches
Gibeciere ...	22523	For continuous working we require —— miners' inches
Gibelino ...	22524	What is the total supply in miners' inches
Gibelotte ...	22525	Have now —— miners' inches of water
Giberne ...	22526	**Minimum**
Giblets ...	22527	Is the minimum
Giboulee ...	22528	What is the minimum
Giboyeux ...	22529	As a minimum figure
Gicheroso...	22530	Minimum ever reached was
Giddily ...	22531	The minimum hitherto has been
Giebelfeld	22532	**Mining** (*See also* "Hydraulic," "Property.")
Gielamento	22533	Mining outfit
Giereagle ...	22534	Mining property
Gierigkeit...	22535	Mining tools
Giesser ...	22536	Is a reliable practical mining expert
Giessform...	22537	Mining costs —— per ton
Giesskanne	22538	What is the estimated cost of mining alone
Giessofen ...	22539	The cost of mining may be taken at
Giferada ...	22540	What is the estimated cost of mining and milling
Giftbecher	22541	The cost of mining and milling the ore may be taken at [—— per ton
Giftedly ...	22542	The cost of mining is ——, and milling —— per ton
Giftstoff ...	22543	The cost of mining and milling would be reduced at least
Giftzahn ...	22544	There is every facility for economic mining [—— per ton
Gigantazo ...	22545	There are little or no facilities for economic mining
Gigantessa	22546	As soon as I can resume mining
Gigantic ...	22547	Hope to resume mining within —— weeks
Gigantilla...	22548	Mining matters generally are improving
Gigantizar	22549	The mining has hitherto consisted of
Giganton ...	22550	No attention has been paid to systematic mining in times past
Giggling ...	22551	**Mining engineer(s)** (*See also* "Expert.")
Gighardo ...	22552	What is your opinion of —— as a mining engineer
Gigliato ...	22553	Has not the reputation of a mining engineer of standing
Gigliozzo ...	22554	Could you send competent mining engineer to examine and report
Gignendus	22555	Is said to be a mining engineer of repute [(us)
Gignor ...	22556	May be a very good mining engineer but is not known to me
Gigotter ...	22557	Can you recommend —— as a competent mining engineer
Gilecuelco...	22558	Mining engineer has examined the property and confirms [statements in reports

Gilguero ...	22559	Mining engineer has examined the property but does not con-[firm statements in reports
Gilmaestre	22560	Has an excellent reputation as a mining engineer and is a man [of unimpeachable honesty
Giltig ...	22561	Has good technical reputation as a mining engineer but is said
Gimblette...	22562	**Mint** [to be biassed by his personal interests
Gimcrack ...	22563	At the mint
Gimelga ...	22564	To the mint
Gimlethole	22565	The assay at the mint is
Gimnasio ...	22566	Forwarded to the government mint at
Gimnica ...	22567	**Minus** (See also "Plus.")
Gimotear ...	22568	Is this minus or plus
Gimpel ...	22569	It is minus (the)
Gimping ...	22570	It is not minus (the)
Ginebra ...	22571	Should be minus
Gineprajo...	22572	Must be minus
Ginestreto	22573	Minus cost of
Gingembre	22574	Minus commission
Gingerish...	22575	Minus out of pocket expenses
Gingerly ...	22576	Minus charges for
Gingiber ...	22577	Minus depreciation
Gingidio ...	22578	Minus the following
Gingivas ...	22579	Minus —— but plus ——
Gingivula...	22580	**Minute(s)**
Ginglarus ...	22581	On the minutes
Gingriator	22582	Any minute
Gingritus ...	22583	Require(s) copy of minutes certified by chairman
Ginguet ...	22584	Minute Book
Giojosetto...	22585	Per minute (See also "Speed.")
Giomelia ...	22586	**Minutely** (See also "Details.")
Giorgeria ...	22587	**Minutiæ**
Giornata ...	22588	**Misapprehension**
Giostrante	22589	Do not act under any misapprehension
Giovanello	22590	Owing to some misapprehension
Giovanile ...	22591	Would appear to have acted under a misapprehension
Giovanotta	22592	Is there no misapprehension
Giovativo ...	22593	There is no misapprehension
Giovatrice	22594	So long as there is no misapprehension
Giovenca ...	22595	**Miscalculate(d)**
Giovevole ...	22596	Was (were) miscalculated
Gioviale ...	22597	Was (were) not miscalculated
Gipsfigus ...	22598	**Miscalculation(s)**
Gipsoso ...	22599	Owing to some miscalculation
Giracapo ...	22600	Take care there is no miscalculation
Giraffe ...	22601	To guard against miscalculation
Giraldete ...	22602	**Mischief** (See also "Damage," "Injury.")
Giraldilla ...	22603	**Misconception**
Giramento	22604	**Misconduct**
Girandula...	22605	Said to have been dismissed for misconduct
Girapliega	22606	Was (were) dismissed for misconduct
Girasal ...	22607	Guilty of grave misconduct
Giratorio ...	22608	The alleged misconduct consisted of
Giravolta ...	22609	**Misfortune(s)**
Girazione ...	22610	It would be a great misfortune at the present moment to
Girdles ...	22611	Is not at all a misfortune
Girdling ...	22612	Has (have) had the misfortune to
Girellajo ...	22613	This (which) would be a great misfortune
Girelletta ...	22614	**Mislead**
Girgillus ...	22615	Has (have) done all he (they) can to mislead
Girifalte ...	22616	Do you consider that —— is trying to mislead

Girino	...	22617	To mislead
Giriren	...	22618	**Misleading**
Girlhood	...	22619	Very misleading
Girlish	...	22620	Is (are) misleading
Girofina	...	22621	Not misleading
Gironado	...	22622	**Mismanage(d)**
Girondiste		22623	Badly mismanaged
Girpear	...	22624	Alleged to have been mismanaged
Gisement	...	22625	Undoubtedly mismanaged
Gitanada	...	22626	**Mismanagement**
Gitanear	...	22627	Through mismanagement
Gitanesco	...	22628	**Miss**
Gitanillo	...	22629	You must not miss
Gitanismo		22630	Am not at all likely to miss
Gitano	...	22631	Do not miss
Gittajone	...	22632	To miss
Gitterig	...	22633	In case I (we) should miss
Gittone	...	22634	In case you (——) miss
Giubba	...	22635	You should not miss
Giubbette	...	22636	Shall miss
Giubbone	...	22637	Which caused me (us) to miss
Giubilare	...	22638	Which caused me (us) to miss seeing
Giubilio	...	22639	In which case it would miss
Giucatore	...	22640	**Missed** (*See also* "Mail," "Steamer.")
Giudaico	...	22641	Has (have) missed
Giudicata	...	22642	Has (have) not missed
Giudiciale	...	22643	· Should have missed but for
Giudicioso		22644	Missed the
Giuggiare	...	22645	Missed connection with
Giugulare	...	22646	**Missing**
Giuladro	...	22647	Cable what is missing
Giulebbe	...	22648	The following is a list of the missing
Giulianza	...	22649	Is (are) missing
Giulivetto	...	22650	Letter still missing
Giulivita	...	22651	The remainder is (are) missing
Giulleria	...	22652	Your letter dated —— received but documents are missing
Giumella	...	22653	Your letter dated —— received but enclosure relating to ——
Giuncheto		22654	**Mistake** (*See also* "Error.") [is missing
Giuncoso	...	22655	Mistake in cable
Giunipero	...	22656	Are you quite sure that there is no mistake
Giuntatore		22657	Is there not some mistake
Giuocaccio		22658	There is no mistake
Giuocolare		22659	Is not —— a mistake
Giurante	...	22660	—— is a mistake ; please correct to
Giuratorio		22661	You have made a mistake
Giuridico	...	22662	The mistake was
Giurista	...	22663	To prevent any further mistake(s)
Giusarma	...	22664	There is some mistake
Giustacore		22665	That a mistake has been made seems certain
Giustezza	...	22666	Has the mistake been found out
Gizzard	...	22667	I (we) have made a mistake
Glabella	...	22668	Please correct mistake immediately
Glabraria	...	22669	Is it possible that there is any other mistake
Glabresco	...	22670	Has mistake been corrected
Glabretum		22671	Has mistake been explained
Glabriones		22672	Do (does) not explain mistake
Glacial	...	22673	**Misunderstand**
Glaciated	...	22674	Do not misunderstand me (us)
Glaciatus	...	22675	If you misunderstand
Gladden	...	22676	**Misunderstood**

Gladiolo ...	22677	Altogether misunderstood
Gladlar ...	22678	Has (have) misunderstood
Gladsome...	22679	Instructions sent were misunderstood
Glaieul ...	22680	You (——) seem(s) to have misunderstood
Glaiseux ...	22681	**Mix(ed)**
Glaisiere ...	22682	Is (are) mixed up with —— in the matter
Glandage ...	22683	Avoid being mixed up with
Glandarius	22684	Is alleged to have been mixed up with
Glanders ...	22685	Mixed up with
Glandifero	22686	So as to avoid being mixed up with
Glandiform	22687	—— is mixed up with a somewhat shady lot
Glandium	22688	Is (was) supposed to be mixed up with the —— lot
Glandule ...	22689	**Model(s)**
Glandulous	22690	Model of
Glanzend ...	22691	Model should show
Glanzkohle	22692	Could you send a model
Glaphyrus	22693	Will forward working model and description
Glapir ...	22694	Shall I (we) send a model
Glapissant	22695	Unless you can send a model
Glareola ...	22696	Want model showing
Glareosus...	22697	**Moderate**
Glasartig ...	22698	Any moderate demand
Glasdeckel	22699	Only moderate
Glaseado ...	22700	Very moderate in quantity
Glaserkitt...	22701	Of moderate quality
Glasern ...	22702	**Modification(s)**
Glasfluss ...	22703	Without any modification
Glasglocke	22704	Admit(s) of no modification
Glashutte ...	22705	With some slight modifications
Glaskasten	22706	With the necessary modification(s)
Glasperle ...	22707	**Modified**
Glasseye ...	22708	Can be modified
Glasshouse	22709	Cannot be modified
Glassiness	22710	Can be modified so far as to admit of
Glastinus ...	22711	**Modify**
Glastorum	22712	Modify terms if possible
Glasuren ...	22713	Cannot modify terms in any way
Glaswaare	22714	Should he (——) not modify his terms
Glattstahl	22715	**Moment**
Glattzahn...	22716	Expect every moment to hear
Glauben ...	22717	At the last moment
Glaubiger	22718	Any moment
Glaucio ...	22719	Not a moment to lose
Glauciscus	22720	**Monday** (*See also* "Days.")
Glaucoma...	22721	About Monday week
Glaucous ...	22722	Every Monday
Glazed ...	22723	Every alternate Monday
Glazier ...	22724	Last Monday
Gleamy ...	22725	Next Monday
Gleaning ...	22726	Next Monday week
Glebarius ...	22727	On Monday
Gleboso ...	22728	On Monday morning
Gleeful ...	22729	On Monday afternoon
Gleetune ...	22730	During Monday
Gleichlaut	22731	During Monday night
Gleichniss...	22732	—— Monday in each month
Gleichsam	22733	**Money** (*See also* "Forfeited," "Funds," "Impossible," ["Sterling.")
Gleichung...	22734	Money on deposit
Gleissner ...	22735	Money on loan
Gleiten ...	22736	What is the money required for

Gletscher ...	22737	The money is required for
Gleucinum	22738	What is the balance of the money required for
Gliconico ...	22739	The balance of the money is required for
Glidingly ...	22740	Who will furnish the money for
Gliederbau	22741	—— will furnish all the necessary money
Gliederig ...	22742	—— refuses to furnish any money at all
Glimmering	22743	—— has supplied the money necessary
Glimmers ...	22744	When is the money to be paid
Glimpflich	22745	Money to be paid on or before
Glimpses ...	22746	What money have you available for
Glirarium	22747	The only money available is
Gliscerus ...	22748	All the money I (we) have is
Glissando...	22749 +	Do you require any money
Glissement	22750	In case you should require any money apply to
Glisseur ...	22751	—— will supply you with such money as may be necessary
Glissicato	22752	Have you sufficient money for
Glissoire ...	22753	Have instructed —— to pay you ——
Globate ...	22754	Have cabled you ——
Globettino	22755	What money has been already subscribed
Globosity ...	22756	Sufficient money has not been subscribed
Globulous	22757	The money subscribed only amounted to
Glociens ...	22758	My (our) money is nearly exhausted; please cable —— at once
Glocitatio ...	22759	My (our) money is nearly exhausted; shall require —— before [can proceed
Glockchen	22760	My (our) money will suffice until I (we) reach ——. Please
Glockengut	22761	What money do you require for it　[cable —— to that place
Glockner ...	22762	Require money for —— at once
Glomeralis	22763	What is so large an outlay of money required for
Glomerosus	22764	A large outlay of money will be required to (before)
Glomulus ...	22765	Failure to comply with these conditions will mean forfeiture
Gloomily ...	22766	A forfeitable money deposit　[of all moneys paid
Gloriandus	22767	Refuse(s) to consent to a forfeitable money deposit
Gloriarse ...	22768	Must consent to a forfeitable money deposit
Gloriette ...	22769	Do not consent to a forfeitable money deposit　[the market
Glorificar ...	22770	It would be difficult to raise the money in the present state of
Glorified ...	22771	Quite easy to raise the money at the present moment
Gloriole ...	22772	If you are satisfied with the value of the property there would [be no difficulty in raising the money
Gloriuzza ...	22773	If your report is satisfactory will guarantee to raise the money
Glorreich ...	22774	The money should be available by
Glosador ...	22775	Remit the money to
Glosilla ...	22776	Will remit the money to
Glossario ...	22777	Have remitted the money to
Glossateur	22778	Is there any money in it
Glossema ...	22779	There is money in it
Glossology	22780	There is big money in it
Glottis ...	22781	There is no money in it
Glotzen ...	22782	What money have you in hand
Glouglou ...	22783	Have money in hand at the present moment amounting to
Glouteron...	22784	Have at the present moment —— as money in hand but of this [require —— to pay immediate liabilities
Glowingly	22785	Which will leave me without any money for contingencies
Gluant ...	22786	Should have money by
Glucken ...	22787	Shall not want money if
Gluckhenne	22788	Send all the money you can
Glucklich...	22789	In which case no money will be required
Gluckselig	22790	Do not want any money
Gluckskind	22791	What money will you be able to send
Gluckspilz	22792	Can the payment of the money be deferred; if so, for how long

Glucksrad	22793	When is the next instalment of money due
Gluckstaff	22794	The next money instalment is due on
Glucose ...	22795	When money may be expected to be easier
Gluhwein ...	22796	When money may be expected to be dearer
Glutinamen	22797	Money is easy
Glutinator	22798	Money is scarce
Glutineux...	22799	Money is very tight
Glutton ...	22800	Money will be very tight
Gluttonize	22801	The supply of money has increased
Gluttonous	22802	The supply of money is diminishing
Glycerine ...	22803	The supply of money is increasing
Glycoltic ...	22804	The supply of money is still scarce
Glyconium	22805	Money is cabled through ——
Glyoxylic ...	22806	Money to be paid against
Glyph ...	22807	Money is no object (provided that)
Glyptics ...	22808	Must find (have) the money
Gnaccare ...	22809	Money required for wages
Gnacchera	22810	Must have the money not later than
Gnaciate ...	22811	No money yet to hand
Gnadenakt	22812	No money is yet to hand, please cable
Gnadenbrod	22813	Do you think the money is all right
Gnadenlohn	22814	So far as I can ascertain the money is all right
Gnafalio ...	22815	You need have no fear, the money is all right
Gnaphalium	22816	I have reason to fear the money is lost
Gnaruris ...	22817	Unless you take prompt steps the money will be lost
Gnashing ...	22818	Take necessary steps to secure the money
Gnatone ...	22819	Take any steps you think necessary to recover the money
Gnaulare ...	22820	Stop all money payments
Gnaviter ...	22821	Have stopped all money payments
Gnawed ...	22822	—— was instructed to pay the money on
Gnognotte	22823	In the event of the money being still unpaid
Gnomico ...	22824	Have instructed —— to pay the money
Gnomonique	22825	Who will pay you the money
Goading ...	22826	The money will be paid by
Goatsmilk	22827	The money will not be paid unless
Gobbetto ...	22828	What amount of purchase money is required
Gobbling ...	22829	Will take —— of purchase money in fully paid shares
Gobelet ...	22830	The purchase money is —— payable on
Gobelotter	22831	Either in money or shares
Goberge ...	22832	The money to be payable in instalments of ——
Gobernado	22833	Can I draw upon —— for money required
Gobernalle	22834	For any money required draw upon ——
Gobernar ...	22835	What money was realised
Gobierno ...	22836	The money realised amounted to
Gocciare ...	22837	Could not realise sufficient money in time
Gocciolato	22838	Could you realise any money from
Gocciolone	22839	Could only realise say —— which would be no good
Godailler ...	22840	Could not realise more money than
Godchild ...	22841	Could realise —— from sale of —— if you think it judicious
Godelureau	22842	I (we) have sufficient money in hand for
Godenot ...	22843	I (we) have not sufficient money in hand for
Godereccio	22844	I (we) have only sufficient money in hand to defray
Godevole ...	22845	Has paid money
Godfather...	22846	Refuses to part with the money
Godiche ...	22847	—— refuse(s) to pay the money
Godiveau ...	22848	Claim(s) money for
Godmother	22849	What is the amount of money owing
Godsend ...	22850	Still owe(s) money for
Godson ...	22851	The money was really
Goeland ...	22852	I am (we are) entirely without money

Goelette ...	22853	Will keep you supplied with money
Goffaggine	22854	Unless I am at once supplied with money it will be necessary to
Goffamente	22855	Unable to send more money at present
Goffrido ...	22856	Which is all the money I (we) have to send
Gognolino	22857	Have no money to send
Goguenard	22858	Owing to want of money
Goguettes...	22859	Cannot discharge men until I have money for wages
Goinfre ...	22860	Failure to pay the money means
Goitrous ...	22861	It is very important that the money be paid on
Golaccia ...	22862	Unless the money is paid
Golafre ...	22863	Have sent money as requested
Goldbeater	22864	Will send money as requested
Golddust ...	22865	In the event of your money running short
Goldfinch ...	22866	Have drawn upon you for passage money
Goldfuchs...	22867	Have resumed money payments
Goldgehalt	22868	When will you (they) be able to resume money payments
Goldgrund	22869	Moneys are coming in from shipments of ore (bullion)
Goldhaltig	22870	Is reported to have made his money by
Goldkind ...	22871	Money now in hand amounts to —— require a further ——
Goldleaf ...	22872	It means throwing good money away
Goldleaves	22873	**Monopoly**
Goldmacher	22874	Government monopoly
Goldprobe	22875	To secure monopoly
Goldsize ...	22876	Which will give me (us) the monopoly
Goldstuck	22877	Has (have) secured monopoly
Goldwolf ...	22878	Has (have) prevented his (their) gaining monopoly
Goleggiare	22879	Cannot secure monopoly
Golfclubs...	22880	**Month(s)** (*See also* " Days," " Fortnight," " Week.")
Golfillo ...	22881	For the month(s) of
Golfplayer	22882	On the first of next month
Golillero ...	22883	After the month (of)
Golleria ...	22884	About the month of
Golmagear	22885	Before the month of
Golondrina	22886	Since the month of
Golondro ...	22887	At the beginning of the month
Golosazo ...	22888	About the middle of the month
Golosinar...	22889	At the end of the month
Golpeadero	22890	During the present month
Golpecico ...	22891	During next month
Golusmiero	22892	During the month after next
Gombina ...	22893	Each alternate month
Gomecillo...	22894	Last month
Gomitolare	22895	Next month
Gommage...	22896	This month
Gommeux...	22897	For the month of
Gommifero	22898	For the month ending
Gondel ...	22899	From the month of
Gondola ...	22900	In the month of
Gondoletta	22901	In —— months
Gondolier...	22902	For —— months
Gonfiato ...	22903	Per month
Gonfiatura	22904	Within a month from date
Gonfiezza ...	22905	Within —— months from date
Gonflement	22906	One month
Gonfler ...	22907	Two months
Gongorino	22908	Three months
Gongorista	22909	Four months
Gongorizar	22910	Five months
Goniaster ...	22911	Six months
Goniometro	22912	Seven months

Gonnellone	22913	Eight months
Gonnerin ...	22914	Nine months
Gonorrea ...	22915	Ten months
Goodbyes...	22916	Eleven months
Goodluck ...	22917	Twelve months
Goodnight	22918	What are your payments for the month of
Gooseberry	22919	The working expenses for the current month are
Goosestep...	22920	During the past month there has been (we have) paid [is ——
Gophers ...	22921	The estimated value of concentrates obtained for current month
Gorbion ...	22922	The return for the current month I think will be equal to that
Gordiflon ...	22923	Net profit for the month [of the past one
Gordolobo	22924	Will send you statement of cost for current month by next mail
Gordura ...	22925	Will send you statement of cost and returns for current month
Gorgear ...	22926	During the latter part of the month [by next mail
Gorgeria ...	22927	During the next two months
Gorghetto	22928	Generally our worst month is
Gorgione ...	22929	Each month should be treated by itself
Gorgoglio...	22930	What are the expenses for the month of
Gorgojarse	22931	Expenses for the month of —— amount to
Gorgoran ...	22932	What are the returns for the month of
Gorgorita...	22933	Returns for the month of —— amount to
Gorgotero	22934	What do you estimate your expenses for the next two months
Gorguerin	22935	Estimate that expenses for next two months will total about
Gorguz ...	22936	Send duplicate statement for —— month
Gorjal ...	22937	First half of the month
Gormand ...	22938	Last half of month
Gormandise	22939	For the first half of this month
Gorrada ...	22940	For the last half of this month
Gorretada...	22941	For the first half of last month
Gorrionera	22942	For the second half of last month
Gorrista ...	22943	For the first half of next month
Gorronal ...	22944	For the last half of next month
Gorullo ...	22945	At what do you estimate the total expenditure for the
Gorzaretto	22946	Estimated total cost for the month(s) of [month(s) of
Goshawk ...	22947	What was the actual cost for the month of
Gosier ...	22948	**Monthly** (*See also* "Expenditure.")
Gosling ...	22949	Monthly statement
Gospelized	22950	Monthly pay-roll
Gossamer ...	22951	Monthly cost
Gossampin	22952	Monthly run
Gossip ...	22953	Monthly payment(s)
Gossipers ...	22954	By monthly payments
Gossipinus	22955	Monthly shipment(s) of ore
Gossipion...	22956	Monthly shipments average
Gotaccia ...	22957	Mail monthly statement of
Gotellina ...	22958	Mail monthly statement showing
Gothamite	22959	Omitted to include in monthly statement
Gothic ...	22960	What do you estimate the monthly expenses at
Gothicism	22961	Monthly expenses are now
Gothique ...	22962	What do you estimate the monthly returns at
Gotteshaus	22963	Monthly returns are now
Gottheit ...	22964	Monthly expenses will be increased owing to
Gottlich ...	22965	A monthly statement of
Gottselig ...	22966	A monthly statement of cash payments and receipts
Gotuzza ...	22967	A monthly statement of work done and progress made
Gotzenbild	22968	Include in your monthly statement
Gouache ...	22969	In order to provide for increased monthly cost
Gouailler ...	22970	**More**
Goudron ...	22971	Any more
Goueppeur	22972	No more

Gouffre ...	22973	As much more as possible
Goujat ...	22974	As little more as possible
Gouliafre ...	22975	A little more
Goulument	22976	A great deal more
Goupille ...	22977	As much more as you are able
Gourmander	22978	Are you (they) likely to require more
Gourmette	22979	Am (are) not likely to require more
Gouttiere ...	22980	Am only likely to require more in the event of
Gouvernail	22981	Considerably more
Governance	22982	Considerably more than
Governess...	22983	Have no more to send
Governime	22984	Equal if not more
Gownsman	22985	How much more will it amount to
Gozoso ...	22986	How much more
Gozque ...	22987	It is not possible to do more
Grabado ...	22988	It is not possible to —— more
Grabadura	22989	Is it possible to —— more
Grabataire	22990	Is much more
Grabatulus	22991	It is much more
Grabazon ...	22992	Is it much more
Grabgesang	22993	Is it likely to cost much more
Grabhugel	22994	Is not likely to cost more
Grablied ...	22995	Is likely to cost considerably more
Grabmal ...	22996	Is certain to be more
Grabrede ...	22997	Is less instead of more
Grabscheit	22998	In the event of which should require more
Grabstatte	22999	In case more is required
Grabstein ...	23000	In case more is required telegraph at once
Grabuge ...	**23001**	No more required
Gracchiare	23002	More than
Gracculo ...	23003	No more than
Gracefully	23004	More if possible
Gracejante	23005	May be a little more
Gracejar ...	23006	Not much more
Graceless ...	23007	Only in the event of there being more
Graciable ...	23008	Will only amount to a little more
Gracidare...	23009	Will amount to —— more
Gracieux ...	23010	Will be very much more
Gracilente	23011	Will cost more than
Gracilesco...	23012	Will not cost more than
Gracilita ...	23013	What more do you want
Gracilus ...	23014	Will be more
Graciola ...	23015	Will not be more
Gradacion...	23016	Will it (this) be more
Gradaggio	23017	**Morning** (*See also* "Day.")
Gradare ...	23018	Morning shift
Gradarius...	23019	At —— o'clock this morning
Gradatim ...	23020	In the morning
Gradazione	23021	This morning
Gradecer ...	23022	To-morrow morning
Graderia ...	23023	Yesterday morning
Gradient ...	23024	Each morning
Gradilla ...	23025	Only in the morning
Gradimento	23026	Not until the morning
Gradinar ...	23027	Arrived on the morning of the ——
Gradivus ...	23028	Left on the morning of the ——
Gradleiter	23029	**Mortar(s)** (*See also* "Battery," "Stamps.")
Graduado...	23030	Mortar boxes
Graduating	23031	Lining(s) for mortars
Grafila ...	23032	Mortar(s) to be made in sections for transport

Grafioles ...	23033	Fixed below the mortar(s)
Grafometro	23034	**Mortgage(s)(d)** (*See also* "Foreclose.")
Grafschaft	23035	By means of a mortgage
Gragea ...	23036	Can you arrange a mortgage
Grainetier...	23037	Can you arrange the following settlement of mortgage
Grainmills	23038	Have arranged mortgage on the following terms
Grainstore	23039	Send mortgage on title
Graissage ...	23040	In the event of mortgage not being paid off
Graisseux ...	23041	Mortgage must be paid off
Grajero ...	23042	Intend(s) to foreclose mortgage
Grajuelo ...	23043	First mortgage bonds
Grajugna ...	23044	First mortgage bonds series " A "
Grallator ...	23045	First mortgage bonds series " B "
Gramallera	23046	As a mortgage on the property
Gramaticon	23047	Mortgage on [interest per annum
Gramatista	23048	Of which —— could remain on mortgage at —— per cent.
Gramercy ...	23049	Raise(d) by means of a mortgage on the property
Gramignato	23050	So as to pay off mortgage
Gramineo ...	23051	Unless the mortgage is paid off
Graminosus	23052	There is no mortgage whatever
Grammar ...	23053	To provide money to pay off mortgage
Grammarian	23054	There is said to be a mortgage of
Grammateu	23055	There is a (are) mortgage(s) on the property amounting to a
Grammicus	23056	The mortgage must be arranged for [total of
Gramolaro	23057	Which practically amount(s) to a mortgage on the property
Gramuffa ...	23058	—— has a mortgage on the property amounting to
Granajolo ...	23059	**Mortgagee(s)**
Granarium	23060	Cable full name(s) of mortgagee(s)
Granary ...	23061	The name(s) of mortgagee(s) is (are)
Granate ...	23062	Ascertain claims of mortgagee(s)
Granatino...	23063	Mortgagee(s) claim(s)
Granatuzza	23064	Mortgagee(s) is (are) willing
Granazon ...	23065	Mortgagee(s) threaten(s) to foreclose
Granbestia	23066	Mortgagee(s) demand(s) instant payment
Grancassa	23067	**Most(ly)**
Grancevola	23068	At most
Granchio ...	23069	By far the most
Grandam ...	23070	Is the most I (we) can do
Grandanime	23071	Most of the
Grandaria ..	23072	Most of the work was completed on
Grandazo ...	23073	Most of the work is now finished
Grandelet ...	23074	Most of your instructions already attended to
Grandement	23075	The most
Grandescit	23076	What is the most you can send
Grandetto...	23077	Most important
Grandeur ...	23078	Probably most
Grandigia ..	23079	Most strongly advise
Grandillon	23080	**Mould(s)**
Grandinare	23081	Bullion mould(s) to cast of bar of —— ounces
Grandioso...	23082	Cupel mould(s)
Granditas ...	23083	Ingot mould(s) to cast a bar of
Grandjury	23084	**Mountain(ous)** (*See also* "Hills.")
Grandmere	23085	Side of mountain
Grandoncle	23086	Summit of mountain
Grandsire...	23087	Foot of mountain
Grandtante	23088	At the base of mountain
Granducato	23089	**Mouth**
Grandura ...	23090	Mouth of
Granelloso	23091	At the mouth of
Granevano	23092	At the mouth of tunnel

Granfatto ...	23093	At the mouth of drift
Grangeria...	23094	At the mouth of shaft
Grangusto	23095	**Move(s)**
Granifer ...	23096	To move
Granigione	23097	To move the
Granitique	23098	Could you move
Granitoid ...	23099	Impossible to move
Granitura...	23100	Endeavour to move
Granivoro...	23101	Will move
Granizada	23102	Will not move
Granmerce	23103	Could you move the trial to
Granuja ...	23104	Will attempt to move
Granujoso	23105	When do you intend to move in the matter
Granule ...	23106	Decline(s) to move in the matter
Granulous	23107	Shall not move in the matter for the present
Granzen ...	23108	If anything is to be done ought to move in the matter at once
Granzlinie	23109	Could you move it (this) from
Granzones	23110	Unless I (we) move
Granzsaule	23111	I (we) should have to move
Granzstein	23112	I (we) should require first to move
Granzwache	23113	Do not move
Grapeshot	23114	Would suggest that you move
Graphicus	23115	Move in the matter
Grapnel ...	23116	What is to be the next move
Grappiller	23117	Will be the next move
Grappin ...	23118	The next move should be to
Grappling	23119	The next move will probably be that
Grappolo ...	23120	**Moved**
Grasartig ...	23121	To be moved
Grasdouble	23122	Might be moved
Graseza ...	23123	Cannot be moved
Grasflech ...	23124	Successfully moved
Grasgarten	23125	**Movement(s)**
Grashalm...	23126	Report any movements
Grasmucke	23127	Keep me (us) informed as to your movements
Grasplatz ...	23128	Will keep you informed as to my movements
Grassaccio	23129	No movement
Grassandum	23130	Slight movement upwards
Grassatio ...	23131	Slight movement downwards
Grassatura	23132	Strong movement
Grassello ...	23133	**Moving**
Grassgreen	23134	Not moving
Grassiren ...	23135	Now moving
Grasslich ...	23136	Is —— moving at all in the matter
Grassplot ...	23137	—— is not moving in the matter
Gratamente	23138	Is there anything to prevent our moving later
Gratanter...	23139	It would not prevent your moving later
Gratel ...	23140	It would altogether prevent your moving
Grateolens	23141	Is (are) already moving in the matter
Graticcia ...	23142	**Much**
Gratificar ...	23143	Too much
Gratify ...	23144	Want(s) too much
Gratiner ...	23145	How much
Gratisdato	23146	Not much
Gratissime	23147	How much shall you require
Gratitude...	23148	Much more
Gratonada	23149	Much more than
Grattacapo	23150	How much have you in hand
Grattagia ...	23151	How much can you obtain
~attatura	23152	How much more do you expect

Gratteleux	23153	Do not expect much more for the present
Grattoir ...	23154	As much as
Grattugina	23155	As much as possible
Gratuito ...	23156	As much as you are able
Gratular ...	23157	Much more time
Gratulatio	23158	Much less
Grauelthat	23159	Much less than I thought
Graukopf ...	23160	Much more than I thought
Graulich ...	23161	Get as much as you can
Graupeln ...	23162	Get as much more as you can
Grausam ...	23163	Shall get as much as
Grausig ...	23164	Shall get as much as I expected
Gravamen	23165	Shall get as much as I can
Gravandus	23166	This (which) is much more than I expected
Gravanza ...	23167	Without much more
Gravativo...	23168	Without much loss of time
Gravazione	23169	Will not be much more
Gravedad ...	23170	Will not be much longer now
Gravedine	23171	Very much
Gravedoso	23172	It would not be much
Graveless ...	23173	**Multiply(ing)** (*See also* " By.")
Gravelpits	23174	To multiply
Gravelure...	23175	Should require to multiply
Gravescens	23176	Should not require to multiply
Gravescit ...	23177	**Mundic** (*See also* " Iron," " Mineral.")
Graveside...	23178	Iron mundic
Graveyard	23179	Arsenical mundic
Gravidatus	23180	**Murder(ed)(s)**
Gravidezza	23181	Was murdered on
Gravidor ...	23182	Owing to recent murder(s)
Graviren ...	23183	**Must**
Gravitare ...	23184	If you must
Grayling ...	23185	Must I (we)
Graziato ...	23186	Must I (we) go
Graziosita	23187	I (we) must
Graznador	23188	I (we) must not
Graznido ...	23189	I (we) must know at once
Greaves ...	23190	If you mean to do it (this) you must
Grecisco ...	23191	He (they) must
Grecizante	23192	He (they) must not
Grecizar ...	23193	Must be
Grecque ...	23194	Must be quick
Gredinerie	23195	Must not be
Greekfire ...	23196	Must not be longer than
Greenhorn	23197	Must this be
Greenhouse	23198	Must this be kept quiet
Greenishly	23199	Must be done
Greensward	23200	Must be paid on or before
Greenwood	23201	You must not
Greffeur ...	23202	You must not lose sight of
Gregalizar	23203	You must
Gregario ...	23204	You must proceed
Gregatim ...	23205	You must send
Gregeois ...	23206	You must not proceed (unless)
Greggiuola	23207	You must not send (unless)
Gregorian...	23208	Must go (to)
Gregorillo...	23209	You must go immediately to
Gregueria...	23210	You must send immediately to
Greguescos	23211	You must come immediately to
Greinen ...	23212	Must be held responsible

Grellheit ...	23213	Must be replaced smartly
Grelotter ...	23214	**Mutilate(d)** (*See also* "Cable," "Message.")
Gremial ...	23215	Arrived mutilated
Gremigna ...	23216	Was (were) mutilated
Gremium ...	23217	Was (were) not mutilated
Grenadier...	23218	Owing to it having been mutilated
Grenadille	23219	The mutilated portion is from the word —— to **the word** ——
Grenailler...	23220	The mutilated portion is from the word —— to **the end**
Greneler ...	23221	The mutilated portion is from the beginning to **the word** ——
Grenouille	23222	**Mutual(ly)**
Grenuela ...	23223	If mutually agreeable
Gresca ...	23224	On the understanding that it was mutual
Gresserie ...	23225	Believed to have undertaken mutually
Gressus ...	23226	Must be mutual
Gretola ...	23227	To our (your) mutual advantage
Greuge ...	23228	**My**
Grevement	23229	My opinion is
Greyhound	23230	My impression is
Gribar ...	23231	My intention is
Gricciolo ...	23232	My authority is
Gricenia ...	23233	My lawyer(s) advise(s)
Gridamento	23234	My own holding is
Gridatore ...	23235	My draft
Gridiron ...	23236	My signature
Griego ...	23237	My limit
Griesgram	23238	**Mynpacht**
Griesmehl ..	23239	The mynpacht covers an area of —— acres
Grietoso ...	23240	For mynpacht
Grieving ...	23241	**Myself**
Grievous ...	23242	Important to myself
Grifagno ...	23243	Myself and personal friends
Grifalto ...	23244	As I am at present by myself
Griffbret ...,	23245	Entirely by myself
Griffel ...	23246	Shall be by myself until
Griffonner	23247	When I hope to be by myself
Grignoter...	23248	When I shall not be by myself
Grillageur	23249	**N**
Grillanda...	23250	**Name(s)**
Grillera ...	23251	Name of
Grilletes ...	23252	In the name of
Grillig ...	23253	Now standing in the name(s) of
Grillolino ...	23254	In whose name
Grillones ...	23255	In my (our) name
Grimace ...	23256	Has (have) long had a name for
Grimalkin	23257	When will you be able to name a date for
Griminess...	23258	Cannot name any date
Grimoire ...	23259	Ascertain the name(s) of
Grimpereau	23260	Had better remain in your name for the present
Grimpeur...	23261	Can you identify the name(s) of
Grimpola ...	23262	Cannot identify the name(s) of
Grinalde ...	23263	In my (our) own name(s)
Grincement	23264	In the following name(s)
Gringalet ...	23265	Under the name of
Gringotter	23266	What is (are) the name(s) of
Grinsen ...	23267	Do not know the name(s)
Grinzetta ...	23268	All very good names
Griottier ...	23269	Name(s) very well known
Griphus ...	23270	Names thoroughly respected
Grisaille ...	23271	Can you discover name(s) of
Griseta ...	23272	Cannot discover name(s) of

Grisoller ...	23273	In whose name is it (are they) registered
Grisopazio	23274	Is (are) registered in the name(s) of
Gritador ...	23275	Can you suggest any name(s)
Griteria ...	23276	Previously known under the name of
Grivele ...	23277	—— stand(s) for the present in the name of
Groaning ...	23278	—— is (are) still standing in the name of
Groats ...	23279	Might stand in your name
Grobheit ...	23280	Telegraph the name(s) of
Groblich ...	23281	Telegraph full christian names of ——
Grocire ...	23282	Telegraph full christian name(s) of —— and address(es)
Grognard ...	23283	Mail full christian name(s) of —— and address(es)
Grognement	23284	What is the name of chairman
Grogneur ...	23285	What is the name of secretary
Grogram ...	23286	What is the name of mine superintendent
Gromatice	23287	What is the name of foreman
Grommeler	23288	What is the name of millman
Grondajo ...	23289	What is the name of company
Grondante	23290	What is the name of mine
Gronderie...	23291	What is the name of property
Grondeuse	23292	The name(s) you require is (are)
Groomsman	23293	The name(s) of —— is (are)
Grooved ...	23294	**Named**
Groppetto	23295	As named by yourself
Groppiera...	23296	As named in your letter dated
Grosca ...	23297	The person named is very well known to me (us)
Grosedad ...	23298	The person named has a very good reputation
Grosella ...	23299	The person named has only a fair reputation
Grosellero...	23300	The person named has no reputation for
Grosphos ...	23301	What are the terms named
Grossaccio	23302	The terms named are
Grossartig	23303	In the event of any other terms being named
Grossfurst	23304	**Namely**
Grossiere ...	23305	**Naphtha**
Grossmaul	23306	**Narrow**
Grossmuth	23307	Is (are) narrow
Grossness...	23308	Too narrow
Grossolano	23309	Too narrow to pay
Grossotto...	23310	Very narrow
Grossoyer...	23311	Both narrow and poor
Grossthat...	23312	Is (are) narrow but rich
Grossulus...	23313	Is (are) becoming more narrow
Grossvater	23314	Is (are) not quite so narrow
Grotesque	23315	The margin of profit is too narrow
Grottesco ...	23316	Has become narrow
Groundbait	23317	Become(s) narrow in length
Grounded...	23318	Become(s) narrow in depth
Groundnuts	23319	As the difference between us (——) is so narrow
Groundrent	23320	A narrow valley
Grouping ...	23321	A narrow strip of ground
Grouse ...	23322	**Narrowing**
Grubchen...	23323	Narrowing to
Grubelei ...	23324	**Narrowly**
Grudgingly	23325	**Native(s)**
Grueras ...	23326	Carrying native gold
Grufolare...	23327	Carrying native silver
Gruger ...	23328	Carrying native copper
Grugidor ...	23329	Is mostly in the native state
Grugnio ...	23330	Native labour
Gruinus ...	23331	**Natural(ly)**
Grullada ...	23332	**Nature**

Grumblers	23333	What is the nature of ——
Grumbling	23334	Of a dangerous nature
Grumeleux	23335	Of a temporary nature
Grumete ...	23336	What is the nature of ——'s demands
Grumhidos	23337	What is the nature of ——'s complaints
Grumillo ...	23338	Owing to the dangerous nature of the
Grumulus	23339	Owing to the nature of the
Grundbuch	23340	Should be of a permanent nature
Grundfarbe	23341	Until I (we) know the nature of [of the ground
Grundfeste	23342	No examination could be made owing to the dangerous nature
Grundherr	23343	**Navigable**
Grundiebam	23344	**Near**
Grundiendo	23345	Not near
Grundivero	23346	Very near
Grundivit...	23347	Too near
Grundlich	23348	Near the top
Grundlinie	23349	Near the bottom
Grundmauer	23350	Near the end line(s)
Grundriss...	23351	Near the side line(s)
Grundstein	23352	Near the foot wall
Grundstoff	23353	Near the hanging wall
Grundstuck	23354	Not near enough
Grundung	23355	Not quite near enough
Grundwesen	23356	Will be quite near enough
Grundwort	23357	Sufficiently near for the purpose
Grundzug	23358	Sufficiently near to
Grunnitote	23359	When I hope to be sufficiently near to
Grunnitus	23360	In order to get near
Grunspan ...	23361	In the event of your (——) being near
Gruntingly	23362	**Nearly**
Grupera	23363	Nearly completed
Gruppetto	23364	Not nearly completed
Gruppiren	23365	Is (has) now nearly completed
Grussen ...	23366	As nearly as I (we) can judge
Gruyere ...	23367	As nearly as you (they) can judge
Gruzzolo ...	23368	**Necessarily**
Gryllatote	23369	Not necessarily
Gryllavit ...	23370	**Necessary**
Gryllorum	23371	Do(es) not consider it at all necessary
Gryllos ...	23372	Do you (does ——) think it necessary
Gryphis ...	23373	I (we) do not think it necessary
Gryphites...	23374	In case you (——) think(s) it necessary
Gryphosis	23375	At first it will be necessary to
Guacamayo	23376	Only in case it is absolutely necessary
Guachapear	23377	To my mind it is absolutely necessary
Guadagnato	23378	Consult —— and take necessary steps instantly (to)
Guadamacil	23379	Shall at once take necessary steps (to)
Guadanero	23380	Do you authorize me (us) to take the necessary steps (to)
Guadarnes	23381	Authorize you to take all necessary steps
Guadiana...	23382	Cannot authorize you to take necessary steps (until)
Guadijeno	23383	Take all necessary steps
Guagnelo ...	23384	When do you think it will be necessary
Guainajo ...	23385	Will become necessary as soon as
Guajolire ...	23386	If you think it necessary
Gualatina...	23387	Is now more than ever necessary
Gualchiera	23388	How much will be necessary
Gualdado ...	23389	It is necessary that I (we) should be provided with
Gualderas...	23390	Is it absolutely necessary
Gualdon ...	23391	It is absolutely necessary
Gualdrapa	23392	It is not absolutely necessary but very advisable

Gualdrines	23393	Will only become necessary in the event of
Gualercio ...	23394	It will be necessary for some time to come (to)
Guanciata	23395	Under these circumstances it will be necessary
Guancione	23396	If necessary.
Guantelete	23397	If not necessary
Guantiera...	23398	If necessary to take
Guapamente	23399	If not necessary to take
Guapazo ...	23400	If necessary to give
Guapear ...	23401	If not necessary to give
Guapeton ...	23402	It will be necessary to give notice to
Guaracha ...	23403	It has now become necessary
Guaraguato	23404	In the event of this becoming necessary
Guarantees	23405	Will advise you as soon as necessary
Guarapo ...	23406	Telegraph as soon as you think it necessary
Guardable	23407	Telegraph full details of everything necessary
Guardador	23408	To do what is absolutely necessary
Guardagote	23409	The necessary expenditure will be at least
Guardaja ...	23410	The first thing necessary is
Guardamano	23411	Which rendered it necessary
Guardante	23412	This has been rendered necessary by
Guardapies	23413	Which will provide the necessary means
Guardasol	23414	This will render it necessary
Guardatura	23415	This will not render it necessary
Guardboats	23416	This has made it necessary that I (we) should
Guardeth ...	23417	It has been necessary to devote
Guardingo	23418	It is most necessary that
Guardless	23419	Everything necessary should be done before
Guardships	23420	It is necessary that you
Guarentare	23421	It is necessary that I (we)
Guaribile ...	23422	Not unless you believe it to be absolutely necessary
Guarigione	23423	**Necessitate**
Guarnacca	23424	**Necessity(ies)**
Guarnello ...	23425	Is there any necessity
Guarnir ...	23426	There is no necessity
Guasconata	23427	There is a great necessity
Guascotto...	23428	In the event of this becoming a necessity
Guatatrice	23429	There is at present no necessity for
Guatterino	23430	In case of necessity
Guattire ...	23431	Unless compelled by absolute necessity
Guayacana	23432	Should not have done so unless compelled by absolute necessity
Guayaco ...	23433	The necessity arose through
Guayadero	23434	This will obviate the necessity of
Guayapil ...	23435	Will not this obviate the necessity
Guazzatojo	23436	Would impress upon you the necessity of
Guazzerone	23437	Impress upon —— the necessity of
Gubernabat	23438	Have been unable to impress —— that any necessity exists
Gubernamus	23439	**Need(s)**
Gubernandi	23440	Need not
Gubernaris	23441	I (we) do not need
Gubernatio	23442	I am (we are) likely to need
Gubernatur	23443	In much need of
Gubernent	23444	Should you need this (it)
Gubernetis	23445	Shall not need
Gubernium	23446	Shall not need until (unless)
Guberno ...	23447	There is no need now
Gubiadura	23448	Telegraph how much you (——) need(s)
Guckkasten	23449	Telegraph what (how many) you need
Gudgeons	23450	You need not reply except
Guedeja ...	23451	You need not
Guedejilla...	23452	Need not proceed further with the matter

Guedejudo	23453	Shall certainly not need
Gueltre ...	23454	Is there any need for
Guenille ...	23455	There is no need at all for
Guenuche	23456	No need at present for
Guepier ...	23457	Am (are) much in need of
Guerdon ...	23458	In case of need you (——) can apply to
Guergione	23459	**Needful**
Guerisseur	23460	Have you everything needful
Guermeces	23461	Have everything needful
Guernito ...	23462	Have everything needful except
Guerreador	23463	Have you provided the needful
Guerresco...	23464	**Needless(ly)**
Guerriare ...	23465	**Negative(ly)**
Guerrilla ...	23466	Reply whether negative or affirmative
Guerroyer...	23467	Decision likely to be negative
Guessing ...	23468	In the negative
Guetrier ...	23469	For the negative
Gueulard ...	23470	My information is entirely negative
Gueusaille	23471	My information is practically negative
Gueusarie...	23472	**Neglect(ful)**
Gugliata ...	23473	Can you explain this neglect
Guiadera ...	23474	Was not due to any neglect
Guiamiento	23475	Chiefly owing to neglect of
Guidajuolo	23476	Due to neglect of
Guidalesco	23477	Do not neglect to
Guidardone	23478	Very great neglect
Guidatrice	23479	**Neglected**
Guideless ...	23480	Why was it neglected
Guidemain	23481	Was (were) neglected until too late
Guidepost...	23482	Has (have) been entirely neglected
Guidoneria	23483	He has (they have) neglected to
Guidonian	23484	Has (have) neglected to
Guignier ...	23485	Must not be neglected
Guignon ...	23486	Should not be neglected if possible
Guijarral ...	23487	—— neglected to inform me (us)
Guijarreno	23488	**Negligence**
Guijeno ...	23489	Wilful negligence
Guildhall ...	23490	**Negotiable**
Guileful ...	23491	Not negotiable
Guillame ...	23492	Negotiable paper
Guilledin ...	23493	**Negotiate**
Guillemet ..	23494	Negotiate for
Guillocher	23495	Can you negotiate bills on company
Guillotine...	23496	Expect(s) to negotiate
Guiltern ...	23497	Has (have) failed to negotiate
Guimauve...	23498	As soon as you can negotiate
Guimbalete	23499	Could negotiate if
Guimbarde	23500	Can you negotiate for any extension of
Guinchar ...	23501	Cannot see my way to negotiate
Guindalera	23502	I believe can negotiate
Guindastes	23503	Cable if you are likely to negotiate for
Guindola ...	23504	Unable to negotiate
Guineapigs	23505	Are you (is ——) willing to negotiate
Guineas ...	23506	Am (is) (are) quite willing to negotiate
Guingans ...	23507	Authorize you to negotiate for
Guingette...	23508	Do not negotiate
Guinzaglio	23509	Do not negotiate till you receive instructions
Guionage ...	23510	Do not negotiate until you receive letter dated
Guipure ...	23511	Who would you suggest to negotiate
Guirigay ...	23512	Would suggest —— to negotiate

Guirindola	23513	Is open to negotiate
Guirlande...	23514	Might be able to negotiate
Guirnalda	23515	No use attempting to negotiate so long as
Guisante ...	23516	Refuse(s) to negotiate
Guitarrear	23517	Shall try to negotiate
Guitonear...	23518	Will only negotiate on a basis of
Guitoneria	23519	To negotiate
Guizgar ...	23520	Would negotiate on a basis of
Guizque ...	23521	**Negotiations** (*See also* "Complete.")
Gularum ...	23522	What has been the final outcome of negotiations
Gulator ...	23523	The final outcome of negotiations has been
Gulden ...	23524	Immediately upon negotiations
Gullible ...	23525	Do you authorise me (us) to continue negotiations
Gulones ...	23526	Authorise you to continue negotiations on a basis of
Gulositam	23527	In the present state of negotiations
Gulosius ...	23528	Negotiations still pending
Gulping ...	23529	Negotiations are not satisfactory
Gumboil ...	23530	Negotiations are very satisfactory
Gumedra ...	23531	Negotiations promise to end satisfactorily
Gumminos	23532	Negotiations do not seem likely to end satisfactorily for you (us)
Gummiren	23533	Negotiations suspended owing to
Gummitio...	23534	Negotiations practically concluded
Gumption...	23535	Negotiations have fallen through
Gumstick ...	23536	Negotiations altogether successful, details by mail
Gunflints ...	23537	Outcome of negotiations
Gunmetal ...	23538	Telegraph the outcome of your negotiations
Gunnery ...	23539	Postpone negotiations
Gunpowder	23540	Try and revive negotiations
Gunsmith...	23541	Shall resume negotiations as soon as
Gunstig ...	23542	Cable progress of negotiations
Gunstock ...	23543	Has put an end to all negotiations
Gunwale ...	23544	We withdraw from all negotiations
Guracho ...	23545	Withdraw from all negotiations
Gurbion ...	23546	**Neighbour(s)**
Gurgeln ...	23547	**Neighbourhood**
Gurgitem ...	23548	Shall you be in the neighbourhood of
Gurgulio ...	23549	Am likely to be in the neighbourhood about
Gurgustium	23550	Am not likely to be in the neighbourhood
Gurrufero...	23551	Should you be in the neighbourhood
Gurrumina	23552	Shall be in the neighbourhood
Gurtler ...	23553	Is said to be in the neighbourhood
Gurtriemen	23554	In the immediate neighbourhood
Gurumete...	23555	Payable mines in the neighbourhood
Gurupera ...	23556	**Neighbouring**
Gurupetin	23557	**Neither**
Gurvio ...	23558	In neither
Gusanear ...	23559	In neither of
Gusaniento	23560	Neither of them
Gusarapa ...	23561	Neither of them have
Gusepe ...	23562	Neither seen nor heard of
Gusseisen...	23563	Neither one nor the other
Gussregen	23564	Neither do I think that
Gusswaare	23565	Neither more nor less
Gustabam...	23566	Neither —— nor
Gustabunt	23567	**Net** (*See also* "Gross.")
Gustadura	23568	Net proceeds
Gustamini	23569	Net proceeds amount to
Gustandus	23570	What is the net weight (of)
Gustativo ...	23571	The net weight is
Gustatote ...	23572	Net yield

Gustatus ...	23573	Net yield per ton
Gustevolo...	23574	Net amount
Gustillo ...	23575	Net output
Gutachten	23576	Net output for
Guterwagen	23577	Net weight
Guterzug ..	23578	Net per ton
Guthaben...	23579	Net price
Gutigkeit ..	23580	Net result(s)
Gutlich ...	23581	Net figure(s)
Gutmuthig	23582	Cable the net profit you expect
Guttatim ...	23583	This is net after paying all costs
Guttural ...	23584	What was the net yield (from)
Gutturnium	23585	From which the net yield was
Gutturosus	23586	Cable net yield
Gutwillig ...	23587	Net yield amounts to
Guzmanes	23588	Cable net sum
Guzzling ...	23589	As a net sum
Gygarthus	23590	Cable net value
Gymnasium	23591	Are your figures net
Gymnastic	23592	All these figures are net
Gymnicus...	23593	As a net price
Gymnodont	23594	Lowest net price
Gynarchy...	23595	Leaving a net profit of
Gypsabam	23596	Leaving a net balance of
Gypsabunt	23597	Net after allowing for
Gypsanto ...	23598	Net without any deductions for
Gypsatio ...	23599	Net without any deductions
Gypsatote...	23600	Net estimated value
Gypsavisse	23601	Net approximate value
Gypsemur	23602	All weights are net
Gypseux ...	23603	Net tonnage
Gyral ...	23604	What are the net and gross weights
Gyratilis ...	23605	The net weight is —— the gross weight is ——
Gyrating ...	23606	What are the net receipts
Gyration ...	23607	The net receipts are
Gyrgathus	23608	The gross returns for the period ending [to
Gyrgillus ...	23609	What do the gross returns for the period ending —— amount
Gyrinus ...	23610	**Network**
Gyroidal ...	23611	Network of veins
Gyrostat ...	23612	**Neutral**
Gyves ...	23613	Can you prevail upon —— to remain neutral
Habebat ...	23614	Can guarantee that —— will remain neutral
Habemur ...	23615	Refuse(s) to remain neutral
Habendus	23616	Advise you to remain neutral
Habentia ...	23617	Am (are) entirely neutral
Habergeon	23618	I (we) will remain neutral
Haberias ...	23619	Will remain neutral
Haberrohr	23620	Promise(s) to remain neutral except
Habessit ...	23621	Quite neutral
Habetote ...	23622	Wish(es) to remain neutral
Habgier ...	23623	Cannot remain neutral
Habhaft ...	23624	Better remain neutral
Habicht ...	23625	**Neutralise**
Habichuela	23626	**Never**
Habilatis ...	23627	Has never been tried
Habilete ...	23628	It will never do
Habillage...	23629	Was (were) never mentioned
Habitable...	23630	It has never been mentioned (to)
Habitaculo	23631	It can never be done (whilst)
Habitador	23632	I should never have done it except

Habitandus	23633	Never fear as to result
Habitante...	23634	Never mind what —— says
Habitatio ...	23635	Was never attempted before
Habitatrix	23636	You should never
Habitual ...	23637	**Nevertheless**
Habladurin	23638	**New**
Hablantin	23639	I should advise you to replace by new
Hablatista	23640	Has (have) now been replaced by new
Hablerie ...	23641	What is there new
Hablilla ...	23642	The whole entirely new
Habsuchtig	23643	The only thing that is new is ——
Habueram	23644	Nothing new
Habuisti ...	23645	What would be the cost of new
Hacanea ...	23646	The cost of new would be
Hacecico ...	23647	Have you anything new to report
Hacedero ...	23648	The new scheme is
Hacendeja	23649	Shall require to have new
Hacendilla	23650	Not necessary to have new so long as
Hacendoso	23651	All of which (this) was entirely new to me
Hacezuelo	23652	As soon as the new parts arrive
Hachereau	23653	Is entirely new to me (us)
Hachette ...	23654	Is certainly not new
Hachon ...	23655	Ought to have a new
Hachure ...	23656	Practically new
Hacinador	23657	Quite new
Hackbeil ...	23658	Nothing new at all in it
Hackmesser	23659	Said to be new
Hackneys ...	23660	Send immediately new
Hactenus ...	23661	Will require to have new
Hadern ...	23662	Will make a new
Hadrobolum	23663	The whole entirely new and in good condition
Hadrolla ...	23664	**News** (*See also* "Favourable," "Latest.")
Haematoid	23665	What is the latest news generally
Haerescant	23666	What is the latest news of
Haerescitz	23667	The latest news is
Haeresco ...	23668	Have you any news
Haesitabam	23669	I have no fresh news of importance
Haesitandi	23670	Have you any news respecting
Haesitatio	23671	I have no news yet of ——
Hafner ...	23672	News has arrived here to the effect that
Hagelkorn	23673	Cable whether news is satisfactory or not
Hagerkeit ..	23674	Latest news more favourable
Hagerose ...	23675	Latest news not so favourable
Hagestolz	23676	Do not telegraph unless news is satisfactory
Haggard ...	23677	As soon as you have any news
Haggling ...	23678	Have no further news
Hagiografo	23679	We shall be glad to hear the earliest news you can give (of)
Hagiology	23680	Have you any fresh news with respect to
Hahnrei ...	23681	Get all the news you possibly can about
Hailstorm	23682	In consequence of the news that
Haineux ...	23683	News not reliable
Hairbrush	23684	News not correct
Hairiness ...	23685	No news of any importance since
Hairspring	23686	Regret to have news about
Hairstroke	23687	Since the news arrived that
Haissable ...	23688	Send all the news you are able about —— to ——
Hakchen ...	23689	Shall be glad to have news of
Hakelnadel	23690	We are still without news
Halabatur	23691	When I will send you all news
Halabunt ...	23692	When do you expect to have news

Halagador	23693	Very glad to receive news that
Halagueno	23694	News received practically unimportant
Halamini ...	23695	Do not send unless you have important news
Halanto ...	23696	News received particularly important
Halapanta	23697	**Newspaper(s)**
Halbbruder	23698	Insert in local newspapers
Halbburtig	23699	Have inserted in local newspapers
Halbdunkel	23700	Have advertised in local newspapers
Halbeit ...	23701	Local newspapers are full of
Halberd ...	23702	Mail newspapers
Halbinsel ...	23703	Mail newspapers referring to
Halbiren ...	23704	**Next**
Halbkreis ...	23705	What do you advise next
Halbkugal	23706	What is your next step
Halboffen ...	23707	Think the next step will be
Halbran ...	23708	In your next letter
Halbton ...	23709	In your next telegram
Halcon ...	23710	In the next claim
Halconado	23711	In the early part of next year
Halconear	23712	Leaving by next steamer on ——
Halconeria	23713	Will leave by the next steamer
Halcyoneum	23714	Next day
Haldada ...	23715	Next week
Haldear ...	23716	Next month
Halecula ...	23717	Next year
Haleine ...	23718	**Nickel** (*See also* "Mineral.")
Haleur ...	23719	Kupfernickel
Halfblood...	23720	Nickel ore(s)
Halfcast ...	23721	—— per cent. of nickel
Halfmoon...	23722	—— per cent. of nickel by dry assay
Halftruths	23723	—— per cent. of nickel by wet assay
Halieto ...	23724	Arsenide of nickel
Halieutica	23725	Nickel speise
Halimus ...	23726	What is the present price of nickel
Haliotoid ...	23727	Market value of nickel is
Hallazgo ...	23728	Hydrated silicate of nickel and magnesia
Hallebarde	23729	Nickel as determined by electrolysis
Hallier ...	23730	**Night** (*See also* "Hour.")
Hallowing	23731	Both night and day
Hallucinor	23732	By night and day shifts
Hallulla ...	23733	During the night
Haloid ...	23734	Night shift
Halosachne	23735	During the night shift
Halosis ...	23736	Leave to-night for
Halotecnia	23737	Leaving to-morrow night for
Haloza ...	23738	To-night
Halskragen	23739	To-morrow night
Halsspange	23740	Each night
Halstuck ...	23741	Only in the night
Haltbar ...	23742	Last night
Haltere ...	23743	Not until the night
Haltingly...	23744	Cable to-night
Haltung ...	23745	Sunday night
Halunke ...	23746	Monday night
Halyard ...	23747	Tuesday night
Halysis ...	23748	Wednesday night
Hamadriade	23749	Thursday night
Hamadryas	23750	Friday night
Hamaquero	23751	Saturday night
Hamatilis...	23752	**No**

Hamaxogoga	23753	No less
Hamaxor	23754	No more
Hambones	23755	Of no interest
Hambriento	23756	Am (are) inclined to say no
Hameau	23757	Is it definitely no
Hamedis	23758	It is definitely no
Hamiota ...	23759	No ! This is definite
Hamisch ...	23760	**Nominal(ly)**
Hammel ...	23761	**Nominate(d)**
Hammerbar	23762	Can you nominate a good man for (post of)
Hammerhead	23763	Cannot nominate anyone at this moment
Hammering	23764	Do you think —— would care to be nominated
Hammonis	23765	I think it will be best to nominate —— at once
Hampéred	23766	I think it will be best not to nominate
Hampesco	23767	Shall be obliged to nominate someone for the post of
Hamstring	23768	To nominate
Hanche ...	23769	**Nominee(s)**
Handbooks	23770	**Non**
Handbuch	23771	Non payment
Handcuff ...	23772	Non delivery
Handdienst	23773	Non acceptance
Handedruck	23774	Non arrival
Handeisen	23775	Non suit
Handeln ...	23776	**None**
Handfessel	23777	Are there none to be obtained
Handfest ...	23778	There are none to be obtained
Handgallop	23779	In the event of none coming forward
Handgelenk	23780	None of the following have been sent
Handhabe	23781	There is (are) none here
Handicaps	23782	**Noon**
Handicraft	23783	**Normal**
Handkauf...	23784	**North(erly)** (*See also* " South.")
Handkrause	23785	At —— degrees to the north of ——
Handkuss...	23786	In the north end
Handlanger	23787	Coming in from the north
Handlich ...	23788	Dipping north
Handlung	23789	Due north and south
Handmaid	23790	On the north of
Handmill ...	23791	North east
Handpferd	23792	North west
Handpresse	23793	In a north easterly direction
Handschlag	23794	In a north westerly direction
Handschuh	23795	In a northerly direction
Handsome	23796	Has a northerly trend
Handspikes	23797	Turns a little to the north
Handwerk	23798	North part of the mine (property)
Hanega ...	23799	Now going north
Hanfling ...	23800	Lying to the north
Hangeron...	23801	North side line
Hangman...	23802	North end line
Hanneton...	23803	Runs north and south
Hanquilla..	23804	To the north of
Hanscrito...	23805	The most northerly
Hanswurst	23806	The north vein
Happily ...	23807	The north drift
Haquetier	23808	North crosscut
Haraganear	23809	North shaft
Haraldo ...	23810	Driving north and south
Haranguer	23811	Driving north
Harasser ...	23812	North wall

Harbar ...	23813	North winze
Harbouring	23814	North workings
Harceler ...	23815	**Not**
Hardheart	23816	Not yet
Hardiesse...	23817	Certainly not
Hardihood	23818	Can not
Hardiment	23819	Do not on any account
Hardships	23820	If he (they) cannot
Harebrain	23821	If not
Harebueno	23822	Must not
Harelips ...	23823	Not this
Harengere	23824	Not now
Harfener ...	23825	Not this week
Harfenist ...	23826	Not this month
Haricot ...	23827	Why not
Haridelle ...	23828	If not, do so immediately
Harija ...	23829	If not, do not do this (it)
Harinoso ...	23830	Shall not
Hariolatio...	23831	**Notarial(ly)** (*See also* "Attested.")
Hariolus ...	23832	Notarially witnessed and attested
Harmamaxa	23833	**Notary**
Harmlessly	23834	Notary public
Harmlos ...	23835	**Note(s)** (*See also* "Compare.")
Harmonia...	23836	Please note
Harmonical	23837	Please note for future reference
Harmonieux	23838	Note for
Harmonique	23839	In notes
Harmonista	23840	Bank notes for
Harnacher	23841	Having lost my note(s)
Harnais ...	23842	Note all you can
Harnblase	23843	Mailed full note(s)
Harnero ...	23844	Original note(s)
Harpaction	23845	Send full note(s)
Harpagatus	23846	Should be carefully noted
Harpagon...	23847	To note
Harpastum	23848	**Nothing**
Harpist ...	23849	Can do nothing until
Harplike ...	23850	Can do nothing
Harplute ...	23851	Can do nothing until I (we) receive
Harponner	23852	Can nothing be done
Harpooned	23853	Nothing can be done so long as
Harpune ...	23854	Can nothing be done to prevent
Harpuniren	23855	Can do nothing owing to the absence of
Harridans	23856	Do nothing at all
Harshly ...	23857	Do nothing unless
Hartleibig	23858	Do nothing until you have consulted
Hartlick ...	23859	Do nothing until you have seen ——
Hartnackig	23860	Do nothing until you have further instructions
Hartshorn	23861	Can see nothing on account of
Hartura ...	23862	I shall do nothing without
Hasarder ...	23863	I shall do nothing unless (until)
Haselnuss...	23864	Doing nothing
Hasenbalg	23865	Have as yet heard nothing of him (it)
Hasenherz	23866	In case there is nothing suitable
Hasenlager	23867	Nothing more can be done
Haspeln ...	23868	Nothing practically
Hastatus ...	23869	Nothing of consequence worth cabling
Hastio ...	23870	Nothing has yet been done
Hastula ...	23871	Nothing as yet with regard to
Hatajar ...	23872	Nothing yet is known

Hatboxes ...	23873	Nothing to hinder whatever
Hatchments	23874	Nothing doing
Hatchway	23875	Nothing whatever has been done on account of
Hatefully ...	23876	Nothing as yet
Hativeau ...	23877	There is really nothing suitable
Hätscheln...	23878	Nothing extra
Hatters ...	23879	Can get nothing from
Haubert ...	23880	Has (have) heard nothing from
Haubitze ...	23881	**Notice** (*See also* " Give.")
Hauchlaut	23882	Give notice to
Haudegen...	23883	Have given notice to
Haufig ...	23884	Give notice to agent
Haughtily	23885	Give notice to owner
Hauptanker	23886	Give notice upon arrival
Hauptarmee	23887	Give notice when you leave
Hauptbuch	23888	Notice of bill has been given
Haupterbe	23889	Notice of —— has been given
Hauptfeind	23890	Consult ——before giving notice
Hauptfrage	23891	Have consulted —— and given notice
Hauptgleid	23892	What notice is necessary
Haupthaar	23893	Am (are) obliged to give —— days' notice
Hauptlager	23894	Have you received any notice of (from)
Hauptnote	23895	Have received notice that
Hauptpunkt	23896	As we are obliged to give —— days' notice
Hauptstadt	23897	At a moment's notice
Hauptton ...	23898	At —— days' notice
Hauptwerk	23899	Due notice
Haurior ...	23900	Due notice to be given of
Hausarrest	23901	Do not take any notice of
Hausbacken	23902	Has (have) given notice
Hausbrauch	23903	Have given me (us) notice to (that)
Hausflur ...	23904	Has (have) not yet given notice
Hausfreund	23905	Has (have) received due notice
Haushalt ...	23906	Have been served with official notice
Hausherr ...	23907	Give written legal notice
Haushund	23908	Legal notice
Hausirer ...	23909	If you think it worth while to notice
Hausknecht	23910	Owing to notice not being in proper form
Hauslehrer	23911	Really not worth notice
Hausleute...	23912	Shall delay giving notice until
Hauslich ...	23913	With or without notice
Hausrath ...	23914	Without any further notice
Hausteufel	23915	Until further notice
Haustrum	23916	Until you receive further notice
Hausurus...	23917	Unless you receive further notice
Hausvater	23918	Have taken no notice to date
Hauswasche	23919	Of which due notice will be taken
Hauswesen	23920	Take notice
Hauswirth	23921	Before giving —— notice to
Hautain ...	23922	**Noticeable**
Hautboy ...	23923	**Notified**
Hautchen...	23924	Has (have) notified
Hautement	23925	Has (have) not notified
Hautesse ...	23926	**Notify(ies)**
Hauteur ...	23927	To notify
Hautfond ...	23928	Notify to —— that
Hautgout ...	23929	**Notion**
Haversacks	23930	Has (have) no notion of
Hawkeyed	23931	Has (have) a notion to
Hawks ...	23932	**Notorious(ly)**

Hayfields ...	23933	**November**
Hayloft ...	23934	At the beginning of November
Haymaker	23935	About the middle of November
Haymow ...	23936	During the entire month of November
Hayucal ...	23937	For the entire month of November
Hazabra ...	23938	Last November
Hazaleja ...	23939	Next November
Hazaneria	23940	Near the end of November
Hazanoso ...	23941	First day of November
Hazcona ...	23942	Second day of November
Haztealla ...	23943	Third day of November
Headache ...	23944	Fourth day of November
Headdress	23945	Fifth day of November
Headland ...	23946	Sixth day of November
Headstall ...	23947	Seventh day of November
Hearkened	23948	Eighth day of November
Heartburn	23949	Ninth day of November
Heartfelt ...	23950	Tenth day of November
Heartless ...	23951	Eleventh day of November
Heathendom	23952	Twelfth day of November
Heathens ...	23953	Thirteenth day of November
Hebdomada	23954	Fourteenth day of November
Hebebaum	23955	Fifteenth day of November
Hebeisen ...	23956	Sixteenth day of November
Heberger ...	23957	Seventeenth day of November
Hebesco ...	23958	Eighteenth day of November
Hebetar ...	23959	Nineteenth day of November
Hebetatio...	23960	Twentieth day of November
Hebetatrix	23961	Twenty-first day of November
Hebewinde	23962	Twenty-second day of November
Hebilla ...	23963	Twenty-third day of November
Hebraico ...	23964	Twenty-fourth day of November
Hebraisant	23965	Twenty-fifth day of November
Hebraismo	23966	Twenty-sixth day of November
Hebrews ...	23967	Twenty-seventh day of November
Hebroso ...	23968	Twenty-eighth day of November
Hecatomba	23969	Twenty-ninth day of November
Hechizar ...	23970	Thirtieth day of November
Heciento ...	23971	November expenses amount to
Heckzeit ...	23972	November shipments amount to
Hectare ...	23973	**Now**
Hectical ...	23974	Now or never
Hectorco ...	23975	Am (are) now waiting for
Hecyra ...	23976	Am (are) now quite
Hedentina	23977	I think now is a good time to
Hederaceus	23978	I do not think now is a good time to
Hederich ...	23979	It should be done now
Hederiger...	23980	If it is not done now
Hederosus	23981	Is (are) now on the way
Hediondez	23982	If purchased now
Hedrychum	23983	Now ready to start
Hedyosmus	23984	Now is the time for
Hedypnois	23985	Should be purchased now
Hedysmata	23986	—— left on —— and is now at ——
Heedfully...	23987	Do not do it (this) now
Heftigkeit	23988	**Nowhere**
Heftnadel...	23989	**Nugget** (*See also* "Gold.")
Heidekorn	23990	**Null**
Heidekraut	23991	Null and void
Heidenthum	23992	Will become null and void

Heidnisch....	23998	**Nullify**
Heiland ...	23994	**Number(s)** *(See also " Per Cent.")*
Heilbar ...	23995	This number
Heiligthum	23996	Whole number
Heilkraft ...	23997	The number of
Heilkunde	23998	Number and top limit
Heilmittel	23999	This is in addition to number
Heilquelle	24000	The number(s) is (are)
Heimath ...	**24001**	A large number of
Heimfahrt	24002	A small number of
Heimfall ...	24008	Holds a considerable number
Heimgang	24004	Owing to an error in the numbers
Heimgehen	24005	What is the last number of
Heimkehren	24006	What is the number of the last
Heimkunft	24007	What number of
Heimsuchen	24008	Number of certificate
Heinously...	24009	Let me (us) know the number(s) of
Heirathen	24010	What is (are) the consecutive number(s)
Heiress ...	24011	Numbers run consecutively from —— to ——
Heirlooms	24012	What is the consecutive number of last shipment
Heirship ...	24013	The foregoing word is in the singular number
Heiserkeit	24014	The foregoing word is in the plural number
Heladina ...	24015	Is the word —— singular or plural number
Helciarius	24016	The word —— is in the singular number
Helcysma ...	24017	The word —— is in the plural number
Heldenleid	24018	**Numeral(s)**
Heldenmuth	24019	The following word is used as a numeral
Heldenthat	24020	The two following words are used as numerals
Helenismo	24021	The three following words are used as numerals
Helenium ...	24022	The four following words are used as numerals
Helgadura -	24023	The five following words are used as numerals
Heliaco ...	24024	The —— following words are used as numerals
Helianthe ...	24025	The foregoing word is used as a numeral
Heliometro	24026	The two foregoing words are used as numerals
Helldunkel	24027	The three foregoing words are used as numerals
Hellebarde	24028	The four foregoing words are used as numerals
Helleborum	24029	The five foregoing words are used as numerals
Helluatio ...	24030	The —— foregoing words are used as numerals
Helluonem	24031	Is the following word used as a numeral
Helluor ...	24032	The word —— was used as a numeral
Helmbusch	24033	The word —— was not used as a numeral
Helmintico	24084	**Numerical(ly)**
Helmsman	24035	In numerical order
Helots ...	24036	**Numerous**
Helvella ...	24037	Numerous failures
Helvinus ...	24088	Numerous people
Helxine ...	24039	More or less numerous
Hembrica...	24040	How numerous are they
Hembruno	24041	Are not at all numerous
Hemdknopf	24042	Has (have) numerous offers
Hemenciar	24043	Have numerous enquiries
Hemeresios	24044	Numerous complaints
Hemiciclo ..	24045	Owing to numerous complaints
Hemicranea	24046	**O**
Hemina ...	24047	**Oath**
Hemionite	24048	Need not be made on oath
Hemiplegia	24049	Will require to be made on oath
Hemisferio	24050	Refuse(s) to make statement on oath
Hemistiche	24051	Consent(s) to make statement on oath
Hemitonium	24052	**Obedience**

[401]

c o

Hemitrope	24053	In obedience to (with)
Hemlock ...	24054	Has (have) acted in obedience with
Hemmkette	24055	**Obey**
Hemmschuh	24056	To obey
Hemmung	24057	Better obey
Hemorroida	24058	Must obey instructions
Henbane ...	24059	Must obey orders strictly
Henceforth	24060	Must obey orders smartly
Henchidor	24061	**Obeyed**
Henchman	24062	Has (have) obeyed
Hencoop ...	24063	Has (have) not obeyed
Hendedor...	24064	Shall be obeyed
Hendedura	24065	Instructions have been obeyed
Hendiadis...	24066	Orders have been obeyed
Hendiente	24067	Instructions have not been obeyed
Hendrija ...	24068	Orders have not been obeyed
Henogil ...	24069	**Object**
Henpecked	24070	To object
Hepatarius	24071	Object(s) to
Hepatica ...	24072	My (our) object has been (to)
Hepatites ...	24073	In case you do not object
Hepsema ...	24074	Only object I (we) had was
Heptacordo	24075	Ascertain object of
Heptagono	24076	Their only object is at present to
Heptarchy	24077	What reason is there to object
Heptarquia	24078	Reason(s) why object is (are)
Hepteres ...	24079	Do not object
Heptylic ...	24080	Must object
Heracleon...	24081	An additional object is
Heraldica...	24082	Except you object
Heraldo ...	24083	I (we) strongly object to
Herannahen	24084	What is his (their) object
Heraprica...	24085	His (their) object is to
Herbajar ...	24086	What is the object of
Herbalist ...	24087	What is your object
Herbaria ...	24088	You had better object at once
Herbecer ...	24089	**Objected**
Herbeiller...	24090	Objected to
Herberge ...	24091	Absolutely objected to
Herbescens	24092	**Objection(s)**
Herbeux ...	24093	Do you (does ——) know any reason for such an objection
Herbidus ...	24094	I (we) know no reasons for such an objection
Herbiere ...	24095	The only reason for objection is
Herbigkeit	24096	Can you ascertain any reason for objection
Herbivoro...	24097	Will endeavour to ascertain reason for objection
Herbolaria	24098	Have you any objection legal or otherwise
Herboriste	24099	Have no legal objection
Herborizar	24100	Cannot you overcome possible objection(s)
Herbringen	24101	Have overcome all objection(s)
Herbstlich	24102	If there should be no objection
Hercisco ...	24103	No objection if you can do what you say
Herculanus	24104	What is (are) his (your) objection(s)
Herculean...	24105	No objection(s) at all
Heredado ...	24106	Do not raise any objection(s)
Heredera ...	24107	Raise objections at once (to)
Hereditary	24108	As soon as objection(s) is (are) removed
Herejazo ...	24109	Has (have) raised objections (to)
Herencia ...	24110	In consequence of the objection(s) raised
Heretique...	24111	Is likely to succeed with objections
Hergehoren	24112	Is not likely to succeed with objections

Herhalten...	24113	The only possible objection likely to arise is
Herifuga ...	24114	There would be no objection to
Herimiento	24115	No objection to your
Herinaceus	24116	No objection whatever
Herisser	24117	**Obligation(s)**
Heritiere ...	24118	Am under no obligation whatever
Herleiten ...	24119	Avoid any obligation if possible
Hermanable	24120	Cannot undertake the obligation
Hermandad	24121	Cannot undertake further obligation(s)
Hermanuco	24122	The obligation is very slight
Hermedone	24123	Will undertake obligation
Hermelin ...	24124	Will undertake obligation upon following conditions
Hermetical	24125	What are the full obligations
Hermitage	24126	What are my (our) obligations
Hermosear	24127	**Oblige**
Hermosura	24128	Will you oblige me (us) with
Hermupoa	24129	Regret cannot oblige
Hernach ...	24130	Can you oblige —— with
Hernennen	24131	Endeavour to oblige —— (him)
Herniaria...	24132	Does not oblige us to
Hernieder...	24133	Should like to oblige if possible
Herodian ...	24134	Which (this) will oblige us to
Heroico ...	24135	To oblige
Heronniere	24136	This would oblige me (us) to
Herpetico...	24137	By doing this you will greatly oblige
Herradero	24138	**Obliged**
Herreise ...	24139	Am I (are we) obliged
Herrenal ...	24140	You (we) are obliged
Herrenhaus	24141	Shall be obliged
Herrenlos...	24142	To be obliged
Herreron ...	24143	Has (have) been obliged to
Herreruelo	24144	Has (have) obliged —— to
Herretear ...	24145	Have been obliged to take legal proceedings
Herrgott ...	24146	Expect shall be obliged to
Herring ...	24147	Obliged to realize
Herronada	24148	Unless you are absolutely obliged
Herrschaft	24149	Not until absolutely obliged
Herrscher...	24150	**Observation(s)**
Herruhren	24151	From my personal observations
Herstammen	24152	The following observations
Herunter ...	24153	With respect to ——'s observations
Herventar	24154	Will deal with ——'s observations by mail
Hervoroso	24155	**Observe**
Hervorthun	24156	To observe
Herwarts ...	24157	Did you observe
Herzahlen	24158	Did not observe
Herzeleid ...	24159	Observe closely
Herzgrube	24160	Will observe closely and report
Herzinnig...	24161	Should you observe any tendency to
Herzkammer	24162	Should I (we) observe any tendency to
Herzogin ...	24163	**Observed**
Herzogthum	24164	Has (have) been observed
Hesitative	24165	Has (have) not been observed
Hesiter ...	24166	Have observed instructions
Hesperide...	24167	So far as has been observed
Hespero ...	24168	**Obstruct**
Hessian ...	24169	To obstruct
Hesternus	24170	Do not obstruct
Heterarchy	24171	Should —— obstruct
Heterodoxo	24172	Not likely to obstruct

oo2

Hetzhund...	24173	**Obstructed**
Heuboden	24174	Obstructed by
Heuerig ...	24175	Not obstructed
Heugabel...	24176	Should you be obstructed by
Heuhaufen	24177	**Obstruction**
Heulandite	24178	Obstruction removed
Heumonat	24179	Obstruction(s) still continue(s)
Heuretes ...	24180	As soon as the obstruction is removed
Heurter ...	24181	In order to remove the obstruction caused by
Heuschober	24182	A very great obstruction
Heutzutage	24183	In order to prevent similar obstructions
Hexaclinon	24184	**Obtain** (*See also* "Few.")
Hexaedro ...	24185	Can you obtain
Hexagon ...	24186	Can obtain
Hexahedral	24187	Cannot obtain
Hexameter	24188	I (we) can obtain
Hexangular	24189	I (we) cannot obtain
Hexapeda	24190	Obtain if you can
Hexastile ...	24191	Will obtain
Hexyl ...	24192	Endeavour to obtain
Hexylene ...	24193	Will endeavour to obtain
Hiadas ...	24194	Will it be possible to obtain
Hibernian	24195	Expect to obtain
Hibernus ...	24196	Expect to obtain your terms (terms named)
Hibierno ...	24197	Hard to obtain
Hibisco ...	24198	Obtain leave from
Hiccough ...	24199	Obtain estimate(s) of
Hiccups ...	24200	Obtain permission for —— (from)
Hickory ...	24201	Have no hope of being able to obtain
Hidalgarse	24202	Believe I (we) can obtain
Hidalgo ...	24203	How long can you obtain
Hidalguin...	24204	Cannot obtain any longer
Hiddenly ...	24205	What number can you obtain
Hidebound	24206	Cannot obtain any more
Hideous ...	24207	Obtain all you can
Hidragogo	24208	To obtain
Hidrografo	24209	You should obtain
Hidrometra	24210	You must obtain better terms
Hidropesia	24211	You must obtain longer time
Hidropic ...	24212	You must obtain extension of bond
Hiefhorn ...	24213	From whom shall I (we) obtain
Hiematio ...	24214	From which I (we) obtain
Hiematurus	24215	**Obtained**
Hieracites	24216	To be obtained
Hierarch ...	24217	Was (were) obtained
Hierbei ...	24218	Not yet obtained
Hierdurch	24219	Now being obtained
Hierfur ...	24220	Has (have) obtained
Hierherum	24221	Obtained from
Hierhin ...	24222	Should be obtained from
Hiernieden	24223	Should be obtained from it (them)
Hieroglyph	24224	Can it (this) be obtained
Hierograph	24225	What have you obtained from
Hierology...	24226	Can be easily obtained at
Hieronices	24227	Cannot be obtained
Hierophant	24228	Can only be obtained at
Hiersein ...	24229	Can be obtained at the present time for
Hierselbst	24230	Can be obtained at (from)
Hierwider...	24231	Cannot be obtained at (from)
Hiesig ...	24232	Cannot be obtained here

Higgler ...	24233	Might be obtained
Highaltar	24234	Might be obtained if
Highborn ...	24235	Cable if cannot be obtained
Highflyer ...	24236	Cannot be obtained without
Highheels...	24237	Must be obtained at (from)
Highpriest	24238	Have obtained back
Hightides	24239	Have obtained out of
Highwayman	24240	What can —— be obtained for
Higuera ...	24241	Can be obtained for
Higueron ...	24242	**Obtaining**
Hijuelo ...	24243	I believe there is every prospect of obtaining
Hilable ...	24244	Now engaged in obtaining
Hilandera...	24245	I do not believe there is any prospect of obtaining
Hilanza ...	24246	What is the prospect of obtaining
Hilaratus ...	24247	**Obviously**
Hilaresco ...	24248	**Occasion(s)**
Hilarious ...	24249	As occasion offers
Hilariter ...	24250	Is there any occasion for
Hilfreich ...	24251	There is no occasion at all
Hillocks ...	24252	Should there be any occasion
Hillsides ...	24253	The only occasion would be in the event of
Hilvanar ...	24254	On the former occasion
Himbeere ...	24255	On the first possible occasion
Himeneo ...	24256	Should any occasion occur
Himmelbett	24257	What was the occasion of
Himmelblau	24258	**Occasional(ly)**
Himmelweit	24259	Only occasionally
Himnista ...	24260	Only occasionally at first
Himplar ...	24261	**Occasioned**
Hinbegeben	24262	Occasioned by
Hincadura	24263	Not occasioned by
Hincapie ...	24264	**Occupation(s)**
Hinchazon	24265	Can you (——) obtain occupation for
Hindermost	24266	Can obtain occupation
Hinderniss	24267	Want occupation if possible
Hindeuten	24268	Cannot offer any occupation
Hindooism	24269	The only occupation I (we) can offer
Hinfallen ...	24270	What has your (——'s) previous occupation been
Hinfliehen	24271	Occupation since —— has been
Hinfuhren	24272	**Occupied**
Hingebung	24273	What time was occupied in
Hinges ...	24274	The time occupied was
Hiniesta ...	24275	Has (have) been occupied since —— with
Hinkommen	24276	Now occupied with
Hinleben ...	24277	If not otherwise occupied
Hinnehmen	24278	**Occupies**
Hinnible ...	24279	**Occupy**
Hinnibunde	24280	How long will it occupy
Hinniculus	24281	This will occupy at least
Hinnuleus	24282	How long are you likely to occupy yourself at (with)
Hinojal ...	24283	Will occupy me (——) until
Hinraffen...	24284	Will not occupy me (——) after
Hinsein ...	24285	Can you occupy yourself at —— until
Hinsterben	24286	Will occupy
Hinterlist...	24287	Will not occupy
Hintersitz	24288	Should not occupy
Hinterste ...	24289	**Occur** (*See also* "Happen.")
Hinterthur	24290	**Occurred**
Hinuber ...	24291	Ascertain what actually occurred
Hinwieder	24292	Cannot ascertain what actually occurred

Hinzahlen	24293	Will ascertain what actually occurred
Hiperboreo	24294	What actually occurred was
Hiperdulia	24295	Have not heard what actually occurred
Hipiatrica	24296	How was it this occurred
Hipjoints ...	24297	Is said to have occurred through
Hipocampo	24298	Has (have) occurred between
Hipogastro	24299	Ought never to have occurred
Hipoglosa...	24300	Since it occurred
Hipogrifo ...	24301	As soon as possible after it occurred
Hipomancs	24302	Has anything occurred
Hipomoclio	24303	What has occurred meanwhile
Hipoteca ...	24304	Not unless has occurred since
Hipotetico	24305	**Occurrence(s)**
Hippagus...	24306	The occurrence
Hippiatrus	24307	Occurrence is very similar to
Hippodamus	24308	Is it of frequent occurrence
Hippodrome	24309	Is not of frequent occurrence
Hippogryph	24310	Is of frequent occurrence
Hippopera	24311	Very rare occurrence
Hiproof ...	24312	The occurrence is one which
Hirasco ...	24313	Is a very uncommon occurrence
Hircinus ...	24314	Not an uncommon occurrence
Hircipilus...	24315	**Ochre** (*See also* " Mineral.")
Hircosus ...	24316	**O'clock** (*See also* "Hour.")
Hirmar ...	24317	At —— o'clock
Hirnschale	24318	At —— o'clock a.m.
Hirondelle	24319	At —— o'clock p.m.
Hirsebrei ...	24320	**October**
Hirsekorn...	24321	October expenses amount to
Hirsute ...	24322	October shipments amount to
Hirtenamt	24323	At the beginning of October
Hirundio ...	24324	About the middle of October
Hiscens ...	24325	During the entire month of October
Hisopada ...	24326	For the entire month of October
Hisopear ...	24327	Last October
Hispanico ..	24328	Next October
Hispidosus	24329	Near the end of October
Hispidus ...	24330	First day of October
Hissing ...	24331	Second day of October
Histoire ...	24332	Third day of October
Historicus	24333	Fourth day of October
Historieta...	24334	Fifth day of October
Historisch	24335	Sixth day of October
Histrionic...	24336	← Seventh day of October
Hitzkopf ...	24337	Eighth day of October
Hiulco	24338	Ninth day of October
Hoarfrost...	24339	Tenth day of October
Hobachon...	24340	Eleventh day of October
Hobbling ...	24341	Twelfth day of October
Hobebank	24342	Thirteenth day of October
Hobechos ...	24343	Fourteenth day of October
Hobeleisen	24344	Fifteenth day of October
Hobeln ...	24345	Sixteenth day of October
Hobereau ...	24346	Seventeenth day of October
Hobgoblin	24347	Eighteenth day of October
Hoblonera	24348	Nineteenth day of October
Hobnailed	24349	Twentieth day of October
Hochement	24350	Twenty-first day of October
Hochepot ...	24351	Twenty-second day of October
Hochequeue	24352	Twenty-third day of October

Hochgenuss	24353	Twenty-fourth day of October
Hochheilig	24354	Twenty-fifth day of October
Hochland...	24355	Twenty-sixth day of October
Hochlied ...	24356	Twenty-seventh day of October
Hochnasig	24357	Twenty-eighth day of October
Hochschule	24358	Twenty-ninth day of October
Hochstens	24359	Thirtieth day of October
Hochwurdig	24360	Thirty-first day of October
Hochzeit ...	24361	**Odd**
Hocicada ...	24362	Odd numbers only
Hociquillo	24363	Odd and even numbers
Hockerig ...	24364	**Of**
Hocket ...	24365	Of the
Hodgepodge	24366	Of them
Hodiernal...	24367	Of what
Hofbeamte	24368	Of which
Hofdame ...	24369	Of it
Hofdienst...	24370	Of course
Hoffart ...	24371	Of no use
Hoffnung...	24372	Of each
Hofgesinde	24373	**Off**
Hoflich ...	24374	Off for
Hofmeister	24375	How are you off for
Hofnarr ...	24376	I am (we are) badly off for
Hofpartei...	24377	As soon as it clears off
Hofrath ...	24378	It has now left off
Hofschranz	24379	Too far off
Hofstaat ...	24380	Off immediately
Hogano ...	24381	Send off
Hogshead...	24382	Sent off
Hohlweg ...	24383	On and off
Hohnisch ...	24384	**Offence(s)**
Hohnlachen	24385	**Offend**
Hojalatero	24386	To offend
Hojaldre ...	24387	Take care not to offend
Hojaranzo	24388	Will offend
Hojarasca...	24389	**Offensive(ly)**
Hokerin ...	24390	**Offer(s)** (*See also* "Firm," "Open.")
Holanda ...	24391	Shall I (we) accept offer
Holandilla	24392	I (we) think you (——) will do well to accept offer
Holdfasts ...	24393	Close with present offer
Holgorio ...	24394	Should advise you to reject offer
Holgueta ...	24395	Respectfully decline(s) offer
Holladura...	24396	What do you authorize me to offer
Hollander...	24397	Authorize you to offer
Hollenbrut	24398	How long will offer remain open
Hollempein	24399	Offer cannot remain open longer than
Hollybush	24400	What inducement does —— (do they) offer
Holoberus	24401	Offer(s) as a further inducement
Holobryzus	24402	Am I (are we) to withdraw offer
Holocaust...	24403	Am (are) likely to withdraw offer
Holograph	24404	Do not withdraw offer
Holosteon ..	24405	Withdraw offer
Holothuria	24406	You had better withdraw offer
Holperig ...	24407	Do not accept the offer [premium
Holzapfel ..	24408	Would it assist matters if you were to offer the men a
Holzartig ...	24409	Cable if anything suitable offers
Holzern ...	24410	Offer at the same rate for the remaining
Holzessig ...	24411	Am (are) willing to offer
Holzhandel	24412	Am (are) not at all likely to renew offer

Holzkohle...	24413	Are we to understand that the offer is
Holzscheit	24414	A bonâ fide offer
Holzschlag	24415	Best terms can offer
Holzstoss ...	24416	Can you offer any suggestion
Holzwurm	24417	Cannot make better offer
Homage ...	24418	Cannot obtain better offer
Homarrache	24419	Cannot obtain any offer beyond
Hombracho	24420	If you cannot obtain better offer
Hombrada	24421	Can you obtain a firm offer and for how long
Hombrear...	24422	Close with the first good offer
Homebred	24423	Cable terms of offer
Homecillo...	24424	Confirm offer
Homefelt ...	24425	Do you accept offer
Homeless ...	24426	Has (have) made the following offer
Homenage	24427	Has (have) made an offer to
Homeopath	24428	Otherwise must withdraw offer
Homespun	24429	Has (have) withdrawn offer
Homicide ...	24430	Has (have) made no offer to date
Homilia ...	24431	Has (have) refused offer to
Homiliador	24432	I (we) do not think you will improve on offer
Homiliario	24433	I (we) do not consider offer at all reasonable
Homilist ...	24434	I (we) consider offer very reasonable
Homonimia	24435	Is it a firm offer
Homophagia	24436	Make firm offer of
Homousins	24437	Is the best offer I (we) can obtain
Homullus...	24438	Is (are) —— likely to make an offer
Homunculus	24439	If the offer is firm
Hondamente	24440	If you have anything suitable to offer
Hondilla ...	24441	Not likely to offer
Hondonada	24442	Offer accepted
Honestar ...	24443	Offer declined
Honestatio	24444	Offer still open
Honeybag...	24445	Offer subject to
Honeycomb	24446	Offer to stand good until
Honeymoon	24447	Offer received; but too late
Hongoso ...	24448	Offer received; but too low
Hongrer ...	24449	Offer received; will do what I (we) can
Honigbiene	24450	Offer(s) to arbitrate
Honorandus	24451	Open to offers
Honorario...	24452	Reject(s) all offers
Honoratus	24453	Should he (they) offer
Honoripeta	24454	The following offers
Honoured...	24455	The best offer
Honrado ...	24456	The lowest offer
Hontanal ...	24457	This offer is subject to acceptance within
Honteux ...	24458	This offer will remain open until
Hoodwink	24459	Keep offer open
Hooping ...	24460	To offer
Hopalanda	24461	The offer(s) include(s)
Hoplites ...	24462	Would suggest that you make an offer to
Hoppers ...	24463	With firm offer feel sure
Hoquedad	24464	With firm offer am confident of success
Hoquet ...	24465	Will probably renew offer
Horadacion	24466	Will renew offer on condition that
Horadar ...	24467	Have advised —— of the offer
Horambre...	24468	Am (are) obliged for offer but do not see how you can assist at [present
Horarium ...	24469	Make this offer by cable
Horcajadas	24470	Make the following offer by cable
Horchilla ...	24471	Offer declined for the present
Horcon ...	24472	**Offered**

Hordeaceus	24473	Were offered
Hordeia ...	24474	Will be offered
Hordeolus	24475	Was offered for
Hordicalia	24476	As nothing better offered
Horehound	24477	I (we) have offered to go as high as
Horensagen	24478	I (we) have offered
Horfandad	24479	I am (we are) offered
Horiola ...	24480	If anything is offered you
Horizonte...	24481	Never offered
Horloger ...	24482	Offered to
Hormigoso	24483	Only offered to
Hormiguear	24484	I (we) have offered the men a premium
Horminium	24485	Nothing suitable has offered
Horminodes	24486	**Offering**
Hornabeque	24487	Has (have) been offering
Hornacero	24488	Is (are) at present offering
Horned ...	24489	Now offering
Hornisse ...	24490	Nothing suitable offering
Hornless ...	24491	**Office(s)**
Hornotinus	24492	For office use
Hornpipe ...	24493	At the office in
Hornvieh ...	24494	At ——'s office
Horologe ...	24495	To (at) the company's registered office
Horologium	24496	At the office on the property
Horometry	24497	At the office of
Horoscopus	24498	**Officer**
Horquilla...	24499	Formerly an officer of the —— company
Horrendo ...	24500	Officer of the company
Horrescens	24501	**Official(s)**
Horribilis	24502	Official enquiry
Horricomus	24503	This is not official
Horriditas	24504	No official statement has been made as yet
Horrific ...	24505	Official notice of
Horripilo ...	24506	Official quotations
Horrohren	24507	**Officially**
Horrura ...	24508	To officially represent
Horsehair...	24509	Who will officially represent
Horseleech	24510	Officially represented by
Horseshoe	24511	Officially announced
Horsewhip	24512	The shares are quoted officially
Hortal ...	24513	The shares are not quoted officially
Hortamen...	24514	Acting officially
Hortandus	24515	Not acting officially
Hortation	24516	Do not act officially
Hortativus	24517	Must be done officially
Hortatrix ...	24518	Not in any way officially
Hortensius	24519	Was not done officially
Hortera ...	24520	**Officious(ly)**
Hortulan ...	24521	**Offset**
Hosenband	24522	As an offset against
Hosenlatz...	24523	Offset basis
Hospedable	24524	Might be regarded as an offset
Hospederia	24525	**Often**
Hospice ...	24526	How often
Hospiciano	24527	As often as you (——) can
Hospitalis	24528	How often has (have)
Hospituim	24529	Not very often
Hostelage	24530	Not so often
Hostelero ...	24531	The more often the better
Hostelry ...	24532	More often than not

Hostess ...	24533	**Oil**
Hostiario ...	24584	Oil well(s)
Hostiatus...	24585	**Old**
Hosticolum	24536	Old board
Hostifer ...	24537	Old building(s)
Hostigador	24538	Old company
Hostiola ...	24539	Old director(s)
Hostorium	24540	Old dressing floor(s)
Hotbed ...	24541	Old dump(s)
Hotelier ...	24542	Old level(s)
Hotellerie...	24543	Old machinery
Hothouse ...	24544	Old manager
Hotpressed	24545	Old management
Hotspur ...	24546	Old men
Houblon ...	24547	Old mill
Houdah ...	24548	Old pump(s)
Houlette ...	24549	Old shaft(s)
Hounding	24550	Old stope(s)
Hourglass	24551	Old winze(s)
Hourhand	24552	Old working(s)
Hourque ...	24553	New and old
Housedogs	24554	Owner(s) very old
Houseless	24555	Too old to be of use
Housemaid	24556	Very old
Houspiller	24557	Very old and worn out
Houssage...	24558	In the old times
Houssiner...	24559	**Ominous(ly)**
Houssoir ...	24560	**Omission(s)**
Howitzer ...	24561	Any omission will be fatal
Hoyuelo ...	24562	Apologize for omission
Hozadero ...	24563	Owing to omission of
Hozar ...	24564	The omission was due to
Hubbub ...	24565	The omission is not very serious
Huchear ...	24566	The omission has been most serious
Huchoho ...	24567	To prevent similar omission
Huckeback	24568	**Omit**
Huckstered	24569	Better omit
Hucusque...	24570	Caused me (us) to omit
Huelfago ...	24571	Do not omit (to)
Huesarron	24572	I (we) did not omit
Huesoso ...	24573	Shall I (we) omit
Huesped ...	24574	To omit
Huette ...	24575	Take care not to omit
Huevero ...	24576	Was (were) obliged to omit
Hufeisen ...	24577	Will not omit to
Huffish ...	24578	Omit from the word —— to the word ——
Hufschlag	24579	Omit clause —— on page ——
Huftbein ...	24580	**Omitted**
Huftweh ...	24581	Was (were) omitted
Hugelig ...	24582	Why have you (has ——) omitted
Hugonots...	24583	Unintentionally omitted
Huhnchen	24584	Intentionally omitted
Huhnerauge	24585	Omitted in error
Huhnerkorb	24586	Omitted on account of
Huilerie ...	24587	Has (have) been omitted
Huissier ...	24588	Has (have) not been omitted
Huitain ...	24589	Has omitted the most important clause(s)
Huitieme ...	24590	I (we) have omitted
Hujusce ...	24591	It (they) should not be omitted
Huldigung	24592	If possible get it (them) omitted

Humanar ...	24593	Nothing of importance has been omitted
Humanista	24594	Which were omitted from
Humanitas	24595	You have omitted to keep me (us)
Humarazo	24596	**On**
Humatio ...	24597	Payment on account
Humaturus	24598	On the
Humazga ...	24599	On the whole
Humbling	24600	On hand
Humdrum	24601	On my
Humeante	24602	On my behalf
Humectar...	24603	On your behalf
Humectatus	24604	On or about
Humedal ...	24605	On and after
Humesco ...	24606	On or before
Humidity ...	24607	**Once**
Humidulus	24608	At once
Humificus	24609	Only once
Humigatio	24610	Once or twice
Humildad...	24611	Once at least
Humilier ...	24612	Once at most
Humilitas...	24613	Not even once
Humilitudo	24614	**One** (*See also* " Number " and Table at end.)
Humillador	24615	One day
Humillo ...	24616	One week
Humipeta...	24617	One month
Humorada	24618	One half
Humorists	24619	Only one
Humorose	24620	One —— in cash, balance in shares
Humuscula	24621	**Onerous**
Hundeloch	24622	**Only**
Hundestall	24623	At present I (we) have only
Hundisch ...	24624	Can only be done by
Hundsfott	24625	How is it that only
Hundstage	24626	I (we) could only
Hungerig ...	24627	I (we) can only
Hungerted	24628	I (we) shall only
Huntsman	24629	I (we) only intend for the present to
Huraneria	24630	Is the only
Hurano ...	24631	Seems the only thing possible
Hurcion ...	24632	There has been only
Hurenpach	24633	There is (are) only
Hurgonada	24634	Will only remain
Hurgonear	24635	Only for a distance of
Hurkind ...	24636	Only now received
Hurlement	24637	Only in case
Huronera ...	24638	Only now and again
Hurpices ...	24639	**Onus**
Hurricanes	24640	**Onyx** (*See also* " Mineral.")
Hurtagus ...	24641	**Opal** (*See also* " Mineral.")
Hurtaropa	24642	Glassy opal
Hurtigkeit	24643	Fine opal
Husbanding	24644	Noble opal
Husbands...	24645	**Opaque**
Husillero ...	24646	**Open** (*See also* " Offer.")
Huskiness	24647	Am I (are we) open to accept
Husmeador	24648	I am (we are) not open
Husmear ...	24649	Can you keep offer open
Hustings ...	24650	Cannot keep offer open after
Hutburste	24651	Will keep offer open until
Hutform ...	24652	To open

Hutkrampe	24653	Try and keep it open
Hutmacher	24654	**Open cut(s)**
Hyacinth ...	24655	An enormous open cut
Hyades ...	24656	As shown by an open cut
Hyalotheca	24657	By means of an open cut
Hybernatio	24658	Consist(s) only of open cuts
Hybernus...	24659	Owing to the dangerous nature of the open cuts
Hybridous	24660	The open cut is —— feet long and —— feet deep
Hydarides .	24661	The open cut has now fallen together
Hydraulic...	24662	**Opening(s)**
Hydrbromic	24663	As soon as I (we) get an opening
Hydrocele	24664	Have had no opening up to the present time
Hydrogarum	24665	Have no opening at present
Hydrogen...	24666	**Openly**
Hydromel...	24667	Quite openly
Hydropath	24668	But not openly
Hydrophobe	24669	Is it openly stated
Hydropical	24670	It is openly stated that
Hydropisus	24671	It has not hitherto been openly stated
Hydroxyl ...	24672	**Open up**
Hyemalia ...	24673	To open up
Hyematus	24674	So as to open up
Hygian ...	24675	As soon as it (this) is opened up
Hylactor ...	24676	Has opened up
Hymnifer...	24677	By opening up
Hymnodia	24678	Has not been opened up at all
Hymnology	24679	Has opened up well
Hymntune	24680	Is opening up splendidly
Hyosiris ...	24681	Is not opening up at all well
Hypallage	24682	Is opening up badly
Hypenemium	24683	Promise(s) to open up well
Hyperbaton	24684	Should open up
Hyperbole	24685	Will enable us to open up
Hypericon	24686	Lode is opening up well
Hypermeter	24687	Shall proceed to open up
Hyperocha	24688	**Operate(d)**
Hypnotists	24689	To operate
Hypobolum	24690	**Operation(s)** (*See also* "Continuance.")
Hypochysis	24691	When will you commence operations
Hypocondre	24692	Shall commence operations at —— on ——
Hypocrite...	24693	As soon as operations
Hypodytes	24694	As soon as I (we) commence operations
Hypogesum	24695	Commence operations at ——
Hypomnema	24696	Continue operations at —— (until)
Hyporchema	24697	In full operation
Hypostatic	24698	Not in operation
Hypotenufa	24699	Not now in operation
Hypothesis	24700	Has (have) not yet been put into operation
Hysginum	24701	Were put into operation on
Hyssopites	24702	Operations at —— very successful
Hysterics ...	24703	Operations at —— fairly successful
Hystrix ...	24704	Operations at —— not at all successful
Iambic ...	24705	Stop all operations pending
Ianthina ...	24706	What operations do you allude to
Iaspideus ...	24707	Expect to commence operations within next few days
Iasponyx ..	24708	Expect to commence operations at this point (at ——) on ——
Iatronice ...	24709	Operations have proved entirely successful
Iberica ...	24710	Have temporarily suspended operations at this point
Iccirco ...	24711	Want of money stops further operations
Iceblink ...	24712	Necessary that —— should undergo an operation

Iceboat	...	24713
Icebound	...	24714
Icebuilt	...	24715
Icecream	...	24716
Icefield	...	24717
Icehouse	...	24718
Icelander	...	24719
Iceplant	...	24720
Ichneumon		24721
Ichnobates		24722
Icicle	...	24723
Iciness	...	24724
Icnografia	...	24725
Iconicus	...	24726
Iconoclast	...	24727
Iconolater	...	24728
Iconology	...	24729
Icosahedra		24730
Icuncula	...	24731
Idatide	...	24732
Idealists	...	24733
Idealmente		24734
Identify	...	24735
Identique	...	24736
Ideology	...	24737
Idiocrasia	...	24738
Idiomatic	...	24739
Idioms	...	24740
Idiopathy	...	24741
Idiotismus		24742
Idleness	...	24743
Idolator	...	24744
Idolatrer	...	24745
Idolatrico	...	24746
Idolatrous		24747
Idoletto	...	24748
Idolismo	...	24749
Idolize	...	24750
Idoneidad	...	24751
Idulis	...	24752
Idyllium	...	24753
Igitur	...	24754
Iglesia	...	24755
Igmare	...	24756
Ignatone	...	24757
Ignavesco	...	24758
Ignavia	...	24759
Ignavitas	...	24760
Igneous	...	24761
Ignescent	...	24762
Ignescitur		24763
Igniarium		24764
Ignibulum		24765
Ignicion	...	24766
Ignicola	...	24767
Ignicomus		24768
Igniferous		24769
Ignigena	...	24770
Ignipotent		24771
Ignited	...	24772

Operator(s)
Only a small operator
Large operators
A —— operator

Opinion (*See also* " Decisive," " General," " Legal.")
I am (we are) of opinion that
What is your opinion (of)
Is —— still of opinion that
—— is still of opinion that
Am still of the opinion that you should   [dated ——
Do you still hold the same opinion as that expressed in letter
I do not now hold the same opinion
If you are still of the same opinion
Are you still of the same opinion
I am (we are) still of the same opinion
In case you still hold the same opinion
My (our) opinion is
What is ——'s opinion
——'s opinion is
Cannot form any opinion (until)
Can you form any opinion
Cannot form any opinion whatever
Have not yet formed any opinion
When do you expect to cable opinion
What is the general opinion
The general opinion is
Obtain legal opinion
Legal opinion is
Obtain competent opinion as to
Will obtain ——'s opinion
Is (are) of opinion that
Can you give any opinion as to
What is your opinion independently of
Must have an independent opinion
Entirely of your opinion
What is the medical opinion
Medical opinion is
My opinion of the value of
Let me (us) have your opinion frankly
Owing to a difference of opinion
Cannot give an opinion of —— at the present time
I have a very good opinion of
Telegraph your opinion respecting
My opinion is on the whole favourable
My opinion is altogether unfavourable
Have the very highest opinion of
Has (have) a most unfavourable opinion of
Has (have) an unfavourable opinion of
I (we) have formed a very unfavourable opinion of the property
I (we) have formed a very unfavourable opinion of
——, who is a competent engineer, has given as his opinion that
What is your opinion of the intrinsic value of
Can you get reliable opinion of
I (we) wish to have a decided opinion as to the present and
        [prospective value of the property
Opinion expressed by —— is incorrect. The truth is

Opponent(s) (*See also* " Every," " Fraction.")
Should opponent(s)
Who is (are) my (our) opponent(s)
Must consider —— as my (our) opponents

[413]

Ignitegium	24773	All opponents can be dealt with by
Ignivomo ...	24774	Opponents are not very formidable
Ignobilta ...	24775	Opponents are most formidable
Ignobling...	24776	Opponents may be disregarded
Ignominia	24777	Opponents doing well
Ignoramus	24778	Opponents not doing very well
Ignorancia	24779	Opponents hostile ready to purchase
Ignoranton	24780	Opponents friendly ready to purchase
Ignorings...	24781	**Opportune(ly)**
Ignoriren ...	24782	Not opportune
Ignoscens...	24783	Most opportunely
Ignoscor ...	24784	**Opportunity** (*See also* " Favourable.")
Ignoto ...	24785	Do not let the opportunity slip
Ignoturus...	24786	Do not want to let opportunity slip
Ignudato ...	24787	What opportunity is there for
Igualador...	24788	There will be a good opportunity
Igualdad ...	24789	The only opportunity would be
Igualmente	24790	By the first opportunity
Iguana ...	24791	Has (have) missed a good opportunity
Iguarias ...	24792	No opportunity is likely to occur
Ibrige ...	24793	No opportunity has occurred
Ijadear ...	24794	Seize the first opportunity to
Ilapso ...	24795	The opportunity is a very valuable one
Ilarchus ...	24796	Which is a splendid opportunity to
Ilecebra ...	24797	Am (are) waiting an opportunity.
Ilibato ...	24798	**Oppose(s)**
Ilicetum ...	24799	Oppose the (it)
Iliceus ...	24800	Oppose it (him) (them) tooth and nail
Ilimitable...	24801	Oppose at all costs
Iliosus ...	24802	Shall I (we) oppose
Iliquido ...	24803	Do not oppose
Illabens ...	24804	Oppose by every means in your power
Illaboro ...	24805	Can only oppose indirectly
Illacciare ...	24806	Do not let him (them) know I (we) intend to oppose
Illaidire ...	24807	Delay combination to oppose
Illaqueare...	24808	Oppose(s) me (us) all he (they) can
Illatebro ...	24809	To oppose
Illative ...	24810	Will no doubt oppose
Illatratio ...	24811	Will do all I (we) can to oppose
Illaturus ...	24812	**Opposed**
Illaudatus	24813	Am (are) opposed to
Illazione ...	24814	Altogether opposed to
Illbred ...	24815	Is (are) opposed to
Illegible ...	24816	Is (are) not opposed at all to
Illegitime...	24817	Unless you are opposed to
Illepidus ...	24818	Unless you are opposed by —— (him)
Illicitly ...	24819	**Opposite**
Illigator ...	24820	Opposite to
Illimitato ...	24821	**Opposition**
Illimite ...	24822	Expect(s) no opposition
Illinctus ...	24823	Expect(s) opposition from
Illinendus	24824	Meet(s) with great opposition
Illiquefio ...	24825	Meet(s) with no opposition
Illisible ...	24826	There is no opposition at present
Illiterate ...	24827	Cable if you meet with any opposition
Illjudge ...	24828	Am (are) meeting with much opposition
Illnature ...	24829	Have you encountered any opposition from
Illogical ...	24830	Have not met with any serious opposition
Illorsum ...	24831	Should you meet with opposition
Illstarred ...	24832	No opposition likely

Illucesco ...	24833	Opposition still continues
Illuctans ...	24834	Opposition entirely at an end
Illuded ...	24835	**Oppress(ed)**
Illuiare ...	24836	**Oppression**
Illuminer ...	24837	**Oppressive(ly)**
Illusoire ...	24838	**Option**
Illustrarē ...	24839	The option to
Illustrius ...	24840	The option of (for)
Illuvies ...	24841	At my (our) option
Illuviosus ...	24842	At his (their) option
Illwishes ...	24843	At your option
Ilotisme ...	24844	Give option on
Iltiss ...	24845	Give option to
Iluminado	24846	Option(s) expire(s) on
Ilusorio ...	24847	Option expired on
Imadas ...	24848	What is the option worth
Imagery ...	24849	Option may be taken to be worth
Imaginaire	24850	Give for the option
Imaginatif	24851	Renew option
Imaginoso	24852	Option for forty-eight hours
Imaguncula	24853	Option for three days
Imbagnato	24854	Option for —— days
Imbaldire...	24855	Secure option on
Imbandito	24856	Secure option for —— days
Imbardarsi	24857	Can you get an option on
Imbasceria	24858	Can secure option for —— month(s)
Imbeato ...	24859	Has (have) —— month(s) option
Imbeccare...	24860	Have I your authority to secure option on following terms
Imbecile ...	24861	Can you get option extended for
Imbecility	24862	Extension of option
Imbecillis...	24863	I (we) will extend option
Imberbis ...	24864	I (we) will extend option for —— days (if)
Imberuto ...	24865	Get option extended for —— days (if)
Imbiadato	24866	Has (have) no option but to
Imbiber ...	24867	Has (have) no option whatever
Imbiettare	24868	To have the option of
Imbiondire	24869	I (we) should have option to
Imbitumato	24870	With the option to
Imbociato...	24871	Without option unless
Imbolatore	24872	Without any option
Imborrable	24873	Without the option of
Imboschire	24874	Has the option been exercised
Imbosom ...	24875	Had not I (we) better exercise option to
Imbracteor	24876	If the option is not exercised
Imbràttato	24877	Under the terms of my (our) option
Imbrentina	24878	Under an option
Imbreviato	24879	Might be able to get an option
Imbriacone	24880	Am (are) offered an option for
Imbricado	24881	Can you secure an option for
Imbricatim	24882	Within limits of option
Imbricitor	24883	Advise you to secure working option on property
Imbrifer ...	24884	At the option of the lessee(s)
Imbrique ...	24885	**Optional**
Imbroccata	24886	Quite optional
Imbroglio...	24887	If optional
Imbrunito	24888	Not optional
Imbuendus	24889	**Or**
Imbuir ...	24890	Or not
Imbuonire	24891	Whether or not
Imbursar ...	24892	Either one or the other

Imitador ...	24893	Or would you (——) prefer to
Imitamen ...	24894	Or would you advise me (us) to
Imitando ...	24895	Or shall I (we)
Imitateur ...	24896	Either —— or ——
Imitating ...	24897	**Order(s)** (*See also* "Court," "Fill.")
Imitative ...	24898	To the order of
Imitatrice	24899	To the joint order of
Imitaturus	24900	To order
Immacolare	24901	To my (our) order
Immacule...	24902	To your order
Immagrire	24903	You had better order what you want at
Immanente	24904	In good order
Immanitas	24905	In bad order
Immarcesco	24906	Is order to buy in force
Immaturo...	24907	Is order to sell in force
Immeans ...	24908	Order to buy still in force
Immeditato	24909	Order to buy withdrawn
Immensitas	24910	Order to sell still in force
Immensus	24911	Order to sell withdrawn
Immerdar...	24912	Order to remain in force until
Immerens...	24913	Previous order(s)
Immerenter	24914	Previous order cancelled
Immerfort	24915	All previous orders cancelled
Immergeor	24916	Decline(s) the order
Immergrim	24917	Await orders (from)
Immerhin...	24918	Is the whole order to be executed or only a part
Immersatio	24919	Do you give positive orders that I am (we are) to
Immeuble...	24920	I (we) give you positive orders to
Immezzare	24921	Have you any further orders
Immigrator	24922	Have no further orders
Imminutio	24923	Before the order(s) was (were) received
Immirrato	24924	Do not order
Immiscer ...	24925	Do you confirm ——'s order
Immissum	24926	Has (have) given orders
Immittor ...	24927	Keep strictly to ——'s orders
Immobilier	24928	Out of order
Immoderate	24929	Order as quickly as possible
Immodeste	24930	Do not order it (them) at present
Immolandus	24931	Should be put in good order throughout (*See also* " Over-
Immolate ...	24932	Must be put in good order throughout ʃhaul," &c)
Immolatrix	24933	Has (have) been put in order throughout
Immondezza	24934	Is (are) in good order throughout
Immondices	24935	As soon as all is in order
Immoriger	24936	All is now in order
Immorsus...	24937	Presume that everything is in order
Immortalis	24938	The works are getting into better order gradually
Immortel ...	24939	The works are now in good order
Immortire	24940	Have deposited —— subject to your (their) order
Immoulded	24941	The standing orders
Immulgens	24942	Standing orders cancelled
Immunity...	24943	Give strict orders that
Immurmuro	24944	Have given strict orders that
Immussulus	24945	Wait for orders
Immutato...	24946	Am (are) waiting for orders
Immutesco	24947	Can you obtain an order for me (us) to
Impacable	24948	**Ordered**
Impacatus	24949	I (we) ordered
Impadulare	24950	I (we) have already ordered in my (our) own name
Impagliato	24951	Not ordered
Impaired ...	24952	If not ordered

Impallesco	24953	Unless it is (they are) already ordered
Impallidus	24954	**Orderly**
Impalmato	24955	**Ordinary(ily)**
Impalpable	24956	In the ordinary way
Impannata	24957	Take all ordinary precautions
Imparante	24958	All ordinary precautions were taken to
Imparentia	24959	Everything now proceeding as ordinarily
Imparfait ...	24960	**Ore(s)** (*See also* "Assorted," "Average," "Base," "Broken," "Bunch," "Depth," "Develop," "Estimate," "Grade,"
Imparolato	24961	Some good stones of ore ["Improvement," "Large," &c.)
Impassion	24962	Follow the ore
Impastato...	24963	Report on the ore at
Impastus ...	24964	The ore is
Impatience	24965	The ore is altering
Impatriare	24966	The ore is coming in
Impawn ...	24967	The ore is narrowing
Impeach ...	24968	The ore has practically pinched out
Impearl ...	24969	The ore is continuous for a length of
Impeciato...	24970	The ore still continues at
Impedandus	24971	The ore is enough to
Impedatio	24972	Is there not enough ore to pay for its removal
Impeded ,..	24973	There is enough ore
Impedicare	24974	There is not enough ore
Impedido ...	24975	The ore is improving as developed
Impediente	24976	The ore is improving in the drift as we advance
Impeditivo	24977	The ore is improving in the breast at No. —— level
Impegnato	24978	The ore is increasing
Impegolare	24979	The ore pitches to the east
Impelagato	24980	The ore pitches to the west
Impeler ...	24981	The ore pitches to the north
Impellent ...	24982	The ore pitches to the south
Impendium	24983	Refractory ore
Impendulus	24984	The ore is rich, but refractory
Impennarsi	24985	On account of the refractory nature of the ore
Impennatus	24986	Is the ore refractory
Impennis ...	24987	The ore is running poor
Impensado	24988	The ore is somewhat broken and disordered
Imperadore	24989	The ore is similar
Imperativo	24990	Is the ore similar
Imperatum	24991	The ore is not similar
Imperdible	24992	The ore is —— thick
Imperditus	24993	The ore is again widening out
Imperfecto	24994	The ore is difficult to break
Imperialis	24995	The ore is easy to break
Imperiante	24996	The ore in the breast of the level is
Impericia ...	24997	The ore in the breast of the level is very much scattered
Imperitans	24998	The ore is pinching in the breast (is now —— inches thick)
Imperito ...	24999	The ore is widening out in the breast (is now —— inches thick)
Impermisto	25000	The ore in the drift
Impersonal	**25001**	The ore in the drift has improved; it is now
Impertiens	25002	The ore in the drift has improved from
Impetigine	25003	The ore in the drift will average
Impetrable	25004	The ore in the stope is widening out (is now —— inches thick)
Impetrante	25005	The ore in the stope is narrowing (is now —— inches thick)
Impetratio	25006	The ore is narrowing under foot (is now —— inches thick)
Impetritus	25007	The ore is widening out under foot (is now —— inches thick)
Impetrix ...	25008	The ore in the winze
Impetuoso	25009	The ore in the winze has been cut off (by)
Impetus ...	25010	The ore in the winze is improving as we go down
Impeverato	25011	The ore in bottom of winze is not so good as in level above

Impiagato	25012	The ore from
Impiantare	25013	Where is the (this) ore from
Impiatoso...	25014	The (this) ore is from
Impicatus...	25015	The ore from the upper workings
Impiccatto	25016	The ore from the lower workings
Impietrato	25017	The ore above the water level
Impiety ...	25018	The ore below the water level
Impigero ...	25019	The ore yields
Impigrire .	25020	The ore yields a profit of —— per ton
Impinguare	25021	The yield of the ore
Impiombato	25022	Probably the ore will yield
Impious ...	25023	Ore bearing ground
Implacatus	25024	Ore bed
Implanter...	25025	Carbonate ore
Implement	25026	Ore chamber
Impleor ...	25027	Hæmatite ore
Impletion...	25028	No ore whatever
Impleturus	25029	There is no ore that will pay to remove
Implicado...	25030	There is no ore above
Impliquer...	25031	There is no ore below
Imploratio	25032	The only way in which the ore can be profitably worked is to
Implume ...	25033	Ore is very poor

Ore, assay of

Implutus ...	25034	
Impluvia ...	25035	The ore has assayed —— per ton
Impoetarsi	25036	What is the average assay value of the ore
Impoison ...	25037	The assay value of the ore is
Impolite ...	25038	Now in ore, assays average per ton
Impolitus ...	25039	Cable assay of ore as soon as possible
Imponedor	25040	Have struck ore at —— which assays ——

Ore body(ies)

Imponendus	25041	
Imponitore	25042	Large ore body
Impopular	25043	Fine body of ore
Imporcatio	25044	Splendid body of ore
Imporous ...	25045	High grade ore body
Importado	25046	Low grade ore body
Imposable	25047	Near ore body
Imposicion	25048	New ore body
Imposing ...	25049	Develop new ore body
Imposthume	25050	Should develop new ore body(ies)
Impotente	25051	This will open up a fine body of ore
Impounded	25052	Has (have) opened up a large body of high grade ore
Impoverito	25053	Has (have) opened up a fine body of ore
Impransus	25054	Has (have) opened up a large body of low grade ore
Imprecate...	25055	Has (have) struck a rich ore body
Impregnado	25056	Has (have) struck a rich ore body in the —— level
Imprenta ...	25057	Have discovered a good body of ore at
Impressive	25058	Has every appearance of becoming a good body of ore
Imprevisto	25059	Is not much of an ore body
Imprigitas	25060	Appearances in favour of our striking ore body
Imprimente	25061	We expect to strike ore body within the next —— feet
Imprimerie	25062	What are the dimensions of ore body
Imprimis ...	25063	The dimensions of the ore body are —— feet long, —— feet [wide, proved for a depth of —— feet
Imprinted	25064	The ore body is becoming more horizontal
Imprinting	25065	The ore body is becoming more vertical
Imprison ...	25066	The ore body continues to increase in size
Improbador	25067	The ore body continues to improve in quality
Improbatis	25068	The ore body is diminishing in value
Improbity	25069	The ore body is diminishing in size
Improbo ...	25070	What length have you driven on the ore body at

Improbulus	25071	I (we) can confirm the statement made, *i.e.*, as depth is [obtained the ore bodies are more solid and continuous
Impromessa	25072	**Ore broken**
Improntato	25073	Ore broken not shipped
Impropieta	25074	Ore broken not treated
Improprio...	25075	Ore broken and raised from —— level since
Improuver	25076	**Ore, bunch of**
Improvisar	25077	The ore is becoming bunchy
Imprudent	25078	The ore is very bunchy
Impudencia	25079	Has small bunches of rich and poor ore scattered through it
Impudenter	25080	**Ore charges**
Impudeur...	25081	Charges upon the ore
Impugnatus	25082	What are the charges upon the ore
Impugned	25083	Exclusive of freight charges upon the ore
Impuissant	25084	Inclusive of freight charges upon the ore
Impune ...	25085	The total charges upon the ore amount to —— per ton
Impunible	25086	Freight and treatment charges upon ore
Impunidad	25087	**Ore chimney** (*See also* " Chimney.")
Impunitus	25088	The ore occurs only in chimnies
Impuntire	25089	Ore in chimney
Impuritas...	25090	Outside the ore chimney
Imputativo	25091	New ore chimney
Imputresco	25092	**Ore chute**
Inabilita ...	25093	The ore occurs only in chutes
Inabitato ...	25094	What is the dip of the ore chute [horizontal
Inabrite ...	25095	The ore chute is dipping at an angle of —— degrees to the
Inabruptus	25096	The vertical end line of the ore chute
Inacceso ...	25097	The vertical end line of the ore chute should be within —— feet
Inaccurate	25098	Expect to strike ore chute within next —— feet
Inacheve ...	25099	**Ore, class of**
Inacquare...	25100	First class ore
Inaction ...	25101	Second class ore
Inaddietro	25102	Third class ore
Inadequate	25103	What is the number of tons of —— class ore in stock
Inadibilis ...	25104	We have now in stock —— tons of first class ore
Inadustus...	25105	We have now in stock —— tons of second class ore
Inagotable	25106	We have now in stock —— tons of third class ore
Inalesco ...	25107	Number of tons of first class ore
Inalienus ...	25108	Number of tons of second class ore
Inalterado	25109	Number of tons of third class ore
Inamabile...	25110	What is the assay value per ton of —— class ore
Inamaresco	25111	First class ore has an assay value of —— per ton
Inambulans	25112	Second class ore has an assay value of —— per ton
Inamidato	25113	Third class ore has an assay value of —— per ton
Inanellare...	25114	**Ore concentration**
Inanilogus	25115	Number of tons of concentration ore
Inanimalis	25116	The ore is well suited for concentration (by)
Inanimarsi	25117	The ore is not suited for concentration (by)
Inanimito...	25118	The ore is practically valueless without concentration
Inaniter ...	25119	The ore will average —— ozs. per ton without concentration
Inanition ...	25120	**Ore contents**
Inapercu ...	25121	What is the value of the ore contents for ——
Inaplicado	25122	The ore contains —— per cent. of
Inapplique	25123	The ore contains —— per cent. of aluminium
Inapposite	25124	The ore contains —— per cent. of antimony
Inaptly ...	25125	The ore contains —— per cent. of arsenic
Inarched ...	25126	The ore contains —— per cent. of barium
Inardeo ...	25127	The ore contains —— per cent. of bismuth
Inarescens	25128	The ore contains —— per cent. of chromium
Inargute ...	25129	The ore contains —— per cent. of cobalt

Inarticule ...	25130	The ore contains —— per cent. of copper
Inaspectus	25131	The ore contains —— per cent. of gold
Inasprire ...	25132	The ore contains —— per cent. of iridium
Inassuetus	25133	The ore contains —— per cent. of iron
Inaudible ...	25134	The ore contains —— per cent. of lead
Inauditus ...	25135	The ore contains —— per cent. of lime
Inaugural...	25136	The ore contains —— per cent. of magnesium
Inaurato ...	25137	The ore contains —— per cent. of manganese
Inbreathe...	25138	The ore contains —— per cent. of mercury
Inbrunst ...	25139	The ore contains —— per cent. of nickel
Incalciato...	25140	The ore contains —— per cent. of phosphorus
Incalfacio...	25141	The ore contains —— per cent. of platinum
Incallidus ..	25142	The ore contains —— per cent. of silicon
Incamerare	25143	The ore contains —— per cent. of silver
Incammino	25144	The ore contains —— per cent. of strontium
Incandesco	25145	The ore contains —— per cent. of sulphur
Incantatus	25146	The ore contains —— per cent. of tellurium
Incaponire	25147	The ore contains —— per cent. of tin
Incappiare	25148	The ore contains —— per cent. of titanium
Incarnante	25149	The ore contains —— per cent. of tungsten
Incasable ...	25150	The ore contains —— per cent. of zinc
Incastrato...	25151	**Ore crushed**
Incasurus ...	25152	Number of tons of ore crushed
Incatenate	25153	Total weight of ore crushed
Incatolico ...	25154	—— tons of ore crushed has yielded —— ozs. of retorted gold
Incautela ...	25155	The quality and quantity of the ore crushed is equal to average
Incautious	25156	**Ore customs**
Incavated...	25157	**Cut ore**
Incendiary	25158	To cut ore
Incendioso	25159	May cut ore at any day
Incenerito...	25160	**Ore, dimensions of**
Incensario	25161	What are the dimensions of the ore
Incense ...	25162	Dimensions of the ore have never been exceeded
Incentivo ...	25163	Dimensions of the ore are at present
Inceptum ...	25164	**Ore, discovery of**
Incernor ...	25165	Important discovery of ore
Incerteza ...	25166	Is there any new discovery of ore
Incessant ...	25167	There is no new discovery of ore whatever
Incessens ...	25168	Rumour of important discovery of ore at
Incessible...	25169	**Ore dry**
Incestueux	25170	The ore is dry
Incestuoso	25171	**Ore extracted**
Incettato ...	25172	What amount of ore has been extracted
Inchiodato	25173	What is the quantity and value of ore extracted to date
Inchiostro...	25174	We have extracted to date —— tons of ore, approximate [value ——
Inchoandus	25175	Ore extracted during past week
Inchoate ...	25176	Ore extracted during past month
Incidendus	25177	No books have been kept showing quantity of ore extracted
Incidir ...	25178	No figures are available of the ore extracted and treated (sold)
Inciferato...	25179	Have not extracted any ore since
Incinerar ...	25180	It is difficult to extract the ore on account of
Incingor ...	25181	Only a small amount of ore has been extracted
Incipiens ...	25182	A large amount of ore has already been extracted
Incipisso ...	25183	Hope to begin extracting ore on
Incision ...	25184	Rate of extraction of ore
Incitacion...	25185	Past rate of extraction of ore
Incitador ...	25186	Present rate of extraction of ore
Incitateur...	25187	At our present rate of extraction of ore
Incitativo ...	25188	Our present rate of extraction of ore is —— tons per month
Incitega ...	25189	When we expect to increase our rate of extraction of ore to [—— tons per month

Incivil ...	25190	As soon as we can increase our present rate of extracting the [ore
Inclamans	25191	**Ore dump**
Inclamator	25192	Number of tons of ore on the dump
Inclareo ...	25193	What is the average value of the ore on the dump
Inclasped ...	25194	The average value of the ore on the dump is
Inclemente	25195	There is no ore on the dump worth saving
Inclinante	25196	There are —— tons of ore on the dump, worth say
Inclinatus	25197	Ore on the dump is of fair quality
Inclined ...	25198	**Ore found**
Inclining ...	25199	Found ore at
Included ...	25200	To find the ore
Inclutus ...	25201	We have found good ore at
Incluyente	25202	Have found the ore at
Incoactus ...	25203	Have not found the ore
Incoativo ...	25204	No more ore has been found yet
Incobrable	25205	Have not yet found ore in —— level
Incoctilis ...	25206	Find ore [—— feet
Incoerenza	25207	Do not expect to find any ore until we have driven an additional
Incognito ...	25208	Do not expect to find any ore until we have sunk an additional
Incolendus	25209	**Ore, grade of** [—— feet
Incolpato ...	25210	The grade of the ore is not so good
Incolumis...	25211	The grade of the ore is very variable
Incombusto	25212	The grade of the ore varies between —— and ——
Incommodum	25213	The grade of the ore has fallen to
Incomodar	25214	The grade of the ore has risen to
Incompleto	25215	The ore as developed improves in grade
Incompris	25216	We are at present running on —— grade ore
Inconcino ...	25217	No ore below —— in grade can be touched without loss
Inconcitus	25218	There is an abundance of ore of —— grade
Inconcusso	25219	**Ore high grade**
Incondiute	25220	The ore is high grade
Inconfeso ...	25221	The ore is becoming high grade
Inconfusus	25222	Number of tons of high grade ore in stock
Incongruo	25223	What is the value assigned to high grade ore
Inconscius	25224	High grade ore is all ore above —— per ton
Inconsulto	25225	The high grade ore runs
Inconteste	25226	Running on high grade ore
Incordare ...	25227	**Ore second grade**
Incordio ...	25228	The ore is becoming second grade
Incoronato	25229	Number of tons of second grade ore in stock
Incospicuo	25230	What is the value assigned to second grade ore
Incoxans ...	25231	Second grade ore runs between —— and —— ounces per ton
Incrassate	25232	Running on second grade ore
Increanza...	25233	**Ore low grade**
Increatus ...	25234	The ore is low grade
Incredule ...	25235	The ore is low grade but promises
Increible ...	25236	The ore is becoming low grade
Incremento	25237	The ore is of too low a grade for shipment
Increpador	25238	The grade of the ore is too low to be of any value
Increpito ...	25239	What is the value assigned to low grade ore
Incretare ...	25240	Low grade ore is all ore below —— per ton
Incriminer	25241	Number of tons of low grade ore
Incrociare...	25242	Running on low grade ore [ore
Incrojato ...	25243	Recently they have only been raising and running on low grade
Incroyable	25244	Recently I (we) have only been raising and running on low grade ore
Incruento ...	25245	**Ore hauling**
Incrustar ...	25246	Cost of hauling ore amounts to —— per ton
Incubandus	25247	What is the cost of hauling ore
Incubate ...	25248	Cable number of tons of ore hauled
Incubus ...	25249	We have hauled —— tons of ore since

Incudine ...	25250	**Ore house(s)**
Inculcatus	25251	New ore house
Inculpable	25252	Finished erection of ore house
Inculpated	25253	**Ore jig** (*See also* " Jig.")
Incultura ...	25254	Have now —— tons of jig ore
Incumbent	25255	What is your stock of jig ore
Incumbir ...	25256	Estimate jig ore at —— tons
Incunabula	25257	**Ore, leaching of**
Incurably ...	25258	Cost of leaching ore
Incurious ...	25259	The ore leaches well
Incurrens ...	25260	The ore leaches badly
Incurso ...	25261	The ore leaches slowly
Incursurus	25262	The ore leaches quickly
Incurvarsi	25263	**Ore milling** (*See also* "Milling.")
Incurvate ...	25264	Number of tons of ore milled
Incurvesco	25265	Number of tons of milling ore
Incurvus ...	25266	The ore has milled —— per ton
Incussio ...	25267	Is the ore free milling
Incutere ...	25268	The ore is free milling
Incutiens ...	25269	The ore is not free milling
Indable ...	25270	Is the ore milling as you expected
Indagador	25271	The ore is not milling so well as expected
Indaganter	25272	The ore is milling as well as expected
Indagatrix	25273	The ore is milling better than expected
Indágatus	25274	The ore will require milling
Indanajare	25275	What ore are you now milling
Indebido ...	25276	Has the mill been running on high and low grade ore ? and in [what proportions
Indebilire...	25277	The mills have been running on high and low grade ore in [their natural proportions
Indebitum	25278	Mill has been running on high grade ore
Indebolito	25279	Mill has been running on low grade ore
Indebted ...	25280	What is the total cost per ton of mining and milling the ore
Indecenter	25281	The ore can be mined and milled at a low cost
Indecible ...	25282	The ore can be mined and milled at a cost of —— per ton
Indecioso ...	25283	**Ore occurrence**
Indecorum	25284	The ore occurs
Indefectus	25285	The ore occurs in flats [and —— feet in length
Indefenso...	25286	A large bed of ore has been developed for —— feet in width
Indeflexus	25287	The ore occurs in beds which extend for a distance of
Indegnarsi	25288	The ore occurs in chimnies
Indelibere...	25289	The ore occurs in bunches
Indelicat ...	25290	The ore occurrence is a *stockwerk*
Indelt ...	25291	**Ore payable**
Indemnatus	25292	The ore pays
Indemnity	25293	No pay ore
Indemnizar	25294	The ore will pay
Indenture...	25295	The ore will pay if economically handled
Indepisci ...	25296	The ore will pay net per ton
Indesertus	25297	The ore will not pay
Indetonsus	25298	Will the (this) ore pay
Indevotion	25299	The pay ore is confined to say —— tons [depth
Indexes ...	25300	Am (are) of the opinion that pay ore does not run to any
Indiarsi ...	25301	It is extremely probable that pay ore will continue to a further
Indicateur	25302	The ore has ceased to be payable [depth of about —— feet
Indicatura	25303	The pay ore is very pockety
Indice ...	25304	The pay ore has now lasted for a length of —— and a depth
Indicendus	25305	The pay ore is now —— thick [of ——
Indicerole...	25306	The pay ore is as rich as ever
Indiciado ...	25307	We have now pay ore —— wide which averages

Indictio ...	25808	Have not yet found any ore that would pay to extract
Indictivus...	25809	What is the prospect of finding pay ore
Indidem ...	25810	**Ore pipe**
Indienne ...	25811	What are the dimensions of the ore pipe
Indiestro ...	25812	The dimensions of the ore pipe are
Indigence	25813	The ore pipe is dipping at an angle of —— degrees to the [horizontal
Indigentia	25814	**Ore pocket**
Indigesto ...	25815	The ore is pockety
Indigetur ...	25816	The ore is usually found in pockets
Indigite ...	25817	Has (have) struck a pocket of ore
Indignar ...	25818	Is opening out into a rich pocket of ore
Indignidad	25819	Is proving only a small pocket of ore
Indigofera	25820	Have struck a very rich pocket of ore
Indimensus	25821	The pocket of ore shows signs of a pinch
Indipiscor...	25822	The pocket of ore maintains its size
Indiquer ...	25823	The pocket of ore maintains its size and grade
Indireptus	25824	**Ore, production of**
Indiscusso	25825	At present the ore production is
Indisponer	25826	What is the present rate of ore production
Indistinto...	25827	At present producing large quantities of ore . [—— per ton
Individuo ...	25828	At present producing large quantities of ore which will average
Indivinare	25829	We are producing —— tons of ore per —— days
Indivise ...	25830	**Ore prospects**
Indivulsus	25831	Every prospect of getting good ore
Indiziare ...	25832	Every prospect of getting ore
Indocile ...	25833	But little prospect of getting ore in payable quantities
Indocilito...	25834	Every prospect that the ore will continue
Indolencia	25835	We have a good prospect of finding ore but anticipate it will
Indolesco ...	25836	**Ore, to raise** [be low grade
Indomable	25837	Is it necessary to raise the ore
Indompte ...	25838	It is not necessary to raise the ore
Indonnarsi	25839	Raise all the ore you can
Indoppiare	25840	Raise all the ore you can within the next —— month(s)
Indormiens	25841	When we shall be able to raise the ore
Indovinare	25842	When will you be able to raise the ore
Indozzato ...	25843	Do not raise any ore, leave it standing
Indrudire ...	25844	Most of the ore now being raised is from
Indubious ..	25845	The quantity of ore raised will depend on
Indubitado	25846	Cable number of tons of ore raised and forwarded to mill(s)
Inducidor...	25847	Ore raised and forwarded to mill(s) —— tons (since)
Inductive ...	25848	The ore raised since —— amounts to —— tons
Inducturus	25849	**Ore reserves**
Inducula ...	25850	As to ore reserves
Indudable	25851	Ore in reserve
Indugevole	25852	Reserves of ore amount to —— tons
Indugiante	25853	Ore reserves have been largely increased by recent developments
Indugredi	25854	Reserves of ore practically non-existent
Indulcitas	25855	Reserves of ore inconsiderable
Indulger ...	25856	—— tons of ore in reserve
Indulging...	25857	The actual reserves of ore are confined to —— tons
Indultario	25858	The ore actually in reserve is —— tons which should yield a [net profit of
Indumento	25859	Approximate ore reserves —— tons estimated value ——
Indupedire	25860	Approximate ore reserves —— tons cannot estimate value at
Indurabile	25861	The average assay of the ore in reserve is —— per ton [present
Indurate ...	25862	At our present rate of extraction we should take out the whole [of the ore in reserve within the next —— month(s)
Indusiatus	25863	State approximate value per ton of ore in reserve
Indusium ...	25864	Nothing left in the way of ore reserves
Industria ...	25865	Develop ore reserves vigorously

Induttrice	25366	Develop ore reserves, but ship sufficient to cover expenses
Inebrior ...	25367	Develop simply with a view of accumulating ore reserves
Ineditus ...	25368	By reserves of ore, do you mean that it has been opened on [three sides
Ineffable ...	25369	By reserves of ore, I (we) mean that it has been opened on [three sides
Inefficacy ...	25370	By reserves of ore, 1 (we) mean [three sides
Ineficaz ...	25371	I (we) estimate —— tons of ore can be put into reserve at an [expense of —— in —— months
Inegalite ...	25372	The statement that large ore reserves are exposed is not correct
Inelegant ...	25373	**Ore rich** (*See also* "Ore grade of.")
Inemorior	25374	The ore at —— is exceedingly rich
Inemptus ...	25375	Expect to find rich ore deeper
Ineptitude	25376	**Ore sacks**
Inerenza ...	25377	Ore sacked
Inerrancia	25378	**Ore sales**
Inerrante ...	25379	Account sales of ore sold
Inerticula	25380	Examine ore sales
Inertness ...	25381	Ore sales, get total tons and value of ore sold
Inerudito ...	25382	Ore is sold to —— at ——
Inescandus	25383	Who is the ore sold to and where
Inescato ...	25384	Get verified copies of a/c sales of ore
Inesione ...	25385	**Ore sample(s) of**
Inespere ...	25386	Ore sampled
Inespiable...	25387	Ore sampled at
Inestenso ...	25388	Is ore sampled at
Inestimado	25389	Average sample(s) of the ore
Inetichito...	25390	Sample(s) of the ore
Ineundus ...	25391	Selected sample(s) of the ore
Inevitable...	25392	**Ore shipment(s)**
Inevolutus	25393	Shipping ore (*See also* "Shipping.")
Inexacto ...	25394	Ore shipped
Inexcitus ...	25395	Ore shipped to date
Inexistent...	25396	Ore shipped to date amounts to —— tons
Inexorable	25397	The ore shipped has average value of —— per ton
Inexpertus	25398	The ore is shipped to
Infacundo ..	25399	To ship ore
Infaisable...	25400	Shall commence to ship ore on
Infamacion	25401	Shall re-commence to ship ore on
Infamandus	25402	Within what time can you ship ore to the value of
Infamar ...	25403	All ore to be shipped in the name of
Infamatus	25404	In whose name has the ore been shipped
Infamous ...	25405	The ore has been shipped in the following name(s)
Infancy ...	25406	The amount of ore shipped
Infanterie	25407	The ore broken and in stock will sort to —— tons for shipment
Infantile ...	25408	We shall continue to ship high grade ore
Infantulus	25409	We shall continue to ship low grade ore
Infanzon ...	25410	Have you shipped any ore yet from
Infarciens...	25411	Have not shipped any ore (owing to)
Infarcito ...	25412	Have already shipped —— tons of ore
Infarinato	25413	**Ore in sight**
Infatuate ...	25414	Number of tons of ore in sight in the mine
Infatuer ...	25415	Cable number of tons of ore in sight
Infecond ...	25416	Ore in sight amounts to
Infected ...	25417	Ore in sight will last for
Infecting ...	25418	Ore in sight will not last for more than
Infedelita...	25419	Is there any ore in sight
Infederare	25420	There is no ore in sight
Infelicito ...	25421	Practically there is no ore in sight
Inferencia...	25422	What is your estimate of the ore in sight
Inferigno ...	25423	My (our) estimate of the ore in sight is —— tons

Inferir ...	25424	I (we) estimate the ore in sight to amount to —— tons and to [have an approximate value of ——
Infermiere	25425	Amount of ore in sight is stated to be —— tons
Infernado ...	25426	Ore in sight is calculated at
Infernalis ...	25427	Can you confirm estimate of value of ore in sight
Inferocire ...	25428	Cannot confirm estimate of value of ore in sight
Infervesio...	25429	I (we) confirm estimate of value of ore in sight
Infestans ...	25430	**Ore smelting** (*See also* "Smelting.")
Infestator...	25431	The ore is a good smelting ore
Infettivo ...	25432	Is the ore a good smelting ore
Infiammare	25433	The ore is not a good smelting ore
Infiascato ...	25434	Can obtain ample supplies of ore to make a good smelting [mixture
Infibulo ...	25435	The ore can be smelted at a profit
Inficetus ...	25436	Can the ore be smelted at a profit
Inficialis ...	25437	The profit on smelting the ore would not exceed —— per ton
Inficiator ...	25438	The amount of ore smelted
Infidelity ...	25439	**Ore sorted**
Infidels ...	25440	The ore is easy to sort
Infierno ...	25441	The ore is difficult to sort
Infigendus	25442	Shall sort a parcel of ore and ascertain value
Infiggere ...	25443	Ore sorted ready for shipment
Infiltrer ...	25444	Have you any ore sorted
Infilzarsi ...	25445	I (we) have —— tons of sorted ore
Infimates ...	25446	Will give us —— tons of sorted ore
Infingidor...	25447	Shall sort the ore up to a value of —— per ton
Infinidad ...	25448	The ore will pay if carefully sorted
Infinite ...	25449	We have raised —— tons of ore, but have not yet been able [to sort it
Infinitive ...	25450	**Ore sorters**
Infinoche ...	25451	Number of ore sorters employed
Infintura ...	25452	**Ore in stock**
Infiorare ...	25453	Number of tons of ore in stock
Infirmatio	25454	Value of ore in stock [value ——
Infirmerie	25455	We have now in stock —— tons of sorted ore, estimated
Infirmitas ..	25456	We have now in stock —— tons of unsorted ore, estimated [value ——
Infirmly ...	25457	**Ore struck**
Infizzare ...	25458	Ore struck at (in)
Inflagione ..	25459	The ore recently struck averages —— feet wide
Inflamable	25460	The ore recently struck assays
Inflamed ...	25461	Expect to strike ore within the next —— feet
Inflatilia ...	25462	**Ore, tonnage of**
Inflectens ...	25463	Estimated tonnage of ore
Inflection ...	25464	Cannot estimate tonnage of ore
Inflettere ...	25465	Cable estimated tonnage of ore
Inflexible ...	25466	The tonnage of the ore cannot be estimated until
Inflexio ...	25467	**Ore treatment**
Inflicted ...	25468	Cost of ore treatment
Inflictive ...	25469	The ore is difficult to treat
Infligir ...	25470	The ore is easy to treat
Influjo ...	25471	Formerly the ore was treated by roasting
Infocarsi ...	25472	The ore treatment is to roast and then chloridise
Infodiens ...	25473	The ore is treated " raw " in pans
Infodior ...	25474	**Ore, dip of**
Infogliare...	25475	What is the dip of the ore
Inforabile	25476	The dip of the ore is
Inforciado	25477	**Ore, width of**
Informador	25478	What is the average width of ore
Informarsi	25479	The average width of ore is
Informer ...	25480	Cable width and value of ore
Informidad	25481	The width of the ore is ——. The value is ——
Infossato ...	25482	What is the length and width of the ore

Infracteur	25483	**Ore, value of**
Infragilis ...	25484	Ore value $5 per ton or less
Infralire ...	25485	Ore value $5 to $8 per ton
Infrantojo	25486	Ore value $8 to $10 per ton
Infrascato	25487	Ore value $10 to $15 per ton
Infrendeo ...	25488	Ore value $15 to $20 per ton
Infrequent	25489	Ore value $20 to $25 per ton
Infrezione	25490	Ore value $25 to $30 per ton
Infriandus	25491	Ore value $30 to $35 per ton
Infricatio ...	25492	Ore value $35 to $40 per ton
Infrictus ...	25493	Ore value $40 to $45 per ton
Infringed ...	25494	Ore value $45 to $50 per ton
Infringens	25495	Ore value $50 to $60 per ton
Infringir ...	25496	Ore value $60 to $70 per ton
Infruenza ...	25497	Ore value $70 to $80 per ton
Infruscare	25498	Ore value $80 to $90 per ton
Infulas ...	25499	Ore value $90 to $100 per ton
Infundible	25500	Ore has improved in value throughout the mine
Infuocato ...	25501	The ore we have now averages —— in value
Infuriato ...	25502	The ore has hitherto averaged —— in value
Infuscate ...	25503	I (we) estimate the value of the ore at
Infused ...	25504	What is the estimated value of the ore
Infuserato	25505	What is the estimated value of the ore between No. —— level
Infusible ...	25506	The estimated value of the ore is [and No. —— level
Infusorium	25507	The ore averages in value —— per ton
Ingabbiare	25508	What is the value of the ore at present available
Ingannante	25509	The value of the ore at present available is approximately ——
Ingannigia	25510	What is the value of the ore for
Ingannuzzo	25511	The value of the ore for —— is
Ingastada...	25512	What is the value of ore for gold, silver, and copper respectively
Ingavinato	25513	The ore has no value for ——
Ingegnarsi	25514	What is the net value of the ore
Ingegnetto	25515	The net value of the ore is
Ingegnuolo	25516	What is the gross value of the ore
Ingelidus ...	25517	The gross value of the ore is
Ingelosire	25518	Would have to account for the value of all ores extracted
Ingeminans	25519	Value of ore taken out
Ingemisco	25520	Value of ore taken out under trespass
Ingemmato	25521	What is the tonnage and value of the ore taken out under
Ingeniculo	25522	The vein is practically barren of ore of any value [trespass
Ingenieria	25523	**Organization**
Ingenieur...	25524	Organization fair
Ingenuatus	25525	Organization good
Ingenuidad	25526	Organization excellent
Ingeridura	25527	Pending the proper organization of
Ingertar ...	25528	**Organize**
Ingessato ...	25529	Could you (——) organize the —— for
Inghermire	25530	Organize syndicate
Inghiotte ...	25531	Organize company
Ingiellare ...	25532	Organize the work so as to
Ingirted ...	25533	I shall organize the work so as to
Ingiugnere	25534	My first work will be to organize
Ingiuriare	25535	To organize
Inglomero	25536	—— will organize the
Inglosable	25537	**Organized**
Ingluvie ...	25538	All the work is well organized
Ingobbire...	25539	Have organized syndicate
Ingojatore	25540	Have organized company
Ingollare ...	25541	**Origin**
Ingombrato	25542	Discover origin if possible

Ingorbiare	25543	Cannot discover origin
Ingordezza	25544	Of doubtful origin
Ingrafter ...	25545	Origin or cause of
Ingrain ...	25546	**Original(ly)** (*See also* "Compare," "Excess.")
Ingrandire	25547	Original lost
Ingratella...	25548	Original inadvertently destroyed
Ingratitud	25549	Original must be produced
Ingravans	25550	Original has been lost or mislaid
Ingravesco	25551	Original agreement(s)
Ingraziato	25552	Original deed(s)
Ingredient	25553	Original paper(s)
Ingressus ...	25554	According to the original understanding
Ingriffato ...	25555	What was the original understanding
Ingrognato	25556	The original understanding was
Ingroppare	25557	**Originate(d)**
Inguainare	25558	To originate
Ingubbiare	25559	Was (were) originated
Inguistara	25560	Originated by
Ingustable	25561	Said to have been originated for the purpose of
Ingustatus	25562	Never could have originated from
Inhabitado	25563	No doubt originated from
Inhabited ...	25564	**Ostensible(ly)**
Inhallable...	25565	**Other(s)**
Inhalor	25566	All other
Inhiatio	25567	Other people willing to take
Inhibendus	25568	Can you (——) suggest any other means
Inhonestas	25569	I (we) cannot suggest any other means
Inhonorar...	25570	Do you know any other suitable means for
Inhorreo ...	25571	I do not know any other or more suitable means
Inhumanus	25572	What other steps do you mean
Inibitorio ...	25573	The other steps I mean are
Inidoneita...	25574	Is there any other
Inimicarsi...	25575	I do not think there is any other
Inimiciter ...	25576	From other
Inimicizia...	25577	In no other way
Inimitable	25578	In all other ways
Inimitie ...	25579	I do not see any other way
Iniquitire ...	25580	Will any other
Iniquitous	25581	On the other hand
Initialis ...	25582	Other than
Initiation ...	25583	If any other
Initior ...	25584	If any other means are available
Initurus ...	25585	**Otherwise**
Inizzato ...	25586	Cable if otherwise
Injected ...	25587	Otherwise it will be of no use
Injecturus	25588	Otherwise it will be necessary at once to
Injucundus	25589	Otherwise you should immediately
Injunctus ...	25590	If otherwise
Injungor ...	25591	Or otherwise
Injurieux ...	25592	Otherwise than to
Injurioso ...	25593	**Ought**
Injusticia ...	25594	Certainly ought to
Inkhorn ...	25595	Ought not to
Inkiness ...	25596	Ought to act at once
Inkstand ...	25597	Ought to have done
Inlandisch	25598	Ought to have been done before
Inlecito ...	25599	Ought never to have been done
Inliegend ...	25600	Ought to have been provided against
Inlividire ...	25601	Ought not to have been omitted
Inmemorial	25602	Which (this) ought

Inmenso ...	25603	Ought I (we)
Inmentre ...	25604	You (——) ought
Inmiscible	25605	Both ought
Inmudable	25606	**Ounce(s)** (*See also* "Assay," "Gold," "Pennyweight" and [Table at end.)
Inmunidad	25607	Per ounce
Innacible ...	25608	Each ounce
Innacquato	25609	Of an ounce
Innalbare ...	25610	Equal to —— per ounce for ——
Innamarsi	25611	Less than one ounce per
Innamidare	25612	Less than —— of an ounce will not pay
Innamorata	25613	—— of an ounce will pay
Innanimato	25614	—— of an ounce and over ——
Innantiche	25615	Cost(s) —— per ounce
Innaridito	25616	Ounce(s) of gold per ton of 2,000 lbs.
Innascoso...	25617	Ounce(s) of gold per ton of 2,240 lbs.
Innasprire	25618	Ounce(s) of silver per ton of 2,000 lbs.
Innatatio ...	25619	Ounce(s) of silver per ton of 2,240 lbs.
Innaturale	25620	The value of gold is taken at —— per ounce
Innaurare...	25621	The value of silver is taken at —— per ounce
Innaverato	25622	What is the value of the gold taken at per ounce
Innavigo ...	25623	What is the value of the silver taken at per ounce
Innebbiato	25624	Weighing —— ounces (troy)
Innector ...	25625	Weighing —— ounces (avoirdupois)
Innegable...	25626	**Our(s)**
Innerhalb...	25627	Our cable
Innigkeit ...	25628	Our letter dated
Innkeeper...	25629	Our company
Innocenter	25630	Our interests
Innocuous	25631	Our best plan would be
Innodatus...	25632	**Ourselves**
Innodiare ...	25633	Only ourselves
Innotesco ...	25634	Ourselves and
Innovated...	25635	You and ourselves
Innovation	25636	**Out**
Innumerus	25637	Out and away
Innuovare	25638	In and out
Innupta ...	25639	Altogether out of the question
Innutrio ...	25640	Out of
Innutritus	25641	Out of which
Inoblitus ...	25642	Do what you can to carry out my (our) (——'s) wishes
Inobscuro...	25643	Will do all in my power to carry out wishes expressed
Inoccatus ...	25644	How much do you expect to turn out
Inocciduns	25645	Ought to turn out at least
Inoccupe ...	25646	Entirely out of
Inocencia ...	25647	To carry out
Inocentado	25648	Not got out more than
Inoculador	25649	Considerably out of pocket by it
Inoculatio	25650	**Outcrop** (*See also* "Croppings.")
Inoculer ...	25651	Outcrop of lode
Inoculista...	25652	The outcrop
Inodore ...	25653	From the outcrop for a depth of
Inodorous	25654	Picked samples of the outcrop assay
Inofenso ...	25655	Various samples from the outcrop assay
Inoffensus	25656	Average samples of the outcrop assay
Inojeta ...	25657	The outcrop is bold and well defined
Inolire ...	25658	The outcrop can be traced for
Inolmarsi ...	25659	The outcrop in places is —— wide
Inominalis	25660	The vein outcrops like a wall
Inondante...	25661	The outcrop of the vein shows for a distance of
Inonesta ...	25662	The outcrop of the vein may be traced for a distance of

Inonorato ...	25663	Ore taken from the outcrop shows
Inopacus ...	25664	Quartz taken from the outcrop assays ——
Inoperante	25665	**Outfit** (*See also* "Appliances.")
Inopertus ...	25666	The necessary outfit for
Inopinatus	25667	In order to provide the necessary outfit
Inopiosus ...	25668	Cost of necessary outfit will amount to
Inoportuno	25669	Outfit should include the following
Inorganico	25670	Have arranged for outfit
Inorior ...	25671	**Outgoing(s)**
Inorridire...	25672	**Outlay**
Inospite ...	25673	The present outlay must be curtailed
Inprimis ...	25674	The outlay on —— will require to be large
Inquantum	25675	Cable if in your opinion present appearances justify an outlay
Inquests ...	25676	Present appearances justify an outlay of [of
Inquietare	25677	Present appearances do not justify heavy outlay
Inquilino ...	25678	The outlay is fully justified by present appearances
Inquinar ...	25679	What do you estimate will be the outlay for
Inquinatio	25680	I expect an outlay of —— will enable you to
Inquirer ...	25681	An outlay of
Inquisitor...	25682	I think you are justified in increasing your outlay to
Inradiare ...	25683	Owing to the outlay required
Inramo ...	25684	The outlay on plant has been very heavy
Inregolare	25685	The outlay has not been needlessly heavy
Inremisse ...	25686	Will require considerable outlay for
Inresoluto...	25687	The outlay has been very large
Inretire ...	25688	No large outlay will be required for some time to come
Inrossare ...	25689	**Outlier(s)**
Insaccato ...	25690	**Outlook** (*See also* "General.")
Insaciable...	25691	The general outlook is good
Insalatina...	25692	As to the present outlook
Insalubre ...	25693	**Outlying**
Insalutato	25694	The outlying portion
Insaniens ...	25695	**Output**
Insanity ...	25696	What do you expect output will be
Insaponare	25697	Expect output will be at least
Insatietas ...	25698	Output for month ending
Insatious ...	25699	Output for year ending
Insaziata ...	25700	Can you approximately state the output for
Inscalpo ...	25701	Cannot approximately state the output for
Inscendo ...	25702	Should approximate the output at
Inschrift ...	25703	The output has been limited to
Insciente ...	25704	What is the present output
Inscitus ...	25705	The present output is at the rate of —— tons per
Inscribed ...	25706	The output has been —— tons during the past —— months
Inscribens	25707	Can you maintain an output of
Inscripto ...	25708	To maintain this output we must
Inscrivere...	25709	It is not possible to maintain an output of more than
Insculped ...	25710	Taking the output at
Insculptus	25711	Which will enable us to raise the output to ——
Insecandus	25712	Can you increase the output
Inseccion ...	25713	Cannot increase output
Insectans ...	25714	I can increase the output [per week
Insectile ...	25715	I (we) shall be able to increase the output of ore to —— tons
Insecutus ...	25716	I cannot increase the output until
Insediare ...	25717	Can you estimate the probable output for the month of
Insegnato...	25718	The regular output from the mine is —— tons
Inselvarsi...	25719	What is the present output of the mine(s) per month
Insembra ...	25720	The present output is ——
Inseminor...	25721	Output for the month of —— is
Insensates	25722	The output has been comparatively small

Insensilis ...	25723	The output has not amounted to more than —— tons per —
Insepulto ...	25724	**Outside** (*See also* "Inside.")
Inserted ...	25725	Outside of
Insertim ...	25726	What are the outside figures
Inservible...	25727	Outside figures
Inservitum	25728	At the outside
Inseverito...	25729	On the outside of
Inshore ...	25730	Outside our
Insibilo ...	25731	Outside our boundaries
Insiccatus...	25732	What are the outside dimensions
Insicium ...	25733	The outside dimensions are
Insideor ...	25734	Outside the timbers
Insidiador	25735	**Outsiders**
Insidieux ...	25736	Outsiders are holding
Insieparsi...	25737	Outsiders are buying
Insiliens ...	25738	Outsiders are selling
Insimular...	25739	Outsiders must be kept in ignorance of
Insincerus	25740	What are outsiders doing
Insinuante	25741	Quite an outsider
Insinuar ...	25742	**Outstanding**
Insinuated	25743	Cable amount of outstanding liabilities
Insinuatus	25744	To defray outstanding liabilities
Insipidez ...	25745	Mail particulars of outstanding accounts
Insipidire...	25746	All outstanding accounts were paid on ——; our liabilities now
Insipience...	25747	Accounts outstanding amount to [only consist of
Insisted ...	25748	There are no outstanding accounts
Insistenza...	25749	After we have paid all outstanding accounts
Insistir ...	25750	**Outward(s)**
Insitituis ...	25751	**Oval**
Insobriety	25752	Forms a basin-shaped oval
Insofern ...	25753	Oval in form
Insolatio ...	25754	Has (have) worn oval
Insoldable	25755	**Over**
Insolencia...	25756	Over draft
Insolesco ...	25757	Over due
Insolidum	25758	Over sold
Insollito ...	25759	Over bought
Insolutus ...	25760	To pick over
Insolvent ...	25761	Must stand over for the present
Insomnio ...	25762	Can you come over
Insonciant	25763	Will come over as soon as I (we) have arranged
Insorgere ...	25764	Cannot come over
Inspecting	25765	Strongly advise you in your own interests to come over
Inspectio ...	25766	**Overburden** (*See also* "Burden," "Hydraulic.")
Insperatus	25767	Still stripping the overburden
Inspergor...	25768	Shall finish removal of overburden about [burden
Inspettore	25769	We are employing all our force for the removal of the over-
Insphere ...	25770	**Overcharge(s)**
Inspiciens...	25771	**Overcome**
Inspicior ...	25772	To overcome
Inspirador	25773	Are you likely to overcome
Inspuor ...	25774	Am (are) not likely to overcome
Instabilis ...	25775	Am (are) sanguine shall be able to overcome
Installed ...	25776	As soon as I (we) have overcome
Instamment	25777	Have overcome all difficulties
Instancia ...	25778	The difficulties to be overcome are serious
Instaturus	25779	There is no serious difficulty to overcome
Instigato ...	25780	Unable to overcome
Instillare ...	25781	So as to overcome
Instincts ...	25782	Provided that I (we) can overcome

Instinto ...	25783	**Overdraft** (*See also* "Bank.")
Instipulor...	25784	**Overdrawn**
Instituens...	25785	Has (have) overdrawn his (their) credit
Instituir ...	25786	Have already overdrawn account
Institute ...	25787	**Overdue** (*See also* "Due.")
Instratum...	25788	Now overdue
Instrictus...	25789	Not overdue
Instruido ...	25790	**Overhaul** (*See also* "Boiler," "Carefully.")
Instrument	25791	To overhaul
Insuasum...	25792	Overhaul at once
Insuavita ...	25793	**Overhauled** (*See also* "Order.")
Insuccatus	25794	Should be thoroughly overhauled
Insucidare	25795	Has (have) been thoroughly overhauled
Insuflar ...	25796	Has (have) not been overhauled
Insulaire ...	25797	**Overhauling**
Insularius	25798	Now overhauling
Insulator ...	25799	Overhauling stamps
Insulous ...	25800	Overhauling engine
Insulsez	25801	When will you finish overhauling
Insulsitas...	25802	Hope to finish overhauling about
Insultador	25803	Finished overhauling the —— on ——
Insultante	25804	Require(s) complete overhauling
Insulting ...	25805	**Overlap**
Insultura ...	25806	The claims overlap
Insurgent...	25807	Do not overlap
Insusurro...	25808	The overlap amounts to an area of
Intabesco ...	25809	**Overlapped**
Intactilis ...	25810	Overlapped by
Intacto ...	25811	Not overlapped
Intagliato...	25812	Slightly overlapped
Intaille ...	25813	Not correct if shown as overlapped
Intamolare	25814	Send plan showing amount overlapped
Intanfarsi...	25815	**Overlapping**
Intantoche	25816	Shown as overlapping
Intantum ...	25817	A correct survey shows the —— claim overlapping
Intastura ...	25818	A correct survey shows no overlapping
Intavolato	25819	**Overload(ed)**
Integellus...	25820	Overloaded with
Integrante	25821	Not overloaded
Integrasco	25822	**Overlook(ed)**
Integratus	25823	Have you (has ——) overlooked
Integrizia ...	25824	Unable to overlook
Intelecto ...	25825	Will overlook
Intellego ...	25826	Do not overlook
Intemerata	25827	Has (have) not been overlooked
Intemperie	25828	**Overshot**
Intendanza	25829	**Oversight**
Intended ...	25830	Regret oversight
Intenerire...	25831	Quite an oversight
Intensidad	25832	Oversight was due to
Intentato ...	25833	**Overweight(s)**
Intentona ...	25834	Overweight(s) amount(s) to
Intentus ...	25835	**Owe(s)**
Intepidire...	25836	**Owing**
Interaneus	25837	Owing to
Intercalar...	25838	What was it (this) owing to
Intercede ...	25839	Could it have been owing to
Intercesor...	25840	Was owing to
Intercetto ...	25841	Was not owing to
Interclamo	25842	May have been owing to

Interdire ...	25843	Quite unavoidable, owing to
Intererro ...	25844	Owing to breakdown of
Interesse ...	25845	Owing to the decrease of
Interficio ...	25846	Owing to the increase of
Interieur ...	25847	**Own(s)**
Interjaceo...	25848	Do(es) not own it
Interjeter ...	25849	Would it be any advantage to own
Interlido ...	25850	Would be a great advantage to own
Interligne...	25851	Is it very necessary for you (us) to own
Interlope ...	25852	Do (does) not own the whole
Interlunio...	25853	By their own
Interluor ...	25854	Ought to own
Intermedio	25855	Who owns
Intermisto	25856	Ought we to own
Intermural	25857	We ought to own
Interniteo...	25858	**Owned**
Internonce	25859	Not owned
Interpelar...	25860	Is owned
Interpetre...	25861	Owned by
Interplico...	25862	Is (are) owned by
Interpolis...	25863	**Owner(s)** (*See also* "Behalf," "Bond," "Inform.")
Interporsi...	25864	Owner(s) is (are) short of cash
Interpresa	25865	Owner(s) is (are) practically bankrupt
Interputo...	25866	Get owner(s) to agree to
Interrasus	25867	Submit the following proposal to owner(s)
Interregno	25868	Owner(s) refuse(s) to
Interrex ...	25869	Owner(s) refuse(s) to negotiate
Interritus...	25870	Owner(s) refuse(s) to permit
Interrogar	25871	Owner(s) consent(s) to
Interrotto...	25872	Owner(s) is (are) considerably in debt
Interrumpo	25873	Owner(s) will not extend time for completion of purchase
Intersecar...	25874	Owner(s) is (are) poor and will be glad to take
Intersisto ...	25875	Owner(s) has (have) plenty of means and will certainly not
Interstruo...	25876	During time of present owner(s) [take less than
Intertexo ...	25877	Have seen the owner(s)
Intertrigo...	25878	Have had interview with the owner(s) who
Interturbo	25879	Have had interview with the owner's representative
Intervallo ...	25880	— Is the owner of —— of the property
Intervenir...	25881	Owner(s) accept(s)
Interverto...	25882	Owner(s) agree(s) to the following terms
Intervireo...	25883	Is held by —— owner(s)
Intessuto ...	25884	The owner(s) of the
Intestinal ...	25885	Owner(s) would be willing to
Intextus ...	25886	Owner(s) will accept —— cash and —— shares
Inthrall ...	25887	Owner(s) of the mine will meet you at
Intignare ...	25888	The present owner(s) of the property
Intimacion	25889	Was (were) never the owner(s)
Intimatore	25890	Whom I have ascertained is (are) practically owner(s) of the
Intimement	25891	The previous owner(s) [property
Intimidad...	25892	Who is (are) the owner(s)
Intimorire	25893	Owner(s) refuse(s) lower terms
Intinctio ...	25894	Owner(s) refuse(s) proposal of ——
Intingolo ...	25895	Owners are willing to make a reduction of —— for immediate
Intitulata ...	25896	I do not see how owners can help themselves [cash payment
Intolerant...	25897	Is property worth entertaining ? Owner here
Intonacato	25898	The owners are reputed to be wealthy
Intonatura	25899	As the owners are not by any means wealthy
Intondeo ...	25900	**Ownership**
Intone ...	25901	Private ownership
Intoppare...	25902	Under ——'s ownership

Intorneare	25903	The mine(s) has (have) frequently changed ownership
Intorniato	25904	**P**
Intorquens	25905	**Pack**
Intortus ...	25906	Pack mules
Intoxicate...	25907	To pack
Intraciso ...	25908	Shall commence to pack on
Intrafine ...	25909	A pack train
Intramento	25910	**Package**
Intramuros	25911	No package or piece to exceed
Intrandus...	25912	No package or piece to be less than
Intrasegna	25913	No package missing
Intraturus	25914	Of the package(s) is (are) missing
Intrearsi ...	25915	Owing to improper package
Intreated ...	25916	Package containing —— mailed on ——
Intreguare	25917	When was package mailed
Intremisco	25918	**Packed**
Intrepido ...	25919	Not packed
Intrescato...	25920	Packed according to instructions
Intributio...	25921	To be carefully packed
Intricate ...	25922	Packed in
Intricatus...	25923	To be packed and marked as follows
Intrigante	25924	**Paddock**
Intrigue ...	25925	At the paddock
Intrinseco...	25926	A portion of the reef in the paddock
Intrinsic ...	25927	**Page**
Intristare ...	25928	Clause —— on page ——
Intritum ...	25929	On page number
Introcludo	25930	What is number of page
Introcque...	25931	**Paid** (*See also* "Deposit," "Fine," "Forfeit.")
Introcurro	25932	Paid by
Introdotto	25933	Not paid
Introducir	25934	Still remain(s) unpaid
Introiens ...	25935	Has (have) —— paid you
Intromit ...	25936	—— has (have) paid me on your account
Introniser...	25937	Why have you not paid
Introrsum	25938	Was (were) paid on —— by ——
Introrumpo	25939	Cannot be paid until
Introverso	25940	Freight to be paid at (by)
Introvocor	25941	Has (have) already been paid
Intruders ...	25942	Has (have) not paid
Intruonare	25943	Has (have) not yet paid
Intruppato	25944	Has (have) not been paid because
Intrusive ...	25945	Has (have) paid on your account
Intubaceus	25946	Must be paid
Intueor ...	25947	Must not be paid
Intufare ...	25948	Must be paid on or before
Intuition ...	25949	Should be paid
Intumorito	25950	Should not be paid
Inturbatus	25951	To be paid
Intursium	25952	To be paid into Court
Intwist ...	25953	To be paid as follows
Inudito ...	25954	To be paid in —— instalments
Inuguale ...	25955	To be paid in advance
Inumbrans	25956	To be paid on delivery
Inumeridad	25957	Unless paid on or before delivery
Inumidire...	25958	Expenses will be paid
Inunctio ...	25959	Expenses will not be paid
Inundante	25960	Expenses to be paid by ——
Inundated	25961	Expenses to be paid by you
Inundator...	25962	I have now paid on your account a total of

Inurbano ...	25963	Please cable whether you have paid
Inusable ...	25964	Paid to-day
Inusitado ...	25965	When will it (——) be paid
Inutil ...	25966	When must it (——) be paid
Inutilizar ...	25967	Unless —— is paid beforehand
Invadeable	25968	Unless —— is paid down before you leave
Invadendus	25969	The total amount paid was
Invadir ...	25970	The total amount to be paid is
Invagarsi ...	25971	Which amount must be paid on
Invaghito ...	25972	Will require to be paid at once
Invalentia...	25973	Is reported to have paid
Invaletudo	25974	Has paid to date
Invalidad ...	25975	The men are all paid off
Invalidite ...	25976	Are the men paid and discharged
Invalorire...	25977	Mining crew not to be paid off
Invaluable	25978	Crew paid off on
Invasion ...	25979	Crew to be paid off on
Invasurus...	25980	Crew will be paid off on
Inveceria ...	25981	I have paid debts amounting to
Invectiva ...	25982	Should —— not have already paid
Invedorito	25983	Should you not have already paid
Inveggiare	25984	**Paint(ing)**
Inveighed...	25985	**Palæozoic**
Invelenire...	25986	**Palpable(ly)**
Invendible	25987	**Paltry**
Invenditus	25988	**Pamphlet**
Invenesato	25989	**Pan(s)** *(See also "Amalgamation.")*
Invenomed	25990	Pan gearing
Inventeur ...	25991	Necessary pans and gearing
Inventing...	25992	Cast-iron dies for pans
Inventora...	25993	Mullers for pans
Inventrice...	25994	Housing for pans
Invergens ...	25995	Drawing showing disposition of pans and settlers
Invernada...	25996	Cost of necessary pans
Inversely ...	25997	Power for driving pans
Investigar...	25998	By pan amalgamation
Inveterate...	25999	Cost per ton of pan amalgamation
Inveterer ...	26000	Assay of pulp entering pans
Inveziono...	**26001**	Pans with settlers
Inviamento	26002	Pans without settlers
Inviatore ...	26003	Yield from pan(s)
Invidendo...	26004	Clean-up pan(s)
Invideor ...	26005	Clean-up from pan(s) yielded
Invidietta	26006	**Panic**
Invietito ...	26007	No absolute panic
Invievole ...	26008	Owing to a panic as regards
Invigilar ...	26009	Panic on the Stock Exchange
Invigorire...	26010	Panic imminent
Inviolate ...	26011	Panic raging
Inviolatus...	26012	Panic subsiding
Inviolento...	26013	Panic still continues
Invironare	26014	Panic quite subsided
Invirtuoso	26015	Panic has caused much mischief
Inviscato ...	26016	Have been trying to produce panic
Invitandus	26017	**Panned** *(See also "Concentrates.")*
Invitatura	26018	**Pannings**
Inviting ...	26019	**Papers** *(See also "Books," "Burnt," "Deposited.")*
Invixiato ...	26020	Have found papers
Invocador...	26021	Papers mailed on
Invocated...	26022	Papers all in order

Invocation	26023	Papers lodged at
Invokingly	26024	Papers all duly signed
Involgere ...	26025	Return all the papers
Involito ...	26026	Local papers
Involtino ...	26027	Legal papers
Involucro ...	26028	Have mislaid the papers
Involutato	26029	Please send a duplicate set of papers
Involvens ...	26030	Papers will reach you about
Involvulus	26031	Deposit all papers with
Invoquer ...	26032	Shall mail on —— papers relating to
Invulgatio	26033	See notices in papers
Inweave ...	26034	There is a paragraph to this effect in the —— paper
Inwohnend	26035	**Par**
Inyungir ...	26036	Par value
Inzigare ...	26037	What is the par value
Iodate ...	26038	The par value is
Iodide ...	26039	Should shares touch par
Iodoform ...	26040	Now at par
Iotacismus	26041	Do not sell below par
Iperdulia ...	26042	Present price is par
Ipocistide...	26043	Shall I (we) buy at par
Ipocondria	26044	Am (is) buying at par
Ipocresia ...	26045	At par
Ipocritone	26046	At par or lower
Iposarca ...	26047	Can be obtained at —— below par
Ipotetico ...	26048	In order to raise the shares above par
Ippocampo	26049	Whilst the shares are above par
Ippocrene...	26050	**Parallel**
Ippogrifo ...	26051	Parallel with
Ipsemet ...	26052	Parallel to
Ipsissimus	26053	To run parallel with
Ipsola ...	26054	Runs parallel with our boundary
Iracundia...	26055	Runs parallel for a distance of —— feet
Irascencia...	26056	At right angles to a line drawn between —— and —— and
Irascens ...	26057	A parallel case [parallel to
Irascible ...	26058	Do you know a parallel case
Irefully ...	26059	Do not know a parallel case
Irenarca ...	26060	The only parallel case is that of
Irenarches	26061	**Parcel** (*See also* "Package.")
Irenicon ...	26062	A parcel of ore
Irenicus ...	26063	Parcel of ore ready for shipment —— tons
Irgendein...	26064	Shall have a parcel of ore ready for shipment on
Iricolor ...	26065	Have sold a parcel of ore weighing —— tons, realized ——
Iridium ...	26066	Have a dispute as to last parcel of ore
Irlandais ...	26067	**Pare**
Irnella ...	26068	Pare of men
Ironclads ...	26069	**Part**
Ironheart ...	26070	Part of
Ironique ...	26071	Am (is) willing to part with
Ironmaster	26072	Is unwilling to part with
Ironmould	26073	Do not part with
Ironstone ...	26074	Do not part with it (them) below
Ironware ...	26075	Shall not part with
Irradiated...	26076	Equal parts
Irradiatio ...	26077	In part payment
Irraucesco	26078	On the part of
Irredux ...	26079	Only require(s) a part of
Irreflechi ...	26080	The best part
Irregolato	26081	The greater part
Irregulier ...	26082	The lesser part

Irrenhaus ...	26083	**Partial(ly)** (*See also* "Confirm.")
Irrepertus	26084	**Participate(d)**
Irrequieto	26085	**Particular(s)** (*See also* "Description.")
Irresolute ...	26086	Mail particulars of and value
Irretito ...	26087	With all particulars
Irretortus...	26088	Full particulars were cabled on
Irreverens...	26089	Await further particulars [points
Irrgang ...	26090	I (we) want the latest and fullest particulars on the following
Irrglauber	26091	Send the fullest particulars and latest information respecting
Irrichire ...	26092	Particulars should give [—— on ——
Irridendus	26093	Will be able to give you full particulars
Irrigated ...	26094	Be very particular about
Irrigateur ..	26095	Papers with full particulars mailed
Irrigidito ...	26096	Have forwarded by mail leaving —— all the particulars you
Irriguus ...	26097	Send full particulars about it [require
Irrision ...	26098	Cannot learn any particulars
Irrisorio ...	26099	Send full particulars to —— who is at ——
Irritamen...	26100	The only particulars I (we) have relating to
Irritation ...	26101	Telegraph full particulars
Irrlehre ...	26102	Give me (us) further particulars
Irroboro ...	26103	Give me (us) further particulars as to the extent and value as
Irrogatus ...	26104	Have mailed full particulars [quickly as possible
Irrorandus	26105	Anxiously awaiting full particulars as to
Irroresco ...	26106	As soon as I can learn particulars will inform you
Irrstern ...	26107	Ascertain full particulars and cable
Irrthum ...	26108	No particulars are yet known
Irrubeo ...	26109	Give —— full particulars
Irruginito...	26110	Await additional particulars
Irrumpens	26111	Send additional particulars by mail
Irrupturus	26112	Send additional particulars by cable as soon as possible
Irrwisch ...	26113	Cannot learn any particulars whatever
Irsuzia ...	26114	Later particulars are to the effect that
Irtiola ...	26115	Refuse(s) additional particulars
Isagoge ...	26116	Cannot act without further particulars
Isagogicum	26117	Be very particular in following instructions
Ischiacus ...	26118	Be very particular in giving instructions
Ischiade ...	26119	Be very particular as to
Ischium ...	26120	If anything too particular
Ischnotes ...	26121	Was not particular enough
Iscrivere ...	26122	—— will give you all particulars
Isegrimm ...	26123	Take particular notice
Iserine ...	26124	**Particularly**
Isidoriano	26125	Most particularly
Isinglass ...	26126	Particularly as regards
Islamites ...	26127	Most particularly request you (to)
Islandlike...	26128	Generally as regards —— but particularly respecting ——
Isleta ...	26129	**Parties**
Isoamyle ...	26130	Parties doubtful of
Isobars ...	26131	Parties inclined to suspect that
Isoceles ...	26132	Other parties
Isocrona ...	26133	The parties are
Isolators ...	26134	Can you ascertain who the parties referred to are
Isolement...	26135	See if possible parties connected with
Isomeric ...	26136	Have seen all the parties connected with
Isopleuro ...	26137	Do you know the parties' names
Isopyron ...	26138	Learn from parties here that
Ispida ...	26139	Parties here prepared to
Issued ...	26140	Parties here not satisfied with
Issuing ...	26141	Delay on your part is dangerous, cannot hold parties much longer
Istactenus	26142	Parties here are said to be interested

Istantaneo	26143	Certain parties here
Istesso ...	26144	**Partly**
Isthmiacus	26145	Am (is) (are) partly
Isthmus ...	26146	Partly made up of
Istigatore...	26147	Only partly
Istinenza ...	26148	Partly true
Istiusmodi	26149	Partly false
Istorietta ...	26150	**Partner(s)**
Istorlomia	26151	Are partners
Istorsum ...	26152	Are not partners
Istratto ...	26153	Could only see —— of partners
Istrionica ..	26154	Formerly a partner with
Istruzione...	26155	Telegraph if possible names of ——'s partners
Istupidito...	26156	——, who is a partner, is now at
Itaconic ...	26157	——, who is a partner, will meet you at
Italicize ...	26158	Cannot decide in the absence of my partner
Italique ...	26159	Will decide at once on the return of my partner, whom I ex-
Iterable ...	26160	Will send partner [pect about ——
Iteration ...	26161	**Partnership**
Itinerant ...	26162	Partnership formed
Itinerario ...	26163	Partnership dissolved
Itterizia ...	26164	Notice of dissolution of partnership
Iviritta ...	26165	No legal partnership
Ivory ...	26166	**Party** (*See also* "Parties.")
Ivrognerie	26167	**Pass**
Ivygrown...	26168	To pass
Ivyplant ...	26169	To pass over
Izaga ...	26170	To pass under
Izquierdo ...	26171	Will pass under
Jabalcon ...	26172	Will pass over
Jabalina ...	26173	Better allow it to pass
Jabardear...	26174	Will pass through
Jabardillo	26175	Expects to pass through here on or about
Jabardo ...	26176	Ore pass
Jabberer ...	26177	Pass book
Jabeguero...	26178	**Passage(s)**
Jabeque ...	26179	Secure passage(s) for
Jabonado ...	26180	Have secured passage(s) for
Jabonadura	26181	Cannot secure passage(s)
Jaboter ...	26182	Passage out and home
Jacebatur...	26183	**Passed**
Jacerina ...	26184	Has (have) passed
Jachali ...	26185	Has (have) not passed
Jaciendus...	26186	Passed through here on
Jacinto ...	26187	Passed through
Jacior ...	26188	Passed over
Jaciturus ...	26189	Passed under
Jackal ...	26190	**Past**
Jackanapes	26191	In the past
Jackboots...	26192	Judging from past experience
Jackdaw ...	26193	Past all chance of recovery
Jackketch	26194	During the past few days
Jackknife ...	26195	During the past —— week(s)
Jackstaves	26196	During the past —— month(s)
Jacktowels	26197	For the past year
Jacobinism	26198	**Patch(es)**
Jacobite ...	26199	In patches
Jaconas ...	26200	The ore occurs in patches
Jacquot ...	26201	**Patent(s)** (*See also* "Claim," "Invention.")
Jactancy ...	26202	Patent notice

Jactandus...	26203	Patent claim
Jactarse ...	26204	Patent survey
Jactatrix ...	26205	United States patent
Jactitans ...	26206	Will guarantee United States patent
Jactitatio ...	26207	Have not yet obtained the patent
Jactuose ...	26208	Have not yet obtained the patent and have no advices
Jacturalis...	26209	Have not yet obtained the patent, advices are unfavourable
Jaculamen	26210	Have not yet obtained the patent but advices are favourable
Jacularis ...	26211	Patent(s) has (have) been applied for
Jaculator ...	26212	Patent(s) will be applied for
Jaculum ...	26213	Patent(s) will be guaranteed
Jadear ...	26214	What will be cost of patent
Jaecero ...	26215	Cost of patent will be about
Jagdbar ...	26216	Has (have) agreed to defray cost of patent
Jagdflinte	26217	Must secure patents for all claims
Jagdhorn ...	26218	Undertake(s) to secure patent(s)
Jagdhund	26219	Pending examination of patent(s)
Jagdrevier	26220	Patent(s) are now being examined
Jagdtasche	26221	Examination of patent(s) quite satisfactory
Jagerin ...	26222	Examination of patent(s) not at all satisfactory
Jaggedly ...	26223	Except you (——) can obtain patent(s)
Jaguadero	26224	Except you (they) (——) will guarantee patent(s)
Jaharrar ...	26225	Must insist on patent(s) being obtained
Jahlings ...	26226	No patent, only a specification filed
Jahrbuch ...	26227	No patent or specification
Jahreszeit...	26228	Patent(s) granted
Jahrgang ...	26229	Patent(s) not yet obtained
Jahrlich ...	26230	Patent(s) cannot stand if contested
Jahrmarkt	26231	Patent(s) are all in proper order
Jahrzehend	26232	Owing to a flaw as regards patent
Jahzorn ...	26233	Title to property is United States patent
Jailbird ...	26234	Will take —— month(s) to complete patent(s)
Jailfever ...	26235	Should satisfy yourself that patent conveys
Jalapa ...	26236	Do work necessary for patent
Jalbegado	26237	All work necessary for patent has been done
Jaldado ...	26238	I (we) have contracted for patent surveys
Jaletina ...	26239	**Patented**
Jaljacote ...	26240	Not patented
Jallonner...	26241	Is the property patented
Jallulo ...	26242	The property is not yet patented
Jalmero ...	26243	The property is patented
Jalousie ...	26244	The property is now being patented
Jamacuco ...	26245	The most important part of the property is not patented
Jamavas ...	26246	Is (are) the —— claim(s) patented
Jambage ...	26247	The whole of the claim(s) are patented
Jambonneau	26248	Specify which of the claims are patented
Jamborlier	26249	The following claims are patented, viz. :—
Jambrar ...	26250	The following claims are not patented, viz. :—
Jamdudum	26251	The most important claim is patented
Jamerdana	26252	Each claim is patented
Jameteria ...	26253	Advise you not to touch property unless patented
Jamila ...	26254	Cannot touch property unless patented
Jammed ...	26255	The invention is not patented
Jamona ...	26256	**Patentee(s)**
Jampots ...	26257	**Patience** (*See also* " Exercise.")
Jampridem	26258	It will be necessary to exercise considerable patience
Jamuscar ...	26259	**Patient(ly)**
Janglingly	26260	Must be more patient
Janissaire...	26261	**Pattern(s)**
Janitor ...	26262	**Pay(s)** (*See also* " Disburse," " Impossible.")

Janitrices ...	26263	Provided that —— will pay
Janitrix ...	26264	Shall I (we) offer to pay .
Jannequin	26265	Do not offer to pay
Jansenist ...	26266	Offer(s) to pay at once
Jantolina ...	26267	Pay particular attention (to)
Janvier ...	26268	Will pay particular attention (to)
Japanned ...	26269	In case of refusal to pay cable
Japanning	26270	Has (have) promised to pay on or before ——
Jappement	26271	You must not pay more than ——
Jaqueca ...	26272	Cannot pay more than
Jaquelado...	26273	Do not think can pay more than
Jaquemart	26274	Will this pay you (——)
Jaqueton ...	26275	It cannot pay
Jaquette ...	26276	Agree(s) to pay
Jaquima ...	26277	Am (are) without instructions to pay
Jarabear ...	26278	Have received instructions to pay
Jaracuo ...	26279	Do not pay any more
Jaramago...	26280	How do you (does ——) propose to pay
Jarapotear	26281	Is (are) unable to pay
Jardinage...	26282	In order to pay for assessment work
Jardinet ...	26283	On the understanding that "no cure no pay"
Jardiniere...	26284	Please pay to the order of ——
Jargonels ...	26285	Please pay this sum (the sum of ——) to
Jargonner...	26286	Would it be advisable to pay
Jarife ...	26287	Will pay for reply
Jaropar ——	26288	Provided that —— is (are) willing to pay
Jarragin ...	26289	Provided that —— do(es) not pay
Jarretiere ...	26290	To pay expenses for the month of
Jasamine ...	26291	Please cable —— to pay me (us)
Jaspeado ...	26292	Have cabled —— to pay you
Jaspeadura	26293	Who will pay expenses
Jasperate ...	26294	—— will pay expenses
Jaspoidal ...	26295	Please pay on my account (to ——)
Jattanza ...	26296	Require to pay on or before ——
Jauchzen ...	26297	Must pay
Jaugeage ...	26298	Cannot pay
Jaugeur ...	26299	Do not pay
Jaunatre ...	26300	To pay
Jaundiced...	26301	Pay to
Jaunissant	26302	Who is to pay
Jauntily ...	26303	Will not have to pay
Jaurado ...	26304	Will pay you
Javaline ...	26305	Not to pay less than —— per cent.
Jawort ...	26306	**Payable**
Jayanazo ...	26307	Any ore assaying —— is payable
Jazminorro	26308	Payable at
Jealousy ...	26309	Payable here
Jecusculum	26310	Payable to
Jedermann	26311	When and where is it payable
Jedesmal ...	26312	Payable at —— on ——
Jedoch ...	26313	How is it to be payable
Jedweder ...	26314	To be payable in fully paid shares
Jeeringly ...	26315	To be payable —— in cash and —— in fully paid shares
Jeglicher ...	26316	To be payable —— in cash; the balance of —— can remain
Jejunatio ...	26317	Payable in cash [at —— per cent. interest per annum
Jejunely ...	26318	Payable in cash; balance in bill(s) at —— months
Jejunium ...	26319	Payable in cash on documents being signed
Jellied ...	26320	Payable in —— month(s) from signing of contract
Jellybags ...	26321	Payable in —— instalments of ——
Jenabe ...	26322	Payable to the order of

Jenneting ...	26323	Payable at the bank of
Jenseitig ...	26324	To be payable
Jentaculum	26325	To be payable on
Jeopardy ...	26326	Has anything payable been met with (*See also* "Ore.")
Jerarchia ...	26327	Nothing payable has been met with as yet
Jeremiad ...	26328	A large quantity of payable stone
Jerezano ...	26329	The payable stone is confined to
Jerkingly ...	26330	This will exhaust the chances of finding payable ore in this
Jernotte ...	26331	**Payee(s)** [direction
Jerofile ...	26332	**Paying** (*See also* "Concern.")
Jerquilla ...	26333	Are you (is ——) paying attention to
Jersera ...	26334	Am (—— is) paying special attention to
Jesters ...	26335	What are you paying for
Jesting ...	26336	Am (are) now paying
Jesuita ...	26337	A dividend paying concern
Jesuitical ...	26338	A splendidly paying property
Jesuitism ...	26339	At present paying —— per cent. per annum
Jesusear ...	26340	Formerly paying
Jetblack ...	26341	Not paying cost at present time
Jettison ...	26342	By paying —— in cash
Jettyhead...	26343	**Payment(s)** (*See also* "Deferred," "Demanded," "Final.")
Jeuneur ...	26344	Enforce payment
Jewelbags...	26345	Payment refused
Jewellery ...	26346	Refused payment
Jewesses ...	26347	Payment must not be delayed
Jewsharp ...	26348	Payment cannot be made until ——
Jibboom ...	26349	To meet all payments
Jiferia ...	26350	First payment of —— due on ——. Will agree to no reduc-
Jiguilete ...	26351	Who will guarantee payment of [tion
Jijallar ...	26352	Bank guarantee(s) payment(s)
Jilosteo ...	26353	—— guarantee(s) payment(s)
Jimenzar ...	26354	What payments have you to meet before
Jingling ...	26355	The only cash payment is
Joaillier ...	26356	Stop payment of
Jobard ...	26357	Have stopped payment (of)
Joblots ...	26358	All payments to be made by
Jobmaster	26359	All payments to be made to
Jocabundas	26360	√ Arrange for immediate payment
Jocaliter ...	26361	Immediate payment absolutely necessary
Jochholzer	26362	Immediate payment very advisable
Jockeyed ...	26363	Payment should be made immediately if
Jockeyism	26364	In part payment
Jockeyship	26365	If part payment is made at once (on ——)
Jocosely ...	26366	Payment in full
Jocoseness	26367	These payments have been left undischarged
Jocosidad...	26368	Cable —— to make payment instantly [been made
Jocrisse ...	26369	⋎ Inform me by cable at once whether the (these) payments have
Joculor ...	26370	What arrangement have you made for payment
Jocundity...	26371	Must suspend payment
Jofaina ...	26372	Has (have) suspended payment
Jogging ...	26373	By deferred payments
Jogtroter ...	26374	For what cash payment
Jogtroting	26375	**Pay Ore** (*See also* "Ore.")
Johnodory	26376	**Pay roll** (*See also* "Cost sheet(s).")
Joignant ...	26377	What is the amount of pay roll for month of
Joinhand ...	26378	Pay roll amounts to
Jointheir ...	26379	Duplicate of pay roll
Jointress ...	26380	Monthly pay roll
Jointstool...	26381	**Pay-streak** (*See also* "Gold," "Streak.")
Jointure ...	26382	The pay-streak has entirely died out

Jokishly ...	26383	The pay-streak averages —— per ton, the average width is ——
Jollyboat ...	26384	Pay-streak is well defined
Jolthead ...	26385	What is the width of the pay-streak at
Jonchaie ...	26386	The width of the pay-streak is ——
Jonchets ...	26387	What is the average width of pay-streak
Jonglerie ...	26388	What is the average value of pay-streak
Jongleurs...	26389	**Peculate**
Jonjoli ...	26390	**Peculation**
Jonquil ...	26391	**Peculiar(ly)**
Jorgina ...	26392	**Penalty(ies)**
Jornalero ...	26393	No penalty
Jorobado ...	26394	What is the penalty
Joselasar ...	26395	Legal penalty is
Jostrado ...	26396	**Pending**
Jouable ...	26397	Pending further advice
Journal ...	26398	Pending arrival of
Journalist ..	26399	Pending more complete particulars
Jovenado ...	26400	Pending more complete instructions
Jovial ...	26401	Pending legal decision
Jovialidad	26402	Pending erection of
Joviality ...	26403	Pending settlement of arbitration
Joyeusete...	26404	Pending settlement of
Joyfully ...	26405	Pending completion of necessary formalities
Joyousness	26406	Pending completion of arrangements
Joyuela ...	26407	Now that it (this) is so long pending
Juaguarzo	26408	Which is now pending
Juanete ...	26409	**Penetrate(d)**
Juanetudo	26410	Has (have) been completely penetrated with
Juardoso ...	26411	**Penetration**
Jubelfeier	26412	To prevent penetration of (by)
Jubeln ...	26413	**Pennyweight(s)** (*See also* Table at end.)
Jubeor ...	26414	About one pennyweight
Jubertar ...	26415	Less than one pennyweight
Jubeteria ...	26416	Pennyweights per ton of 2,000 lbs.
Jubilacion	26417	Pennyweights per ton of 2,240 lbs.
Jubilar ...	26418	1 pennyweight per ton
Jubonero ...	26419	1½ pennyweights per ton
Juchoir ...	26420	2 pennyweights per ton
Jucunditas	26421	2½ pennyweights per ton
Jucundor ...	26422	3 pennyweights per ton
Judaique ...	26423	3½ pennyweights per ton
Judaismus	26424	4 pennyweights per ton
Judaizante	26425	4½ pennyweights per ton
Judaskuss	26426	5 pennyweights per ton
Juderia ...	26427	5½ pennyweights per ton
Judgeship	26428	6 pennyweights per ton
Judgment ..	26429	6½ pennyweights per ton
Judicante...	26430	7 pennyweights per ton
Judicassit...	26431	7½ pennyweights per ton
Judicatory	26432	8 pennyweights per ton
Judicatrix	26433	8½ pennyweights per ton
Judiciario...	26434	9 pennyweights per ton
Judicieux ...	26435	9½ pennyweights per ton
Judihuelo...	26436	10 pennyweights per ton
Judisch ...	26437	10½ pennyweights per ton
Jueguecico	26438	11 pennyweights per ton
Jugadera ...	26439	11½ pennyweights per ton
Jugalis ...	26440	12 pennyweights per ton
Jugarius ...	26441	12½ pennyweights per ton
Jugarreta...	26442	13 pennyweights per ton

Jugatorius	26443	13½ pennyweights per ton
Jugend ...	26444	14 pennyweights per ton
Jugendlich	26445	14½ pennyweights per ton
Jugendzeit	26446	15 pennyweights per ton
Jugerum ...	26447	15½ pennyweights per ton
Jugglery ...	26448	16 pennyweights per ton
Juglaresa ...	26449	16½ pennyweights per ton
Jugosidad	26450	17 pennyweights per ton
Jugoso ...	26451	17½ pennyweights per ton
Juguete ...	26452	18 pennyweights per ton
Jugulandus	26453	18½ pennyweights per ton
Jugularis ...	26454	19 pennyweights per ton
Jugumentum	26455	19½ pennyweights per ton
Juiceless ...	26456	—— ounce(s) —— pennyweights per ton
Juillet ...	26457	—— ounce(s) —— pennyweights —— grains per ton
Juiverie ...	26458	**Penthouse**
Jujubier ...	26459	Until a penthouse has been constructed
Julianise ...	26460	Shall fix penthouse in position on
Julica ...	26461	**Per**
Julienne ...	26462	Per contra
Jumbling ...	26463	Per day
Jumeau ...	26464	Per week
Jumelos ...	26465	Per month
Jumentil ...	26466	Per annum
Juncetum ...	26467	Per foot
Junciana ...	26468	Per fathom
Juncino ...	26469	Per ton
Juncturus ...	26470	As per
Junculus ...	26471	**Per cent.** (*See also* "Assay," "Gold.")
Jungendus	26472	1 per cent.
Jungfrau ...	26473	1¼ per cent.
Junglada ...	26474	1½ per cent.
Jungles ...	26475	1¾ per cent.
Juniors ...	26476	2 per cent.
Juniperus ...	26477	2¼ per cent.
Junketing	26478	2½ per cent.
Junquera ...	26479	2¾ per cent.
Junquitos ...	26480	3 per cent.
Juntador ...	26481	3¼ per cent.
Juntorio ...	26482	3½ per cent.
Juramentar	26483	3¾ per cent.
Jurandum	26484	4 per cent.
Juratoria ...	26485	4¼ per cent.
Jurdia ...	26486	4½ per cent.
Jurejuro ...	26487	4¾ per cent.
Jurgiosus ...	26488	5 per cent.
Juridico ...	26489	5¼ per cent.
Jurugo ...	26490	5½ per cent.
Jurulentus	26491	5¾ per cent.
Jurymast ...	26492	6 per cent.
Jurymen ...	26493	6½ per cent.
Jusbarba ...	26494	7 per cent.
Jusquesito	26495	7½ per cent.
Jusquiame	26496	8 per cent.
Jussionem	26497	8½ per cent.
Justamente	26498	9 per cent.
Justesse ...	26499	9½ per cent.
Justicia ...	26500	10 per cent.
Justiciero ...	26501	10½ per cent.
Justificar ...	26502	11 per cent.
Justissime ...	26503	12 per cent.
Justitium ...	26504	13 per cent.
Juttingly ...	26505	14 per cent.
Juvaminis ...	26506	15 per cent.
Juvandus ...	26507	16 per cent.
Juvaturus ...	26508	17 per cent.
Juvenalis ...	26509	18 per cent.
Juvenculus	26510	19 per cent.
Juvenesco ...	26511	20 per cent.
Juvenile ...	26512	25 per cent.
Juventud ...	26513	30 per cent.
Juwelier ...	26514	35 per cent.
Juxtaposer	26515	40 per cent.
Juzgante ...	26516	45 per cent.
Kabeltau ...	26517	50 per cent.
Kachelofen	26518	55 per cent.
Kaffeehaus	26519	60 per cent.
Kaffeesatz	26520	65 per cent.
Kahlheit ...	26521	70 per cent.
Kahmig ...	26522	75 per cent.
Kaiserin ...	26523	80 per cent.
Kaiserthum	26524	85 per cent.
Kalbfell ...	26525	90 per cent.
Kalbleder ...	26526	95 per cent.
Kaltblutig	26527	100 per cent.
Kaltsinn ...	26528	Per cent. per annum
Kamille ...	26529	Per cent. above
Kammerche	26530	Per cent. discount
Kammergut	26531	Per cent. of
Kammerrath	26532	Per cent. of moisture
Kammertuch	26533	Per cent. of loss

Kammsetzer	26534	Per cent. of profit
Kampfen ...	26535	This is equal to a saving of —— per cent.
Kampfplatz	26536	In my (our) experiments I (we) have succeeded in obtaining
Kangaroo ...	26537	**Percentage(s)** [—— per cent. of the gold
Kanguruh	26538	Percentage of ore
Kaninchen	26539	Percentage of metal
Kannevas ...	26540	What percentage are you figuring on
Kanzellist...	26541	Figuring upon a percentage of
Kaolinite ...	26542	A considerable percentage (of)
Kapaun ...	26543	A moderate percentage (of)
Kapelle ...	26544	A small percentage (of)
Kaperbrief	26545	The percentage figures are
Kappzaum	26546	What percentage will it yield
Karglich ...	26547	Will yield a percentage of
Karrengaul	26548	The percentage results show
Karrner ...	26549	Owing to the low percentage of
Kartoffel ...	26550	Which will increase the percentage of —— to ——
Kaseform ...	26551	What is the percentage composition
Kasemilbe	26552	The percentage composition is
Kasserne ...	26553	What percentage of the value of the ore do (did) you obtain
Kastanie ...	26554	**Perceptible(ly)**
Kasteien ...	26555	If perceptible
Kattun ...	26556	Not perceptible
Kaufherr	26557	Unless perceptible
Kaufladen	26558	**Peremptory(ily)**
Kauflente...	26559	Was very peremptory
Kaufmann	26560	Instructions are peremptory
Kebsweib ...	26561	Are instructions peremptory
Keckheit ...	26562	Instructions not peremptory
Kedger ...	26563	**Perfect(ed)**
Keelhauled	26564	As soon as perfect
Keelson ...	26565	Not quite perfect
Keeneyed ...	26566	As nearly perfect as possible
Keepsake ...	26567	**Perfectly**
Kegelbahn	26568	Perfectly well
Kegeln ...	26569	Perfectly understand
Kegelspiel	26570	It must be perfectly understood (that)
Kehlkopf ...	26571	It is perfectly understood that
Kehraus ...	26572	**Perforate(d)**
Kehren ...	26573	Perforated plates
Kehrseite ...	26574	**Perform(ed)**
Keinerlei ...	26575	So as to perform
Kelchglas...	26576	To perform
Kellerei ...	26577	Cannot perform
Kellnerin ...	26578	Will perform all that was promised
Kennbar ...	26579	Would not promise anything which he could not perform
Kennels ...	26580	**Perhaps**
Kerbstone	26581	Whether perhaps
Kermesse ...	26582	Perhaps —— might
Kernobst ...	26583	Or perhaps
Kernspruch	26584	If not —— perhaps ——
Kettledrum	26585	**Peril(ous)(ly)**
Ketzerei ...	26586	**Permanent(ly)**
Ketzerisch	26587	Permanent plant
Keuschheit	26588	Permanent plan of
Keyboard ...	26589	As soon as a permanent plan has been decided upon
Keyhole ...	26590	**Permian**
Keyseating	26591	**Permissible**
Keystones ..	26592	**Permission**
Kickshaw ...	26593	Grant permission for

Kidnappers	26594	Obtain permission for examination by
Kidneys ...	26595	Obtain permission for inspection by
Kielholen ...	26596	Who am I to apply to for permission to
Kielwasser	26597	Get permission from (for)
Kienfackel	26598	Permission to see mine refused to all
Kienholz ...	26599	Can I (we) grant permission to
Kienruss ...	26600	Permission cannot be granted
Kiessand ...	26601	Obtain permission
Kilderkin ..	26602	Will not grant permission
Kilndried ...	26603	Better refuse permission
Kilnshaped	26604	Has (have) refused permission
Kilogram ...	26605	Do not give permission
Kindbett ...	26606	Has (have) already granted permission
Kinderfrau	26607	Request(s) permission to
Kindermagd	26608	Without asking permission
Kindeskind	26609	You have full permission (to)
Kindheit ...	26610	Has (have) given permission to
Kindling ...	26611	Get permission for —— to examine
Kindtaufe	26612	Refuse(s) permission
Kinetics ...	26613	Will readily grant permission
Kingcraft...	26614	Give permission for
Kingcup ...	26615	Give permission for examination by
Kingfisher	26616	Give permission for visit to
Kingsevil ...	26617	**Permit(s)**
Kinkingly	26618	Permit —— to
Kinnbacken	26619	Will not permit me (us) to see mine
Kinnkette	26620	Will not permit me (us) to see mine or works
Kinnlade ...	26621	Will you permit
Kinswoman	26622	Cannot permit
Kiosque ...	26623	Will permit
Kippered ...	26624	Is it advisable to permit
Kirche ...	26625	It is not advisable to permit
Kirchengut	26626	Can you obtain a permit for —— to ——
Kirchgang	26627	Can you give —— a permit to
Kirchspiel	26628	Do not permit
Kirchthurm	26629	Do not permit inspection by
Kirren ...	26630	In case you cannot permit
Kirschbaum	26631	Please permit —— to have full access to
Kirschkern	26632	Please permit —— to examine and report on
Kitchens ...	26633	In order to permit of easy access to
Kittiwake	26634	Permit —— to see works
Kitzelig ...	26635	Permit —— to inspect mine
Kladde ...	26636	**Permitted**
Klaftern ...	26637	Cannot be permitted
Klagbar ...	26638	Is not permitted
Klagerin ...	26639	**Perpendicular(ly)**
Klammern	26640	**Persevere**
Klatsche ...	26641	Advise you strongly to persevere
Klausner ...	26642	Cannot advise you to persevere
Kleberig ...	26643	To persevere
Klecksen ...	26644	**Persist(ed)(ing)**
Kleeblatt ...	26645	If you are convinced that there is good in persisting
Kleesalz ...	26646	**Person**
Kleesaure...	26647	Each person
Kleiden ...	26648	**Personal** (*See also* "For.")
Kleinheit ...	26649	Is a personal friend of
Kleinlaut ...	26650	Stated he was a personal friend of
Kleinlich ...	26651	From personal knowledge
Kleinmuth	26652	From personal inspection
Kleister ...	26653	Have you (has ——) any personal interest at all

Klempner...	26654	**Personally**
Klettern ...	26655	Personally what is your opinion
Klimatisch	26656	Personally my opinion is
Klingklang	26657	Personally I am against
Klippig ...	26658	Personally I am strongly in favour of
Klippklapp	26659	Personally I have no knowledge of
Klopfen ...	26660	You had better see —— (him) personally
Klopplerin	26661	Have seen —— (him) personally
Klotzig ...	26662	In case you cannot attend to this personally
Klugelei ...	26663	Shall be attended to personally
Klugheit ...	26664	If it is for yourself personally
Klumperig	26665	If it is not for yourself personally
Klumpfuss	26666	For myself personally
Klystier ...	26667	Personally I am satisfied (that)
Knacken ...	26668	Personally I am not at all satisfied (that)
Knackwurst	26669	Do not know personally and cannot ascertain anything reliable
Knallerbse	26670	**Persuade(d)**
Knapsack...	26671	Endeavour to persuade
Knaupeln...	26672	Cannot persuade
Knauserig	26673	Cannot you persuade —— to
Knavery ...	26674	Has (have) persuaded
Knavishly	26675	Has (have) not persuaded
Knebeln ...	26676	**Peter**
Knecht ...	26677	Looks as if it would peter out
Kneeholly	26678	**Petered**
Kneepan ...	26679	Has quite petered out
Kneipzange	26680	**Petering**
Knickerig...	26681	Is petering out rapidly
Knicknack	26682	Petering out
Knieband...	26683	**Petition(s)**
Kniefall ...	26684	To petition
Kniekehle...	26685	Petition to
Kniestuck	26686	Preparing to petition
Knifeboxes	26687	To petition government (authorities)
Knightly ...	26688	When will you present petition
Knirps ...	26689	Petition was presented on ——
Knirschen	26690	Petition will be presented on ——
Knistern ...	26691	Since the presentation of the petition
Knittable...	26692	Petition local authorities for
Knoblauch	26693	Am (are) about to petition local authorities for
Knopfloch	26694	As soon as petition is granted
Knorpelig...	26695	Petition has been granted
Knotgrass	26696	Should petition be refused
Knotted ...	26697	Petition has been refused
Knottiness	26698	A joint petition
Knowledge	26699	Present counter petition
Knuckled...	26700	Oppose petition as much as you possibly can
Knuffen ...	26701	Support ——'s petition
Kobold ...	26702	Suggest that you petition against
Kochbuch...	26703	Cannot support the petition of
Kochkunst	26704	The petition has been dismissed with costs [own costs
Kochloffel	26705	The petition has been dismissed, but each party to bear their
Kochsalz ...	26706	The petition has been dismissed, the company to pay costs
Kochtopf ...	26707	**Petroleum**
Kohler ...	26708	Borehole has tapped petroleum at a depth of —— feet
Kohlrabi ...	26709	The petroleum is good quality
Kokette ...	26710	The petroleum is only fair
Kokettiren	26711	The strata is very favourable for petroleum
Komiker ...	26712	**Pick(s)** (*See also* "Gad.")
Komodiant	26713	To pick

Konigin ...	26714	Pick out
Koniglich...	26715	Pick up
Konigthum	26716	If you can pick up
Konkurs ...	26717	Impossible to pick out
Kopfhanger	26718	Miners' picks
Kopfkissen	26719	**Picked**
Kopfputz ...	26720	Picked up by
Kopftuch ...	26721	Numbers —— to —— are picked stones, the remainder are
Kopiren ...	26722	Not picked in any way [average samples
Korkzieher	26723	Of picked ore
Kornahre ...	26724	Picked specimens
Kornblume	26725	The samples were all picked
Kornboden	26726	They are all picked men
Kornchen...	26727	Men should be carefully picked
Kornrose ...	26728	**Picker**
Kornwurm	26729	**Pillar**
Korperbau	26730	Pillar of ground
Korperlich	26781	Pillar of ore
Korpermass	26732	If we remove pillar
Korperwelt	26733	Shall have to leave a pillar of ground
Kostbar ...	26734	Unless we leave a pillar of ground
Kostganger	26735	**Pinch(ed) (ing)**
Kostlich ...	26736	We have passed through the pinch in the vein; it has now
Krabbeln ...	26737	**Pioneer** (*See also* "Exploration.") [opened out to —— feet
Krachzen ...	26738	Pioneer level
Kraftigen...	26739	As a pioneer level
Kraftmehl	26740	To drive No. —— as a pioneer level
Kraftsuppe	26741	**Pipe(s)**
Krahenauge	26742	Have completed pipe line to
Krahwinkel	26743	What diameter of pipes do you require
Krakeel ...	26744	The pipes should be —— diameter
Kramerei ...	26745	Could bring in a line of pipes from
Krampfhaft	26746	Hydraulic pipes burst
Kranich ...	26747	Owing to leak in pipes
Krankheit	26748	Pipe line
Krankung	26749	Steam pipes
Kranzchen	26750	Steel pipes
Kratzfuss	26751	Spiggot and faucit pipes
Krause ...	26752	—— feet of wrought iron pipes
Krauskohl	26753	—— feet of cast iron pipes
Krawall ...	26754	—— feet of steel pipes
Krebsgang	26755	**Piping**
Kreditiren	26756	**Piston**
Kreisamt ...	26757	Piston rings
Kreisel ...	26758	**Pit(s)**
Kreislauf ...	26759	Only a shallow pit
Kreislinie...	26760	The vein has been tested by numerous shallow pits
Kreisstadt	26761	**Pitch(es)**
Kreuzfeuer	26762	Pitches south
Krenzgang	26763	Pitches north
Kreuzigen	26764	Pitches east
Kreuzweg...	26765	Pitches west
Kreuzweise	26766	**Pitman(men)**
Kriegsfuss	26767	Require a good pitman
Kriegsrath	26768	Is an excellent pitman
Kritisch ...	26769	Send good pitman as soon as possible
Kritisiren...	26770	**Pitwork**
Krittlich ...	26771	The pitwork is all in good order
Kritzeln ...	26772	The pitwork would require some slight repairs
Kronanwalt	26773	The pitwork is old

rongut ...	26774	The pitwork is now completed to a depth of
ronprinz	26775	Cost of new pitwork would amount to
ronung ...	26776	Destroying the pitwork in the shaft for a depth of
ropfgans	26777	Shall commence to fix pitwork in shaft on
rumelig ...	26778	When will you have the new pitwork placed in the shaft
rummstab	26779	**Place(s)**
uchlein ...	26780	Place(s) for
ugelfest...	26781	Can you place
ugelform	26782	Can place
uheuter ...	26783	Cannot place
uhlfass ...	26784	Who would you suggest in place of ——
uhlofen ...	26785	Have no one at present who could fill ——'s place
uhltrank	26786	Believe —— would be competent for the place
uhlung ...	26787	Who will take your (——'s) place
uhmilch...	26788	—— will take my (——'s) place
uhnheit ...	26789	Shall you require anyone to take —— (his) place
ulisse ...	26790	Shall not require anyone in —— (his) place
ummerlich	26791	Ought to have someone at once in place of ——
ummervoll	26792	Where shall you place
undigen...	26793	Could you place any of the shares? If so, how many
unftig ...	26794	Could place —— shares
unstler ...	26795	What sum could you place
unstreise	26796	I think —— could place
unstwerk	26797	In several places
upferig ...	26798	At the following places
upplerin	26799	At each place
urassier...	26800	At what (which) place(s)
urbiss ...	26801	To this place
urschner	26802	Later on would propose to place
urzathmig	26803	When would you propose to place
urzlich ..	26804	Could place immediately
urzweilen	26805	In place of
utscher ...	26806	To take the place of the present
utschiren	26807	The nearest place is
yanize ...	26808	The place is very suitable for
yrielle ...	26809	The place is altogether unsuitable for
Labascor	26810	Place very little credit in
Labbiale ...	26811	To be substituted in place of
Labbrone ...	26812	To place
Labdace ...	26813	Places all here in a very unsatisfactory position
Labecula ...	26814	**Placed**
Labefacio ...	26815	What amount (number) have you placed
Labeffitto ...	26816	I (we) have placed
Labeonem...	26817	Have not placed any
Laberinto...	26818	How many shares have you placed
Labially ...	26819	Has (have) already placed —— shares
Labiernago	26820	Badly placed
Labiosus ...	26821	Well placed
Laborador	26822	Could be readily placed at this moment
Laborante...	26823	Might be placed at about
Laboratory	26824	To be placed
Laborear ...	26825	To be placed at or near
Laboremur	26826	This has placed me (us)
Laborieur...	26827	**Placer** (*See also* "Hydraulic.")
Laborifer ...	26828	Placer ground
Labourable	26829	Placer working(s)
Labouring	26830	A placer claim
Labradero	26831	Property comprises —— placer claims
Labranza ...	26832	Placer deposit(s)
Labratum...	26833	**Placing**

Labriego ...	26834	For placing this (it)
Labrusca ...	26835	Commission for placing the property
Labsal ...	26836	**Plain(ly)**
Laburnum	26837	Send in plain words
Lacargama	26838	Send in plain figures
Lacayuelo...	26839	**Plaintiff(s)**
Lacchetta ...	26840	**Plan(s)** (*See also* " Elevation.")
Lacciola ...	26841	Send rough plan
Lacerable ...	26842	Sketch plan
Lacerandus	26843	Send plan showing position of
Laceration	26844	Plan is perfectly feasible
Laceratore	26845	What are your plan(s) for
Laceratrix	26846	Please mail progress plans and sections to date
Lacerioso ...	26847	Plans were mailed on ——
Lacernulam	26848	Plans will be mailed on ——
Lacerosus...	26849	Have received plans but you have not shown
Lacertulus	26850	Plan(s) showing —— mailed
Lacessens ...	26851	Will mail plans showing what you require on ——
Lacessitus	26852	Letter explaining plans forwarded on ——
Lacessor ...	26853	Send tracing of your mine plan (showing)
Lacewoman	26854	Send tracing of your plan and section
Lachanisso	26855	Have prepared plan and section of mine
Lachanum	26856	I think your best plan would be (to)
Lacheln...	26857	My plan would be to
Lacherlich	26858	From the plan(s) supplied
Lachrymal	26859	Has (have) rendered it necessary to change plans
Lachter ...	26860	Keep me advised of any change of plan(s)
Laciniado...	26861	Seem(s) to have changed his (their) plan(s)
Laciniatim	26862	Mail at earliest moment possible plan(s)
Lacivioso ...	26863	Plans very misleading
Lackaday ...	26864	Reliable plan very much wanted
Lackbrain	26865	Shown on the plan sent you on ——
Lackiren ...	26866	Should not be shown on any plans issued to the public
Lackwit ...	26867	There are practically no plans at all
Laconic ...	26868	Do you wish me to plan
Laconique	26869	Better plan everything so that
Laconism ...	26870	Will plan everything so that
Lacotomus	26871	On the plan received
Lacquer ...	26872	Has altogether upset my plans
Lacrear ...	26873	Mail plan of proposed works
Lacrimando	26874	I (we) will finish plans as soon as possible
Lacrimetta	26875	That the plan is perfectly sound
Lacris ...	26876	Can you devise some plan by which
Lacrymosus	26877	Cannot devise any plan by which
Lactainic ...	26878	Plans not arrived
Lactancia ...	26879	Have plan corrected (to)
Lactario ...	26880	On your plan
Lactatote ...	26881	On official plan
Lactavisse	26882	**Plant** (*See also* " Engine.")
Lacteous ...	26883	Machinery and plant at
Lacteribus	26884	Complete plant including everything necessary (for)
Lacticinio..:	26885	What plant is there
Lacticolor...	26886	A very efficient plant (consisting of)
Lactifagos	26887	The plant is very poor
Lactifero ...	26888	All the plant
Lactoid ...	26889	Does schedule include all the plant
Lactometer	26890	Plant not included in schedule
Lactucula...	26891	Not including plant.
Lactumen...	26892	All the plant is in very fair order
Laculatus...	26893	General condition of plant is very poor

Laculor ...	26894	The plant is practically worn out
Lacunavit	26895	Plant is very much crowded
Lacunosam	26896	A complete schedule of the plant
Lacusculus	26897	Entirely new plant
Lacustre ...	26898	Expenditure on plant will amount to
Lacuturris	26899	The cost of the necessary plant
Laddering	26900	Proceeding with erection of plant
Ladderway	26901	With present plant
Ladeado ...	26902	The plant necessary for
Ladenpreis	26903	Complete air compressing plant with ——drills
Ladestock	26904	Complete air compressing plant consisting of
Ladiernago	26905	The whole of the plant (at)
Ladovunque	26906	Would not be advisable to put in permanent plant at present
Ladramente	26907	Concentrating plant should be capable of dealing with
Ladrerie ...	26908	Owing to limited capacity of plant
Ladrillado	26909	Would increase the capacity of plant to
Ladrillera	26910	Amalgamation plant
Ladronaja	26911	Concentration plant
Ladronesco	26912	Dressing plant
Ladruccio...	26913	Smelting plant
Ladybird ...	26914	**Plat**
Ladylike ...	26915	Cutting plat
Ladyship ...	26916	Plat of 　　　　　　　　　[additional in the shaft
Laedebatur	26917	Shall commence cutting plat as soon as we have sunk —— ft.
Laedendus	26918	We have been employed in cutting plat
Laedetur ...	26919	Shall start at once to cut plat
Laedevant	26920	**Platform(s)**
Laedimini	26921	**Platinum**
Laedistis ...	26922	Have samples examined for platinum
Laesuram...	26923	Samples sent contain platinum
Laffette ...	26924	Samples sent do not contain platinum
Laganoso ...	26925	Considerable quantities of platinum
Lagarejo ...	26926	Platinum is found along with
Lagartado	26927	Platinum has been found on the property
Lagartija ...	26928	What is the present price of platinum
Laggingly	26929	**Pledge**
Laghettino	26930	Do not pledge yourself
Lagnarsi ...	26931	Will you pledge yourself
Lagnevole...	26932	Cannot pledge myself (ourselves)
Lagonam ...	26933	**Pledged**
Lagopus ...	26934	Pledged to
Lagrimable	26935	Are you in any way pledged
Lagrimear	26936	Am (are) absolutely pledged to
Lagrimetta	26937	Am (are) absolutely pledged to do this
Laguncula	26938	Not pledged in the slightest
Lagunero ...	26939	**Pleistocene**
Lahmung ...	26940	**Plentiful(ly)**
Laical ...	26941	Is there a plentiful supply of
Laichen ...	26942	There is a plentiful supply of
Laichzeit ...	26943	The supply is not very plentiful
Laidamente	26944	Is very plentiful
Laideur ...	26945	Is not very plentiful
Laidezza ...	26946	Do not expect a plentiful supply before
Lainage ...	26947	When we may expect a plentiful supply
Lainerie ...	26948	**Plenty**
Laitance ...	26949	Plenty of
Laldabile ...	26950	Can you obtain plenty of
Laldatore ...	26951	Can obtain plenty of
Laldotto ...	26952	There is still plenty of space for
Lalisionem	26953	Which will leave plenty of space for

Lambebas...	26954	**Pliocene**
Lambel ...	26955	**Plunder(ed)**
Lambente...	26956	Plundered to the extent of
Lambiccare	26957	**Plunger** (*See also* "Pump.")
Lambiner ...	26958	Plunger lift
Lambitivo	26959	Plunger pump
Lambitum	26960	Plunger pole
Lambkin ..	26961	Plunger pole case
Lambourde	26962	Plunger pump —— inches diameter, —— ft. stroke
Lambrequin	26963	What is the speed of plunger
Lambrisser	26964	Plunger makes —— strokes per minute
Lambrusca	26965	Give diameter of plunger and length of stroke
Lambswool	26966	**Plural**
Lamedura...	26967	**Plus** (*See also* "Minus.")
Lamellate...	26968	It is plus (the)
Lamentable	26969	Is it plus (the)
Lamentanza	26970	It is not plus (the)
Lamentato	26971	Should be plus
Lamented	26972	Must be plus
Laments ...	26973	Plus cost of
Lameplatos	26974	Plus commission
Lameron ...	26975	Plus out of pocket expenses
Lametada...	26976	Plus charges for
Lamiente ...	26977	Plus depreciation
Laminated	26978	Plus the following
Laminatojo	26979	—— + ——
Laminera ...	26980	**Plutonic**
Laminosus	26981	**Pocket**
Lamiscar ...	26982	Out of pocket expenses
Lamiznero	26983	Pocket of
Lampacear	26984	Pocket of ore (*See also* "Ore.")
Lampadaire	26985	We have taken —— tons from one pocket
Lampadis...	26986	Every indication of a nice pocket of ore at this place
Lamparin ...	26987	**Pockety** (*See also* "Ore.")
Lamparista	26988	The vein is a very pockety one
Lampasado	26989	A pockety vein
Lampblack	26990	**Point(s)**
Lampenruss	26991	At what point
Lampetra ...	26992	At this point
Lampiste ..	26993	At the point of contact
Lamplight	26994	Points to
Lampooning	26995	Points to the same conclusion
Lampoons	26996	On the following points
Lamprey ...	26997	At the several points
Lamproie ...	26998	**Pointblank**
Lampsana	26999	Refuse(s) pointblank
Lampuga ...	27000	Pointblank whether
Lampurus	**27001**	Ask —— pointblank
Lampwick	27002	Did you ask —— (him) pointblank
Lanapena ...	27003	Did not ask pointblank
Lancearius	27004	Ask(ed) pointblank
Lanceheads	27005	**Policy(ies)** (*See also* "Insurance.")
Lanceola ...	27006	As a matter of policy
Lancetadas	27007	Pending a change of policy on the part
Lancettina	27008	The present policy of the Board is to
Lanchar ...	27009	Shall I renew policy(ies)
Lanchonero	27010	Fire policy(ies)
Lanciabile	27011	Will attend to insurance policy(ies)
Lanciarsi ...	27012	Insurance policy(ies)
Lanciatore	27013	Insurance policy(ies) has (have) expired

Lancifer ...	27014	Insurance policy(ies) expire(s) on
Lancinante	27015	Insurance policy(ies) expire(s) on —— shall I renew
Lancinatus	27016	**Poll**
Lanciotto ...	27017	Has (have) decided to take a poll
Lancoir ...	27018	What has been the result of the poll
Lancurdia	27019	—— shareholders polled their votes in favour of
Landagents	27020	—— shareholders polled their votes against
Landbau ...	27021	A poll has been taken with the result that
Landbirds	27022	Avoid a poll if possible
Landesherr	27023	Impossible to avoid a poll
Landeuge ...	27024	Transfers must be registered two months prior to a poll
Landgrave	27025	So as to control poll [control poll
Landgut ...	27026	Sign transfers leaving transferee's name in blank so as to
Landhaus	27027	We are practically sure to win in case of a poll
Landkarte	27028	We are practically sure to lose if a poll is demanded at the
Landlaufer	27029	It is very unwise to risk a poll [present time
Landlied ...	27030	**Pool**
Landlubber	27031	Pool has been formed to buy
Landpartie	27032	Pool has been formed to sell
Landplage	27033	**Poor** (*See also* " Grade," " Quality.")
Landrath ...	27034	Every end is at present poor
Landrilla ...	27035	Generally the ends are poor
Landscape	27036	Generally the ends are not so poor
Landslip ...	27037	Not quite so poor
Landstrich	27038	The returns are very poor
Landsturm	27039	The returns for the present month will be poor
Landtax ...	27040	Too poor to pay
Landvolk ...	27041	Very poor offer
Landwein...	27042	Very poor
Landwirth	27043	The prospect is a very poor one (of
Laneria ...	27044	The show is only poor
Lanestris ...	27045	**Poorer**
Langage ...	27046	If anything poorer
Langaruto	27047	Not poorer
Langmuth	27048	If poorer
Langoureux	27049	Unless poorer
Langouste	27050	**Poppet heads**
Langsamer	27051	At the poppet heads
Langstens	27052	Have erected poppet heads
Language	27053	For the poppet heads
Languebam	27054	Timbers for the poppet heads
Languente	27055	**Porphyry(itic)**
Languesco	27056	A dyke of porphyry
Languidez	27057	The hanging wall is porphyry
Languidore	27058	The footwall is porphyry
Languor ...	27059	The country rock is porphyry
Languria ...	27060	**Port(s)**
Laniamento	27061	The nearest port is
Laniarium	27062	What is the nearest port for
Lanicutis ...	27063	Port charges
Lanificio ...	27064	There are several convenient ports
Lanionius	27065	There is no port
Lanipendia	27066	**Portable**
Lanosorum	27067	Portable boiler
Lantejuela	27068	Portable engine
Lanternajo	27069	Portable engine and boiler
Lanternfly	27070	Semi-portable
Lanternier	27071	Would not be sufficiently portable
Lanternone	27072	**Portion** (*See also* " Part.")
Lanuggine	27073	What portion can you secure

Lanzadera	27074	Have been able to secure you a portion
Lanzon ...	27075	As my (our) portion
Lanzuela ...	27076	Am offered a portion of
Lapachar ...	27077	A considerable portion of which
Lapathum	27078	Consent(s) to retain a large portion
Lapdog ...	27079	Will give up a portion of
Lapelled ...	27080	For one half portion
Lapereau ...	27081	For one third portion
Lapicidina	27082	For one fourth portion
Lapidabant	27083	From the upper portion of the mine
Lapidandi...	27084	From the lower portion of the mine
Lapidaria ...	27085	In the lower portion of
Lapidatote	27086	In the upper portion of
Lapidavers	27087	Into —— equal portions
Lapidavit ...	27088	Only a very small portion of which
Lapidemini	27089	The greater portion of which
Lapideo ...	27090	Take(s) as his (their) portion
Lapidifico...	27091	**Position(s)** (*See also* "Legal.")
Lapidosus...	27092	Inform —— of the position of affairs
Lapizar ...	27093	Have informed —— of the position of affairs
Lapjoints ...	27094	Shall I inform —— of the position of affairs
Lappaceus	27095	Do not inform anyone of the position of affairs
Lappern ...	27096	Cable present position of affairs
Lappolone	27097	The position has very much improved
Lapstone ...	27098	What is the position of
Lapsurus ...	27099	The position is serious
Lapwork ...	27100	The position is difficult but not serious
Laquais ...	27101	Position practically hopeless
Laqueato ...	27102	In a very dangerous position
Laquelle ...	27103	The position of
Laqueolus	27104	Judging from the present position of the (this) affair
Larbason ...	27105	Cable any change in the position
Larcenies ...	27106	Cable any serious change in the position to —— immediately
Lardaccio ...	27107	Position not altered in any way
Lardarium	27108	Cable if —— is in a position to
Lardaruolo	27109	Cable when you are in a position to
Lardatojo ...	27110	Are you in a position (to)
Lardellare...	27111	Am (are) not in a position (to)
Lardoire ...	27112	Am (are) in a position to
Largement	27113	When I (we) hope to be in a position to
Largess ...	27114	What position have you taken up in the matter of
Larghetto...	27115	My position is this
Larghita ...	27116	Cannot understand the position of
Largificus...	27117	In order to strengthen my (our) position
Largitas ...	27118	What is the position held by ——
Largitorem	27119	Decline(s) the position of
Largitrice...	27120	I should be in a position
Largomira	27121	This (it) is ready to be lowered into position
Largueado	27122	Present position intolerable
Laricino ...	27123	**Positive**
Larifugam	27124	Is not at all positive
Larigot ...	27125	Is quite positive that
Laringe ...	27126	Is —— quite positive that
Larmglocke	27127	Are you positive that
Larmier ...	27128	I am (we are) positive
Larmoyant	27129	Cannot be positive until
Larruped ...	27130	Without being positive I believe
Larvosus ...	27131	Is (are) positive
Laryngean	27132	As soon as I am (we are) positive
Laryngitis	27133	As soon as anything positive is known (arranged)

Lasamento	27134	Nothing positive is at present known (arranged)
Lascar ...	27135	If you are positive
Lasciarsi ...	27136	If you are not positive
Lascibile ...	27137	In the absence of positive proof
Lascito ...	27138	Something positive should be settled
Lascivanza	27139	Unless you are quite positive
Lascivete ...	27140	**Possession** (*See also* "Got.")
Lascivia ...	27141	Possession will be given
Lasciviens	27142	When will possession be given
Lascivulus	27143	Possession cannot be given until
Laserpicio	27144	Who is now in possession
Lasquenete	27145	Am now in legal possession
Lassamini...	27146	Is (are) now in possession
Lassantur...	27147	Did you get possession
Lassativo ...	27148	Demand immediate possession
Lassatote ...	27149	Cannot obtain possession of
Lassavisse	27150	Refuse(s) to give possession of
Lassemur ...	27151	Possession will be given in exchange for
Lassescit ...	27152	From papers now in my (our) possession
Lassezza ...	27153	Possession of
Lassitude ...	27154	In possession of
Lassreis ...	27155	Not in possession
Lassulus ...	27156	Hope to be in possession of all information shortly
Lasterhaft	27157	Possession undisputed
Lastermaul	27158	Put —— in possession of all information
Lastimoso	27159	—— is in possession of full information
Lastretta ...	27160	Retain possession whatever you do
Lastricato...	27161	Will retain possession at all costs
Lastrone ...	27162	**Possibility**
Lastthier ...	27163	Is hardly a possibility
Lastwagen	27164	Is only the merest possibility
Lasurblau	27165	Not likely to become more than a possibility
Latanier ...	27166	The only possibility
Latchkeys	27167	Is there any possibility of
Latebram...	27168	There is no possibility
Latebroso...	27169	**Possible(ly)**
Lateramen	27170	Would it be possible to
Lateraria ...	27171	It is not possible at present
Laterculum	27172	Is it possible
Laterensis	27173	If possible
Lateritius...	27174	If not possible
Laternula...	27175	If this is not possible please cable
Laterones...	27176	If this is not possible you had better
Lathebed ...	27177	Do you think it possible
Lathechuck	27178	No longer possible
Latialis ...	27179	As promptly as possible
Latibulo ...	27180	As much as possible
Laticlavis...	27181	As soon as it is possible
Latifolius	27182	When it should be possible to
Latigadera	27183	When will it be possible to
Latiguear ...	27184	The earliest moment possible
Latinidad...	27185	**Post** (*See also* "Mail.")
Latinisme...	27186	Altogether unfitted for the post
Latinuccio	27187	Do you care to apply for the post of
Latitantes	27188	For the post of
Latitatio ...	27189	Have missed the post leaving
Latitudine	27190	Should reach you by the post due about
Latomus ...	27191	In course of post
Latonero ..	27192	Now in the post
Latrabam ...	27193	**Postal**

Latrabrent	27194	Postal address
Latratore ...	27195	Postal facilities
Latravero ...	27196	**Posted** (*See also* "Keep.")
Latrines ...	27197	Specification posted on ——
Latrocinio	27198	Keep me (us) posted up as regards any change
Latronem...	27199	Keep me (us) well posted up as regards affairs
Latschen ...	27200	**Postpone**
Lattajuolo	27201	To postpone
Lattermath	27202	Postpone until
Latteruolo	27203	Postpone action
Lattich ...	27204	Do not postpone
Lattimoso...	27205	Can you postpone
Lattovaro ...	27206	Unable to postpone later than
Laturarius	27207	Unable to postpone meeting later than
Latwerge ...	27208	Shall I (we) postpone
Laubholz ...	27209	Postpone leaving until
Laubig ...	27210	Will postpone leaving until
Laubsage ...	27211	Postpone alterations to
Laudabilis	27212	**Postponed**
Laudable ...	27213	Postponed until
Laudandus	27214	Must be postponed
Laudativus	27215	Was postponed through
Laudatore	27216	Is to be postponed owing to
Laudemio	27217	Is to be postponed until
Laudevole...	27218	Stands postponed
Laufbahn ...	27219	Examination must be postponed
Laufend ...	27220	Underground work may be postponed until
Lauffeuer ...	27221	**Postponement**
Laufgraben	27222	**Pound(s)** (*See* Table at end.)
Laugen ...	27223	Pounds per ton
Laugensalz	27224	Pounds of
Laughable	27225	Only a few pounds weight
Laughing...	27226	**Powder** (*See also* "Cartridge," "Explosive.")
Launched	27227	Giant powder
Laundress	27228	As soon as I can obtain any powder
Launque ...	27229	No powder to be obtained nearer than
Laureando	27230	Powder magazine
Laureate ...	27231	**Power** (*See also* "Horsepower.")
Lauredal ...	27232	If it is in your (——'s) power
Laureled ...	27233	It is not in my power
Laureolam	27234	It is in the power of —— to
Laurezione	27235	It is in ——'s power
Laurices ...	27236	It is not in —— 's power
Lauricomo	27237	Is in the power of
Laurigera...	27238	Is not in the power of
Lautenzug	27239	Is —— of sufficient power
Lauterkeit	27240	Is (are) not of sufficient power
Lavabris ...	27241	Is (are) of sufficient power
Lavacapo ...	27242	Not of sufficient power for my (our) purpose
Lavacaras	27243	Has (have) no power
Lavacias ...	27244	Has (have) considerable power
Lavacrum...	27245	Has (have) considerable power in the district
Lavadura ...	27246	Should be of ample power for (to)
Lavamanos	27247	Will be of ample power
Lavandiere	27248	Will require machinery of more power
Lavaplotos	27249	Will require much more power
Lavareto ...	27250	What power will you require
Lavativo ...	27251	Have you sufficient power
Lavatorio	27252	Will then give me (us) sufficient power for
avatrice ...	27253	To develop sufficient power to

Lavaturus	27254	**Power Drills** (*See also* "Drill.")
Lavazione...	27255	**Power of Attorney** (*See also* "Attorney," "Power of
Laveggio ...	27256	Cable if you require Power of Attorney [Attorney," page 56.)
Lavender ...	27257	Mail Power of Attorney
Lavendola	27258	Cable name in full in which Power of Attorney is to be made
Lavernio ...	27259	Give Power of Attorney to [out
Lavishness	27260	Have you mailed Power of Attorney
Lavoraccio	27261	Apply to —— for Power of Attorney
Lavoratura	27262	Have given —— Power of Attorney
Lavoretto ...	27263	Power of Attorney mailed on
Lavoriera ...	27264	Power of Attorney mailed on —— appointing ——
Lawbook ...	27265	Power of Attorney too limited
Lawine ...	27266	Power of Attorney mailed in favour of —— on ——
Lawlords ...	27267	Will mail Power of Attorney within next —— days
Lawmaker	27268	Will mail Power of Attorney at once ,
Lawmonger	27269	Shall you require Power of Attorney before you can act
Laxamento	27270	Power of Attorney cancelled
Laxandus...	27271	Power of Attorney mailed does not cover
Laxidad ...	27272	Power of Attorney should provide for
Laybrother	27273	Power of Attorney recovered
Layclerk ...	27274	Duplicate Power of Attorney mailed on ;——
Layetier ...	27275	Power of Attorney to be made out in name of
Layfigure ...	27276	In the absence of Power of Attorney
Lazareto ...	27277	Pending arrival of Power of Attorney
Lazarillo ...	27278	Who holds Power of Attorney
Lazarlike ...	27279	**Practicable**
Lazeggiare	27280	Is it practicable (to
Lazulite ...	27281	It is practicable
Lazzeretto	27282	It is not practicable
Leadashes	27283	Please say whether you consider it (this) practicable
Leadminer	27284	It might be practicable (if)
Leafless ...	27285	As soon as it is practicable
Leafstalk ...	27286	When will it be practicable (to)
Leakages ...	27287	I do not think it is practicable
Lealmente	27288	**Practical(ly)**
Lealtad ...	27289	If practical
Leapfrog ...	27290	Practically all
Leapyear ...	27291	Practically none
Learnedly...	27292	**Practice**
Leaseholds	27293	Follow the usual practice
Leather ...	27294	What is the usual practice
Lebbrolina	27295	The usual practice is to
Lebeche ..	27296	This is not the general practice
Lebemann	27297	The practice is generally
Lebendig ...	27298	**Pre-Cambrian**
Leberthran	27299	**Precaution(s)**
Leberwurst	27300	What precautions have you taken against
Lebewohl...	27301	Have taken ample precautions
Lebhaft ...	27302	Take every precaution against (as regards)
Lebkuchen	27303	Every precaution has been taken to secure
Lebraston...	27304	In spite of every precaution
Lebzeiten ...	27305	Owing to neglect of proper precautions
Lecanoric...	27306	Take every precaution to check
Leccamento	27307	Take every precaution against "salting"
Leccardo ...	27308	Take every precaution to avoid interference
Leccatore ...	27309	**Precedent(s)**
Lecchetto...	27310	What precedent is there for ——
Lecconcino	27311	No precedent
Lecconeria	27312	According to precedents
Lechada ...	27313	**Preceding**

Lechefrite	27314	In preceding clause (paragraph)
Lechoso ...	27315	See preceding
Lechugado	27316	**Precise(ly)**
Lechzen ...	27317	Be most precise
Leckerhaft	27318	In precise terms
Leckermaul	27319	Cable precisely what happened
Lecticario,...	27320	**Preclude(s)**
Lecticula ...	27321	To preclude
Lectitalus...	27322	Will preclude
Lectoria ...	27323	Will not preclude
Lectulus ...	27324	Will this (it) preclude me (us) from
Lecythus ...	27325	**Precluded**
Ledgers ...	27326	**Precluding**
Lediglich ...	27327	**Predominate(ing)**
Leerheit ...	27328	**Prefer** (*See also* " Like.")
Leeringly ...	27329	Prefer to
Leeshore ...	27330	Do not prefer to
Leeside ...	27331	Very much prefer to
Leeward ...	27332	Telegraph which (what) you (——) prefer(s)
Lefthand ...	27333	Would prefer (to)
Legaccio ...	27334	Would prefer at present to
Legaggione	27335	Would you prefer
Legajo ...	27336	Would not prefer
Legalidad...	27337	I (we) would prefer that
Legalised ...	27338	In case you should prefer
Legamoso...	27339	If possible should prefer
Legarium ...	27340	Should have preferred giving no opinion until
Legarsi ...	27341	Prefer that you should act as you think best
Legataire ...	27342	**Preferable(ly)**
Legatarius	27343	**Preference**
Legatine ...	27344	Have no preference, leave matter entirely with
Legativum	27345	In preference shares
Legatorio ...	27346	Have issued preference shares amounting to
Legaturina	27347	What dividend do the preference shares carry
Legendario	27348	The preference shares carry a dividend of
Legerement	27349	In order to pay dividend on preference shares
Legerete ...	27350	**Prejudice(ial)**
Leggendajo	27351	Avoid creating a prejudice
Leggiaccia	27352	Must be without prejudice
Leggiadro...	27353	Am gradually overcoming prejudice
Leggiere ...	27354	Owing to native prejudice
Leghenne ...	27355	Without prejudice
Legicrepa...	27356	Without prejudice to my (our) claim
Legierung...	27357	There is a great prejudice against
Legionario	27358	There is a great prejudice in favour of
Legirupa ...	27359	**Preliminary(ies)**
Legista ...	27360	Legal preliminaries
Legitimate	27361	As a preliminary (to)
Legitimist	27362	As a preliminary test
Legnaggio	27363	As a necessary preliminary
Legnajuolo	27364	In the preliminary stage
Legnerello	27365	Merely preliminary
Legorizia ...	27366	Preliminary contract agreed to
Legracion...	27367	As soon as the preliminary work is completed [with
Leguleius ...	27368	As soon as the necessary preliminaries have been complied
Legulejo ...	27369	Preliminaries to be complied with are only of a formal nature
Legumineux	27370	**Premature**
Legumiste	27371	Do not be premature
Lehenbar ...	27372	Would it not be premature at the present time (to)
Lehenfrei ...	27373	Somewhat premature

ehengut ...	27374	Owing to the premature discharge of
ehenherr	27375	**Prematurely**
ehenrecht	27376	Do not act in any way prematurely
ehensmann	27377	In my (our) opinion has (have) acted prematurely
ehmgrube	27378	**Premise(s)**
ahmig ...	27379	**Premium**
ehnen ...	27380	Extra premium
ehnsessel	27381	Require an extra premium of
ehramt ...	27382	What is the premium
ehrerin ...	27383	At a premium of
ehrjahre...	27384	Sell when they reach —— premium
ehrling ...	27385	Are expected to reach —— premium
ehrreich...	27386	Are already at a premium
ehrsaal ...	27387	The premium is too heavy
ehrstunde	27388	The premium is not sufficient
eibarzt ...	27389	Premium is fictitious
eibbinde...	27390	Premium is not fictitious
eibhaftig	27391	Premium will not last
eibrente ...	27392	Except at a premium
eibrock ...	27393	**Prepaid**
eibwache	27394	Need not be prepaid
eichenzug	27395	Must be prepaid
eichnam...	27396	**Preparation(s)**
eichtlich	27397	We are now making preparations (for)
eichtsinn	27398	We are now making preparations for opening out at
eidwesen	27399	**Prepare**
eihhaus ...	27400	To prepare
eimruthe	27401	Prepare to
eimsieder	27402	Prepare —— for
einsamen	27403	Prepare everything for
einweber	27404	Prepare as quickly as possible
eiostreum	27405	Before I (we) can prepare
eistung ...	27406	So as to prepare
eisurely ...	27407	What will you require to prepare for
eitfaden ...	27408	You should prepare for (to)
eithammel	27409	It is necessary for me (us) to prepare
eitriemen	27410	**Prepared**
eitstern ...	27411	Prepared for
eitton ...	27412	Are you prepared to accept offer of
ejedumbre	27413	Am (are) not prepared to (for)
ejivial ...	27414	Am (are) quite prepared to (for)
ejuelos ...	27415	Cable as soon as you are prepared
embulus	27416	Am (are) not quite prepared
emniscus	27417	You should be prepared for —— (the)
emonade	27418	Everything is prepared and in readiness for ——
emonrind	27419	Has (have) prepared to (for)
emosin ...	27420	When I shall be prepared to
endel ...	27421	Be prepared to
endenlahn	27422	**Preparing**
endiculus	27423	Am (are) now preparing so as to
endinella	27424	Preparing for (to)
endinoso	27425	**Preponderate(ing)**
endore ...	27426	The former preponderating
endrera ...	27427	The latter preponderating
engthily...	27428	**Presence**
enguarada	27429	My (——'s) presence essential
enguaraz	27430	Your (——'s) presence very desirable
enguear ...	27431	Unless my presence is essential
enguetero	27432	**Present(s)**
eniendus	27433	At present

Leniente ...	27434	For the present
Lenificar ...	27435	Not at present
Lenitive ...	27436	Up to the present
Lenitudo ...	27437	At the present time
Lenizar ...	27438	As things are at present
Lenksam ...	27439	Do not stop at present
Lenocinio...	27440	Shall stop for the present
Lenonius ...	27441	That may present itself
Lentaggine	27442	Should anything present itself
Lentandus	27443	Nothing presents itself at this moment
Lentarsi ...	27444	**Presented**
Lentejuela	27445	Has (have) not been presented
Lenticchia	27446	Was (were) presented on
Lenticular	27447	Unless already presented
Lentilleux	27448	As soon as presented
Lentiscal ...	27449	**Preserve(d)**
Lentisque...	27450	To preserve
Lentitud ...	27451	Preserve silence as long as possible
Lentoidal ...	27452	Must be preserved
Lentulus ...	27453	Can no longer be preserved
Lenzato ...	27454	**President**
Lenzuelo ...	27455	Who is the president of
Leoncello ...	27456	The president is
Leonessa ..	27457	The president and chief officials are in favour of
Leonine ...	27458	The president and chief officials are antagonistic to
Leontice ...	27459	Who has the ear of the president
Leonuro ...	27460	The present president of the company
Leopardine	27461	**Press(ed)**
Leopidium	27462	Am (are) at present pressed for time
Leopidotes	27463	Press for settlement
Lepidezza...	27464	**Pressing**
Lepidolite	27465	Pressing for
Leporajo ...	27466	**Pressure**
Leporarium	27467	What is the pressure
Leporinus...	27468	To stand a pressure of
Lepreria ...	27469	Average pressure in cylinder
Lepreux ...	27470	Average working pressure
Leproserie	27471	Maximum pressure
Leprosidad	27472	Minimum pressure
Leprosy ...	27473	—— lbs. to the square inch pressure
Leprottino	27474	Now working at a pressure of —— lbs. to the square inch
Leprously...	27475	**Presumably**
Lepusculi...	27476	**Presume**
Lerciare ...	27477	To presume
Lesepult ...	27478	May I (we) presume
Leserlich ...	27479	May presume that
Lesestunde	27480	If you hear nothing further you may presume that
Leseubung	27481	**Pretence**
Lesewelt ...	27482	On pretence that
Lesinerie ...	27483	**Pretext**
Lesineux ...	27484	The pretext was
Lessatura ..	27485	Under the pretext of
Lessened ...	27486	**Prevail**
Lessive ...	27487	Can you prevail on —— (him) to
Lesueste ..	27488	Cannot prevail on —— (him) to
Letamajo ...	27489	Try to prevail on —— (him) to
Letaminato	27490	Hope to prevail on —— (him) to
Letania ...	27491	Unless you can prevail on —— (him) (them) to
Letavero ...	27492	**Prevent(s)**
Letavisse ...	27493	To prevent

Lethalis ...	27494	Prevent him (——)
Lethaliter ..	27495	Cannot prevent
Lethargic ...	27496	Endeavour to prevent
Lethean ...	27497	Unable to prevent
Lethificus...	27498	Impossible to prevent
Leticoso ...	27499	In order to prevent
Letifero ...	27500	In order to prevent loss of time
Letiggine ...	27501	Must do all you can to prevent
Letiziante...	27502	Unless can prevent
Letraderia	27503	Which will prevent my (our)
Letrina ...	27504	Endeavour to prevent formation of
Lettaccio ...	27505	Until weather prevents
Letterario...	27506	The greatest possible care will have to be taken to prevent
Letteretta ..	27507	Difficulties have arisen which will prevent
Letterone ...	27508	**Prevented**
Letteruzza	27509	Unless prevented by,
Letticello ...	27510	Have been prevented by
Lettiera ...	27511	Could have been prevented if
Lettuccino	27512	Impossible to have prevented
Letztere ...	27513	Have been prevented through
Letzthin ...	27514	This (which) has prevented me from
Leucanthes	27515	Block on railway prevented arrival of
Leucaspide	27516	Block on railway prevented dispatch of
Leuchtgas	27517	**Preventing**
Leucocruta	27518	**Prevention**
Leucoion ..	27519	**Previous**
Leuconotus	27520	The previous
Leumund ...	27521	What occurred previous to
Leutessa ...	27522	The only thing previous was
Leutselig ...	27523	Previous to
Levaldina...	27524	Previous to this
Levamine ...	27525	Since the previous
Levandus ...	27526	Was (were) the previous owner(s)
Levantada	27527	By the previous
Levarsi ...	27528	This was previous to
Levatura ...	27529	Against the previous
Leveche ...	27530	On a previous occasion
Leveret ...	27531	**Previously**
Leviathan...	27532	Was not previously
Levidensis	27533	Long previously
Levigar ...	27534	As previously reported
Levigated ...	27535	Has (have) not previously
Levitico ...	27536	Previously examined by
Levitique ...	27537	Does not appear to have been previously examined by
Lexico ...	27538	**Price(s)** (*See also* " Bedrock," " Changed," " Cost," " Dear,"
Lexiconic ...	27539	Closing prices [" Fall," " High," " Rise.")
Leyenda ...	27540	A fall in price(s) is imminent
Lezarder ...	27541	Be prepared for a fall in prices
Lezioncina	27542	At the price named
Liaison ...	27543	At this price
Liancha ...	27544	About the price
Liarder ...	27545	Beyond this price
Libaminis...	27546	What is the price (of)
Libanotis ...	27547	Price prohibitive
Libarius ...	27548	Must reduce the price
Libation ...	27549	Will he (——) come down in price
Libatorium	27550	Will not come down in price
Libecciata	27551	Expect an advance in price
Libelar ...	27552	Last price is fully maintained
Libellista ...	27553	Lowest price for —— is ——

Libellous ...	27554	At present price
Libenter ...	27555	Cable present price of
Libentina...	27556	The price asked is
Liberalize...	27557	Cable prices for my private information
Liberandus	27558	Prices show upward tendency
Liberatore	27559	Prices show downward tendency
Liberavit ...	27560	Prices merely nominal
Libercolo ...	27561	Prices unchanged
Liberrimo...	27562	What do you (does ——) consider a fair price
Libertad ...	27563	I (——) consider(s) —— a fair price
Libertate ...	27564	Is the price reasonable
Liberties ...	27565	The price asked is reasonable
Libertine ...	27566	The price asked is too high
Libiconoto	27567	Price asked excessive considering that
Libidine ...	27568	Reserve price
Libidinous	27569	The reserve price is
Libistio ...	27570	There is no reserve price
Libitum ...	27571	The highest price paid was ——
Libonotus...	27572	The lowest price paid was ——
Libraccio ...	27573	Ascertain lowest price
Libraino ...	27574	At lowest price possible
Librairie ...	27575	Dear at any price
Libralis ...	27576	Endeavour to get price reduced
Librarium	27577	The price now asked is
Libremente	27578	Bedrock price
Libreria ...	27579	Mine price
Libretto ...	27580	Prices may go up again
Libripens ...	27581	Prices may go down again
Liburnica...	27582	At what price have you bonded ..
Licenciado	27583	At what price have you sold
Licencieux	27584	Is well worth (the money) price asked
Licensed ...	27585	Is not worth (the money) price asked
Licenziare	27586	Now fetching good prices
Lichen ...	27587	What is the price asked
Lichtbild ...	27588	What price do you want for
Lichterloh	27589	What is (are) to-day's price(s) for
Lichtglanz	27590	Would get a good price at this moment
Lichtmesse	27591	What price can I go to
Lichtputze	27592	What is your price f.o.b. for
Lichtseite...	27593	What is your price c.f. for
Lichtvoll ...	27594	What is your price c.i.f. for
Licinus ...	27595	What is your price ex ship for
Licitador ...	27596	What is your price on rails at
Licitatrix ...	27597	What is your price delivered at
Licitezza ...	27598	Price f.o.b.
Liciturus ...	27599	Price c.f.
Lickerish ...	27600	Price c.i.f.
Licopodio ...	27601	Price ex ship
Licorista ...	27602	Price on rails at
Licoroso ...	27603	Price delivered at
Lictorius ...	27604	Let me know your private idea as to price
Licuable ...	27605	Send prices and particulars
Liebaugeln	27606	Send price list(s) for (of)
Liebesgott	27607	Better wait for improved prices
Liebhaber...	27608	Better wait for lower prices
Liebkosen...	27609	So as to bring down the price of the stock
Lieblos ...	27610	In order to run up the price
Liebraston	27611	In order to run down the price
Liebreich ...	27612	The price of the shares has run up on account of
Liebschaft	27613	The price of the shares has run down entirely through

Liederlich...	27614	The effect will be to run down the price
Lieferung...	27615	The effect will be to run up the price
Liegemen ...	27616	At what price can you buy out lessee(s)
Liencecico	27617	At what price can you negotiate
Lienicus ...	27618	**Prill(s)**
Lientera ...	27619	Prills weigh
Lieutenant	27620	**Primarily**
Lievitare ...	27621	**Primary**
Lifeblood ...	27622	**Principal(ly)**
Lifebuoy ...	27623	The principal points
Lifegiver ...	27624	Is the principal owner of
Lifeguard...	27625	Have seen the principal owner(s)
Lifelessly ...	27626	Have examined the principal points of interest
Lifelike ...	27627	One of the principal men at
Lifetime ...	27628	**Principle**
Liftingly ...	27629	On principle
Ligaculum	27630	On what principle
Ligadas ...	27631	**Print(ed)**
Ligagamba	27632	Now in print
Ligamento	27633	Has appeared in print
Ligature ...	27634	**Private(ly)**
Ligellum ...	27635	Private information
Ligereza ...	27636	Private opinion
Lighters ...	27637	Ascertain and inform me privately
Lighthouse	27638	For your private information I may tell you
Lightning	27639	Have learned privately that
Lightsome	27640	What is your private address
Ligistrare...	27641	My private address is
Lignarium	27642	What is your private opinion (of)
Ligneux ...	27643	My private opinion is (that)
Lignipes ...	27644	Keep this private until you hear from
Ligomela ...	27645	This must be kept quite private
Ligonizo ...	27646	This is strictly private and confidential
Liguilla ...	27647	**Probability**
Ligurio ...	27648	Consider and report by cable on the probability of
Liguritor ...	27649	What probability is there that —— is ——
Ligustico ...	27650	No probability whatever
Likelihood	27651	**Probable**
Lilacbush...	27652	Probable value
Lilactree ...	27653	Probable cost
Lilacwood	27654	Is this at all probable
Liliacco ...	27655	Is it probable that
Lilietum ...	27656	It is very probable
Lilyhands...	27657	Not very probable
Limabile ...	27658	As soon as it appears probable
Limande ...	27659	It appears very probable now that
Limatezza	27660	It does not seem very probable that
Limatula ...	27661	**Probably**
Limberness	27662	Is probably
Limbicco ...	27663	May probably
Limekiln ...	27664	Will be here (at ——) probably on (by)
Limepits ...	27665	**Procedure**
Limicola ...	27666	Consult —— as to the best procedure
Liminare ...	27667	—— cannot advise as to procedure
Liminium...	27668	Procedure is illegal
Limiste ...	27669	Procedure is perfectly legal
Limitaneus	27670	Procedure will be to
Limitrofe ...	27671	What is the legal procedure
Limning ...	27672	**Proceed**
Limonadier	27673	To proceed

Limoncello	27674	Proceed immediately (to)
Limonera ...	27675	Can you proceed at once
Limoniates	27676	Can proceed immediately
Limoniere...	27677	Can proceed immediately if you obtain permission of
Limoscapo	27678	Cannot proceed to —— before
Limosna ...	27679	Will proceed as instructed
Limpiadera	27680	Do you mean me to proceed to —— before
Limpidetto	27681	You need not now proceed with
Limpidite	27682	Instruct —— to proceed to (with)
Limpidness	27683	Cable as soon as you are ready to proceed
Limpieza ...	27684	Am (are) now ready to proceed
Limpingly	27685	Shall be ready to proceed about
Limpion	27686	If you are ready to proceed go at once
Limure ...	27687	Unless you are ready to proceed not later than
Linagista...	27688	Shall I proceed alone
Linajuda ...	27689	You had better not proceed without
Linaloe ...	27690	Do not proceed to —— unless you are satisfied
Linamen ...	27691	Cannot proceed to
Linceul ...	27692	In case —— should refuse to proceed
Lindano ...	27693	Refuse(s) to proceed
Linderung	27694	Must proceed immediately with
Lindeza ...	27695	Proceed very cautiously with
Lineage ...	27696	When I shall proceed to
Linealis ...	27697	You will have to proceed with great tact
Lineatura	27698	Proceed to —— to take over ——
Linfatico ...	27699	**Proceeding(s)** (*See also* " Defend," " Legal.")
Lingerie ...	27700	Do (does) not advise proceedings as could not recover expenses
Lingering ...	27701	At the present stage of the proceedings
Lingote ...	27702	**Proceeds**
Linguaccia	27703	Gross proceeds
Linguadro	27704	Net proceeds
Lingual ...	27705	Proceeds of
Linguatus	27706	Proceeds of sale
Linguist ...	27707	What are the estimated proceeds
Lingulaca...	27708	The proceeds amount to
Linimentum	27709	The proceeds will be sufficient to
Linipulus...	27710	Telegraph proceeds of ——
Linkboy ...	27711	Proceeds of the —— amount to
Linking ...	27712	**Process(es)**
Linkisch ...	27713	The process is very tedious
Linositas ...	27714	The process will be very tedious
Linotte ...	27715	What is your experience of the —— process
Linquendus	27716	My experience of the —— process is (that)
Linseed ...	27717	Tried the —— process but rejected it
Linstock ...	27718	Employ the —— process extensively
Linteamen	27719	The process has hitherto given very indifferent results
Lintean ...	27720	The process is very costly
Lintearius	27721	Is the process suitable for us
Linterna ...	27722	The process is not suitable
Lintiggine	27723	The process is not at all new
Liocorno ...	27724	The process possesses great merit
Liofante ...	27725	By this (which) process
Lionlike ...	27726	Can you test the process
Lipiria ...	27727	Said to employ the —— process
Lipotimia...	27728	Visit —— and inspect the —— process
Lippidoso...	27729	What process do you suggest
Lippiens ...	27730	**Procure**
Lipservant	27731	To procure
Liquabilis	27732	Procure as much as possible
Liquare ...	27733	Procure as soon as possible

iquativo ...	27784	**Procured**
iquefacer	27785	Have procured a new
iquefarsi	27736	**Produce**
iquefying	27737	What will you be able to produce
iquesco ...	27738	Expect to be able to produce
iquidable	27739	Hope shortly to produce
iquidez ...	27740	Should produce
iquirizia...	27741	When I (we) shall be able to produce
iquoretto	27742	Estimated produce
iquorice ...	27743	Cannot produce
iquoriste	27744	**Produced**
iressa ...	27745	Have produced
iripipium	27746	Have produced during the past —— days
irondo ...	27747	Have produced during the past week
iscezza ...	27748	Have produced during the past month
isciatore...	27749	Have produced per week
iserage ...	27750	Have produced per month
iseron ...	27751	**Producer(s)**
isible ...	27752	Producer gas
isimaquia	27753	Large producer(s) of
isirvite ...	27754	Was formerly a very large producer
isongero...	27755	Unless can secure co-operation of main producers
isonjear ...	27756	Producers are suspicious
ispeln ...	27757	**Production**
issoir ...	27758	Production has been very large
isteado ...	27759	How have you estimated production
istener ...	27760	Production based upon
istening ...	27761	Production will be increased to
istlessly ...	27762	To increase the production
istoneria	27763	Cannot increase production until (unless)
itacion ...	27764	To maintain present rate of production
itamaccia	27765	Rate of production
itargirio...	27766	What is your estimate of production
iterarius...	27767	Production for the current month will probably exceed
iteratura	27768	What has been your total production since
iterero ...	27769	**Profit(s)** (*See also* "Expect," "Income," "Narrow.")
ithanicus	27770	Divide all profits equally
ithocolla...	27771	We will split the profits
ithotomus	27772	What are the gross profits
itiere ...	27773	The gross profits are
itigante ...	27774	What is net profit after payment of all expenses
itigatrix...	27775	Net profit after payment of all expenses
itigieux ...	27776	What is net profit to company
itofago ...	27777	Net profit to company
itografia...	27778	What profit are the mines now yielding per month
itoralis ...	27779	What is last month's profit
itoricus ...	27780	Profit for last month
itotomia...	27781	Please cable estimated month's profit
itteraire ...	27782	Estimated profit
itteram ...	27783	Estimated profit —— per ton
ittlego ...	27784	Profit will be at least
ituraris ...	27785	Estimated profit for month(s) (of)
iturgic ...	27786	What profit will there be
iturgus ...	27787	No profit at all
ivellare ...	27788	What profit has there been
ivelong ...	27789	A profit of
iveried ...	27790	Not sufficient profit
iverwort...	27791	What is the margin of profit
iveryman	27792	Profit will not exceed
ivescere ...	27793	In calculating profit have you allowed for

Liviandad...	27794	No reliable data for calculating profit
Livianos ...	27795	At what rate do you estimate the profits
Lividastro	27796	Unless you can see your way to make a profit
Lividezza ...	27797	In order to make a profit
Lividness ...	27798	At a profit of
Lividulus...	27799	Leaving a profit of
Liviritta ...	27800	Leaves no profit
Livraison...	27801	Leaves too small a profit
Lixabunda	27802	Have been working at a profit since
Lixiviate ...	27803	Profit since
Lizardlike	27804	Is said to have made a profit
Llagador ...	27805	Which will leave a considerable profit
Llamada ...	27806	Will show a profit of
Llamativo...	27807	Estimated profit not less than
Llamazar ...	27808	Revised estimate of profit
Llanten ...	27809	The net profit for the year
Lloriquear	27810	Ore blocked out should yield a profit of
Lloronas ...	27811	Is (are) receiving large profits from the mine
Llovediza...	27812	Profit and loss account
Lloviznar ...	27813	**Progress** *(See also " Good.")*
Lluvioso ...	27814	Progress of drivages
Loable	27815	Progress of
Loadstar ...	27816	Making good progress
Loafingly ...	27817	Making fair progress
Loafsugar	27818	Making poor progress
Loanda ...	27819	Now making rapid progress
Loathfully	27820	What progress have you made (in) (with)
Loathness...	27821	Hope soon to make some progress against
Lobanillo ...	27822	Are you making any progress with
Lobbyists...	27823	We are making good progress with
Lobezno ...	27824	Have made no progress as yet
Lobgesang	27825	Telegraph immediately the progress you have made (with) (at)
Lobpreisen	27826	Good progress is being made with this (it) (at)
Lobredner	27827	Can you not increase progress
Lobuno ...	27828	Will endeavour to increase progress
Lobworms	27829	What is the present rate of progress
Locabamur	27830	Good progress is being made in all departments
Locabunt ...	27831	Make all the progress you can
Localidad...	27832	Progress has become slower
Localist ...	27833	This will materially accelerate our progress
Localiter ...	27834	Our slow progress is owing to
Localmente	27835	Next week we hope to make better progress
Locandiere	27836	Cable progress of
Locandus...	27837	General progress
Locarium ...	27838	Very little progress has been made here owing to
Locataire ...	27839	Also report progress you have made with
Locatote ...	27840	Progress at —— appears very slow
Locaturus...	27841	Our progress will continue slow until
Locavisse ...	27842	Cable on —— what progress you have made up to that date
Locellaris ...	27843	Cable on —— what progress you anticipate making up to ——
Locherig ...	27844	Cable progress and when complete cable
Lockage ...	27845	Will cable progress from time to time
Lockerheit	27846	**Prohibit(ed)**
Lockgates...	27847	Has it (have they) been prohibited
Lockjaw ...	27848	Has (have) been prohibited
Locksides...	27849	I am (we are) prohibited
Lockspeise	27850	When will it be prohibited
Lockung ...	27851	Will be prohibited on and after ——
Lockvogel	27852	Will probably be prohibited
Locomoteur	27853	Was prohibited on

Locomotive	27854	**Prohibitive**
Locuples ...	27855	**Prolong(ed)**
Locustfly ...	27856	**Promise** (*See also* "Broken.")
Locusts ...	27857	Can you promise
Locutorio ...	27858	Cannot promise
Lodabilita	27859	Will you be able to fulfil promise
Lodativo ...	27860	Regret cannot fulfil promise
Lodatrice ...	27861	Have every reason to believe can fulfil promise
Lodazal ...	27862	Should like to fulfil my promise if possible
Lodevole ...	27863	In order to fulfil promise
Lodoletta ...	27864	Will it (this) prevent you fulfilling promise
Lodoners ...	27865	Which prevented my fulfilling promise
Lodretto ...	27866	Promise(s) exceedingly well
Loftiness ...	27867	Do(es) not promise
Logbook ...	27868	**Promised**
Logbuch ...	27869	Promised me (us) personally
Logement...	27870	—— has promised to
Logeur ...	27871	—— has not promised to
Logique ...	27872	I (we) have promised
Logistica ...	27873	In spite of what was promised
Logline ...	27874	**Promising**
Loglioso ...	27875	More promising
Logogriph	27876	Not so promising
Logomachy	27877	The rest of the quartz is very much more promising
Logoratore	27878	**Promote** (*See also* "Company.")
Logreria ...	27879	**Promoter(s)**
Loguccio ...	27880	**Promotion**
Lohgerber	27881	Cable what progress you have made with promotion
Lointain ...	27882	What will be about the cost of promotion
Loliaceus ...	27883	All expenses of promotion up to allotment
Lolligine ...	27884	Promotion expenses should include allowance for
Lollipop ...	27885	**Prompt**
Lombaire...	27886	For prompt delivery
Lombardic	27887	Be as prompt as you know how
Lombricato	27888	Has (have) been as prompt as possible
Lombricone	27889	When is the prompt date
Lomentum	27890	The prompt date is
Lomiancho	27891	Prompt reply necessary
Lomoso ...	27892	**Promptly**
Lonchitis ...	27893	As promptly as possible
Londiga ...	27894	Must be done promptly
Loneliness	27895	I (we) will do this as promptly as possible
Longabo ...	27896	Please act promptly
Longanimis	27897	It will be necessary to act promptly
Longevidad	27898	Promptly owing to
Longevite...	27899	Advise you (them) to act promptly
Longincue	27900	Unless you act promptly
Longipes ...	27901	Either promptly or not at all
Longiscet...	27902	**Proof(s)**
Longitude	27903	Proof positive
Longmetre	27904	Have you obtained any proof
Longnosed	27905	Can you obtain any proof of it
Longprimer	27906	Have obtained positive proof of
Longshanks.	27907	Have no proof
Longtail ...	27908	Have no legal proof
Longtemps	27909	Stronger proof is necessary before
Longuement	27910	Without further proof
Longurius	27911	What proof exists
Lonjista ...	27912	As a proof of this (it)
Lontananza	27913	Require(s) further proof

Lontanarsi	27914	The proof is
Lontanetto	27915	The only additional proof required is
Looming ...	27916	Cannot give any proof
Loophole ...	27917	There is every proof.
Loopline ...	27918	Does not constitute any real proof
Loosened ...	27919	Constitute(s) a convincing proof of
Lopicia ...	27920	Could you transmit legal proof of
Loquace ...	27921	Proof sheets shall be mailed
Loquacita...	27922	**Proper(ly)**
Loquaculus	27923	In proper order
Loquelaris	27924	Unless properly done
Loquentia	27925	**Property(ies)** (*See also* "Attachment," "Bonded," "De- [veloped," "Estate," "Finally," "Firmly," "Hydraulic," ["Inspected," "Mining." ["Patented," &c.)
Loqueteau	27926	Where is the property situated
Loquillo ...	27927	The property is situated at
Loquitor ...	27928	What does the property consist of
Lorbeer ...	27929	The property consists of the following claims
Lordingly...	27930	Property consists of
Lordizia ...	27931	The property contains
Lordling ...	27932	What is the lowest sum —— will take for the property
Loretum ...	27933	Is the lowest sum will take for the property
Loricated ...	27934	In my opinion the property is worth
Loricemur	27935	What is your opinion of the value of the property
Lorigado ...	27936	To prove the value of the property
Lorimers ...	27937	The property covers an area of
Loriquillo...	27938	A considerable extent of the property is
Lorsque ..	27939	On account of the large area of the property [working
Losanje ...	27940	How is the property placed for economic development and
Losbrechen	27941	The property is well placed for economic development and
Loschhorn	27942	The property is badly situated for [working
Loschkohle	27943	Has been represented to me as a very valuable property
Losdrucken	27944	The property is a very valuable one
Losgehen ...	27945	In my (our) opinion the property is not so valuable as has [been stated
Loskaufen	27946	I (we) do not think the property will prove a valuable one
Loskommen	27947	I (we) do not think the property is worth more than
Loslassen ...	27948	Consider property is worth
Losplatzen	27949	I (we) consider the property likely to become very valuable
Lossein ...	27950	I (we) consider the property well worthy of your attention
Lossuriare	27951	I (we) fully believe there is a splendid future for the property
Lotolente ...	27952	I (we) fully believe there is a fair future for the property
Lotometra	27953	During your absence leave —— in charge of the property
Lottatore ...	27954	During my absence I shall leave —— in charge of the property
Lotulentus	27955	Who shall I leave in charge of the property [property
Lotusbean	27956	The following development works are in progress on the
Lotustree ...	27957	No developments have been made on the property practically
Lousewort	27958	The further development of the property is very advisable
Loustic ...	27959	What further developments do you advise
Loutishly ...	27960	Advise the following developments of the property
Louveteau	27961	Does the property include
Louvoyer ...	27962	The property does not include
Loveapple	27963	Was (were) not included in the property
Lovefeasts	27964	Several properties [property
Loveknot ...	27965	Am (are) well pleased so far with what I (we) have seen of the
Loveletter...	27966	I (we) fear property will prove a disappointment
Lovelorn ...	27967	Are you fully satisfied with the intrinsic value and prospects of
Lovesick ...	27968	The property was offered [the property
Lovesong ...	27969	Can you report favourably on property as a whole
Lovesuit ...	27970	Would you entertain the offer of a —— property for ——
Lovetoken	27971	Should you meet with a good property, let me (us) know [lowest cash price and terms

Lovetrick ...	27972	Are you satisfied that the property is worth the price asked
Lovingly ...	27973	The property is well worthy of further investigation
Lowborn ...	27974	The property is not worthy of investigation
Lowering ...	27975	I advise you to pay —— not later than —— or lose the property
Lowermost	27976	Delay on your part is dangerous ; the property should not be
Loxodromy	27977	Is there any danger of my (our) losing the property [lost
Loyallike ...	27978	There will be no danger of your not getting the property
Lozanecer ...	27979	Think it wise to secure property
Lozania ...	27980	Think it wise to secure property adjoining
Lozenge ...	27981	Cannot secure property
Lubberly ...	27982	Cannot secure property on any terms
Lubentia ...	27983	Cannot secure property on reasonable terms
Lubricabat	27984	Cannot secure property for less than
Lubricanto	27985	Can you secure property for
Lubricar ...	27986	Can you secure property for —— (or not exceeding ——)
Lubricite ...	27987	Am endeavouring to secure property
Lucanar ...	27988	The future of the property depends upon
Lucanicus ...	27989	The value of the property is entirely prospective
Luccetto ...	27990	The actual value of the property at this moment is
Lucchesino	27991	The prospective value of the property at this moment is
Luccichio ...	27992	Cable what you know of property, owner here
Lucciolato...	27993	Property has been reported upon by
Lucellum ...	27994	Do you know the following property
Lucentezza	27995	We should be glad to sell property
Lucerius ...	27996	Do you consider the property worth entertaining
Lucernal ...	27997	I consider it a most valuable property
Lucerniere...	27998	I did not think the property good enough for you
Lucernuzza	27999	The property has been worked to a very considerable extent
Luchador ...	28000	The property has not been worked to any great extent
Lucherare ...	**28001**	Require remittance of —— to bond property which I consider [very promising. Terms of bond as follows
Luchillo ...	28002	The property can be economically worked
Lucible ...	28003	At the time that —— examined the property
Lucidarium	28004	I am not sufficiently acquainted with the property to answer
Lucidato ...	28005	I am sufficiently acquainted with the property to reply that
Lucidulus ...	28006	The property you will have to examine is situated in
Lucifers ...	28007	Cannot reach property to examine it within the time stated : [would require —— days longer
Lucifuga ...	28008	This (it) relates to the property at
Lucigena ...	28009	How long would you require for survey and examination of
Lucinium ...	28010	I have carefully examined the property [the property
Lucisator ...	28011	—— has personally examined the property
Luciscit ...	28012	If you can pick up a good property at a reasonable price, do so
Luckless ...	28013	The property is well placed (for)
Lucrifacio ...	28014	The property is badly placed (for)
Lucriones ...	28015	From this portion of the property [you of
Lucripeta ...	28016	—— is sufficiently acquainted with the property to inform
Luctamine...	28017	Could you suggest anything to make the property a good [paying concern
Luctisonus	28018	Telegraph all such details as will enable us to form our views [as to the value of the property
Luctuosa ...	28019	The general opinion of all who have visited the property is
Lucubrar ...	28020	Who originally owned and worked the property [tion
Lucumones	28021	I consider it a valuable property and a very desirable acquisi-
Ludibrium	28022	I have visited the property, but have not made any technical [examination
Ludibundus	28023	Could you examine the other properties at the same time
Ludificare ...	28024	Can examine the other properties at the same time
Luendus ...	28025	**Proportion(s)**
Luftball ...	28026	In about equal proportions

Luftchen ...	28027	In the same proportion
Luftdruck	28028	In the following proportions
Luftloch ...	28029	In equal proportions
Luftpumpe	28030	What proportion of
Luftraum ...	28031	What will my proportion be
Luftrohre...	28032	Your proportion would be
Luftsprung	28033	Only a very small proportion
Lugarazo ...	28034	In a fair proportion
Lugendos...	28035	What do you regard as a fair proportion
Lugenhaft	28036	I (we) regard —— as a fair proportion
Lugenmaul	28037	Is (are) out of all proportion
Luggagecar	28038	Out of all proportion to the risk taken
Lugger ...	28039	To be divided in the following proportions
Lugliatico	28040	A considerable proportion has been
Lugliolo ...	28041	Contains a considerable proportion of (it) (this)
Lugnerisch	28042	A large proportion
Lugsail ...	28043	The greater proportion
Lugubre ...	28044	Divided into —— equal proportions
Lugubriter	28045	In what proportion is it (this) to be divided
Luicion ...	28046	What proportion does it bear per
Luissimo ...	28047	The percentage proportion is
Luiturus ...	28048	In its (their) own proportion(s)
Lujarse ...	28049	Were they in their correct proportions
Lujuriar ...	28050	They were in their correct proportions
Lullaby ...	28051	They were not in their correct proportions
Lumachella	28052	**Proportionate**
Lumacone	28053	At a proportionate rate
Lumbellus	28054	**Proposal(s)**
Lumbrada	28055	Decline(s) proposal(s) made
Lumbricus	28056	Accept(s) proposal(s) made
Lumectum	28057	Cable proposal made by
Lumeggiare	28058	—— has made the following proposal
Lumettino	28059	Are you still open to a proposal
Lumiere ...	28060	I am (we are) still open to a proposal
Lumignon	28061	I am (we are) not open to a proposal for
Luminary...	28062	In the absence of any proposal from
Lumineux...	28063	Await written proposal
Luminosita	28064	Waiting for your proposal
Luminoso...	28065	Am (are) not clear as to precise proposal
Lummelhaft	28066	Is proposal perfectly clear
Lumpishly	28067	Proposal is quite clear
Lunaison ...	28068	Cannot accept proposal of
Lunanco ...	28069	Will accept proposal of
Lunated ...	28070	Do not accept proposal
Lunatique	28071	The amended proposal is as follows
Lunettier ...	28072	Better request —— to make a final proposal
Lunganimo	28073	Decline(s) to accept the proposal
Lungfever	28074	The final proposal is
Lunghetto	28075	Cannot entertain proposal made until
Lungitano	28076	Do you entertain proposal
Lungura ...	28077	Do not entertain proposal
Lunicorno	28078	Cable whether proposal is likely to be entertained
Luniforn ...	28079	Proposal likely to be entertained
Lunisolar ...	28080	Proposal not likely to be entertained
Luogaccio	28081	Will cable soon whether proposal is or is not entertained
Lupacchino	28082	Must send a more definite proposal
Lupanarium	28083	I (we) cannot make definite proposal until (before)
Lupatello ...	28084	Not in a position to make definite proposal
Lupercalis	28085	Would you approve of proposal on the following lines
Lupicia ...	28086	Would such a proposal be entertained

Lupinaceos	28087	Such a proposal would be entertained
Lupinajo ...	28088	Such a proposal would not be entertained
Luppolo ...	28089	Have you any further proposal to make
Lupulatus	28090	Shall I (we) accept proposal
Luquete ...	28091	You had better accept proposal
Lurcher ...	28092	Do not accept ——'s proposal unless (until)
Lurching ...	28093	——'s proposal has been accepted
Lurcinor ...	28094	——'s proposal has been declined
Lurcone ...	28095	Unless you accept my (our) proposal(s)
Luridus ...	28096	Is (are) —— likely to accede to my (our) proposal
Luronne ...	28097	I consider the proposal a very fair one
Lusciniola	28098	Has (have) made a proposal that (to)
Lusignuolo	28099	Has (have) requested —— to formulate his (their) proposal(s)
Lusingante	28100	I (we) make the following proposal
Lusorium...	28101	To your proposal
Lussazione	28102	To my proposal
Lussoriare	28103	**Propose**
Lussurioso	28104	To propose
Lustern ...	28105	Will propose
Lustigkeit	28106	Propose(s) to
Lustrandus	28107	Do (did) not propose to
Lustrated...	28108	How do you propose to deal with
Lustratore	28109	I (we) propose to deal with
Lustreise ...	28110	Do not propose to deal with it (this) (him)
Lustreless...	28111	When do you propose to deal with the
Lustremini	28112	What do you propose to do with respect to
Lustricus ...	28113	What do (does) —— propose to do with respect to
Lustring ...	28114	I (we) propose to act as follows
Lustroso ...	28115	—— propose(s) to act at once
Lustspiel ...	28116	Would propose to
Lutanist ...	28117	As soon as you have anything definite to propose
Lutarius ...	28118	Could you propose anything better
Lutatura ...	28119	I (we) think the best thing to propose would be that I (we)
Lutherien...	28120	I (we) propose in the first place to
Luthier ...	28121	Refuse(s) to propose anything
Lutifigolo...	28122	Have you anything to propose
Lutiner ...	28123	I (we) would only propose that
Lutteur ...	28124	I (we) have nothing to propose
Lutulento...	28125	**Proposed**
Luxabatur	28126	The proposed plan
Luxamini ...	28127	Proposed by
Luxantur ...	28128	Has (have) proposed to
Luxation ...	28129	Has (have) not proposed to
Luxaveno ...	28130	What has (have) —— proposed
Luxemur ...	28131	**Proposition** (*See also* " Proposal.")
Luxueux ...	28132	Pending receipt of definite proposition
Luxurians	28133	Cannot entertain any such proposition
Luxuriosus	28134	Cannot entertain proposition of
Luxurist ...	28135	Proposition entertained
Luzerne ...	28136	Proposition definitely accepted
Lychnites...	28137	Much opposed to the proposition
Lychnobius	28138	Your proposition too costly
Lycopods ...	28139	If I (we) entertain your proposition
Lycopsis ...	28140	**Proprietary**
Lymphamini	28141	**Proprietor(s)**
Lymphans	28142	**Prosecute**
Lymphatic	28143	To prosecute
Lymphemur	28144	Will prosecute
Lynceus ...	28145	Will not prosecute
Lynched ...	28146	Shall I (we) prosecute

Lynchlaw ...	28147	Shall commence to prosecute at once
Lyncurium	28148	Do not prosecute
Lynxeyed ...	28149	Take immediate steps to prosecute
Lyricen ...	28150	To prosecute the enquiry
Lyrichord...	28151	If you wish me to prosecute you must
Lyricismal	28152	They were in duty bound to prosecute
Lyrique ...	28153	Would certainly prosecute
Lyrisch ...	28154	So as to prosecute
Macaque ...	28155	Do (does) —— intend to prosecute
Macareno ...	28156	Intend(s) to prosecute
Macaroons	28157	Has (have) not decided at present whether to prosecute
Macarsi ...	28158	**Prospect(s)** (*See also* "Every," "Expenditure," "Fair,"
Macaw ...	28159	Prospect for ["Favourable," "Ground.")
Maccatella	28160	A mere prospect
Maccherone	28161	No prospect whatever (of)
Macchietta	28162	Cable prospects of
Macchinoso	28163	Whether any prospect
Maccidibus	28164	What are the present prospects of
Maceador ...	28165	The present prospects are
Macebearer	28166	If present prospects can be relied upon
Macedoine	28167	On the present appearance and prospects of
Macedonian	28168	Will prospects strongly justify this (these) figure(s)
Macellajo ...	28169	Is there any prospect of
Macellesco	28170	There is just a slight prospect that
Macellum ...	28171	There is no prospect at present (of)
Macerabam	28172	As soon as I (we) see any prospect of
Macerantur	28173	Do not see any prospect of
Macerar ...	28174	What prospect is there that I (we)
Maceratio ...	28175	What are your prospects as regards
Maceratote	28176	I (we) believe that there is a good prospect of
Maceries ...	28177	Should you see no prospect of success
Maceriolam	28178	Unless you see fair prospect of success
Macerone ...	28179	Prospect is more hopeful
Macescens	28180	Prospect is not so hopeful
Maceton ...	28181	Prospects generally are brighter
Machalath	28182	Prospects are decidedly encouraging
Machefer ...	28183	Prospects are most encouraging
Macherlohn	28184	Prospects are grand
Machicot ...	28185	Prospects are undoubtedly good
Machiega ...	28186	Prospects not sufficiently encouraging to
Machinale	28187	Are prospects encouraging enough for
Machinatio	28188	Present prospects very discouraging
Machinete	28189	What prospect is there of improvement
Machinist...	28190	There is every prospect of improvement
Machionem	28191	As prospects are improving
Machonner	28192	As prospects are not improving
Machowa ...	28193	Prospects of anything better are very slight
Machthaber	28194	There is every prospect that worse will follow
Machute ...	28195	Prospect thoroughly and report [(during)
Macicez ...	28196	I (we) shall prospect this portion of the property thoroughly
Macilenza...	28197	The prospect is enticing
Macinante	28198	There seems every prospect of
Macinatura	28199	There seems very little prospect of
Macinello ...	28200	Have obtained prospects
Maciullare	28201	Considered as a "prospect" it is very promising
Macizar ...	28202	There is just a prospect that
Mackerel ...	28203	What future prospect is there of
Macolatore	28204	Report as to actual money prospects
Maconnage	28205	Report as to speculative prospects
Maconnerie	28206	What prospect is there of your being able to do it (this)

Macredo ...	28207	Provided that you have a distinct prospect of
Macreuse ...	28208	Unless prospects materially improve I (we) would suggest that
Macriculam	28209	Unless prospects materially improve in the meanwhile
Macritas ...	28210	Our prospects are undoubtedly good
Macrobius	28211	The prospects generally continue to improve
Macrochira	28212	If prospects do not improve
Macrocosmo	28213	No improvement in prospects whatever
Macrologia	28214	Affords some little prospect of improvement
Macruisti ...	28215	The prospects would be very encouraging but for
Mactabilis	28216	Future prospects are fair
Mactandus	28217	Future prospects bright
Mactavisse	28218	Is there any immediate prospect of ore
Macteola ...	28219	What are the prospects as regards ore
Macticus ...	28220	We have a very good prospect of finding ore at
Maculated	28221	Prospects moderate
Maculature	28222	Our mining prospects continue very favourable
Maculoso ...	28223	Has a very promising prospect
Maculuzza	28224	Every prospect of a decline
Macuquino	28225	Every prospect of a rise
Madapolam	28226	The gravel prospects well
Madbrain ...	28227	The mine is a mere " prospect "
Madcap ...	28228	Continue to prospect at
Maddened	28229	Would advise strongly that you continue to prospect
Madefatto...	28230	**Prospected**
Maderada...	28231	Has (have) been thoroughly prospected
Madereria...	28232	Has (have) not been prospected yet to any extent
Maderista...	28233	As soon as I (we) have prospected the ground in this direction
Madernale	28234	Until I (we) have thoroughly prospected
Madhouse...	28235	Should be thoroughly prospected
Madidans ...	28236	**Prospecting**
Madidatote	28237	No prospecting
Madifico ...	28238	Prospecting for
Madonnetta	28239	Prospecting with
Madrastra	28240	Prospecting in
Madrear ...	28241	Vigorous prospecting
Madreclavo	28242	A prospecting shaft
Madrens ...	28243	The work consists of —— prospecting shaft(s)
Madrepore	28244	Prospecting shaft now —— feet deep
Madreselva	28245	When shall you commence prospecting
Madrevite...	28246	Shall commence prospecting at once
Madrigal ...	28247	What prospecting has been done
Madrilla ...	28248	Have sunk a prospecting shaft —— feet deep
Madronal ...	28249	Has (have) been prospecting since —— on this vein
Madrugada	28250	A considerable amount of prospecting has been done with the [following results
Madrugon	28251	Little or no prospecting has been done up to the present time
Maduradero	28252	I am (we are) prospecting
Madurante	28253	Has (have) been prospecting (for)
Madurativo	28254	Better limit prospecting to
Maesil ...	28255	Better cease prospecting until (unless)
Maesterio...	28256	Has (have) ceased prospecting
Maestevole	28257	Shall cease prospecting
Maestoso ...	28258	Shall cease prospecting until (unless)
Maestradgo	28259	Shall continue prospecting
Maestranza	28260	Shall continue prospecting in this direction (at)
Maestrear ...	28261	Strongly suggest further prospecting
Maestressa	28262	Do you advise further prospecting
Mafattore...	28263	Do not advise any further prospecting
Mafortium	28264	Stop all prospecting
Magacen ...	28265	Am (are) prospecting in the hope of discovering lead

Magagnato	28266	In consequence of large amount of prospecting work
Magazine ...	28267	**Prospector(s)** (*See also* "Diggers," "License.")
Magazzino	28268	Prospector's outfit
Magdaleon	28269	**Prospectus**
Magdaliam	28270	For prospectus
Magencar ...	28271	If issued in a prospectus
Magenkrebs	28272	Require sufficient details for prospectus
Magensaft	28273	When will prospectus be issued
Magerkeit	28274	Prospectus will be issued about
Magestad ...	28275	Prospectus was issued on
Magestuoso	28276	Please mail prospectus of
Magganum	28277	Will mail prospectus
Maggesato	28278	Have mailed prospectus
Maggiorana	28279	The prospectus was issued but the public did not subscribe
Maggiore ...	28280	For prospectus purposes
Maggoty ...	28281	Do not issue prospectus until you receive
Magically ...	28282	Before you issue prospectus
Magicien ...	28283	Must have these particulars before issue of prospectus on
Magionetta	28284	Do(es) not agree with statement(s) in prospectus
Magismo ...	28285	Explain(s) discrepancy in prospectus
Magistery...	28286	**Protect**
Magistrate	28287	To protect
Magliato ...	28288	To protect my (our) interests
Magliolina	28289	In order to protect
Magmatibus	28290	Will protect
Magnalmo	28291	Cannot protect
Magnanerie	28292	Consent(s) to protect
Magnanimo	28293	Refuse(s) to protect
Magnarius	28294	Will this be sufficient to protect
Magnetique	28295	Will not be sufficient to protect
Magnetism	28296	You should protect
Magnetized	28297	You must protect yourself(ves)
Magnidicus	28298	I (we) shall have to protect myself (ourselves)
Magnifacio	28299	It will be necessary to take every means to protect
Magnificar	28300	Please protect my (our) draft for
Magnified	28301	Will protect your (their) draft for
Magniloquo	28302	Do everything necessary to protect my (our) interests
Magnipendo	28303	Will do everything necessary to protect your interests
Magnitude	28304	**Protected**
Magnolier...	28305	Protected by
Magnopere	28306	Protected from
Magolato ...	28307	Protected against
Magpie ...	28308	Fully protected
Magretto ...	28309	Has (have) been protected
Magrujo ...	28310	Am (are) protected against
Magudaris	28311	Was (were) protected on
Maguillo ...	28312	Are not protected at all
Magullado	28313	Not sufficiently protected
Maharon ...	28314	Must be protected
Mahlen ...	28315	Was (were) not protected at all
Mahomedan	28316	Provided that my (our) interests are fully protected
Maibaum ...	28317	Cable whether I am (we are) protected against
Maidenhair	28318	**Protection**
Maidenlike	28319	No protection whatever
Maidens ...	28320	Will it be sufficient protection
Maigrelet ...	28321	What protection is there against
Maigreur ..	28322	You have practically no protection
Maikäfer ...	28323	There is ample protection
Mailboats ...	28324	As protection against
Mailloche ...	28325	Must have ample protection against

[472]

[ailmatter	28326	Every needful protection
[aimonetes	28327	**Protest(s)**
[aindeck ...	28328	To protest
[ainel ...	28329	Must protest
[ainforte	28330	—— protest(s) that
[ainlevel	28331	Before I (we) protest
[ainmast...	28332	Before you protest
[ainsail ...	28333	Unless he (they) should protest
[ainsheet	28334	Better lodge formal protest at once
[aintained	28335	Am (are) compelled to protest against
[aintenant	28336	Has (have) been paid under protest
[aintien ...	28337	It would be no use to protest
[aintop ...	28338	You had better pay, but do so under protest
[ainyard ...	28339	Protest(s) strongly against
[airesse ...	28340	Has (have) signed under protest
[aisempre	28341	Sign under protest
[aitinante	28342	Was signed under protest
[aitriser ...	28343	I (we) strongly protest against
[ajadal ...	28344	Under protest
[ajaderia...	28345	Protest useless
[ajamiento	28346	Has (have) lodged a protest
[ajarrana	28347	Protest against you (him) (them) doing so
[ajencia ...	28348	Protest mailed
[ajesta ...	28349	Protest forwarded for your signature
[ajestical	28350	Extend protest
[ajolar ...	28351	Extend protest before leaving
[ajolica ...	28352	**Protested**
[ajorasco...	28353	Draft for —— has been protested
[ajorat ...	28354	Has (have) protested against
[ajordomo	28355	Was (were) protested on
[ajuela ...	28356	Has (have) protested draft
[ajuscule	28357	Has (have) not protested as yet
Makeln ...	28358	**Protract(ed)**
Makulatur	28359	**Prove(s)**
Malaccorto	28360	To prove
Malachin ...	28361	As soon as I (we) can prove
Malachites	28362	To prove the existence of
Malacisso ...	28363	This will prove
Malactico ...	28364	In order to prove
Malacuenda	28365	Can you prove anything against him (them)
Maladetto...	28366	Cannot legally prove anything, but have strongest suspicion
Maladicere	28367	When I (we) shall be able to prove [that
Maladroit...	28368	Impossible to prove anything against
Malafatta ...	28369	Really proves nothing
Malagana ...	28370	I (we) can certainly prove
Malagevole	28371	Unless you can absolutely prove
Malagiato...	28372	What can you (——) prove
Malaginus	28373	Unable to prove
Malaisance	28374	When I (we) expect to be able to prove
Malalingua	28375	Provided that you (——) can prove
Malanconia	28376	Prove(s) to be more than I (we) anticipated
Malandato	28377	May prove to be
Malandazza	28378	You should prove to —— that
Malapert ...	28379	And afterwards prove
Malaquites	28380	**Proved**
Malarious	28381	Proved a failure
Malassetto	28382	Proved a tolerable success
Malaticcio	28383	Proved a great success
Malatolta ...	28384	Not proved
Malaurioso	28385	Has been proved again and again

Malavoglia	28386	This has proved
Malavrezzo	28387	Unless it has been proved to the contrary
Malaxabam	28388	Unless it has been proved
Malaxabunt	28389	Unless it can be proved that
Malaxamini	28390	Has (have) been proved
Malaxantur	28391	Has (have) proved very successful
Malaxavit	28392	Not proved as yet
Malbati ...	28393	Can it be proved that
Malcaduco	28394	Fear it cannot be proved
Malcarado	28395	When it was fully proved that
Malcaso ...	28396	Has (have) hitherto proved most reliable
Malcomido	28397	Has (have) hitherto proved unreliable
Malconcio...	28398	**Provide(s)**
Malcriado...	28399	Only provide(s) for
Malcubato	28400	To provide for
Maldecidor	28401	Consent(s) to provide
Maldicente	28402	Refuse(s) to provide
Maldicho ...	28403	Should not provide
Maldita ...	28404	To provide
Malebolge...	28405	To provide for contingencies
Malecon ...	28406	In order to provide
Maledetto	28407	When will it be necessary to provide
Maledicor...	28408	It will be necessary to provide
Maledictus	28409	It is necessary to provide at once for
Maledire ...	28410	Will you provide necessary funds
Malefactor	28411	To provide necessary funds for
Maleficiar...	28412	Cannot provide additional funds
Malefidus ...	28413	Will provide whatever may be necessary
Maleic ...	28414	Provide —— with what he (they) require(s)
Malemerito	28415	Can you provide
Malentendu	28416	I (we) can provide
Malerische	28417	I am (we are) unable to provide
Malerstock	28418	How much can you provide
Malestruo	28419	Do all that you can to provide against
Malevedere	28420	I (we) will take every care to provide against
Malevolent	28421	Does this provide for
Malevolo ...	28422	This provides for
Malfaisant	28423	This does not provide for
Malfattore	28424	Is —— willing to provide anything
Malfondato	28425	How much is —— willing to provide
Malgama ...	28426	How do you intend to provide for
Malgastar...	28427	If I am (we are) to provide
Malgoverno	28428	Will provide it (this)
Malgradito	28429	Provide everything necessary for
Malhablado	28430	**Provided**
Malhecho ...	28431	Fully provided
Malherir ...	28432	To be provided by
Malheureux	28433	Has (have) provided for
Maliarda ...	28434	Has (have) not provided for
Malicia ...	28435	Should be provided with
Malicieux...	28436	Provided that
Malicordem	28437	Has (have) been provided for
Malicorium	28438	Better be provided for
Malificio ...	28439	Has (have) not been provided for
Malignant	28440	Not provided in any way
Malignatis	28441	You should be provided for (with)
Malignidad	28442	Have you provided for
Malignity...	28443	Has (have) not provided against
Maligno ...	28444	Provided that —— will extend the time of
Maliloquax	28445	Provided that —— will give sufficient guarantee

Malincorpo	28446	Everything needful has been provided
Malinteso ...	28447	Nothing practically has been provided at all
Maliscalco	28448	Provided it (this) can be done
Malistalla	28449	Provided that the cost is not excessive
Malitiose ...	28450	Have you provided for
Malitorne ...	28451	What have you provided for
Maliziare ...	28452	Am (are) completely provided with
Malizietta...	28453	When I shall be completely provided with
Mallard ...	28454	**Providing**
Malleabile	28455	Providing that
Malleate ...	28456	**Province**
Malleolus ...	28457	**Provision(s)**
Malletes ...	28458	As a provision for
Mallevato ...	28459	What provision have you made against
Malleveria	28460	Provision should be made for placing
Malmenare	28461	Provision should be made for
Malmettere	28462	No provision was made for placing
Malmirado	28463	Has (have) not made provision for
Malmsey ...	28464	Quite sufficient provision at present for
Malodours	28465	Not enough provision for
Malograr ...	28466	What provision has been made for
Malparida	28467	Ample provision has been made for
Malparto ...	28468	Too late to make any provision for
Malpeigne	28469	The necessary provision would cost
Malpiglio ...	28470	Subject to due provision being made for
Malpratice	28471	Subject to the following provisions
Malpropre	28472	I (we) have ample provisions
Malpulito ...	28473	I (we) have really no provisions
Malquerer	28474	Can any provision be made for
Malrotar ...	28475	Cannot make any provision for
Malsano ...	28476	Every provision is made against [for
Malseant ...	28477	There is considerable difficulty in the way of making provision
Malsonnant	28478	There is considerable difficulty in getting provisions
Maltalento	28479	Have contracted for supply of provisions
Maltdust ...	28480	All provisions are cheap
Malteur ...	28481	Provisions are very dear
Maltfloor ...	28482	The cost of provisions amounts to —— per month
Malthouse	28483	What is the monthly cost of provisions
Malting ...	28484	Provisions must be provided for the winter
Maltornito	28485	**Provisional**
Maltotier ...	28486	Provisional agreement
Maltraiter	28487	Provisional contract
Maltrato ...	28488	On the expiration of provisional agreement
Maltreated	28489	Provisional contract signed
Maltster ...	28490	As a provisional arrangement
Malucho ...	28491	Will endeavour to make a provisional agreement
Malusato ...	28492	Endeavour to come to a provisional understanding
Malvaceus	28493	**Provisionally**
Malvagia ...	28494	Have arranged provisionally that
Malvagione	28495	Have contracted provisionally
Malvavisco	28496	**Proviso**
Malveduto	28497	**Proximity**
Malversar	28498	I think we are in close proximity to
Malvissuto	28499	**Proximo** (*See also* "January," "February," &c., &c.)
Malvivente	28500	On the —— proximo
Malvoluta	28501	**Proxy(ies)**
Malzdarre...	28502	Please send proxy in favour of
Mamadera	28503	Proxy in favour of —— mailed on
Mamaluke	28504	Get all the proxies you can
Mamante ...	28505	Unless we have a sufficient number of proxies

Mamario ...	28506	Require proxies representing —— shares
Mamellado	28507	Has (have) promised me his (their) proxy(ies)
Mamiferos	28508	Refuses to sign proxy
Mamillare	28509	Proxies received to date, representing —— shares
Mammalian	28510	How many proxies do you require in order to be secure
Mammalucco	28511	Require —— proxies representing —— shares in order to be
Mammeatus	28512	**Prudent** [secure
Mammella	28513	Be prudent
Mammiculam	28514	I (we) consider it prudent to
Mammifere	28515	I (we) consider it prudent not to
Mammoletto	28516	Consider you have acted very prudently
Mammonist	28517	Am afraid you have (—— has) not acted altogether prudently
Mammoth	28518	You should be very prudent how you act
Mamotreta	28519	Be very prudent as regards
Mampara ...	28520	Cable if you think it would be prudent to
Mamphula	28521	I (we) do not think it would be prudent to
Mampirlan	28522	I (we) think it would be prudent to
Mampostear	28523	Should be more prudent
Mampresar	28524	Not quite prudent enough
Mamullar ...	28525	Tell —— to be very prudent as to
Manacles ...	28526	As soon as I (we) consider it prudent
Manacling	28527	As soon as you consider it prudent
Manadera...	28528	**Public(ly)**
Manager ...	28529	On public lands
Manakin ...	28530	For the public
Manantial...	28531	The British public
Manatella...	28532	Before the public
Mancamento	28533	Has been before the public since
Mancando	28534	—— stated in public that
Mancatore	28535	It was not stated in public but privately
Manceba ...	28536	It was stated in public that the
Manceppare	28537	Is about to be put before the public
Mancerina	28538	Prior to being offered to the public
Manchado	28539	At the present time the public would undoubtedly take it
Manchette	28540	At the present time the public would not look at it
Manchevole	28541	Should be made public at once
Manchot ...	28542	Do not make this public in any way
Mancipar ...	28543	Has not yet been made public
Mancipatus	28544	Take immediate steps to make it public
Manciples...	28545	Has been stated in the public press
Mancomun	28546	It has been stated in the public papers here that
Mancornar	28547	It (this) will shortly be made public
Mancupium	28548	Will not be offered to the public
Mandabat...	28549	We shall be compelled to make it public
Mandadera	28550	Do not announce anything publicly until
Mandamini	28551	The public mainly subscribed
Mandandus	28552	The public hardly subscribed at all
Mandantur	28553	Do not inform the public
Mandarin...	28554	Will not inform the public
Mandatario	28555	**Publish**
Mandatory	28556	Publish on
Mandatote	28557	Will publish
Mandatrice	28558	Will not publish
Mandatulus	28559	Better publish at once
Mandavero	28560	Do not publish
Mandement	28561	To publish
Mandemur	28562	Should I (we) publish your report
Mandible ...	28563	Should you publish my report
Mandibular	28564	Intend to publish report in full
Mandilejo...	28565	Will only publish synopsis of report

[476]

Mandioca ...	28566	On condition that you do not publish it
Mandoline	28567	Propose to publish
Mandora ...	28568	Do not on any account publish
Mandracho	28569	Do not publish this until
Mandragore	28570	Threaten(s) to publish
Mandrake...	28571	Will undoubtedly publish
Mandrarum	28572	Do not think will publish
Mandriez ...	28573	Should —— publish
Manducar...	28574	Do not publish it for the present
Manducatio	28575	**Published**
Mandunt ...	28576	To be published
Maneater ...	28577	Has (have) been published
Manebitur	28578	Has it (this) been published
Manedum...	28579	Has not yet been published
Maneggiare	28580	In the event of it being published
Maneggio...	28581	Was published before arrival of your cable
Manejado...	28582	Will be published on
Maneota ...	28583	As soon as it was published
Manescalco	28584	Is it advisable that this should be published
Manesis ...	28585	It is not advisable that this (it) should be published
Manfanile...	28586	It is very advisable that it (this) should be published
Manfulness	28587	Before it (this) was published
Mangajarro	28588	Since it (this) was published
Manganate	28589	Who first published it
Manganilla	28590	Was published by
Mangeaille	28591	Provided that it is not published
Mangeoire	28592	**Pulley(s)** (*See also* "Blocks.")
Mangiapelo	28593	What is the speed of pulley(s)
Mangiatoja	28594	The speed of pulley(s) is —— feet per second
Manginess	28595	Send pulley(s) for
Mangione...	28596	Owing to the breakage of pulley(s)
Mangled ...	28597	Split pulley(s)
Mangling ...	28598	With fast and loose pulley
Mangonear	28599	Wire rope pulley
Mangonicus	28600	Pulley for hemp rope
Mangonium	28601	Face of pulley to be turned straight
Mangotree	28602	Pulley to have a round face
Mangual ...	28603	**Pulp**
Manguitero	28604	No samples of the pulp were taken
Mangusta	28605	Please forward average sample of the pulp (say about —— lbs.)
Manhole ...	28606	**Pulp assays**
Marrialbo ...	28607	Samples of the pulp assay
Maniaque...	28608	Pulp assays since —— average
Maniatico...	28609	Pulp assays from —— to —— inclusive average
Manicaccia	28610	Please cable average of pulp assays since
Manicarsi...	28611	Have arranged to take average samples of pulp and will report
Manicatore	28612	Average of pulp assays [assays
Manicheist	28613	**Pulverizer**
Manichetto	28614	Pulverizer trial
Manicorto...	28615	After the stuff has been through the pulverizer
Manicristo	28616	Have purchased pulverizer
Manido ...	28617	Have erected pulverizer
Maniement	28618	Have discontinued use of pulverizer
Manieriste	28619	Each pulverizer requires —— actual horsepower
Manierlich	28620	**Pump(s)** (*See also* "Aitchpiece," "Boiler," "Clack,"
Manierona	28621	Direct acting steam pump ["Depend," "Plunger.")
Manifacero	28622	What size pumps have you at
Manifestly	28623	What pumps have you on the mine
Manifesto...	28624	What size pumps do you require for [per hour —— ft.
Maniglia ...	28625	The pumps required should be capable of raising —— gallons

Manigolda	28626	Cornish pump
Maniguetas	28627	Pump column has given way at [weeks
Manilahemp	28628	To replace pump column and unwater —— level will take ——
Manilargo	28629	Working vigorously at repairs to pumps
Manilarope	28630	Shall not be able to advance matters until arrival of pump(s)
Manimesso	28631	Until repairs to pump are completed
Manimorcia	28632	Have obtained estimate for a new pump amounting to
Maniplaris	28633	Estimate for pumps is —— to include
Maniplus ...	28634	Steam pump
Manipodio	28635	Prefer steam pump
Manipular	28636	Horizontal steam pump
Maniqueo...	28637	Vertical steam pump
Maniscaleo	28638	Owing to the failure of steam pump
Manivacio...	28639	H piece
Manivelle ...	28640	H piece door
Manjelin ...	28641	H piece for
Manjorrada	28642	Drawing of H piece
Mankiller ...	28643	The pumps are in good condition
Mankind ...	28644	The pumps are very much in need of repair
Manlevar ...	28645	Owing to a breakage of the pumps
Manliana ...	28646	The pumps cannot deal with the incoming water
Mannajetta	28647	Shall have to supplement pumps
Mannajone	28648	Ought at once to erect new pumps
Mannequin	28649	When shall you require new pump
Mannerism	28650	Send —— feet of —— inch pumps
Manniglich	28651	Does this amount include cost of pumps
Mannsalter	28652	Exclusive of cost of pumps
Mannsleute	28653	Pumps will have to be obtained
Mannulus ..	28654	Inclusive of cost of pumps
Manobrero	28655	Main pump rod
Manoeuvre	28656	The angle bob of pump
Manojear ...	28657	Windbore for —— inch pumps
Manometro	28658	Working barrel for —— inch pumps
Manorhouse	28659	Plunger pole and case for —— inch pumps
Manorial ...	28660	We have had to repack the plunger of pump
Manoteado	28661	Have you sufficient pumping power
Manovaldo	28662	How deep will your present pumping power carry you
Manovrare	28663	What description of pump do you require
Manpleaser	28664	I (we) advise the erection of —— pump
Manquear...	28665	Until we can put in permanent pump
Manquillo	28666	Should not put in permanent pumps
Mansamente	28667	Would strongly advise purchase of permanent pumps
Mansarde ...	28668	Purchase and erect pump as soon as possible
Mansejon ...	28669	What will the cost of pump amount to
Mansion ...	28670	Pump itself will cost —— to which add —— for freight
Manslayer	28671	Pump(s) to be erected by
Manstealer	28672	What is the capacity of your present pump
Manstutor	28673	Present pump capable of raising
Mansucius	28674	Pump is now raising —— gallons (English) per hour —— feet
Mansuefare	28675	What is the power and condition of pumps
Mansuesio	28676	The pumps and machinery requested for
Mansuetudo	28677	Examine and report on condition of pumps
Mantacare	28678	How long can you depend on the pumps
Mantacozzo	28679	The lowest lift of the pump
Manteca ...	28680	The No. —— lift of the pump
Mantecoso	28681	At the bottom of the pump column
Manteleria	28682	Pumps now working —— strokes a minute
Mantelet ...	28683	Delay —— hours through repairs to pumpwork
Manteling	28684	The pump will just keep the water at ——
Mantelium	28685	Fear pumps will be unable to control water

Mantellare	28686	Pumps quite able to control water
Mantellina	28687	Great strain on pumps may be unable to control water
Mantelloto	28688	Bottom pump drowned
Mantenedor	28689	Water is gaining on pump(s)
Mantenente	28690	Pump(s) gaining on water [present pump
Mantenersi	28691	We will probably be able to sink —— feet additional with
Mantequera	28692	Shall not be able to do anything until the pumps are fixed
Manticetto	28693	**Pumped**
Manticiaro	28694	When do you expect that the water will be pumped out
Manticora...	28695	Water was pumped out on
Manticulor	28696	Expect that the water will be pumped out about
Mantiglia...	28697	Until the water is pumped out
Mantillon...	28698	As soon as the water is pumped out
Mantisam...	28699	Shall not be able to get the water pumped out without
Manton ...	28700	**Pumping**
Mantrap ...	28701	Not pumping
Manuable...	28702	Pumping engine
Manualis ...	28703	A permanent pumping plant
Manualiter	28704	Begin pumping
Manubrium	28705	When shall you begin pumping
Manuccia ...	28706	I (we) began pumping on
Manucordio	28707	Hope to begin pumping on
Manuductor	28708	The moment we cease pumping
Manufactus	28709	What are you pumping at present
Manuleato	28710	We are pumping —— gallons (English) per twenty-four hours
Manumiss...	28711	Better cease pumping
Manumittor	28712	Shall I (we) cease pumping
Manured ...	28713	Have ceased pumping
Manuring...	28714	Do not cease pumping
Manuscrito	28715	We have ample pumping power for present needs
Manutener	28716	We shall require additional pumping power
Manysides	28717	Breakdown of pumping engine
Manzana ...	28718	For repairs to pumping engine
Manzanillo	28719	When will you complete repairs to pumping engine
Manzotta ...	28720	As soon as we have completed repairs to pumping engine
Mapalia ...	28721	Shall have completed repairs to pumping engine by
Mapamundi	28722	Have you boiler power for pumping and hoisting
Mapletree...	28723	I have boiler power for both pumping and hoisting
Maplewood	28724	I have not boiler power for both pumping and hoisting
Mappamonda	28725	Machinery broken down have had to stop pumping
Mappulam	28726	Pumping charges amount to —— per month
Maquereau	28727	Pumping charges
Maquignon	28728	What do pumping charges amount to per month
Maquila ...	28729	Pumping machinery
Maquinaria	28730	Pumping machinery destroyed by collapse of shaft
Marabout...	28731	**Pumpman** (*See also* "Pitman.")
Marachella	28732	**Punctual(ly)**
Maraicher...	28733	**Purchase** (*See also* "Completed," "Confirm.")
Marangone	28734	To complete purchase
Marasmo ...	28735	From present purchase price
Marasquin ...	28736	Unless you complete purchase
Marathrum	28737	Purchase confirmed
Maraudeur	28738	Purchase repudiated
Marauding	28739	Purchase authorized
Maravedi ...	28740	Purchase not authorized
Maravillar	28741	To purchase
Marbete ...	28742	Will purchase on the following terms
Marbreur ...	28743	Will not purchase
Marcador ...	28744	Do not purchase
Marcasite ...	28745	The purchase of

Marcassin...	28746	The purchase and erection of
Marcebat ...	28747	What is the purchase price
Marcescens	28748	Cannot arrange terms of purchase
Marchamar	28749	Have arranged terms of purchase
Marchante	28750	Purchase amount
Marchepied	28751	What amount (quantity) (number) are you willing to purchase
Marchesato	28752	Am (are) willing to purchase
Marchette...	28753	Unable to purchase more than
Marching ...	28754	With an option to complete purchase for
Marchitez .	28755	With an option of purchase within —— months
Marciata ...	28756	An option to purchase
Marcidus ...	28757	Can obtain option to purchase at
Marcigione	28758	Will —— give the option to purchase
Marciume...	28759	Is willing to give the option to purchase
Marcola ...	28760	The purchase of
Marcotter ...	28761	Defer completion of purchase until
Mareaje ...	28762	I (we) have the cash ready if you advise purchase
Marecageux	28763	Do you advise purchase
Marejada ...	28764	I (we) strongly advise you to purchase
Maremmano	28765	I (we) cannot advise you to purchase
Marero ...	28766	The purchase to be completed on or before
Marestails	28767	When will the purchase be completed
Maretazo ...	28768	When will the purchase require to be completed
Marfaga ...	28769	As soon as the purchase is completed
Marfileno ...	28770	Provided that the purchase is completed by
Margallon...	28771	The purchase must be completed not later than
Marganesa	28772	The purchase cannot be completed until
Margaridem	28773	The purchase is not yet completed
Margarita...	28774	The purchase was completed on
Margelle ...	28775	Will take —— of the purchase money in shares
Margenar ...	28776	Will take the whole of the purchase money in shares
Marginado	28777	Has (have) paid the whole of the purchase money
Marginal ...	28778	Has (have) received the whole of the purchase money
Marginatus	28779	As soon as have settled preliminaries of purchase
Marginetta	28780	I am (we are) anxious to purchase
Margolato	28781	The purchase price should not exceed
Margottare	28782	Trying to negotiate for a purchase of
Margrave ...	28783	Delay purchase until you receive my (our) letter dated
Marguerite	28784	Will seriously interfere with purchase
Marhojo ...	28785	Will not interfere with purchase
Marial ...	28786	Will it (this) interfere with purchase
Maricon ...	28787	Am prepared to pay purchase money on learning that you are
Maridable...	28788	Purchase for joint account [satisfied with value of property
Maridanza	28789	Purchase for account of
Maridillo ...	28790	Purchase will be completed as soon as possible [advisable
Marigold ...	28791	I (we) do not believe that purchase upon the terms stated is
Marimacho	28792	Confer with —— before completing purchase
Marimanta	28793	Completion of purchase
Marimorena	28794	Cable immediately whether the purchase has been completed
Marinade ...	28795	The purchase amount should be reduced by ——
Marinerado	28796	**Purchased**
Marinesco...	28797	Purchased by
Mariniren...	28798	Can be purchased for
Mariolare ...	28799	Purchased for
Mariona ...	28800	Cannot be purchased
Mariperez...	28801	Why have you not purchased
Mariquetas	28802	Why did you not purchase
Mariscal ...	28803	Has (have) been purchased by
Maritaccio	28804	Was (were) purchased by
Maritandus	28805	Is (are) believed to have been purchased by.

Maritarsi ...	28806	Can be purchased out and out for
Maritimar	28807	Was purchased in —— for
Maritornes	28808	Cannot be purchased now under
Marittimo	28809	**Purchaser(s)**
Mariuolo ...	28810	Purchaser(s) to take over
Marjolaine	28811	Purchaser(s) will not complete sale until
Marjoleta...	28812	Purchaser(s) willing to pay money at once
Marjoram...	28813	Purchaser(s) wish to let —— remain at —— per cent. per
Marketdays	28814	Purchaser(s) to give guarantee of [annum interest
Markethall	28815	The purchaser(s) is (are) stated to be
Marketing	28816	Have discovered who the purchaser(s) is (are)
Markgraf ...	28817	To be returned to purchaser(s)
Markiren ...	28818	Would it (this) be returned to purchaser(s)
Marksman	28819	Would not in any case be returned to purchaser(s)
Marktbude	28820	**Purport(ed)(ing)**
Marktpreis	28821	What is the main purport of
Marlstone...	28822	Which purported to be
Marmaglia	28823	Cable purport of
Marmalade	28824	**Purpose(s)**
Marmaritis	28825	For present purposes
Marmeggia	28826	My present purpose is to
Marmella ...	28827	Will answer all purposes
Marmiton...	28828	For what purpose do you require
Marmochio	28829	For the purpose of
Marmonner	28830	Their purpose seems to have been
Marmoraria	28831	For no purpose whatever
Marmoratum	28832	Quite good enough for the purpose
Marmoreo...	28833	Is it good enough for the purpose
Marmoriren	28834	Not quite good enough for the purpose
Marmorosus	28835	On purpose
Marmoset...	28836	Appears to have been done on purpose
Marmotear	28837	Does it appear to have been done on purpose
Marmotta...	28838	Does not appear to have been done on purpose
Marmuscule	28839	Might answer the purpose
Marneron ...	28840	Has (have) not answered the purpose
Marneux ...	28841	So as to answer my (our) purpose
Marobbio ...	28842	Has (have) fully answered my (our) purpose
Maroma ...	28843	Not suitable for the purpose required
Marooned...	28844	Cable purpose you require this sum for
Maroquin...	28845	The chief purpose is for
Maroufle ...	28846	Not sufficiently suitable for my (our) purpose
Marplot ...	28847	Nothing here suitable for your purpose
Marquant...	28848	**Purser**
Marquetry	28849	A competent and reliable man to act as purser
Marquez ...	28850	Mine purser
Marquisate	28851	Similar to the purser of a Cornish mine
Marraga ...	28852	**Pursuance**
Marraine ...	28853	In pursuance of
Marranalla	28854	**Push(ed)**
Marraneta	28855	Push ahead with
Marregon ...	28856	Shall I (we) push
Marrillo ...	28857	Do not push
Marronage	28858	I (we) shall push
Marroneto	28859	To push
Marronnier	28860	To push forward
Marrowbone	28861	Push towards the (this)
Marrowless	28862	You must push on with
Marrucajo	28863	Push this work (matter) all you can
Marrullero	28864	Will push this work (matter) to every extent in my (our) power
Marschall...	28865	Push ahead with this (it)

Marselles ...	28866	When I (we) shall push ahead with
Marshgas ...	28867	You must certainly push on quickly
Marshweeds	28868	Do not try to push
Marsouin ...	28869	Do not expect to push it through
Marspiter ...	28870	Expect to push it through
Marstall ..	28871	Do you expect to push it through
Marsupium	28872	Am (are) afraid shall not be able to push matters faster
Martagon ...	28873	Push forward with
Martellata	28874	Should push on now as rapidly as possible
Martello ...	28875	Shall push it (this) all I (we) can
Martialis ...	28876	If I am (we are) to push the business
Marticola ...	28877	To enable me (us) to push the business
Martigena	28878	There is no need at present to push it
Martinello	28879	There is every need to push this (the)
Martinete...	28880	Is there any reason to push the matter
Martingale	28881	Should be pushed as rapidly as possible
Martiniega	28882	**Put** *(See also " Give.")*
Martirizar	28883	To put
Martoriare	28884	Will put
Martraza ...	28885	I (we) shall put
Martyr ...	28886	Shall I (we) put
Martyrdom	28887	Do not put
Martyred ...	28888	Might be put
Martyriser	28889	So as to enable me (us) to put
Marvelled...	28890	Do not think it very wise to put
Marzacotto	28891	Is it wise to put
Marzadga...	28892	Better put up with it
Marzemino	28893	Shall have to put up with it
Marzipan ...	28894	Will put in my (our) next letter
Masadero ...	28895	Put in your next
Mascabado	28896	Has (have) been put in the hands of
Mascarade	28897	Will have to be put off until (unless)
Mascarero...	28898	Can it be put off
Mascarpsi...	28899	Should not be put off
Mascellone	28900	Might be put off until
Maschera ...	28901	Put off for the present
Maschig ...	28902	Put off payment
Mascujar ...	28903	Put off all the payments you can
Masculate	28904	How long can you safely put it (this) off
Masculesco	28905	Cannot be put off
Masculine...	28906	Put on
Masecoral...	28907	Can you put on more men
Mashtubs...	28908	Put on as many more men as possible
Maskenball	28909	Will put on as many men as I (we) can
Maskers ...	28910	Put on the biggest force at your disposal to
Masnadiere	28911	Have put on all the force I (we) can
Masonic ...	28912	Put up
Masoritico	28913	Put up with him (it) at present
Masque ...	28914	To be put in
Masquerade	28915	Propose to put in
Massaccia	28916	Not to be put in
Massacrant	28917	Have put in
Massacred	28918	Should not put in
Massacring	28919	No need to put in
Massage ...	28920	Where do you propose to put
Massaliter	28921	To be put at
Massaretta	28922	Recommend you to put up
Massepain	28923	You had better put in a clause to the following effect
Masserizia	28924	A clause has been put in
Massgabe ...	28925	A clause will be put in

Massima	...	28926	Must be put in order
Massregel	..	28927	Require(s) to be put in order
Mastello	...	28928	**Putting**
Masterful	...	28929	Putting in
Masterhand		28930	When do you propose putting in
Masterkey		28931	**Pyrites** (*See also* "Auriferous," "Mineral," "Quartz.")
Mastermind		28932	Iron pyrites
Masterwork		28933	Copper pyrites
Mastheaded		28934	Iron and copper pyrites
Masticate	...	28935	Iron and copper pyrites carrying —— per cent. of silver
Mastiff	...	28936	Argentiferous pyrites
Mastiffdog		28937	Auriferous pyrites
Mastins	...	28938	Arsenical pyrites
Mastiquer	...	28939	The pyrites carries the precious metals
Mastodon	...	28940	The pyrites carries no precious metals
Mastoidal	...	28941	—— per cent. of pyrites
Mastranto		28942	A sample of the pyrites assayed —— silver per ton of 2,240lbs.
Mastruca	...	28943	The veinstone carries —— per cent. of pyrites
Mastrupor		28944	One —— of the gold is carried by the pyrites
Masurka	...	28945	The gold is contained in the pyrites
Matacandil		28946	An average sample of the stone contained —— per cent. of pyrites, [the latter assayed gold ——, silver ——, per ton of 2,240lbs.
Matachin	...	28947	An average sample containing pyrites assayed gold ——, silver [——, per ton of 2,240lbs.
Matafuego		28948	The concentrated pyrites assayed gold ——, silver ——, per [ton of 2,240lbs.
Matalahuga		28949	Massive pyrites
Matalan	...	28950	Propose to calcine and chlorinate the pyrites
Matalobos		28951	Pyrites containing —— per cent. of copper
Matalotage		28952	Treatment of pyrites
Matamore	...	28953	In pyrites carrying silver
Matarife	...	28954	The pyrites carries no gold, only a little silver
Matassetta		28955	For the present the pyrites will be stored
Matchgirls		28956	We have now —— tons of pyrites in stock. Estimated value
Matchless	...	28957	**Q**
Matchwood		28958	**Qualification(s)**
Matelasser		28959	Qualification —— shares
Mateless	...	28960	What are your (——'s) qualifications for ——
Matelotte	...	28961	Possessing the necessary qualifications
Matematica		28962	The following qualification(s) is (are) necessary
Mateolas	...	28963	**Qualified**
Materassa	...	28964	Fully qualified
Matercula	...	28965	Not qualified in the least
Materiaux		28966	Unless fully qualified
Materiell	...	28967	You have (—— has) ceased to be qualified
Maternal	...	28968	**Qualify**
Maternidad		28969	In order to qualify
Maternity	...	28970	**Quality** (*See also* "Common," "Finest," "Grade," "Medium.")
Matertera	...	28971	Cable what is the quality of the ore
Mathematic		28972	The quality of the ore is
Mathesis	...	28973	Medium quality
Matiere	...	28974	Good quality
Matiguelo	...	28975	Usual quality
Matineux	...	28976	Inferior quality
Matinier	...	28977	The quality of the ore is not so good
Matins	...	28978	The quality is improving
Matinsong		28979	The quality of the ore is better
Matitatojo		28980	Divide the ore into the following qualities
Matizado	...	28981	Cable the amount of each quality you have in stock
Matorral	...	28982	Only ship the best quality
Matralis	...	28983	Quality too low to ship

Matraquear	28984	Is only of medium quality
Matresco ...	28985	**Quantity(ies)** (*See also* " Great.")
Matricario	28986	This quantity
Matricide ...	28987	What quantity of —— have you available
Matricular	28988	Telegraph me (us) the quantity required
Matrignare	28989	What quantity do you want
Matrimony	28990	What quantity of
Matrimus...	28991	The quantity is limited
Matronalia	28992	The quantity is practically unlimited
Matronatus	28993	A large quantity of
Matrose ...	28994	A small quantity of
Mattaccino	28995	What quantity can you obtain
Mattapane	28996	Let me (us) know the quantity of
Matteola ...	28997	What is about the quantity you have
Matterello	28998	What is the total quantity
Matteria ...	28999	The total quantity is
Matterone	29000	What quantity will you require
Mattinata...	**29001**	Average quantity
Mattolina...	29002	Please cable approximate quantity of
Muttonato	29003	Can you increase the quantity
Mattoniero	29004	Will endeavour to increase the quantity
Mattress ...	29005	Cannot increase the quantity
Mattutino...	29006	Shall be able to increase the quantity as soon as
Maturandus	29007	Can increase the quantity to
Maturango	29008	Accumulate meanwhile as large a quantity as possible
Maturation	29009	The quantity will be less than for the past —— month(s)
Matured ...	29010	Impossible to determine quantity of ore
Maturemur	29011	A large quantity has undoubtedly been extracted
Maturescit	29012	Only a small quantity
Maturezza	29013	The quantity is less than reported
Maturity ...	29014	It is impossible to show the quantity in the time
Maturrime	29015	What is the largest quantity you can show in the time
Maturuisti	29016	What quantity have you of
Maturuit ...	29017	The quantity and quality of the ore
Matutear ...	29018	**Quarrel(s)**
Matutinal...	29019	Owing to a quarrel between
Maudire ...	29020	There has been no quarrel
Maudlin ...	29021	Which (this) has arisen out of the quarrel between—— and——
Mauerkalk	29022	Avoid any quarrel if possible
Mauern ...	29023	Is it not possible to prevent quarrel
Mauersque	29024	Impossible to prevent quarrel
Mauerwerk	29025	Quarrel amicably settled
Maugre ...	29026	Endeavour to settle quarrel
Maulaffe ...	29027	**Quarrelled**
Maulesel ...	29028	Have —— and —— quarrelled
Maulheld ...	29029	—— and —— have quarrelled
Maullador	29030	**Quarried**
Maulstick...	29031	Can be quarried at a cost of —— per ton
Maulthier...	29032	**Quarry(ies)**
Maulwurf...	29033	Large quarries of
Maunque ...	29034	The ore deposit is practically a quarry
Mauricatim	29035	Through the caving in of the sides of the quarry
Mausefalle	29036	The deposit can be worked as an open quarry
Mausegift...	29037	**Quarter(s)(ly)**
Mausestill	29038	One quarter (of)
Mausezeit...	29039	Three quarters (of)
Mausoleum	29040	During the first quarter of
Maussade...	29041	During the second quarter of
Mauvais ...	29042	During the third quarter of
Mauviette...	29043	During the last quarter of

Mavortius...	29044	**Quartz** (*See also* "Barren," "Ferruginous," "Lode.")
Mawkish ...	29045	Gold quartz
Maxilar ...	29046	Have met with quartz in the breast of the level
Maxillaire	29047	What is the width of the quartz
Maxillary ...	29048	The quartz is —— feet wide
Maximitas	29049	What is the average thickness of the quartz
Maximopere	29050	The average thickness of the quartz is ——
Maximus ...	29051	—— level is now in quartz
Mayal ...	29052	Numerous veins of quartz
Maybloom	29053	The quartz is practically barren
Mayday ...	29054	The quartz carries a little mineral
Mayduke ...	29055	We have selected the quartz and rejected one —— part
Mayflower	29056	Available quartz
Mayfly ...	29057	Concerning available quartz
Maygame ...	29058	What quartz have you available for milling
Maylady ...	29059	The only quartz available for milling is —— tons
Maymorning	29060	I (we) have —— tons of quartz available for milling
Mayonnaise	29061	There is no quartz available for milling
Mayoralty	29062	Free milling quartz
Mayorazga	29063	Quartz is almost free from base ores
Mayoress ...	29064	The quartz is decomposed for a depth of —— feet
Mayoridad	29065	The quartz carries —— per cent. of pyrites
Maypole ...	29066	The quartz is very rich
Mayuscula	29067	Specimens of the quartz yielded
Mayweed ...	29068	The matrix is quartz
Mazacote ...	29069	The quartz is very compact
Mazagatos	29070	The quartz is friable
Mazamorra	29071	A quartz leader
Mazapan ...	29072	Ferruginous quartz
Mazarine ...	29073	Quartz mill
Mazette ...	29074	No quartz below —— will pay
Maziness ...	29075	Quartz containing —— leaves a profit of —— per ton
Maznar ...	29076	Decomposed pyrites and quartz [iron sand
Mazonadura	29077	The deposit consists of quartz pebbles cemented with black
Mazoneria	29078	The quartz is of a soft and friable nature
Mazonomum	29079	There is really only a patch of quartz, containing at the out-
Mazote ...	29080	Average value of quartz reported to be [side —— tons
Mazzachera	29081	There is but little quartz between the walls
Mazzamurro	29082	The quartz is much stained with iron
Mazzasette	29083	—— tons of quartz taken from the several workings have been [crushed, with a result of —— retorted gold
Mazzeranga	29084	The quartz is well charged with pyrites
Mazzero ...	29085	Uniformly disseminated through the quartz
Mazzettino	29086	Average value of quartz
Mazzicare	29087	Quartz will average about —— per ton
Mazziculo...	29088	Chiefly quartz with
Mazzocchio	29089	**Quartzite**
Mazzolino...	29090	In a quartzite formation
Meabilis ...	29091	The hanging wall is quartzite
Meadows ...	29092	The footwall is quartzite
Meagrely ...	29093	**Quartzose**
Meagrims...	29094	**Quay**
Meajuela ...	29095	**Queer**
Mealman ...	29096	**Question(s)**
Mealtime ...	29097	Entirely out of the question
Meandering	29098	What is the question
Meaperros	29099	The question now is
Measled ...	29100	It is a question whether
Measured ...	29101	It is out of the question for the present
Meatdish ...	29102	Is there any question as to

Meatoven ...	29103	There can be no question
Meatpies ...	29104	Please answer questions contained in my (our) cable of ——
Meauca ...	29105	Please cable answer to this question immediately
Mecanica ...	29106	Please answer the following questions
Mecaniquez	29107	Cannot reply to your question(s) before
Mecastor ...	29108	The question has arisen whether
Mecedura ...	29109	To try and solve the question
Mecenate ...	29110	Will try and solve the question
Mechador ...	29111	It is a very serious question whether
Mechamment	29112	Consider it a serious question
Mechancete	29113	Do not consider it a serious question
Mechanics	29114	In case any question should arise [letter dated ——
Mechaniker	29115	The answer(s) to your question(s) is (are) contained in my
Mecher ...	29116	Question(s) has (have) been put to me (us) whether
Mechinal ...	29117	In case of any question arising refer to me (us) (——)
Mechoacan	29118	To settle the question
Mechonidem	29119	Cable to —— and obtain his (their) replies to the following
Mechoso ...	29120	Remain until the question is settled [questions
Mecompte...	29121	**Questionable**
Meconites	29122	Is believed to have been mixed up in some very questionable
Mecontent	29123	Value is very questionable [transactions
Medaglia ...	29124	Consider it questionable
Medaglista	29125	**Quick**
Medaillier...	29126	Be as quick as you can
Medallion	29127	Will be as quick as possible
Meddlesome	29128	How quick will you be about it
Medecin ...	29129	Was a little too quick
Medela ...	29130	Not sufficiently quick
Medendus	29131	**Quickly**
Medesimo	29132	Please reply quickly
Medetur ...	29133	As quickly as possible
Medialem ...	29134	Push the work as quickly as possible
Medianeria	29135	This had better be done as quickly as possible
Medianista	29136	Must be completed quickly
Medianus ...	29137	Travel as quickly as you can to
Mediastine	29138	Ascertain as quickly as possible whether
Mediatizer	29139	Forward as quickly as possible
Mediatore	29140	Very quickly
Mediatrice	29141	Unless you act quickly
Mediazione	29142	If this is done at all it must be done quickly
Medicable...	29143	How quickly can you get to
Medically ...	29144	Advise you to act quickly
Medicament	29145	Nothing here can be done very quickly
Medicastro	29146	Cannot be done more quickly
Medicatus	29147	Should be done as quickly as possible
Medicea ...	29148	**Quicksand(s)**
Medicinale	29149	**Quicksilver** (*See also* "Cinnabar," "Mercury," "Mineral.")
Medicone ...	29150	The ore contains —— per cent. of quicksilver
Medicosum	29151	The quicksilver is found associated with
Medieval ...	29152	What is the present quotation for quicksilver
Medimnus	29153	A quicksilver mine
Mediocre ...	29154	First hand quicksilver is —— per bottle
Mediocrita	29155	Second hand quicksilver is —— per bottle
Mediopano	29156	Please forward as soon as possible —— bottles of quicksilver
Medioxume	29157	There is a great loss of quicksilver
Medipontus	29158	Causes a great loss of quicksilver
Medisance	29159	The loss of quicksilver per ton of ore is at least
Meditans ...	29160	The quicksilver ore is distributed in stringers and pockets
Meditation	29161	**Quiet**
Meditative	29162	Things are pretty quiet here just now

Mediter ...	29163	Look about on the quiet
Meditrina	29164	Am looking about on the quiet
Medrar ...	29165	Everything is now quiet
Medrosia ...	29166	Keep this quite quiet
Medular ...	29167	Must be kept quiet
Medullaris	29168	Will keep it quite quiet
Medullitus	29169	This had better be kept quiet
Medullose	29170	Expected to remain quiet
Medullula	29171	**Quietly**
Meerbusen	29172	As quietly as possible
Meerenge ...	29173	Quietly if possible
Meereswoge	29174	Have a look at the mine quietly and report
Meerhorn ...	29175	Have a look at the machine(s) quietly and report
Meerrettig	29176	**Quintal(s)**
Meerschaum	29177	**Quit**
Meerufer ...	29178	Quit claim
Meetness ...	29179	Quit claim deed
Mefiance ...	29180	Threaten(s) to quit
Mefitico ...	29181	Better give notice to quit
Megalesia...	29182	Have given notice to quit
Megalium	29183	Have received notice to quit
Megarde ...	29184	Is he (are they) likely to quit
Megaspores	29185	He is (they are) likely to quit
Megisserie	29186	He is (they are) not likely to quit
Megistanes	29187	Better quit work
Megliorare	29188	**Quite**
Mehlteig ...	29189	It is quite as much
Mehlthau ...	29190	Is it quite sufficient
Mehlwurm	29191	It is quite sufficient
Mehrheit ...	29192	Is this quite right
Mehrmalig	29193	It is quite right
Meiden ...	29194	Would it be quite agreeable for you (them)
Meilleur ...	29195	It would be quite agreeable for me (them)
Meineidig	29196	Are you quite sure
Meischen ...	29197	I am quite sure (that)
Meisseln ...	29198	I am not quite sure
Meistens ...	29199	Not quite so much
Meisterin ...	29200	Quite as much as
Mejicana ...	29201	You have done quite right
Mejillon ...	29202	Quite out of the question
Mejorar ...	29203	Quite out of the question unless
Melacchino	29204	Would be quite near enough
Melacitola	29205	Is quite near enough
Melaconite	29206	**Quotation(s)**
Meladucha	29207	The quotation(s) is (are) merely nominal
Melagrana	29208	What are the quotations for
Melampus	29209	Cable lowest quotations for
Melampyron	29210	Cable to-day's quotations of
Melancholy	29211	The following is (are) to-day's quotation(s)
Melandrys	29212	Since last quotation(s)
Melangola	29213	Quotation(s) too high
Melangue ...	29214	Quotation(s) too low
Melanism ...	29215	What are the official quotations for
Melanteria	29216	There is no quotation for —— shares at all
Melanthion	29217	The last quotation for these shares was
Melanurus	29218	Can you get quotation for
Melaphyre	29219	Your quotation must be f.o.b.
Melarancia	29220	Your quotation must be c.& f.
Melcocha ...	29221	Your quotation must be c.f.& i.
Meldung ...	29222	Quotation is (was) f o.b.

Meleagris ...	29223	Quotation is (was) c.& f.
Melecina ...	29224	Quotation is (was) c.f.& i.
Melenudo ..	29225	Unable to give quotation
Melessa ...	29226	Quotation for lead is
Meleteus ...	29227	Quotation for silver is
Melgacho ...	29228	Quotation for copper is
Meliceria ...	29229	Quotation for zinc is
Melichino ...	29230	Get me quotations of
Melichros ...	29231	Other quotations higher
Melicrator	29232	Other quotations lower
Melifero ...	29233	Stock Exchange quotations
Meliloto ...	29234	**Quote**
Melimeli ...	29235	To quote
Melindre ...	29236	What shall I (we) quote
Melioresco	29237	Quote as low as possible
Meliphylla	29238	Quote high
Melissic ...	29239	What do —— quote for
Melitensis...	29240	Quote best price for
Melitites ...	29241	**Quoted**
Meliturgus	29242	Quoted at
Meliuscule	29243	I (we) quoted you for
Melizomum	29244	Cable what are the shares quoted at now
Melkhuh ...	29245	Are now quoted at par
Mellado ..	29246	Quoted at —— premium
Melliculum	29247	Quoted at —— discount
Mellifer ...	29248	The shares are quoted nominally, there is no business
Mellificus ...	29249	Shares are not quoted on the Stock Exchange
Melligenus	29250	—— shares are now being quoted at
Mellonajo ...	29251	**R**
Mellowly ...	29252	**Radius**
Melmoso ...	29253	Within a radius of
Melodia ...	29254	What is the required radius
Melodicon	29255	**Rail(s)** (*See also* "Crosscut," "Go.")
Melodieux	29256	Send tracing showing section of rail
Melodinam	29257	Steel rails —— pounds per yard
Melodisch...	29258	Steel rails
Melodized ..	29259	To be finished with T rails complete
Melodrama	29260	**Railway(s)** (*See also* "Line.")
Melofoliam	29261	On —— railway
Melograph	29262	There is a railway within —— miles
Melomanie	29263	There is a railway close up to the property
Melomelum	29264	The —— railway crosses a portion of the property
Melonniere	29265	A railway is projected to be completed within —— months, [which will come within —— miles of the property
Melons ...	29266	A railway is projected to join
Melopepo ...	29267	There is a railway between —— and —— [way is anticipated
Melophare	29268	The weather is becoming very severe and a block on the rail-
Melopiano	29269	Before the weather stops traffic on the railway
Melosidad	29270	When will the snow block on the railway be removed
Melotritis...	29271	Anticipate that the railway will be open again for traffic in about [—— days
Melpomene	29272	When do you think the railway will be open for traffic
Melting ...	29273	The railway has been opened since
Meluggine	29274	The railway is now open
Meluzza ...	29275	Shall commence shipping ore as soon as the railway is opened
Members ...	29276	Thence by railway —— miles
Membrane	29277	Accumulate as much ore as possible and ship as soon as railway [is open
Membranula	29278	Survey for railway
Membratim	29279	Your railway proposition is
Membretto	29280	Your railway proposition is too costly

Membrilla	29281	Railway blocked by
Membro ...	29282	**Rain(s)**
Membrolino	29283	As soon as the rains begin
Membrosus	29284	During the rains
Membrudo	29285	Until after the rains
Memecylon	29286	Rain has now commenced
Memento ...	29287	Owing to the scarcity of rain
Memoirise	29288	We have only sufficient water after a heavy rain
Memorabile	29289	After a heavy rain we have —— miners' inches of water
Memoranda	29290	Cannot forward on account of the rains
Memoratrix	29291	The rain has been excessive [working
Memorevole	29292	Although the rain has been heavy we have been able to continue
Memoriale	29293	Even with heavy rain the supply of water is only —— miners'
Memorioso	29294	No rain has fallen since [inches
Memoriter	29295	We cannot commence to crush until the rains begin
Menaced ...	29296	In consequence of the heavy rains
Menagery...	29297	Are now having heavy rains
Menarrosto	29298	Cannot expect continuous rain for —— months
Menatina ...	29299	The rains have been very heavy during the past week
Menatrice...	29300	Have had incessant rain since my last
Mendacious	29301	Rain has been falling since
Mendicant	29302	The absence of rain is becoming very serious
Mendicatio	29303	Washed away by the rain
Mendicidad	29304	Was (were) more or less washed away owing to the heavy rains
Mendicite...	29305	Considerable damage has been done by the rains
Mendiculus	29306	**Rainy** (See also "Commenced.")
Mendicum	29307	**Raise** (See also "Rise.")
Mendigar ...	29308	To raise
Mendiguez	29309	How much can you raise
Mendius ...	29310	Can raise about
Mendrugo	29311	Can you raise
Meneador...	29312	Cannot raise more than
Menestral...	29313	Can easily raise
Menetrier...	29314	If you can raise
Mengajo ...	29315	If you are unable to raise
Menguante	29316	Endeavour to raise
Meniana ...	29317	Will endeavour to raise
Meniantes	29318	Expect to raise about
Menimato...	29319	Raise as high as possible
Meninge ...	29320	Raise as much as possible
Meningitis	29321	How much (many) can you raise per day of twenty-four hours
Menique ...	29322	Can raise per day of twenty-four hours —— tons
Menjunge...	29323	The raise in the back —— level
Menomanza	29324	Estimate we shall raise next week —— tons
Menomuccio	29325	As soon as we begin to raise ore [during next ——
Menoscabar	29326	State approximate tonnage and value of ore expect to raise
Menotisa ...	29327	We have not been able to raise any ore owing to
Menotte ...	29328	**Raised**
Menovale ...	29329	What quantity of ore have you raised since
Mensagero	29330	—— tons have been raised since
Menschlich	29331	Have you raised
Mensetta ...	29332	I (we) have raised
Mensonge...	29333	They have raised
Menstrual...	29334	How much have you (they) raised since ——
Mensula ...	29335	Will be raised
Mentastro...	29336	**Raising**
Mentecatez	29337	Raising per day
Mentibor ...	29338	What are you raising per day
Mentidero...	29339	We are now raising —— tons per ——
Mentiens ...	29340	Are now raising

Mentiginem	29341	Raising upon the average
Mentionner	29342	When will you begin raising ore
Mentitrice	29343	**Ramify(ies)**
Mentiturus	29344	**Rapid(ly)**
Mentosto ...	29345	As rapidly as possible
Mentovato	29346	**Rash(ly)**
Mentulatus	29347	**Ratchet**
Menuaille...	29348	Ratchet wheel
Menuceles	29349	Ratchet gear
Menudear...	29350	Send six ratchet wheels
Menudillo	29351	**Rate(s)**
Menuiserie	29352	Rates falling
Menuisier...	29353	Rates rising
Menuzar ...	29354	Rate of exchange
Menzionato	29355	At the rate of
Menzognere	29356	At what rate
Meollada ...	29357	At any rate
Mephitic ...	29358	What are the rates for
Mephiticus	29359	At what rate can (could) you
Meprisable	29360	What rate are you bidding for
Mequetrefe	29361	The rates are very high
Meraculus	29362	The rate for freight seems high
Meramente	29363	What is the present rate of extraction
Meraviglia	29364	The present rate of extraction is
Mercabilis	29365	At our present rate of extraction
Mercadante	29366	Threaten(s) to increase the rate(s)
Mercaderia	29367	Expect(s) that the rate(s) will be lessened
Mercancia...	29368	Cannot get a better rate
Mercandus	29369	Rate of speed
Mercantile	29370	Present rate of driving
Mercantone	29371	Present rate of sinking
Mercaptan	29372	Can you not increase the present rate of (for)
Mercatale...	29373	Will endeavour to increase the present rate
Mercatanza	29374	Unable to increase the rate (owing to)
Mercedivus	29375	At what rate do you expect to ship
Mercedula	29376	Expect to ship at the rate of
Mercenario	29377	What rate are you paying for
Mercennajo	29378	This is a very low rate
Mercennume	29379	At the present low rate
Mercers ...	29380	Endeavour to get lower rate
Mercimonio	29381	Lowest rate for —— is ——
Mercoledi ...	29382	**Rather**
Mercredi ...	29383	Which would you rather do
Merculino...	29384	Rather than
Mercurial ...	29385	I (we) would rather that you
Mercyseat...	29386	I (we) would much rather
Merdellon...	29387	Would rather
Merecedor	29388	Would rather not
Meremur ...	29389	Rather better
Merendar ...	29390	Rather worse
Merendone	29391	**Ratification**
Merengue...	29392	**Ratify**
Meretriz ...	29393	**Ratio**
Mergansar	29394	**Ravine(s)**
Meridialis...	29395	A deep ravine
Meridien ...	29396	At the bottom of the ravine
Meridional	29397	Separated by a ravine —— feet deep
Merienda ...	29398	In order to cross ravine
Meriggiana	29399	Crossing ravine saves a distance of
Meriggio ...	29400	From the side of the ravine

Meritabunt	29401	**Raw**
Meritamus	29402	**Reach(es)**
Meritantur	29403	—— will in all probability reach —— on ——
Meritatote	29404	When do you expect to reach
Merited ...	29405	I (we) expect to reach —— on or about
Meritentis	29406	As soon as I (we) reach
Meritevole	29407	Cable as soon as you reach
Meritorius	29408	In case the letter does not reach you (dated ——)
Merkbar ...	29409	Should be posted not later than —— if it is to reach me at ——
Merklichen	29410	Have mailed instructions to-day which should reach you at (on)
Merkwurdig	29411	Will reach you at
Merlato ...	29412	Is (was) to reach you at
Merlatura...	29413	Reaches from —— to ——
Merlin ...	29414	If you cannot reach —— before —— cable instructions as to
Merlotto ...	29415	**Reached**
Merluche ...	29416	Has (have) reached me
Mermaid ...	29417	Has (have) not yet reached me
Merobibus	29418	Can be reached by
Meroctes ...	29419	Cannot be reached without
Merodear ...	29420	Has (have) almost reached the
Merodista...	29421	**Reaction**
Meropidis...	29422	Reaction has undoubtedly commenced
Merrain ...	29423	There will no doubt be a speedy reaction
Mersatus ...	29424	Cable me at first sign of reaction
Merulento	29425	There are already signs of reaction
Mesaconic	29426	Reaction imminent
Mesallier ...	29427	There is no sign of reaction at present
Mesancylum	29428	Owing to the reaction
Mesaula ...	29429	**Read**
Meschiare...	29430	Read our cable of —— as follows
Meschinita	29431	For —— read ——
Mescibile ...	29432	Omit the following code words and read instead
Mesciroba...	29433	Should read thus
Mescitore ...	29434	To be read at
Mescolanza	29435	Read the next word as a number
Mescolato...	29436	Read the first two words as numbers
Mesegueria	29437	Read the third word as a number
Mesentery	29438	Read the fourth word as a number
Meshworked	29439	Read the fifth word as a number
Mesiazgo ...	29440	Read the sixth word as a number
Mesillo ...	29441	Read the seventh word as a number
Mesmerism	29442	Read the eighth word as a number
Mesnadero	29443	Read the ninth word as a number
Mesocarps	29444	Read the tenth word as a number
Mesochorus	29445	Read the —— word as a number
Mesolabum	29446	**Readiest**
Mesoleucus	29447	What do you consider is the readiest way
Mesomelas	29448	The readiest way is
Mesonage...	29449	**Readily**
Mesonanta	29450	**Readiness**
Mesonista...	29451	Hold yourself in readiness to
Mesopodio	29452	Am (are) holding myself (ourselves) in readiness to
Mesotypes	29453	**Reading**
Mesoxalate	29454	What is the true reading
Mesozoic ...	29455	Is the true reading
Mespilus. ...	29456	Is not the true reading
Mesquin ...	29457	**Readjust(ed)**
Messagerie	29458	**Readjusting**
Messaggio	29459	**Ready** (*See also* "Get," "Getting.")
Messbude...	29460	When do you expect to be ready

Messeant ...	29461	We have been ready since
Messengers	29462	Please cable as soon as you are ready
Messerino...	29463	As soon as everything is ready
Messiato ...	29464	I (we) expect to be ready about
Messieurs...	29465	Everything is now ready
Messingen	29466	Everything can be ready not later than
Messopfer...	29467	Must be ready by
Messruthe	29468	Are you ready
Messtable...	29469	Have everything ready
Messtisch ...	29470	Nothing is practically ready
Messzeit ...	29471	Not yet ready
Mestenco ...	29472	All ready
Mesticare ...	29473	Hope to get everything ready in three days
Mestichino	29474	Will shortly be ready
Mestizia ...	29475	I am (we are) quite ready to begin
Mestoletta	29476	When will —— (he) be ready
Mestolone...	29477	Advise —— (him) as soon as you are ready
Mestura ...	29478	Must be ready by —— certain
Metacarpal	29479	Will be ready by —— certain
Metadella ...	29480	You had better be ready to leave at any moment
Metairie ...	29481	Cannot possibly be ready before
Metaketone	29482	Shall not be ready until
Metalepsis	29483	Will cable you as soon as I am (we are) ready
Metalifero	29484	You should have everything ready before you begin to
Metallen ...	29485	Can be ready in time to ship on
Metalliere...	29486	Cannot be ready in time to ship on
Metallique	29487	Ready to (for)
Metalloïd ...	29488	Ready to purchase
Metalurgia	29489	Everything is ready for
Metaphor ...	29490	As soon as everything is ready for
Metaphrast	29491	Have everything ready by the time he arrives
Metaplasmo	29492	Have everything ready by the time I arrive
Metastasis	29493	When ready cable
Metastatic	29494	If all ready
Metatesi ...	29495	Are you (is ——) all ready for
Metaturas	29496	As soon as you (they) are all ready for
Metayere ...	29497	**Real**
Meteduria	29498	**Realization(s)**
Metellus ...	29499	Realization of
Meteore ...	29500	**Realize**
Meteorique	29501	How much are you likely to realize (from)
Meteorite ...	29502	I am (we are) likely to realize
Metheglin	29503	Expect to realize
Methide ...	29504	Will realize somewhere about
Methodical	29505	Am (are) endeavouring to realize
Methodize	29506	Would it be a good time to realize
Methoxyl ...	29507	I do not think it would be a good time to realize
Methylenic	29508	Would probably be a good time to realize
Methylic ...	29509	Would you advise me (us) to realize
Meticcio ...	29510	Have not been able to realize
Meticuleux	29511	Will not realize more than
Meticuloso	29512	Cannot advise you whether to realize or not
Metiendus	29513	Shall I (we) begin to realize
Metimiento	29514	Realize all available assets and mail accounts
Metitionem	29515	Realize all ore possible
Metodico ...	29516	**Realized**
Metonymy	29517	Has not realized
Metopion ...	29518	Sale has realized
Metralla ...	29519	What has it (have they) realized
Metrically	29520	It (they) realized

Metrocomia	29521	Think it (they) ought to have realized more
Metrology...	29522	Am (are) satisfied with what it has (they have) realized
Metromania	29523	By which time we shall have realized
Metropole	29524	All ores to be realized
Mettable ...	29525	**Really**
Mettersi	29526	**Reappoint(ed)**
Mettiloro ...	29527	**Reappointing**
Metuens ...	29528	**Reason(s)** (*See also* "Know.")
Metzeln ...	29529	My reason(s) is (are)
Metzger ...	29530	What are your (——'s) reasons for
Meubler ...	29531	Cable your reason for requiring
Meucheln ...	29532	Give(s) as a reason
Meuchlings	29533	Telegraph your reasons for declining
Meuliere ...	29534	The reason(s) was (were)
Meurtrier ...	29535	Do you know any reason
Mewing ...	29536	The only reason I know is
Mezclable...	29537	Do not know any reason why
Mezcladura	29538	The reason is
Mezereon ...	29539	The reason generally believed is
Mezquindad	29540	Can you ascertain the reason (why)
Mezzajuolo	29541	Will endeavour to ascertain the reason (why)
Mezzalana	29542	Anything in reason
Mezzanetto	29543	There is reason to anticipate
Mezzanita	29544	There is no reason to anticipate
Mezzatinta	29545	For the reasons already given
Mezzedima	29546	What is the reason
Mezzettino	29547	The reason of —— is
Mezzobusto	29548	Out of all reason
Miagar ...	29549	**Reasonable(ly)** (*See also* "Expense.")
Miagolare...	29550	It is reasonable to expect
Miasmatic	29551	Is it reasonable to expect
Miaulement	29552	It is not reasonable to expect
Micalete ...	29553	If —— will take a reasonable price
Miccianza...	29554	It is not reasonable
Miccichino	29555	It is very reasonable
Michaelmas	29556	Perfectly reasonable
Micidia ...	29557	I think the offer is a very reasonable one
Micotrogus	29558	Can you not induce —— to be more reasonable
Micrasters	29559	I (we) think —— offer quite a reasonable one
Microcosm	29560	I do not think you will get a more reasonable one (offer)
Microlites...	29561	It is only reasonable that
Microphony	29562	Is willing to accept any reasonable offer
Middlemen	29563	Am (is) (are) quite ready to do anything reasonable
Midheaven	29564	It is hardly reasonable
Midleg ...	29565	It is not reasonable to expect otherwise at this time
Midolloso ...	29566	Is it reasonable to suppose that
Midriff ...	29567	It is reasonable to suppose that
Midshipman	29568	**Reassure(d)**
Midwifery	29569	**Reassuring**
Miembro ...	29570	**Rebate(s)**
Miercoles ...	29571	To rebate
Miethen ...	29572	Rebate of
Miethleute	29573	Must have a rebate of at least
Miethling	29574	Is willing to give a rebate
Miethzeit ...	29575	No rebate will be allowed
Mietitore ...	29576	Has (have) allowed a rebate of
Mietitrice ...	29577	Refuse(s) to give a rebate
Migaja ...	29578	Subject to a rebate of
Migdolibs...	29579	Rebate insufficient
Mightiness	29580	Cannot increase rebate

Migliajo ...	29581	Unable to obtain increased rebate
Migliarina	29582	**Rebuild**
Migliorare	29583	Will it be necessary to rebuild
Mignarder	29584	It will be necessary to rebuild
Mignardise	29585	It will not be necessary to rebuild
Mignello ...	29586	When do you commence to rebuild
Mignolare ..	29587	Hope to commence to rebuild on or about ——
Mignonette	29588	Have already commenced to rebuild
Mignoter ...	29589	Shall commence to rebuild as soon as I can get in the necessary
Migrabunt	29590	Rebuild without delay [supplies
Migraine ...	29591	Shall commence to rebuild immediately
Migranimi	29592	**Recall**
Migrantur	29593	To recall
Migrassit ...	29594	Had I (we) not better recall
Migratory...	29595	It will be necessary to recall
Migraturus	29596	Suggest that you recall
Migravero	29597	Must first recall
Migravisti	29598	**Recalled**
Migrazione	29599	Likely to be recalled
Migremur...	29600	—— is (are) likely to be recalled
Mijauree ...	29601	Has been recalled
Mijediega...	29602	In the event of your being recalled
Milagrero...	29603	**Recapitulate(d)**
Milchbart	29604	**Receipt(s)**
Milchcow ...	29605	Am (are) in receipt of your letter dated
Milcheimer	29606	Is (are) in receipt of your letter dated
Milchglas...	29607	What are the total receipts for the month of
Milchsaft ...	29608	The total receipts for the month of —— are
Mildewed ...	29609	What were the receipts during
Mildthatig	29610	Receipts hitherto have been nil
Milenario ...	29611	Receipts hitherto
Milenrama	29612	The receipts were
Milepora ...	29613	Expenses are about equalled by receipts
Milesius ...	29614	Receipts exceed cost by
Milestones	29615	Cost exceeds receipts by
Milfoil ...	29616	Immediately on receipt
Milgrana ...	29617	As soon as you are in receipt of this (it) cable
Milhojas ...	29618	Cable your receipts for
Miliaceam...	29619	Our receipts for —— amount to ——
Miliarium...	29620	Without including last month's receipts
Miliciano ...	29621	Inclusive of receipts for current month
Militaire ...	29622	Estimated receipts
Militant ...	29623	Please acknowledge by cable receipt of this (to)
Militaron ...	29624	Until receipt of
Militatore...	29625	Acknowledge receipt of remittance value —— sent on ——
Militiolam	29626	Arrange(d) with —— to cable receipt of money
Militorio ...	29627	**Receive**
Milkfever ...	29628	To receive
Milkmaid ...	29629	Did you receive
Milkpan ...	29630	Did not receive
Milkscore...	29631	Which you will receive
Milksop ...	29632	Cannot receive it (them) before
Milkwhite	29633	The moment you receive it (them)
Milkwort ...	29634	When may I expect to receive
Milkyway	29635	You may expect to receive it (them) on or about
Millantare	29636	You will receive full instructions by mail
Millefolia ...	29637	As I did not receive
Millenary ...	29638	Should you not receive
Millennial...	29639	In case I do not receive
Millepede ...	29640	You will receive additional

Millesime ...	29641	When do you expect to receive
Millet ...	29642	When shall I (we) receive the document(s)
Millhands...	29643	When will you be ready to receive
Millhorse ...	29644	Hope to be ready to receive —— before
Milliarde ...	29645	In case you should receive
Milliner ...	29646	Telegraph the moment you receive the money
Millrace ...	29647	As soon as I (we) receive from
Millwheels	29648	Unless you receive —— to be paid before you start
Miltitibus...	29649	**Received**
Miluogo ...	29650	Has (have) received your letter dated ——
Milvina ...	29651	Has (have) not received your letter dated ——
Mimallones	29652	Have you received
Mimbrear ...	29653	Has (have) not been received
Mimbroso...	29654	Has (have) not yet received
Mimetical...	29655	Do not act until you have received
Mimetist ...	29656	I (we) shall not act until I (we) have received
Mimiambus	29657	Have received orders from —— (to)
Mimically...	29658	Will by this time have received
Mimicker ...	29659	Enclosure referred to not received
Mimique ...	29660	In case you should not have received
Mimograph	29661	Have you received any notice of
Mimologia	29662	Have received notice of
Minacciare	29663	Have received official notice of
Minaciter ...	29664	Have not received any notice at all
Minaret ...	29665	Have not received this (it)
Minatory ...	29666	Received foregoing from —— (since when)
Minauder...	29667	The following has been received since
Mincemeat	29668	Only just received from
Minchione	29669	Not yet received from
Mindern ...	29670	We have not received any —— since
Mindestens	29671	Have not received it (this). How was it sent ?
Mineralise	29672	Have you received and paid
Minerval ...	29673	Have received —— and paid the same to
Minestrare	29674	None received since
Minestrino	29675	I (we) have not received any tidings of
Minever ...	29676	Have you received any tidings of
Mingled ...	29677	Which you have received from
Mingon ...	29678	Which you have already received
Miniaceus ..	29679	Have —— been received by you ? They were mailed on
Miniatrice	29680	Has (have) received several cables from
Miniatulus	29681	**Receiver**
Miniature...	29682	Apply for a Receiver to be appointed
Minimista	29683	Have applied for a Receiver to be appointed
Minimized	29684	Receiver not yet appointed
Ministerio...	29685	Receiver has been appointed
Ministrant	29686	Official Receiver
Ministril ...	29687	**Recent**
Minorar ...	29688	Recent improvements
Minorasco	29689	Recent developments
Minorativo	29690	Has this been recent
Minoridad	29691	Quite recent.
Minoringo	29692	So recent as
Minorkey ...	29693	What is the most recent information regarding
Minormente	29694	The most recent information regarding
Minotaur ...	29695	Recent movements
Minstrels ...	29696	Cable the most recent change
Minthos ...	29697	The most recent change(s) is (are)
Minting ...	29698	**Recently**
Minucia ...	29699	Developments recently made have proved
Minuendus	29700	Which have been recently begun

Minuettina	29701	Have you recently been on the property
Minuetto ...	29702	I have recently been on the property
Minurio ...	29703	Who has (have) recently visited the property
Minuscolo...	29704	Not been very recently
Minutaglia	29705	Not at all recently
Minutatim	29706	Has only recently begun
Minutegun	29707	Was (were) recently at
Minutero ...	29708	There was recently
Minutieux	29709	—— is said to have recently
Minuzzame	29710	**Recess**
Minuzzolo	29711	A recess should be left to allow for
Minyantes	29712	Send exact dimensions of recess
Miocene ...	29713	So as to form a recess
Mioche ...	29714	Recess will admit of
Miografia ...	29715	Shall have to enlarge recess in order to
Miologia ...	29716	Cannot enlarge recess beyond
Mirabel ...	29717	**Recharge(d)**
Mirabile ...	29718	Must be recharged
Mirabolano	29719	**Reciprocate(d)**
Mirabundus	29720	**Reckless(ly)**
Miracles ...	29721	**Reckon(s)**
Miracolone	29722	How did you reckon
Miraculam	29723	You should not reckon on
Miraculous	29724	Can we reckon on
Miradura ...	29725	You may reckon on
Mirage ...	29726	It is useless to reckon that
Miraglio ...	29727	How many (much) did you reckon for
Miramiento	29728	How many (much) did you reckon as
Mirasol ...	29729	**Reckoned**
Mirationis	29730	Reckoned as
Miratore ...	29731	Reckoned in the following way
Mirificus ...	29732	Formerly I (we) reckoned that
Mirinaque	29733	Was reckoned for (as)
Mirlarse ...	29734	To be reckoned as
Mirliflore ...	29735	**Recognize**
Mirmidon...	29736	Cannot recognize
Mirmillo ...	29737	To recognize
Miroiterie...	29738	Refuse(d) to recognize
Mirolla ...	29739	Do not recognize
Mirtetum ...	29740	Refuse(s) to recognize any claim
Mirthfully	29741	In case they refuse to recognize
Mirthless ...	29742	Has (have) refused to recognize any claim
Mirtidano...	29743	If he (they) will not recognize
Mirtiforme	29744	Has promised to recognize any claim if just
Misagiato...	29745	I think you (——) ought to recognize the fact
Misaiming	29746	**Recognizing**
Misantropo	29747	Recognizing and confirming
Misattend...	29748	**Recollect**
Misbegot ...	29749	Do you recollect
Misbehaved	29750	I (we) recollect perfectly well
Miscadere...	29751	Cannot recollect perfectly but have a notion that
Miscall ...	29752	Cannot recollect at all
Miscalled ...	29753	See if —— can recollect
Miscella ...	29754	**Recommence**
Mischanced	29755	Recommence work
Mischen ...	29756	Recommence driving
Mischiante	29757	Recommence raising
Miscibile ...	29758	Recommence shipping
Miscontrue	29759	Recommence sinking
Miscounted	29760	Recommence stoping

RECOMMENCE (*continued*). Mis

Miscuglio ...	29761	Recommence buying
Miserabile	29762	Recommence selling
Miseraccio	29763	When will you recommence
Miseraica ...	29764	Shall recommence —— on
Miserandus	29765	So as to recommence
Miseranter	29766	Will recommence immediately
Miseratio ...	29767	Will recommence at the earliest possible moment
Miserello ...	29768	You must recommence at once to
Miseretur ...	29769	Cannot recommence whilst
Miseritudo	29770	Shall recommence within the next —— days
Miserlike ...	29771	You (——) had better recommence at once
Miserly ...	29772	Recommence it (this)
Miserrimo	29773	Recommence both
Miserulus ...	29774	Do not recommence until
Misfatto ...	29775	Do not recommence until you have seen
Misfortune	29776	Shall not recommence until
Misgiving...	29777	**Recommenced**
Misgrown...	29778	Have recommenced driving
Misionero...	29779	Have recommenced raising
Misjudging	29780	Have recommenced shipping
Mislain ...	29781	Have recommenced sinking
Mislayer ...	29782	Have recommenced stoping
Mislealta ...	29783	Have recommenced work
Mismatch...	29784	Have already recommenced
Misogamist	29785	Have you recommenced
Misogyny ...	29786	Should you not already have recommenced
Misplaced ..	29787	**Recommencing**
Mispresa ...	29788	**Recommend(s)**
Misprints ...	29789	To recommend
Misquote ...	29790	Recommend you to
Missalbook	29791	—— recommend(s) that
Missbranch	29792	I (we) can strongly recommend
Missdeuten	29793	Recommend before doing this to
Missfallen	29794	Recommend putting up
Missgonnen	29795	I (we) would recommend purchase upon the following terms
Misshellig	29796	Can you recommend a good man
Missiculo ...	29797	I (we) cannot recommend a good man at this moment
Missitatus	29798	What would you recommend
Missklang	29799	Cable if you can recommend
Misslauten	29800	Ascertain from —— whether he (they) can recommend
Misslingen	29801	I (we) can safely recommend —— (him)
Missrathen	29802	You can safely recommend —— (him)
Misston ...	29803	Would you recommend —— (him)
Mistagoga	29804	I hardly like to recommend —— (him)
Mistamente	29805	Do you strongly recommend me (us) to accept
Mistarius ...	29806	Strongly recommend you to accept this (it)
Mistbeet ...	29807	**Recommendation**
Mistela ...	29808	Have you any further recommendation
Misterioso	29809	**Recommended**
Mistgabel ...	29810	Has (have) been strongly recommended (by)
Mistgrube	29811	Has (have) been recommended to avoid
Misthaufen	29812	Was (were) not recommended
Mistichita...	29813	Strongly recommended by
Mistilineo ...	29814	Were certainly not recommended by
Mistletoe ...	29815	As recommended by
Mistrust ...	29816	Can be recommended to
Mistrusted	29817	**Reconcile**
Misturato ..	29818	How do you (does ——) reconcile
Misusage ...	29819	**Reconsider**
Misused ...	29820	Think you had better reconsider

[.497] II

Misvenire...	29821	Would it not be advisable to reconsider
Mitayo ...	29822	Reconsider the matter
Mitbesitz ...	29823	Would —— (he) reconsider the matter
Mitbruder	29824	It would be fruitless to ask —— to reconsider the matter
Mitburger	29825	Have asked —— to reconsider the matter, expect his reply [within —— days
Mitdasein...	29826	It would certainly be worth while to reconsider

Reconsideration

Miterbe ...	29827	**Reconsideration**
Mitescens...	29828	After reconsideration
Mitgift ...	29829	Reconsideration useless
Mithalten...	29830	The only object of reconsideration would be
Mithilfe ...	29831	What is the object of reconsideration
Mithin ...	29832	Cannot see any object in reconsideration
Mithras ...	29833	**Reconsidered**
Mithridax...	29834	Cannot be reconsidered
Mitificare ...	29835	Must be reconsidered
Mitigacion	29836	Now being reconsidered
Mitigandus	29837	Have you (has ——) reconsidered
Mitigate ...	29838	Has (have) reconsidered
Mitigating	29839	Has (have) not reconsidered
Mitiger ...	29840	Has (have) been fully reconsidered
Mitlaut ...	29841	As soon as it (this) has been reconsidered
Mitleidig ...	29842	When will it be reconsidered
Mitones ...	29843	Will be reconsidered on
Mitonner ...	29844	Will be reconsidered as soon as
Mitraille ...	29845	When the whole matter will be reconsidered
Mitred ...	29846	**Reconstruct** (*See also* " Reorganize.")
Mitridato ...	29847	**Reconstruction** (*See also* " Reorganization.")
Mitschuler	29848	**Record(s)** (*See also* "Deed.")
Mittaglich	29849	Can you find any record of
Mittelbar ...	29850	Cannot find any record of
Mittelwort	29851	The only record I (we) can find is
Mittendus	29852	There is no record
Mittler ...	29853	Previous to any record being kept
Mittwoch ...	29854	It will be necessary to carefully record
Mitunter ...	29855	The abstract of the record shows
Mitwelt ...	29856	I (we) learn from the record (that)
Mitwirken	29857	The deeds should be placed on record
Mitzahlen...	29858	Hope to record deeds not later than
Mixturar ...	29859	Look up records of
Mizzling ...	29860	Carefully search the records
Moanful ...	29861	Have searched the records
Mobcap ...	29862	Will have records carefully searched
Mobilato ...	29863	**Recorded** (*See also* "Deed.")
Mobile ...	29864	The deed does not seem to be recorded
Mobiliare ...	29865	It is recorded
Mobilier ...	29866	Has (have) not been recorded
Mobilise ...	29867	All deeds have been duly recorded in the name of
Mobilitas ...	29868	When do you expect to get deeds recorded
Mocadero ...	29869	The deeds will be recorded on or before
Mocajardo	29870	The deeds were recorded on
Moccasin ...	29871	**Recorder**
Moccatojo	29872	Recorder at
Moccicare...	29873	Before the Recorder
Moccicoso...	29874	County Recorder
Moccolino...	29875	**Recover**
Mocedad ...	29876	What are you likely to recover
Mochada ...	29877	Expect to recover about
Mochilero ...	29878	Is he (are they) likely to recover
Mockable ...	29879	Ought to recover

Mockgold ...	29880	Hardly expected to recover
Mocking ...	29881	Expect to recover the whole amount
Mockishly	29882	Expect to recover the best part of
Mockturtle	29883	Only expect to recover a small amount (part)
Mocosidad	29884	Is it worth while to try and recover
Modaccia ...	29885	It is not worth while to try and recover
Modality ...	29886	It is certainly worth while to try and recover
Modanatura	29887	Can you recover
Modelar ...	29888	Cannot recover more than
Modellato...	29889	You must recover if possible
Modelling...	29890	Cannot recover the damage
Modelliren	29891	Should you not be able to recover more than
Modenarr ...	29892	It will be very difficult to recover
Moderamen	29893	It was very difficult to recover
Moderarsi...	29894	I (we) shall endeavour to recover
Moderatrix	29895	**Recoverable**
Moderig ...	29896	**Recovered**
Moderner ...	29897	The whole is likely to be recovered
Modernism	29898	Only a small part is likely to be recovered
Modestia ...	29899	Anything recovered
Modewaare	29900	Recovered slightly
Modicellus	29901	Little, if anything, will be recovered
Modicite ...	29902	**Recovering**
Modificar ...	29903	Steadily recovering
Modista ...	29904	**Recovery**
Modolare ...	29905	What is the chance of recovery
Modorrar ...	29906	No chance of recovery
Modulamen	29907	Fair hope of recovery
Modulating	29908	**Rectification**
Modulator	29909	**Rectified**
Moelleux ...	29910	Cannot this be rectified
Mofadura...	29911	Should be rectified at once
Mofetizado	29912	Try and have it rectified immediately
Moffette ...	29913	Will try and have it rectified immediately
Mofletudo...	29914	It was rectified almost immediately after it occurred
Mogeles ...	29915	Cannot now be rectified
Moggiata ...	29916	Should be rectified at all costs
Mogiganga	29917	Must be rectified
Mogigatez	29918	Would not aid us if it was rectified
Mogliama...	29919	Would it aid us to have it rectified
Moglich ...	29920	It would aid us materially to have it rectified
Mogrollo ...	29921	**Rectify**
Mohair ...	29922	**Recurrence**
Moharrache	29923	So as to prevent any recurrence
Mohawk ...	29924	Has there been any recurrence
Mohiento ...	29925	There has not been any recurrence
Mohnsaft ...	29926	There has been only one recurrence
Mohoso ...	29927	There is not likely to be another recurrence
Mohrin ...	29928	There has been a recurrence (of)
Moignon ...	29929	**Redress**
Moineau ...	29930	To seek redress
Moiniere ...	29931	Can you get no redress for
Moinillon...	29932	Our only redress is to
Moirage ...	29933	Redress must be insisted upon
Moisissure	29934	What redress can we obtain
Moissine ...	29935	If necessary seek legal redress
Moissonner	29936	Will seek legal redress at once
Moistened ..	29937	Shall I seek redress
Moistness...	29938	Intend(s) to seek redress
Moiteur ...	29939	Redress refused

Mojabana...	29940	Redress granted
Mojarrilla...	29941	**Reduce** (*See also* "Expense.")
Mojonar ...	29942	To reduce
Molarius ...	29943	Try and reduce
Molasses ...	29944	Shall try and reduce
Moldeador	29945	Must manage to reduce expenses
Moldurar ...	29946	Reduce expenses as far as possible
Molecule ...	29947	How much will it (this) reduce expenses by
Moledor ...	29948	It is absolutely necessary to reduce
Moleeyed ...	29949	Cannot reduce
Molehill ...	29950	Will endeavour to reduce expenses (until)
Moleskins...	29951	Will reduce
Molestador	29952	This will reduce
Molestatio	29953	So as to reduce
Molestful ...	29954	Cannot reduce lower than
Moletraps...	29955	What is the lowest to which you can reduce (the)
Molibdena	29956	The lowest to which I (we) can reduce
Molienda ...	29957	Reduce as much as possible
Molimentum	29958	Reduce as low as possible
Molinello ...	29959	By this we shall reduce cost to
Molinera ...	29960	You must reduce estimate for —— month by ——
Molinismo	29961	How much can you reduce the estimate for —— month by
Molitivo ...	29962	**Reduced** (*See also* "Fine.")
Molivisse ...	29963	Should be reduced
Molleja ...	29964	Will be reduced to
Mollejuela	29965	Has (have) been reduced to
Mollentar...	29966	Has (have) been reduced all round
Molleron ...	29967	Has (have) not reduced
Mollesco ...	29968	Reduced at least
Mollestra ...	29969	Were only reduced owing to
Mollicicco...	29970	Can be reduced (if)
Molliculus	29971	Could be reduced (if)
Molliendus	29972	Cannot be reduced
Mollient ...	29973	Must be reduced (if)
Mollificit ...	29974	Estimates will have to be reduced
Mollified ...	29975	Estimates cannot be reduced
Mollior ...	29976	If the cost can be reduced
Mollipedem	29977	Purchase amount should be reduced
Mollipes ...	29978	**Reducing**
Mollissime	29979	**Reduction** (*See also* "Extraction.")
Mollitivo ...	29980	A reduction of
Molliznar...	29981	What reduction can be made in
Molltonart	29982	What reduction will be made
Molluscan	29983	Considerable reduction will be made
Mollusque	29984	Considerable reduction must be made
Moloche ...	29985	Endeavour to get reduction
Molochinus	29986	A considerable reduction will be made if
Molondro...	29987	A large reduction would be made for cash
Molorchus	29988	Try and get some reduction
Molten ...	29989	Endeavour to get a further reduction
Moltiparo...	29990	The reduction is altogether insufficient
Moltura ...	29991	Will be a very considerable reduction
Molybdate	29992	Cannot get a reduction
Molybditis	29993	Reduction of price
Momentaneo	29994	Reduction of cost
Momentum	29995	No further reduction can be made
Momeria ...	29996	Great reduction will have to be made in
Momordiga	29997	A reduction in price of one ——
Momperada	29998	**Reduction Works**
Monacetic...	29999	The reduction works are in very good order

Monachal...	30000	Reduction works are in a very dilapidated state
Monachetta	**30001**	Owing to repairs necessary at reduction works [repair
Monachino	30002	What would it cost to put the reduction works in complete
Monacillo...	30003	The reduction works require —— spending to render them [efficient
Monacordio	30004	The cost of an efficient reduction works (plant) to consist of [—— would be
Monadic ...	30005	This will give us a very efficient reduction works
Monarcale	30006	Improvements to reduction works
Monarchie	30007	Shall commence overhauling reduction works at once
Monarquia	30008	The reduction works are very well arranged
Monastery	30009	Cannot extend the reduction works
Monastican	30010	This will increase the capacity of the reduction works to
Monatlich...	30011	**Reef(s)**
Monatstag	30012	Reef formation
Monaulus...	30013	A reef has been found
Monaut ...	30014	A fall of reef
Moncherino	30015	Quartz reef
Mondaceie	30016	Banket reef
Mondador	30017	A new reef
Mondain ...	30018	A reef —— feet thick
Mondanite	30019	On the line of the reef [about
Mondatura	30020	The cost of exploring the reef to a depth of —— feet would be
Mondejo ...	30021	Owing to a recent fall of reef
Mondhell ...	30022	Falls of reef are very frequent
Mondkalb...	30023	How many loads of reef have you hauled since
Mondonga	30024	Loads of reef hauled since
Mondonguil	30025	What is the hauling cost of reef per load
Mondozzajo	30026	The cost of hauling reef per load is
Mondualdo	30027	What is the number of loads of reef hauled (since)
Monedage...	30028	—— loads of reef hauled (since)
Monelleria	30029	The reef is becoming pinched up
Monetaggio	30030	Have struck a new reef measuring —— feet wide
Monetalis...	30031	Outcrop of reef
Monetiere...	30032	The reef at the outcrop assays
Monetized	30033	The reef shows a well defined body of quartz for a length
Moneybag	30034	The reef is now wider than the drive [of —— feet
Moneywort	30035	The reef is not so wide as the drive
Monferina	30036	The (this) portion of the reef
Monforte ...	30037	The reef has improved in quality
Mongia ...	30038	The reef has lessened in value
Mongibello	30039	The reef is very promising but we have not met with any
Mongrel ...	30040	**Re-election** [payable stone
Monicaco ...	30041	Not eligible for re-election
Monicongo	30042	**Re-examination**
Monigote ...	30043	On re-examination
Moniliform	30044	The re-examination has shown
Monilla ...	30045	**Re-examine(d)**
Monipodeo	30046	To re-examine
Monishment	30047	Suggest that you (——) re-examine
Monition ...	30048	Rigorously re-examine(d)
Monitorius	30049	**Refer**
Monitress...	30050	Please refer to
Monizione	30051	Please refer to —— for
Monkeys ...	30052	To refer
Monkhood	30053	May I (we) refer to you
Monnayage	30054	You may certainly refer to me
Monnayeur	30055	Can I (we) refer him (them) to you
Monnosino	30056	You can refer him (them) to me [information
Monnuccia	30057	Whom would you suggest that I (we) should refer to for

Monoacidic	30058	In case of need you may refer to
Monobasic	30059	Would rather that you did not refer to
Monobihlos	30060	Refer to my (our) letter of
Monocerote	30061	Refer to my (our) cable of
Monochord	30062	Refer the matter to
Monochrome	30063	To which do you refer
Monogamy	30064	I (we) would refer him (——) to my (our) report dated
Monograph	30065	**Referee(s)**
Monolith ...	30066	Appointment of official referee
Monologo ...	30067	**Reference**
Monomachia	30068	Without further reference
Monomanie	30069	Must have a reference
Monomio ...	30070	Reference given is satisfactory
Monopadium	30071	Reference given is unsatisfactory
Monopastos	30072	This has no reference whatever to
Monopetalo	30073	With reference to
Monophone	30074	No reference was made to
Monopireno	30075	The reference was not a good one
Monopoleur	30076	This is in reference to my (our) letter dated
Monopolist	30077	This is in reference to my (our) cable dated
Monopteron	30078	What are your instructions with reference to
Monostico	30079	Cable what has been settled in reference to
Monothism	30080	In reference to your cable of —— please communicate with
Monoxylus	30081	**Referred**
Monsenor ...	30082	Have you referred the matter to
Monsignore	30083	Have referred the matter to
Monsoons...	30084	Have not referred the matter to
Monstrans	30085	Has been referred for confirmation to
Monstratio	30086	Has been referred for settlement to
Monstrifer	30087	Referred to in your letter dated
Monstrosus	30088	Referred to in your cable dated
Monstrueux	30089	Referred to in the following words
Monstruo ...	30090	**Refined**
Montagnard	30091	Must be refined
Montagneux	30092	Refined bullion
Montanera	30093	Ounces of refined bullion
Montantada	30094	The refined bullion is —— fine
Montaraz ...	30095	It is refined
Montatojo	30096	Yields —— per cent. refined
Montazgar	30097	It is not refined
Monterey ...	30098	Is now being refined
Montesino	30099	As soon as it has been refined
Monthling	30100	What do you estimate will be the yield in refined bullion
Monticule...	30101	**Refinery(ies)** (See also " Refining Works.")
Montiera ...	30102	**Refining**
Montirung	30103	Loss on refining
Montivagus	30104	What is the loss on refining
Montoya ...	30105	Cost of refining
Montuoso...	30106	What is the cost of refining
Monument	30107	Refining charges
Monzicchio	30108	**Refining Works**
Monzon ...	30109	On completion of refining works
Moonbeam	30110	To take charge of refining works
Mooncalf ...	30111	Now in charge of refining works at
Mooneyed...	30112	Capital site for refining works
Moonlight	30113	Capacity of refining works
Moonshine	30114	The capacity of the refining works is
Moonstruck	30115	What is the capacity of refining works
Moorgame	30116	Owing to the limited capacity of the refining works
Moorhen ...	30117	At the principal refining works

Moorlands	30118	**Refractory** (*See also* "Ore.")
Mopishly ...	30119	The ore is very refractory
Mopsey ...	30120	On account of the refractory nature of the ore
Moquear ...	30121	The ore is a refractory one
Moquetear	30122	Is somewhat refractory
Moquifero	30123	If he (it) should become refractory
Moracho ...	30124	Is becoming more refractory
Morailles ...	30125	Is not so refractory
Moraines ...	30126	**Refrain**
Moraleja ...	30127	To refrain
Moralidad	30128	Consent(s) to refrain
Moralisch ...	30129	Refuse(s) to refrain
Moraliseur	30130	Advise you strongly to refrain from
Moralite ...	30131	Provided that —— will refrain from
Moralizar ...	30132	Do you advise me (us) to refrain from
Moralmente	30133	Refrain if possible from any interference
Morastig ...	30134	Will gladly refrain
Moravian ...	30135	**Refund**
Morbidez ...	30136	To refund
Morbidness	30137	You had better demand that —— refund(s) the money
Morbifero	30138	Refuse(s) to refund
Morbleu ...	30139	Will not refund unless (until)
Morbonia ...	30140	Must refund the amount paid for
Morboso ...	30141	Will —— (they) refund
Morcella ...	30142	Promised to refund
Morchioso	30143	Will no doubt refund
Mordacetto	30144	Owing to my (our) having to refund
Mordacity...	30145	Will have to refund
Mordaculus	30146	Will not have to refund
Mordante ...	30147	**Refunded**
Mordenten	30148	**Refusal**
Morderin ...	30149	Try and get a refusal of
Mordicar ...	30150	Cannot get refusal of
Mordiente	30151	Has (have) obtained a refusal of —— for —— days
Mordihui ...	30152	Since its refusal by
Mordiller ...	30153	Endeavour to postpone refusal
Mordisco ...	30154	Do not accept ——'s refusal as final
Morditrice	30155	Do not formally accept ——'s refusal
Morditura	30156	Shall I (we) accept refusal
Mordore ...	30157	Cannot accept refusal
Morelle ...	30158	Will take no refusal
Morenillo ...	30159	Has (have) obtained refusal of the property until —— for ——
Moresque ...	30160	Have had an interview with —— to whom I have conveyed
Morfondre	30161	**Refuse(s)** [your refusal to
Morganatic	30162	Refuse offer
Morgenbrod	30163	Refuse(s) to
Morguene...	30164	Refuse to do so
Moribund...	30165	To refuse
Moricaud ...	30166	Why do (did) you refuse
Moricino ...	30167	Am (are) compelled to refuse as I (we)
Morigerar	30168	Should —— refuse
Morinelo ...	30169	Had to refuse on account of
Moringic ...	30170	Positively refuse(s) to
Morioncino	30171	Should advise you to refuse
Morisqueta	30172	Refuse(s) to have anything to do with it
Moriturus	30173	Refuse(s) to interfere
Morlaco ...	30174	Refuse(s) to permit me (us) to interfere
Mormonite	30175	They distinctly refuse
Mormorante	30176	It is probable they will refuse
Mormoroso	30177	Refuse(s) to take less

Mormullo ...	30178	If we refuse we ought at once to
Mormyra ...	30179	—— refuse(s) to hand over the paper(s)
Mornifle ...	30180	Refuse(s) to hand over
Moroide ...	30181	Am I (are we) to refuse
Morologus	30182	Await your instructions before I (we) finally **refuse**
Moroncho	30183	As refuse
Morosely ...	30184	**Refused**
Morosite ...	30185	Has he (have they) refused
Morphine ...	30186	He has (they have) refused
Morphnus...	30187	He has (they have) not yet refused
Morsana ...	30188	Must be refused
Morsicare ...	30189	Has (have) been refused
Morsilis ...	30190	Was (were) distinctly refused
Morsure ...	30191	I (we) never have refused
Mortadela...	30192	Which (this). I (we) have refused
Mortaise ...	30193	Why was it refused
Mortajetto	30194	Refused because of
Mortajone	30195	**Refute(d)**
Mortalidad	30196	**Refuting**
Mortality ...	30197	**Regard(s)**
Mortamente	30198	As regards
Mortarium	30199	Without any regard to
Mortarmill	30200	With regard to
Mortecino	30201	Pay no regard whatever to
Morteruelo	30202	Paid no regard whatever to
Mortgaged	30203	Due regard must be paid to
Morticinus	30204	How do you regard it
Mortifier ...	30205	Was got up without any regard to
Mortine ...	30206	Regard it (this) as most important
Mortoria ...	30207	With all due regard for
Mortuaire	30208	As regards the following points
Mortualia	30209	Without any regard to the truth
Mortuarius	30210	Without any regard to the cost
Morueca ...	30211	Without any regard to the consequences
Morveux ...	30212	**Regarded**
Morvido ...	30213	Was (were) regarded as
Mosaical ...	30214	Was (were) not regarded as
Moscadato	30215	Regarded as perfectly safe
Moscadella	30216	Regarded as altogether unsafe
Moscajola...	30217	**Regardless** (*See also* " Expense.")
Moscardon	30218	Regardless of
Moscatel ...	30219	**Register**
Moschatus	30220	To register
Moscherino	30221	Do not register
Moscheuton	30222	Register closed
Mosciana ...	30223	In the share register
Moscoleato	30224	**Registered** (*See also* " Name.")
Mosillos ...	30225	In whose name is the property registered
Moslemo ...	30226	The property is registered in the name of
Mosqueador	30227	Has the property been duly registered in the name of
Mosquetazo	30228	Has (have) been registered
Mosquito ...	30229	Was (were) not registered
Mossgrown	30230	Has (have) never been registered
Mossiness...	30231	Should be registered immediately
Mossroots	30232	What is ——'s registered address
Mossroses ...	30233	——'s registered address is
Mostacchio	30234	I do not know ——'s registered address
Mostacilla	30235	Should have a registered address
Mostaza ...	30236	Was sent in a registered letter, posted on ——
Mostear ...	30237	Should be sent in a registered letter

Mostellum	30238	Is this (are these) properly registered
Mostrable...	30239	As soon as it is (these are) registered
Mostranza	30240	Registered in the name of
Mostrenco	30241	Not registered in the name of
Motacen ...	30242	Should be registered in the name of
Motacilla ...	30243	**Registrar**
Motejador	30244	Official registrar
Motette. ...	30245	The registrar of company
Motheaten	30246	Have seen registrar of company
Motherless	30247	Registrar of company has consented to
Motilar ...	30248	Registrar of company has declined
Motioning	30249	**Registration**
Motiveless	30250	**Regret**
Motivity ...	30251	Regret that
Motolita ...	30252	With much regret
Motoneria...	30253	Sincerely regret what has happened
Motril ...	30254	Regret to have to report that
Motteggio	30255	**Regular(ity)**
Mottuzzo ...	30256	Regular pattern
Moucheron	30257	Must be more regular with
Moucheture	30258	Will endeavour to be more regular with
Mouchoir ...	30259	Unless you can make sure of being more regular
Moufette ...	30260	With regularity and despatch
Mouflon ...	30261	**Regularly**
Mouillage ..	30262	Send regularly
Mouldable	30263	Report regularly
Moulinage	30264	Advise me (us) regularly as regards
Moulinet ...	30265	Will advise you regularly
Moulting ...	30266	**Regulate(d)**
Mounted ...	30267	To regulate
Mournfully	30268	Was (were) to regulate
Mousehole	30269	You had better regulate
Mousetrap	30270	To regulate the output
Mousseline	30271	This will regulate
Moustache	30272	This will enable me (us) to better regulate
Moustique	30273	So as to regulate
Moutardier	30274	In order to better regulate
Mouthing...	30275	**Regulating**
Mouthpiece	30276	**Regulation(s)**
Moutonner	30277	Government regulation(s)
Mouvant ...	30278	**Reimburse(d)** (*See also* " Repay.")
Mouvement	30279	To reimburse
Movibile ...	30280	Who will reimburse me (us)
Moviente ...	30281	Just sufficient to reimburse you for
Movilidad ..	30282	Will reimburse you for all out of pocket expenses
Movimiento	30283	Have arranged that you shall be satisfactorily reimbursed
Movitore ...	30284	**Reissue**
Movitrice ...	30285	To reissue
Moyennant	30286	About to reissue
Moyuelo ...	30287	Cannot reissue
Mozalbete...	30288	Cannot reissue without the following formalities, viz. :—
Moznado ...	30289	Can you reissue
Mozzamento	30290	When is it proposed to reissue
Mozzicone	30291	**Reissued**
Mucciare ..	30292	Has (have) been successfully reissued
Muccinium	30293	**Reiterate(d)**
Muccosus ...	30294	**Reject(ed)**
Mucesco ...	30295	To reject
Muchacha	30296	It was necessary to reject
Mucilagine	30297	How much (many) was it necessary to reject

Muckheaps	30298	Could not reject
Mucosidad	30299	Compelled to reject
Mucosite ...	30300	Reject any that are not absolutely sound
Mucousness	30301	Do not reject
Mucronated	30302	Propose to reject
Muculentus	30303	In case you reject
Mudable ...	30304	**Rejecting**
Mudanza ...	30305	**Relation(s)**
Mudfish ...	30306	So as not to jeopardise our relations with
Mudholes ...	30307	Amicable relations
Mudigkeit	30308	**Relative**
Mudsucker	30309	Relative to
Mueble ...	30310	What is this relative to
Muellage ...	30311	This is relative to
Muerdago...	30312	Does not seem to me (us) to be relative to
Muermera...	30313	Relative to which please note
Muermoso	30314	Should anything be said relative to
Muffetto ...	30315	**Relax(ed)**
Muffins ...	30316	Do not relax
Mugavero...	30317	Will not relax
Mugeracha	30318	Must not be relaxed
Mugercilla	30319	**Release**
Mugeriego	30320	To release
Mugerona ..	30321	Endeavour to procure release (of)
Mugghiare	30322	Means to procure release
Muggiolare	30323	Should you procure release
Muggish ...	30324	Will —— release me (us) from
Mugiebat ..	30325	Will not release you (them)
Mugiente ...	30326	Will only grant release upon condition that
Mugilis ...	30327	Desire(s) release from engagement
Muginator	30328	Cannot release you until
Mugivisse...	30329	Which (this) will release
Mugliare ...	30330	How much will this release
Mugnajo ...	30331	Release has been mailed
Mugnitore	30332	When may I (we) expect release to be mailed
Mugron ...	30333	Release should
Mugweed ...	30334	**Released**
Muhlbach...	30335	Has (have) been released
Muhlgraben	30336	Was (were) released on
Muhlrad ...	30337	Is (are) not released
Muhsam ...	30338	Have been released under
Muhselig ...	30339	If —— can be released from
Mulacchia...	30340	Released through
Muladar ...	30341	Can be released immediately
Mulatero ...	30342	When may I (we) expect to be released
Mulberry ...	30343	When is he (——) likely to be released
Mulcamini	30344	**Reliability**
Mulcanto ...	30345	Has (have) no great reputation for reliability
Mulcatote...	30346	**Reliable**
Mulcatus ...	30347	Is it (he) reliable
Mulcebunt	30348	Is reliable
Mulcedo ...	30349	Is not reliable
Mulcemur...	30350	—— is (are) perfectly reliable
Mulcendus	30351	This information is perfectly reliable
Mulciber ...	30352	Ascertain if information is reliable
Mulctrale...	30353	Of a reliable nature
Mulctrum...	30354	To a reliable extent
Muledriver	30355	I do not know a sufficiently reliable man
Mulenda ...	30356	**Reliance**
Muleteam...	30357	What reliance can be placed upon

Muliaca ...	30358	No reliance can be placed upon
Muliebre ...	30359	You may place every reliance upon
Muliebrity	30360	Personally, I should have no reliance whatever in him (——)
Mulierare...	30361	Personally, I should place the very greatest reliance in [him (——)
Muliercula	30362	Do not place any reliance in what you may hear concerning
Mulierosus	30363	Every reliance can be placed in
Mulinare ...	30364	**Relied**
Mulinello ...	30365	Quite relied upon you
Mulionius...	30366	Is he (——) to be relied upon
Mulishly ...	30367	To the best of my belief he (——) may be absolutely relied
Mulishness	30368	I do not think he (——) can be relied upon [upon
Mullein ...	30369	Unless he (——) can be relied upon absolutely
Mulleolus ...	30370	**Relieve(d)**
Mullidor ..	30371	So as to relieve
Mullioned...	30372	Must be relieved from
Mulseus ...	30373	Should be relieved as early as possible
Mulsuram	30374	**Relieves**
Multanime	30375	**Relinquish(ed)**
Multatio ...	30376	Unless I am (we are) to relinquish
Multesimus	30377	Do you relinquish
Multibibus	30378	Do not relinquish
Multicavus	30379	Need not be relinquished
Multicia ...	30380	Must now be relinquished
Multicolor	30381	**Relinquishment**
Multifacio	30382	**Relocate(d)**
Multiform	30383	Relocated on (by)
Multigener	30384	Has (have) not been relocated
Multijugis	30385	Is it likely to be relocated
Multinodus	30386	Is not likely to be relocated
Multinomio	30387	Claim(s) has (have) been relocated, everything is now in order
Multipede	30388	**Reluctant(ly)**
Multiplex ...	30389	**Rely**
Multiplier	30390	To rely upon
Multiscius	30391	I (we) rely upon you
Multivagus	30392	May I rely upon
Multivalve	30393	You may rely upon
Multoties ...	30394	Do not rely upon
Mulvianus	30395	You had better not rely upon
Mumbler ...	30396	You may rely upon me (us) doing as much as I (we) can
Mummeries	30397	I should advise you not to rely upon
Mummery	30398	I shall rely upon you to
Mummified	30399	In any case you may rely upon
Mumpishly	30400	You may rely upon me
Mumps ...	30401	Could you rely upon
Muncher ...	30402	I believe that I can rely upon
Mundane ...	30403	I do not think it safe to rely upon
Mundation	30404	How much (many) can I (we) rely upon
Mundialis...	30405	When may I (we) rely upon receiving it (the)
Mundicina	30406	You may rely upon having —— before ——
Mundificar	30407	**Relying**
Mundinovi	30408	Am (are) relying upon you for the facts
Munditer ...	30409	**Remain(s)**
Mundities...	30410	To remain
Mundleim...	30411	Am I to remain here
Mundlich ...	30412	How long am I (are we) to remain (at)
Munerare ...	30413	How long will you remain (at)
Munerarius	30414	How long will —— remain (at)
Munerosus	30415	Expect to remain until
Municipe ...	30416	Could not remain over

Municipium	30417	Shall be obliged to remain here until
Munifex ...	30418	Nothing remains now except
Munifico ...	30419	Nothing, however, remains to be done
Munimentum	30420	You had better remain where you are
Munitions	30421	⌐ Remain ᵣ⁺ —— until you hear from me (us)
Munitoria...	30422	Will remain here until
Muniturus	30423	You should not remain longer than
Munterkeit	30424	Shall not remain longer than I am obliged
Munuscolo	30425	Shall not remain after
Munusculum	30426	What is the latest date to which I can remain
Munychion	30427	Should very much like to remain here a further —— days
Munzfuss ...	30428	You may remain an additional —— days
Munzwesen	30429	Remain until
Muovente ...	30430	✓ Remain until I (we) cable you again
Muoversi ...	30431	In any case do not remain after
Muradal ...	30432	Let things remain as they are till further instructed
Muralla ...	30433	All that now remains is
Muramento	30434	It only now remains to me (us)
Muratore ...	30435	How long will you require to remain in order to complete work
Murciegalo	30436	Can I remain here until
Murciolum	30437	Remain at —— for the present
Murderous	30438	**Remainder**
Murecillo ...	30439	What remainder will there be
Murginari	30440	What shall I do with remainder
Murgisonem	30441	There is no remainder
Muriatic ...	30442	The weight of the remainder is
Muriccia ...	30443	Remainder will be shipped about
Murice ...	30444	Remainder will reach you not later than
Muricidus...	30445	The remainder (is) are worthless
Murmugear	30446	When will remainder be forwarded
Murmullar	30447	Remainder will be forwarded about
Murmuratio	30448	How shall I dispose of the remainder
Murmureo	30449	Dispose of the remainder by
Murmurillo	30450	There is still a remainder of —— to be dealt with
Murmuring	30451	What is the quality of the remainder
Murrhina ...	30452	The quality of the remainder is good
Murrian ...	30453	The quality of the remainder is no better
Murrisch ...	30454	The quality of the remainder is worse
Murtatum	30455	The remainder is (are)
Murtilla ...	30456	Of the remainder
Murucuya	30457	To the remainder must be added
Musachino	30458	To take the remainder
Musaraigne	30459	For the remainder of the term
Musarana...	30460	The remainder of
Musarder ...	30461	For the remainder of
Muscadine	30462	**Remained**
Muscarium	30463	Has (have) remained
Muscerda ...	30464	Has (have) not remained
Muschietto	30465	From having remained
Muscino ...	30466	Remained under water
Muscipula	30467	**Remaining**
Muscles ...	30468	Still remaining
Muscoletto	30469	Nothing remaining
Muscovy ...	30470	What is there remaining
Musculado	30471	What is the distance remaining undriven between —— and ——
Musculeux	30472	Have arranged with —— as to remaining at
Musculosus	30473	**Remark(s)**
Museliere ...	30474	To remark
Muserolle ...	30475	Is there anything to remark in connection with
Museruola	30476	I (we) have nothing to remark

Musgano ...	30477	I (we) should like to remark
Mushroom	30478	This has no reference to my (our) remarks in letter dated ——
Musical ...	30479	In reference to the remarks contained in your letter dated ——
Musicbook	30480	Wish(es) to make some remarks having reference to
Musichino	30481	Some remarks might be made with reference to
Musicone ...	30482	**Remarkable(ly)**
Musikant ...	30483	**Remedied**
Musiksaal...	30484	Should be remedied immediately
Musimonem	30485	Will be remedied (by)
Musique ...	30486	Can only be remedied (by)
Musitar ...	30487	Cannot now be remedied
Musivarius	30488	**Remedy**
Musivum ...	30489	Have we no remedy
Muskapple	30490	Our only remedy is to
Muskate ...	30491	Can you suggest any remedy
Muskcherry	30492	If I am (we are) to remedy
Muskelig ...	30493	**Remember**
Muskiness	30494	To remember
Muskmelon	30495	Remember to
Muskoxen...	30496	Unfortunately do(es) not remember
Muskpear	30497	Be sure that you remember to
Muskplant	30498	**Remembered**
Muskrat ...	30499	Was (were) not remembered in time
Muskrose ...	30500	Has (have) remembered everything
Muskseed...	30501	Remembered everything except
Muskwood	30502	**Remind(ed)**
Muslin ...	30503	Am (are) instructed to remind you that (of)
Musoliera...	30504	Please remind —— to
Musquash	30505	**Reminder**
Musquerola	30506	As a reminder
Mussatote...	30507	**Remit**
Mussavero	30508	To remit
Mussitator	30509	Promise(s) to remit
Mustacea ...	30510	Will remit about ——
Mustard ...	30511	Cannot remit at present
Mustela ...	30512	Cannot remit before
Mustelinus	30513	Cannot remit more than
Mustellino	30514	If —— does not remit by
Musterung	30515	You must remit immediately
Mustricula	30516	Remit by cheque
Mutabilita	30517	Remit by cable
Mutable ...	30518	When do you expect to remit
Mutatore ...	30519	Expect to remit
Mutatorius	30520	Except you remit
Mutatrix ...	30521	Why do you not remit
Mutescit ...	30522	When will you remit
Mutevole ...	30523	Will remit to-morrow
Muthmassen	30524	Will remit you not later than
Muthwillig	30525	What is the most you can remit
Mutilatio ...	30526	Cannot remit more than —— at the present time
Mutilators	30527	Do not remit until
Mutilavit ...	30528	You must remit by telegram instantly to ——
Mutinerie...	30529	You should remit at once
Mutinous ...	30530	Must remit by cable direct to
Mutinying	30531	I (we) will remit to-morrow but do not wait for this
Mutiren ...	30532	Remit as promptly as possible
Mutolezza	30533	Remit by draft on
Mutonialus	30534	Remit not later than
Mutterer ...	30535	Will remit with the least delay possible
Mutterlich	30536	How much can you remit and when

Muttermaal	30537	I can remit —— on ——
Mutterwitz.	30538	I can remit —— on —— and a further sum of —— on ——
Muttonchop	30539	I will remit as promised on ——
Muttonfist	30540	Remit by telegram as much as you can not later than -
Mutuarius	30541	How much can you remit on or before
Mutuatario	30542	**Remittance(s)** (*See also* " Deferred," "Depend.")
Mutuiter ...	30543	Forward remittance not later than
Muzarabe ...	30544	Expecting a remittance from you daily
Myacibus ...	30545	A remittance is absolutely necessary
Myagros ...	30546	The usual remittance was sent on
Mycetias ...	30547	Increase amount of remittance to
Myobarbum	30548	Increased remittance required owing to
Myoctonos	30549	Why do you require the increased remittance
Myoparo ...	30550	Make the remittance payable to
Myophonos	30551	Remittance should reach here (——) not later than
Myopie ...	30552	Remittance should be sent per
Myosotidem	30553	Remittance was sent per
Myrapium	30554	Remittance was sent through usual channel
Myriad ...	30555	Can you not make the usual remittance suffice
Myriapode	30556	Has (have) received no remittance since
Myricam ...	30557	The usual remittance will be enough
Myristicus	30558	The remittance mentioned
Myrmecites	30559	I should advise you for the present to withhold remittance
Myrmecoleo	30560	When can you send remittance
Myrmidon	30561	Send further remittance
Myrmillo ...	30562	Remittance awaits you (at ——)
Myropolium	30563	Remittance not yet received
Myrrh ...	30564	Have not yet received a remittance for this month
Myrrhapium	30565	I (we) rely on further remittance
Myrrhidem	30566	Expect remittance from you on
Myrrhinus	30567	Remittance as per your cable of —— received
Myrsineum	30568	Please let me have remittance at once to cover cost of
Myrsinites	30569	Will require further remittance of —— to carry out your
Myrtaceus	30570	Your last remittance of —— has been received [instructions
Myrtetum...	30571	Have not yet received any advice of remittance
Myrtidanus	30572	The last remittance from you was received on
Myrtuosus	30573	The last remittance from —— was received on
Mystagogue	30574	**Remitted** (*See also* " Fine.")
Mysteres ...	30575	Remitted by
Mysterieux	30576	Should be remitted at once
Mystical ...	30577	Must be remitted at once
Mysticism	30578	Has (have) been remitted
Mystique ...	30579	Was remitted on
Mythically	30580	Have remitted —— to
Mythologie	30581	Have not remitted yet
Nabato ...	30582	Could you not have remitted
Nabina ...	30583	In case you have not remitted
Nabissare...	30584	What amount of money do you require to be remitted
Nablionem	30585	Have remitted —— through
Nablium ...	30586	Have remitted to you to-day by cable —— per ——
Naboblike...	30587	Have remitted to you to-day through —— the sum of ——
Nabobs ...	30588	**Remonstrate(d)**
Nacaire ...	30589	Has (have) personally remonstrated against
Nacarado ...	30590	Remonstrate most strongly
Nacaron ...	30591	No use whatever to remonstrate
Naccherino	30592	**Remote(ly)**
Nachaffen...	30593	**Removal**
Nachahmen	30594	Demand immediate removal of ——
Nachbeten	30595	Pending removal
Nachbild ...	30596	**Remove**

Nachdenken	30597	To remove
Nachfrage	30598	Expect to remove to —— about
Nachfullen	30599	When are you likely to remove
Nachgeburt	30600	Remove everything
Nachgerade	30601	Remove anything that will pay to do so
Nachgiebig	30602	**Removed**
Nachholen	30603	Removed to
Nachklang	30604	Removed by
Nachkommen	30605	Has (have) been removed
Nachlass ...	30606	Has (have) not been removed
Nachmachen	30607	Could be removed
Nachmittag	30608	Was (were) removed
Nachsagen	30609	Should not be removed
Nachschuss	30610	In case they have already been removed
Nachsinnen	30611	Might be removed from
Nachspahen	30612	Might be removed to
Nachspuren	30613	Might be removed from —— to ——
Nachstens	30614	Have removed everything of value
Nachsuchen	30615	**Remunerate(d)**
Nachteule...	30616	**Remuneration**
Nachthaube	30617	Not sufficient remuneration
Nachtheil ...	30618	Will this be sufficient remuneration
Nachthorn	30619	What is your (——'s) idea of remuneration
Nachtigall	30620	Must offer sufficient remuneration to induce
Nachtlich ...	30621	**Remunerative**
Nachtragen	30622	It is hardly sufficiently remunerative
Nachweis ...	30623	Do you consider it will prove remunerative
Nachwinter	30624	I (we) strongly believe that it will be remunerative
Nachwirken	30625	I (we) do not see how it can (could) possibly be remunerative
Nachzug ...	30626	Very remunerative
Nacido ...	30627	By no means remunerative
Naciente ...	30628	Ultimately remunerative
Nackend ...	30629	I feel sure it will be remunerative as soon as
Nacreous ...	30630	Has (have) accepted a remunerative engagement
Nadaderas	30631	Has (have) been very remunerative in the past
Nadador ...	30632	Has (have) never been remunerative
Nadelholz...	30633	Has (have) never been remunerative owing mainly to
Nadelstick	30634	To make the property remunerative
Naderia ...	30635	**Render(ed)**
Nadrenas ...	30636	To render
Naevulum	30637	Render all the assistance you can
Nafalio ...	30638	I shall be happy to render any assistance in my power
Nagelfest ...	30639	Regret cannot render any assistance
Nagelneuen	30640	Do not render
Nagethier...	30641	Shall I (we) render any assistance
Naguela ...	30642	Render your account(s)
Nagyagite	30643	Will proceed to render every assistance
Naherung...	30644	**Rendering**
Nahkissen	30645	**Renew**
Nahrstand	30646	To renew
Nailbrush...	30647	Please renew
Nailery ...	30648	Will only renew for
Nailmaker	30649	Cannot renew
Naissance...	30650	Will you renew
Naivetat ...	30651	Consent(s) to renew
Naked ...	30652	Refuse(s) to renew
Nakedness	30653	Wish(es) to renew
Nalgatorio	30654	Will renew the agreement on more favourable terms
Nalguear ...	30655	Will renew the bond
Nameless ...	30656	Endeavour to get —— to renew the bond

Namenstag	30657	**Renewable**
Namentlich	30658	**Renewal**
Namesake ..	30659	**Renewed**
Namhaft ...	30660	Will be renewed
Namore ...	30661	Has (have) been renewed
Namque ...	30662	Unable to get renewed
Nancisor ...	30663	Was (were) to have been renewed
Nanerello ...	30664	As soon as it is (they are) renewed
Nankeen ...	30665	**Reorganization**
Nanking ...	30666	Reorganization scheme
Nantar ...	30667	Cable details of reorganization scheme
Napello ..	30668	What are your views as to reorganization
Naphtalin...	30669	Cable your adherence to reorganization scheme
Naphtas ...	30670	Fully approve of reorganization
Napinam ...	30671	Do(es) not approve of reorganization
Napkin ...	30672	Holders of —— shares in favour of reorganization
Napperon ...	30673	How many holders are in favour of reorganization
Nappone ...	30674	Success of reorganization scheme assured
Naranjado	30675	Reorganization scheme cannot succeed .
Narbig ...	30676	The only alternative is reorganization
Narcissine	30677	Consent(s) to reorganization scheme
Narcissus ...	30678	What is my (our) position under reorganization scheme
Narcotique	30679	Induce —— to give consent to reorganization ·
Narcotism	30680	—— refuse(s) consent to reorganization
Nardifera...	30681	Have obtained ——'s (his) consent to reorganization
Nardinus ...	30682	Cannot obtain ——'s (his) consent to reorganization
Narguer ...	30683	Unless you can obtain ——'s (his) consent to reorganization
Narigal ...	30684	Does the reorganization scheme provide for
Narizado ...	30685	The reorganization scheme provides for
Narquois ...	30686	The reorganization scheme does not provide for
Narrabilis...	30687	Unless the reorganization scheme provides for
Narrable ...	30688	**Reorganize**
Narragione	30689	To reorganize
Narrandus	30690	It will be necessary to reorganize the company
Narrante ...	30691	If we are to avoid having to reorganize the company ·
Narrativa ...	30692	Cannot avoid having to reorganize the company
Narrator ...	30693	It will be absolutely necessary to reorganize
Narratorem	30694	You should reorganize
Narratrice	30695	Do you see your way clear to reorganize
Narraturus	30696	Shall commence to reorganize
Narrenhaus	30697	Has (have) commenced to reorganize
Narria ...	30698	To thoroughly reorganize
Narrisch ...	30699	**Reorganized**
Narthecia ..	30700	As soon as it (this) has been reorganized
Narthex ...	30701	Will certainly have to be reorganized
Narwhal ...	30702	As soon as I (we) have been able to get this reorganized
Nasality ...	30703	Thoroughly reorganized
Nasalized ...	30704	**Repaid** (*See also* "Repay.")
Nasallant...	30705	**Repair(s)** (*See also* "Bridge.")
Nasardo ...	30706	To repair
Nascebar ...	30707	Out of repair
Nascemini	30708	Repairs highly necessary
Nascentem	30709	Has (have) been obliged to stop for repairs
Nascher ...	30710	The —— require(s) extensive repairs
Naschwerk	30711	Can you repair at once
Nascimento	30712	What will the cost of repairs amount to
Nascondere	30713	When will repairs be completed
Nasenbeln...	30714	You had better have all repairs done before you leave
Nashorn ...	30715	All repairs necessary should be completed as soon as possible
Nasillard ...	30716	All repairs to be done at the expense of

Nasilleur ...	30717	Can easily do everything necessary in the way of repairs myself
Nasiterna...	30718	Repairs will cost about
Nassaggine	30719	Repairs can be readily made within —— days
Nasskalt ...	30720	Repairs very serious and extensive
Nastriera ...	30721	Do not repair
Nasturcio...	30722	Repairs are nearly completed
Nasturtion	30723	Repairs will be completed within —— days
Nasutiore...	30724	Please estimate cost of repairs
Nasutulus	30725	Estimated cost of repairs is
Natabam ...	30726	Is the plant generally in good repair
Natabunt ...	30727	The plant generally is not in good repair
Natalicio ...	30728	The plant generally is in good repair
Natandi ...	30729	Some small repairs will be necessary to the plant
Natantur ...	30730	The repairs should be finished not later than
Natatil ...	30731	How are you getting on with the repairs
Natation ...	30732	The repairs were not finished on account of
Natatoria ...	30733	Send a revised estimate of repairs
Nateron ...	30734	Have made a revised estimate of repairs
Natilla ...	30735	The revised estimate of repairs gives as a total amount
Natinatio ...	30736	Get all necessary repairs done at once
National ...	30737	Have you commenced the repairs
Natividad...	30738	Have not yet commenced the repairs (as)
Nativity ...	30739	Am (are) pushing repairs with vigour
Natrice ...	30740	Repairs were commenced on
Nattier ...	30741	Why have you not commenced repairs
Nattiness ...	30742	Has (have) had to be sent to —— for repairs
Naturaccio	30743	Now engaged on repairs
Naturaleza	30744	You must postpone repairs until
Naturalist	30745	Delay repairs until arrival of ——
Naturarsi...	30746	Shall have to stop for repairs on
Naturgabe	30747	Shut down for repairs
Naturistic...	30748	How long will it take to complete repairs
Naturkraft	30749	Expect repairs will be finished by
Naturlich ...	30750	Expect repairs will cause a delay of
Naturtrieb	30751	Get on with repairs smartly
Nauculam	30752	Can only manage temporary repairs
Naufragar	30753	**Repaired(ing)**
Naufragium	30754	To be repaired
Naufragoso	30755	Can it (they) be repaired
Naughtily	30756	Am afraid it (they) cannot be repaired
Naulium ...	30757	Can readily be repaired
Naumachia	30758	Shall I (we) have it (them) repaired
Naupegus...	30759	Damage already repaired
Nauseate ...	30760	Will send —— (it) (them) to be repaired
Nauseating	30761	Will be repaired within the next —— days
Nauseous ...	30762	Cannot be repaired
Nautica ...	30763	Will be repaired at once
Nautically	30764	Should not be repaired until
Nautilus ...	30765	Cannot be repaired here
Nautonier...	30766	After I (we) have repaired
Navaja ...	30767	**Reparation**
Navajero ...	30768	**Repay** (See also "Reimburse," "Repaid.")
Navajonazo	30769	When do you (does ——) expect to repay
Navalestro	30770	To repay
Navandus...	30771	Will repay
Navarchus	30772	Will fully repay present outlay
Navegar ...	30773	Can never repay
Navelwort	30774	Will this repay
Naveresco...	30775	It will repay
Navette ...	30776	It will not repay

[513]

Navicante...	30777	In order to repay
Navicella ...	30778	Consent(s) to repay
Navichiere	30779	Refuse(s) to repay
Navichuelo	30780	Should repay
Navicular	30781	**Repayable**
Navideno ...	30782	**Repayment**
Naviero ...	30783	Being repayment of
Navifragus	30784	**Repeat**
Navigable...	30785	If you can repeat
Navigans ...	30786	If you cannot repeat
Navigated	30787	Repeat the first —— word(s) of your cable
Navigating	30788	Repeat the last —— word(s) of your cable
Navigators	30789	Please repeat entire cable
Navigiolum	30790	Do not understand your cable, please repeat
Naviglio ...	30791	Do not repeat
Navities ...	30792	Repeat, using other code words
Navrant ...	30793	Repeat, using more explanatory words
Nayada ...	30794	Repeat, using plain words
Nazarene ...	30795	Repeat first word of cable
Nazula ...	30796	Repeat second word of cable
Neanmoins	30797	Repeat third word of cable
Neaptide ...	30798	Repeat fourth word of cable
Nearness ...	30799	Repeat fifth word of cable
Nearsight ..	30800	Repeat sixth word of cable
Neatherd ...	30801	Repeat seventh word of cable
Nebbione ...	30802	Repeat eighth word of cable
Nebeda ...	30803	Repeat ninth word of cable
Nebelfleck	30804	Repeat tenth word of cable
Nebelig ...	30805	Repeat eleventh word of cable
Nebelregen	30806	Repeat twelfth word of cable
Nebenfrage	30807	Repeat thirteenth word of cable
Nebenlinie	30808	Repeat fourteenth word of cable
Nebenrolle	30809	Repeat fifteenth word of cable
Nebenwort	30810	Repeat sixteenth word of cable
Neblina ...	30811	Repeat seventeenth word of cable
Nebridas ...	30812	Repeat eighteenth word of cable
Nebrites	30813	Repeat nineteenth word of cable
Nebula ...	30814	Repeat twentieth word of cable
Nebulatus	30815	Repeat twenty-first word of cable
Nebuletta...	30816	Repeat twenty-second word of cable
Nebuleux ...	30817	Repeat twenty-third word of cable
Nebulist ...	30818	Repeat twenty-fourth word of cable
Nebulosity	30819	Repeat twenty-fifth word of cable
Nebulous ...	30820	Repeat twenty-sixth word of cable
Necantur ...	30821	Repeat twenty-seventh word of cable
Necaturus	30822	Repeat twenty-eighth word of cable
Necavero ...	30823	Repeat twenty-ninth word of cable
Necavisti ...	30824	Repeat thirtieth word of cable
Necedad ...	30825	Repeat —— word of cable
Necesitado	30826	Message unintelligible; what do you mean by
Necessario	30827	You (they) must repeat
Necesse ...	30828	Repeat message from the word —— to the end
Necessiter...	30829	Repeat message from —— to —— neither of which words
Neckband...	30830	Repeat your telegram dated [need be repeated
Neckcloth...	30831	Repeat this telegram back to inform me (us) that it has
Necken ...	30832	**Repeated(ly)** [reached you intact
Necklace ...	30833	**Repetition**
Necklets ...	30834	Repetition of [can act
Necktie ...	30835	Must await the repetition of message from —— before I (we)
Necrology	30836	Must await its repetition

[514]

Necromancy	30837	**Replace**
Necropolis	30838	To replace
Necrosis ...	30839	Shall I (we) replace
Necrotomy	30840	Do not replace
Nectareal ...	30841	Expect(s) can replace
Nectarine ...	30842	It is necessary to replace
Necunquem	30843	Endeavour to replace
Necydalus	30844	Will replace
Needlebook	30845	Will not replace
Needleful ...	30846	This will enable me (us) to replace
Needlework	30847	When do you expect to replace
Nefando ...	30848	**Replaced**
Nefarius ...	30849	Must be replaced
Nefaste ...	30850	Can it be replaced
Nefendezza	30851	Can be replaced at an expense of
Nefendita ...	30852	Can be replaced but will cause a delay of
Neflier ...	30853	Should be replaced as soon as possible
Nefrendis ...	30854	Will be replaced almost immediately
Nefritico ...	30855	Was (were) replaced almost immediately
Negabundus	30856	Have you replaced it (them)
Negantis ...	30857	Have replaced it (them)
Negation ...	30858	Cannot be replaced until
Negatived...	30859	**Replete**
Negativus...	30860	**Reply**
Negatorius	30861	To reply
Negatory ...	30862	Reply to
Negatrix ...	30863	Reply at my (our) expense
Negerin ...	30864	Reply paid
Negghieza	30865	Please reply promptly
Neghittoso	30866	Reply is satisfactory
Neglectful	30867	Reply is not satisfactory
Neglectim ..	30868	Try and get a reply from —— as to
Neglexisse	30869	Cannot get any definite reply
Neglezione	30870	Cannot make any definite reply (until)
Negligent...	30871	Can you get a reply from
Negligible	30872	What reply did you get from
Negligor ...	30873	Have not had any reply from
Negociado	30874	The reply I received from —— was to the effect that
Negocier ...	30875	Have received reply from
Negotialis...	30876	Waiting a reply as to —— from ——
Negotiant...	30877	Anxiously waiting reply as to
Negotiator	30878	Await reply as to
Negotiolum	30879	Please let me (us) have a reply as speedily as possible
Negotium...	30880	Will reply by cable immediately
Negozietto	30881	Reply by cable immediately
Negozioso ...	30882	As soon as the reply is given by
Negral ...	30883	Subject to a reply within the next —— days
Negreguar	30884	Subject to a reply within the next —— hours
Negrerie ...	30885	Subject to reply in twenty-four hours
Negress ...	30886	No reply to
Negrigenza	30887	In reply to
Negrilla ...	30888	Why do you (does ——) not reply (to)
Negromante	30889	Have received no reply to my (our) cable sent on
Neigeux ...	30890	Reply fully by letter
Neighing ...	30891	Reply by cable
Neigungen	30892	Must have a reply not later than
Nemboso ...	30893	Must have a reply immediately if I am (we are) to
Nemicare ...	30894	Should you not reply I (we) shall consider you decline
Neminis ...	30895	Should not reply be sent to
Nemoralis ..	30896	I (we) will reply within the next few (——) days

Nemoroso	30897	When you reply please give further information with regard to
Nennwerth	30898	Will reply as soon as I have seen
Nenufar ...	30899	Reply should be sent to care of
Neocomian	30900	This is in reply to
Neocorus ...	30901	Cannot understand your reply, do you mean
Neofito ...	30902	No reply having been received from you
Neogamist	30903	Subject to reply by wire
Neografo ..	30904	Reply to my (our) telegram of
Neolithic ...	30905	Delay reply until
Neologism	30906	Reply quickly to these questions
Neomenia...	30907	Expect to get a reply not later than
Neophyte ..	30908	When do you expect to get a reply
Neoterico ...	30909	I hope to be able to reply
Neozoic ...	30910	Please reply by telegraph to my (our) last cable
Nephews ...	30911	Please reply by telegraph to my (our) telegram sent on
Nephritem	30912	Has (have) no reply to make
Nepitella ...	30913	Your prompt reply is necessary as —— will leave in a few days
Nepotalis ...	30914	Do not fail to reply to-day ⸢for
Nepotinus	30915	I will reply to-morrow
Nepticulam	30916	Await reply from —— to my (our) letter dated
Neptunian	30917	Reply categorically to questions in the following order, viz. :—
Nequalia ...	30918	Reply categorically to questions in strict numerical order
Nequando...	30919	Cannot reply categorically to your questions
Nequedum	30920	Will reply to your questions within next three days
Nequeor ...	30921	Will reply to your questions as soon as I have seen ——
Nequiens ...	30922	**Replying**
Nequissime	30923	Delay replying to —— until
Nequitanza	30924	**Report(s)** (*See also* "Caution," "Confirm," " Descriptive," ⸢" Despatch," "Examination," "False," " Favourable,"
Nequities ...	30925	Report by　　　　　　　　　　　　　　　 ⸢" Fee," &c.)
Nerbare ...	30926	Report by cable
Nerborino..	30927	Report by letter
Nereggiare	30928	Must have your report on or before
Nericante ...	30929	Mail copy of report (by)
Neronianus	30930	Send report on —— for
Nerprun ...	30931	To report
Nervalibus	30932	Report at once respecting
Nervecells...	30933	Report for week ending
Nerveless ...	30934	Report for past four weeks
Nerviceus ...	30935	Report generally favourable
Nervine ...	30936	Report very favourable
Nervioso ...	30937	Report generally unfavourable
Nervorum...	30938	Report is considered unfavourable
Nervosita ...	30939	Report distinctly unfavourable
Nervously...	30940	Please cable whether your report is generally ⸢unfavourable favourable or
Nervudo ...	30941	Please cable whether I may report on
Nescentia ...	30942	—— writes me to report on property at
Nescience ...	30943	It is not advisable that you should report on
Nescitote ...	30944	Obliged to refuse my (our) consent for you to report on
Nescitur ...	30945	You may certainly report on
Nespera ...	30946	Report any change
Nespilo ...	30947	There is no change to report
Nespolina...	30948	The only change to report is
Nessuno ...	30949	Send duplicate copy of your report (to)
Nestacessi	30950	When is report likely to be issued
Nestajuola	30951	Report will be issued about
Nestegg ...	30952	A report has been circulated to the effect
Nestidis ...	30953	Ascertain whether there is any truth in the report that
Nestorian...	30954	There is no truth in the report that
Netezuèlo ...	30955	Contradict report on my (our) authority

ethermost	30956	There is a slight amount of truth in the report
etmakers	30957	The report is quite true
ettapanni	30958	Send further report as to
ettareo ...	30959	Report received on ——
ettatojo ...	30960	Have not received any report
ettement	30961	There is a report that —— has (have)
ettigkeit	30962	Has —— made any report
ettles ...	30963	—— has not made any report
ettoyer ...	30964	Since last report
ettunio ...	30965	Before my next report
eubacken	30966	Report may be relied upon
eublau ...	30967	Report is misleading as to
euerdings	30968	Report is absolutely unfounded
eugeborem	30969	Regret that there is some foundation for report
eugierde	30970	Cable résumé of your report
euheit ...	30971	Hope to forward report on
eumatico	30972	When may I (we) expect your report on
eumond ...	30973	In the event of your confirming ——'s report
eunfach ...	30974	Can you confirm ——'s report
eunmalig	30975	Am generally able to confirm ——'s report
eunzig ...	30976	Regret cannot confirm ——'s report
euricus ...	30977	What (who) has given rise to report
eurismo ...	30978	Report as soon as possible as to
Neurobata	30979	Shall leave for —— on —— to report on property for
Neuroides...	30980	Be very cautious in any report you may make for
Neurologia	30981	When could you report on property for me (us)
Neuropter	30982	Examine and report fully as to the present condition of the [underground workings
Neutiquam	30983	Examine and report fully on the present state of machinery
Neutral ...	30984	Recent reports very unfavourable
Neutrality	30985	Recent reports are said to be very favourable
Neutrobi ...	30986	Recent reports are said to be very unfavourable
Neuvieme...	30987	When will you mail your report
Nevadilla ...	30988	My report was mailed on
Nevereta ...	30989	Will report as soon as possible
Nevicoso ...	30990	Can you report for —— and when
Neviscar ...	30991	I should be very glad to report but I cannot leave here until
Nevischia...	30992	Will you make a joint report with
Nevralgia ...	30993	Do you wish to have a joint or separate report
Nevrotomia	30994	Prefer a separate report
Newborn ...	30995	Prefer a joint report
Newcoined	30996	You cannot rely on any reports made by
Newfangled	30997	You can place every reliance on ——'s reports
Newsboy ...	30998	No alteration since last report at
Newsman...	30999	Draw your report with great caution as it will be published
Newsmonger	31000	Nothing material to report [in extenso
Nexibilis ...	**31001**	Report is required as quickly as possible
Nexionis ...	31002	Excellent report
Niaiser ...	31003	Reliable reports
Nibbed ...	31004	Current reports
Nibbiaccio	31005	Has given a very favourable report
Nibblingly	31006	Has made a very fair report
Nicchiare ...	31007	Examine and report by letter
Nicchietta	31008	Examine and report by cable
Niccolino ...	31009	Wait for my complete report
Nicerobino	31010	Have received your report, how shall I (we) remit
Niceterium	31011	Could you conveniently examine and report quickly on the pre- [sent value and prospects of —— mine, situated at —— ? [If so, when could you leave and what would be your fee ? [Cable reply to

Niceties ...	31012	Intend having special report
Nichet ...	31013	Report as to our prospects in —— ground
Nichilita ...	31014	No report from you
Nichoir ...	31015	Very damaging reports are current here
Nichtig ...	31016	Damaging reports are being circulated by
Nicknames	31017	Your last report was dated ——, since when we are without [news. Cable how things are
Nicociana...	31018	I consider the report a very fair and correct one
Nicophores	31019	I do not think the statements contained in ——'s report are [correct
Nictaculus	31020	Report is absolutely untrue
Nictalope ...	31021	Report most misleading
Nictantur...	31022	The report is entirely false and misleading
Nidada ...	31023	Report should be as impartial as possible
Nidamentum	31024	Can he (——) be relied upon to give an impartial report
Nidificium	31025	I do not think he (——) can be relied upon to give an impartial [report
Nidiuzzo ...	31026	Since my last report on the mine
Nidorosity	31027	In preparing report
Nidulor ...	31028	Require report on
Niebla ...	31029	Obtain immediately umpire's report
Niederlage	31030	I (we) have no report to date
Niederung	31031	Examine and report upon
Niedrig ...	31032	Report upon mining property at
Nientemeno	31033	Report upon hydraulic property
Niespera ...	31034	Please instruct —— to report upon
Nigauder ...	31035	Please instruct —— to report weight
Nigellus ...	31036	Can you arrange for —— to report on
Niggardish	31037	Cannot arrange with —— (him) to report
Niggardly...	31038	Could arrange for —— (him) to report
Nightbird...	31039	Will endeavour to arrange for —— (him) to report upon
Nightborn	31040	Have arranged with —— (him) to report
Nightcap ...	31041	Await copy of report and letter
Nightdog ...	31042	Have you received —— report
Nightdress	31043	On the whole report (is) generally satisfactory
Nightfire ...	31044	On the whole report (is) very unsatisfactory
Nightfly ...	31045	On the whole the report is decidedly unfavourable
Nightgown	31046	Keep the two reports carefully separate
Nightmare	31047	Have mailed report on ——
Nightshade	31048	When did you mail report
Nightspell	31049	Half-yearly report
Nightward	31050	Annual report
Nigreflo ...	31051	Decline the (this) report
Nigrescens	31052	I (we) shall not be able to report before next
Nigricans ...	31053	Discouraged by reports
Nigrine ...	31054	Reports received very unfavourable
Nigrities ...	31055	In the event of your report being unfavourable
Nigritudo...	31056	Is your report likely to be unfavourable
Nihildum ...	31057	Report is likely to be unfavourable
Nihilistic ...	31058	Will forward report from —— as soon as I receive it
Nihility ...	31059	You had better go as quickly as possible to —— and report
Nilpferd ...	31060	I am at liberty to examine and report on property named and [await your instructions to do so. Can start within —— days
Nimbatus ..	31061	Regret that I (we) cannot undertake to report on property
Nimbifer ...	31062	Could report on property but cannot get there until
Nimblefoot	31063	The report has originated from
Nimbleness	31064	The report has originated through
Nimiamente	31065	Can you discover how the report originated
Nimicato ...	31066	Will endeavour to discover how the report originated
Nimicizia ...	31067	Report as promptly as possible on
Nimiopere	31068	See report dated
Nimirum ...	31069	Await report

Nimmersatt	31070	Am (are) anxious to receive your report quickly
Nincompoop	31071	Report on the value and prospects of
Ninefold ...	31072	Report fully as to
Ninepins ...	31073	Is report likely to be favourable
Ninfea	31074	Report is likely to be favourable
Ninferno ...	31075	Report is not likely to be favourable
Ninguidus	31076	**Reported(ing)**
Ningulam	31077	Reported with
Ninnarella	31078	Has (have) been reported on by
Ninnolare...	31079	Has (have) not been reported on by
Ninullos ...	31080	Has it been reported on by
Niobite ...	31081	Reported as having
Nipotemo...	31082	Reported to be
Nippingly	31083	It has been reported here that
Niptrum ...	31084	The property has already been reported upon by
Niquel ...	31085	The property has not previously been reported upon by any
Niquitoso...	31086	Who is said subsequently to have reported [technical expert
Nirgend ...	31087	**Reprehensible**
Niscondere	31088	**Represent**
Nispola ...	31089	Do you know anyone who could represent me (us)
Nitedula ...	31090	Has (have) been appointed to represent
Nitelinus ...	31091	Will represent me (us)
Nitella ...	31092	Who will represent me (us)
Nitentius ...	31093	Cannot represent me (us) owing to
Nitidabain	31094	—— cannot represent me (us); will explain by letter
Nitidabunt	31095	If —— cannot, try and secure —— to represent me (us)
Nitidamini	31096	If —— cannot represent us shall I try and secure ——
Nitidatote...	31097	**Representation**
Nitidezza ...	31098	**Representative**
Nitiditas ...	31099	**Represented**
Nitido ...	31100	**Reprimand**
Nitouche ...	31101	**Reprint(s)**
Nitrates ...	31102	**Repudiate**
Nitreria ...	31103	To repudiate
Nitreux ...	31104	Repudiate all claims
Nitrify ...	31105	Repudiate any such liability(ies)
Nitrogen ...	31106	Repudiate any responsibility for further cost
Nitrosita ...	31107	**Repudiation**
Nivalis ...	31108	Possible repudiation of
Nivaticum	31109	There is every prospect of repudiation
Nivelacion	31110	There is no prospect of repudiation
Nivelador...	31111	What is the prospect of repudiation
Niveleur ...	31112	**Repurchase**
Nivesco ...	31113	Willing to repurchase
Nivifera ...	31114	Not willing to repurchase
Nivoso ...	31115	Would be glad to repurchase at
Noachian ...	31116	Offer to repurchase at
Nobilis ...	31117	Might be able to repurchase at
Nobilitato...	31118	Worth while to repurchase if
Nobilities ...	31119	**Repurchased**
Nobiscum	31120	Has (have) repurchased at
Nobleman	31121	Has (have) not repurchased
Noblemente	31122	**Reputation**
Noblesse ...	31123	—— has a poor reputation
Nocchiroso	31124	Has he (——) the reputation of a first-class mining engineer
Noccinola ...	31125	What is his (——'s) reputation
Nocenter ...	31126	—— has a fair reputation as a practical man
Nocentino...	31127	—— has a poor reputation as a practical man
Nocevole ...	31128	—— has a good reputation as a practical man
Nochebueno	31129	—— has an excellent reputation as a practical man: can be [thoroughly relied up~

Nocimiento	31130	**Repute(d)**
Nocitore ...	31131	**Request(ed)** (*See also* "Ask.")
Nociturus...	31132	At whose request
Noctambulo	31133	At my (our) request
Noctesco ...	31134	At the request of
Nocticolor	31135	At your request
Nocticulus	31136	To request
Noctifer ...	31137	Your request cannot be granted
Noctilugus	31138	Your request is granted with pleasure
Noctipuga	31139	Your request will receive attention
Noctivago...	31140	You had better request
Noctuinus	31141	Request —— at once to
Nocturne ...	31142	—— request(s) me (us) to
Nocumentum	31143	See request
Nocuous ...	31144	See request in letter dated
Nodabilis ...	31145	Your request as to accounts shall be attended to
Nodding ...	31146	**Require(s)**
Noderoso ...	31147	To require
Nodosamia	31148	How much (many) do you require
Nodosity ...	31149	Have you all that you require for
Nodribile ...	31150	Let me (us) know what you require
Nodritore ...	31151	Will do what you require
Nodritrice	31152	Will not require
Nodriza ...	31153	About what time (date) will you require
Nodulus ...	31154	What is it especially that you require
Noemical ...	31155	Should you require
Noguena ...	31156	Should you not require me (us)
Noguerado	31157	I (we) shall require
Noiratre ...	31158	Will probably require
Noirceur ...	31159	Should you require an(y) additional
Noiseless ...	31160	Do(es) not require an(y) additional
Noisome ...	31161	Will require at once
Noleggiare	31162	As to what —— may require
Noliser ...	31163	Will require to be
Nolunto ...	31164	Urgently require
Nomaccio ...	31165	Have had to require —— (him) to
Nomadist...	31166	Can you not require —— (him) to do it (this)
Nomadized	31167	Cannot require —— (him) to do anything except on personal [grounds
Nombradia	31168	Should I (we) require
Nombrar ...	31169	Who may require
Nombreux	31170	Would you require me to
Nomignolo	31171	When (what) are you likely to require
Nominalis...	31172	Do you require
Nominally	31173	Is it correct that you require
Nominandus	31174	Will require considerable tact to bring about
Nominative	31175	Forward statement showing for what purpose you require
Nomino ...	31176	**Required**
Nomisma ...	31177	To be required
Nomocanon	31178	When will it be required
Nomografo	31179	Will not be required before
Nonageni ...	31180	Is very much required at the present time
Nonagesimo	31181	Will be required as soon as
Nonagies ...	31182	Should it be required before
Nonaginta	31183	Will not be required at all now (that)
Nonarius ...	31184	Should be required (to)
Nonato ...	31185	If required could you
Nonchalant	31186	Most urgently required
Noncovelle	31187	Required as soon as possible
Noncria ...	31188	Will probably be required before
Noncurante	31189	**Requirement(s)**

Nondemanco	31190	Present supplies exceed requirements
Nondormire	31191	Present supplies not sufficient to meet requirements
Nonelect ...	31192	**Requisite(s)**
Nonesuch...	31193	It is absolutely requisite to
Nonetto ...	31194	It will be requisite to
Noningenti	31195	Do not get anything that is not absolutely requisite
Nonjuror ...	31196	Have you the requisite machinery for
Nonnain ...	31197	Cannot obtain the requisite
Nonnannome	31198	In order to get the requisite
Nonnunquam	31199	With everything requisite for
Nonobstant	31200	**Requisition**
Nonpareil...	31201	**Rescind**
Nonsuited...	31202	To rescind
Nonuncium	31203	Cannot rescind
Nonylene ...	31204	Do your best to induce —— to rescind
Noontime...	31205	Is (are) willing to rescind (if)
Noquero ...	31206	**Rescinded**
Norabuena	31207	Was (were) rescinded on
Noramalis	31208	Has (have) not yet been rescinded
Nordestear	31209	Unless it is (they are) rescinded
Nordlich ...	31210	Consider previous orders rescinded
Nordovest...	31211	Cannot under any circumstances be rescinded
Nordpol ...	31212	**Rescission**
Norial ...	31213	**Rescue**
Nortear ...	31214	To rescue
Northstar...	31215	Failed to rescue
Northwind	31216	**Rescued**
Noscendus	31217	Safely rescued
Noscitans...	31218	Successfully rescued
Nosebags ...	31219	**Resent(ed)**
Nosegay ...	31220	**Reservation**
Nosocomion	31221	Without reservation
Nostalgia ...	31222	Only reservation is (was)
Nostrano ...	31223	**Reserve(s)** (*See also* "Ore.")
Nostrapte...	31224	Reserve for
Nostratim...	31225	To reserve
Nostrum ...	31226	At what do you estimate the reserves
Notabilite .	31227	Give tonnage and approximate value of reserves
Notaire ...	31228	Actual reserves of ore do not exist
Notajesco ...	31229	Cannot estimate the value of the reserves
Notajuolo...	31230	I estimate that we have in reserve [worth ——
Notamment	31231	I estimate that our ore reserves are at least —— tons
Notando ...	31232	There are —— tons of ore in reserve, but I cannot approximate [the value (until)
Notariato ...	31233	Cable the number of tons and approximate value of ore in
Notatura ...	31234	Prospective reserves [reserve
Notebook ...	31235	These developments will increase our reserves of ore by —— [tons and —— value
Notenpult...	31236	An additional —— tons of ore in reserve
Noterella ...	31237	The reserves of ore are undoubtedly very large
Noteur ...	31238	The reserves of ore exist between —— and —— levels
Nothanker	31239	—— has estimated the ore reserves at —— tons, worth say [——. Can you confirm
Nothdurft	31240	I fully confirm —— estimate of —— tons, approximate value
Nothfall ...	31241	Confirm —— estimate as to tonnage, but not value [——
Nothigen ...	31242	Cannot confirm —— estimate either as to tonnage or value
Nothluge ...	31243	What will you (——) reserve for me
Nothstand	31244	I (——) intend(s) to reserve —— shares for you
Noticeable	31245	I rely upon you to reserve —— shares for me
Noticiar ...	31246	Must have an undertaking from —— to reserve

Notificado	31247	Are you (is ——) keeping anything in reserve
Notionist ...	31248	Write fully and without reserve
Notissime...	31249	Cable me (us) fully and without reserve
Notizietta...	31250	You should reserve to yourself the option (of)
Notola ...	31251	—— reserve(s) to himself (themselves) the option (of)
Notoletta ...	31252	I (we) reserve to myself (ourselves) the option (of)
Notoriedad	31253	Without any reserve whatsoever
Notoriete ...	31254	The only reserve (is) [have a good prospect in
Notorious ...	31255	The present reserves will last —— months; in addition we
Notricare ...	31256	Draw on the reserves
Notriles ...	31257	There are no reserves of ore in the technical sense of the term
Nottivago...	31258	I (we) shall reserve
Nottolata ...	31259	I (we) shall reserve —— for future treatment
Nottolone...	31260	**Reserve Account**
Noueux ...	31261	**Reserve Fund** (*See also* "Fund.")
Nougat ...	31262	Should be placed to reserve fund
Nourisher	31263	Now standing as reserve fund
Nourrice ...	31264	Will diminish reserve fund
Nourrisson	31265	Will increase reserve fund
Nourriture	31266	**Reserved**
Nouveaute	31267	To be reserved
Novacion ...	31268	Should be reserved entirely (for)
Novacula ...	31269	Will be reserved for
Novandus...	31270	Has (have) been reserved for
Novantena	31271	Ought to have been reserved for
Novastro ...	31272	In consequence of not having reserved
Novatore ...	31273	You should not have reserved
Novatrix ...	31274	You should have reserved
Novaturus	31275	All former rights reserved
Novecento	31276	Have reserved to myself (ourselves) the right of
Novedad ...	31277	Has (have) reserved to himself (themselves) the right of
Noveleria ...	31278	**Reservedly**
Novelette ...	31279	**Reserving**
Novelist ...	31280	**Reservoir(s)**
Novellarsi...	31281	**Reship(ped)**
Novelletta	31282	**Resident**
Novellizia...	31283	Resident agent
Novelty ...	31284	Resident director
Novenarius	31285	Resident director and general manager
Novennial...	31286	**Residue(al)**
Novensiles	31287	**Resign**
Noventa ...	31288	To resign
Noventeno	31289	You (——) had better resign at once
Noverare ...	31290	Would it be advisable for me (——) to resign
Novercalis	31291	If anything further of a like nature transpired I should resign
Noviciate ...	31292	Wish(es) to resign [at once
Novicio ...	31293	I (we) (——) do(es) not wish to resign
Novilla ...	31294	Is expected to resign
Novillejo ...	31295	Am (are) obliged to resign owing to
Novilunio ...	31296	Should resign
Novitatis ...	31297	Should not resign
Novitiolus...	31298	Refuse(s) to resign
Nowhere ...	31299	Consent(s) to resign
Noxalis ...	31300	**Resignation**
Noxitudo ...	31301	Has (have) not sent in resignation
Noyale ...	31302	Has (have) sent in resignation
Nozzles ...	31303	Am (is) not likely to send in resignation
Nozzoline ...	31304	Cannot accept your resignation
Nuageur ...	31305	It is very desirable that you (——) should cancel resignation
Nuancer ...	31306	Refuse(s) to accept resignation

Nubada ...	31307	Consent(s) to accept resignation
Nubarron...	31308	Cable resignation
Nubecula ...	31309	Imperative that you cable resignation
Nubiaduna	31310	——— has (have) to-day tendered his (their) resignation
Nubifer ...	31311	Beg to tender my resignation
Nubifugus	31312	**Resigned**
Nubigena ...	31313	Has ——— resigned
Nubilarium	31314	Has resigned
Nubilatur	31315	Has not resigned
Nubiletta ...	31316	**Resigning**
Nubiloso ...	31317	**Resist(ed)**
Nublosidad	31318	**Resistance**
Nucalibus...	31319	**Resisting**
Nuchtern ...	31320	**Resolute(ly)**
Nucifraga...	31321	**Resolution(s)**
Nuciprunum	31322	Failed to come to any resolution
Nucleoid ...	31323	Passed a formal resolution to
Nucleum ...	31324	Can only be done by formal resolution
Nudamente	31325	Formal resolution has been passed to reconstruct the company
Nudity ...	31326	Formal resolution has been passed to raise additional capital
Nudoso ...	31327	Formal resolution has been passed to issue an additional ——— [shares
Nuegados...	31328	Formal resolution has been passed to go into liquidation
Nuestramo	31329	Resolution(s) passed at the meeting on ——— has (have) been
Nugacitem	31330	No such resolution(s) was (were) passed [confirmed
Nugatorio	31331	Resolution(s) has (have) not been confirmed
Nuggety ...	31332	Until resolution(s) has (have) been formally confirmed
Nugivendus	31333	As a special resolution
Nugolaglia	31334	**Resolved**
Nugolato ...	31335	Am (is) (are) resolved to
Nugolosita	31336	When it was resolved to
Nugoluzzo	31337	It has been resolved to
Nuisance ...	31338	Have directors resolved to
Nuisible ...	31339	Directors have resolved to
Nulidad ...	31340	Directors have not resolved to
Nullatenus	31341	Should directors have resolved to
Nullement	31342	What have you (has ———) resolved to do
Nullezza ...	31343	I (we) have (——— has) resolved to
Nullite ...	31344	Is stated to have resolved to
Nullusdum	31345	Is ——— (are you) quite resolved to
Numen ...	31346	Has ——— (have you) resolved upon any line of action
Numerandus	31347	I am (we are) not at all resolved to
Numerario	31348	**Resource(s)**
Numerical	31349	Resources are very considerable
Numerique	31350	Resources altogether satisfactory
Numerist ...	31351	Resources beginning to get exhausted
Numerosam	31352	The resources are being rapidly exhausted
Numerosita	31353	Resources of the property are very great
Numerotage	31354	Resources of the property are limited
Numidiana	31355	What are the resources of the property
Numidicus	31356	Present resources are limited to
Numismatic	31357	Our last resource
Numskull...	31358	Can you suggest any other resource
Numularia	31359	I cannot suggest any other resource
Nunciante	31360	As a last resource
Nunciar ...	31361	As a last resource I (we) would suggest
Nunciature	31362	So as not to exhaust all resources
Nuncubi ...	31363	What are the available resources
Nuncupans	31364	The only available resources are
Nuncupatim	31365	In the event of all other available resources being exhausted

Nundiale ...	31366	**Respect(s)**
Nundinal ...	31367	Further information is required with respect to
Nundinator	31368	Do you know anything in respect of (to)
Nunnery ...	31369	Will inform you further with respect to it (this)
Nunquando	31370	With respect to
Nunquidnam	31371	I shall be glad to hear from you in respect to
Nunquis ...	31372	Is (are) in every respect liable
Nuntiavit ...	31373	In every respect
Nuotare ...	31374	In no respect
Nuovamente	31375	In all respects equal
Nupcial ...	31376	With due respect to
Nuptialis ...	31377	Pay every respect to
Nupturio ...	31378	I am (we are) very uneasy with respect to
Nuriculam	31379	**Respectable**
Nursemaid	31380	Consult a respectable
Nursery ...	31381	Is (are) considered most respectable
Nurtured ...	31382	Not altogether respectable
Nuscitio ...	31383	Is he (are they) considered respectable
Nussbaum	31384	Not considered very respectable
Nutante ...	31385	Do you personally consider him (them) respectable
Nutaturus	31386	**Respecting**
Nutbrown	31387	Shall be glad to hear from you respecting
Nutgall ...	31388	Further information desirable respecting
Nuthook ...	31389	Give —— any information you can respecting this matter
Nutjobber	31390	Shall I (we) communicate with —— respecting
Nutmeg ...	31391	You had better not communicate with —— respecting
Nutribile ...	31392	You had better communicate with —— at once respecting it
Nutricarsi...	31393	Is there anything new respecting
Nutricator	31394	Telegraph what I am to do respecting ——
Nutricula ...	31395	**Respective(ly)**
Nutriebat ...	31396	**Respond**
Nutriendus	31397	**Response**
Nutrimento	31398	**Responsibility**
Nutrition ...	31399	You must undertake the whole responsibility as regards
Nutritura ...	31400	In the joint responsibility of
Nutshell ...	31401	**Responsible**
Nuttree ...	31402	Responsible for
Nutzlich ...	31403	Who is responsible for
Nuvoletta...	31404	—— is (are) responsible for
Nuvolone ...	31405	I am (we are) responsible for
Nuvoluzzo	31406	You will be held responsible
Nyctalops...	31407	Must hold —— responsible
Nycticorax	31408	Are very responsible people
Nympharena	31409	Cannot be held responsible (for)
Nymphe ...	31410	Repudiate(s) being responsible
Nymphlike	31411	Do you think —— is (was) responsible
Oakapple ...	31412	Threaten(s) to hold me (us) responsible for any
Oakbark ...	31413	Give legal notice to hold him (them) responsible for [for
Oaktree ...	31414	Have given legal notice that shall hold him (them) responsible
Oakum ...	31415	Have received legal notice that I (we) shall be held responsible
Oarsman ...	31416	I (we) will not be responsible for [for
Oasis ...	31417	To be jointly responsible
Oatcake ...	31418	Will not be responsible for any cost incurred after ——
Oatmalt ...	31419	Give notice that shall hold him (them) responsible for any
Oatmeal ...	31420	Would require to become responsible for [damage caused by
Obacerbo ...	31421	Contend(s) that he is (they are) not responsible
Obacht ...	31422	You must contend that he is (they are) responsible
Obambulans	31423	**Rest**
Obambulo	31424	**Restrain(t)**
Obarator ...	31425	**Restrict(ed)**

Obaresco ...	31426	**Restriction(s)**
Obarmavi ...	31427	Until present restrictions are removed
Obaudio ...	31428	Unless present restrictions are removed
Obauratus	31429	Am trying to get restrictions removed as to
Obbedire ...	31430	Have succeeded in getting restrictions mitigated
Obbietto ...	31431	Have not succeeded in getting restrictions removed
Obbiezione	31432	As soon as restrictions have been removed
Obbliare ...	31433	**Result(s)** (*See also* "Disappointing," "Expect," "Experi-
Obbligarsi	31434	Please cable the result [ment," "Final.")
Obbliquare	31435	What is likely to be the result
Obblivioso	31436	The result
Obbrianza ...	31437	The most likely result
Obbrobbio	31438	No result
Obbruteo ...	31439	Result most satisfactory
Obbumbrare	31440	Result so far satisfactory
Obcalleo ...	31441	Result not at all satisfactory
Obcantatus	31442	Result disappointing
Obcecado ...	31443	Result encouraging
Obcordate	31444	Result has been different to what was anticipated
Obdormio ...	31445	The present result is *nil*
Obducor ...	31446	To the present result has been
Obductam	31447	It will probably result in
Obdurabat	31448	The result cannot but be disappointing
Obduracy ...	31449	In the result of
Obduravit ...	31450	Should this be the result
Obduresco	31451	Whatever may be the result
Obduretur	31452	The anticipated result
Obedecer ...	31453	Result is
Obedience ...	31454	Result has been to
Obeditur ...	31455	What has been the result of your
Obeisance ...	31456	Result is not very evident at present
Obejaruco ...	31457	Result is already evident
Obeliscal ...	31458	Should this result
Obelisk ...	31459	Little or no result
Obelisque ...	31460	Will cable you the result the moment I am (we are) able
Obencadura	31461	Will cable you the result not later than
Obenhin ...	31462	Waiting anxiously to know the result of
Obanques ...	31463	When do you expect to cable results
Obequito ...	31464	With very fair results
Oberbett ...	31465	Do you accept ——'s results
Oberflache	31466	Do not accept ——'s results
Obergewalt	31467	Accept ——'s results [factory
Oberhemd ...	31468	I have every hope that result of present work will be satis-
Oberjager ...	31469	I (we) shall confirm the results
Oberkleid ...	31470	Will send result as soon as possible
Oberlippe ...	31471	**Resulted(ing)**
Oberstimme	31472	Resulted in
Obertheil ...	31473	Nothing has so far resulted
Oberwahnt	31474	Has (have) resulted so far in
Oberwasser	31475	**Resume**
Oberwerk ...	31476	To resume
Obescent ...	31477	Resume work at
Obeseness ...	31478	Resume operations at
Obesidad ...	31479	Resume operations as soon as possible
Obesite ...	31480	Resume drivage(s)
Obeying ...	31481	Resume sinking
Obfirmate ...	31482	When do you expect to resume
Obfuscate ...	31483	Expect to resume operations on or before
Obgannio ...	31484	Shall not be able to resume much before
Obgleich ...	31485	As soon as I (we) can resume

Obherbesco	31486	To resume work
Obhorreo ...	31487	To resume drivage (at)
Obinanis ...	31488	To resume sinking the shaft
Obinducto	31489	Will resume operations at —— as soon as
Obirascens	31490	Shall resume immediately
Obispado ...	31491	Do not propose to resume until (unless)
Obispalia ...	31492	**Resumed**
Obispillo	31493	Have resumed work at (on)
Obitual ...	31494	Have resumed the crossout
Obituario ...	31495	Have resumed the drivage
Objacens ...	31496	Have resumed sinking
Objacuit ...	31497	Have resumed sinking winze
Objecter ...	31498	**Resumption**
Objecting ...	31499	**Re-survey**
Objecturus	31500	Make entirely new re-survey
Objicibus ...	31501	As shown by re-survey
Objiciens ...	31502	**Retain(s)**
Objurgate...	31503	Retain the best counsel
Objurgueo	31504	You had better retain at once
Oblada ...	31505	Should be very glad if I (we) could retain
Oblapie ...	31506	You are quite at liberty to retain
Oblateness	31507	To retain
Oblatione ...	31508	Do not retain
Oblatrans...	31509	To retain until
Oblatrare ...	31510	Will retain
Oblaturus...	31511	Endeavour to retain
Oblectatio	31512	Not advisable to retain —— later than
Obleniebo...	31513	Will not retain —— later than
Oblenitote	31514	Retain —— pending
Oblicuidad	31515	Retain sufficient funds to meet expenses of
Obliegen ...	31516	To retain an interest in the mine
Obligandus	31517	Willing to retain a considerable interest
Obligante ...	31518	Retains a very considerable interest
Obligato ...	31519	**Retained(ing)**
Obligeant ...	31520	Has (have) not retained the slightest interest
Obligemur	31521	Opponents have retained
Obliging ...	31522	**Retaliate**
Obligurio ...	31523	**Retard(ed)**
Oblimatus	31524	This (which) has retarded me (us) considerably
Obliquatio	31525	Will probably retard
Obliquely ...	31526	Has (have) retarded
Obliquita ...	31527	Has (have) not retarded
Obliterado	31528	Owing to my (our) being retarded by
Obliterer ...	31529	Provided that I am (we are) not retarded by
Oblitesco ...	31530	**Retarding**
Oblivion ...	31531	Retarding all progress
Obliviosus	31532	Considerably retarding
Obliviscor...	31533	Temporarily retarding
Oblocantur	31534	**Retire(d)(s)**
Oblocatus...	31535	Will you retire at the next meeting of shareholders
Oblocutor...	31536	Retire(s) at the next meeting of shareholders
Oblong ...	31537	Am (are) not inclined to retire
Oblongness	31538	Am (are) quite prepared to retire
Oblongule...	31539	Who is (are) the director(s) to retire at the next meeting
Oblongulus	31540	Retire(s) at the next meeting and is (are) eligible for re-election
Obloquy ...	31541	Retire(s) at the next meeting and is (are) not eligible for
Obluctans...	31542	**Retiring** [re-election
Obmann ...	31543	The retiring director(s)
Obmolior ...	31544	**Retort** (*See also* " Amalgam.")
Obmovent...	31545	Mercury retort

Obmurmuro	31546	Mercury retort and furnace
Obmutesco	31547	Capacity of retort is
Obniger ...	31548	Complete mercury retort with furnace and condenser
Obnoxious	31549	Mercury retort, horizontal type ; —— inches by —— inches [internally
Obnubilo ...	31550	Mercury retort, vertical type ; diameter at top —— inches ; [diameter at bottom —— inches ; height —— inches (all
Oboista ...	31551	**Retorted** (*See also* "Gold.")　　 [internal dimensions)
Obolebatur	31552	Retorted quicksilver
Obolemus ...	31553	All the quicksilver should be carefully retorted before com-
Oboluisti ...	31554	**Retorting** [mencing
Oborior ...	31555	Not enough to commence retorting
Obosculor	31556	As soon as I have sufficient to commence retorting
Obradura ...	31557	Now engaged retorting
Obragero ...	31558	Before retorting
Obrepticio	31559	After retorting
Obrigesco...	31560	At the retorting house
Obrigkeit ...	31561	**Retrench**
Obrizo ...	31562	**Retrenchment**
Obrogatur	31563	**Return(s)** (*See also* "Expense.")
Obruendus	31564	Return with
Obruisse ...	31565	Return to
Obrumpo ...	31566	Can you return to
Obrussus ...	31567	To return
Obryzatus	31568	On the return of
Obsaluto ...	31569	Do not return
Obscene ...	31570	On your (——'s) return from
Obscurado	31571	Can you call at —— on your return
Obscurant	31572	Will endeavour to call at —— as I (we) return
Obscurecer	31573	Cannot call at —— as I (we) return
Obscuritas	31574	As I (we) return
Obsecrate ...	31575	Nothing can be done until the return of
Obsecuente	31576	When are you likely to return to
Obsecundo	31577	Expect to return to —— about
Obsepior ...	31578	Will probably return
Obseptum...	31579	Will probably return in a few days
Obsequela...	31580	You must return immediately
Obsequiar	31581	Return immediately if you wish to see
Obsequieux	31582	Shall you return by way of
Obsequium	31583	Shall return by way of
Obseratus	31584	Shall not return by way of
Observable	31585	You must return home at once
Observador	31586	You must return home at once ; —— seriously ill
Observant...	31587	You must return home at once ; —— is dead
Obseso ...	31588	I (we) will return home immediately
Obsession ...	31589	Then return home direct
Obsessurus	31590	Immediately upon your return
Obsibilo ...	31591	As soon as he (——) returns
Obsideor ...	31592	Return as soon as you conveniently can
Obsidiana	31593	There is no absolute need for you to return before
Obsidional	31594	Shall I return
Obsidium ...	31595	Shall I return it (them) to
Obsignatus	31596	You had better return it (them) to
Obsignor ...	31597	There is no need to return it (them)
Obsistente	31598	Have had to return owing to
Obsistitur...	31599	Had to return owing to difficulties arising with
Obsolesco...	31600	Do not expect to return much before
Obsoletus ...	31601	Expect to return not later than
Obsonator	31602	Shall certainly not return before
Obsonium...	31603	Instruct —— to return here without delay

Obsorbeo ...	31604	Return immediately to England
Obstantia ...	31605	Instruct —— to return to England as speedily as possible
Obstaturus	31606	**Returns**
Obstbaum	31607	Cable returns for the week ending
Obsterno ...	31608	Cable returns for the month ending
Obstetric ...	31609	Cable returns for the —— ending
Obstgarten	31610	Returns for the week ending —— amount to ——
Obsthoker	31611	Returns for the month ending —— amount to ——
Obstinacy...	31612	What are your returns for the month of
Obstinado ..	31613	The returns for the month of —— amount to
Obstinate ...	31614	Returns for the —— ending amount to ——
Obstinatum	31615	Shall not be able to maintain present returns
Obstineo ...	31616	Our returns for the year just closed
Obstitum ...	31617	Must include any returns to
Obstmus ...	31618	As soon as the returns are to hand
Obstrepens	31619	But the actual returns are not yet in
Obstrictus	31620	As soon as the returns are received
Obstringo	31621	Telegraph as soon as any returns are known
Obstruct ...	31622	The returns from ore
Obstruir ...	31623	Until returns are received from ore already shipped [made
Obstrusus...	31624	A further expenditure of —— required before returns can be
Obstupesco	31625	Returns are not yet to hand
Obstupidus	31626	When do you expect to know the returns
Obstwein ...	31627	When do you expect to make returns
Obstzeit ...	31628	Expect to make returns within —— month(s)
Obtegendus	31629	Expect to make returns within next three months
Obtemperar	31630	Returns cannot be expected much before
Obtencion...	31631	Returns considered satisfactory
Obtendens	31632	Returns not at all satisfactory
Obtento ...	31633	This will not cause any delay in making returns
Obtenturus	31634	Will it (this) cause any delay in making returns
Obtestans...	31635	Please cable returns of
Obtestatio	31636	At present can only estimate the returns
Obticentia	31637	Estimated returns
Obtineor ...	31638	What returns do you estimate will be received from
Obtingit ...	31639	No returns
Obtorpeo ...	31640	The returns indicate (that)
Obtritus ...	31641	**Returned**
Obtruder ...	31642	Has —— returned to
Obtruncor	31643	—— has returned to
Obtrusive...	31644	Should be returned at once
Obtundere	31645	Shall be returned at once
Obtunsio ...	31646	Has (have) already been returned
Obturbatur	31647	Cannot be returned until
Obturbo ...	31648	Has not been returned owing to
Obturgesco	31649	He (they) (——) has (have) just returned
Obtuseness	31650	Has (have) not yet returned
Obtusius ...	31651	By which time he (——) will probably have returned
Obumbrans	31652	To be returned in good condition
Obumbro ...	31653	**Returning**
Obuncus ...	31654	Returning charges
Obundatio	31655	Previous to returning
Obusier ...	31656	**Revenue Account**
Obustam ...	31657	Expenditure on revenue account
Obvagio ...	31658	To be charged to revenue account
Obvallatus	31659	Expenditure on revenue account must be kept distinct from
Obventio ...	31660	Send statement showing your expenditure on revenue account
Obversatus	31661	What is the balance of revenue account [to date
Obverse ...	31662	The balance of revenue account is
Obvertor ...	31663	Which leaves —— as the balance of revenue account

Obviar ...	31664	Should this be charged to revenue account
Obvolutus	31665	Should be charged to revenue account
Obwalten ...	31666	Has (have) been charged to revenue account meanwhile
Obyecto ...	31667	We have expended in addition on revenue account
Ocasionado	31668	Mail statement showing expenditure on revenue account since
Occallatio ...	31669	Amount you have (—— has) expended on revenue account
Occallesco...	31670	Approximate expense on revenue account
Occaminis	31671	**Reverberatory** (*See also* " Furnace.")
Occasurus	31672	**Revised**
Occatorius	31673	Cable revised estimate
Occavero ...	31674	**Revoke** (*See also* " Cancel.")
Occensus ...	31675	To revoke
Occepto ...	31676	Threaten(s) to revoke
Occhiaccio	31677	Must revoke
Occhiata ...	31678	**Revoked**
Occhiatura	31679	Not yet revoked
Occhietto ...	31680	Will be revoked at the next meeting of
Occhiolino	31681	Was revoked on (by)
Occidendus	31682	**Revoking**
Occidentem	31683	**Revolution(s)** (*See also* " Speed.")
Occiditore...	31684	What is the number of revolutions per minute at (of)
Occiduous	31685	—— revolutions per minute
Occinens ...	31686	Unless we run at —— revolutions per minute
Occipital ...	31687	Necessary to run at —— revolutions per minute
Occipitium	31688	**Revolutionary**
Occipizio ...	31689	Revolutionary movement
Occiput ...	31690	Revolutionary movement likely to be successful
Occlamito...	31691	Revolutionary movement cannot be successful
Occluding...	31692	If the revolutionary movement is successful
Occludor ..	31693	Provided the revolutionary movement is not successful
Occoltare ..	31694	**Revolve(d)**
Occorrente	31695	**Revolving**
Occulco ...	31696	**Reward(ed)**
Occultatio	31697	Should be rewarded
Occultness	31698	As a reward for
Occultus ...	31699	Claim(s) a minimum reward of
Occumbens	31700	If you think fit, offer a reward for discovery of
Occupandus	31701	Has (have) offered a reward for discovery of
Occupant ...	31702	Have you (has ——) offered a reward for discovery of
Occuparsi...	31703	Has (have) offered no reward whatever
Occupatore	31704	**Rich** (*See also* " Exceedingly," " Ore.")
Occupier ...	31705	Have discovered a rich streak of ore at —— which assays
Occurritur	31706	There is a rumour current that a rich streak of ore has been [found at ——; cable what truth there is in rumour
Occursans...	31707	There is no truth in the rumour that a rich streak of ore has [been cut
Occursio ...	31708	The rumour that a rich streak of ore has been cut is true; it
Oceanic ...	31709	Rich ore [assays ——
Ocellated ...	31710	Very rich
Ochavado...	31711	Fairly rich
Ochavear ...	31712	With rich ore occasionally in pockets
Ochenton ...	31713	The rich ore has come to an end
Ochlocracy	31714	The ore is gradually opening out into a rich pocket
Ochosen ..	31715	The rich ore amounts to inside of —— tons
Ochreous ...	31716	Cable assay of rich ore
Ochsig ...	31717	Does the rich ore continue
Ocinium ...	31718	Cable width and length of rich shoot of ore
Ociosidad ...	31719	The rich ore shoot is, as at present developed, —— feet long
Ocquinisco	31720	Not so rich [by —— feet wide
Ocreatus ...	31721	**Richer** (*See also* " Ore.")

Ocroto ...	31722	Still richer
Octachord	31723	Have nothing richer
Octaedro ...	31724	Cable whether the ore is becoming richer or **poorer**
Octagonal ..	31725	The ore is becoming richer
Octahedron	31726	In depth the ore is becoming richer [richer
Octangular	31727	As the breast of the level is advanced, the ore is becoming
Octaphorum	31728	**Richly**
Octastylos	31729	**Richness**
Octavario ...	31730	**Rid**
Octaviante	31731	As soon as I am (we are) rid of
Octavilla ...	31732	Unless (until) I (we) can get rid of
Octavum ...	31733	If I am (we are) ever to get rid of
Octennial ...	31734	Do not get rid of him (——) for the present
Octillion ...	31735	Should prefer to get rid of —— rather than ——
Octingenti	31736	Should be very glad to get rid of
Octobass ...	31737	**Riffles**
Octodecim	31738	From the riffles
Octogeni ...	31739	—— ozs. of amalgam from the riffles
Octogesimo	31740	**Right(s)**
Octogies ...	31741	Quite right
Octojugis ...	31742	All right
Octonarius	31743	Everything is going on all right
Octonary ...	31744	Mining right(s)
Octopetala	31745	Agricultural right(s)
Octopus ...	31746	Water right(s)
Octostilo ...	31747	Agricultural and mining rights
Octroyer ...	31748	My (our) rights
Octuple ...	31749	Your rights
Octussis ...	31750	His (their) rights
Octylic ...	31751	If right
Ocular ...	31752	If not right
Ocularius ...	31753	Are you all right
Oculens ...	31754	Thought it was all right
Oculiform...	31755	What right has —— to
Oculista ...	31756	—— has (have) no right to
Oculitus ...	31757	Cable whether this is right
Ocultable ...	31758	Cable whether this is the right interpretation
Ocultador...	31759	Is it right
Ocupacion	31760	It is right
Ocurrencia	31761	It is not right
Odalisque...	31762	It is not altogether right
Oddity ...	31763	Would it be right to
Oddlooking	31764	It would be quite right to
Odiatore ...	31765	It would not be right to
Odibile ...	31766	Found everything all right
Odieux ...	31767	Is everything all right? Cable
Odievole ...	31768	Is it quite right to
Odinolyon	31769	Do you consider it right that
Odiosetto ...	31770	I (we) consider it quite right that
Odiosicus ...	31771	I (we) do not consider it quite right that
Odiosidad...	31772	The sole right to (of)
Odiousness	31773	The right thing would be to
Odische ...	31774	If you are satisfied that everything is right
Odometro...	31775	I am quite satisfied that everything is right
Odontalgia	31776	I am not at all satisfied that things are right
Odontides...	31777	What would be the right place for
Odontoid ...	31778	The right place would be
Odontology	31779	Is not in the right place
Odorabile ...	31780	Do whatever you think right
Odoramen	31781	Intend to assert my (our) rights

Odorandus	31782	You had better take legal steps to assert our rights te
Odorato ...	31783	Have already taken legal steps to assert our rights
Odorazione	31784	—— is about to take legal steps to assert his rights
Odorifero ...	31785	**Rigid(ly)**
Odorously	31786	**Rigorous(ly)**
Odoruzzo ...	31787	**Rigour**
Odourless...	31788	**Riot(ers)**
Odrecillo ...	31789	**Rise** (*See also* "Raise.")
Odreria ...	31790	To rise
Odrina ...	31791	Will rise
Oeconomia	31792	Will not rise
Oedicnemo	31793	Will put in a rise
Oefter ...	31794	To connect with the rise (at)
Oeillade ...	31795	Will connect with the rise (at)
Oelbaum ...	31796	The rise is now up —— feet
Oelfarbe ...	31797	Cannot rise before
Oelgemalde	31798	The vein in the rise
Oellampe ...	31799	The ore in the rise
Oelmalerei	31800	Rise is now within —— feet of surface
Oelsuss ...	31801	Rise is now within —— feet of the —— level
Oenanthe ...	31802	Rise is within —— feet of the winze
Oenate ...	31803	Shall commence to rise upon the vein at once
Oenopolium	31804	An average sample from the rise assays
Oenothera	31805	From the rise
Oertlich ...	31806	The price is not likely to rise
Oesophage	31807	Is the price likely to rise
Oesterlich	31808	The price is almost certain to rise
Oestrus ...	31809	The price of the shares should rise at least
Oesypum ...	31810	There has been no rise in the price
Oeuvre ...	31811	There is not likely to be any rise in the price
Ofendedor	31812	How high is the water likely to rise
Ofengabel	31813	Will probably rise to ——
Ofenkrucke	31814	**Risen**
Ofenloch ...	31815	Has (have) risen
Ofenschirm	31816	Has (have) not risen
Oferente ...	31817	The water has risen —— feet during the last twenty-four hours
Offatim ...	31818	How high has the water risen
Offenbar ...	31819	The water has risen up to
Offenceful	31820	The water had risen —— feet up to —— o'clock to-day
Offenheit ...	31821	The water had risen up to the —— level [your cable
Offensanza	31822	The price of the shares had risen previous to the receipt of
Offensatio	31823	Owing to the price of the shares having already risen
Offenseur ...	31824	Has the price risen
Offensive ...	31825	The price has risen
Offensore ...	31826	The price has not risen
Offensum ...	31827	Has (have) already risen
Offerable ...	31828	**Rising**
Offerenda ...	31829	Is already rising
Offertory ...	31830	Is the water still rising
Offhanded	31831	The water is still rising
Officialis ...	31832	The water has stopped rising [water from rising
Officiate ...	31833	At what level do you expect you will be able to keep the
Officieux ...	31834	Hope to stop the water from rising beyond
Officine ...	31835	Have stopped the water rising beyond
Officioso ...	31836	**Risk(s)**
Offirmatus	31837	What risk do I (we) run by
Offocandus	31838	There is no risk incurred at all
Offrande ...	31839	The risk you would incur is simply
Offringor ...	31840	To risk
Offscour ...	31841	Will risk

Offspring ...	31842	Will not risk
Offucia ...	31843	You will risk
Offuscato ...	31844	Any delay means serious risk
Offusquer ...	31845	If you delay you will run great risk of losing the property
Oficializo ...	31846	What risk is there (of)
Oficiar ...:	31847	There is no risk at all practically
Oficinal ...	31848	The risk will be very small
Oficinista ...	31849	The risk is very great
Ofrecedor ...	31850	In the event of your deciding to risk
Ofrenda ...	31851	In case you should decide not to risk
Oftalmia ...	31852	I (we) strongly advise you not to risk
Ofuscar ...	31853	You run a very great risk by
Oggannio ...	31854	The risk is comparatively trifling
Oggetto ...	31855	Am (are) willing to take the risk if not more than
Oggigiorno	31856	There will be no risk
Ogling ...	31857	The risk is
Oglionte ...	31858	If you are satisfied we do not run any risk of losing
Ognindi ...	31859	Is it worth the risk
Ognorache	31860	It is worth the risk
Ogress ...	31861	It is not worth the risk
Ohnmacht	31862	If it can be managed without much risk
Ohrenzeuge	31863	Will you guarantee me (us) against any risk
Ohrfinger ...	31864	Will guarantee you against any risk
Ohrloffel ...	31865	Will guarantee you against risk to the extent of
Oilcake ...	31866	Cannot guarantee you as regards risk
Oilcloth ...	31867	It would not do to run any risk
Oilcolour ...	31868	The only risk would be in case of
Oiliness ...	31869	Before incurring any risk
Oilmen ...	31870	**Risky**
Oilpaint ...	31871	Very risky business
Oilshop ...	31872	Not at all risky
Oiltank ...	31873	If it is in the slightest degree risky
Oilwells ...	31874	Do nothing risky
Ointment ...	31875	Will do nothing risky
Oiseau ...	31876	Has (have) done nothing risky
Oisillon ...	31877	**River** (*See also* " Bed," " Water.")
Oisivete ...	31878	The property is bounded by the —— river
Oislo ...	31879	The ground rises from the —— river
Ojaladera ...	31880	Property is situated on the —— river
Ojalar ...	31881	Property is situated near the —— river
Ojeada ...	31882	There are several rivers on the concession
Ojeadura ...	31883	In the bed of the river [purposes
Ojeriza ...	31884	The —— river distant —— would give ample water for milling
Ojeteado ...	31885	The —— river distant —— would give ample water for power
Ojialegre ...	31886	**Rivet(s)** [and milling purposes
Ojimoreno	31887	**Road(s)**
Ojinegro ...	31888	Now on the road
Ojuelo ...	31889	On the road to
Olandilla ...	31890	There is a good road from —— to the mine(s)
Oldage ...	31891	The road between —— and the mine(s) is very bad
Oldfashion	31892	A very bad road
Oldmaids ...	31893	The gradient of the road between —— and the property is very
Oldstyle ...	31894	The road has a very steep gradient for —— miles [slight
Oleaceus ...	31895	Is —— miles by road (from)
Oleaginoso	31896	Owing to the road(s) being blocked up (by)
Oleamentum	31897	On account of the bad state of the road(s)
Oleandre ...	31898	When do you expect the road(s) will be opened
Olearider ...	31899	Expect the road(s) will be open on or about
Olearius ...	31900	A road would require to be made
Oleaster ...	31901	What would the cost of a road amount to

Olecranon...	31902	The cost of a suitable road would be about —— and could be [finished within —— weeks of commencement
Oledero ...	31903	Does your estimate include roads
Olefine ...	31904	Estimate does not include roads.
Oleograph	31905	It will be necessary to make a road from —— to the property
Oleomiel ...	31906	The road will be finished within the next —— days
Oleosidad ...	31907	Roads impassable between the months of —— and ——
Olezzante ...	31908	The roads are in excellent condition between —— and ——
Olfactans ...	31909	The roads are impassable through —— [months (inclusive)
Olfactatus ...	31910	The roads are impassable from —— to ——
Olfactory ...	31911	The roads are impassable
Olfactrix ...	31912	Before the roads become impassable
Oliandolo...	31913	The condition of the road is too bad for transporting heavy
Olibrius ...	31914	Inclusive of roads [freights
Oliente ...	31915	The road would be required to be repaired
Oligarch ...	31916	The road(s) is (are) in splendid condition
Oligarquia	31917	The gradient of the road is too steep for
Oligocene ...	31918	Several bad pieces of road
Olimpiada	31919	**Roast(ed)** (*See also* "Calcine," "Concentrates.")
Olivaison ...	31920	**Roaster** (*See also* "Furnace.")
Olivarda ...	31921	Ought to at once purchase and erect mechanical roaster at mill
Olivarius ...	31922	When do you expect you will complete erection of mechanical [roaster
Olivastro ...	31923	The mechanical roaster will be erected and ready for use about
Olivetree ...	31924	**Robber(y)**
Olivettes ...	31925	**Rock** (*See also* "Barren," "Changed," "Geological," "Hard,"
Olivetum ...	31926	The rock is not at all hard ["Mineral.")
Olivifer ...	31927	The rock is exceedingly hard
Olivilla ...	31928	Rock has become much softer
Olivitas ...	31929	Rock has become much harder
Ollaos ...	31930	The country rock is
Olluela ...	31931	On account of the excessive hardness of the country rock
Olocausto	31932	The rock is good for machine boring
Olografo ...	31933	Surface rock [from
Olorifico	31934	Should be glad if you would send specimen samples of the rock
Olorinus ...	31935	The rock is becoming harder in the shaft
Oloroso ...	31936	The rock at —— is becoming softer
Oltramodo	31937	The rock forming the hanging wall of the vein is
Oltrarsi ...	31938	The rock forming the footwall of the vein is
Oltreche ...	31939	Owing to bars of hard rock
Oltremare	31940	As the rock has now become softer
Oltremonti	31941	Alum-schist
Olusculum	31942	Anamesite
Olvidadizo	31943	Andesite
Olvidar ...	31944	Anhydrite
Olympian ...	31945	Aphanite
Omaccino...	31946	Aphanite-porphyry
Ombelico ..	31947	Augite-andesite
Ombliguera	31948	Augite-porphyry
Ombraculo	31949	Augite-rock
Ombrager ...	31950	Augite-schist
Ombragione	31951	Augite-syenite
Ombratura	31952	Basalt
Ombrelle ...	31953	Basaltic-porphyry
Ombrifero	31954	Basalt-wacke
Ombrilungo	31955	Breccia
Ombrometre	31956	Calcareous rock
Ombrosita	31957	Carboniferous limestone
Omelete ...	31958	Chalk
Omened ...	31959	Chalk-marl

Omental ...	31960	Chalk-rock
Omentatus	31961	Chlorite-schist
Omettere ...	31962	Clay
Omicidio ...	31963	Clay-slate
Omicron ...	31964	Clinkstone
Ominans ...	31965	Conglomerate
Ominator ...	31966	Crystalline limestone
Ominosus ...	31967	Dacite
Omiomeria	31968	Diabase
Omissible ...	31969	Diabase-porphyry
Omissive ...	31970	Diabase-schist
Omissurus	31971	Diallage-rock
Omittendus	31972	Diorite
Ommesso ...	31973	Diorite-porphyry
Omnibus ...	31974	Diorite-slate
Omniformis	31975	Dolerite
Omnigenus	31976	Dolomite
Omnimodo	31977	Domite
Omniparens	31978	Elvanite
Omniparity	31979	Felsite-rock
Omniscient	31980	Felspar-porphyry
Omniscio ...	31981	Felstone
Omnivagus	31982	Gabbro
Omnivorous	31983	Gneiss
Omogeneita	31984	Granite
Omologo ...	31985	Granite-porphyry
Omophacius	31986	Granite-gneiss
Omoplato ...	31987	Granulite
Oncejera ...	31988	Greenstone
Onceno ...	31989	Greisen
Onchets ...	31990	Guano
Oncinetto ...	31991	Hornblende-porphyrite
Onctuosite	31992	Hornblende-schist
Ondeado ...	31993	Hypersthene-andesite
Ondeggiare	31994	Itacolumite
Ondoyer ...	31995	Killas
Ondule ...	31996	Kyanite-rock
Onduliren...	31997	Laterite
Oneeyed ...	31998	Lava
Oneness ...	31999	Leucite-rock
Oneraire ...	32000	Leucite-porphyry
Onerandus	**32001**	Lignite
Onerario ...	32002	Limestone
Oneraturus	32003	Magnesian limestone
Oneroso ...	32004	Marble
Onesided ...	32005	Melaphyre
Onestato ...	32006	Mica-trap
Onestura ...	32007	Mica-schist
Onfacino ...	32008	Micaceous porphyry
Ongarese ...	32009	Mountain limestone
Onguent ...	32010	Nepheline-dolerite
Onionbulb	32011	New Red Sandstone
Onionplant	32012	Old Red Sandstone
Onionseed...	32013	Oolite
Oniscus ...	32014	Phonolite
Onochilus...	32015	Pitchstone
Onoclea ...	32016	Pitchstone-porphyry
Onocrotalo	32017	Porphyrite
Onomancia	32018	Porphyritic dolerite
Onopordon	32019	Porphyritic granite

Onorabile ...	32020	Porphyritic syenite
Onoratore	32021	Porphyry
Onoratrice	32022	Quartz
Onoretto ...	32023	Quartz-breccia
Onorifico ...	32024	Quartzite
Onotaure ...	32025	Quartz-porphyry
Onrushing	32026	Quartz-schist
Onslaught	32027	Rhyolite
Ontaneto ...	32028	Rock-salt
Ontologist	32029	Sand
Onychitis ...	32030	Sandstone
Onzavo ...	32031	Sanidine-trachyte
Oogala ...	32032	Schist
Oolitic ...	32033	Schorl-rock
Opacidad ...	32034	Schorl-schist
Opalesce ...	32035	Serpentine
Opaline ...	32036	Shale
Opeconsiva	32037	Slate
Openeyed ...	32038	Syenite
Openhand...	32039	Syenitic-gneiss
Openheart	32040	Syenite-granite
Openmouth	32041	Tachylite
Operable ...	32042	Talc-schist
Operaccia ...	32043	Tourmaline-schist
Operador ...	32044	Trachyte
Operagione	32045	Trachyte-porphyry
Operaglass	32046	Tufa
Operateur	32047	**Rock Borer** (*See also* " Drill.")
Operatic ...	32048	**Rock Breaker**
Operating...	32049	The rock breaker jaws
Operatrice	32050	Send —— pair(s) of rock breaker jaws
Operculo ...	32051	Mail tracing of rock breaker jaws
Operetta ...	32052	**Rods** (*See also* " Connecting.")
Operiendus	32053	**Roll(s)** (*See also* " Crusher.")
Operiere ...	32054	Steel shells for rolls
Operista ...	32055	A set of Cornish rolls
Opernhaus	32056	High speed steel rolls
Operose ...	32057	—— sets of crushing rolls
Operositas	32058	Krom's rolls
Opertaneus	32059	**Roofing**
Opertorium	32060	Sheet iron roofing
Opertum ...	32061	**Room**
Opferherd...	32062	Plenty of room
Opferthier	32063	Reserve room for
Opferung ...	32064	Will reserve room for
Ophicleide	32065	Have reserved room for
Ophidion ...	32066	**Rope** (*See also* " Chain.")
Ophiuchus	32067	Wire rope —— inches in circumference —— ft. long
Ophthalmia	32068	Capstan rope
Opiates ...	32069	Rope for winze kibble
Opificium ...	32070	Good Manilla rope —— in. in circumference —— ft. long
Opilacion ...	32071	Flat wire rope —— feet long, —— in. wide and —— in. thick
Opilativo ...	32072	Flat Manilla rope —— feet long, —— in. wide and —— in. [thick
Opimaco ...	32073	**Rotate(d)**
Opimianus	32074	**Rotation**
Opimitas ...	32075	**Rough(ly)**
Opinabilis	32076	Too rough to
Opinable ...	32077	Very rough
Opinant ...	32078	Mail a rough estimate
Opinatio ...	32079	A rough estimate is all that is required

Opiniatre ...	32080	As a rough estimate
Opinionist	32081	Will send you a rough draft
Opiparis ...	32082	**Round(ly)**
Opitulatio	32083	In round figures
Opitulor ...	32084	What do you think it would amount to in round figures
Opobalsamo	32085	I think it would probably amount to —— in round figures
Opodeldoc	32086	**Route**
Opoponaca	32087	En route
Oporotheca	32088	Now en route for
Oportuno ...	32089	Cable best route
Opositor ...	32090	You will receive full particulars as to route from
Opossum ...	32091	Would suggest as an alternative route
Oppango	32092	The quickest route is
Oppector ...	32093	The safest route is
Opperiens...	32094	A quicker route is viâ
Oppetendus	32095	**Routine**
Oppetitus...	32096	**Royalty**
Oppiato ...	82097	Upon a basis of a —— per cent. royalty
Oppidanus	32098	**Rubbish** (*See also* " Debris.")
Oppidatim	32099	**Ruby(ies)**
Oppilatio ...	32100	Small rubies have been found on the property
Oppleor ...	32101	Rubies are reported to have been found at
Oppliare ...	32102	The ruby mines are situated at
Opponent...	32103	Can you visit and report upon ruby mines at
Opporemuto	32104	The rubies are found associated with
Opposable	32105	The rubies have been valued at
Opposing ...	32106	The rubies have no market value
Oppositus...	32107	**Rugged**
Oppressato	32108	**Ruin(s)(ed)**
Oppresseur	32109	In ruins
Oppressive	32110	Ruined by
Opprimente	32111	Ruined by mismanagement
Opprobre ...	32112	Owners practically ruined
Opprobrium	32113	**Ruinous(ly)**
Oppugnare	32114	The general condition is simply ruinous
Oppugnatio	32115	Present expenditure ruinous
Oppugning	32116	In order to prevent ruinous extravagance
Opresivo ...	32117	**Rumour(ed)** (*See also* " Failed.")
Oprobioso...	32118	A rumour has been circulated here to the effect that
Opsidianus	32119	Please ascertain and cable what truth there is in the rumour
Opsonator...	32120	There is no truth in the rumour at all [that
Optabilis ...	32121	The only truth in the rumour is
Optative ...	32122	Have you heard any rumour as to
Optativus...	32123	Have not heard the slightest rumour
Optical ...	32124	I heard a (the) rumour but paid no attention to it
Optigraph	32125	The parties amongst whom the rumour was started are very
		[disreputable
Optiker	32126	I have no doubt that the rumour is essentially correct
Optimates	32127	Do(es) not place any credence in the rumour
Optimism ...	32128	The rumour has been repeated
Optionatus	32129	**Run(s)**
Optique ...	32130	Shall run until
Opugnador	32131	On completion of run
Opulemment	32132	What is your estimate of the present run
Opulency ...	32133	I (we) estimate this run will yield
Opuntia ...	32184	I (we) estimate this run will last us
Opuscule ...	32135	So long as continue to run above
Oquedal ...	32136	Some of it runs as high as
Orach	32137	On the run of the lode
Oracional...	32138	The run of the lode is

Oracular ...	32139	**Running**
Oraculous...	32140	In running measure
Orageux ...	32141	Running day and night
Oraison ...	32142	Shall cease running on ——
Oramentum	32143	Ceased running on ——
Orange ...	32144	When will you begin running
Orangeade	32145	Shall begin running
Orangeman	32146	Cannot begin running before
Orangepeel	32147	Running most satisfactorily
Orangepip	32148	Not running quite so satisfactorily
Orangerie...	32149	**S**
Orangista...	32150	**Saccharoid**
Orangotan	32151	**Sack(s)**
Orateur ...	32152	How many sacks of ore (——) have you shipped
Oratorial ...	32153	I (we) have shipped —— sacks
Oratrice ..	32154	Ore sacks
Oraturus ...	32155	What is the weight of each sack
Orbayar ...	32156	The weight of each sack is about
Orbicolato	32157	We have shipped —— sacks, weighing about —— pounds
Orbicular ...	32158	A sample of one sack has assayed
Orbiculine	32159	In double sacks
Orbite ...	32160	**Sacked**
Orbitual ...	32161	Sacked up ready for transport
Orcaneta ...	32162	Sacked ore
Orcetto ...	32163	Now sacked
Orchard ...	32164	Not yet sacked
Orchestra...	32165	As soon as sacked
Orchilla ...	32166	**Sacrifice(d)**
Orcinianus	32167	Willing to make a considerable sacrifice
Orcinic ...	32168	Would you have to sacrifice
Orciolago ...	32169	Would have to sacrifice
Orcioletto...	32170	Would not have to sacrifice
Orcotomia	32171	If any sacrifice is to be made
Orcynus ...	32172	Necessary to sacrifice
Ordainer ...	32173	**Sacrificing**
Ordaining...	32174	**Safe**
Ordalia ...	32175	Safe investment
Ordeata ...	32176	Safe purchase
Ordenada ...	32177	Safe for the next three months
Ordenante	32178	Safe for the next —— months
Ordentlich	32179	Sufficiently safe to
Ordeum ...	32180	I think it is a very safe thing
Ordiendus	32181	I do not think it at all safe
Ordigno ...	32182	Do you think it would be safe to rely upon
Ordinal ...	32183	I think it would be quite safe (for)
Ordinance	32184	Will (would) it be safe (to)
Ordinarius	32185	It will (would) not be safe
Ordination	32186	I (we) do not consider it safe to
Ordinator...	32187	I (we) do not think it is (they are) safe
Orditajo ...	32188	Perfectly safe
Ordnung ...	32189	The workings are not safe
Ordonner ...	32190	You should make everything safe
Orduxier ...	32191	As soon as it is (they are) safe
Orecchia ...	32192	It is (they are) quite safe
Orecchione	32193	Is it (are they) quite safe
Orecchiuto	32194	It is (they are) not safe
Oregano ...	32195	Think you would be quite safe in
Oreillette ...	32196	Do not think you would be safe in
Oreillons ...	32197	It would be safe (to)
Orelland ...	32198	It would not be safe to act at present

Oreoselino	32199	Should be quite safe to
Orfandad ...	32200	Is it not safe to
Orfanello ...	32201	It is not safe to
Orfebreria	32202	As soon as it is safe to
Organcase	32203	**Safeguard**
Organero ...	32204	To safeguard my (our) interests
Organical ...	32205	**Safely**
Organique	32206	Arrived here (at ——) safely on
Organizer...	32207	Can safely proceed with (to)
Organloft ..	32208	Cannot at present proceed safely with (to)
Organpipe	32209	May be safely worked
Organstop	32210	Cannot be safely worked
Orgelchor ...	32211	If it can be done safely
Orgelet ...	32212	In case it (this) cannot be done safely
Orgelplatz	32213	**Safety** (*See also* "Fuse.")
Orgelzug ...	32214	Safety lamp(s)
Orgoglioso	32215	Safety-valve
Orgulto ...	32216	Patent safety arrangement
Oribandolo	32217	All in perfect safety
Orichalcum	32218	With due regard to the safety of the men
Orichicco ...	32219	**Said**
Oricilla ...	32220	It has been said (that)
Oricrineto	32221	It is being said
Oriental ...	32222	This was reported to have been said by
Orientiren	32223	Cable who it was said by and to whom
Orificeria ...	32224	It was said by —— to ——
Oriflama ...	32225	Has he (——) said
Oriflambic	32226	Do you know exactly what was said
Origanum...	32227	Agree(s) exactly with what was said by
Originado...	32228	**Sail**
Originaire	32229	Propose to sail on
Originator	32230	Do not sail until
Originitus	32231	Sail for —— with the least delay
Origliare ...	32232	**Sailed**
Orinaletto...	32233	Sailed on
Oriniento ...	32234	Not yet sailed
Orinque ...	32235	Has just sailed for
Oriolajo ...	32236	**Salary** (*See also* "Give.")
Oripeau ...	32237	What salary would you (——) expect
Oriscello ...	32238	Can expect a salary of —— per annum
Orison ...	32239	Can only pay a small salary for the present
Orizzonta ...	32240	Business only admits of small salary
Orliccio ...	32241	Salary too high
Orlop ...	32242	At a salary of —— per annum
Ormatore ...	32243	What is the present salary of.
Orminale ...	32244	Had previously a salary of —— per annum
Orminiaco	32245	What is the usual salary paid to a competent man
Ormolu ...	32246	You should not pay a salary of more than
Ornabeque	32247	On account of salary
Ornado ...	32248	Salary insufficient
Ornamentar	32249	Salary insufficient; want(s) at least —— per month
Ornately ...	32250	Salary to be increased at end of first year
Ornatrice ...	32251	**Sale(s)** (*See also* "Account," "Confirm," "Disposal.")
Ornatulam	32252	Sale completed at
Ornaturus	32253	Examination will help sale
Orniere ...	32254	Examination will not help sale
Ornithias ...	32255	Prevent sale
Ornithon ...	32256	Public sale
Ornitolita ...	32257	The following sales have taken place
Ornitologo	32258	When will sale take place and where.

)robanche	32259	The sale is to take place on —— at ——
)robathion	32260	Sale will take place about
)robias ...	32261	A public sale is announced for
)robitis ...	32262	Sale(s) has (have) been made
)rochicco ...	32263	Sale on private terms
)rometria ..	32264	Sale by public auction
)rondo ...	32265	Terms of sale
)ropelero ...	32266	The following are the terms and conditions of sale
)ropesa ..	32267	Ascertain terms and conditions of sale
)ropimente	32268	When do you expect to complete sale
)rpellajo ...	32269	Hope to complete sale on or about
Orphanage	32270	Has (have) completed sale of
Orphanboy	32271	As soon as the sale is completed
Orphangirl	32272	The(se) mine(s) is (are) now for sale
Orpharion	32273	Will probably be for sale shortly
Orphelin ...	32274	In case a sale should be brought about
Orrery ...	32275	Have effected a sale of (for)
Orridetto ...	32276	The property has been for sale since
Orsaccio ...	32277	The property is again for sale
Orsicello ...	32278	The property has been offered for sale several times
Ortaglia ...	32279	Should the property be for sale cable lowest terms and price
Orteñca ...	32280	Better withdraw sale
Ortega ...	32281	Shall I (we) withdraw sale
Orthisch ...	32282	Has (have) withdrawn sale
Orthoclase	32283	Is (are) for sale at —— on the following terms
Orthocolus	32284	Was offered for sale but no bidders
Orthodox ...	32285	Was offered for sale but withdrawn at
Orthoepy ...	32286	Sale of
Orthominum	32287	Mail full particulars of sale(s)
Orthopedy	32288	Account sales of ore
Orthostyle	32289	Account sales of —— tons of ore show value realized
Orticheto ..	32290	Mail account sales of all ore sold as soon as possible
Ortivus ...	32291	Account sales of ore were mailed on [them
Ortodossia	32292	Account sales of ore will be mailed as soon as I (we) receive
Ortogonio ...	32293	Account sales of ore showing actual realization of —— tons
Ortografo ...	32294	Please mail account sales of ore [were mailed on ——
Ortolan ...	32295	In order to effect a sale it will be necessary to have
Ortologia ...	32296	There was only one sale at that figure
Ortopedia ...	32297	Push the sale of
Ortopnea ...	32298	Will push forward the sale of
Ortschaft ...	32299	What are the prospects of effecting a sale
Ortygiam ...	32300	There is every prospect of effecting a sale
Orvietano ...	32301	In view of short sales
Oryctology	32302	Conditions of sale will be forwarded by first mail
Orzaderas...	32303	Conditions of sale will be forwarded as soon as possible
Orzajuolo ...	32304	**Saleable**
Orzuelo ...	32305	Now saleable
Osadamente	32306	If saleable
Osalida ...	32307	**Salt**
Osambre ...	32308	There is a plentiful supply of salt (at)
Osannare ...	32309	The cost of salt at present is —— per lb.
Oscedinem	32310	Can obtain any quantity of salt for (at)
Oscenita ..	32311	Can you obtain a plentiful supply of salt
Oscilante ...	32312	A bed of salt —— feet thick
Oscillated ...	32313	We can pump any quantity of salt brine from ——
Osciller ...	32314	Am arranging to put down a bore hole for salt
Oscitancy ...	32315	What is the present depth of the bore hole for salt
Oscitanter...	32316	The bore hole for salt is now down —— feet
Oscitation...	32317	Salt was struck by a bore hole at a depth of —— feet
Osculandus	32318	Owing to the scarcity of salt

Osculare ...	32319	Have contracted for a supply of salt at —— per lb.
Osculatory	32320	**Salted** (*See also* "Sample.")
Osculo ...	32321	Have you any suspicions that the samples were salted [salted
Oscurabile ...	32322	I have grave suspicions that the samples marked —— were
Oscuratore	32323	You will have to take every precaution that the samples are [not salted
Oscuretto ...	32324	Reject samples marked —— as I am convinced that they have [been salted
Oseille ...	32325	There can be no doubt that the samples that were mailed on [—— were salted
Osifraga ...	32326	There is little doubt that the mine (property) was salted
Osiride ...	32327	Should you have any suspicion that things are being salted
Osmazone...	32328	**Salting** [you had better
Ospedale ...	32329	Examine carefully and be on the alert against salting
Ospiziare ...	32330	**Same**
Ospraturam	32331	From the same
Osprey ...	32332	Is it the same
Ossaccio ...	32333	It is the same
Ossatura ...	32334	About the same
Ossements	32335	Is (are) the same as
Osseous ...	32336	Same as
Ossequiare	32337	It is likely to be the same
Osservanza	32338	Is most probably the same
Osservato ...	32339	Cannot be the same
Ossiacanta	32340	It is very likely that it is the same
Ossicle ...	32341	Continue for the present the same
Ossiculum	32342	The same in every respect
Ossificato ...	32343	Not the same
Ossifrage ...	32344	The same quality
Ossify ...	32345	Of much the same quality
Ossilegium	32346	Practically the same as
Ossuaire ...	32347	The same as believed
Ossuarium	32348	The same as reported
Ostalage ...	32349	The same as before
Ostatore ...	32350	On the same terms as before
Ostelliere ...	32351	By the same
Ostendens...	32352	Just the same
Ostensible	32353	Offer him (them) (——) the same terms
Ostension ...	32354	Not exactly the same terms
Ostensoir ...	32355	In the same way
Ostentador	32356	Much about the same
Ostentatio	32357	The same clique are believed
Ostentavi ...	32358	With the same result
Ostentoso ...	32359	The same parties have
Osteocope ...	32360	By the same parties
Osteologic	32361	Cannot you do the same
Osteotomia	32362	Shall I (we) do the same
Osterfest ...	32363	Better do exactly the same
Ostermesse	32364	The same or better
Ostetrice ...	32365	**Sample(s)** (*See also* "Assay," "Average," "Selected.")
Ostilmente	32366	Send sample
Ostinato ...	32367	Sample sent
Ostiolum ...	32368	Please send sample of —— to ——
Ostracism...	32369	Forward samples for examination
Ostracties...	32370	Forward samples for complete analysis
Ostrearium	32371	Forward samples for assay
Ostreosus ...	32372	To sample
Ostrera ...	32373	Has (have) sampled
Ostrich ...	32374	I (we) have not yet received any samples [you
Ostricone ...	32375	Samples received will be assayed and results communicated to

Ostrifero ...	32376	Is it necessary that all the samples should be assayed
Ostrinus ...	32377	Samples to be assayed are marked
Ostruttivo	32378	Samples have assayed as follows
Ostupefare	32379	Samples will be sent as soon as possible
Ostwind ...	32380	All your samples should be taken in duplicate
Osudo ...	32881	Can you forward a duplicate sample of
Otacusta ...	32382	When will you be able to send samples of
Oteador ...	32383	Samples should reach you on or about
Othone ...	32384	An average sample from —— tons assayed
Otiandum...	32385	A sample from it (of this) assayed
Otograph ...	32886	An average sample of tailings assayed
Otorgador...	32387	An average sample from the old dumps assayed
Otorgancia	32388	An average sample from the waste heaps assayed
Otraccio ...	32389	It is not possible to take a fair sample of it (this)
Otramente	32390	It would be very difficult, if not impossible, to obtain a fair
Otrello ...	32891	Send samples of them [sample of the ore in the mine
Otriato ...	32392	An average sample representing the natural proportion of the
Otricetto ...	32393	An average sample [different grades of ore has yielded
Otrosi ...	32394	Samples of the outcrop of the lode have yielded
Ottalmico...	32395	Have taken an average sample of —— tons
Ottanzette	32396	Send samples to be assayed at one of the government offices
Ottativo ...	32897	Will forward samples to-morrow
Ottemole ...	32398	A sample containing no visible gold assays
Ottenible ...	32399	Have forwarded a sample of —— tons of ore
Otterhunt...	32400	Samples taken away
Otters ...	32401	Has (have) reason to believe the samples were salted
Ottoageno	32402	Has (have) no reason to believe the samples were salted
Ottodecimo	32403	Samples forwarded
Ottoman ...	32404	Samples will be forwarded as soon as possible
Ottonario ...	32405	What would be the cost of having a —— ton sample crushed
Ottusetto ...	32406	Can you arrange to get a —— ton sample crushed [ton of
Ottusione...	32407	Have arranged to get a —— ton sample crushed at a cost per
Ouaille ...	32408	Obtain a true average sample of the lode and have it assayed by
		[unimpeachable assayer
Oubliettes	32409	An average sample of —— to —— tons
Oublieux ...	32410	The average value of samples is —— per ton
Ouragan ...	32411	Have had samples assayed by —— (at ——) with following
Ourdissage	32412	**Samplers** . . [results
Ourlet ...	82413	**Sampling Mill**
Outardeau	32414	**Sampling Works**
Outargued	32415	Public sampling works
Outbidden	32416	At the public sampling works at
Outbrave ...	32417	Sold by auction at the public sampling works at
Outbreak ...	32418	I (we) have now shipped —— tons of ore to the sampling works
Outbuilt ...	32419	The returns from the sampling works should
Outcursed	32420	Not yet received returns from sampling works
Outdoing ...	32421	Sampling works are closed down through
Outflank ...	32422	Sampling works will re-open on or about
Outgeneral	32423	As soon as the sampling works are open [—— days
Outherod ...	32424	Shall ship —— tons to the sampling works during the next
Outhouse ...	32425	As soon as we receive returns from sampling works,
Outillage ...	32426	**Sanction**
Outjested ...	32427	You have the sanction of
Outjuggle...	32428	You have my (our) sanction to
Outlawed ...	32429	Cannot sanction (it)
Outleap ...	32430	Cannot give my (our) sanction unless
Outliver ...	32431	Has the sanction of —— been obtained
Outparish...	32432	With the sanction of
Outposted...	32433	Without the sanction of
Outrageux	82434	Will you sanction

Outrance ...	32435	Should be very glad if you can get —— to sanction
Outremer ...	32436	Cannot do this (it) unless I have the (your) sanction (of)
Outrider ...	32437	Will endeavour to obtain ——'s sanction and will cable you
Outrigger...	32438	Court refuses to sanction [again
Outshine ...	32439	Court will sanction if I (we) at once
Outskirts ...	32440	**Sanctioned**
Outvoted ...	32441	Not sanctioned
Outwatch ...	32442	**Sand**
Outweighed	32443	Can obtain sand for fluxing from
Ouvrable ...	32444	There is a plentiful supply of suitable sand for fluxing purposes
Ouvreur ...	32445	Sand for fluxing would cost —— per ton delivered
Ouvriere ...	32446	**Sandstone**
Ovante ...	32447	In sandstone
Ovary ...	32448	At present in sandstone
Ovationem	32449	Overlaid by a bed of sandstone
Ovejuela ...	32450	As soon as we have cut through the sandstone
Ovenshelf...	32451	Micaceous sandstone
Overacted...	32452	A rib of sandstone
Overalls ...	32453	**Sanguine**
Overarch ...	32454	Too sanguine
Overatore...	32455	Not to take too sanguine a view
Overbear ...	32456	Am (are) very sanguine that I (we) shall
Overdose ...	32457	Without being sanguine
Overdriven	32458	Am not at all sanguine
Overflown...	32459	**Sapphire(s)**
Overfond ...	32460	Small sapphires have been found on the property
Overissued	32461	Sapphires are reported to have been found at
Overlain ...	32462	The sapphire mines are situated at
Overpoise ...	32463	Can you visit and report on sapphire mines at
Overripe ...	32464	The sapphires are found associated with
Overshot ...	32465	The sapphires have been valued at
Overstrung	32466	The sapphires have no market value
Overtrade...	32467	**Sarcasm**
Overture ...	32468	Sarcasm intended
Overvalued	32469	Sarcasm not intended
Overvoted...	32470	Was sarcasm intended
Overweight	32471	**Sardonyx**
Oviaricus ...	32472	**Satisfaction**
Ovidutto ...	32473	Everything gives me (us) the greatest satisfaction
Oviluccio ...	32474	**Satisfactorily**
Oviparous...	32475	Most satisfactorily
Ovispillo ...	32476	**Satisfactory** (*See also* "Explanation.")
Ovraggio ...	32477	Fairly satisfactory
Ovunque ...	32478	Would this be satisfactory to you (——)
Ovviatore...	32479	It would be quite satisfactory
Owlet ...	32480	Will be satisfactory
Owllike ...	32481	Will not be satisfactory
Oxalite ...	32482	It would be more satisfactory if
Oxalme ...	32483	On satisfactory security(ies) being lodged
Oxamide ...	32484	Will the following security(ies) be satisfactory
Oxatylic ...	32485	Quite satisfactory
Oxeador ...	32486	Can you offer some satisfactory explanation
Oxeye ...	32487	Has (have) not proved altogether satisfactory
Oxiacanta...	32488	If not quite satisfactory will endeavour to
Oxicrato ...	32489	The security(ies) is (are) not altogether satisfactory
Oxicroceo...	32490	You should take care that everything is in satisfactory order
Oxidation ...	32491	It will be quite satisfactory if [before you begin
Oxigenado	32492	Do you consider it satisfactory if
Oxigono ...	32493	If you consider it satisfactory
Oximaco ...	32494	I (we) consider it quite satisfactory

Oxlip ...	32495	I (we) do not consider it satisfactory
Oxstall ...	32496	Satisfactory to both
Oxyblatta...	32497	Satisfactory to either
Oxycedros	32498	Satisfactory to neither
Oxyder ...	32499	The most satisfactory arrangement would be
Oxydiren ...	32500	A more satisfactory arrangement
Oxygarum	32501	Can you suggest a more satisfactory arrangement
Oxygen ...	32502	Not at all satisfactory
Oxygenous	32503	Have received your despatch, everything satisfactory
Oxymel ...	32504	Satisfactory intelligence
Oxymircine	32505	**Satisfied**
Oxymoron	32506	Everybody satisfied
Oxyporium	32507	Are you satisfied that (with)
Oxytone ...	32508	I am (we are) quite satisfied to
Oyster ...	32509	I (we) should be more satisfied if
Oysterman	32510	I am (we are) fully satisfied that (with)
Oziosetto ...	32511	I am (we are) fully satisfied with everything up to the present
Oziosita ...	32512	Is —— satisfied
Ozzimato ...	32513	Demand is not yet satisfied
Paarung ...	32514	Demand is now satisfied
Paarweise...	32515	Are you satisfied that
Pabellon ...	32516	Is —— (are you) fully satisfied that
Pabilo ...	32517	Cable as soon as you are satisfied as to
Pabulant ...	32518	I am (we are) not at all satisfied (that)
Pabularis ...	32519	—— is satisfied
Pabulator	32520	Not satisfied
Pabulose ...	32521	Quite satisfied
Pabulum ...	32522	It will be necessary that —— should be satisfied as to
Pacager ...	32523	What would —— require before he was (they were) satisfied
Pacandus...	32524	If you are satisfied with
Pacatezza	32525	If you are not satisfied with
Pacchiare ...	32526	Personally, I am quite satisfied
Pacciame ...	32527	Personally, I am not satisfied
Pacciotta ...	32528	Should be satisfied with
Pacedero ...	32529	Should be satisfied if you could obtain
Paceficare	32530	Shall not be satisfied unless you can obtain
Pachalic ...	32531	Trust you will be satisfied with what I (we) have done
Pachorrudo	32532	As soon as you are satisfied
Pachten ...	32533	**Satisfy**
Pachyderm	32534	So as to satisfy
Paciencia ...	32535	Unless I (we) can satisfy
Pacificans	32536	Cannot satisfy
Pacifier ...	32537	Will you (——) agree to satisfy
Pacifique ...	32538	**Saturday**
Pacifying ...	32539	On Saturday
Paciscor ...	32540	Last Saturday
Package ...	32541	Next Saturday
Packehen ...	32542	—— Saturday in each month
Packerei ...	32543	Every Saturday
Packetboat	32544	Every alternate Saturday
Packetship	32545	During Saturday night
Packpapier	32546	About Saturday week
Packthread	32547	Next Saturday week
Packwagen	32548	On Saturday morning
Packwax ...	32549	On Saturday afternoon
Pacotilla ...	32550	On Saturday night
Pactar ...	32551	During Saturday
Pactilibus...	32552	**Save**
Pactiser ...	32553	What do you expect to save
Pactitius ...	32554	Will it (this) save

Paddlebox	32555	This (it) will save
Padellajo ...	32556	Will not save
Padelletta	32557	Hope to save
Padiglione	32558	To save
Padilla ...	32559	Endeavour to save
Padlocks ...	32560	Will in future save
Padoana ...	32561	Impossible to save more
Padrastro	32562	This will save the cost of
Padrona ...	32563	Can you (——) arrange to save
Padroncino	32564	Can only save
Padroneria	32565	Will probably be able to save
Padulesco...	32566	Will enable me (us) to save
Paesaccio ...	32567	Would enable me (us) to save
Paesello ...	32568	**Saved**
Paesista ...	32569	The amount saved is equal to —— per cent.
Paflon ...	32570	Very little has hitherto been saved
Pagadero ...	32571	Now being saved
Pagaduria	32572	In future all this will be saved
Paganalia	32573	There will be nothing saved for the present
Paganicus	32574	There would be nothing saved by it
Paganised	32575	**Saving**
Paganizm	32576	What will be the saving by
Pagare ...	32577	The saving will be
Pagatim ...	32578	It would be a great saving if (to)
Pagatrice ...	32579	By saving the
Pagatura ...	32580	I am (we are) at present saving all the
Pageantry	32581	Is —— (are you) saving the
Pagecico ...	32582	There is very little saving
Pagellam ...	32583	Gold saving appliances
Pageria ...	32584	Gold saving plant
Paggetto ...	32585	Gold saving
Pagination	32586	Monthly saving
Paginula ...	32587	A great saving would result
Paglietana	32588	A great saving has resulted
Pagliolaja	32589	Saving —— per cent.
Pagliuzza...	32590	As a saving clause
Pagnotta ...	32591	**Saw** (*See also* ".See.")
Pagoda ...	32592	—— reports that he saw
Pagonazza	32593	Saw personally
Pagoncello	32594	Unless you (——) saw personally
Pagonessa	32595	Saw nothing
Pagurus ...	32596	Saw all he (they) had to show
Paillard ...	32597	Hand saw(s)
Pailleux ...	32598	Circular saw
Pailon ...	32599	**Sawmill(s)**
Paisage ...	32600	Circular sawmill
Paisanage...	32601	Circular sawmill with engine
Paisible ...	32602	Circular sawmill with engine and boiler complete
Pajarear ...	32603	Sawmill to deal with logs —— × —— × ——
Pajarilla ..	32604	A sawmill would effect considerable saving
Pajarota ...	32605	Have erected sawmill at
Pajolata ...	32606	**Sawn**
Pajuelero ...	32607	Sawn timbers —— inches × —— inches × —— feet
Pajuncio ...	32608	Sawn lumber —— is delivered on property for ——
Palabrada	32609	**Sawyer(s)**
Palabreso	32610	**Say(s)**
Palabrista	32611	To say
Palabunde	32612	Can certainly say
Palace ...	32613	Can only say that
Palaciego ...	32614	Cannot say yet

Paladar ...	32615	What am I (are we) to say as regards
Paladino ...	32616	All you can say is
Palafitta ...	32617	Decline(s) absolutely to say anything
Palafren ...	32618	I (we) can only go so far as to say
Palagetto...	32619	People here say
Palagonite	32620	It is difficult to say
Palajuolo ...	32621	It is practically impossible to say
Palamallo...	32622	I (we) should say
Palamenta	32623	I (we) should say at this moment
Palancada	32624	Would certainly say
Palandrana	32625	Would you say
Palandus ...	32626	Must say either "yes" or "no" on or before ——
Palangas ...	32627	To enable me (us) to say "yes" or "no"
Palanqueta	32628	Can you (they) say anything about
Palanquin	32629	Cannot say anything about
Palatably...	32630	Do not say anything
Palatinado	32631 ✔	Do not say anything to —— about ——
Palatinus ...	32632	Say(s) that he (they) will
Palatione ...	32633	Says that there is
Palatium ...	32634	Says that there is not
Palatualis...	32635	Says that there will be
Palaver ...	32636	Says that there will not be
Palazon ...	32637	Says that he cannot
Palazzacio	32638	Says that he can easily
Palazzista...	32639	—— says that
Palcuccio ...	32640	What does —— (he) say
Paleador ...	32641	**Scale** *(See also "Fixed.")*
Paleatus ...	32642	On a small scale
Paleeyed ...	32643	On a small scale for the present
Paleface ...	32644	Everything is on a very large scale
Palenque ...	32645	Is really on an immense scale
Paleograph	32646	**Scarce**
Paleology...	32647	Is likely to be scarce
Palesato ...	32648	Is it likely to be scarce
Palestrico ..	32649	Is not likely to be scarce for some time to come
Paletada ...	32650	Extremely scarce
Paletilla ...	32651	Is at present somewhat scarce
Palette ...	32652	Very scarce owing to
Palettina ...	32653	Water is very scarce for —— months of the year
Palfrey ...	32654	Water is scarce all the year round
Paliacion ...	32655	Water is scarce only between —— and —— months
Palietto ...	32656	Timber for mining purposes is scarce
Palificata ...	32657	Timber for fuel is scarce
Palillero ...	32658	Provisions generally are scarce
Palimpissa	32659	Is (are) not at all scarce
Palindrome	32660	Is (are) now scarce
Palinsesto	32661	Continue(s) to be scarce
Palique ...	32662	Is (are) becoming very scarce
Palisade ...	32663	**Scarcely**
Palisser ...	32664	Scarcely anything at all doing
Palitante ...	32665	Scarcely the right time for
Palitroque	32666	Scarcely any to be obtained
Paliurus ...	32667	Scarcely any to be discovered
Palizada ...	32668	Is (are) scarcely known
Pallacana...	32669	Scarcely finished
Palladium	32670	**Scarcity**
Pallescens	32671	There is a great scarcity of
Palleta ...	32672	There is no scarcity at all
Palliate ...	32673	Anticipate scarcity of
Pallidetto...	32674	In consequence of present scarcity

Pallidly ...	32675	To what is the scarcity owing
Pallidness	32676	The scarcity is chiefly owing to
Pallidume	32677	When the present scarcity ends
Palliolum ...	32678	**Scare**
Pallonare ...	32679	As soon as the present scare has disappeared
Palloncino	32680	So long as the present scare lasts
Palloribus	32681	Has (have) caused a considerable scare
Pallottola ...	32682	Likely to cause a considerable scare
Palmarium	32683	Not likely to cause any scare
Palmary ...	32684	**Scared**
Palmatiam	32685	Been considerably scared by
Palmatoria	32686	No need to be (feel) scared
Palmatus ...	32687	**Scatter**
Palmeado...	32688	**Scattered**
Palmejar ...	32689	The property is very much scattered
Palmesia ...	32690	Very much scattered
Palmetto ...	32691	The ore is very much scattered in the vein
Palmhouse	32692	The vein material is scattered
Palmier ...	32693	The alluvial deposit is somewhat scattered
Palmifero...	32694	Now all scattered
Palmilla ...	32695	Scattered throughout
Palmipede	32696	Scattered very sparingly
Palmipibus	32697	**Schedule(s)**
Palmistry...	32698	A complete schedule of same
Palmitate ...	32699	Please send schedule of
Palmitieso	32700	A schedule of
Palmone ...	32701	The schedule does not give
Palmosus ...	32702	Omitted from schedule
Palmotear	32703	Will forward a complete schedule by next mail (on ——)
Palmtrees...	32704	Have you included in schedule
Palmzweig	32705	Are all included in schedule
Palombaro	32706	Why have you included in schedule
Palombina	32707	Why have you not included in schedule
Palomeria...	32708	Forward without delay complete schedule of
Palomino ...	32709	All schedules to be signed by you
Palonnier ...	32710	Mail complete schedule of liabilities signed by yourself
Palourde ...	32711	**Scheme(s)**
Palpable ...	32712	There is a scheme on foot to (for)
Palpadura	32713	What do you (does ——) think of ——'s scheme
Palpamen...	32714	I (we) do not think much of the (——'s) scheme
Palpandus	32715	I think the scheme a very good one
Palpatrice	32716	The original scheme was to
Palpebra ...	32717	Would you approve of such a scheme
Palpitate ...	32718	Have you developed your scheme for
Palpiter ...	32719	Would you identify yourself with a scheme to
Paltonato...	32720	State more fully what the scheme is
Paltoquet...	32721	The scheme at present is to
Paltriness...	32722	The (their) scheme has hitherto been to
Paludaccio	32723	What is his (their) scheme
Paludatus	32724	It is part of their scheme to
Paludello ...	32725	To carry out the scheme would mean
Paludifere	32726	Will you assist in carrying out the scheme
Palumbes...	32727	Am (are) compelled to withdraw from the scheme
Palumbinus	32728	Cannot assist in carrying out the scheme (for)
Palustre ...	32729	Can you devise any scheme for
Palvesaro ...	32730	Upon the following scheme
Pamenia ...	32731	Owing to the original scheme having failed
Pampanada	32732	The new scheme is to
Pampano ...	32733	**Schist**
Pampered...	32734	The formation is schist

Pamphlet ...	32735	Hornblendic schist
Pampinatus	32736	Micaceous schist
Pampinor ...	32737	Talcous schist
Pamplina ...	32738	Much associated with schist
Pamula ...	32739	Decomposed schist with branches of quartz
Panacher ...	32740	Through very hard schist
Panaderia...	32741	**Schistose**
Panariolum	32742	Schistose matter
Panarius ...	32743	**Scoriaceous**
Panattiera	32744	**Screen(s)** *(See also* " Grate," " Stamp.")
Pancaccia ...	32745	Screens for
Pancakes ...	32746	Wire cloth screens —— mesh —— wire
Pancarpia...	32747	Perforated copper screens
Pancera ...	32748	Steel screens
Pancerone	32749	**Screw(s)**
Panchetta...	32750	**Scrip** *(See also* " Certificate.")
Panchros ...	32751	When will the scrip be issued
Panciolle ...	32752	The scrip will be issued as soon as
Pancratice	32753	The scrip should be accompanied by
Pancrazio...	32754	The scrip is accompanied by
Pancreas ...	32755	Has (have) forwarded scrip, together with
Pancreatic	32756	He (——) hold(s) the scrip
Pancturus	32757	The scrip is held mainly by (in)
Pandatus ...	32758	Who holds the scrip
Pandean ...	32759	—— holds —— worth of scrip
Pandendus	32760	The scrip is at present practically in the hands of
Panderazo	32761	Apply to —— for scrip
Pandering	32762	Refuse(s) to hand over scrip
Pandiculor	32763	Has (have) received scrip
Pandora ...	32764	Retain the scrip until further orders
Pandorgona	32765	Will retain the scrip until further orders
Pandurizo	32766	**Scrupulous(ly)**
Panecico ...	32767	**Sea**
Panegyric	32768	Is within —— miles of the sea
Panelling ...	32769	The nearest seaport is
Panetas ...	32770	To the sea
Paniaccio ...	32771	The nearest way to the property is by sea to —— (and thence
Paniaguado	32772	The property is situated near the sea coast [by)
Paniceus ...	32773	The sea coast
Panichina...	32774	**Seal(ed)**
Paniculo ...	32775	Under the seal of the company
Panierino ...	32776	Notarially attested and sealed
Panieruzzo	32777	**Seam(s)**
Panifex ...	32778	Thin seams of
Panificado	32779	A seam of —— inches thick
Panificem...	32780	On a seam of
Panificium	32781	Seams of —— intercalated with
Panivorous	32782	Owing to the thinness of the seams
Panlargo ...	32783	Has (have) struck a seam of
Pannage ...	32784	A seam of coal
Pannajuolo	32785	Several seams of —— aggregate thickness
Pannello ...	32786	**Search(ed)**
Pannibus ...	32787	To search
Pannicolo...	32788	Shall continue to search
Panniculus	32789	Continue(s) to search
Pannier ...	32790	You had better make a strict search
Pannilino ...	32791	Has (have) made a strict search but discovered nothing
Pannosus ...	32792	Repeat search
Pannulos ...	32793	Has (have) repeated search with the result that
Panonceau	32794	You should search for

anoplia ...	32795	To search for
anopticon	32796	Will search
anslavist	32797	Make a thorough search
antaleone	32798	Have not yet had time to make a thorough search
'antaloon...	32799	As the result of the search
'antanoso	32800	What has the search resulted in
'antenne ...	32801	The search has resulted in
'anterana	32802	Make a search and enquiry as to
'anterreno	32803	**Searching**
'antheist ...	32804	A most searching enquiry
'antheon ...	32805	Searching for
'anthier ...	32806	Am (are) searching for ore body
'anticinor	32807	**Season(s)**
'antile ...	32808	Wet season
Pantoffel ...	32809	Dry season
Pantofola...	32810	Shipping season
Pantograph	32811	During the wet season
Pantometra	32812	During the dry season
Pantomime	32813	When does the wet season commence
Pantophagy	32814	When does the dry season commence
Pantoque ...	32815	The wet season commences about
Pantuflazo	32816	The dry season commences about
Panzerhemd	32817	During the winter season
Panzern ...	32818	During the summer season
Panzeruola	32819	About —— is the best season for
Panziera ...	32820	Before the season is too far advanced
Paoncino ...	32821	The season has already too far advanced to (for)
Paonessa ...	32822	Otherwise the season will be too far advanced
Papacy ...	32823	The season is hardly sufficiently advanced yet (for)
Papafigo ...	32824	The present time is the best season for
Papageno...	32825	The present time is the worst season for
Papahigos	32826	Season will begin late this year
Papalist ...	32827	Season likely to begin early this year
Papalize ...	32828	Season will finish early this year
Papamoscas	32829	Season likely to finish early this year
Papanatas	32830	Exceptionally trying season(s)
Papandujo	32831	Exceptionally trying wet season(s)
Paparabias	32832	Compliments of the season
Paparismo	32833	**Seasonable**
Papasal ...	32834	**Seat**
Papavereus	32835	With a seat on the Board
Papazgo ...	32836	Will disqualify you for a seat on the Board
Papeleador	32837	**Second** (*See also* "Ore.")
Papelejo ...	32838	Second in command
Papeleria ...	32839	Second quality
Papelon ...	32840	Second class ore
Paperasser	32841	What is the value of the second class ore
Paperclips	32842	The value of the second class ore is between —— and ——
Paperello ...	32843	How much second class ore have you in stock
Papermaker	32844	We have —— tons of second class ore in stock
Papermill...	32845	Shall begin shipping second class ore on
Papetier ...	32846	For the future our second class ore will run about
Papiergeld	32847	**Secondary**
Papilione ...	32848	Quite secondary
Papillate ...	32849	**Secondhand**
Papilletta ..	32850	**Secret**
Papilloter ...	32851	This must be kept perfectly secret from
Papirolada	32852	It is no longer any secret that
Papisme ...	32853	This had better be kept secret until
Papistical	32854	Keep this for the present a secret

Papizzare ...	32855	They have endeavoured to keep it secret
Pappagallo	32856	It will be impossible to keep this (it) a secret after
Pappalardo	32857	Has (have) secret information that
Pappatore	32858	**Secretary**
Pappolones	32859	The secretary of the company
Papstlich ...	32860	I have been appointed secretary to
Papstthum	32861	Are you willing to apply for post of secretary to
Papudo ...	32862	Should suggest that you write the secretary in reference to
Papyraceus	32863	Send secretary's full name
Papyrean ...	32864	The full name of the secretary is as follows
Papyrifer ...	32865	The secretary to
Papyrius ...	32866	Who is the secretary to
Paquebot ...	32867	Am (is) willing to act as secretary
Paquerette	32868	Am (is) not willing to act as secretary
Parabilis ...	32869	Is (are) about to appoint a new secretary
Parabolano	32870	Have just appointed a new secretary
Parabolic ...	32871	**Secretly** (*See also* " Secret.")
Paraboloid	32872	**Section** (*See also* " Plan.")
Parachute...	32873	Plan(s) and section(s) [corrected to latest date
Paracleto ...	32874	Mail as soon as possible tracings of mine plan and section
Paracresol	32875	Have forwarded tracings of mine plan and section corrected
Paradera ...	32876	A longitudinal section [to ——
Paradies ...	32877	A transverse section
Paradigmas	32878	A section showing
Paradoja ...	32879	A section of
Paradoxal...	32880	Together with plan(s) and section(s)
Paradromis	32881	This section of the property (mine)
Parafrasi ...	32882	In this section of the country
Parafraste	32883	When will you be able to forward plan and section
Paraganda	32884	Will forward plan and section about
Paragoge ...	32885	Each section
Paragrafo...	32886	To be shown in section
Paragram...	32887	Send section showing —— shaft in its relation to
Paraguas ...	32888	**Sectional**
Paraitre ...	32889	**Secure** (*See also* " Fraction.")
Paralaje ...	32890	To secure
Paralatic ...	32891	Secure at once
Paralelo ...	32892	How much can you secure
Paralencic	32893	Expect to secure about
Paralipsis...	32894	How much do you wish me to secure on your account
Paralisia ...	32895	Endeavour to secure on my account
Parallax ...	32896	Am (are) able to secure
Paralogism	32897	Has (have) not been able to secure
Paramentar	32898	Secure as much as you can
Paramese ...	32899	I (we) consider it best to secure
Parametro	32900	With difficulty have been able to secure
Paramosche	32901	It would not be difficult to secure
Paramount	32902	Think you had better secure at once
Parancero...	32903	You should not fail to secure
Parandus ...	32904	In case you cannot secure
Parangon ...	32905	Do you consider it secure
Paranites ...	32906	Consider it perfectly secure
Paranympha	32907	Sufficiently secure for
Paranza ...	32908	Secure sufficient for
Paraocchi...	32909	In order to secure control
Parapegma	32910	You should secure control at once
Parapetto ...	32911	If you are going to secure control
Parapherna	32912	We must secure control of the property (mine)
Paraphoron	32913	Secure as much time as you can
Paraphrast	32914	Hope to secure

Parapiglia	32915	•Should be glad to secure the services of
Parapsis ...	32916	Cannot secure
Pararayo ...	32917	Can you secure
Pararius ...	32918	You should secure it at once
Parasceve...	32919	Will endeavour to secure
Paraselene	32920	Do(es) not secure
Parasitic ...	32921	If you are able to secure
Parasol ...	32922	In the event of your not being able to secure
Parassito ...	32923	In the event of your being able to secure
Parastades	32924	Should advise you to secure it (them) without delay
Parathesis	32925	Did you secure
Paratitla ...	32926	At what price can I (we) secure
Paraturas...	32927	At what reduction can you (——) secure
Parauso ...	32928	**Secured**
Paravent ...	32929	Has (have) secured
Paraveredi	32930	As soon as you have secured
Parazonio...	32931	Are you fully secured in respect to
Parboiled...	32932	To what amount are you (we) secured
Parcamente	32933	Have secured all that was available
Parcelling...	32934	Am (is) (are) amply secured
Parcemiqui	32935	Partially secured
Parceria ...	32936	Secured to the extent of
Parchemin	32937	Secured against [payable in cash on ——
Parching ...	32938	Can be secured on a —— months working option for ——
Parchment	32939	Can be secured for —— months on payment of —— in cash
Parcial ...	32940	Should have been secured
Parcidad ...	32941	Has (have) not been secured
Parcimonia.	32942	Can still be secured
Parciter ...	32943	Cannot be secured after
Pardujo ...	32944	Was (were) secured
Pardalios ...	32945	Was (were) already secured
Pardoner ...	32946	To be secured by
Pardoning	32947	**Securely**
Pardusco ...	32948	**Security(ies)**
Parecchi ...	32949	As security
Pareciente	32950	As security for
Paredano ...	32951	As security against
Paredilla ...	32952	No security at all
Pareggiare	32953	What security have you against
Pareglio ...	32954	The security is very good
Paregoria...	32955	Security is practically valueless
Pareille ...	32956	What security can you (——) offer
Parelcon ...	32957	What security can you (——) obtain
Parelia ...	32958	Must give security for costs
Parenesis...	32959	Retain all security(ies) possible
Parentage...	32960	Must have better security
Parentally	32961	Security offered and accepted
Parentatur	32962	Security offered but refused
Parentella	32963	What security have you received
Parenteria	32964	The security(ies) received amount(s) to
Parentless	32965	Get the most material security you can
Parergon ...	32966	Try and get increased security
Paresseux...	32967	Willing to give more security
Parfait ...	32968	Do(es) not wish to give me (us) much security
Parfiler ...	32969	Is willing to deposit as security the following, viz.:—
Parfondre...	32970	Is (are) —— willing to give security(ies)
Parfumerie	32971	Quite willing to give security
Pargamino	32972	If any security
Pargetting	32973	Am (are) compelled to decline security offered
Pargoletto	32974	Endeavour to obtain better security

Pargolo ...	32975	The securities held have a market value of
Parhelion...	32976	**Sediment**
Parhippus	32977	**Sedimentary**
Parhypate	32978	**See(s)** (*See also* " Saw.")
Pariahlike	32979	See about
Parianus ...	32980	See after
Pariatio ...	32981	See clause
Paricidium	32982	See number
Pariendus	32983	See page
Pariente ...	32984	To see
Parietaria...	32985	Will see
Parietina ...	32986	Cannot see
Parieur ...	32987	You had better see —— at once
Parihuela...	32988	Am (are) to see —— on ——
Parilitas ...	32989	Was (were) not able to see
Pariren ...	32990	Can you by any possibility see
Parisians ...	32991	Should be glad if you would see after him (it)
Paritudo ...	32992	Will see after him (it) at once
Parjure ...	32993	Can you see your way to
Parlacocco	32994	Cannot at present see my way
Parladillo...	32995	Can see my way clearly enough as far as regards
Parlador ...	32996	By which time I hope to see my way more clearly
Parladuria	32997	You should at once call and see
Parlagione	32998	Has (have) been to —— but was not able to see
Parlando ...	32999	Has (have) made an appointment to see
Parlantina	33000	Has (have) not yet been able to make an appointment to see
Parlatorio	**33001**	Endeavour to see how matters stand
Parlatrice...	33002	See what you can do
Parlement	33003	When I will see what I can do
Parleron ...	33004	If you can see your way clear go ahead
Parletico ...	33005	Unless you can see your way clear you had better not attempt
Parlevole ...	33006	When shall you see about
Parleyed ...	33007	When I shall see about
Parliere ...	33008	I (we) shall see about it (this) at once
Parloir ...	33009	Better see about it (this) at once
Parlotear ...	33010	See that everything is in order
Parmesan...	33011	See that everything is in order before you begin (to)
Parnassico	33012	See what it is that is not in order
Parochial ...	33013	When I (we) will see what is not in order
Parochus ..	33014	Came to see —— (him)
Parodico ...	33015	Is to come to see —— (him) on ——
Parodied ...	33016	Refused to see —— (him)
Parodists ...	33017	Am not at all anxious to see —— (him)
Paroffia ...	33018	Should like you to see
Paroisse ...	33019	Should like to see
Parolajo ...	33020	I (we) did not see
Paroles ...	33021	See —— when you are in ——
Parolina	33022	Was unable to see ——
Paroluzza...	33023	Expect to see you in London about
Paroniquia	33024	Shall see —— about it (this)
Paronychia	33025	You must see —— at once about
Paronymes	33026	Do not omit to see
Paropsidem	33027	You had better see —— at once and arrange about
Paroquet ...	33028	I (we) shall be glad to see ——
Parosismo	33029	**Seem(s)**
Paroxysm...	33030	How does it seem to you
Parpadear	33031	It seems to me (——) that
Parpalla ...	33032	Seems to be falling off
Parquetage	33033	Does not seem at all likely to
Parqueteur	33034	Seems very likely to

Parquetry	33035	Seems almost certain
Parrafo· ...	33036	It seems uncertain both as regards —— and ——
Parricide ...	33037	Seem(s) as if
Parrocchia	33038	Seem(s) to be going along all right
Parroco ...	33039	Seems to be all right as regards
Parrucca ...	33040	Seems to be anything but right
Parsimony	33041	**Seeming**
Parsing ...	33042	**Seemingly**
Parsley ...	33043	**Seen**
Parsnip ...	33044	Have you (——) seen
Parsonical	33045	I (we) have seen
Partageant	33046	I (we) have not seen
Partaker ...	33047	I (we) have not as yet seen
Partenaire	33048	As soon as you have seen
Partencia ...	33049	When can —— be seen
Parterre ...	33050	—— can be seen on
Parthenice	33051	—— cannot be seen until
Parthenon	33052	Will report to you fully as soon as I (we) have seen
Partiarius	33053	This shall be seen to at once
Particeps ...	33054	Had better be seen to as soon as possible
Participar...	33055	Shall be seen to as soon as it has been·determined whether
Particula ...	33056	Should be seen to at once
Partiendus	33057	Must be seen to at once
Partisan ...	33058	Could not be seen to until
Partition ...	33059	Should have been seen to before
Partitive ...	33060	Have seen —— (him) and made the following arrangement
Partorire ...	33061	**Segment(s)**
Partout ...	33062	To be made in segments
Partowned	33063	Each segment should be carefully marked
Partridge...	33064	What is the weight of segments
Partumeius	33065	The weight of each segment is —— lbs.
Parturiate	33066	Can be transported only in segments
Parturiens	33067	No segment should exceed —— lbs. in weight
Partyman...	33068	One segment is missing
Parulis ...	33069	Send duplicate of No. —— segment
Parumper...	33070	Segment(s) broken
Parunculus	33071	**Segregate(d)**
Parvedad ...	33072	**Seize**
Parvenza ...	33073	To seize
Parvificio ...	33074	Threaten(s) that he (they) will seize
Parvolino ...	33075	**Seized**
Parvulez ...	33076	Has (have) been seized
Parzoniere	33077	Has (have) not been seized
Pasable ...	33078	Has (have) been seized by
Pasacalle ...	33079	Has this (——) been seized
Pasadillo ...	33080	Was (were) seized on
Pasamanear	33081	Would suggest that the property be seized
Pasamiento	33082	In order to prevent the property being seized
Pasaporte...	33083	Liable at any moment to be seized
Pasavoleo...	33084	**Seizure**
Pascasio ...	33085	So long as there is no risk of seizure
Pascebat ...	33086	What is the risk of seizure
Pasceolus ...	33087	There is daily risk of seizure
Pascersi ...	33088	There is not the slightest risk of seizure
Paschalis ...	33089	In order to prevent seizure
Paschen ...	33090	Impossible to prevent seizure
Pascitrice...	33091	Must remit —— in order to prevent seizure
Pascolare ...	33092	Legal seizure
Pascua ...	33093	Illegal seizure
Pascuilla ...	33094	**Seldom**

Paseante ...	33095	**Select**
Pasicorto ...	33096	To select
Pasilargo ...	33097	Could you select
Pasion	33098	You can select
Pasitrote ...	33099	You should select at once
Pasmoso ...	33100	Will select
Pasquare ...	33101	As soon as you have been able to select
Pasquinade	33102	**Selected** (*See also* "Sample.")
Passacorde	33103	Have you (has ——) yet selected
Passaggio....	33104	I (we) have not selected
Passagier ...	33105	In case (——) has (have) not yet been selected
Passameso	33106	Selected ore
Passarsi ...	33107	Selected samples
Passatojo ...	33108	Were the samples selected in any way
Passavant...	33109	Samples were not selected in any way
Passbooks	33110	Has (have) already selected
Passedroit	33111	Has (have) been selected
Passelacet	33112	Has (have) not been selected
Passend ...	33113	Was (were) selected prior to receipt of
Passenger...	33114	Had not been selected
Passepied...	33115	Had been selected previously
Passepoil ...	33116	Had not been selected owing to
Passeran ...	33117	Could you not have selected
Passernice	33118	Could not have selected
Passerotto	33119	Could have selected if I had known you wished it
Passgang ...	33120	Must not be in any way selected
Passionato	33121	Was (were) not in any way selected
Passionner	33122	Who has been selected for
Passive ...	33123	Selected by
Passivity ...	33124	Was (were) selected
Passover ...	33125	Was (were) not selected
Passports ...	33126	**Selection**
Passuro ...	33127	Send a selection of
Password ...	33128	Has (have) sent a selection of
Pastaccia ...	33129	**Self** (*See also* "Myself.")
Pastareale	33130	For self alone
Pasteboard	33131	**Sell**
Pasteleria...	33132	To sell
Pastelon ...	33133	Will sell
Pasticcio ...	33134	Will not sell
Pastiche ...	33135	Take advantage of the present price to sell (at)
Pastiglia ...	33136	Think you had better sell
Pastillico ...	33137	Would you advise me (us) to sell
Pastimes ...	33138	Cannot advise you whether to sell or hold
Pastinaca...	33139	I (we) would advise you to sell
Pastinator	33140	I (we) would advise you not to sell
Pastinum ...	33141	When I shall be able to advise you whether to sell or hold
Pastoforio	33142	Can you sell and at what price
Pastomis ...	33143	I (we) can sell (at)
Pastophori	33144	Could you sell
Pastoral ...	33145	Do not sell
Pastorius ...	33146	Did he (they) sell
Pastorizia...	33147	Difficult to sell
Pastorship	33148	Should be glad to sell
Pastoso ...	33149	Expected to sell
Pastoureau	33150	Had I (we) not better sell
Pastrycook	33151	Sell —— shares in —— company
Pastryshop	33152	Unable to sell at your limit
Pasturage...	33153	If necessary you must sell at a loss [name
Pasturing...	33154	Shall I (we) sell any more beyond the number (quantity) you

Patache ...	33155	If you can sell any additional number (quantity) let me know [it by cable
Patagalana	33156	Can you sell any more
Patagiatus	33157	Do not sell any more
Patagon ...	33158	Sell as many more as you can up to
Pataguim ...	33159	Sell as many (much) as you can at
Patatal ...	33160	You should sell as quickly as possible
Patatras ...	33161	You should sell as quietly as possible
Patauger ...	33162	It does not matter whether you sell quietly or not
Patched ...	33163	What do you wish to sell at
Patching ...	33164	Sell at
Patchwork	33165	Sell at not less than
Patefacio ...	33166	Cable in case you wish to sell and how many (much)
Patenotre...	33167	Should be glad to sell if I could obtain not less than ——
Patentirt ...	33168	Do not sell for a few days if you think there is any chance of [their going better
Patereccio	33169	May perhaps sell better within the next —— days
Paternal ...	33170	Not likely to sell better
Paternitas	33171	Cannot possibly say whether they will sell better or otherwise
Patesca ...	33172	Can you increase your order to sell
Patescens...	33173	Can most likely sell
Patetical ...	33174	Will most likely sell
Patheque ...	33175	There is very little chance of my (our) being able to sell
Pathetisch	33176	At what profit are you willing to sell
Pathicus ...	33177	At what price are you willing to sell
Pathogeny	33178	Will sell if I (we) can get a net profit of
Pathology	33179	At what limit may I (we) sell
Patiancho	33180	The limit at which you can sell is
Patibulo ...	33181	Shall I (we) sell
Patienter ...	33182	I (we) cannot sell more than
Patilla ...	33183	I (we) can sell at least
Patimazizo	33184	In case you can sell, please cable
Patimento	33185	In case you cannot sell, please cable
Patinar ...	33186	Cannot sell
Patinarius	33187	Do not sell unless —— concurs
Patisserie...	33188	Do not sell until (unless)
Patochada	33189	Do not sell on any account
Patologico	33190	It would be best, I think, for you to sell
Patrana ...	33191	I strongly advise you not to sell
Patrandus	33192	Can you discover whether —— has agreed to sell
Patraque ...	33193	—— has agreed to sell
Patraturus	33194	—— is believed to have arranged to sell
Patriarch ...	33195	I have no doubt that —— has arranged to sell
Patriciado	33196	Can only sell at a loss of
Patriedad...	33197	Do not sell at any loss
Patrigno ...	33198	Am (are) willing to sell provided loss does not exceed
Patrimus ...	33199	Can you sell
Patriota ...	33200	Authorize you to sell
Patrocinar	33201	Sell by public auction and take the best price that offers
Patrolled ...	33202	You should send —— (him) a Power of Attorney to sell or [buy on your account
Patronatus	33203	You should send me (us) a Power of Attorney to buy or sell [on your account
Patronear...	33204	Please sell for my account
Patroniser	33205	Please sell for account of
Patronless	33206	Shall I (we) sell for your account
Patronymie	33207	Sell at once
Patrouille...	33208	Sell sufficient to cover
Patruelem	33209	You can begin to sell (at)
Patrulla ...	33210	Have not been able to sell as you wished
Patsche ...	33211	Have not been able to sell within your limits
Pattering ...	33212	Have not been able to sell at all

Pattoche ...	33213	Should you sell, please cable
Pattovire ...	33214	Should you not sell, please cable
Pattuglia ...	33215	Should you be able to sell
Pattypan ...	33216	Should you not be able to sell
Patullar ...	33217	How many (much) have you still left to sell
Paturnia ...	33218	Please confirm instructions to sell
Paucissime	33219	I (we) now confirm instructions to sell
Paucitas ...	33220	Cancel the instructions given you on —— to sell
Pauculas ...	33221	Your cancelling instructions not to sell will be attended to
Pauken ...	33222	Your cancelling instructions not to sell came too late; had
Paulatino...	33223	Why do you not sell [already sold
Paulisper ...	33224	Instructions to sell contained in my (our) letter dated
Paullatim	33225	Sell at par or even at a small loss
Paumier ...	33226	Sell if you can without any loss
Pauperatus	33227	Am (are) not at all anxious to sell
Paupercula	33228	Sell discreetly
Pauperism	33229	Sell at whatever price you can get
Paupiere ...	33230	Sell if you can get the net cost
Paurevole...	33231	You should not be in a hurry to sell
Pauroso ...	33232	Cannot sell any more at the present time
Pausado ...	33233	Sell for delivery next account
Pausairt ...	33234	Sell for delivery after meeting
Pausingly	33235	Sell as near to my limit as you can
Pausiren ...	33236	Await further instructions before you sell
Pauvresse ..	33237	How much (many) do you agree to sell
Pavefatto ...	33238	How much (many) have you (they) agreed to sell
Pavement...	33239	I (we) have agreed to sell
Paventante	33240	They have agreed to sell
Paventato...	33241	Not agreed to sell any
Paventoso...	33242	Would you be willing to sell (if)
Pavesadas	33243	Sell the mine (property) for what it will fetch, or otherwise
Pavesajo ...	33244	Sell —— shares [abandon it, selling all tools and materials
Pavibundo	33245	Sell 5 shares
Pavicula ...	33246	Sell 10 shares
Pavilion ...	33247	Sell 15 shares
Paviota ...	33248	Sell 20 shares
Pavipollo ...	33249	Sell 25 shares
Pavitatio ...	33250	Sell 30 shares
Pavonaceus	33251	Sell 35 shares
Pavonada...	33252	Sell 40 shares
Pavoncella	33253	Sell 45 shares
Pavonear ...	33254	Sell 50 shares
Pavoninus	33255	Sell 55 shares
Pavordear...	33256	Sell 60 shares
Pavoroso ...	33257	Sell 65 shares
Pawning ...	33258	Sell 70 shares
Pawnshop	33259	Sell 75 shares
Pawnticket	33260	Sell 80 shares
Paxillus ...	33261	Sell 85 shares
Payaso ...	33262	Sell 90 shares
Payclerks...	33263	Sell 95 shares
Payday ...	33264	Sell 100 shares
Payoffice ...	33265	Sell 200 shares
Paysagiste	33266	Sell 300 shares
Pazienza ...	33267	Sell 400 shares
Pazpuerco	33268	Sell 500 shares
Pazquato	33269	Sell 600 shares
Pazzarello...	33270	Sell 700 shares
Pazzeresco	33271	Sell 800 shares
Pazzerone...	33272	Sell 900 shares

Pazziuola ...	33273	Sell 1000 shares
Peaceable ...	33274	**Seller(s)**
Peacemaker	33275	Are you (is ——) a seller of
Peachick ...	33276	Am (is) not a seller of
Peagero ...	33277	Sellers are firm
Peahen ...	33278	There are very few sellers
Peaking ...	33279	There are plenty of sellers
Pearlashes	33280	No sellers
Pearliness	33281	Sellers are to pay all charges
Pearlwort ...	33282	**Selling**
Pearmain ...	33283	Is (are) selling at
Peartree ...	33284	Is (are) not selling at
Peascod ...	33285	Is (are) believed to be selling largely
Peausserie	33286	Is (are) selling largely
Pebbled ...	33287	Is (are) not selling
Pebete ...	33288	Continue(s) selling
Pecaminoso	33289	Cease selling
Pecante ...	33290	Has (have) ceased selling
Pecatriz ...	33291	Begin selling
Peccable ...	33292	Believed to be selling at
Peccadillo	33293	Believed to be selling because of
Peccamen'...	33294	Why is —— (are you) selling
Peccancy ...	33295	Can you discover who is (are) selling
Peccatore ...	33296	Have discovered that —— is (are) selling
Peccatrice...	33297	—— is (are) selling at
Peccaturus	33298	Am (is) (are) selling because
Pecchiare ...	33299	People generally are selling
Pecezuelo ..	33300	**Selvage(s)**
Pechar ...	33301	The footwall has a clay selvage —— inches thick
Pecheresse	33302	The hanging wall has a clay selvage —— inches thick
Pechfackel	33303	**Semi**
Pechigonga	33304	**Semiannual(ly)**
Pechina ...	33305	**Send**
Pechugon	33306	To send
Peciento ...	33307	Will send
Pecilgar ...	33308	Refuse(s) to send
Peciluengo	33309	Before I (we) send
Pecoraccia	33310	Before you send
Pecorosus...	33311	Able to send
Pectinated	33312	Unable to send
Pectinatim	33313	When I (we) shall be able to send
Pectoral ...	33314	When shall you be able to send
Pecuario ...	33315	Until I am (we are) able to send
Pecuinus ...	33316	How much (many) will you be able to send
Peculator ..	33317	The most I (we) shall be able to send is
Peculiaris...	33318	When I will send as much (many) as I am able
Peculietto	33319	Can send you
Peculio ...	33320	Can you send
Peculiosus	33321	Can send you sufficient to meet your needs on
Pecumoso...	33322	Cannot send you money before
Pecuniario	33323	Will it be prudent to send
Pecunious...	33324	I (we) advise you to send
Pedaggiere	33325	I (we) advise you on no account to send
Pedagnuolo	33326	Has (have) to send the ore to
Pedagogic...	33327	Do not omit to send
Pedagra ...	33328	Send in addition to foregoing
Pedales ...	33329	Send all the
Pedalharp...	33330	Send all the —— you are able
Pedaliera ...	33331	Will send —— from there
Pedalnote...	33332	Will send —— to

Pedalpoint	33333	Did you send
Pedamentum	33334	Can send
Pedaneo ...	33335	Cannot send
Pedanteria	33336	Do not send
Pedantesco	33337	Will not forget to send
Pedantic ...	33338	Do not forget to send
Pedantisch	33339	Do not send unless (until)
Pedantry ...	33340	Will not send unless (until)
Peddlery ...	33341	Do not send anything further until
Pedernal ...	33342	Do not send until you hear from me (——) again
Pedestrian	33343	Shall not send again until I hear from you (——)
Pedetentim	33344	Should you not be able to come, send ——
Pedicello ...	33345	If you can send
Pedicox ...	33346	If you cannot send
Pedicular...	33347	If I (we) cannot send
Pedignone	33348	Send without delay particulars relating to
Pedigree ...	33349	May I (we) send
Pedigueno	33350	You had better not send
Pediluvio ...	33351	Shall I (we) send
Pedimanous	33352	In case you can send ——
Pediment ...	33353	In case you cannot send
Pediolus ...	33354	Please send a new —— at the earliest moment possible
Pedissequo	33355	Please send it (this) immediately
Peditatus...	33356	Shall I (we) send a new
Pedometer	33357	Cable whether I (we) shall send
Pedometric	33358	Send full postal address of
Pedonaggio	33359	Where shall I (we) send it (——) to
Pedorrar ...	33360	Send reply to my (our) last letter
Pedorrevas	33361	Send reply to enquiries contained in my (our) letter dated ——
Pedregal ...	33362	You should send without fail
Pedrégoso	33363	Shall not be able to send until
Pedriscal ...	33364	You are to send
Pedrusco ...	33365	You are not to send
Peduculum	33366	Send it (them) addressed " care of "
Pedulis ...	33367	Will send it (them) to you as soon as possible
Peduncle ...	33368	Send the fullest and latest details (respecting)
Peephole ...	33369	Send by ——
Peerage ...	33370	Send by first steamer
Peevish ...	33371	Send by express
Peewit ...	33372	Will it be possible for you (——) to send
Pegadura...	33373	It will be easy for me to send
Pegamiento	33374	It will be impossible for me to send
Pegante ...	33375	Recommend you to send a competent man at once
Pegascius...	33376	Advise you to send
Pegaseo ...	33377	What (who) do you propose to send
Pegatista ...	33378	I (we) propose to send
Peggiorare	33379	Propose to send all I (we) possibly can
Pegmaris ...	33380	Propose to send as little as possible until
Pegtop ...	33381	You should not send too much (many)
Pegujalero	33382	Do not send too few
Pegujon ...	33383	Shall have to send to —— for
Peguntar ...	33384	As I (we) have had to send to —— for
Peignage ...	33385	Send not later than
Peigneur ...	33386	When I (we) shall be able to send further details
●Peignures...	33387	When will you be able to send
Peinada ...	33388	When will you be able to send the particulars of
Peinadura	33389	Until I am (we are) able to send news that
Peiniger ...	33390	How shall I (we) send it (them)
Peinlich ...	33391	The best way would be to send it (them)
Peitsche ...	33392	Will send it (them) at once

Pejemuller	33393	Will send it (them) to-morrow
Pejepalo ...	33394	Will send it (them) next week
Pejeratus ...	33395	Please send copy of —— (this) to
Pelacane ...	33396	Will send copy of —— to
Peladillos ...	33397	Will send to-day
Pelafustan	33398	Do not omit to send to-morrow latest details of · (for)
Pelagatos...	33399	**Sending**
Pelaghetto	33400	Am (are) sending
Pelagicus...	33401	If you are sending
Pelagosaur	33402	Sending for
Pelaire ...	33403	Sending to
Pelambrar	33404	Propose sending
Pelandusca	33405	Not sending
Pelantrin ...	33406	**Senseless**
Pelapiedi ...	33407	**Sensible(ly)**
Pelapolli ...	33408	**Sent**
Pelargonic	33409	Sent to
Pelaruecas	33410	Sent for
Pelatina ...	33411	Sent by
Pelatojo ...	33412	Sent under cover to
Peldefebre	33413	Sent with
Peleante ...	33414	Not sent with
Pelechar ...	33415	I (we) sent you this month
Pelecinus ...	33416	I (we) sent you this week
Peleona ...	33417	Have you sent
Pelerinage	33418	Has (have) sent
Pelerine ...	33419	Has (have) —— sent
Pelgar ...	33420	Has (have) not sent
Peliagudo...	33421	Should be sent without fail
Peliblanco	33422	Should be sent to
Pelicabra ...	33423	Unless —— can be sent before —— will be no use
Pelican ...	33424	Have not sent owing to
Pelicorto ...	33425	If it (they) have not already been sent, do not forward
Peliforra ...	33426	How was it (were they) sent and when
Peligroso ...	33427	Was (were) sent
Pelilloso ...	33428	Was (were) not sent
Pelirojo ...	33429	Was (were) not sent because of
Pelisse ...	33430	Was (were) sent addressed as follows
Pelitieso ...	33431	Was (were) sent per —— on
Pelitre ...	33432	Was (were) sent addressed " care of "
Pelitrique...	33433	Was (were) sent to —— but refused
Pellabor ...	33434	Has (have) not been sent yet
Pellaccia ...	33435	Will be sent
Pellectus ...	33436	Will not be sent
Pellegrina	33437	Will be sent as soon as possible
Pellejeria ...	33438	I (we) (——) sent you particulars by mail on
Pellejudo ...	33439	Particulars shall be sent by mail
Pellicatio ...	33440	Full details should be sent by mail
Pellicella ...	33441	Should be sent to —— instructing him to
Pelliciato ...	33442	**Sentence(d)**
Pellicius ...	33443	Sentence commencing with the word
Pellicle ...	33444	Sentence finishing with the word
Pelliculor...	33445	Sentence to finish
Pellijero ...	33446	Sentence to commence
Pellitory ...	33447	A new sentence
Pellizcar ...	33448	Strike out the entire sentence
Pellmell ...	33449	Sentence number —— page ——
Pellonia ...	33450	Quite approve of sentence
Pellosita ...	33451	Do not approve of sentence
Pellucid ...	33452	**Separate**

Pelluzgon...	33453	To separate
Pelolino ...	33454	Will separate
Peloris ...	33455	Can separate
Pelosilla ...	33456	Cannot separate [separate from ——
Pelotear ...	33457	Your expenditure in connection with —— must be kept
Pelotonner	33458	Has your expenditure in connection with —— been kept [separate from ——
Pelouse ...	33459	The expenditure has been carefully kept separate
Peltasta ...	33460	The expenditure has not been kept separate
Peltingly ...	33461	Will send statement showing separate expenditure by next mail
Peltrero ...	33462	For the future must be carefully kept separate
Pelucher ...	33463	Will be kept separate from
Pelucon ...	33464	Please instruct —— to separate —— from ——
Peluquera	33465	Should be kept separate owing to
Pelusa	33466	Will be kept separate in future
Pelzmantel	33467	To keep separate
Pelzmatze...	33468	Keep them separate
Pelzwerk ...	33469	Must be kept separate
Pemmican	33470	Cannot be kept separate
Penadillo ...	33471	Need not be kept separate
Penalmente	33472	It is difficult to exactly separate
Penalogise	33473	Will separate them as far as I am (we are) able
Penaria ...	33474	Unable to separate
Penates ...	33475	It will be necessary to separate
Penatigero	33476	Keep separate accounts for
Penaud ...	33477	Keep —— entirely separate from
Penchement	33478	**Separated**
Pencilling	33479	Has been separated from
Pencuria ...	33480	Not easily separated
Pendaglio...	33481	Easily separated
Pendaison	33482	Can be separated but will require some care
Pendanga...	33483	Can only be separated with the greatest difficulty
Pendency...	33484	Can be separated but the cost is too heavy
Pendevole...	33485	**Separately**
Pendiente...	33486	Should be kept and treated quite separately
Pendiller ...	33487	Will be kept and treated quite separately
Penditur ...	33488	**Separation**
Pendol ...	33489	**September**
Pendolage...	33490	At the beginning of September
Pendolero...	33491	About the middle of September
Pendolista	33492	During the entire month of September
Pendolon ...	33493	For the entire month of September
Pendulous	33494	Last September
Pendura ...	33495	Next September
Penerata ...	33496	Near the end of September
Penetrable	33497	First day of September
Penetrador	33498	Second day of September
Penetralis...'	33499	Third day of September
Penetratus	33500	Fourth day of September
Penetror ...	33501	Fifth day of September
Penguin ...	33502	Sixth day of September
Penholder	33503	Seventh day of September
Penicillus...	33504	Eighth day of September
Penigero ...	33505	Ninth day of September
Penisla ...	33506	Tenth day of September
Penitent ...	33507	Eleventh day of September
Penitus ...	33508	Twelfth day of September
Penknife ...	33509	Thirteenth day of September
Penmanship	33510	Fourteenth day of September
Pennacchio	33511	Fifteenth day of September

Pennajuolo	33512	Sixteenth day of September
Pennamatta	33513	Seventeenth day of September
Pennello ...	33514	Eighteenth day of September
Penniferum	33515	Nineteenth day of September
Penniless ...	33516	Twentieth day of September
Pennoniere	33517	Twenty-first day of September
Pennuccia	33518	Twenty-second day of September
Pennyroyal	33519	Twenty-third day of September
Penorcon ...	33520	Twenty-fourth day of September
Pensabilis	33521	Twenty-fifth day of September
Pensagione	33522	Twenty-sixth day of September
Pensandus	33523	Twenty-seventh day of September
Pensativo ...	33524	Twenty-eighth day of September
Pensatrice	33525	Twenty-ninth day of September
Pensaturus	33526	Thirtieth day of September
Pensevole ..	33527	September expenses amount to
Pensiculo ...	33528	September shipments amount to
Pensierato	33529	**Sequel**
Pensility ...	33530	**Sequence**
Pensionary	33531	In proper sequence
Pensitatio	33532	**Sequestrate(d)**
Pensum ...	33533	**Series**
Pentachord	33534	In series
Pentacolo ...	33535	Series number ——
Pentad ...	33536	**Serious(ly)** (*See also* "Complication.")
Pentadoron	33537	Serious matter
Pentagloto	33538	Is it serious
Pentagonus	33539	It is serious
Pentangulo	33540	It is not serious
Pentapody	33541	Not at all serious
Pentarchy	33542	May (might) become very serious
Pentateuco	33543	Condition becoming a little serious
Pentathlum	33544	Do not think it (this) likely to become serious.
Pentatonic	33545	I (we) think it likely to become serious
Pentecost ...	33546	Should it become serious, please cable
Pentolata ...	33547	Is not at all likely to become very serious
Pentoletta	33548	Will advise you (——) should it become serious
Pentorobon	33549	Is (are) in a very serious condition
Pentylic ...	33550	Is not in a serious condition
Penuarius	33551	It will be a serious matter if
Penulatus...	33552	It will be a serious matter unless
Penultima	33553	It will not be a very serious matter (even **if**)
Penumbra	33554	The situation is just a little serious
Penzolone...	33555	The situation is becoming much more serious
Peonage ...	33556	The situation is much less serious than hitherto
Peonza ...	33557	Not so serious as was at first thought
Peopled ...	33558	Much more serious than was at first thought
Peormente	33559	Would only become serious in the event of
Pepajuola ..	33560	**Serpentine**
Pepastico ...	33561	The predominant rock is serpentine
Pepian ...	33562	In serpentine rock
Pepinazo ...	33563	**Serve**
Pepitoria ...	33564	Will serve
Pepitoso ...	33565	Will not serve
Peplide ...	33566	Will serve for the present.
Peposci ...	33567	May serve until I (we) receive
Pepperbox	33568	Will it serve your purpose
Peppercorn	33569	Will not serve my purpose
Peppering	33570	Serve —— with formal notice to (if)
Peppermint	33571	**Served**

Pepsine ...	33572	Has (have) hitherto served admirably
Pepticus ...	33573	Has (have) been served with
Pequenez ...	33574	Not yet been served
Peracer ...	33575	May be served at any moment
Peracturus	33576	Unless immediately served
Peragendus	33577	**Service(s)**
Peragitor ...	33578	Has rendered me (us) very great service
Peragratio	33579	Has (have) been of much service
Peragror ...	33580	Will be of very great service
Peraile ...	33581	Would be of much service
Peralbus ...	33582	Would only be of service in the event of
Peraleda ...	33583	A very valuable service
Peraltar ...	33584	Is it (this) of any service
Peramanter	33585	It is of no service for
Peramplus	33586	Would it (this) (——) be of any service to you
Peranton ...	33587	The service(s) rendered was (were)
Peraridus...	33588	For services rendered
Perarmatus	33589	Any services rendered
Perastute...	33590	What were the services rendered
Peraticum	33591	Is at present in the service of
Perattente	33592	What would you fix as the value of the services rendered
Perbacchor	33593	Should fix the value of the services rendered at (not to exceed)
Perbenigne	33594	Consider value of services rendered to be
Perbibesia	33595	Will not be of much service
Perblandus	33596	Will be of no service (until)
Perbonus ...	33597	Am entirely at your service
Perbrevis ...	33598	Professional services
Percaline ...	33599	Is no longer in the service of the —— company
Percalleo .	33600	Left the service of the company named about
Percatar ...	33601	Secure services of
Percebir ...	33602	**Serviceable**
Perceiver ...	33603	More serviceable
Percellor ...	33604	Less serviceable
Percement	33605	Could be made serviceable
Percepteur	33606	Could it (this) be made serviceable
Perceptive	33607	Is (are) still quite serviceable
Percerpo ...	33608	Is it still serviceable
Percezione	33609	Is (are) not serviceable
Perchador	33610	Would be more serviceable if
Perchloric	33611	Can be made serviceable by
Perchon ...	33612	Cannot be made serviceable by
Percingo ...	33613	Can be made serviceable but will require (cost)
Perciocche	33614	Is (are) in good and serviceable condition
Percipiens	33615	If you can make it (him) (——) serviceable
Percipior ...	33616	**Session**
Percivilis ...	33617	Now in session
Percoceria	33618	Session commences on
Percoctus...	33619	Session commenced on —— and will terminate about ——
Percolate ...	33620	**Set**
Percomis ...	33621	To set
Percontans	33622	To set up
Percoquor	33623	Is (are) set up
Percorrere	33624	Is (are) not yet set up
Percoessura	33625	Cannot be set up
Percrassus	33626	Can be set up
Percrebuit	33627	Will be set up (near to)
Percrucio ...	33628	Should be set up
Percupidus	33629	Might be set up
Percurrens	33630	Is set in
Percussion .	33631	Has (have) set in

Percussuto	33632	Has (have) not yet set in
Percutior ...	33633	Is expected to set in about
Perdecorus	33634	Is set beside
Perdelirus	33635	To be set aside for
Perdendo ...	33636	Should be set aside for
Perder ...	33637	Should be set aside for the present
Perdespuo	33638	Will probably be set aside
Perdidizo ...	33639	Might be set aside for the present
Perdigana	33640	Propose to set it aside for the present (until)
Perdigon ...	33641	**Set-off**
Perdiguera	33642	As a set-off against
Perdimento	33643	**Sets**
Perdiscor ...	33644	Sets of timber
Perdition ...	33645	Have put in —— sets of timber
Perditrice...	33646	**Sett**
Perditurus	33647	Mining sett
Perdoceor...	33648	Boundaries of mining sett
Perdomisco	33649	Lease of mining sett
Perdrix ...	33650	**Settle**
Perduaxint	33651	To settle
Perductus	33652	Will settle
Perduellio	33653	Will not settle
Perdulario	33654	Expect(s) to settle
Perduto ...	33655	Do(es) not expect to settle
Pereales ...	33656	Endeavour to settle the matter as best you can
Perecear ...	33657	Will try and settle the matter
Perecedero	33658	How do you (does ——) propose to settle the matter
Perecido ...	33659	Can you settle the matter
Pereciente	33660	Unable to settle
Peregre ...	33661	Was (were) too late on —— to settle the terms
Peregrinar	33662	Must first settle
Perejilon ...	33663	If you (——) can settle the matter in a friendly manner
Perelegans	33664	Am (are) quite willing to settle everything in a friendly manner
Peremptor	33665	There is no chance of our being able to settle the matter in a [friendly manner
Perendeca	33666	Consent(s) to settle
Perendinus	33667	Refuse(s) to settle
Perennal ...	33668	Is willing to settle upon the following basis
Perennidad	33669	On what basis (terms) is it proposed to settle
Perentorio	33670	To settle the matter
Perequito ..	33671	Will this settle the matter finally
Pererratus	33672	This will settle the matter finally
Pereza ...	33673	This will settle the matter for the present
Perfabrico	33674	Shall I (we) settle on terms offered
Perfacilis ...	33675	Offer(s) to settle upon the following terms
Perfecting	33676	Better settle at once on terms offered
Perfectivo...	33677	Settle the matter on the best terms you can
Perfectrix...	33678	**Settled**
Perferor ...	33679	Have it settled
Perfervid ...	33680	The matter is finally settled
Perficere ...	33681	Everything should be settled up before you (——) leave(s)
Perficiens ...	33682	Everything shall be settled up before I (we) (——) leave(s)
Perfidelis ...	33683	Before I (we) (——) left it was settled to
Perfidia ...	33684	My (our) impression was that it had been settled
Perfidious	33685	Must be settled one way or the other
Perfilado ...	33686	Has (have) been settled
Perflatus ...	33687	Has (have) been satisfactorily settled
Perfluctuo	33688	Has (have) not been settled
Perfoliado	33689	Get matter(s) settled up as quickly as possible
Perforatus	33690	Should have everything settled before
Perforce ...	33691	Should proceed to get matters settled up forthwith

Perfossor ...	33692	Should any question arise it should be settled on the spot
Perfricans	33693	There is not much chance of its being settled so long as
Perfrictio ...	33694	The question must be settled before
Perfrigero...	33695	As soon as anything is settled upon, please cable me (us)
Perfringor	33696	As soon as anything is settled, I (we) will cable
Perfruidor	33697	The moment it is (they are) settled
Perfugio ...	33698	Gradually becoming more settled
Perfumado	33699	Was discussed but never settled
Perfume ...	33700	Not yet settled
Perfuming	33701	It is settled
Perfumista	33702	Is it settled
Perfundens	33703	Was (were) settled
Pergament	33704	Can you get it settled at a cost of
Pergamino	33705	Anticipate it will be settled very soon
Pergandeo	33706	Am (is) (are) quite willing that it should be settled in a
Pergiurare	33707	What have you settled upon (about) [friendly way
Perglisco ...	33708	Has (have) settled upon
Pergnarus	33709	Nothing settled definitely
Pergoletta	33710	Expect it will be settled
Pergrandis	33711	Amicably settled
Perhibeor ...	33712	Has (have) been settled amicably
Perhiemo ...	33713	Expect it will be settled amicably
Perhorreo...	33714	Cannot it be settled amicably
Perhumanus	33715	**Settlement**
Periancio ...	33716	Provided you will apply for a Stock Exchange settlement
Periboetos	33717	A Stock Exchange settlement has been granted
Pericardio...	33718	A Stock Exchange settlement has been refused until the [following information has been supplied
Pericarpum	33719	Until a Stock Exchange settlement has been granted
Periclase ...	33720	Offer in full settlement of claim to
Pericliter ...	33721	Has (have) made the following settlement with
Periclum ...	33722	What prospect is there of settlement and when
Pericoloso...	33723	There is no prospect of any settlement
Pericor ...	33724	There is every prospect of satisfactory settlement
Pericraneo	33725	There is considerable prospect of an early settlement
Peridoneus	33726	Immediately a satisfactory settlement has been come to
Peridoto ...	33727	In full settlement of claim(s)
Peridromo	33728	Until a settlement is arrived at with respect to
Perifollo ...	33729	As a basis of settlement
Perifrasi ...	33730	Delay settlement until
Perigeo ...	33731	Avoid settlement (until)
Periglioso...	33732	Avoid settlement meanwhile
Perigourd...	33733	I (we) cannot see any prospect of an early settlement
Perihelio ...	33734	I (we) will accept the sum of —— in full settlement of claim
Perileucos...	33735	I (we) must give a receipt in full settlement of claim
Perillan ...	33736	Must give a receipt in full settlement of claim
Perilleux ...	33737	Try and effect settlement
Perilous ...	33738	**Settler(s)** (*See also* " Pan.")
Perilsome ...	33739	**Sever**
Perilustre ...	33740	To sever
Perimetro...	33741	**Several**
Perinfamis	33742	For several reasons
Perinique ...	33743	From several places
Perinteger	33744	On several occasions
Perinvisus	33745	It will be several
Periodical...	33746	It will take several
Periodico ...	33747	I (we) shall still require several
Periodisch	33748	For several hours
Periostio ...	33749	For several days
Peripato ...	33750	For several weeks

Periphery ...	33751	For several months
Peripsema ..	33752	**Severe**
Peripuesto	33753	Very severe
Periscelis ...	33754	Promise(s) to be very severe
Periscios ...	33755	**Severely**
Periscopic	33756	Has set in severely
Perishable	33757	**Shackle(s)**
Perishing ...	33758	**Shaft(s)** (*See also* " Brace," " Cage," " Climbing-way," " Com-
Peristroma	33759	Shaft station [menced," " Connect," " Filled," " Footway.")
Peristyle ...	33760	Collar of shaft
Perituro ...	33761	What are the dimensions of the shaft (at ——)
Periwig ...	33762	The dimensions of the shaft within timbers are —— by ——
Periwinkle	33763	The shaft is round and —— diameter
Perizonium	33764	Incline shaft
Perjudicar	33765	The shaft is divided into —— compartments
Perjurador	33766	Each compartment in the shaft measures
Perjurio ...	33767	The shaft is provided with a double skipway
Perlabor ...	33768	The shaft has only a single skipway
Perlapsus ...	33769	Vertical shaft
Perlatico ...	33770	New shaft
Perlaturus	33771	Old shaft
Perldruck...	33772	In the old shaft
Perlectus ...	33773	Engine shaft [inclined on the vein —— feet
Perlepide ...	33774	The shaft is downright for a depth of —— feet and is then
Perleria ...	33775	The shaft is inclined on the vein and has reached a depth of
Perleviter ..	33776	What is the present depth of the shaft at
Perlhuhn ...	33777	What will be the extreme depth of the shaft
Perlibrans...	33778	The present depth of the shaft is —— feet
Perlicio ...	33779	It is intended to sink the shaft to a depth of —— feet
Parlier ..	33780	In the climbing-way of the shaft
Perlitatum	33781	Shall use this shaft only as a climbing-way
Perlongar ...	33782	What is the condition of the shaft
Perlucidus	33783	The shaft is in very fair condition
Perlustro ...	33784	The shaft is in an excellent condition
Permacero	33785	The shaft is much in need of repair [an entirely new one
Permagnus	33786	The shaft is in very bad condition ; it will be advisable to sink
Permaloso...	33787	When will you commence the repairs to the shaft
Permanasco	33788	Shaft repairs now in progress
Permanenza	33789	Shall commence to repair the shaft almost immediately
Permansion	33790	Have already begun to repair shaft
Permarinus	33791	Shall begin to repair shaft as soon as
Permeabile	33792	Whilst the repairs of the shaft are in progress
Permeans ...	33793	The shaft is now timbered down to
Permeated	33794	Shall begin to cut plat in shaft for No. —— level on ——
Permetior...	33795	Main shaft
Permettre ...	33796	In the main shaft
Permetuens	33797	The main shaft has been sunk to a depth of —— feet
Permingo ...	33798	This (it) will constitute our main shaft
Perminutus	33799	Where do you propose to locate the main shaft
Permiscens	33800	When do you propose to commence sinking new shaft
Permisivo ...	33801	Propose to commence sinking shaft at once (about ——)
Permisor ...	33802	Propose to place shaft at
Permixtus	33803	The shaft should intersect the lode at a depth of
Permodicus	33804	The shaft will be vertical [new shaft
Permoleste	33805	Shall obtain estimates for hoisting and pumping machinery for
Permollis ...	33806	The estimates of hoisting and pumping equipments for shaft
		[amount to
Permoveor	33807	Has (have) been developed to a depth of —— feet by a shaft
		[sunk on the vein
Permulcens	33808	Has (have) been developed to a depth of —— feet by a vertical
		[shaft

Permutably	33809	In the shaft (it is)
Permutato	33810	From the shaft (it is)
Pernada ...	33811	Right and left of the shaft
Pernavigor	33812	North and south of the shaft
Perneador	33813	East and west of the shaft
Pernegans	33814	North of the shaft
Pernegatio	33815	South of the shaft
Perneria ...	33816	East of the shaft
Perniborra	33817	West of the shaft
Pernicieux	33818	In order to connect with the shaft
Pernicioso	33819	As soon as I (we) connect with the shaft
Pernicitas .	33820	By a level driven to connect with the shaft
Pernimium	33821	At the bottom of the shaft
Pernobilis	33822	Owing to the shaft being full of water
Pernoctar...	33823	Owing to water in the shaft below No. —— level
Pernonis ...	33824	There are —— shafts on the property
Pernotesco	33825	The shaft will be continued an additional —— feet including [—— feet for sump
Pernotint ...	33826	The new shaft is projected to intersect the ore body at a
Pernoxius...	33827	Now sinking shaft at [depth of ——
Pernumero	33828	What is the speed at which you are now sinking shaft
Pernuzzo ...	33829	Average speed of sinking shaft for the last month has been [—— inches per day of twenty-four hours
Perobscure	33830	Total depth sunk in the shaft since —— has been —— feet
Perodiosus	33831	The water in the shaft is steadily rising
Peronatus...	33832	The water in the shaft stands at
Peronnelle	33833	We are beginning to gain upon the water in the shaft
Peroptato...	33834	We are steadily gaining on the water in the shaft
Perorar ...	33835	Could not be seen owing to water in the shaft
Peroration	33836	During my visit the shaft(s) was (were) free from water
Peroreur ...	33837	Have sunk a new shaft
Peroriga ...	33838	At the new shaft
Peroxide ...	33839	On the line of shaft
Perpanculi	33840	North of the incline shaft
Perparvus	33841	South of the incline shaft
Perpejana	33842	East of the incline shaft
Perpendens	33843	West of the incline shaft
Perpensius	33844	Developed by shaft(s) for a total aggregate depth of —— feet
Perpessio ...	33845	Deep shaft
Perpetrare	33846	Depth of shaft
Perpetuar...	33847	To straighten the shaft [the shaft
Perpetuite	33848	There is a good deal of ground to be cut in order to straighten
Perpiano ...	33849	How long will it take to straighten the shaft and what will be [the approximate cost
Perpictus ...	33850	I (we) estimate time required to straighten the shaft at ——
Perplaceo ...	33851	The shaft is choked with debris [days; approximate cost ——
Perplexed...	33852	To sink a vertical shaft
Perplexing	33853	I (we) expect to reach the shaft about
Perpolio ...	33854	Shaft collapsed owing to
Perpolitus	33855	Now repairing shaft
Perpopulor	33856	Now re-timbering shaft
Perpotatio	33857	Have completed re-timbering shaft
Perpressus	33858	What is your estimate of cost of repairs to shaft
Perpugnax	33859	I (we) estimate that the repairs to shaft will cost about
Perpulcher	33860	Shall sink shaft a further —— feet before commencing to drive
Perpunte ...	33861	At what depth should proposed shaft intersect vein
Perpurgor	33862	Proposed shaft should intersect vein at a depth of —— feet
Perquiesco	33863	Have received following tenders for sinking the shaft
Perquiror ...	33864	Have let the contract for sinking the shaft at
Perquisite	33865	I (we) have commenced sinking the shaft

Perramente	33866	In your next letter give the inside dimensions of shaft
Perrillo ...	33867	Recommencing sinking of shaft (at)
Perrimosus	33868	From the collar of the shaft
Perrogatus	33869	Report present depth of shaft
Perrucke ...	33870	Shaft sunk during —— month —— feet
Perrumpens	33871	The shaft is vertical and fitted with double cage
Perruno ...	33872	The shaft is vertical and fitted with single cage
Perruptus...	33873	To prevent shaft from falling in
Perruque ...	33874	In the bottom of the shaft the vein carries
Persaluto ...	33875	A prospecting shaft [vigour
Persapiens	33876	This will enable us to push the sinking of the shaft with
Perscindor	33877	Shaft will shortly be completed to a depth of
Perscribo ...	33878	**Shafting**
Persecatio	33879	Shafting for
Persecutor	33880	**Shaking Table(s)**
Persedeo ...	33881	**Shale**
Persegnis	33882	Beds of shale
Persequens	33883	Through the overlying shale
Persequir ...	33884	**Shall**
Perservio ...	33885	When shall you
Persevante	33886	When shall I (we)
Persevered	33887	Shall I (we)
Perseverus	33888	I (we) shall
Persiana ...	33889	I (we) shall not
Persicum ...	33890	What shall I (we) do
Persienne ...	33891	When shall I (we) leave
Persifleur ...	33892	When shall I expect you to arrive
Persimplex	33893	When shall you (——) decide
Persislage...	33894	**Shallow**
Persistent...	33895	**Shape** (*See also* " Good.")
Persistir ...	33896	**Shaping**
Persolata ...	33897	**Share(s)** (*See also* "Accept," "Bought," "Buy," "Buyers," ["Capital," "Company," "Discount," "Get," "Held," ["Issued," "Place," "Preference," "Price," "Rise," ["Risen," "Sell," "Sold," &c.)
Persolido ...	33898	Fully paid shares
Persolutus	33899	In fully paid shares
Persolvere	33900	Will take —— in fully paid shares
Personatur	33901	To share
Personcina	33902	Refuse(s) to share
Personeria	33903	Consent(s) to share
Personify ...	33904	Will you share
Personilla...	33905	Am (are) willing to share
Personnel...	33906	Am (are) not willing to share
Persorbens	33907	Not to share
Perspergor	33908	Per share
Perspicas ...	33909	Of a share
Perspicior...	33910	What is (will be) my (our) share
Perspiring	33911	What share(s) have you agreed to take
Perstandum	33912	What share will you take
Persternor	33913	Will take one —— share
Perstimulo	33914	What share will you take in it
Perstratus	33915	My (our) share is (one ——)
Perstringo	33916	My (our) share would be (one ——)
Persuadir...	33917	Your share would be (one ——)
Persuasiva	33918	I (we) should require a share of
Persuasore	33919	Shall certainly require to share
Persultans	33920	Are you (is ——) willing to take a share
Pertaining	33921	Am (is) willing to share to the extent of
Pertempo ...	33922	Will see that you have a share
Pertenecer	33923	Vendors' shares

Pertenuis ...	33924	Founders' shares
Perterebro	33925	Partly paid shares
Perterreor	33926	Please instruct me (us) as to shares
Perticone ...	33927	Have you (has ——) any shares in —— ? if so, how many
Pertiguear	33928	—— has —— shares
Pertimesco	33929	I (we) have —— shares
Pertinente	33930	I (we) have no shares at all
Pertness ...	33931	Do you wish to apply for any shares
Pertolero ...	33932	I do not care to apply for any shares
Pertorqueo	33933	Can I apply for any shares
Pertratto ...	33934	Please apply on my account for —— shares
Pertristis ...	33935	Have applied on your account for —— shares
Pertugada	33936	—— shares have been allotted to you
Pertugetto	33937	Shares have been allotted to
Pertugiare	33938	The shares are all taken up
Pertundor	33939	There is no demand for the shares
Perturbato	33940	There is a good demand for the shares
Perturber ...	33941	Ascertain how many shares are registered in the name of
Perturbing	33942	—— shares are registered in the name of
Peruano ...	33943	There are no shares registered in the name of
Peruggine	33944	What market is there for the shares
Peruke ...	33945	There is no market for the shares
Peruleso ...	33946	The shares have been freely dealt in
Perunctio ...	33947	By which time there will be a market for the shares
Perurbanus	33948	The greater number of shares
Perurgeo ...	33949	—— holds the greater number of the shares
Perutilis ...	33950	Please buy on my account —— shares in the (this)
Pervaded ...	33951	I have obtained —— shares on your account
Pervalidus	33952	I have so far not been able to obtain any shares [absorbed
Pervasurus	33953	You should instruct me quickly as the shares are being rapidly
Pervenche	33954	You should instruct me not later than —— if you wish to have
Pervenente	33955	How many shares have you obtained [any shares
Pervenibo...	33956	I have obtained —— shares
Perveniens	33957	I have not obtained any shares
Pervenitur	33958	How many shares have you sold
Perversite...	33959	I have sold —— shares at —— per share, am I to continue
Perverting	33960	I have not sold any shares [selling
Pervesperi	33961	Have you bought shares (as per)
Pervestigo	33962	What are the —— shares now worth
Pervigilio ...	33963	The shares have no market value [market are unsaleable
Perviridis...	33964	I believe the shares are worth —— but in the present state of
Pervolvor ...	33965	Cable selling price per share (of)
Pesadez ...	33966	Cable buying price per share (of)
Pesadilla ...	33967	Please buy —— shares [—— per share
Pesamment	33968	Please buy if possible —— shares but do not give more than
Pesamondi	33969	Do not give more than —— per share
Pesaroso ...	33970	Has (have) bought —— shares at ——
Pescadazo	33971	Have sold —— shares at ——
Pescaderia	33972	Ascertain if there is any dividend due upon the —— shares
Pescatello...	33973	There is no dividend due upon the —— shares
Pesceduova	33974	The last dividend on the —— shares was paid on ——
Pesciolina...	33975	If you can obtain —— please sell —— shares
Pesciotto ...	33976	Shares are now realizing
Pesciuolo ...	33977	Shares are at —— premium
Pescola ...	33978	Shares are at —— discount
Pescozudo	33979	Shares are just about par
Pescuno ...	33980	I (we) believe the shares are well worth holding
Pesebron ...	33981	I (we) think it would be best to sell the shares
Pespuntar	33982	Please sell —— shares
Pesquera ...	33983	Please sell all my shares

Pesquisar ...	33984	Advise you to sell your shares immediately
Pessarius ...	33985	Please sell shares at once
Pessimist ...	33986	Sell shares at what they will fetch
Pessulus ...	33987	Have sold —— shares at a loss of
Pessundare	33988	Have sold your shares; total net realization
Pestanear ...	33989	Have sold —— shares, cannot obtain a bid for any more at
Pestapepe...	33990	Not able to obtain a bid for the shares [present
Pestatojo ...	33991	The best bid for the shares is ——; shall I sell
Pestbeule ...	33992	Transfer —— shares to
Pesterer ...	33993	Wish to transfer —— shares into the name of
Pestering ...	33994	Send signed transfer for —— shares
Pestifero ...	33995	Send signed transfer for —— shares; should be witnessed by
Pestilent ...	33996	Signed transfer for —— shares mailed [notary public
Pestilitas ...	33997	Signed transfer for —— shares mailed; witnessed by notary
Pestorejo ...	33998	Shares were transferred to —— on —— [public
Petacchina	33999	Give me precise instructions as to shares
Petalaceo ...	34000	A call on the shares is likely to be made [payable on ——
Petalism ...	**34001**	A call of —— per share was made on shares registered on ——
Petarade ...	34002	Please pay call on shares and debit me with the amount
Petardear...	34003	Have paid call on shares to the amount of
Petardista	34004	Shares lodged with
Petasetto ...	34005	Have instructed —— to hand you —— shares
Petaurum...	34006	Would take —— shares in part payment of
Petechial ...	34007	There have been no dealings in the shares since
Petendus ...	34008	The only value the shares have would be in case of a recon-
Petequias ...	34009	The shares are jointly held by [struction
Petereccio...	34010	The first issue of shares will be
Petersilie ...	34011	Of the first issue of the shares
Peticano ...	34012	The first issue of shares has been all taken up
Petilius ...	34013	Transfer for —— shares mailed
Petimetra...	34014	Am willing to take a share to the extent of
Petirojo ...	34015	On payment of an equal share of expenses
Petissens ...	34016	Shares are now ——; do accounts justify
Petitement	34017	Shares are now ——; do you know any particular reason for
Petitioned	34018	Hold the balance of shares to my order
Petitoria ...	34019	The balance of shares for disposal is
Petitrix ...	34020	The fully paid shares will be distributed as a bonus
Petiturus ...	34021	The shares have been assessed with
Petonciano	34022	The shares cannot be assessed with any further amount
Petoritum...	34023	A number of shares
Petraria ...	34024	Shares not saleable until one year after registration of company
Petrel ...	34025	Shares not saleable until —— after the registration of company
Petricosus	34026	Cable present price for (of) —— shares
Petrificar ...	34027	All shares were forfeited
Petrisea ...	34028	All his (——'s) shares have been forfeited
Petrissage	34029	Does not hold a single share
Petrole ...	34030	Cable instructions if I am to buy shares on your account
Petrosilex...	34031	Sudden buying shares
Petruciola	34032	Sudden selling shares
Petschaft ...	34033	**Shareholder(s)** (*See also* "Information.")
Pettegola ...	34034	Cable information required for shareholders' meeting
Pettinare ...	34035	Dissatisfied shareholders of —— shares
Pettirosso...	34036	Will not inform the shareholders
Pettitoes ...	34037	Has (have) been obliged to inform the shareholders
Petulancia	34038	On behalf of the shareholders
Petulanter	34039	At a meeting of the shareholders held on —— it was resolved
Petulcus ...	34040	A committee of enquiry consisting of —— of the largest
		[shareholders has been appointed
Petunsa ...	34041	Would you serve on a committee of shareholders
Peucedano	34042	Shareholders are pressing as to (for)

Peujalero ...	84043	Shareholders are getting anxious as to returns
Peuplier ...	84044	Is (are) —— shareholder(s) in (of)
Peverada ...	84045	Is (are) shareholder(s) in (of)
Peverino ...	84046	Is (are) not shareholder(s) in (of)
Pewseats ...	84047	Is a shareholder to the extent of —— shares
Pewterer ...	84048	—— (he) is one of the largest shareholders of
Pexitas ...	84049	A shareholder in (of)
Pezolada ...	84050	The shareholder(s) in (of)
Pezuelo ...	84051	Wish to issue news to shareholders
Pezzaccio ...	84052	Send particulars of —— for shareholders' meeting
Pezzendo ...	84053	Otherwise shareholders will give trouble
Pezzettino	84054	Subject to confirmation by shareholders
Pfahlban ...	84055	Has been confirmed by shareholders
Pfahlen ...	84056	Do not inform the shareholders　[be issued to shareholders
Pfalzgraf ..	84057	This information is required for circular (report) proposed to
Pfand ...	84058	Suggest that you issue circular (report) to shareholders
Pfandbrief	84059	Propose to issue circular (report) to shareholders
Pfandrecht	84060	I (we) wish to send out a circular to shareholders
Pfandung	84061	At a meeting of shareholders it has been decided to wind up
Pfarrer ...	84062	**Sharp(ly)**　　　　　　　　　　[the company
Pfarrkind...	84063	Very sharp
Pfauhenne	84064	Sharp practice
Pfeifer ...	84065	Be sharp
Pfennig ...	84066	Look sharp
Pferchen ...	84067	Unless you (——) look(s) sharp
Pferdearzt	84068	**Sharpness**
Pferdebahu	84069	**Shatter**
Pferdehuf...	84070	**Shattered**
Pfingsten ...	84071	**Shattering**
Pfirsiche ...	84072	**Sheave(s)**
Pflanze ...	84073	Sheave(s) for
Pflanzholz	84074	Send as quickly as possible sheave(s) to replace
Pflastern ..	84075	What are the dimensions of sheave(s)
Pflaume ..	84076	Sheave(s) —— inches diameter
Pflegekind	84077	Now placing sheave in position
Pflichtig ...	84078	**Shed(s)**
Pflocken ...	84079	**Sheriff**
Pflugeisen	84080	By order of the sheriff
Pflugschar	84081	**Shift(s)** (*See also* "Day.")
Pfortner ...	84082	It will be necessary to shift
Pfriem ...	84083	It will not be necessary to shift
Pfropfen ..	84084	Will it be necessary to shift
Pfrundner	84085	Shall not shift
Pfundweise	84086	Do not shift
Pfuschen ...	84087	**Ship**
Pfutzig ...	84088	Ship viâ
Phalangium	84089	You must ship
Phalanx ...	84090	Will ship
Phalarica ...	84091	Expected to ship
Phaleratus	84092	When will you be able to ship
Phalerides	84093	Shall begin to ship as soon as
Phanaticus	84094	Shall begin to ship
Phantasmal	84095	To ship
Phantasy ...	84096	Can you ship
Phantom ...	84097	Cannot ship
Pharaon ...	84098	In case you can ship
Pharetra ...	84099	In case you cannot ship
Pharias ..	84100	You should not ship
Pharicien	84101	Ship as much as you can not later than
Pharmacy...	84102	Expect to be able to ship viâ —— during the next three months

Pharnaceon	34103	About what time can you ship
Pharyngeal	34104	Ship as speedily as possible this number
Phaselinus	34105	Ship as much as you possibly can
Phasganion	34106	Cable how much you are likely to ship up to [or before
Phasiana ...	34107	Do you anticipate being able to ship to the value of —— on
Phellodrys	34108	If you can ship this quantity cable probable tonnage and value
Phenakite...	34109	Hope to ship before —— at least —— tons approximate value
Phengites	34110	Will ship at least —— on or before
Phenomatic	34111	Will ship as much as I (we) possibly can
Phenomenon	34112	Have not been able to ship owing to
Phenylene	34113	Will have to ship the ore to
Phenylic ...	34114	Shall be able to ship the ore (——) (viâ)
Pheretrum	34115	Shall you be able to ship the ore (——) (viâ)
Phials ...	34116	Shall not be able to ship the ore (——) (viâ)
Phiditia ...	34117	What quantity and approximate value of ore will you be able to [ship up to (before)
Philautia ...	34118	What quantity (value) of bullion will you be able to ship [up to
Philetes ...	34119	Will be able to ship —— tons of ore approximate value
Philibeg ...	34120	Will be able to ship —— ozs. of bullion approximate value
Philippic ...	34121	At what rate do you expect you can ship
Philologia...	34122	Shall be able to ship at the rate of —— per month
Philomath	34123	When can you ship the
Philomel ...	34124	Shall be able to ship the —— not later than
Philomusus	34125	Send by first ship
Philosophy	34126	Ship as early as possible
Philyra ...	34127	Ship by quickest route
Phlebotomy	34128	Ship by the cheapest route
Phlegm ..	34129	Ship part immediately, remainder to follow afterwards
Phlegmatic	34130	Have arranged to ship part immediately, remainder about
Phlegmona	34131	Unable to ship at the present time
Phlegontis	34132	Should you be unable to ship
Phloginos...	34133	I am (we are) quite unable to ship
Phlogiston	34134	Do not ship until you receive further instructions
Phlorol ...	34135	When do you expect to ship freely
Phonascus	34136	Will it pay to ship
Phonograph	34137	Will not pay to ship
Phormion...	34138	What will pay to ship
Phosphate	34139	Will pay to ship
Phosphoric	34140	**Shipment(s)** (*See also* " Keep," " Last.")
Photogene	34141	Crowd the shipments as much as possible
Photometer	34142	What is the amount of your shipments for the past week
Phragmis ...	34143	What is the amount of shipments for the past month
Phraseless	34144	In future all shipments
Phraseur ...	34145	When will you make the next shipment(s)
Phrasing ...	34146	Shipments maintained
Phrenesis ...	34147	Shipments about average
Phrenology	34148	Shipments increasing
Phrygianus	34149	Shipments decreasing
Phrygio ...	34150	Shipments delayed through
Phthisical...	34151	What has caused (is causing) delay of shipment
Phthisique	34152	Will not cause any delay in shipments for the future
Phthitarus	34153	Stop all shipments until
Phthongus	34154	What do the total shipments since —— amount to
Phycitis ...	34155	Total shipments since —— amount to
Phygethlon	34156	Do all you can to expedite the shipment of
Phylacista	34157	Next shipment will be made not later than
Phylactery	34158	Cannot make any shipments meanwhile (until)
Phylarchus	34159	Shipment will be made as soon as the roads permit
Phyletics ...	34160	Am (are) now ready for shipment

Phyrama ...	84161	Report tonnage and approximate value ready for shipment
Physeter ...	84162	I (we) have —— tons approximate value —— ready for [shipment
Physician	84163	Continue shipments
Physics ...	84164	Discontinue shipments meanwhile
Physiker ...	84165	Continue shipments steadily
Physique ...	84166	Continue shipments; cable any stoppage
Phyteuma	84167	You should arrange for shipments before —— to the value of
Phytology	84168	When will you realize shipments [not less than
Piacentare	84169	What have shipments to —— realized
Piacersi ...	84170	Monthly shipments of bars average [returns
Piaceruzzo	84171	Shipments during the month of —— will amount to —— net
Piacevole ...	84172	Shipments during the month of —— will amount to —— gross [returns
Piache ...	84173	The value of shipments for the present month will amount to
Piacimento	84174	The value of shipments for the month of —— amount to
Piacularis...	84175	Please send particulars of shipments
Piaculous...	84176	Shipments suspended
Piadoso ...	84177	How long are shipments likely to be suspended
Piafador ...	84178	Every indication of suspension of shipments
Piagato ...	84179	Shipments delayed through present severe weather
Piaggiare ...	84180	Shipments delayed owing to
Piaghetta...	84181	Large shipments are now being made
Piagnente	84182	Payable one-third on shipment; balance on ——
Piagnisteo	84183	Payable two-thirds on shipment; balance on ——
Piagnitore	84184	Same as last shipment
Piagnoloso	84185	Cable shipments
Piaguzzia...	84186	Cable shipments for last month
Piailler ...	84187	Cable shipments for current month
Piallaccio...	84188	Shipments this month amount to —— tons
Piallatore...	84189	Shipments last month amounted to —— tons
Piamadre ...	84190	Shipments this week
Piamater ...	84191	Shipments last week
Piamentum	84192	Shipments this year to date
Pianamente	84193	Duplicate last shipments
Piandus ...	84194	Delay shipments until further advised
Pianellata	84195	Delay shipments as long as you can
Pianetto ...	84196	When do you expect to begin shipments
Piangendo	84197	Hope to begin shipments not later than
Piangevole	84198	When shall you (will they) commence shipments of
Piangitore	84199	I (we) cannot commence shipments on account of
Piangoloso	34200	Cable number of last shipment
Pianigiano	34201	Cable full particulars and value of shipments
Pianissimo	34202	Shipments stopped owing to
Pianist ...	34203	Shipments stopped as teams cannot haul on account of roads
Pianoforte	34204	Cease all shipments
Pianograph	34205	Expected shipments to —— to total —— tons
Piantabile	34206	Telegraph when you will complete whole of shipment
Piantadoso	34207	We shall commence shipment of ——
Piantatore	34208	Is shipment begun
Pianura ...	34209	Shipments are now being realized; will report as soon as I am
Piariego ...	34210	Shipments to —— have realized [(we are) able to
Piastra ...	34211	What is the net value of the shipments
Piastrella ...	34212	The net value of the shipments is
Piastrino ...	34213	Push shipments forward as much as you can
Piatire ...	34214	What is your opinion as to prospective shipments
Piatteria ...	34215	**Shipped** (*See also* "Ballast.")
Piattola ...	34216	When was it shipped
Piattolone	34217	Was shipped on —— per ——
Piattonata	34218	How much have you shipped
Piaulard ...	34219	The quantity shipped is

Piazza ...	34220	Will be shipped not later than ——
Piazzetta ...	34221	Will be shipped not later than this week
Pibroch ...	34222	Will be shipped
Picacero ...	34223	Have already shipped —— tons
Picadillo ...	34224	Should you not have already shipped
Picadura ...	34225	Have you shipped
Picagrega...	34226	I (we) have shipped
Picante ...	34227	I (we) have not shipped
Picapiojos	34228	Must be shipped not later than
Picaposte ...	34229	Will be shipped at once
Picarazo ...	34230	I (we) have shipped all there is
Picaresca ...	34231	On the —— inst., I (we) shipped
Picaron ...	34232	How much have you shipped since
Picatus ...	34233	Have you shipped any ore since
Picayune ...	34234	Have shipped since
Piccarsi ...	34235	Have shipped —— tons of ore to mills since
Picchiere ...	34236	What quantity of ore have you shipped since —— and what
		[does the value amount to
Piccinacco	34237	Have shipped —— tons since ——, estimated value ——
Piccolello ...	34238	Have shipped —— tons since last advice
Piccolezza	34239	Expected to have shipped more but have been prevented by
Picconajo...	34240	What is the tonnage and approximate value of ore shipped
		[this year
Picconiere	34241	Since January 1st we have shipped —— tons, approximate
Piccozzino	34242	**Shippers** [value ——
Piceaster ...	34243	Who is (are) the shipper(s)
Pichel ...	34244	Shipper(s) is (are)
Picheleria...	34245	Informed by shipper(s)
Pichenette	34246	**Shipping** (*See also* "Finished.")
Pickaxes ...	34247	As soon as we can commence shipping
Pickerel ...	34248	When will you commence shipping
Pickling ..	34249	When do you expect to recommence shipping
Picklock ...	34250	Shall commence shipping on or about
Pickpocket	34251	Commence shipping on or about
Picnicker ...	34252	Recommence shipping on or about
Picnostilo...	34253	Shall not recommence shipping until
Picoteado...	34254	Shipping as rapidly as possible
Picotillo ...	34255	We are now shipping —— tons per day
Picramic ...	34256	We are now shipping to the mills —— tons of ore per day
Pictatium...	34257	**Shoot** (*See also* "Chimney," "Chute," "Ore Chute," &c.)
Pictilis ...	34258	The shoot has gradually died out
Pictorial ...	34259	Hope to meet shoot within another —— feet
Pictorius ...	34260	The shoot is improving
Picturatus	34261	**Shore(d)**
Pictured ...	34262	On shore
Picudilla ...	34263	To shore up
Pidientero	34264	Has (have) been shored up meanwhile
Pidocchio...	34265	**Short(s)**
Piebald ...	34266	Short of
Piecework	34267	Short about
Piedad ...	34268	It is (they are) too short
Piedness	34269	Owing to short supply of
Piegamento	34270	Short shift
Pieghetta ...	34271	Are you (is ——) at all short of
Pieghevole	34272	Am (is) not at all short of
Piegolina ...	34273	By which time I (we) shall be short of
Pielago ...	34274	Can you complete within the short time available
Pienamente	34275	Cannot complete in so short a time
Pienso ...	34276	The time is a little too short
Pierglass ...	34277	The time is short, but will do my (our) best

Pierhead ...	34278	The time is far too short
Pierraille ...	34279	Cannot possibly be done in so short a time
Pierreries...	34280	I am (we are) getting anxious, as the time is now so short
Pierreux ...	34281	Will then be short of
Pietanza ...	34282	Am (are) not short of funds
Pietism ...	34283	Am (are) very short of
Pietistic ...	34284	Should you run short you had better
Pietosetto	34285	Can only stay a short time
Pietrame ...	34286	Regret my (our) time is too short to call
Pietrella ...	34287	In a short time
Pieusement	34288	Too short by
Pieviale ...	34289	Not short enough by
Pifano ...	34290	Prompt action necessary as time is short
Pifferello ...	34291	A short line
Pifferina ...	34292	Could you not construct a short line between —— and ——
Pigargo ...	34293	**Shorten**
Pigendus ...	34294	**Shortening**
Pigeonnier	34295	**Shortest**
Pigeons ...	34296	On the shortest line possible
Piggery ...	34297	Shortest line possible
Piggiorare	34298	What is the shortest line
Piggishly ..	34299	The shortest line is
Pigheaded	34300	**Shortly**
Pigherta ...	34301	**Shortness**
Pigiatore ...	34302	**Should**
Pigliare ...	34303	Should have
Piglievole...	34304	Should not have
Pigmean ...	34305	Should you (——)
Pignataro...	34306	Should you not
Pignatello	34307	You should certainly
Pigneratus	34308	You should certainly not
Pigneror ...	34309	Should be
Pignocher	34310	Should not be
Pignorato...	34311	Should have been
Pignoticos	34312	Should not
Pignut ...	34313	Should not —— be ——
Pigolone ...	34314	Should not have been
Pigramente	34315	Should be done immediately
Pigrezza ...	34316	In case I (we) should not
Pijote ...	34317	In case I (we) should
Pikeman ...	34318	In case you should
Pikestaff ...	34319	In case you should not
Pilastrata...	34320	This should enable me (us)
Pilastrone	34321	This should suffice
Pilchard ...	34322	This should have been seen to
Pildora ...	34323	Should be with you about
Pileatus ...	34324	**Shovel(s)**
Pileolum ...	34325	—— dozen shovels
Pilferer ...	34326	**Show(s)**
Pilfering ...	34327	To show
Pilgern ...	34328	Consent(s) to show
Pilgrimage	34329	All —— (he) could show was
Pililudius...	34330	Only show(s) that
Pillage ...	34331	I (we) should like to show
Pillared ...	34332	You can show
Pillastro ...	34333	You had better not show
Pillion ...	34334	When I (we) shall be able to show
Pilloletta ...	34335	Does not this show
Pillorize ...	34336	Would seem to show that
Pillottato ...	34337	It certainly shows

Pillowcase	34338	I (we) do not think it shows
Pilonero ...	34339	In case —— will not show
Pilorcio ...	34340	In case —— will show you
Pilorier ...	34341	Who will show me (us)
Pilotage ...	34342	—— will show you
Pilotfish ...	34343	This should show you
Piloting ...	34344	This will show you (how)
Pilotry ...	34345	He (——) did not show.
Piltraca ...	34346	Unable to show
Pimbeche...	34347	Able to show
Pimelic ...	34348	You might show it (this) to
Pimentado	34349	It would not be safe to show anything
Pimentero	34350	Please show him (——) all attention
Pimpant ...	34351	Show him (——) every politeness but do not let him see more
Pimpernel	34352	Refuse(s) to show [than you can help (of)
Pimpinella	34353	I (we) have refused to show
Pimpled ...	34354	Would it be wise to refuse to show
Pimpollar...	34355	It would not be wise to refuse to show
Pinabete ...	34356	Do (did) not intend to show
Pinacoteca	34357	Do you intend to show
Pinaculo ...	34358	Shows up very well
Pinafore ...	34359	Does not show up at all well
Pinariego...	34360	Show him (them) my letter dated
Pincelote ...	34361	May I show —— your letter dated
Pincerna ...	34362	Do not show —— my letter dated
Pincettes ...	34363	**Showed**
Pinchauvas	34364	Showed him every attention
Pinching ...	34365	This (it) showed immediately that
Pincho ...	34366	Which showed
Pinchpenny	34367	—— showed plainly enough
Pindaresco	34368	**Showing** (See also " Fine.")
Pindaric ...	34369	A better showing
Pineapple...	34370	Require a better showing
Pinetum ...	34371	Has a better showing than I anticipated
Pinewool ...	34372	Excellent showing
Pingajo ...	34373	**Shown** (See also " Exclusively.")
Pinganitos	34374	**Showy**
Pingente ...	34375	Very showy
Pingersi ...	34376	**Shrewd**
Pinguedine	34377	Reputed to be very shrewd
Pinguiter...	34378	**Shut**
Pinguitudo	34379	Shut out
Pinholed ...	34380	Must be shut out
Pinifero ...	34381	Has (have) been shut out
Pinioning...	34382	Not shut out
Pinite ...	34383	Is trying to shut out
Pinjante ...	34384	Trying to shut out
Pinmaker...	34385	You must take care not to be shut out from
Pinmaking	34386	**Shut down**
Pinmoney...	34387	To shut down
Pinnace ...	34388	Shut down owing to
Pinniger ...	34389	Has (have) shut down
Pinnirapus	34390	Has (have) not shut down
Pinnula ...	34391	Will be shut down until
Pinocha ...	34392	Has (have) been shut down since
Pinpoints...	34393	You had better shut down the mine
Pinsitor ...	34394	Has (have) been obliged to shut down for repairs
Pintacilgo	34395	At present shut down for repairs
Pintamonas	34396	During which time the —— will be shut down for repairs
Pintarojo...	34397	How long will the —— be shut down for repairs

Pin—Pis

Pintica ...	34398	Will be shut down for —— days.
Pintiparar	34399	Have been obliged to shut down for —— days, owing to
Pintorrear	34400	Before you shut down (the)
Pinzacchio	34401	Arrange this before you shut down
Pinzas ...	34402	**Shut up**
Pinzote ...	34403	It will be necessary to shut up
Piocher ...	34404	Visited —— and found that everything was shut up
Pioggioso...	34405	**Sick**
Piojento ...	34406	Is (are) sick from
Piojeria ...	34407	We have now —— men very sick (with)
Piojicida ...	34408	Has (have) been a little sick, but is (am) quite well again
Piojillo ...	34409	Is sick and unable to attend to his duties
Piombaria	34410	Is sick and obliged to leave for
Piombatura	34411	Is sick and anxious to return to
Pioneered...	34412	Have granted sick leave for
Pionnier ...	34413	Is very sick, doctors fear serious result
Piorno ...	34414	Am sick and think it would be wise to go to —— and recruit
Piovanato...	34415	Family sick
Piovevole ...	34416	Sick of the whole business
Pipefish ...	34417	**Sick List**
Piperack ...	34418	How many men have you now on the sick list
Piperia ...	34419	Sick list increasing daily, we have now —— men down
Piperitis ...	34420	Sick list lessening, we have now only —— men down
Pipestem ...	34421	**Sickly**
Pipilare ...	34422	**Sickness**
Pipitana ...	34423	**Side(s)**
Pippionata	34424	Engage(d) on our side
Piquenique	34425	Engaged on the other side
Piquetero...	34426	On which side is
Piragon ...	34427	On one side of
Piramidal...	34428	On the north side
Piramista ...	34429	On the south side
Piratear ...	34430	On the east side
Piraterie ...	34431	On the west side
Piratical ...	34432	By the side (of)
Pirausta ...	34433	At the side (of)
Piroetta ...	34434	On the side (of)
Piromancia	34435	From the side (of)
Pironomia	34436	From both sides (of)
Pirotecnia	34437	From one side (of)
Pirronico ...	34438	From the other side (of)
Pirschen ...	34439	On the other side of the
Pisador ...	34440	On each side (of)
Pisafalto	34441	Side line to the —— drift
Pisauvas ...	34442	On the north side line
Pisaverde...	34443	On the south side line
Piscarius ...	34444	On the east side line
Piscatory ...	34445	On the west side line
Piscatrix ...	34446	On which side are you driving
Pisciacane	34447	On your side
Pisciatura	34448	Side line
Pisciceps ...	34449	End and side lines
Pisciculus...	34450	End of side line
Piscina ...	34451	**Sieve(s)** (See also " Grate," " Screens.")
Piscinalis ...	34452	**Sight** (See also " Reserve.")
Pisellajo ...	34453	In sight
Piselletto ...	34454	Not in sight
Pisillum ...	34455	Draw at —— days' sight
Pisonear ...	34456	Do not draw at sight
Pisoteo ...	34457	Have drawn on you at seven days' sight

Pispiglio ...	34458	Have drawn on you at thirty days' sight
Pispissare...	34459	Have drawn on you at sixty days' sight
Pispoletta	34460	Likely to lose the sight of one eye
Pisseleon ...	34461	Has destroyed the sight of one eye
Pissoceros	34462	Has destroyed the sight of both eyes
Pistacia ...	34463	Not in sight at present
Pistagnone	34464	Report the tonnage and value of the ore in sight
Pistolenza	34465	There is no ore actually in sight
Pistolete ...	34466	The quantity of ore in sight is only —— tons
Pistoresa ..	34467	Estimated value of the ore in sight
Pistorius ...	34468	What is the approximate value of the ore in sight
Pistrage ...	34469	Shall require to make my own survey before I can determine [the tonnage of the ore in sight
Pistrensis...	34470	Shall not be able to report the tonnage of the ore in sight until
Pistrino ...	34471	Estimate(s) the ore in sight at —— tons, approximate value [——, do you confirm this
Pitafflo ...	34472	Can confirm estimate as to the tonnage and value of ore in sight
Pitahaya ...	34473	Can confirm estimate as to the tonnage, but not as to the [value of the ore in sight
Pitanceria	34474	Cannot confirm ——'s estimate either as to the value or as to
Pitanoso ...	34475	Nothing in sight [the tonnage of the ore in sight
Pitapat ...	34476	**Sign(s)** (*See also* " Falling.")
Pitarra ...	34477	To sign
Pitchfork ..	34478	Not to sign
Pitchpipe...	34479	Will sign
Pitetto ...	34480	Refuse(s) to sign
Pitezna ...	34481	Do not sign
Pithaules ..	34482	Have you met with any sign of
Pithecium	34483	There is no sign at present of
Pithiness ...	34484	There is every sign that we are closely adjacent to
Pitiless ...	34485	Should you see any sign
Pitizione ...	34486	Had better not sign until you receive further instructions
Pitoccare ...	34487	Refuse(s) to sign the contract
Pitocchino	34488	Has (have) arranged to sign the contract on
Pitofero ...	34489	Do not sign any contract before
Pitonissa ...	34490	Refuses to sign unless he receives
Pitoyable ...	34491	Before you sign you must insist upon
Pittagoreo	34492	Have arranged to meet at —— to sign deeds
Pittance ...	34493	Shall require a Power of Attorney from —— to sign contract
Pittorello ...	34494	Refuse(s) to sign any transfer
Pittrice ...	34495	Sign for me
Pituitaria...	34496	You can sign for ——
Pituitoso ...	34497	Will —— sign
Pitylisma...	34498	—— will sign
Pityocampa	34499	—— will not sign
Piumacetto	34500	**Signature(s)**
Piumato ...	34501	Your signature is required
Piuvicare ...	34502	The following signature(s) is (are) required
Piviere ...	34503	All signatures must be certified by
Pivoine ...	34504	Send specimen signature(s) for
Pivotted ...	34505	Have sent specimen signature(s) for
Pixide ...	34506	Signature(s) improperly attested
Pizarral ...	34507	All signatures must be notarially attested
Piscar ...	34508	**Signed**
Pizcolabis...	34509	Signed by
Pizmiento	34510	Signed on account of
Pizzicante	34511	Was (were) signed
Pizzicotto...	34512	Was (were) not signed
Placabilis...	34513	Has (have) not been signed
Placable ...	34514	Has (have) the document(s) been signed

Placarder ...	84515	Could not be signed owing to
Placativo ...	84516	Hope to get everything signed on
Placaturus	84517	Will no doubt be signed
Placear ...	84518	Get it (them) signed if you possibly can
Placeman ...	84519	Will get it (them) signed if I (we) possibly can
Placentero	84520	Will be signed
Placero ...	84521	Will not be signed
Placidita ...	84522	Should be signed by
Placidly ...	84523	Has (have) been signed by
Placidulus	84524	Has (have) not been signed by
Placiente ...	84525	Who is it (are they) signed by
Placitum ...	84526	Should be signed without delay
Plackerei ...	84527	Transfer signed by the transferor and witnessed by a notary [public should be mailed at once
Plackesel ...	84528	Transfer duly signed mailed on
Plafonnage	84529	Signed and witnessed transfer(s) required; name of trans-
Plafonneur	84530	**Significance** [feree(s) should be left blank
Plagalisch	84531	**Significant(ly)**
Plagegeist	84532	The most significant features
Plagiarism	84533	Is it not significant that
Plagiat ...	84534	Not at all significant
Plagueful...	84535	**Signified**
Plaguespot	84536	Not yet signified
Plagusia ...	84537	Has (have) —— signified
Plaideur ...	84538	Has (have) not signified
Plaidoyer ...	84539	Provided that —— has signified
Plaindre ...	84540	Provided that —— has not signified
Plaintless...	84541	**Signifies**
Plainwork	84542	Only signifies to this extent, viz.:—
Plaisance ...	84543	**Signify**
Planador ...	84544	Do(es) not signify
Planchada	84545	Does it (do they) signify
Planchear...	84546	Do(es) not signify in the slightest degree
Planchette	84547	**Signing**
Planchuela	84548	On signing document(s)
Planeiron ...	84549	Previous to my (our) signing
Planetary ...	84550	Previous to —— (his) signing
Planetree ...	84551	**Silence**
Planga ...	84552	Your (——'s) silence is
Plangens ...	84553	Your (——'s) silence is very embarrassing to the Board
Planicie ...	84554	**Silica**
Planifolio...	84555	**Siliceous**
Planipedia	84556	**Silurian**
Planipes ...	84557	**Silver** (*See also* " Argentiferous," " Assay," " Gold.")
Planished	84558	In silver coin
Plankler ...	84559	Silver mine
Planlos ...	84560	Chloride of silver
Planmassig	84561	Quotation of the day for silver is —— per ounce
Planoplano	84562	Ounces of silver to the ton
Planschen	84563	Ounces of silver per ton of 2,240 lbs.
Plantador...	84564	Ounces of silver per ton of 2,000 lbs.
Plantario ...	84565	—— ingots of silver, weight —— ounces
Plantation	84566	The silver is —— fine
Plantear ...	84567	Horn silver
Plantiger ...	84568	Ruby silver
Plantillar ...	84569	Sulphide of silver
Plantoir ...	84570	Antimonial sulphide of silver
Planudo ...	84571	Sulphide of silver associated with
Plapperer	84572	The silver occurs in carbonate of lead
Plaquer ...	84573	The silver occurs in galena

Plashing ...	34574	Is a very rich silver ore
Plasmador	34575	The deposit is very rich in silver but is pockety
Plasmante	34576	The enclosing matrix of the silver ore is
Plasmatura	34577	A native alloy of gold and silver
Plasterer ...	34578	Some very rich samples of silver ore have been found
Plastering	34579	The silver ore is found in limestone
Plasticare	34580	The silver is valued at —— per ounce
Plasticity ...	34581	The silver has been sold at —— per ounce
Plastico ...	34582	What is the present price of silver per ounce
Plastron ...	34583	**Silver-lead**
Plataforma	34584.	—— tons of silver-lead containing —— ozs. of silver
Platanetto	34585	—— pigs of silver-lead
Plataninus	34586	**Similar**
Platanista	34587	Is it similar
Platanon ...	34588	It is very similar in appearance to
Platazo ...	34589	It is not in any way similar to
Platbord ...	34590	Not similar to
Platebande	34591	Can you obtain any more —— similar to
Plateglass	34592	Let it (them) be as similar as possible to
Plateresco	34593	Very similar to what I (we) had at (in)
Plateria ...	34594	**Similarly**
Platicante...	34595	**Simple**
Platificar ...	34596	**Simplest**
Plating ...	34597	**Simplified**
Platonico ...	34598	**Simplify**
Platoon ...	34599	To simplify matters
Platrage ...	34600	Will not this simplify matters
Platreux ...	34601	This (it) will simplify matters
Platschen...	34602	This (it) will not simplify matters
Platucha ...	34603	Cannot you simplify matters
Platzen ...	34604	Would it simplify matters to
Platzregen	34605	It would considerably simplify matters (if)
Plaudendus	34606	It would simplify matters very little indeed
Plaudern ...	34607	So as to simplify matters
Plauditur...	34608	So as to simplify the accounts
Plausible ...	34609	**Simply**
Plausito ...	34610	**Simultaneous(ly)**
Playacting	34611	Can it (this) be done simultaneously with
Playade ...	34612	Can be done simultaneously
Playbill ...	34613	Cannot be done simultaneously
Playday ...	34614	Provided that this (it) can be done simultaneously
Playgoers	34615	Will proceed simultaneously
Playhouse	34616	**Since**
Playmate ..	34617	Long since
Playwright	34618	Since when
Pleadable...	34619	This is since
Pleadingly	34620	Since last report
Pleamar ...	34621	Since last advice
Plebaglia ...	34622	Since I (we) arrived
Plebano ...	34623	**Sine quâ non**
Plebeaccio	34624	It is a sine quâ non that
Plebecula...	34625	Is it a sine quâ non that
Plebeian ...	34626	It is not a sine quâ non that
Plebiscite ...	34627	Unless it is a sine quâ non that
Plectilis ...	34628	**Single**
Plectrum ...	34629	Either single or double
Pledger ...	34630	**Singly**
Plegadera	34631	Taken singly
Pleinement	34632	Has (have) taken singly
Pleites ...	34633	Should be taken singly

Pleitista ...	34634	**Singular** (*See also* "Number.")
Plenamente	34635	The foregoing word is in the singular number
Plenarily ...	34636	The following word is in the singular number
Plenilunio	34637	**Sink** (*See also* "Begin," "Farther," "Shaft.")
Plenitude ...	34638	To sink
Plenteous...	34639	Think it would be well to sink
Pleonasmus	34640	When and where do you propose to sink
Pleonastic	34641	Think that the best place to sink would be at
Plerique ...	34642	Sink in order to
Plethoric ...	34643	As soon as you can commence to sink
Pleura ...	34644	You had better postpone commencing to sink
Pleurisy ...	34645	Postpone commencing to sink for the present
Pleuritico...	34646	Shall require to sink
Pleuvoir ...	34647	How far have you still to sink
Pliant ...	34648	We have still to sink —— feet
Plicature ...	34649	Sink until
Pliegue ...	34650	Sink shaft
Plinthis ...	34651	Shall at once commence to sink shaft at ——
Plissement	34652	To sink a shaft
Plocamos ...	34653	Must sink the shaft
Plodder ...	34654	Sink winze
Plodding ...	34655	Shall recommence to sink
Plomada ...	34656	When we shall recommence to sink
Plomazon...	34657	Sink upon
Plombagina	34658	To sink in order to
Plomberie	34659	Cannot sink deeper with present appliances
Plongeon ...	34660	Cannot sink deeper without engaging more men [per month
Plorandus	34661	Cannot sink deeper without increasing our expenses at least ——
Plorante ...	34662	Cannot sink deeper without increasing our boiler power
Ploratrix ...	34663	Cannot sink deeper until the —— is altered
Plostellum	34664	Cannot sink deeper until arrival and erection of new machinery
Plotzlich ...	34665	Cannot sink deeper until I (we) have increased pumping
Ploughboy	34666	Cannot sink deeper until shaft is straightened [capacity
Ploughing	34667	Cannot sink deeper until shaft is repaired
Ploughman	34668	Cannot sink deeper until I (we) have increased hoisting tackle
Ploughtail	34669	Cannot sink deeper until I (we) can secure better air
Ploxemum	34670	How much deeper can you sink if
Plucked ...	34671	I am (we are) commencing to sink at this point
Plucking ...	34672	How much further do you propose to sink before
Plumage ...	34673	**Sinking** (*See also* "Commence.")
Plumageria	34674	Commence sinking
Plumario ...	34675	Approve of vigorous sinking
Plumassier	34676	Stop sinking
Plumaturus	34677	Shall begin sinking
Plumbarius	34678	Sinking a winze
Plumblines	34679	Sinking a (the) shaft
Plumbosus	34680	Sinking shaft
Plumcake...	34681	Continue sinking
Plumear ...	34682	Shall continue sinking until
Plumeless...	34683	Shall continue sinking until I (we) receive further instructions
Plumetis ...	34684	Cost of sinking
Plumifero...	34685	Now sinking at the rate of
Plumion ...	34686	Can you not increase rate of sinking
Plumipes ...	34687	Have stopped sinking until
Plumista ...	34688	Stopped sinking through lack of funds
Plummets	34689	Have been obliged to stop sinking because of
Plumpheit	34690	Sinking the (a) vertical shaft
Plumpie ...	34691	Sinking the (an) incline shaft
Plumpness	34692	Shall recommence sinking
Plumtree ...	34693	In order to continue sinking

Plundered	84694	This will enable us to continue sinking
Plundering	84695	If I am (we are) to continue sinking
Pluperfect	84696	Shall stop sinking
Pluralidad	84697	What is the present rate of sinking
Pluralist ...	84698	Our present rate of sinking is —— feet per week
Plurativus	84699	The speed in sinking during the past —— days has been ——
Plurimum	84700	When we shall be able to resume sinking [feet per day
Plusieurs ...	84701	We shall stop sinking in order to
Pluspres ...	84702	During the last —— feet we have been sinking in
Plutocrats	84703	On which side are you sinking
Pluvial ...	84704	Further sinking will be impossible until (unless)
Pluvieux ...	84705	**Sinking Fund** (*See also* "Reserve Fund.")
Plynteria ...	84706	**Siphon(s)**
Pneumatic	84707	Inverted siphon
Pneumonic	84708	Has (have) connected the ditch and siphon
Poacher ...	84709	Has (have) commenced siphon
Poaching ...	84710	No. —— siphon
Pobeda ...	84711	Siphon at
Pobelhaft...	84712	Can be traversed by a siphon
Poblacho ...	84713	**Site(s)** (*See also* "Mill.")
Poblacion...	84714	Suitable site for
Poblador ...	84715	Cost of site
Pobrar ...	84716	Including —— acres for site
Pobremente	84717	Has (have) secured site for
Pobreria ...	84718	Plan showing proposed site
Pobrismo ...	84719	Present site
Pocciare ...	84720	Near the present site
Pocetta ...	84721	Extension of present site
Pochette ...	84722	**Situated**
Pochettim	84723	Situated near
Pochim ...	84724	Where is it (are they) situated
Pochmuhle	84725	Should be so situated as to [on the —— railway
Pocico ...	84726	The mine(s) is (are) situated at ——, near to ——, a station
Pocilga ...	84727	The mine(s) is (are) situated —— miles from ——, a station [on the —— railway
Pocillator...	84728	The property is situated —— miles from
Pocketed ...	84729	Is situated —— miles from the town of
Pocofila ...	84730	**Situation** (*See also* "Inaccessible.")
Pocolina ...	84731	The situation of the property generally is excellent
Poculentus	84732	The situation is a very bad one owing to
Poculo ...	84733	Owing to the present unfortunate situation
Podadera ...	84734	Owing to the inaccessible situation of the property
Podagra ...	84735	On account of the facilities of this (the) situation
Podagrico	84736	Report fully on present situation
Podargus...	84737	Until the situation changes
Podatario...	84738	Situation practically unchanged
Podenco ...	84739	Report any change in situation
Poderetto...	84740	Will advise you of any change in the situation
Poderoso ...	84741	**Size**
Podestadi...	84742	What is about the size
Podesteria	84743	What is the present size of
Podismus...	84744	The present size is —— by ——
Podocarps	84745	What size do you require
Podrecer ...	84746	Cable the size of
Podricion...	84747	Send full particulars as to size
Podrir ...	84748	Should be the same size as the last
Poelonnee	84749	The size of —— is
Poemetto ...	84750	Any size
Poesia ...	84751	Is of no great size at present
Poetaccio ...	84752	Should it assume any size

Poetants ...	34753	**Sketch**
Poetarsi ...	34754	Please send a sketch showing
Poetaster ...	34755	Have sent a sketch
Poetesse ...	34756	Will send a sketch by next mail
Poetical ...	34757	Will send you sketch by next mail
Poetilla ...	34758	Please send sketch as soon as possible
Poetisch ...	34759	Pen and ink sketch
Poetizar ...	34760	**Sketched**
Poeton ...	34761	**Skilled**
Poetuzzo ...	34762	Skilled labour
Poggerello	34763	**Skip**
Poggiato ...	34764	The dimensions of skip are
Poggiolino	34765	Accident to the skip
Poggiuolo	34766	Self-dumping skip
Pogonias ...	34767	The capacity of the skip is —— pounds
Poignarder	34768	**Skipway** (*See also* "Shaft.")
Pointedly ...	34769	The skipway is in perfect order [to repair
Pointement	34770	The skipway is defective, would cost —— and take —— weeks
Pointeur ...	34771	Shall commence to put in the skipway in the shaft
Pointiller ...	34772	**Slag**
Pointless ...	34773	**Slag-heaps**
Pointsman	34774	Old slag-heaps
Poisoner ...	34775	**Slagpot**
Poisonous	34776	Cast iron slagpot to hold
Poissard ...	34777	**Slander**
Poitrail ...	34778	Slander of title
Poitrine ...	34779	**Slant(ing)**
Poivriere ...	34780	**Slate**
Pokeln ...	34781	The hanging wall is slate
Polacca ...	34782	The footwall is slate
Polaristic....	34783	The country rock is slate
Polarize ...	34784	I am (we are) now driving through slate [formation
Polarstern	34785	I (we) have driven out of the lode and am (are) now in slate
Poleadas ...	34786	The formation is slate
Poleaxe ...	34787	Ordinary clay-slate
Polecat ...	34788	**Sleigh(s)**
Poledrino ...	34789	By means of sleighs
Poleita ...	34790	**Slickenside(s)**
Polemical...	34791	Slickensides are frequent
Polemique	34792	Good slickensides
Polemonio	34793	**Slide(s)** (*See also* "Snow.")
Polestar ...	34794	Apprehend danger from slides
Poliandria	34795	Land slide
Poliantes ...	34796	Land slide has occurred at
Poliarquia	34797	**Slight**
Policarpo ...	34798	A slight advantage
Polidero ...	34799	There is just a slight chance (that)
Poliendus...	34800	There is not even a slight chance (that)
Poligala ...	34801	At present the chances are very slight
Poliglota ...	34802	Would be a slight compensation
Poligono ...	34803	Causing slight injury(ies)
Poligrafia ...	34804	Only slight
Polihedro...	34805	The difference is only slight
Polillera ...	34806	**Slightest**
Polilogia ...	34807	Not the slightest
Polimatia...	34808	Not the slightest advantage
Polimentum	34809	There is not the slightest chance of your
Polipetalo	34810	Is there the slightest chance
Poliphant...	34811	Is there the slightest probability (that)
Polipodio ...	34812	There is not the slightest probability (that)

[581]

Polirstahl...	34813	Has not caused the slightest injury
Polishable	34814	**Slightly**
Polishing ...	34815	Slightly inclined
Polisilabo...	34816	Slightly hurt
Polispermo	34817	Only slightly
Polissage ...	34818	Slightly better if anything
Polissoire ...	34819	**Slime(s)**
Politeismo	34820	Assay slimes
Politeness...	34821	Assay of slimes
Politezza	34822	Have assayed slimes, contents negligible
Politica ...	34823	Assay of slimes gives —— gold —— silver
Politician ...	34824	**Slimepits**
Politicone...	34825	**Slip**
Politiker ...	34826	To slip
Politisch ...	34827	To slip away
Politulus ...	34828	Do not let the opportunity slip
Polizetta ...	34829	Will not let the opportunity slip
Polka ...	34830	**Slipped**
Pollajone ...	34831	Slipped away
Pollajuolo...	34832	Slipped through
Pollanca ...	34833	Is supposed to have slipped
Pollarded ...	34834	**Slope(s)**
Pollebbro ...	34835	On a slope of
Pollezzola...	34836	The ground slopes away to the
Pollicaris ...	34837	**Sloping**
Polliceor ...	34838	**Slow**
Pollicitus ...	34839	Much too slow
Pollinctor...	34840	Not too slow
Pollinejo ...	34841	Will be more slow
Polltax ...	34842	Will not be nearly so slow
Pollubrum	34843	The work has been very slow owing to
Polluctura	34844	Progress is very slow at
Polluelo ...	34845	Progress is very slow on account of
Polluendus	34846	How is it that your progress has been so slow
Pollute ...	34847	At the present slow speed
Polluzione	34848	Continue(s) to be very slow
Polmonare	34849	Very slow indeed
Polnischer	34850	**Slowly**
Polografia...	34851	Not so slowly
Polonaise ..	34852	Slowly increasing
Polpaccio ...	34853	Getting on slowly
Polputello	34854	How is it that you are getting on so slowly
Polstern ...	34855	You appear to be progressing very slowly
Poltacchio	34856	Slowly diminishing
Poltiglia ...	34857	More slowly if anything
Poltronear	34858	Slowly improving
Poltroon ...	34859	**Slowness**
Poltruccio	34860	**Sluice(s)**
Poluto ...	34861	As soon as sluices are prepared
Polvareda...	34862	What length of sluices have you
Polveriera...	34863	Can you not increase the length of sluices
Polverino ...	34864	The length of sluices is —— feet
Polveruzza	34865	As soon as I (we) get the new sluice boxes in position
Polvificar ...	34866	Propose to add —— feet of new sluice boxes
Polvillo ...	34867	Cannot increase length of sluices owing to
Polvinar ...	34868	Shall increase length of sluices as soon as
Polvorear...	34869	Sluice boxes
Polvorista	34870	Shall clean up sluice boxes on
Polyandry	34871	Being the proceeds of —— feet of sluices
Polybasic ...	34872	**Sluicing**

Polybutes...	84873	Shall commence sluicing (on) (at)
Polycnemon	84874	Shall stop sluicing (on) (at)
Polygamy...	84875	Commenced sluicing on
Polyglot ...	84876	When shall you commence sluicing
Polygonal...	84877	—— hours sluicing
Polygonius	84878	Shall have to stop sluicing
Polygraph	84879	Sluicing stopped on account of
Polyhedral	84880	**Small**
Polyhistor	84881	Is only small at present
Polyloquus	84882	Will have to be very small
Polymelus	84883	How small should it be
Polymeric...	84884	The chances are somewhat small
Polymorph	84885	Although somewhat small
Polymyxos	84886	Too small
Polyphonic	84887	Too small to justify
Polypodium	84888	Not small enough
Polyptoton	84889	It is too small
Polysperm	84890	**Smaller**
Polytheism	84891	**Smallest**
Polythrix ...	84892	The smallest I (we) have yet had
Polzella ...	84893	**Smelt**
Pomade ...	84894	To smelt
Pomander ..	84895	Recommence to smelt
Pomellato...	84896	As we have to smelt
Pomerium	84897	Is there any necessity to smelt
Pometo ...	84898	Until we have enough to smelt
Pomfolige...	84899	When do you expect to commence to smelt
Pomiciare...	84900	Shall commence to smelt about
Pomifero ...	84901	Shall not be able to smelt before
Pomilius ...	84902	**Smelter(s)**
Pommel ...	84903	From this must be deducted smelter's charges
Pommeraie	84904	Including smelter's charges
Pompatus...	84905	Have you included smelter's charges
Pompearse	84906	Inclusive of smelter's charges
Pomphaft...	84907	Have not received any returns from smelters
Pompholyx	84908	Have you received any returns from smelters
Pompilos ...	84909	Have received the following returns from smelters, viz.:—
Pomposity	84910	**Smelting** (*See also* "Concentrates," "Free.")
Poncage ...	84911	Smelting ore
Poncela ...	84912	Is it a smelting ore
Ponchon ...	84913	Is it not a good smelting ore
Poncteur ...	84914	Fluxes for smelting
Ponderador	84915	For smelting the ore
Ponderatus	84916	Fuel and fluxes for smelting
Ponderer ...	84917	Smelting furnace
Pondeuse ...	84918	Smelting charges
Ponente ...	84919	Smelting plant
Ponentino...	84920	Shut down the smelting plant
Poniard ...	84921	Rates for smelting
Ponitore ...	84922	Now smelting —— tons per day of twenty-four hours
Pontazgo ...	84923	When do you expect to commence smelting
Pontefice ...	84924	Expect to commence smelting on
Ponticita ...	84925	As soon as I (we) begin smelting
Pontiff ...	84926	Contract for smelting ore
Pontificio ...	84927	**Smelting Cost**
Pontonajo...	84928	Add smelting cost of —— per ton
Pontonier...	84929	Deduct smelting cost of —— per ton
Pontura ...	84930	The cost of smelting is
Ponzonar ...	84931	What is the total cost of smelting per ton
Poorhouse	84932	**Smelting Works**

Poorlaws ...	34933	To the smelting works at
Popamiento	34934	Shipped to the smelting works (at)
Popejoan ...	34935	—— tons of ore shipped to the smelting works
Popelens ...	34936	It will be advisable to erect smelting works
Popeseye ...	34937	It would not be advisable to erect smelting works
Popgun ...	34938	Would you advise the erection of smelting works [miles
Popillo ...	34939	The nearest smelting works are situated at —— distant ——
Popinalis ...	34940	Returns from smelting works
Popinator...	34941	What is the proposed capacity of smelting works [would cost
Poplin ...	34942	The plant for smelting works to deal with —— tons per week
Popolaccio	34943	The cost of erection of the necessary plant for smelting works [would amount to
Popolato ...	34944	To this must be added freight of ore to smelting works
Popolesco ...	34945	From this should be deducted freight of ore to smelting works

Smith (*See also* "Blacksmith.")

Popolezza...	34946	
Popoloso ...	34947	Must be a good smith
Poponcino	34948	As general smith
Popote ...	34949	Can you secure a good local smith
Poppaccia...	34950	Have engaged a good smith
Poppatojo	34951	Cannot find a good smith
Poppellina	34952	Complete set of smith's tools
Poppyseed	34953	Smith's anvil
Poppysmus	34954	Smith's anvil, weight about ——

Smooth(ly)

Populace ..	34955	
Populandus	34956	Everything running smoothly
Populatim	34957	Everything was running quite smoothly (when)
Populeon ...	34958	Not at all smoothly

Snow(s) (*See also* "Filled," "Train.")

Populifer ...	34959	
Populneus	34960	Snow blockade
Populous ...	34961	To snow
Poquedad...	34962	Destroyed by snow-slide
Poquisimo	34963	Mine cannot be examined owing to the snow
Porcaccio ...	34964	The snows during the winter are very severe
Porcal ...	34965	There is very little snow
Porcarius ...	34966	Have been delayed owing to snow
Porcastro ...	34967	There is considerable probability of my being kept at —— by
Porcelain ...	34968	Owing to a snow block at [the snow
Porcellana	34969	Traffic entirely disorganised through snow
Porchaison	34970	The traffic is entirely stopped through snow
Porche ...	34971	Have had a heavy fall of snow
Porcheria ...	34972	Snow is now falling heavily
Porchetto ...	34973	Owing to the telegraph wires being broken down by snow
Porcine ...	34974	During a severe snow storm
Porcipelo ...	34975	Lost in the snow
Porculata...	34976	Cannot work on account of the snow
Porculetum	34977	Snow is now —— feet deep on the level
Porcupine...	34978	Cannot travel from here (to ——) on account of the snow
Pordiosear	34979	The snow is beginning to melt
Porfia ..	34980	The roads are impassable from snow-slides
Porfioso ...	34981	It will not be possible to do anything until the snow melts
Porgadero	34982	We shall do this (it) as soon as the snow melts
Porgente ...	34983	We shall have to get supplies in before the snow begins
Porgimento	34984	The snow has entirely gone
Porisma ...	34985	A snow-slide
Porismatic	34986	A snow storm

Snowed up

Porosidad...	34987	
Porousness	34988	The mine is practically snowed up for —— months of the
Porphyrio...	34989	Snowed up, cannot travel to [year
Porpoise ...	34990	How long do you expect to be snowed up
Porporato...	34991	Shall probably be snowed up for another —— weeks

Porquera ...	34992	**Snowing**
Porraceo ...	34993	Now snowing persistently
Porracina...	34994	If snowing continues we shall be blockaded
Porrectio ...	34995	So long as snowing continues
Porreria ...	34996	**So**
Porridge ...	34997	So called
Porrilla ...	34998	So as to
Porringer ...	34999	So long as
Portacappe	35000	If so
Portadera...	**35001**	If not so
Portafogli	35002	Should this not be so
Portafusil	35003	Is this so
Portaguion	35004	**Soda**
Portalazo...	35005	**Sodium**
Portamorso	35006	Sodium amalgam
Portanario	35007	Concentrated sodium amalgam
Portantina	35008	Have you tried sodium amalgam [forward —— pounds
Portanuela	35009	The effect of sodium amalgam is very beneficial; can you
Portapaz ...	35010	Have tried sodium amalgam, but no beneficial effect
Portarsi ...	35011	Chloride of sodium
Portatil ...	35012	Carbonate of sodium
Portatore ...	35013	Hyposulphite of sodium
Portatrice	35014	Nitrate of sodium
Portaturus	35015	Sulphate of sodium
Portcullis...	35016	Sulphide of sodium
Porteballe	35017	**Soft**
Porteclef ...	35018	Very soft
Portecroix	35019	The rock is comparatively soft
Portefaix ...	35020	The rock is becoming more soft
Portemeche	35021	The rock is quite soft and easily mined
Portend ...	35022	The rock is soft and requires to be heavily timbered
Portendere	35023	The rock becomes soft after a short exposure
Portension	35024	Soft enough for
Portentoso	35025	**Softer**
Portepipe...	35026	Progress quicker as the rock has become gradually softer
Porteplume	35027	Not softer
Portequeue	35028	**Sold** (*See also* " Bought," " Buy," " Sell."')
Porterage...	35029	Sold by order of the sheriff
Porteress ...	35030	Have you (has ——) sold
Porteur ...	35031	Should you (——) have sold
Portevent...	35032	Should you (——) not have sold
Portfire ...	35033	I (we) have sold
Portfolio ...	35034	I (we) have not yet sold
Porthmeus	35035	For whom have you sold
Porthole ...	35036	Could not be sold
Porticale ...	35037	Should not be sold
Portiere ...	35038	Must not be sold
Portinajo ...	35039	Not yet sold
Portioned...	35040	Had better be sold
Portioning	35041	Had better be sold at any price it will fetch
Portique ...	35042	Had better be sold by public auction
Portliness...	35043	Had better be sold if possible by private contract
Portrait ...	35044	Will try to get it sold by public auction
Portrayer...	35045	Has (have) been sold by public auction and has (have) realized
Portreeve ...	35046	Has (have) been sold by private contract and has (have)
Portside ...	35047	How much (many) of it (them) have you sold [realized
Portugues	35048	Have you (has ——) sold all of it (them)
Portulaca...	35049	To whom has it (have they) been sold
Portuosus...	35050	When is it likely to be sold
Porvenir ...	35051	Will probably be sold about

Porvida ...	35052	Do you think it likely to be sold
Posamento	35053	I (we) think it very likely to be sold
Posatezza...	35054	So far as I can find out it was previously sold for
Posatuccia	35055	Is reported to have been sold to
Posaune ...	35056	Should it have been sold
Posavergas	35057	In case it has not already been sold
Posciache...	35058	Was sold before your message arrived
Poscritta ...	35059	Was sold at the price named
Posdata ...	35060	Had better be sold if you can get anything above
Poseedor ...	35061	Sold at your limit
Poseido ...	35062	Has (have) sold on your account
Posesorio ...	35063	Has (have) sold above your limit
Poseyente...	35064	Could not be sold at your limit; will you reduce
Posfecha ...	35065	Cannot be sold at
Positional	35066	Cannot be sold; no bids
Positivist ...	35067	Will be sold by
Positivus ...	35068	Is to be sold immediately
Posolatura	35069	Sold for
Posolina ...	85070	Is reported to have been sold by private contract
Posparts ...	35071	Cable how much (many) you have sold
Pospierna...	35072	Everything is to be sold
Posponer ...	35073	Everything has been sold
Posseder ...	35074	Should it be sold will you authorize me to bid up to
Posseduto...	35075	If it is to be sold, I (we) (——) authorize you to bid for (up
Possessus...	35076	Cannot find out whether it is sold or not [to ——)
Possestrix...	35077	Will endeavour to find out whether it is sold or not
Possevole...	35078	Please discover and report whether it is sold or not
Possideo ...	35079	Must not be sold for less than
Postant ...	35080	Will not be sold until
Postcard ...	35081	Have sold —— shares
Postcenium	35082	Have sold 5 shares
Postchaise	35083	Have sold 10 shares
Postdated...	35084	Have sold 15 shares
Posteaquam	35085	Have sold 20 shares
Postelero ...	35086	Have sold 25 shares
Postemato	35087	Have sold 30 shares
Postergar...	35088	Have sold 35 shares
Posteridad	35089	Have sold 40 shares
Posteriore...	35090	Have sold 45 shares
Posthabeo	35091	Have sold 50 shares
Posthaste...	35092	Have sold 55 shares
Posthorn ...	35093	Have sold 60 shares
Posthumous	35094	Have sold 65 shares
Posticcia ...	85095	Have sold 70 shares
Postiche ...	35096	Have sold 75 shares
Posticium...	35097	Have sold 80 shares
Postierli ...	35098	Have sold 85 shares
Postigo ...	35099	Have sold 90 shares
Postilador	35100	Have sold 95 shares
Postillato ...	35101	Have sold 100 shares
Postillion ...	35102	Have sold 200 shares
Postilloso...	35103	Have sold 300 shares
Postlude ...	35104	Have sold 400 shares
Postmark...	35105	Have sold 500 shares
Postmitto...	35106	Have sold 600 shares
Postmodum	35107	Have sold 700 shares
Postparto...	35108	Have sold 800 shares
Postponed	35109	Have sold 900 shares
Postponing	35110	Have sold 1,000 shares
Postquam...	35111	Will certainly not be sold

Postracion	35112	All to be sold as they stand
Postremas	35113	Over-sold
Postremior	35114	Under-sold
Postrer ...	35115	**Solely**
Postrimero	35116	Solely for your own use
Postschiff...	35117	**Solicitor(s)** (*See also* "Company," "Lawyer.")
Postscribo	35118	Do you know a good firm of solicitors at ——
Postulador	35119	Are very good solicitors at ——
Postulant...	35120	You had better engage a good solicitor
Postulatio	35121	Can I engage a good solicitor
Posturize ...	35122	Take advice of a good solicitor and report
Postutto ...	35123	What does solicitor advise
Postwagen	35124	Solicitor advises us (you) to proceed
Postzug ...	35125	Solicitor advises us (you) to compromise at anything under ——
Posvedere...	35126	Solicitor strongly advises me (us) to compromise
Potable ...	35127	Solicitor thinks our case is very weak
Potaggio ...	35128	Solicitor thinks that we have a very strong case
Potagier ...	35129	Am (are) to have an interview with solicitor on
Potamantis	35130	——'s solicitor is of opinion that
Potashes ...	35131	——'s solicitors are [arrangement
Potasio ...	35132	——'s solicitor has met ours and they have come to the following
Potations..	35133	Could our solicitor come to any arrangement with ——'s
Potatoes ...	35134	Should be drawn up by solicitor
Potatory ...	35135	Do nothing except upon advice of solicitor
Potboy ...	35136	Our solicitors wish to retain ——, his fee is
Potencial ...	35137	You had better arrange with solicitor to retain
Potentado	35138	My solicitor(s) is (are)
Potentatus	35139	Have placed the matter in the hands of my (our) solicitor(s)
Potentilla...	35140	Otherwise shall be compelled to place the matter in the hands [of my (our) solicitor(s)
Potently ...	35141	Are ——'s solicitors taking any steps in the matter
Potenziale	35142	So far ——'s solicitors have not taken any steps at all
Poterium ...	35143	Have been served with a notice from ——'s solicitors
Poterna ...	35144	Who is (are) acting as solicitor(s) to the owner
Potestad ...	35145	Solicitor(s) advise(s) that I (we) cannot
Potesteria	35146	**Solid**
Pothanger	35147	**Soluble**
Potherb ...	35148	**Solution**
Pothook ...	35149	—— solution would I believe be very effectual
Potionatus	35150	A solution process
Potiron ...	35151	**Solvency**
Potisimo ...	35152	**Solvent**
Potiuncula	35153	Is (are) perfectly solvent
Potlid ...	35154	Is (are) believed to be solvent, but I (we) have grave doubts
Potorius ...	35155	Must ascertain if he is (they are) perfectly solvent
Potranca ...	35156	Have ascertained that he is (they are) perfectly solvent
Potrilla ...	35157	Do you consider him (them) solvent
Potroso ...	35158	Is (are) considered perfectly solvent
Potsherd ...	35159	Is (are) —— solvent
Potstone ...	35160	What solvent is employed
Pottasche...	35161	Employ as a solvent
Pottering...	35162	Solvent employed
Potulentus	35163	**Some**
Potvaliant	35164	Some time
Poucettes ...	35165	Can I have some
Poudrette...	35166	Do you know some one who
Pouffer ...	35167	Can you find some one
Pouflasse ...	35168	Will try to find some one
Pouilleux ...	35169	Some one
Poulaille ...	35170	For some

Poularde ...	35171	For some time
Poulette ...	35172	For some time past
Pouliche ...	35173	For some time to come
Pouliniere	35174	Can you advise some means to
Poulterer ...	35175	Some means to
Poulticing	35176	By some way or other
Poumon ...	35177	Endeavour in some way
Pouncebox	35178	From some or other
Poundage...	35179	Some more
Pounding...	35180	Some of it
Poupard ...	35181	Should be glad to have some
Pourboire...	35182	Some other means to
Pourparler	35183	Some other method
Pourquoi ...	35184	**Somehow**
Pourriture	35185	**Something**
Pourvoyeur	35186	Will endeavour to do something immediately in it
Pouvoir ...	35187	Something should be settled
Poveraglia	35188	When will something be settled
Poverello ...	35189	Something ought to be done at once
Poverty ...	35190	Something ought to be done at once or trouble will ensue
Powdered...	35191	Something would seem to be wrong with
Powdering	35192	Unless something can be done
Powerful ...	35193	Can you suggest something better
Poyatos ...	35194	Something has occurred which
Pozanco ...	35195	Cable whether you think that something can be done with it
Poziorita ...	35196	**Somewhat** [(this)
Pozzolana	35197	Somewhat like
Prachtig ...	35198	**Son**
Practicar ...	35199	Is a son of
Practised ...	35200	Is —— a son of
Pradal ...	35201	Is not a son of
Praderoso...	35202	**Soon**
Pragestock	35203	As soon as
Pragmatist	35204	As soon as possible
Prahler ...	35205	Is this too soon
Prahlhans	35206	Is too soon yet
Prairie ...	35207	Is not too soon
Praktikant	35208	How soon will you be able to
Praktisch...	35209	How soon will you be able to do this
Praliner ...	35210	How soon can you let him (us) have it
Pranced ...	35211	Will let you have it as soon as possible
Prandipeta	35212	Must be done soon if it is to be done at all
Prandium...	35213	It will be soon enough for this (if)
Pranger ...	35214	Will be soon enough for this
Pranking ...	35215	Will this be too soon
Pransorius	35216	It will be too soon
Pranzare ...	35217	It will not be too soon
Prasinatus	35218	How soon will you be ready for
Prasiniani	35219	How soon must I (we)
Prasoides ...	35220	How soon will you be ready to
Prasseln ...	35221	How soon will it (they) be required
Pratajuola	35222	You must do this as soon as you possibly can
Pratellina...	35223	Will be quite soon enough
Pratensis ...	35224	Will not be soon enough
Prateria ...	35225	Will this be soon enough
Praticare ...	35226	If anything it is too soon
Praticello...	35227	If not soon enough
Praticien ...	35228	**Sooner**
Pratingly...	35229	Sooner than
Pratique ...	35230	Sooner than anticipated

Pratolino ...	35231	The sooner the better
Prattler ...	35232	The sooner you can leave the better
Pravedad ...	35233	The sooner you can settle matters the better
Pravicors ...	35234	By —— at latest; if possible sooner
Pravitas ...	35235	**Soonest**
Prayerbook	35236	**Sorry**
Prayerless	35237	You will be sorry to learn (that)
Preaching	35238	You will be sorry to learn that ——'s illness has terminated
Preachment	35239	I am (we are) very sorry to learn (that) [fatally
Preadamite	35240	I am (we are) very sorry to have to cable that
Prealable ...	35241	Very sorry to know
Preambulo	35242	Very sorry I (we) cannot accept
Prebendary	35243	I am (we are) very sorry that you cannot see your way to
Prebendier	35244	Sorry to see
Prebestad	35245	Sorry to hear
Precandus	35246	**Sort**
Precario ...	35247	To sort
Precatory ...	35248	Will sort
Precatrix ...	35249	Cannot sort
Precaver ...	35250	What sort of man do you want
Preceder ...	35251	The sort of man required is one who
Precepteur	35252	Would —— (he) be the sort of man you want
Precepto ...	35253	Is just the sort of man
Precesion ...	35254	Is hardly the sort of man
Precessore	35255	Is it necessary to sort out
Precettivo	35256	It is not necessary to sort
Precher ...	35257	**Sorted**
Preciador ...	35258	As soon as it is sorted
Precidere ...	35259	It is necessary that the ore should be carefully sorted
Precieuse ...	35260	I (we) have now —— tons of ore sorted and ready for shipment
Precincts ...	35261	Ore broken but not sorted
Precintas ...	35262	Ore broken, not sorted, —— tons, approximate value
Preciosa ...	35263	Please cable the tonnage of ore sorted [and not sorted
Preciously	35264	Please cable the tonnage and approximate value of ore broken
Precipicio...	35265	We divide the sorted ores into —— grades
Precipitar	35266	**Sorters**
Precisado...	35267	I (we) have now —— sorters engaged
Preciser ...	35268	Shall increase ore sorters to
Preclaro ...	35269	Shall require —— additional ore sorters
Precluded...	35270	**Sorting**
Precocity ...	35271	Sorting ore
Preconceit	35272	Without any sorting
Preconizar	35273	Now sorting
Precordial	35274	Not sorting
Precorrere	35275	In sorting house(s)
Precoz ...	35276	**Sought**
Precursor...	35277	Sought for
Predamento	35278	Sought after
Predation...	35279	Much sought for
Predatore...	35280	Not much sought for
Predatrice	35281	Is (are) sought after
Predecesor	35282	Is it (are they) at all sought after
Predefinir	35283	Is (are) not sought after to any extent
Predellone	35284	Likely to be sought after
Predestine	35285	Not at all likely to be sought after
Predial ...	35286	In the event of it (this) being sought after
Predicable	35287	It (this) should be sought after (for)
Predicador	35288	Should it (this) be sought after (for)
Predicanza	35289	In case it (they) should not be sought after
Predicho ...	35290	**Sound(ly)**

Predict ...	35291	Not sound
Predigen ...	35292	Perfectly sound
Predilecto...	35293	Not at all sound
Prediolo ...	35294	Found to be perfectly sound
Predire ...	35295	Has (have) every appearance of being quite **sound**
Predominar	35296	Only a small portion is sound
Preeligido	35297	Only a small portion was sound
Preescelso	35298	Could not have been sound when sent
Preexistir...	35299	A perfectly sound casting
Prefaced ...	35300	**Source**
Prefacio ...	35301	The source is (was) a reliable one
Prefectura	35302	Do you consider the source reliable
Preferente	35303	The source is (was) not in any way reliable
Preferible...	35304	What is the source of
Prefiggere	35305	**South(erly)** (*See also* "North.")
Prefigurar	35306	South part of the mine (property)
Prefijar ...	35307	South cross-cut
Prefixing ...	35308	South drift
Pregaria ...	35309	Due north and south
Pregevole...	35310	South east
Pregheria...	35311	South west
Pregiabile	35312	In a southerly direction
Pregiarsi ...	35313	In a south easterly direction
Pregiatore	35314	Has a southerly trend
Pregionato	35315	South of
Preglacial ..	35316	To the south of
Pregnancy	35317	At —— degrees to the south of
Pregnezza...	35318	South end line
Pregonar ...	35319	South side line
Pregoneria	35320	On the south of
Pregunta ...	35321	Turns a little to the south
Pregustare	35322	The south vein (lode) (reef)
Prehendens	35323	South shaft
Prehensile	35324	In the south end
Prehnitic ...	35325	Driving south
Preinserto	35326	Now going south
Preisen ...	35327	Coming in from the south
Preisfrage	35328	Dipping south
Prejuger ...	35329	Lying to the south
Prejuicio ...	35330	The most southerly
Prelacy ...	35331	South wall
Prelasser ...	35332	South winze
Prelatical ...	35333	South workings
Prelatist ...	35334	**Space**
Prelection	35335	**Spacious**
Prelever ...	35336	**Spare**
Prelibare ...	35337	To spare
Preliminar	35338	Can you spare
Prellerei ...	35339	Cannot spare
Prelodato...	35340	When will you be able to spare
Prelusion ...	35341	Shall be able to spare —— about
Prelusory ...	35342	For how long will you be able to spare
Prematica...	35343	As soon as you can spare
Prematuro	35344	As soon as I (we) can spare
Premettere	35345	How much time can you spare
Premiador	35346	Can only spare —— days
Premiativo	35347	When I expect to be able to spare
Premisa ...	35348	How much (many) can you conveniently **spare**
Premitir ...	35349	Could spare us
Premocion	35350	Cannot spare any

Premorire...	35351	Do not spare yourself
Premunito	35352	Do not spare any expense
Premutare	35353	Will not spare myself
Prenable ...	35354	Spare parts for
Prenarrare	35355	Spare parts of
Prendador	35356	A spare machine
Prendedero	35357	**Sparingly**
Prenderia...	35358	Sparingly associated with
Prendibile	35359	**Speak**
Prendido ...	35360	To speak
Prenditoro	35361	Speak to —— about
Prenotar ...	35362	Will speak to —— about
Prensadura	35363	No need to speak about
Prensatio ...	35364	**Special(ly)**
Prensista ...	35365	Very special
Prensurus	35366	Not special
Prenuncio...	35367	Special clause
Preocupar	35368	Has (have) specially retained
Preopinar ...	35369	This (it) is of special importance
Preordain...	35370	Must regard this as a special case
Preparar ...	35371	Have special information
Preposito ...	35372	Is there any special reason for
Prepostero	35373	There is no special reason for
Prepotente	35374	Special reason
Prepucio ...	35375	Take special care of
Prepuesto...	35376	I (we) will take special care
Prerutto ...	35377	Did you (he) take special care as to
Presageful	35378	Special care was bestowed upon it (this)
Presagiar ...	35379	Special attention should be paid to
Presagioso	35380	Special attention will be paid to
Presbita ...	35381	Special attention was paid to
Presbyter ...	35382	Have you anything special to report
Prescient ...	35383	Have nothing special to report
Prescindir	35384	The only thing special is
Presciutto	35385	If anything special
Prescripto	35386	**Specie** (*See also* " Coin," " Money.")
Prescrire ...	35387	Payable in specie
Presencial...	35388	Remit in specie
Presentato	35389	Specie arrived
Presenter ...	35390	Box(es) of specie forwarded "care of "
Preservar ...	35391	Specie advised on —— not arrived
Preserving	35392	Specie advised on —— duly received
Presiccio ...	35393	**Specific**
Presidenta	35394	For the specific purpose
Presidiary...	35395	As a specific condition
Presidio ...	35396	**Specific Gravity**
Presilla ...	35397	What is the specific gravity
Presion ...	35398	The specific gravity is
Presomptif	35399	Due to the specific gravity
Presopopea	35400	Depends for its action on specific gravity
Presque ...	35401	**Specifically**
Pressage ...	35402	**Specification(s)** (*See also* " List.")
Pressatura	35403	Complete specification(s)
Pressbed ...	35404	Complete specification(s) mailed
Pressentir...	35405	Complete specification(s) must be furnished
Pressezza ...	35406	Plans and specifications not received, please mail duplicates
Pressgang	35407	Plans and specifications received on
Pressier ...	35408	Is not according to plan(s) and/or specification(s)
Pressmoney	35409	Cannot give specifications required
Pressoche ...	35410	Have complete specifications made out without loss of time

Pressurage	35411	Send specification
Pressureur	35412	Have sent specification
Prestadizo	35413	When will you be able to send specification
Prestador ...	35414	Full specification and estimate
Prestamera	35415	Specification giving following details
Prestamo ...	35416	Obtain from —— specification and estimate for
Prestetto ...	35417	Drawing for specification
Prestigiar ...	35418	**Specified**
Prestinos ...	35419	Unless otherwise specified
Presumenza	35420	Should be distinctly specified
Presuntivo	35421	In specified terms
Presuroso ...	35422	As specified
Pretaccio ...	35423	As specified in line —— page ——
Pretajuolo	35424	Was (were) not specified
Pretatico ...	35425	**Specify(ies)** (*See also* " Expense," " Include.")
Pretended...	35426	To specify
Pretensore	35427	You should specify in your indent
Pretermit ...	35428	You should specify
Pretestar ...	35429	Will fully specify
Pretina ...	35430	Do(es) not specify
Pretinero ...	35431	Please specify for
Pretiosus ...	35432	Will specify for
Pretoirien...	35433	Before you specify
Pretorium	35434	**Specimen(s)**
Pretraille ...	35435	As a specimen
Pretresse ...	35436	Only specimen samples
Prettiness...	35437	Send me (us) specimens of (from the)
Preture ...	35438	Some specimens have been shown to me (us)
Prevailing	35439	From specimens
Prevalenza	35440	Only specimens
Prevalerse	35441	Can you obtain a specimen of
Prevaloir ...	35442	Will obtain and forward specimens
Prevaluto ...	35443	Cannot obtain any specimens
Prevaricar	35444	Have you any other specimens
Prevedere...	35445	Consider it a very good specimen
Prevenant	35446	It is only a poor specimen
Prevenido...	35447	Can you send me good specimens of
Prevertire...	35448	Specimens received
Previlejar...	35449	Specimens not yet to hand
Previsor ...	35450	Selected specimens
Prevoir ...	35451	Only selected specimens assay
Prevostura	35452	Was a specimen only, not intended as an average sample
Prevoyance	35453	**Specious(ly)**
Prewarned	35454	**Speculate(s)**
Prezzabile...	35455	To speculate
Prezzaccio	35456	Do not care to speculate
Prezzatore	35457	Should advise you not to speculate
Prezzemolo	35458	Shall you speculate
Prezzolato	35459	Shall speculate personally to the extent of
Priapismo	35460	Shall not speculate
Priapus ...	35461	Cannot speculate owing to
Prickles ...	35462	**Speculating**
Pridianus...	35463	**Speculation**
Priegare ...	35464	Has (have) been concerned in a (the) speculation
Priegiona ...	35465	Has (have) not been concerned in a (the) speculation
Priestess ...	35466	Just a small speculation
Priesthood	35467	Nothing but a blind speculation
Priestlike ...	35468	What is the outcome of the speculation
Primacia ...	35469	Do you care to join me (us) in a (this) speculation
Primaire ...	35470	Cannot join you in a speculation at present

Primamente	35471	Am (are) afraid the speculation is likely to terminate badly
Primarius...	35472	I (we) think the speculation will terminate well
Primavera	35473	Think it a poor speculation
Primazgo ...	35474	Think it a very good speculation
Primaziale	35475	Advise you to keep out of all such speculations
Primcarse...	35476	Speculation promises well
Primeriza...	35477	Speculation has been very successful
Primeval ...	35478	Speculation has not been at all successful
Primevo ...	35479	The speculation has terminated in a loss of
Primichon	35480	Is not really a speculation
Primicial ...	35481	There is a considerable amount of speculation going on in
Primigenio	35482	The speculation has turned out
Primilla ...	35483	Will join in speculation if
Primipilo ...	35484	Should be glad to join you in any speculation
Primisimo	35485	As a speculation it is most risky
Primitive ...	35486	Through speculation in
Primodum	35487	Entirely through speculation
Primordial	35488	**Speculative**
Primorear	35489	More than speculative
Primpara...	35490	**Speculator(s)**
Primrose ...	35491	A large speculator
Primtone ...	35492	Formerly a large speculator
Princelike	35493	**Speed** (*See also* "Revolution.")
Princess ...	35494	What speed are you making at
Principada	35495	What speed do you anticipate making at ——
Principe ...	35496	Our present speed is
Principino	35497	Average speed per
Pringada ...	35498	Can you not increase speed
Pringon ...	35499	Cannot increase speed until
Pringuera	35500	Hope to increase speed as soon as
Printanier	35501	I hope to maintain this speed [future
Printemps	35502	This (it) will enable us (——) to maintain better speed in
Printing ...	35503	Until this is done I (we) cannot get better speed
Printshop...	35504	**Speedily**
Prinzessin	35505	As speedily as possible
Prinslich ...	35506	**Spend**
Priorate ...	35507	Will require to spend
Prioratico...	35508	How much will you require to spend in order to
Prioress ...	35509	Do not spend
Prioridad ...	35510	**Spending**
Priorship ...	35511	At what rate are you (is ——) spending
Prioste ...	35512	Now spending at the rate of —— per month
Priseur ...	35513	**Spent**
Prismatic...	35514	Having spent all available funds
Prisonbase	35515	Practically all spent
Prisonnier	35516	Leaves —— still to be spent
Pristimos ...	35517	**Spite**
Prisuelo ...	35518	In order to spite
Pritsche ...	35519	In spite of
Privadero ...	35520	In spite of everything
Privagione	35521	**Splendid**
Privanza ...	35522	Looks splendid
Privarsi ...	35523	A splendid chance
Privateer ...	35524	A splendid time for
Privaticus	35525	**Split(s)**
Privative ...	35526	Splits up
Privatrice...	35527	Appears to have split up
Priverus ...	35528	Is proved to have split up
Privigno ...	35529	**Spot**
Privilege ...	35530	Spot cash

Privilegio ...	35531	What is the spot quotation
Privyseal ...	35532	The spot quotation is
Prizefight...	35533	The price quoted was for spot
Proagogium	35534	**Spread**
Proamita ...	35535	This is to be spread over
Proauctor...	35536	If spread over —— months
Proavitus ...	35537	To be spread over the next four months
Probabilis	35538	**Spring**
Probador ...	35539	In the spring of this year
Probatica ...	35540	During the present spring
Probatory...	35541	About last spring
Probaturus	35542	This spring
Probestern	35543	Last spring
Probestuck	35544	Next spring
Probezeit ...	35545	In the early part of next spring
Probidad ...	35546	**Spy**
Probiren ...	35547	To spy out the land
Probiter ...	35548	Acted as a spy
Problema ...	35549	**Spying**
Problemino	35550	Engaged spying about
Proboscis ...	35551	Has (have) been spying around
Procacetto	35552	**Square**
Procacidad	35553	In order to square up.
Procaciter	35554	**Squarely**
Procastria	35555	Has not acted at all squarely
Procciam ...	35556	Has (have) acted quite squarely
Proccurare	35557	Must act squarely
Procedente	35558	Fairly and squarely
Proceditur	35559	**Stability**
Procedure...	35560	Reports to hand as to the stability of —— are unfavourable
Proceduto	35561	As to the stability of
Procella	35562	**Stable(s)**
Proceloso ...	35563	We should require stables for —— horses
Proceritas	35564	The stables are very much dilapidated
Procerulus	35565	The cost of repairs to stables would amount to
Procesado...	35566	**Stack**
Prochiros ...	35567	To stack
Procidens ...	35568	Smoke stack
Procinctus	35569	**Stacked**
Procinto ...	35570	Ore stacked ready for shipment
Proclamans	35571	Ore stacked ready for treatment
Proclinor ...	35572	Ore stacked ready for concentration
Proclive ...	35573	**Staff**
Proclivita...	35574	The staff has become thoroughly demoralised
Proconsolo	35575	**Stage**
Proconsul...	35576	Stage road
Procreador	35577	Stage coach
Procreer ...	35578	Thence by stage coach to —— distant —— miles
Proctors ...	35579	The stage coach runs daily to
Procubitor	35580	By stage coach leaving on
Proculcor...	35581	**Stamp(s)** (*See also* "Battery," "Blanket," "Cam," "Mill," ["Mortar," &c.)
Procumbens	35582	Steam stamps
Procuojo ...	35583	Pneumatic stamps
Procurante	35584	Ordinary Californian revolving stamps
Procuratio	35585	Stamps battery
Procureur...	35586	Stamp mill (*See also* "Mill.")
Prodegeris	35587	Grates for stamps
Prodezza ...	35588	Stamp head(s)
Prodicor ...	35589	Weight of stamp head
Prodigal ...	35590	Stamps of —— pounds each

[594]

Prodigieux	35591	What weight of stamp head are you using
Prodigioso	35592	Stamp head weighs
Prodigitas	35593	Stamp head with shoe lifter and tappit complete, weighs ——
Prodiguer...	35594	Stamp lifter(s) [pounds
Prodigy ...	35595	What is the drop given to stamps
Prodispero	35596	Stamps have —— inches drop
Proditrix ...	35597	Ore is reduced by stamps [hours
Proditurus	35598	What weight of ore is reduced per stamp head per twenty-four
Prodromus	35599	The weight of ore reduced per stamp head per twenty-four
Producente	35600	Stamps are running [hours is —— pounds
Producible	35601	Stamps are running fairly
Producing	35602	Stamps are running extremely well
Producteur	35603	Stamps are not running well
Produire ...	35604	How many stamps have you now running
Produomo	35605	We have —— heads of stamps running
Produttivo	35606	We have —— batteries of —— stamps each running
Produzione	35607	—— stamps running [retorted gold —— ounces
Proejar ...	35608	—— stamps running —— days crushed —— tons, yield of
Proemial ...	35609	—— heads of stamps running —— days yielded —— ounces
Proeminent	35610	Stamps screens [of bullion
Proeza ...	35611	Russian sheet iron screens for stamps
Profanador	35612	Punched copper screens for stamps
Profanatio	35613	Slot punched screens for stamps
Profanely...	35614	Wire wove screens for stamps
Profanidad	35615	Steel screens for stamps
Profaris ...	35616	To stamp
Profazar ...	35617	Commenced to stamp on
Profendare	35618	When will you commence to stamp
Proferente	35619	Hope to commence to stamp within the next —— weeks
Proferire ...	35620	When I (we) shall commence to stamp
Professor ...	35621	When will you recommence to stamp
Profestus ...	35622	Hope to recommence to stamp on
Profeta ...	35623	Recommenced to stamp on
Profetessa	35624	Would you suggest erection of more stamps, if so, how many
Profetico ...	35625	I would not suggest the erection of more stamps at present
Profetizar...	35626	I am prepared to suggest the erection of —— stamps as soon
Profferer ...	35627	Ought certainly to increase the stamps [as possible
Profferito ...	35628	The erection of new stamps proceeding vigorously [days
Proficiens...	35629	Hope to have the new stamps running within the next ——
Proficuo ...	35630	When will you be able to have the new stamps running
Profilist ...	35631	To enable us to put up more stamps
Profiteor ...	35632	There is an excellent site for stamps at
Proflatus ...	35633	There is enough ore to supply —— stamps
Profligar ...	35634	The ore at present in sight would not keep —— stamps
Profluens ...	35635	**Stamped** (*See also* "Mill.") [running continuously
Profluvio ...	35636	We have stamped all the quartz (ore) available
Profond ...	35637	Each document should be stamped with
Profondato	35638	Each document must be stamped with a stamp (value ——)
Profondeur	35639	Owing to documents being improperly stamped
Profoundly	35640	**Stand(s)**
Profringo ...	35641	Better take everything as it stands
Profugium	35642	How shall we stand
Profumare	35643	**Standard**
Profumiera	35644	What is the standard
Profundar	35645	The standard is
Profundens	35646	Is the standard
Profusive ...	35647	Of standard value
Profusor ...	35648	Of standard fineness
Profuturus	35649	**Standing**
Progeneror	35650	Now standing

Progenic ...	35651	The matter is standing over pending
Progenitus	35652	**Standstill**
Progermino	35653	Am (are) at a standstill for want of money
Progestans	35654	Am (are) at a standstill for want of
Progettare	35655	The works have been at a standstill since
Progigno ...	35656	The whole matter is now at a standstill
Proglottis...	35657	**Start** (*See also* "Expedition.")
Prognare ...	35658	To start
Prognosis	35659	To start work
Prognostic	35660	Shall start immediately
Programa	35661	Shall not be able to start before
Progredior	35662	Refuse(s) to start
Progresivo	35663	Start as soon as you can
Prohedri ...	35664	Do not start until
Prohibeor	35665	To enable me (us) to start
Prohibitio	35666	Hope to start almost immediately
Prohijador	35667	Can start work not later than
Prohombre	35668	Will start to-morrow to do this (it)
Proibente...	35669	Before you start for —— you had better
Proibitore	35670	Expect to start not later than
Projectile ...	35671	If I (we) can get the start of ——
Projeter ...	35672	Appear to have got the start of them
Projicior ...	35673	Appear to have got the start of you
Projimo ...	35674	Am (are) quite ready to start as soon as I (we) receive instruc- [tions to do so
Prolabios ...	35675	I fully expect if everything goes well to start the machinery
Prolagare...	35676	Will start again in a few days [within the next —— days
Prolapsing	35677	I expect to be able start again by ——
Prolapso ...	35678	**Started**
Prolatatio...	35679	Will be started by
Proletary ...	35680	Has (have) already started
Prolibor ...	35681	Has (have) already started to do it (this)
Prolific ...	35682	Has (have) not yet started
Prolijidad	35683	Has (have) —— started
Prolissite ...	35684	Was (were) started
Prolitas ...	35685	Have started to
Prolixity ...	35686	Started for —— on the
Prolixness	35687	In case he (——) has not already started
Prolocutor	35688	**Starting**
Prologue ...	35689	As I (we) (——) was (were) starting for
Prolonga ...	35690	On starting the machinery
Proloquium	35691	When do you propose starting
Proloquor	35692	Propose starting on
Prolugeo ...	35693	**State(s)**
Proluvies ...	35694	To state
Promediar	35695	Report on the general state of
Promenade	35696	The general state of —— is very bad
Promeneur	35697	The general state of —— is fairly good
Promercium	35698	The state is worse than I (we) anticipated
Promerens	35699	What is the present state of
Promeritum	35700	Is in a very dangerous state
Prometedor	35701	Is in a very bad state
Promettre	35702	Is it (are they) in a very bad state
Prominent	35703	In the same state as when I wrote last
Prominulus	35704	You do not state
Promiscuo	35705	In a (the) state of
Promisorio	35706	In what State or Territory is it situated
Promissum	35707	State time and price
Promonstra	35708	Please state at once what you suggest
Promontory	35709	Please state more fully what you want
Promotrice	35710	State how much (many) you want

Promouvoir	85711	State what quantity (quality) you want
Prompted	85712	In a fair state of repair
Promulgar	85713	The general state of —— is vile
Promuovere	85714	Could not possibly be in a worse state
Promutato	85715	Owing to the state of
Pronacion...	85716	You should state fully
Proneidad	85717	Please state precisely
Proneness...	85718	In the present state of
Pronepote...	85719	In what state do (did) you find
Pronghorn	85720	Can you (——) state positively what occurred
Pronomen	85721	Am (are) not able to state positively
Pronominor	85722	Can you state positively
Prononcer	85723	I cannot state positively
Pronoun ...	85724	I can state positively and emphatically that
Prontarsi ...	85725	States positively
Pronteza ...	85726	I (we) can state
Prontuario	85727	Cannot state
Pronubus ...	35728	If what he (——) states is true
Pronunzia	35729	Is still in an unfinished state
Proofsheet·	35730	On account of the unfinished state of
Propagador	85731	State approximate value of
Propagande	85782	Everyone who has been there (to ——) states
Propagatio	35733	Owing to the depressed state of
Propaggine	85734	**Stated** (*See also* "Expressly.")
Propaladia	85735	As stated by you in
Propalar ...	85736	As stated by you in report No. —— (dated ——)
Propalatus	85737	As stated by you in prospectus
Propartida	85788	Stated in evidence
Propatruus	85739	You have not stated
Propediem	85740	Was fully stated in my letter mailed on
Propel ...	85741	It has been officially stated (to be)
Propemodum	35742	Now stated to be false
Propensato	35743	—— is said to have stated that
Propension	35744	No limit was stated
Properatus	35745	**Statement(s)** (*See also* "Attested," "Completed," "Confirm,"
Prophano ...	85746	Address statement to ["False," "Found.")
Prophecy ...	85747	Sign statement as
Prophesier	85748	Also statement giving
Prophetis ...	35749	Statement(s) altogether extravagant
Propicio ...	85750	Please send a careful statement as to
Propienda	85751	The statement made was to the effect that
Propinar ...	85752	The (this) statement is official
Propinquo	85753	Has any official statement been made
Propionate	85754	No official statement has been made
Propitians	85755	The only official statement made was
Propiziare	85756	The statement has been denied
Proplasma	85757	Have I (we) your permission to deny the statement
Propnigeum	85758	You have full permission to deny the statement
Propoleos...	85759	Statement mailed on —— is incorrect, please revise
Proponente	85760	Please draw up and mail a statement showing
Proportion	35761	Full statement will be mailed
Proposed ...	85762	Full statement mailed on
Proposito ...	85763	Can you find out if the statement is true
Propoxyl ...	85764	Have discovered that the statement is false
Proprement	85765	Have no doubt but that the statement is perfectly true
Propreso ...	35766	Please send a statement up to and inclusive of
Proprieta ...	85767	Please send statement showing
Propritim...	85768	Statement appears to be wrong
Propterea...	35769	Statement is right except that
Proptosis ...	35770	You should draw up and send a statement with vouchers

Propuesta...	35771	Mail statement of accounts to —— at the earliest possible
Propugnare	35772	Statement and vouchers mailed on [moment
Propulseur	35773	Statement is correct
Propulsion	35774	Statement is not correct
Propylene...	35775	Can you confirm ——'s statement in all respects
Propylic ...	35776	In the event of your being able to confirm ——'s statement
Proquojo ...	35777	Unless ——'s statements can be confirmed by
Proratear ...	35778	Can fully confirm ——'s statements
Proripens...	35779	—— statements are not correct
Proripior ...	35780	—— statements are very misleading
Prorogable	35781	Can confirm ——'s statements except with respect to
Prorogar ...	35782	I (we) cannot confirm ——'s statements with respect to
Prorogatio	35783	Owing to my (our) having been misled by statements made
Prorogued	35784	Please discover what truth there is in the statement
Prorotto ...	35785	A statement has been circulated to the effect
Prorumpir	35786	—— statement is true as far as my knowledge goes
Prosaique	35787	Statement is incorrect as to
Prosaist ...	35788	I have not been able to determine that ——'s statement is true
Prosapia ...	35789	Am (are) inclined to agree with statements and estimates made
Proscenio ...	35790	I think the statements made to you very exaggerated
Proscindo	35791	I think the statements made to you somewhat exaggerated
Prosciolto...	35792	Mail statements showing for what purpose you require the
Proscribir	35793	Statement with full details mailed [sum of ——
Proscrit ...	35794	Mail statements of all monies received and how disbursed
Prosectus ...	35795	There is no ground for the statement made
Prosecutor	35796	Has (have) made very damaging statements
Prosedamum	35797	Render statements accompanied by vouchers showing
Proseguir...	35798	Statements must be accompanied by vouchers
Proselyte ...	35799	Mail statements showing
Prosequens	35800	Mail statements showing expenditure on revenue account since
Prosevante	35801	In my opinion the statements made as to —— are somewhat
Prosicies ...	35802	I am (we are) making full statement [exaggerated
Prosista ...	35803	Has (have) made a sworn statement
Prositum ...	35804	Refuse(s) to make a sworn statement
Prosodial ...	35805	Please render full statement showing
Prosodique	35806	There is only too much ground for the statement you have
Prosody ...	35807	Formal statement [noticed
Prosperar...	35808	Send very short formal statement
Prosperoso	35809	Must add to your statement a list of
Prospimano	35810	The statements set forth are not in accordance with the
		[evidence before me, or the facts as they present themselves
Prosternor	35811	The general statements as set forth are approximately correct,
		[and can be fairly borne out by evidence and existing facts
Prosteso ...	35812	**Station**
Prostibula	35813	Station pump
Prostilo ...	35814	Pump station
Prostituta	35815	Station No. ——
Prostrarsi...	35816	At No. —— station
Prostrato ...	35817	Feet from No. —— station
Prosubigo	35818	Shall commence to cut station
Prosumere	35819	As soon as I (we) have finished station
Prosutto ...	35820	Will take —— days to complete station
Protagon ...	35821	Station is within —— miles of the mine(s)
Protasis ...	35822	Nearest station is
Protaticus	35823	What is the nearest station
Protean ...	35824	**Stationary**
Protected...	35825	Quite stationary
Protecteur	35826	Stationary engine
Proteger ...	35827	At present stationary
Protelatus	35828	**Stationed**

Protendere	35829	Stationed at
Protermino	35830	Formerly stationed at
Proterreo ...	35831	**Stationery**
Protervia ...	35832	Books and stationery
Protestant	35833	Office stationery
Protettore	35834	**Statistical**
Protezione	35835	Statistical information
Prothymia	35836	Forward any statistical information you can obtain relating to
Protocol ...	35837	**Statistics**
Protollor ...	35838	Reliable statistics
Protonoe ...	35839	Statistics are not reliable
Protoplast	35840	Published statistics show
Prototomus	35841	There are no statistics obtainable
Prototype...	35842	Latest and most reliable statistics
Protracted	35843	**Statute(s)**
Protractus	35844	In order to comply with the statutes
Protrahens	35845	According to the statutes of
Protrarre ...	35846	**Statutory**
Protropum	35847	Statutory requirement(s)
Protruded	35848	Statutory declaration
Protrusive	35849	**Stay**
Protubero...	35850	Stay at
Proturbor...	35851	To stay
Protutela ...	35852	How long do you propose to stay (at)
Protzwagen	35853	Do not propose to stay after
Proudness	35854	Should be glad if I could stay until
Provabile ...	35855	Do not stay
Provamento	35856	Do not stay longer than you can help
Provanza ...	35857	Do not stay later than
Provativo...	35858	Stay as long as you are able
Provecho ...	35859	Must stay until
Provedere...	35860	Stay until
Proveduto	35861	Do not stay unless (until)
Provenance	35862	Should be glad to stay
Provender	35863	Stay at —— until you receive letter mailed on
Proveniens	35864	Will stay at —— until I receive your further instructions
Provenir ...	35865	You had better stay a few days longer
Proverbium	35866	Limit your stay at —— to —— days
Proviant ...	35867	Regret that I (we) cannot stay any longer
Providente	35868	How long do you intend to stay
Provideor...	35869	Do not intend to stay after
Provigner ...	35870	How long will —— stay
Provincia	35871	—— will not stay
Proviseur ...	35872	—— cannot stay later than
Provision ...	35873	At what hotel will you stay at in ——
Provisoria	35874	Shall stay at the —— hotel
Provisto ...	35875	**Steadily**
Provisurus	35876	Steadily falling
Prevocador	35877	Steadily rising
Provocante	35878	Steadily increasing
Provoke ...	35879	Steadily progressing
Provolutus	35880	I (we) have been steadily
Provolvens	35881	**Steady** (*See also* "Man.")
Provoquer	35882	Steady and industrious
Provorsum	35883	Do you know a good steady man
Provulgo ...	35884	**Steam** (*See also* "Boiler," "Engine," "Machinery.")
Provvisare	35885	Steam power (for)
Prowler ...	35886	Get up steam and await orders
Prowling ...	35887	To be driven by steam
Proxeneta	35888	Steam power to be supplementary

Proximatus	35889	Please cable whether you intend to employ steam or water
Proximidad	35890	Either steam or water power [power
Proyectar ...	35891	Would require to be driven by steam
Prudemment	35892	By steam only
Prudencia	35893	**Steamer** (*See also* "Go," "Missed.")
Prudential	35894	There is a steamer for
Prudery ...	35895	There is a steamer twice a week, between —— and ——
Prudish ...	35896	When will the next steamer leave for
Prudore ...	35897	The next steamer leaves for —— on ——
Prueba ...	35898	By what steamer will the machinery be consigned
Prueggio ...	35899	Steamer refuses to take
Prugelei ...	35900	There is a steamer several times a week
Pruinoso ..	35901	The connection between —— and —— is by steamer ..
Prunaga ...	35902	Proceed from —— to —— by steamer
Pruned ...	35903	Do you know the steamer in which —— has sailed
Prunelaie ...	35904	—— sailed by the steamer ——
Prunellier...	35905	Meet —— on arrival of steamer
Prunello ...	35906	Is believed to be on the —— steamer
Pruning ...	35907	Cable when steamer leaves
Prunken ...	35908	Steamer leaves
Pruriens ...	35909	The machinery was sent by the steamer which left on —— [bills of lading have been made out in the name of ——
Prurigine ...	35910	**Steel** (*See also* "Stamp.")
Prurito ...	35911	Cast steel
Prusiato ...	35912	To be made of steel
Prussique...	35913	To be tipped with steel
Pryingly ...	35914	Of the best quality of steel
Prytaneum	35915	Cable cost if made of steel
Prytanis ...	35916	Cost if made of steel would be ——
Psallette ...	35917	Crucible steel
Psalmist ...	35918	Tool steel
Psalmodic	35919	Drill steel
Psalterion	35920	Mild steel
Psaltery ...	35921	Should be good steel for welding purposes
Psatonius...	35922	**Steep**
Psautier ...	35923	Very steep
Psephisma	35924	Owing to the steep and precipitous nature of
Pseudolus...	35925	On the side of a steep hill
Pseudonym	35926	**Stem(s)**
Pseudorcin	35927	**Step(s)**
Psicologia...	35928	Have you (has ——) taken any steps to
Psidracium	35929	Has (have) not taken any steps up to the present time
Psilothrum	35930	What steps do you propose to take ..
Psittacus ...	35931	Prepare to take steps at once to
Psoalgicus	35932	Before you take any further steps
Psychist ...	35933	Steps should be taken at once to
Psychosis...	35934	Steps have been taken to
Psyllion ...	35935	Has (have) taken no steps whatever
Ptarmigan	35936	Before taking any further steps you had better consult with
Pternix ...	35937	Take such steps as you deem best
Pterodon ...	35938	Can you suggest what steps should be taken
Pteromata	35939	Take steps at once
Pterygium	35940	Has (have) taken immediate steps to
Puanteur ...	35941	Any steps you may take will be
Pubertad ...	35942	Any steps you may take should be
Pubescente	35943	No steps whatever
Pubescer ...	35944	Are the steps already taken approved of
Publicador	35945	The steps taken are not approved of (by)
Publican ...	35946	The step is a most arbitrary one
Publicanus	35947	**Sterling** (*See also* "Money.")

'ublicatio	35948	**Still**
'ublicist ...	35949	Still continue(s)
'ublicola .	35950	Shall still continue to
'ublikum...	35951	Do you still
'ublished...	35952	**Stipulate**
'ucelana ...	35953	To stipulate
'uceron ...	35954	Will stipulate
'uchada ...	35955	You had better stipulate
'uchecilla	35956	Do not stipulate
'ucherito...	35957	Did you stipulate
'uches ...	35958	You should certainly stipulate for
'uckered ...	35959	Expressly stipulate(s)
'uddler ...	35960	Stipulate for
'uddling ...	35961	Shall I stipulate for
Pudelmutze	35962	**Stipulated**
Pudeln ...	35963	Have stipulated for
Pudibundo	35964	It was carefully stipulated that
Pudicizia ...	35965	Was (were) stipulated for
Pudiente ...	35966	—— has (have) stipulated that
Pudique ...	35967	**Stipulation(s)**
Pudricion...	35968	There was no stipulation at all
Pudridero	35969	There was no actual stipulation, but it was understood that
Pudrigorio	35970	The only stipulation was
Puellario ...	35971	You should make a stipulation that
Puericia ...	35972	No such stipulation(s) was (were) made
Puerile ...	35973	What was (were) the actual stipulation(s)
Puerility ...	35974	The actual stipulation(s) was (were)
Puerpera ...	35975	**Stock(s)**
Puerperium	35976	To stock
Puffball ...	35977	How much (many) do you keep in stock
Puffiness ...	35978	Have none in stock
Puffingly ...	35979	Have only —— in stock
Puffspill ...	35980	Is at present out of stock
Pugilado ...	35981	Have plenty in stock
Pugilism ...	35982	Have very little in stock
Pugilistic...	35983	Stock on hand is running short
Pugillares	35984	We ought to have a good supply in stock against the coming [winter
Pugnacidad	35985	Sufficient stock for
Pugnaciter	35986	Sufficient in stock, provided that
Pugnalata	35987	Stock becoming exhausted
Pugnalone	35988	The stock is heavily watered
Pugnante ...	35989	A fall in stocks is imminent
Pugneletto	35990	Demand the stock immediately
Pugnello ...	35991	Stocks are depressed
Pugneus ...	35992	—— is (are) selling all his (their) stock
Pugnimento	35993	What is the tonnage and estimated value of ore in stock
Pugnitivo	35994	Our stock consists of
Pugnituya	35995	The stock has been manipulated
Pugnuolo...	35996	The stock has not been manipulated
Puisance ...	35997	Is said to be manipulating the stock
Puisatier ...	35998	Is the stock likely to be manipulated
Puissant ...	35999	**Stockbroker(s)** (*See also* "Broker," "Buy," "Sell,"
Pujadero ...	36000	The official stockbroker to the Company ["Share.")
Pujame ...	**36001**	**Stock Exchange** (*See also* "Exchange.")
Pujamiento	36002	On the London Stock Exchange
Pujavante	36003	Stock Exchange quotation applied for
Pulcelloni	36004	Stock Exchange quotation granted
Pulcesecca	36005	Stock Exchange quotation refused
Pulchellus	36006	Write details of documents required in order to apply for a {quotation on your Stock Exchange (the Stock Exchange [at ——

Pulchralis...	36007	Would prevent our obtaining a Stock Exchange quotation
Pulchritas	36008	Would this prevent a Stock Exchange quotation being obtained
Pulciaceum	36009	Would not prevent a Stock Exchange quotation being obtained
Pulcinella...	36010	**Stockjobber**
Pulcritud ...	36011	**Stolen**
Puledrino...	36012	Has (have) been stolen
Puleggia ...	36013	Were stolen on
Pulegium ...	36014	Is believed to have been stolen
Pulgarada	36015	Which was stolen on
Pulgoso ...	36016	Was (were) not stolen
Pulguera ...	36017	**Stone**
Pulicaria ...	36018	Very good stone
Pulimentar	36019	Fair stone
Pulingly ...	36020	Poor stone
Pulitezza ...	36021	The stone is worth —— ounces per ton
Pulitore ...	36022	**Stone Breaker** (*See also* "Crusher," "Rock Breaker.")
Pullarius ...	36023	**Stop** (*See also* "Close," "Expenditure.")
Pullastra ...	36024	To stop
Pullices ...	36025	To stop the (this)
Pullolare ...	36026	Will stop
Pullulante	36027	Will not stop
Pulluler ...	36028	Will it stop
Pulmentum	36029	Consent(s) to stop
Pulmon ...	36030	Refuse(s) to stop
Pulmonary	36031	Do not stop
Pulmoneus	36032	Can stop until
Pulperia ...	36033	Cannot stop after
Pulpeton ...	36034	Stop payment at once
Pulpeux ...	36035	How long will it stop you
Pulpit ...	36036	Will stop me (us) —— days
Pulpitino ...	36037	Can you stop
Pulsabulum	36038	Can stop
Pulsador ...	36039	Cannot stop
Pulsated ...	36040	Can you not put a stop to it
Pulsatile ...	36041	Will endeavour to put a stop to it
Pulsatory ...	36042	As soon as I (we) can put a stop to it
Pulseless ...	36043	So as to put a stop to it
Pulsera ...	36044	Has (have) put a stop to it
Pulsilogio...	36045	Stop can be removed
Pultarium	36046	Do not remove stop
Pulticula ...	36047	Cannot get stop removed
Pultifagus	36048	Stop removed; can present the draft
Pulver ...	36049	You had better stop at —— until you receive further cable
Pulveratio	36050	Stop at once all work
Pulverhorn	36051	Stop at once all non-paying work
Pulverizar	36052	Stop all expenditure immediately
Pulverous...	36053	Stop all expenditure except that which may be absolutely
Pulvillus ...	36054	Stop when [necessary to hold property
Pulvinulus	36055	You had better stop
Pulzone ...	36056	Stop for the present
Pumiceus ...	36057	Has (have) had to stop
Pumicosus	36058	Shall be obliged to stop work on —— owing to want of funds
Pumpchain	36059	I have thought it advisable to stop work at
Pumproom	36060	Stop every expense
Punaise ...	36061	Stop everything
Punchbowl	36062	Had better stop proceedings until
Punctillo ...	36063	Had better stop proceedings at once
Punctuate	36064	Shall we stop
Punctured	36065	**Stope(s)**
Pundonor...	36066	Stope above

Punganes ...	36067	To stope
Pungello ...	36068	From the stope at
Pungente ...	36069	In this (the) stope
Pungitivo ...	36070	As an underhand stope
Pungolare	36071	In the back of the stope
Punible ...	36072	There is a very fine stope of ore at
Punicanus	36073	From the stope above level (number ——)
Puniendus	36074	The stopes above level (number ——)
Punigione	36075	Payable ore is confined to stope(s) at
Puniness ...	36076	There is no payable ore left to stope
Punishable	36077	Can you not begin to stope
Punished ...	36078	Commence to stope at
Punitrice ...	36079	Shall commence to stope as soon as
Punktirte ...	36080	Shall commence to stope
Punktlich...	36081	Has (have) commenced to stope
Punschnapf	36082	Have already commenced to stope
Punster ...	36083	I hope to commence to stope not later than
Puntaglia ..	36084	When are you likely to begin to stope
Puntaletto	36085	Shall start the stope at this point almost immediately
Puntapil ...	36086	How are the stopes looking
Puntato ...	36087	How is this (the ——) stope looking
Puntazza ...	36088	The stopes generally are
Punteadura	36089	The stopes are looking if anything better
Puntear ...	36090	This refers to stope (at ——)
Puntellato	36091	The stopes are looking rather worse
Punterol ...	36092	All the stopes are at present poor
Puntilla ...	36093	The stope looks very well
Puntilloso...	36094	Stopes looking exceedingly well
Puntoso ...	36095	Stopes looking grand
Puntualita	36096	The ore in the stope now measures —— feet by ——
Punzellare	36097	Stopes still continue good
Punzoncino	36098	. The stopes above the —— level are practically exhausted
Punzoneria	36099	Draw on the stopes
Punzonetto	36100	The (this) stope is becoming very poor and will be abandoned
Pupilage ...	36101	All the stopes are generally about the same value
Pupilero ...	36102	The yield from the stopes continues about the average
Pupillary ...	36103	The stopes now show
Pupilletta...	36104	The stope in the back of the —— level is now producing ore
Pupillus ...	36105	Stopes exhausted [worth —— per ton
Pupitre ...	36106	We have holed through to the —— level from the stope below
Puppets ...	36107	Promises to become a very fine stope of ore
Puppyism...	36108	A sample from the stope has assayed
Puramente	36109	The stopes at —— are all showing good ore
Purblind ...	36110	At present rate of extraction stopes will last
Purefacio ...	36111	The stope has been extended
Pureza ...	36112	We are extracting ore from the stopes to their full capacity
Purgabilis	36113	The stope averages —— tons of ore per fathom
Purgable ...	36114	The prospective value of the stopes
Purgamen	36115	The stope has widened
Purgante ...	36116	Cable whether present shipments fairly represent prospective
Purgation	36117	**Stoped** [value of stopes
Purgative...	36118	Stoped out
Purgatorio	36119	Stoped up for a height of —— feet
Purgatrice	36120	Entirely stoped away
Purghetta	36121	We have not stoped any part of the vein
Puridad ...	36122	**Stoping**
Purificans ..	36123	Overhead stoping
Purisme ...	36124	Underhand stoping
Puritanic ...	36125	Commence stoping
Puriter ...	36126	No stoping to be done

Purlieu ...	36127	No stoping has been done
Purloined ...	36128	No stoping is being done at the present time
Purported	36129	**Stoppage(s)**
Purpurante	36130	How long will stoppage last
Purpurasco	36131	Will cause a stoppage of —— days
Purpureo ...	36132	No stoppage
Purpurisso	36133	A stoppage of
Purpurroth	36134	A stoppage has taken place
Purriela ...	36135	So as to prevent any stoppage of
Purring ...	36136	Could not the stoppage have been prevented
Purseproud	36137	Stoppage could have been prevented by (if)
Pursiness ...	36138	Do not see how the stoppage could have been **prevented**
Purslane ...	36139	So as to avoid any stoppage of production
Pursuance	36140	During the stoppage of
Pursuivant	36141	The actual length of stoppage was —— hours
Purulento...	36142	What was the actual length of stoppage
Purveyance	36143	Will it (this) necessitate any stoppage
Purview ...	36144	It will necessitate a stoppage of
Purzelbaum	36145	It will not necessitate a stoppage of
Pusignare...	36146	You must limit the stoppage as much as possible
Pusillita ...	36147	Will do all I (we) can to shorten stoppage
Pustula ...	36148	Is it possible to avoid a stoppage
Pustuletta	36149	It is not possible to avoid a stoppage
Pustuleux...	36150	Will it mean a complete stoppage
Putaismo ...	36151	It will not mean a complete stoppage
Putamen ...	36152	It will mean a complete stoppage of
Putatif ...	36153	Cannot avoid slight stoppage
Putativus...	36154	Cannot avoid stoppage
Putatorius	36155	What has caused stoppage
Puteal ...	36156	Stoppage was caused by
Puteanus ...	36157	The stoppage was mainly due to
Puterhahn	36158	Causing frequent stoppages
Puteria ...	36159	This will lessen the chance of future stoppage
Puticuli ...	36160	**Stopped**
Putidore ...	36161	Payment has been stopped
Putiglioso...	36162	We shall be stopped —— hours
Putolente ..	36163	The —— will be stopped for —— days
Putredinal	36164	All work has been stopped
Putrefacio	36165	All expenditure except —— per month has been **stopped**
Putrefarsi	36166	Has (have) been stopped since
Putrefatto	36167	When was it stopped
Putrefied ...	36168	Has (have) stopped
Putridez ...	36169	Should be stopped at once
Putridite ...	36170	Why have you stopped work at
Puttaccio ...	36171	Why have you stopped the drivage at
Puttanella	36172	Work was stopped because
Puttanesco	36173	The drivage was stopped because
Puttaniere	36174	Has (have) not been stopped
Puttello ...	36175	Has (have) stopped because of
Putstisch...	36176	Has (have) not yet stopped
Putzwaaren	36177	Should not be stopped until
Puzzare ...	36178	As soon as it has been stopped
Puzzevole...	36179	Was (were) only stopped until
Puzzled ...	36180	Was (were) only stopped
Puzzlingly	36181	Stopped for want of
Puzzola ...	36182	Stopped for want of funds
Puzzolente	36183	Work has been stopped at —— in the absence of
Pycnitis ...	36184	Have you stopped
Pycnoticus	36185	Has (have) been recently stopped
Pyctacium	36186	**Storage**

Pygargul ...	36187	What is the storage capacity of
Pyjamas ...	36188	**Store(s)** (*See also* "Material," "Supplies.")
Pyracanth	36189	To store
Pyramidic	36190	Ought to store sufficient
Pyrausta ...	36191	Have now in store
Pyrethrum	36192	We have enough in store to last us during the coming winter
Pyriform ...	36193	Do not purchase any to store
Pyritous ...	36194	The mine keeps a store
Pyrocorax...	36195	The annual profit on the store amounts to
Pyrogallic	36196	Have you any store of
Pyrolusite	36197	There is (are) no store(s) at all
Pyrotechny	36198	There is a pretty good store of
Pyroxene ...	36199	For cost of stores
Pyrrhicha...	36200	Inclusive of stores
Pyrrhonist	36201	Exclusive of stores
Pyruvic ...	36202	Store supplies
Pythaules...	36203	Store house(s)
Pythonisse	36204	Is now removing stores
Pyxidatus...	36205	Am (are) now purchasing necessary stores
Pyxidicula	36206	**Stored**
Quackery ...	36207	Would require to be stored
Quacking ...	36208	Has (have) stored
Quacquere	36209	If stored would entail additional cost of
Quadernale	36210	**Stout(ly)**
Quadrabile	36211	Stoutly built
Quadrageni	36212	Stoutly deny(ies)
Quadragies	36213	**Straight** (*See also* "Fair.")
Quadrangle	36214	Has (have) —— acted perfectly straight
Quadrario...	36215	Has (have) acted perfectly straight
Quadrat ...	36216	Has (have) not acted straight at all
Quadrating	36217	**Straighten** (*See also* "Shaft.")
Quadrature	36218	**Strain**
Quadretto...	36219	To strain
Quadriceps	36220	Do not strain
Quadriglia	36221	Will it strain
Quadrilles	36222	It (this) will strain
Quadrinus	36223	Will not strain
Quadruccio	36224	So long as it does not strain
Quadrumane	36225	Take care not to strain
Quadruped	36226	Will be a strain upon our resources
Quaffer ...	36227	Will it be a strain upon your resources
Quaggiuso	36228	Will not be a strain upon our resources
Quaggy ...	36229	**Strange** [done
Quagliare ...	36230	It seems a little strange that —— should have acted as he has
Quagmire...	36231	I do not think it at all strange that —— has acted as he has
Quaiche ...	36232	The strange part would have been [done
Quailing ...	36233	**Strangers**
Quailpipe .	36234	With strangers
Quaintness	36235	Perfect strangers
Quaker ...	36236	In the hands of strangers
Quakerish	36237	If in the hands of strangers they might do much mischief
Qualifier ...	36238	Even if in the hands of strangers they cannot do any mischief
Qualitat ...	36239	**Strapping Plates**
Qualmish ...	36240	Send sketch with figured dimensions of strapping plates
Qualora ...	36241	**Strata (Stratum)**
Qualsisia ...	36242	The strata are conformable to each other
Qualubet ...	36243	The strata are unconformable to each other
Qualunque	36244	The general dip of the strata is about —— degrees to the
Quamobrem	36245	Horizontal strata [horizontal
Quampridem	36246	The strata are contorted in every direction

Quamquam	36247	In a stratum of
Quamvis ...	36248	The strata consist of
Quandary...	36249	The strata are
Quandoche	36250	From the dip of the strata

Stratification

Quantillum	36251	
Quantisper	36252	Owing to peculiar stratification
Quantopere	36253	No appearance of stratification

Stratified

Quantulus	36254	
Quantumvis	36255	Stratified deposit of
Quapropter	36256	Distinctly stratified

Streak

Quarantine	36257	
Quarrels ...	36258	A streak of mineral —— to —— inches wide
Quarried ...	36259	Have struck a streak of ore assaying
Quarrying	36260	There is a pay streak —— inches wide
Quartarium	36261	The streak runs right through the vein
Quartband	36262	The pay streak is from —— to —— inches wide and assays
Quartering	36263	The pay streak has come to an end
Quartette ...	36264	The pay streak continues
Quartieren	36265	The pay streak is limited to .
Quartuccio	36266	A pay streak
Quassandus	36267	A streak of ore
Quatefacio	36268	Streak is opening out
Quatenus ...	36269	Streak is diminishing

Stream (*See also* " Miners' Inches," " Water.")

Quaterdeni	36270	
Quaternary	36271	There is no stream, only freshets
Quaterne ...	36272	There is a good stream of water on the property
Quaternion	36273	The stream would supply —— miners' inches for —— months
Quaternity	36274	The stream entirely dries up in summer [of the year
Quatrain ...	36275	The stream is dry except after a heavy rain
Quattragio	36276	There is no stream at all
Quaverer ...	36277	There are several small streams
Quavering	36278	In winter the stream yields only —— gallons per minute
Queasiness	36279	In the winter the supply from the stream is abundant
Quebrajoso	36280	What is the volume of water in the stream
Quebrantar	36281	What is the fall in the stream
Quebrar ...	36282	There is only a slight fall in the stream
Queche ...	36283	Between —— and —— the stream falls —— feet

Street

Quedito ...	36284	
Queenbee ...	36285	What is the name of the street
Queenlike...	36286	The name of the street is

Strength

Quehacer ...	36287	
Queiscum ...	36288	Of sufficient strength to withstand
Quejarse ...	36289	Was (were) not of sufficient strength

Strengthen

Quejicoso ...	36290	
Quejigal ...	36291	To strengthen
Quelconque	36292	Will strengthen
Quellen ...	36293	Propose to strengthen
Quelque ...	36294	Would it not strengthen
Queltanto...	36295	Shall proceed at once to strengthen (the)
Quemadero	36296	Would strengthen our position considerably
Quemante...	36297	Would it (this) strengthen our position at all
Quenchless	36298	Would not much strengthen our position

Strengthened

Quenelle ...	36299	
Quenotte ...	36300	Has (have) strengthened
Quenouille	36301	As soon as I (we) have strengthened
Quentchen	36302	Ought to be strengthened
Quequier ...	36303	Has strengthened our position greatly
Querarium	36304	Has not strengthened our position at all
Querbalken	36305	Have it (this) strengthened

Strengthening

Quercicus...	36306	

Querciuola	36307	For the purpose of strengthening
Querelato ...	36308	As soon as I (we) have completed strengthening
Querelleur	36309	**Strenuous(ly)**
Querencia...	36310	After strenuous exertions
Querer ...	36311	Make strenuous efforts to
Querflote ...	36312	In spite of strenuous efforts to the contrary
Quergasse	36313	**Stress**
Querlinie ...	36314	Owing to stress of weather
Querneus ...	36315	Owing to great stress from
Querocha ...	36316	Due to stress caused by
Querpfeife	36317	A stress of —— tons per square inch
Querquerus	36318	**Stretch**
Quersack ...	36319	Stretch a point if possible
Querstand	36320	Persuade —— to stretch a point
Querstrich	36321	**Stretcher Bar(s)** (*See also* "Drill.") [—— inches diameter
Queruber ...	36322	Forward promptly a stretcher bar 4 feet (when closed) and
Querulous	36323	Forward promptly a stretcher bar 5 feet (when closed) and
		[—— inches diameter
Quesadilla	36324	Forward promptly a stretcher bar 6 feet (when closed) and
		[—— inches diameter
Quesear ...	36325	Forward promptly a stretcher bar 7 feet (when closed) and
		[—— inches diameter
Questesso...	36326	Forward promptly a stretcher bar 8 feet (when closed) and
		[—— inches diameter
Questeur ...	36327	Forward promptly a stretcher bar 9 feet (when closed) and
Question ...	36328	**Strict** [—— inches diameter
Questoria...	36329	Be very strict as regards
Quetarsi ...	36330	Not at all strict
Queveis	36331	**Strictly**
Quibbler ...	36332	As strictly as possible
Quibey ...	36333	As strictly as you can
Quibitta ...	36334	Too strictly
Quicial ...	36335	Not too strictly
Quiciritta...	36336	Most strictly
Quickening	36337	**Strike** (*See also* "Lock-out.")
Quickeyed	36338	Expect to strike
Quicklime	36339	The strike began through
Quickmatch	36340	The strike was mainly owing to
Quickset ...	36341	Strike still continues; men demand
Quicquid ...	36342	You had better for the present meet demands of men on strike
Quidam ...	36343	Men on strike refuse offer made to
Quidnunc...	36344	The strike is not expected to last very long
Quiebra ...	36345	Strike over, men gradually returning to work
Quietacion	36646	The strike is extending to
Quietador...	36847	The strike has terminated, have given in to the men
Quietanza	36848	The strike is likely to last a considerable time
Quietativo	36849	Now on strike
Quietism ...	36850	If we are to prevent the strike it will be necessary to
Quietistic...	36851	Have been on strike since
Quietorium	36852	A strike is threatened amongst the miners
Quietud ...	36853	A strike is threatened amongst the labourers
Quijarudo	36854	A strike is threatened amongst the mill men
Quijoteria	36855	In order to avert strike
Quilatador	36856	Pitmen are likely to strike
Quilifero ...	36857	Owing to a strike amongst the men
Quilificar ...	36858	The strike is general throughout
Quillier ...	36859	There has been an important strike in
Quillotro ...	36360	Cable any new strike of ore at once
Quiloso ...	36361	The (this) strike is nearly east and west
Quilting ...	36362	The (this) strike is nearly north and south

Quimbombo	86363	Hope to strike the vein within the next —— feet
Quimerista	86364	Should we not strike the vein within the next —— feet
Quimerizar	86365	Ought to strike the vein within the next —— feet
Quimico ...	86366	Expect to strike the vein within next —— feet
Quinamonte	86367	As soon as we strike the ore
Quinarius...	86368	Cable as soon as you strike ore
Quinary ...	36369	A rich strike is rumoured at
Quinavalle	86370	A rich strike has been made at
Quincalla ...	86371	The strike is not so good as reported
Quinconce	86372	**Strikers** (*See also* "Lock-out," "Strike.")
Quincuatro	86373	Better clear out all the strikers
Quincuplex	86374	I do not see how we can escape giving in to the strikers
Quincurion	86375	Meeting of managers has decided to oppose strikers
Quincussis	86376	Meeting of managers has decided to concede all strikers' [demands
Quindecima	86377	I (we) think it would be wise to accept strikers' conditions
Quindejas	36378	**Stringent**
Quindici ...	86379	Have not been sufficiently stringent
Quinetiam	86380	**Stringer(s)**
Quinientos	86381	There are several stringers of quartz
Quinine ...	86382	There are several stringers of quartz in the level
Quinisco ...	86383	There are several stringers of quartz in the shaft
Quinolas ...	86384	The vein is divided into several stringers
Quinolear...	86385	Will probably prove to be a stringer
Quinquenal	86386	There is (it is) a very fair stringer of ore
Quinquet ...	86387	A stringer of quartz [seem to justify development
Quinquevir	86388	We have passed several small stringers, but not one that would
Quinquies...	86389	**Stroke(s)**
Quintadeno	86390	—— strokes per minute
Quintalada	86391	**Stromeyerite** (*See also* "Mineral.")
Quintanar	86392	**Strong** (*See also* "Feeling.")
Quintaton	86393	Fairly strong
Quintavolo	86394	Very strong
Quinterne...	86395	Quite strong enough
Quintetto ...	86396	Not strong enough
Quinticeps	86397	Should be sufficiently strong
Quintoire ...	86398	Is not quite strong enough
Quintsaite	86399	There is a strong tendency to
Quintuplo	86400	Do you consider it strong enough for
Quinultuno	86401	Should be made as strong as possible
Quinzaine...	86402	There is a very strong feeling that
Quiosca ...	86403	There is a strong indication of
Quiprocuo	86404	**Stronger**
Quiragra ...	86405	Must be made stronger
Quirinal ...	86406	Have been made stronger
Quirister ...	86407	Stronger if anything
Quiritans ...	86408	Stronger than ever
Quiritta ...	86409	**Strongest**
Quirkiah ...	86410	**Strongly**
Quiroteca...	86411	Strongly advise(s)
Quirurgica	86412	I am (we are) strongly in favour of
Quisquilla ...	86413	I am (we are) strongly against
Quitaguas	86414	I (we) strongly urge
Quitaipon...	86415	Strongly oppose(s)
Quitasol ...	86416	Represent strongly that
Quittancer	86417	Strongly deprecate
Quittiren ...	86418	**Struck** (*See also* "Water.")
Quittung ...	86419	Have struck a flow of water
Quivered ...	86420	Have struck for an increase of wages
Quixotic ...	86421	Have struck against new regulations

Quizzical ...	36422	Have struck for less hours
Quizzing ...	36423	Have struck against proposed
Quoadusque	36424	Which was struck
Quodammodo	36425	Was struck on
Quodlibet...	36426	Has (have) struck ore
Quodpiam	36427	Struck an important body of ore
Quojajo ...	36428	Have struck pay ore in shaft, looks like holding down
Quomimus	36429	Have struck pay ore in
Quondam...	36430	Have not yet struck any ore
Quotation...	36431	Has (have) struck upon
Quotient ...	36432	—— feet in we struck
Quotite ...	36433	Struck a seam of
Quotuplex	36434	Struck a good body of ore
Quousque...	36435	Struck ore assaying
Rabacchino	36436	Struck a very rich body of ore
Rabachage	36437	Owing to our having struck
Rabacheur	36438	Have struck a strong body of water
Rabaniza ...	36439	Have so far struck no water at all
Rabanna ...	36440	Have struck a bed of
Rabarbero	36441	Will cable as soon as ore is struck
Rabatjoie ...	36442	Have struck vein, but no mineral
Rabatt ...	36443	Have struck mineral
Rabasuz ...	36444	**Structural**
Rabbassare	36445	Structural alteration(s)
Rabbescame	36446	**Structure**
Rabbin ...	36447	Of the following structure
Rabbinical	36448	What is the structure of
Rabbinista	36449	The structure changes from —— to ——
Rabbits ...	36450	The structure of the rock is
Rabboccare	36451	The structure of the rock is agglomerated
Rabbondare	36452	The structure of the rock is amygdaloid
Rabbonito	36453	The structure of the rock is banded
Rabbuffato	36454	The structure of the rock is brecciated
Rabduchus	36455	The structure of the rock is cavernous
Rabenstein	36456	The structure of the rock is cellular
Rabiatar ...	36457	The structure of the rock is clastic
Rabican ...	36458	The structure of the rock is concretionary
Rabicorto...	36459	The structure of the rock is conglomerated
Rabidly ...	36460	The structure of the rock is crystalline
Rabilargo...	36461	The structure of the rock is coarse-crystalline
Rabioso ...	36462	The structure of the rock is crypto-crystalline
Rabiosulus	36463	The structure of the rock is fine-crystalline
Rabiseco ...	36464	The structure of the rock is micro-crystalline
Rabizar ...	36465	The structure of the rock is fibrous
Rabona ...	36466	The structure of the rock is foliated
Raboseada	36467	The structure of the rock is granitoid
Rabotear ...	36468	The structure of the rock is granular
Rabougrir	36469	The structure of the rock is gritty
Rabudo ...	36470	The structure of the rock is horny (flinty)
Racaille ...	36471	The structure of the rock is massive
Raccattare	36472	The structure of the rock is muddy
Raccertato	36473	The structure of the rock is oolitic
Racchiuso...	36474	The structure of the rock is pegmatoid
Raccolta ...	36475	The structure of the rock is perlitic
Raccomiare	36476	The structure of the rock is pisolitic
Racconcio...	36477	The structure of the rock is porphyritic
Raccerd ...	36478	The structure of the rock is pumiceous
Raccoupler	36479	The structure of the rock is scoriaceous
Raccourcir	36480	The structure of the rock is segregated
Raccozzato	36481	The structure of the rock is spherulitic

Raccroc ...	36482	The structure of the rock is stratified
Racculare...	36483	The structure of the rock is streaked
Racecourse	36484	The structure of the rock is vesicular
Racehorse...	36485	The structure of the rock is vitreous
Raceles ...	36486	**Study**
Racemarius	36487	To study a new method for
Racemic ...	36488	**Stull(s)**
Racemifero	36489	Stull timbers
Racemoso...	36490	Stulls given way
Rachetable	36491	Will take —— days to replace stull timbers
Rachgierig	36492	**Stultified(s)**
Rachitique	36493	Completely stultified
Rachitis ...	36494	**Stultify**
Rachsucht	36495	So as not to stultify
Racimado...	36496	**Style**
Racimolare	36497	What style do you want
Racionable	36498	The style suggested is satisfactory
Racionista	36499	**Sub-agent**
Rackers ...	36500	**Sub-committee**
Racketing	36501	**Sub-divide(d)**
Rackrails ...	36502	**Subject** (*See also* "Hold.")
Rackrent ...	36503	To be subject to
Rackwork...	36504	Subject to a —— of
Racleur ...	36505	Is this subject to any deduction
Racloire ...	36506	It is not subject to any deduction
Racolage ...	36507	Subject to a deduction of
Racoon ...	36508	What is this (it) subject to
Racquetare	36509	Subject to
Racquit ...	36510	It is subject to
Radachse ...	36511	Not subject to
Raddensare	36512	On the subject of
Raddolcato	36513	Will be subject to
Raddutrice	36514	Will not be subject to
Radean ...	36515	Subject to a rebate of
Radehane...	36516	Subject to a return of
Raderemur	36517	Subject to a discount of
Radfelge ...	36518	Subject to approval of
Radiabam...	36519	Subject to your approval
Radiabatur	36520	Should be subject to approval of
Radiabunt	36521	Subject to your approval I (we) propose
Radiance ...	36522	In future this will be subject to
Radiantly...	36523	In future this will not be subject to
Radiar ...	36524	Please report on this subject
Radiated ...	36525	Will report almost immediately on the subject of
Radiation...	36526	Subject to confirmation by
Radiative...	36527	Subject to a confirmation by telegram
Radiatote...	36528	Subject to the following conditions
Radiavero...	36529	Please cable with reference to this (the) subject (of)
Radicality	36530	The subject will be considered and further instructions sent
Radicals ...	36531	Am (is) continually subject to
Radicchio...	36532	Will be for the future subject to
Radicetta ...	36533	**Sublet**
Radicitus ...	36534	Can I (we) sublet
Radicoso ...	36535	Can sublet
Radicula ...	36536	Cannot sublet
Radimadia	36537	To sublet
Radiolaria	36538	You should arrange that the contract contains a clause to [sublet
Radiometro	36539	To sublet the contract
Radiosus ...	36540	To sublet the lease
Radirnadel	36541	Have good offer to sublet

Radoterie ...	36542	Upon what terms have you sublet
Radouber ...	36543	Do(es) not allow —— to sublet
Radschuh...	36544	Will not allow —— to sublet
Radspeiche	36545	Have already allowed —— to sublet
Radspur ...	36546	Can sublet as a whole or partly
Radunanza	36547	Cannot sublet as a whole
Radunato...	36548	**Submit**
Raedizo ...	36549	To submit
Raedura ...	36550	Will submit
Rafaga ...	36551	Cannot submit
Raffidarsi ...	36552	As soon as I have been able to submit
Raffinade ...	36553	Refuse(s) to submit
Raffinerie...	36554	Consent(s) to submit
Rafflers ...	36555	Will not submit
Raffling ...	36556	You had better submit
Raffoler ...	36557	You had better submit the matter to
Raffondare	36558	Before I (we) submit
Rafforzato	36559	To enable me (us) to submit
Raffreddo...	36560	If —— will submit
Raffrenare	36561	If —— will not submit
Raffuscato	36562	Recommend that you submit to it
Raffuter ...	36563	Should prefer not to submit the matter to
Raffzahn ...	36564	Solicitor(s) will submit the case to counsel
Rafistoler ...	36565	Submit as quickly as you can
Rafraichir	36566	Will submit as quickly as possible
Raftered ...	36567	When will you be able to submit
Raftering...	36568	Who will submit to you
Raftsman...	36569	Submit to —— and send copy here
Ragadia ...	36570	Submit to —— and send copy to ——
Ragamuffin	36571	**Submitted**
Ragazzame	36572	Cable replies to question(s) submitted on
Ragazzetto	36573	Have you (has ——) submitted
Ragazzola	36574	Has (have) submitted
Rageur ...	36575.	Have not submitted
Ragfair ...	36576	Has not been submitted
Raggedness	36577	Was (were) submitted on
Ragghiare	36578	Should not be submitted
Raggiata ...	36579	If you have not already submitted the matter
Raggirante	36580	Has been submitted by
Raggravare	36581	Has (have) recommended that it be submitted to
Raggruppo	36582	Have submitted it to —— whose opinion is
Ragguaglio	36583	Solicitors have submitted the case to —— whose opinion is
Ragguardo	36584	**Subordinate**
Ragingly ...	36585	Not subordinate
Ragionale...	36586	Was formerly subordinate
Ragioniere	36587	As a subordinate
Ragliare ...	36588	The position although a subordinate one involves considerable [responsibility
Ragnaja ...	36589	**Subordinated**
Ragnatela	36590	Must be subordinated to
Ragontant	36591	Should not be subordinated
Ragoter ...	36592	Entirely subordinated
Ragpicker	36593	**Subpœna**
Ragrafer ...	36594	Has (have) been served with a subpœna)
Ragrandir	36595	Better subpœna
Ragrement	36596	Cannot serve subpœna
Ragunante	36597	**Subpœnaed**
Ragunatore	36598	**Subscribe**
Ragwort ...	36599	To subscribe
Raidillon ...	36600	Will you subscribe
Raidir ...	36601	Will not subscribe

Raifort	36602	Will —— subscribe
Raigal	36603	—— will subscribe
Raigambre	36604	—— will not subscribe
Railingly	36605	Should be glad if you could see your way to subscribe
Raillery	36606	Do not see my (our) way to subscribe
Railroad	36607	Shall be glad to subscribe
Rainbow	36608	**Subscriber(s)**
Raincloud	36609	List of subscribers
Raingauge	36610	Subscribers to the Memorandum and Articles of Association
Raininess	36611	Send names of subscribers
Rainure	36612	Subscriber's(s') name(s) is (are) as follows
Rainwater	36613	**Subscription**
Raiponce	36614	Subscription list
Raisins	36615	Subscription list opens on —— and closes on ——
Raisonner	36616	How long will subscription list remain open
Raitare	36617	Subscription list will remain open until
Rajadillo	36618	Subscription list closed
Rajadura	36619	**Subsequent(ly)**
Rajahship	36620	Was it subsequent to
Rajeta	36621	Not subsequent to
Rajeunir	36622	Subsequent to
Rajouter	36623	In a subsequent interview
Rakish	36624	Should subsequent investigation
Rakishness	36625	On subsequent examination
Ralement	36626	**Subside**
Ralentir	36627	As soon as the floods subside
Raleon	36628	Until waters subside
Ralladera	36629	**Subsided**
Rallar	36630	Has (have) considerably subsided
Rallargato	36631	Has (have) completely subsided
Rallegrare	36632	Has (have) subsided sufficiently to admit of
Rallentato	36633	**Subsiding**
Rallievare	36634	Now rapidly subsiding
Rallonge	36635	Show(s) no sign(s) of subsiding
Rallumer	36636	**Subsidize**
Rallying	36637	To subsidize
Ramaccio	36638	Will it be necessary to subsidize
Ramaigrir	36639	It will not be necessary to subsidize
Ramaje	36640	**Subsidized**
Ramajolo	36641	Has (have) been subsidized
Ramalazo	36642	Subsidized by
Ramanziere	36643	Are believed to be subsidized by
Ramanzina	36644	Have all been subsidized by
Ramasser	36645	As soon as —— has (have) subsidized
Ramatata	36646	**Subsidy**
Ramatella	36647	**Substance**
Ramazzotta	36648	Cable substance of
Ramberga	36649	Cable substance of what was said
Rambles	36650	Cable substance of letter
Ramblingly	36651	**Substantial(ly)**
Ramentum	36652	Substantially true
Rameria	36653	Well and substantially built
Ramicella	36654	**Substitute** (*See also* " Following.")
Ramicosus	36655	As a substitute
Ramificare	36656	Will arrange for substitute
Ramified	36657	Have arranged for substitute
Ramigno	36658	Cannot arrange for substitute
Ramillete	36659	Wish(es) to substitute
Rammanzo	36660	Cannot substitute
Rammarico	36661	**Substituted**

Rammassato	36662	To be substituted for
Rammblock	36663	Received too late to be substituted
Rammendare	36664	As soon as I (we) have substituted
Rammezzato	36665	Should be substituted as soon as possible
Rammish ...	36666	**Substituting**
Rammollire	36667	When substituting
Rammontato	36668	If I (we) begin substituting
Ramognare	36669	**Substitution**
Ramoitir ...	36670	In substitution
Ramonage	36671	What is the proposed substitution
Ramonear...	36672	The proposed substitution is —— for ——
Ramoruto	36673	**Substratum**
Ramosita ...	36674	A substratum of
Rampage ...	36675	What is the substratum
Rampancy	36676	**Succeed**
Rampicare	36677	Did they succeed
Rampinete	36678	They did succeed
Rampion ...	36679	To succeed
Rampiste ...	36680	Can you succeed in
Rampogna	36681	I am (we are) likely to succeed
Rampognoso	36682	Are we likely to succeed
Rampollare	36683	Are you likely to succeed
Rampollo ...	36684	Am (are) not likely to succeed
Ramrod ...	36685	Believe I (we) shall succeed
Ramuccio...	36686	Am (are) certain to succeed
Rancajada	36687	Will succeed
Ranchear ...	36688	Will not succeed
Ranciadura	36689	Will it succeed
Ranciarse...	36690	Cannot possibly succeed
Rancidezza	36691	Would it be more likely to succeed if
Rancidity...	36692	Would be much more likely to succeed if
Rancidness	36693	Should it (this) succeed
Rancidulus	36694	Should it (this) not succeed
Rancidume	36695	This (it) will almost certainly enable me to succeed
Rancioso ...	36696	Am (are) very much afraid it cannot succeed
Rancissure	36697	In case you do not succeed
Ranconner	36698	In case you should succeed
Rancorous	36699	Should I (we) succeed
Rancour ...	36700	I (we) hope you will succeed (with)
Rancunier	36701	So as to succeed
Rancurarsi	36702	Can you in any way succeed in (with)
Randagine	36703	Should I (we) succeed
Randaje ...	36704	Do you think —— will succeed
Randellare	36705	My opinion is that —— will succeed
Randello ...	36706	My opinion is that —— will not succeed
Randera ...	36707	There is only a remote chance that I (we) shall succeed
Randione ...	36708	**Succeeded**
Random ...	36709	Has (have) not succeeded
Randomshot	36710	Have you succeeded
Rangership	36711	Has (have) —— succeeded
Rangifero	36712	As soon as I (we) have succeeded in (with)
Ranging ...	36713	Which has perfectly succeeded
Rangolare	36714	Cable whether —— (you) have succeeded
Rangoloso	36715	In case it (this) has not succeeded
Rangstreit	36716	**Success** (*See also* "Confident," "Hope.")
Rangulo ...	36717	Cable what success you have met with
Ranilla ...	36718	It has been a great success
Raninas ...	36719	It has only been a partial success
Rankevoll	36720	Is (are) almost sure to be a success
Rankness...	36721	Should it not prove a success

Rannestare	36722	Success is now assured
Ranniere ...	36723	Success is very doubtful
Rannocchia	36724	Have (had) a great success with
Rannodare	36725	Must do your best to make it a success
Ranny ...	36726	Will do my (our) best to make it a success
Ransack ...	36727	Cable what success you have had with (in)
Ransomer	36728	Must be made a success if in any way possible
Ransomless	36729	If it cannot be made a success
Ranter ...	36730	Promises to be a brilliant success
Rantingly...	36731	Anything but a success
Rantipole...	36732	Has always been a success
Ranuncolo	36733	Has never been a success
Ranunculus	36734	Was (were) not a success at first
Ranuzza ...	36735	Has only lately become a success
Ranzonare	36736	—— has achieved considerable success with
Rapacejo ...	36737	Has —— ever obtained any success with
Rapaceria	36738	A continuous success
Rapacidad	36739	Am sanguine of ultimate success
Rapacious	36740	Am by no means sanguine of success
Rapadura...	36741	**Successful** (*See also* "Experiment.")
Rapagon ...	36742	Not yet successful
Rapatelle ...	36743	More successful
Rapatriage	36744	Not so successful as was at first reported
Rapatrier ...	36745	Has not been at all successful
Rapazada...	36746	**Successfully**
Raperilla ...	36747	Quite successfully
Raperonzo	36748	**Such**
Rapeseed ...	36749	Some such
Rapetasser	36750	From such
Raphaninus	36751	By such
Raphides ...	36752	Such as
Rapicuis ...	36753	Such a source as
Rapieceter	36754	Such is (are)
Rapiego ...	36755	Just such an one
Rapiendus	36756	**Suction** (*See also* "Hose.")
Rapimento	36757	Ordinary suction pump
Rapinador	36758	**Sudden**
Rapine ...	36759	**Suddenly**
Rapinoso ...	36760	It has been suddenly arranged that
Rapitore ...	36761	Has been suddenly announced
Rapitrice ...	36762	Too suddenly
Raponchigo	36763	Very suddenly
Rapontico	36764	**Sue** (*See also* "Suing.")
Raposear ...	36765	To sue
Rappaciare	36766	Wish to sue
Rappagarsi	36767	Shall I sue
Rappagato	36768	Do not sue
Rapparier...	36769	You had better sue at once
Rappartito	36770	You had better sue for damages
Rappee ...	36771	It is useless to sue
Rappeler ...	36772	Will sue
Rappezzare	36773	Will not sue
Rappinnare	36774	Should sue —— (him) at once
Rapport ...	36775	**Sued**
Rapporteur	36776	To sue or be sued
Rapprendre	36777	If sued
Rappresso	36778	If sued you had better
Rapprocher	36779	**Suffice**
Rappurare	36780	To suffice
Rapsodia ...	36781	Will it (this) suffice

SUFFICE *(continued).* **Rap–Ras**

Rapsodiste	36782	Will suffice
Raptandus	36783	Will not suffice
Rapturist ...	36784	Should it not suffice
Rapturous	36785	A pen and ink sketch showing main points would suffice
Rapunzel ...	36786	This will suffice until the re-arrangement of —— can be effected
Raqueta ...	36787	**Sufficient(ly)**
Raquetero...	36788	As sufficient
Raquettier	36789	You must keep sufficient money to pay
Raquitico ...	36790	Had I (we) not better keep sufficient money to pay cost of
Rareeshow	36791	What will be sufficient
Rarefactus	36792	It will be quite sufficient if I (we) have
Rarefatto ...	36793	It is hardly sufficient
Rarefiable...	36794	Will be hardly sufficient
Rarefy ...	36795	Has been hardly sufficient
Rarement...	36796	This is not sufficient for
Rarescens ...	36797	Will be sufficient to go on with for the present
Raridad ...	36798	Not sufficient time
Rarificar ...	36799	Has (have) sufficient time for
Raripilus ...	36800	Has not sufficient time
Rarissime ...	36801	A sufficient quantity
Rasamente	36802	A sufficient quantity for (of)
Rasaminem	36803	There is not sufficient for
Rascadura	36804	There is sufficient for
Rascalino ...	36805	Is there sufficient for
Rascality ...	36806	Not in sufficient quantities
Rascals ...	36807	Not sufficient money
Rascazon ...	36808	Has (have) sufficient money for
Rascheit ...	36809	Has not sufficient money
Rascheln ...	36810	Have just sufficient money in hand to
Raschiare...	36811	Have you sufficient money in hand to
Rasciugare	36812	Have not sufficient money to
Rascunar ...	36813	Will give me sufficient
Rasegesang	36814	You had better purchase sufficient
Raselied ...	36815	Not having sufficient (of)
Rasenplatz	36816	Have not sufficient
Rasentare...	36817	Have quite sufficient
Rasete ...	36818	Should you not have sufficient
Rasgado ...	36819	Shall have sufficient if
Rasgueado	36820	Only just sufficient
Rasguno ...	36821	Not sufficient to pay
Rashness ...	36822	Will be sufficient to pay
Rasibus ...	36823	But not sufficient for
Rasiera ...	36824	**Suffocate**
Rasoir ...	36825	**Suffocated**
Rasojaccio	36826	**Suffocation**
Rasorius ...	36827	Died from suffocation
Raspadera	36828	**Suggest**
Raspadillo	36829	Can you suggest
Raspante ...	36830	Suggest that you
Raspato ...	36831	Cannot suggest anything better
Raspatura	36832	What do you suggest
Raspberry	36833	I do not know that I (we) can suggest anything further
Rasperella	36834	Can you suggest anything
Raspinegro	36835	To suggest
Raspollare	36836	Can you suggest any other way
Rasqueta ...	36837	The only thing I (we) can suggest is
Rassade ...	36838	Will act as you suggest
Rassalire ...	36839	Cannot suggest anything
Rassasier ...	36840	Cannot suggest any better way
Rasseggato	36841	Shall be glad to hear of anything you can suggest

[615]

Rassegnare	36842	Cannot act exactly as you suggest
Rassembler	36843	Cannot act as you suggest because
Rasserener	36844	Should suggest that
Rassieger ...	36845	**Suggested**
Rassigno ...	36846	As already suggested
Rassodare...	36847	Has (have) suggested to —— (that)
Rassortir ...	36848	Never was suggested
Rastel ...	36849	Is alleged to have suggested
Rastellum...	36850	**Suggestion(s)** (*See also* " Inconsistent.")
Rastiare ...	36851	Please make suggestions
Rastiatojo	36852	Have you any suggestions to offer
Rastiatura.	36853	Would offer the following suggestions
Rastillar ...	36854	Have no suggestion to offer
Rastlos ...	36855	Will adopt any suggestion you may make
Rastrallar	36856	Arrange to carry out suggestions of
Rastreador	36857	**Suing** (*See also* " Sue.")
Rastrello ...	36858	Now suing for
Rastrojero	36859	**Suit**
Rasttag ...	36860	To suit
Rasure ...	36861	Will it (they) suit
Ratafia ...	36862	Will not suit
Ratarias ...	36863	Will suit very well
Ratatat ...	36864	Will not suit at all
Ratatiner ...	36865	Would suit much better
Ratcatcher	36866	Would not suit nearly so well
Ratebook ...	36867	Should it (they) not suit
Ratelage ...	36868	Have you anything that would suit
Rateleur ...	36869	Do you know anyone who would suit
Rateria ...	36870	Do not know anyone likely to suit
Rathgeber	36871	The only thing I can suggest as being likely to suit (is)
Rathhaus ...	36872	**Suitable**
Rathsam ...	36873	Not at all suitable
Rathschlag	36874	Would it be suitable
Rathsherr...	36875	Would be most suitable
Ratiere ...	36876	Can be made suitable if
Ratificare ...	36877	Not suitable in any way
Ratigar ...	36878	Suitable in every way
Ratiocinor	36879	If anything more suitable
Rationalis	36880	Unless you can suggest something more suitable
Rationnel...	36881	Which would you think would be the more suitable
Rations ...	36882	The most suitable course would be
Ratissage ...	36883	Is not considered quite suitable
Ratissoire...	36884	**Sulphate**
Ratlins ...	36885	Sulphate of
Ratonar ...	36886	**Sulphide** (*See also* " Mineral.")
Ratsbane ...	36887	Sulphide of
Rattaccare	36888	Sulphide of antimony
Rattamente	36889	Sulphide of arsenic
Rattans ...	36890	Sulphide of bismuth
Rattarpare	36891	Sulphide of copper
Ratteindre	36892	Sulphide of iron
Rattenersi	36893	Sulphide of lead
Rattengift	36894	Sulphide of silver
Rattenuto	36895	Sulphide of zinc
Rattezza ...	36896	Mixed sulphides of
Rattizzare	36897	**Sulphur**
Rattles ...	36898	The sulphur mine
Rattoppato	36899	—— per cent. of sulphur
Rattorcere	36900	Crude sulphur
Rattraere ...	36901	Can deliver crude sulphur to —— at —— per ton

Rattratto ...	36902	**Sulphuret(s)** (*See also* "Concentrates.")
Raturer ...	36903	The quartz contains —— per cent. of sulphurets
Rauber ...	36904	Shall stock the sulphurets for the present
Rauberisch	36905	Contained in the sulphurets
Raubmord	36906	Cannot treat the sulphurets for the present
Raubritter	36907	**Sum(s)**
Raubstatt...	36908	Sum of
Raubthier	36909	To sum up
Raubvogel	36910	A lump sum of
Raucedine	36911	For the lump sum of
Raucedo ...	36912	What is the sum named
Raucherig	36913	The sum named is
Rauchfang	36914	Do you think it worth the sum named
Rauchtabak	36915	I (we) think it well worth the sum named
Raucisonus	36916	I (we) do not think it worth the sum named
Raudal ...	36917	The sum is too large
Raudamente	36918	What is the sum total of
Raufbold ...	36919	Would not be too large a sum for
Raumiliare	36920	In my opinion the sum is much too large
Raumlich...	36921	The sum named is too large by
Raumung...	36922	In my opinion the sum would not be too large if
Raunare ...	36923	I (we) think the sum a very fair one
Raunatrice	36924	Considerable sums have been spent on
Rauncinato	36925	The following sums
Rauschen ...	36926	The sum named was
Rauschgold	36927	No sum was named
Rauspern ...	36928	What sum have you now in hand
Ravager ...	36929	**Summer**
Ravaging ...	36930	About last summer
Ravaglione	36931	This summer
Ravalement	36932	Next summer
Ravandage	36933	During the present summer
Ravanderie	36934	Last summer
Ravanello ...	36935	At the end of the summer weather
Ravelings...	36936	The weather is exceedingly hot during the summer
Ravenelle ...	36937	During summer the climate is very unhealthy
Ravening ...	36938	During summer the weather although hot, is healthy
Ravenous ..	36939	In the summer of this year
Raverusto...	36940	**Summit**
Ravigote ...	36941	On the summit of
Ravilir ...	36942	From —— to the summit
Ravisante...	36943	To avoid crossing the summit
Ravisher ...	36944	At the summit the altitude is
Ravisseur...	36945	To the summit
Ravvedersi	36946	**Summon(s)**
Ravveduto	36947	To summon
Ravvinto ...	36948	Better at once summon
Ravvisare...	36949	**Summoned**
Ravvolgere	36950	Summoned to
Ravvolto ...	36951	Have you summoned
Rawboned ...	36952	Have summoned
Rawness ...	36953	Have not summoned
Rayano ...	36954	Must be summoned at once
Rayeta ...	36955	**Sump** (*See also* "Bottom," "Sunk.")
Rayonner...	36956	Sump shaft
Raynelo ...	36957	At the bottom of the sump
Raziocinio	36958	Sump is now —— feet deep
Razonable	36959	What is the depth of the sump below the bottom level
Razonador	36960	Shall clear out sump and recommence sinking at once
Razorbill ...	36961	**Sunday**

Razors	36962	On Sunday
Razzaccia	36963	Last Sunday
Razzegiare	36964	Next Sunday
Razzese	36965	Next Sunday week
Razzimato	36966	Every Sunday
Razzolare	36967	Every alternate Sunday
Razzuolo	36968	—— Sunday(s) in each month
Reabsorbed	36969	On Sunday morning
Reachable	36970	On Sunday afternoon
Reacio	36971	On Sunday night
Reactively	36972	During Sunday
Readably	36973	During Sunday night
Readjust	36974	About Sunday week
Readmettre	36975	**Sundry**
Readmitir	36976	For sundry reasons
Readopto	36977	From sundry causes
Readornar	36978	**Sunk**
Reafficher	36979	Now being sunk
Reagente	36980	Was sunk to a depth of —— feet
Reagravar	36981	—— feet have been sunk through
Reagudo	36982	As soon as we have sunk a further —— feet
Reajourner	36983	How deep have you sunk
Realenjo	36984	Have sunk
Realgar	36985	Have sunk —— feet (for)
Realidad	36986	Have sunk —— feet since
Realillo	36987	Sunk on the vein
Realisiren	36988	Sunk in the country rock
Realism	36989	Sunk on the vein —— feet
Realistic	36990	Sunk in country rock —— feet
Realized	36991	After —— feet have been sunk
Realmente	36992	After —— has been sunk
Reanimar	36993	The vertical depth sunk is —— feet
Reapposer	36994	The inclined depth sunk is —— feet
Reapretar	36995	From —— to —— inclusive we have sunk —— feet
Reaquistar	36996	Sunk entirely in pay ore
Reargenter	36997	Sunk entirely in barren rock
Rearguard	36998	Do you consider that you have sunk deep enough to (for)
Rearmost	36999	We have not yet sunk deep enough to (for)
Rearrank	37000	We have now sunk quite deep enough (to prove) [—— feet
Reascent	37001	Shall start to drive as soon as we have sunk an additional
Reasoner	37002	Winze has been sunk
Reasoning	37003	Shaft has been sunk
Reasonless	37004	As soon as we have sunk sufficiently deep for a sump
Reassigner	37005	Several small shafts have been sunk on the vein
Reassunto	37006	This shaft was sunk in order to
Reasumir	37007	**Sun-stroke**
Reasuncion	37008	Has had a sunstroke
Reatadura	37009	Suffering from sunstroke
Reatteler	37010	**Superficial(ly)** (*See also* "Area.")
Reattivo	37011	Covers a superficial area of
Reaventar	37012	What is the superficial area of ——
Reazione	37013	The superficial area is —— acres
Rebaisser	37014	The property contains a superficial area of
Rebalage	37015	—— acres superficial area
Rebalsar	37016	—— yards superficial area
Rebander	37017	**Superfluous**
Rebanego	37018	Quite superfluous
Rebaptised	37019	Would be superfluous at the present time
Rebaptism	37020	**Superintend(s)**
Rebarbatif	37021	To superintend

Rebatina ...	87022	Will superintend personally
Rebattre ...	87023	Could not —— superintend
Rebautizar	87024	Might very well superintend
Rebbiare ...	87025	Could not superintend
Rebelarse ...	87026	Shall send —— to superintend
Rebelde ...	87027	You had better appoint —— to superintend
Rebellans...	87028	Has (have) appointed —— to superintend
Rebellator	87029	Should have a competent man to superintend
Rebeller ...	87030	Do you require anyone to superintend
Rebellious	87031	Do you know a suitable man to superintend
Rebelliren	87032	Will you send a suitable man to superintend
Rebellisch	87033	Shall I (we) send a competent man to superintend
Rebencazo	37034	For the present you must personally superintend
Rebendecir	37035	Will superintend it (this) myself
Rebenque ...	37036	Cannot undertake to personally superintend
Rebenstock	87037	Cannot superintend as
Rebezo ...	37038	Will superintend as far as I am (we are) able
Rebien ...	37039	Whom do you propose to superintend
Rebiffer ...	87040	—— can very well superintend until
Rebinadura	37041	**Superintended**
Rebirar ...	87042	Will be superintended by
Rebisnieta	37043	Was superintended
Reblanchir	87044	Was not superintended
Reboatum	87045	Who superintended
Reboire ...	37046	**Superintendence**
Rebollo ...	87047	Under ——'s superintendence
Reborder ...	37048	Under my personal superintendence
Rebosadero	87049	**Superintendent**
Rebotador...	37050	As joint superintendent
Rebotica ...	37051	A competent superintendent
Reboucher	37052	Was superintendent of
Rebouillir...	37053	Is superintendent of
Rebounded	37054	Will remain superintendent until
Rebramar...	37055	Employ as mine superintendent
Rebrotin ...	37056	As mine superintendent
Rebrousser	37057	General dissatisfaction expressed with mine superintendent
Rebroyer ...	37058	How long will —— remain superintendent
Rebueno ...	37059	Ceased to be superintendent on
Rebuff ...	37060	Resign my position as superintendent
Rebuffade...	37061	**Superior**
Rebuilt ...	37062	Must be superior
Rebuker ...	37063	Must be superior to that (those) hitherto sent
Rebuking ...	37064	Alleged to be very superior
Rebullicio...	37065	Was (were) by no means superior
Rebullir ...	37066	As being (——'s) superior
Reburjar ...	37067	Is the superior officer
Rebuscador	37068	**Supersede(s)**
Rebuses	37069	To supersede
Rebutted ...	37070	Could supersede
Rebuznar ...	37071	Could not supersede
Recabdar ...	37072	Should be competent to supersede
Recacher ...	37073	**Superseded**
Recadero ...	37074	Was superseded by
Recaida ...	37075	Has never been superseded
Recalcitro...	37076	**Supervise(d)**
Recalentar	37077	To supervise
Recalesco ...	37078	Cannot personally supervise
Recalfacio	37079	**Supervision**
Recalled ...	37080	Under my personal supervision
Recalzon ...	37081	Should be under your own supervision

Recamador	37082	In case it cannot be done under your personal supervision
Recambiar	37083	There has been practically no supervision at all
Recanacion	37084	Must be done under efficient supervision
Recantatio	37085	Under efficient supervision
Recanter ...	37086	To be done under efficient supervision
Recapio ...	37087	There would be no difficulty under efficient supervision
Recapitare	37088	The difficulty is to arrange efficient supervision
Recapture...	37089	**Supplement**
Recargar ...	37090	As a supplement to
Recarreler	37091	Will require to supplement
Recarsi ...	37092	As soon as you decide to supplement
Recasser ...	37093	Is it necessary to supplement
Recasurus...	37094	It is necessary to supplement
Recatonazo	37095	It is not necessary to supplement
Recatonear	37096	**Supplementary**
Recatore ...	37097	Must be regarded as supplementary
Recatrice ...	37098	A supplementary report
Recaudador	37099	Supplementary power for
Recchiata...	37100	**Supplemented**
Receipted...	37101	Supplemented by
Recelador...	37102	Could be supplemented later by
Recelement	37103	Intended to be supplemented by
Receleur ...	37104	**Supplied**
Recension...	37105	Could not be supplied
Recensiren	37106	Expect to be fully supplied
Recensitus	37107	Who supplied it (them)
Recental ...	37108	Was (were) supplied by
Recepage ...	37109	Supplied by
Recepisse ...	37110	To be supplied by
Receptacle	37111	Supplied in place of
Receptivo ...	37112	As soon as I am (we are) supplied with
Receptrix ...	37113	Has (have) supplied
Recercler ...	37114	Supplied —— with
Recesit ...	37115	Badly supplied
Recessior ...	37116	Well supplied
Recetero ...	37117	Should be supplied with
Recetoria ...	37118	Should be supplied at once
Receveuse...	37119	Was (were) fully supplied with
Recevoir ...	37120	Are you supplied with
Rechamus	37121	Am (are) amply supplied with
Rechapper	37122	Am practically not supplied at all
Rechaud ...	37123	Could be supplied at
Rechauffer	37124	Cannot be supplied at less than
Rechazador	37125	Cannot be supplied until
Recheat ...	37126	Has (have) not yet been supplied
Rechenbuch	37127	When will it (this) be supplied
Recherche...	37128	Can be supplied within —— days
Rechifla ...	37129	Has (have) already been supplied
Rechigner	37130	All particulars will be supplied by
Rechinante	37131	—— has supplied all necessary information
Rechinar ...	37132	Information supplied by —— is of very little practical value
Rechnung	37133	Information supplied by —— is of considerable value
Rechoncho	37134	**Supplies** (*See also* " Condemned," " Store.")
Rechoosen	37135	Do you need further supplies
Rechteckig	37136	Supplies are needed for
Rechtlich ...	37137	Have contracted for regular supplies (of)
Rechtsfall...	37138	In the absence of further supplies
Rechtsgang	37139	Supplies are running short
Recibidero	37140	What supplies are required
Recibiente	37141	Require the following supplies

Recibir	...	87142	In the absence of the necessary supplies
Recidendus		87143	Further supplies will be sent
Recidive	...	87144	Supplies for the mill
Recinchar		87145	General mining supplies
Reciniatus		87146	Both mining and milling supplies
Recinium	...	87147	Supplies for the smelting works
Recipiens	...	87148	What is the value of supplies in stock
Reciprocar		87149	The total value of supplies in stock is ——
Reciproque		87150	Owing to difficulty in transporting supplies
Recisimo	...	87151	Supplies can be easily transported to the mine from
Recitado	...	87152	Owing to the difficulty of obtaining supplies
Recitandus		87153	Freight of supplies
Recitante	...	87154	The freight of supplies from —— is —— per ton
Recitative	...	87155	Supplies very much needed
Recitatrix	...	87156	When may I (we) expect to receive supplies
Reciter	...	87157	When do you expect to receive supplies
Reciticcio	...	87158	Expect to have further supplies by
Reciura	...	87159	Sell supplies and stores for what they will realize
Recizalla	...	87160	Have sold supplies; they have realized
Reckless	...	87161	The supplies still on hand have no market value
Reckoner	...	87162	Supplies, machinery, tools and fittings
Reclamar	...	87163	All supplies and materials consumed to be paid for
Reclamatio		87164	**Supply** (*See also* "Plentiful.")
Reclanget		87165	For the supply of
Reclinator		87166	To supply
Reclosed	...	87167	Can you supply
Reclusion	...	87168	Can supply
Reclutador		87169	Cannot supply
Reclutare	...	87170	Should supply
Recobrable		87171	Should not supply
Recobrar	...	87172	Shall I (we) supply
Recocer	...	87173	Would you advise me to supply
Recodadero		87174	Would not advise you to supply
Recogedor		87175	To supply the mill
Recogidas	...	87176	Water supply
Recogitare		87177	Would supply at
Recognosco		87178	Refuse(s) to supply
Recoiffer	...	87179	Consent(s) to supply
Recoiling	...	87180	Please supply full instructions (for)
Recoinage	...	87181	Will supply you with all needful instructions
Recolendus		87182	Report on the supply of
Recoleto	...	87183	Sufficient to supply mill for
Recoller	...	87184	There is a good supply of
Recolligor	...	87185	There is an abundant supply of
Recolorado		87186	The supply of —— is abundant for the time of the year
Recombinar		87187	There is a fair supply of
Recomendar		87188	There is a very poor supply of
Recompensa		87189	There is now a regular supply of
Recomponer		87190	Shall have a regular supply of —— so long as
Recompter		87191	The supply of —— is very irregular
Reconcinno		87192	The supply is small but constant,
Reconcomio		87193	Have contracted for a supply of —— at
Recondite		87194	You had better contract for a supply (of)
Reconducir		87195	Have contracted for a supply (of)
Reconfesar		87196	Please send a further supply of
Reconocer	...	87197	Shall I (we) send a further supply (of)
Reconocido		87198	Shall require an additional supply of —— not later than
Recontante		87199	A further supply has been sent
Recontar	...	87200	Can supply you with
Reconvenir		87201	Supply is very short

Reconvert	37202	Have an ample supply on hand
Recopilar ...	37203	Supply on hand will last until
Recoquin ...	37204	Who will take charge of supplies and stores
Recordable	37205	Hold supplies for the present ; mail particulars of value
Recordatus	37206	Have obtained tenders for the supply of
Recorrida ...	37207	Supply on hand will not last more than —— days
Recortado...	37208	A plentiful supply can be obtained from
Recoser ...	37209	Sufficient to supply all demands
Recoudre ...	37210	It will be necessary that you should supply at once
Recoup ...	37211	When can you supply it (them)
Recoupette	37212	Please supply all necessary information
Recourber	37213	Will supply you with all necessary information
Recouvrir ...	37214	Can —— supply any information
Recoveco ...	37215	Before you supply —— with any information
Recracher...	37216	Is —— willing to supply further information
Recrastino	37217	—— is willing to supply further information
Recrearsi ...	37218	—— is not willing to supply further information
Recreative	37219	After which we shall be able to supply —— stamps
Recrecer ...	37220	There is every promise of an abundant supply of
Recreido ...	37221	**Supplying**
Recremento	37222	—— is supplying all the funds
Recrepir ...	37223	Must cease supplying
Recrescens	37224	Cannot continue supplying
Recriminar	37225	Alleged to be supplying
Recroitre ...	37226	Supplying information
Recrossed...	37227	**Support(s)**
Recruit ...	37228	To support
Recruiting	37229	The support(s)
Recruteur...	37230	Owing to insufficient support
Rectamente	37231	You may rely upon my (our) support
Rectangulo	37232	Can I (we) rely upon your support
Rectifier ...	37233	I think —— will require financial support
Rectilineo...	37234	Am (are) willing to support you (them) to the extent of
Rectitude...	37235	Will you support me (us) to the extent of
Rectorial ...	37236	Unless you can support
Rectorship	37237	Must have the support of
Rectrix ...	37238	Owing to the want of proper support(s)
Recuadrar	37239	There was (were) no support(s) at all
Recuarta ...	37240	Owing to the supports having failed
Recubitus	37241	Can you obtain ——'s support
Recudir ...	37242	Has consented to support
Recueillir ...	37243	Has refused to support
Recuestar...	37244	Can I (we) consent to support
Reculement	37245	Is (are) willing to support
Reculones...	37246	Is (are) not willing to support
Recumbence	37247	You had better not support
Recuperar...	37248	Ought certainly to support
Recurator	37249	So as to support
Recurso ...	37250	Requires internal support
Recurvate...	37251	Requires external support
Recurvitas	37252	Authorities promise support
Recusable	37253	Will authorities support
Recusacion	37254	Authorities will not support
Recusancy	37255	Does it need further support
Recutitus ...	37256	Does not need further support
Redabsolvo	37257	**Supported**
Redaccion...	37258	Unless properly supported
Redactor ...	37259	Unless supported by documentary evidence
Redacturus	37260	Can be supported by facts
Redaggia ...	37261	Partially supported

Redambulo	37262	Entirely supported
Redantruo	37263	Hitherto supported
Redardesco	37264	**Suppose**
Redarguire	37265	To suppose
Redargutio	37266	Can only suppose that
Redatrice ...	37267	Has (have) been led to suppose that
Redauspico	37268	Am (are) not sure, but suppose it will be about
Redazione	37269	How much do you suppose
Redbreast...	37270	What reason have you to suppose that (this)
Redcoat ...	37271	I (we) do not suppose for an instant that
Reddendus	37272	Do you still suppose
Reddishly...	37273	Do not now suppose
Reddita ...	37274	**Supposed**
Redditivus	37275	Is (are) supposed to have been
Reddle ...	37276	Is supposed to have taken place
Redeemed...	37277	It is supposed that
Redefaire ...	37278	It is generally supposed
Redekunst	37279	It has never been supposed that
Redemander	37280	It was at first supposed
Redempteur	37281	Is not to be supposed for an instant
Redemptito	37282	**Supposition**
Redemptrix	37283	On the following supposition, viz. :—
Redencion	37284	The merest supposition
Redentor ...	37285	Is no longer merely a supposition
Redentrice	37286	The original supposition was that
Redethiel ...	37287	**Suppress**
Redevable...	37288	To suppress
Redevenir...	37289	Endeavour to suppress
Redhibeor	37290	Will endeavour to suppress
Redhibitum	37291	Was not able to suppress
Redhostio...	37292	Believe —— is trying to suppress
Redhot ...	37293	**Suppressed**
Redicho ...	37294	Has been suppressed
Rediezmar	37295	Has not been suppressed
Redificare...	37296	Has been suppressed by
Redimendus	37297	Unless it can be suppressed
Redimere ...	37298	Before it was suppressed
Redimible	37299	**Suppression**
Redingote	37300	Owing to suppression of the following material facts, viz. :—
Redinteger	37301	Guilty of wilful suppression
Redipiscor	37302	**Supreme**
Rediseur ...	37303	Decision of Supreme Court
Reditaggio	37304	Carry to Supreme Court
Reditiero ...	37305	Will carry to Supreme Court
Redituable	37306	In supreme control
Redituar ...	37307	Must have supreme control
Redivius ...	37308	Unless I (we) can have supreme control
Redletter ...	37309	**Surcharge(d)**
Redlich ...	37310	**Sure**
Rednosed ...	37311	Can you be sure that
Redoblado	37312	I am (we are) sure that
Redoble ...	37313	Quite sure
Redoblegar	37314	Quite a sure thing
Redolency	37315	Not at all sure
Redomazo	37316	Not sure that
Redomitus	37317	Is (are) sure that
Redondear	37318	To be sure
Redondilla	37319	You must be perfectly sure
Redondon...	37320	Are you (is——) quite sure (that)
Redopelo ...	37321	I am (we are) absolutely sure (that)

Redordior...	37322	I am (we are) not at all sure
Redormitio	37323	In order to be quite sure
Redoubt ...	37324	As soon as I am (we are) quite sure
Redowa ...	37325	Is (are) sure
Redpole ...	37326	Is (are) not at all sure
Redresser	37327	Am (are) not so sure
Redrojo ...	37328	Cable as soon as you are sure
Redrojuelo	37329	So as to be sure
Redruna ...	37330	In order to make doubly sure
Redselig ...	37331	Unless you are quite sure
Redshank...	37332	Cable whether you are or are not sure
Redstart ...	37333	Had better first make sure
Redstreak	37334	Do(es) not feel altogether sure
Redtail ...	37335	To enable me (us) to make sure
Redtapist ...	37336	Better make sure of —— (him)
Reducible	37337	Do you still feel sure as regards
Reduciren...	37338	Do not now feel so sure
Reductivo...	37339	Feel just as sure
Reductorem	37340	**Surely**
Reducturus	37341	Surely not
Reduire ...	37342	Will surely be sufficient
Redulceror	37343	**Surety**
Redundante	37344	As surety for
Redundatio	37345	Not sufficient surety
Reduplicar	37346	Decline(s) to become surety
Reduviosus	37347	Consent(s) to become surety
Redwood ...	37348	**Surface** (*See also* " Area," " Indication.")
Reedgrass...	37349	Surface deposit
Reefer ...	37350	The surface
Roefing ...	37351	On the surface
Reelecto ...	37352	Surface indications show
Reelegir ...	37353	From the surface downwards for a depth of —— feet
Reeligible...	37354	From the surface
Reembargar	37355	Along the surface
Reembolsar	37356	Below the surface
Reemplazo	37357	Near the surface
Reemplear	37358	The entire surface is covered with
Reengrave	37359	Is merely a surface show
Reensayar	37360	A complete survey of surface
Reentrant...	37361	A survey of surface boundaries
Reenvidar	37362	Judging from the old workings at surface
Reesperar...	37363	At a depth of —— feet from surface
Reeved ...	37364	All surface work is suspended by severe weather
Reexpedier	37365	All surface work is suspended during —— months of the year
Reexporter	37366	At surface all work is proceeding in a satisfactory manner
Refaccion ...	37367	At surface the work of clearing progresses satisfactorily
Refajeado...	37368	**Surmise**
Refajuolo...	37369	**Surmount**
Refalsado...	37370	In order to surmount
Refashion...	37371	Provided that I (we) can surmount
Refectorio	37372	**Surmounted**
Refellens ...	37373	Has (have) surmounted all difficulties
Referancia	37374	As soon as I (we) have surmounted
Referente ...	37375	Cannot be surmounted
Referible ...	37376	**Surname**
Referiren ...	37377	Require correct surname of
Refermer ...	37378	**Surpass(ed)**
Refertero ...	37379	Has (have) surpassed my (our) expectations
Refervesco	37380	**Surplus**
Refezione ...	37381	The surplus

Refftrager	37382	What surplus
Reficior ...	37383	A surplus of
Refigendus	37384	What surplus will you have
Refigurar ...	37385	What surplus will you have after you have paid all outstand- [ing liabilities
Refilon ...	37386	Shall have no surplus at all
Refiltrer ...	37387	Do not anticipate any surplus
Refinacion	37388	Expect the surplus will amount to
Refinadera	37389	Any surplus to be returned to subscribers
Refingere ...	37390	Any surplus to be used for
Refirmar ...	37391	Any surplus can be devoted to
Refitalero ...	37392	Surplus amounts to
Refitorio ...	37393	There is a considerable surplus
Refitting ...	37394	In case you have any surplus
Reflagito ...	37395	**Surprise**
Reflechir ...	37396	To surprise
Reflectar ...	37397	Is a great surprise
Reflessare	37398	Is no surprise
Reflexible...	37399	Has taken me (us) by surprise
Reflexity ...	37400	**Surprised**
Reflorecer...	37401	Am (are) somewhat surprised that
Reflourish	37402	Do not wish to be surprised with
Refluent ...	37403	Was (were) considerably surprised
Refluire ...	37404	Not much surprised
Refluxus ...	37405	Surprised to find
Refocilar ...	37406	Surprised to learn
Refodior ...	37407	Surprised to discover
Refollar ...	37408	Surprised to receive
Reforger ...	37409	Do not be surprised if
Reformatus	37410	Should not be surprised to learn
Reformiren	37411	**Surrender**
Reformist	37412	Will —— agree to surrender the papers
Reforzada	37413	Will not agree to surrender
Refoseto ...	37414	Has (have) already agreed to surrender
Refossam ...	37415	Do not surrender
Refovendus	37416	**Surreptitious(ly)**
Refoveor ...	37417	**Surround**
Refraction	37418	**Surrounded**
Refragatus	37419	Surrounded by
Refrain ...	37420	Am (is) (are) at present surrounded by
Refrangere	37421	**Surrounding(s)**
Refranillo	37422	From the general surroundings
Refrapper...	37423	The general surroundings are very satisfactory
Refregar ...	37424	The general surroundings are most unsatisfactory
Refrenato ...	37425	The general surroundings leave much to be desired
Refrendata	37426	The surrounding country
Refresco ...	37427	From the mines surrounding
Refreshed...	37428	Under the present surroundings
Refricatio	37429	**Survey** (*See also* "Dial," "Theodolite.")
Refriega ...	37430	To survey
Refrigerar	37431	Has survey been made
Refrigesco	37432	The survey has been made
Refringens	37433	Survey now being made; expect to complete about
Refringir ...	37434	Shall proceed to survey
Refriser ...	37435	When will survey be completed
Refroidir ...	37436	Survey will be completed within —— week(s)
Refuelle ...	37437	Arrange to have survey made at once
Refugee ...	37438	Forward tracing of survey as soon as possible
Refuggio ...	37439	Survey not yet completed
Refugiado...	37440	Is any accurate survey being made of
Refulgent ...	37441	Is there any correct survey of

Refulgidus	87442	No survey whatsoever has been made
Refundir ...	87443	Doubt correctness of survey
Refusar ...	87444	The survey(s) indicate(s) that
Refutable...	87445	Is shown by tracing of survey sent
Refutador .	87446	Survey shows that I am (we are) in the right
Refutatio ...	87447	When can you commence survey of
Regadera ..	87448	Shall commence survey within —— days
Regadio ...	87449	Cannot commence survey until
Regajal ...	87450	Am (are) now engaged on survey
Regalada ...	87451	From survey of old workings
Regaliolus	87452	How long will the survey take
Regaliter ...	87453	The survey will take —— days
Regalon ...	87454	Can you contract for complete survey
Regaluccio	87455	Can contract for complete survey at
Reganador	87456	Survey of surface
Regardant	87457	Underground survey
Regardless	87458	Survey for line of
Regatear ...	87459	Provided that survey is satisfactory
Regatonear	87460	Demand another survey
Regatta ...	87461	Make entire survey
Regayoir ...	87462	What will be the cost of an entire survey
Regazo ...	87463	The entire survey would cost about
Regeletur...	87464	Require entire survey
Regellos ...	87465	Require entirely new survey [me (us)
Regelrecht	87466	Have a survey made immediately, and post original map to
Regenbogen	87467	Have a survey made immediately, and post tracing to me (us)
Regency ...	87468	Separate survey would cost about
Regendach	87469	Only require additions to survey
Regeneracy	87470	Instruct —— to survey at once
Regenerer	87471	Survey now being made
Regenguss	87472	Inclined to think survey is correct
Regentship	87473	Make sure that ——'s survey is correct
Regenzeit...	87474	When will you finish survey
Regermino	87475	Expect to finish survey and forward plans on or about
Reggibile ...	87476	In the event of survey not being satisfactory
Reggitore...	87477	In the absence of attested survey
Reggitrice	87478	Complete survey not necessary, only additions
Regiamente	87479	Complete survey only necessary in case you have doubts as to
Regibado ...	87480	Complete survey very necessary [the accuracy of present plans
Regicide ...	87481	Survey completed
Regidoria...	87482	Survey completed, will mail plans on ——
Regificus ...	87483	Survey completed, plans were mailed on ——
Regifugium	87484	Owing to inaccuracy of survey
Regignor ...	87485	I (we) do not believe survey made of —— is accurate
Regilded ...	87486	Send full particulars of your survey
Regilera ...	87487	**Surveyed**
Regimber...	87488	Has been surveyed by Government surveyor
Regimiento	87489	Surveyed by
Regional ...	87490	Have surveyed several points
Regionatim	87491	Should be surveyed
Regisseur...	87492	Has (have) been surveyed
Registrado	87493	Has (have) not been surveyed
Registro ...	87494	Has (have) the mine(s) been accurately surveyed
Regitivo ...	87495	The mine(s) has (have) been accurately surveyed
Regizzar ...	87496	The mine(s) has (have) never been thoroughly surveyed
Reglado ...	87497	Until the property has been thoroughly surveyed
Reglisse ...	87498	**Surveying** (*See also* "Dialling," "Levelling.")
Reglutino...	87499	Shall commence surveying on ——
Regnatrix...	87500	Have not yet commenced surveying
Regnaturus	87501	Commenced surveying on ——; hope to complete by

Regnicola...	37502	As soon as I (we) have (—— has) finished surveying
Regocijado	37503	Report as to progress of surveying
Regodearse	37504	Surveying operations proceeding satisfactoril
Regodeo ...	37505	Surveying stopped through
Regola ...	37506	Will necessitate postponement of surveying
Regolante...	37507	Shall recommence surveying on or about ——
Regolarsi ...	37508	Have you recommenced surveying
Regolatore	37509	Have not recommenced surveying
Regoldador	37510	Recommenced surveying on ——
Regoletto ...	37511	As soon as the preliminary work of surveying is finished
Regolfar ...	37512	Have engaged —— to assist in surveying
Regolizia ...	37513	Can you engage assistance for surveying
Regoluzzo...	37514	Cannot obtain any assistance for surveying
Regomello	37515	**Surveyor(s)** (*See also* "Dialler.")
Regordete...	37516	Shall have to engage an outside surveyor
Regosto ...	37517	Have engaged good surveyor at —— per day
Regraciar ...	37518	Can you engage competent surveyor
Regradent	37519	Engage surveyor
Regrant ...	37520	Ought to have retained surveyor
Regresar ...	37521	Have engaged surveyor who is also competent to [assays
Regression	37522	Can you find competent man as surveyor who can also make
Regrunir ...	37523	Have found competent man as surveyor who can also
Regsamkeit	37524	Employ as surveyor
Regueldo ...	37525	United States surveyor
Regueron ...	37526	County surveyor
Reguilete ...	37527	What is the surveyor's opinion
Regulador	37528	Surveyor's opinion is
Regulatim	37529	Have obtained formal report from surveyor
Regulus ...	37530	**Survival**
Regungalos	37531	**Survive**
Regurgitar	37532	**Survivor(s)**
Regustatio	37533	**Suspect(s)**
Regyrabo ...	37534	I suspect
Regyratote	37535	To suspect
Rehacer ...	37536	Do you suspect
Rehartar ...	37537	Do(es) —— suspect
Rehausser	37538	Do(es) not suspect
Rehbock ...	37539	I (we) have some reason to suspect
Rehbraten	37540	I (we) have every reason to suspect
Rehearsal...	37541	I (we) have no reason to suspect
Rehecho ...	37542	Suspect(s) that
Rehenchir...	37543	Should you suspect
Rehendrija	37544	Strongly suspect that
Reherir ...	37545	What do you suspect
Rehilete ...	37546	Have you any reason to suspect
Rehogar ...	37547	I am (we are) inclined to suspect that
Rehposten	37548	Whom do you suspect
Rehuida ...	37549	Do not let anybody suspect
Rehurtado	37550	**Suspected**
Reibung ...	37551	Is suspected of
Reibzeng ...	37552	I (we) suspected
Reichlich ...	37553	I (we) have not suspected
Reichsland	37554	Has (have) —— been suspected before
Reichsrath	37555	Was (were) suspected of
Reichstadt	37556	Has (have) been suspected of
Reichthum	37557	Has (have) never been suspected of
Reiculus ...	37558	I (we) have suspected for some time past that
Reidero ...	37559	Is (are) strongly suspected of
Reihen ...	37560	Was (were) suspected, but nothing was proved
Reimposed	37561	Do not let your intention to —— be suspected by ——

Reimprimir	87562	**Suspecting**
Reinante ...	87563	Have you any reasons for suspecting that
Reincidir ...	87564	Have no reason for suspecting
Reindeer ...	87565	What is your reason for suspecting
Reinette ...	87566	**Suspend**
Reinheit ...	87567	To suspend
Reinigung	87568	Will suspend
Reinless ...	87569	Will probably suspend
Reinserer ...	87570	Cannot suspend without
Reinserted	87571	Would it be well to suspend
Reintegrar	87572	It would not be well to suspend
Reinvested	87573	It would be just as well to suspend
Reinvitare	87574	Before I (we) suspend
Reisekarte	87575	Better suspend your judgment until
Reisekleid...	87576	Will suspend judgment until
Reisender ...	87577	Continue to suspend
Reisepass ...	87578	Am (are) likely to suspend
Reisesack ...	87579	Not likely to suspend
Reisewagen	87580	There is no fear at all that he (they) will suspend
Reissblei ...	87581	Better suspend for the present
Reissfeder	87582	Better suspend work until
Reitbahn ...	87583	Suspend any further action
Reiterar ...	87584	Will suspend further action
Reiteratio...	87585	Cannot suspend this (the) work(s)
Reitgerte ...	87586	When did you suspend
Reitknecht...	87587	**Suspended**
Reitkunst...	87588	Suspended until
Reitweg ...	87589	Has (have) been suspended
Reizend ...	87590	Was (were) suspended
Reizlos ...	87591	Has (have) not been suspended
Reizmittel	87592	Suspended between
Reizvoll ...	87593	Not yet suspended
Rejaillir ...	87594	Suspended payment on
Rejecter ...	87595	Cannot be suspended after
Rejeria ...	87596	Should not be indefinitely suspended
Rejetable ...	87597	Has (have) been indefinitely suspended
Rejiculus ...	87598	Entirely suspended
Rejoicer ...	87599	Work wholly suspended (on account of ——)
Rejonazo ...	87600	Will have to be suspended during
Rejoneador	87601	This work has been suspended since
Rejoneo ...	87602	Why have you suspended work at
Rejonir ...	87603	Suspended owing to
Rejuela ...	87604	Has —— (have you) suspended
Rejurar ...	87605	Has (have) not been suspended for one moment
Rekrutiren	87606	**Suspending**
Relache ...	87607	Has had the effect of suspending
Relacionar	87608	Is (are) suspending
Relajador...	87609	Should he (——) think of suspending operations
Relamer ...	87610	Do(es) not think of suspending
Relamido ...	87611	**Suspense**
Relampago	87612	The matter cannot remain in suspense after
Relangui ...	87613	How long must I (we) remain in suspense
Relanqueo	87614	The matter must remain in suspense pending
Relapsing...	87615	Suspense account
Relapso ...	87616	**Suspension**
Relargir ...	87617	The suspension is not likely to cause
Relassare ...	87618	The suspension of —— has been announced
Relatante ...	87619	The suspension of —— daily expected
Relativo ...	87620	Suspension of labour contract
Relatora ...	87621	What suspension has there been of it (this work)

Relavage ...	37622	There has been no actual suspension
Relaxable...	37623	The suspension lasted —— days
Relaxator...	37624	Owing to the suspension of
Relaxed ...	37625	During the suspension of
Releer ...	37626	Has (have) arranged that there shall be no suspension
Relegar ...	37627	So long as suspension lasts
Relegated...	37628	**Suspicion(s)**
Relegatore	37629	To a suspicion of
Relentecer	37630	Suspicions have been aroused as to
Relentasco	37631	Is there any room for suspicion of
Relenting ...	37632	There is no room for any suspicion of
Relentless...	37633	Have you any suspicion of
Relevandus	37634	Considerable suspicion
Relevante ...	37635	There is great suspicion but no certainty that
Relevement	37636	There is not the slightest suspicion about
Relicario ...	37637	Does any suspicion attach to
Relicturus	37638	No suspicion whatever attaches to
Relievo ...	37639	Grave suspicion has been aroused with (by)
Religamen	37640	Is (are) under grave suspicions
Religieuse	37641	Suspicions were caused by
Religioso ...	37642	There is no cause whatever for suspicion
Relimpiar	37643	The only cause for suspicion is
Relinchar ...	37644	What gave rise to your (their) suspicions
Relindo ...	37645	Cannot have any suspicion of the real facts
Relinquish	37646	Has (have) no suspicion of the real facts
Reliquary ...	37647	**Suspicious(ly)**
Reliquatio	37648	Very suspicious
Reliquia ...	37649	Look(s) suspicious [(them)
Reliure ...	37650	Look(s) suspicious, but I do not believe there is anything in it
Rellanar ...	37651	**Sustain**
Relleno ...	37652	What loss shall we sustain
Relligio ...	37653	The loss we shall sustain will amount to
Reloaded ...	37654	We shall not sustain any loss
Reloco ...	37655	The loss we shall sustain will be trifling
Relojeria ...	37656	To enable me (us) to sustain
Reloner ...	37657	How much (many) will it sustain
Reloquus ...	37658	Not competent to sustain
Reluciente	37659	Quite competent to sustain
Relucir ...	37660	**Sustained**
Reluctant...	37661	What loss (damage) has been sustained by (through)
Reluctatus	37662	Has any loss (damage) been sustained by (through)
Relumbrera	37663	Has (have) sustained loss amounting to
Relumine ...	37664	Has (have) sustained considerable damage
Reluquer ...	37665	No loss has been sustained (by)
Reluttanza	37666	No damage has been sustained (by)
Remacero	37667	Has (have) not sustained
Remachado	37668	Cannot be sustained
Remaconner	37669	**Sustaining**
Remacresco	37670	Should be capable of sustaining
Remacruit	37671	Provided he (——) is capable of sustaining
Remador ...	37672	If I (we) can succeed in sustaining it (this) legally
Remaldecir	37673	**Swamp(y)**
Remaledico	37674	Ground is too swampy
Remallar ...	37675	**Swear** (*See also* "Affidavit," "Declaration.")
Remancipor	37676	**Swindle**
Remandatum	37677	The whole affair seems very much like a swindle
Remanecer	37678	Is undoubtedly a swindle
Remanente	37679	Have you any reason to think it a swindle
Remango ...	37680	I have no reason at all to think it is a swindle
Remansado	37681	Should you think it a swindle

Remansurus	87682	Regarded here as a swindle
Remballer	87683	Do you (does ——) regard it as a swindle
Rembalso ...	87684	Do(es) not regard it as a swindle
Remblayer	87685	Should you believe it to be a swindle
Remboiter	87686	Unless you think it a swindle
Rembrunir	87687	**Sworn**
Remeabilio	87688	To be sworn
Remeaculum	87689	Have been sworn
Remecedor	87690	Have the statements sworn to
Remedable	87691	**Syenite** (*See also* "Rock.")
Remedar ...	87692	The hanging wall is syenite
Remediador	87693	The footwall is syenite
Remedialis	87694	The country rock is syenite
Remedium	87695	In syenite-granite
Remeggio	87696	In syenite
Remeligo ...	87697	Mainly syenite
Remelt ...	87698	A boss of syenite
Rememdado	87699	**Syncline(al)**
Rememorar	87700	Synclinal axis
Remercier...	87701	Forms one side of a syncline
Remetior ...	87702	The strata form a regular syncline
Remiche ...	87703	The property lies on one side of a regular syncline
Remigante	87704	**Syndicate** (*See also* "Capitalist.")
Remigatore	87705	A syndicate
Remiglatio	87706	To form a small syndicate
Remigrate	87707	Can you organize a small prospecting syndicate
Remilgarse	87708	Have organized a small prospecting syndicate
Remilgo ...	87709	My (our) syndicate will make an offer to
Remillus ...	87710	My (our) syndicate will take it
Reminder	87711	Has hitherto been worked by a syndicate
Reminiscor	87712	Propose at first to form a small syndicate
Remipedem	37713	Only suitable for a syndicate
Remirar ...	87714	Proposed syndicate would have a capital of —— in —— shares
Remisceo ...	87715	What would be the capital of the syndicate
Remisible...	87716	Has (have) formed a syndicate (to)
Remisoria	87717	As soon as syndicate is formed
Remissor ...	87718	Pending winding-up of syndicate
Remissurus	37719	Now owned by a syndicate
Remmancher	87720	The syndicate is very wealthy
Remmener	87721	What would be the anticipated profit to the syndicate
Remocion ...	87722	The anticipated profit to the syndicate would be
Remodel ...	87723	Leaving as profit to the syndicate
Remojadero	87724	Would you join a syndicate
Remojar ...	87725	Would join a syndicate to the extent of
Remolacha	87726	Cannot join syndicate
Remolinear	87727	**Synopsis**
Remolino ...	87728	Please cable pithy synopsis of your report
Remolitus	87729	Do you wish synopsis to include
Remoller ...	87730	Supplement synopsis by
Remolque	87731	**System**
Remonebat	87732	What system do you propose to adopt
Remoquete	87733	The system I (we) propose to adopt is
Remoramen	87734	A better system of (for)
Remorator	87735	A most complete system of
Remordedor	87736	Cannot adopt a better system of —— than
Remordre ...	87737	Can you not adopt a different system
Remorse ...	87738	Cannot adopt any other system
Remosto ...	87739	The system is a very good one
Remoturus	87740	The system is almost perfect
Remoucher	87741	The system is very indifferent

Remouiller	37742	The system is bad
Remoulade	37743	Better adopt a different system
Remoulded	37744	Must have a different system of (for)
Remouleur	37745	Must have a better system
Removendus	37746	An automatic system
Removeor...	37747	Do not like the system employed
Rempailler	37748	The work is conducted on a very good system
Rempart ...	37749	The system employed is
Remplacant	37750	What is the system employed for
Remplier ...	37751	Hardly any system at all
Remplumer	37752	Under the present system
Rempocher	37753	Will necessitate an entire change in the system employed for
Remprunter	37754	Is really an old system
Remuant ...	37755	Have arranged the work on a new system
Remuement	37756	Until some other system is adopted
Remuggire	37757	Until I have arranged a new system of (for)
Remulcum	37758	What do you object to in the present system
Remullir ...	37759	My (our) objection to present system is that
Remunerar	37760	**Systematic**
Remurmuro	37761	**Systematically**
Remusgo ...	37762	**T**
Remutandus	37763	**Table(s)**
Remutator	37764	Shown in table
Renaccio ...	37765	Will be found in table (on page ——)
Renacer ...	37766	Table showing
Renajolo ...	37767	**Table-land**
Renamed ...	37768	**Tabular**
Renardeau	37769	Tabular statement of
Renardiere	37770	Send tabular statement
Renascent...	37771	Have annexed tabular statement
Renavigo ...	37772	**Tacit(ly)**
Rencaisser	37773	It was tacitly understood
Rencherir...	37774	There was undoubtedly a tacit understanding to
Rencilloso	37775	**Tackle** (*See also* " Appliances.")
Rencionar...	37776	Tackle has been safely received
Rencontrer	37777	Is there sufficient tackle
Rendement	37778	I (we) have not sufficient tackle
Renderer ...	37779	Send out at once tackle capable of lifting —— tons
Rendevole...	37780	I (we) have ample tackle on the property
Rendezvous	37781	Am (are) entirely stopped for want of necessary tackle
Rendicion...	37782	Tackle is in good condition
Rendido ..	37783	Tackle is very much worn
Renditore...	37784	Stopped on account of repairs to lifting tackle
Rendituzza	37785	**Tact**
Rendormir	37786	Require(s) great tact
Rendoubler	37787	Owing mainly to want of tact
Reneiger ...	37788	**Tactical**
Renelta ...	37789	A tactical mistake
Renendus...	37790	A tactical success
Renerved ...	37791	**Tail**
Renfaiter ...	37792	At the tail of
Renfiler ...	37793	Tail race
Renflement	37794	Beyond the tail of
Renflouer ...	37795	**Tailing(s)** (*See also* " Hydraulic.")
Renfoncer...	37796	Send a sample of about —— of the tailings from [from
Rengainer...	37797	Have forwarded a sample weighing about —— of the tailings
Renglada ...	37798	We shall keep these tailings for the present
Renglon ...	37799	An average sample of the tailings assayed
Rengue ...	37800	What do the tailings assay
Renidesco...	37801	The tailings will be re-treated

Reniego ...	37802	The tailings contain sufficient value to be re-worked
Reniement	37803	At present lost in the tailings
Renifleur ...	37804	Can you not diminish loss in tailings
Rennbahn	37805	The assay of tailings shows a loss of
Renneting	37806	Assay all tailings
Rennthier...	37807	Tailings dam
Renodatus	37808	Tailings mill
Renombrado	37809	Treatment of tailings
Renoncule	37810	Obtained from tailings
Renosita ...	37811	Not obtained from tailings
Renoueur ...	37812	Tailings from
Renouveler	37813	Offer for tailings
Renovador	37814	**Take** (*See also* " Care," " Consideration.")
Renovamen	37815	Will take means to
Renovateur	37816	Take means to
Renovating	37817	Take no
Renovero ...	37818	Take on
Renownless	37819	Take off
Renseigner	37820	Had I (we) not better take
Rentilla ...	37821	To take
Rentoiler ...	37822	Do take
Rentoso ...	37823	Do not take
Rentraire ...	37824	Do not take any
Rentrayeur	37825	Is there any need to take
Rentree ...	37826	There is no need to take
Rentroll ...	37827	It is very necessary to take
Renudabunt	37828	Will take
Renudandi	37829	Will take at
Renuencia	37830	It (this) will take
Renuevo ...	37831	Will not take any less
Renunziato	37832	Is (are) disposed to take a little less
Renverser...	37833	Do not take less than
Renvoyer ...	37834	Will not take less than
Reobarbaro	37835	Can take
Reobtain ..	37836	What can you take
Reoctava ...	37837	Can you take any. more
Reojar ...	37838	Cannot take
Reopontico	37839	Should take
Reorganise	37840	Should not take
Repadecer...	37841	Should not take more than —— days
Repagulum	37842	Should be inclined to take
Repajo ...	37843	Ought not to take
Repandium	37844	Ought only to take
Repangor ...	37845	How long will it take (to)
Reparable...	37846	How long will it take to finish
Reparador	37847	How much will it take to
Reparandus	37848	How much will he (they) take for it
Reparavit ...	37849	It will take at least
Reparon ...	37850	It will take too long
Repasadera	37851	It will not take very long (much)
Repasion ...	37852	It will take about —— days to complete
Repassage	37853	It will take some time
Repasseur...	37854	It will take some time to complete
Repastino	37855	To take for
Repayable	37856	Cannot take any more
Repealed	37857	Cannot take the risk
Repechar ..	37858	Decline(s) to take less
Repedir ..	37859	Would probably take less if you would make a firm offer
Repelado ...	37860	To take out
Repeladura	37861	How much can you take out (per ——)

tepelar ...	37862	Can take out —— (per ——)
tepellens ...	37863	So as to take out
tepeloso ...	37864	To take over
tepenetro...	37865	Has (have) arranged to take over
tepensatio	37866	You had better defer to take
tepensurus	37867	When will you take stock
tepentance	37868	Have arranged to take stock on
tepentere...	37869	Take all you can get
tepenting	37870	To take place
tepentinus	37871	When is it likely to take place
tepenton ...	37872	Is to take place on
tepeople ...	37873	Is not likely to take place before
tepercudir	37874	Will evidently be compelled to take
teparibile...	37875	Is (are) willing to take it (if)
teperire ...	37876	Could take additional
tepertory...	37877	Cable how much (many) you are (—— is) willing to take
tepeso ...	37878	Do not care to take any
tepetencia	37879	Do not care to take more than
tepetendus	37880	Take care that
tepetiren ...	37881	Take care to
tepetitivo	37882	Take care not to
tepicar ...	37883	What steps shall you take to
tepignero...	37884	Take no steps for the present
tepigratus	37885	Shall take immediate steps to
tepilogar ...	37886	Will probably take steps (re ——) on or about
tepining ...	37887	You should take care not to disturb
tepintar ...	37888	It will probably take less than —— to
tepiquete...	37889	I (we) will take all blame
tepizear ...	37890	Who will take the blame
teplacer ...	37891	You must take the blame
teplacing...	37892	Take special precautions against
teplantar...	37893	Take any precautions you think necessary
teplatrage	37894	What special precautions do you intend to take
teplatrer ...	37895	You must take into consideration
teplaudo ...	37896	Will take into consideration
teplebat ...	37897	Did you take into consideration
tepledged	37898	Did take into consideration
tepleturus	37899	Did not take into consideration
tepleuvoir	37900	Do not take any responsibility for
teplezione	37901	Shall not take any responsibility for
teplica ...	37902	**Taken**
teplicador	37903	The first steps to be taken are
teplicante	37904	The only steps taken have been to
teplictus ...	37905	Have taken no steps as yet
teplique ...	37906	Has (have) taken steps
teplonger	37907	What steps have you taken with regard to
teplumbo ..	37908	Have you taken any steps to
tepoblar ...	37909	Have you taken any steps to rectify the matter
tepodrir ...	37910	The only steps I (we) have taken are to
tepolish ...	37911	Every precaution possible has been taken
tepolludo...	37912	Measures will be at once taken to
teponche ...	37913	What course do you advise should be taken
tepondant	37914	Consider the course you have taken a very wise one
teportator	37915	Cable whether you do or do not approve of the course taken
teportorio	37916	Approve entirely of the course taken
teposcens	37917	Do not approve of the course taken (unless)
teposconem	37918	Has (have) not taken
tepose ...	37919	I (we) have taken
teposing ...	37920	I (we) have not taken
tepositus ...	37921	As soon as you have taken

Reposoir	37922	How much (many) has it taken (to)
Reposteria	37923	It has taken
Repoussant	37924	It has not taken
Repregunta	37925	A considerable amount has already been taken
Reprenda ...	37926	What (how many) has (have) been taken
Reprension	37927	A considerable amount (quantity) has been taken firm
Represalia	37928	Very little has been taken
Repressif ...	37929	Has been taken up to the present
Reprieved ...	37930	Should be taken every —— hours
Reprimenda	37931	Should be taken at once
Reprimuto	37932	Should not be taken until (unless)
Reprinted ...	37933	Have you taken into account
Reprise ...	37934	Have taken into account
Reprobable	37935	Have not taken into account
Reprobador	37936	Have not taken any responsibility for
Reprobo ...	37937	Have you taken into consideration
Reprochar	37938	Have you taken into consideration the risk involved
Reproducir	37939	I (we) have taken into consideration the risk involved
Repromitto	37940	**Taking**
Reproof ...	37941	Has (have) been taking
Reprouver	37942	I am (we are) now taking stock
Reprueba ...	37943	Not at present taking out
Reptavero...	37944	Not taking out more than
Reptavit ...	37945	Is (are) now taking out
Reptemur ...	37946	Taking out —— tons per day
Reptilian ...	37947	Has (have) been taking out at the rate of
Reptilis ...	37948	There is no use in taking
Repubesco	37949	Is there any use in taking
Republica...	37950	Am (are) taking steps to
Republique	37951	Am (are) taking every precaution against
Repudiar ..	37952	**Talc**
Repudiatus	37953	A considerable quantity of talc
Repudrirse	37954	**Talcous**
Repuerasco	37955	Talcous schist
Repuesta ...	37956	**Talk(s)**
Repugnant	37957	To talk
Repugnator	37958	Talk it over with
Repulgado	37959	Am to talk it over with —— on
Repulido ...	37960	You had better talk it over with ——
Repulisti ...	37961	Will first talk it over with ——
Repulser ...	37962	Is there any talk of
Repulsivo...	37963	There is no talk of
Repulular...	37964	There is some talk of
Repurgans	37965	There is nothing in it but talk
Reputridus	37966	It is all mere talk
Requebrado	37967	Do not talk about it (this) at all
Requemante	37968	Talks too freely
Requemar...	37969	**Talked**
Requemason	37970	Have talked it over with
Requerant	37971	As soon as I (we) have talked it over with
Requerer ...	37972	Have not yet talked it over with
Requeridor	37973	Was talked about but nothing has yet been done in the matter
Requeson ...	37974	Is much talked about
Requibe ...	37975	**Tally**
Requiebro ..	37976	You must keep a careful tally of each
Requiescat	37977	A careful tally will be kept
Requietudo	37978	A careful tally was kept
Requintar...	37979	No tally was kept
Requisito ...	37980	Be very careful as to the tally
Requital ...	37981	Is there any need of tally

Resaigner ...	37982	There is no need of tally
Resaltar ...	37983	It is necessary that they (——) should tally in every respect
Resaludar .	37984	**Tamper**
Resalvandi	37985	**Tampered**
Resalvo ...	37986	**Tampering**
Resanesco ..	37987	**Tamping**
Resangria...	37988	When tamping
Resarcir ...	37989	Before tamping
Resarturus	37990	Insufficient tamping
Resbalante	37991	Tamping rod
Resbalon ...	37992	**Tank(s)**
Rescatador	37993	Tank(s) for
Rescate ..	37994	What is the capacity of tank
Rescindens	37995	Tank to hold —— gallons
Rescissit ...	37996	Tank —— feet diameter, —— deep
Rescissory	37997	Tank —— feet cube
Rescontrar	37998	Tank —— feet deep, by —— feet long, by —— feet wide
Rescriptum	37999	Lixiviation tank(s)
Rescrivere	38000	Cost of necessary tanks
Rescued ..	**38001**	Now erecting tanks
Rescuentro	38002	Have completed tanks, and am (are) proceeding with
Resculpo ...	38003	Water tank at level (Number ——)
Resecacion	38004	**Tantamount (to)**
Resecandus	38005	Consider it is tantamount to a refusal
Resecutus...	38006	Practically it is tantamount to
Resegmen...	38007	**Taper(s)**
Resellante	38008	Holes to be made to taper
Resomblar	38009	To taper
Reseminant	38010	Tapers from —— diameter to —— diameter
Resemino ...	38011	**Tapered**
Resentful ...	38012	Has tapered down to
Resentido...	38013	Need not be tapered
Resequor ...	38014	Tapered —— in an inch
Reserabat ..	38015	The socket end of the rock drills must be tapered —— in an inch
Reserantur	38016	**Tar**
Reservatus	38017	Through upsetting some burning tar
Reserver ...	38018	**Tare**
Resfriado ...	38019	Has the tare for —— been deducted
Resfriante	38020	The tare has not been deducted
Resfriecer...	38021	The tare deducted was
Resguardar	38022	How much does the tare amount to
Reshaped ...	38023	We usually allow —— for tare
Residencia	38024	**Tariff**
Residuare...	38025	Can you obtain and mail copy of tariff
Resiembro	38026	Copy of tariff has been mailed (will be mailed on ——)
Resignabam	38027	A new tariff is likely to be introduced
Resignante	38028	Present tariff is
Resignatio	38029	The rates will be increased under the new tariff
Resilienza ..	38030	The rates will be decreased under the new tariff
Resinaceus	38031	**Task**
Resinifero...	38032	A most difficult task
Resinous ...	38033	Not a very difficult task provided that
Resipiens .	38034	If he (——) prove(s) unequal to the task
Resistant .	38035	**Tax(es)**
Resistero ...	38036	The taxes are very light
Resistidor .	38037	The taxes are heavy
Resistive ..	38038	There is no tax at all
Resistless ...	38039	The taxes amount to —— per annum
Resobrar ...	38040	What are the annual taxes
Resobrino...	38041	What are the taxes on

Resolano ...	38042	The taxes on —— are
Resoluble...	38043	To cover all taxes
Resoluto ...	38044	Is there any tax on ——, if so, how much
Resolvedly	38045	This (the) tax will probably soon be abolished
Resonacion	38046	This (the) tax is likely soon to be increased
Resonance	38047	This (the) tax will undoubtedly be reduced
Resonner ...	38048	To levy a tax on
Resoplar ..	38049	To abolish the tax on
Resorbens...	38050	In order to pay the taxes on
Resorcin ...	38051	Taxes now due on
Resorter ...	38052	Constitute(s) a very heavy tax on
Resource ...	38053	It is necessary to pay at once the taxes amounting to ——
Respectar ...	38054	It is not necessary to pay the taxes before
Respectful	38055	Unless the taxes are paid on
Respekt ...	38056	**Taxing**
Respergor...	38057	Severely taxing my (our) reserves
Respetable	38058	If it is not taxing
Respetador	38059	Is (are) heavily taxing
Respetoso ...	38060	Providing that it (this) is not taxing
Respexit ...	38061	**Team(s)**
Respice	38062	How many teams do you employ
Respicior ...	38063	We are now employing —— teams
Respignere	38064	The cost of teams amounts to —— per month
Respigon ...	38065	The ore team
Respingar...	38066	Have contracted for the supply of sufficient teams
Respiramen	38067	Can haul —— tons per day with one team
Respirante	38068	How much can you haul per day per team
Respiravi ...	38069	We have plenty of work for a second team
Respired ...	38070	Cannot get any more teams at present
Respiremur	38071	Teams will commence about
Resplandor	38072	Teams cannot haul owing to
Resplendeo	38073	We have now —— teams hauling ore (——)
Responder	38074	Teams cannot haul owing to the bad state of the roads
Responsion	38075	**Technical**
Responsum	38076	Owing to a technical flaw in
Respuendus	38077	I (we) (——) require(s) a technical adviser
Respuesta...	38078	The technical accounts
Resquebrar	38079	A thoroughly technical report
Ressasser ...	38080	**Technicality**
Ressecher ...	38081	A legal technicality
Ressembler	38082	**Technically**
Ressentir ...	38083	Technically you are (—— is) right
Ressonder...	38084	Technically you are (—— is) wrong
Ressuer ...	38085	**Telegram(s)** (*See also* " Cable," " Decipher," " Despatch,"
Restagno ...	38086	By a telegram from [" Message.")
Restaurar ...	38087	In a telegram from
Restfully ...	38088	My (our) telegram of
Restiarius...	38089	Send telegram
Restibilis ...	38090	Have sent telegram
Resticula	38091	Your telegram has been received
Restillo ...	38092	Have you received my (our) telegram sent
Restinctus	38093	Have you received any telegram from
Restinga ...	38094	Which telegram do you refer to
Restinquor	38095	There is no reference in your telegram received to-day to
Restipulor	38096	I (we) refer to your telegram which arrived
Restitrix ...	38097	Please reply to my (our) telegram of
Restituens	38098	Please reply to my (our) last telegram
Restituir ...	38099	Cable date of your last telegram
Restively ...	38100	After arrival of telegram
Restored ...	38101	After I (we) had forwarded my (our) telegram dated ——

Retiredly
Retirem'
Retorn'
Rete
Re

Restregar ...	38102	As requested in your telegram dated
Restrenir ...	38103	As requested in ——'s telegram
Restribar ...	38104	In accordance with your telegram
Restrictim	38105	In accordance with my (our) telegram
Restrojera	38106	In accordance with the telegrams ex
Restrojo ...	38107	Before the arrival of ——'s telegram
Resublime	38108	All telegrams should be sent to
Resucha ...	38109	Have sent a telegram to
Resucitar ...	38110	Address all telegrams to —— for the present
Resuello ...	38111	Think it advisable that you should send a telegram to [to
Resulta ...	38112	Do you think it advisable that I (we) should send a telegram
Resultante	38113	Do not think it advisable that you should send a telegram to
Resulting...	38114	Communicate this telegram to
Resumable	38115	Shall I send any telegram to
Resumbruno	38116	Shall I communicate your telegram to ——
Resumendus	38117	Do not communicate my (our) telegram to ——
Resumido...	38118	Have already communicated your (——'s) telegram to ——
Resumptio	38119	Am (are) in receipt of telegram dated
Resuncion	38120	Am (are) in receipt of telegram from
Resuntivo...	38121	Have received a telegram from —— informing me (us)
Resupinado	38122	Have not received any telegram as yet from ——
Resuressi ...	38123	Has (have) received a telegram announcing
Resurgens	38124	Have received from —— the following telegram
Resurtida ..	38125	My (our) last telegram was despatched
Resuscito ...	38126	Please refer to my (our) telegram sent on ——
Retablo ...	38127	Please refer to your telegram sent on ——
Retaceria ...	38128	Why do you not reply to my (our) last telegram
Retahila ...	38129	Anxiously awaiting reply to my (our) last telegram ——
Retailler ...	38130	Your telegram received; I have acted upon it
Retajar ...	38131	Your telegram received, but I cannot act upon it until (unless)
Retaliated	38132	Your telegram received, and shall receive instant attention
Retallecer...	38133	Your telegram received, but arrived too late to make use of
Retamal ...	38134	Your telegram arrived during my absence at
Retamero .	38135	Your telegram was delayed through
Retamilla...	38136	Have only just received your telegram
Retarded ...	38137	Your telegram received yesterday
Retarding...	38138	Did you get my telegram dated ——
Retemblar	38139	Received your telegram dated ——
Retenida ...	38140	Did not receive your telegram dated ——
Retentatus	38141	Do not expect any telegram until
Retente ...	38142	Please cancel my (our) telegram sent on ——
Retentiva ...	38143	On receipt of telegram
Retenzione	38144	Do not act on ——'s telegram
Retesarse ...	38145	The last telegram from you was received on ——
Rethuro ...	38146	The last telegram from you was as follows [telegram of
Reticella ...	38147	Explain at greater length the following words in your
Reticency...	38148	Do not understand what you mean in your telegram
Reticendus	38149	Cannot understand the —— word of your telegram, please
Reticolato...	38150	The word in the telegram which you require is [repeat
Reticule ...	38151	Your telegram received, cannot understand, please repeat
Retificare ...	38152	Have received a telegram from you, cannot understand, please [repeat, using other words
Retiformis	38153	Please repeat your telegram from —— to —— exclusive of [both these words
Retina ...	38154	Please repeat your telegram from the beginning to ——
Retinente ...	38155	Please repeat your telegram from —— to the end
Retineor ...	38156	Please repeat the last —— words of your telegram
Retintin ...	38157	I (we) now send repetition of telegram
Retiolum ...	38158	You had better wait until you receive a telegram from
Retirada ...	38159	Suggest that you await arrival of telegram from

Resolano	38160	Send duplicate of telegram to
Resolvent	38161	Have sent duplicate of telegram to
Resolver	38162	Transmit telegram to
Resorcer	38163	Have forwarded telegram sent on —— to ——
Retorcido	38164	My (our) telegram was in reference to
Retorcijon	38165	Confirm ——'s telegram
Retoricar	38166	Do not confirm ——'s telegram
Retornante	38167	I (we) confirm telegram sent on ——
Retornelo	38168	I (we) cannot confirm telegram sent on
Retorquens	38169	Do (did) you confirm ——'s telegram [confirm
Retorresco	38170	Have received the following telegram from —— ; please
Retorridus	38171	Before the arrival of telegram
Retorsion	38172	After arrival of telegram
Retorting	38173	Before despatch of telegram
Retostado	38174	After despatch of telegram
Retoucher	38175	Have you received any telegram from
Retouching	38176	As I did not receive any telegram from
Retozador	38177	Wait at —— until you receive telegram
Retozona	38178	Waiting for your telegram before I communicate with
Retractans	38179	Immediately on receipt of telegram
Retractile	38180	Why did you not send telegram (as requested)
Retracto	38181	Why did you not answer my (our) telegram of
Retrahunt	38182	Cannot explain in a telegram, am (are) writing
Retraite	38183	Except you receive a telegram from
Retrancher	38184	Await receipt of telegram
Retratable	38185	I (we) await your telegram
Retratista	38186	I (we) await reply to telegram (sent on ——)
Retrayente	38187	What is your address for telegrams
Retremper	38188	My address for telegrams is care of —— at ——
Retribuir	38189	Have sent telegram(s) to your address at
Retributio	38190	Your telegram is not sufficiently definite
Retroacto	38191	Your telegram was forwarded to
Retrocede	38192	Previous to arrival of your telegram
Retrocesso	38193	Your telegrams received up to date are as follows, viz. :——
Retrocitus	38194	With reference to your telegram dated
Retrofendo	38195	Have deferred sending telegram until
Retrogrado	38196	Cannot defer sending telegram very long [the word ——
Retroquida	38197	Referring to my telegram of —— insert the word(s) —— after
Retrorsum	38198	There is an error in my telegram of ——. For —— read ——
Retrosecus	38199	Is not —— in your telegram of —— an error ? Please correct
		[or confirm
Retrospect	38200	The word in my telegram of —— is incorrect. Please
		[substitute the following
Retruecano	38201	The words you enquire about in my telegram are quite correct
Rettamente	38202	Adhere to the terms in my (our) telegram of
Rettezza	38203	**Telegraph** (*See also* "Cable.")
Rettorica	38204	Telegraph, using McNeill's General and Mining Code
Rettrice	38205	Telegraph using ——'s code
Retuerto	38206	Telegraph using cipher code arranged in my (our) letter dated
Retumbar	38207	To telegraph [——
Retundir	38208	Telegraph instantly
Reubarbo	38209	Telegraph promptly
Reumatico	38210	Telegraph as soon as you possibly can
Reunion	38211	If you telegraph at once
Reupontico	38212	If you do not telegraph at once
Reurged	38213	Will telegraph at once
Reussite	38214	Cannot telegraph
Reuvoll	38215	Continue to telegraph daily
Revalatio	38216	Continue to telegraph weekly
evalidar	38217	Do not telegraph until (unless)

Levaloir ...	38218	Will not telegraph until (unless)
Levanche...	38219	Will you telegraph
Levasseur...	38220	Please telegraph confirmation
Levealed ...	38221	Please telegraph "Yes" or "No."
Leveille ...	38222	Please telegraph under any circumstances
Levejecer ...	38223	Please telegraph summary of
Levejido ...	38224	Please telegraph as soon as possible
Levelabile .	38225	Please telegraph whether
Levelateur	38226	Please telegraph whether this is in order
Levenant ...	38227	Please telegraph if this is not in order
Levendedor	38228	Please telegraph me (us) immediately
Levengeful	38229	Please telegraph me (us) as follows
Levenirse ..	38230	Do not telegraph your answer, write fully
Leventazon	38231	Telegraph briefly and write fully
Leverberar	38232	Could not telegraph before owing to
Leverentia	38233	Shall not telegraph until (unless)
Leversions	38234	Shall be unable to telegraph until
Leverter ...	38235	Telegraph what you have (——— has) done respecting
Levesado ...	38236	Telegraph what you have done with respect to it (this)
Levestido...	38237	I (we) will telegraph the moment I am (we are) able
Levezero ...	38238	Please telegraph instructions at once
Levictual ...	38239	Will telegraph instructions as soon as possible
Levicturus	38240	Telegraph to ——— for instructions
Leviernes...	38241	Telegraph more complete details
Reviewed ...	38242	Will telegraph again as soon as possible as to
Reviewing	38243	You can telegraph to me at
Reviler ...	38244	Advise by telegraph
Revinciens	38245	Telegraph price(s) of
Revindicar	38246	Telegraph result(s) of
Revirement	38247	Telegraph if there is any change
Reviseur ...	38248	Will telegraph any change
Revisoria ...	38249	Will telegraph if matters improve
Revistar ...	38250	Telegraph whether you can do this
Revivalist...	38251	Telegraph ——— what you decide upon
Revividero	38252	Telegraph to ——— if you wish him to act
Revivifier ...	38253	——— has asked me to telegraph to you as follows, viz. :— [as to
Revivisco ...	38254	——— has (have) asked me to telegraph to him (them) instructions
Revocable...	38255	Cannot telegraph any instructions to ——— owing to absence of [———
Revocador	38256	Telegraph communication has temporarily broken down [between here and ———
Revocation	38257	Telegraph communication is stopped between ——— and ———
Revolcarse	38258	Telegraph communication has been resumed (between ———
Revolito ...	38259	You had better telegraph ——— to [and ———)
Revolotear	38260	Do not hesitate to telegraph if necessary
Revolter ...	38261	Do not hesitate to telegraph fully
Revoltillo...	38262	Telegraph at my (our) expense
Revolting...	38263	Telegraph immediately if
Revolvedor	38264	Telegraph report immediately
Revomens	38265	What is the nearest telegraph station
Revoque ...	38266	The nearest telegraph station is ——— distant ——— miles
Revuelco ...	38267	It is important to telegraph at once
Revulsive...	38268	I (we) purpose to telegraph as follows
Rewritten...	38269	As soon as you telegraph
Reyerta ...	38270	Telegraph where I can communicate with
Reyezuelo...	38271	Telegraph at once if reply is likely to be negative
Rezadero ...	38272	Telegraph when you will be able to look into
Rezelador	38273	Telegraph earliest date for shipment of the following
Rezelozo ...	38274	Telegraph cost and earliest date of shipment
Rezongador	38275	When you receive this, telegraph to ——— for

Rezumadero	38276	Telegraph as soon as you receive information respecting
Rezumo ...	38277	Telegraph your authority for
Rhabarber	38278	**Telegraphed**
Rhabdos ...	38279	I (we) telegraphed to you on
Rhabillage	38280	I (we) have not telegraphed
Rhacinus ...	38281	— I (we) have telegraphed (to)
Rhagion ...	38282	Have telegraphed to —— for instructions
Rhagoides	38283	Have telegraphed through —— a remittance of ——
Rhamnus ...	38284	**Telegraphic** (*See also* "Telegraph.")
Rhaphanus	38285	Telegraphic communication
Rhapsodic	38286	Telegraphic communication suspended
Rhederei ...	38287	Telegraphic communication resumed
Rheinwein	38288	Pending resumption of telegraphic communication
Rheochord	38289	There are telegraphic facilities to
Rheostat ...	38290	**Telegraphing**
Rheteur ...	38291	When telegraphing
Rhetoric ...	38292	If you are telegraphing to
Rheum ...	38293	**Telephone**
Rheumatism	38294	I have contracted for construction of telephone line [——
Rhinoceros	38295	What would be the cost of telephone line between —— and
Rhizagra ...	38296	Obtain estimates for cost of construction of telephone line [between —— and ——, and licenses for instruments
Rhizopod...	38297	Have mailed estimates for telephone connection
Rhizotomus	38298	The cost of erection of telephone line would be ——
Rhodian ...	38299	Licenses for use of telephone instruments —— per annum
Rhodites ...	38300	Owing to breakdown of telephone connection
Rhodonite	38301	Delay caused through breakdown of telephone connection
Rhomboid	38302	Telephone now in working order
Rhombus ...	38303	I (we) have no communication with him (it) (——) owing to [breakdown of telephone
Rhonchavi	38304	**Tell**
Rhonchisso	38305	To tell
Rhopalon	38306	Shall I (we) tell
Rhubarb ...	38307	Tell him (them)
Rhumatique	38308	Can tell
Rhymeless	38309	Cannot tell
Rhymer ...	38310	Can you tell
Rhymester	38311	Can tell thereby
Rhythmical	38312	Cannot tell thereby
Rhythmisch	38313	You had better tell —— at once to
Rhytion	38314	You had better not tell —— anything about this
Riabbilire...	38315	Be careful what you tell —— (him)
Riabitato ...	38316	Do not tell
Riaccolta ...	38317	Can you tell whether
Riachuelo	38318	When will you be able to tell whether
Riadattare	38319	Shall not be able to tell until
Riaclogare	38320	Cannot as yet tell whether
Rialterare...	38321	As soon as I (we) can tell
Riamicare	38322	Please tell —— to
Riammesso	38323	Cannot tell precisely
Riammonire	38324	Commencing to tell
Riandato ...	38325	Not yet commencing to tell
Riapertura	38326	You can tell
Riarrecare	38327	—— can tell you about it (this)
Riassumere	38328	**Telluride**
Riaversi ...	38329	Telluride of gold
Riavolo ...	38330	A telluride mine
Ribadito ...	38331	The vein carries telluride of gold
Ribaditura	38332	The sample contains telluride of gold
Ribadoquin	38333	A rich telluride ore
Ribagnare	38334	The gold is chiefly as telluride

Ribalderia	38335	**Telpher**
Ribaldone...	38336	Examine and report on telpher system at
Ribaldry ...	38337	Can introduce a telpher system between —— and ——
Ribambelle	38338	What would be the cost of telpher plant
Riband ...	38339	Could purchase complete telpher plant to transport —— tons
		[per day of twelve hours, for ——
Ribattuta...	38340	Cost and erection of telpher plant
Ribbonsaw	38341	Telpher system at —— has been abandoned
Ribeccare ...	38342	Telpher system would not be suitable owing to
Ribecchino	38343	**Temperature** [grade scale
Ribellato ...	38344	The winter temperature averages —— degrees below zero, Centi-
Ribenedire	38345	During winter the temperature has been known to fall ——
Ribera ...	38346	**Temporarily** [degrees below zero, Centigrade scale
Ribereno ...	38347	Has (have) been temporarily obliged to
Riberiego ...	38348	**Temporary**
Ribetear ...	38349	It is likely to be only temporary
Ribible ...	38350	This (these) arrangement(s) is (are) only temporary
Ribobolo ...	38351	Present arrangement(s) understood to be only temporary
Ribollio ...	38352	Will endeavour to make a temporary arrangement to (for)
Riboteur ...	38353	Can you make a temporary arrangement to (for)
Ribuffare ...	38354	Must make some temporary arrangement to (for)
Ributtante	38355	This arrangement is temporary pending
Ributtato...	38356	The (this) suspension is temporary
Ricacho ...	38357	I (we) think this will only be temporary
Ricadente...	38358	As a temporary measure
Ricadioso ...	38359	A temporary way
Ricaduena	38360	Would be a temporary way out of the present difficulty
Ricafembra	38361	The difficulty is more than a temporary one
Ricagnato...	38362	The difficulty is only a temporary one
Ricalcare ...	38363	Merely temporary
Ricalzarsi...	38364	Has (have) made temporary arrangement(s) that (for)
Ricamatore	38365	Require temporary assistance
Ricambiare	38366	The arrangement(s) was (were) meant to be only temporary
Ricanerie ...	38367	We have made a temporary arrangement for
Ricantato...	38368	**Temporize**
Ricapitare	38369	Better temporize with
Ricardare...	38370	If you (——) can temporize with
Ricaricato	38371	**Tenancy**
Ricascante	38372	During my (our) tenancy
Ricatenare	38373	**Tenant**
Riccaccio ...	38374	**Tend**
Riocchezza...	38375	This will tend to
Ricciolino...	38376	Will it (this) not tend rather to
Ricciuto ...	38377	This will not tend in any way to
Ricefields ...	38378	Will certainly tend to
Riceflour ...	38379	Unless it (this) should tend to become
Ricepaper...	38380	**Tendency**
Ricepere ...	38381	A decided tendency to
Ricercata ...	38382	No decided tendency to
Ricettarsi...	38383	No tendency whatever
Ricettato ...	38384	What is the present tendency (of)
Ricevente ...	38385	The present tendency is
Ricevitore	38386	With a tendency to
Richedere...	38387	Is there any tendency to
Richement	38388	There is a slight tendency to
Richiamare	38389	Should you observe any tendency to (of)
Richieduto	38390	There is a considerable tendency to (of)
Richiesto ...	38391	Unless there should be a tendency to
Richinarsi	38392	Present tendency is up
Richiusura	38393	Present tendency is down

[641]

Richly ...	38394	Present tendency doubtful
Richtblei ...	38395	**Tender(s)**
Riciditura	38396	To tender
Ricignere ...	38397	Tender for
Riciniatus	38398	Can you tender for
Ricioncare	38399	Cannot tender
Ricochet ...	38400	Will send detailed tender by mail
Ricogliere...	38401	Shall not tender for
Ricohombre	38402	Shall be glad to tender for
Ricolmare...	38403	Whose tender has been accepted
Ricolorire...	38404	——'s tender has been accepted, the amount is
Ricolto ...	38405	Has (have) received tender(s) from
Ricommesso	38406	Has (have) not received tender(s) from
Ricompera	38407	You should obtain tender(s) from
Ricompiere	38408	Should you tender, you should include
Ricomposto	38409	Should you tender, you should not include
Ricomunica	38410	Shall I (we) ask —— to tender
Riconciare	38411	Have accepted ——'s tender
Ricondito ...	38412	You had better ask the following firms to tender
Ricondotta	38413	Tender accepted
Riconferma	38414	Tender rejected
Riconfitto...	38415	Have received the following tenders
Ricopiato ...	38416	Has (have) not received any tenders
Ricoprire ...	38417	Tenders for the following work, viz. :—
Ricordarsi	38418	Has (have) put in a tender for
Ricoricare...	38419	Do you advise me (us) to tender
Ricoronare	38420	Certainly advise you to tender
Ricorretto...	38421	Do not advise you to tender
Ricoverare	38422	Do not accept tender
Ricrearsi ...	38423	Have accepted my tender
Ricreativo	38424	Have rejected my tender
Ricreatore	38425	Has (have) advertised for tenders [offers
Ricredente	38426	Has (have) advertised for tenders and received the following
Ricredersi	38427	Better advertise for tenders
Ricreduto ...	38428	Tenders have been advertised for, in accordance with instruc-
Ricucito ...	38429	**Tendered** [tions received
Ricucitura	38430	**Tendering**
Ricuperato	38431	**Tenor**
Ricusante ...	38432	What is the tenor of
Ridamare...	38433	Its tenor is as follows
Riddance ...	38434	**Tensile**
Riddler ...	38435	Tensile strength
Riddone ...	38436	**Tenure**
Riderless ...	38437	During his (——'s) tenure of office
Ridestare ...	38438	**Term** (*See also* " Terms.")
Ridevole ...	38439	For a term of
Ridgeplate	38440	For a term of —— years
Ridgepole...	38441	How long a term can you secure
Ridibunbus	38442	The present term of lease has nearly expired
Ridicitore...	38443	Until the end of the present term
Ridiculez ...	38444	At the end of present term
Ridiculing	38445	**Terminable**
Ridiculoso	38446	Terminable at —— hours' notice
Riding ...	38447	Terminable at —— days' notice
Ridingwhip	38448	To be terminable by notice in writing
Ridirsi ...	38449	**Terminate**
Ridividere	38450	To terminate (on)
Ridolersi ...	38451	Likely to terminate fatally
Ridondanza	38452	Give(s) notice to terminate
'dondato	38453	Advisable to terminate the affair as soon as possible

Ridubitare	38454	Would it not be well to terminate the matter
Riducere ...	38455	So as to terminate the matter at once
Riducitore	38456	How is the affair likely to terminate
Riduzione...	38457	The affair is likely to terminate
Riefeln ...	38458	The affair is not likely to terminate
Rielado ...	38459	When is it (this) to terminate
Rielera ...	38460	Wish(es) to terminate
Riemendare	38461	Terminate ——'s agreement immediately
Riempiere...	38462	**Terminated**
Riempitura	38463	Terminated on
Riempiuto	38464	Already terminated
Rienfiare ...	38465	If it (this) has not terminated
Rientrato ...	38466	Terminated by mutual consent
Riescire ...	38467	**Terminating**
Riesenhaft	38468	Terminating in
Rifacibile ...	38469	**Termination**
Rifador ...	38470	The termination of
Rifasciare ..	38471	Upon the termination of
Rifedire ...	38472	Very successful termination
Riferirsi ...	38473	A disastrous termination
Rifermato...	38474	The only termination possible
Riffraff ...	38475	Upon the termination of the present agreement (lease)
Rifiancare...	38476	Upon termination of contract
Rifidare ...	38477	Fear may have a fatal termination
Rifiggere ...	38478	Has had a fatal termination
Rifigliare ...	38479	**Terminus**
Rifinito ...	38480	The terminus would be at
Rifiorente ...	38481	A terminus of the —— railway
Rifiorito ...	38482	**Terms** (*See also* " Better," " Named," " Obtain," " Term.")
Rifirrafe ...	38483	State terms
Rifiutanza	38484	My (our) terms are
Rifiutato ...	38485	Please inform me (us) as to terms
Riflard ...	38486	What are the best terms you can obtain
Rifleball ...	38487	The best terms I (we) can obtain are
Rifleman ...	38488	On the best terms that I (we) can obtain
Riflessare ...	38489	Terms are quite impossible
Riflusso ...	38490	Unless —— will reduce his (their) terms
Rifondare...	38491	Refuse(s) to reduce terms
Riforbirsi...	38492	Will consent to reduce terms
Riformante	38493	Endeavour to induce —— to reduce his (their) terms
Rifragnere	38494	Terms cannot be altered
Rifrattivo ...	38495	Can be secured on satisfactory terms
Rifrazione	38496	Terms offered not satisfactory
Rifreddare	38497	Would strongly advise you to accept terms offered
Rifrenato ...	38498	Cable if you accept these terms
Rifrigerio...	38499	Hope —— will accept terms offered
Rifrondire	38500	Has reduced his terms to
Rifrustare	38501	On the same terms as before
Rifuggente	38502	To come to terms with
Rifuggita...	38503	Endeavour to come to terms with —— respecting [with
Rifulgente	38504	Telegraph if there is any probability of your coming to terms
Rifutare ...	38505	There is every probability he (——) will agree to terms
Rigadoon ...	38506	There seems no possibility of agreeing to terms
Rigaglia ...	38507	Upon the best terms you can get
Rigaligo ...	38508	Are these terms likely to suit
Rigattiere...	38509	Will the terms suit
Rigescima	38510	Terms will not suit at all
Rigettato ...	38511	Terms altogether too high
Rigging ..	38512	Terms not sufficiently precise
Righteous	38513	Terms very much too stringent

Righthand	38514	Terms will suit
Rigiacere ...	38515	Can still be obtained on the same terms
Rigid ...	38516	Has (have) been offered better terms by
Rigidezza...	38517	Can you not improve terms
Rigidity ...	38518	Cannot improve terms
Rigidness...	38519	Is not according to terms agreed upon
Rigincare ...	38520	Upon the terms contained in your (their) letter dated ——
Rigirare ...	38521	Advisable to come to terms at once
Rigmarole	38522	Am (are) willing to agree to terms if
Rigoglio ...	38523	Is willing to agree to your terms
Rigoletto ...	38524	Should these terms not suit —— please suggest others
Rigoleur ...	38525	Should these terms not suit, please advise
Rigonfiare...	38526	Will agree to your terms on condition that
Rigoratus...	38527	No terms were mentioned
Rigoribus...	38528	The terms mentioned were as follows
Rigorismo	38529	Endeavour to obtain better terms
Rigorosita	38530	Decline the terms
Rigoroso ...	38531	Cannot obtain better terms
Rigorously	38532	Do the best you can as to terms
Rigottato ...	38533	Upon the following terms
Rigoureux	38534	Upon the following terms and conditions
Rigradare...	38535	Offer(s) the following terms
Riguardato	38536	Could offer better terms for
Rigurgito ...	38537	Better close on present terms
Riguridad...	38538	Close if you are convinced you cannot obtain better terms
Rilascio ...	38539	Better accept terms offered
Rilassarsi ...	38540	Unless —— can offer better terms
Rilavorare	38541	Do you still advise us to come to terms with
Rileggere ...	38542	Do not now advise you to come to terms with
Rilevarsi ...	38543	Still advise you to come to terms with
Rilevatore	38544	Accept the terms stated, provided that
Rillettes ...	38545	Will you accept these terms
Rilucciare...	38546	Would accept the following terms, viz. :—
Rilustrare	38547	Cannot accept the terms stated
Riluttante	38548	Would advise you to accept the terms
Rimacinare	38549	Provided that the terms are satisfactory
Rimaille ...	38550	In the event of terms named not being satisfactory
Rimandato	38551	What terms have you agreed to
Rimanenza	38552	Have agreed to the following terms
Rimangiare	38553	What are your (——'s) terms for
Rimazione	38554	Cannot agree as to terms
Rimbaldera	38555	Could you not make better terms
Rimbambito	38556	Accept if you cannot obtain better terms
Rimbastire	38557	Terms accepted
Rimbecco ...	38558	Do you know approximately what ——'s terms would be
Rimbercio	38559	——'s terms would probably be about
Rimboccato	38560	I do not think ——'s terms would exceed
Rimbombar	38561	As per terms stated in
Rimbomboso	38562	Terms most liberal
Rimbuono	38563	Terms anything but liberal
Rimediato	38564	Terms not at all liberal
Rimeditare	38565	Consider these terms very liberal
Rimemorato	38566	Terms strictly net
Rimendo ...	38567	**Terrible**
Rimentita...	38568	**Terribly**
Rimisurato	38569	**Territory**
Rimmollare	38570	A territory of
Rimontato	38571	Is this in a territory
Rimorchio	38572	In the territory of
ᴿorire ...	38573	Covers a great territory

Rimovatore	38574	**Tertiary**
Rimovere ...	38575	Of tertiary age
Rimpalmare	38576	In a formation of —— of tertiary age
Rimpazzata	38577	In tertiary formations
Rimpeciare	38578	Covered by tertiary formations
Rimpiatto	38579	**Test** (*See also* "Assay," "Gold," "Mill.")
Rimple ...	38580	To test
Rimugghire	38581	Be careful to test
Rimuginare	38582	Shall test it (this) as soon as possible
Rimuoversi	38583	Repeat test
Rimurato ...	38584	Test pieces
Rimutanza	38585	**Tested** (*See also* "Testing.")
Rimutevole	38586	Has (have) not been tested
Rinarrare ...	38587	Could be thoroughly tested at a cost of ——
Rinascente	38588	Should be tested (before)
Rinascita ...	38589	Have most carefully tested
Rincage ...	38590	**Testify(ies)**
Rincagnato	38591	—— would have to testify
Rincalzare	38592	Could you (——) testify as to
Rinchinare	38593	Could testify
Rincignere	38594	Could not testify
Rinconada	38595	**Testimony**
Rinconero...	38596	Want of testimony
Rincorarsi	38597	In spite of testimony produced
Rincorso ...	38598	Complete testimony to the contrary
Rincrudire	38599	Sworn testimony
Rinculata ...	38600	Could you give testimony if required
Rinderpest	38601	Want testimony to prove that
Rindsleder	38602	**Testing**
Rindvieh ...	38603	For the purpose of testing
Rinettato ...	38604	Now engaged testing
Rinflorare...	38605	As soon as I (we) have finished testing
Rinfocarsi	38606	**Than**
Rinfondere	38607	More than
Rinfranto ...	38608	Less than
Rinfresco ...	38609	Any more than
Rinfuocare	38610	Not less than
Ringbolt ...	38611	Not more than
Ringdove ...	38612	Than it (this)
Ringelchen	38613	Than with
Ringfence...	38614	**Thank(s)**
Ringfinger	38615	Thanks to
Ringformig	38616	To thank
Ringioire ...	38617	Thank —— on my behalf
Ringleader	38618	Thank —— on behalf of
Ringlero ...	38619	Accept the best thanks of
Ringmaster	38620	Accept my (our) best thanks for
Ringojare...	38621	Have passed a vote of thanks to
Ringorango	38622	I (we) thank you sincerely for what you have done
Ringtail ...	38623	A vote of thanks was passed to you and the staff at a meeting [of shareholders held this day
Ringworms	38624	I (we) thank you very much for your attention to this matter [(to the matter of ——)
Rinnestare	38625	**Thanked**
Rinnovanza	38626	**Thanking**
Rinomabile	38627	**That**
Rinovante...	38628	That is to say
Rinsaccare	38629	That is (are)
Rinselvato	38630	That is (are) not
Rintanarsi	38631	Is that
Rintegrato	38632	Will that be all

Rintocco ...	38633	That can easily be done
Rintoppare	38634	That cannot be done
Rintronato	38635	That is all
Rinumidare	38636	You had better do that
Rinunziare	38637	That will do
Rinvenuto	38638	That will not do
Rinvescare	38639	That will not do except
Rinviliare...	38640	That will only be in the event of
Rinvivirsi...	38641	When will that be
Rinvoltura	38642	That will be
Rinzeppato	38643	That will not be
Riolada ...	38644	That will not be before
Rioperare ...	38645	That will not be until
Riordinare	38646	That will be about
Rioteur ...	38647	**The**
Riotously ...	38648	The following
Riottoso ...	38649	The foregoing
Ripaille ...	38650	The first
Riparabile	38651	The last
Riparatore	38652	The next
Riparius ...	38653	The total
Ripasciuto	38654	**Theft(s)**
Ripassato ...	38655	Owing to several thefts having lately occurred
Ripatriare	38656	Was accused of theft
Ripeness ...	38657	Was convicted of theft
Ripentenza	38658	**Their**
Ripentirsi...	38659	Their own
Ripentuto...	38660	On their account
Ripercosso	38661	Is it (this) their own
Riperella ...	38662	Is undoubtedly their own
Ripescare ...	38663	Is not their own
Ripetente ...	38664	Is not believed to be their own
Ripetitore...	38665	Their stock is at present
Ripezzato ...	38666	Undoubtedly their own property
Ripiacere ...	38667	In their favour
Ripiantare	38668	Not at all in their favour
Ripiar ...	38669	By their own
Ripienist ...	38670	By their own showing
Ripieur ...	38671	**Them**
Ripigliare...	38672	From them
Ripilogare	38673	For them
Riplacarsi...	38674	To them
Riponce ...	38675	By them
Ripopolato	38676	Altogether against them
Riporgere ...	38677	Or any of them
Riporsi ...	38678	**Themselves**
Riportato ...	38679	Against themselves
Riposante...	38680	For themselves
Riposatore	38681	By themselves
Riposevole	38682	Was done by themselves
Riposter ...	38683	They have only themselves to blame
Ripostime	38684	They have only themselves to thank for it
Rippenfell	38685	Nobody but themselves
Rippling ...	38686	**Then** (*See also* " Time.")
Ripregato ...	38687	Provided that I am (we are) then able
Ripremere	38688	Will you be able then
Riprensivo	38689	Not until then
Riprensore	38690	By then if not sooner
Riprestare	38691	Will then be able
Riprodurre	38692	Advise you then

Ripromesso	38693	Whether I (we) shall then be able
Riproposto	38694	How do you mean then
Riprova ...	38695	You can then
Ripudiare	38696	I (we) will then
Ripulas ...	38697	You should then
Ripulito ...	38698	**Thence**
Ripulitura	38699	**Theodolite** (*See also* "Dial," "Level," "Survey.")
Ripurgare...	38700	A theodolite suitable for
Riquadrare	38701	Transit theodolite
Rirompersi	38702	Owing to my (our) theodolite having been broken
Risagallo ...	38703	Have unfortunately broken theodolite; will take —— to get
Risaldato ...	38704	-Have not received theodolite [it repaired
Risalttare...	38705	As soon as I (we) receive theodolite
Risaminare	38706	Will send theodolite
Risanabile	38707	Please despatch theodolite as early as possible
Risaputo ...	38708	**Theory(ies)**
Risarcire ...	38709	Have you any theory to account for
Risbaldire	38710	Do you attach any importance to ——'s theory as to
Riscaldato	38711	Do not attach any importance to ——'s theory as to
Riscelio ...	38712	In distinct contradiction to ——'s theory
Riscontro ...	38713	——'s theory explains —— but not ——
Riscoso ...	38714	**There**
Riscrivere	38715	There is a
Riseccaco ...	38716	Is there a
Riseduto ...	38717	There is no
Risegarsi ...	38718	Is there not
Risegatura	38719	Get there as quickly as you can
Risegnato ...	38720	So long as —— is there
Riseguire ...	38721	Is (are) there
Risembrare	38722	There is (are)
Risentirsi ...	38723	There is (are) not
Riserbanza	38724	How much will there be left
Riserbato ...	38725	There will be
Risette ...	38726	There will be about
Risguardo	38727	There will not be
Risibility ...	38728	What should there be
Risigallo ...	38729	There should be
Risitantem	38730	There should not be more than
Risoffiare ...	38731	There should not be less than
Risolvente	38732	There should not be any difficulty
Risonare ...	38733	There will be considerable difficulty
Risorbire ...	38734	There will not be much difficulty
Risorresso	38735	There will be enough to
Risospinto	38736	There will not be enough to
Risotada ...	38737	Will there be enough to
Risparmio	38738	Is there likely to be
Rispazzato	38739	There is likely to be
Rispegnere	38740	There is not likely to be
Rispeltoso	38741	What is there likely to be
Risponsivo	38742	There is (are) some
Risprimere	38743	Is there any
Risquable...	38744	There is not any
Risquer ...	38745	There or thereabouts
Rissoler ..	38746	**Thereby**
Ristagnato	38747	If you (——) can thereby
Ristaurare	38748	Unless you (——) can thereby
Ristillare ...	38749	It might be possible thereby to
Ristituire ...	38750	**Therefore**
Ristorarsi	38751	**Thereof**
Ristretto ...	38752	**Thereto**

Ristudiare	38753	**Thereunder**
Risucitato	38754	**Thermometer** (*See also* "Temperature," "Weather," ["Zero.")
Risultare ...	38755	A Fahrenheit thermometer
Risurgente	38756	A Centigrade thermometer
Risurressi	38757	A maximum and minimum thermometer
Ritagliare...	38758	**These**
Ritardante	38759	These are
Ritardo ...	38760	Are these
Ritemere ...	38761	These are not
Ritenente ...	38762	**They**
Ritenevole	38763	They are
Ritenotojo	38764	They have
Ritessuto ...	38765	They are not
Ritignere ...	38766	They have not
Ritmico ...	38767	They can
Ritondetto	38768	They cannot
Ritorcersi ...	38769	They will
Ritornanza	38770	They will not
Ritornello...	38771	Can they not
Ritortola ...	38772	Will they not
Ritosare ...	38773	Have they not
Ritradurre	38774	It might have been they who
Ritraente ..	38775	Could not have been they who
Ritraggere	38776	**Thick**
Ritrangolo	38777	How thick
Ritrattato...	38778	Very thick
Ritrecine ...	38779	Not so thick
Ritribuire .	38780	Should be sufficiently thick to (for)
Ritropico ...	38781	How thick do you require it
Ritropisia...	38782	A little too thick
Ritrosetto...	38783	Not sufficiently thick
Ritrovarsi...'	38784	Should be thick enough to
Rittergut ...	38785	Was not thick enough to
Ritualism ..	38786	**Thickly**
Ritualiter...	38787	Thickly coated with
Ritually ...	38788	**Thickness** (*See also* "Width.")
Rituffare ...	38789	Please cable thickness of —— required
Riudito ...	38790	An average thickness of
Riungere ...	38791	From a maximum thickness of
Rivalite ...	38792	Generally the thickness does not exceed
Rivalizar ...	38793	**Thin**
Rivalry ...	38794	How thin
Riveditore	38795	Very thin
Riveduto ...	38796	Not so thin
Riveggente	38797	Should be sufficiently thin to
Rivelabile	38798	How thin do you require it
Rivellino ...	38799	Not sufficiently thin
Rivenderia	38800	A little too thin
Rivenirsi ...	38801	Should be thin enough to
Riverain ...	38802	Was not thin enough to
Riverhorse	38803	**Thing(s)** (*See also* "Condition," "Fair.")
Rivestito ...	38804	I (we) concluded that the best thing was
Riveted ...	38805	As a regular thing
Riviere ...	38806	Things generally
Rivilicare...	38807	Things are
Rivoletto ...	38808	Things look
Rivolgente	38809	How do things look
Rivolgersi...	38810	Things look on the whole fairly well
Rivoltuoso	38811	Things do not look so well
Rivoltura ...	38812	Things look very bad

[648]

Rivomitare	38813	It is the only thing to be done
Rivulet ...	38814	Are things in a fair way to
Roadmetal	38815	Things are in a fair way to.
Roadstead	38816	Things have been considerably upset by
Roadway ...	38817	**Think(s)**
Roarer	38818	To think
Roaring ...	38819	Do not think
Robador ...	38820	As soon as you think fit
Robaliza ...	38821	Should you still think of
Robberies	38822	Provided that you think it necessary
Robeccia ...	38823	What do you think necessary
Robinet ...	38824	What do you think of (about)
Roboracion	38825	What do you think of doing
Roborante	38826	Do whatever you think the best
Roborarium	38827	Do you think (that)
Roborativo	38828	Do you still think of
Roboratote	38829	Should you think
Roboravit	38830	I (we) do not think
Roboreus ...	38831	I (we) certainly think
Robredo ...	38832	I (we) think about
Robustecer	38833	I (we) think that it will
Robustly ...	38834	I (we) do not think that it will
Robustus ...	38835	I (we) do not think it would be well to
Rocailleur...	38836	There is considerable reason to think
Rocalla ...	38837	Is there any reason to think
Rocambole	38838	There is no reason to think
Roccellic ...	38839	Have you any reason to think otherwise
Rocchietto	38840	Do you think so
Rocheln ...	38841	I (we) think so
Rochiren ...	38842	I (we) do not think so
Ròciada ...	38843	If —— thinks so
Rocinante	38844	Do you think there will be any difficulty (with)
Rockalum	38845	I (we) think there will be considerable difficulty with
Rockets ...	38846	Do not think there will be any difficulty with
Rockiness	38847	Do you think it (he) would do for you (us)
Rockrose ...	38848	Think it (he) would do for you (us)
Rocksalt ...	38849	Do not think it (he) would do for us
Rockschoss	38850	I (we) think the best plan would be to
Rococo ...	38851	Act as you think best
Rodaballo	38852	If you think well of this, act at once
Rodajilla ...	38853	If you do not think well of this, do not act until
Rodante ...	38854	Do not think that it would suit
Rodapelo ...	38855	Think it (he) would suit you very well
Rodeabrazo	38856	I (we) think it would suit —— very well
Rodelero ...	38857	—— seem(s) to think that
Rodilleras	38858	Do(es) not seem to think much of it (them)
Rodilludo	38859	Ascertain what —— think(s) with regard to
Rodimento	38860	I (we) think it advisable to
Roditrice ...	38861	I (we) think it advisable for the present to
Roditura ...	38862	I (we) do not think it advisable to
Rodomel ...	38863	I (we) do not think it advisable for the present to
Rodomont	38864	Cable what you think with respect to
Rodrigar ...	38865	Cable whether you think
Rodzuela ...	38866	I (we) think that you had better at once
Roebuck ...	38867	Do you think I (we) had better
Rofianear...	38868	Do not think anything of it (him)
Rogamentum	38869	I am (we are) not inclined to think much of it (him) (them)
Rogation ...	38870	If you think there is anything in it (him)
Rogativa ...	38871	If you do not think there is anything in it (him)
Rogatrix ...	38872	I (we) think you had better not

Rogener ...	38873	I (we) think you had better not do anything for the present
Rogitator ...	38874	Think you have acted very wisely
Rognaccia	38875	Think you have acted a little rashly
Rogneux ...	38876	Think —— has (have) been ill advised to act as he has (they
Rognonner	38877	Should you think differently, please cable [have) done
Rognure ...	38878	Cable to —— and ask what he thinks
Rognuzza	38879	—— has cabled that he thinks we had better
Rogoinnie...	38880	When do you think it will be
Roguishly	38881	When I (we) think it will be
Rogumare	38882	How much do you think we shall have by
Rohheit ...	38883	Think it over and cable
Rohrdecke	38884	Will think it over and cable
Rohrflote ...	38885	It will take some time to think over
Rohricht ...	38886	Do you think —— would care to
Rohrkasten	38887	Do not think —— would care to
Rohrnasat	38888	Think —— would very much like to
Rohrquint	38889	Think there is no probability
Rohrwasser	38890	Do as you think best
Rohrwerk	38891	Do you think this unfair
Roister ...	38892	Do not think this at all unfair
Roistering	38893	Think it very unfair
Roitelet ...	38894	What do you think about doing this at once
Rojeante ...	38895	What do you think about immediate erection of
Rojizo ...	38896	Do not do it (this) if you think it unnecessary
Roldana ...	38897	Am (are) inclined to think that —— is altogether unreliable
Rollholz ...	38898	Am (are) inclined to think that —— is working against us
Rollicking	38899	**Thinly**
Rollwagen	38900	**Thinness**
Romagnuolo	38901	**Third(s)**
Romaine ...	38902	Third clause
Romajohno	38903	In thirds
Romanador	38904	One-third
Romancer	38905	Two-thirds
Romancista	38906	**This**
Romanesco	38907	This is
Romanesque	38908	Of this
Romanizar	38909	By this
Romantic ...	38910	To this
Romantisch	38911	From this
Romanziere	38912	By this you will see that
Romarin ...	38913	From this you must deduct
Rombazzo...	38914	To this you must add
Romboidale	38915	Provided that this will suffice
Rombolato	38916	Should this
Romeaggio	38917	Should this not
Romeino ...	38918	Might not this be made
Romerage...	38919	How is this
Romitano...	38920	Why is this
Romitesco	38921	This means
Rompedera	38922	Does this mean
Rompesacos	38923	This does not mean
Rompevole	38924	How far will this carry you
Rompicapo	38925	This will carry us
Rompicollo	38926	What do you think of this
Romping ...	38927	What does this prove
Rompishly	38928	This proves
Rompitrice	38929	This does not prove
Ronceria ...	38930	This is all I (we) can say at present
Ronchioso	38931	This will enable you
Ronchon ...	38932	Will this enable you

Rondalla ...	38933	This should enable you
Rondeletia	38934	When will this be
Rondeur ...	38935	**Thorough**
Rondinella	38936	**Thoroughly**
Rondinetto	38937	Thoroughly exhausted
Ronflant ...	38938	Thoroughly sound
Rongigata	38939	Thoroughly worn out
Ronquear ...	38940	Has (have) thoroughly
Ronquida...	38941	Have you (——) thoroughly
Ronzamento	38942	Has (have) not yet thoroughly
Roodloft ...	38943	As soon as I (we) have thoroughly
Roofing ...	38944	To enable me (us) to thoroughly
Roomily ...	38945	Will most thoroughly
Roominess	38946	Have gone thoroughly into the matter
Rootcrop ...	38947	As soon as I (we) have gone thoroughly into the matter
Roothouse	38948	You must thoroughly examine
Rootlets ...	38949	I (we) have thoroughly examined
Ropalico ...	38950	Thoroughly examine into every detail
Ropavejero	38951	**Those**
Ropedancer	38952	Those who
Ropemaker	38953	Only those
Ropewalk...	38954	Those to whom you refer in your advice of
Ropeyarn ...	38955	**Though**
Roquefort...	38956	Even though
Roquelaure	38957	**Thought**
Roquette ...	38958	Has (have) thought that
Rorastro ...	38959	As —— thought that
Rorescens...	38960	I (we) have thought it necessary to
Rorifluus ...	38961	I (we) have not thought it necessary to
Rorulentus	38962	I thought the best thing to do
Rosaceous	38963	Was not thought of at all
Rosacruz ...	38964	As soon as you have thought it over
Rosaire ...	38965	Has (have) now thought it over and would suggest
Rosaniline	38966	As soon as I (we) have thought it over
Rosariero ...	38967	Has (have) now thought it over and decided to
Roscidorum	38968	Without any thought for
Roscon ...	38969	Thought I should be able to
Rosebud .	38970	Thought you would be able to
Rosecolour	38971	**Thoughtless**
Rosegall ...	38972	Most thoughtless
Roseliere ...	38973	Beyond being thoughtless
Rosellina ...	38974	**Thoughtlessly**
Rosemallow	38975	Acted very thoughtlessly
Rosemary...	38976	Has no doubt acted thoughtlessly
Rosenkranz	38977	**Thoughtlessness**
Rosenroth	38978	Absolute thoughtlessness
Roseolus ...	38979	As a consequence of ——'s thoughtlessness
Roserare ...	38980	**Thousand(s)** (*See also* Table at end.)
Rosetree ...	38981	All the foregoing figures are thousands
Rosewater	38982	All the following figures are thousands
Rosewood...	38983	Read units as thousands
Rosicler ...	38984	Read hundreds as thousands
Rosiere ...	38985	Read thousands as units
Rosmarinus	38986	Read thousands as hundreds
Rosmatino	38987	**Threaten(s)**
Rosojone ...	38988	To threaten
Rosolaccio	38989	Threaten(s) to
Rosolea ...	38990	Will most probably threaten to
Rosquilla ...	38991	Should —— threaten
Rossarzt ...	38992	Would it be well to threaten (to)

Rossbremse	38993	I (we) think it would be well to threaten (to)
Rossignol ...	38994	I (we) do not think it would be any good to threaten (to)
Rossinante	38995	Threaten(s) me (us) with legal proceedings
Rosskamm	38996	Threaten —— (him) with legal proceedings
Rossoretto	38997	You might go so far as to threaten
Rostbraten	38998	**Threatened**
Rostellum	38999	Has (have) threatened to
Rostfarbig	39000	Has (have) not threatened to
Rostigioso	**39001**	Has (have) already threatened to
Rostofen ...	39002	Am (are) threatened with
Rostratus ..	39003	—— is (are) threatened with
Rostrico ...	39004	Has (have) threatened to commence legal proceedings
Rosulente...	39005	**Through**
Rotamente	39006	Through the
Rotatilis ...	39007	Through this
Rotating ...	39008	Mainly through
Rotatoire ...	39009	Entirely through
Roteazione	39010	Not at all through
Rotelletta...	39011	Was (were) caused through
Rotellone ...	39012	Was (were) not caused through
Rotheln ...	39013	Unless it was caused through
Rothkopf ..	39014	Right through
Rothlauf ...	39015	Through from
Rothwild ...	39016	Will see the matter through before I leave
Rotisserie...	39017	Will you see the matter through
Rotondato	39018	Will see the matter through
Rotondezza	39019	Has (have) gone carefully through the affair
Rottenness	39020	To get through
Rotundatus	39021	When do you expect to get through with it
Rotundity	39022	Will speedily be through
Roturier ...	39023	Expect to get through with it within the next —— days
Rouennerie	39024	As soon as you have gone through the details
Rougeaud...	39025	Cannot get through
Rougeole ...	39026	Shall not be able to get through much before
Roughen ...	39027	So as to get through
Roughness	39028	Through the (this) accident
Roughshod	39029	As soon as I (we) have gone through the papers
Rouillure ...	39030	As soon as I (we) get through the
Roulade ...	39031	To carry it through
Roulement	39032	You must carry it through at all hazards
Roulette ...	39033	Will do my (our) best to carry it through
Roundabout	39034	Have no doubt but that I (we) shall be able to carry it through
Roundelay	39035	Am (are) doubtful that —— will be able to carry it through
Roundshot	39036	Carry it through if you can
Roupiller ...	39037	Shall not be able to carry it through unless
Rousingly	39038	Provided that you can carry it through
Rousselet ...	39039	We shall be delayed —— days through
Rouverin ...	39040	Have you (has ——) gone through the figures
Rouvieux ...	39041	Has (have) gone through the figures
Rovaglione	39042	Has (have) not yet gone through the figures
Rovajaccio	39043	Has (have) been sent through
Roventato	39044	Through my (our) assistance
Roventezza	39045	Through ——'s assistance
Roversio ...	39046	Partly through
Rovesciare	39047	Nearly through
Rovigliato	39048	—— feet through
Rovinatore	39049	**Throughout**
Rovistiare	39050	Throughout the entire proceedings
Rowans ...	39051	Throughout the mine
Rowboat ...	39052	Throughout the whole negotiations

Rowlock ...	39053	Throughout the affair
Royalties ...	39054	Throughout the year
Royaume ...	39055	Throughout the winter
Rozadero ...	39056	Throughout the summer
Rozamiento	39057	**Through Rate** (*See also* " Rate.")
Rozarillon	39058	A through rate from —— to ——
Roznido ...	39059	What is the through rate from —— to ——
Rozzaccia ...	39060	The through rate from —— to —— is ——
Rubacuori	39061	At a through rate (of)
Rubaldone	39062	Lowest through rate
Rubatrice...	39063	Through rate would be inclusive of
Rubatura ...	39064	Through rate would be exclusive of
Rubbish ...	39065	Have seen —— and arranged a through rate of —— per ton
Rubecula ...	39066	**Throw(s)** [between —— and ——
Rubedine ...	39067	To throw
Rubefacio...	39068	This will throw
Rubellante	39069	Will it throw
Rubestezza	39070	It will not throw
Rubeta ...	39071	Throw(s) considerable doubt upon
Rubetarius	39072	Do(es) not really throw any doubt upon it
Rubicandez	39073	Can you throw any light on it
Rubicilla ...	39074	Cannot throw any light upon it at the present moment
Rubicund ...	39075	Do(es) —— throw any obstacle in the way of
Rubificar ...	39076	—— is inclined to throw obstacles in my (our) way
Rubigalia ...	39077	—— throw(s) every obstacle that he (they) can in the way of
Rubigine ...	39078	Do not throw any obstacles in the way of
Rubinetto...	39079	Throw all the obstacles you can in the way of
Ruboroso ...	39080	Will throw every obstacle that I (we) can in the way of
Rubric ...	39081	Will not throw any obstacle in the way of
Rubricate...	39082	It will be necessary to throw aside
Rubriciren	39083	Will it be necessary to throw aside
Rubricosam	39084	It will not be necessary to throw aside
Rubsamen	39085	**Throwing**
Ruchbar ...	39086	It is simply throwing money away [trying it
Ruckblick	39087	May possibly be throwing away money but I (we) recommend
Ruckfall ...	39088	So long as I am (we are) not actually throwing away money
Ruckgang	39089	Throwing away
Ruckhalt ...	39090	**Thrown**
Ruckseite...	39091	Thrown up by
Rucksicht...	39092	Thrown out
Ruckwarts	39093	Thrown open
Ructatriz ...	39094	Has (have) been entirely thrown away
Ructuosus	39095	Has (have) not been entirely thrown away
Rudder ...	39096	Has (have) been thrown
Ruddiness	39097	Has (have) not been thrown
Ruderarius	39098	**Thursday**
Ruderbank	39099	—— Thursday(s) in each month
Rudesse ...	39100	About Thursday week
Rudetum ...	39101	Next Thursday
Rudimental	39102	Last Thursday
Rudoyer ...	39103	Every Thursday
Rudusculum	39104	Every alternate Thursday
Ruefully ...	39105	During Thursday
Ruello ...	39106	Next Thursday week
Ruffianare	39107	During Thursday night
Ruffianly...	39108	On Thursday
Ruffling ...	39109	On Thursday morning
Rufianesco	39110	On Thursday afternoon
Rufous ...	39111	On Thursday night
Ruggedly ...	39112	**Tight**

Rugghiante	39113	Not sufficiently tight
Rugginuzza	39114	Too tight
Rugiente ...	39115	Must be tight
Rugimiento	39116	Unless made tight
Rugiolone	39117	Have not succeeded in making the —— tight
Rugosidad	39118	Have succeeded in making the —— tight
Rugosite ...	39119	In case I (we) do not succeed in making the —— tight
Ruhestand	39120	**Tightly**
Ruhestorer	39121	**Timber(s)** *(See also "Board," "Scarce.")*
Ruhmredig	39122	To timber
Ruhrigkeit	39123	Suitable timbers for
Ruidoso ...	39124	The timber on the property is worth
Ruinate ...	39125	The timber on the property is practically of no value
Ruinazione	39126	What is your estimate for new timbers (for)
Ruindad ...	39127	Estimated cost for new timbers at —— will amount to
Ruinosus ...	39128	The timbers in the shaft are rotten [decayed
Ruinously	39129	The mine timbers between —— and —— levels are altogether
Ruiponce ...	39130	Have contracted for a sufficient supply of timber (for)
Ruisseler ...	39131	Is there timber on the property for fuel and mining purposes
Rujada ...	39132	There is an abundant supply of timber on the property for
		[fuel and mining purposes
Rulingly ...	39133	There is a plentiful supply of timber for fuel
Rullando ...	39134	There is a plentiful supply of timber for mining purposes
Rumbadas	39135	There is a good supply of timber for fuel but it is of small
Rumbon ...	39136	Timber is very scarce [size for
Rumbotinus	39137	Timber on the property costs
Rumiadura	39138	Old timbers likely to give out
Rumiante...	39139	Timbers all in good condition
Rumigeror	39140	A set of timbers
Rumigestri	39141	—— sets of timbers
Ruminalis	39142	To re-timber
Ruminantly	39143	Shall require to re-timber (the)
Ruminator	39144	When shall you commence to re-timber
Ruminatrix	39145	Shall commence to re-timber on
Rummaged	39146	Commenced to re-timber on
Rumpeln ...	39147	There is a good supply of mining timber on the property
Rumpsteak	39148	Mining timber on the property is somewhat scarce, but can
Runaway ...	39149	**Timbered** [be had at reasonable rates
Runciglio ...	39150	Now being timbered
Rundlich ...	39151	Timbered down to —— feet from surface
Rundweg ...	39152	Securely timbered
Runghead...	39153	Well timbered
Runic ...	39154	Not at all well timbered
Runkelrube	39155	Requires to be well timbered
Runzelig ...	39156	Do(es) not require to be timbered
Ruotarsi ...	39157	Will have to be re-timbered
Ruotolare...	39158	Will it have to be re-timbered
Rupicapra	39159	Need not be re-timbered at present
Rupicola ...	39160	Should be re-timbered at once
Rupicones	39161	**Timbering**
Rupinoso ...	39162	Timbering shaft
Ruppig ...	39163	Shall recommence timbering
Ruptorio ...	39164	When will you finish timbering
Ruptured ...	39165	Shall finish timbering about
Ruralist ...	39166	Estimate the cost of timbering will amount to
Ruralness...	39167	Estimate cost of re-timbering the shaft will amount to
Ruscello ...	39168	Cable cost of timbering the shaft
Rusenol ...	39169	Does estimate received include cost of timbering
Rushcandle	39170	Estimate includes cost of timbering
Rushlight...	39171	Estimated cost does not include timbering

Rusignuolo	39172	Estimate should include timbering
Russeting...	39173	**Time(s)** (*See also* "Departure," "Did," "Expire," "Expired,"
Russety ...	39174	To time ["Extend," "Give," "Short.")
Rusthaum	39175	In time
Rusticate ...	39176	Note time required
Rusticulus	39177	Will note time required
Rustigkeit	39178	Long time
Rustiques	39179	Next time
Rustling ...	39180	Last time
Rustrir ...	39181	This time
Rutacens ...	39182	At some future time
Rutellum ...	39183	Additional time
Ruthless ...	39184	Another time
Rutilandus	39185	Short time
Rutiler ...	39186	A short time since
Rutilesco ...	39187	Time is a little too short
Rutinario ...	39188	Time is altogether too short
Rutschen ...	39189	A long time since
Rutatto ...	39190	In the time mentioned
Ruvidita ...	39191	In time for
Ruvidotto	39192	Not in time for
Ruvistico ...	39193	Can you (——) alter the time
Ryegrass ...	39194	Cannot alter the time
Saatfeld ...	39195	Shall you have time to
Saatkorn ...	39196	Shall not have time to
Sabado ...	39197	Shall have plenty of time to
Sabajarius	39198	When I (we) expect to have more time
Sabalera ...	39199	If time will allow
Sabandija...	39200	Want more time
Sabanilla ...	39201	How much time will it occupy
Sabbath ...	39202	Will occupy at least —— days' time
Sabbatical	39203	Time is quite long enough
Sabbiare ...	39204	The precise time
Sabbionoso	39205	For some time to come
Sabedor ...	39206	For some time past
Sabeismo ...	39207	At the same time
Sabelhieb ...	39208	At such times
Sabeliano ...	39209	At all times
Sabellica ...	39210	Many times
Sabeln ...	39211	Can you not shorten the time of (for)
Sabiduria...	39212	Will endeavour to shorten the time
Sabiendas ..	39213	Cannot shorten the time of (fer)
Sabiondez	39214	Can you extend the time of (for)
Sables ...	39215	By which time I (we) shall have
Sablier ...	39216	Endeavour to get time extended for (to)
Sablonneux	39217	Will endeavour to get time extended
Sablonnier	39218	Have not been able to get time extended
Sabogal ...	39219	Consents to extend the time an additional —— days
Saborder ...	39220	—— refuse(s) to extend the time
Saboreador	39221	Will see —— and endeavour to get the time extended
Saborete ...	39222	Will —— extend the time to
Saboyana ...	39223	Will not extend the time beyond
Sabretache	39224	Will this be in time (for)
Sabroso ...	39225	This will not be in time (for)
Sabuletum	39226	It (this) will be in time (for)
Saburralis	39227	Should be in time (for)
Sacabala ...	39228	To be in time
Sacabocado	39229	How much time can you give me (us)
Sacabrocas	39230	Will this be sufficient time for
Sacabuche	39231	Has (have) agreed to extend time until

Sacadinero	39232	Cannot get time extended
Sacadura ...	39233	Time has been extended to
Sacafocida	39234	Time to be extended to
Sacamedula	39235	Enough time
Sacamiento	39236	Is there time enough for
Sacamolero	39237	There is time enough for
Sacamuelas	39238	There is not time enough for
Sacanete ...	39239	Is this time enough
Sacapotras	39240	It is time enough
Sacatapon	39241	It will be time enough (if)
Sacatrapos	39242	Usual time
Saccageur...	39243	What is the usual time
Saccarello...	39244	The usual time is
Saccarius ...	39245	Within the (this) time
Saccellus ...	39246	Time is of the utmost importance
Saccentino	39247	Should you have sufficient time
Saccharoid	39248	Should you not have sufficient time
Saccharum	39249	In case I (we) have not sufficient time
Sacchetta ...	39250	Will it (they) be ready at the time mentioned (viz. :—)
Saccomanno	39251	Will be ready by the time mentioned (viz. :—)
Saccomesso	39252	Cannot be done in the time
Sacellanus	39253	In case you (they) (it) cannot be ready within the time
Sacerdios ...	39254	This will give you plenty of time for [mentioned
Sacerdoce...	39255	This will give me (us) plenty of time for
Sacerdotal	39256	Will there be plenty of time for it
Sacerdozio	39257	Must give reasonable time for
Sachem ...	39258	There will be sufficient time
Sachfallig	39259	There is not sufficient time for a thorough examination
Sachkundig	39260	There is barely sufficient time to
Sachwalter	39261	Time to begin on
Saciable ...	39262	Time to end on
Sackbut ...	39263	When does the time expire
Sackgasse...	39264	Time expires on
Sacking ...	39265	Time expired on —— last
Sackpfcife	39266	As soon as the time is completely expired
Sackpipe ...	39267	Before the time expires
Sacoche ...	39268	Time occupied by —— not included
Sacopenum	39269	How has the time been occupied since
Sacrament	39270	Have been occupied most of the time since —— in (by)
Sacrandus	39271	About the same time as
Sacrarium	39272	What is the latest time you can give him (us)
Sacrebleu ...	39273	The latest time I (we) can give him (you) is
Sacredly ...	39274	Can only be worked at certain times
Sacricola ...	39275	At such times it is necessary to
Sacrifex ...	39276	In a month's time
Sacrificar ...	39277	In a week's time
Sacrilege ...	39278	In —— days' time
Sacrimum...	39279	For some considerable time past
Sacripant ...	39280	At what time
Sacristan ...	39281	At the present time
Sacrosanto	39282	What time will you
Sacudida ...	39283	What time will be necessary to devote to it
Sacudidura	39284	You will have to devote about —— days' time
Saddening	39285	About what time do you expect to
Saddlebow	39286	Time is too short to give effect to your instructions
Saddlery ...	39287	Time is too short for me (us) to do anything in the matter
Saddletree	39288	Unless you can give me (us) longer time
Sadiron ...	39289	Is the present a good time for
Saduceismo	39290	The present is a very good time for
Saduceo ...	39291	The present is not a good time for

Saeppolare	39292	You should lose no time if
Saeppolo ...	39293	You must lose no time if you intend to do anything in the
Saetear ...	39294	I (we) will lose no time [(this) matter
Saeton ...	39295	Do not lose any time
Saettame	39296	Do not wish to lose any time
Saettevole...	39297	Do not lose any time in doing this
Saettiere ...	39298	In order that no time may be lost
Saetuzza ...	39299	Some time ago
Saezeit ...	39300	—— days' lost time, owing to
Safeguard	39301	The total remaining time
Saffian ...	39302	What is the time fixed (for)
Safraniere	39303	No time has yet been fixed
Saftigkeit...	39304	The time required for examination would be about
Saftlos ...	39305	Can you report time required to unwater the mine
Safumar ...	39306	The time required to unwater the mine would be at least
Sagacatis ...	39307	By which time I (we) would expect that [—— days
Sagacezza...	39308	Easily by that time
Sagacidad	39309	Some time must necessarily elapse (before)
Sagacity ..	39310	Unless you succeed in getting time extended
Sagamore...	39311	Endeavour to obtain more time
Sagapeno ...	39312	Plenty of time
Sagazmente	39313	Now is the time if you wish to do anything
Sagebock ...	39314	Now is the time to purchase
Sagebush ...	39315	Now is the time to realize
Sagenhaft...	39316	Scarcely time yet
Sagenitic ...	39317	Scarcely time to
Sagespane	39318	Up to the present time
Sagestre ...	39319	Up to that time
Saggetto ...	39320	At the usual time
Saggiatore	39321	It (this) will take some time
Sagginale...	39322	Some time
Saggio ...	39323	Do not consider the proper time has yet arrived
Saggitiere...	39324	If time permits I (we) should much prefer to
Saggiuolo...	39325	The time required would probably be —— weeks
Sagina ...	39326	If time permits
Saginandus	39327	Would the time occupied in waiting be paid for
Sagitario ...	39328	Time occupied in waiting will be paid for
Sagittaire...	39329	Time occupied in waiting will not be paid for
Sagittalis ...	39330	Time is most important
Sagittifer ...	39331	Do not spend much time upon it
Sagittula ...	39332	Spend what time you think absolutely necessary
Sagliente ...	39333	How much time shall I devote to this (it)
Saglimento	39334	Do not spend more time or money than you can help
Sagoutier ...	39335	At what period of time
Sagrariero	39336	How long a period of time
Sagrasione	39337	For the second time
Sagratina ...	39338	Within what time do you expect
Sagrestana	39339	Within what time
Sagulatus...	39340	Could not commence in time
Sahornarse	39341	Could not be forwarded in time
Sahumado	39342	Will take some considerable time
Sahumadura	39343	Some time in the near future
Sahumerio	39344	Not looking so well at the present time
Sahuquillo	39345	Never better than at present time
Saignant ...	39346	By that time I (we) expect
Saignement	39347	Will probably be decided by that time
Sailloft ...	39348	By that time I (we) shall know
Sailyard ...	39349	By that time I (we) shall be able to tell
Saindoux ...	39350	By that time
Sainete ...	39351	By that time at latest

Sainetillo ...	39352	Impossible before that time
Sainfoin ...	39353	Tin (See also "Cassiterite.")
Saintlike ...	39354	Block tin
Saintship ...	39355	Black tin
Sajorna ...	39356	Metallic tin
Salaam ...	39357	Stream tin
Salacon ...	39358	Tin is associated with
Saladero ...	39359	Carrying —— pounds of black tin per ton of ore
Salading ...	39360	Tin ore
Salamalech	39361	Tinplate(s)
Salamandra	39362	Tip
Salamistra	39363	Side tip wagons
Saland ...	39364	End tip wagons
Salapusius	39365	End and side tip wagons
Salariar ...	39366	Title(s)
Salbadern...	39367	Title deeds
Salceda ...	39368	Can give perfect title
Salchicha ...	39369	Is ——'s title to the property good
Salcigno ...	39370	——'s title is not altogether in order
Saldatojo ...	39371	The title is quite good
Saldiren ...	39372	The title is not sound
Salebratim	39373	The title is really of no value
Salebritas...	39374	Pending examination of titles
Salebrosus	39375	Has (have) arranged to have titles examined
Saledizo ...	39376	Titles have been examined and are in perfect order
Saleggiare	39377	Titles have been examined, flaws slight, can be amended, but [will take —— days
Salement ...	39378	A minute examination of the titles must be made at once
Saleroso ...	39379	Owing to a flaw in the title deeds
Salework ...	39380	Owing to a flaw in the title to
Salgamum	39381	Titles perfect
Salgemma	39382	Titles certified by
Salguero ...	39383	Titles guaranteed by
Saliatus ...	39384	In the event of the titles being all in order
Salibile ...	39385	Will arrange to have (give) a sound title
Salicastro ...	39386	Cannot get a sound title
Salicetum ...	39387	Unless you can get a sound title
Salicoque ...	39388	Abstract of titles mailed on
Salicornia...	39389	Mail abstract of titles on
Salicylic ...	39390	In reference to the title
Saliente ...	39391	Owing to a dispute as to title
Saligaud ...	39392	There is no dispute as to title
Salignon ...	39393	Is there any dispute as to title
Salimbacca	39394	Pending settlement of dispute as to title
Salimeter ...	39395	Provided that the titles are in perfect order
Salinator ...	39396	As soon as title has been amended
Salinero ...	39397	The flaw in title will cause a delay of
Salinity ...	39398	The flaw in title is only formal and can be easily remedied
Salique ...	39399	So as to prove the title
Salisatio ...	39400	To clear up the title
Saliscendo	39401	The title to the property is under Government lease
Salissant ...	39402	Do not lose any time in registering the titles
Salissure ...	39403	Have posted full record of title
Salitore ...	39404	Undertakes to convey a clear and perfect title
Salitrado ...	39405	Title is much involved
Salitreria ...	39406	There is a slight modification required as to title
Saliunca ...	39407	The title is now in perfect order
Salivandus	39408	To
Salivary ...	39409	To be
livated ...	39410	Not to be

Salivosus ...	39411	When is it to be
Sallador ...	39412	Ought to be
Sallendus ...	39413	To be sure
Sallow ...	39414	Sure to be
Sallowness	39415	Is not to be at all
Sallyport ...	39416	To the
Salmacidus	39417	To this
Salmagundi	39418	To what
Salmear ...	39419	To whom
Salmiak ...	39420	—— to ——
Salmografo	39421	**To-day**
Salmuera ...	39422	Will be forwarded to-day
Salnitrum...	39423	Unless we receive to-day will be of no use
Salobral ...	39424	Has (have) been published to-day
Salobreno...	39425	Must have to-day
Saloperie ...	39426	Have been told to-day that
Salopygium	39427	To-day if possible
Salpetrig ...	39428	Only received to-day
Salpicar ...	39429	Have been signed to-day
Salpresar ...	39430	**Together**
Salpuga ...	39431	Together with
Salsamen ...	39432	Either together or separately
Salsedine ...	39433	He (——) ask(s) for both together the sum of
Salseron ...	39434	Must be considered together
Salsicium ...	39435	The two concessions together comprise
Salsifis ...	39436	Not together
Salsilago ...	39437	Both together
Salsitudo ...	39438	This together with
Salsuggine	39439	Whether together or apart
Salsugia ...	39440	To put together
Saltabanco	39441	Put together
Saltado ...	39442	Together with cost of
Saltadura...	39443	This is together with cost of
Saltante ...	39444	Is this together with cost of
Saltaregla...	39445	This is not together with cost of
Saltaren ...	39446	Should be together with
Saltaturus	39447	**Told**
Saltcake ...	39448	Who told
Saltcellar ...	39449	Was not told personally
Saltcador ...	39450	Was told personally
Saltellino ...	39451	Were you told personally
Salterello ...	39452	Who was it told you
Saltern ...	39453	Do not recollect who told me
Saltfish ...	39454	Was told by
Saltillo ...	39455	Cannot divulge who told me
Saltless ...	39456	Will report who told me as soon as I have obtained requisite [permission.
Saltmarsh	39457	Told me about
Saltpetre ...	39458	Told him about
Saltpit ...	39459	Told me to
Saltuatim...	39460	Told him to
Saltuosus ...	39461	Was told as an absolute fact that
Salubridad	39462	**To-morrow**
Salubrite ...	39463	Sometime to-morrow
Saludador	39464	To-morrow morning
Salutaire ...	39465	To-morrow evening
Salutatrix...	39466	Will cable to-morrow
Saluter ...	39467	Will be forwarded to-morrow
Salutevole	39468	Cannot reply until to-morrow
Salvachia ...	39469	Expect to complete to-morrow
Salvadera ...	39470	Cannot complete before to-morrow

Salvagez ...	39471	Not expected until to-morrow
Salvaggio...	39472	Not later than to-morrow
Salvagina...	39473	Your cable received, will reply to-morrow
Salvamente	39474	Is (are) to be signed to-morrow
Salvante ...	39475	Unless received to-morrow
Salvaroba...	39476	**Ton(s)** (*See also* Table at end.)
Salvatrice...	39477	Per ton
Salviado ...	39478	Per ton of 2,000 lbs.
Salviatum...	39479	Per ton of 2,240 lbs.
Salvietta ...	39480	On each ton
Salvificus ...	39481	What is the value per ton
Salvigia ...	39482	The value per ton is
Salvohonor	39483	At a value per ton of ——
Salzbruhe...	39484	Weighing about —— tons
Salzgeist ...	39485	Estimated at —— tons
Salzgurke...	39486	The yield per ton is
Salzquelle...	39487	What is the yield per ton
Salzsaure ...	39488	What is the net profit per ton
Salzsole ...	39489	What is the price per ton
Salzwerk ...	39490	The price per ton is
Sambenito	39491	The net profit per ton is
Samblage...	39492	Has advanced in value —— per ton
Sambuceus	39493	At —— per ton
Sambuchino	39494	Have contracted to buy —— tons of
Samenkorn	39495	Have contracted to sell —— tons of
Samenstaub	39496	How many tons
Samiatus ...	39497	How many tons have you shipped since
Sammelwort	39498	Have shipped —— tons since
Sammeten	39499	Tons of ore.
Sammtlich	39500	Grains per ton
Samnitico...	39501	Tons raised this month
Sampogna	39502	Tons raised last month
Samsuchus	39503	Estimated number of tons [assay value per ton ——
Sanabile ...	39504	For current week we have extracted —— tons of ore, average
Sanalotodo	39505	For current week we have extracted and sorted —— tons of ore.
		[average assay value per ton ——
Sanative ...	39506	We have now —— tons ready for the mill
Sanatory ...	39507	**Tonnage** (*See also* "Total.")
Sanaturus	39508	What is the tonnage available
Sanchete ...	39509	The tonnage available is
Sanciendus	39510	What is the tonnage and estimated value of
Sancionar...	39511	The total tonnage amounts to
Sancitur ...	39512	What is the total tonnage of
Sanctifier ...	39513	State approximate value and tonnage of
Sanctimony	39514	Tonnage exposed
Sanctitas ...	39515	What is the tonnage and approximate sale value of
Sanctitudo	39516	What is your idea of available tonnage
Sanctuaire	39517	Tonnage and value
Sandalina...	39518	Tonnage and estimated value
Sandals ...	39519	**Too** (*See also* "Large," "Late.")
Sandalwood	39520	Too cheap
Sandapino	39521	Too dear
Sandaraca...	39522	Too early
Sandaraque	39523	Too few
Sandareses	39524	Too many
Sandastros	39525	Too high
Sandbad ...	39526	Too low
Sandblind	39527	Too quick
Sanddrift ...	39528	Too slow
derling	39529	Too small

Sandez ...	39530	Too large
Sandgries ...	39531	Too soon
Sandhills ...	39532	Not too soon
Sandstorm	39533	If too soon
Sandwich ...	39534	**Tools** (*See also* " Appliances.")
Sandwort ...	39535	A complete set of tools
Sandwuste	39536	What tools will you require
Saneado ...	39537	Carpenters' tools
Sanedrin ...	39538	Blacksmiths' tools
Sanftigen ...	39539	Require a complete outfit of tools
Sangenos ...	39540	Shall require the following tools
Sangerin ...	39541	Tools were shipped on
Sangfroid ...	39542	Tools will be shipped on
Sangiacco ...	39543	All the tools have been lost
Sangioveto	39544	No damage was done to the tools
Sanglant ...	39545	Only a few tools were lost
Sangloter ...	39546	Send tools for
Sangrador	39547	**Top**
Sangsue ...	39548	At the top of
Sangualis ...	39549	On the top of which
Sangueno ...	39550	Just below the top of
Sanguifero	39551	Nearest to the top
Sanguinary	39552	From top to bottom
Sanguineus	39553	From thence to the top
Sanguinita	39554	From the top downwards for a distance of
Sanicle ...	39555	At the top of the shaft
Sanidine ...	39556	**Total(s)** (*See also* " Tonnage.")
Sanificare ...	39557	Approximate total
Sanioso ...	39558	What is the total amount of
Sanjacado ...	39559	What is the total amount required
Sanjuanada	39560	The total amount is
Sannuto ...	39561	The total amount required is
Sansfacon	39562	This gives a total of
Sanskrit ...	39563	The same total
Sansonnet	39564	From a total of
Santalum ...	39565	At what do you estimate the total expenditure
Santamente	39566	Cannot estimate total expenditure until
Santarello ..	39567	Total estimated expenditure is
Santelmo ...	39568	Give(s) the following totals
Santessa ...	39569	What is the total output since
Santiago ...	39570	The total output since —— is
Santiamen	39571	What is (are) the total shipment(s) since
Santidad ...	39572	The value of the total shipment(s) amounts to
Santificar ...	39573	Cable total amount (of)
Santiguada	39574	Total amount cabled on —— is incorrect
Santigueno	39575	Total amount cabled on —— is correct
Santimonia	39576	Total expenses for current month amount to
Santoccio ...	39577	Please cable estimated total expenses for present month
Santolina ...	39578	Total expenses, surface and underground, for current month
Santoral ...	39579	What are the total expenses per month [amount to
Santurron ...	39580	At what do you estimate the total value of
Sapajon ...	39581	Estimate the total value at
Sapevole ...	39582	Please estimate the total expenses to date of developments at
Sapgreen ...	39583	Please cable total expenditure in connection with
Saphir ...	39584	At what do you estimate the total value of the mine and plant
Sapidity ...	39585	I (we) estimate the total value of the mine and plant at
Sapidness ...	39586	Cable total tonnage of ore raised since
Sapiencia ...	39587	The total tonnage of ore raised since —— is —— tons
Sapienter ...	39588	What are the total charges upon the ore
Sapillo ...	39589	The total charges upon the ore amount to —— per ton

Sapineus ...	39590	The total charges upon the ore exclusive of mining, amount to
Sapiniere ...	39591	What would the total expense be [—— per ton
Sapless ...	39592	The total expense would not be less than
Sapling ...	39593	What has been the total expense of
Saponacco	39594	The total expense to date has been
Saponaria	39595	**Totally**
Saponetto ...	39596	Totally unfitted for
Saponify ...	39597	**Touch**
Saporato ..	39598	To touch
Saporifero	39599	Advise you not to touch it
Saporitino	39600	Am (are) not inclined to touch it
Saporosita	39601	Will certainly not touch it
Sapperlot ...	39602	It is hardly advisable to touch it
Sapphicum	39603	Expect it (they) will touch
Sappiente...	39604	Should it (they) touch
Saprophago	39605	**Towards**
Saputona ...	39606	Is coming towards
Sapwood ...	39607	Is not coming towards
Saqueador	39608	Is it coming towards
Saquera ...	39609	Towards them
Saquilada...	39610	Towards us
Sarabanda	39611	Towards the (this)
Saracenico	39612	A little nearer towards
Saracinare	39613	Coming towards
Saraguete	39614	Coming from —— and towards
Sarampion	39615	As we come towards
Sarangosti	39616	Is it towards or away from
Sarbacane...	39617	Towards the beginning of
Sarcasmus	39618	Towards the end of
Sarcastic ...	39619	Towards which
Sarcenet ...	39620	**Town**
Sarchiato ...	39621	The nearest town is ——, distant —— miles
Sarchiella ..	39622	Is the chief town of
Sarciendus	39623	At the town of
Sarcinator	39624	The property is situated near the town of
Sarcinosus	39625	The property is situated within —— miles of the town of ——
Sarclage ...	39626	A small town on the —— railroad
Sarcloir ...	39627	**Township**
Sarcocela ...	39628	Township site
Sarcoderm	39629	**Trace(s)**
Sarcofago...	39630	To trace
Sarcologia	39631	Can you trace
Sarcotico ...	39632	Will endeavour to trace
Sarculatio...	39633	Have not yet been able to trace
Sardagata...	39634	Can trace
Sardelle ...	39635	Cannot trace
Sardesco ...	39636	Is there any trace of
Sardianus	39637	There is no trace of
Sardoine ...	39638	There is only a trace of
Sardonical	39639	A trace of
Sardonyx ...	39640	Only contain(s) trace(s) of gold
Sargado ...	39641	Should be glad if you would try and trace
Sargenta ...	39642	Will do my best to trace
Sargentear	39643	In case you can trace
Sarilla ...	39644	In case you cannot trace
Sarmentar	39645	Will destroy all trace of
Sarmentoso	39646	Better destroy all trace of
Sarnazo ...	39647	Have destroyed all trace of
Sarracina ...	39648	In order to trace
Sarran ...	39649	The trace of

Sarritor ...	39650	**Traced**
Sarroso ...	39651	Can be traced for a distance of
Sartalejo ...	39652	Cannot be traced at all on the surface
Sartenada...	39653	The vein can be traced for a distance of —— yards
Sartiame ...	39654	The vein cannot be traced outside the property
Sartorio ...	39655	Has (have) been traced
Sartrix ...	39656	Has (have) not been traced
Sasafras ...	39657	Have you yet traced
Sashframe	39658	Have traced
Sassajuolo	39659	Have not traced
Sassafrica...	39660	**Trachyte**
Sassettino	39661	The country is trachyte
Sassicello ...	39662	Now driving in trachyte
Sassoire ...	39663	Have driven through the trachyte
Sassolino ...	39664	Still in trachyte
Sastreria ...	39665	As soon as we have driven through the trachyte
Satageus ...	39666	Have you driven through the trachyte
Satagito ...	39667	**Trachytic**
Satanasso...	39668	A trachytic dyke
Sataneismo	39669	**Tracing(s)** *(See also "Plan," "Section.")*
Satanical ...	39670	Tracings of
Satanisch ...	39671	Please send tracings of foundation plans for machinery
Satellite ...	39672	Please mail tracings of mine plans at once
Satellizio ...	39673	Tracings of mine plans were mailed on
Saterion ...	39674	Will mail tracings as soon as I (we) can get them completed
Satiating ...	39675	Progress tracings
Satietas ...	39676	Duplicate tracings
Satinspar...	39677	Tracings have been sent to
Satinwood	39678	When may I (we) expect to receive tracings of
Satiraccia...	39679	When may I (we) expect to receive tracings of mine plans
Satirico ...	39680	Tracings of machinery
Satirilla ...	39681	Mail tracing of —— as soon as possible
Satirizar ...	39682	Tracing mailed on
Satirizing...	39683	Send immediately tracing of
Satisdatum	39684	Will send tracing of —— as soon as completed
Satisfacer...	39685	**Track(s)**
Satisfaire ...	39686	On the track of
Satisfatto ...	39687	Believed to be on the track of
Satolla ...	39688	If you are on the right track
Satollezza...	39689	The track taken was
Satrapia ...	39690	**Tract(s)**
Satrapone...	39691	Mining and agricultural rights over the entire tract of country
Sattelgurt	39692	The concession covers a tract of country of —— area
Satteln ...	39693	A large tract of forest
Sattelzeug	39694	A large tract of which is
Sattigung...	39695	Could secure a large tract of the territory if needed
Saturate ...	39696	**Trade**
Saturitas ...	39697	Trade generally is looking up
Saturnales	39698	Trade generally is dull
Saturnine...	39699	So long as trade remains dull
Satyre ...	39700	Report as to trade prospects
Satyriasis...	39701	Trade prospects
Satyricus ...	39702	**Traffic**
Satyrion ...	39703	**Trail(s)**
Saubern ...	39704	So long as the trail remains open
Saucebox ..	39705	Trails blocked
Saucepan ...	39706	When do you expect trails will be open
Saucers ...	39707	Expect trails may be open about
Sauciatio ...	39708	Trails during the present weather are dangerous
Saucisson...	39709	**Train(s)**

Saucius ...	39710	Goods train
Sauerstoff...	39711	Passenger train
Saufbruder	39712	Owing to an accident to the train
Saugamme	39713	Shall leave by train on
Saugerohre	39714	Trains have ceased running on account of
Saugethier	39715	Trains have ceased running on account of snow blockade
Saugrenu ...	39716	Trains will recommence running about
Sauhirt ...	39717	When do you expect trains will recommence running
Saulengang	39718	You must go by train to ——
Saumoneau	39719	Considerable delay to trains occasioned by
Saumpferd	39720	As soon as everything is in train for
Saumsattel	39721	Put everything in train for
Saunerie ...	39722	Everything is in train for
Saunterer...	39723	Is everything now in train for
Sauquillo...	39724	Accident to train
Saurites ...	39725	Serious accident to train; I have escaped unhurt
Saurodon ...	39726	Serious accident to train; —— has been hurt
Saurussel ...	39727	**Tram**
Sauseln ...	39728	A tram line
Sausewind	39729	Could easily construct a tram road between —— and ——
Saussail ...	39730	What would the cost of tram road amount to
Saustall ...	39731	The cost of tram road would amount to
Sautiller ...	39732	As soon as the tram road is completed
Sauvageon	39733	Should propose to connect —— and —— by a tram road
Sauvagine	39734	How long is the proposed tram road
Sauvetage	39735	Proposed tram road is —— yards long
Savagism ...	39736	There is an easy gradient for the tram between
Savamment	39737	**Tramroad** (*See also* "Tramway.")
Savaterie ...	39738	Tramroad will be necessary to connect —— and ——
Saviezza ...	39739	Tramroad completed
Savione ...	39740	**Tramway** (*See also* "Hill," "Line," "Railway," "Tram,"
Savonnage	39741	Wire rope tramway [" Wire.")
Savorare ...	39742	Cost of wire rope tramway would amount to
Savorevole	39743	Obtain estimate of equipment for wire rope tramway
Savourless	39744	Wire rope tramway would cost
Savoyard ...	39745	The tramway would be —— miles long
Sawdust ...	39746	By means of a tramway
Sawfish ...	39747	The ore is conveyed by means of a tramway from —— to ——
Sawfly ...	39748	The ore could be cheaply conveyed by a tramway
Sawtooth ...	39749	There is an easy gradient for a tramway
Saxatanus	39750	Tramway completed
Saxatil ...	39751	When will tramway be completed
Saxhorn ...	39752	Expect to complete tramway about
Saxificus ...	39753	Tramway working well
Saxifrage...	39754	Tramway is not working at all satisfactorily
Saxigenus...	39755	Tramway is in a fair state of repair
Saxulum ...	39756	Tramway altogether out of repair
Sayaleria ...	39757	Have commenced work on the tramway
Sayalesco ...	39758	Cost of grading for tramway
Sayonazo ...	39759	Cost of operating tramway
Sazgatillo	39760	Complete equipment of tramway to include
Saziabile ...	39761	Charge —— for each ton passed over the tramway
Sazievole ...	39762	**Transact**
Sazonador	39763	To transact
Sbadatello	39764	Will transact
Sbadato ...	39765	Will not transact
Sbagliare ...	39766	Unable to transact
Sbaldore ...	39767	Unable to transact any business
Sbaraglino	39768	When do you expect —— will be able to transact business
Sbarcatojo	39769	Hope(s) to transact business on or before

Sbarleffe ...	39770	Shall not be able to transact any business until
Sbarrarsi ...	39771	Expect to transact
Sbassanza	39772	In order to transact business
Sbattito ...	39773	Shall require a full Power of Attorney before I (we) can [transact business
Sbavamento	39774	Have mailed Power of Attorney so that you (——) can
Sbavatura...	39775	To enable you to transact [transact business
Sbendarsi...	39776	**Transacted**
Sberciare ...	39777	To be transacted
Sbernio ...	39778	Transacted by
Sbiancare...	39779	As soon as you have transacted
Sbietolare...	39780	Has (have) been transacted
Sbiettare ...	39781	Has (have) not been transacted
Sbilancio ...	39782	—— has not transacted
Sbirbato ...	39783	Cannot be transacted owing to
Sbirraglia...	39784	Has (have) been successfully transacted
Sboccatura	39785	**Transaction(s)**
Sboizonare	39786	No transactions whatever
Sbonzolato	39787	There has been a considerable number of transactions
Sborchiare	39788	There have been very few transactions
Sbozzimare	39789	Transaction(s) is (are) quite approved of
Sbraciata ...	39790	Better stop all further transactions
Sbraculato	39791	What transactions have you had with
Sbranatore	39792	Have not had any transactions with
Sbrancato...	39793	The only transaction was
Sbreggacia	39794	Have not learned of any transaction in
Sbrigativo	39795	Mixed up in several doubtful transactions
Sbruffare ...	39796	There are no transactions
Sbucciato ...	39797	Duplicate last transaction
Sbudellato	39798	Would it be a legitimate transaction
Scabbard ...	39799	It would be a legitimate transaction
Scabbiato ...	39800	It is a perfectly legitimate transaction
Scabello ...	39801	**Transfer(s)** (*See also* " Books," " Deed.")
Scabieuse...	39802	To transfer
Scabillum...	39803	Transfer to
Scabinus ...	39804	Share transfer
Scabitudo...	39805	Transfer deed(s)
Scabratus...	39806	You had better transfer
Scabrieux ...	39807	You had better not transfer
Scabritia ...	39808	Do you advise me (us) to transfer
Scabrosita	39809	Advise you strongly to transfer
Scabrous ...	39810	Get transfers executed
Scacazzare	39811	Has (have) transfer(s) been executed
Scaccarium	39812	Transfer(s) has (have) been duly executed
Scacchiere	39813	Send signed and witnessed transfer to
Scaffale ...	39814	Transfer(s) has (have) not yet been executed
Scaffold ...	39815	Transferee's name should be left blank on transfers
Scaggiale ...	39816	When will the transfer be completed
Scagionare	39817	Expect transfer will be completed within the next —— days.
Scaglietta...	39818	Endeavour to hasten completion of transfer
Scagliola ...	39819	Will do my best to hasten completion of transfer
Scagnardo	39820	What is the delay in the transfer due to
Scalable ...	39821	The delay in the transfer is owing to
Scalaccia ...	39822	—— has signed the transfer for his shares
Scalamati ...	39823	Cannot make any remittance until transfer is completed
Scalaris ...	39824	Hope to complete transfer on
Scalatore ...	39825	As soon as transfer is completed
Scalcheria	39826	Would delay completion of transfer
Scalcinato	39827	Is transfer completed
Scaldamane	39828	When do you think transfer will be completed

Scaldatojo	39829	Before transfer can be completed
Scaldhead	39830	Refuse(s) to complete transfer until
Scalding ...	39831	Refuse(s) to transfer except
Scalfitto ...	39832	The transfer of the property
Scallion ...	39833	The transfer of the property has been formally completed. All [the property is now registered in the name of
Scallopped	39834	Pending receipt of formal transfer
Scalogno ...	39835	The transfer must bear a stamp of
Scalpedra ...	39836	The transfer must be properly stamped
Scalpellum	39837	The transfer was never legally completed
Scalpiccio ..	39838	As soon as the transfer is legally completed
Scalpitare...	39839	Refuse(s) to transfer the balance
Scalplocks	39840	Consent(s) to transfer the balance
Scalprum ...	39841	Undertake(s) all charges of transfer
Scalpturio	39842	**Transfer Books**
Scalterito ...	39843	Transfer books will be closed from —— to —— inclusive
Scaltrezza	39844	Transfer books now closed
Scalzatojo...	39845	Transfer books will remain open until
Scalzatura	39846	Transfer books will re-open on
Scambiare	39847	As soon as transfer books are closed
Scamerare	39848	**Transferable**
Scamiciato	39849	Transferable by deed
Scammonia	39850	**Transferee(s)** (*See also* " Transfer.")
Scamnellum	39851	The transferee's name is
Scamojato	39852	Cable transferee's name in full
Scamoneato	39853	**Transferor(s)**
Scampanata	39854	The transferor's name is
Scampanio	39855	Cable transferor's name in full
Scampering	39856	**Transferred**
Scanalare ...	39857	Has (have) been transferred
Scancello ...	39858	Has (have) not been transferred
Scandaglio	39859	Will be transferred to
Scandaloso	39860	Has (have) been transferred to —— meanwhile
Scandendus	39861	Could be transferred to —— if you wish
Scandiana	39862	Has been duly transferred
Scandulaca	39863	Must be transferred before
Scanfardo...	39864	Endeavour to get transferred to
Scanicare	39865	Have the shares transferred to
Scannato ...	39866	Have the property transferred to
Scansatore	39867	Should wish the shares to be transferred to
Scansion ...	39868	Should wish the property to be transferred to
Scansorius	39869	Balance to be transferred to
Scantling ...	39870	Has (have) transferred the whole to
Scantonare	39871	Balance was transferred on ——
Scapegrace	39872	**Transferring**
Scaphandre	39873	Whilst transferring
Scaphium...	39874	As soon as I (we) have finished transferring
Scaphula ...	39875	When will you (——) have finished transferring (the)
Scapitato ...	39876	Shall finish transferring it (the ——) about —— next
Scaponire...	39877	**Tranship**
Scappante	39878	Require to tranship
Scappatina	39879	Do not require to tranship
Scappinato	39880	As I (we) had to tranship the goods at
Scapponeo	39881	**Transhipment**
Scappuccio	39882	Have made all the necessary arrangements for transhipment
Scapulare ...	39883	The transhipment of the goods (machinery) at ——, saves [transhipment at ——
Scarabee ...	39884	**Transhipped**
Scaraffare...	39885	To be transhipped at
Scaramazzo	39886	Need not be transhipped if
Scaramouch	39887	Was (were) damaged whilst being transhipped

Scarcerato	39888	Everything transhipped without loss or damage
Scarecrow	39889	**Transit**
Scarferone	39890	Still in transit
Scarfskin ...	39891	For transit to
Scaricato ...	39892	Owing to an accident to the transit instrument
Scarifier ...	39893	Lost in transit
Scarifying	39894	In the transit
Scarlatina...	39895	Now in transit between —— and ——
Scarlatto ...	39896	Should be safely packed for transit
Scarnarsi ...	39897	Now in course of transit
Scarnatino	39898	**Transition**
Scarnire ...	39899	**Transitional**
Scarole ...	39900	**Translate(d)**
Scarriere ...	39901	**Translation**
Scarrosus ...	39902	Certified translation
Scarsapepe	39903	Translation of
Scarsezza ...	39904	**Transmission**
Scasimodeo	39905	During transmission
Scassato ...	39906	Wire rope transmission
Scatarrare	39907	Hydraulic transmission
Scatebro ...	39908	Electrical transmission
Scatellato ...	39909	Power transmission
Scatenarsi...	39910	**Transmit**
Scatoletta ...	39911	To transmit
Scatoliere ...	39912	Please transmit to
Scatolona ...	39913	Please transmit the following to
Scattatojo...	39914	Shall I (we) transmit (to)
Scattered ...	39915	Do not transmit to
Scaturire ...	39916	**Transmitted**
Scavalcare	39917	To be transmitted to
Scavenger...	39918	Has been transmitted to
Scavezzato	39919	Was not transmitted to
Scegliere ...	39920	Why was it not transmitted
Scelerat ...	39921	Could not be transmitted on account of
Sceleritas ...	39922	**Transmitting**
Scellement	39923	Capable of transmitting
Scelleroso...	39924	Not capable of transmitting even
Scelleur ...	39925	Capable of transmitting on an emergency
Sceloturbe	39926	**Transpire(s)**
Sceltezza ...	39927	Cable should anything transpire relating to
Scematore...	39928	Must not be permitted to transpire
Scempiare...	39929	Will not be permitted to transpire
Scenaccia ...	39930	Do not permit this to transpire
Scenatilis ...	39931	Provided that nothing further transpires
Sceneries ...	39932	**Transpired**
Scenopegia	39933	Has anything further transpired
Scented ...	39934	Nothing further has transpired
Scentless ...	39935	Nothing has transpired as yet
Scepinus ...	39936	Can have transpired only through
Scepticism	39937	Cannot have transpired through
Sceptique ...	39938	It cannot have transpired through him
Sceptred ...	39939	Nothing practically has transpired respecting
Sceptriger...	39940	All that transpired was
Sceptuchus	39941	Has unfortunately transpired
Scerparsi ...	39942	Cable if anything important has transpired
Scettismo ...	39943	**Transport**
Scettrato ...	39944	To transport
Sceverare ...	39945	Can transport
Schabracke	39946	Cannot transport
Schabsel ...	39947	What about transport

Schachbret	39948	As regards transport
Schachern	39949	Arrange to transport
Schachmatt	39950	What are the available means of transport
Schachtel ...	39951	The only means of transport at present are
Schaden ...	39952	Transport is very difficult during
Schadhaft...	39953	Transport is practically stopped from —— to ——
Schaferin ...	39954	The only means of transport consist of
Schaffner ...	39955	Is there any difficulty as regards transport
Schafschur	39956	There is much difficulty as regards transport
Schafzucht	39957	There is no difficulty as regards transport
Schakern ...	39958	Will enable me (us) to transport
Schalkheit	39959	Has (have) arranged for transport of
Schalmeie...	39960	Cannot arrange for transport of
Schalotte ...	39961	Has —— (have you) arranged for the transport of
Schalttag ...	39962	Provided that I (we) can secure means of transport
Schaluppe	39963	Require full particulars as to transport of quartz (ore)
Schamlos ...	39964	The facilities for transport are good
Schamroth	39965	The facilities for transport are very indifferent
Schandbube	39966	**Transported**
Schandlich	39967	Can be transported by —
Schandthat	39968	Cannot be transported by
Schanzkorb	39969	**Transporting**
Scharfsinn	39970	**Transverse(ly)**
Schariner ...	39971	Transverse section (of)
Scharren ...	39972	**Trap**
Scharteke...	39973	Trap rock
Scharwache	39974	A dyke of trap rock
Schasteria...	39975	The country is trap rock
Schattiren	39976	Now driving in trap rock
Schatzchen	39977	Have driven through the trap rock
Schatzung	39978	Have you driven through the trap rock
Schauder ...	39979	Still in trap rock
Schauerig...	39980	As soon as I (we) have driven through the trap rock
Schaufeln...	39981	Have encountered a dyke of trap rock
Schauplatz	39982	**Traveller**
Schauspiel	39983	Overhead traveller to lift —— tons
Scheckig ...	39984	**Travelling** (*See also* " Expense," " Fee.")
Schediasma	39985	Travelling crane
Schedium...	39986	**Traverse(d)**
Scheduled...	39987	Has (have) completely traversed all ——'s statements
Scheggiale	39988	**Treasury**
Scheggioso	39989	What funds have you in the treasury
Scheibchen	39990	The only available funds in the treasury are
Scheiden ...	39991	There is nothing in the treasury
Scheideweg	39992	Funds in treasury amount to
Scheintod	39993	As soon as I (we) have sufficient funds in the treasury
Scheiteln ...	39994	**Treat**
Scheletro ...	39995	To treat
Schellen ...	39996	Can treat only
Schelmisch	39997	Will treat only
Schelsucht	39998	To treat for
Schematise	39999	To treat with
Schematum	40000	Are you prepared to treat for
Scheming ...	**40001**	Not prepared to treat
Scherana ...	40002	On what basis will you treat
Scherflein...	40003	Will treat only on a basis of
Schericato	40004	Consent(s) to treat on the following basis
Schermagli	40005	Refuse(s) to treat except on a basis of
Schermita...	40006	Unable to treat at the present time
ʼrmugio	40007	The only way to treat it (this) would be to

Schernia ...	40008	Are you inclined to treat for
Scheruola...	40009	If you are inclined to treat
Scherzante	40010	Not inclined to treat
Scherzen ...	40011	So as to treat with
Scheuleder	40012	So as to treat the ore
Schiadeus	40013	At present we are unable to treat such ore
Schiaffo ...	40014	Unable to treat with
Schiancio ...	40015	Shall be pleased to treat with
Schiantato	40016	To treat the ore
Schiappare	40017	Unable at present to treat the ore
Schiattona	40018	What quantity can you treat per twenty-four hours
Schiavesco	40019	Can treat —— tons per twenty-four hours
Schiavina ...	40020	**Treated**
Schicklich...	40021	I (we) have now —— tons ready to be treated
Schickung	40022	What quantity have you ready to be treated
Schieber ...	40023	By this means the ore can be treated
Schieferig...	40024	How is the ore treated
Schieland ...	40025	The ore is treated as follows
Schienale ...	40026	The ore has hitherto been treated as follows
Schiencire...	40027	The ore is treated only for the
Schiessen ...	40028	Can you arrange to get —— tons of ore treated
Schifanza ...	40029	Cannot arrange to get any ore treated [of
Schifatore ..	40030	Have arranged to get a —— ton sample of ore treated at a cost
Schifilta ...	40031	Since —— we have treated —— tons of ore yielding —— [pounds of silver-lead containing —— ounces of silver
Schildlans	40032	**Treating**
Schildpatt	40033	Now engaged treating
Schilfrohr...	40034	Method of treating the ore
Schimbecio	40035	Capable of treating —— tons of ore per —— hours
Schimmelig	40036	**Treatment** [to correct
Schimmern	40037	Not satisfied with the treatment; I am (we are) endeavouring
Schimpfen	40038	Do you consider a different treatment would have been more
Schinanzia	40039	Would you suggest any other treatment [successful
Schindel ...	40040	I (we) consider the following treatment would have been more [successful
Schiniera ...	40041	What method have you adopted for the treatment of the ore
Schiomato	40042	The ore treatment to be adopted is
Schippito ...	40043	By this treatment
Schirmen ...	40044	What is the method of ore treatment
Schirmherr	40045	The method adopted for the treatment of the ore is
Schismatic	40046	By the method hitherto adopted for the treatment of the ore
Schiston ...	40047	By this method of ore treatment
Schiudersi	40048	The present treatment of the ore is very unsatisfactory
Schiumante	40049	The present treatment of the ore is very satisfactory
Schiumoso	40050	A new method of ore treatment
Schivare ...	40051	Is a much better method for the treatment of the ore
Schizopod...	40052	What is the proposed method of treatment
Schlache ...	40053	The present method of treatment ...
Schlafchen	40054	Has (have) not decided on method of treatment ...
Schlafer ...	40055	Cost of treatment is —— per ton
Schlafrock	40056	What has the treatment cost
Schlafzeit...	40057	A better mode of treatment must be adopted
Schlagader	40058	Estimated cost of treatment per ton
Schlagbaum	40059	Estimated cost of transportation and treatment per ton
Schlague ...	40060	**Treaty**
Schlagwort	40061	Now in treaty with
Schlammen	40062	In treaty for ——
Schlampig	40063	Treaty negotiations
Schlangeln	40064	Cable progress of treaty negotiations
Schlauch ...	40065	**Tree(s)** (*See also* "Timber.")

Schlecker ...	40066	**Trespass**
Schleichen	40067	To trespass
Schleife ...	40068	You must prevent any trespass upon
Schlendem	40069	Is (are) likely to trespass upon our property
Schleppend	40070	Is alleged to be a case of legal trespass
Schleunig...	40071	Not a trespass
Schlinge ...	40072	So as to prevent any trespass
Schlitten ...	40073	Clearly a case of trespass
Schlosse ...	40074	**Trespassed**
Schluch ...	40075	Has (have) trespassed
Schlummer	40076	Has (have) not trespassed
Schlupfen...	40077	**Trespasser(s)**
Schlussel ...	40078	Alleged to be trespassers
Schmachten	40079	**Trespassing**
Schmahlich	40080	If he (they) succeed(s) in proving that I (we) have been [trespassing
Schmalte ...	40081	Has (have) been trespassing
Schmauchen	40082	Has (have) not been trespassing
Schmaus ...	40083	Has (have) —— been trespassing
Schmecken	40084	**Trestle(s)**
Schmelz ...	40085	Carried on trestles
Schmelzbar	40086	Of which —— feet is on trestles —— feet high
Schmettern	40087	**Trial** (*See also* "Fixed," "Move," "Verdict.")
Schmiede ...	40088	The trial is fixed to take place on —— (at ——)
Schmiegsam	40089	When is the trial fixed for
Schmitz ...	40090	Trial has been postponed (to ——)
Schmollen...	40091	Cable as soon as the result of the trial is known
Schmucken	40092	Will cable as soon as the result of the trial is known
Schmuggeln	40093	The trial will probably take —— days
Schnakisch	40094	The trial is not yet concluded
Schnallen ...	40095	The trial was concluded to-day. Verdict to be given on
Schnappsen	40096	Result of trial
Schnecke ...	40097	Result of trial in favour of
Schneeball	40098	Result of trial in our favour
Schneeweke	40099	Result of trial against us
Schneideln	40100	Is now on trial
Schneider ...	40101	Give it a fair trial
Schnellzug	40102	To give it a fair trial
Schnitzeln	40103	Will give it a fair trial
Schnode ...	40104	Has it had a fair trial
Schnuppfer	40105	I (we) do not think it has had a fair trial
Schnurband	40106	Had the fairest possible trial
Schnurrig...	40107	Trial on the whole satisfactory
Scholarcha	40108	Trial most satisfactory
Scholarly ...	40109	A preliminary trial of
Scholastic...	40110	Trial has shown (that)
Scholiast ...	40111	Until the trial has been made
Scholical ...	40112	The case is in the list for trial
Scholium ...	40113	The trial is not likely to take place before
Schonung...	40114	It is doubtful when the trial will take place
Schoolboy...	40115	Trial may take place any day
Schoolgirl...	40116	The cost of the trial will amount to
Schooling ..	40117	What will the cost of the trial amount to
Schoolman	40118	Estimated cost of trial will not exceed
Schoolroom	40119	A thorough trial of the machinery
Schoppen ...	40120	Defer trial of
Schossreis...	40121	Trial to be under supervision of
Schottern ...	40122	When shall you make the trial
Schranke ...	40123	Trial will be commenced on
Schreck ...	40124	The outcome of the trial is
Schreibart	40125	Engine trial

Schriftzug	40126	Shall make further trial(s) for the purpose of deciding
Schroten ...	40127	Cannot make trial owing to a breakdown of machinery
Schrotkorn	40128	**Triangle**
Schrotmehl	40129	**Triangular**
Schubsack	40130	**Trias**
Schuchtern	40131	**Triassic**
Schuhmass	40132	**Tribute**
Schulbuch	40133	On tribute
Schuldner...	40134	Can be let on tribute
Schuldpost	40135	On a tribute of —— per cent.
Schulfuchs	40136	What is the tribute
Schulgeld ...	40137	How many miners have you working on tribute
Schulhaus	40138	Have —— miners working on tribute
Schulknabe	40139	Have no miners working on tribute [tribute
Schulpferd	40140	Are you willing to let the ground between —— and —— on
Schulstube	40141	What is your idea of a fair tribute
Schultern ...	40142	Am (are) willing to let the miners work on a tribute of [tribute
Schulubung	40143	It would be judicious to have at least —— miners working on
Schuppig ...	40144	It would be injudicious to let the miners work on tribute
Schurfen ...	40145	A reduced tribute
Schurigeln	40146	Increased tribute
Schurkerei	40147	Offer to work on tribute
Schurzfell...	40148	Decline to work on tribute
Schutteln ...	40149	Have leased workings on a tribute of
Schutzrede	40150	**Tributers**
Schutzzoll	40151	The tributers
Schwachung	40152	Some of the tributers
Schwadrone	40153	Have shipped on account of the tributers.
Schwammig	40154	Tributers' ore has realized
Schwangel	40155	What is the net value of the ore shipped by the tributers
Schwarn ...	40156	The total value of the tributers' shipment(s) to you is
Schweben ...	40157	Give notice to tributers to terminate contract
Schweifen...	40158	Shall I (we) give notice to tributers to terminate contract
Schweissig	40159	Do not give notice to tributers to terminate contract
Schwelger	40160	Tributers' contract terminates on ——; shall I (we) renew
Schwerlich	40161	Tributers' contract terminates on ——; advise you to renew
Schwielig ...	40162	Do you advise me (us) to renew tributers' contract
Schwindel	40163	Do not advise you to renew tributers' contract except
Schwitzbad	40164	Tributers have given notice to terminate contract
Schwulstig	40165	Tributers cannot work owing to
Schwur ...	40166	We have now —— tributers at work [ing to company ——
Schytanum	40167	—— tons of tributers' ore shipped and sold for ——, produc-
Sciabordo ..	40168	Tributers have shipped —— tons for week ending
Sciacquare	40169	The tributers' ore produces —— to the company
Sciagura ...	40170	**Tried**
Scialbare ...	40171	Will be tried
Scialiva ...	40172	Will not be tried
Scialuppa...	40173	Cannot be tried until
Sciamachia	40174	The moment it can be tried
Sciamito ...	40175	As soon as it has been tried
Scianranza	40176	Have you tried
Sciapidire...	40177	Has (have) tried
Sciarrata ...	40178	Has (have) not tried
Sciatheras	40179	Will report to you as soon as I (we) have tried
Sciatical ...	40180	Please report on ——> as soon as you have tried
Sciaticus ...	40181	I (we) have tried hard
Sciattezza...	40182	Have tried my hardest to
Scibile ...	40183	Am (are) about to have it tried
Scibitur ...	40184	As soon as it has been tried I (we) will let you know the result
Scibones ...	40185	When it was tried before, it failed

Sciebat ...	40186	Has not to my knowledge been tried before
Sciemment	40187	Has it (this) been tried before
Scientibus	40188	Was tried before (at)
Scientific ...	40189	**Trifling** (*See also* " Sustain.")
Scientiola...	40190	The injury (damage) is trifling
Scientists ...	40191	Altogether trifling
Scienziato...	40192	Not so trifling as was believed
Scierie ...	40193	**Triplicate**
Scificare ...	40194	In triplicate
Scilicet ...	40195	To be sent in triplicate
Scilinga ...	40196	**Tropic(s)(al)**
Scillinus ...	40197	In the tropics
Scillitico ...	40198	In a tropical climate
Sciloppato	40199	During present tropical weather
Scimiotto ...	40200	**Trouble** (*See also* " Hereafter.")
Scimmione	40201	Do not wish to cause you unnecessary trouble
Scimpodion	40202	Will it cause you any extra trouble
Scineoidal	40203	Will not cause any trouble at all
Scindula ...	40204	The trouble will be
Scintiller ...	40205	Trouble will certainly arise
Sciocchino	40206	Is likely to cause considerable trouble
Scioccone ...	40207	The trouble has hitherto been that
Sciogliere ...	40208	This will prevent further trouble
Sciolezza ...	40209	Will this prevent further trouble
Sciolism ...	40210	So as to prevent further trouble
Sciomancy	40211	Is there any trouble as regards
Sciomantia	40212	There is no trouble as regards it (this)
Scionata ...	40213	There is considerable trouble as regards it (this)
Scioperare	40214	We have hitherto had considerable trouble with it **(this)**
Sciopino ...	40215	What is the precise trouble
Sciopodes ...	40216	The trouble is that
Sciorinato	40217	The trouble would cease if
Scioterio ...	40218	We have had constant trouble with
Scipidezza	40219	Do not hesitate to trouble
Scirignata	40220	**Troublesome**
Sciringare	40221	Very troublesome
Sciroppo ...	40222	Has (have) been more or less troublesome since
Scirpetum	40223	Will no longer be troublesome
Scirpices ...	40224	To prevent him (——) being troublesome
Scirpicula ..	40225	**Trough(s)**
Scirrhoma	40226	—— feet of troughs
Scirrosity...	40227	In a series of troughs
Sciscendo ...	40228	By means of troughs
Sciscitans...	40229	**True** (*See also* " Find.")
Scissile ...	40230	It is not true
Scissionis ...	40231	It is quite true
Scissors ...	40232	Should this be true
Scitator ...	40233	Should it (this) not be true
Scittalo ..	40234	The report is perfectly true
Sciugatojo	40235	The report is anything but true
Scivistit ...	40236	Is it true that
Scivolare ...	40237	Not altogether true
Scivoletto...	40238	Should this be true you had better
Sclamato ...	40239	Sufficiently true for
Sclavonic ...	40240	It is only true to the extent of
Scleroderm	40241	Find out and report whether it is true that
Sclerosis ...	40242	Will report whether true or not
Sclerotic ...	40243	See if this is true
˜clodia ...	40244	**Truly**
˜oppetum	40245	**Trust**

Scodellino...	40246	To trust
Scoffing ...	40247	May certainly trust
Scoglietto ...	40248	Do not trust to
Scogliuzzo	40249	Do you still trust —— (him)
Scojattolo...	40250	Do not on any account trust
Scolaretto...	40251	Can you trust —— (him) to
Scolder ...	40252	Can trust —— (him) to
Scoldingly	40253	Cannot trust —— (him) to
Scolecia ...	40254	If you can trust
Scolinio ...	40255	If you cannot trust
Scoliste ...	40256	You had better not trust to
Scollinare ...	40257	Shall not trust entirely to
Scollops ...	40258	Entirely on trust
Scolopax ...	40259	Provided that you can thoroughly trust
Scolorarsi...	40260	Should advise you not to trust
Scolorito ...	40261	I (we) should not trust —— (him)
Scolpire ...	40262	Believe you can trust
Scolymos ...	40263	A deed of trust
Scombavare	40264	It will be necessary that you (——) execute(s) a deed of trust
Scombrus ...	40265	Deed of trust executed
Scommiato	40266	—— must execute a deed of trust
Scomodato	40267	—— has (have) executed a deed of trust
Scomparire	40268	—— refuse(s) to execute a deed of trust
Scomunica	40269	Consent(s) to execute a deed of trust
Sconciarsi...	40270	Is undoubtedly a breach of trust
Sconcordia	40271	**Trusted**
Sconferma	40272	To be trusted
Sconfitta ...	40273	How far can he (they) (——) be trusted
Sconguiro...	40274	Cannot be trusted
Sconquasso	40275	Can be trusted implicitly
Sconsolare	40276	Has (have) been trusted
Scontrare ...	40277	Has (have) not been trusted
Sconvenuto	40278	If you feel sure that —— can be trusted
Sconvolto ...	40279	Do not feel altogether sure that —— can be trusted
Scoopingly	40280	Has (have) trusted to —— to (for)
Scoopnet ...	40281	If he (——) can be trusted
Scooparius ...	40282	Do you know whether —— can be trusted to (with)
Scopatore ...	40283	Personally I do not believe —— can be trusted
Scopertura	40284	In case he (——) cannot be trusted, whom would you suggest
Scopetino ...	40285	Might, I (we) think, be trusted
Scopettato	40286	If —— (he) can be trusted it will not be necessary to
Scopiped ...	40287	If —— (he) cannot be trusted it will be necessary to
Scoppiante	40288	Is —— (are they) to be trusted
Scoprire ...	40289	I (we) have every confidence that —— (they) can be trusted
Scopuloso...	40290	May be trusted to any amount
Scoraggito	40291	**Trustee(s)**
Scoramento	40292	To be placed in the names of trustees
Scorbiare ...	40293	Give full names of the proposed trustees
Scorbutic ...	40294	The following is (are) the full name(s) of the proposed
Scorcher ...	40295	The trustees for [trustee(s)
Scorching...	40296	The trustees for debenture holders
Scordalus ...	40297	Trustees for debenture holders have applied to the court for
Scordarsi ...	40298	Now in the hands of trustees
Scordevole	40299	Our trustees are
Scoreggia ..	40300	Would you care to act as trustee
Scorgitore	40301	Refuse(s) to act as trustee(s)
Scornful ...	40302	Consent(s) to act as trustee(s)
Scorodite ...	40303	Would —— be willing to act as trustee(s)
Scoronare ...	40304	Quite willing to act as trustee(s)
Scorpion ...	40305	Not willing to act as trustee(s)

Scorpiuron	40306	Trustees should be appointed at once
Scorporato	40307	Have trustees been appointed
Scorrenza ...	40308	Trustees have not been appointed
Scorridore	40309	Trustees will be appointed on
Scorritojo...	40310	By order of the trustee(s)
Scorsojo ...	40311	**Trustworthy**
Scorsonere	40312	**Truth**
Scortesia ...	40313	I (we) wish to know the truth
Scorteum ...	40314	What is the truth
Scorticare...	40315	The absolute truth is
Scossetta ...	40316	It is undoubtedly the truth that
Scostare ...	40317	Nothing but the truth
Scotfree ...	40318	Discover and cable what is the truth
Scotimento	40319	Cannot discover what the real truth is
Scotiterra...	40320	I (we) do not think there is any truth in it
Scotitojo ...	40321	Is there likely to be any truth in it
Scotitrice ...	40322	The only truth in the matter is
Scotolato ...	40323	There is no truth whatever in it
Scotoscope	40824	Can be relied upon to tell the truth
Scottante ...	40325	Cannot be relied upon to tell the truth
Scottatura	40326	We must have some one who will tell us the truth
Scotticism	40327	What truth is there in the report that
Scourging...	40328	Entirely devoid of truth
Scoverta ...	40329	As soon as I (we) learn the truth
Scovritura	40330	**Try**
Scowlers ...	40331	To try
Scowling ...	40332	To try to
Scozzonato	40333	Advise you to try
Scragged ...	40334	Will certainly try (to)
Scraggily ...	40335	It is very necessary that you should try to
Scramare ...	40336	There is no need now to try to
Scrambled	40337	Try if you can do without it (this)
Scrambling	40338	Will try to do without it
Scrapbook	40339	Try if anything can be done respecting
Scraping ...	40340	Shall I (we) try to
Scraptia ...	40341	Do you wish me (us) to try to
Scratcher ...	40342	You can certainly try to
Scrawler ...	40343	I (we) will try
Screabilis ...	40344	I (we) should be very glad if you would try to
Screamer ...	40345	Try your best to
Screditato	40346	Try your best to carry it (this) through
Screeching	40347	Will try my best to carry it (this) through
Screechowl	40348	Try again whether
Screening ..	40349	Try again and if necessary a third time
Scremenzia	40350	Am (are) prepared to try as you suggest
Screpolo ...	40351	Try whether you can keep it open until
Screwcaps...	40352	Will try to keep it open until
Screwplate	40353	I am (we are) afraid to try for fear of
Screziato ...	40354	**Trying**
Scribblers...	40355	Trying to
Scribbling	40356	After trying
Scribendus	40357	Do you think —— is really trying
Scriblita ...	40358	Is no doubt trying hard
Scriccio ...	40359	I (we) do not think —— is really trying
Scrigna ...	40360	Am (are) trying to do so
Scrignetto	40361	Since then I (we) have been trying
Scrimmage	40362	Has (have) —— been trying to
Scrimping	40363	Has (have) not been trying
Scrinium ...	40364	Has (have) been trying to
ptilis ...	40365	Will report after trying

Scriptrum	40366	Please report after trying
Scriptural...	40367	You need have no fear in trying
Scrittojo ...	40368	Am (are) now engaged trying to
Scrittoria ...	40369	Is (are) very trying
Scrivener ...	40370	Owing to the trying nature of
Scrizato ...	40371	Under very trying circumstances
Scroccare ...	40372	**Tub(s)** (*See also* "Waggons.")
Scrofaccia...	40373	Tubs for transportation of
Scrofula ...	40374	**Tubbing**
Scrofuleux	40375	Steel tubbing
Scroll ...	40376	Cast iron tubbing for shaft —— feet internal diameter
Scrollwork	40377	The shaft will require tubbing for a depth of —— feet
Scropuloso	40378	Tubbing successfully completed
Scroscio ...	40379	Placing of tubbing is causing great difficulty
Scrostato ...	40380	As soon as the tubbing is completed
Scrubber ...	40381	When do you expect to complete tubbing
Scrubbing	40382	Hope to finish tubbing within the next —— days
Scrupedus	40383	Owing to the tubbing having become displaced
Scrupling...	40384	**Tube(s)**
Scrupule ...	40385	**Tubular** (*See also* "Boiler.")
Scrutabile...	40386	**Tuesday**
Scrutarius	40387	Next Tuesday
Scrutator ...	40388	Last Tuesday
Scrutatrix	40389	On Tuesday
Scrutillus...	40390	On Tuesday morning
Scrutineer	40391	On Tuesday afternoon
Scrutinium	40392	On Tuesday night
Scrutiny ...	40393	Every Tuesday
Scrutoire ...	40394	Every alternate Tuesday
Scudajo ...	40395	About Tuesday week
Scudellaja	40396	Next Tuesday week
Scuderesco	40397	During Tuesday
Scuderia ...	40398	During Tuesday night
Scudiscio ...	40399	—— Tuesday in every month
Scuffiara ...	40400	**Tufa**
Scuffinare...	40401	**Tunnel(s)** (*See also* "Back," "Drive.")
Sculettare...	40402	To tunnel
Scullcap ...	40403	Deep tunnel
Scullery ...	40404	Main tunnel
Sculmato ...	40405	Tunnel site
Sculpens ...	40406	Tunnel number
Sculptile ...	40407	Old tunnel
Sculptor ...	40408	At what depth will the tunnel strike the vein
Sculptured	40409	The tunnel will give us —— feet of "backs"
Scumaruola	40410	How long will the tunnel require to be
Scuoletta ...	40411	The estimated length of the tunnel is —— feet
Scuotersi ...	40412	We have driven in the tunnel from the mouth —— feet
Scuotitore	40413	The tunnel has already been driven a length of —— feet
Scuppers ...	40414	Is the tunnel being driven by machine drills
Scuramente	40415	The tunnel is being driven by hand labour
Scurezza ...	40416	The tunnel is being driven by machine drills
Scurfiness...	40417	Buildings at the mouth of the tunnel
Scuricella...	40418	From the mouth of the tunnel to the dressing floors
Scurrile ...	40419	Closely adjacent to the mouth of the tunnel
Scurrility ...	40420	The dimensions of the tunnel are
Scusabile ...	40421	What are the dimensions of the tunnel
Scusatore ...	40422	How far is the tunnel in
Scusevole ...	40423	The tunnel is now in
Scutiscum	40424	At the forebreast of the tunnel
Scutulatus	40425	At right angles to the tunnel

Scybalum ...	40426	East and west of the tunnel
Scyllarian...	40427	North and south of the tunnel
Scylletum ...	40428	Between the tunnel intersection and
Scyricum ...	40429	From the intersection of this vein by the tunnel
Scythe ...	40430	Several tunnels have been driven into the hill
Scythicus ...	40431	—— tunnels have been driven
Sdebitarsi ..	40432	In the tunnel
Sdegnosita	40433	From the tunnel
Sdegnuzzo	40434	Of the tunnel
Sdiguinare	40435	The tunnel has caved in for a considerable length
Sdimentico	40436	The vein can be worked to a depth of —— feet by means of a [tunnel —— feet long
Sdipignere	40437	The vein has been developed only by a tunnel; present length
Sdoganare	40438	Tunnel rights [—— feet
Sdolcinato	40439	Tunnel rights included
Sdradajato	40440	What do tunnel rights in the district include
Sdrajone ...	40441	The tunnel is driven on the vein —— feet
Sdrucitura	40442	The tunnel was driven
Seaadder ...	40443	Has (have) been taken from the tunnel
Seabeaten...	40444	A tunnel has been driven
Seabird ...	40445	Stop work at tunnel
Seaboard ...	40446	Work at tunnel has been stopped
Seaboys ...	40447	Have had to stop work at tunnel owing to
Seabreeze ...	40448	There is considerable water at the tunnel forebreast
Seabuilt ...	40449	The tunnel is now draining water from
Seacoast ...	40450	There is every indication in the tunnel forebreast that we are
Seadog ...	40451	Have crossed vein in tunnel [approaching the vein
Seaegg ...	40452	Have you cut the vein in the tunnel
Seafarer ...	40453	Have cut the vein in the tunnel
Seafennel ...	40454	Have not cut the vein in the tunnel
Seafowl ...	40455	Have driven through the vein in the tunnel; it is —— feet wide
Seagirt ...	40456	Continue to drive tunnel
Seagull ...	40457	Recommence driving tunnel
Seahole ...	40458	Recommenced driving tunnel on
Seaholly ...	40459	Shall recommence driving tunnel on
Sealegs ...	40460	Mail a sketch of the tunnel showing its position with respect to
Sealion ...	40461	Have accurate survey made of the tunnel, and mail tracing
Seamaid ...	40462	Surveyor now engaged at the tunnel
Seamonster	40463	When will tunnel survey be completed
Seamstress	40464	Tunnel survey will be completed about
Seanettle ...	40465	Have mailed tracing of tunnel survey
Seanymph	40466	North drift from the tunnel
Seaooze ...	40467	South drift from the tunnel
Seaplant ...	40468	East drift from the tunnel
Searchable	40469	West drift from the tunnel
Searching...	40470	Crosscut from the tunnel
Searcloth ...	40471	Machinery at the tunnel mouth
Searobber...	40472	What is the present speed of driving in the tunnel [hours
Searoom ...	40473	We are now driving in the tunnel —— feet per twenty-four
Seasalt ...	40474	Can you not increase the speed at the tunnel
Seaserpent	40475	Cannot increase the speed at the tunnel
Seaside ...	40476	Have three shifts of men now working at the tunnel
Seasonably	40477	We are pushing the tunnel as much as we can
Seasoner ...	40478	The ground in the tunnel has become very hard
Seatern ...	40479	The forebreast of the tunnel is very hard
Seaurchin...	40480	The rock in the tunnel is sometimes hard
Seawalls ...	40481	The rock in the tunnel has become softer
Seawater ...	40482	The rock in the tunnel is so soft as to require timbering
Seaworthy	40483	Have you fixed upon a site for the tunnel
ʼum ...	40484	Would suggest that the (a) tunnel be commenced at

Sebacic ...	40485	Will send plan showing proposed position of tunnel
Sebesten ...	40486	Keep separate statement of tunnel cost
Sebile ...	40487	Will keep separate statement of tunnel cost
Secabilis ...	40488	Will contract to drive tunnel at —— per
Secadal ...	40489	Have let contract to drive tunnel at —— per
Secadillo ...	40490	The tunnel is now costing —— per
Secalicus ...	40491	At the mouth of the tunnel
Secamente	40492	Feet in from the tunnel's entrance
Secandus ...	40493	From the mouth of tunnel for a distance in of —— feet
Secanza ...	40494	**Tunnelled**
Seccatojo ...	40495	Will require to be tunnelled
Seccatrice ...	40496	Will require to be tunnelled for a length of —— feet
Seccedere ...	40497	Has (have) already tunnelled —— feet
Secchezza...	40498	**Tunnelling**
Secchione ...	40499	Now engaged tunnelling
Seccomoro	40500	When do you expect to complete tunnelling
Seceded ...	40501	As soon as I (we) have completed the necessary tunnelling
Secernens ...	40502	**Turbine(s)** (*See also* " Water-wheel.")
Secespita ...	40503	High-pressure turbine
Sechage ...	40504	Low-pressure turbine
Sechemente	40505	Duplicate wheel for turbine
Secheresse	40506	The turbine will be fixed at
Sechoir ...	40507	What will be the available horse-power developed by the turbine
Sechsfach ...	40508	Turbine will develop —— available horse-power
Sechsmal ...	40509	Turbine to develop —— available horse-power
Sechstens ...	40510	Turbine to drive
Sechzehn ...	40511	Pressure box(es) for turbine
Seclusion ...	40512	Pipe to turbine
Secluso ...	40513	Now erecting turbine
Secondary	40514	Have completed erection of turbine
Secondina...	40515	Have connected turbine with
Secondoche	40516	Turbine and machinery running satisfactorily
Secondrate	40517	**Turn(s)**
Secouer ...	40518	To turn
Secourable	40519	To turn on
Secousse ...	40520	To turn out
Secrecy ...	40521	To turn off
Secrestar ...	40522	As soon as the weather turns
Secretaria...	40523	Let me (us) know how it turns out
Secretear ...	40524	Will let you know how it turns out
Secretion ...	40525	Promises to turn out rather badly
Sectaculum	40526	Promises to turn out exceedingly well
Sectateur ..	40527	Seems likely to turn out
Sectatote ...	40528	Does not seem at all likely to turn out well
Sectatrix ...	40529	Should this not turn out well you had better
Sectionis ...	40530	How do you think it (this) will turn out
Sectionize	40531	To turn over
Sectivus ...	40532	Turn over everything to
Secubitus...	40533	**Turned**
Secuencia...	40534	Has (have) turned out
Seculaire ...	40535	Has (have) been turned round
Secularist...	40536	How has it turned out
Secularly ...	40537	It has turned out badly
Seculier ...	40538	It has turned out to be a fraud
Secundario	40539	It has turned out well
Secundus ...	40540	It has turned out exceedingly well
Securanza...	40541	But it turned out otherwise
Securely ...	40542	As soon as I (we) have turned round
Securitas ...	40543	Has (have) quite turned round
Secutuleia	40544	Has (have) turned over

Secuzione...	40545	Has (have) not yet been turned over
Sedabatur	40546	**Turning**
Sedabunt ...	40547	How is it (the ——) turning out
Sedanchair	40548	Turning out rather badly
Sedanina ...	40549	Turning out as well as was expected
Sedanto ...	40550	Turning out splendidly
Sedativo ...	40551	**Turnover**
Sedavisse ...	40552	**Turpentine**
Sedecimo ...	40553	**Tutwork**
Sedecula ...	40554	On tutwork
Sedemini ...	40555	Tutwork bargain
Sedemur ...	40556	**Tuyer**
Sedentary...	40557	At the tuyer
Sedgebird...	40558	**Twice** (*See also* "Table at end.")
Sedicesimo	40559	**Twofold**
Sediento ...	40560	**Type**
Sedigitus ...	40561	Cable what type of —— you require
Sedimentum	40562	Of the type
Seditieux ...	40563	The type hitherto employed has been
Seditiosus...	40564	**U**
Seditore ...	40565	**Ulterior**
Sedizioso ...	40566	**Ultimate**
Seducibile...	40567	What is the ultimate result
Seductilem	40568	The ultimate result is
Seductio ...	40569	Is this your ultimate decision
Seductrice...	40570	This is my (our) ultimate decision
Sedulita ...	40571	**Ultimately**
Sedulous ...	40572	Will you ultimately be able to
Seedbud ...	40573	Will ultimately be able to
Seedcake ...	40574	Will ultimately not be able to
Seedcorn ...	40575	Expect ultimately
Seedpearl ...	40576	Hope to be able ultimately
Seedtime ...	40577	Ultimately it must come to
Seedvessel	40578	**Ultimatum**
Seefahrer ...	40579	As an ultimatum
Seegefecht	40580	Regard this as an ultimatum
Seegras ...	40581	**Ultimo** (*See also* "January," "February," &c., &c.)
Seehafen ...	40582	On the —— ultimo
Seehandel	40583	Received on the —— ultimo
Seekadet ...	40584	Sent on the —— ultimo
Seekrank ...	40585	Dated the —— ultimo
Seekreig ...	40586	**Umpire**
Seekuste ...	40587	To be referred to an umpire
Seelamt ...	40588	To name an umpire
Seeleben ...	40589	What is the umpire's decision
Seelengute	40590	Umpire's decision favourable
Seelenhirt...	40591	Umpire's decision unfavourable
Seelente ...	40592	**Unable**
Seelsorge ...	40593	Unable to
Seemacht ...	40594	Unable at present
Seemingly	40595	Should you be unable to
Seemliness	40596	If unable to do this, cable at once
Seerauber...	40597	Unable to do anything up to the present
Seereise ...	40598	Unable to comply with your request
Seesaw ...	40599	Unable owing to
Seeschiff ...	40600	Unable to continue for want of
Seesoldat ...	40601	If you are unable, do not hesitate to say so
Seestadt ...	40602	Regret that I (we) find myself (ourselves) unable
Seesturm ...	40603	—— regret(s) that he (they) find(s) himself (themselves)
...ether ...	40604	Shall be unable to attend to this until [unable to

[678]

Seewarts ...	40605	Should you (——) still be unable to
Seewessen ...	40606	Am (is) (are) still unable to

Unacceptable
Segable ...	40607	
Segadero ...	40608	Quite unacceptable
Segaligno...	40609	Regret that the offer made is quite unacceptable
Segamento	40610	Unless this (it) is altogether unacceptable

Unaccountable(ly)
| Segaticcio... | 40611 | |
| Segatrice ... | 40612 | At present it (this) is quite unaccountable |

Unadvisable(ly)
Segatura ...	40613	
Segavene ...	40614	Unadvisable at the present time
Segeln ...	40615	Do you (does ——) consider it unadvisable
Segelwerk...	40616	If you (——) consider(s) it unadvisable
Segestre ...	40617	Most unadvisable

Unaffected(ly)
Segetalis ...	40618	
Seggettina	40619	Has (have) remained quite unaffected
Seggiola ...	40620	Quite unaffected
Seggiolino	40621	As long as —— is (are) unaffected

Unanimous(ly)
Seggono ...	40622	
Seglar ...	40623	By a unanimous vote
Segmento ...	40624	By the shareholders unanimously voting
Segnacaso...	40625	Were unanimously of the opinion
Segnalanza	40626	Except you are unanimous
Segnalarsi	40627	The decision of the court was unanimously in our favour
Segnaletto	40628	Is this a unanimous opinion
Segnatore	40629	This (it) is not a unanimous opinion
Segnetto ...	40630	We are all unanimously in favour of
Segnipes ...	40631	The directors are perfectly unanimous

Unanswered
Segnipibus	40632	
Segnitia ...	40633	Still remain(s) unanswered
Segnuzzo ...	40634	Why is (are) question(s) contained in our cable of —— still
Segregator	40635	Must remain unanswered until [unanswered
Segrego ...	40636	Cannot remain unanswered if

Unappropriate(d)
Segretiere...	40637	
Segricis ...	40638	What is the unappropriated balance
Seguente ...	40639	Of this —— is unappropriated
Seguida ...	40640	Leaving —— unappropriated
Seguigio ...	40641	So long as any remain(s) unappropriated

Unassessable
Seguimento	40642	
Seguitante	40643	Shares registered in ——'s name are unassessable
Segullo ...	40644	Are the shares unassessable
Segundon...	40645	The shares are unassessable

Unattainable
| Segurador | 40646 | |
| Segureja ... | 40647 | At present unattainable |

Unauthorized
Seguridad	40648	
Sehfeld ...	40649	Alleged to be unauthorized
Sehkraft ...	40650	Publication was unauthorized
Sehnerv ...	40651	Owing to the unauthorized issue of
Sehnsucht	40652	If unauthorized

Unavoidable(ly)
Sehwinkel	40653	
Seicento ...	40654	Unless absolutely unavoidable
Seidenbau	40655	Will be unavoidable
Seidenwurm	40656	Unavoidable under present circumstances

Unaware
Seigern ...	40657	
Seigneur ...	40658	Was (were) unaware
Seigniory ...	40659	I was (we were) unaware of it, until I (we) heard from

Unbiassed
Seihtuch ...	40660	
Seilerbahn	40661	Want an absolutely unbiassed report
Seiltanzer ...	40662	Incapable of making an unbiassed report
Seinenets ...	40663	Will give an unbiassed report
Seiriasis ...	40664	Entirely unbiassed

Seisavado ...	40665	By no means unbiassed
Seiseno ...	40666	The reverse of unbiassed
Seitdem	40667	**Uncertain(ty)**
Seitenhieb	40668	The market is very uncertain
Seizable ...	40669	My arrival is very uncertain
Seizieme ...	40670	My departure is very uncertain
Sejugatus...	40671	The supply of ore is very uncertain
Sejunctim	40672	It is very uncertain when
Selbander...	40673	It is very uncertain what
Selbige ...	40674	I am (we are) still uncertain
Selbstlaut	40675	Is a little uncertain
Selbstmord	40676	Altogether uncertain whether
Selciato ...	40677	Still quite uncertain as to
Seldom ...	40678	Continue(s) uncertain
Selector ...	40679	It is (they are) most uncertain
Seleniacus	40680	It is still uncertain whether —— can
Sclenite ...	40681	Is becoming very uncertain
Selenitium	40682	Supply remains uncertain
Seleucide ...	40683	Supplies are very uncertain
Selfacting	40684	The only thing that is not uncertain is
Selfdenial...	40685	On account of the uncertain manner in which
Selfless ...	40686	The result will be uncertain until
Selfmade ...	40687	The result is no longer uncertain
Selfwill ...	40688	Provided there is no uncertainty as regards
Selibris ...	40689	The only uncertainty is as regards
Sellaccia ...	40690	**Unchanged**
Selladura ...	40691	Remain(s) practically unchanged
Sellarias ...	40692	Conditions remain practically unchanged
Sellerie ...	40693	Is your opinion still unchanged respecting
Seltenheit	40694	My (our) opinion is still unchanged
Seltsam ...	40695	——'s opinion continue(s) unchanged
Selvaggina	40696	If still unchanged
Selvatico ...	40697	The general condition of things remains unchanged
Selvetta ...	40698	The character of the rock remains unchanged
Semailles ...	40699	**Uncomfortable(ly)**
Semainier...	40700	Not at all uncomfortable
Semanal ...	40701	Most uncomfortable
Semanario	40702	May be described as uncomfortable
Semantica	40703	Has made the situation very uncomfortable
Semaphore	40704	**Uncommon(ly)**
Semaxius	40705	Was (were) very uncommon until
Sembella ...	40706	Formerly very uncommon
Sembiaglia	40707	Most uncommon
Sembievole	40708	**Uncompromising**
Semblable...	40709	Maintain(s) a most uncompromising attitude
Semblante	40710	Advise(s) the most uncompromising hostility
Sembler ...	40711	**Unconcern**
Sembradera	40712	**Unconcernedly**
Sembradio	40713	**Unconditional(ly)**
Semejable	40714	Has (have) agreed unconditionally (to)
Semencera	40715	Will not accept this (it) unconditionally
Sementar ...	40716	Unless you (——) accept(s) unconditionally
Sementicus	40717	**Uncontrollable**
Sementino	40718	**Undecided**
Semenzajo	40719	Cannot remain undecided
Semenzire...	40720	So long as it (this) remains undecided
Semerine ...	40721	At present undecided
Semestrale	40722	Quite undecided whether
Semetros ...	40723	**Undeniable(ly)**
⁓miacid ...	40724	Undeniably the best course to pursue

Semiassus...	40725	Undeniably correct
Semibos ...	40726	Regret to say it is undeniable (that)
Semibovem	40727	**Under** (*See also* "Below.")
Semibreve	40728	This should bring us under
Semicabron	40729	Will it (this) bring us under
Semicanuto	40730	So as to bring us under
Semicaper...	40731	Under the
Semicingo	40732	Under it (this)
Semicircle...	40733	From under
Semicoctus	40734	Driving so as to come under
Semicolon...	40735	So as to come under
Semicremus	40736	Will come in under
Semicroma	40737	Was supposed to come in under
Semicupio...	40738	Not under any necessity
Semideo ...	40739	Are you under any necessity to
Semidoble...	40740	Under whose authority
Semidocto	40741	Under authority given by
Semidolium	40742	Under the head of
Semidragon	40743	Will not work under
Semiermis	40744	Under these conditions
Semifluid ...	40745	Should not come under
Semiformis	40746	A few may be under
Semifultus	40747	A few will run under ——, but most are above
Semifunium	40748	Under these circumstances
Semigold ...	40749	Under no circumstances whatever
Semigravis	40750	Must not be allowed to fall under
Semihians...	40751	**Undercurrent**
Semihombre	40752	Owing to the undercurrent
Semihora ...	40753	There is an undercurrent of feeling in favour of
Semilacer ...	40754	**Undergo**
Semilautus	40755	Will have to undergo
Semilibram	40756	Should certainly undergo
Semillama	40757	There is no need to undergo
Semillero ...	40758	Unless —— should have to undergo
Semimature	40759	**Undergone**
Semimetal	40760	Has (have) undergone
Semimitra	40761	Has undergone great changes
Semimodius	40762	Since —— has undergone
Semimusico	40763	**Underground** (*See also* "Working.")
Seminality	40764	Have just come up from underground
Seminanis	40765	Will go underground and report immediately
Seminatore	40766	In the underground workings
Seminoso ...	40767	Everything underground is
Seminudus	40768	A survey of the underground workings
Semiobolus	40769	The survey of the underground workings shows
Semioctava	40770	Have underground survey corrected to date
Semiorbis...	40771	Submit plan of underground workings to
Semipedal	40772	**Underhand(ed)**
Semiplena	40773	Have nothing to do with any underhand business
Semiplotus	40774	Suspect underhand work
Semipoeta	40775	Has there been any underhand work
Semiprueba	40776	Cannot discover that there has been any underhand work
Semipuella	40777	Has behaved in a very underhand way
Semiquaver	40778	On account of the underhand way in which
Semirasus...	40779	Underhand stope
Semirecto ...	40780	Underhand stoping
Semisabio	40781	**Underlay**
Semisenex...	40782	**Underlaying**
Semisestil ...	40783	**Underlie(s)**
Semisiccus	40784	Underlie shaft

[681]

Semisomnis	40785	What is the depth of the underlie shaft
Semisonans	40786	The depth of the underlie shaft is
Semissalis	40787	What is the underlie of the vein
Semistante	40788	The vein underlies north —— degrees from the vertical
Semisvolto	40789	The vein underlies south —— degrees from the vertical
Semitarius	40790	The vein underlies east —— degrees from the vertical
Semitectam	40791	The vein underlies west —— degrees from the vertical
Semitiero ...	40792	Owing to the underlie of the vein
Semitone ...	40793	The vein changes its underlie considerably
Semituono	40794	**Underlying**
Semivietus	40795	Underlying which is
Semivivas ...	40796	The underlying formation
Semivocal ...	40797	Underlying an area of —— acres
Semivulpa	40798	To the underlying
Semodialis	40799	**Underneath**
Semolina ...	40800	**Underrate(d)**
Semoncer ...	40801	**Undershot** *(See also* " Water-wheel.")
Semoule ...	40802	**Understand(s)** *(See also* " Comprehend.")
Semovendus	40803	To understand
Semoviente	40804	As I (we) understand it
Semper ...	40805	What am I (are we) to understand from
Sempiterna	40806	Do (did) not understand
Semplice ...	40807	I (we) understand that
Sempreche	40808	What did you understand from —— respecting
Sempremai	40809	What did you understand as regards
Sempreviva	40810	So far as I am (we are) able to understand
Senapismo	40811	If you do not perfectly understand this, please **cable**
Senarero ...	40812	Cannot understand
Senariolus...	40813	Do not quite understand
Senateur ...	40814	Do not understand why
Senatorio ...	40815	Do not understand at present how
Senatrice ...	40816	Do not understand what you mean by
Senciente ...	40817	Do not clearly understand your instructions
Sencillez ...	40818	Do not clearly understand your meaning
Senderear...	40819	Do not understand your letter dated
Senechale	40820	Do not understand your cable dated
Semecionem	40821	Difficult to understand
Senecon	40822	Does he understand his business
Senectud ...	40823	Does he understand the situation
Senectutis	40824	Cannot understand your last despatch
Senescalia...	40825	I (we) do not understand the (your) message
Senescens ...	40826	I understand that you require the following
Seneschal ...	40827	Am I to understand that you require
Senility ...	40828	I understand that ——; if I am not correct cable
Seniors ...	40829	I understand that ——, which I shall take to be correct unless
		[I hear from you within the next —— days
Seniscaleo...	40830	Do you know whether —— understand(s)
Senkblei ...	40831	I am afraid —— does not understand
Sennino ...	40832	Has (have) given me to understand
Senogil ...	40833	Has (have) been given to understand that
Sensaluzzo	40834	Make sure that —— (he) (they) clearly understand(s)
Sensarie ...	40835	Understand your instructions perfectly
Sensatezza	40836	Provided that you clearly understand
Sensation ...	40837	Cannot understand the meaning of
Sensement	40838	**Understanding** *(See also* " Final.")
Sensibly ...	40839	Must have a definite understanding (before)
Sensiculus	40840	On the understanding that
Sensifere ...	40841	Provided that we can come to some understanding as regards
Sensificus ...	40842	Is there any private understanding between —— and ——
Sensuality	40843	Is there any understanding between —— and —— as regards

Sentencia ...	40844	There is a private understanding that
Senticar ...	40845	There is no private understanding
Senticetum	40846	Have a private understanding with —— that
Senticibus	40847	The only understanding is that
Senticosus	40848	Must have a clear understanding as regards
Sentiment	40849	Upon a clear understanding that
Sentinelle ...	40850	The understanding is
Sentiscent...	40851	The understanding was to the following effect
Sentito ...	40852	From want of a proper understanding
Sentrybox...	40853	What is the understanding as regards
Senuela ...	40854	Is there any understanding as regards
Senzache ...	40855	There is a clear understanding as regards
Senzapin ...	40856	There is no understanding as regards
Separador...	40857	By a clear understanding with
Separanza...	40858	Formerly there was an understanding that
Separatist...	40859	There has never been any understanding to my knowledge
Separativo	40860	There was never any such understanding
Separatrix	40861	The only understanding was
Separement	40862	Is a violation of our understanding
Sepedon ...	40863	Is not a violation of our understanding
Sepelir ...	40864	**Understood** (*See also* "Explanation.")
Sepelitus ...	40865	Is it clearly understood that
Sepilcula ...	40866	It is clearly understood
Seplasium...	40867	It is not understood
Sepolcrale...	40868	Probably if you understood
Sepolcrino	40869	It was certainly understood that
Seponendus	40870	It (this) was certainly understood
Sepositio ...	40871	Distinctly understood that
Seppellire ...	40872	Would be better understood if
Septaria ...	40873	It was an understood thing
Septemplex	40874	It has always been an understood thing
Septenario	40875	I (we) clearly understood from —— that
Septennate	40876	Provided that this is clearly understood
Septennium	40877	**Undertake** (*See also* "Deliver.")
Septicity ...	40878	To undertake
Septiembre	40879	Do not undertake
Septifore ...	40880	Refuse(s) to undertake
Septimana	40881	Consent(s) to undertake
Septiremis	40882	Shall I (we) undertake
Septuagint	40883	I (we) can undertake
Septuennis	40884	I (we) regret that —— cannot undertake
Septunx ...	40885	If you cannot undertake it yourself, can you recommend
Septuplus	40886	Will you undertake
Sepulchrum	40887	Will —— (he) (they) undertake
Sepulcro ...	40888	Cannot undertake inasmuch as
Sepultador	40889	Cannot undertake the matter
Sepulture ...	40890	Is —— willing to undertake
Sequacitem	40891	—— is willing to undertake
Sequedad ...	40892	—— would prefer not to undertake
Sequence ...	40893	You had better not undertake —— unless (until)
Sequestror	40894	Shall not undertake —— unless (until)
Sequillo ...	40895	To enable me (us) to undertake
Sequitur ...	40896	Advise you to undertake
Serafico ...	40897	Not advisable to undertake
Seralmente	40898	In case I (we) undertake
Serancer ...	40899	In case you should undertake
Serancolin	40900	In case you should not undertake
Seraphine	40901	Cannot undertake to
Serasquier	40902	Do not undertake anything further until
Serbevole ...	40903	Will not undertake anything further until

Serbrar ...	40904	Should you not undertake
Serenabunt	40905	Will only undertake the affair(s) on condition **that**
Serenade ...	40906	Would you be willing to undertake it (this)
Serenatus	40907	**Undertaking**
Serenero ...	40908	Has given an undertaking to
Serfedocco	40909	Has not given an undertaking to
Serfhood ...	40910	Must give an undertaking to
Serfonette...	40911	Has —— given an undertaking to
Sergas ...	40912	**Undertook**
Sergentina	40913	Undertook to arrange all
Sergozzone	40914	Only undertook to
Seriatim ...	40915	**Undervaluation**
Sericarius...	40916	Undervaluation amounts to ——, please correct
Seriedad ...	40917	**Undervalue(d)**
Serinette ...	40918	Was (were) undervalued
Seringat ...	40919	Have you (has ——) not undervalued
Seringuer...	40920	Undervalued rather than over
Seriphium	40921	Alleged to have been undervalued
Seritatis ...	40922	Over rather than undervalued
Sermentoso	40923	**Underwrite**
Sermocinal	40924	To underwrite
Sermollino	40925	Provided you (——) will agree to underwrite
Sermonale	40926	Will you (——) agree to underwrite
Sermonario	40927	Will agree to underwrite
Sermonize	40928	How much will you (——) underwrite
Sermonneur	40929	**Underwriter(s)**
Sermuncule	40930	Cable names of underwriters
Seronero ...	40931	Underwriters are
Serotinus ...	40932	Underwriters accept claim
Serpear ...	40933	Underwriters will not allow claim
Serpentear	40934	Underwriters have agreed to
Serpentino	40935	Underwriters accept
Serpette ...	40936	Underwriters will not accept
Serpicella ...	40937	Underwriters agree on the understanding that
Serpient ...	40938	Give underwriters formal notice that
Serpolet ...	40939	Have given underwriters formal notice that
Serpulla ...	40940	Have you given underwriters formal notice that
Serpyllum	40941	Better inform underwriters at once
Serrabilis ...	40942	Underwriters were informed on
Serraculum	40943	Have informed underwriters
Serradilla ...	40944	What is underwriters' decision
Serraduras	40945	Underwriters have decided to
Serraginem	40946	**Underwriting**
Serraglia ...	40947	Commission for underwriting
Serraniego	40948	What commission can you (——) offer for under**writing**
Serrarius ...	40949	Underwriting letters
Serrateste	40950	Underwriting commission to be paid in shares
Serrature ...	40951	Underwriting commission to be paid in cash
Serrement	40952	Have signed underwriting letters for
Serretas ...	40953	Claim(s) for underwriting
Serrezuela	40954	**Underwritten**
Serrijon ...	40955	Has (have) been underwritten
Serrones ...	40956	The whole has been underwritten
Serrucho ...	40957	—— of the capital has been underwritten
Serrurerie...	40958	Provided at least —— of the capital is underwritten
Sertularia...	40959	To be underwritten
Servabant...	40960	As soon as —— of the capital has been underwritten
Servaccio ...	40961	**Undeserved**
Servador ...	40962	Not undeserved
vandus	40963	Quite undeserved

Servatrice	40964	**Undesirable**
Servaturus	40965	Very undesirable
Serventese	40966	Unless it (this) is considered undesirable
Servible ...	40967	Undesirable in our present circumstances
Servicial ...	40968	Board consider it undesirable (that)
Servidero ...	40969	**Undeveloped** (*See also* "Unexplored.")
Serviendo...	40970	In the present undeveloped state of
Servigetto...	40971	At present undeveloped
Servigiale ...	40972	As an undeveloped property
Servility ...	40973	**Undignified**
Servillata ...	40974	**Undivided**
Servitors ...	40975	One undivided —— part of
Servivisse...	40976	**Undo**
Serviziato...	40977	**Undoubted(ly)**
Sesaminus	40978	Of undoubted merit
Sesamoide	40979	Is (are) undoubtedly
Sescalco ...	40980	Undoubtedly shows the necessity of
Sescenaris...	40981	**Undriven**
Sescuncia ...	40982	What distance in feet still remains undriven
Sescuplum	40983	Still remain(s) undriven
Seselis ...	40984	**Uneasiness**
Sesentena...	40985	So as to prevent any uneasiness in the minds of
Sesgadura	40986	Great uneasiness prevails here as to
Sesgamente	40987	Not the slightest reason for any uneasiness
Sesquate ...	40988	Has (have) caused considerable uneasiness
Sesquihora	40989	Has (have) increased the prevailing uneasiness
Sesquiplex	40990	Great uneasiness prevails as to the future
Sessantina	40991	**Uneasy**
Sesshaft ...	40992	Directors are very uneasy
Sessibulum	40993	Shareholders are becoming uneasy
Sessional ...	40994	Do not be at all uneasy
Sessitabam	40995	Is there any real reason to be uneasy
Sessitare ...	40996	**Unengaged**
Sessitator...	40997	At present unengaged
Sessola ...	40998	**Unequal**
Sestercio ...	40999	Was unequal
Sestertius...	41000	**Unequalled**
Sestiana ...	**41001**	**Unequally**
Sestultimo	41002	**Unexceptionable(ly)**
Sestuplo ...	41003	**Unexpected(ly)**
Setajuolo ...	41004	Was (were) not altogether unexpected
Setanasso...	41005	Has (have) unexpectedly
Setanium ...	41006	Altogether unexpected
Setbacks ...	41007	**Unexplored** (*See also* "Undeveloped.")
Setentrion	41008	Hitherto unexplored
Setolato ...	41009	In the unexplored ground (to the ——)
Setoletta ...	41010	I (we) have still —— feet unexplored
Setscrew ...	41011	Practically remain(s) unexplored
Settaccia ...	41012	Leave nothing unexplored
Settangolo	41013	Practically there is no ground unexplored between —— and
Settegiare...	41014	**Unfailing** [——
Settimana...	41015	**Unfair(ly)**
Settlers ...	41016	Has (have) acted very unfairly
Seudonimo	41017	Has (have) not acted unfairly
Seufzen ...	41018	Consider proposal very unfair
Seulement	41019	To avoid the appearance of acting unfairly
Sevectus ...	41020	Do(es) not wish to act unfairly in any way
Sevenfold ...	41021	Is (are) not at all unfair considering that
Severidad ...	41022	**Unfavourable**
Severitas ...	41023	The present is a very unfavourable time for

Severiter ...	41024	Should you think the present time unfavourable
Severitudo	41025	Not altogether unfavourable
Sevocabo ...	41026	Under somewhat unfavourable circumstances
Sevocent ...	41027	My (our) impression is distinctly unfavourable
Sevreuse ...	41028	Could not have been more unfavourable
Sewage ...	41029	**Unfavourably**
Sewering ...	41030	Reported unfavourably
Sexageni ...	41031	Was mentioned altogether unfavourably
Sexagesima	41032	Unfavourably impressed
Sexaginta...	41033	**Unfinished**
Sexagonal...	41034	Was (were) left unfinished
Sexangular	41035	Was (were) not left unfinished
Sexcenties	41036	At present unfinished
Sexdecim ...	41037	Do not wish to leave any part unfinished
Sexennalis	41038	In the (its) present unfinished state
Sexennium	41039	**Unfit**
Sexless ...	41040	Quite unfit
Sextante ...	41041	Should —— still be unfit
Sextilla ...	41042	Is (are) unfit to
Sextonship	41043	Altogether unfit for use
Sextupler ...	41044	Unfit for our requirements
Sextussis ...	41045	Unfit even for
Sexualize ...	41046	Unfit for
Sexuel ...	41047	**Unfitted**
Sezenos ...	41048	Unfitted for (to)
Sfacimento	41049	**Unforeseen**
Sfaldarsi ...	41050	Through unforeseen circumstances
Sfallente ...	41051	Was (were) quite unforeseen
Sfangato ...	41052	Was (were) unforeseen at that time (at the time of ——)
Sfarzaccio...	41053	**Unfortunate(ly)**
Sfenditura	41054	**Unfounded**
Sfericita ...	41055	Proved to be not altogether unfounded
Sferoide ...	41056	Is (are) quite unfounded
Sferratojo...	41057	Suspicions quite unfounded
Sfiancarsi...	41058	Was (were) not unfounded
Sfibrato ...	41059	Unfounded so far as I am concerned
Sfilaccio ...	41060	Unfounded so far as —— is concerned
Sfoconato...	41061	May prove to be unfounded
Sfogliame...	41062	**Unfriendly**
Sfolgorare	41063	Has (have) behaved in a most unfriendly way
Sforzante ...	41064	**Unguarded(ly)**
Sforzevole	41065	**Unhealthiness**
Sfrangiare	41066	**Unhealthy**
Sfratarsi ...	41067	The situation is somewhat unhealthy
Sfrattato ...	41068	Is (are) decidedly unhealthy
Sfregatojo	41069	The (this) part of the country is very unhealthy
Sfregiarsi...	41070	During the unhealthy part of the year
Sfrondare...	41071	The climate is unhealthy from —— to ——
Sfruttare ...	41072	Unhealthy for white men
Sfuggiasco	41073	Unhealthy only between —— and ——
Sfumatezza	41074	**Unheard**
Sgallinare	41075	A most unheard of proceeding
Sgannato ...	41076	Has hitherto been unheard of
Sgariglio ...	41077	**Unhesitating(ly)**
Sghembo ...	41078	**Unhurt**
Sgombrare	41079	Fortunately escaped unhurt
Sgomentato	41080	Otherwise quite unhurt
Sgonfiarsi...	41081	**Uniform(ly)**
Sgorbiare ...	41082	**Unimpeachable**
Sgovernato	41083	Of unimpeachable honesty

Sgraderole	41084	**Unimportant**
Sgraffione...	41085	So far has (have) been unimportant
Sgravanza	41086	Unless considered unimportant
Sgravidare	41087	Considered unimportant
Sgretolato...	41088	The effect as yet, has been unimportant
Sgricciolo...	41089	Unimportant except as regards
Sgridatore	41090	A few unimportant changes
Sgrignato...	41091	**Uninformed**
Sguagliato	41092	Purposely kept uninformed
Sguainare	41093	State(s) that he was (they were) kept uninformed
Sguancio ...	41094	Has (have) kept me (us) studiously uninformed
Sguarguato	41095	**Unintelligible** (*See also* " Message," " Telegram.")
Sguernire...	41096	Is quite unintelligible to me (us)
Sgufoncare	41097	**Unintentional(ly)**
Sguittire ...	41098	Was quite unintentional
Shabbiest ...	41099	But I (we) unintentionally
Shabbiness	41100	**Uninterrupted(ly)**
Shackling...	41101	**Union**
Shaddock ...	41102	To effect a union with
Shadowing	41103	Am (are) trying to bring about a union between
Shagged ...	41104	Would you approve of a union with
Shagress ...	41105	Should strongly approve of a union with
Shallow ...	41106	Do not like the idea of a union with
Shambles ...	41107	What would be the advantages to us of a union
Shambling	41108	The advantages of such a union would be
Shameless	41109	The disadvantages of such a union would be
Shamrock...	41110	Do not see that the union would have any direct advantage to us
Shapely ...	41111	Propose a union between
Sharking ...	41112	There is some talk of a union with
Sharpened	41113	**Unique**
Sharpset ...	41114	**Unit**
Shavegrass	41115	Per unit
Shearbill ...	41116	Per unit above —— per cent.
Shearling ...	41117	Per unit of copper
Sheathe ...	41118	Per unit of lead
Sheathing	41119	**Unite**
Sheepcote...	41120	Will unite with
Sheepfold...	41121	**United(ly)**
Sheephook	41122	**Universal(ly)**
Sheepishly	41123	**Unjust(ly)**
Sheepwalk	41124	**Unjustifiable(ly)**
Sheerhulk...	41125	**Unknowing(ly)**
Shellfish ...	41126	**Unknown**
Shelter ...	41127	**Unlawful** (*See also* " Legal.")
Sheltering	41128	**Unlawfully**
Shepherds	41129	**Unless**
Sherbet ...	41130	Unless you can advance anything to the contrary
Shibboleth	41131	Unless it (this) should fail
Shielded ...	41132	Unless you are (—— is) able
Shieldless...	41133	Unless I am (we are) forced to
Shifting ...	41134	Unless there is an immediate alteration for the better
Shipboy ...	41135	Unless you can see your way to do so
Shipless ...	41136	Unless I (we) have
Shipmate ...	41137	Unless I (we) have a reply before
Shivery ...	41138	Unless you (they) have
Shoeblack...	41139	Unless you will
Shoebuckle	41140	Unless —— (he) will
Shoestring	41141	Unless it is absolutely necessary
Shoetie ...	41142	Not unless
Shoplifter...	41143	Refuse(s) to do so unless

Shortcake...	41144	Shall not begin unless
Shotbelt ...	41145	Do not go unless
Shothole ...	41146	Shall not go unless
Shotsilk ...	41147	Unless you feel sure that
Showroom	41148	Unless you receive
Shrapnel ...	41149	Cannot unless
Shrewishly	41150	Unless I (we) can
Shrewmouse	41151	Unless otherwise
Shrievalty	41152	**Unlikely**
Shrillness...	41153	It is not at all unlikely
Shrimp ...	41154	It is most unlikely that
Shrinkage	41155	What you suggest is by no means unlikely
Shrouded...	41156	Quite unlikely at present
Shrubbery	41157	**Unlimited**
Shrubless...	41158	The time is not unlimited
Shudder ...	41159	The supply is not unlimited
Shunting ...	41160	Practically unlimited
Siampan ...	41161	**Unloading**
Sibarita ...	41162	Now engaged in unloading
Sibaritico ...	41163	Unloading as fast as possible
Sibilant ...	41164	As soon as I (we) have finished unloading
Sibilatore...	41165	As soon as you have finished unloading
Sibilatrix ...	41166	**Unlucky**
Sibiloso ...	41167	But was most unlucky
Sibylline ...	41168	Unlucky in everything
Sibynam ...	41169	**Unmanageable**
Siccabatur	41170	Has become practically unmanageable
Siccaneus ...	41171	**Unnecessarily**
Siccatif ...	41172	Unnecessarily long
Siccesco ...	41173	Unnecessarily delayed
Siccificus ...	41174	**Unnecessary**
Sicciolo ...	41175	Unless you consider it unnecessary
Siccitas ...	41176	Was (were) unnecessary
Siccitatis ...	41177	An unnecessary precaution
Siccoculus	41178	Would then be unnecessary
Sicelica ...	41179	Unnecessary, as long as
Sicherheit...	41180	**Unneighbourly**
Sicherlich...	41181	**Unnumbered**
Sichtbar ...	41182	**Unobjectionable**
Sicilices ...	41183	**Unobtainable**
Sicilicula ...	41184	Is (are) unobtainable at present
Sicilisso ...	41185	Unobtainable unless
Sicilivit ...	41186	Unobtainable unless you are prepared to give
Sicimina ...	41187	**Unofficial**
Sicinnista...	41188	**Unpack(ed)**
Sickbed ...	41189	At present unpacked
Sickness ...	41190	**Unpaid**
Sicofanta ...	41191	Unpaid bills amount to
Sicologia ...	41192	Leave nothing unpaid
Sicuranza...	41193	Unpaid merchants' accounts
Sicyonius ...	41194	Cable the total amount of accounts unpaid as on ——
Sidearms ...	41195	Inclusive of bills unpaid
Sidebox ...	41196	Exclusive of bills unpaid
Sideglance	41197	To meet unpaid accounts
Sideralis ...	41198	An unpaid acceptance for ——
Sidereal ...	41199	**Unparalleled**
Siderion ...	41200	**Unpleasant(ly)**
Sideritis ...	41201	**Unprecedented**
Sidewalks ..	41202	**Unprincipled**
⁻⁻lewise ...	41203	**Unproductive**

Siebenfach	41204	**Unprofitable**
Siebenmal	41205	Has (have) so far been unprofitable
Siechbett ...	41206	Practically unprofitable
Siedehaus...	41207	Under ——'s (his) management it was unprofitable
Siegegun ...	41208	Unless actually unprofitable
Siegelring...	41209	**Unpromising**
Siegetrain...	41210	Unpromising up to the present time
Siegreich ...	41211	The outlook is very unpromising
Siembra .	41212	**Unpropitious**
Siepone ...	41213	**Unprospected**
Sierosita ...	41214	**Unprovided**
Sietelevar...	41215	Unprovided with
Siffatti	41216	Hitherto quite unprovided
Sifflement...	41217	As I am (we are) unprovided with the necessary
Siffleur ...	41218	**Unqualified**
Sifoncino ...	41219	Has (have) met with the most unqualified
Sighing ...	41220	**Unquestionable(ly)**
Sigilacion...	41221	**Unreasonable**
Sigilado ...	41222	Unreasonable to expect
Sigillare ...	41223	Do you not think it a little unreasonable
Sigillatim...	41224	Do not think it at all unreasonable
Sigiloso ...	41225	Think it most unreasonable
Siglorum ...	41226	It is not unreasonable to expect
Sigmoidal...	41227	Has made most unreasonable demands
Signaculo...	41228	Quite unreasonable
Signaler ...	41229	Do not submit to any unreasonable demands
Signalized	41230	Do not make any unreasonable demands
Signalpost	41231	——'s demands are altogether unreasonable
Signarius ...	41232	I (we) consider it unreasonable to ask
Signataire	41233	What you (——) ask(s) is unreasonable
Signavero...	41234	What you (——) ask(s) is not unreasonable
Signboard	41235	**Unreliable**
Signet	41236	Consider him (——) unreliable
Signifacio...	41237	Very unreliable
Signifero ...	41238	**Unreserved(ly)**
Significem	41239	**Unsafe**
Signora ...	41240	I (we) consider it unsafe
Signoresco	41241	Consider it (them) unsafe on account of
Signpost ...	41242	Decidedly unsafe
Silabario ...	41243	Should you think it unsafe to do this
Silabico ...	41244	It would be a little unsafe at present
Silatum ...	41245	The workings were unsafe
Silbador ...	41246	Provided that it is (they are) not unsafe
Silberzeug	41247	Why do you consider it unsafe
Silenced ...	41248	Has (have) been unsafe since
Silencieux...	41249	It would in my (our) opinion be very unsafe to do so
Silendos ...	41250	Unsafe and must be re-timbered
Silentium ...	41251	Unsafe and must be pulled down
Silescere ...	41252	Unsafe and must be rebuilt
Siletur ...	41253	So long as it (they) remain(s) unsafe
Silguero ...	41254	**Unsatisfactory** (*See also* "Explanation.")
Silhouette...	41255	Reply is considered unsatisfactory
Silicario ...	41256	Must be considered unsatisfactory
Silicate ...	41257	In the event of it (this) being unsatisfactory
Siligineo ...	41258	In the present unsatisfactory condition of
Siliquor ...	41259	Continue(s) very unsatisfactory
Silken ...	41260	**Unsatisfied**
Silkmercer	41261	**Unserviceable**
Silkmill ...	41262	**Unsettled**
Silkweaver	41263	Continue(s) to be unsettled

Silkworm ...	41264	Promise(s) to become unsettled
Sillabare ...	41265	Things generally are very unsettled
Sillepsi ...	41266	As soon as the present unsettled state of affairs improves
Silletero ...	41267	**Unsound**
Silogismo...	41268	**Unsteady**
Silogizar ...	41269	Continue(s) unsteady
Silphium ...	41270	No longer unsteady
Siluisset ...	41271	The moment it becomes unsteady
Silvano ...	41272	Said to be very unsteady
Silvarum ...	41273	Was formerly unsteady
Silvaticus...	41274	His (——'s) habits are very unsteady
Silverfir ...	41275	**Unsuccessful(ly)**
Silverized...	41276	Alleged to have proved unsuccessful
Silvestre ...	41277	Was it (he) unsuccessful
Silvicola ...	41278	Was (were) unsuccessful
Silvigera ...	41279	Was (were) not unsuccessful
Silvulam ...	41280	Without being absolutely unsuccessful
Simagree ...	41281	**Unsuitable(ly)**
Simarouba	41282	Unless quite unsuitable
Simboleita	41283	But was found to be unsuitable
Simetria ...	41284	Unsuitable for
Simiente ...	41285	Report whether suitable or unsuitable
Similaceus	41286	**Unsuspicious(ly)**
Similagat ...	41287	**Unsystematic**
Similaire ...	41288	**Untenable**
Similamen	41289	Position is untenable
Similarity...	41290	**Until**
Similigena	41291	Will remain until
Similitud ..	41292	Shall not do anything until I hear from you again
Similmente	41293	Can manage until
Simoniaque	41294	Can you wait until
Simonious	41295	Cannot wait until
Simonism ...	41296	Better wait until
Simoom ..	41297	If you can wait until
Simpatia ...	41298	If you cannot wait until
Simpatizar	41299	Until I (we) have
Simperer ...	41300	Cannot decide until I (we) have seen
Simpering	41301	Must remain until
Simplaris ...	41302	Until you hear
Simplear ...	41303	Do nothing until
Simpleton...	41304	Shall do nothing until
Simplona ...	41305	Do not commence until
Simposico...	41306	Manage somehow until
Simpulum	41307	Cannot say until
Siuulacro...	41308	Until further advice
Simulated...	41309	Would carry me (us) on until
Simulativo	41310	**Unto**
Simulatore	41311	**Untried**
Simulatrix	41312	**Untrue**
Simultaneo	41313	**Unusual(ly)**
Simultatis	41314	It is somewhat unusual
Sinabafa ...	41315	It is very unusual
Sinalife ...	41316	It is not at all unusual
Sinapinus...	41317	Is it unusual
Sinapismo	41318	Course suggested is unusual
Sinapizat ...	41319	You have acted in a most unusual way
Sincelador	41320	**Unwarrantable(ly)**
Sincerarai...	41321	**Unwell** (*See also* "Health," "Ill.")
Sincerely ...	41322	**Unwilling(ly)**
Sinceridad	41323	Am (are) unwilling

Sinceriter ...	41324	—— is decidedly unwilling
Sincipucio	41325	Unwilling to
Sincopato...	41326	Not at all unwilling
Sincopizar	41327	Am (is) not unwilling if
Sinderesis...	41328	Should not be so unwilling but for
Sindicado...	41329	Am (is) (are) unwilling because of
Sinecure ...	41330	Assent(ed) most unwillingly
Sinecurist...	41331	**Unwise**
Sinedoque...	41332	A little unwise perhaps
Sinedra ...	41333	Most unwise
Sineresi ...	41334	Do you not think it unwise to
Sinestro ...	41335	Do not think it would be unwise
Sinfisis ...	41336	A most unwise course
Sinfonia ...	41337	Unwise at the present time to
Sinfulness...	41338	Unless you think it (this) unwise
Singbar ...	41339	Would be unwise unless
Singhiozzo	41340	I (we) think it very unwise to
Singkunst	41341	**Unwitting(ly)**
Singlehrer	41342	**Up**
Singleness	41343	Up again
Singlon ...	41344	As soon as they go up again
Singozzare	41345	As soon as they go up to ——
Singschule	41346	Up here
Singsong ...	41347	Up there
Singspiel ...	41348	Up to
Singstimme	41349	Up from
Singularis...	41350	How far up
Singulto ...	41351	Both up and down
Siniestro ...	41352	Will probably go up
Siniscalco ...	41353	Is not likely to go up
Sinister ...	41354	Still going up
Sinistimo ...	41355	More likely to go up than down
Sinistrare	41356	Has (have) already gone up
Sinnbild ...	41357	To pick up
Sinnspruch	41358	Should commence to raise up
Sinocal ...	41359	**Uphill**
Sinodatico	41360	Very uphill work
Sinonimia...	41361	Has (have) succeeded although it has been very uphill work
Sinopicus ...	41362	**Uphold**
Sinople ...	41363	If I am (we are) to continue to uphold you
Sinopsis ...	41364	**Upon**
Sinrazon ...	41365	Upon receipt of
Sinsabor ...	41366	Upon the following conditions
Sintetico ...	41367	Upon what conditions
Sintilla ...	41368	Upon which
Sintoma ...	41369	Upon satisfactory terms
Sinuabamur	41370	Upon the following terms
Sinuated ...	41371	**Upper**
Sinuavero	41372	Upper part of
Sinueux ...	41373	Upper and lower
Sinuosity ...	41374	Both upper and lower
Siparium ...	41375	Upper part of mine
Sipedon ...	41376	Upper tunnel
Siphoning	41377	Upper workings
Siphuncle...	41378	In the upper workings (above level number ——)
Siquando ...	41379	**Uppermost**
Siquidem ...	41380	**Upraise(d)** (See also "Raise," "Rise.")
Siquier ...	41381	The upraise has advanced —— feet for the week ending
Sirascosis ...	41382	The upraise has advanced —— feet since
Sirempse ...	41383	Upraise so far shows nothing of value

Sirgadura...	41384	**Upset**
Sirguero ...	41385	Upset if possible
Siringar ...	41386	Very much upset
Sirloin ...	41387	Has (have) upset all my (our) calculations
Sirocchia ...	41388	Take care that you (——) do(es) not upset
Sirocco ...	41389	Unless I (we) can upset
Siroppetto	41390	Unless the (this) decision can be upset
Sirpicula ...	41391	**Upward(s)**
Sirupeux ...	41392	The tendency is upward
Sisimbrio ...	41393	There is an undoubted movement upward
Siskin ...	41394	Have been moving upward since
Sisterhood	41395	Upward movement stopped
Sistilo ...	41396	From —— upward
Sistratus ...	41397	So long as upward movement continues
Sisurnas ...	41398	**Uranium**
Sisyrorum	41399	**Urge**
Sitarchiam	41400	To urge
Sitarzia ...	41401	Urge upon —— (him)
Siterello ..	41402	Will urge upon —— (him)
Sitibundo...	41403	Urge the matter forward
Sitiebant ...	41404	Will urge the matter forward as much as possible
Sitienter ...	41405	Would urge —— to
Sitivit ...	41406	Better not urge
Sittenlos ...	41407	Shall I (we) urge
Sizarship ...	41408	Would strongly urge you to
Skaters ...	41409	Do not urge —— unless
Skeleton ...	41410	Would it be advisable to urge
Sketched ...	41411	Would not be advisable to urge
Skewered	41412	Before I (we) urge
Skimmilk...	41413	**Urgent(ly)** (*See also* " Inform.")
Skindeep ..	41414	There is no urgent need at present
Skinflint ...	41415	There is an urgent need for
Skipjack ...	41416	Is it urgent
Skirmisher	41417	It is most urgent
Skittish ...	41418	Unless it is very urgent
Skittles ...	41419	It is not very urgent
Skizziren ...	41420	Provided it is not urgent
Sklarisch ...	41421	The most urgent need is for
Skrofeln ...	41422	Urgently required
Skulking ...	41423	Funds urgently required
Skyblue ...	41424	The answer is urgently needed
Skycolour	41425	The necessity is not so urgent as was thought
Skylark ...	41426	If urgent, please cable
Skylight ...	41427	Should you consider it urgent
Skyrocket...	41428	Do not consider there is any urgent necessity for
Slacciare ...	41429	The matter is very urgent
Slackened...	41430	The matter is not at all urgent
Slamming...	41431	Which is the most urgent —— or ——
Slandering	41432	The most urgent is ——
Slargarsi ...	41433	**Us**
Slargato ...	41434	For us
Slashingly	41435	Not for us
Slatinare ...	41436	Is one of us
Slaveborn...	41437	Is he one of us
Slavelike ...	41438	Is not one of us
Slaverer ...	41439	Unless you feel sure he is one of us
Slavestate...	41440	Is likely to become one of us
Slazzerare...	41441	**Usage**
Sledding ...	41442	What is the general usage
˜leekness ...	41443	If according to usage

Sleepfully	41444	Quite in accordance with general usage
Sleeveless ...	41445	**Use**
Slegamento	41446	To use
Sleighing ...	41447	Do not use
Slipboard ...	41448	Now in use
Slipknot ...	41449	In use
Slippered ...	41450	In use at
Slippers ...	41451	No use
Slogatura ...	41452	No use for
Sloggiato ...	41453	The only use
Slontanare	41454	It will be absolutely of no use
Slopbasin ...	41455	Is (are) of no use
Sloppily ...	41456	Would be of the greatest possible use
Sloucher ...	41457	Would it be of any use to
Slowness ...	41458	Would not be of any use
Slowworm	41459	Would —— be of any use to (for)
Sluggard ...	41460	Would be of very much use to us
Sluiceway...	41461	Would not be of any use to us
Slumbering	41462	Use every endeavour to
Smacchiare	41463	In case it (this) would be of any use
Smagliante	41464	It would not be of any use
Smagrare ...	41465	What is the use of
Smagratura	41466	What is the use of doing this
Smallage ...	41467	Is of no use at present
Smallbeer...	41468	Is of no use here
Smallhand	41469	When will you be able to make use of
Smaltine ...	41470	Can you use any other means
Smaltitojo	41471	Cannot use any other means
Smancerose	41472	Can you make use of
Smanziere	41473	Cannot use
Smaragdus	41474	Cannot make any use of
Smargiasso	41475	Could make good use of
Smarigione	41476	Shall have to use
Smarrirsi ...	41477	Use your own discretion as regards
Smarten ...	41478	Make every use you can of
Smartness	41479	Refuse(s) to use
Smatterer...	41480	Insist(s) upon the use of
Smattonare	41481	Will have to use
Smecticus...	41482	Has necessitated the use of
Smelato ...	41483	Will be of good use
Smelling ...	41484	If —— can be of use to you
Smembrare	41485	Why are you not making use of
Smemorarsi	41486	Use the utmost vigilance as regards
Smenomare	41487	Will use the utmost vigilance
Smenovito	41488	When we shall be able to use
Smenticato	41489	You can use my name
Smentirsi ...	41490	You had better not use my name
Smeraldino	41491	Do not use my name
Smiacio ...	41492	Can I use your name
Smidollare	41493	**Used** (See also " Using.")
Smilingly...	41494	Has (have) used
Smillanta ...	41495	Has (have) not used
Smimorato	41496	Is it used for
Sminuirsi...	41497	It is used for
Sminuitore	41498	It is not used now at all
Smirched ...	41499	It is not used for
Smisuranza	41500	**Useful(ly)**
Smoccolato	41501	Would be very useful
Smoderato	41502	Can be usefully employed
Smokebox...	41503	Cannot be usefully employed

Smokedry	41504	Would be a very useful man for you
Smokejack	41505	Has proved most useful
Smokeless	41506	**Usefulness**
Smoking ...	41507	Of doubtful usefulness
Smorbato ...	41508	**Useless(ly)**
Smorfioso ...	41509	Rendered useless
Smothering	41510	Has (have) been rendered perfectly useless
Smovitura	41511	Is it quite useless
Smozzicare	41512	It is quite useless
Smudged ...	41513	It is quite useless for you (——) to
Smuggling	41514	It is useless to cable, will write fully
Smussato ...	41515	Quite useless for the particular purpose wanted
Smyrnium	41516	Altogether useless. Cable what you wish done
Snaillike ...	41517	Will be quite useless
Snakeweed	41518	**Uselessness**
Snamorare	41519	**Using**
Snaplocks...	41520	Is (are) using
Snappish ...	41521	Has (have) been using
Snatchers ..	41522	What have you been using
Snaturato	41523	Has (have) not been using
Sneaking ...	41524	At present using
Snebbiare ..	41525	Intend(s) using
Sneezing ...	41526	When do you think of using
Snelletto ...	41527	Why are you not using
Snervarsi ...	41528	Why are you not using the —— at ——
Snidiato ...	41529	**Usual(ly)**
Sniggerer ...	41530	Usual terms
Snippet ...	41531	As usual
Sniveller ...	41532	As usual except that
Snivelling...	41533	Just as usual
Snobbishly	41534	Upon the usual terms and conditions
Snodamento	41535	Subject to usual terms and conditions
Snominare	41536	What are the usual terms and conditions
Snorting ...	41537	The usual terms and conditions are
Snowball ...	41538	It is not quite usual
Snowbroth	41539	Will take the usual means to
Snowdrop...	41540	Will take the usual course
Snowflake...	41541	The most usual thing is
Snowplough	41542	What is the usual thing to do
Snowstorm	41543	At the usual time
Snowwhite	41544	At the usual place
Snubbing ...	41545	Is it usual to
Snubnosed	41546	It is not usual to
Snuffbox ...	41547	It is hardly usual to do so
Snuffling ...	41548	Better adopt the usual course
Snufftaker	41549	Better continue as usual
Snuggery ...	41550	Will continue as usual until
Soaker ...	41551	**Utmost**
Soalzare ...	41552	To the utmost
Soapboiler	41553	Do your very utmost
Soapstone...	41554	Will do my (our) very utmost
Soapsuds ...	41555	Am (are) doing my (our) utmost
Soarrendar	41556	Have done my (our) very utmost (but)
Soasar ...	41557	Has (have) promised to do his (their) utmost
Soavezza ...	41558	Is (are) doing his (their) very utmost
Soavizzare	41559	Will use my utmost endeavours
Sobadero ...	41560	Utmost care
Sobajadura	41561	The utmost care will be necessary as regards
Sobanda ...	41562	Utmost caution
Sobaquera	41563	Use the utmost caution

Sobaquido	41564	Will use the utmost caution
Sobarbada	41565	Do the very utmost to prevent
Sobbing ...	41566	The utmost care was taken to prevent
Sobbissato	41567	The utmost care is necessary to
Sobbolire ...	41568	The utmost care should be taken to avoid
Soberbio ...	41569	I (we) believe —— is (are) doing his (their) utmost to
Sobillare ...	41570	Shall continue to do my (our) utmost
Sobolesco ...	41571	Will do my (our) utmost to assist
Sobornado	41572	What is the utmost limit you can give
Sobradillo...	41573	The utmost possible limit is
Sobrancero	41574	Use the utmost vigilance
Sobrante ...	41575	Will use the utmost vigilance
Sobreaguar	41576	**V**
Sobrealzar	41577	**Vacancy**
Sobreanal...	41578	There is no vacancy at present
Sobrebeber	41579	Should any vacancy occur
Sobreboya	41580	To fill up the vacancy caused by his (——'s) leaving
Sobrecanon	41581	**Vacant**
Sobrecarga	41582	Is (are) vacant
Sobreceno	41583	Is (are) not vacant
Sobrecoger	41584	Is the position vacant
Sobrecutis	41585	**Vacate(d)**
Sobredicho	41586	Do you intend to vacate
Sobrehueso	41587	Do not intend to vacate
Sobrellare	41588	**Vacation**
Sobremesa	41589	Legal vacation
Sobrenadar	41590	**Vacillate**
Sobrepeine	41591	**Vacillating**
Sobreroas ...	41592	**Vacillation**
Sobreronda	41593	**Vague(ly)**
Sobresalir...	41594	Too vaguely
Sobreseer ...	41595	Was (were) vaguely understood to mean
Sobresello	41596	Has (have) but a vague idea
Sobretarde	41597	At present the whole proposition is vague
Sobrevista	41598	No longer vague
Sobriedad	41599	**Valid**
Sobriety ...	41600	Is it valid
Sobrino ...	41601	It is valid
Sobriquet...	41602	It is not valid
Sobuglio ...	41603	Valid for
Socaire ...	41604	Perfectly valid
Socalina ...	41605	Would not be valid unless
Socalinero	41606	Whether valid or not
Socapiscol...	41607	Take solicitor's opinion whether or not it (this) is valid
Socarrar ...	41608	**Validity**
Socarron ...	41609	As to the validity of
Soccagium	41610	There is no question as to the validity of
Soccedere ...	41611	To examine and report upon the validity of the transfer
Socchiuseo	41612	Has (have) occasioned doubt as to its validity (the validity of
Soccifera ...	41613	Pending confirmation of validity [——)
Soccorenza	41614	**Validly**
Sochantre...	41615	Was validly made (transferred)
Sociabant	41616	Was not transferred validly
Sociable ...	41617	**Valley**
Socialists ...	41618	At the bottom of the valley
Socialita ...	41619	In the valley below
Socialness	41620	Along the valley
Sociatrix ...	41621	**Valuable** (*See also* " Deposit.")
Sociennus	41622	Valuable information
Societary ...	41623	Will be more valuable

[695]

Sociniano ...	41624	Believe it to be exceedingly valuable
Sockel ...	41625	Is likely to become more valuable
Soclavero ...	41626	Will undoubtedly become more valuable
Socollada ...	41627	Is likely to become less valuable
Socorditer	41628	Has rendered me (us) very valuable services
Socorredor	41629	Services rendered not valuable
Socrocio ...	41630	Has become a very valuable property
Sodalitium	41631	It is undoubtedly a valuable opportunity
Sodalizio ...	41632	Would only be valuable as (for)
Soddisfare	41633	**Valuation**
Soddotta ...	41634	At ——'s valuation
Sodducere	41635	According to ——'s valuation
Sodduzione	41636	Will make careful valuation
Sodomita ...	41637	Make a careful valuation of
Sodomitico	41638	Valuation made, total amount ——
Soezmente	41639	Better have valuation made at once
Sofaldar ...	41640	Will have valuation made at once
Sofferare ...	41641	Upon the present valuation of the property
Sofferenza	41642	To be taken over at a valuation
Soffermata	41643	What was the valuation of
Sofferuto ...	41644	The valuation was
Soffiante ...	41645	As soon as the valuation, now being made, is completed
Soffietto ...	41646	When will the valuation be completed
Soffittare ...	41647	Valuation will be finished on
Soffolcere ...	41648	Valuation too high
Soffreddo ...	41649	Valuation not complete
Soffregare...	41650	Valuation will exceed
Soffritore ...	41651	Purchasers to take over plant at valuation
Sofisma ...	41652	Purchasers to take over stores at valuation
Sofisticar ...	41653	Purchasers to take over —— at valuation
Soflamar ...	41654	Pending valuation
Sofrenada...	41655	**Value** (*See also* "Appraise," "Commercial," "Cost,"
Sofrito ...	41656	Intrinsic value ["Depreciation," "Destroy," "Higher.")]
Soggettato	41657	Is (are) of no value
Sogghigno	41658	The value of
Soggiacere	41659	Would be of great value to me (us)
Soggolare ...	41660	Do you know the value of
Sogleich ...	41661	Do not know the value of
Sognante ...	41662	What is your estimate of its value (of the value of ——)
Sogueria ...	41663	Estimate the value at
Soguillo ...	41664	What is the actual value of
Sohlleder ...	41665	The actual value is
Soigner ...	41666	What is the value
Soilpipe ...	41667	Of very low value
Soiree ...	41668	Would be of value only in the event of
Soixante ...	41669	The value at present is merely nominal
Sojourned...	41670	Nominal value
Sojuzgador	41671	The value to us would only be for surface extensions
Sojuzgar ...	41672	May be of considerable value, but is altogether unproved
Solacear ...	41673	Of the greatest possible value
Solacing ...	41674	Ascertain the value as soon as you can
Soladura ...	41675	The full value
Solaginem	41676	The market value is
Solamento	41677	Has caused a great rise in the value
Solanazo ...	41678	Will increase the value enormously
Solandus ...	41679	Has (have) an inflated idea of its value
Solangoose	41680	Consider the value to be
Solariego ...	41681	Consider and report as to the prospective value of
Solatiolum	41682	What is the width and estimated value of
Solatium ...	41683	What is the approximate value per ton

Solatrix ...	41684	Get opinion of —— as to the approximate value of
Solazoso ...	41685	Ore in reserve amounts approximately to —— tons estimated
Solcello ...	41686	What is your estimate of the value of [value ——
Solchetto ...	41687	State the value as nearly as you are able
Soldadero...	41688	Continually falling in value
Soldadesca	41689	So as to prove the value of
Soldanella	41690	Cable value at (of)
Soldateria...	41691	Cable estimated value of
Soldatisch	41692	The value is
Solderer ...	41693	The estimated value is
Soldiery ...	41694	Estimated value
Soldling ...	41695	Of little or no value
Solecchio ...	41696	The value would be for
Solecismo...	41697	Believe the value not to exceed
Solecistic ...	41698	Can you ascertain present value
Soleggiare	41699	Will endeavour to ascertain present value
Solejar ...	41700	Value to be determined by
Solemn ...	41701	Have no value unless for
Solemnidad	41702	Do you think the property of sufficient value to
Solemnness	41703	What is the prospective value of
Solemnity...	41704	The prospective value is
Solemnel ...	41705	The value is entirely prospective
Solemnitas	41706	The value depends entirely upon
Solenoid ...	41707	Safe estimated value
Solercia ...	41708	What is the value of ore delivered to buyers
Solevantar	41709	What is the tonnage and value of ore for which you have already
Solevar ...	41710	Surrender value [received sampler's certificates
Solfaing ...	41711	**Valueless**
Solfanaria	41712	Is (are) valueless
Solfanello...	41713	Will then become practically valueless
Solfeador ...	41714	If it (this) is not to become valueless
Solfeggio ...	41715	**Valve(s)**
Solfier ...	41716	Owing to a breakage of one of the valves
Solicano ...	41717	Valve spindle(s)
Solicit ...	41718	**Vanadium**
Soliciting ...	41719	**Variable**
Solicitude...	41720	Continue(s) to be very variable
Solidaire ...	41721	**Variance**
Solidatrix...	41722	Is (are) completely at variance
Solidesco ...	41723	No longer at variance
Solidez ...	41724	**Variation**
Solidifier ...	41725	Variation of
Solidipes ...	41726	No variation since my last report
Solidness ...	41727	There has been considerable variation
Solifuga ...	41728	Cable any important variation
Soligenas ...	41729	What is the magnetic variation
Soliloquio...	41730	The magnetic variation is —— degrees east of north
Solipedo ...	41731	The magnetic variation is —— degrees west of north
Solipugnam	41732	Practically without variation
Solissimo ...	41733	No variation whatever
Solitaire ...	41734	The variation is very slight
Solitario ...	41735	The only variation is
Solitude ...	41736	Without variation
Solitudine	41737	Should there be any considerable variation
Solivagas ...	41738	**Various**
Soliveau ...	41739	Many and various
Sollalzare...	41740	**Vary(ies)**
Sollastre ...	41741	Is it likely to vary
Sollazzoso...	41742	Is almost certain to vary
Sollecito ...	41743	Varies considerably

Solleone ...	41744	Varies very little indeed
Sollevarsi ...	41745	Varies with every foot
Sollievo ...	41746	Varies occasionally to the extent of
Sollispar ...	41747	Varies between
Sollozar ...	41748	Varies in amount between —— and ——
Soloist ...	41749	Varies from day to day
Solomillo ...	41750	**Varying**
Solsequium	41751	Varying from —— to ——
Solstice ...	41752	Varying between
Solsticial ...	41753	**Vastly**
Solstitium	41754	Vastly improved
Solstizio ...	41755	Vastly altered
Soltadizo ...	41756	Is vastly different
Solterona ...	41757	Unless I am (we are) vastly mistaken
Solubility ...	41758	**Vein(s)** (*See also* "Barren," "Bearing," "Branch," " Fissure."
Solutrix ...	41759	The vein(s) is (are) [" Lode," " Ore.")
Soluturus ...	41760	There are —— veins on the property
Solvable ...	41761	What is the average width of the vein
Solvencia ...	41762	The average width of the vein is
Solvendus...	41763	Cable width of vein
Solverant ...	41764	The vein is fully —— feet in width [yards and trends ——
Solviente ...	41765	The vein can be traced at the surface for a distance of ——
Solvimento	41766	The average dip of the vein will take it outside the property
Solvitore ...	41767	Have discovered vein (of) [within the next —— feet
Somaraccio	41768	Have intersected vein (by)
Somaten ...	41769	The vein in the shaft
Sombrage...	41770	The vein in the sink below
Sombreado	41771	The vein in the winze
Sombreness	41772	The vein in the raise
Sombrerera	41773	The vein in the level
Sombriglio	41774	The vein in the tunnel
Sombrilla ...	41775	On the vein
Sombroso ...	41776	The vein is exceedingly irregular
Sombrously	41777	The vein is a very irregular one, both in width and value
Someggiare	41778	The vein in the end is well defined and regular
Somersault	41779	The veinstone is
Someter ...	41780	The vein is strong and well defined
Sommnation	41781	The vein is well defined but small
Sommatore	41782	The vein has a very marked selvage
Sommeiller	41783	The vein filling consists of
Sommelier	41784	The average value of the vein may be taken at
Sommerlich	41785	The vein is perfectly barren
Sommersare	41786	On the course of the vein
Sommersi...	41787	Cable direction and dip of the vein
Sommertag	41788	The direction of the vein is —— and it dips ——
Sommerzeit	41789	Follow the vein
Sommessivo	41790	Expect to cut the vein within the next —— feet sunk
Sommettere	41791	Expect to strike the vein within the next —— feet
Sommista...	41792	The vein is a large one
Sommossa	41793	Outside the vein
Somnambulo	41794	The vein is small but
Somnians ...	41795	The vein is small and poor
Somniatur	41796	True fissure vein
Somnifero...	41797	Beyond this the vein becomes broken up
Somnificus	41798	The footwall is ——, will start immediately to drive in on the
Somnolence	41799	Have cut the vein by the deep tunnel [vein
Somnolist...	41800	Shall begin immediately to drive on the vein
Somonte ...	41801	North and south on the vein
Somorgujar	41802	Flat vein
Sompesar ...	41803	Flat vein —— feet thick

Somptuaire	41804	The vein is becoming very
Sonable ...	41805	From all available points on the vein
Sonacibus...	41806	In order to drain the vein
Sonadera ...	41807	Has drained the vein
Sonagliata	41808	Will the tunnel drain the vein
Sonaglino...	41809	Rise upon the vein
Sonamento	41810	The rise on the vein is now up —— feet
Sonatrice ...	41811	Owing to alteration in pitch of the vein
Sonatura ...	41812	Send full particulars as to vein cut
Sonchos ...	41813	The vein is increasing in size
Sondage ...	41814	The vein is composed of
Sondalesa...	41815	The vein(s) is (are) small
Sonderling	41816	If this vein is the —— vein
Sondieren...	41817	The vein is nearly vertical for a depth of —— feet
Sonetazo ...	41818	Is visible throughout the vein
Sonetin ...	41819	The vein is spotted with ore
Sonettante	41820	The width of the vein is not yet determined
Sonettessa	41821	Consists of a series of veins of
Sonettista...	41822	The vein is very thin and ill defined
Sonevole ...	41823	The vein though thin is between well defined walls
Songecreux	41824	Where the vein becomes thin
Songeur ...	41825	The vein becomes very thin here (at ——)
Songstress	41826	The vein has now widened out to
Sonipedis ...	41827	The vein is very much pinched
Sonitibus ...	41828	The vein is pinching out longitudinally
Sonivius ...	41829	The vein shows signs of a pinch
Sonnabend	41830	The vein has not pinched
Sonnailler	41831	The vein seems to have pinched out in depth
Sonnellino	41832	Where the pinch occurs in the vein
Sonnenbild	41833	This will prove the vein to a depth of
Sonnerello	41834	The vein has been proved for a depth of
Sonnerie ...	41835	The vein has been proved for a length of
Sonneteer ...	41836	The vein has been prospected for a length of
Sonnetist ...	41837	The vein here is small and of little value
Sonnifero ...	41838	The vein appears to have divided into
Sonnolente	41839	The mother vein of the district
Sonnollare	41840	There are —— distinct veins
Sonoridad	41841	The vein appears to have divided into —— branches
Sonorinus...	41842	The vein so far has improved in value with increased depth
Sonorously	41843	The vein shows a marked falling-off in value
Sonreirse ...	41844	Vein maintains its size and value
Sonrodarse	41845	The vein still continues small and poor
Sonrojar ...	41846	The vein is undoubtedly improving
Sonrugirse	41847	The vein is looking
Sonsacador	41848	The vein has every appearance of
Sonsaque ...	41849	Have struck vein but not pay streak
Sonship ...	41850	Have struck vein but so far have not discovered the pay streak
Sonsonete...	41851	We believe that —— veins have united about this position
Sonticam ...	41852	The vein is being prospected in depth by a shaft already sunk [—— feet
Soolwage ...	41853	The vein carries a little mineral
Soothingly	41854	The vein looks poor
Soothsayer	41855	If the vein is becoming poorer
Sootiness ...	41856	The vein(s) has (have) become poorer
Sopaipa ...	41857	On account of the pockety nature of the vein
Sopalancar	41858	A vein of quartz
Soperchia...	41859	The vein is narrow but rich
Soperifero	41860	The vein is narrow and poor for a length —— of feet
Sopero ...	41861	The vein continues narrow
Sopetear ...	41862	Have cut a small vein at this point

[699]

Sophical ...	41863	Numerous small veins
Sophistic ...	41864	The vein so far promises
Sopiebat ...	41865	The vein has a well defined hanging wall
Sopilote ...	41866	The vein has a well defined footwall
Sopivero ...	41867	Bedded vein
Sopladero ...	41868	Contact vein
Soplamocos	41869	Gash vein
Soplante ...	41870	Lenticular vein [it dips ——— degrees to the horizontal
Soponcio ...	41871	The direction of the vein is ——— degrees east of north, and
Soporific ...	41872	The direction of the vein is ——— degrees west of north, and [it dips ——— degrees to the horizontal
Soporoso ...	41873	The vein runs nearly due north and south
Soportable	41874	The vein runs nearly north-east and south-west
Soportal ...	41875	The vein runs nearly due east and west
Soppannato	41876	There is every indication that the vein will maintain its value
Soppassare	41877	There is every indication that the vein will continue its size in
Soppellito	41878	The footwall of the vein is [depth
Soppestare	41879	The hanging wall of the vein is
Soppiatto ...	41880	The vein lies between walls of
Soppidiano	41881	The vein is very regular and lies between clearly defined walls
Soppiegare	41882	A regular network of veins
Sopportato	41883	Shall proceed immediately to sink upon the vein
Soppresso	41884	An average sample from the quartz of the vein has assayed
Soppriore ...	41885	At the intersection of the vein with
Sopracuto...	41886	To the intersection of the ——— vein with the ——— vein
Sopraddire	41887	The vein at ——— (this point) is very much broken up
Sopraffine...	41888	The vein has been faulted by
Soprammodo	41889	The vein has been heaved ——— feet horizontally
Soprano ...	41890	The vein is very much broken up and disturbed
Soprappeso	41891	Begin to doubt whether we are upon the ——— vein
Soprastato	41892	Have now driven ——— feet on the vein
Sopratodos	41893	The average assay of the vein material shows
Sopravanzo	41894	The only developments upon the vein consist of
Soprossuto	41895	The vein has now been developed to a depth of ——— feet [vertically and ——— feet horizontally
Soprumano	41896	This should cut the vein at a vertical depth of ——— feet
Sopuntar ...	41897	To sink on the vein
Soracum ...	41898	Have sunk on the vein ——— feet
Sorbedor ...	41899	**Vendor(s)** (*See also* " Behalf," " Better," " Concession,"
Sorbent ...	41900	Vendor's shares [" Induce," " Insist.")
Sorbetiere ..	41901	As vendor
Sorbettato	41902	Have arranged with vendor(s) that
Sorbible ...	41903	Vendors to take ——— in cash and ——— in fully-paid shares
Sorbicion ...	41904	Vendors will accept bill for ——— at ——— months
Sorbier ...	41905	Vendor(s) willing to apply for shares [correct
Sorbillans...	41906	The representations made by the vendor(s) are substantially
Sorbondare	41907	The representations made by the vendor(s) are very much over
Sorbonical	41908	The vendor(s) agree(s) to [stated
Soroeress ...	41909	If the vendor(s) will not
Sorcery ...	41910	If the vendor(s) will
Sorciaja ...	41911	Vendor(s) will
Sorcoletto	41912	Vendor(s) will not
Sordaggine	41913	Vendor(s) consent(s)
Sordamente	41914	Unless the vendor(s) is (are) willing to
Sordastro ...	41915	Vendor(s) is (are) perfectly willing to
Sordecula...	41916	Vendor(s) is (are) not willing to
Sordidatus	41917	Inasmuch as the vendor(s)
Sordidez ...	41918	Owing to a dispute with the original vendor(s)
Sordidness	41919	Vendor(s) will not agree to
Sordina ...	41920	Have had an interview with the vendor(s)

Sorditudo...	41921	Have had an interview with the vendor(s), it has been agreed
Sordulente	41922	Unless the vendor(s) is (are) willing to defray the cost
Sorellina ...	41923	Am (are) to meet vendors on
Sorgenvoll	41924	Have you seen vendor(s)
Sorgfaltig...	41925	Have not seen vendor(s)
Soricinus ...	41926	Vendor(s) must relinquish
Soriculata...	41927	Vendor(s) will not relinquish
Sormontare	41928	Vendor(s) is (are) perfectly willing to relinquish
Sororcula ...	41929	Vendor(s) wish(es) to retain [of the company
Sororicida	41930	Vendor(s) will retain shares for —— months after incorporation
Sorportato	41931	Will ascertain from the vendor(s) whether
Sorprender	41932	Ascertain from the vendor(s) whether
Sorpresa ...	41933	Have ascertained from vendor(s) that
Sorquidato	41934	Vendors are general merchants at
Sorracus ...	41935	The vendor(s) is (are) really the Bank at ——
Sorregar ...	41936	Will vendor(s) guarantee titles
Sorridere ...	41937	Vendor(s) wish(es) me (us) to become
Sorriego ...	41938	**Ventilate(d)**
Sorriness ...	41939	To ventilate
Sorrowful...	41940	So as to ventilate
Sorrowing	41941	Unless we can ventilate
Sorrowless	41942	To ventilate the matter
Sorsaltare...	41943	Thoroughly ventilate the matter
Sorsettino...	41944	Threaten(s) to ventilate the matter in the public Press
Sortaccia ...	41945	**Ventilating** *(See also " Blower.")*
Sorteador...	41946	Engine used for driving the ventilating fan
Sortilegio ...	41947	For ventilating purposes
Sortilige ...	41948	**Ventilation** *(See also " Defective.")*
Sortiment...	41949	The ventilation is very good
Sortirem ...	41950	The ventilation is somewhat deficient
Sortitorem	41951	Has not improved the ventilation of the mine
Sorvenire ...	41952	For the sole purpose of ventilation
Sorviziato...	41953	Ventilation is now very much better
Sorvolante	41954	We have now excellent ventilation throughout the workings
Sosamente	41955	Owing to the want of ventilation
Sosanar ...	41956	To secure the proper ventilation of
Soscritto ...	41957	Will improve the ventilation of the mine
Soscrivere...	41958	So as to improve the ventilation of the mine
Sosegado ...	41959	As soon as ventilation is re-established
Soslayar ...	41960	**Venture**
Soslinear ...	41961	A blind venture
Sospecha ...	41962	To venture
Sospechoso	41963	To join in the venture
Sospendere	41964	Do not venture
Sospignere	41965	I (we) venture to suggest that
Sospirante	41966	Would you agree to join in the venture
Sospiretto...	41967	Cannot join in the venture
Sospiroso ...	41968	Should like to join in the venture
Sossannare	41969	In case you (they) do not join in the venture
Sostarsi ...	41970	In case I (we) join in the venture
Sostenedor	41971	In case I (we) do not join in the venture
Sostenenza	41972	It is too uncertain a venture
Sostenersi...	41973	Is it worth while to venture
Sostentato	41974	It is worth while to venture
Sostrum ...	41975	It is not worth while to venture
Sotabanco...	41976	Should not venture
Sotacola ...	41977	Would not venture to
Sotadeum ...	41978	What is the result of the venture
Sotalugo ...	41979	The result of the venture is a loss of ——·
Sotanear ...	41980	The result of the venture is a profit of ——

Sotaventar	41981	Result of the venture to date is *nil*
Sotayuda ...	41982	Do you still advise me (us) to venture
Sotechado...	41983	Advise you strongly to venture
Soteriam ...	41984	Do not now advise you to venture
Soterraneo	41985	Would —— consent to venture
Sottecchi ...	41986	Consent(s) to venture
Sottement	41987	Refuse(s) to venture
Sotterrato...	41988	Take care not to venture too far (much) [venture
Sottiletto ...	41989	See —— and ask if —— (he) (they) would care to join in
Sottinteso...	41990	How much will you venture
Sottishly ...	41991	Will venture to the extent of
Sottocalza	41992	Provided that you join in the venture
Sottocoppa	41993	If you do not intend to join in the venture
Sottogola ...	41994	Cable whether you will join in venture and for how much
Sottomesso	41995	Is —— likely to venture to
Sottosopra	41996	Is (are) likely to venture to
Sottovento	41997	Is (are) not likely to venture to
Sottratto ...	41998	They are hardly likely to venture to
Sotuer ...	41999	**Veracity**
Soubresant	42000	Doubt the veracity of
Soubrette ...	**42001**	Will guarantee the veracity of
Souchet ...	42002	**Verbal**
Soucieux ...	42003	The arrangement was only verbal
Soucoupe ...	42004	There was a verbal understanding
Soudainete	42005	Must have something more than a verbal understanding
Soudoyer ...	42006	**Verbatim**
Soufflage ...	42007	A verbatim report of
Souffleur ...	42008	**Verdict** (*See also* " Exonerate," " Favourable," " Trial.")
Souffrant ...	42009	Verdict is for the defendant
Soughing ...	42010	Verdict is for the defendant with costs
Souiller ...	42011	When is the verdict likely to be given
Soulcurer ...	42012	Verdict has been postponed
Soulever ...	42013	Expect the verdict will be given on or before —— [——)
Souligner ...	42014	The verdict has been given in my (our) favour (in favour of
Soulless ...	42015	The verdict has been given against me (——)
Soumettre	42016	Do not hesitate to cable the moment you know the verdict
Soundboard	42017	Shall not hesitate to cable as soon as I (we) know the verdict
Soundness	42018	The verdict is in our favour; shall obtain —— costs
Soupçon ...	42019	Verdict has been given against us; we shall have to pay costs
		[amounting to ——
Soupconner	42020	The verdict is in our favour, but each side has to pay its own
Souplesse ...	42021	Verdict of —— [costs
Soupticket	42022	Verdict of acquittal
Sourciller ...	42023	Verdict of guilty
Sourdaud ...	42024	Verdict deferred
Sourdement	42025	Judges have given unanimous verdict in our favour
Sourdine ...	42026	—— judges out of —— have given verdict in our favour
Sourdock ...	42027	Jury dismissed ; could not agree as to verdict
Sourgourd	42028	Verdict carries damages amounting to
Souriceau...	42029	Should you get favourable verdict
Sourmilk ...	42030	Should you not get favourable verdict
Sourness ...	42031	Pending verdict being pronounced
Sousbarbe...	42032	**Verge**
Souscrire ...	42033	On the verge of
Sousferme	42034	Stand(s) on the verge
Sousgarde...	42035	Practically on the verge of bankruptcy
Souslover ...	42036	**Verification**
Sousmarin	42037	Require(s) verification
Souspied ...	42038	In verification of
Soussigner	42039	Do(es) not require further verification

Soustraire	42040	**Verified**
Soutache ...	42041	Must be verified by you in your capacity of
Soutanelle	42042	To be verified by the official in charge
Souteneur...	42043	All documents must be verified before a notary public
Souterrain	42044	All documents have been verified on oath
Southerner	42045	Pending receipt of verified documents
Soutirage ...	42046	**Verify**
Souvenir ...	42047	To verify
Soverchio ...	42048	Proceed to verify
Sovereign ...	42049	Shall proceed to verify
Sovranzare	42050	Can you verify
Sovrappin...	42051	Cannot verify
Sovratodos	42052	Verify at once
Sovresso ...	42053	As soon as you have been able to verify
Sovvenirsi	42054	As soon as I (we) have been able to verify
Sovvertire...	42055	When will you be able to verify
Sowthistle	42056	Verify statement(s)
Soyeux ...	42057	Cannot verify statement(s)
Sozzezza ...	42058	If you can verify ——'s statement
Sozzopra ...	42059	It will be necessary to verify ——'s statement(s) in every detail
Spaccarsi ...	42060	Should you be able to verify ——'s statement(s)
Spaccatura	42061	Should you not be able to verify ——'s statement(s)
Spaced ...	42062	Unless you are able to verify ——'s statement(s)
Spacieux ...	42063	I (we) can verify
Spaciously	42064	I (we) cannot verify
Spadaccia	42065	Verify titles as soon as possible
Spadassin...	42066	Will verify titles as soon as possible
Spadebone	42067	**Version**
Spaderno ...	42068	What is your (——'s) version of the matter
Spadetta ...	42069	My version of the matter is
Spadiceus...	42070	According to ——'s version of the matter
Spadicose...	42071	Now give(s) another version of the matter
Spadiglia ...	42072	Corroborates ——'s version of the matter
Spadonatus	42073	Has (have) given an altogether different version of
Spadonina	42074	As soon as you have obtained ——'s version of the matter
Spadulare...	42075	Another version is that
Spaghero ...	42076	**Vertical(ly)**
Spagiricus	42077	What is the vertical depth of
Spagliare ...	42078	The vertical depth is
Spajemento	42079	What is the vertical distance between
Spalcato ...	42080	Vertically below
Spallaccia...	42081	The vertical distance between —— and —— is ——
Spallare ...	42082	The distance is —— feet vertical
Spallino ...	42083	The vertical depth is —— feet, giving an inclined depth on the
Spalmatore	42084	Nearly vertical [vein of —— feet
Spalpeen ...	42085	To sink vertically for
Spaltig ...	42086	Is nearly vertical down to the —— level
Spampanata	42087	**Very**
Spandersi...	42088	Very bad
Spanditojo	42089	Very good
Spandrel ...	42090	Very big
Spanferkel	42091	Very small
Spangled ...	42092	Very high
Spanishfly	42093	Very likely
Spannew ...	42094	Very low
Spannkraft	42095	Very much
Spannung	42096	Very many
Spantato ...	42097	Very often
Spappolato	42098	Very rich
Sparabicco	42099	Very poor

Sparadrap	42100	Very soon
Sparagiaja	42101	Very late
Sparagnare	42102	**Vesicular**
Sparapane	42103	**Vessel(s)** (*See also* "Ship," "Steamer.")
Sparatore ...	42104	Cable arrival of vessel
Sparaviere	42105	Will cable arrival of vessel
Spardeck ...	42106	Shall charter a small vessel for explosives
Sparecchio	42107	Small vessels trade between —— and ——
Sparelembo	42108	Expect to secure vessel shortly
Spareness...	42109	Sailing vessel
Sparerib ...	42110	River vessel
Sparganion	42111	Have engaged a vessel to take
Spargendus	42112	Have not yet been able to engage a vessel
Spargersi ...	42113	Vessel sunk
Spargitore	42114	Vessel arrived with
Sparherd ...	42115	Vessel has not yet arrived
Sparingly ...	42116	Vessel expected on
Sparizone ...	42117	What is the name of the vessel
Sparkasse	42118	The name of the vessel is
Sparkish ...	42119	The vessel —— with —— left on
Sparkler ...	42120	The vessel has not yet left
Sparling ...	42121	Has the vessel left
Sparmiare	42122	Vessel is to leave on
Sparniccio	42123	Will cable when vessel leaves
Sparrow ...	42124	**Vested**
Sparrwerk	42125	Is (are) vested
Sparsam ...	42126	To be vested in
Sparsely ...	42127	Should be vested in
Sparseness	42128	Can be vested meanwhile in the hands of
Sparsionem	42129	Vested interests (rights)
Sparsivus ...	42130	Vested in the names of trustees
Spartarium	42131	Now vested in the —— company
Sparteoli ...	42132	**Vexatious(ly)**
Sparterie ...	42133	Delay very vexatious
Spartibile...	42134	Delay is becoming vexatious
Spartito ...	42135	**Viaduct**
Sparutello	42136	**Vibration**
Spasimare	42137	Due to the vibration caused by
Spasmodic	42138	**Vice-Consul**
Spasticos ...	42139	**Vicinity**
Spastojare	42140	Are there any payable mines in the vicinity
Spastriare	42141	The mine is in the vicinity of several paying mines
Spatalari ...	42142	There are no paying mines in the immediate vicinity
Spatalium	42143	In the immediate vicinity
Spathiform	42144	Have inspected several mines in the vicinity
Spatiator ...	42145	On account of the vicinity of
Spatjahr ...	42146	**Videlicet**
Spatsommer	42147	**View(s)**
Spatula ...	42148	With a view of
Spauroso ...	42149	In view of
Spavaldo ...	42150	The views of
Spaventare	42151	What view do you take with respect to
Spavined ...	42152	What is (are) ——'s view(s)
Spawned ...	42153	My (our) view of the matter is
Spazieren...	42154	——'s views are (that)
Spazierweg	42155	Cable your views respecting it
Spazietto ...	42156	What have you in view
Spaziosita...	42157	Have you anything immediately in view for
Spazzatojo	42158	Have nothing immediately in view
Spazzino ...	42159	The only thing in view at the present time is

Speakable...	42160	Take care to keep in view
Speared ...	42161	Continue to keep it (this) in view
Speargrass	42162	Take(s) a sanguine view of
Spearman...	42163	Do(es) not take a sanguine view of
Specchiajo	42164	In view of the necessity for (of)
Speciale ...	42165	Have you anything in view
Specialist ...	42166	Your view is
Speciarias...	42167	Quite agree with your views
Specifique...	42168	Will ascertain ——'s views
Specifying	42169	Will do my best to carry out your views
Specillum ...	42170	Will do my best to carry out ——'s views
Specioso ...	42171	Cannot carry out your views
Speckled ...	42172	Cannot carry out ——'s views
Speckseite	42173	—— has expressed to me his views, which are as follows
Specolante	42174	**Vigilance** (*See also* " Utmost.")
Specolo ...	42175	The utmost vigilance will be necessary to prevent
Spectabat...	42176	In spite of my (our) vigilance
Spectacled	42177	**Vigilant(ly)**
Spectandus	42178	**Vigorously**
Spectant ...	42179	Push ahead vigorously with
Spectator ...	42180	Proceeding vigorously
Spectatrix	42181	**Vigour**
Spectavit ...	42182	With the greatest possible vigour
Spectral ...	42183	Prosecute with vigour
Spectrum ...	42184	**Village**
Speculamen	42185	A small village near
Specular ...	42186	**Vindicate(d)**
Speculated	42187	To vindicate
Spedaletto	42188	Cannot vindicate himself
Spedaliere	42189	Must vindicate yourself
Spedalingo	42190	Cannot vindicate myself
Spedatura...	42191	Partly vindicated
Spediteur ...	42192	Was (were) fully vindicated
Speditivo ...	42193	**Vindication**
Speechify ...	42194	In vindication of
Speechless	42195	Pending complete vindication of
Speediest ...	42196	**Vindictive(ly)**
Speediness	42197	**Vindictiveness**
Spegmam...	42198	**Violate(d)**
Spegnersi...	42199	Do(es) not violate
Spegnibile	42200	Must not violate
Spegnitojo	42201	Shall not violate
Speichel ...	42202	**Violation** (*See also* " Faith.")
Speiler ...	42203	In direct violation of
Speisehaus	42204	**Violent(ly)**
Speiseol ...	42205	**Virtual(ly)**
Speiss ...	42206	Is a virtual admission of
Spelazzino	42207	It amounts virtually to
Spellbound	42208	Virtually there has been no progress whatever
Spelonca ...	42209	**Visible** (*See also* " Gold.")
Speltatis ...	42210	Contains visible gold
Speluncas...	42211	Do(es) not contain any visible gold
Spenden ...	42212	Visible gold
Spennato ...	42213	Visible throughout the stone
Spensaria ...	42214	Visible improvement
Spenzolato	42215	No visible improvement
Sperabile ...	42216	Is any improvement visible
Speranza ...	42217	**Visit** (*See also* "Deferred.")
Speravero...	42218	Visit to
Sperber ...	42219	During visit to

Spermaceti	42220	Expect a visit from
Spermatico	42221	Can you visit —— and give me (us) an idea as to the approxi-
Spermcells	42222	On my second visit [mate value of
Spermoil ...	42223	Cannot visit
Spernacem	42224	Cannot visit —— during this trip
Spernax ...	42225	Cannot visit —— to make report until
Spernitur ...	42226	Leave here to visit the —— property on ——
Speronato...	42227	Is now absent on a visit to
Sperrbaum	42228	Hope to visit
Sperrhaken	42229	May be able to visit
Sperrsitz ...	42230	When are you likely to visit
Sperticato...	42231	Shall not be able to visit —— in addition to ——.
Sperula ...	42232	Shall not be able to visit —— until —— owing to
Spesaccia ...	42233	Better defer visit until
Speserella...	42234	Better hasten visit to
Spetrare ...	42235	Has (have) not been able to visit
Spettativa	42236	Shall certainly visit
Spettatore	42237	When do you expect —— to visit you
Spettorato	42238	Do not expect —— to visit me
Speustica ...	42239	Expect —— to visit me about
Spezielta ...	42240	Will visit
Spezzatura	42241	Pending your visit to
Sphacelist...	42242	**Visited**
Sphacelus ...	42243	Have visited
Sphaeram...	42244	Have you visited
Sphagnum	42245	Have not visited
Spharisch...	42246	Was (were) visited
Sphenoid ...	42247	After I (we) have visited
Spherical ...	42248	Has (have) just visited
Spherique...	42249	As soon as I have visited
Spheroidal	42250	As soon as you have visited
Sphincter ...	42251	**Vital**
Sphingato	42252	I (we) consider it (this) vital
Sphingium	42253	I (we) do not consider it (this) vital
Sphondylus	42254	Do you consider it vital to
Sphragidem	42255	**Vitiate**
Sphragis ...	42256	To vitiate
Spiacente ...	42257	Do nothing to vitiate
Spiacibile ...	42258	Will not do anything to vitiate
Spiaggetta	42259	Nothing has been done to vitiate
Spiagione...	42260	Should you do so it will vitiate
Spiantato...	42261	It would vitiate the
Spiatrice ...	42262	**Vitiated**
Spicanardi	42263	The trial was vitiated through
Spicatum ...	42264	Which has vitiated
Spiccatura	42265	Has (have) not vitiated
Spiccicato...	42266	Has entirely vitiated the result(s)
Spiced ...	42267	**Vitreous**
Spiceum ...	42268	**Vitriol**
Spicewood	42269	Blue vitriol
Spicifer ...	42270	Green vitriol
Spicilegio ...	42271	**Void** (See also " Null.")
Spicknadel	42272	Has practically rendered the agreement void
Spicosity ...	42273	Does not the agreement thereby become void
Spiderish ...	42274	To prevent it (the ——) becoming void
Spidone ...	42275	To be void
Spiegativo	42276	To be void unless (by)
Spiegel ...	42277	**Voided**
Spiegelung	42278	Has (have) voided
Spieggiato	42279	Has (have) not voided

Spielbret ...	42280	**Volcanic**
Spielend ...	42281	Is (are) no doubt of volcanic origin
Spielkarte...	42282	Volcanic rocks
Spieltisch ...	42283	The whole country is of volcanic origin
Spiesser ...	42284	**Volt(s)** (*See also* "Dynamo.")
Spigatura...	42285	Pressure at dynamo terminals ―― volts
Spighetta...	42286	Between ―― and ―― volts
Spigionato	42287	Dynamo to give ―― volts [volts
Spigot ...	42288	With a speed of ―― revolutions per second we only get ――
Spikenard	42289	Volts at motor
Spilikins ...	42290	Volts in primary circuit
Spilletto ...	42291	Volts in secondary circuit
Spilungone	42292	What number of volts do you require
Spinacea ...	42293	Generating dynamo to give ―― volts
Spinally ...	42294	Motor requires ―― volts
Spindel ...	42295	**Voluntarily**
Spinelle ...	42296	**Volunteer(s)**
Spinescent	42297	**Vote(s)** (*See also* "Meeting," "Thank.")
Spinettajo	42298	Vote for
Spingarda	42299	Will you vote for me
Spinigera ...	42300	Will vote for you
Spinnaker	42301	Vote for the resolution in favour of
Spinnerin...	42302	To vote
Spinnhaus	42303	How many votes do you require
Spinnstube	42304	Require ―― votes
Spinosity ...	42305	Shareholders will probably vote unanimously for
Spinosulas	42306	―― votes were given for
Spinstress	42307	―― votes were given against
Spinther ...	42308	**Vote of Thanks** (*See also* "Thank.")
Spinturnix	42309	Vote of thanks to yourself passed with acclamation at Share-
Spiombare	42310	On the motion for a vote of thanks [holders meeting to-day
Spionicus ...	42311	Amendment to vote of thanks carried by majority of those
Spioniren ...	42312	**Vouch** [present
Spiovere ...	42313	To vouch (for)
Spipoletta	42314	Can you vouch for the accuracy (of)
Spirabo ...	42315	Can vouch for the accuracy (of)
Spiraculum	42316	Cannot vouch for its accuracy (the accuracy of ――)
Spiraglio ...	42317	Can certainly vouch for
Spiramento	42318	Can ―― vouch for
Spirifers ...	42319	―― can vouch for
Spirillum ...	42320	―― cannot vouch for
Spiritalis ...	42321	Consent(s) to vouch for
Spiritedly...	42322	Refuse(s) to vouch for
Spiritello ...	42323	**Vouched**
Spiritless ...	42324	Cannot be vouched for
Spiritual ...	42325	Can be vouched for
Spiritueux	42326	Is vouched for by ――
Spirometer	42327	Is not vouched for by ――
Spissatus ...	42328	**Voucher(s)**
Spissitudo	42329	Vouchers required for all payments
Spitefully...	42330	The vouchers for
Spitfire ...	42331	All the accounts must be accompanied by vouchers
Spithamas	42332	Accounts and vouchers mailed on
Spitter ...	42333	Have mailed accounts, vouchers will follow
Spittoon ...	42334	Shall bring necessary vouchers with me
Spitzbube...	42335	Bring vouchers
Spitzig ...	42336	Bring or send all necessary vouchers
Spitzkugel	42337	Vouchers for ―― not to hand, please mail
Spitzname	42338	Have you received the vouchers
Spitzsaule	42339	Have not received the vouchers

Spiumare ...	42340	Vouchers received on
Spizzeca ...	42341	Vouchers received are all in order
Splashy ...	42342	Have not been able to get the voucher for the item
Splayfoot ...	42343	Have obtained a voucher for each item
Splebeire ...	42344	Need a voucher for ——, please mail
Spleenish ...	42345	Have not received a voucher for
Spleissig ...	42346	**Voyage**
Splendens...	42347	The voyage has been a very pleasant one
Splendesco	42348	The voyage has occupied —— days
Splendet ...	42349	The voyage has been exceedingly rough
Splendidus	42350	Died on the voyage to
Splendour	42351	Has (have) been ordered sea voyage
Splenetic ...	42352	The voyage to —— occupies —— days
Spleniato ...	42353	Has (have) been much benefited by the voyage
Splenium ...	42354	Has (have) not been benefited much by the voyage
Splenology	42355	**Vulcanite**
Splintery ...	42356	If made of vulcanite
Splitterig ...	42357	To be of vulcanite
Splutter ...	42358	**Vulcanized** (*See also* " India Rubber.")
Spodestato	42359	To be of vulcanized India rubber
Spodumene	42360	**W**
Spogliante	42361	**Wages** (*See also* " Earn.")
Spogliarsi...	42362	What wages do you pay for
Spogliazza	42363	We are now paying —— wages
Spokesman	42364	The present rates of wages are
Spoletto ...	42365	In order to pay the men's wages
Spoliandus	42366	The wages sheet per month amounts to
Spoliarium	42367	The wages sheet for the current month amounts to
Spoliateur...	42368	Wages per day of twelve hours
Spoliation	42369	Wages per day of —— hours
Spoliatrix ...	42370	Competent miners earn —— per day wages
Spoliavit ...	42371	How much do the wages amount to
Spoliemur	42372	The wages amount to
Spolparsi ...	42373	Wages are very high
Spolverare	42374	Owing to the high rate of wages
Spondaggio	42375	On account of the high wages paid
Spondam ...	42376	Competent men command high wages
Spondeon...	42377	Competent men command —— wages per twelve hours
Spondulo ...	42378	Shall have to increase wages to retain men
Spondylion	42379	To reduce wages
Sponge ...	42380	Cannot safely reduce wages
Spongecake	42381	Can you not economise wages
Spongeous	42382	Can economise wages to the extent of
Spongieux	42383	Cannot economise wages
Sponginess	42384	Has (have) reduced wages
Spongiola...	42385	Wages are very low
Sponsal ...	42386	Expect wages will advance
Sponsorial	42387	Demand increased wages
Spontane ...	42388	**Waggons** (*See also* " Tub.")
Spontibus...	42389	Mine waggons
Spoonbill ..	42390	Steel waggons
Spoonfulls	42391	Waggons to carry
Spoonmeat	42392	Dimensions of waggons
Spoppato ...	42393	End tip waggons
Sporadic ...	42394	Side tip waggons
Sporadique	42395	Wheels and axles for waggons
Sporcizia ...	42396	Steel wheels for waggons
Sporogeus	42397	Steel frames for waggons
Sportella ...	42398	**Wait** (*See also* " Until.")
Sporting ...	42399	To wait

Sportively	42400	Wait for
Sportsman	42401	To wait for
Sportulat ...	42402	Wait until
Sposalizia...	42403	Do not wait
Spostrice ...	42404	Do not wait any longer
Spotestare	42405	How long can you (they) wait
Spotless ...	42406	How long shall I (we) have to wait
Spottelei ...	42407	Do you mean that I am (we are) to wait
Spottpreis,..	42408	Better wait
Spottweise	42409	Better wait until you receive
Spouseless	42410	Better not wait
Spouter ...	42411	Wait until you hear further
Spouting ...	42412	Will wait until I (we) hear further
Spracche ...	42413	No need to wait
Sprachart ...	42414	Refuse(s) to wait after
Spragging	42415	Consent(s) to wait until
Sprangato	42416	Wait for a few days more
Spreadeth...	42417	Will wait until
Sprecatore	42418	Will wait for
Sprecher ...	42419	Will wait until I (we) hear from you again
Spreizen ...	42420	Will wait at —— for instructions
Spremitura	42421	Must wait until
Sprengung	42422	Must wait for
Spretarsi ...	42423	Must wait until —— at this place
Spretionem	42424	Must wait until —— to give him (——) time to reply
Spretoris ...	42425	Shall I (we) wait
Sprezzante	42426	Not to wait
Sprillare ...	42427	Wait to see
Springbox...	42428	Will wait as long as I can
Springhalt	42429	Do you still advise me (us) to wait
Springhead	42430	Do not advise you to wait
Springtime	42431	Advise you strongly to wait
Spritsail ...	42432	Cannot wait
Sprode ...	42433	Cannot wait after
Spromesso	42434	Cannot —— wait
Spronante...	42435	Cannot wait indefinitely
Spronatore	42436	Am (are) compelled to wait for
Spronella ...	42437	You have done right not to wait
Spropiarsi	42438	Can you wait until
Sprossling	42439	Cannot wait until
Sprotetto ...	42440	Can wait until
Sprouted ...	42441	Do not wait too long
Sprovvisto	42442	How long shall I wait before
Sprucebeer	42443	Do not wait later than
Spruceness	42444	Shall I (we) wait at
Sprudeln ...	42445	You had better wait at —— until arrival of mail
Spruffare ...	42446	You had better wait at —— until arrival of cable
Spruhregen	42447	But do not wait for this
Spruneggio	42448	Had better wait until
Spruzaglia	42449	Cannot wait for written replies
Spruzzetto	42450	You have acted wrongly not to wait
Spucellare	42451	**Waited**
Spucknapf	42452	Has (have) waited since
Spugnitoso	42453	Has (have) waited for
Spugnuzza	42454	Has (have) not waited for
Spulezzare	42455	Why have you waited
Spulfass ...	42456	I (we) have waited on account of
Spulicht ...	42457	Should have waited
Spulwasser	42458	Should not have waited
Spulwurm...	42459	Have waited since —— for

Spumesco ...	42460	**Waiting**
Spuminess	42461	Waiting for
Spumosita	42462	Waiting because of
Spundloch	42463	Still waiting
Spuntatura	42464	Do not keep —— waiting
Spuntonata	42465	Are you waiting for anything, if so what
Spuntone ...	42466	Am (are) now waiting only for
Spunyarn	42467	Waiting for instructions
Spurcido ...	42468	Waiting for stores and supplies
Spurcitia ...	42469	Is it any good waiting longer
Spurhund	42470	Do you advise waiting longer
Spurrier ...	42471	Advise waiting a little longer
Sputacchio	42472	Do(es) not advise waiting longer
Sputapepe	42473	Unless you can advise waiting longer
Sputarola ...	42474	Whilst you are waiting for
Sputasenno	42475	Am (are) waiting for you (——) to
Sputation	42476	Is waiting for you to
Sputatondo	42477	Am (are) kept waiting on account of
Sputterer ...	42478	Why are you waiting
Sputtering	42479	Think you will do better by waiting
Spyboat ...	42480	Provided that you are not waiting
Spyglass ...	42481	Am still waiting to hear from you regarding
Squabbler	42482	I am waiting for —— to be sent me by mail (from ——)
Squabbling	42483	I am waiting for this (it) in order to
Squacchera	42484	I am only waiting for instructions to ——, please send by [cable
Squadrare...	42485	**Waive**
Squadrons	42486	On condition that you (——) will waive
Squagliato	42487	Will agree to waive
Squalentia	42488	Has (have) agreed to waive [standing, viz. :—
Squalidly ...	42489	Has (have) agreed to waive all rights on the following under-
Squallore ...	42490	Will on no account waive
Squamatim	42491	To waive all claims
Squammeux	42492	**Waived**
Squamoidal	42493	Has (have) waived
Squanderer	42494	Has (have) not waived
Squarcetto	42495	Has (have) —— waived
Squarcina...	42496	Has (have) waived the right to
Squareness	42497	**Waiver**
Squaresail	42498	The usual waiver clause
Squarish ...	42499	Insert waiver clause
Squarquojo	42500	On the understanding that waiver clause is added
Squarrosus	42501	**Wall(s)** (*See also* " Defined," " Footwall," " Hanging-wall,"
Squashing	42502	The wall still continues good [" Vein.")
Squashy ...	42503	Wall rock
Squasilio ...	42504	Well defined walls
Squatter ...	42505	Both walls are well defined and very strong
Squeak ...	42506	Retaining wall will cost
Squeaking	42507	Proceeding with erection of retaining wall
Squeamish	42508	Brick wall
Squelched...	42509	Stone wall
Squelette ...	42510	**Want(s)**
Squillato ...	42511	To want
Squille ...	42512	Want to
Squinanzia	42513	Do(es) not want
Squinteyed	42514	For want of
Squinting...	42515	A want of
Squireship	42516	No want of (for)
Squirrel ...	42517	Nothing is being done owing to want of [days
Squirter ...	42518	The want of foregoing will keep me (us) idle another ——
Squisito ...	42519	Want more precise reply

Squittire ...	42520	I may personally want you to
Squotolare	42521	How soon will you want
Staatsklug	42522	As soon as you really want
Staatsrath	42523	What will —— want if
Stabbiato ...	42524	What do you want (to)
Stabbing ...	42525	What does —— want (to)
Stabbiuolo	42526	Want mainly
Stabilezza...	42527	—— wants you (them) to
Stabilitas ...	42528	Am (are) much in want of
Stableboy ...	42529	My (our) chief want is:
Stableman	42530	Hardly seem(s) to know what they (he) want(s)
Stableness	42531	Want(s) too much
Stabulario	42532	Want(s) at once
Stabulum ...	42533	Not in want of anything
Staccetto ...	42534	Shall not want more than
Stachel ...	42535	In want of funds
Stackyard...	42536	In want of supplies
Stacula ...	42537	Provided that you do not want
Staderajo ...	42538	Provided that you are in want of
Staderina ...	42539	Owing to a (the) want of
Stadialio ...	42540	Much in want of
Stadtchen...	42541	How much (many) shall you want
Stadtisch ...	42542	Understand that you want
Stadtleute	42543	Unless you particularly want
Stadtmauer	42544	Regret —— cannot do what you want
Stadtrecht	42545	**Wanted**
Stadtwage	42546	Wanted —— to
Staffare ...	42547	I am wanted at
Staffette ...	42548	Wanted you to
Staffhead ...	42549	Wanted me (us) to
Staffilata ...	42550	Is (are) absolutely wanted
Stafisagra	42551	Will be wanted as soon as
Stagbeetle	42552	Will be wanted almost immediately
Stagecoach	42553	Will not be wanted unless
Stageplay ...	42554	Is (are) urgently wanted
Stageyness	42555	What was it, that —— wanted
Staggering	42556	What was it that you wanted —— to do
Staggitore	42557	I (we) wanted
Stagiaire ...	42558	Is (are) not now wanted
Stagliato ...	42559	You are very much wanted at
Stagnant ...	42560	—— is very much wanted
Stagnation	42561	Was not what was wanted
Stagnuolo	42562	Unlikely to be wanted until
Stagonias ...	42563	Not wanted in the least
Stahlern ...	42564	Further particulars much wanted
Stahlstick	42565	Cable precisely what is wanted
Stahlwaare	42566	Provided you are not wanted
Staircase ...	42567	As soon as it is (they are) wanted
Stairrod ...	42568	Understood that you wanted
Stalactite ...	42569	What was it (——) wanted for
Stalagmias	42570	Was (were) wanted
Stalemate...	42571	**Wanting**
Stalked ...	42572	Still wanting
Stalking ...	42573	What is wanting
Stallage ...	42574	Nothing wanting
Stalletta ...	42575	**War**
Stalliere ...	42576	There is considerable prospect of war between —— and ——
Stallified ...	42577	Since the time of the war
Stalljunge	42578	On account of the war
Stalwart ...	42579	What prospect is there of war

Stamajuolo	42580	There seems very little prospect of war
Stambecco	42581	War is considered imminent
Staminal ...	42582	The war is practically at an end
Stamineus	42583	On account of war rumours
Stammbaum	42584	War has been declared between
Stammerer	42585	Should war break out
Stammgut	42586	War will probably continue until
Stammtafel	42587	Fully prepared in the event of war breaking out (to)
Stampabile	42588	**Warehouse**
Stampatore	42589	In warehouse at
Stampeded	42590	Ex warehouse
Stancarsi ...	42591	Warehouse rent
Stanchetto	42592	**Warily**
Stanchion...	42593	**Warm**
Standard ...	42594	**Warmly**
Standhaft	42595	Warmly approve(s) of
Standort ...	42596	**Warn**
Standpoint	42597	To warn
Standrecht	42598	Shall I (we) warn
Standstill...	42599	Better warn
Stangonata	42600	Better not warn
Stanhope ...	42601	Please warn —— that (against)
Stankern ...	42602	Will warn —— against
Stannarius	42603	This is only just to warn you
Stanniol ...	42604	Warn you (——) seriously that
Stannous ...	42605	Only wished to warn you
Stanzetta ...	42606	**Warned**
Stanziante	42607	Has (have) warned
Stanzibolo	42608	Has (have) not warned
Staphyloma	42609	Has (have) been repeatedly warned
Staples ...	42610	Was (were) not warned
Starboard...	42611	Advise you (——) to be warned in time
Starcher ...	42612	**Warning**
Starchness	42613	**Warrant**
Starfish ...	42614	Dividend warrant
Stargazer ...	42615	Dividend warrant for —— mailed on
Starkemehl	42616	Have not received any dividend warrant
Starkend ...	42617	Dividend warrant received
Starlight ...	42618	There is really no warrant for
Starlike ...	42619	Is there sufficient warrant for
Starnutato	42620	Think there is sufficient warrant for
Starostia ...	42621	Do not think there is sufficient warrant for
Starrkopf ...	42622	To warrant
Starters ...	42623	Sufficient to warrant
Startlish ...	42624	Not sufficient to warrant
Starvation	42625	Can warrant
Starveling	42626	Cannot warrant
Starwort ...	42627	Refuse(s) to warrant
Statedly ...	42628	Is there sufficient to warrant further expenditure [penny
Statepaper	42629	There is not sufficient to warrant the expenditure of a single
Stateroom...	42630	Consider there is sufficient to warrant the expenditure of
Statetrial ...	42631	In the absence of anything to warrant
Stathouder	42632	What is there to warrant
Staticulum	42633	Is there sufficient development since —— to warrant
Statigkeit	42634	There is sufficient development to warrant
Statique ...	42635	There is not sufficient development to warrant
Statisch ...	42636	Present indications do not warrant
Statistic ...	42637	Do present indications warrant you
Statoder ...	42638	I (we) do not think there is sufficient to warrant
⁻atthaft ...	42639	There is ample —— to warrant

Statuaccia	42640	**Warranted** (*See also* "Guarantee.")
Statuarius	42641	Provided that it is (they are) warranted
Statuesque	42642	Is it (are they) warranted
Statuetta ...	42643	Is (are) warranted
Statuliber...	42644	Is (are) not warranted
Statumen...	42645	Warranted similar to
Statuminor	42646	**Warrantee**
Statutable	42647	**Warranty**
Statutory ...	42648	**Was** (*See also* "Were.")
Statutum ...	42649	Was it a (an)
Staubchen	42650	It was a (an)
Staubern ...	42651	It was not a (an)
Stavernare	42652	Always was
Staybolt ...	42653	Never was
Staylace ...	42654	Was formerly
Staymaker	42655	I was
Staysails ...	42656	I was not
Staytackle	42657	Until I was certain
Stazzatura	42658	As soon as I was (we were) certain
Stazzonare	42659	He was
Stealthily...	42660	Was he
Steamcocks	42661	He was not
Steamship	42662	Was he not
Stearique ...	42663	**Wash(ed)**
Steatite ...	42664	Washed ore
Steccaja ...	42665	Thoroughly washed
Stecconato	42666	**Washer(s)**
Steckbrief...	42667	Steel washers
Stecken ...	42668	**Washing** (*See also* "Alluvial," "Hydraulic.")
Steeliness...	42669	When do you expect to commence washing
Steelyard ...	42670	Expect to begin washing within the next few days
Steepled ...	42671	Expect to begin washing not later than
Steerage ...	42672	As soon as I (we) begin washing
Steersman	42673	To enable me (us) to begin washing
Stegreif ...	42674	Before I (we) start washing
Stehend ...	42675	You had better try washing
Steigbugel	42676	Any washing
Steigern ...	42677	By washing
Steigung ...	42678	In washing
Steinalt ...	42679	Washing for [better
Steinbild ...	42680	Washing not so good as expected, next one promises much
Steindruck	42681	After washing —— hours, we have cleaned up —— value, from
Steineiche	42682	**Waste** [which you must deduct expenses ——
Steingut ...	42683	The waste
Steinhart ...	42684	The waste in (of)
Steinigen ...	42685	A deplorable waste of
Steinmetz...	42686	There has been a great deal of waste
Steinnuss...	42687	To avoid any waste of time
Steinsalz ...	42688	There has been a considerable waste of time
Steinwurf...	42689	Shall not waste any time
Stellaria ...	42690	Do not waste a moment
Stellatura...	42691	Do not waste any more time
Stellifero ...	42692	There has been no waste of time up to the present
Stellulate ...	42693	Would only be a waste of time
Stelluzz ...	42694	Would not be an entire waste of time, because
Stelzfuss ...	42695	To diminish waste of
Stempel ...	42696	Will do all I (we) can to lessen the waste of
Stemperato	42697	Has (have) caused a considerable waste of
Stench ...	42698	Considerable waste of
Stendente...	42699	Waste of time

Stenditojo	42700	**Waste** of money
Stenebrare	42701	Waste heaps
Stentorian	42702	Waste rock
Stenuativo	42703	The removal of the waste rock
Stepfather	42704	The waste amounts to
Stepmother	42705	There is very little avoidable waste
Steppdecke	42706	A great waste of
Steppnaht	42707	Do not allow any waste of
Steppstich	42708	Will not allow any waste of
Stepson ...	42709	Cotton waste
Stepstone...	42710	**Wasteful**
Sterbefall...	42711	**Wasting**
Sterbejahr	42712	If wasting
Sterblich ...	42713	Think you are only wasting your time
Stercoreus	42714	So long as you are (—— is) not wasting money
Sterculius...	42715	We shall only be wasting money
Stereotype	42716	Not wasting
Stericula ...	42717	**Watch**
Sterilesco ...	42718	To watch
Sterilezza...	42719	Watch for
Sterilito ...	42720	Continue to watch
Sterilized ...	42721	Will continue to watch
Sterminio...	42722	Better keep a strict watch on
Sternchase	42723	Am (are) keeping a watch on
Sternchen...	42724	Is keeping a watch on
Sternendus	42725	Watch for any indication of
Sternness ...	42726	Watch and report any movement of (in)
Sternuens...	42727	Watch —— and report
Sterntutat ...	42728	Watch what he (——) may do
Sternway ...	42729	Watch my (our) interests
Stertorous	42730	I (we) will watch your interests
Stersetto ...	42731	Will watch over our interests meanwhile
Stethoskop	42732	Keep a close watch on all matters concerning
Steuerbar ...	42733	On the watch for
Steuermann	42734	**Watched**
Stewing ...	42735	Must be carefully watched
Stewpan ...	42736	Is (are) being well watched
Stiacciata...	42737	Unless it is (they are) watched
Stiamazzo	42738	**Watchful(ness)**
Stiavina ...	42739	In spite of my (our) watchfulness
Stibadium	42740	Suggest greatest possible watchfulness
Stibiato ...	42741	**Watching**
Stibinus ...	42742	I am (we are) watching your interests
Sticarum ...	42743	Watching every opportunity
Stichblatt...	42744	**Watchman(men)**
Stichwort...	42745	The only expense will be that of a watchman on the property
Stickerin ...	42746	Have engaged —— extra watchman(men)
Stickiness...	42747	Have now —— watchmen
Stickler ...	42748	**Water** (*See also* " Fall," " Flow," " Flume," " Fork," " Gauge," [" Hydraulic," " Miners' Inches," " Pump," " River," " Scarce," [" Struck," &c.)
Stickluft ...	42749	Water for
Stidionata	42750	Water for concentrating purposes
Stiefel ...	42751	Water for milling purposes
Stiefkind ...	42752	We can easily keep the water under
Stiefvater ...	42753	The water is gaining upon us
Stieglitz ...	42754	We are now straining everything in our efforts to keep the [water under
Stiffen ...	42755	Would give us a head of water of —— feet
Stiffness ...	42756	The upper workings are now completely drained of water
Stificare ...	42757	Is the water out of
Stifling ...	42758	The water is now out of

[714]

Stiftsdame	42759	Is the water now out of the —— shaft
Stiftsherr ...	42760	The water is now out of the —— shaft
Stiftung ...	42761	The shaft was drained of water on ——
Stigmaria...	42762	I (we) doubt whether we shall be able to cope with the water
Stigmosus	42763	Shall commence at once to get the water out of the lower work-
Stignere ...	42764	The water in the shaft is now up to within —— feet of [ings
Stilettato ...	42765	The water is gaining on the pumps
Stiliforme...	42766	The pumps are gaining on the water
Stillarium	42767	When do you expect the workings to be free from water
Stillarsi ...	42768	When do you expect to have the lower workings free from water
Stillatore ...	42769	Is (are) now free from water
Stillborn ...	42770	Is (are) now full of water
Stillend ...	42771	Expect the mine will be free from water on or about ——
Stillroom ...	42772	Sufficient water to
Stimabile ...	42773	Not sufficient water to
Stimatrice	42774	Barely sufficient water for
Stimazione	42775	Have you sufficient water for
Stimmfahig	42776	Water is very scarce
Stimmung .	42777	An abundance of water for
Stimolato ...	42778	For hot water
Stimulant...	42779	For cold water
Stimuleus...	42780	Plenty of water for
Stincatura	42781	Is the mine full of water
Stinger ...	42782	It is useless to go to —— unless the mine is free from water
Stingily ...	42788	Water raised —— gallons
Stinginess	42784	Ample water supply for development of electric energy
Stinguere ...	42785	Water is scarce from —— to —— [workings
Stiniere ...	42786	Deep tunnel is draining water from all parts of the upper
Stinkpot ...	42787	The (this) —— level is not yet free from water
Stinkstone	42788	The (this) —— shaft is not yet free from water
Stioppo ...	42789	When will you get the water out of —— level
Stipatus ...	42790	As soon as the water is out of —— level
Stipendary	42791	We are prevented by water in the shaft
Stipettajo...	42792	We have been very short of water during the summer
Stipidire ...	42793	Owing to the mine being full of water
Stippling ...	42794	The water is gradually lessening
Stipticus ...	42795	We have now only —— inches of water
Stipularis...	42796	The water from the mine is very corrosive
Stiratura ...	42797	The water from the mine cannot be utilised for
Stirnhaar ...	42798	Full of water
Stirpame ...	42799	Have lowered the water to
Stirpatore...	42800	Gallons of water per twenty-four hours [hours
Stirpesco ...	42801	We are now pumping —— gallons of water per twenty-four
Stirpitus ...	42802	Heavy influx of water; all underground operations stopped
Stirrer ...	42808	Is water out of No. —— level
Stitching ...	42804	Free from water
Stitcita ...	42805	There can be no trouble with water
Stithy ...	42806	If we are to control the water
Stiticuzzo...	42807	We can get —— miners' inches with a head of —— feet
Stiumoso ...	42808	I am of opinion that the greatest portion of surface water can
Stivalarsi ...	42809	Water to run the [be kept above the base of —— level
Stivaletto ...	42810	**Water, cost of** (*See also* "Water supply.")
Stivamento	42811	Water costs —— per miners' inch
Stlatarius...	42812	Ample water can be obtained at a cost of —— per miners' inch
Stlembus ...	42813	**Water, depth of**
Stlopus ...	42814	What depth of water have you at (in)
Stobern ...	42815	The present depth of water at (in) —— is
Stocchetto	42816	What is the depth of water in the shaft
Stochern ...	42817	The depth of water in the shaft is now —— feet
Stockaded...	42818	**Water ditch**

Stockblind	42819	A ditch to bring in water from —— would cost ——
Stockdegen	42820	What would be the cost of a ditch to bring in the water from
Stockdove...	42821	**Watered** [——
Stockdumm	42822	Well watered
Stockfish ...	42823	The property is well watered
Stockhaus	42824	**Waterfall**
Stockings ...	42825	**Water level**
Stockstill ...	42826	What is the water level
Stocktaub...	42827	Above the water level
Stofflich	42828	Below the water level
Stogliere ...	42829	At the water level
Stoically ...	42830	From the water level in
Stoicism ...	42831	Have lowered the water level to
Stolidetto...	42832	The general water level of the country
Stolidity ...	42833	**Water pipe line** [from ——
Stolpern ...	42834	There is a water pipe line —— yards which brings in the water
Stolziren ...	42835	Can construct a water pipe line to bring in the water from [——. Estimate cost at ——
Stomacante	42836	The water pipe line is in a very bad state of repair
Stomacato	42837	What would it cost to repair the water pipe line
Stomachans	42838	Estimate cost of repairing water pipe line at ——
Stomachico	42839	**Water power** (*See also* "Water supply.")
Stomacuzzo	42840	Pay attention to the question of water power
Stomalgia...	42841	Will deal with the water power question at an early date
Stomatice...	42842	What is the volume of water available for power purposes
Stoneaxe ...	42843	The available water power is sufficient for all present demands
Stoneblind	42844	There is water power sufficient for (to)
Stonechat...	42845	There is water power sufficient to run —— stamps
Stonecrop...	42846	There is water power sufficient to run ——, in addition to
Stonefruit...	42847	Water for power purposes [—— stamps
Stonepitch	42848	I (we) have contracted for water power
Stoneyness	42849	Require full particulars as to water power
Stooper ...	42850	My letter dated ——, gives full particulars as to water power
Stoopingly	42851	The water obtainable for power purposes is approximately —— [gallons per minute ; height of fall —— feet
Stopcock ...	42852	Water power available is —— gallons per minute ; height of
Stopgap ...	42853	Water power available is theoretically —— h.p. [fall —— feet
Stoppaccio	42854	Water for power purposes does not materially diminish in the
Stoppage ...	42855	Water power is not available in the dry season [dry season
Stoppeln ...	42856	Water power varies from —— h.p. available in the wet season, [to —— h.p. in the dry season
Stoppinare	42857	An expenditure of —— is necessary for the construction of [race before water power can be utilised
Stoppione...	42858	An expenditure of —— is necessary for the construction of [pipe line before water power can be utilised
Stopwatch	42859	The water power could conveniently be used for working water [wheel
Storax ...	42860	The water power could conveniently be used for working turbine
Storcersi ...	42861	The water power could conveniently be used for working
Storditivo...	42862	**Waterproof** [hydraulic pressure engine
Storiella ...	42863	**Water question**
Storievole...	42864	Pending settlement of the water question
Storlomia...	42865	**Water rights**
Stormbeat	42866	Have secured water rights
Stormcones	42867	Have you legally secured water rights to company
Storminess	42868	It will be necessary to secure the water rights to
Stornello ...	42869	Now engaged on survey for water rights
Storrato ...	42870	When will you complete survey for water rights
Storrogen...	42871	Will complete survey for water rights within —— days
Stortetta ...	42872	Have completed survey for water rights

Stortilato ...	42873	Unless you secure water rights
Stossweise	42874	Are we running any risk as to water rights
Stoutly ...	42875	Not running any risk as to water rights
Stoutness ...	42876	Unless —— can secure the necessary water rights [risk of
Stover ...	42877	Unless —— can secure water rights there will be considerable
Stoviglie ...	42878	Have secured water rights; there will be no possible chance of [future litigation

Water supply (See also " Water power.")

Stowaway	42879	There is a good supply of water for
Strabere ...	42880	There is a good supply of water for
Strabism ...	42881	Have arranged for a supply of water [miles
Strabuono	42882	There is an ample supply of water at ——, a distance of ——
Straccale ...	42883	There is an ample supply of water on the property
Stracciare ...	42884	There is an abundant water supply
Stracorso ...	42885	There is a plentiful supply of water all the year round
Stracotato	42886	There is a plentiful supply of water from —— to —— months [both inclusive
Stradella ...	42887	What would it cost to obtain a sufficient supply of water (to)
Stradiotto...	42888	At what cost can you obtain necessary water supply and within
Stradoppio	42889	There is generally an abundant water supply [what time
Straduzza	42890	The water has increased, but the supply is still short
Strafatto ...	42891	An ample supply of water can readily be obtained at
Strafelato	42892	Water supply greatly increased
Straffheit ...	42893	Water supply diminishing
Straflos ...	42894	Water supply greatly decreased

Water tank

Straforare...	42895	
Straggler ...	42896	What is the capacity of water tank
Straglio ...	42897	Shall need to construct a new water tank
Stragrave ...	42898	Pending repairs to water tank
Stragula ...	42899	We ought to have water tank capacity for at least ——

Water, volume of

Strahlen ...	42900	
Strainable	42901	What is the volume of water at
Straitly ...	42902	Ascertain the volume of water in winter
Straitness...	42903	The volume of water in winter is
Straletto ...	42904	Ascertain the volume of water in summer
Stralunato	42905	The volume of water in summer is
Stramaturo	42906	The volume of water is increasing
Strambello	42907	The volume of water is still steadily increasing
Stramentum	42908	What is the volume of water flowing from (in)

Water, want of

Stramineus	42909	
Strampeln	42910	Owing to want of water [is only sufficient to last —— days
Stranaccio	42911	Expect I (we) shall have to stop for want of water. There
Strandgut	42912	There is no want of water
Straneare ...	42913	Suspended for want of water
Stranguria	42914	Entirely stopped since —— for want of water
Stranianza	42915	For want of water
Stranuccio	42916	Great want of water

Waterway

Strapagato	42917	

Water-wheel(s) (See also " Turbine.")

Strappata...	42918	
Strapping	42919	Should be thoroughly acquainted with the erection of water-
Strapunto...	42920	Shall put up a water-wheel at [wheels
Strasapere	42921	An overshot water-wheel
Strascino ...	42922	An undershot water-wheel
Stratagem	42923	Pelton water-wheel
Stratified ...	42924	Pelton water-wheel —— feet diameter
Stratiotes ...	42925	Leffel turbine water-wheel
Strattezza...	42926	Owing to an accident at the main water-wheel
Stravasato	42927	Put in a water-wheel for the purpose of

Way (See also " Go.")

Stravedere	42928	
Stravolto ...	42929	On the way out
Strawberry	42930	One way out of the difficulty would be (to)

WAY (continued).

Strawhat ...	42931	The only way out of the difficulty
Strayed ...	42932	If nothing can be done in this way (in the way of ——)
Straziato ...	42933	In the regular way.
Streaking ...	42934	Same way as before
Streamer ...	42935	Can you pass —— on your way to
Streamlet ...	42936	I shall pass —— on my way to
Strebbiare	42937	Shall not pass —— on my way to
Streben	42938	The only way to get to the property (mine) is via ——
Strebligo ...	42939	By way of
Streetdoor	42940	Is it in your way
Strefolare...	42941	It is not in my way
Stregaccia...	42942	Can you put anything in my way
Stregheria	42943	Cannot put anything in your way at this moment
Streichen ...	42944	Which do you consider the best way
Streiferei ...	42945	The best way would I think be to
Streitaxt ...	42946	The way generally adopted is
Stremato ...	42947	The most certain way is to
Strengthen	42948	Will be the easiest way to go
Strenuitas	42949	Whichever is the best way
Strenuous...	42950	Go the shortest way you can
Streperus ...	42951	Which is the best way to go
Strepidire	42952	Is the best way to
Strepitans	42953	**We**
Strepitato	42954	We are
Stress ...	42955	We are not
Strettoino...	42956	Are we to
Strettoja ...	42957	If we are to
Streusand...	42958	We authorize
Striated ...	42959	We do
Striation ...	42960	We do not
Stribbuire...	42961	We have
Stribiligo ...	42962	We have not
Strickerin...	42963	We must
Strictim ...	42964	We must not
Strictures	42965	We shall
Stridevole...	42966	Shall we
Stridoris ...	42967	We will
Stridulo ...	42968	We will not
Striegel ...	42969	**Weak**
Strigatore...	42970	Still very weak
Strigium ...	42971	**Weaken**
Strigliare ...	42972	Do nothing to weaken
Strigosus ...	42973	**Weakened**
Strikingly	42974	My (our) position has been very much weakened by
Strillato ...	42975	Not at all weakened
Stringless	42976	**Wealden**
Strionico ...	42977	**Wealth(y)**
Stripling ...	42978	Is (are) reported to be wealthy
Striscetta...	42979	The reverse of wealthy
Strisciato ...	42980	Very wealthy
Stritolare ...	42981	Formerly very wealthy
Striver ...	42982	Are anything but wealthy at this time
Strivingly...	42983	Known to me (us) as being wealthy
Strobilus ...	42984	In the hands of very wealthy people
Strofinare...	42985	One or two wealthy people are connected with it
Strohdecke	42986	A very wealthy syndicate
Strohhalm	42987	Entirely in the hands of wealthy people
Stroked ...	42988	**Wear**
Strokeoar...	42989	Wear and tear
Stroking ...	42990	Inclusive of wear and tear

Strolagare	42991	Exclusive of wear and tear
Strolch ...	42992	Fair wear and tear
Stroller ...	42993	Allowance to cover wear and tear
Stromauf ...	42994	Have allowed —— for wear and tear
Stromenge	42995	What have you allowed for wear and tear
Stromfall ...	42996	No allowance has been made for wear and tear
Strommitte	42997	**Weather** (*See also* "Frost," "Ice," "Snow," "Thermo-
Stroncato ...	42998	Splendid weather for [meter," &c.)
Stronghold	42999	Weather not at all favourable for
Strongset ...	43000	Weather altogether unsettled
Strongyles	**43001**	During the winter weather
Strophe ...	43002	During the summer weather
Strophium	43003	Until weather prevents
Strosciare...	43004	Whilst the weather will not admit of surface operations
Strozzule ...	43005	The weather is now exceedingly cold
Structilis ...	43006	The weather is now very severe
Structural	43007	The weather is now very warm
Struggente	43008	Cannot leave during the present severe weather
Straggersi	43009	Cannot travel while present weather lasts
Strumatica	43010	On account of sudden and severe changes of the weather
Strumento	43011	As soon as the weather changes
Strumous...	43012	As soon as the weather permits
Struppig ...	43013	There is every indication of a favourable change in the weather
Strutheum	43014	There is every indication of the present weather lasting
Struttura ...	43015	Impossible during the present weather
Struzione ...	43016	Very bad weather
Strychnine	43017	During the present bad weather
Stubbornly	43018	If the present bad weather continues
Stuccatore	43019	The first fine weather
Stucchente	43020	Should present fine weather continue
Stuccoed ...	43021	The weather has been unusually good
Stuckchen	43022	The weather is much better
Stuckkugel	43023	Owing to the state of the weather
Stuckwerk	43024	We have already wintry weather
Student ...	43025	Fair weather
Studhorse	43026	Every prospect of good weather
Studiarsi	43027	Change of weather
Studiatore	43028	Before commencement of cold weather
Studiedly...	43029	Owing to the severity of the weather
Studieux ...	43030	Severe weather lasts for —— months of the year
Studiolino	43031	**Wednesday**
Studying ...	43032	Every Wednesday
Stufatura...	43033	Every alternate Wednesday
Stuhlgang	43034	Last Wednesday
Stultified ...	43035	Next Wednesday
Stultizia ...	43036	Next Wednesday week
Stumbling	43037	On Wednesday
Stummel ...	43038	On Wednesday morning
Stummheit	43039	On Wednesday afternoon
Stumpfnase	43040	On Wednesday night
Stumpy ...	43041	During Wednesday
Stunden ...	43042	During Wednesday night
Stundlich...	43043	—— Wednesday in each month
Stuonante	43044	About Wednesday week
Stuparius...	43045	**Week(s)** (*See also* "Day," "Fortnight," "Month.")
Stupefacio	43046	Per week
Stupefait ...	43047	During the present week
Stupefarsi	43048	During next week
Stupendous	43049	During the week after next
Stupidezza	43050	Last week

Stupidity ...	43051	During the past week
Stupifier ...	43052	Next week
Stupratore	43053	The week after next
Sturbanza	43054	For the week ending
Sturbatore	43055	This week
Sturdily ...	43056	One week
Sturdiness	43057	Two weeks
Sturgeon ...	43058	Three weeks
Sturmhaube	43059	Four weeks
Sturmwind	43060	Five weeks
Stutzig ...	43061	Six weeks
Stuzzicare	43062	Seven weeks
Stygian ...	43063	Eight weeks
Stylet ...	43064	Nine weeks
Stylishly ...	43065	Ten weeks
Styloidal ...	43066	Eleven weeks
Stypteria ...	43067	Twelve weeks
Stypticity...	43068	Within the next week
Stypticus ...	43069	Within —— weeks from date
Suadebat ...	43070	For —— weeks
Suadendus	43071	In —— weeks
Suadetur ...	43072	About a week
Suadir ...	43073	About the beginning of next week
Suadrevole	43074	About the end of next week
Suasible ...	43075	Regularly each week
Suasion ...	43076	Will require at least one week
Suasively...	43077	Will require several weeks more
Suasorio ...	43078	Should be accomplished in about a week
Suasurus ...	43079	Past —— weeks
Suavemente	43080	Before the end of the present week
Suavezza ...	43081	**Weekly**
Suaviator...	43082	Required weekly
Suavidad ...	43083	Weekly statement
Suavidicus	43084	Weekly statement not yet received
Suavillum	43085	Weekly report
Suavitudo...	43086	**Weigh**
Suavizador	43087	To weigh
Subaccuso	43088	Please weigh
Subacetate	43089	No need to weigh
Subacido ...	43090	Weigh again
Subacrid ...	43091	Shall I (we) weigh
Subacturus	43092	Weigh the matter over carefully
Subadjuva	43093	**Weighbridge**
Subalbico...	43094	**Weighed**
Subalpinus	43095	Must be re-weighed
Subaltern ...	43096	Should be weighed very accurately
Subamarus	43097	Has (have) been weighed again and found to be quite correct
Subaqueous	43098	Each one was weighed separately
Subaquilus	43099	Was it (were they) weighed
Subarator...	43100	Was (were) weighed
Subaresco...	43101	Was (were) not weighed, only estimated
Subarguto	43102	Shall be weighed on receipt
Subasta ...	43103	Please have —— weighed on receipt
Subballio ...	43104	Have been weighed and found correct
Subbiare ...	43105	Have weighed the matter over very carefully
Subbietta...	43106	**Weighing**
Subbillare	43107	Weighing over
Subbiloso...	43108	Weighing less than
Subbissato	43109	**Weight(s)** (*See also* "Exceed" and Table at end.)
Subcantor	43110	Dead weight

Subcentral	43111	What is the correct weight (of)
Subcerno ...	43112	The correct weight is
Subcilles ...	43113	The correct weight is —— pounds
Subcingo ...	43114	All weights are given in pounds
Subclavero	43115	All weights are given in tons of 2,240 pounds
Subcoactus	43116	All weights are given in
Subconcave	43117	Provided that the weight(s) do(es) not exceed
Subcrudus	43118	Can take any weight up to
Subcustos	43119	Were the weights given gross or net
Subcutaneo	43120	The weight(s) given was (were) gross
Subdean ...	43121	The weight(s) given was (were) net
Subdeanery	43122	What is the average weight of
Subdebilis	43123	The average weight of —— is
Subdecano	43124	The average weight is about
Subdecuplo	43125	Short weight
Subdelegar	43126	Total weight
Subdiacono	43127	Send memorandum of weights
Subdialis ...	43128	Net weight
Subdito ...	43129	Gross weight
Subdivider	43130	Estimated weight
Subdoctus	43131	**Welcome**
Subduable	43132	Was most welcome
Subduced...	43133	Would be very welcome
Subduer ...	43134	**Weld**
Subduing...	43135	Must weld easily
Subdulcis...	43136	To weld
Subduple ...	43137	**Welding**
Subedit ...	43138	Electric welding plant
Subediting	43139	**Well**
Subentrare	43140	Do you think it is well to do this
Suberic ...	43141	Do not think it would be well
Suberous ...	43142	I (we) think it would be just as well to
Subeundus	43143	It would certainly be just as well
Subfibulo ...	43144	As well as
Subflavus...	43145	Not so well as
Subfletar ...	43146	When will —— be well enough to (for)
Subfrigide	43147	Expect(s) to be sufficiently well to travel by
Subgenus...	43148	Afraid —— will not be sufficiently well to leave before
Subgrandis	43149	Sufficiently well for
Subgrunda	43150	As soon as —— is sufficiently well (to)
Subgutto ...	43151	Well enough for the present
Subhumidus	43152	Is (are) —— well known to you (——)
Subiculum	43153	Very well known
Subiente ...	43154	Very well indeed
Subigendus	43155	Doing very well
Subigito ...	43156	Not doing very well
Subimpetro	43157	Will do perfectly well
Subinanio	43158	**Well(s)**
Subinfero...	43159	From a well
Subintroeo	43160	From wells
Subinvideo	43161	It will be necessary to sink a well
Subirascor	43162	From a well —— feet deep
Subitaneus	43163	A well has been sunk —— feet
Subitanza...	43164	A well has been sunk —— feet without finding any water
Subjacent...	43165	From the wells on the property
Subjecion...	43166	There is an abundance of water from the wells
Subjecting	43167	Can you not obtain water by a well
Subjektiv...	43168	Several wells have already been sunk
Subjiciens	43169	An artesian well
Subjoin ...	43170	Shall require to sink artesian well for water supply

Subjonctif	43171	Have ample supply of water from artesian well(s)
Subjugalis	43172	**Well boring machinery**
Subjugium	43173	Complete plant of well boring machinery, to include
Subjuntivo	43174	**Went**
Sublabro ...	43175	Went on
Sublapsus	43176	Went to
Sublation	43177	Went up
Sublaturus	43178	Went down
Sublevatio	43179	Went out
Sublicius ...	43180	Went in
Sublimado	43181	As soon as —— went
Sublime ...	43182	**Were** (*See also* " Was.")
Sublimidad	43183	We were
Sublimiter	43184	We were not
Sublinitus	43185	They were
Sublivesco	43186	They were not
Sublucanus	43187	Were you (they)
Sublunary	43188	What were we to
Sublustris	43189	We were to
Subluvies ...	43190	We were not to
Submarine	43191	Were we to
Submergor	43192	**West** (*See also* " East.")
Subminia ...	43193	—— degrees west of north
Submittens	43194	Due east and west
Submoneor	43195	West of
Submorosus	43196	To the west of
Submovetur	43197	West vein (lode) (reef)
Subnascens	43198	West drift
Subnector	43199	West crosscut
Subniscus	43200	West shaft
Subnormal	43201	West wall
Subnotatio	43202	West winze
Subnubilus	43203	West working(s)
Suboctuplo	43204	In the west end
Subodiosus	43205	Driving west
Subodoror	43206	Driving east and west
Suboffendo	43207	Now-going west
Subordinar	43208	West end line
Subornatus	43209	West side line
Suborner ...	43210	West part of the mine (property)
Suborniens	43211	Turns a little to the west
Suboxide ...	43212	Coming in from the west
Subpallide	43213	Dipping west
Subpinguis	43214	Lying to the west
Subpolar ...	43215	**Westerly**
Subrancus	43216	In a westerly direction
Subremigo	43217	Runs westerly
Subrenalis	43218	Has a westerly trend
Subrepcion	43219	The most westerly
Subreptive	43220	**Wet**
Subrigens...	43221	Exceedingly wet
Subripior ...	43222	Not quite so wet as before
Subrogar ...	43223	Is more wet
Subrotatus	43224	Wet crushing plant
Subruber ...	43225	At wet mill
Subrutilus	43226	Through becoming wet
Subsalts ...	43227	Is it a wet process
Subsanno...	43228	It is a wet process
Subscribir	43229	It is not a wet process
Subsecivus	43230	**Wharf(ves)**

Subsellium	43231	On the wharf
Subsentio ...	43232	Free on wharf ——
Subsequens	43233	Free ex wharf
Subserve ...	43234	Wharf dues
Subsidence	43235	Shall require to build a wharf at estimated cost of ——
Subsidiary	43236	Can come alongside the wharf at
Subsidium	43237	Could construct a tramway between mine and wharf
Subsidy ...	43238	Should suggest wire ropeway between mine and wharf
Subsigned	43239	The property includes wharf at
Subsimilio	43240	There is a private railway down to the wharf
Subsistent	43241	From the company's own wharf
Subsisting	43242	Includes wharf
Subsoil ...	43243	Does not include wharf
Subsolano	43244	Does it (this) include wharf
Subsortior	43245	**Wharfage**
Substamen	43246	For wharfage and lighterage
Substituir...	43247	To include all wharfage charges
Substraer ...	43248	**What**
Substringo	43249	If so, what
Subsultim	43250	What do you think of it (this)
Subtardus	43251	What do you think about
Subtegmen	43252	Cable what you think is the best thing to be done
Subtenant	43253	What has been decided respecting
Subtender...	43254	Do not understand to what you allude
Subtensa ...	43255	What was the outcome of
Subtenuis ..	43256	What are you (they)
Subtepide...	43257	What do you advise
Subterduco	43258	What shall I (we)
Subterfuge	43259	What are you going to do
Subterlino	43260	What will
Subterreus	43261	What is (are)
Subtervolo	43262	What is it (this)
Subtexurus	43263	What is the
Subtilely ...	43264	What would you
Subtilize ...	43265	What should I
Subtondeo	43266	What will it amount to
Subtraendo	43267	As soon as you have decided what
Subtrahend	43268	Provided what you suggest is
Subtristis...	43269	**Whatever**
Subucula ...	43270	Do whatever you consider best
Subuglio ...	43271	Will be guided by whatever you suggest
Suburban...	43272	Whatever you do
Subveniens	43273	Whatever you do, be careful not to
Subvening	43274	**Whatsoever**
Subvenir ...	43275	**Wheel(s)** (*See also* " Water-wheel.")
Subversion	43276	Wheels and axles
Subvietus...	43277	Steel wheels
Subviridio	43278	By means of gear wheels
Subvolito ...	43279	**Wheel-barrow**
Subway ...	43280	Wheel-barrows for
Subyugar ...	43281	**Wheel-wright**
Succeditur	43282	**When**
Succeduto...	43283	When was it sent
Succensens	43284	When may I (we) expect
Success ...	43285	If so, when
Successeur	43286	When is (are)
Successore	43287	When you are
Succhiare ...	43288	When you are about it (this)
Succiatore	43289	When are you
Succiduous	43290	When are you likely to

Succinate ...	43291	When do you
Succineus...	43292	When do you think
Succino ...	43293	When do you think you will be able to
Succisivum	43294	When do you think —— will
Succollans	43295	When do you think you will begin
Succomber	43296	When can
Succory ...	43297	When can I (we)
Succourer...	43298	When can I (we) start
Succresco ...	43299	When you can
Succulency	43300	When you do
Succumb ...	43301	When I (we) shall be able to
Succumbens	43302	When shall you
Succursale	43303	When do you advise
Succurva ...	43304	When you are sure of
Succussio ...	43305	When and where
Succutior ...	43306	When do
Sucedido ...	43307	When did
Sucement ...	43308	**Whence**
Sucerdas ...	43309	From whence
Sucesible ...	43310	**Whenever**
Sucidume ...	43311	Whenever you can
Suciedad ...	43312	Whenever you think proper
Sucosita ...	43313	Whenever you do this
Sucotrino ...	43314	**Where**
Suction ...	43315	Where is it (the)
Sudabundus	43316	— Where is (are)
Sudamina...	43317	Where there is
Sudariolum	43318	Where you can
Sudatorium	43319	Where can you
Sudatory ...	43320	Where can I (we)
Sudatrix ...	43321	Where do you propose to locate
Suddecani	43322	**Whereabouts**
Suddetto ...	43323	The whereabouts of
Suddiviso...	43324	Whereabouts unknown
Sudelei ...	43325	**Whereas**
Sudiceria ...	43326	**Whereby**
Sudiciume	43327	**Wherefore**
Sudiculum	43328	**Wheresoever**
Sudlich ...	43329	**Whereupon**
Sudoretto ...	43330	**Wherever**
Sudoriento	43331	**Whether**
Sudorifico	43332	Whether or no
Sudoste ...	43333	Whether you will or will not
Sudpol ...	43334	Whether —— or ——
Sudsudest...	43335	Whether " yes " or "no "
Sudueste ...	43336	If so, whether
Sudwarts ...	43337	If not, whether
Sueldas ...	43338	Whether it would be advisable to
Sueroso ...	43339	Whether you can
Suette ...	43340	Whether —— (he) can
Sufferable ..	43341	Whether it is or is not possible to
Sufferance	43342	**Which**
Suffering ...	43343	By which
Suffertim ...	43344	From which
Suffiatis ...	43345	Of which
Suffibulo ...	43346	To which
Sufficed ...	43347	To which I (we) adhere
Suffiendus	43348	Before which
Suffitor ...	43349	Between which
Suffix ...	43350	After which

Sufflamen ...	43351	Until which
Sufflated ...	43352	Pending which
Suffocate ...	43353	Which would you prefer
Suffodior ...	43354	Which is safest
Suffolcere...	43355	**Whichever**
Suffoquer ...	43356	Whichever you think best
Suffrages ...	43357	Whichever you think right
Suffringor	43358	Whichever course is best
Suffuerat ...	43359	**While**
Suffulcrum	43360	**Whilst**
Suffumigio	43361	Whilst you can
Suffused ...	43362	Whilst I am (we are)
Sufocador...	43363	Whilst you (they) are
Sufraganeo	43364	Whilst this is being done
Sufragio ...	43365	Whilst the ground is being prepared (for)
Sufrible ...	43366	Cannot be done whilst
Sufridera ...	43367	Whilst —— is (are) here
Sufriente ...	43368	Whilst —— is (are) with you
Sufusion ...	43369	Whilst under repairs
Sugarbaker	43370	Whilst I am on the property
Sugarcandy	43371	**Whim(s)** (See also "Cage.")
Sugarhouse	43372	Steam whim
Sugarloaf ...	43373	Horse whim
Sugarmill...	43374	By means of a horse whim
Sugarplum	43375	Shall put up a horse whim
Sugary ...	43376	As soon as the —— whim is erected
Sugatto ...	43377	Gearing of horse whim
Sugerente...	43378	Shall arrange to draw with horse whim
Sugerir ...	43379	To replace the horse whim now in use
Suggellare	43380	Whim shaft
Suggerens...	43381	Whim rope
Suggerire ...	43382	**White**
Suggester...	43383	**White vitriol**
Suggestive	43384	**Who**
Suggettino	43385	Who is (are)
Suggingare	43386	Who is it
Suggredior	43387	Who is (are) not
Suggrunda	43388	Who said that
Sughereto...	43389	Who can
Sugillatio ...	43390	Who cannot
Sugliardo ...	43391	Who must
Sugnaccia...	43392	Who should
Sugumera...	43393	Who was (were)
Suicidal ...	43394	Who was (were) not
Suicidio ...	43395	Who will
Suitors ...	43396	Who will not
Suivante ...	43397	Who gave the order for it
Sujetar ...	43398	**Whoever**
Sulcamen ...	43399	**Whole**
Sulcavit ...	43400	Do you (does ——) include the whole
Sulculus ...	43401	Has (have) included the whole
Sulfonete ...	43402	On the whole
Sulfurea ...	43403	The whole of the (this)
Sulkily ...	43404	To obtain the whole of
Sullaturio...	43405	From the whole
Sullenly ...	43406	From the whole bulk
Sullenness	43407	The whole concern
Sullunare ...	43408	The whole property
Sulphamide	43409	Do you mean the whole or only a part
Sulphites ...	43410	I (we) mean the whole

Sulphosalt	43411	I (we) do not mean the whole, but only a part of
Sulphuric ...	43412	**Wholesale**
Sultana ...	43413	**Wholly**
Sumach ...	43414	Either wholly or in part
Sumador ...	43415	Either wholly or not at all
Sumamente	43416	If wholly
Sumario ...	43417	Lost wholly
Sumergir ...	43418	**Whom**
Sumiller ...	43419	By whom
Sumisavoce	43420	From whom
Sumista ..	43421	With whom
Summanalia	43422	Without whom
Summarily	43423	By whom was the order given
Summation	43424	Whom have you selected for
Summergo	43425	Whom did you advise
Summiren...	43426	**Whose**
Summissus	43427	By whose
Summitas ...	43428	From whose
Summomole	43429	With whose
Summoner	43430	Without whose
Summonses	43431	By whose instructions was it done
Summovens	43432	By whose instructions it was done
Sumonte ...	43433	**Why**
Sumoscapo	43434	Why not
Sumptito ...	43435	Why do(es) not ——
Sumptuary	43436	Why do you not
Sumptuous	43437	Why do you not answer
Sumtifeci ...	43438	Why is (are)
Sumulas ...	43439	Why is (are) not
Sumulista...	43440	Why is it necessary to
Sunbeam ...	43441	Why has it (this) been done
Sunburner	43442	Why do (did)
Sunburnt ...	43443	Why do you wish me (us) to
Sunchar ...	43444	The only reason why, was
Sundhaft ...	43445	What is the reason why
Sundial ...	43446	There was no reason why
Sunflower ...	43447	Please explain why
Sunlight ...	43448	Will explain the reason why, by mail
Sunlike ...	43449	**Wide** (*See also* " Broad.")
Sunrise ...	43450	How wide
Sunset ...	43451	Not so wide
Sunshade ...	43452	Too wide
Sunshine ...	43453	Avoid wide fluctuations of
Sunstroke...	43454	**Wider**
Suntuoso ...	43455	Must be made wider
Suocera ...	43456	No wider
Supedaneo	43457	Unless wider
Supeditado	43458	**Widespread**
Supellex ...	43459	**Width** (*See also* " Thickness.")
Superable...	43460	Cable present width of
Superadd ...	43461	The present width of —— is
Superandus	43462	What is the total width of
Superatore	43463	The total width is —— feet
Superatrix	43464	Varies in width from —— to ——
Superavit ...	43465	Varies considerably in width
Superbetto	43466	In width
Superbiare	43467	At its maximum width
Superbiens	43468	The width of the tunnel is
Superbiter...	43469	The width of the drivage is
Superbly ...	43470	Must not exceed —— feet in width

Superbosus	43471	Can I (we) increase the width to ——
Supercargo	43472	Do not increase the width
Superchero	43473	Can increase the width to
Supercilio...	43474	Constantly varies in width
Superduco	43475	From the width
Superegero	43476	Judging from the width
Superemico	43477	For the whole width of the
Superenato	43478	—— feet in width by —— feet long
Superesco ...	43479	What is the average width and value (of)
Superevolo	43480	For the last —— feet the average width has been
Superficie ...	43481	The average width is ——, the average value is ——
Superfino ..	43482	What is the average width of
Superhabeo	43483	The average width is
Superheat	43484	Give width in inches (of)
Superhuman	43485	The width in inches is
Superieur ...	43486	**Wild**
Superiotes	43487	**Wilful**
Superjacto	43488	**Wilfully**
Superlabor	43489	Was not done wilfully
Supermando	43490	Am (are) suspicious was done wilfully
Supernal ...	43491	**Will**
Superobruo	43492	Will not
Superpingo	43493	Will he (——)
Superponor	43494	Will you (they)
Superpose ..	43495	Will it (this) do
Superroyal	43496	Will it cause
Supersero ...	43497	I (we) will
Superstite...	43498	I (we) will not
Supersurgo	43499	He (they) will
Supervacuo	43500	He (they) will not
Supervaler	43501	In case he (they) will
Supervehor	43502	In case he (they) will not
Supervene	43503	In case you will
Supination	43504	In case you will not
Supineness	43505	Will be
Supinitas ...	43506	Will not be
Suplantar ...	43507	Will it (this)
Suplemento	43508	This (it) will not
Suplencia ...	43509	Will probably be with you before
Supletorio	43510	Will probably be here until
Suplicante	43511	When will you be able to
Suplidor ...	43512	When will he (they) be able to
Suponedor	43513	Will you be likely to
Suportar ...	43514	Will be likely to
Suppactus	43515	Will not be likely to
Suppallido	43516	Will this be as you wish
Suppalpor	43517	Will be as I (we) wish
Supparum	43518	Will —— act for me (us)
Suppediano	43519	Will you act for me (us)
Suppentopf	43520	Will act for you
Supperless	43521	Cost of erection will amount to
Suppilato	43522	**Willing**
Suppleness	43523	Am (are) quite willing to
Supplente .	43524	Willing to continue
Suppletive	43525	Willing to act
Suppliance	43526	Willing to incur
Supplicato	43527	Willing to defer
Supplicier...	43528	Are you still willing
Supplicium	43529	Perfectly willing to do the right thing
Supplique...	43530	Would —— be willing to

Supplosio ...	43531	He (——) would be quite willing to
Supporting	43532	He (——) would not be willing to
Supposable	43533	Provided that you are willing
Suppregare	43534	Provided that —— (he) is willing
Supprimer	43535	Am (is) (are) not now willing
Suppromus	43536	As soon as you are willing
Suppurato	43537	—— is (are) quite willing to
Supputatio	43538	—— is (are) not at all willing to
Supraspina	43539	Should you (——) not be willing
Supremacia	43540	Unless you are perfectly willing
Supreme ...	43541	Unless —— is perfectly willing
Supremum	43542	+ Cable whether —— is willing
Supresor ...	43543	Cable whether you are quite willing to
Supriorato	43544	Quite willing to do anything that will help you
Supurante	43545	Quite willing to resign
Supurativo	43546	Is (are) willing to resign, if
Suputar ...	43547	**Willingly**
Surabonder	43548	**Willingness**
Suraign ...	43549	**Win**
Suranne ...	43550	To win
Surbande ...	43551	Intend to win
Surcador ...	43552	Feel that I am (we are) sure to win
Surcharge	43553	Do all you possibly can to win
Surcingle ...	43554	Shall probably win
Surcroit ...	43555	Not at all likely to win
Surculado	43556	**Winch**
Surcularis ..	43557	Steam winch
Surdaster ...	43558	**Wind(s)**
Surdiginem	43559	Heavy gale of wind
Surdissime	43560	During a gale of wind
Surefooted	43561	By the wind
Suretyship	43562	Wind caused great damage
Surexciter...	43563	Wind did not cause any serious damage
Surfacing ...	43564	Damaged during the recent heavy winds [" Hoisting."]
Surfaire ...	43565	**Winding-engine** (*See also* " Drum," " Engine," " Hoist,"
Surfboats...	43566	**Wind up** (*See also* " Court," " Haul," " Liquidation.")
Surfeit ...	43567	To wind up
Surfeiting...	43568	There is nothing to do but to wind up
Surgeless ...	43569	Before finally deciding to wind up
Surgente ...	43570	Do you still advise us to wind up
Surgeon ...	43571	Do not advise you to wind up
Surgical ...	43572	I (we) do not see what you can do except wind up
Surgidero...	43573	Provided that shareholders agree to wind up
Surgitur ...	43574	Formal resolutions have been passed to wind up
Surhausser	43575	Subject to a formal resolution of the shareholders to wind up
Surlonge ...	43576	Should you decide not to wind up
Surmener ...	43577	Should the resolution to wind up be confirmed
Surmised ...	43578	Confirmatory resolution to wind up has been passed
Surmount...	43579	Confirmatory resolution to wind up has not been passed
Surnager ...	43580	The only other course open is to wind up
Surnommer	43581	Is there any other course open than to wind up
Surpasser ...	43582	Unless we wind up
Surplice ...	43583	**Winding up** (*See also* " Court.")
Surplomb...	43584	Defer winding up until
Surplus ...	43585	Has (have) presented a petition to court for winding up
Surprendre	43586	Court has granted winding up petition
Surremit ...	43587	Court has dismissed winding up petition
Surripior ...	43588	Petition for voluntary winding up
Surrogatio	43589	The winding up is to be under the supervision of the Court
..oir ...	43590	The winding up is to be under the supervision of the Board of
		[Trade

Surtaxer ...	43591	**Windlass** (*See also* " Winch.")
Surtidor ...	43592	By means of a windlass
Surtout ...	43593	Through failure of windlass
Surveiller...	43594	**Windmill(s)**
Survenant	43595	Windmill for pumping
Survivance	43596	Windmill for
Susamiel ...	43597	**Winter** (*See also* " Frost," " Season," " Snow.")
Susceptor...	43598	Winter has now set in
Suscettino	43599	In the winter
Suscipiens	43600	Throughout the winter
Suscitar ...	43601	The winter begins about —— and lasts until about ——
Suscitatio...	43602	All outside work is suspended during the winter
Suscriptor	43603	The property is entirely isolated during the winter
Susinetta ...	43604	Supplies for the winter
Suslero ...	43605	The winters are very mild
Susorniare	43606	The winters are exceedingly severe
Suspectful	43607	The winter causes no suspension of work
Suspender	43608	Next winter
Suspendium	43609	Last winter
Suspense ...	43610	Before the winter sets in
Suspensoir	43611	During the winter months
Suspeximo	43612	During the present winter
Suspicato ...	43613	In the winter of this year
Suspirador	43614	**Winze(s)** (*See also* " Deep.")
Suspiratus	43615	Depth of winze
Suspiroso ...	43616	We have sunk a winze
Sussecuto...	43617	The winze is now down —— feet
Susslich ...	43618	How deep is the winze (at)
Sustainer ...	43619	The winze at
Sustaining	43620	In winze No. ——
Sustancial	43621	Samples taken from winze have assayed
Sustantivo	43622	In the bottom of winze
Sustenance	43623	Will be connected by a winze
Sustener ...	43624	Have been connected by a winze
Sustillo ...	43625	In the winze between —— level and —— level
Sustinens...	43626	From winze
Sustituire...	43627	By means of a winze
Sustollens...	43628	Cost of sinking winze is (was) —— per foot
Susurrador	43629	Shall sink winze with all speed
Susurrameu	43630	Have commenced sinking winze in —— level
Susurron ...	43631	Winze in —— level is now down —— feet
Susymbrium	43632	We are still —— feet short sunk in the winze
Suterina ...	43633	There is no ore in the winze
Sutileza ...	43634	The average of the samples from this winze is
Sutilmente	43635	To meet the winze to be sunk from
Sutorius ...	43636	Under the winze sunk from level No. ——
Suttrare ...	43637	Until the winze has been completed
Suverato ...	43638	At the lowest point reached in winze, viz., —— feet
Suversion...	43639	Are you sinking a winze below
Suvvertito	43640	Shall follow the ore down by a winze
Suzerain ...	43641	Have followed the ore down by a winze for —— feet
Suzzatore...	43642	Winze sunk entirely in ore
Svalorito ...	43643	**Wire** (*See also* " Cable," " Telegraph," " Tramway.")
Svampare...	43644	Wire rope for ——
Svantaggio	43645	Wire rope —— inches circumference
Svecchiato	43646	Wire rope tramway
Svelamento	43647	—— feet of steel wire rope —— inches circumference
Sveltezza ...	43648	—— feet of flat steel wire rope, —— inches by —— inches
Svembrato	43649	A wire cable should be sent for the purpose of
Svenevole...	43650	Wire rope complete with shackles

Sventrare ...	43651	Brass wire
Sverginare	43652	Copper wire
Svergogna	43653	Steel wire
Svestirsi ...	43654	**Wirepuller(s)**
Sviatrice ...	43655	**Wire ropeway**
Svigorito ...	43656	What supports do you intend to employ for wire ropeway
Sviluppato	43657	The supports for the wire ropeway to be of timber
Svinatura...	43658	The supports for the wire ropeway to be of iron [ropeway
Sviscerare...	43659	Am preparing plan and section of proposed route for wire
Svivagnato	43660	Have mailed plan and section of proposed route for wire
Svogliato ...	43661	**Wisdom** [ropeway
Svoltatore	43662	Doubt(s) the wisdom of
Swabber ...	43663	**Wise(ly)**
Swaggerer	43664	If you are (—— is) wise
Swains ...	43665	Will it be wise (to)
Swallow ...	43666	It would not be wise
Swallowing	43667	It will not be wise to tamper with
Swampy ...	43668	**Wish(es)**
Swanlike ...	43669	To wish
Swannery...	43670	Do you (does ——) wish
Swansdown	43671	Do(es) not wish
Swanskin ...	43672	Do not wish you to
~~Swarthily~~	~~43673~~	~~Only wish that~~
Swathe ...	43674	Wish(es) that
Swathing ...	43675	What I (we) wish is
Sweatiness	43676	Has (have) expressed a strong wish that
Sweating ...	43677	Has —— expressed any wish to
Swedish ...	43678	Has (have) not expressed any wish to
Sweeper ...	43679	Exactly what you wish
Sweepingly	43680	Wish you (to)
Sweepnet ...	43681	Wish you to do this at once
Sweepstake	43682	Unless you wish otherwise
Sweetbriar	43683	I (we) particularly wish
Sweeten ...	43684	Provided that you do not wish me (us) to
Sweetheart	43685	Why do you wish
Sweetly ...	43686	Wish to have your advice
Sweetmeat	43687	In case you wish
Sweetoil ...	43688	In case you do not wish
Sweetpea ...	43689	Should you wish
Swellmob...	43690	What do you wish
Sweltering	43691	When do you wish
Swerving ...	43692	Where do you wish
Swiftly ...	43693	My (our) only wish is to
Swiftness ...	43694	Unless you should wish me (us)
Swigging ...	43695	Unless you particularly wish
Swiller ...	43696	Unless you should wish me (us) not to
Swilling ...	43697	Wish(es) to know promptly
Swimmingly	43698	Wish this to be done at once
Swineherd	43699	Wish(es) it (this) to be done promptly
Swingboat	43700	Your wishes will have my immediate attention
Swinger ...	43701	**Wishful**
Swinging ...	43702	Most wishful to
Swinishly...	43703	**With**
Switch ...	43704	With it (this)
Switched ...	43705	Was (were) not with
Switchmen	43706	Unless accompanied with
Swiveleye ...	43707	Was (were) not accompanied with
Swooning...	43708	Either with or without
Swoop ...	43709	Was it with
Swordbelt...	43710	Was entirely with

Swordblade	43711	It was with
Swordfight	43712	It was not with
Swordfish...	43713	**Withdraw** (*See also* "Offer.")
Swordgrass	43714	To withdraw
Swordknot	43715	Expect to withdraw
Swordless	43716	I (we) withdraw
Swordsman	43717	Withdraw from
Swordstick	43718	Advise you to withdraw
Syagros	43719	Do you advise me (us) to withdraw
Sybaris ...	43720	Do not advise you to withdraw
Sycaminum	43721	Should advise you to withdraw if you can
Sycitem ...	43722	Are you still determined to withdraw
Sycitibus ...	43723	As soon as you decide to withdraw
Sycomorus	43724	Should you decide to withdraw
Sycophancy	43725	Should you withdraw
Sylbenmass	43726	Should you not withdraw
Syllabatim	43727	I (we) shall withdraw
Syllabic ...	43728	Shall withdraw unless (except)
Syllaceus ...	43729	You cannot very well withdraw now
Syllaturio	43730	Do not withdraw
Syllepsis ...	43731	Please withdraw my (our) name(s)
Sylleptic ...	43732	Will gladly withdraw
Syllogism...	43733	Will withdraw if it will help matters
Syllogizer	43734	Is about to withdraw
Sylphic ...	43735	Wish(es) to withdraw from
Sylphlike ...	43736	Must withdraw offer made
Sylvan ...	43737	Has (have) given notice to withdraw
Symbolic ...	43738	Give —— notice to withdraw
Symbolique	43739	Would like to withdraw if
Symbolized	43740	Refuse(s) to withdraw
Symmetrize	43741	Consent(s) to withdraw
Sympathy	43742	Consent(s) to withdraw action
Symphonize	43743	Refuse(s) to withdraw action
Symphrades	43744	**Withdrawal**
Sympinium	43745	Legal notice of withdrawal
Symplegma	43746	Previous to receiving notice of withdrawal
Symposium	43747	Have you (has ——) received notice of withdrawal
Sympotica	43748	Has (have) received notice of withdrawal
Symptom ...	43749	**Withdrawing**
Synagogue	43750	Begin by withdrawing
Synanche ...	43751	Threaten(s) to begin by withdrawing
Syncellus ...	43752	**Withdrawn**
Synchronal	43753	To be withdrawn
Synchysis...	43754	Was (were) withdrawn
Syncopate	43755	Has (have) not yet withdrawn (offer)
Syncope ...	43756	Has (have) —— withdrawn
Syndrone ...	43757	Have you withdrawn
Synecdoche	43758	Consider offer withdrawn
Synedrion	43759	Has (have) withdrawn (offer)
Synephebi	43760	Has (have) withdrawn from
Syngenesia	43761	Will undoubtedly be withdrawn
Syngrapha	43762	Is (are) not at all likely to be withdrawn
Synochitis	43763	Almost certain to be withdrawn
Synodical ...	43764	All proceedings withdrawn
Synodium...	43765	All proceedings to be withdrawn
Synonymal	43766	Expect to be withdrawn
Synonyme	43767	Should you not already have withdrawn
Synonymous	43768	In the event of your having already withdrawn
Synoptical	43769	Not yet withdrawn
Synoptique	43770	Have withdrawn my name

Syntagma...	43771	Have withdrawn your name
Syntax ...	43772	**Withheld**
Synthesis ...	43773	Have you (has ——) withheld
Syphilitic...	43774	Has (have) withheld
Syriacism...	43775	Has (have) not withheld
Syringites	43776	Have you withheld notice from
Syrmaticus	43777	**Withhold**
Systemize...	43778	To withhold
Systole ...	43779	Do not withhold
Systylos ...	43780	Cannot withhold
Syzygia ...	43781	Better withhold
Tabaccajo	43782	Better not withhold
Tabaksdose	43783	Do you advise me (us) to withhold
Tabalada ...	43784	Advise you strongly to withhold
Tabalear ...	43785	I (we) should advise you for the present to withhold
Tabanazo ...	43786	Must not withhold
Tabanque...	43787	Must withhold
Tabaola ...	43788	**Within**
Tabaquera	43789	Within limits(s) stated
Tabaquista	43790	Within the limit
Tabardete	43791	Is it within
Tabarrino...	43792	It is not within
Tabasheer...	43793	Should this be within
Tabatiere ...	43794	Should this not be within
Tabbycat ...	43795	Unless it is within
Tabbying ...	43796	Not within
Tabefacio ...	43797	Must be kept within
Tabelion ...	43798	Cannot be kept within
Tabellario	43799	Within the space named
Tabelle ...	43800	Within the time
Tabernacle	43801	Within the time agreed
Taberneria	43802	Must keep within the terms accepted
Tabernula	43803	Will keep within the terms accepted
Tabesco ...	43804	Cannot keep within the terms accepted
Tabicar ...	43805	Provided —— keeps within terms of agreement
Tabidulus...	43806	Keep well within
Tabificavi...	43807	Will keep well within
Tabifico ...	43808	Could not keep within
Tabillas ...	43809	If I am (we are) to keep within the limits stated in your letter of
Tabinet ...	43810	**Without**
Tabitena ...	43811	Without the (this)
Tablachina	43812	Not without
Tablado ...	43813	Cannot very well do without
Tablagear...	43814	Can do perfectly well without
Tablature...	43815	Have had to do without the (it) (this)
Tablazon ...	43816	If it can be done without much expense
Tableaux ...	43817	Can be done without any difficulty
Tablebeer ...	43818	Can be done without much cost
Tablebook	43819	Cannot be done without considerable difficulty
Tablecloth	43820	Without further help
Tableland...	43821	Cannot do without further help
Tablelinen	43822	Can do very well for the present without further help
Tabletalk ...	43823	**Withstand**
Tableteado	43824	In order to withstand
Tabletier ...	43825	Has (have) so far managed to withstand
Tablilla ...	43826	**Withstood**
Tabling ...	43827	**Witness(es)** (*See also* "Subpœna.")
Tabloids ...	43828	To witness
Tabularius	43829	To witness trial of
Tabulating	43830	To witness the (this)

Taburacura	43831	Am called as a witness for
Taburete ...	43832	You are wanted as a witness for
Taccagno ...	43833	The (this) witness
Tacciato ...	43834	Can witness
Taccolare ...	43835	Could witness
Tacconcino	43836	Did not witness
Tacebatur	43837	Did you witness
Tacendus ...	43838	Was able to witness
Tacette ...	43839	I have been subpœnaed as a witness (at ——)
Tacheron ...	43840	There are plenty of witnesses to prove
Tachoneria	43841	It would be difficult to find any witness(es) to prove
Tacitly ...	43842	Witness(es) on our side
Taciturno ...	43843	Witness(es) against us
Taconear ...	43844	Can you procure witness(es) to testify
Tactica ...	43845	Have witness(es) ready who can testify
Tactically ...	43846	Unable to find witness(es) to testify
Tactician ...	43847	Without more reliable witness(es)
Tactique ...	43848	In the absence of reliable witness(es)
Tactual ...	43849	**Witnessed**
Tacuisse ...	43850	Must be properly signed and witnessed
Tadelhaft ...	43851	Was (were) not signed and witnessed
Tadellos ...	43852	Signed and witnessed before a notary public
Tadelsucht	43853	**Wolfram**
Tadorno ...	43854	**Won** (*See also* "Appeal," "Case.")
Tadpole ...	43855	Has been won by
Taedebat ...	43856	Was won by
Taedifer ...	43857	Was not won by
Tafanario ...	43858	Cable as soon as you know who have won
Tafelmusik	43859	We have won [—— days; instruct by cable
Tafetan ...	43860	Opponents have won ; notice of appeal must be lodged within
Tafferel ...	43861	**Wonder**
Tafferugia	43862	**Wonderful(ly)**
Taffeta ...	43863	**Wood** (*See also* "Fuel," "Timber.")
Taffrails ...	43864	There is sufficient wood for all our needs
Tafurea ...	43865	There is an abundance of wood for fuel
Tagarino ...	43866	There is a great scarcity of wood for fuel
Tagarotear	43867	The cost of wood delivered to the mine per cord is
Tagearbeit	43868	We consume —— cords of wood per week
Tageblatt ...	43869	Wood for fuel costs —— per cord
Tagelohn ...	43870	The cost of the wood is only the hauling charges (viz. ——)
Tagliabile	43871	There is ample wood for all requirements for some years
Tagliatojo...	43872	Our present boiler(s) consume(s) —— cords of wood per [twenty-four hours
Tagliente ...	43873	The mill requires —— cords of wood per twenty-four hours
Tagliolini ...	43874	The nearest wood to the property is —— miles distant
Tagliuola ...	43875	The property is surrounded by excellent wood
Tagsatzung	43876	Lined with —— wood
Taharal ...	43877	Lined with Californian red wood
Tahureria...	43878	Wood working machinery
Taibeque ...	43879	Circular saw for wood —— inches diameter
Tailblock ...	43880	The annual cost for wood alone has hitherto been
Taillader ...	43881	Owing to the scarcity of wood
Taillant ...	43882	Is there plenty of wood for fuel and mining purposes
Tailleur ...	43883	**Wood spirit**
Taillis ...	43884	**Wooden**
Tailorbird...	43885	To replace present wooden structure
Tailoress ...	43886	Wooden structure
Tailoring ...	43887	On wooden piles
Taimado ...	43888	Wooden sleepers
Taintless ...	43889	**Word(s)** (*See also* "Message," "Number.")

Tajadera ...	43890	Words inclusive
Tajadillo ...	43891	Has kept his word
Tajador ...	43892	Has not kept his word
Tajamiento	43893	The following word is used in the plural number
Takingness	43894	The following word is used in the singular number
Taktfest ...	43895	The foregoing word is not used as a cipher word
Taktmassig	43896	The following word is not used as a cipher word
Taktstab ...	43897	Is the word —— used as a cipher word
Takttheil ...	43898	The word —— is not used as a cipher word
Talabarte ...	43899	The word —— is used as a cipher word
Taladrar ...	43900	Use the word —— as a cipher word
Talamera ...	43901	**Wording (of)**
Talanquera	43902	**Work(s)** *(See also "Complete," "Connect," "Snow.")*
Talantoso ...	43903	To work
Talasomeli	43904	Do not work
Talassio ...	43905	Will not work
Talebearer	43906	To enable the work to proceed
Talegazo ...	43907	When are you likely to begin the (this) work
Talentare ...	43908	Shall commence the work on or about ——
Talented ...	43909	Shall commence the (this) work at once
Taleola ...	43910	Before you commence the work of
Taleteller ...	43911	To commence work at once
Talglicht ...	43912	To commence work within —— days
Talictro ...	43913	Shall begin to work
Talionar ...	43914	When do you begin to work
Talionibus	43915	Do not defer the work a moment
Talipedo ...	43916	Defer this work until
Talisman ...	43917	Shall I (we) defer this work until
Talitrum ...	43918	Now hard at work
Talkative ...	43919	Hope to get to work within the present week
Talkers ...	43920	Work now proceeds throughout the whole twenty-four hours
Tallarola ...	43921	Arrange to work continuously day and night
Tallecer ...	43922	Work proceeding steadily
Tallista ...	43923	Works exceedingly well
Tallness ...	43924	Works fairly well
Tallowish ...	43925	Do(es) not work at all satisfactorily
Tallyho ...	43926	Will not work at all
Tallyman ...	43927	Refuse(s) to work as long as
Tallyshop...	43928	Refuse(s) to work except
Talmente ...	43929	Consent(s) to work
Talmud ...	43930	Men will only work upon the following terms, viz. :—
Talmudico	43931	The additional works necessary for
Talmudista	43932	Development works
Taloche ...	43933	The necessary development works
Talonear ...	43934	Cost of development works
Talonniere	43935	All inside work
Talpana ...	43936	Outside work
Talque ...	43937	All the outside work is now completed
Talus ...	43938	Outside work will be completed about
Taluter ...	43939	When will the outside work be completed
Talvolta ...	43940	Dead work
Tamable ...	43941	Much dead work will be necessary before
Tamandoa	43942	A considerable amount of dead work has been necessary
Tamaras ...	43943	Push ahead with the following work
Tamarindo	43944	Push the work forward as much as you can
Tamarisk ...	43945	The work at present
Tambalear	43946	I (we) advise vigorous prosecution of work at
Tambellone	43947	All mining works
Tambesco...	43948	Cannot do the work
Tambien ...	43949	The works have been continued regardless of cost

Tamborete	43950	Suspension of all work
Tambour ...	43951	Stoppage of all works ordered
Tamburello	43952	Stop the following work
Tamburiere	43953	Have stopped the following work
Tamely ...	43954	Has (have) forbidden the work to be continued
Tameness ...	43955	Have had to stop work on account of ——
Tamenetsi...	43956	Work practically stopped during the winter months
Tamisage ...	43957	The profit from the works is —— per annum
Tamiseur ...	43958	If all works are stopped, shall we sell or warehouse stores
Tammy ...	43959	Have not been able to find any one who will take the work in
Tamnacum	43960	Owing to the important work which is now in progress [hand
Tamorlan ...	43961	Surface work
Tamperer ...	43962	It (this) has caused the entire stoppage of the surface work
Tampering	43963	Will considerably delay our surface works
Tampion ...	43964	Work was stopped —— hours owing to
Tamponner	43965	Stop all work until
Tanaceto ...	43966	You should ask —— for the work
Tanaglia ...	43967	This work is almost completed
Tandem ...	43968	Have not been able to measure the work done, on account of
Tanfanare	43969	Shall require to do the following work before we resume sinking
Tangage ...	43970	Shall require to do the following work before we resume driving
Tangential	43971	When will you finish your work at
Tangible ...	43972	Have ceased work at present
Tangidera...	43973	Shall require this work during the present month
Tangir ...	43974	If work already done is correct, I (we) only require additions
Taniere ...	43975	The work already done is doubtful
Tankard ...	43976	Will not work under
Tannenwald	43977	Take over the whole works as they stand
Tanner ...	43978	The alterations to the insecure work will be completed about
Tanning ...	43979	The work will be completed within —— days
Tanpit ...	43980	I (we) intend doing this work within the next few days
Tanquam ...	43981	This work will be done during the present week
Tantafera...	43982	Work now proposed
Tantalize ...	43983	If quick work is to be done
Tantamount	43984	Quick work is necessary
Tanteador	43985	Decline(s) to work if any reduction is made
Tantillum...	43986	Decline(s) to work
Tantinetto	43987	Decline(s) to work unless (until)
Tantisper ...	43988	Very slow work
Tantivy ...	43989	Systematic work
Tantopere...	43990	Excellent work
Tantrum ...	43991	Cannot work later than
Tantulum...	43992	Report on the position of the works you have at present in
Tantundem	43993	What work have you now in hand [hand
Tanzbar ...	43994	Underground work
Tanzboden	43995	Work should be commenced immediately
Tanzerlich	43996	I am (we are) crowding work on (at)
Tanzkunst	43997	Do not crowd too much work on it
Tanzplatz...	43998	Crowd the work all you can on (at)
Taonner ...	43999	Will crowd this work as much as possible
Tapaboca ...	44000	Have had to suspend work since
Tapadillo	**44001**	Expect to resume full work on
Tapafogon	44002	I (we) have resumed work at
Tapafunda	44003	If work(s) is (are) immediately resumed
Tapageur ...	44004	Preliminary works
Tapatan ...	44005	The necessary preliminary work being completed
Taperness...	44006	What will be the cost of preliminary work
Taperujo ...	44007	The preliminary work will cost at least
Tapestried	44008	The preliminary work should not cost more than
Tapeworm	44009	Provided that the work is continued without interruption

Tapeziren ...	44010	Provided that it causes no interference to work now in hand
Tapferkeit	44011	Do not advise this work
Taphinsius	44012	Can you induce —— to continue this work
Taphole ...	44013	The first work to be undertaken will be
Tapiador ...	44014	Should be quite ready for work early next month
Tapiceria ...	44015	The work is being vigorously pushed in every department
Tapinarsi ...	44016	When will work be resumed
Tapines	44017	Shall not be able to resume work until
Tapinosis ...	44018	As soon as I (we) can resume work
Tapioca ...	44019	Have stopped work at
Tapisote ...	44020	Why have you stopped work
Tapisserie...	44021	**Worked**
Tapissier ...	44022	Now being worked by tribute
Tapoter ...	44023	Has (have) never been worked to a profit
Tappezzare	44024	Has (have) been worked to a large extent
Tappula ...	44025	Has (have) not been worked to any extent
Taproom ...	44026	Is now being worked for
Taquetas ...	44027	Is not now being worked
Taquigrafo	44028	Is worked out
Taquinero...	44029	Was considered to be worked out
Tarabuster	44030	At the present rate of extraction available ore will be worked [out within the next —— months
Taracea ...	44031	Was (were) formerly worked for
Taragallo ...	44032	The whole of the ground down to a depth of —— feet is en- [tirely worked out
Taragontia	44033	Have been extensively worked
Tarambana	44034	Only worked at the surface
Tarantella	44035	The mines have been miserably worked
Tarariva ...	44036	The mines have been worked most efficiently
Tarascar ...	44037	Owing to the bad system upon which the mines were worked
Taravilla ...	44038	Can be worked if
Tarazanal...	44039	Can be worked only by
Tarchiato ...	44040	Should not be worked unless
Tarchon ...	44041	Provided it (they) can be worked without
Tardador ...	44042	**Working(s)** (*See also* "Bottom," "Carefully," "Deep,"
Tardamente	44043	Old mens workings ["Deepest," "Expense," "Underground.")
Tardanza ...	44044	Native workings
Tardecica ...	44045	In the old workings
Tardiness ...	44046	In the upper workings
Tardipedem	44047	In the lower workings
Tarditas ...	44048	The old workings have all fallen together
Tarditudo...	44049	Could not inspect the old workings as they have caved
Tardivoto ...	44050	There are very extensive old workings [together
Tardon ...	44051	Undoubted traces of old workings
Tarentule ...	44052	These workings were then abandoned
Target ...	44053	Recently they have been working at
Targuer ...	44054	In order to recommence working at
Tarifer ...	44055	Cost of working averages —— per ton of 2,240 lbs.
Tarissable...	44056	There is every facility for cheap working
Tarjeton ...	44057	There are no facilities for cheap working
Tarlatana ...	44058	For working the mine
Tarnished...	44059	Under present working conditions
Tarnishing	44060	The working trial
Taroccare ...	44061	As a working result
Tarpaulin...	44062	The result of working to date has been
Tarpigna ...	44063	Has been working steadily in our interests
Tarquinada	44064	The working expenses for the month of —— were
Tarragon ...	44065	Is (are) at present only working —— days per month
Tarraja ...	44066	Is (are) working only on
Tarrier ...	44067	—— feet under the old workings
Tarrying ...	44068	The workings are entirely choked up

Tartaleta ...	44069	The lower workings have been flooded by
Tartamudeo	44070	In order to clear the workings of accumulated rubbish
Tartanelle...	44071	As soon as we have cleared out the old workings
Tartarean ...	44072	As soon as everything is in working order
Tartareous	44073	When will you have everything in working order
Tartaric ...	44074	Expect to have everything in good working order in —— days
Tartarizar...	44075	Is (are) not in good working order
Tartassato	44076	The old workings are full of water
Tartelette ...	44077	Only old workings
Tartrate ...	44078	Below the old workings
Tartuferie...	44079	To come in under the old workings
Tarullo ...	44080	The old workings are very extensive
Tarwater ...	44081	Evidently working for
Tascador ...	44082	Evidently working in the interest of
Tasche ...	44083	The cost of working may be taken at —— (per ——)
Taschetta ...	44084	The cost of working will not exceed
Tasconio ...	44085	The workings are of a very limited extent
Tasimeter...	44086	Good facilities exist for cheap and economical working
Taskmaster	44087	As soon as the workings are unwatered
Tasquera ...	44088	The old workings are full of débris [unsafe
Tassagione	44089	The present condition of the underground workings is very
Tasseau ...	44090	Before the workings can be regarded as safe
Tasselled ...	44091	The distance between these workings horizontally is —— feet
Tastara ...	44092	The distance between these workings vertically is —— feet
Tasteful ...	44093	By this means we shall ventilate the lower workings
Tasteless ...	44094	We are no doubt near ancient workings
Tastiera ...	44095	I (we) believe we are below the ancient workings
Tastolina ...	44096	The old workings are
Tatillon ...	44097	Adjacent workings
Tatonage ...	44098	Now stored in the workings
Tattamella	44099	In upper workings
Tattle ...	44100	**Working capital** (*See also* " Capital," " Company.")
Tattooing...	44101	What working capital do you consider necessary for this
Tauber ...	44102	**Workman** [property
Taubstumm	44103	**Workmanlike**
Taucher ...	44104	In a workmanlike manner
Taudion ...	44105	**Workmanship**
Taufbecken	44106	To be of the best workmanship and quality
Taufbund...	44107	Is of good workmanship
Taufling ..	44108	**Workmen**
Taufname...	44109	Have now —— workmen engaged
Taufpathin	44110	How many workmen have you engaged at
Taufstein ...	44111	Workmen are engaged at
Tauglich ...	44112	Engage necessary workmen for
Taujia ...	44113	Shall I engage necessary workmen for
Taumalin ...	44114	Have engaged necessary workmen for
Taumelig ...	44115	Native workmen
Taunate ...	44116	**Worn**
Taunter ...	44117	Is practically worn out
Tauntingly	44118	Is hardly worn at all
Taupiere ...	44119	Should not be worn
Tauricida ...	44120	Is really worn out
Taurifero ...	44121	Hardly appears to be worn
Taurigena...	44122	Can it be that the —— is worn out
Taurilia ...	44123	The only thing that is worn out is
Taurobolo...	44124	The only place that is worn is
Tausendmal	44125	**Worried**
Tausendste	44126	No need to feel worried
Tautologia	44127	Is (are) much worried about
Tauwerk ...	44128	Personally I am very much worried as to

Tauxia ...	44129	**Worry**
Tavelure ...	44130	Causing much worry and anxiety
Tavern ...	44131	**Worse**
Tavernajo .	44132	Cable should things get any worse
Taverniere	44133	Will cable you if things get worse
Tavolella ...	44134	If anything, things are becoming worse
Tavolotto ...	44135	Is (are) slightly worse
Tawdrily ...	44136	Can hardly be worse
Tawdriness	44137	Worse instead of better
Taxability...	44138	Might be worse
Taxable ...	44139	Unless things are actually becoming worse
Taxativo ...	44140	Is (are) no worse than before
Taxidermy	44141	The property generally is looking worse
Taxillus .	44142	Do you think that the mine looks any worse
Taxingly ...	44143	The mine is certainly not looking worse, but there is no im-
Taxpayer ...	44144	Gradually getting worse [provement
Teachable...	44145	Better rather than worse
Teachest ...	44146	Decidedly worse
Teaching ...	44147	Just a little worse
Teadealer .	44148	**Worst**
Teadrinker	44149	The worst is over
Teapot ...	44150	The worst is not yet over
Tearer ...	44151	The worst of the affair is
Teasaucer...	44152	Let me (us) know the worst
Teaspoon ...	44153	Fear the worst
Teataster ...	44154	**Worth** (*See also* "Having.")
Teathings...	44155	How much is it worth to us
Teatray ...	44156	What is it worth to you
Teatree ...	44157	I (we) estimate it is worth to you at least
Teatrino ...	44158	Not worth more than
Teatrista ...	44159	Would it be worth my (our) while to
Tebertino ...	44160	I (we) think it would be worth your while to
Tecchire ...	44161	Cannot think it would be worth while to
Teccolina ...	44162	Hardly worth while
Techado ...	44163	Do you still think it is worth while
Technical ...	44164	Am still of the opinion that it is worth while
Technici ...	44165	Quite worth while
Technique	44166	Is it worth as much as
Technology	44167	It is not worth more than
Technosus	44168	The sum named is much more than it is really worth
Techumbre	44169	It is worth more on account of
Teclear ...	44170	Would be worth considerably more if it were not for the fact
Tecolithus	44171	In consequence of this, its worth has been materially diminished
Tecomeco ...	44172	Do you think it worth the necessary trouble
Tectonicus	44173	Provided that it is worth
Tectorium	44174	Perhaps —— (it) may be worth
Tedifer ...	44175	As soon as you have determined how much it is worth
Tediosita ...	44176	To enable me (us) to determine exactly what it is worth
Tediously ..	44177	Practically it is not worth a cent
Tedium ...	44178	Worth the price asked for it
Teeming ...	44179	I estimate the mine and the mill are worth together say
Teetotal ...	44180	I estimate the mine itself to be worth, say
Teetotum ...	44181	I consider ——'s (his) services worth
Tegamata...	44182	I consider my services worth
Tegamino...	44183	Is it (——) worth trying
Tegendus ...	44184	**Worthless**
Tegeticula	44185	Absolutely worthless
Tegghina ...	44186	Worthless except in the event of
Tegillum ...	44187	Is it (this) worthless
Tegnenza ...	44188	Would be worthless if it were not for

Tegoletta ...	44189	At the present time it is (they are) worthless
Tegulaneus	44190	Do you mean that the property is practically worthless
Tegumento	44191	**Worthlessness**
Teigneux ...	44192	**Would**
Teinada ...	44193	Would be
Teinoscope	44194	Would it (be)
Tejedora ...	44195	Would it be worth while to
Tejido ...	44196	Would it not be
Tejoleta ...	44197	It would perhaps be
Telamon ...	44198	It would not be
Telarana ...	44199	Would be better (if)
Telaruolo ...	44200	I (we) would
Telefio ...	44201	I (we) would not
Teleosaur ...	44202	Would you
Telephion...	44203	He (they) would
Telescopic...	44204	He (they) would not
Teletarum	44205	Would just as soon
Teleton ...	44206	Would just as soon —— as ——
Teliambus	44207	Would continue
Telimus ...	44208	Would accept that
Tellement...	44209	Would certainly do so, unless
Telltale ...	44210	Provided that —— would
Telluric ...	44211	When would you
Teluccia ...	44212	Why would you
Telurio ...	44213	It would
Tematico ...	44214	It would not
Tembladal	44215	**Wound up** (*See also* " Wind up.")
Tembleque	44216	Now being wound up
Temblon ...	44217	**Wreck**
Temerabat	44218	An entire wreck
Temerario...	44219	Will probably become a total wreck
Temerator	44220	From the wreck
Temeridad	44221	Can you save anything from the wreck
Temeritudo	44222	Nothing is likely to be saved from the wreck
Temerity ...	44223	**Wrecked**
Temeron ...	44224	Which wrecked the
Temnibile...	44225	Would have wrecked
Temoignoge	44226	Was (were) entirely wrecked
Temoin ...	44227	Was (were) not wrecked
Temoniere	44228	Entirely wrecked
Temoroso ...	44229	**Wrecker(s)**
Tempaccio	44230	Professional wrecker(s)
Tempanador	44231	**Wrench**
Tempellare	44232	**Wretched(ly)**
Temperante	44233	**Wretchedness**
Temperatio	44234	**Writ**
Temperavit	44235	Has (have) been served with a writ
Tempestad	44236	Has (have) not yet been served with a writ
Templadura	44237	Solicitors have accepted service of writ
Templier ...	44238	Shall I issue a writ
Temporalis	44239	Better not issue a writ until
Temporize	44240	Issue a writ at once
Tempranal	44241	A writ has been issued against
Temptable	44242	A writ has been issued by
Temptation	44243	Has (have) —— issued a writ
Tempter ...	44244	Writ of ejectment
Temptingly	44245	Issue writ of ejectment
Temulento	44246	Writ of ejectment issued
Tenable ...	44247	Writ of ejectment will be issued cn
Tenacear ...	44248	**Write** (*See also* " Letter.")

Tenacidad	44249	Write fully by first mail
Tenacious...	44250	Write me to the following address
Tenaciter ...	44251	Will write
Tenallon ...	44252	Get —— to write
Tenant ...	44253	Get —— to write up the
Tenantable	44254	Cannot write until
Tenantless	44255	No use to write until
Tenantry ...	44256	When did you write last
Tenasmone	44257	Write fully to —— and inform him of all particulars
Tenazuelas	44258	Write me (us) at once with full particulars
Tencionare	44259	Write me (us) at once respecting
Tenconten	44260	In case of any alteration write fully
Tendalera...	44261	You can write to me care of —— at ——
Tendance ...	44262	There is no time to write; better telegraph
Tendarola...	44263	Write me (us) what you have done with respect to
Tendedor ...	44264	I (we) will write you fully by next mail
Tendelet ...	44265	—— will write you giving full instructions
Tendencia...	44266	Write(s) as follows, viz. :—

Writing

Tenderete ...	44267	
Tenderly ...	44268	Am (are) writing fully
Tenderness	44269	You should have everything in writing
Tendicula...	44270	Absolutely necessary to have everything in writing
Tendiente ..	44271	Am (are) writing —— by this mail
Tendinoso ..	44272	Everything has been put in writing
Tenditore ...	44273	Everything will be put in writing
Tendrement	44274	Nothing was put in writing

Written

Tendril ...	44275	
Tenebellis...	44276	Have you written
Tenebrario	44277	Have not written yet
Tenebricus	44278	—— should be written to at once
Tenebroso ..	44279	Should you not already have written
Teneduria ..	44280	Have written to you care of —— at ——
Tenellulus	44281	—— has written to the following effect
Tenement...	44282	Has (have) written to me (us) that
Tenerello ...	44283	Has (have) never written
Teneritas ...	44284	Why have you never written
Tenersi ...	44285	My last letter to you was written on ——
Teneruccio	44286	Have not yet received your letter written on ——

Wrong

Tenerume...	44287	
Tenesmo ...	44288	What is wrong (with ——)
Tenitojo ...	44289	Altogether wrong
Tennisball	44290	Is (are) quite wrong
Tenuisnet...	44291	There is really nothing wrong
Tenorist ...	44292	The accounts are undoubtedly wrong
Tenseness...	44293	Is there not something wrong with
Tensibilis ...	44294	Something must be wrong with (at ——)
Tensiores ...	44295	Nothing is wrong with (at ——)
Tentacion...	44296	Is anything wrong with (at ——)
Tentalear ...	44297	There is something wrong with
Tentandus	44298	There is nothing wrong with —— except that
Tentateur...	44299	Have not so far found anything wrong
Tentativo ...	44300	Should you find anything wrong do not hesitate to cable
Tentatrice...	44301	It was undoubtedly wrong to
Tentbed ...	44302	Have sent you the wrong ——; please forward it to
Tentenna ...	44303	Have sent you the wrong ——; please re-mail it to me (us)
Tentennone	44304	You have not informed us what is wrong
Tenterhook	44305	Provided that nothing is actually wrong
Tentorium	44306	The moment I discover where the wrong actually lies
Tentpegs ...	44307	Everything is wrong
Tenture ...	44308	Everything seems to have gone wrong

Tenuatim ..	44309	Everything is going wrong
Tenuiculus	44310	**Wrongful(ly)**
Tenuidad ...	44311	For wrongful dismissal
Tenutario ...	44312	**Wrongly**
Tenutella ...	44313	Either rightly or wrongly
Tenzonare	44314	Was (were) wrongly
Teocracia ...	44315	**Wrote** (*See also* "Write.")
Teocratico	44316	**Wrought** (*See also* "Iron.")
Teologal ...	44317	Whether of cast or wrought iron
Teologone...	44318	To be of wrought iron
Teoretico ...	44319	All to be of the best quality wrought iron
Teosofia ...	44320	**X**
Tepefare ...	44321	**Y** [end.)
Tepefatto ...	44322	**Yard(s)** (*See also* "Fathom," "Feet," "Mile," and Table at
Tephritis ...	44323	Cubic yard(s)
Tepidarium	44324	Square yard(s)
Tepidezza...	44325	Per cubic yard
Tepidness...	44326	Per lineal yard
Tepidule ...	44327	Per square yard
Tepificare...	44328	The cost per yard driven
Teporatus..	44329	What is the cost of driving per yard
Teppich ...	44330	The cost of driving per yard is —— (inclusive of ——)
Teramnos ...	44331	How many square yards does it cover
Terapeutas	44332	Covers an area of —— square yards
Teraphim ...	44333	An additional area of —— square yards
Tercamente	44334	**Year(s)** (*See also* "Annual.")
Tercenista...	44335	For the current year
Tercenteni	44336	For one year
Terchio ...	44337	For two years
Tercianela...	44338	For —— years
Terciazon ...	44339	In one year
Terdecies ...	44340	In —— years
Terebate ...	44341	Per year
Terebellum	44342	For the year ending
Terebinto ...	44343	Next year
Terebratio	44344	Last year
Tereniabin	44345	This year
Tergemino	44346	During the present year
Tergiverso	44347	During the past year
Teriones ...	44348	During the next year
Teristro ...	44349	Early in the year
Terjugus ...	44350	Early next year
Termagancy	44351	About the beginning of next year
Termidor ...	44352	About the middle of next year
Terminable	44353	About the end of next year
Terminacho	44354	About the year ——
Terminalia	44355	For all the year round practically
Terminante	44356	For how many years
Terminavi	44357	Will require nearly a year
Termite ...	44358	Has already taken —— years [services for a third year
Termtime...	44359	For two years certain with option to company to retain your
Ternario ...	44360	Am (is) (are) not willing to sign for more than two years
Ternatura ..	44361	Is (are) the worst month(s) of the year
Ternecico ...	44362	For the rest of the year
Terneruela	44363	Can the mine(s) be worked throughout the year
Ternideni ...	44364	The mine(s) can be worked practically throughout the year
Terquedad	44365	At all times of the year [ruptedly
Terraccia ...	44366	Work at the mine can proceed throughout the year uninter-
Terraced ...	44367	Regular work can proceed only during —— months of the
Terradgo ...	44368	First half of the year [y·

Terrafine ...	44369	Last half of the year
Terragero	44370	For the first half of this year
Terraneola	44371	For the last half of this year
Terraplen	44372	For the first half of last year
Terraqueo...	44373	For the last half of last year
Terrazzano	44374	For the first half of next year
Terrefacio	44375	For the last half of next year
Terregoso ...	44376	In the year ——
Terremoto	44377	In the year 1875
Terrene	44378	In the year 1876
Terrenello...	44379	In the year 1877
Terrenidad	44380	In the year 1878
Terrenum ...	44381	In the year 1879
Terrestita ...	44382	In the year 1880
Terrestre ...	44383	In the year 1881
Terretremo	44384	In the year 1882
Terreux ...	44385	In the year 1883
Terribilis ...	44386	In the year 1884
Terribly ...	44387	In the year 1885
Terricola ...	44388	In the year 1886
Terriculum	44389	In the year 1887
Terrier ...	44390	In the year 1888
Terrifico ...	44391	In the year 1889
Terrifying	44392	In the year 1890
Terrigeno ...	44393	In the year 1891
Terrisonus	44394	In the year 1892
Territandi...	44395	In the year 1893
Territoire ...	44396	In the year 1894
Terronazo ...	44397	In the year 1895
Terrontera	44398	In the year 1896
Terroribus	44399	In the year 1897
Terrorize ...	44400	In the year 1898
Terrulens ...	44401	In the year 1899
Tersamente	44402	In the year 1900
Tersely ...	44403	In the year 1901
Terseness ...	44404	In the year 1902
Tersidad ...	44405	In the year 1903
Tersura ...	44406	In the year 1904
Tertianus ...	44407	In the year 1905
Tertiarium	44408	**Yearly** (*See also* "Annually.")
Terticeps ...	44409	If yearly or otherwise
Tertulia ...	44410	Meetings to be held yearly
Teruelo ...	44411	Accounts to be made up yearly
Teruncius ...	44412	At our yearly meeting on ——
Terzaruolo·	44413	Yearly accounts will be mailed about
Terzerol ...	44414	Yearly accounts were mailed on
Terzett ...	44415	Yearly accounts should be accompanied by
Terzone ...	44416	Forward the yearly accounts as early as possible
Tesaureria	44417	This would increase the yearly profit to
Tesauro· ...	44418	Estimated yearly profit
Tesonia ...	44419	**Yes** (*See also* "Affirmative.")
Tesseaux ...	44420	Yes, decidedly
Tesselated	44421	No need to cable unless you can answer "yes"
Tessera ...	44422	Reply in any case either "yes" or "no"
Tesseratus	44423	Shall I (we) reply "yes"
Tesserula ...	44424	Must not reply "yes"
Tessimento	44425	Cannot reply "yes" until
Tessitrice ...	44426	Cable as soon as you can reply "yes"
Testabile ...	44427	Am (are) inclined to say "yes"
Testaceus ...	44428	Is it definitely "yes"

Testacion ...	44429	It is definitely " yes "
Testadora...	44430	Yes, this is definite
		[reply is " yes "
Testamento	44431	In answer to the question contained in your letter of —— the
Testamur ...	44432	In answer to the question contained in your cable received on
		[—— the reply is " yes "
Testarudo	44433	Has (have) —— replied " yes " or " no "
Testator ...	44434	—— has (have) replied " yes "
Testicolo ...	44435	**Yesterday** (*See also* " To-day.")
Testiculus	44436	Yesterday afternoon
Testificar ...	44437	Yesterday morning
Testifier ...	44438	During yesterday
Testimonio	44439	The day before yesterday
Testiness ...	44440	Were forwarded yesterday
Testolina ...	44441	Went yesterday to
Teston ...	44442	Mailed yesterday
Testoncino	44443	Was (were) settled yesterday
Testpaper...	44444	Finished yesterday previous to the arrival of your cable
Testtubes ...	44445	Were paid yesterday
Testudine	44446	**Yet**
Tetanico ...	44447	As yet
Tetanoidal	44448	Not yet
Tetanos ...	44449	Am (are) unable as yet (to)
Tetchily ...	44450	Will not as yet
Tetilla ...	44451	Nothing as yet
Tetracolou	44452	Am (is) not yet prepared to reply
Tetraedro ..	44453	**Yield** (*See also* " Returns.")
Tetragono ..	44454	Gross yield
Tetralix ...	44455	Net yield
Tetrameter	44456	Are the figures sent the gross or net yield
Tetramine	44457	The figures sent are gross (*i.e.:* inclusive of ——)
Tetraphori	44458	The figures sent are net (*i.e.:* exclusive of - ——)
Tetrarca ...	44459	What is the gross yield per ton
Tetrarquia	44460	The gross yield is
Tetraspore	44461	At what do you estimate the net yield per ton
Tetratomic	44462	Estimate the net yield at —— per ton
Tetrethyl ..	44463	The present yield
Tetrices ...	44464	The future yield
Tetriodide	44465	Should yield at least
Tetritudo ...	44466	Do(es) not yield
Tetrobolum	44467	Will not yield
Tetterello ...	44468	Cannot yield
Tettigonia	44469	Can only yield
Tettoja ...	44470	Continue(s) to yield
Tetulit ...	44471	Will no doubt materially increase the yield of
Teuchites ...	44472	Will undoubtedly diminish the yield of
Teucrio ...	44473	Unable to increase the yield
Teufeler ...	44474	Will enable me (us) to increase the yield
Teuthales ...	44475	Yield is light
Teuthrion...	44476	The yield varies between —— and —— per ton of 2,240 lbs.
Teutonic ...	44477	Total gross yield
Textbook ...	44478	The yield from last month's working is
Texthand ...	44479	The yield from last week's working is
Textilis ...	44480	**Yielded** (*See also* " Clean up.")
Textorio ...	44481	General clean up yielded
Textrinum	44482	The mine(s) has (have) yielded
Textual ...	44483	The mines have not recently yielded any profit
Textualist...	44484	Formerly yielded largely
Textuary ...	44485	**Yielding**
Thalamegos	44486	The mines are now yielding a monthly profit of
Thalassius	44487	The mines are now yielding —— tons per month

Thalerus ...	44488	Ceased yielding
Thalictrum	44489	**You**
Thallous ...	44490	Either you or ——
Thane ...	44491	You must decide
Thaneship	44492	By you
Thankfully	44493	From you
Thatcher ...	44494	To you
Thatching	44495	If you
Thatigkeit	44496	Provided that you
Thauwetter	44497	Provided that you will agree
Thawingly	44498	Provided you see no reason to the contrary
Theangelis	44499	Do you still
Theatralis...	44500	Do you not
Theatre ...	44501	If you do not
Theatrical	44502	Unless you
Thebaine ...	44503	It only now remains with you to
Theekessel	44504	—— told me that you
Theestoff ...	44505	**Your**
Theezeng ...	44506	By your
Theiform ...	44507	From your
Theilchen...	44508	To your
Theilung ...	44509	Of your
Theine ...	44510	With your
Theistic ...	44511	Your report
Thelygonum	44512	Your letter
Theobroma	44513	Your cable
Theocracy...	44514	As per your
Theodicy ...	44515	As per your instructions
Theogonist	44516	**Yourself(ves)**
Theogony ...	44517	By yourself
Theologian	44518	Not by yourself
Theorem ...	44519	Do not attempt to do the work by yourself
Theoretic ...	44520	Can you manage to do it (this) by yourself
Theoricien	44521	Anything to be done must be done by yourself
Theorist ...	44522	**Z**
Theosophic	44523	**Zaffres** (*See also* "Cobalt.")
Thereafter	44524	Zaffres containing —— per cent. cobalt, —— per cent. **nickel,**
Theriaque...	44525	**Zeal** (and —— per cent. **arsenic**
Theristrum	44526	Commend —— for his zeal
Thermopile	44527	Has (have) shown much zeal in
Thermopoto	44528	Has (have) not shown to my mind much zeal in
Thesaurizo	44529	Directors appreciate zeal displayed by
Thespesian	44530	Would be glad if more zeal generally was shown
Theuer ...	44531	**Zealous(ly)**
Theurgist...	44532	Should be zealously watched
Theurgy ...	44533	Should be zealously guarded
Thialdine ...	44534	Has (have) worked zealously in our interests (in the **interests**
Thickening	44535	**Zero** (*See also* "Temperature.") **[of ——)**
Thickhead	44536	Now down to zero
Thickset ...	44537	**Ziervogel process**
Thickskin...	44538	Employ the Ziervogel process
Thieftaker	44539	Employ the Ziervogel and Augustin processes **combined**
Thierisch ...	44540	Believe the Ziervogel process could be **advantageously employed**
Thierkreis	44541	A modified Ziervogel process
Thievery ...	44542	The ore is not suitable for the Ziervogel process
Thievish ...	44543	**Zinc** (*See also* "Blende," "Mineral.")
Thimble ...	44544	Zinc blende
Thimbleful	44545	Zinc blende associated with
Thimblerig	44546	Auriferous zinc blende
Thinkable	44547	Owing to the presence of a considerable amount of zinc blende

END OF PART 1.

PART II.

SURVEY OF MINERAL PROPERTIES.

Cipher Word.	No.	
Threescore	44573	Name of mine
Threnodia...	44574	Mining district
Threshers ...	44575	Geographical position
Threshold...	44576	Situation, locality, etc.
Thriftily ...	44577	Date of location
Thriftless ...	44578	Where recorded
Thrill ...	44579	Names of locators
Thrilling ...	44580	Names of present owners
Thriver ...	44581	History
Thrivingly	44582	Present title
Throbbing	44583	Distance to wood
Throned ...	44584	Distance to water
Thronerbe	44585	Distance to ore market
Thronging	44586	Distance to steamer
Thronrede	44587	Altitude, climate, etc.
Throttled ...	44588	Condition of roads
Throwster...	44589	Nearest railway
Thrummed	44590	Nearest waggon road
Thrustpin...	44591	Nearest important town
Thugism ...	44592	Geology
Thumbmark	44593	Topography (mountains, deep ravines, etc.)
Thumbscrew	44594	Trees and grass
Thumbstall	44595	Dimensions of claims
Thumper ...	44596	Description of mine
Thumping	44597	Surface works
Thundered	44598	Machinery
Thundering	44599	Mine openings
Thunlich ...	44600	Character of country rock
Thurangel	44601	Character of gangue
Thurarius	44602	Vein matter
Thurflugel	44603	Strike of vein
Thuribulum	44604	Dip of vein
Thurifer ...	44605	Average width of vein
Thurilegus	44606	Extent of outcrop
Thurklinke	44607	Character of footwall
Thurmchen	44608	Character of hanging wall
Thurschild	44609	Hardness of walls
Thwack ...	44610	Character of selvage
Thwart ...	44611	Character of ore
Thwarting	44612	General occurrence of ore
Thymallus	44613	Pay chutes
Thymelicus	44614	Course and trend of ore bodies
Thymianus	44615	Assays of the ore
Thyrse ...	44616	Gold contents

Cipher Word.	No.	
Thy—Tim		
Thyrsiger ...	44617	Silver contents
Tialismo ...	44618	Lead contents
Tiberium ...	44619	Copper contents
Tibialis ...	44620	Zinc contents
Tibiamente	44621	Other base metallic contents
Tibicine ...	44622	Amount of ore in sight
Tibicinium	44623	Value of ore in sight
Tibieza ...	44624	Tonnage and value of ore extracted and not worked
Tiburtino ...	44625	Tonnage and value of ore extracted to date
Ticketed ...	44626	Ore worked
Tickling ...	44627	Method of reduction
Ticklishly...	44628	Average yield per ton
Tidegate ...	44629	Particulars of underground workings
Tideless ...	44630	Water underground
Tidemill ...	44631	Timbering required
Tidetable ...	44632	Cost of timber and lumber
Tideway ...	44633	Cost of mining or extraction of ore
Tidiness ...	44634	Cost of reduction of ore
Tiefsinn ...	44635	Development work done
Tienniuave	44636	Proportion of developed to undeveloped ground
Tiepidare ...	44637	Reduction works
Tiepidetto	44638	Drainage requirements
Tierce ...	44639	Drainage facilities
Tigercubs...	44640	Cost of transportation
Tigerish ...	44641	Ore prices at nearest market
Tigermoth	44642	Wages
Tightrope...	44643	Contract prices
Tigliata ...	44644	The water supply
Tignamica	44645	The timber supply
Tignosuzzo	44646	General stores and supplies
Tignuola ...	44647	Cost of fuel
Tigrato ...	44648	Profit on previous operations
Tigrinus ...	44649	Profit on present working
Tijerada ...	44650	Probable profit on future working
Tijeretazo	44651	Adjacent mines
Tilbury	44652	Prospective value of mineral belt
Tildar ...	44653	Other information
Tilgung ...	44654	Price asked
Tiling ...	44655	Drawbacks
Tillerrope ..	44656	Probable value of mine
Tilleul ...	44657	Recommendations
Tilter ..	44658	General conclusions
Tilthammer	44659	Time and terms of bond
Tiltyard ...	44660	Any other conditions
Timbalear	44661	Maps and sections
Timballo ..	44662	Recapitulation
Timbertree	44663	Tables
Timberyard	44664	Appendix (ces)

SURVEY OF MINERAL PROPERTIES.

Consecutive Numbers.	Pay particular attention to	Need not pay attention to	Report by cable as to	
	Cipher Word. Tim—Tip	Cipher Word. Tip—Tit	Cipher Word. Tit—Tod	
1	Timbrar ...	Tippling ...	Tithymalus	Name of mine.
2	Timbrels ...	Tipsily ...	Titilar ...	Mining district
3	Timekeeper	Tipstaff ...	Titillate ...	Geographical position
4	Timeliness	Tiptoe ...	Titimaglio...	Situation, locality, etc.
5	Timepiece ...	Tiqueur ...	Titimalo ...	Date of location
6	Timeserver	Tirabala ...	Titivated ...	Where recorded
7	Timeworn	Tirabuzon...	Titlark ...	Names of locators
8	Timiama ...	Tiracabeza	Titlepage ...	Names of present owners
9	Timidetto ...	Tiracuello...	Titmouse ...	History
10	Timidez ...	Tirage ...	Titolaccio ...	Present title
11	Timiditas ...	Tirailler ...	Titolone ...	Distance to wood
12	Timidulus...	Tiralineas ...	Titrated ...	Distance to water
13	Timocracy...	Tiramollar...	Tittering ...	Distance to ore market
14	Timohogia	Tirania ...	Titubanter	Distance to steamer
15	Timonear ...	Tiranizar ...	Titubeante	Altitude, climate, etc.
16	Timoniere ..	Tirannare ...	Titubeo ...	Condition of roads
17	Timorato ...	Tirannello...	Titulado ...	Nearest railway
18	Timorous ...	Tiranneria...	Titularly ...	Nearest waggon road
19	Timoruccio	Tirantez ...	Tituletur ...	Nearest important town
20	Timpanello	Tirapie ...	Titulillo ...	Geology
21	Timpanitis	Tirasser ...	Titulizado...	Topography (mountains, deep [ravines, etc.)
22	Tinajeria ...	Tiratura ...	Tityrus ...	Trees and grass
23	Tinajon ...	Tireballe ...	Tiznar ...	Dimensions of claims
24	Tinchetta ...	Tirebottes ...	Tizoncillo ...	Description of mine
25	Tincone ...	Tirebourre...	Toadeater ...	Surface works
26	Tinctilis ...	Tireclou ...	Toadfish ...	Machinery
27	Tinctorius...	Tiredness ...	Toadflax ...	Mine openings
28	Tincture ...	Tirefond ...	Toadseye ...	Character of country rock
29	Tinderbox ...	Tirelait ...	Toadstool ...	Character of gangue
30	Tinelero ...	Tiremoelle...	Toalleta ...	Vein matter
31	Tineosus ...	Tirepied ...	Toasting ...	Strike of vein
32	Tinette ...	Tireplomb...	Toastrack ...	Dip of vein
33	Tinfloors ...	Tiresome ...	Tobacco ...	Average width of vein
34	Tingente ...	Tireuse ...	Tobaccojar	Extent of outcrop
35	Tinglado ...	Tiritador ...	Tobaja ...	Character of footwall
36	Tiniebla ...	Tiritona ...	Tobillo ...	Character of hanging wall
37	Tinker ...	Tischblatt...	Toboggan ...	Hardness of walls
38	Tinning ...	Tisichezza...	Tobsucht ...	Character of selvage
39	Tinniturus	Tisicuccio ...	Tocamiento	Character of ore
40	Tinshop ...	Tisicune ...	Toccalapis	General occurrence of ore
41	Tinsmith ...	Tisserand ...	Toccapolsi...	Pay chutes
42	Tintamarre	Tissue ...	Toccatina ...	Course and trend of ore bodies
43	Tintement...	Titanio ...	Toccatore ...	Assays of the ore
44	Tintenfass...	Titanitic ...	Toccatrice ...	Gold contents
45	Tintilamo ...	Titanous ...	Tochter ...	Silver contents
46	Tintinnire...	Titbit ...	Tochura ...	Lead contents
47	Tintoreria ...	Titelblatt ...	Tocinero ...	Copper contents
48	Tintouin ...	Titerero ...	Tocsin ...	Zinc contents
49	Tinuela ...	Tithable ...	Tocullio ...	Other base metallic contents
50	Tipografo ...	Tithefree ...	Todavia ...	Amount of ore in sight
51	Tippet ...	Tithing ...	Toddlers ...	Value of ore in sight
52	Tippler ...	Tithingman	Todesangst	Tonnage and value of ore ex-[tracted and not worked

SURVEY OF MINERAL PROPERTIES.

Consecutive Numbers	Having regard to	Confirm information respecting	Require fullest details of	
	Cipher Word. Tod—Tom	Cipher Word. Tom—Top	Cipher Word. Top—Tor	
1	Todesstoss	Tombless ...	Toparchas ...	Name of mine
2	Todestag ...	Tombolare...	Toparquia...	Mining district
3	Todestrafe...	Tomboy ...	Topazium ...	Geographical position
4	Todfeind ...	Tombstone	Topboots ..	Situation, locality, etc.
5	Todillus ...	Tomento ...	Topelhaft ...	Date of location
6	Todkrank ...	Tomfoolery	Topesco ...	Where recorded
7	Todtenkapf	Tomillar ...	Topeton ...	Names of locators
8	Todtlich ...	Tominejo ...	Topetudo ...	Names of present owners
9	Tofaceus ...	Tomolto ...	Topfer ...	History
10	Toffishly ...	Tomtit ...	Topgallant	Present title
11	Togada ...	Tonadica ...	Tophaceus...	Distance to wood
12	Togatarius	Tonatore ...	Topheavy ...	Distance to water
13	Toglimento	Tonchioso ...	Tophinus ...	Distance to ore market
14	Toglitrice ...	Tondamento	Topiarium...	Distance to steamer
15	Togulam ...	Tondatura...	Topically ...	Altitude, climate, etc.
16	Tohalla ...	Tondeuse ...	Topinaria ...	Condition of roads
17	Toilerie ...	Tondichter	Topknot ...	Nearest railway
18	Toilet ...	Tonelete ...	Topless ...	Nearest waggon road
19	Toilsome ...	Tonescit ...	Toplights ...	Nearest important town
20	Tojines ...	Tonfuhrung	Topmast ...	Geology
21	Tokens ...	Tonganuts...	Topografia	Topography (mountains, deep [ravines, etc.)
22	Toldadura...	Tongue ...	Topolino ...	Trees and grass
23	Toldilla ...	Tongueless	Toppetto ...	Dimensions of claims
24	Tolerable ...	Tonguetied	Topping ...	Description of mine
25	Tolerancia...	Tonicella ...	Topple ...	Surface works
26	Tolerandus	Tonitralis ...	Topsail ...	Machinery
27	Tolerate ...	Tonitruo ...	Topsawyer...	Mine openings
28	Toleration...	Tonkunst ...	Topahrouds	Character of country rock
29	Tolladar ...	Tonleiter ...	Topsyturvy	Character of gangue
30	Tollbar ...	Tonsetzer ...	Toqueado ...	Vein matter
31	Tollbooth ...	Tonsilitic ...	Toqueria ...	Strike of vein
32	Tollbridge...	Tonsils ...	Toquilla ...	Dip of vein
33	Tollecer ...	Tonsorium	Toracico ...	Average width of vein
34	Tollendus ...	Tonstrina ...	Torbellino...	Extent of outcrop
35	Tollerante ...	Tonstuck ...	Torbidato ...	Character of footwall
36	Tollgate ...	Tonsurar ...	Torbidezza	Character of hanging wall
37	Tollhouse ...	Tonsured ...	Torcas ...	Hardness of walls
38	Tollkuhn ...	Tonsylbe ...	Torcedero ...	Character of selvage
39	Tolommea...	Tonteria ...	Torceriais ...	Character of ore
40	Tolondro ...	Tontillo ...	Torchboys...	General occurrence of ore
41	Toluidine ...	Tontine ...	Torchepot ...	Pay chutes
42	Toluol ...	Tonzeichen	Torchette ...	Course and trend of ore bodies
43	Tolutaris ...	Toolchest ...	Torching ...	Assays of the ore
44	Toluylic ...	Tooled ...	Torchlight	Gold contents
45	Tolvanera ...	Tooth ...	Torchon ...	Silver contents
46	Tomaclum...	Toothache...	Torcida ...	Lead contents
47	Tomadero ...	Toothless ...	Torcidillo ...	Copper contents
48	Tomahawk	Toothpaste	Torcijon ...	Zinc contents
49	Tomajon ...	Toothpick...	Torcimanno	Other base metallic contents
50	Tomatoes ...	Toothsome	Torcitura ...	Amount of ore in sight
51	Tombak ...	Topadizo ...	Torcoliere ...	Value of ore in sight
52	Tombeau ...	Topador ...	Torculado ...	Tonnage and value of ore ex- [tracted and not worked

SURVEY OF MINERAL PROPERTIES.

Consecutive Numbers.	Pay particular attention to	Need not pay attention to	Report by Cable as to	
	Cipher Word. Tor	Cipher Word. Tor—Tos	Cipher Word. Tos—Tov	
53	Tordella ...	Torreado ...	Tosspot	Tonnage and value of ore ex-[tracted to date
54	Tordilon ...	Torrefier ...	Tostado ...	Ore worked
55	Torero ...	Torrejon ...	Tostadura...	Method of reduction
56	Toreumatum	Torrentada	Tostanezza	Average yield per ton
57	Torffuder ...	Torrentius...	Totalement	Particulars of underground [workings
58	Torgniole ...	Torreon ...	Totalidad ...	Water underground
59	Toriondez ...	Torreznero	Totality ...	Timbering required
60	Torkeln ...	Torridity ...	Totalized ...	Cost of timber and lumber
61	Tormentil ...	Torridzone	Totalness ...	Cost of mining or extraction [of ore
62	Tormenting	Torrigiano...	Totjugus ...	Cost of reduction of ore
63	Tormentoso	Torrontes ...	Totomaglia	Development work done
64	Torminalis	Torsaccio ...	Totovia ...	Proportion of developed to un-[developed ground
65	Tornaboda	Torsade ...	Touaille ...	Reduction works
66	Tornado ...	Torsione ...	Touchable...	Drainage requirements
67	Tornagusto	Tortela ...	Touchhole...	Drainage facilities
68	Tornaletto...	Tortellajo	Touchily ...	Cost of transportation
69	Tornapunta	Torticolis ...	Touchiness	Ore prices at nearest market
70	Tornasolar	Tortillage ...	Touchpaper	Wages
71	Tornatilis ...	Tortillon	Touchstone	Contract prices
72	Tornaviage	Tortoise ...	Touchwood	The water supply
73	Torneante ...	Tortolella ...	Touffu ...	The timber supply
74	Torneria ...	Tortolico	Toughen	General stores and supplies
75	Torniare ...	Tortores ...	Toughening	Cost of fuel
76	Tornillero ...	Tortueux ...	Toughly ...	Profit on previous operations
77	Torniquete	Tortuga ...	Toughness...	Profit on present working
78	Torniscon ...	Tortuosita...	Toujours ...	Probable profit on future [working
79	Tornister ...	Torturer ...	Toupillon ...	Adjacent mines
80	Torondoso...	Torturing ...	Tourbeuse...	Prospective value of mineral [belt
81	Torongil ...	Torvinus ...	Tourelle	Other information
82	Torozon ...	Torvisco ...	Tourist ...	Price asked
83	Torpedo ...	Torviter ...	Tourlouron	Drawbacks
84	Torpescens	Toryism	Tournament	Probable value of mine
85	Torpeur ...	Torzonado...	Tournevis ...	Recommendations
86	Torpidness	Toscamente	Tourniquet	General conclusions
87	Torpiglia ...	Tosegoso ...	Tournoyer...	Time and terms of bond
88	Torporific ...	Tosidura ...	Tousle ...	Any other conditions
89	Torquatus...	Tosolato ...	Toussaint ...	Maps and sections
90	Torqueor ...	Tosquedad	Tousseur ...	Recapitulation
91	Torrajuolo...	Tosserella ...	Toutefois ...	Tables
92	Torrazzo ...	Tossicare ...	Tovaglia ...	Appendix(ces)

SURVEY OF MINERAL PROPERTIES.

Consecutive Numbers	Having regard to	Confirm information respecting	Require fullest details of	
	Cipher Word. Tow—Tra	Cipher Word. Tra	Cipher Word. Tra	
58	Towel	Tracattivo	Trafficker	Tonnage and value of ore ex- [tracted to date
54	Toweling	Tracciare	Traficante	Ore worked
55	Towingpath	Traceable	Trafiere	Method of reduction
56	Towline	Tracement	Trafisso	Average yield per ton
57	Townclerk	Trachali	Trafoglio	Particulars of underground [workings
58	Towncrier	Tracheitis	Traforato	Water underground
59	Townball	Trachiaro	Trafreddo	Timbering required
60	Townhouse	Tracias	Trafugare	Cost of timber and lumber
61	Townlands	Tracista	Trafurello	Cost of mining or extraction of [ore
62	Township	Trackless	Trafusola	Cost of reduction of ore
63	Townsman	Tracocente	Tragacanth	Development work done
64	Towntalk	Tracodardo	Tragacete	Proportion of developed to un- [developed ground
65	Towropes	Tracollato	Tragafees	Reduction works
66	Toxicavit	Tracotanza	Tragaluz	Drainage requirements
67	Toxicology	Tracotto	Traganthes	Drainage facilities
68	Toxicum	Tractable	Tragantona	Cost of transportation
69	Toxique	Tractandus	Tragbahre	Ore prices at nearest market
70	Toyish	Tractarian	Tragbar	Wages
71	Toymaker	Tractatrix	Tragedian	Contract prices
72	Toyman	Tractorium	Tragekorb	The water supply
73	Toyshop	Tracutato	Tragelafo	The timber supply
74	Tozzetto	Tradeguild	Tragemata	General stores and supplies
75	Traantico	Trademark	Tragettare	Cost of fuel
76	Traavaro	Tradendus	Tragheit	Profit on previous operations
77	Trabacca	Tradesfolk	Tragically	Profit on present working
78	Trabadero	Tradesman	Tragico	Probable profit on future [working
79	Trabajador	Tradewinds	Traginar	Adjacent mines
80	Trabaldare	Tradigione	Tragineria	Prospective value of mineral [belt
81	Trabanco	Tradiritto	Tragiogare	Other information
82	Trabarium	Traditor	Tragique	Price asked
83	Trabeato	Traditurus	Tragodie	Drawbacks
84	Trabecula	Tradolce	Tragopanas	Probable value of mine
85	Traben	Traducible	Tragrande	Recommendations
86	Trabiccolo	Traductor	Traguardo	General conclusions
87	Trabilla	Traduire	Tragulas	Time and terms of bond
88	Trabucador	Trafagador	Traharius	Any other conditions
89	Trabucante	Trafagon	Trahison	Maps and sections
90	Trabuquete	Trafalmejo	Traidora	Recapitulation
91	Tracannato	Trafelare	Traimento	Tables
92	Tracasser	Trafficato	Trainable	Appendix(ces)

Cipher Word.	No.	Cipher Word.	No.	Cipher Word.	No.	Cipher Word.	No.
Trainbands	1	Transcend	60	Trariparsi	119	Trasviato	178
Traineau	2	Transcrire	61	Trarotto	120	Trasvolare	179
Trainoil	3	Transduco	62	Trarupato	121	Trasvolto	180
Traitable	4	Transegna	63	Trasabuelo	122	Tratadista	181
Traiteur	5	Transept	64	Trasalire	123	Tratado	182
Traitorous	6	Transeunte	65	Trasandato	124	Tratanza	183
Traitress	7	Transferir	66	Trasavio	125	Trattatore	184
Trajecero	8	Transfixo	67	Trascabo	126	Trattenere	185
Trajected	9	Transfodio	68	Trascanton	127	Traubig	186
Trajecting	10	Transform	69	Trascelto	128	Traudire	187
Trajectura	11	Transfuga	70	Trascocco	129	Trauerflor	188
Trajiciens	12	Transgress	71	Trascorral	130	Trauern	189
Tralatato	13	Transient	72	Trascotato	131	Traufrinne	190
Tralciato	14	Transigir	73	Trascritto	132	Traulizo	191
Tralciuzzo	15	Transilire	74	Trascuarto	133	Traumbild	192
Traliccio	16	Transitivo	75	Trasdoblar	134	Traumbuch	193
Trallern	17	Transitory	76	Trasdosear	135	Traumerie	194
Traloquor	18	Translabor	77	Trasenalar	136	Traumwelt	195
Tralordo	19	Translate	78	Trasero	137	Trauvede	196
Tralucent	20	Translego	79	Trasfregar	138	Travaglia	197
Tralucere	21	Transmigro	80	Trasfusion	139	Travailler	198
Tralucidus	22	Transminar	81	Trasgresor	140	Travalente	199
Tramador	23	Transmoveo	82	Trasguero	141	Travariare	200
Tramail	24	Transmute	83	Trash	142	Travasato	201
Tramazzato	25	Transpareo	84	Trashojar	143	Travatura	202
Trambusta	26	Transponer	85	Trasiego	144	Travedere	203
Tramenato	27	Transtineo	86	Traslapar	145	Traveggole	204
Tramestio	28	Transulto	87	Traslativo	146	Traveller	205
Tramezzare	29	Transvaser	88	Traslatore	147	Travelling	206
Tramitello	30	Transvehor	89	Trasloar	148	Traversed	207
Tramittens	31	Transverso	90	Trasmallo	149	Travertino	208
Trammels	32	Transvider	91	Trasmitido	150	Travestido	209
Trammogia	33	Tranzadera	92	Trasmodare	151	Travesty	210
Tramortito	34	Tranzon	93	Trasmontar	152	Travesura	211
Tramoya	35	Trapacear	94	Trasmutato	153	Traviatore	212
Tramoyista	36	Trapacista	95	Trasnello	154	Travicella	213
Trampal	37	Trapalon	96	Trasnieto	155	Travieso	214
Trampeador	38	Trapanato	97	Trasnochar	156	Travillano	215
Trampler	39	Trapball	98	Trasognare	157	Travisarsi	216
Trampling	40	Trapdoor	99	Trasoneria	158	Travolgere	217
Tramtare	41	Trapecio	100	Trasoriere	159	Travone	218
Tranavero	42	Trapensare	101	Traspadano	160	Trawlboats	219
Trancado	43	Trapezium	102	Trasparere	161	Trawlers	220
Trancahilo	44	Trapezoid	103	Traspaso	162	Trawlnets	221
Trancenil	45	Traphole	104	Traspeinar	163	Trazumarse	222
Tranchant	46	Trapiccolo	105	Trasplante	164	Treachery	223
Tranchoir	47	Trapisonda	106	Traspontin	165	Treader	224
Tranetto	48	Traposta	107	Traspuesta	166	Treadles	225
Trangallo	49	Trapper	108	Trasquero	167	Treadmill	226
Trankchen	50	Trappings	109	Trasteado	168	Treason	227
Tranken	51	Trappistic	110	Trasteria	169	Treasured	228
Tranobile	52	Trappola	111	Trastienda	170	Treatise	229
Tranquera	53	Trapporre	112	Trastornar	171	Treatment	230
Tranquilar	54	Trappreso	113	Trastrigo	172	Trebacis	231
Transactor	55	Trapstick	114	Trastrueco	173	Treballa	232
Transadigo	56	Trapuntato	115	Trastullo	174	Trebedes	233
Transalpin	57	Traquear	116	Trastumbar	175	Trebentina	234
Transanejo	58	Traquenard	117	Trasudere	176	Trebling	235
Transatare	59	Traqueteo	118	Trasversal	177	Trebuchant	236

Cipher Word.	No.	Cipher Word.	No.	Cipher Word.	No.	Cipher Word.	No.
Trebucher	237	Trepanning	296	Tricoteuse	355	Trinkhalle	414
Trebuto	238	Trephine	297	Tricuspide	356	Trinklied	415
Treccheria	239	Trepidante	298	Tricycle	357	Trinoctium	416
Trecchiero	240	Trepidatur	299	Trident	358	Trinomio	417
Trecenario	241	Trepidezza	300	Tridentato	359	Trinquete	418
Trecesimo	242	Trepidulus	301	Triebfeder	360	Triobolum	419
Trecientos	243	Trepigner	302	Triebsand	361	Triocca	420
Tredecimo	244	Trepointe	303	Triefauge	362	Trionfale	421
Treefrog	245	Trepondo	304	Triefen	363	Triorches	422
Treeless	246	Treppello	305	Triemito	364	Triorque	423
Treemoss	247	Trescato	306	Triennial	365	Trioxide	424
Trefedad	248	Tresdoble	307	Triennium	366	Tripartite	425
Treffend	249	Tresmesino	308	Trientalis	367	Tripatinum	426
Trefilerie	250	Tresnal	309	Trifance	368	Tripectore	427
Trefileur	251	Tresorerie	310	Trifariam	369	Tripeman	428
Trefoglio	252	Trester	311	Trifler	370	Triperie	429
Trefoil	253	Tretean	312	Trifling	371	Tripetalo	430
Tregenda	254	Treuherzig	313	Trifolio	372	Tripier	431
Treggione	255	Triacal	314	Triforcato	373	Tripitrape	432
Treibbett	256	Triads	315	Triformis	374	Triplex	433
Treibeis	257	Trialtrip	316	Triftig	375	Triplicado	434
Treibhaus	258	Triangulo	317	Trigamy	376	Triplicity	435
Treibrad	259	Triaquera	318	Trigemini	377	Tripod	436
Treillage	260	Triatomic	319	Triglifo	378	Tripolio	437
Treintanal	261	Tribaldare	320	Triglites	379	Tripotier	438
Treinteno	262	Tribaquio	321	Triglyphus	380	Trippaccia	439
Treizieme	263	Tribbiare	322	Trigonalis	381	Trippingly	440
Trekker	264	Tribolarsi	323	Trigraphic	382	Triptongo	441
Trekking	265	Triboloso	324	Trigueno	383	Triptoton	442
Trellised	266	Triboulet	325	Trihedral	384	Tripudiar	443
Tremadal	267	Tribrachus	326	Trilatero	385	Tripulado	444
Trembler	268	Tribrevis	327	Trilingue	386	Triquetra	445
Trembling	269	Tribuarius	328	Triliteral	387	Triregno	446
Trembloter	270	Tribuebant	329	Trilladera	388	Trireme	447
Tremebundo	271	Tribuendus	330	Trillern	389	Trisagium	448
Tremefacio	272	Tribuir	331	Trilogy	390	Trisaieul	449
Tremendous	273	Tribuisset	332	Trilustre	391	Trisarquia	450
Trementina	274	Tribulante	333	Trimbaler	392	Trisavolo	451
Tremerella	275	Tribulose	334	Trimembris	393	Trisecdor	452
Tremescet	276	Tribunal	335	Trimesic	394	Trisecar	453
Tremielga	277	Tribunesco	336	Trimestre	395	Trisect	454
Tremipibus	278	Tributario	337	Trimmer	396	Trisection	455
Tremiscere	279	Tributim	338	Trimmingly	397	Trispastus	456
Tremolante	280	Tributurus	339	Trimodium	398	Tristacho	457
Tremolina	281	Tricennial	340	Trinacrio	399	Tristanza	458
Tremoroso	282	Tricerbero	341	Trincafiar	400	Tristega	459
Tremplin	283	Trichalcum	342	Trincatore	401	Tristesse	460
Tremulare	284	Tricherie	343	Trincerare	402	Tristities	461
Tremulous	285	Tricheur	344	Trincetto	403	Tristitudo	462
Trencellin	286	Trichitis	345	Trinchante	404	Tristras·	463
Trenchant	287	Trichorum	346	Trinchear	405	Tristuzzo	464
Trencillar	288	Trichotomy	347	Trincheron	406	Trisulco	465
Trennung	289	Trichter	348	Trinciata	407	Trisyllabe	466
Trentaine	290	Tricipete	349	Trincos	408	Tritamente	467
Trentamila	291	Trickster	350	Tringler	409	Tritavos	468
Trentuno	292	Triclinio	351	Trinitaria	410	Trite	469
Trenzado	293	Tricolour	352	Trinket	411	Triteismo	470
Trepan	294	Tricornis	353	Trinkgelag	412	Tritello	471
Trepanner	295	Tricorpor	354	Trinkglass	413	Triteness	472

Cipher Word.	No.	Cipher Word.	No.	Cipher Word.	No.	Cipher Word.	No.
Trithales	473	Tronerar	532	Truffle	591	Tugurio	650
Triticeo	474	Tronfiare	533	Trugbild	592	Tuilerie	651
Trittbret	475	Tronquista	534	Trugiolare	593	Tuition	652
Trittume	476	Trooper	535	Truglich	594	Tuitionary	653
Triturable	477	Troopships	536	Truhaneria	595	Tulip	654
Triturer	478	Tropelia	537	Truism	596	Tulipanero	655
Tritylic	479	Tropezador	538	Trujaleta	597	Tuliptree	656
Triumphant	480	Tropezon	539	Trujamania	598	Tullianum	657
Triumpher	481	Tropfeln	540	Trulleum	599	Tullidura	658
Triumvirat	482	Tropfnass	541	Trullisso	600	Tumbadero	659
Triune	483	Tropfstein	542	Trumpeter	601	Tumbagon	660
Triunfador	484	Trophied	543	Truncado	602	Tumbilla	661
Triunfante	485	Trophy	544	Truncated	603	Tumbler	662
Triunfo	486	Tropical	545	Truncatote	604	Tumbonear	663
Triunviro	487	Tropicarum	546	Truncheon	605	Tumbril	664
Trivalency	488	Tropiezo	547	Trundle	606	Tumescens	665
Trivial	489	Tropologia	548	Trunnion	607	Tumfatto	666
Triviality	490	Troquillo	549	Truppweise	608	Tumidezza	667
Triviritim	491	Trostgrund	550	Truque	609	Tumido	668
Trivolum	492	Trostlich	551	Truquiflor	610	Tumidulus	669
Trocable	493	Trostung	552	Trusatilis	611	Tumoroso	670
Trocaico	494	Trotoneria	553	Truster	612	Tumulandus	671
Trocatinta	495	Trottoir	554	Trustfully	613	Tumult	672
Trocear	496	Trotzig	555	Trustingly	614	Tumultuar	673
Trochaic	497	Troubadour	556	Trustless	615	Tumultueux	674
Trochee	498	Troublous	557	Truthenne	616	Tunanteria	675
Trochilos	499	Troumadame	558	Trutinor	617	Tunbellied	676
Trechisco	500	Troupeau	559	Trychnos	618	Tundente	677
Trochoidal	501	Troupier	560	Trygonis	619	Tundicion	678
Trocken	502	Trousering	561	Tryphera	620	Tundidura	679
Troddel	503	Trousers	562	Trysail	621	Tundizno	680
Trodelhaft	504	Trout	563	Trysting	622	Tungstate	681
Trodelkram	505	Trouvable	564	Tuantem	623	Tunicatus	682
Trodler	506	Trouvaille	565	Tubarius	624	Tunichetta	683
Trofeista	507	Trouvere	566	Tubbing	625	Tuningfork	684
Trogliare	508	Trovatore	567	Tubercle	626	Tunist	685
Troglodyte	509	Trovista	568	Tubereuse	627	Tuppelig	686
Trognon	510	Troxalidem	569	Tuberosa	628	Turaccio	687
Trogoletto	511	Troxalis	570	Tuberosity	629	Turbacion	688
Troisieme	512	Troyano	571	Tubicen	630	Turbamulta	689
Troismats	513	Truant	572	Tubulatus	631	Turbaned	690
Troissix	514	Truantship	573	Tuburcinor	632	Turbary	691
Trojaccia	515	Trubselig	574	Tucetarius	633	Turbatetto	692
Trojero	516	Trucciare	575	Tuchen	634	Turbativa	693
Trollop	517	Truchement	576	Tuchfabrik	635	Turbatore	694
Trollopped	518	Truchsess	577	Tuchhandel	636	Turbatrice	695
Trombadore	519	Trucidar	578	Tuchrahmen	637	Turbella	696
Trombato	520	Trucidatio	579	Tudernis	638	Turbidness	697
Trompada	521	Truciolo	580	Tudesco	639	Turbidulus	698
Trompetazo	522	Trucker	581	Tudesque	640	Turbiedad	699
Trompeten	523	Trucklebed	582	Tudicula	641	Turbinatio	700
Trompicon	524	Truculento	583	Tuerto	642	Turbineus	701
Trompillar	525	Trueblue	584	Tufarada	643	Turbion	702
Tronador	526	Truelove	585	Tuffatore	644	Turbotiere	703
Troncal	527	Trueness	586	Tufted	645	Turbotin	704
Troncativo	528	Trufador	587	Tugendhaft	646	Turbulento	705
Troncatura	529	Trufaidin	588	Tugger	647	Turbystum	706
Tronchado	530	Truffato	589	Tugging	648	Turchesco	707
Tronconner	531	Truffiere	590	Tugurietto	649	Turcimanno	708

Cipher Word.	No.	Cipher Word.	No.	Cipher Word.	No.	Cipher Word.	No.
Turdarium	709	Tweedcloth	768	Ueberblick	827	Ultimas	886
Turdetanus	710	Tweezers	769	Ueberdiess	828	Ultimately	887
Turdiga	711	Twelfthday	770	Uebereck	829	Ultimatum	888
Turdillus	712	Twiggy	771	Ueberfahrt	830	Ultraistic	889
Tureen	713	Twilight	772	Ueberfluss	831	Ultrajador	890
Turfhouse	714	Twinborn	773	Ueberhand	832	Ultrajoso	891
Turfiness	715	Twinge	774	Ueberhaupt	833	Ultroneus	892
Turfing	716	Twinging	775	Ueberklug	834	Ululabilis	893
Turfmoss	717	Twinkle	776	Ueberlegt	835	Ululamen	894
Turfspade	718	Twinned	777	Uebermacht	836	Umackern	895
Turgencia	719	Twister	778	Uebermass	837	Umanderung	896
Turgesco	720	Twittingly	779	Uebernahme	838	Umarbeiten	897
Turgidezza	721	Twoedged	780	Ueberquer	839	Umazione	898
Turgidity	722	Twohanded	781	Ueberreif	840	Umbehalten	899
Turibulum	723	Twopenny	782	Ueberrock	841	Umbela	900
Turificar	724	Tympanicus	783	Uebertrag	842	Umbelico	901
Turkscap	725	Tympaniser	784	Ueberwurf	843	Umbelifera	902
Turkshead	726	Tympanon	785	Ueberzahn	844	Umbellate	903
Turlupin	727	Typed	786	Ueblich	845	Umbilden	904
Turmales	728	Typemetal	787	Uebrigens	846	Umbilicado	905
Turmeric	729	Typemould	788	Ueppig	847	Umbraculum	906
Turmeruela	730	Typestick	789	Ueppigkeit	848	Umbrage	907
Turncoat	731	Typewriter	790	Ufanamente	849	Umbralar	908
Turnip	732	Typhoid	791	Ufaneza	850	Umbravero	909
Turnipseed	733	Typically	792	Ufficiare	851	Umbrechen	910
Turnkey	734	Typified	793	Ufficioso	852	Umbrella	911
Turnkunst	735	Typify	794	Uffizietto	853	Umbrifer	912
Turnout	736	Tyrannic	795	Uggiolare	854	Umbrosity	913
Turnpike	737	Tyranniser	796	Uglified	855	Umbroso	914
Turnspit	738	Tyrant	797	Ugliness	856	Umdrehung	915
Turnstile	739	Tyrunculus	798	Ugnatura	857	Umettabile	916
Turntable	740	Ubbiaccia	799	Ugnetto	858	Umettativo	917
Turnubung	741	Ubbidente	800	Ugnimento	859	Umettoso	918
Turquino	742	Ubbiditore	801	Ugonotto	860	Umfassend	919
Turquoise	743	Ubbriacone	802	Ugualato	861	Umformen	920
Turreted	744	Ubbrigato	803	Uguannatto	862	Unganglich	921
Turronada	745	Uberifero	804	Uhlane	863	Umgegend	922
Turtle	746	Uberius	805	Uhrglas	864	Umgelben	923
Turtledove	747	Uberrimo	806	Uhrkette	865	Umgranzen	924
Turtlefin	748	Ubertoso	807	Uhrmacher	866	Umgurten	925
Turumbon	749	Ubication	808	Uhrwerk	867	Umhullen	926
Tusilago	750	Ubicuidad	809	Ukase	868	Umiliaca	927
Tutamentum	751	Ubicumque	810	Ulcerado	869	Umilmente	928
Tuteador	752	Ubilibet	811	Ulcerated	870	Umkleiden	929
Tutelar	753	Ubiquista	812	Ulcerativo	871	Umlagern	930
Tutiplen	754	Ubiquitous	813	Ulcerieur	872	Umliegend	931
Tutoiement	755	Ubrera	814	Ulceroso	873	Umnehmen	932
Tutoress	756	Uccellante	815	Ulciscens	874	Umoraccio	933
Tutoring	757	Uccelletto	816	Ulcusculus	875	Umoretto	934
Tutorship	758	Uccelliera	817	Uligine	876	Umorosita	935
Tutoyer	759	Uccelluzzo	818	Uliginosus	877	Umpflugen	936
Tuttavolla	760	Ucchiello	819	Ulivastro	878	Umpire	937
Tutulatus	761	Ucencia	820	Ulivella	879	Umpragen	938
Tutumaglio	762	Udandus	821	Ulivigno	880	Umreissen	939
Tututto	763	Uddered	822	Ulmaceous	881	Umringen	940
Tuyanter	764	Udimento	823	Ulmaria	882	Umruhren	941
Twaddlers	765	Uditorato	824	Ulmitriba	883	Umsatteln	942
Twankay	766	Udometre	825	Ulpicum	884	Umschauen	943
Tweak	767	Uebelthat	826	Ulterior	885	Umschiffen	944

Cipher Word.	No.	Cipher Word.	No.	Cipher Word.	No.	Cipher Word.	No.
Umsetzen	945	Unaptness	1,200	Unbiass	4,150	Unclassic	9,200
Umsichtig	946	Unargued	1,250	Unbiegsam	4,200	Uncleanly	9,300
Umspringen	947	Unarmed	1,300	Unbigoted	4,250	Uncleansed	9,400
Umstecken	948	Unarrested	1,350	Unbishop	4.300	Unclench	9,500
Umstehende	949	Unartfully	1,400	Unblamable	4,350	Unclerical	9,600
Umstellung	950	Unartig	1,450	Unblamed	4,400	Uncloaked	9,700
Umsturz	951	Unartistic	1,500	Unbleached	4,450	Uncloister	9,800
Umthun	952	Unashamed	1,550	Unblended	4,500	Unclothe	9,900
Umtrieb	953	Unaspiring	1,600	Unblest	4,550	Unclouded	10,000
Umwalzung	954	Unassailed	1,650	Unblotted	4,600	Uncocked	10,100
Umwechseln	955	Unassisted	1,700	Unblushing	4,650	Uncoil	10,200
Umwerfen	956	Unassuaged	1,750	Unboasted	4,700	Uncoiling	10,300
Umwolken	957	Unassuming	1,800	Unboastful	4,750	Uncoloured	10,400
Umzaunung	958	Unatonable	1,850	Unbodied	4,800	Uncombined	10,500
Umzingeln	959	Unatoned	1,900	Unbolted	4,850	Uncomely	10,600
Unabashed	960	Unattacked	1,950	Unbookish	4,900	Uncompact	10,700
Unabated	961	Unattended	2,000	Unborrowed	4,950	Unconcern	10,800
Unablassig	962	Unattired	2,050	Unbosom	5,000	Unconfuse	10,900
Unabraded	963	Unaudited	2,100	Unbosomed	5,100	Unconjugal	11,000
Unabridged	964	Unavenged	2,150	Unbraced	5,200	Unconsoled	11,100
Unabsehbar	965	Unavowed	2,200	Unbribed	5,300	Unconsumed	11,200
Unabsolved	966	Unawakened	2,250	Unbroken	5,400	Uncontrite	11,300
Unaccented	967	Unaware	2,300	Unbruised	5,500	Uncorrupt	11,400
Unachieved	968	Unawed	2,350	Unbuckle	5,600	Uncouple	11,500
Unaching	969	Unbaffled	2,400	Unburden	5,700	Uncourtly	11,600
Unachtsam	970	Unbagged	2,450	Unburied	5,800	Uncovered	11,700
Unacquired	971	Unbaked	2,500	Unburning	5,900	Uncramped	11,800
Unacted	972	Unbalanced	2,550	Unbutton	6,000	Uncreated	11,900
Unactuated	973	Unbaptized	2,600	Uncandidly	6,100	Uncritical	12,000
Unadapted	974	Unbashful	2,650	Uncanny	6,200	Uncropped	12,100
Unadmired	975	Unbearable	2,700	Uncanonize	6,300	Uncrowded	12,200
Unadorned	976	Unbearded	2,750	Uncanopied	6,400	Unctorius	12,300
Unaffable	977	Unbeaten	2,800	Uncaressed	6,500	Unctuous	12,400
Unaffected	978	Unbecoming	2,850	Uncaria	6,600	Uncultured	12,500
Unafraid	979	Unbedacht	2,900	Uncarpeted	6,700	Uncurled	12,600
Unagitated	980	Unbefangen	2,950	Uncaused	6,800	Uncurrent	12,700
Unahnlich	981	Unbegotten	3,000	Unceasing	6,900	Undabundus	12,800
Unalarmed	982	Unbeguiled	3,050	Uncemented	7,000	Undamped	12,900
Unallied	983	Unbegun	3,100	Uncensured	7,100	Undankbar	13,000
Unallowed	984	Unbeheld	3,150	Unchained	7,200	Undawned	13,100
Unallured	985	Unbelesen	3,200	Unchancy	7,300	Undazzled	13,200
Unalluring	986	Unbelief	3,250	Uncharged	7,400	Undebarred	13,300
Unalter	987	Unbeloved	3,300	Uncharming	7,500	Undebased	13,400
Unamazed	988	Unbemerkt	3,350	Uncharnel	7,600	Undecagon	13,500
Unamiable	989	Unbending	3,400	Unchaste	7,700	Undecayed	13,600
Unamusing	990	Unbenign	3,450	Unchastity	7,800	Undecenary	13,700
Unanalyzed	991	Unbenumbed	3,500	Uncheered	7,900	Undecentum	13,800
Unanchored	992	Unbequem	3,550	Unchided	8,000	Undecided	13,900
Unanealed	993	Unberufen	3,600	Unchurch	8,100	Undecimus	14,000
Unanimans	994	Unbescelt	3,650	Unciarius	8,200	Undecisive	14,100
Unanimated	995	Unbesought	3,700	Uncinare	8,300	Undecked	14,200
Unanimidad	996	Unbespoken	3,750	Uncinello	8,400	Undeclared	14,300
Unannexed	997	Unbestowed	3,800	Uncinulus	8,500	Undecuplo	14,400
Unappalled	998	Unbetrayed	3,850	Uncionario	8,600	Undefaced	14,500
Unapparent	999	Unbetreten	3,900	Uncivilly	8,700	Undefiled	14,600
Unappeased	1,000	Unbewacht	3,950	Unclarify	8,800	Undefrayed	14,700
Unapplied	1,050	Unbewailed	4,000	Unclasp	8,900	Undelaying	14,800
Unapprised	1,100	Unbewiesen	4,050	Unclasped	9,000	Undemanded	14,900
Unaptly	1,150	Unbewitch	4,100	Unclasping	9,100	Undeniable	15,000

Cipher Word.	No.	Cipher Word.	No.	Cipher Word.	No.
Underaged	16,000	Undoubtful	75,000	Unerwartet	440,000
Underbred	17,000	Undoubting	76,000	Unespied ...	450,000
Underbrush	18,000	Undramatic	77,000	Unessayed	460,000
Underclay	19,000	Undraped...	78,000	Unevenly ...	470,000
Undercoats	20,000	Undreamt	79,000	Unevenness	480,000
Undercroft	21,000	Undressed	80,000	Uneventful	490,000
Undercut ...	22,000	Undried ...	81,000	Unexacting	500,000
Underditch	23,000	Undrooping	82,000	Unexampled	510,000
Underdoing	24,000	Undrossy ...	83,000	Unexcised	520,000
Underdrain	25,000	Undular ...	84,000	Unexecuted	530,000
Underfed ...	26,000	Undulated	85,000	Unexempt	540,000
Underfoot	27,000	Undulation	86,000	Unexistent	550,000
Undergird	28,000	Undulatory	87,000	Unexpanded	560,000
Undergone	29,000	Unduldsam	88,000	Unexpect ...	570,000
Underhand	30,000	Unduteous	89,000	Unexposed	580,000
Underived	31,000	Undutiful...	90,000	Unexpunged	590,000
Underleaf	32,000	Unearned...	91,000	Unextinct	600,000
Underling	33,000	Unearthly	92,000	Unfading...	610,000
Underlock	34,000	Uneasiness	93,000	Unfahig ...	620,000
Undermeal	35,000	Uneatable	94,000	Unfainting	630,000
Undermined	36,000	Unebenheit	95,000	Unfairness	640,000
Undermost	37,000	Uneclipsed	96,000	Unfaithful	650,000
Underneath	38,000	Unedel ...	97,000	Unfalcated	660,000
Underpart	39,000	Unedifying	98,000	Unfallow ...	670,000
Underplot	40,000	Uneducated	99,000	Unfamiliar	680,000
Underprize	41,000	Uneffaced	100,000	Unfasslich	690,000
Underrate	42,000	Unehelich	110,000	Unfathered	700,000
Underscore	43,000	Uneinig ...	120,000	Unfatigued	710,000
Undersell ...	44,000	Unelastic ...	130,000	Unfaultily	720,000
Undershot	45,000	Unelated ...	140,000	Unfavoured	730,000
Undershrub	46,000	Unelbowed	150,000	Unfearful	740,000
Undersized	47,000	Uneligible	160,000	Unfeasible	750,000
Undersong	48,000	Unembalmed	170,000	Unfehlbar	760,000
Understate	49,000	Unembodied	180,000	Unfeigned	770,000
Understudy	50,000	Unemphatic	190,000	Unfeminine	780,000
Undertax ...	51,000	Unenchant ,	200,000	Unfenced ...	790,000
Underwent	52,000	Unencumber	210,000	Unfertile ...	800,000
Underwood	53,000	Unendeared	220,000	Unfettered	810,000
Underworld	54,000	Unending	230,000	Unfigured	820,000
Undescried	55,000	Unendlich	240,000	Unfilially ...	830,000
Undesirous	56,000	Unendowed	250,000	Unfilming	840,000
Undeterred	57,000	Unenervate	260,000	Unfirmness	850,000
Undeutlich	58,000	Unengaging	270,000	Unfitly ...	860,000
Undevoured	59,000	Unenglish	280,000	Unfixed ...	870,000
Undevout	60,000	Unenjoyed	290,000	Unflagging	880,000
Undextrous	61,000	Unenlarged	300,000	Unflathig	890,000
Undiademed	62,000	Unenslaved	310,000	Unflawed	900,000
Undigenous	63,000	Unentangle	320,000	Unfledged	910,000
Undigested	64,000	Unentered	330,000	Unfolding	920,000
Undinted	65,000	Unentombed	340,000	Unfolgsam	930,000
Undipped	66,000	Unenvied ...	350,000	Unforbid	940,000
Undismayed	67,000	Unequable	360,000	Unfordable	950,000
Undisono	68,000	Unequalled	370,000	Unforeseen	960,000
Undiverted	69,000	Unerfahren	380,000	Unforetold	970,000
Undivine ...	70,000	Unerhort ...	390,000	Unforfeit ...	980,000
Undivorced	71,000	Unerlaast ...	400,000	Unforgiven	990,000
Undivulged	72,000	Unerlaubt	410,000	Unformlich	1,000,000
Undocked...	73,000	Unerortert	420,000	Unforsaken	2,000,000
Undomestic	74,000	Unerring ...	430,000	Unfostered	—millions

Cipher Word.	s.	d.	Cipher Word.	s.	d.	Cipher Word.	s.	d.
Unfought	0	$0^{1}/_{32}$	Ungnade	1	7	Unicamente	6	6
Unfragrant	0	$0^{1}/_{16}$	Ungoading	1	8	Unicameral	6	7
Unframing	0	$0^{1}/_{8}$	Ungorged	1	9	Unicaulis	6	8
Unfrankirt	0	$0^{3}/_{16}$	Ungoverned	1	10	Unicidad	6	9
Unfrequent	0	$0^{1}/_{4}$	Ungraceful	1	11	Uniclinal	6	10
Unfriable	0	$0^{5}/_{16}$	Ungracious	2	0	Unicolorus	6	11
Unfriedsom	0	$0^{3}/_{8}$	Ungranted	2	1	Unicornuto	7	0
Unfriended	0	$0^{7}/_{16}$	Ungrateful	2	2	Unieme	7	1
Unfrock	0	$0^{1}/_{2}$	Ungrudged	2	3	Unifacial	7	2
Unfrozen	0	$0^{9}/_{16}$	Unguanno	2	4	Unificaba	7	3
Unfrugal	0	$0^{5}/_{8}$	Unguent	2	5	Unificar	7	4
Unfruitful	0	$0^{11}/_{16}$	Unguentary	2	6	Uniformar	7	5
Unfugsam	0	$0^{3}/_{4}$	Unguentous	2	7	Uniformity	7	6
Unfunded	0	$0^{13}/_{16}$	Unguical	2	8	Unigenito	7	9
Unfusing	0	$0^{7}/_{8}$	Unguidedly	2	9	Unigenous	8	0
Ungained	0	$0^{15}/_{16}$	Unguifero	2	10	Unilabiate	8	3
Ungainful	0	1	Unguiform	2	11	Unilateral	8	6
Ungallant	0	$1^{1}/_{8}$	Unguiltily	3	0	Unilocular	8	9
Ungaresca	0	$1^{1}/_{4}$	Unguinosus	3	1	Unimagined	9	0
Ungarina	0	$1^{3}/_{8}$	Ungulate	3	2	Unimbued	9	3
Ungathered	0	$1^{1}/_{2}$	Ungunst	3	3	Unimitated	9	6
Ungeachtet	0	$1^{5}/_{8}$	Unhacked	3	4	Unimpaired	9	9
Ungeared	0	$1^{3}/_{4}$	Unhallowed	3	5	Unimpeach	10	0
Ungeberdig	0	$1^{7}/_{8}$	Unhaltbar	3	6	Unimpeded	10	3
Ungebildet	0	2	Unhandily	3	7	Unimplied	10	6
Ungeboren	0	$2^{1}/_{4}$	Unhandsome	3	8	Unimplored	10	9
Ungefallig	0	$2^{1}/_{2}$	Unhanged	3	9	Unimposed	11	0
Ungehauer	0	$2^{3}/_{4}$	Unhappy	3	10	Unimposing	11	3
Ungehobelt	0	3	Unharassed	3	11	Uninclosed	11	6
Ungemach	0	$3^{1}/_{4}$	Unharbour	4	0	Uninduced	11	9
Ungenauen	0	$3^{1}/_{2}$	Unhardened	4	1	Uninfected	12	0
Ungenerous	0	$3^{3}/_{4}$	Unharmful	4	2	Uninflamed	12	3
Ungenial	0	4	Unharness	4	3	Uninjured	12	6
Ungently	0	$4^{1}/_{4}$	Unhatched	4	4	Uninspired	12	9
Ungenugsam	0	$4^{1}/_{2}$	Unhazarded	4	5	Uninured	13	0
Ungepruft	0	$4^{3}/_{4}$	Unhealthy	4	6	Uninvaded	13	3
Ungerecht	0	5	Unheavenly	4	7	Uninvented	13	6
Ungesauert	0	$5^{1}/_{4}$	Unheeded	4	8	Uninviting	13	9
Ungesellig	0	$5^{1}/_{2}$	Unheedful	4	9	Uninvoked	14	0
Ungestalt	0	$5^{3}/_{4}$	Unheeding	4	10	Unioculus	14	3
Ungestraft	0	6	Unheilsam	4	11	Unionist	14	6
Ungetheilt	0	$6^{1}/_{2}$	Unheimlich	5	0	Uniparous	14	9
Ungetreu	0	7	Unhelmed	5	1	Uniquely	15	0
Ungewandt	0	$7^{1}/_{2}$	Unhelpful	5	2	Uniquement	15	3
Ungewitter	0	8	Unheroic	5	3	Uniqueness	15	6
Ungeziefer	0	$8^{1}/_{2}$	Unhinge	5	4	Uniradiate	15	9
Unghiato	0	9	Unhoard	5	5	Unisexual	16	0
Unghiella	0	$9^{1}/_{2}$	Unhoflich	5	6	Unisonance	16	3
Ungilded	0	10	Unholiness	5	7	Unisson	16	6
Ungimiento	0	$10^{1}/_{2}$	Unhonoured	5	8	Unitable	16	9
Ungiran	0	11	Unhopeful	5	9	Unitamente	17	0
Ungirded	0	$11^{1}/_{2}$	Unhostile	5	10	Unitarian	17	3
Ungirding	1	0	Unhoused	5	11	Unitedly	17	6
Ungiven	1	1	Unhumanize	6	0	Uniterra	17	9
Unglaubig	1	2	Unhumbled	6	1	Unitized	18	0
Unglazed	1	3	Unhusked	6	2	Unitrice	18	3
Ungleich	1	4	Uniaxial	6	3	Unituoso	18	6
Ungluck	1	5	Unibilita	6	4	Univalve	18	9
Unglued	1	6	Unicalamus	6	5	Universal	19	0

Cipher Word.	£	s.	d.	Cipher Word.	£	s.	d.	Cipher Word.	£	s.	d.
University...	0	19	3	Unmarried	1	14	0	Unorganise	2	17	6
Universo ...	0	19	6	Unmasked	1	14	3	Unoriginal	2	18	0
Univocal	0	19	9	Unmassig ...	1	14	6	Unorthodox	2	18	6
Unjealous ...	1	0	0	Unmeaning	1	14	9	Unpacific ...	2	19	0
Unjointed ...	1	0	3	Unmeant ...	1	15	0	Unpacked ...	2	19	6
Unjoyous ...	1	0	6	Unmeddling	1	15	3	Unpainful...	3	0	0
Unjudged ...	1	0	9	Unmeditate	1	15	6	Unpanoply	3	1	0
Unkempt ...	1	1	0	Unmeetly ...	1	15	9	Unparadise	3	2	0
Unkennbar	1	1	3	Unmeetness	1	16	0	Unpardoned	3	3	0
Unkennel ...	1	1	6	Unmellowed	1	16	3	Unpasslich	3	4	0
Unkindly ...	1	1	9	Unmelted ...	1	16	6	Unpastoral	3	5	0
Unkindness	1	2	0	Unmensch...	1	16	9	Unpathed ...	3	6	0
Unkinglike	1	2	3	Unmerciful	1	17	0	Unpathetic	3	7	0
Unklarung	1	2	6	Unmerited...	1	17	3	Unpaved ...	3	8	0
Unklugheit	1	2	9	Unmerklich	1	17	6	Unpawned...	3	9	0
Unknightly	1	3	0	Unmetallic	1	17	9	Unpeaceful	3	10	0
Unknot ...	1	3	3	Unmilitary	1	18	0	Unpenitent	3	11	0
Unknowable	1	3	6	Unmilked...	1	18	3	Unpeopled...	3	12	0
Unknowing	1	3	9	Unminded...	1	18	6	Unperjured	3	13	0
Unkosten ...	1	4	0	Unmindful	1	18	9	Unpervert ...	3	14	0
Unkundig...	1	4	3	Unmingle ...	1	19	0	Unpetrify ...	3	15	0
Unlaboured	1	4	6	Unmingling	1	19	3	Unpillared	3	16	0
Unladen ...	1	4	9	Unmistaken	1	19	6	Unpiloted ...	3	17	0
Unladylike	1	5	0	Unmixing ...	1	19	9	Unpinked ...	3	18	0
Unlamented	1	5	3	Unmoaned	2	0	0	Unpitied ...	3	19	0
Unlarding...	1	5	6	Unmodest ...	2	0	6	Unpitiful ...	4	0	0
Unlaunched	1	5	9	Unmodified	2	1	0	Unpitying...	4	1	0
Unlaurel ...	1	6	0	Unmodishly	2	1	6	Unplagued	4	2	0
Unlavish ...	1	6	3	Unmodulate	2	2	0	Unpleasant	4	3	0
Unlawful ...	1	6	6	Unmoglich	2	2	6	Unpliable ...	4	4	0
Unlearned...	1	6	9	Unmolested	2	3	0	Unpliant ...	4	5	0
Unleidlich...	1	7	0	Unmonied...	2	3	6	Unploughed	4	6	0
Unlenksam	1	7	3	Unmoored...	2	4	0	Unpoetic ...	4	7	0
Unlesbar ...	1	7	6	Unmoralize	2	4	6	Unpoetical	4	8	0
Unlessened	1	7	9	Unmotherly	2	5	0	Unpolarize	4	9	0
Unlevelled...	1	8	0	Unmounted	2	5	6	Unpolished	4	10	0
Unlicensed	1	8	3	Unmovable	2	6	0	Unpollute ...	4	11	0
Unlicked ...	1	8	6	Unmoving ..	2	6	6	Unpopular	4	12	0
Unlighted...	1	8	9	Unmuffle ...	2	7	0	Unportion...	4	13	0
Unlikeness	1	9	0	Unmundig	2	7	6	Unpotable...	4	14	0
Unlimber ...	1	9	3	Unmusical...	2	8	0	Unpraised...	4	15	0
Unlineal ...	1	9	6	Unmuthig...	2	8	6	Unprecise .	4	16	0
Unliquored	1	9	9	Unmuzzle ...	2	9	0	Unprelatic...	4	17	0
Unlively ...	1	10	0	Unnameable	2	9	6	Unpriestly...	4	18	0
Unloaded ...	1	10	3	Unnatural...	2	10	0	Unprincely	4	19	0
Unlocked ...	1	10	6	Unneedful...	2	10	6	Unprisoned	5	0	0
Unloving ...	1	10	9	Unnerve ...	2	11	0	Unprofaned	5	2	6
Unluckily ...	1	11	0	Unnobled ...	2	11	6	Unprolific ...	5	5	0
Unlustrous	1	11	3	Unnoticed...	2	12	0	Unprompted	5	7	6
Unlusty ...	1	11	6	Unnumbered	2	12	6	Unprovoked	5	10	0
Unmachten	1	11	9	Unnurtured	2	13	0	Unpruned ...	5	12	6
Unmagnetic	1	12	0	Unobjected	2	13	6	Unpublic ...	5	15	0
Unmaidenly	1	12	3	Unobliging	2	14	0	Unpunctual	5	17	6
Unmaimed	1	12	6	Unobscured	2	14	6	Unpunished	6	0	0
Unmakable	1	12	9	Unobvious...	2	15	0	Unpurged ...	6	2	6
Unmake ...	1	13	0	Unoffended	2	15	6	Unpurified	6	5	0
Unmanly ...	1	13	3	Unopposed	2	16	0	Unpursued	6	7	6
Unmannlich	1	13	6	Unorderly ...	2	16	6	Unquaffed...	6	10	0
Unmantled	1	13	9	Unordnung	2	17	0	Unquailed...	6	12	6

Cipher Word.	£.	s.	d.	Cipher Word.	£.	s.	d.	Cipher Word.	£.	s.	d.
Unquailing	6	15	0	Unrounded	26	10	0	Unslaked ...	63	0	0
Unquelled...	6	17	6	Unroyally ...	27	0	0	Unsleeping	64	0	0
Unquenched	7	0	0	Unruffled ...	27	10	0	Unslung ...	65	0	0
Unquietly ...	7	2	6	Unruhmlich	28	0	0	Unsmirched	66	0	0
Unransomed	7	5	0	Unruliness	28	10	0	Unsmoked	67	0	0
Unrathlich	7	7	6	Unsaddle ...	29	0	0	Unsoaped ...	68	0	0
Unravaged	7	10	0	Unsafeness	29	10	0	Unsociable	69	0	0
Unrazored...	7	12	6	Unsafety ...	30	0	0	Unsocket ...	70	0	0
Unreadable	7	15	0	Unsaglich ...	30	10	0	Unsoiling ...	71	0	0
Unreality ...	7	17	6	Unsailable...	31	0	0	Unsoldered	72	0	0
Unreasoned	8	0	0	Unsaluted ...	31	10	0	Unsolid ...	73	0	0
Unrebuked	8	2	6	Unsanitary	32	0	0	Unsolvable	74	0	0
Unrecanted	8	5	0	Unsaturate	32	10	0	Unsorglich	75	0	0
Unrecht ...	8	7	6	Unsauft ...	33	0	0	Unsorrowed	76	0	0
Unredeemed	8	10	0	Unsavoury	33	10	0	Unsorted ...	77	0	0
Unredlich ...	8	12	6	Unscaly ...	34	0	0	Unsouled ...	78	0	0
Unrefined ...	8	15	0	Unscanned	34	10	0	Unsoundly	79	0	0
Unreformed	8	17	6	Unscared ...	35	0	0	Unsparing...	80	0	0
Unrefuted ...	9	0	0	Unschlitt ...	35	10	0	Unspecious	81	0	0
Unregsam ...	9	2	6	Unschooled	36	0	0	Unsphere ...	82	0	0
Unreinlich	9	5	0	Unschuld ...	36	10	0	Unspiked ...	83	0	0
Unrelated ...	9	7	6	Unscorched	37	0	0	Unsplit ...	84	0	0
Unrelaxing	9	10	0	Unscoured...	37	10	0	Unspoiled ...	85	0	0
Unrelieved	9	12	6	Unscreened	38	0	0	Unspoken ...	86	0	0
Unremedied	9	15	0	Unscrew ...	38	10	0	Unsquared	87	0	0
Unremitted	9	17	6	Unscrewing	39	0	0	Unstable ...	88	0	0
Unremoved	10	0	0	Unsearched	39	10	0	Unstained...	89	0	0
Unrenowned	10	10	0	Unseasoned	40	0	0	Unstamped	90	0	0
Unrepaired	11	0	0	Unsecret ...	40	10	0	Unstarched	91	0	0
Unrepented	11	10	0	Unsecular ...	41	0	0	Unstatig ...	92	0	0
Unrepining	12	0	0	Unseemly ...	41	10	0	Unsteadily	93	0	0
Unreproved	12	10	0	Unseitigen	42	0	0	Unsteeped...	94	0	0
Unrequited	13	0	0	Unseldom ...	42	10	0	Unsting ...	95	0	0
Unrescued	13	10	0	Unselfish ...	43	0	0	Unstinted ...	96	0	0
Unresented	14	0	0	Unserige ...	43	10	0	Unstored ...	97	0	0
Unresigned	14	10	0	Unserved ...	44	0	0	Unstreitig...	98	0	0
Unresisted	15	0	0	Unshackle...	44	10	0	Unstrung ...	99	0	0
Unresolved	15	10	0	Unshapable	45	0	0	Unstudied...	100	0	0
Unrespited	16	0	0	Unshaved ...	45	10	0	Unstuffed ...	105	0	0
Unrestful ...	16	10	0	Unsheath ...	46	0	0	Unsubdue ...	110	0	0
Unresting ...	17	0	0	Unshielded	46	10	0	Unsuborned	115	0	0
Unrestored	17	10	0	Unshifting	47	0	0	Unsucked ...	120	0	0
Unrevealed	18	0	0	Unshocked	47	10	0	Unsugared	125	0	0
Unrevenged	18	10	0	Unshrined...	48	0	0	Unsuited ...	130	0	0
Unrevered...	19	0	0	Unshrunk...	48	10	0	Unsuiting ...	135	0	0
Unrevised ...	19	10	0	Unsicher ..	49	0	0	Unsullied ...	140	0	0
Unrevoked	20	0	0	Unsifted ...	50	0	0	Unsunned .	145	0	0
Unrhymed	20	10	0	Unsightly...	51	0	0	Unsurgical	150	0	0
Unrichtig ...	21	0	0	Unsilvered	52	0	0	Unswathe ...	155	0	0
Unriddle ...	21	10	0	Unsinewed	53	0	0	Unswayable	160	0	0
Unrigged ...	22	0	0	Unsingled...	54	0	0	Unswept ...	165	0	0
Unripe ...	22	10	0	Unsinkable	55	0	0	Unswerving	170	0	0
Unripeness	23	0	0	Unsinking...	56	0	0	Unsworn ..	175	0	0
Unrivalled ..	23	10	0	Unsinnig ...	57	0	0	Untabamos	180	0	0
Unrivet ...	24	0	0	Unsisterly...	58	0	0	Untack ...	185	0	0
Unrobe ...	24	10	0	Unsittlich ...	59	0	0	Untadura ...	190	0	0
Unromantic	25	0	0	Unsizable ...	60	0	0	Untaken ...	195	0	0
Unroofing ...	25	10	0	Unskilful ...	61	0	0	Untamable	200	0	0
Unroot ...	26	0	0	Unskilled ...	62	0	0	Untamiento	210	0	0

Cipher Word.	£.	Cipher Word.	£.	Cipher Word.	£.
Untando ...	220	Untroubled	2,100	Unwohlsein	8,000
Untangled...	230	Untrussed ...	2,200	Unwohnlich	8,100
Untastbar ...	240	Untruth ...	2,300	Unwomanly	8,200
Untasted ...	250	Untruthful	2,400	Unwonted ...	8,300
Untasteful	260	Untuchtig...	2,500	Unwooed ...	8,400
Untaught ...	270	Untugena ...	2,600	Unworldly ..	8,500
Untauglich	280	Untunable...	2,700	Unworth ...	8,600
Untaxed ...	290	Untuosidad	2,800	Unwounded	8,700
Untempered	300	Untutored...	2,900	Unwrap ...	8,800
Untempting	310	Untwine ...	3,000	Unwrenched	8,900
Untenable...	320	Untwister ...	3,100	Unwrinkled	9,000
Untenderly	330	Unuberlegt	3,200	Unwrought	9,100
Unterbauen	340	Unumrenden	3,300	Unwurdig ..	9,200
Unterbett ...	350	Ununited ...	3,400	Unyielded ...	9,300
Unterdruck	360	Unupheld ...	3,500	Unyoke ...	9,400
Untergang	370	Unurged ...	3,600	Unyoking ...	9,500
Untergeben	380	Unvacated...	3,700	Unzartheit	9,600
Unterhalt ...	390	Unvaried ...	3,800	Unzeitig ...	9,700
Unterholz ...	400	Unveralten	3,900	Unziemlich	9,800
Unterkleid	410	Unverburgt	4,000	Unzollbar ...	9,900
Unterkunft	420	Unverdant...	4,100	Unzoned ...	10,000
Unterlage ...	430	Unverhofft	4,200	Unzucht ...	10,100
Unterlippe	440	Unvermogt	4,300	Unzulassig	10,200
Untermann	450	Unverruckt	4,400	Upanishad	10,300
Unterpfand	460	Unversed ...	4,500	Upblown ...	10,400
Unterricht	470	Unverwandt	4,600	Upbraider ...	10,500
Unterrock ...	480	Unviolated	4,700	Upbringing	10,600
Untersagt...	490	Unvirtuous	4,800	Upcast ...	10,700
Unterst ...	500	Unvisited ...	4,900	Upcheered ..	10,800
Untertasse	525	Unvitiated...	5,000	Upcoiled ...	10,900
Unterwegs	550	Unvizard ...	5,100	Upcurling ...	11,000
Unthankful	575	Unvoweled	5,200	Upgrown ...	11,100
Unthatig ...	600	Unwahrheit	5,300	Upheaval ...	11,200
Unthawed...	625	Unwakened	5,400	Upholder ...	11,300
Untheilbar	650	Unwariness	5,500	Upholstery	11,400
Unthier ...	675	Unwarlike...	5,600	Upiglio ...	11,500
Unthinking	700	Unwarmed	5,700	Uplanders..	11,600
Unthorny ...	725	Unwarping	5,800	Uppishly ...	11,700
Unthread ...	750	Unwasted ...	5,900	Uppishness	11,800
Unthrifty ...	775	Unwavering	6,000	Uprightly ...	11,900
Unthriving	800	Unweaponed	6,100	Uprising ...	12,000
Unthrove ...	825	Unwearied ...	6,200	Uproarious	12,100
Unthunlich	850	Unwearying	6,300	Uprouse ...	12,200
Unticcio ...	875	Unwedded ..	6,400	Upstart ...	12,300
Untidiness...	900	Unweighing	6,500	Upstrokes ...	12,400
Untidy ...	925	Unweise ...	6,600	Uptake ...	12,500
Untiefe ...	950	Unwelcome	6,700	Upthrown ...	12,600
Untiled ...	975	Unwept ...	6,800	Uptraced ...	12,700
Untimely ...	1,000	Unwerthe ...	6,900	Upwhirled...	12,800
Untireable...	1,100	Unwetter ...	7,000	Upwound ...	12,900
Untiringly	1,200	Unwhipt ...	7,100	Uracano ...	13,000
Untomb ...	1,300	Unwille ...	7,200	Uranfange...	13,250
Untouched	1,400	Unwilling ...	7,300	Urania ...	13,500
Untowardly	1,500	Unwiped ...	7,400	Uranitic ...	13,750
Untracked...	1,600	Unwirksam	7,500	Uranology ...	14,000
Untrained...	1,700	Unwirthbar	7,600	Urbanatim	14,250
Untrenched	1,800	Unwisdom...	7,700	Urbanidad...	14,500
Untrimmed	1,900	Unwithered	7,800	Urbanity ...	14,750
Untrodden...	2,000	Unwittily ...	7,900	Urbanized ...	15,000

Cipher Word.	£.	Cipher Word.	£.	Cipher Word.	£.
Urbewohnen	15,250	Usattim ...	55,000	Utriaca ...	170,000
Urbicapus ...	15,500	Uscetto ...	56,000	Utricida ...	175,000
Urbicremus	15,750	Usciere ...	57,000	Utriculus ...	180,000
Urbild ...	16,000	Usciolino ...	58,000	Utrobique ...	185,000
Urbildlich ...	16,250	Uscitura ...	59,000	Utrolibet ...	190,000
Urceolaris ...	16,500	Usefulness...	60,000	Utterable ...	195,000
Urceslate ...	16,750	Usenoria ...	61,000	Utterance ...	200,000
Urchilla ...	17,000	Usher ...	62,000	Utterer ...	210,000
Urchinlike...	17,250	Usherine ...	63,000	Uttermost ...	220,000
Urdidera ...	17,500	Ushership ...	64,000	Uvayema ...	230,000
Urdiembre...	17,750	Usignuolo ...	65,000	Uvilla ...	240,000
Urdira ...	18,000	Usiria ...	66,000	Uvularia ...	250,000
Urdireon ...	18,250	Usitato ...	67,000	Uxorculo ...	260,000
Urdiriamos	18,500	Usofrutto ...	68,000	Uxoricide ...	270,000
Ureltern ...	18,750	Usoliere ...	69,000	Vacada ...	280,000
Urendus ...	19,000	Usowissel ...	70,000	Vacanteria...	290,000
Urenkelin ...	19,250	Usquebaugh	71,000	Vacantly ...	300,000
Ureteres ...	19,500	Usquequo ...	72,000	Vacarme ...	310,000
Ureteritis ...	19,750	Ustedor ...	73,000	Vacatura ...	320,000
Urethra ...	20,000	Ustolare ...	74,000	Vaccarella ...	330,000
Urfarben ...	20,500	Ustorius ...	75,000	Vaccaruis ...	340,000
Urgemische	21,000	Ustricula ...	76,000	Vacchetta ...	350,000
Urgrossung	21,500	Ustulandus	77,000	Vaccinable	360,000
Urheber ...	22,000	Ustulation...	78,000	Vaccinate ...	370,000
Urinantem...	22,500	Usualiter ...	79,000	Vaccine ...	380,000
Urinarius ...	23,000	Usualmente	80,000	Vaccinium...	390,000
Urinolo ...	23,500	Usualness ...	81,000	Vacerrosus	400,000
Urinometer	24,000	Usuario ...	82,000	Vacherie ...	410,000
Urkunde ...	24,500	Usucapio ...	83,000	Vaciabais ...	420,000
Urkundlich	25,000	Usucapiria...	84,000	Vaciadero ...	430,000
Urlatore ...	26,000	Usucatton ...	85,000	Vaciadizo ...	440,000
Urlauber ...	27,000	Usufruct ...	86,000	Vaciaremos	450,000
Urnacht ...	28,000	Usurajo ...	87,000	Vaciero ...	460,000
Urnicion ...	29,000	Usureabais	88,000	Vacilante ...	470,000
Urogallo ...	30,000	Usurear ...	89,000	Vacilaria ...	480,000
Uroscopia ...	31,000	Usureaste ...	90,000	Vacillacao ...	490,000
Urquell ...	32,000	Usurious ...	91,000	Vaciller ...	500,000
Urruncum...	33,000	Usurpacao...	92,000	Vacivitas ...	525,000
Ursacchio ...	34,000	Usurpador...	93,000	Vacuefacio...	550,000
Ursache ...	35,000	Usurpateur	94,000	Vacuetto ...	575,000
Urschrift ...	36,000	Usurpatory	95,000	Vacuidad ...	600,000
Ursidas ...	37,000	Usurper ...	96,000	Vacuista ...	625,000
Ursiform ...	38,000	Usurpingly	97,000	Vacunaba ...	650,000
Ursprung ...	39,000	Usurpiren ...	98,000	Vacunador...	675,000
Urstandig ...	40,000	Utensilio ...	99,000	Vacunaras...	700,000
Urstoff ...	41,000	Uterino ...	100,000	Vacuum ...	750,000
Ursulines ...	42,000	Utilidad ...	105,000	Vadeabais ...	800,000
Urtheilen ...	43,000	Utilisms ...	110,000	Vadeable ...	900,000
Urticaire ...	44,000	Utiliteit ...	115,000	Vademecum	1,000,000
Urtication ...	45,000	Utilizaba ...	120,000	Vaderschap	2,000,000
Urticosus ...	46,000	Utilizaron ...	125,000	Vadimonium	3,000,000
Urverleger...	47,000	Utilize ...	130,000	Vadoso ...	4,000,000
Urwald ...	48,000	Utilizing ...	135,000	Vadzigheid	5,000,000
Usabile ...	49,000	Utilmente ...	140,000	Vaferrimo ...	6,000,000
Usagre ...	50,000	Utopian ...	145,000	Vafricies ...	7,000,000
Usamento ...	51,000	Utopianist...	150,000	Vafrous ...	8,000,000
Usanaccia ...	52,000	Utopique ...	155,000	Vagabond ...	9,000,000
Usance ...	53,000	Utopiste ...	160,000	Vagada ...	10,000,000
⸺ ᵉmos ...	54,000	Utrarius ...	165,000	Vagante ...	—millions

Cipher Word.	$ cents.	Cipher Word.	$ cents.	Cipher Word.	Dollars.
Vagaremos ...	0 1	Valicato ..	0 60	Vaneando ...	20
Vagaroso ...	0 2	Validabais ...	0 61	Vanecerse ...	21
Vagatore ...	0 3	Validacion ...	0 62	Vaneggiare ...	22
Vagatrice ...	0 4	Validando ...	0 63	Vanerello ...	23
Vagellajo ...	0 5	Validemens ...	0 64	Vangaccia ...	24
Vagellone ...	0 6	Validez ..	0 65	Vangajuole ...	25
Vagheggino ...	0 7	Validismo ...	0 66	Vangatura ...	26
Vaghezza ...	0 8	Validita ...	0 67	Vangelico ...	27
Vagimento ...	0 9	Validness ...	0 68	Vangile ...	28
Vaginant ...	0 10	Valiente ...	0 69	Vanguard ...	29
Vaginarius ...	0 11	Valigetta ...	0 70	Vanidad ...	30
Vagisco ...	0 12	Valigias ...	0 71	Vanidicus ...	31
Vagliare ...	0 13	Valigiotto ...	0 72	Vanidoso ...	32
Vagliatura ...	0 14	Valimiento ...	0 73	Vanillier ...	33
Vagrancy ...	0 15	Valinch ...	0 74	Vanilocuo ...	34
Vaguccio ...	0 16	Valise ...	0 75	Vanished ...	35
Vagueante ...	0 17	Valkenier ...	0 76	Vanisimo ...	36
Vaguedad ...	0 18	Valkenkap ...	0 77	Vanistorio ...	37
Vaguement ...	0 19	Valkenmist ...	0 78	Vaniteux ...	38
Vagueness ...	0 20	Valkennet ...	0 79	Vanity ...	39
Vaguisimo ...	0 21	Valkyrean ...	0 80	Vannage ...	40
Vagulatio ...	0 22	Valladear ...	0 81	Vanquisher ...	41
Vahanero ...	0 23	Vallame ...	0 82	Vansire ...	42
Vaharina ...	0 24	Vallecico ...	0 83	Vantail ...	43
Vaheabais ...	0 25	Vallecula ...	0 84	Vantajoso ...	44
Vahearia ...	0 26	Vallejueto ...	0 85	Vantamento ...	45
Vahuno ...	0 27	Vallettina ...	0 86	Vantatrice ...	46
Vaillance ...	0 28	Valletto ...	0 87	Vanterie ...	47
Vaincre ...	0 29	Vallicella ...	0 88	Vantevole ...	48
Vainement ...	0 30	Vallico ...	0 89	Vanvera ...	49
Vainglory ...	0 31	Valligiano ...	0 90	Vapeur ...	50
Vainica ...	0 32	Vallonota ...	0 91	Vapiditas ...	51
Vainqueur ...	0 33	Valoir ...	0 92	Vapidly ...	52
Vaishnava ...	0 34	Valones ...	0 93	Vapidness ...	53
Vaisseau ...	0 35	Valorabas ...	0 94	Vaporaccio ...	54
Vaisselle ...	0 36	Valorous ...	0 95	Vaporante ...	55
Vaiven ...	0 37	Valsaba ...	0 96	Vaporarium	56
Vaivodata ...	0 38	Valsarido ...	0 97	Vaporativo ...	57
Vajezza ...	0 39	Valsavias ...	0 98	Vaporavit ...	58
Vajolato ...	0 40	Valsente ...	0 99	Vaporeux ...	59
Vajuolo ...	0 41	Valseuse ...	1 0	Vaporific ...	60
Valblok ...	0 42	Valstrik ...	2 0	Vaporizer ...	61
Valbrug ...	0 43	Valuator ...	3 0	Vaporosita ...	62
Valdeur ...	0 44	Valvasor ...	4 0	Vaporoso ...	63
Valeggio ...	0 45	Valveseat ...	5 0	Vapourable ...	64
Valentacho ...	0 46	Valvula ...	6 0	Vapourbath	65
Valenteria ...	0 47	Vambrace ...	7 0	Vapourish ...	66
Valentine ...	0 48	Vampeggio ...	8 0	Vapponibus	67
Valentumo ...	0 49	Vampirist ...	9 0	Vapulabas ...	68
Valenza ...	0 50	Vampiro ...	10 0	Vapulamos ...	69
Valerate ...	0 51	Vamplate ...	11 0	Vapularan ...	70
Valerian ...	0 52	Vanadate ...	12 0	Vapularis ...	71
Valeroso ...	0 53	Vanagloria ...	13 0	Vapulaste ...	72
Valetaille ...	0 54	Vanamente ...	14 0	Vapulation ...	73
Valetudo ...	0 55	Vandalic ...	15 0	Vapuleo ...	74
Valeureux ...	0 56	Vandalismo ...	16 0	Vaqueriles ...	75
Valiantly ...	0 57	Vandoise ...	17 0	Vaqueriza ...	76
Valicable ...	0 58	Vandola ..	18 0	Vaquetear ...	77
Valicare ...	0 59	Vandyke ...	19 0	Vaquilla ...	78

Cipher Word.	Dollars.	Cipher Word.	Dollars.	Cipher Word.	Dollars.
Varaderos ...	79	Vaseux ...	138	Veduno ...	197
Varador ...	80	Vasilhame	139	Veeduria ...	198
Varangues...	81	Vasistas ...	140	Veeringly ...	199
Varapalo ...	82	Vassaled ...	141	Vegetable ...	200
Varasceto ...	83	Vastabas ...	142	Vegetality	201
Varbasco ...	84	Vastacion ...	143	Vegetamen	202
Varchilla ...	85	Vastamente	144	Vegetandus	203
Vardascazo	86	Vastandus	145	Vegetarian	204
Vareabamos	87	Vastaremos	146	Vegetate ...	205
Vareabaron	88	Vastarian ...	147	Vegetatif ...	206
Vareage ...	89	Vastatrix ...	148	Vegetation	207
Vareasteis...	90	Vastbakken	149	Vegetevole	208
Varejon ...	91	Vastedad ...	150	Veggente ...	209
Varengage...	92	Vastissime	151	Vegghiante	210
Varenmos...	93	Vastitude ...	152	Vegghieria	211
Varenne ...	94	Vaterland ...	153	Veggiolo ...	212
Variabas ...	95	Vatermord	154	Vegliatore...	213
Variably ...	96	Vaterstadt	155	Vegliuccia...	214
Variado ...	97	Vaticanist...	156	Vegrandis ...	215
Variamente	98	Vaticide ...	157	Vehemencia	216
Variante ...	99	Vaticinar ...	158	Vehement ...	217
Variarent ...	100	Vatidico ...	159	Vehicle ...	218
Variation ...	101	Vaudeville...	160	Vehicular ...	219
Varicelle ...	102	Vaultage ...	161	Veiller ..	220
Varicitus ...	103	Vauntful ...	162	Veilleuse ...	221
Varicosity...	104	Vauntingly	163	Veillotte ...	222
Varicoso ...	105	Vauntlay ...	164	Veineux ...	223
Variedade...	106	Vauntmure	165	Veinless ...	224
Variegado...	107	Vaurien ...	166	Veinster ...	225
Variegated	108	Vautrait ...	167	Veintavo ...	226
Variegetur	109	Vavasory ...	168	Veintenar ...	227
Variformed	110	Vecchiaja ...	169	Veintidos ...	228
Varillage ...	111	Veccioso ...	170	Veintinua ...	229
Variole ...	112	Vececonte ...	171	Veinzend ...	230
Variolique...	113	Veceria ...	172	Veisle ...	231
Variolitic ...	114	Vechtkunst	173	Veitsdans ...	232
Varioloid ...	115	Vechtperk	174	Vejaban ...	233
Variorum ...	116	Vecinal ...	175	Vejacion ...	234
Variously ...	117	Vecindado	176	Vejamen ...	235
Variqueux	118	Vecorditer...	177	Vejaremos...	236
Varkenskot	119	Vectabilis ...	178	Vejecito ...	237
Varletry ...	120	Vectarius ...	179	Vejentana ...	238
Varnish ...	121	Vecteux ...	180	Vejestorio ...	239
Varnishing	122	Vectigales ...	181	Vejezuelo ...	240
Varona ...	123	Vedabamos	182	Vejigacion...	241
Varraco ...	124	Vedamiento	183	Vejigon ...	242
Varraquear	125	Vedanga ...	184	Vejiguero ...	243
Varredura...	126	Vedarian ...	185	Velabile ...	244
Varvassore	127	Vedegambre	186	Velabrum ...	245
Varvicite ...	128	Vedejudo ...	187	Velacho ...	246
Vasallage ...	129	Vederbal ...	188	Velador ...	247
Vasarium ...	130	Vedette ...	189	Veladura ...	248
Vascello ...	131	Vedijuela ...	190	Velambres...	249
Vascoloso ...	132	Veditore ...	191	Velarte ...	250
Vascuence ...	133	Vedovaggio	192	Velatura ...	251
Vascular ...	134	Vedovale ...	193	Velazione ...	252
Vaseline ...	135	Vedovatico	194	Veldarbeid	253
Vasellajo ...	136	Vedovello ...	195	Veldbloem...	254
Vaselletto ...	137	Vedovona ...	196	Veldflesch...	255

Cipher Word.	Dollars.	Cipher Word.	Dollars.	Cipher Word.	Dollars.
Veldflint	256	Vendeja	315	Venthole	374
Veldgewas	257	Vendemmia	316	Venticello	375
Veldgodin	258	Vendendus	317	Ventiduct	376
Veldklaver	259	Venderache	318	Ventiera	377
Veldnimf	260	Venderesse	319	Ventigenus	378
Veldslang	261	Vendettas	320	Ventilabro	379
Veldspin	262	Vendeur	321	Ventilaran	380
Veleidad	263	Vendibilis	322	Ventilator	381
Velenosita	264	Vendicarsi	323	Ventilavit	382
Velerhande	265	Vendicato	324	Ventiler	383
Velettajo	266	Vendicion	325	Ventinove	384
Velfalla	267	Vendiente	326	Ventiscar	385
Velicacion	268	Vendimiado	327	Ventiscoso	386
Velicaste	269	Vendittrix	328	Ventisette	387
Veliferous	270	Venditurus	329	Ventjager	388
Velificare	271	Vendivel	330	Ventolera	389
Velilla	272	Vendredi	331	Ventolino	390
Velitaris	273	Veneer	332	Ventosear	391
Velivolans	274	Veneering	333	Ventosity	392
Velivolent	275	Veneficiar	334	Ventouser	393
Vellecillo	276	Venenario	335	Ventraccio	394
Velleite	277	Veneneux	336	Ventrada	395
Vellendus	278	Venenoso	337	Ventrecha	396
Vellicate	279	Venerable	338	Ventricose	397
Vellocino	280	Venerador	339	Ventriculo	398
Vellonero	281	Venerandus	340	Ventriere	399
Vellorita	282	Venerante	341	Ventriglio	400
Vellosidad	283	Veneration	342	Ventriosus	401
Vellumina	284	Venereous	343	Ventroso	402
Vellutero	285	Venerien	344	Venturero	403
Veloce	286	Veneruela	345	Venturiere	404
Velocipede	287	Venetian	346	Venturilla	405
Velocitare	288	Venezolano	347	Venturing	406
Velocity	289	Venganza	348	Venturon	407
Velonera	290	Vengativo	349	Venuculum	408
Velonis	291	Vengeance	350	Venudator	409
Veloutier	292	Vengeful	351	Venusbild	410
Velozmente	293	Vengiadore	352	Venustas	411
Velutinous	294	Venialidad	353	Venustidad	412
Veluzzo	295	Veniality	354	Venzette	413
Velveteen	296	Venialness	355	Vepallida	414
Velveting	297	Venicula	356	Veprajo	415
Velvety	298	Venideros	357	Veprecula	416
Venabulum	299	Venison	358	Vepretum	417
Venadero	300	Veniticcio	359	Verachting	418
Venaison	301	Venitur	360	Veracidad	419
Venaje	302	Venomous	361	Veracious	420
Venalidad	303	Venora	362	Veraltet	421
Venaliter	304	Ventaglia	363	Veramente	422
Venalitium	305	Ventajoso	364	Veranada	423
Venalogia	306	Ventalle	365	Veranadero	424
Venatical	307	Ventanazo	366	Verandahs	425
Venation	308	Ventanera	367	Verargen	426
Venatrice	309	Ventarron	368	Verarming	427
Vencedor	310	Ventaruola	369	Veratrine	428
Vencimento	311	Ventavolo	370	Veraussern	429
Vendange	312	Venteadura	371	Verbaccio	430
Vendaval	313	Venteando	372	Verbale	431
Vendedor	314	Venterello	373	Verbaliser	432

Cipher Word.	Dollars.	Cipher Word.	Dollars.	Cipher Word.	Dollars.
Verbalisms	433	Verdigris	492	Verging	755
Verbality	434	Verdina	493	Verglazen	760
Verbanaca	435	Verdinegro	494	Vergnugt	765
Verbannung	436	Verditure	495	Vergoden	770
Verbasco	437	Verdognolo	496	Vergognare	775
Verbasterd	438	Verdolaga	497	Vergognoso	780
Verbatim	439	Verdoppeln	498	Vergolato	785
Verbazend	440	Verdorren	499	Vergolder	790
Verbedding	441	Verdoyant	500	Vergramd	795
Verbena	442	Verdoyer	505	Vergreifen	800
Verbenatus	443	Verdrangen	510	Verguenza	805
Verberaron	444	Verdreven	515	Verguilla	810
Verberate	445	Verdrossen	520	Verguizer	815
Verbereus	446	Verdrukte	525	Verguld	820
Verbergung	447	Verduften	530	Vergulding	825
Verbeurder	448	Verdunkeln	535	Verguldmes	830
Verbiage	449	Verdunning	540	Verguldsel	835
Verbigero	450	Verdure	545	Vergutung	840
Verbinden	451	Verdurita	550	Verhaften	845
Verbittern	452	Verdursten	555	Verhandeln	850
Verblasen	453	Verduwing	560	Verhard	855
Verbleiben	454	Verecundia	565	Verharding	860
Verbluffen	455	Veredario	570	Verhasst	865
Verblutung	456	Veredlung	575	Verheeren	870
Verboksen	457	Verehren	580	Verhelfen	875
Verbosely	458	Vereinige	585	Verhemelte	880
Verbosita	459	Vereinzeln	590	Verhitten	885
Verboso	460	Vererblich	595	Verhitting	890
Verbrauch	461	Veretrum	600	Verhungern	895
Verbrennen	462	Verewigen	605	Verhuten	900
Verbriefen	463	Verfallen	610	Vericueto	905
Verbroseln	464	Verfarben	615	Veridical	910
Verbruid	465	Verfechter	620	Veridico	915
Verbundete	466	Verfehlen	625	Veridique	920
Verburgen	467	Verfeinern	630	Veriest	925
Verbursten	468	Verfeuert	635	Verifiable	930
Verdacho	469	Verfliegen	640	Verificar	935
Verdachtig	470	Verflucher	645	Verifiers	940
Verdadero	471	Verfmolen	650	Veriloquio	945
Verdaging	472	Verfolger	655	Verimonia	950
Verdaliero	473	Verfpot	660	Verirren	955
Verdammung	474	Verfwinkel	665	Verisimil	960
Verdanken	475	Vergadoro	670	Veritable	965
Verdantly	476	Vergahren	675	Veritevole	970
Verdatre	477	Vergangen	680	Verity	975
Verdaulich	478	Vergeblich	685	Verjagen	980
Verdecillo	479	Vergelden	690	Verjaging	985
Verdeckbar	480	Vergella	695	Verjahrung	990
Verdegay	481	Vergeltung	700	Verjongen	995
Verdelger	482	Vergenoegd	705	Verjuice	1,000
Verdemarco	483	Vergeta	710	Verkalken	1,010
Verdemezza	484	Vergeteado	715	Verkauf	1,020
Verderben	485	Vergettes	720	Verkehrt	1,030
Verderers	486	Vergeure	725	Verkennen	1,040
Verderol	487	Vergeven	730	Verketterd	1,050
Verdesecco	488	Vergezicht	735	Verketzern	1,060
Verdezuelo	489	Verghetta	740	Verklagen	1,070
Verdicante	490	Vergiften	745	Verklarung	1,080
Verdienst	491	Verginello	750	Verkleiner	1,090

Cipher Word.	Dollars.	Cipher Word.	Dollars.	Cipher Word.	Dollars.
Verkleumd	1,100	Vermicular	9,500	Verponding	28,500
Verknagen	1,110	Vermiforme	9,750	Verprassen	29,000
Verknocht	1,120	Vermifugal	10,000	Verpulvern	29,500
Verknupfen	1,180	Vermifugo	10,250	Verquellen	30,000
Verkochen	1,140	Vermil	10,500	Verraquear	30,500
Verkorene	1,150	Vermilion	10,750	Verrassend	31,000
Verkorpern	1,160	Verminaca	11,000	Verrathen	31,500
Verkorting	1,170	Verminatio	11,250	Verrechnen	32,000
Verkregen	1,180	Vermindern	11,500	Verreisen	32,500
Verkrompen	1,190	Vermineux	11,750	Verrek	33,000
Verkummern	1,200	Verminken	12,000	Verrenkung	33,500
Verkwisten	1,225	Verminly	12,250	Verrerie	34,000
Verladen	1,250	Verminous	12,500	Verrettata	34,500
Verlaging	1,275	Vermiparo	12,750	Verrimpeld	35,000
Verlaksel	1,300	Vermisseau	13,000	Verrinare	35,500
Verlakt	1,325	Vermitteln	13,250	Verriondez	36,000
Verlamd	1,350	Vermocane	13,500	Verrocal	36,500
Verlangern	1,400	Vermogend	13,750	Verrollen	37,000
Verlarven	1,450	Vermolmen	14,000	Verrostet	37,500
Verlating	1,500	Vermorsen	14,250	Verroterie	38,000
Verlauwen	1,550	Vermoulure	14,500	Verrotting	38,500
Verlechzen	1,600	Vormuffen	14,750	Verruca	39,000
Verledene	1,650	Vermummung	15,000	Verrucaria	39,500
Verleggen	1,700	Vermuth	15,250	Verrucose	40,000
Verleiden	1,750	Vernacular	15,500	Verrucula	40,500
Verleihung	1,800	Vernageln	15,750	Verrugoso	41,000
Verlept	1,850	Vernal	16,000	Verruguera	41,500
Verletzer	1,900	Vernaliter	16,250	Verrukken	42,000
Verleugnen	1,950	Vernally	16,500	Verruto	42,500
Verleumder	2,000	Vernant	16,750	Versable	43,000
Verlichten	2,250	Vernarbung	17,000	Versabunde	43,500
Verliebt	2,500	Vernation	17,250	Versado	44,000
Verlobniss	2,750	Verneinend	17,500	Versagen	44,500
Verlofpas	3,000	Verneming	17,750	Versalilla	45,000
Verlokster	3,250	Vernicato	18,000	Versammeln	45,500
Verloop	3,500	Vernichten	18,250	Versant	46,000
Verlootdag	3,750	Verniciare	18,500	Versatile	46,500
Verlothen	4,000	Vernicle	18,750	Verschalen	47,000
Verloving	4,250	Verniers	19,000	Verschil	47,500
Verluiden	4,500	Vernilis	19,250	Verschot	48,000
Verlumpt	4,750	Vernisseur	19,500	Verseman	48,500
Verlustig	5,000	Vernuft	19,750	Versement	49,000
Vermageren	5,250	Vernuftig	20,000	Versetto	49,500
Vermahlung	5,500	Veromberen	20,500	Versicolor	50,000
Vermaining	5,750	Veroncello	21,000	Versicula	50,500
Vermaken	6,000	Veronica	21,500	Versierder	51,000
Vermauern	6,250	Veronique	22,000	Versifier	51,500
Vermehren	6,500	Verordnen	22,500	Versify	52,000
Vermeil	6,750	Veroverd	23,000	Versigeln	52,500
Vermeint	7,000	Verpacken	23,500	Versilbern	53,000
Vermelden	7,250	Verpanden	24,000	Versipelle	53,500
Vermenella	7,500	Verpestung	24,500	Versista	54,000
Vermeology	7,750	Verpfanden	25,000	Verslagen	54,500
Vermerken	8,000	Verpflegen	25,500	Verslapt	55,000
Vermesser	8,250	Verpichen	26,000	Verslaving	55,500
Vermetto	8,500	Verpinning	26,500	Verslempe	56,000
Vermicelli	8,750	Verplanten	27,000	Verslinden	56,500
Vermiceous	9,000	Verplet	27,500	Versmacht	57,000
Vermicide	9,250	Verplicht	28,000	Versmading	57,500

Cipher Word.	Dollars.	Cipher Word.	Dollars.	Cipher Word.	Dollars.
Versmolten ...	58,000	Vertueux ...	87,500	Vesicate ..	550,000
Versneld ...	58,500	Vertuschen ..	88,000	Vesication	575,000
Versnerken ...	59,000	Veruben ..	88,500	Vesicatory	600,000
Versoffen ...	59,500	Veruntamen	89,000	Vesiculeux	625,000
Versorio ...	60,000	Vervactum ...	89,500	Vespajoso	650,000
Verspaten ...	60,500	Vervagabo ...	90,000	Vesperbell	675,000
Versperd ...	61,000	Vervagaret ...	90,500	Vesperbrod	700,000
Versperren ...	61,500	Vervain ...	91,000	Vespertina	725,000
Verspunden	62,000	Vervaldag ...	91,500	Vesperugo	750,000
Verst ...	62,500	Vervanger ...	92,000	Vespiary	775,000
Verstaler ...	63,000	Verveceus ...	92,500	Vespices ...	800,000
Verstampen	63,500	Vervecinus ...	93,000	Vessatore	825,000
Verstandig ...	64,000	Vervels ...	93,500	Vessignon	850,000
Verstarken ...	64,500	Vervolg ...	94,000	Vessillo ...	875,000
Verstehen ...	65,000	Vervolgens ...	94,500	Vestaccia	900,000
Versterf ...	65,500	Verwachten	95,000	Vestal ...	925,000
Verstimmen	66,000	Verwahrung	95,500	Vestetta ...	950,000
Verstohlen ...	66,500	Verwaist ...	96,000	Vestiaire	1,000,000
Verstomd ...	67,000	Verwandeln ...	96,500	Vestiarium	1,100,000
Verstoring ...	67,500	Verwante ...	97,000	Vestibular	1,200,000
Verstort ...	68,000	Verwarming	97,500	Vestibulo	1,300,000
Verstramd ...	68,500	Verwasemen	98,000	Vesticeps	1,400,000
Verstreuen ...	69,000	Verwassern...	98,500	Vestidura	1,500,000
Versuchen ...	69,500	Verwebt ...	99,000	Vestigatio	1,600,000
Versuft ...	70,000	Verweigern...	99,500	Vestigium	1,700,000
Versurus ...	70,500	Verweisung	100,000	Vestiglo	1,800,000
Versussung	71,000	Verwelf ...	105,000	Vestimenta	1,900,000
Versute ...	71,500	Verwelven ...	110,000	Vesting ...	2,000,000
Vertagis ...	72,000	Verwerthen	115,000	Vestiplica	2,100,000
Vertakking...	72,500	Verwerving	120,000	Vestirsi...	2,200,000
Vertalmen ...	73,000	Verweslich	125,000	Vestitello	2,300,000
Vertandeln...	73,500	Verwickeln ...	130,000	Vestitrix ..	2,400,000
Vertebral ...	74,000	Verwirrung	135,000	Vestment	2,500,000
Vertebrate ...	74,500	Verwischen	140,000	Vestry ...	2,600,000
Vertedor ...	75,000	Verwittwet ...	145,000	Vestrymen	2,700,000
Vertellos ...	75,500	Verwohnen ...	150,000	Vestuario	2,800,000
Vertendus ...	76,000	Verwormd ...	155,000	Vesture ...	2,900,000
Vertenfelt ...	76,500	Verwulfsel ...	160,000	Vesuvian	3,000,000
Verterend ...	77,000	Verwundbar	165,000	Vetachtig	3,100,000
Vertering ...	77,500	Verwundern	170,000	Vetaturus	3,200,000
Vertex ...	78,000	Verwuster ...	175,000	Vetches ...	3,300,000
Vertheilen ...	78,500	Verzagen ...	180,000	Vetchling	3,400,000
Verthun ...	79,000	Verzaking ...	185,000	Veterano	3,500,000
Vertible ...	79,500	Verzarteln ...	190,000	Veterband	3,600,000
Vertibutum	80,000	Verzehren ...	195,000	Veteretum	3,700,000
Verticilos ...	80,500	Verzeid ...	200,000	Vetergat	3,800,000
Verticity ...	81,000	Verzeihung	225,000	Veterinary	3,900,000
Vertiefung ...	81,500	Verzetten ...	250,000	Veternosus	4,000,000
Vertiente ...	82,000	Verzicare ...	275,000	Vetillerie	5,000,000
Vertigine ...	82,500	Verzicola ...	300,000	Vetoed ...	6,000,000
Vertigo ...	83,000	Verzinnen ...	325,000	Vetoists ...	7,000,000
Vertinsel ...	83,500	Verzinster ...	350,000	Vetonica...	8,000,000
Vertrackt ...	84,000	Verzollung ...	375,000	Vetpuist...	9,000,000
Vertraging ...	84,500	Verzuckt ...	400,000	Vetriato	10,000,000
Vertrapt ...	85,000	Vesciaja ...	425,000	Vetriciajo	20,000,000
Vertrauter ...	85,500	Vescicoso ...	450,000	Vetsalade	30,000,000
Vertretung ...	86,000	Vescicuzza ...	475,000	Vettajuolo	40,000,000
Vertrieb ...	86,500	Vescovado ...	500,000	Vetturale	50,000,000
Vertrodeln ...	87,000	Vesicaria ...	525,000	Vetturino	— millions

Cipher Word.	Inches.	Cipher Word.	Ft. In.	Cipher Word.	Ft. In.
Vetuste ...	·01	Vicicilin ...	0 2 3/4	Vierhanten	2 1
Vetustesco	·02	Vicieux ...	0 2 7/8	Vierhoekig	2 2
Veuvage	·03	Vicinage ...	0 3	Viermalig ...	2 3
Vexandus	·04	Vicinanza ...	0 3 1/8	Viersitzig ...	2 4
Vexation ...	·05	Vicinitas ...	0 3 1/4	Vierspan ...	2 5
Vexatoire ...	·06	Vicioso ...	0 3 3/8	Viersprong	2 6
Vexillary ...	·07	Viciously ...	0 3 1/2	Viertel ...	2 7
Vexillatio ...	·08	Vicisitud ...	0 3 5/8	Viervoeter...	2 8
Vexingly ...	·09	Vicissatim...	0 3 3/4	Viervorst ...	2 9
Vexiren ...	·10	Vicitatore ...	0 3 7/8	Vierwielig...	2 10
Vezzosetto	·25	Vicoletto ...	0 4	Vietabile ...	2 11
Viability ...	·50	Vicomtesse	0 4 1/8	Vietamento	3 0
Viable ...	·75	Vicontiel ...	0 4 1/4	Vietativo ...	3 1
Viaduct ...	1/32	Victim ...	0 4 3/8	Vietatore ...	3 2
Viaggetto ...	1/16	Victimario	0 4 1/2	Vietatrice ...	3 3
Viaggiante	3/32	Victimated	0 4 5/8	Viewers ...	3 4
Viajante ...	1/8	Victimise ...	0 4 3/4	Viewing ...	3 5
Viajata ...	5/32	Victorear ...	0 4 7/8	Viewless ...	3 6
Viandista ...	3/16	Victorial ...	0 5	Viewly ...	3 7
Viands ...	7/32	Victorieux ...	0 5 1/4	Viezevazen ..	3 8
Viareccio ...	1/4	Victory ...	0 5 1/2	Vigecuplo ...	3 9
Viarecta ...	9/32	Victress ...	0 5 3/4	Vigente ...	3 10
Viarian ...	5/16	Victualien...	0 6	Vigesimus...	3 11
Viaticum ...	11/32	Victualler ...	0 6 1/4	Vigil ...	4 0
Viatorio ...	3/8	Victuals ...	0 6 1/2	Vigilancia ...	4 1
Viatrice ...	13/32	Victurus ...	0 6 3/4	Vigilandus	4 2
Vibices ...	7/16	Vicuna ...	0 7	Vigilanter ...	4 3
Vibium ...	15/32	Videlicet ...	0 7 1/4	Vigilarius ...	4 4
Vibonem ...	1/2	Videndus ...	0 7 1/2	Vigilativo ...	4 5
Viborera ...	17/32	Vidimiren ...	0 7 3/4	Vigilatur ...	4 6
Viborezno ...	9/16	Vidinius ...	0 8	Vigliaccio ...	4 7
Vibrabilis ...	19/32	Vidriado ...	0 8 1/4	Vigliatura...	4 8
Vibracula ...	5/8	Vidrieria ...	0 8 1/2	Vigliuolo ...	4 9
Vibrandus...	21/32	Viduage ...	0 8 3/4	Vignazzo ...	4 10
Vibratile ...	11/16	Viduatus ...	0 9	Vigneron ...	4 11
Vibration ...	23/32	Viduertas ...	0 9 1/4	Vignettes ...	5 0
Vibratory ...	3/4	Vidulum ...	0 9 1/2	Vigogne ...	5 1
Vibrisso ...	25/32	Viehstall ...	0 9 3/4	Vigorar ...	5 2
Viburnum...	13/16	Viehweide .	0 10	Vigorezza ...	5 3
Vicar ...	27/32	Viehzucht...	0 10 1/4	Vigoroso ...	5 4
Vicarage ...	7/8	Vieillard ...	0 10 1/2	Vigorously	5 5
Vicareria ...	29/32	Vieillerie ...	0 10 3/4	Vigoureux...	5 6
Vicariatus...	15/16	Vieillot ...	0 11	Vihaia ...	5 7
Vicarious ...	31/32	Viejarron ...	0 11 1/4	Vihuelista...	5 8
Vicarship ...	1	Viejazo ...	0 11 1/2	Viking ...	5 9
Vicecomes ...	1 1/16	Vieldentig...	0 11 3/4	Vilachtig ...	5 10
Viceconsul	1 1/8	Vieldo ...	1 0	Vilement ...	5 11
Vicedios ...	1 1/4	Vielecki ...	1 1	Vilifier ...	6 0
Vicegerent	1 3/8	Vielfras ...	1 2	Vilify ...	6 1
Vicelegato...	1 1/2	Viellure ...	1 3	Vilipendio ...	6 2
Vicemadre...	1 5/8	Vielmal ...	1 4	Vilipeso ...	6 3
Vicenarius...	1 3/4	Vielsagend	1 5	Villadiego ...	6 4
Vicenary ...	1 7/8	Vielseitig ...	1 6	Villageois ...	6 5
Vicennale ...	2	Vielwisser...	1 7	Villaggio ...	6 6
Vicennium	2 1/8	Vientre ...	1 8	Villain ...	6 7
Vicerector ...	2 1/4	Vierbeinig...	1 9	Villainous...	6 8
Viceroy ...	2 3/8	Vierdeport	1 10	Villanage ...	6 9
Vicesimani	2 1/2	Vierderlei ...	1 11	Villananza	6 10
Viciarium ...	2 5/8	Vierdubbel	2 0	Villanchon .	6 11

* See also "Dimensions" p. 178; "Fathom" p. 231; "Feet" p. 235; "Foot" p. 244; "Inch" p. 29;
"Mile" p. 365; "Yard" p. 741; &c., &c.

c c c

Cipher Word.	Ft.	In.
Villancio ...	7	0
Villanello ...	7	1
Villaneria ...	7	2
Villanesco...	7	3
Villanotto ...	7	4
Villarsia ...	7	5
Villarsite ...	7	6
Villaticus ...	7	9
Villazgo ...	8	0
Villicato ...	8	3
Villivina ...	8	6
Villorin ...	8	9
Vilmente ...	9	0
Vilordo ...	9	3
Viltmuts ...	9	6
Viltwever ...	9	9
Vilucchio ...	10	0
Vilumetto ...	10	6
Vimbrera ...	11	0
Viminalia ...	11	6
Vimineo ...	12	0
Vinaceous ...	12	6
Vinagera ...	13	0
Vinagrillo ...	13	6
Vinagross ...	14	0
Vinaigrer ...	14	6
Vinateria ...	15	0
Vinatico ...	15	6
Vinattiere ...	16	0
Vincastra ...	16	6
Vincevole ...	17	0
Vincheto ...	17	6
Vincibilis ...	18	0
Vincibosco ...	18	6
Vinciglio ...	19	0
Vincimen ...	19	6
Vincipremi ...	20	0
Vincitore ...	20	6
Vincitrice ...	21	0
Vincolato ...	21	6
Vinctionem ...	22	0
Vinculable ...	22	6
Vinculetur ...	23	0
Vinculum ...	23	6
Vindangeur ...	24	0
Vindemario ...	25	0
Vindemiate ...	26	0
Vindemiola ...	27	0
Vindemitor ...	28	0
Vindicable ...	29	0
Vindicatio...	30	0
Vindiciren...	31	0
Vindicta ...	32	0
Vindictive...	33	0
Vindster ...	34	0
Vinearius ...	35	0
Vineclad ...	36	0
Vinegar ...	37	0
Vinegrub ...	38	0

Cipher Word.	Ft.	In.
Vineyard ...	39	0
Vingerlid ...	40	0
Vingtaine ...	41	0
Vinicole ...	42	0
Viniebla ...	43	0
Vinipotor ...	44	0
Vinitorius...	45	0
Vinkennest	46	0
Vinkenslag	47	0
Vinnulus ...	48	0
Vinolencia...	49	0
Vinomele ...	50	0
Vinosidad ..	51	0
Vinosity ...	52	0
Vintage ...	53	0
Vintner ...	54	0
Vinucchio...	55	0
Vinylic ...	56	0
Viocurrus ...	57	0
Violabilis ...	58	0
Violable ...	59	0
Violaceous	60	0
Violamento	61	0
Violario ...	62	0
Violateur ...	63	0
Violation ...	64	0
Violative ...	65	0
Violatore ...	66	0
Violatrice ...	67	0
Violaturus	68	0
Violazione	69	0
Violemment	70	0
Violence ...	71	0
Violentare...	72	0
Violescent...	73	0
Violetta ...	74	0
Violinete ...	75	0
Violinista ...	76	0
Violoncelo...	77	0
Viottola ...	78	0
Viperajo ...	79	0
Viperalis ...	80	0
Viperetta ...	81	0
Viperino ...	82	0
Viperous ...	83	0
Viragine ...	84	0
Viraginity...	85	0
Viraton ...	86	0
Virazoues ...	87	0
Virectum ...	88	0
Vireinato ...	89	0
Virescent ...	90	0
Virgator ...	91	0
Virgidemia	92	0
Virgilian ...	93	0
Virginal ...	94	0
Virgineus ...	95	0
Virginidad	96	0
Virginity ...	97	0

Cipher Word.	Yds.	Ft.
Virgolare ...	0	98
Virgulatus	0	99
Virgule ...	0	100
Virgulilla ...	0	110
Virgulto ...	0	120
Virguncula	0	130
Viridario ...	0	140
Viriditas ...	0	150
Viriliter ...	0	160
Virilmente	0	170
Viripotens...	0	180
Virotazo ...	0	190
Virtuality ...	0	200
Virtueless ...	0	210
Virtuoso ...	0	220
Virtuously	0	230
Virtuozen ...	0	240
Virulence ...	0	250
Virulentus	0	300
Visaged ...	0	350
Visceral ...	0	400
Visceratim	0	450
Vischakte	0	500
Vischangel	0	550
Vischarend {	0	600
	=200	0
Vischben ...	250	0
Vischioso ...	300	0
Vischjager	350	0
Vischketel...	400	0
Vischknit ...	450	0
Vischkorf ...	500	0
Vischschub	550	0
Vischwant	600	0
Viscidity ...	650	0
Visciolato ...	700	0
Viscolina ...	750	0
Viscontado	800	0
Viscosetto...	850	0
Viscosidad	900	0
Viscosity ...	950	0
Viscount ...	1,000	0
Visettino ...	1,050	0
Visibility ...	1,100	0
Visigoth ...	1,150	0
Visionario ...	1,200	0
Visionist ...	1,250	0
Visionless ...	1,300	0
Visirial ...	1,350	0
Visitable ...	1,400	0
Visitacion ...	1,450	0
Visitant ...	1,500	0
Visiteur ...	1,550	0
Visiting ...	1,600	0
Visitorial ...	1,650	0
Visitors ...	1,700	0
Vislumbrar	1,750	0
Visnomist ...	One mile	
Visored ...	— miles	

Cipher Word.	Lbs.	Ozs.	Cipher Word.	Lbs.	Cipher Word.	Tons.	Cwts.	Lbs.
Visoreino ...	0	1	Vivaciteit ...	45	Vlugzand ...	0	0	104
Visorio ...	0	2	Vivacity ...	46	Vobiscum ...	0	0	105
Vispera ...	0	3	Vivagno ...	47	Vocabolo ...	0	0	106
Visqueux ,...	0	4	Vivajetto ...	48	Vocabulary ...	0	0	107
Visschen ...	0	5	Vivamente ...	49	Vocabulum ...	0	0	108
Vista ...	0	6	Vivandero ...	50	Vocalist ...	0	0	109
Vistillas ...	0	7	Vivandetta ...	51	Vocaliter ...	0	0	110
Vistomente ...	0	8	Vivandiere ,,...	52	Vocalizing ...	0	0	111
Vistoso ...	0	9	Vivant ...	53	Vocally ...	0	1	0
Visualize ...	0	10	Vivaquear ...	54	Vocalmente ...	0	2	0
Vitaccia ...	0	11	Vivaracho ...	55	Vocalness ...	0	3	0
Vitalicio ...	0	12	Vivario ...	56	Vocativo ...	0	4	0
Vitalists ...	0	13	Vivency ...	57	Vocaturus ...	0	5	0
Vitalitas ...	0	14	Viveres ...	58	Voceador ...	0	6	0
Vitando ...	0	15	Viveuse ...	59	Voceraccia ...	0	7	0
Vitebianca ...	1	0	Vivevole ...	60	Voceria ...	0	8	0
Vitelina ...	2	0	Vivianite ...	61	Vochtweger ...	0	9	0
Vitellary ...	3	0	Vividly ...	62	Vociferar ...	0	10	0
Vitelletta ...	4	0	Vividness ...	63	Vociferous ..	0	11	0
Vitellinus ...	5	0	Vivienda ...	64	Vocificans ...	0	12	0
Vitelotte ...	6	0	Vivificar ...	65	Vocingkear ...	0	13	0
Vitesse ...	7	0	Vivified ...	66	Vocitare ...	0	14	0
Vitiate ...	8	.0	Vivifying ...	67	Vocitatus ...	0	15	0
Vitiating ...	9	0	Vivipare ...	68	Vocolezza ...	0	16	0
Viticchio ...	10	0	Viviparity ...	69	Voculatio ...	0	17	0
Viticella ...	11	0	Viviparous ...	70	Vocule ...	0	18	0
Vitigineus ...	12	0	Viviradix ...	71	Voederbak ...	0	19	0
Vitiligo ...	13	0	Vivoroso ...	72	Voelhoren ...	1	0	0
Vitiositas ...	14	0	Vivoter ...	73	Voerman ...	2	0	0
Vitisator ...	15	0	Vixenish ...	74	Voerting ...	3	0	0
Vitoperio ...	16	0	Vixenly ...	75	Voetbode ...	4	0	0
Vitorear ...	17	0	Vizcacha ...	76	Voetdeksel ...	5	0	0
Vitrarius ...	18	0	Vizcondado ...	77	Voeteuvel ...	6	0	0
Vitrause ...	19	0	Vizcondesa ...	78	Voetganger ...	7	0	0
Vitreamina ...	20	0	Viziato ...	79	Voetknecht ...	8	0	0
Vitreous ...	21	0	Vizierate ...	80	Voetpunt ...	9	0	0
Vitrerie ...	22	0	Viziosita ...	81	Voetstrik ...	10	0	0
Vitrescent ...	23	0	Viznaga ...	82	Voetzoeker ...	11	0	0
Vitrificar ...	24	0	Vlakgangen ...	83	Vogatore ...	12	0	0
Vitrified ...	25	0	Vlakkerig ...	84	Vogatrice ...	13	0	0
Vitriform ...	26	0	Vlasboer ...	85	Vogavante ...	14	0	0
Vitrine ...	27	0	Vlashekel ...	86	Vogelbauer ...	15	0	0
Vitriolado ...	28	0	Vlaskleur ...	87	Vogelbek ...	16	0	0
Vitriolic ...	29	0	Vlasmarkt ...	88	Vogelchen ...	17	0	0
Vitriolize ...	30	0	Vlasveld ...	89	Vogelhaus ...	18	0	0
Vitriuola ...	31	0	Vlaswinkel ...	90	Vogelhecke ...	19	0	0
Vittoriare ...	32	0	Vlechtband ...	91	Vogelherd ...	20	0	0
Vittrice ...	33	0	Vlechtsel ...	92	Vogeljacht ...	21	0	0
Vittuaglia ...	34	0	Vlechtwerk ...	93	Vogelknip ...	22	0	0
Vitulino ...	35	0	Vlekpapier ...	94	Vogelnest ...	23	0	0
Vituperar ...	36	0	Vlengelig ...	95	Vogelslag ...	24	0	0
Vituperium ...	37	0	Vlierboom ...	96	Vogliente ...	25	0	0
Vituperoso ...	38	0	Vlierhout ...	97	Voglievole ...	26	0	0
Vitzucht ...	39	0	Vliarthee ...	98	Vogliolina ...	27	0	0
Viudal ...	40	0	Vlietgod ...	99	Voglioso ...	28	0	0
Viudedad ...	41	0	Vloeking ...	100	Vogliuzza ...	29	0	0
Viudita ...	42	0	Vloerbalk ...	101	Voiced ...	30	0	0
Vivacezza ...	43	0	Vloerbezem ...	102	Voiceless ...	31	0	0
Vivacious ...	44	0	Vlotgras ...	103	Voidable ...	32	0	0

Cipher Word.	Tons.	Cipher Word.	Tons.	Cipher Word.	Tons.
Voidance ...	33	Volsella ...	92	Voranstalt ...	355
Voidness ...	34	Voltabile ...	93	Voratrice ...	360
Voilerie ...	35	Voltaic ...	94	Voratura ...	365
Voisinage ...	36	Voltallig ...	95	Vorazmente ...	370
Voiture ...	37	Voltameter	96	Vorbauen ...	375
Voiturier ...	38	Voltante ...	97	Vorbehalt ...	380
Vokalmusik ...	39	Voltapile ...	98	Vorbesagt ...	385
Voladera ...	40	Voltaplast ..	99	Vorbeugung ...	390
Voladizo ...	41	Voltario ...	100	Vorbild ...	395
Volaille ...	42	Voltatype ...	105	Vorbote ...	400
Volandas ...	43	Voltazione...	110	Vorbringen ...	405
Volantica ...	44	Volteador ...	115	Vordatiren ...	410
Volanton ...	45	Voltejear ...	120	Vordem ...	415
Volapie ...	46	Voltereta ...	125	Vorderfuss ...	420
Volaterio ...	47	Voltigeur ...	130	Vorderhand ...	425
Volatilixe ...	48	Voltolarsi ...	135	Vordermann ...	430
Volatinear ...	49	Voltolone ...	140	Vordersitz ...	435
Volatizar ...	50	Voltzite ...	145	Vordrucken ...	440
Volbloedig ...	51	Volubilate .	150	Voreilig ...	445
Volbouwen ...	52	Volubility ...	155	Vorfahren ...	450
Volcable ...	53	Volucris ...	160	Vorfinden ...	455
Volcanic ...	54	Volulite ...	165	Vorfordern ...	460
Volcanique ...	55	Volumed ...	170	Vorfrage ...	465
Volcaniser ...	56	Volumetric	175	Vorganger ...	470
Volcanoes ...	57	Volumetto...	180	Vorgaukeln ...	475
Voldragen ...	58	Voluminoso	185	Vorgebaude ...	480
Voleggiare ...	59	Volumist ...	190	Vorgebirge ...	485
Volentieri ...	60	Voluntad ...	195	Vorgeblich ...	490
Voleter ...	61	Voluntary .	200	Vorgemach ...	495
Volgare ...	62	Volunteer ...	205	Vorgestern ...	500
Volgeling ...	63	Voluptor ...	210	Vorgestrig ...	510
Volgitojo ...	64	Voluptuary	215	Vorhaben ...	520
Volgziek ...	65	Voluptuoso	220	Vorherig ...	530
Volharding ...	66	Voluta ...	225	Vorjahrig ...	540
Volhouder ...	67	Volutabrum	230	Vorkampfer ...	550
Volitioned ...	68	Volutavit ...	235	Vorkaufen ...	560
Volitivo ...	69	Volutedly ...	240	Vorkehren ...	570
Volkreich ...	70	Volvible ..	245	Vorkosten ...	580
Volksblad ...	71	Volvox ...	250	Vorlage ...	590
Volksfest ...	72	Volvulus ...	255	Vorlangst ...	600
Volkslied ...	73	Volwichtig	260	Vorlassung ...	610
Volksmacht ...	74	Vomicato ...	265	Vorlegen ...	620
Volkssage ...	75	Vomicosus...	270	Vorlesbar ...	630
Volkwerver ...	76	Vomique ...	275	Vorlesung ...	640
Vollblutig ...	77	Vomitador	280	Vorliebe ...	650
Vollenden ...	78	Vomiting ...	285	Vormachen ...	660
Vollerei ...	79	Vomitive ...	290	Vormalig ...	670
Vollfuhren ...	80	Vomitona ...	295	Vormela ...	680
Vollheit ...	81	Vomitorius	300	Vormittag ...	690
Volljahrig ...	82	Vomitory ...	305	Vormkracht ...	700
Vollmacht ...	83	Vondeling...	310	Vorname ...	710
Vollmond ...	84	Vonkelend...	315	Vornehmen ...	720
Volltonend ...	85	Vonnothen	320	Vorplatz ...	730
Vollziehen ...	86	Vorabend ...	325	Vorposten ...	740
Volontar ...	87	Voraciter ...	330	Vorrecht ...	750
Volontiers ...	88	Voragine ...	335	Vorrucken ...	760
Volpetta ...	89	Voraginoso	340	Vorschein ...	770
Volpicini ...	90	Vorahnung	345	Vorschlag ...	780
Volprezen ...	91	Voraltern. ...	350	Vorsehung ...	790

Cipher Word.	Tons.	Cipher Word.	Tons.	Cipher Word.	Tons.
Vorsetzen ...	800	Vuilniskar	4,900	Wagenkrat	58,000
Vorsichtig ...	810	Vulcanite...	5,000	Wagenlens	59,000
Vorsorge ...	820	Vulcanized	5,500	Wagenplein	60,000
Vorspielen ...	830	Vulgacho ...	6,000	Wagenrad	61,000
Vorsprung ...	840	Vulgaire ...	6,500	Wagenspil	62,000
Vorstadt ...	850	Vulgaridad	7,000	Wagenstar	63,000
Vorstechen ...	860	Vulgarism	7,500	Wagenweg	64,000
Vorstossen...	870	Vulgarly ...	8,000	Wagenwinde	65,000
Vorstpan ...	880	Vulgarness	8,500	Wagerecht	66,000
Vorsturzen	890	Vulgate ...	9,000	Wagered ...	67,000
Vortanque ...	900	Vulgaturus	9,500	Waggery ...	68,000
Vortanzer ...	910	Vulgivagus	10,000	Waggish ...	69,000
Vortarist ...	920	Vulkan ...	11,000	Waggoner	70,000
Vortexes ...	930	Vulkanisch	12,000	Wagonage	71,000
Vortheil ...	940	Vulnerable	13,000	Wagonette	72,000
Vortice ...	950	Vulneraria	14,000	Wagstuck	73,000
Vorticetto ...	960	Vulnerose	15,000	Wagtail ...	74,000
Vorticoso ...	970	Vulnisicus	16,000	Wahlbezirk	75,000
Vortraben ...	980	Vulpanser	17,000	Wahlfahig	76,000
Vortritt ...	990	Vulpecula	18,000	Wahlliste	77,000
Voruber ...	1,000	Vulpibus ...	19,000	Wahlrecht	78,000
Vorvater ...	1,100	Vulpicauda	20,000	Wahlspruch	79,000
Vorwalten ...	1,200	Vulpinite ...	21,000	Wahlstatt	80,000
Vorweg ...	1,300	Vulpino ...	22,000	Wahnsinn	81,000
Vorwenden	1,400	Vulticula ...	23,000	Wahrheit...	82,000
Vorwinseln	1,500	Vulturism	24,000	Wahrnehmen	83,000
Vorwitzig ...	1,600	Vulturno ...	25,000	Wahrwolf	84,000
Vorzeit ...	1,700	Vulturous	26,000	Waiflike ...	85,000
Voskleurig...	1,800	Vulviform	27,000	Wailful ...	86,000
Vossenhol ...	1,900	Wabble ...	28,000	Wailingly...	87,000
Vossevel ...	2,000	Wabblingly	29,000	Wainbote	88,000
Votahorse ...	2,100	Wachfeuer	30,000	Wainhouse	89,000
Votacesso ...	2,200	Wachhabend	31,000	Wainrope ..	90,000
Votagione ...	2,300	Wachposten	32,000	Wainscot ...	91,000
Votaress ...	2,400	Wachsbild	33,000	Waisengeld	92,000
Votive ...	2,500	Wachsern...	34,000	Waistbands	93,000
Vouching ...	2,600	Wachskerze	35,000	Waistcoat	94,000
Vouchment	2,700	Wachslicht	36,000	Waitresses	95,000
Vouchsafe ...	2,800	Wachsstock	37,000	Wakefully	96,000
Vouloir ...	2,900	Wachsthum	38,000	Wakening	97,000
Voussure ...	3,000	Wachstube	39,000	Wakerobin	98,000
Vowelled ...	3,100	Wachtel ...	40,000	Waldchen	99,000
Vowels ...	3,200	Wachtelnet	41,000	Waldhorn	100,000
Voyager ...	3,300	Wachtgeld	42,000	Waldstrom	105,000
Voyaging ...	3,400	Wacker ...	43,000	Waldteufel	110,000
Voznar ...	3,500	Wadcutter	44,000	Walengang	115,000
Vrachtkar ...	3,600	Waddling...	45,000	Walkable	120,000
Vraiment ...	3,700	Wadhook...	46,000	Walkererde	125,000
Vratigheid ...	3,800	Wadsett ...	47,000	Walkmill ...	130,000
Vredebode ...	3,900	Wafelmeid	48,000	Walkmuller	135,000
Vredekrans	4,000	Waffel ...	49,000	Walkroon	140,000
Vredestaf ...	4,100	Waffenrock	50,000	Walkstok	145,000
Vredevorst	4,200	Waffenthat	51,000	Wallach ...	150,000
Vriespunt ...	4,300	Waftage ...	52,000	Wallcress	155,000
Vroegbeurt	4,400	Waftured	53,000	Wallerite ...	160,000
Vroegkerk ...	4,500	Wagebalken	54,000	Wallet ...	165,000
Vueleo ...	4,600	Wagehals...	55,000	Walleyed ...	170,000
Vuesenoria...	4,700	Wagenachse	56,000	Wallfuhrer	175,000
Vuestro ...	4,800	Wagenburg	57,000	Wallfisch ...	—Tons

SUNDRY WEIGHTS AND MEASURES.

BRITISH AND FOREIGN.

* Consecutive numbers continued from page 747

Cipher Word.	No.	
Wal—Wap		**BRITISH.**
Wallflower	44665*	Inch(es)
Wallfruit ...	44666	Square inch(es)
Wallmoss ...	44667	Cubic inch(es)
Wallnut ...	44668	Foot
Wallop ...	44669	Feet
Wallpaper	44670	Square foot (feet)
Wallplates	44671	Cubic foot (feet)
Wallrath ...	44672	Fathom(s)
Wallsided	44673	Cable length(s) (= 120 fathoms)
Walltrees ...	44674	Yard(s)
Wallwort ...	44675	Square yard(s)
Walrus ...	44676	Cubic yard(s)
Walrustand	44677	Rod(s) = pole(s) = perch(es)
Waltzed ...	44678	Furlong(s)
Waltzing ...	44679	Mile(s)
Walzwerk ...	44680	Square mile(s)
Wanbegrip	44681	League(s)
Wanbeleid	44682	Link(s)
Wandelbar	44683	Square link(s)
Wandellos	44684	Chain(s)
Wandelpad	44685	Square chain(s)
Wandelrit	44686	Rood(s)
Wandering	44687	Acre(s)
Wanderjahr	44688	Grain(s) (Troy or Avoirdupois)
Wanderoo	44689	Pennyweight(s)
Wanghee ...	44690	Ounce(s) (Troy)
Wangtooth	44691	Ounce(s) (Avoirdupois)
Wangunstig	44692	Pound(s) (Troy)
Wanhoop ...	44693	Pound(s) (Avoirdupois)
Wanhopend	44694	Quarter(s)
Wankaut ...	44695	Centner(s) (100lbs. English)
Wankeling	44696	Hundredweight(s) (112lbs. English)
Wankelmuth	44697	Ton(s) (2,000lbs. English)
Wanklank	44698	Ton(s) (2,240lbs. English)
Wanness ...	44699	Pint(s)
Wanthaler	44700	Quart(s)
Wantonized	44701	Gallon(s) (10lbs. English)
Wantonly ...	44702	Gallon(s) American (8¹/₃lbs. English)
Wantonness	44703	Cord(s) (128 cubic feet)
		FRENCH.
Wantrowarg	44704	Millimètre(s)
Wapacut ...	44705	Centimètre(s)
Wapenbord	44706	Décimètre(s)
Wapenfeit	44707	Mètre(s)
Wapenkamer	44708	Décamètre(s)
Wapenrek	44709	Hectomètre(s)
Wapenshaw	44710	Kilomètre(s)
Wapensmid	44711	Myriamètre(s)
Wapentake	44712	Centiare(s)
Wappenbuch	44713	Deciare(s)

Cipher Word. Wap - Was	No.	FRENCH (*continued*).
Wappet ...	44714	Are(s)
Warbling ...	44715	Decare(s)
Warcry ...	44716	Hectare(s)
Wardance...	44717	Stère(s)
Wardcorn...	44718	Millilitre(s)
Wardein ...	44719	Centilitre(s)
Wardenship	44720	Décilitre(s)
Wardingly	44721	Litre(s)
Wardmote	44722	Décalitre(s)
Wardpenny	44723	Hectolitre(s)
Wardrobe	44724	Kilolitre(s)
Wardroom	44725	Milligramme(s)
Wardstaff	44726	Centigramme(s)
Wardwit ...	44727	Décigramme(s)
Warefully	44728	Gramme(s)
Warehouse	44729	Décagramme(s)
Warfare ...	44730	Hectogramme(s)
Warfields ..	44731	Kilogramme(s)
Warhorse...	44732	Myriagramme(s)
Warklomp	44733	Quintal(s)

SPANISH AND MEXICAN.

Warlike ...	44734	Linea(s)
Warlocks ...	44735	Linea(s) cuadrada(s)
Warmblutig	44736	Linea(s) cubica(s)
Warmingpan	44737	Pulgada(s)
Warmness	44738	Pulgada(s) cuadrada(s)
Warmpfanne	44739	Pulgada(s) cubica(s)
Warmstein	44740	Pie(s)
Warmtestof	44741	Pie(s) cuadrado(s)
Waroffice ...	44742	Pie(s) cubico(s)
Warpaint ...	44743	Vara(s)
Warpath ...	44744	Vara(s) cuadrada(s)
Warpingly	44745	Vara(s) cubica(s)
Warplumes	44746	Cuadra(s)
Warproof ...	44747	Cuadra(s) cuadrada(s)
Warrelwind	44748	Legua(s)
Warrener ...	44749	Legua(s) cuadrada(s)
Warriors ...	44750	Marco(s)
Warsong ...	44751	Onza(s)
Warstruik	44752	Ochavo(s)
Wartung ...	44753	Grano(s)
Warwhoop	44754	Castellano(s)
Warwolves	44755	Tomine(s)
Warworn ...	44756	Almud(es)
Warzuchtig	44757	Fanega(s)
Wasachtig	44758	Cuartilla(s)
Wasboom...	44759	Carga(s)
Waschdag	44760	Adarm(es)
Waschfrau	44761	Libra(s)
Waschgeld	44762	Arroba(s)
Waschketel	44763	Quintal(es)
Waschleine	44764*	Tonelada(s)

Consecutive numbers continued on page 780.

LETTERS.*

In reference to my (our) letter dated	In reference to your (——'s) letter dated	Have you received my (our) letter dated	Have received your (——'s) letter dated	
Cipher Word.	Cipher Word.	Cipher Word.	Cipher Word.	
Was—Wat	**Wat**	**Wat—Wav**	**Wav—Wea**	
Waschmeid	Watchtower	Watermacht	Wavemotion	The ——
Waschtobbe	Watchword	Watermark	Waveringly	The 1st
Waschtrog	Waterader	Watermelon	Waveson ...	The 2nd
Washandel	Waterbel ...	Watermeter	Waxcandles	The 3rd
Washball	Waterbird	Waternimf	Waxcloth...	The 4th
Washboard	Waterbron	Waterouzel	Waxlights	The 5th
Washhouse	Waterbug	Waterpeper	Waxmoth...	The 6th
Washingtub	Waterbutt	Waterpipes	Waxmyrtle	The 7th
Washpot ...	Watercart	Waterplant	Waxpalms	The 8th
Washstand	Waterclock	Waterpomp	Waxworks	The 9th
Waspbite ...	Watercraft	Waterproof	Waybilled	The 10th
Waspish ...	Watercrane	Waterrail...	Waybread	The 11th
Wassail ...	Watercress	Waterschat	Wayfaring	The 12th
Wassailcup	Watercure	Watershed	Waylay ...	The 13th
Wasserbau	Waterdamp	Waterside	Waymark	The 14th
Wasserfall	Waterdeck	Waterslang	Wayside ...	The 15th
Wasserig ...	Waterdicht	Watersnake	Wayward...	The 16th
Wasserkopf	Watereppe	Watersnip	Waywardish	The 17th
Wasserwage	Waterflood	Waterspout	Waywise ...	The 18th
Wastebook	Waterfowl	Waterstof	Waywode...	The 19th
Wastefully	Watergall	Watertank	Weakener	The 20th
Wastegate	Watergod...	Watertight	Weakeyed	The 21st
Wasteness	Watergolf	Waterveld	Weakside	The 22nd
Wastepipe	Watergruel	Watervlot	Wealsman	The 23rd
Wasteweir	Waterhen...	Watervogel	Wealthily	The 24th
Watchcases	Wateriness	Waterworn	Weaponed	The 25th
Watchdog	Waterkant	Waterzak...	Weaponless	The 26th
Watchglass	Waterkunde	Watscheln	Wearable ..	The 27th
Watchhouse	Waterland	Wattiren ...	Wearisome	The 28th
Watchkey	Waterlily ...	Wavelets ...	Weasand ...	The 29th
Watchmaker	Waterline ..	Wavelike ..	Weasel ...	The 30th
Watchnight	Waterloop	Waveloaf ...	Weathered	The 31st

* *See also* "Date(d)," page 151; "Letter," page 331; &c., &c.

LETTERS.

In reply to your (——'s) letter dated	Waiting for reply to my (our) letter dated	Will reply to your letter about	Cancel my (our) letter of	
Cipher Word.	Cipher Word.	Cipher Word.	Cipher Word.	
Web—Weg	**Weg—Wei**	**Wei**	**Wei—Wel**	
Webbing ...	Weggehen	Weibsvolk	Weinschenk	The ——
Webfooted	Weggras ...	Weichling	Weinstock	The 1st
Wechsler ...	Weghatten	Weideland	Weinsuppe	The 2nd
Weckuhr ..	Wegkapern	Weidenbaum	Weintraube	The 3rd
Weddingday	Wegkratzen	Weidenkorb	Weinwage	The 4th
Wedeln ...	Weglating	Weideplatz	Weinzoll ...	The 5th
Wedergade	Weglocken	Weiderecht	Weirdness	The 6th
Wedergroet	Wegmachen	Weidmann	Weissager	The 7th
Wedergunst	Wegmeter	Weidmesser	Weissbier ...	The 8th
Wederhelft	Wegmussen	Weidtasche	Weissbrod	The 9th
Wederkant	Wegnehmen	Weigering	Weissdorn	The 10th
Wederkomst	Wegraffen	Weighhouse	Weissfisch	The 11th
Wederloon	Wegrucken	Weightless	Weissnahen	The 12th
Wederspalt	Wegscheren	Weihkessel	Weisswein	The 13th
Wedged ...	Wegsegeln	Weihwedel	Weiterung	The 14th
Wedlock ...	Wegspulen	Weinbauer	Weitlaufig	The 15th
Weedery ...	Wegstehlen	Weinbeere	Wekstem ...	The 16th
Weedless ...	Wegwalzen	Weindunst	Welbedacht	The 17th
Weekblad...	Wegwandern	Weinerlich	Welbeklant	The 18th
Weeklacht	Wegweiser	Weinfass ...	Welbemind	The 19th
Weepingly	Wegwerping	Weingarten	Welcherlei	The 20th
Weevil ...	Wegwerpsel	Weingegsen	Welcome ...	The 21st
Weevilled...	Wegwollen	Weingeist	Welcoming	The 22nd
Wegbegeben	Wegzaubern	Weinhandel	Weldable ...	The 23rd
Wegblazen	Wehklage ..	Weinheber	Welfare ...	The 24th
Wegbleiben	Wehrgelt ...	Weinkenner	Welgeboren	The 25th
Wegbrennen	Wehrstand	Weinkuper	Welgegrond	The 26th
Wegdrogen	Weiberhass	Weinlaube	Welgewild	The 27th
Wegessen ...	Weiberhemd	Weinprobe	Welkin ...	The 28th
Wegfahren	Weiberlist	Weinranke	Welladay ...	The 29th
Wegfeilen	Weibername	Weinreich	Wellaimed	The 30th
Wegfischen	Weiberrock	Weinsaufer	Wellbeing	The 31st

CABLES.*

In reference to my (our) cable dated	In reference to your (——'s) cable dated	Have you received my (our) cable dated	Have received your (——'s) cable dated	
Cipher Word. **Wel**	Cipher Word. **Wel—Wer**	Cipher Word. **Wer—Wet**	Cipher Word. **Wha—Whi**	
Wellborn ...	Weltwunder	Wernerian	Whacked ...	The ——
Wellbred ...	Welvaren...	Werpanker	Whacking	The 1st
Welldoer ...	Welwezen...	Werpgaren	Whalebone	The 2nd
Welldoing	Welwillend	Werpspies	Whaleman	The 3rd
Wellliked ...	Welzalig ...	Werptol ...	Wharfinger	The 4th
Wellmarked	Wencher ...	Werptros ...	Wharfside	The 5th
Wellmeant	Wendekreis	Werthlos ...	Whatlike ...	The 6th
Wellnigh ...	Wendepunkt	Werthvoll	Whatnot ...	The 7th
Welloff ...	Wenigstens	Wervelbeen	Wheatear...	The 8th
Wellpaid ...	Wenteling	Wervelwind	Wheatfield	The 9th
Wellpump	Wentelstok	Wervelziek	Wheatmoth	The 10th
Wellread ...	Wenteltrap	Wesentlich	Wheedled...	The 11th
Wellspent	Wentelzuil	Weshalve ...	Wheelchair	The 12th
Wellspoken	Werbeliste	Wespennest	Wheeling ...	The 13th
Wellspring	Werbeplatz	Wesshalb ...	Wheelless...	The 14th
Welltimed	Weregild ...	Westergang	Wheelmen	The 15th
Wellustig...	Wereldbol	Westerkerk	Wheelrace	The 16th
Wellwisher	Wereldrond	Westing ...	Wheelwork	The 17th
Welriekend	Wereldstad	Westseite...	Whelk ...	The 18th
Welsher ...	Werfgast ...	Wetbreker	Whereabout	The 19th
Welsmakend	Werfschint	Wetbreuk	Whereunto	The 20th
Weltalter ...	Werkdadig	Wetdocked	Whetstone	The 21st
Weltburger	Werkeltag	Wetenschap	Wheyish ...	The 22nd
Weltering	Werkjongen	Wetgevend	Whiffle ...	The 23rd
Welthandel	Werkknecht	Wethouder	Whiggery	The 24th
Weltklug ...	Werkkring	Wetnursed	Whiggish...	The 25th
Weltkunde	Werkloon...	Wetteifer ...	Whimpering	The 26th
Weltleute...	Werkmeid	Wetterdach	Whimpers	The 27th
Weltmann	Werkmiddel	Wetterhahn	Whimrope	The 28th
Weltmarkt	Werkpak ...	Wettpreis...	Whimsey ...	The 29th
Weltmeer...	Werkster ...	Wettrennen	Whimsical	The 30th
Weltweiser	Werkthatig	Wetzstahl	Whimwham	The 31st

* See also "Cable," p. 85; "Message," p. 363; "Telegram," p. 636; "Telegraph," p. 638; &c., &c.

CABLES.

In reply to your (——'s) cable dated	Waiting for reply to my (our) cable dated	Will reply to your cable about	Cancel my (our) cable of	
Cipher Word.	Cipher Word.	Cipher Word.	Cipher Word.	
Whi	**Whi—Wid**	**Wid—Wil**	**Wil**	
Whinchat ...	Whitethorn	Widespread	Wildeman	The ——
Whinyard	Whitewash	Widgeon ...	Wilderness	The 1st
Whipcord ...	Whitewood	Widower ...	Wildfang ...	The 2nd
Whipgraft	Whiting ...	Widowhood	Wildfire ...	The 3rd
Whiphand	Whitlow ...	Widowish...	Wildfowl ...	The 4th
Whiplash ...	Whitsun ...	Widowlike	Wildfremd	The 5th
Whipmakers	Whittle ...	Widowwail	Wildgoose	The 6th
Whipping...	Whitybrown	Wiedergabe	Wildleder...	The 7th
Whipsaw ...	Whizzed ...	Wiederkehr	Wildlichen	The 8th
Whipstaff...	Whizzing ...	Wiederthun	Wildmint...	The 9th
Whipster ...	Wholeness	Wiedster ...	Wildoats ...	The 10th
Whipstitch	Wholesome	Wiegekap...	Wildpern ...	The 11th
Whipstock	Whopping	Wiegenlied	Wildschur	The 12th
Whirligig ...	Whorlebut	Wiegezang	Wilfully	The 13th
Whirlpool	Whortle ...	Wielding ...	Wilfulness	The 14th
Whirlwind	Wichsen ...	Wierooking	Wilgeboom	The 15th
Whiskered	Wickedly ...	Wierookvat	Wilgenbast	The 16th
Whiskey ...	Wickedness	Wievielste	Wilgenteen	The 17th
Whiskeyjar	Wickeln ...	Wiewohl ...	Wilgetak ...	The 18th
Whisten ...	Wickeltuch	Wifehood...	Willemite	The 19th
Whistling	Wickerwork	Wifelike ...	Willenlos ...	The 20th
Whistspel...	Wideawake	Wigless ...	Willfahren	The 21st
Whitebait...	Widening ...	Wigmaker	Willigen ...	The 22nd
Whitebeans	Widerhaken	Wigvormig	Willkommen	The 23rd
Whiteboys	Widerhalt	Wigwam ...	Willowbark	The 24th
Whitecrops	Widerlager	Wildachtig	Willowed ...	The 25th
Whitefaced	Widerpart	Wildbad ..	Willowgall	The 26th
Whitefriar	Widerrede	Wildboar ...	Willowherb	The 27th
Whitelead	Widerrufen	Wildbraten	Willowish	The 28th
Whitemeat	Widersinn	Wildcat ...	Wilskracht	The 29th
Whitemetal	Widerspiel	Wik'dieb ...	Wilsome ...	The 30th
Whitetail ...	Widerstand	Wildduck ..	Wilsuiting	The 31st

Windages...	44765*	African Banking Corporation, Limited
Windbag ...	44766	Agra Bank, Limited
Windbeutel	44767	Alexander, Fletcher & Co.
Windbound	44768	Alexanders & Co., Limited
Windbruch	44769	Allan T. H. & Co.
Windehest	44770	Anglo-Argentine Bank, Limited
Windegg ...	44771	Anglo-Austrian Bank
Windeln ...	44772	Anglo-Californian Bank, Limited
Windfahne	44773	Anglo-Egyptian Bank, Limited
Windfall ...	44774	Anglo-Foreign Banking Company, Limited
Windflower	44775	Anglo-Italian Bank, Limited
Windgauge	44776	Armstrong & Co.
Windhandel	44777	Australian Joint Stock Bank
Windhatch	44778	Banco do Brazil
Windhaver	44779	Banco Nacional de Mexico, Mexico
Windhund	44780	Banco sud Americano de Buenos Aires
Windiness	44781	Bank of Adelaide
Windingly	44782	Bank of Africa, Limited
Windkolik	44783	Bank of Australasia
Windlade...	44784	Bank of British Columbia
Windlicht	44785	Bank of British North America
Windmacher	44786	Bank of China, Japan, and the Straits, Limited
Windmill...	44787	Bank of Egypt, Limited
Windowbar	44788	Bank of England
Windowsash	44789	Bank of France
Windowsill	44790	Bank of Ireland
Windpipe...	44791	Bank of Liverpool, Limited
Windrose...	44792	Bank of Montreal
Windseite	44793	Bank of New South Wales
Windstill ...	44794	Bank of New Zealand
Windstoss	44795	Bank of Scotland
Windsucht	44796	Bank of Tarapaca and London, Limited
Windtight	44797	Bank of Victoria, Limited
Windvang	44798	Banque Commerciale
Windward	44799	Banque de Constantinople
Windzeiger	44800	Banque de l'Indo Chine
Winebibber	44801	Barclay, Bevan, Tritton, Ransom, Bouverie & Co.
Winebin ...	44802	Baring Brothers & Co., Limited
Winecask ...	44803	Barnsley Banking Company, Limited
Winecellar	44804	Beckett & Co.
Wineglass	44805	Belfast Banking Company, Limited
Winemaker	44806	Biggerstaff, W. & J.
Winepress	44807	Birmingham District & Counties Banking Co., Limited
Winevaults	44808	Blake, Boissevain & Co.
Wingcease	44809	Blydenstein B. W. & Co.
Winkelgeld	44810	Bolitho, Williams, Foster, Coode, Grylls & Co., Limited
Winkelkast	44811	British Bank of South America, Limited
Winkelmass	44812	British Linen Company Bank
Winkingly	44813	Brooks & Co.
Winnowed	44814	Brown Brothers & Co. (New York)
Winnowing	44815	Brown, Janson, & Co.
Winsomely	44816	Brown John & Co.
Winstbejag	44817	Brown, Shipley, & Co.
Winterhaft	44818	Burnett & Co.
Winterkorn	44819	Burt Frederick & Co.
Winterly ...	44820	Bywater, Tanqueray & Phayre, Limited
Winterpear	44821	Caledonian Banking Company, Limited
Winterrok	44822	Canadian Bank of Commerce (New York)
Wintrily ...	44823	Capital and Counties Bank, Limited

* Consecutive numbers continued from page 775.

Winzerei ...	44824	Carlisle and Cumberland Banking Company, Limited
Wipbrug ...	44825	Chartered Bank of India, Australia and China
Wipgalg ...	44826	Chartered Mercantile Bank of India, London, and China
Wipplank...	44827	Chemical National Bank (New York)
Wirbelwind	44828	Chick Alfred Y. & Co.
Wiredrawer	44829	Child & Co.
Wirefenced	44830	City Bank, Limited
Wiregauge	44831	City of Melbourne Bank, Limited
Wireworm	44832	Clydesdale Bank, Limited
Wirkeisen ..	44833	Cocks, Biddulph & Co.
Wirklich ..	44834	Colonial Bank
Wirkung ...	44835	Colonial Bank of New Zealand
Wirrkopf ...	44836	Commercial Bank of Australia, Limited
Wirrseide ...	44837	Commercial Bank of Scotland, Limited
Wirthbor ...	44838	Commercial Banking Company of Sydney
Wirthshaus	44839	Comptoir National d'Escompte de Paris (Paris)
Wiseacre ...	44840	Comptoir National d'Escompte de Paris (London)
Wiseling ...	44841	Consolidated Bank, Limited
Wishwash	44842	Coulon, Berthoud & Co.
Wiskunde	44843	Coutts & Co.
Wiskunstig	44844	Cox & Co.
Wispeln ...	44845	Crédit Lyonnais (Paris)
Wisselkans	44846	Crédit Lyonnais (London)
Wisselvak...	44847	Cunliffe Roger, Sons, & Co.
Wistarias ...	44848	Delhi and London Bank, Limited
Wistfully ...	44849	Del Mar Walter & Co.
Witchcraft	44850	De Nationale Bank Der Zuid-Afrikaansche Republiek, Beperkt
Witcheln ...	44851	Derenberg and Meyer
Withamite	44852	Deutsche Bank (Berlin)
Witharig ...	44853	Devon and Cornwall Banking Company, Limited
Withering	44854	Discount Banking Company of England and Wales, Limited
Withernam	44855	Dobree Samuel and Sons
Withers ...	44856	Dosseur M. & F.
Withholden	44857	Drexel, Morgan & Co. (New York)
Withinside	44858	Drummond Messrs.
Witkleurig	44859	Duff Wm. & Co.
Witstarver	44860	Dünkelsbühler Bernard
Witterung	44861	Eives and Allen
Wittfrau ...	44862	English Banking Co., Limited
Witticism	44863	English, Scottish and Australian Chartered Bank
Wittiness ...	44864	English and Italian Banking Corporation, Limited
Wittingly...	44865	Erlanger Emile & Co. (Paris)
Witwenjahr	44866	Erlanger Emile & Co. (London)
Witwensitz	44867	Eugene Kelly & Co. (New York)
Witzigen ...	44868	Federal Bank of Australia, Limited
Witzwort ...	44869	First National Bank, Denver (Colorado)
Wizardlike	44870	First National Bank (New York)
Wizardry ...	44871	German Bank of London, Limited
Wizened ...	44872	Gibbs Antony & Sons
Woadmill ...	44873	Gillett Brothers & Co.
Wochenbett	44874	Glyn, Mills, Currie & Co.
Wochenlohn	44875	Gordon, Smith & Co.
Wochentag	44876	Goslings and Sharpe
Wochnerin	44877	Granger (Paul) & Co.
Wodwich ...	44878	Grindlay & Co.
Woebegone	44879	Halifax Joint Stock Banking Company, Limited
Woefully ...	44880	Hallett & Co.
Woefulness	44881	Heidelbach, Ickelheimer & Co. (New York)
Wohlauf ...	44882	Henry Ch. & Co.
Wohlfeil ...	44883	Herries, Farquhar & Co.

Wohlgebaut	44884	Hickie, Borman & Co.
Wohlgehen	44885	Hill & Sons
Wohlgeruch	44886	Hoare Messrs.
Wohlklang	44887	Holt & Co.
Wohlstand	44888	Hong Kong and Shanghai Banking Corporation
Wohlthater	44889	Hopkinson Charles & Sons
Wohlweise	44890	Horton H. L. & Co., Limited
Wohlwollen	44891	Imperial Bank of Persia
Wohnhaft	44892	Imperial Ottoman Bank
Wohnstatt	44893	Inch James & Co.
Wohnstube	44894	International and Mortgage Bank of Mexico
Wohnzins...	44895	International Bank of London, Limited
Woldragend	44896	Ironmonger and Heale
Wolfdog ...	44897	Jay & Co.
Wolffish ...	44898	Joseph and Bergel
Wolfhound	44899	Keyser A. & Co.
Wolfhunt ...	44900	King Henry S. & Co.
Wolfram ...	44901	Knauth, Nachod & Kühne (New York)
Wolfsangel	44902	Kountze Brothers (New York)
Wolfsbane	44903	Kuhn, Loeb & Co. (New York)
Wolfseinde	44904	Kulb, A. & Co.
Wolfsfalle	44905	Lancashire and Yorkshire Bank, Limited
Wolfsgras	44906	Land Mortgage Bank of India, Limited (Credit Foncier Indien)
Wolfsgrube	44907	Lazard Brothers & Co.
Wolfsleger	44908	Leeds Joint Stock Bank, Limited
Wolfsmagen	44909	Liverpool Union Bank, Limited
Wolfskin ...	44910	Lloyds Bank, Limited
Wolfszahn	44911	London and Brazilian Bank, Limited
Wolkchen	44912	London and County Banking Co., Limited
Wolkenlos	44913	London and Hanseatic Bank, Limited
Wolkenzug	44914	London and Midland Bank, Limited
Wolkigheid	44915	London and Provincial Bank, Limited
→ Wollboden	44916	London and River Plate Bank, Limited *address all communications*
Wollenband	44917	London and San Francisco Bank, Limited
Wollengarn	44918	London and South Western Bank, Limited
Wollenzeug	44919	London and Westminster Bank, Limited
Wollfarber	44920	London and Yorkshire Bank, Limited
Wollkammer	44921	London Bank of Mexico and South America, Limited
Wollkopf ...	44922	London Banking Corporation, Limited
Wollmarkt	44923	London Chartered Bank of Australia
Wollsack ...	44924	London Joint Stock Bank, Limited
Wollsammet	44925	Luke Thomas & Co., Limited
Wollschnur	44926	Macfadyen P., & Co.
Wollstaub	44927	McGrigor Sir C. R. Bart., & Co.
Wollustig ...	44928	Manchester and County Bank, Limited
Wolvenbeet	44929	Manchester and Liverpool District Banking Co., Limited
Wolvendak	44930	Martin's Bank, Limited
Wolvennet	44931	Matheson & Co.
Wolverine	44932	Melville, Fickus & Co., Limited
Womanhater	44933	Merchant Banking Company, Limited
Womanhood	44934	Metropolitan, Birmingham, and South Wales Bank, Limited
Womanish	44935	Miéville Frank & Son
Womankind	44936	Miners' and Merchants' Bank, Ouray (Colorado)
Womanlike	44937	Morgan J. S. & Co.
Womanly ...	44938	Morgan Thomas & Co.
Wombat ...	44939	Morrison William H.
Women ...	44940	Murrieta, C. de, & Co., Limited
Wonach ...	44941	Natal Bank, Limited
Wonderer...	44942	National Bank, Limited
Wonderheid	44943	National Bank of Australasia

Wonderkind	44944	National Bank of China, Limited
Wonderland	44945	National Bank of India, Limited
Wonderment	44946	National Bank of New Zealand, Limited
Wonderstuk	44947	National Bank of Scotland, Limited
Wondzalf...	44948	National Park Bank (New York)
Wonnemonat	44949	National Provincial Bank of England, Limited
Wontedness	44950	Netter Albert
Woodapples	44951	New English Bank of the River Plate, Limited
Woodashes	44952	New Oriental Bank Corporation, Limited
Woodbine...	44953	North and South Wales Bank, Limited
Woodborer	44954	Oppenheim E. L. & Co. (New York)
Woodchat...	44955	Oppert E. D. & Co.
Woodchuck	44956	Paley, Scriven & Co.
Woodcut ...	44957	Parr's Banking Company and the Alliance Bank, Limited
Woodcutter	44958	Peabody, Henry W., & Co.
Woodenish	44959	Pierce, Wright & Co.
Woodenly...	44960	Post, Martin & Co.
Woodland	44961	Prescott, Dimsdale, Cave, Tugwell & Co., Limited
Woodlark...	44962	Provincial Bank of Ireland, Limited
Woodlouse	44963	Queensland National Bank, Limited
Woodmites	44964	Reinhardt Charles, & Co.
Woodmote	44965	Robarts, Lubbock & Co.
Woodnymph	44966	Rothschild N. M., & Sons
Woodpecker	44967	Royal Bank of Ireland, Limited
Woodpigeon	44968	Royal Bank of Queensland, Limited
Woodruff ...	44969	Royal Bank of Scotland
Woodscrews	44970	Rüffer A., & Sons
Woodshock	44971	Russian Bank for Foreign Trade
Woodsmen	44972	Samuel Montagu & Co.
Woodsorrel	44973	Schafer Brothers (New York)
Woodworker	44974	Schulz and Ruckgaber (New York)
Woodwort	44975	Schuster, Son & Co.
Wooingly ...	44976	Scott Sir Samuel, Bart., & Co.
Woolcomber	44977	Segalla Brothers
Wooldyer...	44978	Seligman Brothers
Woolfell ...	44979	Seyd (Julius), Bishop, Johnson & Co., Limited
Woolliness	44980	Silver S. W., & Co.
Woolpacker	44981	Simond & Co.
Woolstock	44982	Smith, Payne & Smiths
Wordbooks	44983	Société Générale de Paris
Wordily ...	44984	Standard Bank of Australia, Limited
Wordless ...	44985	Standard Bank of South Africa, Limited
Worftenne	44986	State National Bank, Denver (Colorado)
Workaday	44987	State National Bank
Workbags	44988	Stillwell and Sons
Workbox ...	44989	Third National Bank (New York)
Workfellow	44990	Truninger & Co.
Workfolk...	44991	Tweedie, A. F., & R. W.
Workhouse	44992	Union Bank of Australia, Limited
Workman...	44993	Union Bank of London, Limited
Workpeople	44994	Union Bank of Manchester, Limited
Workshop	44995	Union Bank of Scotland, Limited
Worktable	44996	Union Bank of Spain and England, Limited
Workwoman	44997	Union Discount Company of London, Limited
Worldling	44998	United States National Bank (New York)
Worldwide	44999	Watson William, & Co.
Wormeaten	45000	Wells, Fargo & Co.
Wormfence	**45001**	Western Australian Bank
Wormgear	45002	Williams Deacon and Manchester and Salford Bank, Limited
Wormholed	45003	Yokohama Specie Bank, Limited

Wormkruid	45004	Advance Corporation, Limited
Wormlike...	45005	Adventurers of Mexico, Limited
Wormstekig	45006	African and General Exploring Co., Limited
Wormul ...	45007	African Exploration and Investment Co., Limited
Wormwheel	45008	African Investment Corporation, Limited
Wormwood	45009	Agency and Exploration Co. of Australasia, Limited
Worrier ...	45010	Agency, Land, and Finance Co. of Australia, Limited
Worringly	45011	Alliance Economic Investment Co., Limited
Worsening	45012	Alliance Investment Co., Limited
Worship ...	45013	Alliance Mortgage and Investment Co., Limited
Worshipful	45014	Alliance Trust and Investment Co., Limited
Worshipper	45015	American Association, Limited
Worsted ...	45016	American Debenture Co.
Worsteling	45017	American Exploration and Development Corporation, Limited
Wortarm ...	45018	American Freehold-Land Mortgage Co. of London, Limited
Worterbuch	45019	American Investment Trust Co., Limited
Wortfolge	45020	Anglo-American Debenture Corporation, Limited
Wortfugung	45021	Anglo-American Exploration and Development Co., Limited
Worthily ...	45022	Anglo-American Land Mortgage and Agency Co., Limited
Worthiness	45023	Assets Founders' Share Co., Limited
Worthite ...	45024	Assets Realisation Co., Limited
Wortkarg...	45025	Atlas Investment Trust, Limited
Wortreich	45026	Australasian Mortgage and Agency Co., Limited
Wortspiel ...	45027	Australian Mortgage, Land, and Finance Co., Limited
Worunter ...	45028	Bechuanaland Exploration Co., Limited
Woudezel ...	45029	British and American Mortgage Co., Limited
Woudgodin	45030	British & American Trustee & Finance Corporation, Limited
Wounder ...	45031	British and Australasian Trust and Loan Co., Limited
Wounding	45032	British North Borneo Co.
Woundless	45033	British South Africa Co.
Woundwort	45034	Canadian Agricultural, Coal, and Colonisation Co., Limited
Wourali ...	45035	Canadian and American Mortgage and Trust Co., Limited
Wowider ...	45036	Central African and Zoutpansberg Exploration Co., Limited
Wrackful...	45037	Chiapas Zone Exploration Co., Limited
Wrackgrass	45038	Colonial and United States Mortgage Co., Limited
Wrackgut	45039	Colonial Debenture Corporation, Limited
Wraiths ...	45040	Consolidated Gold Fields of South Africa, Limited
Wrakgoed	45041	Consolidated Trust, Limited
Wrakhout	45042	Debenture Corporation, Limited
Wrangled...	45043	Dutch Guyana Exploration Syndicate, Limited
Wrangling	45044	Empire of India Corporation, Limited
Wrappage	45045	Exploration Company, Limited
Wrappers...	45046	Exploring Company, Limited
Wraprascal	45047	Foreign and Colonial Debenture Corporation, Limited
Wrasse ...	45048	Foreign and Colonial Investment Trust Co., Limited
Wrathfully	45049	Glasgow and South African Co., Limited
Wrathless	45050	Globe Industrial and General Trust Corporation, Limited
Wraul ...	45051	Gold Fields of Siam, Limited
Wreakful ...	45052	Gold Fields of South Africa, Limited
Wreakless	45053	Hudson's Bay Company
Wreathen...	45054	Hyderabad (Deccan) Company, Limited
Wreckage...	45055	Imperial British East Africa Co.
Wrencher...	45056	Imperial Colonial Finance and Agency Corporation, Limited
Wrenching	45057	Indian and General Investment Trust, Limited
Wrestler ...	45058	Industrial and General Trust, Limited
Wrestling...	45059	International Trustee, Assets, & Debenture Corporation, Ltd.
Wriggler ...	45060	Loan and Finance Corporation, Limited
Wrightia ...	45061	London and Australasian Debenture Corporation, Limited
Wringbolt	45062	London and Colonial Finance Corporation, Limited
Wringstave	45063	London and General Exploration and Developing Co., Limited

Wrinkle ...	45064	London and South African Exploration Co., Limited
Wristband	45065	London Scottish American Trust, Limited
Wristlet ...	45066	London Share and Debenture Co., Limited
Writable ...	45067	Lower California Development Co., Limited
Writership	45068	Manitoba Mortgage and Investment Co., Limited
Writhle ...	45069	Mashonaland Agency, Limited
Writingink	45070	Matabeleland Company, Limited
Writingpen	45071	Mercantile Investment and General Trust Co., Limited
Wrongdoer	45072	Merchants' Trust, Limited
Wrongfull	45073	Mexican Company of London, Limited
Wronging	45074	Mexican Explorations, Limited
Wrongless	45075	Mexican General Land Mortgage and Investment Co., Limited
Wrongous	45076	Mexican Investment Corporation, Limited
Wrymouth	45077	Mines Company, Limited
Wrynecked	45078	Mines Contract Co., Limited
Wryness ...	45079	Mines Selection Syndicate, Limited
Wucherer	45080	Mines Trust, Limited
Wucherhaft	45081	Mining Shares Investment Co., Limited
Wuftheid	45082	Mozambique Company
Wulstig ...	45083	Natal Prospecting Co., Limited
Wundarzt	45084	National Discount Co., Limited
Wundbalsam	45085	National Financial Corporation, Limited
Wundenmahl	45086	Nobel-Dynamite Trust Co., Limited
Wunderbar	45087	Northern Transvaal Lands Co., Limited
Wunderbild	45088	Oceana Development Co., Limited
Wundergabe	45089	Oceana Transvaal Land Co., Limited
Wunderlich	45090	Pacific Loan and Investment Co., Limited
Wunderthat	45091	Patents, Mining, and Financial Trust, Limited
Wunderwerk	45092	Pioneers of Mashonaland Syndicate, Limited
Wundfieber	45093	Premier Concessions of Mozambique, Limited
Wundmahl	45094	Scottish American Investment Co., Limited
Wundpulver	45095	Scottish Australian Investment Co., Limited
Wundsalbe	45096	Silati River Gold Mining and Prospecting Co., Limited
Wurdevoll	45097	South African Argonauts, Limited
Wurdigen	45098	South African Gold Trust and Agency Co., Limited
Wurdigkeit	45099	South African Loan, Mortgage, and Mercantile Agency, Limited
Wurfkraft	45100	South African Trust and Finance Co., Limited
Wurflinie	45101	South American and Mexican Co., Limited
Wurfnetz ...	45102	Southern Land Co., Limited
Wurfspiess	45103	Straits Prospecting Syndicate, Limited
Wurfwaffe	45104	Transvaal Gold Exploration and Land Co., Limited
Wurmfrass	45105	Transvaal Lands Co., Limited
Wurstmaul	45106	Transvaal Minerals, Limited
Wurzelkeim	45107	Transvaal Mortgage, Loan, and Finance Co., Limited
Wurzelwort	45108	Transvaal Prospecting Co., Limited
Wurzhaft	45109	Trust and Agency Company of Australasia, Limited
Wuthend ...	45110	Trustees, Executors, & Securities Insurance Corporation, Ltd.
Wutherich	45111	Union Debenture Co., Limited
Wychelm ...	45112	Union Discount Co., of London, Limited
Wychhazels	45113	United African Lands, Limited
Wyvern ...	45114	United Kingdom and Foreign Investment & Finance Co., Ltd.
Wyvernish	45115	United States and South American Investment Trust Co.,
Xangti ...	45116	United States Debenture Corporation, Limited [Limited
Xanthate ...	45117	United Trust, Limited
Xanthein ...	45118	Vancouver Land and Securities Corporation, Limited
Xanthidium	45119	Virginia Development Co., Limited (Philadelphia)
Xanthocon	45120	West Australian Land Co., Limited
Xanthosia	45121	West Australian Mortgage and Agency Corporation, Limited
Xenelasian	45122	Worcester Exploration and Gold Mining Co., Limited
Xenodochy	45123	Wyldsdale Gold Exploration and Developing Co., Limited

Cipher Word.	No.	To be Substituted for.
Xenotime ...	45124	Diamantina
Xerasia ...	45125	Fumil
Xeroderm ...	45126	Mandanha
Xeromyrum	45127	Pocão de Moreira ✓
Xerophagy	45128	Rio de Janiero
Xerotes ...	45129	Sete Lagoas
Xylanthrax	45130	Jequitinhonha River
Xylite ...	45131 ✓	Dredging
Xylograph	45132	Dredger
Xyloid ...	45133	This telegraph office leaks
Xyloidine ...	45134	Telegraph office at —— leaks
Xylophaga	45135	Pouso Alto
Xyster ...	45136	Rio Congonhas
Yaccawood	45137	Conceicão
Yacht ...	45138	River or Placer testing plant
Yachtclub	45139	Keystone Driller Co., Beaver Falls, Pa
Yachtsman	45140	Serro
Yaciente ...	45141	Lagoa Seco
Yactura ...	45142	Cascalha
Yambico ...	45143	Strong current
Yanking ...	45144	— feet below surface of water to cascalha
Yanolite ...	45145	Pipes drive freely
Yantar ...	45146	Pipes do not drive freely
Yapocks ...	45147	Pipes pull up easily
Yardarm ...	45148	Pipes pull up hard
Yardstick ...	45149	Left hand side of river
Yardwand	45150	Right hand side of river
Yarrish ...	45151	Boa Vista
Yataghan ...	45152	Pot hole
Yaupers ...	45153	

Cipher Word.	No.	To be Substituted for.
Yawl	45154	Can be carried by Ox teams
Yawning	45155	Cannot be carried by Ox teams
Yearbook	45156	It will be necessary to pack on mules
Yearlings	45157	Send by cable immediately to Banco da Republica do Brazil dollar
Yearningly	45158	Send by cable immediately to the London and Rivo Plate Bank dollar
Yeastiness	45159	Rio Vaccaria
Yeastplant	45160	Rio Salinas
Yeasty	45161	Rio Macahubas
Yeguada	45162	Rio Itacambirassú
Yeguero	45163	Rio Pardo
Yellowbird	45164	Rio Arassuahy
Yellowboy	45165	Rio Setubal
Yellowish	45166	Rio Capavery
Yellowness	45167	Cadete Justimano F. de Azevedo
Yellowwort	45168	Francalino Senior
Yelmeria	45169	Francalino Junior
Yeoman	45170	Filisberto Dariel
Yeomanlike	45171	Nelson F. Humphrey
Yerbamate	45172	B. S. Pray
Yermer	45173	F. Milton Johnson
Yernecico	45174	John B. Humphrey
Yeseria	45175	American Minister
Yewtrees	45176	Consul at Rio de Janeiro
Yezidees	45177	Consul at Bahia
Yggdrasil	45178	Cannievieras
Yieldance	45179	Belmonte
Yieldingly	45180	Black Diamond
Yogin	45181	Bolt
Yokefellow	45182	Port of Entry
Yokemate	45183	Naptha

Cipher Word.	No.	To be Substituted for.
Yonker ...	45184	Gasoline
Youngish ..	45185	Naptha Launch
Youngling	45186	Steam Launch
Youngster	45187	Read 7 words ahead
Youthful ...	45188	Read 7 words back
Youthhood	45189	Meyer William George
Youthsome	45190	Roy McCutchan
Yttrious ...	45191	M.P. Almeida, 28 Main St. Winter Hill Somerville
Yuleblock ...	45192	Exploring expedition by launch
Yulelogs ...	45193	Prospecting expedition by ——
Yuletide ...	45194	Systematic prospecting & sampling in river bed
Yunque ..	45195	Systematic prospecting & sampling on river banks
Yunteria ...	45196	Preliminary prospecting of river bed.
Yusano ...	45197	Preliminary prospecting of river banks
Zaadachtig	45198	Country adjoining Arashuaty River favorably situated for Hydraulic Mining
Zaadbal ...	45199	Country adjoining Arashuaty River not favorably situated for Hydraulic Mining
Zabattiero...	45200	Bedrock in river - meets all requirements of Dredge
Zabbelen ...	45201	Bedrock in river - does not meet all requirements Dredg
Zabida ...	45202	Boston & Colombia Gold Dredging Co
Zabism ...	45203	J.L. Hayward
Zabistic ...	45204	Please translate and mail to my wife
Zabordar ...	45205	Please translate and telegraph to my wife
Zabucar ...	45206	Please translate and forward to ——
Zabullida ...	45207	De Beers
Zacapela ...	45208	Carney, Senior,
Zacatin ...	45209	Jesse (?) Carney, Junior
Zaccagna ..	45210	Gale Francis
Zaccarale ...	45211	Anselmi.
Zaccaro ...	45212	Touseau & Co, 31 St. Swithins Lane, London
Zacchera ...	45213	Farbutt, Son &Co (T&S. Syndicate)

Cipher Word.	No.	To be Substituted for.
Zaccheroso	45214	The T & S Property (8-X and 13-18)
Zaccho ...	45215	Rothchilde
Zacconato ...	45216	Robinson
Zachtheid ...	45217	Sao Joao de Chapada
Zackig ...	45218	Sojza
Zadelboom	45219	Minas do Chupé
Zadeldek ...	45220	Pau de Fructa
Zadelknop...	45221	Dattas
Zadelmaker	45222	Risdon 3/4 ft Bucket Dredge
Zadelpaard	45223	" 5 " " "
Zadelriem ...	45224	Bucyrus 3/4 ft " "
Zadelrug ...	45225	" 5 " " "
Zafacoca ...	45226	With tailings stacker
Zafareche ...	45227	Diamond Washing Plant
Zaferia ...	45228	Machinery for diamond washing plant only
Zaffamento	45229	Centrifugal Pump with Engine
Zaffardoso...	45230	" " " Boiler & Engine
Zaffatura ...	45231	Knocked down for mule packing
Zafferano ...	45232	Number — Non Fraction
Zaffetica ...	45233	Testing Plant with propellerwheel
Zaffiretto ...	45234	" " " " " & scow
Zaffirino ...	45235	Testing Plant without propeller wheel or scow
Zaffrone ...	45236	'Traction Road Engine
Zafiamente	45237	— Wagons for traction road
Zafiedad ...	45238	De Beers Consolidated Mines Limited
Zafrau ...	45239	De Beers Mines
Zagaglia ...	45240	Crater formations
Zagaie ...	45241	True Diamond Mine
Zagalejo ...	45242	Oxidized portion of crater
Zagersbok...	45243	Penetrated below oxidized zone of crater

Cipher Word.	No.	To be Substituted for.
Zaghaft ...	45244	Area of crater at surface
Zaguanete...	45245	Area of crater at level of "hard rock"
Zahareno ...	45246	Contains — carats of diamonds per load of 16 cu. ft.
Zaheridor ...	45247	Contains — carats of diamonds per cu. yd
Zahigkeit .	45248	Will average — stones per carat
Zahinar ..	45249	The percentage of stones over one carat is
Zahlbar ...	45250	" " " " " two " "
Zahlfrist ...	45251	" " " " " three " '
Zahlperle ...	45252	" " " " " four " "
Zahlreich ...	45253	" " " " " five " '
Zahlung ..	45254	Will average — in gold per cubic yd
Zahlwerth ...	45255	Test No — shows — in gold per cu yd
Zahmbar ...	45256	Exploration results are satisfactory at
Zahmheit ..	45257	Exploration results are not satisfactory at
Zahnfaule ..	45258	To reach — — it will be necessary to portage — times above water fall
Zahnfieber...	45259	Myer's list of unbonded properti
Zahnhohle...	45260	Myer's list of bonded properties
Zahnlucke...	45261	Everybody and Everything is all right here
Zahnpulver .	45262	
Zahnwurzel	45263	
Zahonado ...	45264	
Zahorra ...	45265	
Zahumador	45266	
Zahumerio	45267	
Zahurda ...	45268	
Zainetto ...	45269	
Zakgeld ...	45270	
Zakhorloge	45271	
Zakspiegel	45272	
Zalaccas ...	45273	

Cipher Word.	No.	To be Substituted for.
Zalfactig ...	45274	
Zalfolie ...	45275	
Zalfpot ...	45276	
Zaliger ...	45277	
Zaligheid ...	45278	
Zaliging ...	45279	
Zalmboer ...	45280	
Zalmforel ...	45281	
Zalmzegen	45282	
Zamang ...	45283	
Zambracca	45284	
Zamia ...	45285	
Zamouse ...	45286	
Zampetta ...	45287	
Zampiletto	45288	
Zampilio ...	45289	
Zampillare	45290	
Zampogna	45291	
Zanajuolo ..	45292	
Zancato ...	45293	
Zandberg ...	45294	
Zanderig ...	45295	
Zandgrond	45296	
Zandheuvel	45297	
Zandkoker	45298	
Zandkorrel	45299	
Zanghelden	45300	
Zangnimf ...	45301	
Zangschool	45302	
Zangstem ...	45303	

Cipher Word.	No.
Zangvogel...	45304
Zaniker ...	45305
Zankapfel ...	45306
Zankisch ...	45307
Zannetta ...	45308
Zanonia ...	45309
Zanzaretta	45310
Zanzariere	45311
Zapaton ...	45312
Zapfen ...	45313
Zapfenbier	45314
Zaphara ..	45315
Zapotilla ...	45316
Zappadore...	45317
Zappeln ...	45318
Zappettare	45319
Zappettina	45320
Zappone ...	45321
Zapuzar ...	45322
Zaquizami	45323
Zarabanda	45324
Zarabutero	45325
Zaradion ...	45326
Zaragatona	45327
Zaragoci ...	45328
Zaramago ...	45329
Zarambeque	45330
Zaramullo...	45331
Zarandajas	45332
Zarandillo...	45333

Cipher Word.	No.
Zarapallon	45834
Zarapatel ...	45835
Zarapito ...	45836
Zarcillo ...	45837
Zarebas ...	45838
Zarevitz ...	45839
Zariano ...	45840
Zarnich ...	45841
Zarpazo ...	45842
Zarracatin ..	45843
Zarramplin	45844
Zarriento ...	45845
Zartheit ...	45846
Zartlich ...	45847
Zartsinn ...	45848
Zarzahan ...	45849
Zarzaidea ...	45850
Zarzamora	45851
Zarzuela ...	45852
Zascandil ...	45853
Zatheid ...	45854
Zatiquero ...	45855
Zattera ...	45856
Zauberer ...	45857
Zauberisch	45858
Zauberstab	45859
Zaudern ...	45860
Zaumen ..	45861
Zaunkonig	45862
Zauntritt ...	45863

E E E

Cipher Word.	No.
Zavardarsi	45364
Zavorrare ...	45365
Zazzeretta ..	45366
Zazzerino ...	45367
Zealful ...	45368
Zealless ...	45369
Zealot ...	45370
Zealotist ...	45371
Zealously ...	45372
Zebra ...	45373
Zebralike ...	45374
Zebraplant	45375
Zebrawood	45376
Zecchiere ...	45377
Zechbruder	45378
Zecher ...	45379
Zechfrei ...	45380
Zechstein ...	45381
Zedenkunde	45382
Zedenles ...	45383
Zedenwet ...	45384
Zedigheid ...	45385
Zedoaria ...	45386
Zegedicht ...	45387
Zegegalm ..	45388
Zegekar ...	45389
Zegekoets ...	45390
Zegekrans...	45391
Zegelgeld ...	45392
Zegeling ...	45393

Cipher Word.	No.
Zegelloon ...	45394
Zegellak ...	45395
Zegelmerk...	45396
Zegelpers ...	45397
Zegelrecht...	45398
Zegelring ...	45399
Zegenbede...	45400
Zegeoffer	45401
Zegepralen	45402
Zegetocht ..	45403
Zegsman ...	45404
Zehenender	45405
Zehent ...	45406
Zehnerlei	45407
Zehnfach ...	45408
Zehntens ...	45409
Zehrgeld ...	45410
Zeichnen ...	45411
Zeichnung...	45412
Zeidler ...	45413
Zeilage ...	45414
Zeilmaker ..	45415
Zeilwind ...	45416
Zeisig ...	45417
Zeitalter ...	45418
Zeitangabe	45419
Zeitdauer ..	45420
Zeitgeist ...	45421
Zeitherig ...	45422
Zeitigen ...	45423

Cipher Word.	No.
Zeitlaufe ...	45424
Zeitlebens ..	45425
Zeitmangel	45426
Zeitmesser	45427
Zeitraum ...	45428
Zeitweilig ...	45429
Zelamina ...	45430
Zelateur ...	45431
Zelatrice ...	45432
Zeleras ..	45433
Zelfbedrog	45434
Zelfbelang...	45435
Zelfbewust	45436
Zelfkanten	45437
Zelfkennis...	45438
Zeltdecke ...	45439
Zeltstange	45440
Zemindary	45441
Zendbode ...	45442
Zendbrief ..	45443
Zendster ...	45444
Zenith ...	45445
Zenzalino ...	45446
Zenzontle ...	45447
Zeolites ...	45448
Zephyr ...	45449
Zeppamento	45450
Zeppatore ...	45451
Zerbersten	45452
Zerbineria...	45453

Cipher Word.	No.				
Zerblauen ...	45454				
Zerbrechen	45455				
Zerfasern ...	45456				
Zergehen ...	45457				
Zerhacken...	45458				
Zerklopfen	45459				
Zerknicken	45460				
Zerlegbar ...	45461				
Zerlegung ...	45462				
Zerlumpt ...	45463				
Zermalmen	45464				
Zernagen...	45465				
Zernichten	45466				
Zerplatzen	45467				
Zerpulvern	45468				
Zerqualen...	45469				
Zerrbild ...	45470				
Zerreisen ...	45471				
Zerrupfen ...	45472				
Zersetzung	45473				
Zerspalten	45474				
Zerstieben	45475				
Zerstorbar	45476				
Zerstorung	45477				
Zerstreut ...	45478				
Zertheilen ...	45479				
Zertrennen	45480				
Zesregelig ...	45481				
Zestiende ...	45482				
Zestigtal ...	45483				

Cipher Word.	No.
Zetetico ..	45484
Zethamer ...	45485
Zeticula ...	45486
Zettelbank	45487
Zettelchen	45488
Zettorario ...	45489
Zeughaus ...	45490
Zeugmatous	45491
Zevenblad ...	45492
Zevenjarig	45493
Zezeyer ...	45494
Zibaldone ...	45495
Zibeline ...	45496
Zibellino ...	45497
Zickzack ..	45498
Ziegelofen ..	45499
Ziegenbock	45500
Ziegenkase	45501
Ziehkind ...	45502
Zielenadel ...	45503
Zielsangst ...	45504
Zielsgenot ...	45505
Zielsrust ...	45506
Zieltogen ...	45507
Zieltoging ...	45508
Ziemlich ...	45509
Zierbengel	45510
Zierrath ...	45511
Zigofilo ...	45512
Zigrino ...	45513

Cipher Word.	No.
Zigzag ...	45514
Zigzagging	45515
Zilorgano ...	45516
Zilverglid ...	45517
Zilvermunt	45518
Zimalogia ...	45519
Zimbellare...	45520
Zimbello ...	45521
Zimmarrone	45522
Zimmer ...	45523
Zimmeraxt	45524
Zimmerholz	45525
Zimologia ..	45526
Zimperlich	45527
Zinalino ...	45528
Zincage ...	45529
Zincamyl ...	45530
Zincbloom	45531
Zincethyl ...	45532
Zincwhite ...	45533
Zincwork ...	45534
Zingaresca	45535
Zinghinaja	45536
Zinguerie ...	45537
Zinkenite ...	45538
Zinkstuk ...	45539
Zinnern ...	45540
Zinnober ...	45541
Zinsfuss ...	45542
Zinsnede ...	45543

Cipher Word.	No.
Zinzanioso	45544
Zipizate ...	45545
Zipoletto ...	45546
Zipperlein ...	45547
Zirconite ...	45548
Zirkelrund	45549
Zirlamento	45550
Zirletto ...	45551
Zither ...	45552
Zitkamer ...	45553
Zitteraal ...	45554
Zizanador ...	45555
Zizanero ...	45556
Zobelpelz ...	45557
Zoccalojo ...	45558
Zocchetto ...	45559
Zoccolante	45560
Zoccoletto ...	45561
Zodenbank	45562
Zodenwerk	45563
Zodiacale ...	45564
Zodiaco ...	45565
Zoeotrope ...	45566
Zogerung ...	45567
Zogling ...	45568
Zoilist ...	45569
Zolfanello ...	45570
Zolfatara ...	45571
Zolfino ...	45572
Zolfonaria...	45573

Cipher Word.	No.
Zolforato ...	45574
Zollbar ...	45575
Zollbeamte	45576
Zolletta ...	45577
Zollipar ...	45578
Zollsiegel ...	45579
Zollstab ...	45580
Zolltarif ...	45581
Zollverein ...	45582
Zollwesen ...	45583
Zolocho ...	45584
Zombamente	45585
Zombatore	45586
Zombolato	45587
Zonceria ...	45588
Zoneless ...	45589
Zonzorrion	45590
Zoochemy ...	45591
Zoofago ...	45592
Zooforica ...	45593
Zoografia ...	45594
Zoographer	45595
Zoolatria ...	45596
Zoologique	45597
Zoologist ...	45598
Zoology ...	45599
Zoomorphic	45600
Zoonomia ...	45601
Zoophagon	45602
Zoophyte ...	45603

Cipher Word.	No.
Zoosperm ...	45604
Zootomia ...	45605
Zopilote ...	45606
Zopiters ...	45607
Zoppettino	45608
Zoppicante	45609
Zoppicone ...	45610
Zoqueteria...	45611
Zoquetudo	45612
Zornig ...	45613
Zorrastron	45614
Zorrillo ...	45615
Zorrocloco ..	45616
Zorruela ...	45617
Zorzalena ...	45618
Zotichetto ..	45619
Zotteln ...	45620
Zouave ...	45621
Zoutmaking	45622
Zoutmeter...	45623
Zoutpacht ..	45624
Zoutsteen ...	45625
Zoutzolder	45626
Zubehor ...	45627
Zubereiten	45628
Zubinden ...	45629
Zubusse ...	45630
Zuccajo ...	45631
Zuccajuola	45632
Zuccherajo	45633

Cipher Word.	No.
Zucconare ..	45634
Zuccotto ...	45635
Zuchthaus	45636
Zuchtigen ..	45637
Zuchtlos ...	45638
Zucken ...	45639
Zuckerbrot	45640
Zuckerkand	45641
Zuckerrohr	45642
Zuckersatz	45643
Zudecken ...	45644
Zuderia ...	45645
Zueignen ...	45646
Zufahren ...	45647
Zufallig ...	45648
Zufertigen	45649
Zuffettina ..	45650
Zufluss ...	45651
Zufolatore...	45652
Zufoletto ...	45653
Zufolge ...	45654
Zufolone ...	45655
Zufubren ...	45656
Zugbrucke	45657
Zugeben ...	45658
Zugehoren...	45659
Zugellos ...	45660
Zugemuse ...	45661
Zugesellen...	45662
Zugethan ...	45663

Cipher Word.	No.
Zughalten ...	45664
Zugluft ...	45665
Zugochs ...	45666
Zugolino ...	45667
Zugvogel ...	45668
Zugwind ..	45669
Zuidpool ...	45670
Zuidpunt ...	45671
Zuigeling ..	45672
Zuigpapier	45673
Zuklappen...	45674
Zuklinken ..	45675
Zuknoppen	45676
Zukommen	45677
Zulangen ...	45678
Zulaque ...	45679
Zulassig ...	45680
Zullenco ...	45681
Zumacar ...	45682
Zumachen...	45683
Zumbido ...	45684
Zumbooruk	45685
Zumeist ...	45686
Zumessen ...	45687
Zumiento ...	45688
Zumillo ...	45689
Zumuthen	45690
Zunageln ...	45691
Zunden ...	45692
Zundloch ...	45693

Cipher Word.	No.
Zunehmen	45694
Zuordnen ...	45695
Zupichen ...	45696
Zurcidera ...	45697
Zurdear ...	45698
Zurichten ..	45699
Zuriegeln ...	45700
Zurita ...	45701
Zurlato ...	45702
Zurlites ...	45708
Zurraco ...	45704
Zurrapilla ...	45705
Zurraposo ...	45706
Zurriaga ...	45707
Zurribanda	45708
Zurronero ...	45709
Zurrusco ...	45710
Zuruck ...	45711
Zurufen ...	45712
Zurustung	45713
Zusammen	45714
Zusatz ...	45715
Zusehends	45716
Zusichern ...	45717
Zusiegeln ...	45718
Zuspeise ...	45719
Zusperren ...	45720
Zuspitzen ...	45721
Zusprache	45722
Zustandig ...	45723

r Word.	No.
.llen ...	45724
.opseln	45725
tutzen .	45726
.tappen ...	45727
athulich ...	45728
.utragen	45729
Zutraulich	45730
Zutreffen ..	45731
Zutrinken ...	45732
Zuversicht	45733
Zuvorderst	45734
Zuwachs ..	45735
Zuwenden ..	45736
Zwanglos ...	45737
Zwanziger	45738
Zwartbont	45739
Zwartkop ...	45740
Zwartsel ...	45741
Zwavelbad	45742
Zwavelerts	45743
Zweifach ...	45744
Zweifellos ...	45745
Zweigbahn	45746
Zweimalig	45747
Zwelging ...	45748
Zwemkleed	45749
Zwemkunst	45750
Zwemvogel	45751
Zwicken ...	45752
Zwieback ...	45753

Cipher Word.	No.
Zwiebeln ...	45754
Zwielicht ...	45755
Zwiespalt ...	45756
Zwietracht	45757
Zwillich ...	45758
Zwirnband	45759
Zwirnfaden	45760
Zwolftens ...	45761
Zygomatic ..	45762
Zymologist	45763
Zymoscope	45764
Zymosis ...	45765
Zymotechny	45766
Zymotic ...	45767

𝕷ondon:

PRINTED BY WHITEHEAD, MORRIS & Co., LTD.,
9, FENCHURCH STREET, E.C.

McNEILL'S CODE.

EXTRACTS FROM PRESS OPINIONS.

Glasgow Herald.

"Is a very elaborate work, manifesting a vast amount of painstaking and care. It should prove of great service to engineers, mining directors, bankers, stock brokers, solicitors, and indeed to all business men."

Morning Post.

"Of the many publications designed to meet such requirements, none is more complete, is more conveniently arranged than McNeill's Code, which, while primarily intended for use in connexion with mining affairs, really covers nearly every possible contingency that is likely to occur in any mercantile or financial relations. This admirable Code is the work of Mr. Bedford McNeill."

Financial News.

"McNeill's 'Mining and General Code' appears to have been carefully compiled. The author knows his subject, and his experience in this respect has been turned to good account in his book."

St. James's Gazette.

"The book as a whole is by far the most complete thing of the kind which has yet been published, and bears ample testimony to the thorough grasp of his subject which Mr. McNeill has acquired. The volume, which is arranged in a clear and convenient form, will be a valuable addition to the office library of all who have business in the mining world."

Financial Times.

"Mr. Bedford McNeill has produced an elaborate Telegraph Code, which includes the technical terms and sentences required by the mining, metallurgical, and civil engineer, by the mine directors, and by those connected with the direction or management of mining and smelting companies. The Code is the outcome of considerable industry and ingenuity. It will undoubtedly prove very useful, and a source of much economy to the classes for whom it is designed."

Industries.

"Mr. McNeill's work, covering 807 pages, and containing 45,767 phrases, will undoubtedly be warmly welcomed by those connected with the direction of mining companies. The author's ripe experience and high professional qualifications as a mining engineer are evidence of the accuracy of the technical terms, whilst the financial part of mining and the needs of the financier have not been neglected. The Code contains a very complete schedule of the phrases likely to be required in reports upon mineral properties. Mr. McNeill's compilation is undoubtedly the most complete technical code existing, and, as a striking example of industry, patience, and skill, is deserving of unqualified praise."

Electrician.

"More than usual care has been taken in the selection of the Code words, which, from a casual survey, appear less liable to telegraphic error than is frequently the case."